"THE EMPIRE
OF THE
BRETAIGNES", 1175–1688

"THE EMPIRE OF THE BRETAIGNES", 1175–1688

The Foundations of a Colonial System of Government

Select Documents on the Constitutional History of the British Empire and Commonwealth, Volume I

Edited by
FREDERICK MADDEN
with
DAVID FIELDHOUSE

Documents in Imperial History, Number 1

Greenwood Press
Westport, Connecticut • London, England

Library of Congress Cataloging in Publication Data
Main entry under title:

Select documents on the constitutional history of the
  British Empire and Commonwealth.

  (Documents in imperial history, ISSN 0749-4831 ;
no. 1-)
  Includes index.
  Contents: v. 1. "The Empire of the Bretaignes",
1175-1688.
  1. Commonwealth of Nations—Constitutional history—
Sources.   2. Great Britain—Colonies—Constitutional
history—Sources.   3. Great Britain—Constitutional
history—Sources.   I. Madden, Frederick.
II. Fieldhouse, D. K. (David Kenneth), 1925-   .
III. Series: Documents in imperial history ;
no. 1, etc.
KD5025.S45   1985   342 '.029 '09171241   84-21213
                       342.22909171241
ISBN 0-313-23897-9 (lib. bdg. : v. 1)

Library of Congress Catalog Card Number: 84-21213
ISBN: 0-313-23897-9
ISSN: 0749-4831

First published in 1985

Greenwood Press
A division of Congressional Information Service, Inc.
88 Post Road West, Westport, Connecticut 06881

Printed in the United States of America

10 9 8 7 6 5 4 3 2 1

CONTENTS

xviii   Contents

PREFACE

In the last days of empire, in a period when that very word is fraught with emotional response - often (if not always) ignorant and ill-judged - and when fashion tends so overwhelmingly to concentrate narrowly on the ideologies of the last half century of decolonisation, it is right and necessary for Commonwealth historians to consider once more (and perhaps fully, even for the first time) the whole impressive record of eight hundred years of English experience of imperial rule: Norman-English indeed at first, though later the Welsh, Scots and Irish made substantial contribution as rulers or colonists to the operations of colonial machinery of government. For that rich experience did not of course begin with a United Kingdom in 1800 - or indeed a Great Britain in 1707; nor even (as traditionally supposed) still a century earlier with the East India or Virginia companies. Indeed, when governmental instruments had to be found for the distant provinces of a New World, the Crown's servants, lawyers and clerks, looked obviously and inevitably to the earlier precedents they had at hand in what had been - until the loss of Calais - an English medieval empire in the British Isles and Western Europe.

For what is the characteristic nature of an *imperial* government? The exercise of rule from a metropolis over outlying frontiers. At its root it is concerned with distance. But distances are of course in no way absolute: they may be reduced by technological progress in communication or emphasised fitfully by the relative strength of character, resolve or resource of ruler or frontiersmen. There will always be a difference - maybe a disjunctive delay or blurred understanding - between what the metropolis proposes and what the frontier tolerates: central intention will be eroded by local circumstances. In a sense this same phenomenon is common to all government: it is not otherwise in the continuing dialogue between federal and provincial authorities, or between capital and district. The source of legitimate power may nominally be central, but the facts and the reluctance to comply, stubbornly local. The tension inherent in this separation of power exists in a United Kingdom as it does in an Empire. What distinguishes an *imperial* rule from other forms of government is not therefore a matter of kind, but only of degree. Distance to Dublin, Durham or Cornwall may have been considerably shortened, but once upon a time they were virtually beyond the king's writ: the time then taken by a royal command was comparable with that which in later centuries complicated rule across the Atlantic or half way round the world. So in looking closely at the beginnings of imperial experience we are thrust back into the many centuries before Elizabethan adventurers looked away from continental Europe beyond Ireland to America. And both contemporary administrators and later pamphleteers saw the relevance of that pre-Elizabethan experience and used it.

The dominant and perennial problem so characteristic of
imperial government, then, concerns how the metropolitan power,
attempting to expand its rule over remote regions, can secure an
acceptable, if changing, balance between *imperium* and *libertas*:
that is, between central unity and local autonomy; or between
similarity and diversity, assimilation and autochthony, authority
and justice, interdependence and independence *etc*. If there were to
be an empire, if a kingdom's responsibility were extended hopefully
(if maybe vainly) to increase stability, security or opulence, there
was clearly a need for some common purpose, estimated naturally in
the interest of the realm but identified (in a paternal imperial
way) as government for the good of all, not just the few: but this
impulse was matched by a realisation that imperial rule would be
impossible without some colonial cooperation and collaborators, who
could insist on their own terms for any contract or partnership,
which inevitably would mean a considerable degree of self-government
on the frontier. So centuries before Balfour in 1926 put the two
words side by side into a single phrase to describe 'dominion
status', there was need to embrace both 'freedom' and 'association'.
This is the theme that runs through these volumes: a continuing,
organic evolution as policy and institutions responded and adjusted
to challenge and need. The first English empire saw the Crown,
sometimes tactically afforced by Parliament, trying to secure some
authority on outlying parts of the British Isles as well as on the
continent of Europe. Then in the first British empire in America
there was an empire of settled plantations, conceived in discontent,
self-exile, and disobedience to regimes in the realm, where imperial
authority was diluted by distance, where local aspiration challenged
central instructions, and where confrontation finally drifted into
secession and war. Certainly from that experience the lesson was
learnt that unity did not mean uniformity, that conformity was
improbable, that authority could not be enforced, and that
differences had to be tolerated as inevitable. In the second
British empire, taken up 'in a fit of absence of mind' after 1783,
there developed an unintentional dichotomy between a number of
diverse conquests under crown colony government (as devised by
Carleton for Quebec) and in the deep freeze of trusteeship (as
propounded by Burke for India) on the one hand, and several settled
colonies moving, with Canada as pioneer and pacemaker, to full self-
government in a pattern maybe similar to, but not identical with,
Westminster. A third British empire, or a first Commonwealth, emerged
of self-governing colonies (since 1907 called Dominions) moving towards equality of status but (like the pigs in *Animal Farm*) still
unequal in function with Britain; and finally after the Second
World War a second Commonwealth (like its predecessor largely the
creation of Dominion leaders): a multi-racial association of fully
sovereign nations, nominally equal now in function as in status, but
where independence and responsibility have often proved to be unreal
and elusive among an increasing welter of small states, frustrated
by both lack of power and resources.
        In this volume of our collection of documents illustrative of
the priorities, devices and frustrations in the British experience
of imperial government, we have brought together some of that
earlier evidence which is so fundamental to its understanding. We

could of course have shown similar phenomena and problems in still
earlier, ancient empires, or other rival, alien ones: the ubiquity
of the alternatives of 'direct' or 'indirect' rule, the thwarting
of metropolitan policy by local 'civil disobedience', or the bland
assumptions of the imperial capital being questioned, put aside,
neglected, evaded or resisted on the frontier: indeed, the very
unreality of empire and of imperial tyranny - for rule over 'dependencies' - was often no more than a fictitious aspiration, a grand
illusion, kept alive by a mutual conspiracy of metropolitan ministers and colonial élites.

    The historiography of European colonial empires has tradition-
ally concentrated on four major themes: why colonies were acquired;
how they were governed; how their economic life was regulated;
and why they eventually won(or were granted)independence. The relative
importance given to each of these has varied from one time to
another, reflecting in part some contemporary preoccupation with
different aspects of the problem of empire. But if political
scientists and publicists are thus influenced by changing fashion,
historians must remain firmly dedicated to learn what happened, and
to understand and clarify what they observe. It is no argument to
suppose that, since in the aftermath of decolonisation so much of
the political systems and constitutional forms of empire was
destroyed, the study of the governments provided by metropolitan
powers is unworthy of careful research: it matters not, historic-
ally, that many of these institutions and usages were apparently
written on the sands and were obliterated by the tide. Again,
though it is natural that in the retreat from empire new successor
regimes should reject colonial precedents, disclaim any debt to the
historical past, and assert indigenous root and origin for their
institutions and practices - for any brave new world must be seen
to be liberated and autochthonous -, it must not cloud the vision
of the political analyst to observe that there is a considerable
degree of legal and constitutional continuity between the imperial
past and the post-independence present. Just as in a sense the new
federal United States was heir in the 1780s to the practical balance
of power between capital and colony in the Old Colonial System, so
too, as the years since the moment of freedom roll by, we can see
much of the same old patterns of government persisting. Whatever
they may proclaim, by no means have all new states broken the
continuity of constitutional and legal evolution (which is the main
theme of these volumes): and some of the most important of them
(the United States and India among them) still carry the imprint of
a British approach to government and law. This continuity may
indeed have little to do narrowly with empire as such; but where
there is a sense of assurance in what is known and a premium on
pragmatic convenience, it has a great deal to do with history.
Where the possible options, which are available in political
science and constitutional engineering to deal practically with a
persistent problem within a national society, are limited, then it
is not surprising that similar devices will be used.

    The case then for studying the constitutional history of the
British empire (along with that of other one-time imperial systems)
remains as strong as ever. This collection may reveal something of
the remarkable variety and wealth of the imperial experience of a

European off-shore archipelago with its many dependencies; it
stands firmly in its own right as a theme of compelling and
fascinating absorption. Indeed, whatever the present situation or
passing fashion, imperial history can only be properly interpreted
on the basis of the closest understanding of public law and
institutions in Britain and her colonies for this, more than any
other single factor, remains the essence of formal empire. Commercial systems - mercantilism, free trade, neo-mercantilism - might
come and go as economic forces or intellectual fashions changed.
Attitudes to the imperial mission also had their secular and
cyclical fluctuations. But as long as it remained a British dependency, a colony had to be seen in some way to be provided with a
government, and a system of recognised law had to be administered.
To settler, native and British official alike the institutions
through which these obligations were fulfilled and the principles
on which government was based were critical for the very life of
the colony. It is not surprising then that most of the great
issues and crises in British imperial history - the American
revolution, the granting of responsible government in the mid-
nineteenth century, the federation of groups of colonies, the
gradual transfer of power in tropical possessions during the
twentieth century - were all constitutional in character, nor that
so much of the contemporary archives, pamphlets and historical
literature on empire should have been concerned with these overriding problems. Temporarily unfashionable as they may perhaps be,
constitutional issues must always remain (as they were) central to
the study of the history of the changing relationship of Britain
and her erstwhile possessions.
      Constitutional history within an imperial context has a
unique character which makes it both more difficult and demanding
and at the same time intrinsically more interesting than that of a
single autonomous state. This is because every principle and practice was the product of at least three forces - one British,
another imperial, the third specific to the individual colony.
Some of the literature recognises this fact, though often it makes
assumptions with hindsight about the evolution of the contemporary
British constitutions which are not warranted: but the main
difficulty has always been to get the balance of these forces right.
There are indeed several dimensions which have to be borne in mind
when studying the constitutional history of any one dependency:
the stages of evolution of British constitutional convention and
usage which conditioned any new form of colonial government (for
after all the metropolis could hardly grant what was not yet opera-
tional and tested at home); the direct influence of British
authority and domestic political pressures on the colony; those
forces within the colony which gave its institutions and laws a
unique character, even if they had come originally from a common
imperial stock; and the external influence of contemporary practices and developments in other British possessions, and (in the
twentieth century) the allegedly 'world view' of empire in the
League or United Nations. Historiographically the greatest weight
has normally been given either to a broadly imperial, or to a
colonial viewpoint: there has been little consideration of the
others, either because the relevance of the stage of the contem-

porary British constitution has been forgotten or dismissed as too
complicated a tangle to unravel, or because multilateral comparative
influences from other dependencies would make the narrative too
complex. In the literature generated after a colony has achieved
independence the outlook has tended to be narrowed further by a
zenophobic 'funnel vision', so that one gains the impression that a
particular colony existed in a vacuum locked in isolated constitutional combat with the metropolis. This has become more evident
recently with the balkanisation of imperial history into area,
regional, continental, or more absurdly 'Third World', history. But
even in mature ex-colonies like Canada and Australia, departments of
history regard with evident pride their ignorance of the parallel
histories of other colonies within the common imperial experience.

It is one primary aim of this collection of documents to
establish a better balance between these several forces. The documents have been chosen and arranged thematically, so that at every
stage ideas, policies and actions emanating from England are balan-
ced by those evolving in individual colonies; and by setting together evidence on many of those colonies which shared similar problems, it is intended to show how much was in common between them and
how much experience in any one of them might affect others. Obviously
it would not be economic of space to print at length almost identical
documents for all or most of the colonies. But it is hoped that by
judicious selection this collection may for the first time demonstrate the true relationship between constitutional developments and
ideas in Britain, individual colonies and the empire at large.

The other main purpose of these documents is to make available
material which has not previously been published or which is not
readily available except in specialised libraries or printed collections with a limited, often regional, focus. Well-known and often
used material which is central to the subject has, of course, been
included; but most of the material is either taken from manuscript
sources or from comparatively rare publications. The main technical
problem was to decide how much material to print concerning any one
theme or territory. At one extreme it was important not merely to
illustrate arbitrarily chosen themes with appropriately over-selected
extracts: it was essential to provide enough evidence to demonstrate
points conclusively, and this has involved including some roughage.
We have also attempted to include as much evidence as possible relating to individual colonies so that the collection could be used for
the study of the autonomous constitutional history of many dependencies. At the other extreme we were faced by the problem of length:
to have reproduced any larger proportion of the many filing cabinets
of material we collected would have been beyond the possibilities of
modern publication. The result is necessarily a compromise. It
might have seemed convenient to cover the whole topic in a single
volume, but this would have involved selecting and truncating documents to the point at which they could no longer speak for themselves. We have therefore planned a series of four volumes, each
dealing with a coherent period and theme, and we have tried to exercise a firm self-discipline in selection, requiring every document
or clause to justify itself. The first volume considers the origins
of the English colonial empire, mainly in the Americas, to about 1688,
placing particular emphasis on the early English origins of imperial

constitutional principles and practices. The second will deal with
the period 1689 to 1783, ending with the independence of the United
States, but excluding material on new colonies acquired in and after
1763. The third will cover the period 1763 to about 1870, concentra-
ting on the development of the 'second British empire'. A final
volume will provide material on the years 1870 to 1931, concluding
with the Statute of Westminster on the ground that vastly more
material is already available in print on the following half century.
That there must be these divisions into separate volumes is a cause
for regret. On the contrary we hope that we have demonstrated that
the First, the Second or the Third Empires, the First or Second
Commonwealths should not be studied in segregated isolation but that
the whole process – alive, resilient, changing – has been a *continuum*
of evolution: not torn fragments, but a seamless garment.

     A final comment is necessary on the principles adopted in
annotating the documents. It is arguable that, if the material is
selected with sufficient care, it should tell its own story and that
editorial comment may even mislead. While we accept the validity of
this argument we decided that fairly detailed annotation was desirable on two grounds. First, there is at present (until AFM provides
one, as is a necessary part of this project) no reasonably detailed
general constitutional history of the British empire to provide
background information and interpretative comment. Second, since
many of the concepts reflected in the documents are unfamiliar, it
seemed essential to provide sign-posts whenever necessary. We have
therefore often included short introductory notes to many sections
of the documents to indicate the broad themes to which they relate,
and some extensive footnotes both to clarify the points at issue and
to provide background facts. If we have succeeded, this collection
should be capable of being used independently by anyone who has at
least a preliminary knowledge of the history of the British empire
and Commonwealth.

     At the moment when formal empire is coming to an end with forty
eight full Members of the Commonwealth having achieved independence
and only a handful of small almost irreducible colonies left, it is
opportune to demonstrate and document the wealth of this imperial
experience. For AFM this work constitutes over a quarter of a century of research, copying, collection, editing, cutting and annotation. DKF, less immediately involved, has provided an indispensable
external eye, and has imposed a disciplined structure and severe
surgery on what has been collected. We hope that the volumes which
should emerge from Greenwoods over the next few years will prove useful in revealing something of the richness of the quarry in which we
have worked and will encourage others to continue to research therein.

                                                          A.F.M.
                                                          D.K.F.

     In making transcripts from the documents we have attempted
largely to retain spelling and capitalisation to preserve something
of the flavour of the originals, but punctuation has often been
modified to make understanding easier. The translations are largely
mine. For research assistance in a few fat years we are grateful to
the Leverhulme Trust, the Beit Fund and the Oxford University's
Higher Studies Fund: for painstaking help in collecting documents I
wished to include in this first volume I must thank Audrey Martin
and Janet Clarke for copying and typing extracts in Bodley, the

British(Museum)Library and the Public Record Office in days before
the xerox machine: for fair typing of the butchered extracts and
explanatory notes, Lyn Yates, Audrey Skeats - and my wife, Margaret
(who also laboured devotedly with the proofs) -; and for undertaking
the formidably exacting, and disciplined, responsibility of producing
camera-ready copy for the publishers, our daughter Janet. Much more
than the token acknowledgment should be given to the staffs of the
Public Record Office, of the British Museum, of the Bodleian, the
Widener and Congress libraries and most particularly of Rhodes House
where once I was an assistant librarian. Volumes in preparation for
some thirty years would never have been published without the concern
and initiative of Professor Robin Winks, Master of Berkeley College,
Yale; nor without generous grants for the typing of this work by the
Administrators of the Beit Fund, the Rhodes Trustees, the British
Academy and Nuffield College.

My debt must also be readily admitted to R.L. Schuyler's
Parliament and the Empire (1929) and to Julius Goebel's 'Matrix of
Empire' in J.H. Smith's *Appeals to the Privy Council* (1950) which
pointed me so fatally in the direction demonstrated in the first
sections of this first volume and added some half-a-dozen years to
my own research. In pursuit of such clues, I am well aware that I
have strayed into unfamiliar, even sacred, groves. Medieval historians may well wince at what may seem to them an insensitive projec-
tion backwards of modern concepts and words alien to their usage or
meaning - not least 'imperial' or 'colonial' - and the rehearsal of
plausible similarities which they cannot accept as precedents: my
only excuse is that later pamphleteers used them (often quite inac-
curately) as ammunition in their polemics: indeed, they blazed a path to
an exclusive zone, into which in ignorant innocence I have trespassed.
Any student of colonial America will recognise what my footnotes owe
to those two great American historians, C.M. Andrews and H. Osgood,
who opened up that subject with such magisterial largeness of mind
over so many individual colonies: they gave a lead which I am proud
to have followed. Vincent Harlow, Kenneth Robinson, Nicholas
Mansergh, Richard Southern, Geoffrey Elton, Jack Gallagher and
Michael Brock supported me with their belief in the importance of
this mammoth project; Sheila Fieldhouse and Gowher Rizvi always had
confidence that we would one day find a publisher. Finally, I would
like to record my thanks for a final correction of proofs to Sir
Edgar Williams who has supervised my written work with so sharp an
eye for verbal infelicities for almost fifty years; and my lasting
debt to the late Sir Kenneth Wheare, our mutual friend, who encouraged me to resist specialisation and to use any time, spare from
teaching as Reader in Commonwealth Government, to tackle the enormous span and rich variety of the Commonwealth experience of rule
in the very broadest historical dimension.

A.F.M.
August 1984

ABBREVIATIONS

Add.MSS.	Additional Manuscripts (B.M.)
Adm.	Admiralty archives (P.R.O.)
Amer. Ant. Soc.	American Antiquarian Society
A.G.	Attorney General
A.P.C.	Acts of Privy Council (Colonial)
B.	Baron of Exchequer Court
B.M.	British (Museum) Library
Bull., I.H.R.	Bulletin, Institute of Historical Research
C.B.	Chief Baron of Exchequer Court
Cal. Pat. Rolls	Calendar of Patent Rolls
C.S.P.	Calendar of State Papers (Colonial, or Ireland)
Ch.	Chancery records
C.J.	Chief Justice; or Commons' Journals
Coll.	Collections
C.O.	Colonial Office archives (P.R.O.)
C.P.	Common Pleas
H.M.C.	Historical Manuscripts Commission
Hist. Rev./Stud.	Historical Review/Studies
Journ. Jam. Ass.	Journal of Jamaican Assembly
J.C.P.C.	Judicial Committee of Privy Council
J.P.B.	Jersey Prison Board, report and evidence, 1891
K.B.	King's Bench
L.C.	Lord Chancellor
L.J.	Lords' Journals
L.O.	Law Officers (A.G. & S.G.)
Mass. Hist. Soc.	Massachusetts Historical Society
N.Y. Hist. Soc.	New York Historical Society
Parl. Hist.	Parliamentary History (debates)
Parl. Rolls	Parliamentary Rolls
P.C.	Privy Council archives (P.R.O.)
Proc.	Proceedings
P.R.O.	Public Record Office (London)
Rot. parl.	Rotuli parliamentorum
S.G.	Solicitor General
St. T.	State Trials
St. of R.	Statutes of the Realm
Treas.	Treasury archives
Y.B.	Year Book

BIBLIOGRAPHICAL NOTE

Most of the documents previously in print and quoted here from the
Calendar of State Papers (Colonial), the Acts of the Privy Council
(Colonial) *etc*; from J.R. Bartlett (ed.) *Records of...Rhode Island
and Providence plantation* (1856-); J.R. Brodhead (ed.), subsequently
E.B. O'Callaghan, and then B. Fernow, *Documents relative to the
colonial history...of New York* (1856-); W.H. Browne (ed.) *Archives
of Maryland* (1883-); C.J. Hoadley (ed.) *Records...of New Haven*
(1857-); S.M. Kingsbury (ed.) *Records of the Virginia Company*
(1905-); W.L. Saunders (ed.); *Colonial records of North Carolina*
(1886-); N.B. Shurtleff (ed.) *Records of the governor and company
of Massachusetts Bay* (1853-) and *Records of New Plymouth* (1856-)
J.H. Trumbull (ed.) *Public records of...Connecticut* (1850-); and
W.A. Whitehead (ed.) *Documents relating to...New Jersey* (1880-);
also from the Massachusetts Historical Society, *Collections* (1806-)
and *Proceedings* (1879-) and the New York Historical Society,
Collections (1811-) and from the selections in W. Macdonald's
Select Charters (1899) and F.N. Thorpe's *Federal and State
Constitutions* (1909) have been taken from, and checked with, the
manuscripts themselves; but for the convenience of those who wish
to consult the whole document where we have had space to print only
an extract, we have generally given reference to the main published
source which, though long since out of print, is still more readily
available in libraries than the original.

I. THE CONSTITUTIONAL FOUNDATIONS OF EMPIRE

(A) PRECEDENTS AND MODELS WITHIN THE BRITISH ISLES

Before ever any Elizabethan adventurer set foot in the New World there were five centuries or more of precedents stored away in the minds and archives of English officials. Issues had been joined, questions asked, expedients tried, a system found; and such experience was hardly irrelevant in the subsequent history of the British empire. The history of governance overseas began near at home both in the British Isles and indeed on continental Europe: the English medieval empire was the seedbed of forms used later. To inheritance of dominions outside the realm of England (and these included the pre-Conquest Norman empire of the Channel Islands) were added by marriage, inheritance, conquest and plantation, an empire not only in France, consisting of Anjou, Aquitaine and Gascony, but on the perimeter of England in Ireland, Wales and the Isle of Man. Though all the continental possessions were lost to the English Crown (Calais last of all) by the mid-sixteenth century, the traditions and usages deriving therefrom passed into British colonial practice in the modern period.

First, it was established that the monarchy was unitary and that 'dominions' were possessions of the Crown of England. Secondly, these dependencies might retain their own laws and customs, except in so far as common law, ordinance, or statute might be imposed on them by the authority of the realm. Thirdly, both the king-in-council and the king-in-parliament might legislate for 'dominions' though in fact it was usually the king (with or without the advice of his council) who did so. But Acts of the English Parliament, in which they were not represented, could bind the subjects in 'dominions' and indeed tax them. Though few did, many Acts purported to do so and some seem to have been obeyed. Fourthly, the king in council could hear appeals from his dominions and indeed often did so.

Nevertheless, it had also been established that on the frontier, almost beyond effective control, 'dominions' in march and palatinate possessed a considerable amount of sturdy local self-government with legislatures of their own. It was government at a distance and on

the cheap. It was politic to leave local issues to local men. The
Crown could grant or revoke power, could check its use (as by *quo
warranto*), and could assert its remedial jurisdiction.   To distant
marcher lords or prelates, (such as the bishop of Durham on the
Scottish border), to merchants overseas in Flanders or Calais ,(in
identical phrases to those to guilds in England) it could delegate
powers of self-government.   Nominally at least ,local legislation
might be at times subject to royal initiative (as under Poynings'
Law in Ireland), but more probably to royal veto.   For the most part
the Crown, not wishing to get directly involved, was content to exercise some supervision only.   In practice local autonomy would depend
largely on the relative strength or resolution of the king, the
marcher lord or the local leaders in the frontier provinces: and
inevitably this might be dominated by the distance between the metropolis and the 'dominion'.

    Thus, long before 1600 England had a colonial system in embryo.
Moreover, she had experience of the crucial dilemma of imperial
government: how to secure a reasonable and inexpensive balance
between central unity and local diversity, between interdependence
and independence, between a continuing association and freedom.

    For a fuller discussion of the significance of the documents in
this introductory section, see F. Madden,'1066, 1776 and all that':
the relevance of English medieval experience of 'empire' to later
imperial constitutional issues-in *Perspectives of Empire* ed. J.
Flint and G. Williams (1973).

(1) PARLIAMENT AND THE DOMINIONS

    Probably the most important, and subsequently controversial, con-
stitutional principle concerning the relations between England (after
1707 Great Britain and after 1801 the United Kingdom) and the'dominions' of the Crown outside this 'realm' was that the English
Parliament claimed unlimited authority over them, even though they
were not represented in it.   This principle was challenged from time
to time by the Irish, Americans and others on various grounds: but
normally that the existence of a local legislature in these dominions and the absence of their representatives at Westminster inhib-
ited Parliament from passing laws relating to their domestic affairs.
The documents in this section are intended to illustrate the later
claim that, from at least the thirteenth century, Parliament had
been involved in the exercise of the right to legislate for all dominions of the Crown,even though these might have been permitted
subordinate legislatures and irrespective of whether they sent representatives to the house of commons.

    Perhaps there should be a note of caution in the study of these
documents.   It is true they constitute the substance of the precedents used, and indeed abused, by later pamphleteers in the debate on
metropolitan power in the seventeenth and eighteenth centuries.   But
the attempt to divide the authority of Parliament and Crown is anachronistic: and the divisions made here in these first two sections
could be misleading.   Later protagonists used medieval precedent

as precept for their own time or cause: this is as true of Coke as
of Darcy, Mayart or Molyneaux or of Otis, Wilson or John Adams. But
it should be remembered that until some time in the fifteenth century
all legislation was formally in the king's name, though he might
claim the advice and assent of Parliament and 'bills' technically
long remained petitions for the king's consent. Many things were
done in Parliament which were not done by Parliament: what the king
had power to do, with or without the advice of the council, might
however have more apparent and effective authority if done in the
presence of Parliament. In other words,it may for long have been
the power of the king which was being exercised in these statutes;
with Parliament only as the convenient channel of expressing that
authority.

1. (a) ORDINANCE FOR THE COLLECTION OF THE 'NEW CUSTOMS' UPON WOOL
        etc, EXPORTED FROM ENGLAND, IRELAND AND WALES, 1275.[1]
   In the new custom, which is granted by all the magnates
of this realm and at the request of the commonalty of
merchants of all England, it is provided that in each
county - in the largest town of which there is a port -
there be elected two of the most loyal and most powerful
men who shall have charge of one part of the seal,and one
man who will be designated by the King shall have another
part,and they shall be sworn loyally to receive and answer
for the King's money: namely half a mark[2]from each sack
of wool[3]and half a mark from each 300 [*wool*] fells that
make a sack, and one mark from each last of hides which
will leave the kingdom in Ireland and in Wales as well

---

1. F. Palgrave (ed.) *Parl. Writs* I.1: Rot.fin. 3 Ed.I m.24d. Trans
from French. This ordinance, made in an unwontedly full and representative 'parliament', imposed new duties on exports from
England and from the dominions of Wales and Ireland. By agreement
with communities of merchants Edward I was replacing the 'new'
customs of 1266 which had been widely opposed, by this more satisfactory and rewarding substitute whereby duties were paid in London
and thirteen other ports to local officials under the supervision of
royal financial advisers. Presumably these duties would be passed
on to the foreign buyers. Though the ordinance was an expression
of royal authority, the presence of so many representatives assenting thereunto was a symptom of the new understanding between the king
and merchants in pursuit of a common 'national' policy. What the
Crown had power to do, it had power to do more effectively in
Parliament, and this included the imposition of taxation. Neither
Wales nor Ireland were yet annexed to the realm of England. Nevertheless the Statute of Merchants (1285) and the Ordinance of the
Staple (1326) were applied to Ireland and ordinances were sent by
the king and council in 1293, 1323 and 1325. The Statute of Merchants expressly included Ireland: '*par tut sun reaume de Engleterre
e de Irlaunde*' (13 Ed.I stat.3) without any suggestion that ratification was necessary by the Irish Parliament.
2. One mark was 13s. 4d. or 66p.
3. i.e. 26 stone or 364 lbs.

as in England within and without franchise. Moreover in
each port out of which ships can go there shall be two
honest men sworn not to permit wool, [*wool*] fells or
leather to leave without letters patent under the seal
which shall be [*kept*] at the chief port in the same
county ....

1. (b) WRITS TO THE JUSTICIAR RELATING TO THE COLLECTION IN IRELAND
OF THE 'NEW CUSTOMS', 25 May 1275.[1]
    The King to his trusty and well beloved Galfridus
[*Geoffrey*] de Genvill, Justiciar of Ireland, greeting.
We send you the form for a grant freely made to us by
the archbishops, bishops, abbots, priors, counts, greater magnates and the whole commonalty of our realm, of
half a mark on every 300 wool fells and one mark on
every last of hides exported from our kingdom of England
as well as our land of Wales....
    [Another writ of the same day specified that 'These moneys are
    to be collected in every port of our land of Ireland both out-
    side the liberties and within them by our agents and bailiffs
    who are to have sealed authority to do so from the magnates
    signing the grant'.]
    And since we wish that the aforesaid customs may be
granted to us and collected in our land of Ireland in
like manner, we command you to require (by what manner
seems to you expedient) that the archbishops, bishops,
abbots, priors, counts, magnates and the commonalty of
merchants of the said land[2], grant to us similar customs
in the prescribed form for the same land.
    We send you Luke of Lucca and his merchant partners
from Lucca [and certain Florentine merchants] whom we have
appointed our agents in all matters relating to the collection and expenditure of the aforesaid customs in the
said land, and whatever seems fitting under the authority of our seal to do shall be done....
    [The justiciar was to give all assistance and advice in the
    collection of the customs 'as they or certain attorneys of theirs
    may indicate to you in our name. You are also to inform us as
    soon as possible how you have carried out our orders'.][3]

1. *Parl. Writs.*I p.1 (No.3 & 4). Trans. from Latin.   If the king
in parliament in England could impose customs duties on 'dominions'
- and there is evidence that they were collected forthwith (*Cal.
docs. rel to Ireland,*ed.H.S. Sweetman *1254-84,*p.243; *1285-92,*p.9)
- the consent of the chief prelates, magnates and merchants in
Ireland might in practice seems desirable.   A similar procedure
was used in 1285 to extend the Statutes (I & II) of Westminster
and Gloucester.   Sometimes an Irish Parliament positively confirmed English statutes (e.g. in 1320, 13 Ed.II cap.2).
2. Twelve Irish magnates were in attendance at the Parliament in
Westminster: a reminder that by encouraging petitioners to come to
his parliaments from his 'dominions', Edward I was already making
the English Parliament 'imperial'.
3. One of the first calls on the revenues obtained was for the king's

2. (a) NAVIGATION ACT, (5 Rich.II St.1 cap.3) 1381
   Item, to increase the navy of England which is now
greatly diminished, it is assented and accorded That
none of the King's liege people do from henceforth ship
any merchandise in going out or coming within the realm
of England in any port, but only in ships of the King's
liegance[1] [on pain of forfeiture of merchandise to the king.][2]

2. (b) NAVIGATION ACT, (14 Rich.II cap.6) 1390.
   Item, That all merchants of the realm of England
shall freight in the said realm the ships of the said
realm and not strange ships; so that the owners of the
said ships take reasonable gains for the freight of the
same.

2. (c) NAVIGATION ACT, (32 Hen.VIII cap.14) 1540.
   Forasmuch as it is evidently and notoriously knowen
that the most parte of this our soveraine lorde the
Kinges realme of Inglaund and the confynes and dominions
of the same is and ben compassed and invironed by and
with the grete seas, so that neither the kinges liege
people and subjects of this his said realme nor yet anny
other of anny foren realmes or Countries can or may convey or transporte their Wares, goodes, marchaundises and
commodities into and from the said realm alongest the
said sees but only by shippes, And where the Navy or
multitude of Shippes of this realme in tymes past hath
ben and yet is verie profitable, requisite, necessarie
and comodiouse as well for the entercourse and concurse
of marchaunts transporting and conveying their wares and
marchaundises as is above said, and a greate defence and
suerty of this realme in tyme of warre as well to offend
as defende, and also the maynetenance of many maisters,
maryners and seemen making them expert and coniving in
the arte and science of shippmen and sayling, and they,
their wifes and children have had their lyving of and by
the same, and also hathe ben the chief mayntenance and
supportacion of the Cities, Townes, villages, havens and
creekes nere adjoyning unto the see coastes, and the
King's subjectes,bakers, bruers, butchers, smythes,
ropers, shipwritters, taillours, showemakers and other
vitallers and handycraftes men inhabiting and dwelling
near unto the said coastes have also had by the same a
greate parte of their lyving,...
   [and since the navy was in decay, ships needed repair, and men
   were unemployed and impoverished, and statutes 5 Rich.II St.1

Welsh war (*ibid.1285-92*, pp.35 ff.300).
1. The following year an Act (6 Rich.II St.1 cap.8) provided that,
where no English ships were available, others might be used. Nevertheless, Parliament was already showing concern for the navigation
of the realm.
2. One-third was to be paid to the informer.

cap.3; 6 Rich.II St.1 cap.8;   4 Hen.VII cap.10 and 23 Hen.VIII
cap.7 had been neglected, these Acts were now confirmed and would
be enforced: freight rates <u>in the realm and its dominions</u> were
laid down, goods carried for aliens in English ships would have
preferential rates and those using foreign ships would pay
higher rates.]

3. (a) CALAIS REVENUES ACT, (1 Hen.V cap.9) 1413.[1]
     [Although by ordinance and statute Edward III and Richard II
had assigned all royal revenues within the town and marches of
Calais to the maintenance of that dominion, the security of the
realm itself, no less than the upkeep of that town, had been
endangered by subsequent grants 'by divers letters patent to
divers persons' for reduction of, and even exemption from, rent.]
     ...Our Lord the King, wishing to eschew such damage
in time to come, with the advice and assent aforesaid and
at the request of the said Commons, wills and has ordained and established That all the letters patent made to
captains, and any other persons whatsoever of all manner
of rents, lands, tenements, customs, fisheries as well
as of any other revenues, profits and commodities whatsoever in the said town and marches as of the offices of
collectors of all rents, customs, revenues, profits and
commodities to them thereof made before this time against
the ordinances aforesaid, be entirely revoked and annulled and that the said revenues, profits and commodities
be resumed into the hands of our said Lord the King and
expended upon the upkeep of the payments and charges
belonging to the said town and marches....

3. (b) CALAIS STAPLE ACT, (2 Hen.VI cap.4) 1423.[2]
     Item, whereas the noble King Edward the Third did
ordain his staple to be at Calais, and that the whole

---

1. Trans from French. In 1536, when negligence had again caused
alarm over the decay of the defences of Calais, a further statute
(27 Hen.VIII cap.63) provided for the observation of certain detailed ordinances for its administration, provisioning and defence.
Burgesses were to be elected to Parliament. Calais was referred to
in the preamble as 'one of the mooste pryncipall treasours to this
Realm of England as well for his defense of this his Realm and of
the narowe Sees whereof his royal Majestie is...Lorde and Kyng, as
also for the spedy and sure Passage of all his subjects havyng
entercourse of Marchandyse or otherwyse travaylyng in to the Dominions of Foreyne Prynces and Potentates'. Calais was a conquered
dominion from which the native inhabitants had been removed. The
ability to speak English was a necessary qualification for certain
posts and professions.
2. A 'staple' (the word used first in English here) was a place
appointed by the Crown in which a body of merchants were thereby
to enjoy the exclusive right to purchase certain goods for export.
These staples could be in England; as, for example, when in 1353
Edward III had named ten English towns (together, incidentally, with
Carmarthen, Dublin and three other Irish ports) and had provided

repair of wools, woolfels, leather, lead, tin, butter,
cheese, and other merchandise, except woolen cloths, and
red herring, passing out of the realm of England, and his
lands of Wales and Ireland, and his town of Berwick upon
Tweed, should be at the said town of Calais[1] [and subsequent
statutes of Richard II, Henry IV and V had confirmed Calais as the
site of the staple] ....

Nevertheless, the leather, and founded tin, called
shoten tin, bought and provided here in England, have not
been brought to the said staple of Calais, after the form
of the said statutes, but doth pass into Flanders, Holl-
and and Zealand to the great damage and diminishing of
the customs and subsidies due to the King, if they were
brought to the town of Calais. The King, willing to
eschew the damage and diminution, by the advice and
request aforesaid, hath ordained and established, That
all the statutes thereof made and not repealed, be holden
and kept, and put in due execution. And that the whole
repair of wools, woolfels, leather, lead, whole tin, and
shoten tin and all other merchandise pertaining to the
staple, passing out of the realm of England, and of the
countries of Wales, and Ireland, be at the said place of
Calais, and at none other place beyond the sea, as long
as the said staple shall be at Calais, upon pain of forfeiture of the very value of the merchandises, which shall
pass elsewhere but to the parts towards the west, named
in the said statutes thereof made. And that no licence
from henceforth be granted to the contrary: except for
wool, fells, and leather of Northumberland, Westmorland,
Cumberland and the bishoprick of Durham, saving the King's
prerogative....

4. (a) ACT IN RESTRAINT OF APPEALS, (24 Hen.VIII cap.12) 1533.[2]
Where by divers sundry old authentick Histories and
Chronicles, it is manifestly declared and expressed, that

---

regulations for their government and commerce. The word came to
mean the authorised place for a trade, a depot or a factory; and
later by transference, the main commodity dealt with by a particular
company, port or colony.
1. Calais had been made in 1348 the foreign staple for certain
goods. In 1363 the staple in wool - 'the sovereine merchandise'
of the realm - was established there under the Company of Merchants
of the Staple; though, at various periods since, that monopoly
had been withdrawn due to the strength of merchant opinion in
England which was at times in favour of keeping the staple in the
realm itself.
2. In 1536 the 'pretended power and usurped authority of the bishop
of Rome' was extirpated by statute (28 Hen.VIII cap.10) 'out of
this realm and other his Grace's dominions'. Parliament was again
legislating beyond the realm, claiming to exclude papal authority
from the 'dominions'.

this realm of England is an Empire,[1] and so hath been
accepted in the World, governed by one supreme Head and
King, having the Dignity and Royal Estate of the Imperial
Crown of the same; unto whom a body politic, compact of
all sorts and degrees of people... be bounden and owe to
bear next to God a natural and humble obedience; ...
In consideration whereof [i.e. the delays incurred by the hearing of appeals in Rome] the King's Highness, his Nobles and
Commons...doth therefore by his royal assent and by the
assent of the Lords spiritual and temporal and the Commons in this present Parliament assembled, and by authority of the same, enact...That all causes, testamentary,
causes of matrimony and divorces, rights of tithes,
oblations and obventions...within this realm or within
any of the King's dominions or marches of the same or
elsewhere,...shall be from henceforth...determined within
the King's jurisdiction and authority and not elsewhere....

4. (b) ACT OF SUPREMACY, (26 Hen.VIII cap.1) 1534.
    Albeit the King's Majesty justly and rightfully is
and oweth to be the supreme head of the Church of England,
and so is recognised by the clergy of this realm in their
Convocations; yet nevertheless for corroboration and confirmation thereof...Be it enacted by the authority of
this present Parliament...That the King our Sovereign
Lord, his Heirs and Successors, Kings of this Realm,
shall be taken, accepted and reputed the only supreme
Head in Earth of the Church of England, called *Anglicana
Ecclesia*; (2) and shall have and enjoy, annexed and united
to the Imperial Crown of this Realm, as well the Title
and Stile thereof, as all Honours, Dignities, Preheminences, Jurisdictions, Privileges, Authorities, Immunities,
Profits and Commodities to the said Dignity of supreme
Head of the same Church belonging and appertaining....

---

1. In defying the Papacy and challenging the authority of the Holy
Roman Emperor (Charles V, nephew of Catherine of Aragon) Henry VIII
was persuaded that history validated a claim for Britain to be an
empire: a state recognising no superior.   Had not the emperor
Constantine been the son of a British princess and was not he
proclaimed emperor in Britain?   Was there not some evidence that
King Arthur had a seal engraved with the title *imperator*?   If the
Holy Roman Empire could claim such a title, then certainly, with
its new sense of national confidence and territorial expansion on
the perimeters of England, Britain could also.   'The empire of the
Bretaignes' was a phrase too in Ralegh's prayer, though by its
reference to the 'attendant daughter islands about her' presumably
he meant Ireland, Man and the Channel Islands [see section 4, below].
    It might be noted that in the aftermath of the successful assert-
ion of their independence from Britain, some Americans referred to
'the American empire' which they had established. 'The United
States, in the minds of its revolutionary founders, was born an imperial republic': see R.W. Van Alstyne, *The American Empire* (1960).

5. LEATHER EXPORTS CUSTOMS ACT, (27 Hen.VIII cap.14) 1535.[1]

Where great Quantity and much Abundance of Leather is daily conveyed out of this Realm, as well by Strangers, as also by Tanners, and other the King's Subjects, inhabited in divers Parts of this Realm, towards the Sea Coasts, and in specially out of Wales[2] Cheshire and Cornwal, where little or no Custom is paid for the same, which Leather is commonly packed by the said Strangers, Tanners and other the King's Subjects in their Houses, and so conveyed into the Ports and Havens where they intend to ship the same; which Packs, so conveyed and brought to such Ports and Havens to be shipped, be never there unpacked, to be viewed what Number of Leather is contained in any such Pack, but entered in the Customers Books by and upon the Information and Report of the said Strangers, Tanner or other Person, Transporter of the same Leather; (2) and albeit that the King's Highness in such Places and Ports hath very little Custom paid for the same, yet forasmuch as in such Places there is no better Search nor View had for the perfect Knowledge of the Number and Quantity of the Leather so by them packed, the King's Grace is much deceived of such his Customs as sought therefore to accrue to his Highness ....

[In London the counting and weighing of hides exported was supervised and controlled, but the evasion of customs in Wales, etc. meant both lower and unfairly competitive prices and greater overseas exports from these areas.]

Be it enacted...That from henceforth no manner of Stranger or Denizen shall pack, or cause to be packed, any manner of Leather to be conveyed or shipped over the Sea, out of this Realm, Wales, or other the King's Dominions, otherwise than in this Act is expressed, that is to say, that all such Leather shall be hereafter packed by a Packer sworn in every such Port where any Leather shall be shipped to be conveyed out of this Realm, Wales, or other the King's Dominions, upon Pain of Forfeiture of all such Leather as hereafter shall be packed contrary to the Purport of this Act, or of the Value thereof; (8) and also that from henceforth every Stranger and Denizen, which shall ship, send or convey any Leather over the Sea, out or from any Port of this Realm, Wales, Cheshire, or other the King's Dominions, shall pay like Custom for the same as is used to be paid within the Port of London, that is to say, every Stranger to pay for every Dicker[3] of Leather for Custom *iv.s.ix.d.* and every Denizen *iv.s.i.d.*....

---

1. Similarly in 1566 by 8 Eliz.I cap.3, Parliament made it an offence to export live sheep from the 'realm of England, Wales or Ireland or out of any of the Queen's Highness dominions'.
2. Wales was annexed to the realm of England in 1536 [see below No.89a].
3. i.e. 10 hides.

6. TITHES ACT, (27 Hen.VIII cap.20) 1535.

(3)...That every of his subjects of this realm of
England, Ireland, Wales and Calais, and marches of the
same, according to the ecclesiastical laws and ordinances
of this church of England, and after the laudable usages
and customs of the parish or other place where he dwell-
eth or occupieth, shall yield and pay his tythes, offer-
ings and other duties of Holy Church:...

7. ACT CONCERNING THE USE OF CROSSBOWS AND HANDGUNS, (33 Hen.VIII
cap.6) 1542.[1]

[Since inconveniences had been caused by these weapons their
use was strictly regulated.]

XXIII. Provided always, and be it enacted by the authority aforesaid, That this present Act, nor anything
therein contained, shall in any wise extend or be prejudicial unto the King's subjects resident or inhabiting near
unto the coasts of the sea, in any part of this realm,
their houses being not above five miles distant from the
said coasts; (2) nor also to any of the King's said
subjects inhabiting within twelve miles of the borders
of Scotland;[2] (3) nor to any of the King's subjects inhabitants of the town and marches of Calais; (4) nor to
any of the inhabitants of the isles of Jersey, Guernsey,
Anglesey and the isles of Wight and Man; (5) but that it
shall be lawful for every of these said inhabitants at
all times hereafter to have, exercise and use their handguns, hagbuts and demi-hakes, of the length abovesaid,
within the limits and isles above said, so that, it be
at no manner of deer, heron, shovelard, pheasant, part-
ridge, wild swine or wild elk, or any of them: this
present Act or any thing therein contained to the contrary notwithstanding.

8. ACT TRANSFERRING THE ISLE OF MAN FROM CANTERBURY TO YORK,
(33 Hen.VIII cap.31) 1542.

The diocese of Chester, and the diocese of Man in the
isle of Man,[3] shall be united to the province and archbishoprick of York, and shall be dissevered from the
archbishoprick of Canterbury....

---

1. This Act has been used in support of the case that Parliament
cannot legislate without local assent for the Channel Isles; but
that it expressly excluded the Borders, coastal areas and off-
islands seems rather to argue strongly that Parliament was making
these exemptions specifically for defence purposes in 'frontier'
regions, and that its power to bind these areas by its statutes was
undoubted.
2. This section was partly repealed by 4 Jac.I cap.1
3. The Isle of Man, a fief of the Crown of England granted to the
Stanleys by Henry IV, was not part of the realm. But Parliament
settled the question of succession in 1610 and re-invested the government of the island in the Crown in 1765: it claimed therefore
to be able to bind a dependency of the Crown if it were expressly

9. ROYAL STYLE AND TITLES ACT, (35 Hen.VIII cap.3) 1544.
   Where our most dread natural and gracious Sovereign
Leige Lord the King hath heretofore been, and is justly,
lawfully and notoriously known, named, published, and
declared to be, King of England, France and Ireland,
Defender of the Faith, and of the Church of England, and
also of Ireland, in Earth Supreme Head: and hath justly
and lawfully used the Title and Name thereof, as to his
Grace appertaineth: Be it enacted...That all and singular
his Grace's Subjects and Resiants, of or within this his
Realm of England, Ireland, and elsewhere within other his
Majesty's Dominions, shall from henceforth accept and
take the same his Majesty's Stile, as it is declared and
set forth in Manner and Form following, that is to say,
in the Latin Tongue by these Words, *Henricus Octavus Dei
Gratia, Angliae, Franciae & Hiberniae Rex, fidei Defen-
son, & in terra ecclesiae Anglicanae & Hiberniae
supremum Caput*; and in the English Tongue by the Words,
Henry the Eigth, by the Grace of God King of England,
France and Ireland, Defender of the Faith: and of the
Church of England, and also of Ireland, in Earth the
Supreme Head: And that the said Stile, declared and set
forth by this Act, In Manner and Form as is above-
mentioned, shall be from henceforth, by the Authority
aforesaid, united and annexed for ever to the Imperial
Crown[1] of his Highness Realm of England....

10. ACT REPEALING ANTI-PAPAL LEGISLATION, (1 & 2 Phil. & Mary cap.8)
                                                           1554.[2]
   ...II We, the Lords Spiritual and Temporal and the
Commons, assembled in this present Parliament, representing the whole body of the Realm of England, and the dominions of the same[3]....

11. ACT OF SUPREMACY, (1 Eliz.I cap.1) 1559.
   ...That where in Time of the Reign of your most dear
Father, of worthy Memory, King Henry the Eighth, divers
good Laws and Statutes were made and established, as well
for the utter Extinguishment and putting away of all
usurped and foreign Powers and Authorities out of this
your Realm, and other your Highness Dominions and Countries,[4] as also for the restoring and uniting to the
Imperial Crown of this Realm, the ancient jurisdictions,

---

named in a statute [see section 4 (e) below].   1.cf.No.4 (a).
2. i.e. all statutes passed against the see of Rome since the twentieth year of the reign of Henry VIII.
3. Note that the English Parliament was again claiming to represent,
and to legislate for, both realm and dominions.[Contrast the wording in the Acts of 1649: No.211 below.]
4. The Irish Parliament provided for similar oaths to the Queen as
'supreme governor' the following year (2 Eliz.I cap.1).[See also
the earlier Act of 1537, p.108 below.]

authorities, superiorities and pre-eminences to the same
of right belonging and appertaining ....
    [Parliament repealed 1 & 2 Phil. and Mary cap.8. which had
    restored such powers to the Pope, and revived 23 Hen.VIII cap.9,
    24 Hen.cap.12 etc. against such external authority.   The Crown
    was invested with its 'ancient jurisdiction over the estate
    ecclesiastical and spiritual within these your realms of England
    and Ireland, or any other your Highness' dominions or countries',
    and 'all foreign powers repugnant to be same' were 'clearly
    abolished out of this realm and all your Highness' dominions for
    ever'.   All clerics, judges, mayors and royal officials within
    the realm or dominions had to take an oath to the Queen as
    'supreme governor' of the realm and dominions in matters spiritual.
    Anyone writing, printing, teaching, or expressing a defence of
    papal authority would for a second offence incur the pains of the
    Statute of Provision and Praemunire (16 Rich.II cap.5).][1]

12. TONNAGE AND POUNDAGE ACT,(1 Jac.I cap.33) 1604.[2]
    [Since kings of England had 'tyme out of mind' been granted
    subsidies by Parliament for the defence of the realm 'and the
    keeping and safeguards of the Seas for the intercourse of Merch-
    andize safelie to come into and passe out of the same', and
    Parliament desired such 'furniture' to be kept in readiness for
    the speedy suppression of invasion,]
    ...Wee doe give and graunte to you our Supreme Liege
Lorde and Soveraigne, one Subsidie called Tonnage: That
is to say, Of everie Tonne of Wine that is or shall come
into this Realme or any your Majesties Dominions by way
of Merchandise, the summe of Three Shillings...;   And
alsoe one other Subsidie called Poundage, That is to say,
Of all manner of Goods and Merchandise of everie Merchant
Denizen and Alien caried or to be caried out of this

---

1. In 1563 5 Eliz.I cap.1 - due to dangers 'grown to marvellous Out-
rage and licentious Boldness' - the defence of papal authority was
made treasonable for a first offence for 'any Person or Persons
dwelling...within this Realm or within other the Queen's Dominions,
Seignories or Countries or in the Marches of the same or elsewhere
within or under her Obedience and Power'. Statutes to retain subjects in due obedience (23 Eliz.I cap.1) , against Jesuits (27 Eliz.
I cap.2) and against recusants (35 Eliz.I cap.2) were among many of
those which included reference to the 'dominions'. So too did the
Act of Uniformity (1 Eliz.I cap.2) e.g. §ii and §xiv : on the significance of this statute for the religious issues in Quebec,see below
Vol.III.
2. Similarly in 1641 by 16 Car.I cap.8, tonnage and poundage was
imposed on the realm and dominions by Parliament. The statutes
requiring thanksgiving to God every 5th of November (3 Jac.I cap.1)
and punishing profanation of Sundays by sports and pastimes (1 Car.I
cap.1) explicitly included 'the realm of England and the dominions
of the same'. That Parliament claimed to legislate and to impose
taxes does not, of course, imply that such statutes were enforced.

Realme or any your Majesties Dominyons, or to be brought
into the same, by way of Merchandize, of the Value of
everie Twentie Shillings of the same Goods and Merchandize, Twelve Pence....

(2) THE ROYAL PREROGATIVE AND THE DOMINIONS

In the subsequent history of the Empire, the prerogative authority of the Crown, fundamental to control of its dominions, was second
only to that of the omnicompetent sovereignty of king-in-parliament.
The prerogative was that special power which enabled the king to
perform his function of governing: it was granted to the king by
the law of the realm and permitted expressly for that purpose. In
earlier centuries of course (as we have noted) Parliament itself was
also a means of expressing royal power and indeed derived from it.
Long after its prerogative had been curtailed or canalised in internal affairs at home, the Crown remained the supreme source of authority overseas.

These documents illustrate the establishment of the supremacy of
the king's jurisdiction as 'sovereign lord over all'; the Crown's
right to delegate powers of jurisdiction to admirals or government
to merchants, and to supervise foreign commerce and external policy;
and its right to question the use of (and to resume) powers delegated. It should also be noted that.even before 1607, there were
several important assumptions which concerned the prerogative power:
that, where there was doubt about the extent of the prerogative, it
could be defined by the judges in the courts of common law and could
be both defined and extended by an Act of the king-in-parliament;
that the need for flexibility in the continuous problems of government required that the king should have exceptional (and emergency)
powers, including the right to legislate by proclamation (with or
without the advice of his council[1]); that, though he might constitutionally exercise a dispensing power, he could not disregard, overrule or repeal a statute; that his actions must be consistent with
the law as it stood; and that any delegation (by grace) of powers
to individuals or groups - commissions, letters patent etc - derived
from the king's personal prerogative as sovereign.

13. (a) STATUTE OF MARLBOROUGH, (52 Hen.III cap.19) 18th November
1267.[2]

    ... None from henceforth except our Lord the King
shall hold in his Court any plea of false judgement,

---

1. The notion of the king-in-council was, indeed, somewhat illusory
before the Restoration. The Statute of Proclamations (31 Hen.VIII
cap 8), asserting that, 'those same shall be obeyed, observed and
kept as though they were made by Act of Parliament', referred to such
legislation as being made 'with the advice of his honourable Council';
but the councillors were mentioned as a means of enforcing the king's
legislative will, - a device which proved cumbersome; and the Statute
was repealed after eight years without effect (it would seem) on the
use, legality or number of proclamations.
2. The conquest of England by the duke of Normandy meant no sudden

given in a Court of his tenants; for such plea specially
belongs to the Crown and dignity of our Lord the King....

13. (b) STATUTE OF WESTMINSTER I, (3 Ed.I cap.17) 1275.
   [There was provision for recovery of beasts impounded in castles
   or fortresses and for punishing those guilty of such a crime
   'where the King's writ lieth.']
   (8) And if that be done in the Marches of Wales or in
any other Place where the King's Writs be not current,
the King who is Sovereign Lord over all, shall do right
there unto such as will complain.[1]

13. (c) STATUTE OF GLOUCESTER, (6 Ed.I cap.1) 1278.[2]
   Whereas the Prelates, Earls, Barons and others of
the Kingdom, claim to have divers Franchises, for the
Examination and Judgement whereof the King had appointed
a day to the said Prelates, Earls, Barons, and others:
It is provided and granted with one accord, that the
aforesaid Prelates, Earls, Barons, and others, may use
such sort of Franchises, so that nothing accrue to them
from..Usurpation or Occupation, and that they occupy nothing against the King, until the next coming of the King
through the County, or the next coming of the Justices
in Eyre for Common Pleas...And hereof Writs shall be
issued to the Sheriffs, Bailiffs and others, in Behalf
of every Demandant; and the Form of the Writ shall be
changed according to the Diversity of the Franchises
that each man claimeth.

---

break in the laws which were observed. William I, though Conqueror,
claimed his new kingdom by right of descent which was accepted by the
Witan. He emphasised the continuity of his succession by accepting
the existing customary laws (Mercian, West Saxon, Danish, Jutish, *etc.*)
and the shire, hundred and manorial courts. He confirmed the Laws of
Edward the Confessor – perhaps because Norman-Frankish law was in no
importable, codified form. But the mark of the Norman conquerors
became evident in time by the greater centralisation and greater eff-
iciency of government, the clarification of tenures, the assertion
of the king's direct and dominant overlordship, the emphasis on security and military service, and the process of surrender and regrant.
   These three statutes illustrate the establishment of the supremacy of the king's jurisdiction in the realm.
1. i.e. appeals would lie to the king from the marches which lay
beyond his writ.
2. This section of the statute illustrates the use and the origin of
the *quo warranto* writ, some of the uncertainties of which were further cleared up in 1290 (18 Ed.I). The Statute of Westminster II
(13 Ed.I) was also expressly a continuation of this Statute of
Gloucester: it provided that no man should depart without remedy
from the king's court (cap.50). There are many examples of *quo
warranto* cases in Bracton's Note Book (e.g. No.241,268,862,1111,
1119) and in*Placita de Quo Warranto temporis Edw.I,II and III in
Curia receptae Scaccarii West . asservata*(1818) e.g. William and
Alice Latimer of Sutton, Sneton and Potton (p.2).
   For the voiding of the Virginia charter in May 1624, and the
difficulty of employing the *quo warranto* process against Massachus-

And the Sheriffs shall cause to be commonly proclaimed throughout their Bailliwicks, that is to say, in
Cities, Boroughs, Market Towns and elsewhere, that all
those who claim to have any Franchises by the Charters
of the King's Predecessors, Kings of England,or in other
manner, shall come before the King or before the Justices
in Eyre, at a certain day and place, to shew what sort of
Franchises they claim to have, and *by what Warrant* ....

14. *CHARTERS TO MERCHANTS OVERSEAS*:
  (a) LETTERS PATENT FROM EDWARD III TO THE MERCHANTS OF THE
                 STAPLE IN FLANDERS, 1 July 1359.[1]
  [The king 'after careful consideration with the magnates and
  others of our Council' had reversed an earlier ruling (Statute
  of Staples, 1354) whereby wool merchants could not engage in the
  export trade. However, they then alleged that they were suffering financial hardship, owing to the debasement of the Flanders
  coinage and the loss of their earlier franchises in the towns
  there; and the king initiated negotiations with these towns. As
  a result the Count of Flanders had issued new provisions, by the
  common assent of his county, and particularly at the request of
  the citizens of Bruges,]
  ...that they may have and use under the jurisdiction of
a Governor, all the franchises and liberties they used
to have in time past, notwithstanding that the staples
are in addition separated from the said country of Flanders and placed in our said kingdom of England...And we
have consequently given leave and power to our said merchants by our letters patent to last as long as it pleases us, to elect among themselves a suitable Governor
whenever it shall please them and it is necessary to hold
among themselves in the town of Bruges their meetings and
assemblies to the end that they may have and enjoy their
franchises and privileges, thus granted to them again by
the Count of Flanders, in such a manner that neither
amidst their assemblies and meetings nor for any other
cause shall our said staples established in our said
kingdom of England be in any way disturbed, debased or
impaired; and that no ordinance or communal regulation
shall be made by the aforesaid Governor and company in
the said town of Bruges or elsewhere to interfere with
our merchants or their apprentices or servants that they

---

etts in 1681-3, see below Nos. 168, 281 and 284.
1. W. Cunningham, *The growth of English industry and commerce*...
(1890) I App.pp. 544-5 Trans from French. The staple established at
Bruges in 1341 had been awarded by statute to foreign merchants in
1354 at a time when English exporters had insufficient capital and
the king's credit was poor. Nevertheless within the next few years
English merchants had crept back into the staple trade and virtually
dominated it once more. In 1363 it was moved to the more convenient
port of Calais : [see above No.3].
The Crown was hereby granting limited rights of self-government to
merchants overseas.

may not freely and peacefully sell and buy their goods
at whatever time it shall please them and to whatever
person, where they shall best see their profit without
interference or hinderance from anyone....

14. (b) LETTERS PATENT FROM EDWARD III TO THE MERCHANTS OF THE
                        STAPLE AT CALAIS, 1 March 1363.[1]
    ... Know that we, by the assent of the bishops, mag-
nates and others of our Council, have ordained that the
staple of wool and other merchandise which are exported
out our realm of England and our lands of Wales, Ireland
and Scotland, be held at our town of Calais and that
twenty-six English merchants[2]...may be there to govern
the town, the people and the goods which are sold there;
and that the said twenty-six English merchants may consist of two mayors and twenty-four aldermen by whom the
citizens and others who sell at the said town may be
received and governed; and that they may constitute
among themselves a commonalty and have a common seal and
have power to make such ordinances as they wish....
    That the heirs of the mayors, aldermen and burgesses
who thus dwell in and shall inhabit the said town and
eskyvynage[3], born in our dominion there, shall be accepted as heirs denizen of England, and shall enjoy their
inheritances in the said realm of England as if they had
been born in England, by descent or remainder, or by
whatever other way they may hold the right to their said
inheritances; and also that the heirs of the said mayors,
aldermen and burgesses, born in England, shall have their
inheritances in the said town and eskyvynage, and elsewhere in our dominion there, in the manner aforesaid, and
that descent of lands, tenements and rents, and of mov-
ables, shall be determined and used there according to
the law of England.
    We will grant that the said mayors and aldermen, or
four, three, or two of them,chosen and appointed by the
said mayors and aldermen by their common consent, may
and shall have power to hold pleas before them concerning
debts, accounts, covenants and contracts, according to
the law merchant, and also concerning arson, felonies,
mayhems and trespasses, however committed, as well on
land as at sea, in the said town, eskyvynage, and port,
and elsewhere outside our dominion; and concerning fines
and recognizances of lands, rents and tenements, in the
said town and eskyvynage, according to the laws of England, or the custom of the country; and that they may,

---

1. Rymer's *Foedera* (1830) Vol.III pt.ii,p.690. Trans from French.
In H. Knighton's *Chronica* (IV.2626) it was stated that the merchants
were to provide six men-at-arms and four archers. They were to
collect the *maletote* on leather, wool and woolfells exported, and
for each woolfell they were to collect 40d. for the defence of Calais.
2. These were named in the patent.
3. i.e.bailiwick - the area under an échevin(French alderman).

by virtue of their offices, without other warrant, inquire, hear and determine, as well at our instance as at
the instance of a party, all manner of legal points and
disputes which are to be investigated in eyre of justices,
or at our bench in England, in the aforesaid places;....
and on this [*recognizance of debt*] they may draw up letters of
obligation according to the manner of the *Statutes of
Merchants* in England,[1] and to have them enforced, in all
our dominions, according to the law of the staple in
England....
    We will that all the merchants, whether of our own
nation, or foreigners, coming to and staying in the said
town of Calais with their goods, shall be under the government and jurisdiction of the said mayors and aldermen,
to give franchises and liberties to foreign merchants for
their sojourn with their merchandise in the said town....

> [In cases of crimes committed against burgesses or their ser-
> vants, the case was to be brought before the mayors and aldermen,
> to be tried by good loyal men, 'according to their laws and
> usages'. Where the offence concerned denizens, or denizens and
> foreigners, and was committed within the franchise, the trial was
> to be by denizens. Where it concerned foreigners and denizens,
> and was committed outside the franchise, the trial was to be half
> by denizens and half by foreigners, before the mayors, aldermen,
> and authorities of the place where the crime was committed.]

14. (c) LETTERS PATENT FROM HENRY IV TO THE MERCHANTS IN HOLLAND,
                  ZEALAND, BRABANT, AND FLANDERS, 5 February 1407.[2]
    Henry, by the grace of God King of England and France
and Lord of Ireland, to all to whom these present letters
shall come, greeting.
    Know ye that, Whereas, according as we are informed,
through want of good and discreet rule and government,
sundry damages, strifes, oppressions and wrongs oftentimes
heretofore have been moved and committed among the merchants of our kingdom of England, and of other of our dominions, remaining and sojourning in the parts of Holland,
Zeland, Brabant and Flanders, and in whatsoever other
parts beyond the seas being in amity with us, and greater
hereafter (which God forbid) are feared to be like to
fall out, unless we speedily put to our helping hands for
the procuring of better government to be maintained among
the said merchants, We, heartily desiring to prevent the
perils and dangers which are like to fall out in this
case, and that the said merchants and others which travel
out of our said realm and dominions into the parts aforesaid may justly and faithfully be ruled and entreated, Do
will and grant, by the tenor of these presents, to the
said merchants, that they may freely and whensoever they
please, assemble in some convenient and fitting place,
where they shall think good, and that they may choose and

---

1. 11 Ed.I St.1 and 13 Ed.I St.3 (1283 and 1285).
2. C.P. Lucas, *The beginnings of English overseas enterprise* (1917)
pp. 184-7.

elect among themselves certain sufficient and fit persons
for their Governors in those parts at their good liking;

And furthermore we give and grant to the said Governors which are in such sort to be chosen by the aforesaid
merchants, as much as in us lieth, special power and
authority to rule and govern all and singular the merchants our subjects remaining in those parts and which
hereafter shall come and repair to those parts, either by
themselves or by their sufficient deputies, and to do
unto them and every one of them in their causes and quarrels whatsoever, which are sprung up or shall hereafter
spring up among them in the parts aforesaid, full and
speedy justice....

And, by the common consent of the aforesaid merchants
our subjects, to make and establish statutes, ordinances
and customs as shall seem expedient in that behalf for
the better government of the state of the said merchants
our subjects,

And to punish reasonably according to the quantity of
their offence in that behalf all and singular the merchants our subjects which shall withstand, resist or disobey the aforesaid Governors so to be chosen, or their
deputies, or any of them, or any of the aforesaid statutes, ordinances and customs....

And furthermore, by the tenor of these presents, we
straitly command all and singular the aforesaid merchants
our subjects, that they attend, advise, obey and assist,
as it becometh them, the said Governors so to be chosen,
and their deputies, in all and singular the premisses and
other reasonable things, which any way may concern in
this behalf their rule and government....

14. (d) LETTERS PATENT FROM HENRY VII TO THE MERCHANT ADVENTURERS
AT CALAIS, 28 September 1505.[1]

...whereas we have been credibly informed that for
default of good, saad[2] and politique Rule and Governance
divers harmes, dissensions and greeves between the said
Merchants Adventurers repairing, conversant and abedeing
at our Towne of Calays and in the parts of Holland,Zeland,
Brabant, Flanders and other places abroad...Wee...Give
and graunt unto our said Merchants Adventurers Power,
Licence, Libertie, and Authority That they as often and
whensoever it shall please them shall meete freely and
lawfully in places convenient and honest within our said
Towne of Calais and Marches of the same when it shall
please them; Assemble themselves and then elect and
choose a Governor or Governors of themself at their Libertie and pleasure. And also at the election of such
said Governor or Governors to choose name and appoint

1. G.Cawston and A.H.Keene, *The early chartered companies* (1896),
pp.249-54.
2. (also 'sadd') meaning 'wise'.

Four and Twenty of the most sadd, discreet and honest
Persons of divers Fellowships of the said Merchants
Adventurers, and the same Foure and Twentie to be called
and named foure and twenty Assistants to the said Governor or Governours....

    [The governor and assistants were given 'full power and auth-
ority To make.... Statutes, Ordinances and Customs'.]

15. *ADMIRALTY JURISDICTION*:
   (a) ACT DEFINING THE EXTENT OF ADMIRALTY JURISDICTION
               (13 Rich.II St.1 cap.5) 1389.[1]

   Item, Forasmuch as a great and common Clamour and
Complaint hath been oftentimes made before this Time, and
yet is, for that the Admirals and their Deputies hold
their Sessions within divers Places of this Realm, as
well within Franchise as without, accroaching to them
greater Authority than belongeth to their Office, in prejudice of our Lord the King, and the common Law of the
Realm, and in diminishing of divers Franchises, and in
Destruction and impoverishing of the common People; it
is accorded and assented, That the Admirals and their
Deputies shall not meddle from henceforth of any thing
done within the Realm, but only of a Thing done upon the
Sea, as it hath been used in the Time of the noble Prince
King Edward, Grandfather of our Lord the King that now
is.

15. (b) ACT FURTHER DEFINING ADMIRALTY JURISDICTION
                      (15 Rich.II cap.3) 1391.[2]

   [In response to the 'great and grievous Complaint of all the
Commons' against the encroachment by the Admirals,]
   ... it is declared, ordained and established, That of

---

1. The system of admiralty courts (implied, for example, in the later
Navigation Act of 1696, § 6) had existed at least as early as the
mid-fourteenth century. With the inadequacy of the common law
courts to deal with piracy, with the increase in the volume of foreign trade, and with naval victory at Sluys in 1340, the Crown had
granted jurisdiction to royal officials, particularly (and more effectively) admirals, to deal with piracy and disputes in coastal waters
which had many similarities with civil law. The fact that common law
was not used and there were no juries led to the unpopularity of
admiralty courts.
   The series of statutes included here illustrate limitations being
imposed on this prerogative jurisdiction by the king-in-parliament.
   This Act, sub-titled 'What things the Admiral and his Deputy shall
meddle', sought to define and limit the area of admiralty jurisdiction, and to prevent encroachments on the vested interests of borough,
manor and royal courts. For admiralty cases in the fourteenth century, see R.G. Marsden, *Court of Admiralty: select cases...*(1894) and
also more generally his *Documents relating to the law and custom of
the sea* (1915) and F.R.Sanborn,*The origins of early English maritime
and commercial law* (1933).
2. This Act, though more precise than that of 1389, still contained

all Manner of Contracts, Pleas, and Quarrels, and all
other Things rising within the Bodies of the Counties,
as well by Land as by Water, and also of Wreck of the
Sea, the Admiral's Court shall have no manner of Cognizance, Power nor Jurisdiction; but all such manner of
Contracts, Pleas, and Quarrels, and all other Things
rising within the Bodies of Counties, as well by Land
as by Water, as afore, and also Wreck of the Sea, shall
be tried, determined, discussed, and remedied by the Laws
of the Land, and not before nor by the Admiral, nor his
Lieutenant in any wise. Nevertheless, of the Death of a
Man, and of a Mayhem done in great Ships, being and hov-
ering in the main Stream of great Rivers, only beneath
the Bridges of the same Rivers nigh to the Sea, and in
none other Places of the same Rivers, the Admiral shall
have Cognizance, and also to arrest Ships in the great
Flotes for the great Voyages of the King and of the
Realm; saving always to the King all Manner of Forfeitures and Profits thereof coming; And he shall have also
Jurisdiction upon the said Flotes, during the said Voyages only, saving always to the Lords, Cities, and
Boroughs their Liberties and Franchise....

15. (c) ACT AGAINST PIRACY (27 Hen.VIII cap.4) 1535.[1]
     Where Pirates, thieves, robbers and murtherers upon
the sea, many times escape unpunished because the trail
of their offences hath heretofore been ordered before
the Admiral or his Lieutenant or Commissary after the

---

no penalty for breach of its provisions and the admirals ignored it.
Not until 1400 (2 Hen.IV cap.11) were statutory penalties prescribed.
However, during the fifteenth century with the internal Wars of the
Roses and the loss of naval supremacy, piracy again increased; and
not until the Tudors - and Henry VIII in particular - did the creation of a more powerful navy give a new effectiveness to admiralty
courts. Furthermore, the peace with France after 1526 provided the
opportunity for renewed efforts against pirates in the Channel.
1. This statute provided that cases should be tried not by civil but
by common law, to secure more convictions. The 'commissaries' were
becoming known as 'vice-admirals of the coast' and in 1536 the first
formal patent as 'vice-admiral' was issued by the Crown to William
Gonson for the coasts of East Anglia. His courts dealt variously
with quarrels, wrecks, salvage, trespass, confiscations, obstruction
of havens and fairways, and breaches of fishing custom and rights.
     But in the early seventeenth century the growth of admiralty
jurisdiction became once more a grievance. It was indeed one of the
issues which Sir Edward Coke, a champion of the common law, pressed
against the civil lawyers. The system and the issues were exported,
nevertheless, to the New World. To secure fishing rights and national trade monopolies the vice-admiralty jurisdiction was a recognised
weapon: a beginning was made as early as 1615 when the attempt to
extend it to Newfoundland was included in a royal charter. See
H.J. Crump, *Colonial admiralty jurisdiction in the seventeenth
century* (1931).

course of the civil laws, the nature whereof is that
before any judgement of death can be given against the
offenders either they must plainly confess their offence
(which they will never do without torture or pains)...
or else their offences be so plainly and directly proved
by witnesses indifferent, such as saw their offences
committed which cannot be gotten but by chance at few
times because such offenders commit their offences upon
the sea and at many times murther and kill such persons
... which should bear witness against them in that
behalf...[and because common seamen could not easily be brought to
testify 'without protraction of time and great cost', Be it enacted]

That all such offences done in or upon the sea or in
any other haven, river, or creek where the Admiral or
admirals pretend to have jurisdiction, shall be inquired,
heard and determined in such shires and places in this
realm as shall be limited by the King's Commission to be
directed for the same in like form and condition as if
such offences had been done upon the land, and that such
Commissions shall be had under the King's Great Seal
directed to the Lord Admiral or Admirals or to his or
their Lieutenant, deputy or deputies and to three or four
such other substantial persons as shall be named by the
Lord Chancellor...to hear and determine such offences
after the common course of the laws of the land used for
felonies done and committed within this realm....
    [The procedure of trial by jurors from the shire, of judgement
    and forfeiture of property was prescribed.]

16. SIR THOMAS SMITH ON THE PREROGATIVES OF THE CROWN, 1565.[1]
    The Prince whom I nowe call...The Monarch of England,
King or Queene, hath absolutelie in his power and authoritie of warre and peace, to defy what Prince it shall
please him and to bid him warre and againe to reconcile
himselfe and enter in league or truce with him at his
pleasure or the advice onely of his privie counsell.
His privie counsell be chosen also at the Prince's pleasure ....
    [from the nobles, knights and esquires whom he consulted daily
    or when weighty matters of the realm required]
The Prince doth participate to them all or so many of
them as he shall thinke good, such legations and messages
as come from forren Princes, such letters or occurentes as
be sent to himselfe or his secretaries, and keepeth so
many ambassades and letters sent unto him secret as he
will....In warre time and in the field the Prince hath

1. *De republica Angelorum*, 1583 (Facsimile Amsterdam 1973) pp.43-7.
Sir Thomas Smith had been professor in civil law at Cambridge, had
served as a diplomat and followed William Cecil as secretary of state
briefly in 1572:[no relation to his namesake who had interests in
the Levant, Virginia, the East Indies and Ireland]. *De republica
Angelorum: the maner of government, or policie of the Realme of
England* was first published in 1581 and had allegedly been 'compiled'
by Smith almost twenty years earlier; but it has been also ascribed

also absolute power so that his worde is a law; he may
put to death or to other bodilie punishment whom he shall
thinke so to deserve, without processe of lawe or forme
of judgement.   This hath been sometime used within the
Realm before any open warre in sudden insurrections and
rebellions, but that not allowed of wise and grave men...
[who believed that only 'present necessitie' would justify punishment not 'done by order of lawe'.] This absolute power is called
martial law [which must be used when time and place prevented due
process and required speedy execution.]
     The Prince useth also absolute power in crying and
decrieing the mony of the realme by his proclamation
onlly....
          [It was stamped with his image and title: he determined
     its weight and form].
     The Prince useth also to dispence with lawes made,
whereas equitie requireth a moderation to be had and
with paynes for transgression of lawes where the payne
of the lawe is applied onely to the Prince.   But where
the forfeite (as in popular actions[1] chaunceth many times)
is part to the prince, the other part to the declarator,
detector or informer, there the prince doth dispence for
his owne part onely.   Where the criminall action is intended by the inquisition[2] (that maner is called with us
at the Prince's suite) the Prince giveth absolution and
pardon....The Prince giveth all the chiefs and highest
offices or magistracies of the realme, be it of judgement or dignitie, temporall or spirituall and hath the
tenthes and first fruites of all ecclesiasticall promot-
ions, except in the universities and certain colledges
which be exempt.   All writs, executions and commaund-
ments be done in the Prince's name, [though there had been
exceptions in times past in the palatines and marches].... The
supreme justice is done in the Kinges name and by his
authoritie onely.   The Prince hath the wardship and first
marriage of all those that hold landes of him in chiefe
And also the government of all fools naturall or such as
be made by adventure of sickness and so continue, if they
be landed....
     Diverse other rights and preeminences the Prince hath
which be called prerogatives royalles or the prerogative
of the king, which be declared particularly in the books
of the common laws of England.   To be short the Prince is
the life, the head and the authoritie of all thinges that
be done in the realme of England.   And to no Prince is
done more honour and revenue than to the King and Queen
of England.... [The prince was spoken to and served bareheaded

---

to William Stafford who published *A discourse on the common weal* also
in 1581.
1. i.e. actions by private informers against those who violated the
penal statutes.
2. i.e. inquest by a grand jury

'in reverence and kneeling',]   This is understood of the subjects of the realme;   for all strangers be suffered there
and in all places to use the maner of their countrie such
is the civilitie of our nation....

17. *BATE'S CASE*, November 1606.[1]
   Fleming (C.B.):   To the King is committed the government
of the realm and his people;   and Bracton saith that for
his discharge of this office God has given to him power,
the act of government and the power to govern.   The King's
power is double, ordinary and absolute, and they have
several laws and ends.   That of the ordinary is for the
profit of particular subjects, for the execution of civil
justice, and determining of *meum* ;   and this is exercised
by equity and justice in ordinary courts, and by the
Civilians is nominated *jus privatum*, and with us Common
Law: and these laws cannot be changed without Parliament,
and although that their form and course may be changed
and interrupted, yet they can never be changed in substance.   The absolute power of the King is not that which
is converted or executed to private use, to the benefit
of any particular person, but is only that which is applied to the general benefit of the people and is *salus
populi* ;   as the people is the body and the King the head;
and this power is *[not]* guided by the rules which direct
only at the Common Law, and is most properly named policy
and government;   and as the constitution of this body
varieth with the time, so varieth this absolute law
according to the wisdom of the King for the common good;
and these being general rules and true as they are, all
things done within these rules are lawful.   The matter in
question is material matter of State, and ought to be
ruled by the rules of policy;   and if it be so, the King
hath done well to execute his extraordinary power.   All

---

1. 2 St.T. 389ff.   The Crown's heavy - and not always carefully con-
sidered-expenses (including the colonisation of Ireland), the large
annual deficit on existing revenues, the parsimony of the Commons
and their attack on feudal dues and monopolies, prompted James I to
follow the advice of his lord treasurer, Robert Cecil, and increase
impositions: additional customs duties, over and above tonnage and
poundage, which in the protection and regulation of trade, was an
undoubted and essential part of the Crown's prerogative in foreign
affairs.
   John Bate refused to pay the additional imposition on currants on
the grounds that it was non-parliamentary taxation.   Previously such
duties had been paid by non-members to companies (first the Venetian,
then the Levant) which paid an annual grant to the Crown for their
monopoly patent.   But these companies had failed and impositions had
continued to be levied on currants imported.   There is no doubt that
Bate had no case in law: both Popham and Coke accepted the decision
against him in the Exchequer Court as just, but the *dicta* seems to
give wide powers to the Crown.   Fleming was chief baron of the court
of exchequer: [see also p.30].

customs, be they old or new, are no other but the effects
and issues of trade and commerce with foreign nations;
but all commerce and affairs with foreigners, all war and
peace, all acceptance and admitting for current, foreign
coin, all parties and treaties whatsoever, are made by
the absolute power of the King; and he who hath power of
causes hath power also of effects. No exportation or importation can be but at the King's ports, they are the
gates of the King, and he hath absolute power by them to
include or exclude whom he shall please; and ports to
merchants are their harbours and repose, and for their
better security he is compelled to provide bulwarks and
fortresses, and to maintain for the collection of this
custom and duties collectors and customers; and for that
charge it is reason that he should have this benefit. He
is also to defend the merchants from pirates at sea in
their passage. Also by the power of the King they are
to be relieved if they are oppressed by foreign
princes....
It is said that an imposition may not be upon a subject without Parliament. That the King may impose upon
a subject I omit; for it is not here the question if the
King may impose upon the subject or his goods; but the
impost here is not upon a subject, but here it is upon
Bate , as upon a merchant who imports goods within this
land charged before by the King; and at the time the
impost was imposed upon them they were the goods of the
Venetians and not the goods of a subject, nor within the
land, but only upon those which shall after be imported;
so that all the arguments which were made for the subject
fail. And where it is said that he is a merchant, and
that he ought to have the sea open and free for him, and
that trades of merchants and merchandise are necessary
to export the surplus of our commodities and then to
import other necessities, and so is favourably to be respected; as to that, it is well known that the end of
every private merchant is not the common good but his
particular profit,which is only the means which induceth
him to trade and traffic. And the impost to him is nothing, for he rateth his merchandise according to that ....
The commodity of currants is no commodity of this land,
but foreign. And whereas it is said that it is victual
and necessary food, it is no more necessary than wine,
and impost for that that been always paid without contradiction; and without doubt there are many drinkers of
wine who are also eaters of currants. That which should
be said [to be] victual for the commonwealth is that which
ariseth from agriculture and of the earth within this
land, and not nice and delicate things imported by merchants, such as these currants are....
And whereas it is said that if the King may impose, he
may impose any quantity what he pleases, true it is that
this is to be referred to the wisdom of the King, who
guideth all under God by his wisdom, and this is not to

be disputed by the subject; and many things are left to
his wisdom for the ordering of his power, rather than
his power shall be restrained, The King may pardon any
felon; but it may be objected that if he pardon one
felon he may pardon all, to the damage of the commonwealth, and yet none will doubt but that is left in his
wisdom...And the wisdom and providence of the King is
not to be disputed by the subject; for by intendment
they cannot be severed from his person, and to argue *a
posse ad actum* to restrain the King and his power because
that by his power he may do ill is no argument for a
subject. To prove the power of the King by precedents
of antiquity in a case of this nature may easily be done,
and if it were lawful in ancient times it is lawful now,
for the authority of the King is not diminished and the
Crown hath the same attributes that then it had....
    Now for restraint of commodities many precedents are
to prove it. [After considering the precedents he summed up:]
All these statutes prove expressly, that the King had
power to increase the impost, and that upon commodities
of the land, and that he continually used this power notwithstanding all acts of Parliament against it....Where-
fore I think, that the King ought to have judgement....[1]

18. *PROHIBITIONS DEL ROY* (Michaelmas Term), 1607.[2]
    [On 10 November 1607 Archbishop Bancroft had argued in relation
    to prohibitions in matters ecclesiastical that] the King him-

---

1. By contrast with Clarke (B) who had emphasised the Crown's indisputable prerogative to have revenues necessary for 'the weal of the
King *[which]* is the public weal of the people', Fleming (CB) seemed
to distinguish (as did Americans later in the 1760s) those duties
imposed for the regulation of trade from those for the increase of
revenues.
2. 12 Coke Repts.65.Sir Edward Coke, chief justice in the court of
common pleas since 1606 and later of the king's bench, was concerned
to advance the claims of the common law [see p.20]. Since common law
judges were finding the letters patent issued to the court of high
commission under the Act of Supremacy (1 Eliz.I cap.1 § viii) to be
too loosely and generally phrased both as to offences and punishments,
they had been restricting the jurisdiction of the ecclesiastical
courts by the frequent use of writs of prohibition which virtually
meant that many cases were diverted to, and determined by, the court
of common pleas. The judges were asserting that,as with other statutes, § viii of the Act of Supremacy should be interpreted in the
common law courts. The house of commons too were objecting particularly to the high commission's use of the *ex officio* oath and were
trying to abolish it. In 1607 James I was asserting, at the prompt-
ing of the archbishop of Canterbury, his right to arbitrate between
the jurisdictions of his bishops and his judges: a claim which Coke
firmly rejected (see also *Institutes*, pt.14 cap.74). In the next
four years so many writs of prohibition were issued by the court of
common pleas that the very existence of the high commission, and by
implication of other prerogative courts, seemed threatened. A com-

self may decide it in his Royal person and that the Judges
are but the delegates of the King and that the King may
take what causes he shall please to determine from the
determination of the Judges and may determine them himself.   And the Archbishop said, that this was clear in
divinity, that such authority belonged to the King by
the word of God in the Scriptures.

To which it was answered by me *[Sir Edward Coke]*,in the
presence and with the clear consent of all the Judges of
England and Barons of the Exchequor, that the King in his
own person cannot adjudge any case either criminal, as
treason, felony etc., or betwixt party and party, concerning his inheritance, chattels or goods etc. but this
ought to be determined and adjudged in some Court of Justice, according to the law and custom of England and
always judgements are given, *ideo consideratum est per Curiam*,
so that the Court gives judgement; and the King hath his
Court, viz. in the Upper House of Parliament, in which he
with his Lords is the supreme Judge over all other Judges;
for if error be in the Common Pleas, that may be reversed
in the King's Bench; and if the Court of the King's
Bench err, that may be reversed in the Upper House of
Parliament, by the King with the assent of the Lords
Spiritual and Temporal without the Commons....
        [The King might sit in King's Bench or the Star Chamber]
And it is commonly said in our books, that the King is
always present in Court in the judgement of law,[1] and
upon this he cannot be nonsuit; and the judgements are
always given *per Curiam*; and the Judges are sworn to execute

---

promise, generous to high commission, was reached in 1611 when new
letters patent defined offences and punishments more exactly, but
hostility and suspicion continued. In 1641 by 16 Car.I cap.11 the
court of high commission was abolished: [see p.646].
1. Therefore the king is present in any of the courts of his dominions. The Crown,which was the final source for redress, was also
the essential source of power in, and the motive force of, each government under the Crown. The unity of the empire and Commonwealth
derived from (and was symbolised by) this unity of the Crown. Later
in 1861 it was held in *In re Holmes* (2 Johnson and Hemming 527) in
a case from Canada, concerning a petition to Queen Victoria for the
restoration of an estate invested in the Crown for the construction
of the Rideau canal by Acts of the provincial legislature, that 'as
holder of Canadian land for the public purposes of Canada the Queen
should be considered as present in Canada and out of the jurisdiction
of this Court (i.e. Chancery in Britain)'. The petitioners had argued
that the queen was present in Chancery and amenable by the British
Petition of Right Act, (1860) to the jurisdiction in chancery. But
that Act did not claim to extend to Canada or to acquire jurisdiction
over colonial cases. Judgement therefore affirmed that 'when land in
Canada is vested in the Queen not by prerogative but under an Act of
the Provincial Legislature for the purposes of the province..., the
Queen is not to be regarded as within the jurisdiction of this
Court'.

judgement according to law and the custom of England....
[The king could not delay justice or take any cause out of his Courts to give judgement on it himself.]
And the Judges informed the King, that no King after the Conquest assumed to himself to give any judgement in any cause whatsoever which concerned the administration of justice within this realm but these were solely determined in the Courts of Justice....
[The king could not arrest any man for the party aggrieved had no remedy against the king. No case might go to the king and his council unless from a judgement.]
The King said that he thought the law was founded upon reason and that he and others had reason as well as the Judges: to which it was answered by me, that true it was, that God had endowed His Majesty with excellent science and great endowments of nature; but His Majesty was not learned in the laws of England, and causes which concerned the life or inheritance or goods or fortunes, of his subjects are not to be decided by natural reason, but by artificial reason and judgement of law, which law is an act which requires long study and experience before a man can attain to the cognizance of it: that the law was the golden mete-wand and measure to try the causes of the subjects; and which protected His Majesty in safety and peace. With which the King was greatly offended and said that then he should be under the law, which [it] was treason to affirm, as he said. To which I said, that Bracton saith, *quod Rex non debet esse sub homine, sed sub Deo et lege.*[1]

(3) NATIONALITY IN THE DOMINIONS

The concept of a single uniform nationality was fundamental to the British empire; and these documents (extended well beyond 1608 to show the later evolution of the principle involved) demonstrate the roots of this principle. *Calvin's Case*, finally decided in that year to rule on the consequences of the union of Crowns, incidentally resulted in clear statements concerning the character of different possessions of the king of England - separate kingdoms united only in his person as contrasted with dominions of the Crown of England - and also the distinction between dominions inherited and those conquered. The principles laid down in this case relating to conquered colonies formed the basis of English law during the eighteenth century and were given clear expression in Lord Mansfield's

---

1. In July 1641 by a statute of the Long Parliament (16 Car.I cap.10) prerogative jurisdiction within 'the realm of England or dominion of Wales' ceased. The Act establishing the Star Chamber (3 Hen.VII cap. 1) was repealed and the other prerogative courts in the marches of Wales, Chester, Lancaster and the North were abolished. But certain appeals, particularly from the Channel Islands continued to be heard by committees of the privy council - presumably as part of 'the ordinary course of the law' referred to in § iii of the 1641 Act - and thereby provided precedents for the extension of the Crown's appellate jurisdiction at the Restoration [see section 4(f),and pp.646ff].

verdict in the case from the ceded island of Grenada in 1774:
Campbell v. Hall [see Volume III].

19. (a) ACT CONCERNING THOSE BORN IN THE KING'S OVERSEAS DOMINIONS
                            (25 Ed.III St.2) 1350.[1]
  [The children of the king, wherever they were born, and
  other children born out of the allegiance, named or to be named
  by the king, might inherit as English subjects.]
  And that all children heritors which from henceforth
shall be born without the ligeance of the King, whose
fathers and mothers at the time of their birth be and
shall be in the faith and ligeance of the King of England,
shall have and enjoy the same benefits and advantages to
have and bear their inheritance within the same ligeance,
as the other inheritors aforesaid in time to come....[2]

19. (b) NATURALISATION ACT (42 Ed.III cap.10) 1368.
  Item, upon Petition put in the Parliament by the
Commons desiring that Infants born beyond the Sea within
the Seigniories of Calais *[Guines and Gascony]* and elsewhere,
within the Lands and Seigniories that pertain to our Lord
the King beyond the Seas, Be as able and heritable of
their heritage in England as other infants born within
the Realm of England: It is accorded,*[and assented]*, That
the common Law and the Statute upon the same point

---

1. It is clear from Bracton that, even in the late thirteenth century, the law acknowledged that a man might be a subject and tenant
both of the French and of the English king; and for generations a
Bruce (for example) held lands on both sides of the Anglo-Scottish
border. The personal obligations of a tenant to a lord became transferred to the relationship of a subject and a king. Moreover, with
the beginning of a sense of national identity, and of enmity to
France or Scotland, the doctrine of allegiance - part personal, and
part territorial - became the basis of the law of nationality:
birth within the allegiance came to mean within a defined territory,
realm or dominion, and a capacity to inherit and own land there the
mark of subjecthood.
  Following a discussion of the law on the matter of subjecthood
in 1343, this statute was passed since it was becoming accepted that,
while the prerogative might grant the incidents of status, status
itself could be acquired only by parliamentary enactment. In 1425
(Year Book. 3 Hen.VI Trin.30) it was declared that only Parliament
could make an alien a subject: '*la dit Alice per autorite del dit
Parliament fuit fait person able a purchaser terre et tenements
enheritances, come chescun auter legel home que fuit deins le
Royaume*': and in 1454 (Year Book. 32 Hen.VI Hil.13) it was stated
by Fortescue (C.J.) that only the king-in-parliament could deprive
his subject of the benefit of common law - '*Le Roy sans Parlement
ne poit prendre son lige home de droit*'.
2. It seems soon to have been accepted that such children had been
given by the statute not only the right of inheriting land, but all
the other privileges of natural-born subjects.

another time made, be holden *[and kept]*.[1]

20. *CALVIN'S CASE*, Trinity Term, 1608; a synopsis.[2]
    [Commissioners appointed severally by the Crowns of England
and Scotland[3] had agreed in December 1604 on Articles for a Union
and proposed (1) the repeal of all mutually hostile legislation,
(2) the provision on reciprocal terms of mutual free trade and
(3) the declaratory naturalisation reciprocally of 'all born in
either nation sithence his Majesty was king of both' (*post-nati)*
together with the statutory naturalisation (within certain limits)
of those born before (*ante-nati*).[4] Impatient for Union, however,
James VI and I had already on 20 October 1604[5] issued a proclamation assuming a new title as King of Great Britain and, though
the English Parliament had refused to enact such a title, he
enforced its use among his Scots subjects against their express
wishes. Not until two years later did the English Parliament
have an opportunity to discuss the proposed Articles of Union.
With the support of the Lords in England, James I by proclamation
declared 'the law to be as the Commissioners had proposed', but
the Commons, while agreeing (under strict conditions and with
some reluctance) to the first two proposals, refused to accept
reciprocal naturalisation and of course repudiated prerogative
legislation.
    At a conference held jointly with the Lords on 25-26 February
1607 Sir Francis Bacon had stated for the Commons that they could
not regard the royal proclamation as preventing their questioning
of its alleged justification on the ground of support, not by the
judges, but merely by 'divers sages of the law', and that they
feared recourse to a declaratory statute as a double-edged weapon.
The question (he said) was not what was fit to be the law, but
what was the law; not *de bono*, but *de vero*. Others in the group
of Commons lawyers (which included Sir Edwin Sandys) asserted
variously on grounds of international, natural, civil and common
law, that naturalisation derived from two distinct allegiances to
separate bodies of law operating in two precincts without extra-
territoriality: the ruling of the parliament of Paris was cited
by which the duke of Brabant was permitted, by virtue of the title
to Brabant, to ally himself with the English, although his possession of the earldom of Flanders necessitated his allegiance to
the king of France; though Gascony was united to England by

1. The additional words in square brackets are not found in Pickering's *Statutes at large*, but are in the *Statutes of the Realm*.
2. 2Howell St.T 559-695. The length of this important case which
considered naturalisation in the context of precedents from the
English medieval empire may justify this precis.
3. The English statute (1 Jac.I cap.2) authorised them 'to treat for
the weal of both kingdoms' (see also 3 Jac.I cap.3). The Scottish
statute in July 1604 is printed in I C.J. 319.
4. Private English Statutes for naturalisation of individual Scots
in 1603 included the treasurer of Scotland, Sir George Howme, the
Earl of Mar and Sir Edward Bruce, see also *Acts of the Privy Council*
10 Car.I *passim*.
5. See below No.96.

marriage, a statute of 1374 referred to Gascons as aliens;[1] and
when Mary of Scots married Francis II of France naturalisation
did not follow *ipso jure* but a Scottish statute was necessary to
provide for it.

Dodridge, the king's solicitor, Lawrence Hyde and other common
lawyers argued that the *post-nati* were not naturalised in
England.][2]

The 4 and 5 Reason, that the great seal of England,
which is the organ by which the law is conveyed, is not
powerful nor binding in Scotland; therefore those born
in Scotland [are] not inheritable to the laws of England,
nor to be born subjects of England, when they cannot be
commanded by the great seal of England.

6. Reason, that in subordinate kingdomes, dukedomes
or seignories, as Ireland, Gascoigne, Aquitaine, Angois,
the great seal of England is passable, and the parliament
of England hath power; as is proved by that a writ of
error may be brought in the Kings-bench of a judgement
in Ireland, and the parliament of England may make a
statute to bind in Ireland, if Ireland be specially
named, but without special nameing it doth not bind....
An Habeas Corpus hath been directed under the great seal
of England into Gascoigne, as appeareth by records of
the Kings-bench. And the islanders do send petitions
and make proctors to the parliament of England, as is
still put in use to this day. By which it appeareth,
that the case is not like between England and these
kingdomes and dukedomes subordinate to England, as it is
between England and Scotland; Scotland being a distinct
kingdom not subordinate, and as ancient as England
itself....

[Therefore, being neither a subordinate kingdom like Ireland,
nor an incorporated territory like Wales, where writs would run
and privileges be communicated, Scotland was a distinct and co-
ordinate kingdom.

Lord Popham (C.J.)[3], Sir E. Coke of common pleas, and Sir J.
Fleming of the exchequer, however, stated on the contrary that
allegiance was personal to the king - not to the body politic,
and was not confined to the realm. When and wherever the king
went outside his realm, allegiance (they said) followed his
protection, and it could remain when territories ceased to
belong to him: 'in nations conquered there are no laws, yet is
there present allegiance; and after allegiance gotten, it is
secondary for the king to deliver laws to the people of his
allegiance'. Scots could not have dignities of honour or

---

1. 42 Ed.III cap.8 and 43 Ed.III cap.2 referred to Gascons as
'aliens'; but 37 Ed.III cap.16 stated that Gascony was 'in the
allegiance of the King' and 28 Hen.VI cap.5 referred to those in
Gascony and Guienne as 'liege merchants'.
2. The law officers had, however, earlier in 1604 declared that
post-nati were at English common law 'as little aliens as if born
in Exeter or York'.
3. Sir John Popham was one of those who had taken the initiative in
securing the first Virginia charter in 1606.

places in the Lords in England so long as the laws stood distinct
in separate realms,but by the union of Crowns they were naturalised subjects , not aliens, in England.

The Commons were prepared in May 1607 to repeal hostile laws
(4 Jac.I cap.1),[1] but they refused to accept the Commissioners'
opinion that the *post-nati* were naturalised at common law and
would not enact a statutory naturalisation unless there were
a union of law in the two kingdoms, and Scots were made subject
to English duties.

Recourse was therefore had to the courts for a decision. In
a collusive suit to test the law, Robert Calvin (or Colvil), an
infant born in Edinburgh on 5 November 1605 (i.e. after - *post-
natus* - the accession of James VI to the English throne) claimed
through his guardians to be '*pro jure* by the law of England a
natural-born subject to purchase freehold, and to bring real
actions within England'. His action was against the Smith brothers who had possession of his lands in Shoreditch and Bishopsgate.
Bacon's argument as counsel for Calvin.[2]
The central problem he said was that, although the realms were
united in the person of the sovereign, the laws remained separate: did naturalisation depend on the former or the latter?
The king might be considered as (a) a father, (b) a shepherd and
(c) God. In a monarchy the law reinforced the original simple
submission, of which there were four types. The laws were the
sinews of the body politic.

There were four degrees of persons in the question of naturalisation - alien enemies, alien friends, denizens 'adopted' by
royal charter, and natural subjects by birth or by Act of Parliament. From this analysis emerged three points relevant to the
case. The *ante-nati* could not be considered in the same light
as the *post-nati*, because the law was not retrospective; since
one could be only alien or natural-born, and Scots, if not natural
born, must therefore be aliens and *on a par* with any alien friends
of England; the status of aliens (friends or enemies) was determined by the exercise of prerogative, and even natural-born status
depended on the king.]

...in all the distributions of persons, and the degrees
of abilities or capacities, the king's act is all in all,
without any manner of respect to law or parliament. For
it is the king that makes an alien enemy, by proclaiming
a war, wherewith the law or parliament intermeddle not.
So the king only grants safe-conducts, wherewith law and
parliament intermeddle not. It is the king likewise
that maketh an alien friend, by concluding a peace, wherewith law and parliament intermeddle not. It is the king

---

1. In August 1607 by an Act 'anent the Union' the Scottish Parliament were ready to assent to the Commissioners' scheme provided the
English Parliament did. The Scots were desirous of sharing in an
expanding English market; but the English were afraid that Scotland,
a poor undeveloped country with no staple export, would be a drain
on her trade.
2. Bacon became solicitor general in June 1607. He and Hamilton had
been given by the other Commissioners the responsibility of drafting

that makes a denizen by his charter, absolutely of his
prerogative and power, wherewith law and parliament intermeddle not. And therefore it is strongly to be inferred,
that as all these degress depend wholly upon the king's
act, and no ways upon law or parliament;[1] so the fourth
[naturalised subjects]although it comes not by the king s
patent, but by operation of the law, yet that the law, in
that operation, respecteth only the king's person, without respect of subjection to law or parliament....
   [The arguments of the opposition might, he said, be refuted
under four heads:-
1. The proposition that naturalisation follows allegiance, and
that allegiance follows the kingdom.
   The argument that naturalisation depended on English law, which
had no force in Scotland could be countered by citing the extra-
territorial force of English law in regard to laws of treason and
of contempt, and also in a statute of Edward III (1350)[2] naturalising children born anywhere in the world of English parents still
in allegiance. The opposition's use of statutes might be challenged: that the metaphorical use of territorial designations
('England' for 'king of England') could not be construed to exclude allegiance to the person; that the post-nati Scots, like
Irishmen, might commonly be deemed aliens, but (as by a statute
of 1541)[3] might be considered 'born within the king's obedience';
that a statute - enacting, not declaratory - had been necessary
in 1340 [4] to separate allegiance to the English and French crowns
in the event of their union in one person, but no such statute
existed or had been sought relative to a joint allegiance of the
Scots. Case law was unreliable and of limited value, and the
examples cited by the opposition were misleading, he declared.
2. The argument drawn from the rule of civil law 'cum duo jura',
that when two rights meet in one person they remain distinct.
   The correct interpretation was that the two jurisdictions became
one, because, where there was one man, there was one soul, one homage, one conscience.
3. The argument based on the alleged inconveniences arising from
general naturalisation, ipso jure.
   These inconveniences did not really exist. The alleged loss of
revenue to the king was insignificant.]
   As for the confluence of Scotsmen, I think we all
conceive the spring-tide is past at the king's first
coming in. And yet we see very few families of them

---

the proposed Articles for Union.
1. This argument was used by American pampheteers in the mid eighteenth century to claim that subjects of the king were not necessarily
subject to Parliament.
2. 25 Ed.III St.2 [see above No.19].
3. 32 Hen.VIII cap.16. The opposition had argued that the phrase
'aliens out of the King's obedience' implied that there were aliens
born within that allegiance too.
4. 14 Ed.III St.5, which asserted that the realm of England 'ought
never to be in subjection' to the king of France.

throughout the cities and boroughs of England. And for
the naturalising of the Indes, we can readily help that
when the case comes; for we can make an act of parliament of separation, if we like not their consort....[1]
[4. *Alleged distinction between countries acquired by descent and
by conquest.*

   The opposition argued (i) *that while countries acquired by
descent did not become subject to England and English law, a
country conquered by English power became a part of England.*
But what happened if the conquest were by a mixed army of English
and Scots in a condominium? (ii)*That a conquered country was
subject to English law.* This was <u>not</u> so;]

   ...it shall suffice to say that...the laws of England
are not superinduced upon any country by conquest; but
that the old laws remain until the king by his proclamation or letters patent declare other laws;[2] and then, if
he will, he may declare laws which be utterly repugnant
and differing from the laws of England. And here of many
ancient precedents and records may be shewed, that the
reason why Ireland is subject to the laws of England is
not *ipso jure* upon conquest, but grew by a charter of
king John, and that extended but to so much as was then
in the king's possession; for there are records in the
time of king E*[dward]* I and II, of divers particular grants
to sundry subjects of Ireland and their heirs,[3] that they
might use and observe the laws of England....
(iii) *That it is desirable in a conquered colony to assimilate the
new subjects, by transplantation and by garrisons.*
   And certainly I suppose it will sound strangely in the

---

1. cf. Commonwealth Immigration Act, 1962. Spokesmen for English
merchants seemed somewhat paradoxically to fear both Scottish poverty and Scottish competition: they suspected that Scots would
compete for jobs and trade and avoid English duties (I C.J. p.327).
On 14 February Fuller argued strongly that there were too many English graduates and merchants already for the opportunities available
and that English towns were over-populated. Furthermore he declared
that the argument of naturalisation stemming from a single head would
have meant, if Philip and Mary had had a son, that Spaniards and
Sicilians would be naturalised too (*ibid.*pp.334-5). Bacon in reply
(*ibid.*pp.336-7) had pointed to the great opportunities overseas in
lands and fisheries in the New World. 'If we be pent in England,
there is Room abroad &c - Ireland, Virginia &c'. The union of the
two kingdom would 'with Shipping maintained' lead to 'the greatest
Empire that hath been heard of in many Ages', he said; but 'surety,
... not wealth' was the prize (see also I Parl. Hist. 1081-1096).
Bacon said England was not over-populated 'but thin sown with
people'. He also argued that, since Poynings' laws, not all English
laws applied to Ireland, but English law did not deny naturalisation
to the Irish, or to Manxmen and Channel Islanders (1087-8).
2. This was Mansfield (C.J.)'s maxim in *Campbell v. Hall*, 1774 whereby he upheld the continuance of French law in Quebec.
3. See below section 4 (a) 1 § (i).

hearing of foreign nations, that the law of England
should *ipso facto* naturalise subjects of conquests and
should not naturalise subjects which grow into the king
by descent: that is, that it should confer the benefit
and privilege of naturalisation upon such as cannot at
the first but bear hatred and rancour to the state of
England and have had their hands in the blood of the subjects of England, and should deny the like benefit to
those that are conjoined with them by a more amiable mean;
and that the law of England should confer naturalisation
upon slaves and vassals (for people conquered are no better in the beginning) and should deny it to freemen...
there is a difference that the law of England never
knew....
(iv) *That conquest is more irrevocable than descent.*

> [But present law could not be influenced by future possibilities.
> Bacon therefore declared that naturalisation would flow, in the
> case of Scotland as in Ireland, from the union in person of the
> king.

> *Exposition of the case that 'post natus of Scotland is by the
> law of England natural' rested on three types of proof.*
> 1.*Favour of law.*

> All national laws had to be considered as part of the law of
> nature: by the law of England, a subject was naturalised by
> being born in England or of English parents.]

In such sort doth the law of England open her lap to
receive in people to be naturalized: which indeed sheweth the wisdom and excellent composition of our law, and
that it is the law of a warlike and magnanimous nation
fit for empire. For look, and you shall find that such
kind of estates have been ever liberal in point of naturalisation whereas merchant-like and envious estates have
been otherwise....

> [2. *Reasons and authorities of law.*

> Allegiance was to the person of the king, and not to the king-
> dom, and it was not limited by the boundaries of the kingdom.
> The presence of a single king, with natural as well as political
> capacities, had an effect on his two kingdoms. Five statutes
> might be adduced to support this case. (i) The Despensers had
> asserted 'the damnable and damned opinion' that homage was due
> to the Crown and not to the person of the king. This distinction
> was denied by the statute (1322) banishing them.[1] (ii) An Act of
> the first year of James I [2] referred to a single Imperial Crown,
> though not to single monarchies. (iii) Earlier legislation of
> James I had acknowledged that the union of the two kingdoms had
> already begun in His Majesty's person.[3] (iv) A special Act of
> Parliament would have been needed to override the common law
> rule that the addition of a new kingdom to the king of England

---

1. D. Pickering, *Statutes at large,* I 362-8.
2. 1 Jac.I cap.1. There were three references to 'one imperial
crown'.
3. 4 Jac.I cap.1 repealing hostile laws.

brought about a new union of the Crowns and kingdoms themselves. (As in 1340, 14 Ed. III St.5, *vide supra*). (v) The Act of 1368[1] on the right of infants born in the land of the king beyond the seas to inherit land within England was declaratory and derived from common law.

3. *Precedents*

The valid precedents of union might be reduced to those of Gascony, Anjou and Guienne from Henry II to John, and from John to the 17th year of Edward II, *Praerogativa Regis* (1324).[2] After John (when the king was king *de jure* and not *de facto*), nevertheless those who did not commit treason continued to inherit lands within the realm of England until the statute of 1324 destroyed this right. Guienne and Gascony were not governed by English laws, but retained their own. The alleged extra-territorality of English law (of writs and of Acts of Parliament) did not in fact concern subjects of Gascony, but only English interests and persons in that dominion.

Coke's Report of Calvin's Case.

The case rather 'for weight than difficulty' had been adjourned to the Court of Exchequer where it was ruled that there was a *prima facie* case for hearing the suit in England: the lord chancellor and 12 judges concurred in judgement for Calvin.

The main arguments for the case fell under five heads:

1. *Ligeantia* (Allegiance)

Copious learned evidence was adduced to prove that allegiance was general over all kingdoms and dominions in peace and in war, and that it could not be local and confined to the realm, being a quality of the mind. These arguments were based not on modern invention, but on ancient precedent.][3]

For we are but of yesterday (and therefore had need of the wisdom of those that were before us) and had been ignorant, if we had not received light and knowledge from our forefathers, and our days upon the earth are but a shadow in respect of the old ancient days and times past wherein the laws have been by the wisdom of the most excellent men, in many succession of ages, by long and continual experience, the trial of right and truth, fined and refined which no man, being of so short a time, albeit he had in his head the wisdom of all men in the world

---

1. See above No.19 (b).
2. 17 Ed.II caps 1-16 esp. cap.12.
3. Sandys' argument on 28 February 1607 (I C.J. p.345) is worth notice. It related to the comparatively recent advent of the concept of the nation state. Early precedents, he said, were misleading: the times were different from those when allegiance was strong and nationality weak. 'States were then no more than Heaps of People. Policies were not framed nor distinguished; then Subjection made a Naturalisation'. But 'Sithence Kingdoms are more distinct, more formal, more regular'. He further argued that the political map of Europe was fluid and unstable: 'Kingdoms rend and divide and after glew again....Out of Rome sprang Thirty Kingdoms: Within these Hundred Years, Eleven Kingdoms in Europe; now, but Six'.

in any one age could ever have effected or attained to.
And therefore...no man ought to take upon him to be wiser
than the laws....

> [Allegiance was to the natural person of the king, who held his
> kingdom of England by birthright and not by any act of coronation.
> The use of the name of the country for the name of the ruler was
> merely metonomy.
> 2. *Leges* (Laws)
> Natural law rendered allegiance due to the king, and that law was
> incorporated in the law of England. Natural law preceded judicial
> or municipal law and was immutable.]

Wherefore to conclude this point...if the obedience and
ligeance of the subject to his sovereign be due by the
laws of nature, if that law be parcel of the laws, as well
of England as of all other nations, and is immutable, and
that Postnati and we of England are united by birth-right
in obedience and ligeance, which is the true cause of
natural subjection - by the law of nature it followeth,
that Calvin the plaintiff,being born under one ligeance
to one king, cannot be an alien born....

> [3. *Regna* (Kingdoms).
> The union of the two kingdoms took four forms: one king; all-
> egiance due to that one king; protections required by subjects of
> both kingdoms; the purely heraldic. Similarly four forms of sep-
> aration existed: two kingdoms; two laws; two parliaments; two
> peerages.]
> 4. *Alienigena* (Alien birth).

An alien is a subject that is born out of the allegiance
of the king and under that of another, and can have no real
or personal action concerning land....

> [Every man was either a subject born, or (temporarily or perpet-
> ually) an alien friend or similarly an alien enemy. All pagans
> were perpetual enemies to Christendom in law and the law presumed
> they will not be converted.]

And upon this ground there is a diversity between a
conquest of a kingdom of a Christian king, and the conquest of a kingdom of an infidel; for if a king come to a
Christian kingdom by conquest, seeing that he hath '*vitae
et necis potestatem*', he may at his pleasure alter and
change the laws of that kingdom, but until he doth make
an alteration of those laws, the ancient laws of that kingdom remain. But if a Christian king should conquer a kingdom of an infidel, and bring them under his subjection,
there *ipso facto* the laws of the infidel are abrogated;
for that they be not only against Christianity, but against
the law of God and of nature, contained in the Decalogue:
and in that case, until certain laws be established amongst them, the king by himself, and such judges as he shall
appoint, shall judge them and their causes according to
natural equity, in such sort as kings in ancient time did
with their kingdoms, before any certain municipal laws
were given, as before hath been said. But if a king hath
a kingdom by title of descent, there seeing by the laws of
that kingdom he doth inherit the kingdom, he cannot change

those laws of himself, without consent of parliament.
Also if the king hath a Christian kingdom by conquest, as
Henry II had Ireland, after John had given unto them, being under his obedience and subjection, the laws of England for the government of that country, no succeeding
king could alter the same without parliament. And in that
case while the realm of England and that of Ireland were
governed by several laws, any that was born in Ireland
was no alien to the realm of England. In which precedent
of Ireland three things are to be observed.
1. That then there had been two descents, one from Henry
II to Richard I , and from Richard to John, before the
alteration of the laws. 2. That albeit Ireland was a
distinct dominion, yet, the title thereof being by conquest, the same by judgement of law might by express words
be bound by act of the parliament of England. 3. That
albeit no reservation were in king John's Charter, yet by
judgement of law a writ of error did lie in the King's
Bench of England of an erroneous judgement in the King's
Bench of Ireland. Furthermore, in the case of a conquest
of a Christian kingdom, as well those that served in wars
at the conquest, as those that remained at home for the
safety and peace of their country, and other the king's
subjects, as well Antenati as Postnati, are capable of
lands in the kingdom or country conquered, and may maintain any real action, and have the like privileges and
benefits there, as they may have in England....
   [There were three essential incidents to a subject born: his
   parents must have been under the obedience of the king; the
   place of his birth must have been within the king's dominion;
   and the time of his birth was important to establish that right
   of ligeance. Aliens could not inherit land in England, on the
   grounds of the possible danger to the security and stability of
   the realm.
   Precedents from Gascony, though a separate and distinct kingdom
   with distinct titles and laws beyond the jurisdiction of the chancery of England, showed that a Gascon in the king's allegiance was
   not regarded as an alien born in respect of lands in England.[1]
   Similar examples occurred in the cases of Guienne and Aquitaine.
   Also]
   ...those that are born in Guernsey and Jersey (though
those isles are no parcel of the realm of England, but
several dominions enjoyed by several titles, governed by
several laws) are inheritable and capable of any lands
within the realm of England....
   [Other precedents included Wales; the Isle of Man, 'an ancient
   and absolute kingdom' out of the power of Chancery but whose inhabitants were capable of inheriting lands in England; and Calais,
   part of the kingdom of France, but a conquest in which subjects
   could inherit lands in England. King John had given a charter to
   conquered Ireland for the introduction of English law, though since

1. 39 Ed.III cap.16 and 28 Hen.VI cap.5 (7 *Coke Repts*. 20a).

it had a separate Parliament it had some distinct laws and usages and must be regarded as a 'distinct dominion' - yet Irishmen might inherit in England.

In the case of Scotland itself, there were earlier examples of
the right to inherit English lands being regarded as compatible
with the fact that different laws were in operation (e.g. 42
Ed.III cap.2) in the two kingdoms.

5. *Legal inconveniences.*

As far as duties and liabilities accompanying the ownership of
land in England were concerned, *post-nati* and men born out of
the realm of England (whether in Ireland, Man or the Channel
Islands) were in the same position as Englishmen.

The judgement was that the Smith brothers (who had possession
of the lands in Shoreditch and Bishopsgate)[1] must answer to
Robert Calvin's case.]

Ellesmere (L.C.)'s speech in the Exchequer Chamber
Mine opinion is...that these Post-nati are not Aliens
to the king, nor to his kingdome of England, but by their
birth-right are liege subjects to the king, and capable
of estates of inheritance and freehould of landes in England; and may have and maintaine as wel reall as personall actions for the same, and that therefore the now com-
plainant Robert Calvine ought to bee answered....

[This opinion was based on recent statutes, the proclamations,
whose authority he defended, and the opinions of judges both in
court and in the Parliament, which he regarded as of equal weight.

The first problem was how the case should be judged; clearly
not by Parliament, since the case had now come for decision to
chancery, to be judged according to common law. This in turn
raised the problem of what was common law.]

The common law of England is grounded upon the law of
God, and extendes itselfe to the originall laws of nature,
and the universall lawe of nations... it is the common
custome of the realme...and it standeth upon two main
pillars....

[namely, on certain fixed maxims and unchallenged principles,
and on former judgements and precedents. If these were absent,
the rule may be relied upon that no-one should go to chancery
without finding a remedy; it was incumbent upon chancery to
produce one. It should not be necessary to wait for a Parliament,
which was not in any case 'to be called for the wrong of a few
private subjects'. Lastly,there was the general rule in civil
law that when necessary, the judges must enunciate the fundamental principles on which judgements were to be grounded. Statute
and common law were necessarily impermanent and subject to revision in order to bring them up to date. There were precedents
(e.g. in the reign of Edward III) where the judges had consulted
the king's privy council on matters of law,before making a judgement.]

---

1. Lawrence Hyde was counsel for the defence.

Thus *arbitria iudicum* and *responsu prudentum* have been received, allowed and reverenced in all times as positive lawe; and so it must be still; for, otherwise much mischiefe and great inconvenience will ensue. For new cases happen every day; no lawe ever was, or ever can be made, that can provide remedie for all future cases, or comprehend all circumstances of humane actions which iudges are to determine....

[Examination of the previous possessions of the Crown, by descent and by conquest brought us to the question - if subjects born in such lands were not aliens, and if subjects born now in Ireland, Guernsey and Jersey were similarly not accounted aliens, why should not the same apply to subjects born in Scotland? In all material points, the analogy was valid. This might be seen from an analysis of the contrary arguments, to which it might be answered; that the idea that in respect of laws there was a difference between lands acquired by descent and lands acquired by conquest was erroneous, for]

...those that are borne in Ireland, and those that are borne in Scotland, are all alike for their birth within the king's dominions, and are borne under the like subiection and obedience to the king and have the like bond; nay even the same bond of allegiance; that is, they are borne *ad fidem regis* ....[*Furthermore*] the king may by his great seale commaund all his subjects that bee under his obedience, wheresoever they bee in the world; so he did in Normandie; so he did in Aquitany; so he did in that part of Scotland that he had in possession....So hee may commaund his subjects, if they be in France, Spaine, Rome, or Turkie, or the Indies....when these countries came into the king's possession, the kinges continued several seales in them both for the administration of iustice; but as subordinate to the great seale of England....

[The existence of different laws (in Normandy, Aquitaine, the Channel Isles or the palatines) could make no difference to sovereignity and allegiance.]

...and none of them can be aliens to the king so none of them can bee aliens or strangers in any of his kingdome or dominions; nor aliens or strangers one to another no more than a Kentish man to a Cheshire man....Therefore all that have bin borne in any of the kinges dominions since hee was king of England, are capable and inheritable in all his dominions without exception....

[The argument used against allowing aliens to hold land in England, that it would be a drain on the economy, did not apply in this case, where there was one king of both England and Scotland, any more than it could serve against those born in Ireland or the Channel Islands.

When Edward III established his claim to the larger and more magnificent throne of France, there had been concern whether the kingdom of England should be demoted to a vice-royalty, as Ireland had been. (14 Ed.III St.5)].

But in this new learning, there is one part of it so strange, and of so dangerous consequent, as I may not let

it passe *viz.* that the king is as a king divided in himself; and so as two kings of two severall kingdomes; and
that there be severall allegeances and severall subject-
ions due unto him respectively in regarde of his severall
kingdoms, the one not participating with the other. This
is a dangerous distinction betweene the king and the
crowne, and betweene the king and the kingdome:[1] it reach-
eth too farre; I wish every good subject to beware of it
...So then since there is but one king and souveraigne to
whome this faith and allegeance is due by all his subjects
of England and Scotland, can any humeane policie divide
this one king and make him two kings?....

    [Could there be war between the king of England and the king of
Scotland? Could a man be loyal to one king and traitor to the
other? The king must have 'intire and perfect obedience of all
his subjects and subjects ought to have all the privileges pertaining to their birthright in all the king's dominions'. If it
should be a difficult legal point, then the king 'by sentence of
the most religious, learned and judicious king that ever this
kingdome or island had', could resolve it: his prerogative was
a certain rule, part of the civil law and ancient common law of
England. (Presumably therefore a proclamation in Ellesmere's
opinion was sufficient.) As for the fears of a flood of Scots
immigrants, had this happened with regard to Wales or Ireland?
Nor was it likely that the king would permit the depopulation of
so 'ancient, noble and famous' a nation.

Conclusion: Calvin and all *post-nati* in Scotland were 'in reason
and by the common lawe of England naturall-borne subjects within
the allegeance of the King of England and innabled to purchase
and have freehould and inheritance of lands in England; and to
bring reall actions for the same in England'. If not, what had
been gained by this 'blessed and happie union'. Therefore he
gave judgement in chancery for the defendants to answer Calvin's
suit for the lands he claimed: and eight of his nine fellow
judges concurred.][2]

---

1. The source for this distinction, the metaphor of the king's politic
and his natural bodies, and the concept of the Crown as a corporation,
seem largely to have obtained currency in this period from a treatise
written in 1566 by a Catholic lawyer of the Middle Temple, Edmund
Plowden, in support of Mary Stuart's claim to the English throne. Published in 1571 as *Les Comentaries ou les reportes* (its English edition
is dated 1816), it was used by Plowden's son after 1603 to advance the
case for union favoured by James VI and I. (See article by Marie
Axton in *Huntington Library Quarterly* Vol.37 1974). The distinction
between king and Crown had proved unacceptable as a 'damnable heresy'
when made by the Despensers in the 1320s; and James I's Parliament
rejected both the metaphor and the union. Of course it became constitutional orthodoxy after 1688; and in the 1950s the separation of
the Crowns and the recognition of the person as 'Head' became an acceptable doctrine of the modern Commonwealth.
2. The judgement in *Calvin's Case* was claimed by James Wilson in his
Considerations (1774) as proof that a subject of the king was not

21. *CRAW v. RAMSAY*, 1670.[1]
   *Whether a naturalization in Ireland will naturalize the person
   in England?*
   If it will, then whether by that Act for naturalizing
the antenati of Scotland[2] any, his brothers, had title to
inherit the Earl of Holdernes in the lands in question?
....
   It is admitted, and will easily appear, that one nat-
uralized in Scotland since the Union cannot inherit in
England.
   Ireland then differs from Scotland, in a common dif-
ference with Gernsey, Jersey, Isle of Man, Berwick, and
all the English plantations, for that they are dominions
belonging to the Crown of England, which Scotland is not.
   If this difference, which was never discussed in
Calvin's case, alter not the case from a naturalizing in
Scotland, it remains, whether by Act of Parliament of
England, though not extant, Ireland in this matter be
not differenc'd from other dominions belonging to England?....
   No laws made in any other dominion acquired by conquest, or new plantation, by the King's lieutenants, substitutes, governours, or people there, by virtue of the
King's letters patents, can make a man inherit in England, who could not otherwise inherit: for what the
King cannot do by his letters patents, no delegated power
under him can do by his letters patents.
   It follows likewise upon the same reason, that no
tenure of land, by homage, fealty or other service in any
other dominion of the Kings, acquired by conquest, or
otherwise by any grant of letters patents, can make a man
inherit in England, who could not otherwise inherit, for
that is not *homagium ligeum*, but *feodale*, as is rightly distinguished....

---

subject to Parliament. This same emphasis, however, on the personal
tie of allegiance to James VI and I was important for the future law
of the Empire and Commonwealth with the sovereign as source and bond
of union. It established the rule for a common subjecthood throughout the realm and dominions, so that there was a common status, not
separate and distinct ones. Inhabitants of lands, which by descent,
cession or conquest came under the Crown, became subjects. Subjects
who went to settle colonies overseas took their subjecthood with
them. Neither emigration, nor loss of territory by the Crown could
dissolve the bond; *nemo potest exuere patriam*: the status of subject
was permanent and indelible. Though the loss of the American colonies showed the inconvenience, and the Great Trek of Boer farmers the
impossibility, of its strict enforcement, this remained the rule at
common law till the Naturalisation Act of 1870.
1. Vaughan 274. The case concerned an action by <u>Craw</u> for trespass
and ejection from the Ramsey inheritance in Holderness, and turned on
whether <u>Ramsay</u> was naturalized in England and could lawfully inherit
those lands.
2. Such an Act had been passed in the Irish Parliament in July 1634.

A subject born in any dominion belonging to the Crown
of England, is inheritable in England as well as native
Englishmen. So the natural born subjects of Ireland,
Gernsey, Jersey, Berwick and all the English plantations
inherit; but the specifique reason of their inheriting
in England is not because they are born in dominions belonging to the *Crown* of England, for if so, none could inherit who wanted that, and then the postnati of Scotland
should not inherit, for Scotland is not a dominion belonging to the *Crown* of England, but to the *King* of England.
   It remains then, according to the resolution and reasons
of *Calvin's case*, that the specifique and adequate cause,
why the 'King's subjects of other his dominions than England, do inherit in England is, because they are born his
natural subjects as the English are, he being actually
King of England at the time of their birth,when their subjection begins and so are born liege-men to the same
King'....

   [Vaughan (C.J.) asked why an 'act of law' could not have the
   same effect. Because, he argued, naturalisation was a 'fiction
   of law' only accepted as 'true law' where law makers had such
   power - in Ireland or Scotland but not in England: an act in
   another kingdom to which England had not assented could not be
   accepted as law in England. 'The law of England is that no alien
   can be naturalised but by Act of Parliament with the assent of
   the whole nation'.]

   And speaking of Ireland among other things, he *[Coke]*
saith that albeit no reservation were in King John's
Charter, yet by judgement of law a writ of error did lye
in the King's Bench of England, of an erroneous judgement
in the King's Bench in Ireland.
   A writ of error lies not therefore to reverse a judgement in Ireland by special Act of Parliament, for it lies
at common law to reverse a judgement in any inferior dominions; and if it did not, inferior and provincial governments, as Ireland is, might make what laws they
pleas'd; for judgements are laws when not to be revers'd....
   Though Ireland have its own Parliament, yet it is not
absolute, and *sui juris* , for if it were, England had no
·power over it, and it were as free after conquest and
subjection by England as before. That it is a conquer'd
kingdom is not doubted....
   What things the Parliament of Ireland cannot do.
1. It cannot alien itself, or any part of itself, from
being under the dominion of England, nor change its
subjection.
2. It cannot make itself not subject to the laws of, and
subordinate to, the Parliament of England.
3. It cannot change the law of having judgements there
given, revers'd for error in England, and others might be
named ....

   [He listed laws made in the Parliament of England which bound
   Ireland and he shows how kings in council in England had given

instruction for the observance of English laws in Ireland. Coke's
opinion that they were accepted by 'parliaments' in Ireland –
that, for example, King John's promulgation of English law was
done in an assembly *de communi omnium de Hibernia consensu* – was,
he believed, a misuse of the word.

In his judgement one of his fellow judges had argued that]...
Ireland is a distinct kingdom from England, and therefore
cannot make any law obligative to England.

That is no adequate reason, *[declared Vaughan]* for by that
reason England,being a distinct kingdom, should make no
law to bind Ireland, which is not so. England can naturalize, if it please, nominally a person in Ireland, and
not in England.

That is no adequate reason....But he recover'd by saying that Ireland was subordinate to England and therefore
could not make a law obligatory to England.

Secondly he *[the same fellow judge]* said England and Ireland were two distinct kingdoms, and no otherwise united
than because they had one Sovereign. Had this been said
of Scotland and England it had been right, for they are
both absolute kingdoms, and each of them *sui juris*.

But Ireland *[was]* far otherwise; for it is a dominion
belonging to the Crown of England and follows that it
cannot be separate from it, but by Act of Parliament of
England, no more than Wales, Gernsey, Jersey, Berwick, the
English plantations, all which are dominions belonging to
the realm of England, though not within the territorial
dominion or realm of England, but follow it, and are part
of its Royalty....

[Vaughan declared that a union of distinct kingdoms required a
statute: by such legislation he alleged Edward III had united
his French possessions to the English crown.]

Wales, after the conquest of it by Edward the First,
was annext to England..., but at first received laws
from England, as Ireland did, but not proceeded by writs
out of the English Chancery, but had a Chancery of his
own, as Ireland hath; *[Wales]* was not bound by the laws
of England, unnamed until 27 H.8.[1] no more than Ireland
now is.

Ireland in nothing differs from it, but in having a
Parliament, *gratia Regis*, subject to the Parliament of
England; it might have had so, if the King pleas'd; but
it was annext to England. None doubts Ireland, as conqu-
er'd , as it; and as much subject to the Parliament of
England, if it please.[2]
The Court was divided, viz. the Chief Justice and Tyrrell for the
plaintiff: Wylde and Archer for the defendant.

22. EDWARD RANDOLPH TO THE COMMISSIONERS OF CUSTOMS, 7 December 1695.[3]
   ... I now lay before your Honours an Account of the

---

1. 27 Hen.VIII cap.26 [see below No.89].
2. See section (4)(a) II.
3. C.O. 324/5 pp. 353-8. Randolph had been sent in 1676 by the

present State of his Majesty's Colonies and Provinces
upon the North Coast of America, in relation to a Scotch
Act *[1695]* which is lately past, In which Act under pretence of Erecting an East India Company in that Kingdome
[the Darien Company] They do...Engage themselves with Great
Sums of Money in an American Trade, a Trade which has
already for Severall Years been carried on by Scotchmen
under pretence of being Persons born within the allegiance
of his Majesty, as by the Act of 12 Car.2^d.[1] They claim
liberty to do, and altho' in the Act of the 14th of the
said King,[2] only English, Irish and Subjects in the Plantations are to be accounted English, as to the Navigating
of Ships; Yet they take on them to come from Scotland
under the notion of Supra-Cargos and Merchants and seldome
faile of Counterfeit Masters.... They *[the Company]* have
liberty to Plant Colonies &c. in or upon places not Inhabited,[3] and...make & conclude Treaties of Peace and
Commerce with the Governors and Proprietors, paying only
to his Majesty's out of Scotland the Yearly acknowledge-

---

lords of trade to investigate the breaches of the trade laws in New
England, and in 1678 he was appointed collector of customs in Massachusetts. In 1693 a Scottish Act had sought to encourage Scottish
trade, and in 1695 the Darien Company ('the Company of Scotland trading to Africa and the Indies') was formed.
1. 12 Car.II cap.18 – the Navigation Act of 1660 [see below No .252].
2. 13 & 14 Car.II cap.11.§ vi. Scottish trade undoubtedly suffered
from the English connection, especially with the increasing acceptance of mercantilist orthodoxy at the Restoration. But the geographical position of Scotland favoured her share in illicit trade.
3. The Company disregarded the fact that Darien was in the centre of
Spanish territories and was 'uninhabited' because of the pestiferous
climate.   'The Company of Scotland' had begun in part as a gamble on
the anomalies of the Anglo-Scottish relationship. Merchants in London
wishing to challenge the English East India Company's monopoly as
interlopers under a separate flag, had been encouraged to use Scotland's nominal independence as a base.   Scots merchants were interested in finding new markets: so far their operations imperially had
been limited to supporting the colonial enterprise of England.Though
William III as king of Scotland in 1693 had promised to support Scottish ventures for increased overseas trade, especially in the Indies,
jealous pressure from the English lords of trade and Parliament seemed
to turn his goodwill to hostility; the king had to side with the
stronger realm. When the king sought to obstruct the enterprise and
English shareholders were forced to pull out by the English government, resentment in Scotland made the wild foolish Darien enterprise –
the emporium at the crossroads of the world – an extraordinarily national, defiantly anti-English enthusiasm. When it failed so catas-
trophically,it was not the stupidity and ignorance of the directors
which rankled, but the double-dealing of the king and the selfish
obstructiveness of the English government. In January 1699 the king
had sent a circular to colonial governors warning them to see that
no help or countenance would be forthcoming for the'rash and foolish'
Scots whose lawlessly irresponsible buccaneering in Spanish America

ment of one hogshead of Tobacco.[1] And although they forbid
all other Scotts than those of their Company to touch on
any Plantations which they shall acquire on pains of confiscation, Yet they allow all Such Scotts to Trade in
Tobacco & Sugar elsewhere:that is to say amongst the
English, They paying for what they so bring home, such
duties as are now Established in Scotland.

By all which it may be presumed how they project to
let themselves into the Trade of all his Majesties Plantations, and 'tis Probable they meditate either the Purchasing a Settlement in one of the 3 Lower Countys of
Newcastle, Kent or Sussex, on the Southern Shore of Delaware bay as being no part or Parcell of the Land Granted to Mr. Penn in his Province of Pensilvania.- Or in
some one or more Islands nigh the Continent, by which
Expedient if acquired they might in a short time make a
Staple, not only of all Sorts of European Manufacturers
but also of the Enumerated Plantation Commodities even
as it is this day practiced with great abuse at the small
Dutch Island of **Carasaw** *[Curaçao]*....

    [He suggested 'for the prevention of so great a Mischief to
England', that S. Carolina (with its settlement of Scots Covenanters)[2] and the Bahamas should be united directly under the Crown;
that N. Carolina should be annexed and governed by Virginia; that
West Jersey should be taken over by Pennsylvania; that East
Jersey (with a Scots settlement) and Connecticut should be annexed to New York, and Rhode Island to Massachusetts.]

That no Projectior,Planter or other person whatsoever,
presume to alien or Transfer any Island Plantation &c.
To any Scotch Agent Factor or other Forreigner whatsoever
under the Penalty of High Treason, the whole Tract from
32° to 44° being His Majesties Dominion and annexed to
the Crown of England ....

I think where any Proprietary or Charter Colony -
shall refuse in this time of danger to accept his Majesties Government,they should be obliged both to accept
and Maintegn Such Officers as may be needfull to preserve the Trade of England and the Deputys to his Majesty....[3]

---

might provoke war with the king's ally.   See G.P. Insh , *The Company
of Scotland* (1932).
1. The exemption from duties for 21 years gave the Company of Scotland a considerable advantage over the English East India Company.
2. See G.P. Insh , *Scottish Colonial Schemes, 1620-86* (1922).
3. To tackle these evasions, and especially the carrying of enumerated commodities to Ireland and Scotland, a new Navigation Act (7 &
8 Will.III cap.22) was passed in 1696: 'by the artifice and cunning
of ill-disposed persons', it said, 'great abuses' were 'daily being
committed to the prejudice of English navigation and the loss of a
great part of the plantation trade of this kingdom'. [see Volume II].

As its contribution to the 'cold war' of mutual sanctions between
England and Scotland, the English parliament in 1705 in the Aliens
Act (3 and 4 Anne cap.7) enacted that, unless by Christmas Day that

23. ACT FOR NATURALIZING FOREIGN PROTESTANTS (7 Anne cap.5) 1708.[1]
   Whereas the Increase of People is a Means of advancing
the Wealth and Strength of a Nation[2] and whereas many
Strangers of the Protestant or reformed Religion out of
due consideration of the happy Constitution of the Government of this Realm would be induced to transport themselves and their Estates into this Kingdom, if they might
be made Partakers of the Advantages and Privileges which
the natural-born Subjects thereof do enjoy. Be it enacted...
   All Persons taking the Oaths and making and subscribing the Declaration appointed by 6 Anne cap.23[3] shall
be deemed natural-born Subjects[4] ....
   All the Children of natural-born Subjects born out of
the Ligeance of her Majesty...shall be deemed to be
natural-born Subjects of his Kingdom to all Intents, Constructions and Purposes whatever [5]....
   [The Act was to apply to Ireland.]

---

year the Scottish parliament had agreed to accept the Hanoverian
succession in a union of kingdoms, 'no person or persons being a
native or natives of the kingdom of Scotland (except such as are
now settled inhabitants within the kingdom of England or the dominions thereunto belonging...) shall be capable to inherit any
lands...within this kingdom of England or the dominions thereunto
belonging or to enjoy any benefit or advantage of a natural born
subject of England', but shall be regarded as 'an alien born out of
the allegiance of the Queen of England'. Scots would not be
supplied with arms or horses; no Scottish coal or cattle would be
imported. Later in 1705 (4 Anne cap.3) this Act was repealed.
1. The subsequent Act of 1740 for naturalising foreign Protestants
settling in the American colonies (13 Geo.II cap.7) had a somewhat
more extended and explicit list of the attractions of British subjecthood - the 'lenity' of British government, the 'purity' of
religion, and 'benefit' of law, the 'advantages' of trade and the
'security' of property. Those resident in British colonies for
seven years who took the prescribed oaths and declarations were
granted British nationality. Quakers could affirm, and Jews could
be excused from certain Christian expressions.
2. By contrast with mid-seventeenth and early nineteenth century
attitudes, this non-Malthusian view about population as a source of
power was characteristic of the eighteenth century. It led to
measures to prevent the emigration of skilled men.
3. This Act required Scottish peers to swear allegiance, to abjure
papal jurisdiction and the Jacobite cause, and to make a declaration
against transubstantiation.
4. This section was repealed three years later.
5. This section was reaffirmed in 1731 (4 Geo.II cap.21). In 1773
(13 Geo.III cap.21) it was extended to the next generation's children. Among the private acts each year the naturalisation of individuals continued steadily throughout this period: see D. Pickering,
Statutes at Large, VII *passim*.

24. PRIVY COUNCIL'S OPINION ON THE POWER OF A COLONIAL ASSEMBLY
REGARDING NATURALISATION, 19 May 1773.[1]
...That there is nothing in the Act which is repugnant
to the Act of the thirteenth of King George the second,
cap.7, but they are of opinion that the privileges which
this Act offers to Confer, are considerably more Extensive than any Provincial Assembly hath authority to give.
That it hath been doubted whether the Parliament of Ireland, which is a Kingdom and of great Antiquity, could
naturalize to any Effect; and proved irrefragably, that
it could not give, as this Act Imports, all the privil- .
eges of a Natural-born Subject in any other place than
that Island. The Doubt was conceived upon this, that the
King cannot naturalize, and it had never been Used before
the tenth of King Charles the first: which objections
apply much more distinctly in point of Fact and History
to the American Colonies. But supposing they are thought
Competent to Naturalize to Effects merely local[2] and which
don't interfere with the Laws of Great Britain, the Act
now under Consideration, is Exceptional,because it pur-
ports to give all the Qualities of a Natural-born Subject
of Great Britain and particularly the Liberty of Trading
contrary to the plantation Act.

25. *THE CASE OF THE INDIAN CHIEF*, 5 March, 1801.[3]
...Another ground is, that he was not resident in a
British territory, for that the sovereign of this country
is not in possession of Bengal with the same imperial
right as belong to the Mogul. It is contended on this

---

1. A.P.C.(Col.)V.251. A Pennsylvanian Act, passed to invest W.
Kembell of Philadelphia 'with the privileges of a natural-born subject of this province', had been referred to the law officers by the
privy council. The law officers considered the Act *ultra vires*. Now
the privy council concurred.
2. In 1826 a British statute (7 Geo.IV cap.68) enabled the legislative council of Upper Canada to naturalise persons there so that they
could vote and be elected in the province: any such provincial naturalisation bill was however required to be reserved for H.M's assent.
In 1830 a similar Act (1 Will.IV cap.53) was passed for Lower Canada.
In the event both provincial councils legislated to naturalise those
aliens residing seven years previously as British subjects,and those
resident since as British subjects within the colony after they had
completed seven years residence and had taken the oath of allegiance.
3.3 C.Rob. 31 (High Court of Admiralty). The case concerned a British
prize ship captured by the Spaniards and recaptured by the British
with the American consul at Calcutta aboard. One question concerned
whether he was still a British subject , having been born before the
Revolution - though he claimed to be an American. In his judgement
Sir William Scott declared that, even if the consul were an alien, he
was certainly a British merchant while he traded within the Company's
protection in India, and that,having traded with the enemy, he was
liable to have his goods lawfully confiscated.

point that the King of Great Britain does not hold the
British possessions in the East Indies in the right of
sovereignty and therefore that the character of British
merchants does not necessarily attach on foreigners locally resident there.   But taking it that such a paramount
sovereignty on the part of the Mogul princes really and
solidly exists and that Great Britain cannot be deemed to
possess a sovereign right there, still it is to be remembered, that wherever even a mere factory is founded in
the eastern parts of the world, European persons trading
under the shelter and protection of those establishments
are conceived to take their national character from that
association under which they live and carry on their
commerce....

   [In Europe merchants mixed with and became incorporated in the
   local society; in the East they remained strangers and were dependent upon the protection of the factory which was necessary to
   make their trade possible.]

   ...though the sovereignty of the Mogul is occasionally
brought forward for purposes of policy, it hardly exists
otherwise than as a phantom: it is not applied in any
way for the actual regulation of our establishments. The
country exercises the power of declaring war and peace
which is among the strongest marks of actual sovereignty
and if...this empyrean sovereignty of the Mogul is sometimes brought down from the clouds as it were, for purposes of policy, it by no means interferes with the
actual authority which this country and the East India
Company, a creature of this country, exercises there with
full effect.[1]   The law of treason, I apprehend, would
apply to Europeans living there in full force: it is
nothing to say that some particular parts of our civil
code are not applicable to the religious or civil habits
of the Mahomedan or Hindoo natives;   and that they are,
on that account, allowed to remain under their own laws
[just as the Jews might retain their own particular laws in England.]

(4) BRITISH PRECEDENTS FOR OVERSEAS COLONISATION
(a) IRELAND

   In the middle of the twelfth century Erin was a kingdom without
a capital, revenue or government. The High Kingship (*Ard-ri*) was
the prize of nominal supremacy, like the *bretwalda* in the heptarchy
of Anglo-Saxon England: an honour competed for among the half dozen
sub-monarchies and the many feuding princes, chiefs, clans and septs.

---

1. The fiction of Moghul sovereignty did not long survive,however.
Section xcv of the Act renewing the East India charter in 1813 (53
Geo.III cap.155) stated 'that nothing in this Act contained shall
extend or be construed to extend to prejudice or affect the undoubted
sovereignty of the Crown of the United Kingdom of Great Britain, and
Ireland in and over the said territorial acquisitions' of the Company.

The Church, once so dedicated, cultured and evangelistic, now seemed to Rome, in the aftermath of Hildebrand's disciplinary zeal, a scandal to Christendom. In 1155 the pope authorised Henry II to invade Ireland to assert law and order and to reform its Church and people; but Henry was reluctant to act directly, as again he was when Dermot, king of Leinster, in 1166 appealed to him for help against the High King, the kings of Connaught and Meath, and other rivals. But he permitted Dermot to recruit among the Norman-Welsh in South Wales. After early successes these adventures faltered and, faced with a rallying among his Irish enemies and afraid of being cut off, Strongbow, earl of Pembroke and now king of Leinster, pleaded with Henry II again, offering homage and submission on Henry's terms in return for assistance. At this point in October 1171 Henry II invaded Ireland, not to conquer so much as to ensure that the gains of Strongbow and the Geraldines should depend on the Crown of England. He annexed Dublin and its adjacent coast; gave a municipal charter to Dublin; garrisoned Dublin, Wexford and Waterford; demanded homage from Norman barons and Irish chiefs for their lands; and established a justiciar (or viceroy) with a council of magnates to govern for him. Leaving after six months, he made his papal title, 'Lord of Ireland', over to his youngest son in 1177, and when John in 1199 succeeded him on the English throne that Lordship became merged in the Crown of England.

Though thereby Ireland became a dependency of the Crown, it was only a partial, even a paper, conquest. An expatriate Anglo-Norman garrison with a small enclave within 'The Pale' round Dublin and an uncertain and varying influence over the surrounding districts - ('cantreds'); a group of settler magnates ('the middle nation') becoming more Irish each year; and the kings, chiefs and tribesmen ('the wild Irishry') themselves - such was the 'dominion' of Ireland. It was a large offshore island, for the most part quite unaffected by its nominal conquerors, who even within the region round the capital where they clung to some of the trappings of *imperium*, found themselves, more often than not, being conquered in turn by their environment.

I ENGLISH LAW
The main theme of the documents in these first sections is the extension of English rule in Ireland: the establishment and the developing organisation of the structure of government; the imposition and acceptance - if at first only as a vague criterion - of English common law in place of Irish *brehon* custom; and the questions about appeals from courts in Ireland to the king's privy council, king's bench, or the house of lords in England.

§ (i) *The extension of English government and law*
26. POPE ALEXANDER III TO HENRY II, 20 September 1172.[1]
[The pope welcomed news that Henry II had 'extended over that barbarious and uncouth people the plenitude of your peace'. The Irish were a vicious and pagan race: their monstrous custom accepted immorality between relatives: they reverenced neither

---

1. T. Hearne (ed.) *Liber niger scaccarii* (1728) I pp.44-7 Trans. from Latin. By the bull *Laudabiliter* of 1155 Adrian IV, the English pope,

churches nor priests; they ate meat in Lent and paid no tithes.
He gave thanks that]
   ...the forbidden things which were done in that land
might now begin to be discontinued; that the seeds of
virtue might be planted in place of the weeds of vice;
and that, with the aid of God, this people might through
you be brought to abjure the foulness of their sins, and
to submit themselves to the discipline of Christian practice. Thus might you deserve an imperishable crown of
eternal glory and this race be brought to salvation...
And since(as in the excellence of your Majesty) the
Roman Church has fuller rights of jurisdiction over islands than it has over main-lands,[1]we trusting in your
fervent devotion, now hope that you will not only maintain the rights of that Church but also increase them....
   [Therefore the pope exhorted him to continue his good work.] [2]

---

had sanctioned Henry II's projected invasion of Ireland 'to subject
its people to law and to root out from them the weeds of vice',
reserving to the Church its rights and the annual 'Peter's pence'.
But it was not till 1172 that the king's invasion took place and
at the synod of Cashel the leaders of the Church of Ireland accepted the English king as the instrument of their reformation and his
title as conqueror and 'Lord of Ireland'. In March 1213 King John
accepted papal suzerainty over both England and Ireland together
with tribute money and an oath of homage.
1. This claim was based in the apocryphal Donation of Constantine.
2. In their remonstrance to John XXII later in 1317, O'Neill of
Ulster and Tyrone, claiming to be hereditary 'King of Ireland', and
other chiefs rehearsed the crimes committed by the English under
guise of Adrian IV's bull: Ireland had been 'rent by teeth more
cruel than any beasts'; the Irish had been driven to mountains and
bogs to live like dogs - indeed it was 'no more sin to kill an Irishman than a dog'; the English had striven 'to wipe our nation out
entirely and utterly to extirpate it'; and English justice was
partial and oppressive and was denied to the Irish. The worst in
perfidy were the settlers, 'the English of the middle nation' different,indeed,from the English of England: they murdered guests: they
paid no 'Peter's pence'; they divided Irishmen,brother from brother,
and stood arrogantly between the king and his people. Nothing had
been heard from Edward II in reply to their request for him to partition Ireland by reasonable agreement between the Irish and the
English colonists. Therefore in taking up arms and throwing off the
yoke of slavery, the Irish princes were doing nothing unlawful, but
rather meritorious: for the invader had not kept the terms of the
papal bull requiring 'justice and moderation'. (E. Curtis and R.B.
McDowell, *Irish historical documents* (1943) pp,38-46). This later
Irish independence movement had been stimulated by Edward Bruce's
attempt to form an anti-English alliance and by the Scottish victories. But when Bruce was killed at the battle of Faughart, the
alliance collapsed;and English'lordship'was restored by 1319:a dependence which (instead of one on the Scottish Crown) some septs (e.g.
the O'Maddens) clearly preferred.

27. TREATY OF WINDSOR BETWEEN HENRY II AND RODERIC O'CONNOR,
7 October 1175.[1]

...1. Henry, King of England, has granted to the aforesaid Roderic his liegeman, King of Connaught, as long as
he shall faithfully serve him that he shall be king under
him, ready to do him service as his man. 2. And he shall
hold his land as fully and peacefully as he held it before the Lord King of England entered Ireland, rendering
tribute to him. 3. And he shall have all the rest of the
land and its inhabitants under him and shall bring them
to account so that they shall pay full tribute to the
King of England by his hand while they may preserve their
rights to him. 4. And those who hold tenures by any
means may hold them in peace as long as they remain in
fealty to the King of England and continue to pay him
faithfully and fully his tribute, and the other rights
they own him by the hand of the King of Connaught, saving
in all matters the right and honour of the Lord King of
England and himself [i.e. Roderic]....

> [Roderic was to judge and remove those who threw off their all-
> egiance: he might call upon the assistance of the king of Eng-
> land's Constable in Ireland if necessary. Roderic should pay
> tribute of one hide of every ten beasts killed, 'acceptable to
> the merchants'. The king of England retained in his dominion
> and that of his barons - Dublin and its pale; Meath; Wexford
> with the whole of Leinster; and Waterford with its territories
> and Dungarvan. In these domains Roderic was not to meddle.]

28. LETTERS PATENT FROM JOHN TO THE JUSTICIAR REGARDING WRITS,
2 November 1204.[2]

THE King[3]...&c, to his Justiciar, barons, knights,

---

1. Rymer's *Foedera* I pp.41-2. Trans. from Latin. Roderic was High
King (*Ard-ri*) of Connaught. He had offered the Earl of Pembroke,
'Strongbow', the kingdom of Leinster under him, but the offer was
refused. Strongbow claimed the kingdom by marriage and conquest and
when he heard that Henry II was on the way to Ireland by way of Pembroke, he chose to make submission to the English king. Rory now
submitted too.
2. H.F. Berry (ed.) *Early Statutes of Ireland* (1907) I p.3. The justiciar was chief justice, commander of the feudal levy,and royal
political agent. He was answerable to the king for carrying out instructions sent from England. It was alleged that,by the 'statute of
Henry Fitz Empress',Henry II gave the council of magnates in Ireland
the right temporarily to choose a justiciar when a vacancy occurred
and before the king's nomination was known: a right used in 1425,
1470 and 1477, abolished by Poynings' Parliament in 1494,and enacted
by the Irish parliament in 1541 (33 Hen.VIII sess.2 cap.2). In the
absence of the king from England, England too was ruled by the justiciar.[For the election of an Irish justiciar, see p.114].
3. King John had been appointed 'Lord of Ireland' by his father in
1177. Indeed, Henry as *'Dominus terrae'* had already asserted his
right as feudal overlord and supreme landlord, and had introduced
English feudal law into his grants of Leinster and Meath.

and all his faithful subjects of Ireland,...&c, Know ye
that we have granted authority to our Justiciar of Ireland, and his writs shall run throughout our entire land
and dominion of Ireland, namely - the writ of Right, or
half a knight's fee and less; and of *Mort d'ancestor* likewise of half a knight's fee and less; and the limitation
of *Mort d'ancestor* shall be after the passage of King Henry
our father, from Ireland into England; and the writ of
Novel Disseisin shall have its limitation after our first
coronation at Canterbury, and the writ of Fugitives and
Villeins shall have its limitation after the taking of
Dublin; and the writ for making bounds between two
vills; and so we command and strictly enjoin that you
cause these things to be done and firmly observed throughout our entire jurisdiction of Ireland.[1] *Westminster*

29. LETTERS PATENT FROM HENRY III TO THE JUSTICIAR REGARDING ENGLISH
LAW, 29 June 1226.[2]
    The King to his beloved and faithful G *[eoffrey]* de
Marisco, Justiciar of Ireland, greeting. We command you
that you keep and cause to be kept the laws and customs
of our land of England in our land of Ireland, as the
lord King John, our father enjoined them to be kept when
he was last in that land. [3]

Windsor.

1. On the king's last expedition to Ireland in 1210 ('12 King John')
he decreed that the laws of England should be observed in Irish
courts. It was asserted that this was done at the request of 'all
the men of Ireland', meaning of course not the Gaelic chiefs but the
Anglo-Norman magnates ‒ the leaders of the colonists. The right to
English law and liberties remained a useful claim for the Anglo-Irish
to make. In 1217 **Magna** Carta was sent over to Ireland and published
there, confirming to the Anglo-Normans those rights as if they had
been born in England.
2. H. Berry (ed.) *op.cit.* I p21. On 17 May 1222 Henry III had reminded
the Archbishop of Dublin 'as you well know that the laws of our land
of Ireland and of England are and ought to be the same'. *ibid.* I p20.
In 1228 he directed that King John's charter for English laws should
be proclaimed throughout the counties in Ireland.
3. Patent Rolls, 11 Hen.III, recorded that when King John came to
Ireland he brought with him 'discreet' men skilled in laws,by whose
concurrent advice at the request of the Irish,'he commanded the laws
of England to be observed'. (Walter Harris ed. *Hibernica* II (1750)
pp. 1-2). In 1229 by the 'Statute of Ireland', the king in council
enacted that in his Dominion of Ireland the questions relating to
female inheritance and knight service should be determined, not by
Irish customary law (*brehon*) but by English common law. The rule of
succession by *tanistry* which provided for an heir to be chosen within
the sept, not merely on grounds of birth but of seniority and worth,
provided a complication for it created secure personal estate only for
the lifetime of the elected chief or captain. So did Irish *gavelkind* which might mean repeated divisions of lands on the death of any
member of a sept. Furthermore, the common protection and trust which

30. LETTERS PATENT FROM HENRY III TO THE JUSTICIAR, 9 September 1246.[1]

Foreasmuch as for the common benefit of the land of Ireland and the unity of the King's dominions, the King wills and by the Common Council of the King it is provided, That all laws and customs which are observed in the kingdom of England should be observed in Ireland, and the said land should be subject to the said laws, and should be ruled by the same as the lord, King John, when he was last in Ireland, ordained and ordered to be done. Forasmuch also as the King wills that all writs of common right which run in England should likewise run in Ireland under the King's new seal, which is commanded to the Archbishops *etc.* that for the peace and quiet of the said land they permit them to be ruled and governed by the same laws and follow them in all things.

Woodstock.

31. LETTERS PATENT FROM EDWARD I TO THE JUSTICIAR, 1277.[2]

Edward, by the grace of God, King of England, lord of Ireland, duke of Aquitaine, to his beloved and trusty Robert de Ufford, his justiciar in Ireland, greeting.

Concerning the improvement in the condition and peace of our land of Ireland, about which you have recently informed us through your letters, we rejoice and are exceedingly glad; and, commending greatly your diligence in this respect, we hope that (with the help of God) you will in the future continue successfully and energetically, so far as you are able, the work you have so far laudably undertaken there.

Furthermore concerning this, since the commonalty of Ireland present to us 8,000 marks on this account, that we should grant to them the enjoyment of English laws in the land aforesaid, know you that we, because the laws which the Irish possess are detestable to God and are contrary to all right, to such an extent that they ought not to be considered laws;

We have on this matter treated carefully and deliberated more fully with our council, and it appears sufficiently expedient to us and our council to grant to the said people the enjoyment of English laws;[3] provided

could be ensured for the sept as a whole by Irish custom, was threatened by the individualisation of tenure when the chief (for example) was admitted to the rights of English law. By contrast with Wales, where law was territorial (and Welsh law was pleaded in the kings' courts), in Ireland law was accepted as personal: some claimed the 'privilege' of English laws; others not.

1. *Foedera* I p.266 Trans. from Latin.
2. *Foedera* I (1816 ed.) p.540. Trans from French. Robert d'Ufford, the justiciar, had reported to the king the desire of 'the Irish' for 'the common laws of the English'.
3. Admission to English law was granted to individual Irish and resident English inhabitants from time to time (e.g. H.S.Sweetman, *Cal. of docs. relating to Ireland 1285-92* pp.33,38.[see also below, No.34.]

nevertheless that in this there is a common agreement
running among the people, or at least among the prelates
and magnates of that land who are well disposed.[1]

On account of this, we order you that, after deliber-
ating with them on the matter, and carefully examining
the wishes of the people, those prelates and the magnates
well disposed to us, and reaching agreement between you
and them concerning the highest sum of money which you
can obtain, you shall arrange with them, on the basis of
these promises and in our name, for the full payment to
us for that reason by the agreement of all, or at least
of the greater and more responsible section of them,
according as it seems to your judgement most expedient
for our honour and convenience.

Provided nevertheless that they shall agree to provide good and brave footsoldiers, up to a certain number,
which you may decide upon with them, for us once only,
ready to come to us, when we shall issue orders for
them.[2]

32. WRIT FROM EDWARD I TO THE JUSTICIAR FOR THE OBSERVANCE OF
CERTAIN ENGLISH STATUTES, 14 September 1285.[3]

Be it remembered that on Friday, the Feast of the
Exhaltation of the Holy Cross, 14 September in the 13th
year...&c., at Winchester, were delivered to Roger Bretun,
clerk of the Venerable Father W.(recte Stephen) bishop of
Waterford, then Justiciar of Ireland, certain Statutes
by the King and his council made and provided, namely,
the Statutes of Westminster made immediately after the
King's coronation, and the Statutes of Gloucester and
the Statutes made for Merchants, and the Statutes of
Westminster in the parliament of the King at Easter in
the said year provided and made, to be brought into
Ireland and there to be proclaimed and observed.[4]

---

1. Edward I realised he had not the power or authority in Ireland to
enforce the total acceptance of English law.
2. Though there was doubt about the extension of English law, it was
often referred to as a criterion. The king's council declared in
1285,in relation to certain Irish customs about inheritance, that
'the land of Ireland ought to be governed by the laws and customs
used and approved in the Kingdom' (ibid.p.31); and again in 1289, in
respect of the rights of Geoffrey de Geynville in his liberty, the
phrase occurs - 'in every liberty of England to whose laws the land
of Ireland ought to conform'. (ibid.p.241).
3. H.F. Berry (ed.) op.cit.I p.47. In 1324 (ibid.p.295), more detailed instructions were given concerning the way in which English ordinances for Ireland were to be made known to officials and judges there.
They were to be enrolled in the Irish chancery under the Irish seal.
For the form of a summoning of an Irish Parliament in 1297, see E.
Curtis and R.B.McDowell, Irish Historical Documents (1943)pp.32-8 .
4. Thereby the main features of Edward's legal code contained in 3,
6 & 13 Ed.I were ostensibly introduced into Ireland: the system of
courts, writs, franchises, tenures, debt, pardon etc.

33. (a) STATUTE OF YORK (12 Ed.II St.1) 20 October 1318.[1]
Forasmuch as divers people of the realm of England and
of the land of Ireland have heretofore often times suffered mischiefs and disherisons by reason that in some
cases where there was default in the law no remedy was
ordained; and also forasmuch as some points of the statutes heretofore made have need of clarification, our Lord
the King Edward son of King Edward, desiring that full
right be done to his people at his parliament held at
York, the third week after Michaelmas in the twelfth year
of his reign, by assent of the prelates, earls, barons
and commonalty of his realm there assembled hath made
these Acts and Statutes here following the which he wills
to be strictly observed in the said realm and the said
land....

33. (b) WRIT FROM EDWARD II TO CHANCELLOR OF IRELAND, 10 September
1320.[2]
...Certain statutes made by us in our parliament called at York with the assent of the prelates, earls, barons and the whole commonalty of our realm there being,
for the common weal of the people of the said realm and
of our land of Ireland, We do send to you signed under
our seal, commanding that these statutes you do cause to
be kept in our aforesaid chancery and to be enrolled in
the rolls of the said chancery and under our seal which
we use in Ireland in form patent to be exemplified; and
to every one of our courts in the said land and into every
county of that same land to be sent by our writs under the
same seal; commanding our officials of those courts and
the sheriffs of the said counties, that the aforesaid
statutes in their presence they do cause to be published
and the same in all and every article as much as to
every one of them appertains, to be observed....

34. LETTERS PATENT FROM EDWARD II TO THE LORD-LIEUTENANT REGARDING
ENGLISH LAW OF LIFE AND LIMB, 20 January 1321.[3]
Know you that whereas in the time of lord Edward

Similarly on 4 April 1307,by a writ to his justiciar,Edward I sent
copies of certain statutes 'made in our Parliament at Carlisle...
for the common utility of the people of our realm and the improvement
of the state of our entire dominion'. These Acts 'sealed under our
seal of England' the justiciar was to publish and was commanded to
enforce in Ireland: (H.F. Berry (ed.) I p.241). Thereby the king disregarded the Parliament of Ireland and assumed that his English Parliament had a sufficient, imperial authority to make laws for Ireland.
1. This preamble is followed by six different heads of legislation,
relating mainly to tenures and legal process.
2. D. Pickering (ed.),*Statutes at Large* I, 357. Trans from Latin.
3. H.F. Berry (ed.) *op. cit.* I p.292. The viceroy, Roger Mortimer,
was now styled lord-lieutenant, not justiciar. In the aftermath of
the failure of the Bruce invasion, there was little revenge taken
against rebels, but rather appeasement, as exemplified in these

of famous memory, formerly King of England, our father,
and afterwards in our time, it has been frequently shown
to our said father and to us, with heavy complaint, that
because the Irish admitted to English law in the said
land did not previously enjoy the said law concerning
life and limbs, our peace in the said regions was disturbed in many ways and evil-doers there not being punished
were emboldened to commit divers felonies, to the grevious
injury to our people of the said regions,and [whereas]at
length in our Parliament summoned at Westminster in the
octave of St. Michael last past, prayer was made to us
that we should cause a remedy to be applied thereupon,
We therefore, wishing to provide for the peace and quietness of our said people, will That all the Irish previously admitted to English law and those who hereafter
shall happen to be admitted thereto, do use henceforth
the said law concerning life and limbs, and by these
presents we command that the Irish so admitted and to be
admitted to the said law, as well within liberties as
without, be treated according to the custom of the English [always saving the lord's rights in the chattels of *betaghes*,
or native villeins.]

35. 'STATUTES OF KILKENNY' (40 Ed.III), 18 February 1366.[1]
    Whereas at the conquest of the land of Ireland and
for a long time after the English of the said land used
the English language, mode of riding and apparel and were

---

letters patent; but it was of course impossible to enforce this
policy generally, even in the Pale. Nevertheless,there were some in
remote areas, like the O'Maddens of Galway, who asked for and were
granted English law.
1. H.F. Berry (ed.) *op. cit.* I. pp.435-7. Trans from French. Edward
III's son Lionel, earl of Ulster and lord of Connaught, who had been
sent as his father's lieutenant with full powers to pacify and secure
Ireland generally, summoned this Parliament of colonists in a final
effort to secure at least the loyal English in the organised counties and liberties of the east and south-east. These statutes marked
the end of attempts to reduce the whole island to Anglo-Norman law
and dominion. A large part of Ireland was abandoned to Gaelic law
and custom. The chiefs and tribes there were placed beyond the reach
of English law and redress in all courts as the king's 'Irish enemies'. A vain attempt was made to prevent the inroads of Gaelic cul-
ture on the so-called 'degenerate English' of the marches (though of
course they were largely by origin French and by assimilation Irish):
but the separation of cultures proved impossible to enforce. Indeed,
the use of the English tongue and custom continued to decline among
the Anglo-Irish; only Irish living among the English in the 'obedient shires' could be admitted as an individual act of favour to
rights under English law; the 'servile Irish' outside those shires
were outlawed and rightless.
This statute was confirmed by the Irish parliament in 1495 (10 Hen.
VII cap.8). Though a 'statute', its contents had been largely an-
ticipated by an 'ordinance' in the great council of Ireland in 1351.

governed and ruled, they and their subjects, called *betaghes*, by the English law; in which time God and Holy
Church and their franchises according to their conditions
were maintained and they themselves lived in due subjection....

 [but now many 'degenerate' English settlers had given up the
use of English language, dress, law and usage for that of the
Irish 'enemies' and had intermarried with these native Irish to
the detriment of the king's allegiance, homage and service, the
king in his Irish Parliament ordained under prescribed penalties,
the freedom of Holy Church, the prohibition of intermarriage and
the use of English names and dress.]

 IV. Also, whereas diversity of government and divers
laws in one land cause diversity of allegiance and disputes among the people, it is agreed and established,
that no English having disputes with other English,
henceforth make distraint or take pledge, distress or
vengeance against any other at the common law, and that
no English be governed in the settlement of their disputes by March or *Brehon* law, which by right ought not to
be called law, but bad custom: but that they be governed,
as right is, by the common law of the land, as the lieges
of our lord the King; and if any do to the contrary, and
there-of be attaint, that he be taken and imprisoned, and
adjudged as a traitor. And that no difference of allegiance henceforth be made between the English born in Ireland, and the English born in England, by calling them
English hobbe, or Irish dog, but that all be called by
one name, the English lieges of our lord the King, and
that he who shall be found doing to the contrary be punished by imprisonment for a year, and afterwards fined,
at the King's will; and by his ordinance it is not the
intention of our lord the King but that it may be lawful
for any one who can, to take distress for services and
rents due to them, and for damage *feasant* as the common
law requires....

 [War was to be undertaken only on the authority of the king's
council with the advice of the magnates and commons of the county
where the issue arose. The English were not to stir up wars:
they were not to sell arms or war horses to the Irish, or even
food in war time: they were not to entertain Irish minstrels and
poets who acted as spies in 'a land...at war'. They must practice
the bow, and use the English tongue. Only in the marches should
kerns and hired soldiers be maintained. Every chieftain of English lineage[1] was made responsible for the punishment of his foll-
owers and retainers as 'captains of their nations'. There should
be 'one peace and one war' throughout Ireland: but in every peace-

---

1. e.g. the Butlers, Burkes and Geraldines, who were now lords over
about one-third of the island and who played a prominent part in the
Gaelic recovery and renaissance. As earls of Ormond, Desmond and
Kildare these leaders of 'the middle nation' came to rule large autonomous palatinate-like areas, partly as feudal seigneurs and partly
as Gaelic kings.

ful county - the 'obedient shires' of Louth, Meath, Trim, Dublin,
Kildare, Kilkenny, Wexford, Waterford and Tipperary, - there would
be keepers of the peace to review the loyal English for militia
duties. Labourers were not to pass beyond the seas: and the
king's officers were not to be hindered.   Those breaking these
statutes would be excommunicated.][1]

36. ACT AGAINST *BREHON* LAW (10 Hen.VII cap.11) 1495.[2]
     Item, prayen the commons of this land of Ireland, that
where it is used by divers of the said land for the death
of any of their friends or kinsmen to bren,[3] slay,or
robbe, as many as beareth the name of him that is slain,
whereas his next heir should sue appeal of death in the
King's Court for that murder, and by reason of such damp-
nable wayes will compel all such persons as been of the
same name that he is of, that was causer of that murder,
howbeit that he was never of his blood, to pay assaut,
that is to say, to depart with the most part of their
goods by way of amends: Wherefore it be ordeyned, enacted and established by authority of this present Parliament, That if any person or persons from this time
forward doe challenge or cause any of the King's subjects
to pay any assaut or have amends, otherwise than the
king's lawes will in that behalfe, that he or they that
so shall offend, and thereof to be convicted,have judgement *de vie* &c. *de member* ....
     [The hue and cry authorised by the Statute of Winchester should
     be levied in cases of murder and robbery; and the provisions of
     the same statute should be duly carried out as 'it hath been in
     old time past within the said land'.]

37. STATE PAPER ON THE CONDITION OF IRELAND, 1515.[4]
     ...Ther byn more then 60 countryes, called Regyons,

---

1. In 1375 Edward III summoned 60 representatives of the Irish Parliament to come before his council in England; and, though they complied, they asserted that they were 'not bound to send such representatives' to England and they reserved to themselves 'the right of
assenting to any subsidies made in their name'. It was now accepted
as prudent, in this period of aristocratic Home Rule, that taxes
should be sanctioned by the Irish Parliament; but that Parliament
dwindled in numbers and soon became representative of little more
than parts of Leinster, Meath and a few towns.
For the declaration by the Irish Parliament a century later that
Ireland was governed by Irish law and by statutes made or confirmed
in the Irish Parliament,see below No.46.
2.*Irish Statutes* I p.50:the Act prohibiting such custom'other than the
King's laws will'.The last notable *brehon* judgment was probably in 1584.
It concerned a land dispute in Lower Ormond,where it lingered longer
than elsewhere(e.g.E.Curtis,*Calendar of Ormond deeds* (1841) for a deed
between Maurus Mc an Gown and Donald O'Meara and the rights of McDonn-
ail Buy to redeem the lands 'according to the old Irish charters'.)
3. To spoil or to foul - also to burn.
4. State Papers II: Henry VIII pt.iii (1834) pp.1-30. This unsigned

in Ireland, inhabyted with the Kinges Irishe enymyes,some
region as bygge as a shyre, some more, some lesse, unto
a lytyll,...where reygneith more than 60 Chyef Capytaynes,
whereof some callyth themselffes Kynges, some Kynges
Peyres in ther langage, some Pryncies, some Dukes, some
Archdukes, that lyveyth onely by the swerde and obeyeth
to no other temperall person, but onely to himself that
is stronge: and every of the said Capytaynes makeyth
warre and peace for hymself, and holdeith by swerde, and
hathe imperiall jurysdyction within his rome, and obeyeth
to noo other person, Englyshe ne Iryshe, except only to
suche persones, as maye subdue hym by the swerde....
   Also, ther is more than 30 greate captaines of the
Englyshe noble folke, that folowyeth the same Iryshe
ordre....
        [The names of the counties, which 'obey not the Kinges lawes',
    were listed. Although the operation of the King's laws was
    effective only in parts of Uryell, Meath, Dublin and Kildare, the
    former number of officials had not been correspondingly reduced,
    while the chaotic financial situation was causing great hardship
    to the English resident there.   It was now proposed that, to
    remedy the situation,]
 ...every of the sayd Iryshe greate landlordes, and chyefs
of every greate nation, that shall dyspend by the Kinges
graunts 1000 markes yerely, by estimation, be create and
made Lord of the Kinges Parlyament and Greate Counsayll,
and to answer to the Kinges Parlyament and Great Counsayll, as ofte as they shalbe callyd to such placeys, as
shallbe please the Deputye to retayne the same....
   Also, that the chyef of every pety nation of every
Iryshe country, that shall dyspend by the Kinges graunte
the some of 500 markes, to him and his heyres for ever,
be, at the wyll and dyscressyon of the deputye and the
sayd captaine, made Knight, and shall injoye the honour
and worsship of thordre of Knyghthodd, as other Englyshe
Knyghtes dothe.
   Also, that every Iryshe landlord, and every chyef
captaine of his nation, greate or small, shalbe barbeyd
and roundeyed,[1] after th Englyshe maner, and not after
the Iryshe maner; and he that shalbe presume to the
contrary, to lose and forfet to the King £20 *tociens quo-
ciens*; and over that none of the sayd landlordes, greate
or small, suffyr any other person, horsman or foteman, on
the aforesayd payne, to use the contrarye of this the
Kinges statute; and he that shalbe fortune to be incorry-
gyble in the premisseis in despyceing the Kinges statute,

---

paper contained many details relating to the state of Ireland for
the young king to consider. It also somewhat enthusiastically suggested plans for Ireland's reformation and development, and optimistically estimated the revenues from Ireland to be greater than those
of England.
1. Peter the Great of course similarly considered facial hair a
matter of civilised and governmental concern.

to lose his goodes and his landes from hym and his heyres
for ever.

Also, that the Bysshop, and the chyef landlord of
every Iryshe countrey, subgett to the King, be ordayned
allwaye by the Kinges deputye to be Justyces of the
Kinges Peace within the same contrarye, with power and
autotyrie to inquyre for the King, and to punyshe all
maner ryottes, felonyes, and all other transgressions
don within the same countrye, and for thexecution of
the same to have power and auctorytie to call them Englyshe or Iryshe, whom they lyste, after ther dyscretion,
so that all the complaintes of the sayd countrye shalbe
determyned within them selffes,...

Also, that every landelord, greate or small, of every
Iryshe countrey, subget to the King, put his sonne and
heyre to Dublyn, or to Drogheda, or to some other Englyshe towne, to lerne to wryte and rede, and to speke
Englyshe, to lerne also the draught and maners of Englyshe men,...

Also, for a fynall conclusyon, yf the land were put
in ordre...the Kinges revenues of this lande wolde be
unto lytyll, or nought, lesse then the revenues of
Ireland,...

[considering how profits would grow 'by the meanes' and how
customs, fees, tollages, poundage, wardships, forfeitures, amercements, *etc.* would increase[1] 'if the King would cast his loke
thereon and to streche his arme to accomplyshe and performe the
same'. Prophecy had said that war in the land would cease, and
God would favour the king backed by the English and Irish armies
to subdue France, rescue Greece, recover Constantinople, vanqu-
ish the Turk, win the Holy Cross and the Holy Land, and die Emperor of Rome.

'Notwithstanding the said mysordre of Ireland', men already
wish to go and live there.]

If this lande were put ones in ordre as aforesaid,
hyt wolde be none other but a very Paradyce, delycious
of all plesaunce in respect and regard to any other land
in this worlde.... [1]

38. (a) ELIZABETH I TO SIR HENRY SIDNEY, 11 June 1567.[2]
    [She welcomed the arrest of the earl of Desmond. The opportun-

---

1. An early example of promotional wishful-thinking. Enthusiasts
for empire with incorrigible and irrepressible optimism have always
made exaggerated claims to secure support, interest and capital and
have tended to inflate expectations and oversell claims. The 'puff-
ing' of foolish bubbles in the brochures of adventurers has misled
many historians and later theorists of imperialism to accept these
dreams as realities.
2. P.R.O: State papers (Ireland) XXI No.10; see also Calendar of
State Papers (Ireland) 1509-73 p.335. These documents attempt to
illustrate the debate on how best to exercise control in Ireland.
The methods of indirect rule - government by the Gaelic chiefs
('captains of the nations') or by Norman-Irish magnates with 'palat-

ity should be taken to grant 'to the gentlemen of those parts'
that their estates should be immediately dependent on the Crown.]
    ...the captains of the Irishry *[were]* to be encouraged
to surrender their estates and receive grants of them by
way of inheritance and by this means to reduce the number
of men of war kept by them. Care to be taken in drawing
the grants that the estates be included within the jurisdiction of some county, and that such inconveniences as
were found to arise from the grants to the Earls of Ormond and Desmond may be avoided. A fit person to be appointed president of Munster, and if that answer, a similar course to be followed for Connaught. The insufficiency of the Bench to be remedied by the appointment of
judges from England with increased salaries....Purpose
to plant Ulster with obedient subjects ....
    [Sidney was to be principal minister, and Captain Humfrey Gilbert
    was to assist him in the plantation.]
Has determined to plant certain counties with English...]¹
    [She complained that she disliked the querulous tone in Sidney's
    letters.]²

___

ine 'jurisdictions had not been successful: the tyrannies of Desmond in Munster and O'Neill in Ulster had proved unreliable instruments of English rule. Direct rule was a heavy burden on the Crown.
Garrison colonies on the Irish frontier in the King's and Queen's
Counties in the mid-sixteenth century had been shown to be an expensive means of retaining conquered areas; and Sir Henry Sidney, an
able administrator, who had been appointed lord deputy in 1565, was
anxious to promote some private plantations as an alternative to
direct Crown action: Richard Grenville, Humfrey Gilbert and Thomas
Smith all became interested in schemes for the colonisation of Munster, and of Ulster too when the murder of Shane O'Neill in June 1567
was known.
1. In part this was an attempt to keep out the Scots (C.S.P.XX No.41
p.327). Sidney and Gilbert (who was negotiating terms on behalf of a
west-country interest) favoured - and the queen came to approve (6
July 1567: *ibid.*XXI no.49 p.340) - that 'some gentlemen of good
houses within our realm here may be induced to come over with their
own tenants and friends and to have assigned to them such portions of
territories there, as yielding for the same small rent at the beginning with an increase reasonable after some years' possession, and so,
by the continuance of time, establish those counties with English
birth and government'. It would be expensive; there must be surveys,
fortifications, and division into shires, but Elizabeth I saw it
would place burdens on other shoulders than hers. They must recruit
'the best sort you can': in time the forts could be handed over to
loyalist English gentlemen-planters. Thomas Smith's plans for more
forcible planting would be too costly. As for the Irish, she felt it
necessary to win their obedience by training those who had suffered
Irish tyranny 'to feel and taste of the sweets of civil order and
justice. So that which is wished and cannot be perfected may by
preparation be made ready hereafter to succeed'.
2. The latter part of this letter may have been drafted by Sir William Cecil, who privately advised Sidney to show ' patience and sin-

38. (b) SIR HENRY SIDNEY TO SIR WILLIAM CECIL, 12 November 1568.[1]
   Nowe for the mayne of Ulster, - to trewe it is that
the charges willbe intollerable for her Majestie as I
feare either to defend that Province by Souldioures, or
to plante it with People at her owne charges, and yet
one of these ii waies must nedes be taken before reformacion or Revenue can be loked for. And therefore in my
opinion persausion woolde be used emonges the nobiletie
and principale gentlemen of England that there might be
sondri mens charges, without exhausting of the Princes'
particuler purse, be induced here some Collany....
       [Ulster might be peopled with a colony of 2000 men 'where there
       liveth not the 200th man that might be nourished'. Nevertheless,
       it might in time provide an annual revenue of £5000; but the
       gentlemen undertakers would have to provide money, apparel, vic-
       tuals, tools and seed, for they would find there 'nothing else
       but earthe'.][2]

cerity under the correction of the queen's letter'. (*ibid.*XXI No.13)
When Sidney informed her of O'Neill's death she was eager to have a
careful map of 'the demesnes of our earldom of Ulster....properly
belong[*ing*] to us' so that she could initiate loyalist plantations.
Though she knew 'all would come by conquest', she wanted to know what
lands were held by service tenure and what by rent, for 'in conscience' distinction must be made and recognised. (*ibid.*XXI No.10).
Elizabeth did not wholly trust Sidney's advice: indeed, since he
was also lord president of the council of Wales from 1559 to 1586,
she might have been jealous of his authority. Certainly,though both
for financial reasons ruled out direct rule, Sidney favoured a
stronger central control of any power delegated to earls, presidents,
chiefs or undertakers, than the queen herself did.
1. C.S.P. (Ireland)XXVI. No.18 p.393: see also R. Dunlop in *Scottish
Hist. Rev.* XXII pp.51ff, 115ff and 192ff. Sidney was recommending the
establishment of English presidencies in Munster and Connaught to
replace the quasi-palatine jurisdictions of the Norman-Irish earldoms; the reduction of chiefly autonomy by the abolition of coign
and livery; the imposition of tenures direct from the Crown by surrender and re-grant; and the gradual anglicisation of Ireland by
'planting' loyal English colonists. Sir William Cecil was the
queen's principal secretary of state from 1558 to 1572. While he,
Sidney and the queen all rejected the costly policy of direct rule
advocated by Edmund Tremayne, clerk to the council (B.M. *Titus B*
XII p.358) and many others, the queen did not fully back Sidney in
his policy of more control and greater supervision. Elizabeth I was
prepared to give the earls and chiefs another chance and to leave new
responsibilities to the'undertakers'. The Irish Parliament by statute
set up presidencies in Munster and Connaught in 1570 and passed an
Act to abolish coign and livery.
2. But the earls , chiefs and owners of the soil - Anglo-Irish as well
as Irish - resisted appropriation; and armed plantation by the private
enterprise of Carew, Smith, Essex and others proved bloody, expensive
and ineffective in Leinster, Munster, Ards and Antrim during the next
decade; as did similar attempts by Raleigh, Grenville and others in
Munster during the years after 1586 when the Desmond estates were

39. EDMUND SPENSER: A VIEW OF THE STATE OF IRELAND, c.1596.[1]
     It *[Brehon law]* is a rule of Right unwritten, but deliv-
ered by tradition from one to another, in which oftentimes there appeareth great shew of Equity, in determining the Right between Party and Party, but in many things
repugning quite both to God's Law, and Man's....there
be many wide Countries in Ireland, which the Laws of
England were never established in, nor any acknowledgment of Subjection made; and also even in those which
are subdued, and seem to acknowledge Subjection, yet the
same *Brehon* Law is practised among themselves, by reason,
that dwelling as they do, whole Nations and Septs of the
Irish together, without any Englishman among them, they
may do what they list, and compound or altogether conceal
amongst themselves their own Crimes, of which no notice
can be had by them, which would and might amend the same,
by the Rule of the Laws of England....
     [It was a 'wicked law' not least in the mere imposition of a
  fine for murder. It had been extending its hold at the expense
  of Englishry and English law.]
     The common Law of England is...of itself most right-
ful and very convenient (I suppose) for the Kingdom for
which it was first devised; for this (I think) as it
seems reasonable that out of the Manners of your People
and Abuses of your Country for which they were invented,
they take their first Beginning or else they should be
most unjust; for no Laws of Man (according to the
straight Rule of Right) were just but as in regard of
the Evils which they prevent and the Safety of the Com-
monweal which they provide for...Now, then, if these
Laws in Ireland be not likewise applied and filled for
that Realm, they are sure very inconvenient....
     [He instanced as a defect of the common law the abuse of trial
  by jury by prejudiced Irish jurors.]

40. RESOLUTION OF JUDGES CONCERNING IRISH CUSTOM OF *GAVELKIND*,
                                     (Hilary Term), 1605.[2]
     [The division of the lands of the 'mere Irish', and the custom of
  succession by *tanistry* or *gavelkind* was described. Such law
  prevented development and improvement. *Gavelkind* in Ireland

---

forfeited to the Crown.
1. pp.7-8, 33 (1763 ed.) Edmund Spenser was a clerk in the Irish
chancery and then to the council of Munster. He had been appointed
secretary to the lord lieutenant, Lord Grey of Wilton, in 1580. The
second part of *The Faerie Queene* was completed and published in 1596.
Though he accepted that the totality of English law was appropriate
only in England where it had developed, he believed that its gradual
introduction into Ireland would be beneficial and just to the Irish.
2. Sir John Davies, *Les reports des cases...en les courts de roi en
Ireland* (1674) 49-0. Trans. from French. This resolution at the
order of the Deputy was recorded in the acts of the Irish council.
The rights of those inheriting land by Irish custom before James I's
accession were safeguarded. Two years later in king's bench (*ibid.*

was different from the custom in Kent;[1] for example, it permitted
bastards to inherit in preference to legitimate heirs. It res-
embled more the custom in North Wales which was reformed in 1284
(12 Ed.I) and abolished in 1543 (34 & 35 Hen.VIII cap.26).]

For these reasons and because all the said Irish
counties and inhabitants of them were formerly to be governed by the rule of the English common law, it was resolved and declared by all the judges that the said Irish
custom of *gavelkind* was void in law, not solely for its
inconvenience and irrationality, but also since it was
a more personal custom and should not alter the descent
of inheritance.

And all lands in these Irish counties were adjudged
to descend according to the rules of common law and that
women may be endowed and sons may inherit in those lands,
any Irish usage and custom notwithstanding....

41. FYNES MORYSON: THE COMMONWEALTH OF IRELAND, c. 1610.[2]
  [His account of the 'wild or mere Irish' emphasised their readiness to resort to force rather than law, their turbulence, feuds,
  idleness; their immorality, gambling and drunkenness; their lack
  of respect for order, etc. The system of elective succession
  (*tanistry*) led to licence, disorder, demagogery &. The Anglo-
  Irish were equally lawless, dirty and degenerate: recent settlements had attracted the drop-outs and misfits; the plantation of
  Munster following Desmond's rebellion in 1586 had made Ireland
  'the sink of England'.]
Touching the laws. The mere Irish from of old to the
very end of the war had certain judges among themselves,
who determined their causes by an unwritten law, only
retained by tradition, which in some things had a smack
of right and equity, and in some others was contrary to
all divine and human laws. These judges were called
Brehons , altogether unlearned, and great swillers of
Spanish sack (which the Irish merrily called the King of
Spain's daughter). Before these judges no probable or
certain arguments were available to condemn the accused,
but only manifest apprehensions in the fact. A murder
being committed, these judges took upon them to be inter-
cessors to reconcile the murderer with the friends of the
murdered, by a gift vulgarly called Iriesh *[eric]*.[3] They

___

40) *tanistry* was declared abolished as repugnant to common law; it
differed (it was said) from the peculiar custom of Denbigh which had
been explicitly permitted by statute and from that of Kent where
gavelkind and English common law both antedated the Conqueror. In
Ireland it was revived as an instrument against Catholic landlords by
an Act of 1704.
1. For statutory acceptance and modification of the law of *gavelkind*
in England see 31 Hen.VIII cap.3. It was not entirely abolished in
Kent till 1926.
2. From his *Itinerary II*, Chapter 5, printed in C.L. Falkiner, *Illustrations of Irish History* (1904), pp.241-281. Moryson was secretary
to Charles Blount, lord Mountjoy, as lord deputy of Ireland.
3. This was a fine prescribed for violent crime, including murder,

did extort unreasonable rewards for their judgement, as
the eleventh part of every particular thing brought in
question before them.   For the case of incontinency,
they exacted a certain number of cows (which are the Irish
rewards and bribes) from the married and unmarried, though
they lived chastely (which indeed was rare among them),
yet more from the married and chaste than from others.
Myself spoke with a gentleman then living, who affirmed
that he had paid seven cows to these judges, because he
could not bring witnesses of his marriage, when he had
been married fifty years. Among other their barbarous
laws, or rather customs and traditions, I have formerly
spoke of their tenure of land, vulgarly called *themistry*,
or *tanistry*, whereby not the eldest son but the elder uncle,
or the most valiant (by which they understand the most
dissolute swordsman), of the family succeeded the deceased by the election of the people, whereof came many murders and parricides and rebellions, besides great wrongs
done to the state, as in this particular case:— If the
predecessor, of free will or constrained by arms, had
surrendered his inheritance to the King, and had taken it
back from the King's grant by letters patents upon rent
and other conditions for the public good, they at his
death made this act void, because he had no right but for
life. By these judges and by these and like laws were
the mere Irish judged to the end of the last rebellion,
though the English laws had long before been received in
Ireland by consent of the three states in Parliament.
    For in the tenth year of King Henry VII, by consent of
the three states in Parliament, the barbarous *Brehon* judges
and laws, and this particular law of *themistry* by name, were
all abrogated, and the common law and statutes of Parliament made to that day in England, were all established
in Ireland ,[1] And from the first conquest to that time and
long after, the states of Ireland were called to the Parliament by the King's writs, and the laws there made were
sent into England, and there allowed or deaded in silence
by the King; and so the approved were sent back to the
Lord Deputy, who accordingly confirmed them for Acts of
that Parliament, and rejected the other by the king's
authority, by which also the Lord Deputy, according to his
instructions from the King, prorogued or dissolved the
Parliaments. But if the worthy progenitors of our late
kings should revive, and see the face of these Parliaments
changed, and the very English-Irish backward to make laws
of reformation, they would no doubt repent their wonted
leniency in making them lawgivers to themselves, and free-
ing them from constraint in that kind. At first this government was fatherly to subjects being as children, but if
they were now degenerated, should not the course of government be made suitable to their changed affections?....

similar to the *wergeld* (blood-money) of Teutonic and Anglo-Saxon law.
1. Presumably an inaccurate reference to Poynings' Laws;[see No,57,69.]

[The pacification and plantation after the recent rebellion
provided an opportunity 'to stretch the King's power to the utter-
most north, to bring the lords to civil obedience, to enrich them
by orderly rents, and to fill the King's coffers out of their
abundance': above all,for the judges to bring about the subjecting of tyrannical lords and chiefs to the king's 'equal justice,'
and to teach the common people 'they were not slaves but free
men'. But the influx of English lawyers frustrated these hopes:
they connived with the 'barbarous lords' to defraud the king of
his rights and to oppress the common people.]

I formerly showed that King Henry VII established the
English laws in Ireland, yet the common law, having not
his due course in the time of the rebellion, most civil
causes were judged according to equity at the council tab-
les, as well at Dublin as in the provinces of Munster and
Connaught, and by military governors in several counties.

42. SIR JOHN DAVIES ON THE APPLICATION OF ENGLISH LAW, 1612.[1]
...the Crown of England did not from the beginning
give Laws to the Irishry, whereas to give laws to a conquered people is the principal mark and effect of a perfect conquest. For albeit King Henry the Second, before
his return out of Ireland, held a Council or Parliament
at Lismore, *Ubi leges Angliae ab omnibus sunt gratanter receptae,
et juratoria cautione praestita confirmatae*, as Matthew Paris
writeth.

And though King John, in the twelfth year of his reign,
did establish the English laws and customs here, and
placed sheriffs and other ministers to rule and govern
the people according to the law of England, and to that
end, *Ipse duxit secum viros discretos et legis peritos, quorum
communi consilio statuit et praecepit leges Anglicanas teneri in
Hibernia*, &c., as we find it recorded among the Patent-
Rolls in the Tower, 11 Henry III m.3; though, likewise,
King Henry the Third did grant and transmit the like
charter of liberties to his subjects of Ireland as himself and his father had granted to the subjects of England, as appeareth by another record in the Tower, 1 Hen.
III Pat.m.13; and afterwards by a special Writ, did
command the Lord-Justice of Ireland, *Quod convocatis Archie-
piscopis, Comitibus, Baronibus, etc. Coram eis legi faceret Chartam
Regis Johannis: quam ipse legi fecit et jurari a Magnatibus Hiberniae, de legibus et Constitutionibus Angliae observandis, et quod
leges illas teneant et observent*, 12 Hen.III, claus.m.8....
Notwithstanding, it is evident by all the records of this
kingdom that only the English colonies [sic] and some few
septs of the Irishry which were enfranchised by special

---

1. H. Morley (ed.), *Ireland under Elizabeth and James I* (1809) pp.
259-337 *passim*. Davies was attorney general of Ireland and dedicated
his pamphlet to James I. It was published in 1612. In the preface
to his *Reports des Cases* (1674) pp. 3-4, he stated that King John
'did order and settle the Government here in all points according to
the modell of the Commonwealth of England':which was not of course true.

charters were admitted to the benefit and protection of
the laws of England, and that the Irish generally were
held and reputed aliens, or rather enemies to the Crown
of England, insomuch as they were not only disabled to
bring any actions, but they were so far out of the protection of the law as it was often adjudged no felony to
kill a mere Irishman in the time of peace....

From the fortieth year of Edward the Third...till the
reign of King Henry the Eighth...Statutes speak of English rebels and Irish enemies, as if the Irish had never
been in condition of subjects, but always out of the
protection of the law..,by divers heavy penal laws the
English were forbidden to marry, foster, to make gossips
with the Irish, or to have any trade or commerce in their
markets..,it is manifest that such as had the government
of Ireland under the Crown of England did intend to make
a perpetual separation and enmity between the English
and Irish, pretending no doubt that the English should
in the end root out the Irish;...

True it is that King John made twelve shires in Leinster and Munster, namely Dublin, Kildare, Meath, Uriel,
Catherlough, Kilkenny, Wexford, Waterford, Cork, Limerick, Kerry, and Tipperary; yet these counties did
stretch no farther than the lands of the English colonies did extend. In them only were the English laws published and put in execution, and in them only did the
itinerant judges make their circuits and visitations of
justice, and not in the countries possessed by the Irishry, which contained two-third parts of the kingdom at least...

By the Statute of Kilkenny[1]...the Brehon Law was condemned and abolished, and the use and practice thereof
made high treason, But this law extended to the English
only, and not to the Irish....

For the space of two hundred years at least after the
arrival of Henry the Second in Ireland the Irish would
gladly have embraced the laws of England, and did earnestly desire the benefit and protection thereof, which
being denied them, did of necessity cause a continual
bordering war between the English and the Irish ····

The next error in the civil policy...did consist in
the distribution of the lands and possessions which were
won and conquered from the Irish. For the scopes of
land which were granted to the first adventurers were
too large, and the liberties and royalties which they
obtained therein were too great for subjects...many of
these lords to whom our Kings had granted these petty
kingdoms did, by virtue and colour of these grants,
claim and exercise *jura regalia* within their territories,
insomuch as there were no less than eight Counties Palatines in Ireland at one time....

These absolute Palatines made Barons and Knights, did
exercise high justice in all points within their territ-

---

1. see No.35.

ories, erected courts for criminal and civil causes and
for their own revenues, in the same form as the King's
Courts were established at Dublin; made their own judges, seneschals, sheriffs, coroners, and escheators, so
as the King's Writ did not run in those counties, which
took up more than two parts of the English colonies....
   They did fear that if the Irish were received into the
King's protection and made liegemen and free subjects,
the State of England would establish them in their possessions by grants from the Crown, reduce their countries
into counties, ennoble some of them, and enfranchise all,
to make them amenable to the law...they persuaded the
King of England that it was unfit to communicate the laws
of England unto them; that it was the best policy to
hold them as aliens and enemies....
   [The success of the recent settling of Ulster had prompted the
   further extension of the English judicial system.]
   The streams of the public justice were derived into
every part of the kingdom, and the benefit and protection
of the law of England communicated to all, as well Irish
as English, without distinction or respect of persons;
...the common people were taught by the justices of assize that they were free subjects to the Kings of England,
and not slaves and vassals to their pretended lords;....
   Moreover, these civil assemblies at assizes and sessions have reclaimed the Irish from their wildness, caused
them to cut off their glibs[1] and long hair, to convert
their mantles into cloaks, to conform themselves to the
manner of England in all their behaviour and outward
forms. And because they find a great inconvenience in
moving their suits by an interpreter, they do for the
most part send their children to schools, especially to
learn the English language....

43. THE CIVIL ARTICLES OF THE TREATY OF LIMERICK, 3 October 1691.[2]
   1. The Roman catholics of this kingdom shall enjoy
such privileges in the exercise of their religion, as
are consistent with the laws of Ireland, or as they did
enjoy in the reign of King Charles II, and their majesties, as soon as their affairs will permit them to summon
a parliament in this kingdom, will endeavour to procure
the said Roman catholics such further security in that
particular, as may preserve them from any disturbance
upon the account of their said religion.
   2. All the inhabitants or residents of Limerick, or
any other garrison now in the possession of the Irish,

---

1. A matted fringe of hair.
2. E. Curtis and R. B. McDowell, op.cit.pp.172-5. See also Irish
Hist. Stud. VIII pp.37 ff. These terms were agreed by Godard van
Reede-Ginkel (later earl of Athlone), the commander-in-chief of the
English army, and the Lords justices of Ireland with Patrick Sars-
field and his lieutenants of the Irish army of James II.

and all officers and soldiers, now in arms, under any
commission of King James, either in the English quarters
or the counties of Limerick, Clare, Kerry, Cork, Mayo ['and
*all such as are under the protection in these counties']*1 or any
of them *[and'all members of Irish regiments]* ...who shall return
and submit to their majesties' obedience, and their and
every of their heirs, shall hold, possess and enjoy all
and every their estates of free-hold, and inheritance,
and all the rights, titles, and interests, privileges and
immunities, which they, and every, or any of them held,
enjoyed, or were rightfully and lawfully entitled to in
the reign of King Charles II, or at any time since, by
the laws and statutes that were in force in the said
reign...Provided also, that no person whatsoever shall
have or enjoy the benefit of this article, that shall
neglect or refuse to take the oath of allegiance made by
act of parliament in England, in the first year of the
reign of their present majesties, when thereunto required....

    [Such soldiers, and merchants returning to Ireland, would have
a general pardon of all attainders, outlawries, trespasses etc.
and Ginkel and the lords justices promised to use their best endeavours to get Parliament to repeal any attainders and to ratify
these articles. The oath to be administered would be that of
allegiance and no other.[2]   The terms would be ratified by their
Majesties within the year and would be confirmed in Parliament.][3]

.1. This clause was 'casually omitted' in the copy William III signed
in February 1692, but he reinserted it and reaffirmed it in a codicil.
Presumably it would embrace not merely the soldiers but the civilian
population generally in those counties.
2. That is, not that of supremacy, nor that against papal spiritual
power. But there was no explicit promise to repeal the Elizabethan
penal code.
3. These were generous terms to the vanquished; but the Irish protestant Parliament would not consider itself bound by them, at least
not to their spirit. Their Act of Confirmation (9 Will.III cap.2)
ratified 'so much of them as may consist with the safety and welfare
of your Majesty's subjects of this Kingdom'; indeed some of the
Irish Lords protested on 23 September 1697 because 'not one of the
said Articles is therein...fully confirmed' and because changes in
wording altered 'both the Sense and Meaning of some Parts of the
Articles'. Though the omitted clauses, and a few articles were ignored, the changes themselves however were not substantial; but,
despite William III's efforts to reduce the number of attainders and
the amount of land confiscated, within the decade the Catholics had
the freehold only of about one-eighth of the island and the Irish
Parliament was engaged in a series of penal laws against Catholics
which effectively excluded them from government, the professions,
guilds, and corporations, even from buying or leasing new lands, and
finally (in 1727) from the franchise. It was the English parliament,
however, in 1691, (3 Will.III cap.2), which had extended to the members
of both Houses of the Irish Parliament the requirement of oaths which
excluded Catholics [see No.65 (b)].Certainly by limiting the number

§ (ii) *Appeals*
44. AN APPEAL TO HENRY III, 4 June 1223.[1]
    The King to the Archbishop of Dublin, Justiciar of
Ireland greeting. We have considered the record, authenticated under the seal of those who were present, of
those arguments concerning the five carucates[2] of land
with appurtenances at Dalkey which were in dispute between Geoffrey de Marsh and Eva his wife, the petitioners,
and Reginald Talebot, the tenant. In which it is contained among other things that, when the aforesaid Reginald
had answered what was objected to him, he showed a charter of the Lord King John our father which he had concerning the same land and by reason of the same charter asked
to be left in peace till we *[the King]* came of age.[3]
Furthermore he also called us ourselves to warranty and
since he did not (as was seen in Court) have us to warranty on the stated day, the aforesaid Geoffrey and Eva
his wife by judgement of the same court recovered the
seizin of the land. On this matters therefore a conference was held between our loyal magnates and legal ex-
perts, and their sentence was that there was error on
two grounds. 1st.Because Reginald did not have peace
till we came of age, which he ought to have had by reason
of the said charter according to the custom of our realm.
2nd, because when any one summoned to plead in our courts
concerning land and has made the plea of warranty concern-

of Irishmen protected by the Treaty, by reviving religious statutes
which had not been enforced under Charles II, and by enacting legislation to exclude Catholics from any office and influence, the two
Parliaments broke the terms of the Treaty. Just as leaving the im-
plementation of the Declaration of Breda (4 April 1660) to Parliament
had unexpected results for English nonconformity, so it was the English and Irish legislatures which robbed Irish Catholics of a reasonably honourable and non-vindictive settlement.
1. *Rot. litt. claus.*I 549. Trans. from Latin. On 21 February 1218
(*ibid.*I 1353) the king had commanded Geoffrey de Marsh(Marisco), then
justiciar of Ireland, to send under seal the written record of a
complaint he had heard and judgement he had made between Eva de Ber-
mingham , his own wife (and widow of Gerald FitzMaurice) and Reginald
Talebot over land in Dalkey. Geoffrey had decided in his wife's
favour and Reginald appealed to the king. It is an example of an
appeal from a dependency, perhaps; but illustrates the fact that the
king's court (i.e. as delegated to the justiciar in Ireland) was not
superior to the king. The reversal of the justiciar's judgement
seems to have had nothing to do with the later rule that no man could
judge in his own cause, but was probably due to the fact that Geoffrey
de Marsh was out of favour and had been replaced as justiciar. He
was thought to have retained royal revenues for his own use. He was
later held responsible for the death of Richard, the earl marshal
and earl of Pembroke, in 1234.
2. A piece of land which could be tilled by one plough in a year.
3. Henry III was nine at his father's death.

ing it, it is not in the power of the claimant or indeed
for the court, that a person called to warranty should be
summoned and by due manner and custom compelled to appear
to warrant for that land or to show why he ought not to
do so. If therefore we did not appear for a warranty on
the day fixed it ought not to be considered a error or
defect as our Court *[i.e.the justiciar's court]* is not above
us to summon and compell us unless we wish it. Wherefore a error lies in this too. And therefore we command
you forthwith without accusation to cause the aforesaid
Reginald to be re-seized in the same land and appurtenances which seizin he lost by an unjust judgement. *[In the
council at Westminster]*.

45. *THE CASE OF THE PRIOR OF LANTHON*, 1430.[1]
    8 Hen.VI... This is a memorable petition concerning an
Erroneous Judgement given in the Parliament of Ireland
*[before James Botiller the Lord Lieutenant, and the lords spiritual
and temporal of Ireland]* upon a Writ of Error there brought
and certified into the King's Bench in England which had
no power to reserve it: on the Petition suggested and
therefore prayed it might be removed into the Parliament
and Lords House in England to redress it....
    [The petition to the Lords in England asked them to see that
    justice was done 'according to the Law and Custom of the Realm
    of England'.]
    To which Petition there is no answer entred in the
Parliament Roll, but only the Petition itself at the end
of the Roll. By which Petition it seems the Judges of
the King's Bench in England were of Opinion that they
could not reverse an Erroneous Judgement given in the
Parliament of Ireland, but only the King and Lords house
in the Parliament of England.

46. STATUTE OF DROGHEDA (38 Hen.VI), 21 July 1460.[2]
    [Franchises and liberties heretofore granted to the Church,
    'the land of Ireland' and certain cities were confirmed. The

---

1. William Prynne, *Brief animadversions on....the Fourth Part of the
Institutes* (1669) 313-4. Prynne accepted this as evidence that the
English House of Lords had final appellate jurisdiction, but Moly-
neax thought that on the contrary the absence of judgement by the
English Lords was proof that there was no appeal from the Irish Lords
to the English House.
2. H.F. Berry (ed.) *Statute rolls of the Parliament of Ireland*; Henry
VI (1910) pp. 645-7. This declaration was a move by the Anglo-Irish
colonists to secure 'home rule'- Irish legislative independence under
the Crown (as later 'Grattan's Parliament' did briefly after 1783).
When attainted by the English Parliament, Richard, duke of York, previously lord lieutenant, had fled back to Ireland where he and the
cause of the White Rose were popular. The Anglo-Irish lords made him
virtually a king of Ireland and welcomed his son, Edward IV, as one
of themselves when he succeeded to the English crown in the following
year. In 1467 Edward IV's attempt to crush the home-rule aristocracy

powers of the duke of York as the king's'lieutenant and governor
of his land of Ireland wherein he represents in the absence of
our said sovereign lord out of the same land his right noble
person and estate' were enacted by Parliament so long as he
resided in Ireland; he should enjoy the same reverence and obedience as was due to the king.]
...VI. Also, at the request of the Commons: That
whereas the land of Ireland is and at all times has been
corporate of itself, by the ancient laws and customs used
in the same, freed of the burthen of any special law of
the realm of England, save only such laws as by the Lords
spiritual and temporal and the Commons of the said land
had been in Great Council or Parliament there held, admitted, accepted, affirmed and proclaimed, according to
sundry ancient statutes thereof made, And whereas also
of ancient custom, privilege and franchise of the said
land, there is and at all times has been the seal of the
King current, by which the laws there and also the King's
subjects of the same land are guided and directed...alth-
ough there are in the said land and of ancient custom
have been a constable and marshal, yet divers persons of
the same land have oftentimes heretofore sued and procured, of great malice, many of the King's subjects of
the same to be sent for, to come into England by colour
of such appeals, in great derogation and prejudice of
the said liberty and franchise. Whereupon the premises
considered: It is ordained, enacted and established in
the said Parliament and by authority thereof, That henceforth no person or persons being in the said land of Ireland, be by any command given or made under any other
seal than the said seal of the same land, compelled to
answer to any appeal or any other matter out of the said
land. And that no officer or minister of the same land
to whom any such command comes, put that command or any
proclamation or any other thing contrary or prejudicial
to the said ancient custom privilege or franchise in execution [on pain of forfeiture, or fine] ...It is also ordained
by the said authority that any appeal of treason taken in
this land be determined before the Constable and the Marshal of the said land for the time being, and within the
said land, and in no other place....
[Since 'the defence of the English nation of this land from the
danger and malice of the Irish enemies of the same land rests and
depends on English laws', tenants were required to provide archers
in proportion to their holdings 'with bows and arrows fit for war
according to the English fashion'. The Irish coinage was also
regulated.]

---

by attainting the earls of Desmond and Kildare proved premature. Thereafter the Kildares became *de facto* supreme rulers in Ireland until
Henry VIII made a successful counter-attack on their power in 1534
when his excommunication by the pope prompted a rising on the plea
that Ireland could no longer be held as a papal fief under an English
king who was a heritic. This statute was repealed by the Irish Parl-

47. ACT OF APPEALS (28 Hen.VIII cap,6), 1537.[1]
   [Whereas 'good' statutes had been made in England against
   appeals to Rome and since Ireland was]
   ...the King's proper dominion of England, and united,
knit and belonging to the imperial crown of the same
realm which Crown of itself and by itself is fully, wholy,
intirely and rightfully endowed and garnished with all
power, authority and preheminence, sufficient to yield
and render to all and singular subjects of the same full
and plenarie remedies in all causes of strife, debate,
contention or division without any suite, provocation,
appeale or any other process to be had, made or sued, to
any forein prince or potentate spiritual or temporal...
   [such appeals were therefore abolished. All cases which previously would have been appealed to Rome should henceforth go]
   ...to the King of England and lord of Ireland...or to
his...lieutenant, deputie, justice or other governour...
of this land of Ireland for the time being, to his...
court of chauncerie within the same realm of England or
land of Ireland....
   [The chancellor of England should delegate authority to commissioners to hear and determine such cases.]

48. PROCEDURE IN CASES OF TREASON BY IRISH PEERS, 1578.[2]
   Gerrards, Chancellor of Ireland, moved this question
to the Queen's Council, whether an Earl or Lord of Ireland who commits treason in Ireland by open rebellion
can be arraigned and put to his trial in Ireland for the
offence by the statutes of 28 Hen.VIII cap.13, 32 Hen.VIII
cap.4, 35 Hen.VIII cap.2 and 5 Edw.V cap.11. And it was
holden by Wray, Dyer and Gerrards, Attorney General, that
he cannot; for he cannot have his trial here by his peers
nor by any jury of twelve because he is not a subject of
England but of Ireland; and therefore his trial shall be
there. And it is said that the usage there of attainting
a peer is by parliament and not by peers.

49. DECLARATION AND PROTESTATION OF THE IRISH PARLIAMENT,
                                24 May 1641.[3]
   ...For the avoiding of any Doubt or Ambiguity which

iament in 1495 (10 Hen.VII cap.23).
1. *Irish Statutes at large*. Similarly 28 Hen.VIII cap.13 legislated
against papal authority to bring Irish laws into conformity with the
'good' statutes made in England.
2. 2 Dyer 360b. In *O'Rourke's* case (1591) all the judges agreed that
23 Hen.VIII cap.33 made Irishmen indictable for treason in English
courts: (1 And. 262). Strafford claimed in his trial (1641) that
Ireland as a conquered country was not bound by English statutes
(1 St.T. 730,738-9), and argued that his case should have been heard
by the Irish House of Lords. It was resolved, however, not only that
he was an English peer but that' Parliament of England had jurisdiction over all things done in Ireland.' See also the case of *Lord
Conner Maguire* (8 St.T. 354).
3. Commons Journal (Ireland) I pp.212-3. Sir Matthew Hale, however,
claimed a quarter of a century later that a final appeal lay on a
writ of error to the English House of Lords from a 'judgement given

might be moved or stirred against the Power of Judicature
of the high Court of Parliament in this Realm, and to
manifest and declare a most clear, undoubted, and unden-
iable Truth to all Posterity, the lords spiritual and
temporal and Commons, in Parliament assembled, do
hereby declare and protest, that the said Court of Parliament of this Kingdom hath always had and ought to have
full Power and Authority to hear and determine all Treasons and other Offences, Crimes, Causes, and Things whatsoever, as well capital and criminal as civil, contrived,
perpetrated, done, or happened within this Realm, and
likewise to inflict condign Punishment upon all Offenders, and to administer equal Justice unto all Persons
whatsoever in the said Realm according to the ancient
Course and Rights of Parliament, in all Times and Ages
used and exercised within the said Realm of England, and
that all other Courts of Justice, and all Magistrates,
Judges, Offices, and Subjects of any Estate, Degree,
Quality, or Condition whatsoever, of the said realm of
Ireland, are liable to the Resolutions, Orders, and
Judgements of this said Court of Parliament of this Realm,
and that the said Court of Parliament is the supreme Judicatory in the said Realm.

50. DECLARATORY ACT OF THE IRISH PARLIAMENT, May 1689.[1]
     [No English Acts were binding in Ireland.][2]
     ...Be it hereby enacted...That no writ of error shall
be hereafter brought out of England, in order to remove
any record, or transcript of record, out of his majesty's
court of king's bench in Ireland, or out of any other
court of record here into England, in order to reverse
any such judgements, But in regard judgements to be given
in his majesty's court of king's bench in Ireland may
happen sometimes to be erroneous, Be it enacted...other
than where the king's majesty shall be party, plaintiff
or defendant or other person or persons against whom any
such judgements shall be given may at his election sue
forth out of the high court of chancery in Ireland, a
special writ of error...to cause the said record, and all
things concerning the said judgements, to be brought
before the justices of the common pleas, and barons of
the exchequer....
     And whereas of late times several persons have brought
appeals before the house of lords in England, in order
to reverse decrees granted in the high court of chancery
in Ireland, which tend to be great trouble, charge and

in the lords house of parliament in Ireland'.
1. E. Curtis and R.B.McDowell, *op.cit.* pp.169-71. This 'Patriot
Parliament' was the last in which Catholics were represented until
after the repeal of the Union. By its Act of Attainder it sought
to condemn some thousands of Protestant landlords to confiscation
and death – a policy which James II opposed but ineffectually. He
did, however, firmly refuse to accept the repeal of Poynings' Law.
2. For this section of the Act, see No.64.

vexation to such of his majesty's subjects as have obtained such decrees, and is an apparent new encroachment upon
the fundamental constitutions of this realm,...Be it
further enacted...That no person or persons whatsoever,
do hereafter presume to sue out any such appeals, or to
tender or produce any such appeal to the lord chancellor,
or lord keeper of Ireland, or to any of the officers of
the said court of chancery, and that such appeals shall
be void, and that no appeal whatsoever (to reverse any
decree or sentence passed, or to be passed in Ireland)
shall be brought into England neither before the house of
lords there, or any commissioner or delegates of appeal,
and that all such appeals shall be disallowed....

51. *ANNESLEY v. SHERLOCK*, 1716-19.
     [Maurice Annesley reclaimed lands in Ireland from Hester Sher-
     lock. In the Irish court of the exchequer he won a favourable
     verdict, but Sherlock appealed to the Irish House of Lords where
     on 19 June 1716 the judgement was reversed and the sheriff of
     County Kildare was instructed to see that she obtained the title
     to the lands.
     Annesley therefore appealed to the House of Lords in England
     on 7 May 1717: he did not 'complain of the Want of Jurisdiction
     in the Hours of Lords in Ireland, but only that he is aggrieved
     by the Decree made by their Lordships'. (L.J. XX.484) On 31
     May 1717 the committee of the Lords reported that in May 1698
     resolutions of their House had in respect of the Bishop of Derry's
     case instructed the Irish Court of Chancery to disregard appeals
     to the Irish Lords and to see that appeals should lie to the House
     of Lords in England.[1] Since Annesley did not deny the jurisdict-
     ion of the Irish Lords, but claimed only error, they did not enter-
     tain his appeal.]
12 June 1717.[2]
     Upon reading...the Petition and Appeal of Maurice
Annesley...; the said Petition and Appeal setting forth
(amongst other things) "That the Petitioner is advised,
no Appeal lies to the House of Lords in Ireland from any
Decree of the Court of Exchequer in that Kingdom; but
that all Appeals ought to be prosecuted immediately before this House, as being the Supreme Court of Judicature;
and if in case such Appeal did lie to the House of Lords
in Ireland, yet the Petitioner conceives himself aggrieved
by their Lordships Decree, made the 19th of June 1716,
upon hearing the Cause upon the said Hester Sherlock's
Appeal, so far as the same hath varied and reversed the
said Decree in the Exchequer", and praying "That the
Proceedings of the Lords in Ireland may be set aside:"...[3]

---

1 . The English House of Lords had declared the proceedings in the
Irish Lords to be *coram non judice*.
2. L. J. XX.495. This second appeal by Annesley was now accepted as
satisfactory.
3. Hester Sherlock refused to answer in the Lords in England and appealed again to the Irish Lords who again confirmed her claim to the

[On 1 February 1718 the house of lords agreed that the land
should be restored to Annesley (594). When the Irish Court of
the Exchequer attempted to execute that judgement and fined the
sheriff who disregarded their instruction, the Irish Lords resolved that no appeal lay from the Irish courts to the Lords in
Great Britain:[1] they imprisoned the judges of the Irish Court
of Exchequer; and they addressed the king asserting their final
appellate jurisdiction.
   The Lords in England on 23 January 1719 again resolved that the
proceedings in the Irish Lords were *coram non judice* and null
and void'. (XXI.55).]   28 January 1719.[2]
Resolved by the Lords Spiritual and Temporal in Parliament assembled, That Jeffry Gilbert Esquire, Lord Chief
Baron of His Majesty's Court of Exchequer in Ireland,
and John Pocklington Esquire and Sir John St. Leger Knight
the other Barons of the said Court, in their Proceedings
in the Cause between Annesley and Sherlock, in Obedience
to the Orders of this House, have acted with Courage,
according to Law, in Support of His Majesty's Prerogative,
and with Fidelity to the Crown of Great Britain....
   [They asked the king to confer some favour on these judges who
   had suffered for doing their duty.]
ORDERED, That a Bill be brought in, for the better
securing the Dependency of Ireland upon the Crown of
Great Britain; and that the Judges do prepare a Bill
accordingly, upon the Debate of the House.

52. REPRESENTATION OF IRISH HOUSE OF LORDS TO GEORGE I, 1719.[3]
   [They claimed that Irish Acts (including 11 Eliz.I cap.1)[4] had
   demonstrated that Henry II, in return for the homage and allegiance of Irish princes *etc.* 'given of goodwill and without war',
   gave the laws and institutions of England to Ireland: a 'concession and compact' which attracted English immigrants. They recognised the king's right to have final jurisdiction,but regarded the
   claim of the Lords of Great Britain as a novel invasion of that
   prerogative. They repudiated the resolution of the English Lords
   that they had no lawful jurisdiction.]
Upon which occasion, we cannot but observe, that the
parliament of Ireland (as the constitution thereof has
been for some hundreds of years) being convened by the
same authority and writs of summons, and consisting of
like members, and distinct houses of peers and commons,
and the former having the same assistance and attendance
from the judges of the several courts and masters of
chancery, as in England or Great Britain, either some
record, act of parliament or ancient usage must be shewn,
whereby to make a difference (which has never yet been

---

lands.
1. See No.52 below .
2. L. J. XXI.214.
3. L. J. (Ireland) II 655-0.[See the declaration of 1641:No.60 below].
4. See below No.81: the Act attainting O'Neill.

attempted) or else, from our very constitution, it must, as we conceive, appear, that whatever power of judicature is lodged in the English or British parliament, with respect to that kingdom and its inferior courts, the same must also be allowed to be in the parliament of Ireland, with like respect to the kingdom and courts thereof. And if it be looked upon as illegal for any inferior court in Great Britain to act in direct opposition to, or contempt of, the orders and decrees of the house of lords in parliament there assembled, the same must also be concluded upon the like opposition given or contempt shown, to such parliamentary orders and decrees, as are or shall be made within this kingdom....

It is, under God, the great security of this your majesty's kingdom of Ireland, that by the laws and statutes thereof, the same is annexed and united to the imperial crown of England, and declared to be depending upon, and for ever belonging to, the same. But if all judgements, decrees and determinations made in this your majesty's highest court within this kingdom, are subject to be nulled and reversed by the lords in Great Britain, the liberties and properties of all your subjects of Ireland, must thereby become finally dependent on the British peers, to the great diminution of that dependence, which, by law, we always ought to have immediately upon the crown itself.

That your majesty has, by the constitution of this your realm of Ireland,the full power of judging and determining all causes that belong to it alone *in pleno parliamento*, is what no man hitherto has ventured openly to deny or doubt of.

But, if in all cases that relate to this kingdom, the dernier resort (as some of late have affected to speak) ought to be to the house of lords in Great Britain, however this your majesty's power may still in words be acknowledged, the force and effect of it is in reality taken away and wholly vested in the British peers....

It is notorious, that the lords of Great Britain have not in themselves, either by law or custom, any way of putting their decrees in execution within this kingdom,of which they have given most undoubted evidence by their late application to your majesty to cause such their decrees to be executed by an extraordinary interposition of your royal power. And should your majesty think fit to yield to this their desire, we humbly presume to think it would highly affect the liberty of your majesty's loyal subjects of this kingdom,...

And we further represent to your majesty, that these proceedings of the lords of England have greatly embarrassed your parliament and disquieted the generality of your most loyal protestant subjects of this your kingdom, and must of necessity bring all sheriffs and officers of justice under great hardships, by reason of the clashing of different jurisdictions. Nor can we but with grief

observe, that whilst many of the peers and commons who
sat in parliament were papists, their judicature was
never questioned. But of late, since only protestants
are qualified to have a share in the legislature, their
power and the right of hearing causes in parliament hath
been denied, to the great discouragement and weakening
of the protestant interest in Ireland....

    [They affirmed the dependence of Ireland upon the Crown and the
    king's undoubted prerogative within Ireland to hold parliaments
    there and to determine Irish cases there. They deplored the ass-
    istance given by the judges in the Irish exchequer recently to
    the encroachments on that jurisdiction.]

53. DECLARATORY ACT OF BRITISH PARLIAMENT (6 Geo.I cap.5)   1719.[1]
1. WHEREAS the House of Lords of Ireland have of late,
against Law, assumed to themselves a Power and Jurisdiction to examine, correct and amend the Judgements and
Decrees of the Courts of Justice in the Kingdom of Ireland. Therefore for the better securing of the Dependency of Ireland upon the Crown of Great Britain, May it
please your most Excellent Majesty that it may be declared, and be it declared by the King's most Excellent Majesty, by and with the Advice and Consent of the Lords
Spiritual and Temporal, and Commons, in this present
Parliament assembled, and by the Authority of the same,
That the said Kingdom of Ireland hath been, is, and of
Right ought to be subordinate unto and dependent upon
the Imperial Crown of Great Britain, as being inseparably
united and annexed thereunto; and that the King's Majesty, by and with the Advice and Consent of the Lords
Spiritual and Temporal, and Commons of Great Britain in
Parliament assembled, had, hath, and of Right ought to
have full Power and Authority to make Laws and Statutes
of sufficient Force and Validity, to bind the Kingdom and

---

1. This Act was, of course, the exact model for that of 1766 (6 Geo.
III cap.12) relating to America. It should be noted that while the
right of the British parliament is 'declared', the denial of the
Irish Lords to have appellate jurisdiction - a much more recent British claim - was 'declared and enacted'. The British government
exercised control of the dependent kingdom nominally through a Lord
Lieutenant who was appointed by, and was accountable to, the secretary of state. But the Lord Lieutenant was in Ireland only for the
biennial sessions of Parliament required to obtain supplies to pay
the English army; so in practice two or three Lords justices and
a group of expatriate English officials ('the Castle') governed Ireland in the interest of Britain and the Irish Anglican minority with
the assistance of the machinery of Poynings' Law and the influence
of the 'Undertakers' who managed the Irish Parliament. Nevertheless,
in the course of time it was among the privileged Anglicans that an
anti-Castle party emerged to challenge on patriotic as well as selfish grounds the presumptions of Westminster. The very success of
American protest against the Declaratory Act gave them encouragement
and opportunity in the 1780's.

People of Ireland.[1]
    II. And be it further declared and enacted by the
Authority aforesaid, That the House of Lords of Ireland
have not, nor of Right ought to have any Jurisdiction to
judge of, affirm or reverse any Judgement, Sentence or
Decree, given or made in any Court within the said Kingdom, and that all Proceedings before the said House of
Lords upon any such Judgement, Sentence or Decree, are,
and are hereby declared to be utterly null and void to
all Intents and Purposes whatsoever.

II THE DEBATE ON THE AUTHORITY OF THE ENGLISH AND IRISH PARLIAMENTS
    A problem of considerable concern for American and other colonists
later was the authority of the Westminster Parliament over dominions
and dependencies of the English Crown. The question of the relations
of the English and Irish parliaments was crucial to any case to be
made on this issue. Was Ireland bound by English statutes whether
those Acts had been ratified or confirmed in Dublin or not,or whether Ireland was explicitly named in the Act or not? Was the English
Parliament the supreme legislature for Ireland, though no representatives from Ireland were members of it?

54. *PILKINGTON'S CASE*, 1441.[2]
    [John Pilkington had brought a writ of *scire facias* against
    A, requiring A.to show cause why letters patent from the king
    granting him an office in Ireland should not be set aside,since
    the king had previously granted the same office for life to
    Pilkington.]
    A's defence. Ireland is and always has been a realm
separate and distinct *[separe et severe]* from that of England, ruled and governed by the customs and laws of that
same land *[Ireland]*. The magnates of that land (which are
of the King's Council) have used from time to time in the
absence of the King, to elect a justiciar with power to
pardon and punish all felonies, trespasses etc., and to
call a parliament of magnates and commonalties etc. to
pass statutes etc. and to do all other things appertaining to the role of a parliament, It was enacted by this
parliament that every office-holder in that country must
occupy his office personally before a certain day otherwise he forfeits it. The said John *[Pilkington]* filled the
office with a deputy and since he did not in his own person come to take up that office before the *[appointed]* day,
the office was vacant. The King therefore by letters
patent gave the office to A. A.pleads that letters patent should be found valid and not be revoked...,
    [One judge, Yelverton, argued that the Parliament of Ireland
    cannot make binding laws in a matter involving the loss *[disherit-
    ance]* to the King: to annul the first grant by accepting the
    validity of the statute against deputies would be such a loss.]

---

1. See documents on the debate on the legislative authority of the
Irish Parliament: section 4(a) II, following.
2. Year Book 20 Hen.VI ff.8-9. Trans. from the French. The case was

Fortescue (J). This power to prescribe is vested in
no persons in Ireland but resides in the King himself....
     [Otherwise there would be an analogy with the Chancellor of
     England presenting to benefices of which the King was patron:
     even the Chancellor holds his office only at the King's pleas-
     ure.]
Also the land of Ireland is separated from the realm of
England because, if a tithe or a fifteenth were granted
here, it would not bind those of Ireland even if the
King promulgated this same statute in Ireland under his
great seal, unless they wished in their own parliament
to approve it; but if they wished to approve it, then
it would be upheld there and they would be bound by it.
Thus this prescription *[title]*is good, for which reason
the letters patent *[to A]* will be deemed valid....
     Portington (J). And also, as to what Fortescue has
said, that if a tithe or a fifteenth were granted in the
Parliament here *[in England]* that would not bind those of
Ireland I concur; for they have no order by our writ to
come to our Parliament; but it is not because the land
is separate from England,but because a tithe granted *[by
the English parliament]* would not bind those of Durham or of
the county palatine of Chester and they are not separate
from this realm ....
     [The other judges, Markham and Ascough, seemed to argue in fav-
     our of Pilkington's claim, but the record does not show them
     either supporting or denying the *obiter dicta* of Fortescue or
     Portington. There is no judgement.][1]

55. IRISH ACT RATIFYING ENGLISH STATUTES (8 Ed.IV cap.70), 1468.[2]
     ...Having consideration how the learned people of
this land are of different opinions whether the said
statute made in England should be in force in this land
without a confirmation had upon the said statute in this
land; in avoidance of every inconvenience and mischief
which might happen by reason of the ambiguity about the
said statute, It is enacted confirmed and ratified by
authority of the said Parliament, That the said statute
be adjudged and approved in its force and strength....
And that henceforth the said act and all other statutes

---

heard in England. It concerned the question whether an Irish statute against absentee officials might void a grant made by the king
to Pilkington and confirm a re-grant made to another , A —.
1. Yelverton and Portington seem to have considered the letters patent to A. void : Fortescue, Markham and Ascough that they were valid.
2. H. F. Berry (ed.) *op.cit.* Ed.IV p.619. Trans. from French. The
question was whether the English statute relating to rape (6 Rich.II
cap.6) applied without being ratified in the Irish Parliament. Later
pamphleteers like Darcy, Bolton and Molyneaux regarded this preamble
as a statutory declaration of a constitutional law. See also the
declaration of independence in law by the Drogheda Parliament, 1460
[see above No.46].

and acts made by authority of Parliament within the
realm of England of all manner of rapes, be ratified and
confirmed...by the authority of this said Parliament.

56. THE CASE OF *THE MERCHANTS OF WATERFORD*,1485-6.
(a) The first judgement: in the Exchequer[1]
    ...Moreover the matter concerned two questions. Namely
one, whether an incorporated town in Ireland and the other inhabitants in Ireland were bound by the statutes made
in England. And the second question was whether the King
could grant a licence contrary to a statute *etc.* and
particularly when it is now ordained by statute that the
man who discovers the crime may have one half [of the goods
involved] and the King the other.
   To resolve these questions, etc. all the judges were
assembled in the Exchequer Chamber. There, concerning
the first question it was said that the lands of Ireland
itself have a parliament and courts of every sort, as in
England,and that by that parliament they make and change
the laws and are not bound by statutes of England because
here they do not have knights of parliament *(quia hic non
habent Milites parliamenti)*. But it is understood to affect
only the lands and property in that land, but the persons there are subjects of the King and as subjects are
bound to anything done outside that land[2] contrary to
such statutes; just as inhabitants of Calais, Gascony,
Guienne etc., while they were subjects and likewise under
obedience, were under the jurisdiction of the Admiral of
England for deeds done on the high seas. Likewise a
writ in error of judgement lies from Ireland to the court
of King's Bench here in England ....
     [As for the second question it was argued that a licence from
     the king was valid, provided it did not make possible the commiss-
     ion of what was a felony at common law.]
(b) The second judgement: in King's Bench[3]
   Hussey, the chief justice, said that statutes made in

---

1. Year Book 2 Rich.III fol.12. Trans. from Latin. An English stat-
ute(2Hen.VI cap.4) had provided that wool and other staples should
be exported from Ireland, as well as from England, only to Calais
on pain of forfeiture. Certain merchants of Waterford, however, had
consigned wool to Sluys in a ship which put in at Calais where it was
seized by the treasurer, Sir Thomas Thwaites. The merchants petitioned the king in council for restitution, claiming that the licence
from Edward III gave them the right to ship merchandise whither they
pleased.
2. The argument was therefore that Irish were liable for breaches of
English statutes outside Ireland; that is, that English statutes
have extra-territoriality.
3. Year Book I Hen.VII fol.3. Trans from French. All the judges were
present including the lord chancellor and the lord privy seal - and
this time, the lord chief justice too. There had been considerable
deliberation and research in the recess and Henry Tudor had replaced
Richard III as king.

England did bind those in Ireland: an opinion which was
not seriously denied by the other judges, notwithstanding
that some of them had been of the contrary opinion last
term in his absence. He then said that the statutes must
be considered, and how the statutes and their letters[1]
may stand together ....

> [But the judges appeared to have agreed that the king could
> grant a licence (with a *non-obstante* clause) contrary to a stat-
> ute, if such a licence - as in this case - permitted what was not
> a felony at common law.]

57. POYNINGS' ACT CONFIRMING ENGLISH STATUTES (10 Hen.VII cap.22) 1495.[2]

ITEM, prayen the commons, that forasmuch as there been
many and diverse good and profitable statutes late made
within the realm of England by great labour, studie, and
policie, as well in the time of our sovereign lord the
king, as in the time of his full noble and royal progenitors, late Kings of England, by the advise of his and
their discreet counsail, whereby the said realm is ordered and brought to great wealth and prosperity, and by
all likelyhood so would this land, if the said estatutes
were used and executed in the same: Wherefore it be ordeyned and established by authority of this present Parliament by the assent of the lords spirituall and temporall, and commons assembled in the same, That all estatutes, late made within the said realm of England, concerning or belonging to the common and publique weal of
the same, from henceforth be deemed good and effectuall
in the law, and over that be acceptyd, used, and executed
within this land of Ireland in all points at all times
requisite according to the tenor and effect of the same;
and over that by authority aforesaid, that they and every
of them be authorized, proved, and confirmed in this said
land of Ireland. And if any estatute or estatutes have
been made within this said land, hereafter to the contrary, they and every of them by authority aforesaid be
adnulled, revoked, voyd, and of none effect in the law.

58. IRISH ACT UNITING THE CROWNS (33 Hen.VIII cap.1) 1542.[3]

An Act that the King of England, his Heirs and Suc-

---

1. A licence to the citizens of Waterford granted by Edward III and
confirmed by Edward IV and Richard III.
2. This statute clarified an important matter of Irish administration,
denying the claims made in 1460 [see No.46]. These were the first
Irish statutes to be passed in the English language.
3. Irish statutes,I pp. 176-7. Henry was advised by his Irish council to assume the title since the Irish claimed the Lordship of the
English King 'to be but a governance under the obedience' of the
Pope. The Parliament which enacted this statute was a fuller one
than many for a long time and included some who had been absent for
generations, but it represented only the English parts of Ireland.
This unilateral Act of the Irish Parliament was paradoxically both

cessors, be Kings of Ireland.

FORASMUCH as the King our most gracious dread soveraign lord, and his grace's most noble progenitors, Kings of England, have bin Lords of this land of Ireland, having all manner kingly jurisdiction, power, pre-eminences, and authoritie royall, belonging or appertayning to the royall estate and majestie of a King, by the name of Lords of Ireland, where the King's majestie and his most noble progenitors justly and rightfully were, and of right ought to be, Kings of Ireland, and so to be reputed, taken, named, and called...Be it enacted, ordeyned, and established by authoritie of this present Parliament, That the King's highnesse, his heyres and successours, have the name, stile, title, and honour of the King of this land of Ireland with all maner honours, preheminences, prerogatives, dignities, and other things whatsoever they be to the estate and majestie of a King imperiall appertayning or belonging; and that his majestie, his heyres and successours, be from henceforth named, called, accepted, reputed, and taken to be Kings of this land of Ireland, to have, hold and enjoy the said stile, title, majestie, and honours of King of Ireland,...as united and knit to the imperial crown of the realm of England....

[Provision was made for proclamations to be made relating to the union of the Crowns and for penalties of high treason to be enforced against those who did not accept it.]

59. SIR JOHN DAVIES: SPEECH ON THE ORIGINS OF THE IRISH PARLIAMENT, 1613.[1]

...Doubtless, though the rest of the ordinary Courts of Justice began with the First Plantation of the English Colonies here, yet the Wisdom of the State of England thought it fit, to reserve the Power of making Laws to the Parliaments of England, for many Years after.

So as this high extraordinary Court was not established in Ireland, by Authority out of England, for many Years after, in the Form that now is, till towards the declining of King Edward the Second's Reign:...

[Nevertheless it was incorrectly but] expressly declared by two Statutes [32 Hen.IV cap.19 and 2 Rich.III cap.8] the Usage of holding Parliaments in Ireland, was from the immediate coming in of the English - 'That all the liege People of Ireland had, and used to hold Parliaments without Interruption, from the Conquest of the said Land by

---

a recognition of their need for the Tudor alliance and English protection, and an assertion that it was not a subordinate legislature.
1. *Tracts* Vol 32 (1770) No.9 pp.27-37. *The usage of holding parliaments in Ireland etc. stated from record by Mr. Lodge*, keeper of the rolls. Davies was now elected speaker of the Irish Parliament.

For an English judicial opinion on the limited powers of the Irish Parliament half a century later, see *Craw v. Ramsay* [No. 27 above, pp. 42-3].

the most noble King, Henry Fitz- Emprys,[1] to the present
Time'. - Likewise, in a certified Bill, [19 Hen.VI cap.6]
it is recited 'That the Land of Ireland is your Lordship's
of olde Tyme, annexed to your Crown: in the which Land,
ye and all your Progenitors, some Tyme Kinges of England
and Lordes of Ireland, of the Tyme that none Myn renueth,
have had Courtes, that is to say, Chancery, Kinge's Benche
and Eschequer: and other Courtes reall, that is to say
Parliamentes and great Conseilles'....

    [The first writ of summons to a parliament, he said, however,
    was dated 1 January 1366: there were others on 18 January 1369
    and 22 January 1378. In 1456 a representative was to be sent
    from each of 4 counties.]

...these Records...refute the received Opinion, that
'from Henry II to Henry VII the King's Deputies frequently
held Parliaments, and enacted such Laws, as they thought
advantageous for the Publick, without any particular
Directions or Authority from the Crown for that Purpose'.

60. (a) DECLARATION AND QUESTIONS OF IRISH HOUSE OF COMMONS,
                          16 February 1641.[2]
    Inasmuch as the Subjects of this Kingdom are free,
loyal and dutiful Subjects of his most excellent Majesty
their natural liege Lord and King to be governed only[3]
by the common laws of England and Statutes of Force in
this Kingdom [in the same manner as his English subjects were
and claim as their 'birthright and best inheritance', the knights,
citizens and burgesses asked the Lords to put questions to judges
on these matters] not for any Doubt or Ambiguity which may
be conceived or thought of...but for Manifestation and

---

1. i.e. Henry II.
2. C. J. (Ireland) I 174-5. In November 1640 (*ibid.* 162) the Irish
Commons had voted a Remonstrance against various recent acts of
Strafford as lord deputy and had asserted the rights of the people
of Ireland, 'being now for the most part derived from British ancestors', to be governed, in 'the happy subjection of this kingdom to
the imperial crown of England', by the 'fundamental laws of England'
and by other statutes 'here enacted and declared'. In the articles
of impeachment against Strafford in January 1641, it was alleged
by the English Commons that he had threatened the fundamental laws
of Ireland by declaring that the king could do as he pleased there
since it was a conquered territory. Both Parliaments were making
common cause against Strafford. This declaration and the questions
asked were part of further protest against his regime of 'Thorough'.
3. In reply on 25 May the judges declared that Irish subjects were
free and 'for the general' to be governed 'only by the Commons Laws
of England and Statutes of this Kingdom'; but they quibbled about
'only', for laws grew obsolete and judges, they argued, interpreted
and re-made law. Furthermore, many of the questions concerned the
royal prerogative which they were sworn to protect; and some dealt
with matters not of law but of policy, of which they were not judges.
They did not give an opinion whether Ireland was subject to the supremacy of the English parliament, for that question had not been
expressly asked.

Declaration of a clear Truth and of the said Laws and
Statutes already planted and for many Ages past settled
in this Kingdome ....

    [The Commons prayed the Lords to ask the judges certain quest-
ions relating to the jurisdiction of the Irish privy council, or
of the power of the governor to act alone; the grant of monopolies; the power of the lord lieutenant to punish; the proclaim-
ation of martial law; appeal to the king in England; the immunity of juries, *etc.* including particularly,]

    1. Whether the Subjects of this kingdome be a free
people and to be governed only by the Common Lawes of
England and Statutes of force in this kingdom?

60.(b) DECLARATION OF IRISH HOUSE OF COMMONS, 26 July 1641.[1]

    It is voted upon Question *nullo contradicente* that the
Subjects of this his Majesty's Kingdom are a free people,
and to be governed only according to the Common Law of
England and Statutes made and established by Parliament
in this Kingdom of Ireland and according to the lawful
Custom used in the same[2]....

60. (c) DEMANDS OF IRISH REBELS TO THE COUNCIL, 3 February 1642.[3]

    [They asked for the restoration of lands confiscated under
Elizabeth and James I, for Catholic commanders of militia,and for
a Catholic Deputy.]

    VII. That the Merchants and Traders of the Irish Nat-
ion may be as free in their Trade and have as much priviledge and favour in their Customes either in England or
Scotland, as the Scots of late are granted in England or
the English in Scotland....

    IV. That they may enjoy entirely all the Priviledges
and Franchises granted them by Edward the fourth[4]....

    XII. That they may have a Trienniall Parliament as in
England, and that the Catholiques may have the choice of
their Parliament men.

60. (d) REMONSTRANCE OF GRIEVANCES OF THE CONFEDERATE IRISH
                          CATHOLICS, 17 March 1643.[5]

  12. That whereas this your Majestie's kingdom of Ireland

---

1. C.J. (Ireland) I p.269.
2. No claim to initiate legislation was made. The declaration continued with impugning the judges for their quibbling opinion, with
indicting the council as 'no judicatory', and with denouncing proclamations and *quo warranto* as means of governing Ireland.
3. *Tracts relating to the Irish rebellion*, 1641-66, No.25.
4. Edward IV virtually abandoned Ireland to the pro-Yorkist earls –
especially (after 1471) to Kildare, who became a palatine lord to
the Anglo-Irish and an *Ard-Rí* to the Gaelic chiefs.
5. J.T. Gilbert (ed), *Richard Belling's History of the Irish Confederation* (1882) II pp. 226-242. Catholic fears for the suppression
of their faith by an English Puritan Parliament prompted the Irish
rebellion of October 1641 under Rory O'More. Statutes in the Long
Parliament,providing for large-scale confiscation and sale of the

in all succession of ages since the raigne of King Henry
the Second sometimes King of England and Lord of Ireland,
had Parlyaments of their owne, composed of Lords and Commons in the same manner and forme qualified with equall
liberties, powers, priviledges, and immunities with the
Parlyament of England and onely dependant of the King and
Crowne of England and Ireland:and for all that time noe
prevalent record or authentique president can be found,
that any statute made in England could or did bind this
kingdome before the same were here established by Parlyament...[Yet,notwithstanding, recent Acts (16 Car.I cap.33,34,35,37)
   had declared Irishmen 'unsummoned, unheard' to be rebels and had
   confiscated 2½ million acres for sale to Undertakers. 'The scope,
   seeminge to ayme att Rebells only' and their estates, was so widely worded that all the lands of the kingdom were threatened without any consideration of their owners. All tenures under the Crown
   and most of the Crown's revenues were taken away by such Acts : and
   the Crown was deprived of its prerogatives of issuing pardons and
   making grants of land 'a president that noe age can instance the
   like'.]
      ...Against this Act the said Catholiques doe protest
as an Act against the fundamentall lawes of this kingdome
and as an Act destructive to your Majestie's rights and
prerogatives, by cullor whereof, most of the forces sent
hither to infest this kingdom by sea and land disavowed
any authoritie from your Majestie but doe depend uppon
the Parlyament of England.

60. (e) ADDITIONAL PROPOSITIONS MADE BY THE CONFEDERATE IRISH
                         CATHOLICS, 29 March 1644.[1]
   [Poynings' Act should be suspended and a free Irish parliament
   summoned. Offices of profit should be conferred on Catholic Irishmen 'in equality and indifference with your Majesty's other subjects'. Only those 'estated and residenced' within Ireland should

---

lands of Irish rebels to pay for their suppression,stiffened Catholic
resistance to the claims of the English Parliament to legislate for
Ireland. Protestants in the Irish Parliament, following the advice
of the two 'parliamentarian' lords justices, excluded Catholics from
both Houses: and at a general assembly in October 1642 at Kilkenny
a Catholic Confederation was established. Darcy took a lead in
drafting its constitution: a supreme council, two houses, and four
subordinate provincial councils. For seven years the Confederate
Supreme Council organised forces, taxation, negotiations, etc. and
was the *de facto* government in many parts of Ireland. In negotiations
with the king they claimed for Ireland co-ordinate status with Scotland and England with its separate parliament and laws (cf. *ibid*. III
pp. 336-9).
The Remonstrance was presented to the king's commissioners at Trim.
The king was not unsympathetic to their claims for legislative independence,but was forced to be circumspect in his relations with the
English Parliament (*ibid*. II pp. 141-3).
1. J.T. Gilbert, (ed.) *op.cit*. III P.130. These eighteen new demands
were annexed to those in the Remonstrance of 17 March 1643 (*ibid*.II

vote in the Irish Parliament.]

11. That an Act shall be passed in the next Parliament declaratorie that the Parliament of Ireland is a free Parliament of itselfe, independent of and not subordinate to the Parliament of England; and that the subjects of Ireland are immediately subject to your Majesty as in right of your Crowne; and that members of the sayd Parliament of Ireland and all other the subjects of Ireland are independent, and in no way to be ordered or concluded by the Parliament of England and are only to be ordered and governed within that kingdom by your Majesty and such Governors as are or shall be there appointed and by the Parliament of that kingdome according to the lawes of the land.[1]

60. (f) ORMOND'S ANSWER, September 1644.[2]

...To the eleventh Proposition: His Majestie conceives the substance of this Proposition which concerneth the fundamentall rights of both kingdomes, fitt to be referred to the free debate and expostulation of the two Parliaments, when it shall please God that they may freely and safely sitt, his Majestie being so equally concerned in the priviledges of either that hee will take care to the uttmost of his power that they shall both conteyne themselves within their proper limitts, his Majestie being the head and equally concearned in the rights of both....[3]

---

pp.226 ff.).
1. The protestant counter-propositions demanded an Act of the English Parliament attainting the rebels and 'according to the presidents of former times' that such a statute 'be in due forme of law transmitted and passed in Ireland' (*ibid*.III p.146); but they did not commit themselves 'how far laws made in England may bind in Ireland' - a matter best resolved by'records and presidents'.
2. J. T. Gilbert, *op.cit*.III p.296 (cf.177). James Butler,earl of Ormond, was appointed commander in chief by the king in 1639 and lord lieutenant in 1642. He was appointed by the king to negotiate for him with the Confederates. Both sides would seem to have agreed that Ireland was not subject to English parliamentary supremacy, but Charles I was reluctant to assent to an Irish statute declaring such legislative autonomy,as it would weaken his own support in England. He hoped that resolutions of both houses of the Irish Parliament would be sufficient. In January 1649 Ormond and the Irish Parliament agreed on this compromise (*ibid*.VII p.194). In August 1649 Cromwell arrived with a considerable army to reduce and conquer Ireland, to seek punishment for the massacres in Ulster,and to enforce the Acts of 1642 (16 Car.I caps.33 *etc*.). In August 1652 by an Act of Settlement the Parliament of England legislated for Irish confiscations and penalties to pay for the conquest - 'they (the labourers and craftsmen) submitting themselves to the Parliament of the Commonwealth of England'.
3. Nevertheless on 28 September 1644 (*ibid*.pp.310-311) the Confederates answered again that the Irish Parliament was 'independent' of the

61. (a) PATRICK DARCY: *AN ARGUMENT*..., 9 June 1641.[1]
   [He argued that 'in all precedent ages, lawes cleare in themselves-
   for their greater honor and countenance, they have beene declared
   and enacted in parliament'.]
   ...The Law declared by Magna Carta was cleare before,
yet it was enacted 9 Hen.III and in thirty Parliaments
since...and the statute of 25 Ed.III of treasons is declaratory and so are many statutes. Adam eate the forbidden fruite; Cain killed his brother. God demaunded whether this was done yet he could not be ignorant of the
fact. This first article in the Civill and Canon law
Courts is whether there is such a law, all this is done
for illustrations sake....
   This Question is short and yet comprehensive: that
we are a free people, is confessed to my hands: to that
part of the answer I doe not except, the second part of
the Question is, whether wee are to be governed by the
lawes of England and statutes in force onely. First
though I need to prove it, yet it is cleare, we ought to
be so governed....
   [English common law, general custom and 'beneficial statutes'
   had long been received, but]
   ...for the statutes of England, general statutes were
received in this kingdome, some at one time, some at
another, and all generall statutes by Poynings Act *anno*
10 Hen.VII, but no other statute or new introducing law
untill the same be first received and enacted in Parliament in this kingdome and thus may appeare by two dec-
larative statutes, the one 10 Hen.IV [*1409*] and the other
29 Hen. VI [*1451*].[2]

61. (b) SIR RICHARD BOLTON: *A DECLARATION*, April 1644.[3]
   [He quoted precedents relating to the extension of English law

---

English Parliament 'without which independency, this realme could be
no kingdome, nor any Parliaments here necessary, nor any subject of
this kingdom sure of his estate, life or liberty other than at the
will and pleasure of a Parliament, wherein neither Lords, Knights
nor burgesses of this kingdom have place or vote'.
1. *An argument delivered by Patrricke Darcy; by the express order
of the House of Commons....* printed 1643: re-printed 1764, pp. 67-0.
Darcy had been appointed by the Irish House of Commons as their pro-
locutor (or advocate) in discussions with the Lords relating to the
judges 'pretended answers'.
2. 10 Hen.lV declared, it was claimed, 'That the Statutes made in England should not be in force in this Kingdome unless they were Allowed
and Published in this Kingdome by Parliament' (similarly 29 Hen.VI).
But these statutes were lost, though Bolton claimed to have seen them
once in the Treasury in Waterford.
3. *A declaration, setting forth how, and by what means, the laws and
statutes of England from time to time, came to be of force in Ireland.*
Walter Harris (ed.) *Hibernica II* (1750) pp. 1-21. Bolton was lord
chancellor of Ireland; but Harris believed this anonymous pamphlet,
which the Irish Lords and Commons considered carefully in April 1644,

to the Irish of the counties - John, Henry III *etc*. - and considered that, while two categories of law - common law and local
custom of township or manor - applied, the question of the third
category would depend on whether they were declaratory and therefore applied without confirmation, or whether they were introductory.]

 ...The third sort are Statute Laws, made in Parliament
by the King, the Lords spiritual and temporal, and the
Commons, which are the representative body of the Commonwealth: And of this sort, some are general laws, extending to all parts of the kingdom, and some are particular,
extending only to particular places or persons. And of
the general laws, some are introductory and positive, and
some are declaratory, declaring the common law in some
doubtful and ambiguous point, and some are mutatory, to
alter and repeal some former laws in part or in the whole.
But the Common Laws are general customs, and the particular customs were only of force in England in the time
of King John; for all the statute laws now of force in
England have been made since that time, *viz*.in the reign
of Hen.III and in the reigns of other succeeding Kings;
So as the laws established by King John in Ireland, in the
twelfth year of his reign,[1] were only these general customs, which are now called the Common Laws. And the
particular and local customs, which are limited to persons or places, which could not be transferred or applied
by any general words to the Kingdom of Ireland; where
the person or places, whereunto these particular customs
were limited and confined, are not to be found, and concerning the Statute Laws, which have been made since the
time of King John, so many of them as concern particular
persons, and particular places in England, cannot by any
general confirmation or approbation become to be laws of
force in Ireland; where no such places or persons are to
be found; but all such statutes as have been made since
the time that King John established the laws of England
in the kingdom of Ireland, which are only declaratory of
the Common Laws, are of force in Ireland, without any
other confirmation or approbation, but only the first establishment. And of this Sort are the statutes of Magna
Charta, made in the 9th year of Hen.III,the statute made
in 14th of Hen.III called *Statutum Hiberniae*, and the statute of 25th of Edw. III called the *Statute de Proditionibus*,
and many other statutes of the like kind. But such statutes as have been made in England since the 12th of King
John, and are introductory and positive, making new laws,
or any ways altering, adding unto, or diminishing the
ancient Common Laws, have not been binding, or any ways
of force in Ireland, until such time as they have been
enacted, allowed, and approved of, by act of Parliament,
in Ireland....

---

was by Darcy. *N.B.*These pamphlets were reprinted in 1750 and 1764.
1. This refers to John's grant, as conqueror, of English law to

[for example, the confirmation in Irish parliaments of the Statutes of Merton, Marlborough, Gloucester and Westminster I. The
arguments in Pilkington's case and the decisions in the Merchants
of Waterford case were cited.]

By this...it is apparent that none of those statutes
made in England from the 12th year of King John until 10
Hen.VII (which were introductory or positive) have been
received or put in execution as laws in the realm of Ireland until the same were approved and enacted by several
acts of Parliament in Ireland....

It is true that since 10 Hen.VII there have been many
Acts of Parliament made in England of great importance
both for the government of the Common-wealth, and the administration of justice between party and party, which
are now of force in Ireland: but none of them were ever
received as laws in Ireland, until the same were enacted
by several Parliaments holden in Ireland....

But it may be objected, that although such Acts of
Parliament as have been enacted in England, wherein no
mention hath been made of Ireland, do not bind and are
not of force in Ireland; yet all such acts as have been
or shall be made in England, wherein Ireland is particularly named are and shall be of force there without any
confirmation or approbation by Act of Parliament in Ireland....

[Some of these he dismissed as being declaratory and explanatory only; others as ordinances of the king's council and contrary to the original grant of the king as conqueror; others as
being disregarded and of no legal effect in Ireland anyway.]

And now, in as much as the laws of England and Ireland
do not admit of any inconveniences; it is to be considered, what inconveniences may follow, if the Kingdom of
Ireland should be bound by any statute made in England,
and not confirmed by Act of Parliament in Ireland. First,
the Parliament of Ireland should be nugatory and superfluous, if by naming Ireland in any statute made in
England, Ireland should be bound; then all these Parliaments which have been holden in Ireland since 12 King
John, for the space of about 400 years, should have been
needless and superfluous, which is not to be imagined.
Secondly, if the statutes made in England, by expressing
Ireland, should be binding, then by the same reason, a
statute made in England may repeal, alter, or change, all
the laws and statutes, which hitherto have been made and
approved, or hereafter shall be made or approved in Ireland, which were a thing marvelous inconvenient for that
Kingdom:...

[Furthermore two Parliaments might make conflicting laws; and
the laws made by those in Ireland, who best knew its needs and
conditions, should not be legally inferior to those made in England. Each kingdom had its own separate Parliament and distinct
laws, equal and co-ordinate. The fact that an appeal lay from

Ireland in 1210; for doubts about this 'grant',see pp.51-2,66-7,91-2.

Ireland to king's bench in England meant no more than that the
judges in England would consider whether by the laws of Ireland,
not of England, there had been error. Henry II's conquest enabled
him as conqueror to establish lawfully whatever government and law
he pleased: it did not make Ireland subordinate to the English
parliament. Henry II divested himself of all his regal power in
Ireland by an[alleged]grant to John in 1177 of a separate kingdom
there. When John succeeded to the English Crown, there was a
union of Crowns but not of realms. Nor did a grant of English
law in 1210 imply a subordination of Ireland to the realm of England any more than it would to Scotland if John had decided to
grant Scottish law.

He affirmed that (1) Henry II as a conqueror had permitted Irish
laws to continue for 28 years,and Ireland was not subordinated-as
England had not been subordinated to Normandy. (2) If his 'conquest' of Ireland had united the realms automatically, as he said
it did not necessarily do, then Henry II divided them in 1177.
(3) When John had established the government of Ireland according
to the laws of England, he did so not by power through descent
through his brother,but by that regal power donated by his father
in 1177.

Many important records, however, he admitted, had 'miscarried
in those troublesome and distempered times' and could not be found
(p.4). These would be conclusive proof, especially Irish acts of
1326 and 1451 which, he claimed,declared that English statutes
were not in force unless confirmed in the Irish parliament.][1]
Ireland is a kingdom distinct of itself and so declared
by Act of Parliament in 33 Hen.VIII cap.1, the government
thereof being established according to the model of England[2] which was, and is, not only regal but also politick:
so as by that establishment Ireland became a body politick
of itself as England was then: consisting of the King's
Majesty as supreme head and of the Peers and Commons as
members of the same, in such sorts that the Peers and
Commons of England are not, nor cannot be any parliament
or member of this body politic of Ireland no more than
the Peers or Commons of Ireland are and can be members of
the body politick of England: therefore it cannot stand
either in law or common reason that the one body politick
should be subordinate or subject to the controul of the
other; - for then the King's Majesty which is the head of
the one and also of the other should be both superior and
inferior to himself in his royal and politick capacity
within itself which are altogether repugnant....

[Ireland would acknowledge England's 'precedency and seniority
in politick government', but the superiority of, and its subjection to, the king alone].

1. i.e. 19 Ed.II and 29 Hen.VI which,however,he said were not to be
discovered in the parliamentary rolls.
2. The Act uniting the Crowns did not, of course,explicitly state
this. Any similarity with the Westminster model was largely coincid-
ental; see F. Madden,'Not for export' in *The first British Common-*
wealth ed. Hillmer and Wigley (1980).

61. (c) SIR SAMUEL MAYART: ANSWER TO A BOOK ENTITLED A DECLARATION.[1]
[The historical evidence for a grant made by Henry II in an
Oxford Parliament of 1177 to Prince John of a separate Kingdom of
Ireland was wholly absent, unreliable, inexact or second-hand.
The alleged historians did not categorically state it in the terms
stated: contemporaries did not mention it; loose references by
chroniclers must be considered as being made by those who, like
the monks, had no careful training in the use of legal terms and
instruments, or in constitutional law. If Henry II did not give
powers of absolute government to his eldest son, why should he
have done so to a boy of four as John was in 1177?]
   ...Ireland was always united to England and governed
by the laws of England....Ireland was annexed to the
Crown of England before King John came to the Crown and
...he assumed the title of *Dominus Hiberniae*, which land
was annexed to the Crown of England before and to which
title he stuck and not to his being created King of Ireland before by his Father: for if he had, questionless
he would have taken the stile of King of Ireland when he
came to be King of England....
   [In accordance with the express terms of the grant which Henry
III made of the whole land of Ireland,Edward I stated, in letters
patent of lands granted on 6 February 1294, that these same lands
should be held of· him and his heirs for ever '*ita quid non sep-
araretur a Corona Angliae*' p.32.]
   It may be therefore granted as it is likely to be true
...that King John had a great and large power granted to
him, yet not absolute but limited...but not anywhere doth
it appear that the kingdom was absolutely granted to King
John or that (as the Author saith) he held it as a separate and distinct kingdom severed apart from the Kingdom
of England and of which Henry II was divested which if
any should have said, yet there must be better authorities than those of chronicles to guide a case of this high
and weighty concernment or else the Author will miss much
of what he would have ....
   [Ireland from the Conquest was united to England. John ruled
it as part of his kingdom and made grants of Irish land. In 1279
[?1277: No.31] Ed.III ordered there to be 'one and the same law in
Ireland as in England'...not just common law but '*omnes leges et
consuetudines teneantur et eisdem legibus subjaceat*'. In 1537
(28 Hen.VIII cap.6) appeals to the king for remedial justice were
asserted because 'this land of Ireland is the King's proper dominion of England and united, knit and belonging to the Imperial
Crown of the same realm': in 1537 (28 Hen.VIII cap.3) the Statute against absentees affirmed that the kings of England held
great possessions there in right of the English crown; and in
1542 (33 Hen.VIII cap.1) the Statute uniting the Crowns declared
that the lordship of Ireland had been united to the English Crown.
   ' A Declaration' had argued that English law was observed only
in the counties of Leinster and Munster until, in late Tudor times,

---

1. Printed in Walter Harris, *Hibernica II* (1750) pp.23-131. Mayart
was justice in the Irish courts of common pleas in the 1640s.

the machinery of county government had been extended to Ulster and
Connaught. Mayart claimed that county organisation existed
throughout all Ireland and the king's writs were current in the
thirteenth century,until English rule collapsed with the encroachment of Gaelic septs and *brehon* law.
  The author of *' A Declaration'* had argued that English statutes
would apply without re-enactment in Ireland, only if they were
declaratory.   If he admitted that the English Parliament might
bind by any declaratory law,then his whole argument failed.]
  ...For he saith, that the statutes of England, as that
of 25th Ed.III, &c. *[de Proditionibus]* which are only declaratory, are of force in Ireland without any other confirmation. And if they have power by a statute there to
declare what is law which shall bind in Ireland, why
should they not as well have power to make a new law to
bind it? For if a declaratory law binds, it binds as it
is a statute: for the declaratory statute saith, the
law shall be thus or thus taken. Therefore, if they
should not bind in other cases, where positive laws (as
he calls them) are made for Ireland as well as in these,
you must say the Parliament of England, has power to bind
Ireland by a statute made in England, and yet it has not
power to bind Ireland: and yet it is one and the same
power, which makes declaratory laws and new laws, and so
it is understood in the Parliament of York, 12 Ed.II [the
preamble of which stated that because of the 'defaults' in some
laws and the obscurity of certain statutes, the king in parliament had enacted the necessary statutes of clarification. Parliamentary legislation, even if thus declaratory, must have some
positive significance,or there would be no need by statute to
clarify the law. How if an Irish statute should declare the law
to be different? If a declaratory statute bound, so too must
other statutes. The alleged differentiation between declaratory
and introductory statutes was 'a distinction and a division of a
thing which is in truth indivisible'.
  Statutes which mentioned Ireland specifically or the 'dominions'
generally,and those which made mention of neither, were extended
and observed in Ireland from the conquest. From court records he
showed how section by section the Statute of Westminster II (1285)
- an introductory Act - was applied before any re-enactment in
Ireland by 13 Ed.II. So were the Statutes of Mortmain (1279), of
Provisors (1351),and of Staples (1354).][1]
  By these records it appears that Ireland antiently was
so far from being accounted a Kingdom separated and divided from the Government of England that it was esteemed
in the nature of a county belonging to England: the Jus-

1. e.g. The Irish Parliament only as late as 1454 (32 Hen.VI cap.1)
declared the many English Statutes of Provisors (from 25 Ed.III cap.
22 to 3 Hen.V cap.4)were to be in force; but clearly these statutes
were regarded as being in force before,since the preamble states that
they were being disregarded in Ireland 'more now than before this
time'. In 1411 Henry IV sent the Statutes of Provisors of 1351 and
1390 to Ireland to be enrolled there.

tice *[justiciar]* of Ireland but, as it were, a kind of
Sheriff to execute the process sent out of the courts of
Justice of England ....

[Records showed that English statutes enacted exclusively for
Ireland (e.g. that against absentees, 1380) were observed in Ireland without confirmation in the Irish Parliament; so too were
certain English statutes enacted for England (e.g. that of Mortmain, 1279).]

The main and chief end in raising all these records
is to prove, that before any confirmation of the statutes
of England in Ireland by Parliament there, they were there
received and executed and that notwithstanding those statutes which the Author supposes were made there, whereby
the statutes of England should not be binding in Ireland
without consent of the Parliament there, yet after that
statutes made in England for Ireland only were received
and executed there, notwithstanding any such supposed
statute as the Author speaks of: and therefore, if any
such there were, yet, even by the Judges of Ireland, were
they esteemed void also, would they not some time or
other, have made question of the executing the statutes
of England there? ...

[The English Parliament could bind Ireland,but the Irish Parliament could not bind England: therefore Ireland was subject to
English statutes,and the resolutions of the 'free' Irish Parliament in 1641 and the suspension of Poynings' Laws were of no
effect. English statutes had been sent regularly to the chancellor of Ireland to be enrolled in the Irish chancery and published to be obeyed: Mayart gave examples. *Pilkington's Case* was
indecisive: two judges took one view, two the contrary. The
matter of the English Parliament's being non-representative was
irrelevant: it had legislated effectively for Wales, Chester and
Calais, 'for the statutes of England do bind many places from
whence there are no Knights or Burgesses'. Representation might
be of significance in matters relating to land, but not of persons;
for law-making it was necessary to have consent of the three
estates - king, lords and commons; but it was not necessary to
have representatives from every seignory, dominion or county.
Corporations and cities made by-laws which bound themselves, but
they were subordinate to the law of the land and could not exclude
the right of the English Parliament to make laws to bind them:
'Ireland no more than in the former case of corporations'. The
author of *'A Declaration'* had argued that the Statute of Ireland
(14 Hen.III) was 'no introductory law but an explanation of the
common law' to which we only say that, admit it to be so, yet that
the power to make a declaratory law is one and the same with the
power to make an introductory law,as we have shown before: otherwise if they have power to make one kind of law, they have power
to make the other'. Calvin's case showed that Ireland could be
subject to English law and to the writ of error on appeal to the
king's bench in England: judges might be interpreting Irish custom
as they might *gavelkind* in Kent, but custom in Ireland and Kent
might be altered by Act of Parliament. 24 Hen.VIII cap.12 relating to appeals, and 26 Hen.VIII cap.3 relating to first fruits,both

mentioned 'the dominions': they were both applied to Ireland
before confirmation in the Irish parliament respectively by 28
Hen.VIII cap.6 and cap.14. Mayart mentioned that the careful
procedures laid down by Poynings' Law were of great wisdom and
good for Ireland. Scotland was no parallel: it was not conquered
nor subject to the realm or Crown of England; and it never received English laws.   Ireland was conquered, annexed and united:
English law was communicated to Ireland and counties formed before
King John in 1210 put the grant in writing.]

If the King of England should conquer any territories
beyond the sea and give them the law of England and annex
them to the Crown of England, I think none will say that
the distance of place will shake off the Power of the
Government of England: no more will it do that of Ireland ....

[Ireland was as much knit into the English body politic as the
palatines or the City of London and like them was subject and
subordinate to Parliament.][1]

62. THE INSTRUMENT OF GOVERNMENT,16 December 1653.[2]

The government of the Commonwealth of England, Scotland,
and Ireland, and the dominions thereunto belonging.

I. That the supreme legislative authority of the Commonwealth of England, Scotland, and Ireland, and the dominions thereunto belonging, shall be and reside in one
person, and the people assembled in Parliament: the style
of which person shall be the Lord Protector of the Commonwealth of England, Scotland, and Ireland ....

[The 'chief magistracy and the administration of the government'
would be in the Lord Protector assisted by a council.]

IX. That as well the next as all other successive Parliaments shall be summoned and elected in manner hereafter
expressed; that is to say, the persons to be chosen within England, Wales, the Isles of Jersey, Guernsey, and the
town of Berwick-upon-Tweed, to sit and serve in Parliament,
shall be, and not exceed, the number of four hundred. The
persons to be chosen within Scotland, to sit and serve in
Parliament,shall be, and not exceed, the number of thirty;
and the persons to be chosen to sit in Parliament for Ireland shall be, and not exceed the number of thirty ....

[Parliament would be summoned by writ,sent under the great seal
of England, to sheriffs. If writs were not issued,then sheriffs

---

1. See also Vaughan (C.J.)'s opinion in *Craw v. Ramsay*,1670, No.21.
2. S.R. Gardiner, (ed.) *Constitutional documents of the Puritan revolution* (1906) pp. 405-417. The United Commonwealth of England,
Ireland, Scotland and Wales established in this written constitution,
depended on the success of the army of the English Parliament and on
military force and conquest. The distribution of seats according to
population was a radical idea, but the members elected in Ireland and
Scotland were largely government nominees and army officers,and supported the Protector as loyally as members for royal pocket-boroughs
did the king's ministers in the unreformed Parliament during the
next century.

of counties *etc*. within England, Wales, Scotland and Ireland
should take action to cause members to be chosen. Chief officers
of state were to be chosen by the approbation of Parliament. Those
with estate valued at £200 could vote _ though royalists and Catholics were disqualified.][1]

63. REPORT FROM A COMMITTEE OF THE ENGLISH HOUSE OF COMMONS,
26 November 1670.[2]

The great dispute was concerning the power of charging Ireland by the parliament of England.

1. It was said that we have the same power to charge
Ireland that we have of other plantacions....

To this it was answered.

That Ireland was not a plantacion[3] but a distinct Kingdome, governed by lawes and parliaments of its owne. That
it seemeth inconsistent with the nature of a government
by kings, lords, and Commons to be charged by any other
power than the parliament of that kingdome they having
no representatives in this.

That we do not yet offer to tax our plantacions which
is in kindness to them, that they may grow up and thrive
under them, and certainly Ireland is more to be cherished
in all respects than either of them.

64. DECLARATORY ACT OF IRISH PARLIAMENT, May 1689.[4]

Whereas his majesty's realm of Ireland is, and hath
been always a distinct kingdom from that of his majesty's
realm of England, always governed by his majesty and his
predecessors, according to the ancient customs, laws and
and statutes thereof, and as the people of this kingdom
did never send members to any parliament ever held in Eng-

---

1. For the first time the territories, kingdoms, principality, dominions and nations of what was to become the United Kingdom were brought
together temporarily into a single state.
2. L. F. Stock,*Proceedings and debates of the British Parliament*(1924)
I pp.367-8. The United Commonwealth under the Protector was dissolved
at the Restoration, as too was the free trade which Ireland had had
with the colonies. The English Parliament legislated for Ireland in
the Navigation Act (12 Car.II cap.18); in the prohibition of woollen
exports to foreign countries from Ireland - and the Channel Isles too
- (12 Car.II cap.32; 14 Car.II cap.18) and in the prohibition of
tobacco planting (12 Car.II cap.34; 15 Car.II cap.7).
3. The argument was motivated by a desire to exclude Ireland, a commercial rival, from the privileges a plantation enjoyed under the Navigation Acts in relation to ships and seamen and the carrying trade.
4. E. Curtis and R.B.McDowell, *op.cit.*169-71. The earl of Tyrconnell,
James II's deputy, had by 1689 secured Catholic majorities in both houses of the Irish Parliament. James saw Ireland as a stepping-stone
back to the throne in England: the Irish Catholics saw James as a
weapon against the Protestants and as a rallying point for Irish pat-
riotism. This Act asserted both legislative and judicial autonomy.
James, however, refused to assent to a twin bill which would have repealed the Poynings'Law procedure and granted Ireland a legislative

land, but had their laws continually made and established
by their own parliaments, so no acts passed in any parliament held in England were ever binding here, excepting
such of them as by acts of parliament passed in this kingdom were made into laws here, yet of late times (especially in the times of distractions) some have pretended, that
acts of parliament passed in England, mentioning Ireland,
were binding in Ireland:...Be it therefore enacted...That
no act of parliament passed,or to be passed in the parliament of England, though Ireland should be therein mentioned, can be, or shall be any way binding in Ireland;
excepting such acts passed, or to be passed in England,as
are or shall be made into law by the parliament of Ireland....

   [No appeals from Irish cases were to go to the English House
of Lords.][1]

65. (a) ENGLISH ACT FOR THE BETTER SECURITY OF PROTESTANT SUBJECTS
                   (1 Will. & Mary III sess. 2 cap.9), 1689.
   WHEREAS the Kingdome of Ireland is (as well by the law
of this Kingdome, as those of Ireland) annexed and united
to the imperiall Crown of England, and all Acts, Judgements Sentences Orders Decrees or other Proceedings of
what kinde soever there had made or done without or
against the authoritie of the Kings or Queens of this
Kingdome of England are absolutely null and void,And all
persons in Ireland that oppose or submitt not to the Government of the Crowne of this Realme are Rebells and
guilty of High Treason,Notwithstanding which severall
persons since the happy Accession of their Majestyes King
William and Queene Mary to the Imperiall Crowne of this
Realme have beene lately assembled at or neere the City
of Dublin in the Kingdome of Ireland without any authoritie from their said Majesties pretending to be or calling themselves by the Name of a Parlyament and in such
Rebellious Assembly have made and passed severall pretended Acts or Statutes in manifest opposition to the Soveraignty and to the inherent Rights and Dignities of the
Crowne of this Realme and to the generall Prejudice and
Violation of the Rights and Properties of their Majestyes

---

initiative.
1. See. No.50 above.
2. In the Bill of Rights (1 Will.III sess. 2 cap.2) the English'Convention Parliament' had declared William and Mary to be King and
Queen 'of England, France and Ireland and the Dominions thereunto
belonging according to the resolution...of the said Lords and Commons': that is, the English Parliament gave away the title to the
united Crowns of England and Ireland. This the Irish protestant Parliament accepted in 1692:[see below No.66].
By contrast, and perhaps in a spirit of defiance of the English, the
Scots Convention had drawn up their own 'Claim of Right' and, with no
pretence of any 'abdication',positively deposed James II for attacking the 'fundamental constitution' of Scotland; but Scotland and

good Subjects of that Kingdome[1], and although all the said
Proceedings are absolutely null and void in themselves yet
neverthelesse for the more plain and expresse declareing
and asserting the Soveraignty Rights and Dignities of the
Crowne of England and for the clearing all Doubts and
quieting the Minds of their Majestys good Subjects of
that Kingdome and alsoe for the remedying preventing and
avoiding the several Mischiefs and Inconveniences intended
by this Act to be provided against, Bee it enacted and declared by the King and Queens most excellent Majesties by
and with the advice and consent of the Lords spirituall
and temporall and Commons in this present Parlyament assembled and by authoritie of the same That the Persons now or
of late assembled at Dublin without any authoritie derived from their Majestyes pretending to be or calling themselves by the Name of a Parlyament, were not nor are a Parlyament but an unlawfull and rebellious Assembly And that
all Acts of Attainder and all other Acts and Proceedings
whatsoever had made, done or passed, or to be had made, done
or passed in the said pretended Parlyament shall be taken
deemed and adjudged to be and are hereby declared to be
absolutely null and void to all Intents, constructions and
purposes whatsoever, And alsoe that noe Act, Statute, judgement, Outlawry, Decree, Sentence, Order, or other Proceedings,
Matter, or thing whatsoever since the thirteenth day of
February in the year of our Lord one thousand six hundred
eighty eight had made, passed, given, pronounced, or done, or
hereafter to be had made passed given pronounced or done
by any person or persons whatsoever by colour of any Commission, Writ, Power, or Authority as hath beene or shall be
given by or derived from or under their Majestyes, Shall
be of any Strength, Force, Vertue, or Effect, but that the
same to all intends, constructions, and purposes shall be
and are hereby declared and adjudged to be absolutely
null and void ....

  [II. Cities and corporations were to be in same state as 1683,
  notwithstanding *Quo warranto* s, *etc*., which were now declared void.[2]
  III. No Protestants were to be prejudiced by their absence *etc*.
  between 1685-1688 during the completion of the reduction of Ireland. IV. Protestants were restored to their possessions.]

65. (b) ENGLISH ACT FOR ABROGATING THE OATH OF SUPREMACY IN IRELAND,
                          (3 Will.III & Mary cap.2) 1691.[3]
     [Reference was made to the Elizabethan Act of Supremacy in

---

England were separate realms.
1. This refers to the Acts of the Irish 'Patriot Parliament' which
restored lands to Catholic families deprived of them since the rebellion of 1641 and which attainted some 2,400 Irish Protestants of
treason.
2. By reconstructing such corporations, Tyrconnell had secured the
return of Catholic M.Ps.
3. 6 St. of R.254-7. This Act of the English Parliament was extended
to Ireland when Lord Sidney as William III's lord lieutenant summoned

1560.][1]
....IV. And forasmuch as great disquiet and many dangerous attempts have been made to deprive their Majesties
and their royal predecessors of the said realm of Ireland by the liberty which the popish recusants there have
had and taken to sit and vote in Parliament, Be it enacted....That from and after the last day of January next
no person that is or shall be hereafter a peer of that
realm or member of the House of peers that shall vote or
make his proxy in the said House of Peers, or sit there
during any debate in the said House, nor any person that
after the said day of January shall be a member of the
House of Commons shall be capable to vote in the said
House or sit there during any debate in the same after
their Speaker is chosen, unless he first take the oaths
herein....

   [There followed the form of the oaths to be administered, including a denial of the doctrine of transubstantiation.]

66. IRISH ACT CONFIRMING THEIR MAJESTIES' RIGHT TO THE IRISH CROWN
(4 Will.III & Mary cap.1), 1692.[2]
   FORASMUCH as this kingdom of Ireland is annexed and
united to the imperial crown of England and by the laws
and statutes of this kingdom is declared to be justly
and rightfully depending upon, [3] and belonging, and for
ever united to the same; and the Kings and Queens of
England are by undoubted right Kings and Queens of this
realm, and ought to enjoy the stile, title, majesty,
power, preheminence, jurisdiction, prerogative and authority of Kings and Queens of the same....we the lords
spiritual and temporal and commons in Parliament assembled, as we are in duty bound, do recognize and acknowledge,
that the kingdom of Ireland, and all titles, stiles,
royalties, jurisdictions, rights, privileges, prerogatives, and preheminences-royal thereunto belonging,

an effectively Protestant Parliament for Ireland in 1692.
1. This Irish statute had been enacted in similar terms to the English
one for the previous year. The Crown's prerogative, however was employed on a considerable scale to grant dispensation for officials
from penalties for not taking the oath.
2. The Irish Parliament was now exclusively Protestant. By an English statute (3 Will.III cap.2) the former oath of supremacy provided
by an Irish statute (2 Eliz.I cap.1) - which members of the Irish
Parliament had been exempted from taking - had been replaced by a
declaration against transubstantiation and an abjuration of the authority of the pope, which members were now required to take. Opening
the Irish Parliament in October 1692,the lord lieutenant, Lord Sidney.
told them that the goal must be 'the firm settlement of this country
upon a Protestant interest'. (II C.J.10).
3. This is a clear acknowledgement by the Irish Parliament of its
subordination: typical of the general insistence on the dependence of
'dominions' and 'plantations' since the Commonwealth Act of 1649,
[see No.221 (b).]

are most rightfully and lawfully vested in their Majesties King William and Queen Mary, and that their most excellent Majesties were, are, and of right ought to be
King and Queen of England, Ireland, Scotland, and France,
and the dominions and territories thereunto belonging;
in and to whose princely persons the royal state, crown,
and dignity of the said realms, with all honours, stiles,
titles, regalities, prerogatives,powers, jurisdictions,
and authorities to the same belonging and appertaining,
are more fully, rightfully and intirely invested and incorporated, united and annexed....

67. (a) WILLIAM MOLYNEAUX: *THE CASE OF IRELAND'S BEING BOUND BY
        ACTS OF PARLIAMENT IN ENGLAND*, 1689.[1]
    [He questioned whether Ireland could ever rightly be consid-
    ered as having been 'conquered' by Henry II or (for example,in
    suppression of rebellions) by any kings since. Rather was there
    voluntary acceptance of English institutions, the concession of
    subsequent liberties, and the right of holding a separate Irish
    Parliament on the English model (p.32). If ever there were an
    'original compact', it was that between Henry II and the people
    of Ireland.]
    ...Here we have a free Grant of all the Liberties of
England to the people of Ireland. But we know the Liberties of Englishmen are Founded on that Universal Law of
Nature, that ought to prevail throughout the whole World,
of being Govern'd only by such Laws to which they give
their own Consent by their Representatives in Parliament
....[2]
    [He argued that in 1177 John was given a separate Kingdom of
    Ireland and when he became king of England, Ireland was annexed
    to the Crown but not to the realm of England. He used the mis-
    sing statutes of 10 Hen.IV (1409) and 29 Hen.VI (1451) to affirm
    that English Acts did not apply until confirmed in the Irish
    Parliament (p.58).]
    ...We shall next Enquire, Whether there are not other
Acts of the English Parliament, both before and since
the 10th of Henry the Seventh, [*i.e. Poynings Law*] which
were and are of Force in Ireland, tho' not Allow'd of by
Parliament in this Kingdom. And we shall find, That by
the Opinion of our best Lawyers, there are divers such;
but then they are only such as are Declaratory of the
Antient Common Law of England , and not introductive of
any New Law: For these become of Force by the first

---

1. Molyneaux, an Irish protestant M.P. who had taken refuge in England during the régime of James II's deputy, Tyrconnel, dedicated
this pamphlet to William III. The occasion was the bill pending in
the English parliament to prohibit the export of Irish wool and wool-
en manufactures to any foreign country (10 Will.III cap.16):[see also
Vol.II section 1]. A disciple of Locke, Molyneaux emphasised the necessity,according to natural law, for consent-by representation-in
legislation. Otherwise this argument(and facts)follow closely those
of Bolton's *Declaration* [see above No.61 (b)].
2. See also *ibid*.pp.113,150, for further Lockean argument.

General Establishment of the Common Laws of England in
this Kingdom, under Henry the Second, King John, and Henry
the Third; and need no particular Act of Ireland for
their Sanction.

As to those English Statutes since the 10th of Henry
the Seventh, that are Introductive of a New Law, it was
never made a Question whether they should Bind Ireland,
without being Allow'd in Parliament here; till of very
late years this Doubt began to be moved; and how it has
been Carried on and Promoted, shall Appear more fully
hereafter....

[He denied the opinion of Hussey and Coke that Ireland can be
bound if named specifically, or generally as a 'dominion'. The
Statutum Hiberniae (14 Hen.III) was only a certificate of common
law; the ordinance for the state of Ireland (17 Ed.I) was only
an order of the king in council, not a statute, and was never observed, etc. If Ireland became subject to the authority of the
English legislature by conquest, was England bound by the Norman
conquest to laws made by the duke's overlord in Paris? (p.94). If
English-made laws were accepted in Ireland, it was because the
balance of convenience and reason at certain times was for such
acceptance.]

There have been other Statutes or Ordinances made in
England for Ireland which may reasonably be in force here
because they were made and assented to by our Representatives ...

[e.g. a writ of 1281 (9Ed.I) which, at the request of Lords
and Commons of Ireland, applied to Ireland certain declaratory
statutes made at Lincoln and York in explanation of the common
law which 'manifestly shews that the King and Parliament of
England would not Enact Laws to Bind Ireland without the Concurrence of the Representatives of this Kingdom'.]

Formerly When Ireland was but thinly Peopled and the
English law not fully Currant in all parts of the Kingdom,
'tis probable that then they could not frequently Assemble
with conveniency or safety to make Laws in their own Parliament at home and therefore during the Heat of Rebellions
or Confusion of the Times they were forced to Enact Laws
in England. But then this was always by their proper
Representatives...This sending of Representatives out of
Ireland to the Parliament of England on some occasions
was found, in process of time, to be very Troublesome and
Inconvenient; and this we may presume, was the Reason,
that afterwards, when Times were more settled, we fell
again into our old Track and regular Course of Parliament
in our own Country ....

[He claimed that no introductory statute had ever been passed
by the English Parliament to apply to Ireland till the Acts of
1641 (16 Car.I cap.33 etc.) for confiscation and sale of rebel
lands: this was a necessary emergency measure, Ireland was aflame
with rebellion, and no Irish Parliament could meet, so the English
Parliament acted 'for our Relief and Safety'.[1]

1. Molyneaux of course wrote with protestant bias.

But, he said, these Acts were repealed by the Irish Parliament at
the Restoration. The commercial legislation of Charles II's reign-
superfluous, evaded or observed- could not deprive the Irish of
500 years' liberty.

The recent English Act for the security of Irish Protestants
(1 Will.III sess.2 cap.9) was confirmed in the Irish parliament
(7 Will.III cap.3) and had been passed at Westminster only as a
necessary emergency measure at the request of Irish Protestant
refugees in England: they had 'recourse to this Means as the
only which could then be had'. Similarly he accepted recent English statutes (1 Will.III sess.1 caps. 29 and 34) as emergency
legislation to which the Irish owed merely voluntary submission
since it was 'pleasing': they did not have binding authority
(p.112). If they had, the'Glorious Revolution' would imply the
loss, not the confirmation, of rights and liberties.

That a writ of error lay from the Irish to the English court of
king's bench did not imply subordination: it existed only by
enactment of an Irish Parliament 'which is lost', and the suit
was to the king himself as the king of Ireland.]

[But] this does not argue that Ireland is therefore
Subordinate to England, for the People of Ireland are the
Subjects of the King to whom they appeal. And 'tis not
from the Country where the Court is held, but from the
Presence and Authority of the King...that the Pre-eminence
of the Jurisdiction does flow, And I question not, but in
former times when these Courts were first Erected and when
the King Exerted a greater Power in Judicature than he
does now, and he used to sit in his own Court, that if he
had Travell'd into Ireland, and the Court had follow'd
him thither, Erroneous Judgements might have been remov'd
from England into his Court in Ireland, since the Court
Travell'd with the King. From hence it appears that all
the Jurisdiction that the King's Bench in England has
over the King's Bench in Ireland arises only from the
King's Presence in the former [1]....

[To assert Ireland to be bound by English statutes was against
reason, against natural right, against English common law and
certain English statutes and Irish statutes (e.g. 10 Hen.IV and
29 Hen.VI), against several charters of liberties granted to Ireland, against the King's regality and prerogative, and against
traditions of former ages. It would also be inconvenient and
confusing.]

67. (b) RESOLUTIONS OF ENGLISH HOUSE OF COMMONS, 27 June 1698.[2]
...Resolved, *Nemine contradicente*, That the Book, intituled,

---

1. This argument would also support the superiority of the English
Parliament where kings were present longer than in king's bench, and
the king's personal veto was still in 1698 a real factor. Molyneaux
realised his was a double-edged argument (*ibid*. p.138); but his answer
that the English Parliament was claiming a legislative authority
apart from the King was blatantly untrue.

2. C.J.XII.330. On 30 June they sent an Address to the king warning
him against the danger of Ireland's shaking off its subjection to Eng-

"The Case of Ireland's being bound by Acts of Parliament
in England stated," is of dangerous Consequence to the
Crown and People of England, by denying the Authority of
the King and Parliament of England, to bind the Kingdom
and People of Ireland; and the Subordination and Dependence that Ireland hath, and ought to have, upon England, as being united and annexed to the Imperial Crown
of the Realm.
    Resolved, That the Bill, intituled, An Act for the
better Security of his Majesty's Royal Person and Government, transmitted under the Great Seal of Ireland, whereby an Act of Parliament made in England, expressly to bind
Ireland, is pretended to be reenacted, and Alterations
therein made; and divers things enacted also, pretending
to oblige the Courts of Justice, and the Great-Seal of
England, by the Authority of an Irish Parliament, has
given Occasion and Encouragement to the forming and publishing the dangerous Positions contained in the said
Book....[1]

III THE PROCEDURES OF THE IRISH PARLIAMENT
    By the mid-thirteenth century kings of England were ready, when
convenient, to summon representatives of landholders and knights of
the counties to their council for Ireland. Thereby Ireland secured
a Parliament of its own at Dublin, though its role was passive and
from 1495 under the régime of their own Poynings' Law its initiatives
and procedure were restricted.

68. WRIT FROM EDWARD I FOR THE COLLECTION OF A SUBSIDY FOR THE
    SCOTTISH WAR, 18th January 1300.[2]
    ...Know that whereas for the safety of our royal Crown
and the common advantage of our kingdom and of our lands,

---

and by reason of Molyneaux's book, and, assuring him of their assistance 'in a Parliamentary way' to maintain that dependence.
1. In asserting the claim of the English house of lords to final
appellate jurisdiction in the Declaratory Act of 1719 (6 Geo.I cap.5)
the British Parliament also declared its right to bind Ireland by
statutes [see No.53].
2. H. F. Berry (ed.) *op.cit.*p.229. Trans. from Latin. The writ was
addressed to 'the earls, barons, knights and other his faithful
people established throughout the land of Ireland'; on account of
which the justiciar caused to be summoned a general Parliament at
Dublin a fortnight before Easter. In addition to the magnates, the
counties sent 2,3 or 4 elected representatives,and the cities 2 or 3
to represent the communities.
The Irish Parliaments began (as did their English prototypes) as afforced meetings of the king's council in Ireland which was the natural
way of administering a dominion. The king (or his representative)
did not have to call a council to advise him, still less tenants-with
or without approval of council or Parliament; and this remained true
in principle till the late fifteenth century: the ordinances of 1323,
1357 and 1361 were made on the authority of the king and his council
in England. But it was prudent to request advice,and supplies,of

we have ordained, and also we purpose to be, on the next
feast of the Nativity of S. John the Baptist *[i.e. 24 June]*
at Carlisle *[with an armed force]* ...to set out therefrom to
repress...the rebellion of the Scottish enemies and our
rebels: for the more successful execution of which business we need your assistance and aid...

> [the justiciar and chancellor were to request 'the subsidy which
> shall appear suitable to the successful issue of so serious an
> undertaking and to the advantage and honor of us and you'. Simil-
> ar writs had been sent to other cities and boroughs in Ireland.][1]

69. POYNINGS' ACT ON PROCEDURES FOR IRISH PARLIAMENTARY LEGISLATION,
(10 Hen.VII cap.4), 1495.[2]
    ITEM, at the request of the commons of the land of
Ireland, be it ordained, enacted and established, That

Irishmen. Gradually the common council of prelates and magnates
included a secret (privy) inner council of senior officials.
Not till 1264 did an Irish 'Parliament' meet: an assembly of tenants-in-chief representing the commonalties of landholders - officials, councillors, magnates, prelates and knights of the counties
(who were not then elected). These last had little but a passive
role to play and were called only when it was politic to do so (see
E. Curtis and R.B.McDowell *op.cit.*,pp.32-38). Business remained
virtually indistinguishable from that dealt with by the council -
grievances, taxes, the maintenance of the king's peace and common
law; and there seems no rationalisation in distinguishing councils
from Parliaments. Not till 1370 did it become normal to summon representative commoners with their petitions into the enlarged assembly. Substantially the Parliament did little but register decrees
prepared by the lord lieutenant.
Furthermore it should be remembered that petitioners went to English
Parliaments from the 'dominions', and Edward I particularly encouraged them to do so. The Statute of Absentees (1380) was passed by
the English Parliament on the presentation of a message from Ireland (Parl.Rot. III.85-6).
The first so-called'Statutes'in *Irish Statutes* (1786) were made in
1310 at a Parliament in Kilkenny: then there is a gap until the
middle of the fifteenth century. As for H.F.Berry's edition of
Early Statutes (1907) it included for the most part writs from the
king, ordinances of the English and Irish councils, enrolments and
memoranda (e.g. in 1285 extending the Statutes of Westminster,
Gloucester and Merchants to Ireland), a few subsidies granted in
Irish Parliaments and the confirmation of English statutes. See
especially H.G. Richardson and G. O. Sayles, *Parliament and Council
in Medieval Ireland* (1947) and *The Irish Parliament in the Middle
Ages* (1967).
1. Before this Irish 'Parliament' met some boroughs had agreed to
pay subsidies. The Parliament excused itself from making a subsidy
but asked the justiciar to make a tour and collect the subsidy from
the communities. To these the magnates would contribute. Parliament
agreed that no money was to be carried out of Ireland 'without special warrant'.
2. <u>Sir</u> <u>Edward</u> <u>Poynings</u> was sent as deputy with a small armed force

at the next Parliament that there shall be holden by the
King's commandment and licence, wherein amongst other,
the King's grace entendeth to have a general resumption
of his whole revenues sith the last day of the reign of
King Edward the second, no Parliament be holden   hereafter
in the said land, but at such season as the King's lieut-

---

to reduce the 'Lordship' to obedience and put an end to virtual 'Home
Rule' wherein the Irish Parliament was the mere tool of the lord
lieutenant. He came with English officials whose tenure of office
was not for life, but during pleasure only. Henry VII was determined
to resume both the Crown's right to appoint the great officers of
state in Ireland,and its revenues lost or usurped since 1327. Poynings' success in these matters was ephemeral:'Home Rule' was restored
under Kildare, and half the Irish lands could not be confiscated
merely by a Resumption Act. But the Irish Parliament was made subordinate to a firm control from England by this, its own Act.
Though later denounced as the instrument of its legislative enslavement, this procedural Act of Poynings' Parliament at Drogheda was
regarded in the Irish Parliament (until the lord deputyship of Strafford) as a safeguard: it was the Irish executive council in 1585, or
1613, which sought to suspend the Act as inconvenient and procrastin-
atory. In 1495 it was passed to curb the overmighty Irish-born lord
lieutenant and officials who were out of control of the king and the
Irish Parliament (and abused Irish autonomy and colonial 'nationalism'
for their own interest and power); to avoid a repetition of the Sim-
nel affair when the pretender was crowned in a common council in
Dublin as 'Edward VI', and to prevent there being a legal Parliament
in Yorkist Ireland to give authority to an illegitimate Yorkist
'king'; and to free the Irish Parliament from a burdensome mass of
petty administrative detail by clarifying its legislative work.
Furthermore, the Act was nominally a confirmation of articles agreed
in an afforced council two years earlier and advocated by petitions
from representative commoners.
As for the device of royal control of parliamentary legislation,this
was no real departure from the procedures expected: it was for a
Parliament to obey the king's wishes and to make possible his policies. It must be remembered that not till the late sixteenth century
did the English House of Commons win an initiative. The king sent
his bills to his English Parliament and expected them to be enacted.
By Poynings' Law the Irish Parliament reduced the lord lieutenant's
veto, removed from him the summoning of Parliament and the initiative in legislation, associated with him a council of officials, and
gave the final word to the king and council in England. The Irish
Parliament could reject measures and they did so; but their power
to amend was limited. Moreover, in the period between 1534 and 1615
they used the Act against the Tudor bureaucracy as a means of obstruction and delay. That the Act was a frustrating curb on parliamentary initiative only became obvious when its effect in freezing the
Irish Parliament in a static posture of subservience to the king was
contrasted with the organic evolution made by its prototype model in
England during the next century and a half. In 1495 both Parliaments
were subordinate to, and controlled by, the Crown.

enant and counsile[1] there first do certifie the King,
under the great seal of that land, the causes and considerations, and all such acts as them seemeth should pass
in the same Parliament, [2] and such causes, considerations,
and acts affirmed by the King and his counsail to be good
and expedient for that land, and his licence thereupon,
as well in affirmation of the said causes and acts, as to
summon the said Parliament under his great seal of England had and obtained: that done, a Parliament to be had
and holden after the form and effect afore rehearsed:
and if any Parliament be holden in that land hereafter,
contrary to the form and provision afordsaid, it be deemed void and of none effect in law.

70. (a) PROCEDURES FOR SUMMONING AN IRISH PARLIAMENT, 14 November
1497.[3]

Right worshupfull and myn especiall gode Lorde, I
commaund me unto you with all due reuerance certyfyng you
that maister Topclefe, chefe Justice here, is send by my
lorde of Kildare[4], the kyngs depute here, to the kyngs
highnes for diuers matirs or in especiall to have licence
of the kyng to hold a parlement here, wherfor I wold avise
you to laboure to the kyng to have a prouiso for youre
lordeship putt in the said licence And that ye be not
slow therein, for my lorde depute is well dispossit to
you therein.[5]

70. (b) CERTIFICATION BY HENRY VII FOR AN ACT EXEMPTING ORMOND FROM
THE ACT OF RESUMPTION, 26 June 1498.[6]

By the King, Moste Reverende father in God, trustie and

---

1. This council was not actually defined, but seemed to have included
the great officers of state and some magnates. The lord lieutenant
might still be able to select bills to be sent to England, but lost
his veto on bills certified by the king.
2. That draft bills should be sent to the king and his council in
England for approval, and licenced certification presumably might imply
that the king could not add further bills or even amend them; and that
no new bills could come from Ireland during a session. But none of
these implications seem to have been accepted in practice.
3. E. Curtis (ed.) *Calendar of Ormond Deeds* IV pp.333-4. From Walter
Champfleur, abbot of St. Mary's and agent for the earl of Ormond, to
his patron who was an absentee.
4. Kildare, having been attainted in 1495, was restored as deputy
'since all Ireland cannot rule this man, this man must rule all Ireland'.
5. Ormond had not been exempted from the earlier Act of Resumption in
1479, and now through Champfleur was seeking protection from the king.
Henry VII was prepared to do this by his prerogative, but Ormond wanted an Act in addition. This clause sufficiently indicates there was
no doubt that the Crown could add to bills.
6. E. Curtis (ed.) *op.cit.*IV pp.337-0. Henry VII sent this certification for a bill to the lord chancellor of Ireland to be passed in the
Irish Parliament. The bill had been drafted by Ormond and had been

right entierly welbeloved, We grateyou hartlye well, And
sende unto you herein enclosed the tenour and effecte of
a certain Acte whiche the Comens of our lands of Irlande
have instantly besought us may passe in our Parliament
nowe holden within our said lande.[1] Whereupon We being
agreable unto the said Acte woll and chardge you that,
under our great seale being in your warde,ye do make our
lettres sufficiently to be directed unto our right trusty
and right welbiloved Cousin,therle of Kildare, Deputie
Lieutenaunte of our said lande, Yeving unto him full power and auctoritie by the same to suffre the said Acte to
passe in our said Parliament according to the tenour and
effecte aforesaid, As we specially trust you, And there
our lattres shalbe your sufficient dischardge in that
behalf.   Yeven under our Signet at our Castell of Wynde-
sor,the XXVI day of June *[1498]*.
     [The Act itself stated:]
     ...We woll and chardge you that emonges suche articles
as we have appointed to passe undre our great seale into
our lande of Irlande to be enactid at the Parliament nowe
holden there, that this Article following be made and
sealed undre oure great seale in the fourme following...
it was ordeyned by an Acte of Parliament holden at Dro-
ogheda in this lande of Irlande... *[in]* the Xth yereof the
Reigne of our souverain lord Henry the VIIth*[1495]* before
Sir Edward Poynynges knight,then deputie of this said
lande of Irlande to our souverain lord king Henry the
VIIth...that there shulde be resumed, seised, and takyn
into the King our said souverain lordes hands,all maner
honours, manours, lordships, Castells...hereditaments,
and comodities whereof our souverain lorde the King or
any of his noble progenitours, kings of Englande, was at
eny time seised of in Fee simple or Fee taill from the
last day of the Reigne of King Edwarde the seconde to
this present Acte...And where the Kings said highness
not willing the said Erle to be Prejudiced, endamaged,
ne hurte by reason of the said Acte, Therefore Be it enactid, ordeyned and establisshed by the auctoritie of this
present Parliament the same Acte of Resumpsion and every
other Acte or acts made in the said Parliament as far as
they or any of theme be prejudiciall or hurtefull or concerneth the said Erle of Ormonde and his heires or any
feoffee or feoffees to his use or their heires,be revoked,
repeled and demed voide and of noon effect in lawe. And
the said Thomas Erle of Ormonde...by the same auctoritie
be ennabled and restorid to his name,dignytie and estate
honour,and preemynence that he had or was of the first

---

sent straight to the king.
1. This was a fiction since the Irish Parliament did not meet until
after this certification arrived in Ireland. But it shows that bills
might arise in the deliberations of the Irish Parliament and be
sent for approval by the king after Parliament had met.

day of the said Parliament....And also it is ordeyned...
That all lettres patents, confirmacions and graunts [of
land etc] made to any person or persons by our said souverain lorde, and his deputie and deputies of our said souverain lord the King said lands of Irland aftre the for--
said Resumpsion Acts...be utterlye voide and of noon effect on lawe...Provided alwaies that the two parts of all
the revenues, ysses and proficts of the premises by cause
of thabsent of the said Erls of Ormonde...out of the said
land of Irlande be and remayne to the use of our said
souverain lorde the King for the defence of the said lande
according to tholde ordenance, use and custume of the
same....

70. (c) DISPENSING ACT FOR FAILURE TO OBSERVE POYNINGS' LAW, 1537.[1]
    For the great trust and confidence that the King's
highnesse hath in his deputie and counsaile of this his
land of Ireland, and in the nobles spiritual and temporal,
and the commons his loving subjects of the same, his Majestie is pleased and contented, that it be enacted by
authority of this present Parliament, That this present
Parliament summoned, begun and holden, and every Act, ordinance, provision, thing or things, of what nature, name,
condition, or quality it be of, had, done, made or established, by authority thereof, shall be good and effectual
to all intents and purposes according to the tenour and
effect of the said acts, ordinances, and provisions...
[despite failure to observe 10 Hen.VII cap.4].
    II. Provided alway, ...no Act, ordinance, provision,
thing or things...be enacted or established by virtue or
authority of this present Parliament, but only such Acts,
ordinances, and provisions, thing or things, as shall be
thought expedient for our soveraigne lord the King's
honour, and encrease of his grace's revenues and profites,
and the common weale of this his land and dominion of
Ireland.

71. IRISH ACT OF SUPREMACY (28 Hen.VIII cap.5) 1537.[2]
    LIKE as the King's Majesty justly and rightfully is
and ought to be supreme head of the church of England,
and so is recognised by the clergie, and authorised by

1. Statutes at Large (Ireland)I. pp.89-90. This Irish statute made
lawful the recent anti-papal legislation passed by the Irish Parliament, though the procedure in Poynings' Law had not been followed.
With the fall of the Kildares and the end of Irish aristocratic 'Home
Rule' in 1534, the Irish government became more immediately under English control. The new English officials found the procedure under the
1495 Act inconvenient just as the Irish Parliament was to find it use-
fully protective and obstructionist. In 1569 an Irish statute enacted that no bill suspending Poynings' Law should be sent to England
without its express consent.
2. Statutes at Large (Ireland) I p.90.

an Act of Parliament made and established in the said
realm: So in like maner of wise, forasmuch as this land
of Ireland is depending and belonging justly and rightfully to the imperial crown of England, ...Be it enacted
by authority of this present Parliament, That the King
our sovereign lord, his heyres and successors, Kings of
the said realm of England, and lords of this said land
of Ireland, shall be accepted, taken, and reputed the
only supream head in earth of the whole church of Ireland,
...and shall have and enjoy, annexed and united to the
imperial crown of England, as well the title and stile
thereof, as all honours, dignities, preheminences, jurisdictions, priviledges, authorities, immunities, profites,
and commodities to the said dignitie of supreme head of
the same church belonging and appertayning,...

72. ACT INTERPRETING POYNINGS' ACT (3 and 4 Phil. and Mary cap.4),
                                                1556.[1]

Where at a Parliament holden at Drogheda...in the
tenth year of the reign of the late King of famous memory,
Henry the seventh...before Sir Edward Poynings, knight,
then lord deputy of this realm of Ireland, an Act among
other things was enacted and made for and concerning the
order, manner, and form of Parliament to be from henceforth holden and kept in this realm of Ireland...and by
the said Act [10 Hen.VII cap.4] more at large doth appear:
for as much as sithence the making of the said Act diverse
and sundry ambiguities and doubts have been made and risen
upon the true understanding and meaning of the same; for
the avoiding of the which doubts and ambiguities, and for
a full and plain declaration of the true meaning and understanding of the said Act, Be it ordained, enacted, and
established by authority of this present Parliament, That
the said Act, and every clause and article therein contained, shall from the first day of September last past
be expounded, understanded, and taken, as hereafter followeth; that is to say, That no Parliament be summoned
or holden within this realm of Ireland, until such time
as the lieutenant, lord deputy...and the council of this
said realm of Ireland, for the time being, shall have certified the King and Queen's Majesties...under the great
seal of this said realm of Ireland, the considerations...
and ordinances, as by them shall be then thought meet and
necessary to be enacted and passed here by Parliament, and
shall have also received again their Majesties' answer,
under their great seal of England, declaring their pleasure, either for the passing of the said acts, provisions,
and ordinances, in such form and tenor as they shall be
sent into England, or else for the change or alterations
of them, or any part of the same.

---

1. By this Irish statute the procedures of Poynings' Law were clarified and amended. The king could approve draft bills during a session
and could license Parliaments without the advice of the Irish council.
The right to amend and initiate new legislation was now expressly

II. And be it further enacted by the authority aforesaid, That after such return made, and after licence and
authority to summon a Parliament within the said realm of
Ireland, granted under the great seal of England unto the
said lieutenant or lord deputy...and not before, the same
lieutenant...shall and may summon and hold a Parliament
within this realm of Ireland, for passing and agreeing
upon such acts, and no other, as shall be so returned
under the said great seal of England.

III. And forasmuch as many events and occasions may
happen during the time of the Parliament, the which shall
be thought meet and necessary to be provided for, and yet
at or before the time of the summoning of the Parliament,
was not thought nor agreed upon: therefore Be it further
enacted and established by authority of this Parliament,
That as well after every such authority and licence sent
into this realm of Ireland, as also at all times after
the summons, and during the time of every Parliament to
be hereafter holden within the said realm of Ireland, according to the tenor and form of this Act, the lieutenant...
and council of the same realm of Ireland for the time being shall and may certify all such other considerations,
causes, tenors, provisions, and ordinances, as they shall
further then think good to be enacted and established, at
and in the same Parliament within the same realm of Ireland, to the King and Queen's Majesties...under the great
seal of this said realm of Ireland, and such considerations...and ordinances...as shall be thereupon certified
and returned into the said realm, under the great seal
of England, and no others, shall and may pass and be enacted here in every such Parliament within this said
realm of Ireland, in case the same considerations *[etc.]*...
be agreed and resolved upon by the three estates of the
said Parliament; any thing contained in this present Act,
or in the foresaid Act made at Drogheda to the contrary
notwithstanding.

IV. Provided always, and be it further enacted by the
authority of this present Parliament, That all and every
Parliament and Parliaments summoned, kept and holden within this realm of Ireland,since the making of the said former Act, in the said tenth year of the reign of the said
late King Henry the seventh,and all and every Act...passed,
ordained, and enacted in the same,shall be and remain in
such and the same force...as if this Act had never been
had ne made: this Act, or any thing therein contained to
the contrary notwithstanding....

73. JUDGES' OPINION ON THE IRISH HOUSE OF COMMONS' CLAIM ON MONEY
                              BILLS, 14 February 1693.[1]
   [They had considered the procedures in 10 Hen.VII cap.4 and 11
   Eliz.I sess.3 cap.8 and found that the lord lieutenant and council
   alone were empowered to prepare all bills and that the Irish Parl-

asserted.   1.See p.111 n.1.

iament could not be summoned to consider bills until they had been
certified by the king under the great seal of England: furthermore 4 Phil. and Mary cap.4 empowered the king in council in England to amend draft bills, and the lord lieutenant and council to
prepare and certify additional bills when the Irish Parliament
was in session. In 1614 the Irish Commons expressly acknowledged
'the sole right and authority to transit such Bills into England
as are to be propounded in Parliament, to rest in the Lord Deputy',
though they requested the deputy to consult with their committee
in drafting bills; and in 1661 they claimed no exclusive privilege to advise the deputy but appointed a joint committee with the
Lords to consult on a money bill.][1]
   Upon consideration of all which statutes, journals,
transmisses, and other proceedings of Parliament, we are
unanimously of opinion:
   First, That it is not the sole right of the Commons
of Ireland, in Parliament assembled, to prepare heads of
bills for raising money.
   Secondly, That the Chief Governor and Council may prepare bills for raising of money, and certify, and transmit the same to their Majesties and the Council of England, to be returned under the Great Seal of England, and
afterwards sent to the Commons, although the heads of such
bills have not their first rise in the House of Commons.[2]

IV THE PREROGATIVE
   This final section of Irish documents attempts to illustrate the
part played in Ireland by the king's representative (*justiciar*, *lord
lieutenant*, or *lord-deputy*) and the manifestations of the king's
prerogative powers (charters, letters patent, commission, instructions, writs, orders *etc.*).

---

1. *Tracts [Godwin Pamphlets]* Vol.32. No.2 Appendix. On 3 November
1692 the supply bill was rejected (II C.J.35) and the Irish Parliament was prorogued. This opinion on legal procedures was delivered
by the eight Irish judges. Twelve English judges gave an identical
opinion in June 1693. Money bills continued to be prepared in consultation between the English and Irish privy councils every two
years. The Parliament did not meet again for three years and then
accepted immediately the preparation of a money bill on the lines
advocated by the lord lieutenant.
2. After 1692 the Irish Parliament acquired a very limited initiative by a new procedure whereby 'heads of bills' might be proposed in
either House and, if certified by the lord lieutenant and council and
passed by both Houses, would be sent to the king in council in England for assent, amendment or rejection: such bills would then be
returned to the Irish Parliament to be passed or rejected in full.
This was the Irish form of reservation of laws to the Crown as
practised elsewhere in the colonies. (For committees of the House
considering and preparing 'heads of bills', reporting on 'lawes
needful, and proposing the acceptance of certain English statutes',
see II C.J.19,26,35).

74. CHARTER FROM HENRY II TO THE MEN OF BRISTOL, 1171.[1]
Know ye that I have given and granted, and by the present charter have confirmed, to my men of Bristol my city
of Dublin for them to inhabit. Wherefore I will and
firmly command that they shall inhabit it and hold that
of me and of my heirs well and in peace, freely and quietly, entirely and fully and honourably with all the liberties and free customs [2] which the men of Bristol have at
Bristol and throughout all my land.

75. CHARTER FROM HENRY II TO JOHN FITZ GEOFFREY, 5 August 1252.[3]
...Know ye we have given, granted, and confirmed by
this our charter, on our own behalf and of that of our
heirs, to our beloved and faithful John Fitz Geoffrey in
return for his homage and service all the cantred of the
Islands in Thothmon in Ireland with all its appurtenances,
To be possessed and held by the said John and his heirs of
us and our heirs, quietly, well and in peace with all its
vills, demesnes, rents, services from free men and vill-
ein-services in woods and fields, marshes, meadows and
pastures, waters, fisheries, fish-ponds and mills with
the presentations of churches, and all liberties and
free pastures belonging to the said cantred without any
limitation. In return for a rent to be paid to us and
our heirs at our exchequer in Dublin of forty-three marks.
viz. to the Michaelmas exchequer, twenty-one and one half
marks, and to the Easter exchequer twenty-one and one half
marks and for doing the service of the fee of two knights
to us and our heirs which is to cover every service, custom and demand....
    [Fitz Geoffrey and his heirs were granted immunity in their
    cantred from actions in the sheriff's courts, should exercise
    jurisdiction similar to the sheriff's within the *cantred*, and
    should be answerable directly to the jurisdiction of the king's
    justices.]

76. LETTERS PATENT FROM EDWARD III TO THE JUSTICIAR, 15 February
                                                    1359.[4]
    Edward, King of England, *etc.*, to his dear and faith-
ful cousin James le Botiller, Justiciar of Ireland, greeting. Know that we confiding in your wisdom and fidelity,
have given you by the tenour of these presents the power

---

1. N.D. Harding, editor, *Bristol Charters* 1155- 1373, (Bristol,1930)
pp.6-7.
2. Or 'services'.
3. E.Curtis (ed.) *op.cit.*Vol I, 1172-1350. (Dublin 1932) No.118.
4. E. Curtis ed. *op.cit.*II. The king's representative ('vice-roy')
was called *justiciar* till the beginning of the fourteenth century:
he acted for the king of England as Lord of Ireland. From 1316 he was
named *Lord Lieutenant*. During the period of Irish aristocratic 'home
rule' in the latter half of the fifteenth century, the king's lieutenant left effective rule in Ireland to the powerful local earls,-
Ormond, Desmond and Kildare - as deputies. With Tudor assertion of
the king's authority *Lords deputy* were appointed from England.

to remove sheriffs, constables, bailiffs and all other
ministers whatsoever in our land of Ireland, whom you
have found unsuitable and to put others suitable in their
places, by council and advice of our Chancellor and Treasurer of Ireland as often as need shall be and as for our
greater advantage you shall deem fit. We do not wish however that Justices or Barons of the Exchequer or other
our ministers in the said land, whose offices we have
granted them by letters patent under our Great seal of
England, shall under pretext of this present power given
you by us be removed by you from their offices.... *(portion
of Great seal.)*

77. *THE LORD LIEUTENANT:*
   (a) LETTERS PATENT FROM HENRY VI TO THE LORD LIEUTENANT,
                             10 February 1429.[1]
    [The earl of Ormond was appointed lieutenant for two years.
    The king granted him power]
    ...to guard our peace and the laws and customs of that
land and to do all and sundry to bring into our peace
both English and Irish of that land and to punish them
according to the laws and customs of that land or according as may seem best to him for our profit in the rule of
our said land and of our lieges and subjects there. And
to summon and convoke parliaments and councils in said
land as often as shall seem necessary in places where it
seems best to hold them, summoning before him to parliament prelates, magnates and others who ought to come to
such parliaments to make statutes and ordinances there
for the good rule of the land, according to the custom
of the same, by assent of prelates, magnates and others
aforesaid.
    Also to proclaim in the said land by our writs of the
same our royal services and all such services according
to the due custom of the same and to punish those who
are delinquent. Also to proclaim as often as shall be
necessary that all and sundry who have any annuities or
fees of our gift or of our predecessors shall be prepared
to set forth to ride and to labour with the said lieutenant within the said land for receiving and admitting
to our peace both English and Irish who are rebels to our
said land and customs....
    [The powers were granted to punish those who refuse 'to come
    to justice, with royal power if necessary'; to pardon; to grant
    confiscated lands to suitable loyalists 'at farm or by reasonable
    rent' by advice of the council.]

1. Printed in E. Curtis and R.B.McDowell *op.cit.* pp.70-2;including
the indenture relating to fees to be claimed by Ormond. The earl
ruled virtually from 1416 to 1462 and secured the Desmond power in
the south west. Since Henry VI was still a minor, this letter patent was witnessed by Humfrey, duke of Gloucester as 'Guardian of
England'. These documents should be compared with the commissions
and instructions to colonial governors later.

...Also full power to supervise all ministers or officers
in Ireland, to remove those who are useless, and to put
others who are useful and suitable in their places....

77. (b) ACTS RELATING TO THE ELECTION OF A JUSTICIAR, 1494-1542.[1]
     Forasmoche as contynually sethens the conquest of this
realme of Irlande it hathe bene used in the same realme of
Irlande, That at eny such tyme as it hath chaunsed the same
realme to be destitute of a Lieutenant, Deputie, Justice
or other hed governour by deth, surrendre, or departure
out of the same realme of otherwise, the Counsaill of this
realme, etc., forthe tyme being have used by the lawes and
usages of the same to assemble them selfes togither to choise and elect a Justice to be the ruler and governour of
the realme till the Kinges highnes had deputed and ordeyned
a Lieutenant, Deputie or other governour for the same realme[2].... [Poynings' Act of November 1494,making the treasurer justiciar in any such vacancy,had been repealed in 1497 after his departure; but records having been 'imbeaselid' and lost, there were many
uncertainties; so in 1542 (33 Hen.VIII cap.2)]... for the remedy
whereof and establyshement of a certain ordre to be had for
thelection, *etc.*, Be it enacted and established by auctoritie of this present Parliament That, imediately upon tha-
voidaunce of eny the Kinges Lieuteuauntes, Deputies or Justice of this realm...the Kinges Chauncellor of this realme
or Keper of his graces great seale for the tyme being,
shall by the kinges writt or writtes call or assemble togither at suche place as the said Chauncellor *etc.*, shall
think convenyent, the kinges counsaillors [from all the
shires of the Pale, the south and the south-west] to electe and
choise oon suche person as shalbe an Englishman and borne
within the realm of England[3], being noo spirituall person,
to be Justice and governour of this realme, etc., during
the kinges highnes pleasure,...And yf there be noo suche
person then within this realme, then they to electe and
choise twoo persons of the said counsaill of English blode
and surname,.. [the chancellor being hereby authorised 'according
to the ancient usage' to make letters patent under the Irish great
seal.]

77. (c) INSTRUCTIONS FROM HENRY VIII TO THE DEPUTY, 1530.[4]
     [The deputy was to deliver the king's credentials and instruct-

---

1. E. Curtis (ed.) *op.cit.*III pp.275-7 where the date given (1494) is
clearly wrong.With a few minor changes, this is the form enacted in
1542 (Irish St.I pp.207-9).
2. By the alleged 'statute of Henry FitzEmpress', the Irish council
believed it had the right to elect to a vacant justiciarship, and had
done so several times (e.g. Kildare in 1470). The Irish Parliament had
under Kildare's influence confirmed this claim in an Act of 1485. Poynings had temporarily asserted the king's right in 1494, but Kildare
had secured the repeal of his Act in 1497. In 1542 having broken the
Kildare power and assumed the Irish Crown [No.58], Henry VIII was making a gracious but careful gesture.
3. To exclude the self-perpetuating *caucus* of Anglo-Irish magnates.
4. Printed in E. Curtis and R. B. McDowell, *op. cit.* pp. 79-81 Sir
William Skeffington was deputy for the lord lieutenant, the duke of

ions to the chancellor and council of Ireland, and to consult
with them on policies for 'the surety, weal and defence of that
land' and the peace, law and order therein. He was provided with
200 horsemen and money, and was to have special concern for any
'grudges and displeasures' among the earls whose powerful assistance was so vital to resist the king's Irish enemies and preserve
his land. He was not to invade the lands of the 'wild Irishry'
without the express agreement of the council nor to use Irish
revenues for that purpose without their consent.]
     The said deputy shall also take with him the letters
patent, under the king's seal of Ireland, devised upon
all such articles and points, as there were thought good
to be enacted and passed by authority of the parliament
of his said land: which parliament the said deputy shall
call and convoke with as good diligence as he shall see
to be necessary and requisite, endeavouring him, with
the assistance of the residue of the said council, to
the establishment, enacting and passing of such acts, by
the authority aforesaid, as by the king's highness shall
be devised, and to the due certificate to be made unto
the king's highness thereof, as is accustomed, and semb-
lably to the execution and performance of the same, after
such sort and manner, as may be to the weal of the king's
said people and land, and after such form as the said
articles do purport. The discreet ordering whereof, for
attaining them to pass, the king's highness committeth
to the wisdom and endeavour of the said deputy, with the
assistance of the residue of the council as is aforesaid.
     [His first urgent object would be to obtain a subsidy for the
     king's purposes, if possible even before the Irish parliament met.[1]
     The deputy might put men under the command of the earl of Kildare
     in his promised 'excourses' on 'the King's rebellious subjects of
     the wild Irishry'.][2]

Richmond and Somerset. The council in Dublin was a small pro-English
junta.
1. See, for example, No.68.
2. The overmighty Kildares, however, proved unreliable instruments
for the king's purpose. After their fall and the collapse of the
Geraldine league, Henry VIII was determined to reduce the power of
the Anglo-Irish lords, to replace his nominal and somewhat indirect
overlordship by a more efficient and direct rule by officials from
England and to make an effective kingdom (see No.80) of his Irish
dominion (he was grandson of the popular Richard of York). Resolutely
but circumspectly the frontiers of English power were extended in
Meath and Leinster. St. Leger as deputy was notably successful in
winning over Anglo-Irish and Gaelic chiefs to accept royal government
and to receive Crown titles for their lands by a conciliatory policy
of treaties, surrender and re-grant. After defeat Conn O'Neill, the
hereditary king of Ireland who had been crowned at Tara, submitted to
St. Leger in December 1541, accepting Henry VIII as king, holding his
lands by knight service of the Crown, and promising to attend the
Irish Parliament as earl of Tyrone.
     But the Tudor machinery of government was inadequate for direct

Finally, the said deputy shall from time to time as
well by his letters apart, as also jointly with the residue of the king's said council, advertise the king's
highness of the state and successes of the affairs in the
said land of Ireland; endeavouring himself always with
diligence to those things, which,by common advice of the
said council, shall be thought good, both for administration of justice, punishment of transgressors and malefactors, good order, quiet, and rule to be observed in
the said land, with the dimission and letting of the farms,
wards, marriages, and other the king's profits there, by
common advice, as well of the king's said deputy, as of
the council aforesaid, and also for the resistance of the
malice and temerity of the king's said rebellious subjects;
using all politic provisions, as well by appointments to
be taken with them,when the case shall require, as by
force and other good and discreet ways as shall be thought
convenient; and, generally, shall do, observe, and accomplish all such things, as to the office, authority, and
trust, which the king's highness of special confidence,
hath and doth put him in, shall appertain; whereby he
shall more and more deserve the king's special favour and
thanks, to be hereafter remembered to his weal accordingly.

77. (d) COMMISSION TO LORD MOUNTJOY, 12 April 1603.[1]
[His powers as deputy general of Ireland which he was to hold
during pleasure were listed:-]to protect the peace,laws and
customs of all liege subjects english and irish, to punish all persons offending, to ordain with the advice of
the counsell ordinances and statutes, to make proclamations and demand the due execution thereof...to grant
with the advice of the counsell full pardon to all seeking the same...to do justice to all persons according to
the laws and customs aforesaid...to levy the king's subjects...to reserve with the advice of counsell an annual
rent upon every...lease and allotment...to constitute all

rule in Ireland. Henry VIII had to act as a foreign *Ard-Ri* (high
king) using the great lords and chiefs as 'captains of the nations'
accountable to him. These chiefs for the most part governed their
lands by Irish custom,but their link (by surrender and re-grant)with
the king did tend to weaken their responsibility to their vassals,to
leave the clansmen without rights and protection, and to individual-
ise clan tenures contrary to Irish custom and inheritance laws. The
most effective way of extending English law proved to be by plantation of English settlers [see Nos.38,83]. Confiscations of land had
begun under Queen Mary in 1556; so did armed resistance.to them.
1. J.C. Erik, *The repertory of the inrolments of the patent rolls of
Chancery in Ireland* (1846) Vol.I p.17. Mountjoy's office of deputy
general and governor had been renewed on 9 April following the demise
of Elizabeth I. The systematic conquest of Ireland carried out by
adequate forces maintained from England was the new policy: its aim_
to make the king's writ run everywhere and replace *brehon* land law
by common law tenures ;[see above p.64n].

officers [chancellor, treasurer, justices, law officers *etc.*
excepted] ...to receive the homage of all tenants spiritual
and temporal and of all subjects...to summon and hold one
parliament only when most expedient, the king's consent
in that behalf being first had, to prorogue and adjourn
said parliament as there shall be necessity; and fully
to determine, dissolve and end it within two years from
the time of its beginning...to make all accountable officers account,_the treasurer and sub-treasurer only
excepted...to exercise and ordain everything which by
right, use and custom belongs to the office of deputy
general and are necessary for the good government and
custody of the peace of said land, the quietness of the
people and the recovery of the king's rights, to do and
execute all other things in the king's name which His
Majesty should or ought to do, if he were there in his
own person [including right to purvey and commandeer, and exercise martial law.]

78. ACT CONFIRMING THE CROWN'S RIGHT OF RESUMPTION (38 Hen.VI cap.
33), 1460.[1]

...XXXIII. Also, at the request of the Commons, That
whereas the King our sovereign lord, has retained to his
Highness from time to time divers Lords Lieutenants and
Governors of his land of Ireland, granting to them yearly
for the same great sums of money to be paid to them for
their salaries, as it appears of record by the Indentures
thereof between our said sovereign lord and the said
lieutenants severally made; which sums for many years
back have not been paid because of the piteous and lament-
able diminution of the revenues, commodities and profits
appertaining to the Crown of England, from which the
said salaries yearly accrued, to the great defence, increase and enrichment of the said land, the protection
and defence whereof depend now solely upon the revenues
of the said land, and upon such forfeitures as the law
gives to his Highness;...
        [which revenues were of no great value and wholly insuffic-
    ient to meet defence expenditure]
                        Whereupon the premises considered,
It is ordained, established and enacted in the said Parliament, that by authority thereof, the King do resume
take and seize into his hands, from the feast of Saint
Martin last past, all manors, castles, lordships, towns,
villages, lands, tenements, rents, revenues, annuities,
services, fees, fee farms, with their appurtenances whatsoever, and all other things profits, possessions and
advantages in the said land by him from the first day of

---

1. H. F. Berry (ed.), *Early Statutes of Ireland*. King Henry VI. (Dublin
1910). pp.719-21. The Irish Parliament was being used to reverse
grants previously made by the Crown which it could not have done
without recourse to legal action in the Courts.

his reign to any person or persons by his letters patents,
by authority of Parliament or otherwise, granted for term
of life term of years or in fee, in any manner...And
further that all licences of absence made to any person
or persons of the said land be made void, revoked, repealed and of no force virtue or effect....[The revenues of all
lordships *etc*. seized by the king were to revert to the king.] and
the revenues, issues and profits thereof *[were to]* be
employed upon the said defence from the said feast during
one year, unless that the said person or persons be in his
own person or in their persons within the said land between this and the feast of Easter next coming, there to
remain upon the defence thereof for the said year....

79. LETTERS PATENT FROM HENRY VII TO WILLIAM CASSHENE, 18 March 1502.[1]
    ...Know that of our special grace and with the assent
of our very dear kinsman, Gerald, Earl of Kildare, our
deputy, and of our dearest second son, Henry, Duke of
York, our lieutenant of our land of Ireland, we have
granted, on our own behalf and that of our heirs, as far
as in us lies, to William Casshene, son of Thaddeus Casshene, or by whatever other name he is known, who, it is
said, is a man of Irish birth and blood, that he and all
his issue, both begotten and to be begotten, are to be of
the estate and condition of free men, exempt from every
servile burden of the Irish. That they shall sue and be
sued in all other courts, and those of our heirs, and
those of all other men whatsoever just as Englishmen do
in our land of Ireland; and that they shall be under
our laws and shall be able to enjoy those laws freely
just as our liegemen of English birth enjoy and use those
laws. That they shall be able in perpetuity to acquire
for themselves and their heirs and to hold for their
heirs lands, tenements, rents, services and offices of
any kind....Provided that the said William Casshene and
his said issue behave themselves towards us, our heirs,
and our subjects as our faithful liegemen and so bear
themselves for the future. In witness of which we have
caused these letters patent to be made out.[2]

---

1. E. Curtis (ed.) *op.cit.* III, 1413-1509 (1935) no.306. Trans, from
Latin. The letters patent were given under the great seal of Ireland and witnessed at Dublin.
2. Another example of the methods of securing local collaboration
and support can be seen in the indenture between the deputy Lord
Gray and Thady O'Byrne, 'chief captain of his nation'. On January
22 1535 O'Byrne agreed, as proof of his obedience and loyalty to
Henry VIII to provide 20 horsemen and 20 *galloglasses* ('footmen')
according to the usage of his country at his own charges' and in
case of necessity and emergency a further 128 armed *galloglasses*
for up to three months. (Cal. Pat. Roll 28, 29, 30 Hen.VIII:
Rotulorum patentium et clausorum Cancellariae Hiberniae Calendarium
p.14 LXXII).

80. ACT AGAINST ABSENTEES (28 Hen.VIII cap.3) 1537.[1]

Forasmuch as it is notorious and manifest, that this the King's land of Ireland, heretofore being inhabited and in due obedience and subjection unto the King's most noble progenitors, Kings of England, who in those daies in the right of the crown of England had great possessions, rents, and profits within the same land, hath principally growan into ruine, desolation, rebellion, and decaie, by occasion that great dominions, lands and possessions within the same land as well by the King's graunts as by course of inheritance and otherwise descended to noblemen of the realm of England and especially the lands and dominions of the earldoms in Ulster and Leinster;

[who 'having the same both they and their heirs by process of time, demouring within the said realm of England and not providing for the good order and suritie of the same their possessions there in their absence and by their negligences suffered those of the wild Irishrie, being mortal and natural enemies to the Kings of England and English dominion, to enter and hold the same without resistance'. Such behaviour had led to the decay of towns and castles, the loss to the Crown of dominion and revenue, the strengthening of the king's enemies and their encroachment on his dominion:[2] and reconquest had cost king and loyal residents 'charges inestimable'.]

Be it enacted, established and ordained by the King our sovereign lord, the lords spiritual and temporal, and commons in this present parliament assembled,...That the King, his heires and assignes, shall have, hold, and enjoy as in the right of the crown of England all honors manors, castles, seigniories, hundreds, franchise...and all the singular other possessions, hereditaments, and all other profites as well spiritual as temporal,... whereunto they *[the absentees]*...have lawfull right, title, possession or clause of entre.

81. ACT OF ATTAINDER AGAINST O'NEILL (11 Eliz.I Sess.3,cap.1),1569.[3]

...which rebel,*[Shane O'Neill]* to the perpetual damage

---

1. Statutes at large, Ireland (1786) I pp.84-6. The inadequacy of the English forces for the defence of the English conquests there made the Anglo-Irish lords have recourse to Irish custom of 'coign and livery'; and this quartering on the tenants of retainers (*kerns*, *bonnaughts* and Hebridean *galloglasses*) caused English yeomen settlers to return to England. So did many landowners. Those who remained accepted Irish tenants whose services were prescribed by *brehon* law, and became virtually Irish chiefs, adopting Irish customs. Furthermore they resisted the encroachments of the king's law which would have given their tenants some protection against them.
2. For an earlier English ordinance of 1368 and an English statute of 1380 ordering all having lands in Ireland to reside there, see E. Curtis and R.B.McDowell *op.cit.*pp.59-61n; and H.F.Berry (ed.) *op.cit.* II p.476. Two-thirds of the absentee landlord's profits could be confiscated and appropriated to the defence of the colony [as in the Act of Resumption, 1460: No.78].
3. Statutes at Large, Ireland I pp.323-330. O'Neill had made his

and infamy of his name and linage, refusing the name of
a subject, and taking upon him as it were the office of
a prince, hath proudly, arrogantly, and by high and perilous practices enterprised great stirs, insurrections, rebellions, and horrible treasons against your royal Majesty your crown and dignity ...to deprive your Highness,
your heirs and successors, from the real and actual possession of this your Majesty's kingdom of Ireland, your
true, just, and ancient inheritance...our intent and
earnest desire is to entitle your Majesty, your heirs
and successors, by Parliament, to the dominion and territories of Ulster, as a foundation laid for your Highness
to plant and dispose the same for increasing of your
revenue, strengthening of us, and confirmation of this
your realm....

> [Ancient Irish chronicles showed that Irish kings and princes,
> of their own free will and without war, had taken oaths of fealty
> to Henry II and had become his liege subjects; and that he in
> turn had gived them the laws as in England and a separate Parl-
> iament.][1]

82. WRIT ESTABLISHING THE COURT OF CASTLE CHAMBER IN IRELAND,
                                              15 April 1581.[2]
    II. Forasmuch as by unlawful maintenance, embraceries,
confederacies, alliances... [and other breaches of the law]
the policy and good rule of that our realm is well near
subverted, and for not punishing of these inconveniences
and by occasion of the premisses nothing or little is or
may be found by enquiry; whereby the laws of that our
realm in execution do and must take little or no effect
...for the better remedy whereof...We have thought meet
to appoint that a particular court for the hearing and
determination of these detestable enormities...shall be
holden within our Castle att our City of Dublin in that
our realm of Ireland or in such other place where the
ordinary term shall be kept in that our realm, and that
the same Court shall be called the Castle Chamber of our

---

submission to the queen in 1562, but was an uncompromising opponent
of the extension of English law into his lands. As captain of Tyrone he was pledged to keep the queen's peace within the province and
to support the lord deputy,but he sought to extend his own rule in
Ulster against the O'Donnells and the Antrim Scots by a campaign of
terrorism and tyranny and was killed in a drunken brawl in June 1567.
Sir Henry Sidney as lord deputy now urged the confiscation, the anglicisation, and the shiring of Ulster [see No.38] but the queen was
prepared to let O'Neill's *tanist* succeed to the lands. This Act declared three counties forfeit. It was passed in Parliament where there
was now a considerable loyal opposition party of Catholic lawyers and
gentry who were ready enough to attaint rebels on condition that penal
laws against Catholics were not pressed.
1.The Act also explicitly reserved Irish native lands from confiscation on the grounds that O'Neill's personal tyranny over the Irishry
had been so overwhelming and demanding.
2. G. W. Prothero, *Statutes and other Constitutional Documents of the*

said realm of Ireland.

III. ...We do by these presents appoint and constitute you and such as shall in your offices for the time execute, or any three of you, whereof the said Lord Deputy Lieutenant Justice or Justices, Lord Chancellor or Keeper of our said great seal or Lord Treasurer to be one, our Commissioners and Justices of our said Court of our Castle Chamber, together with such as by authority hereof shall be to you associate in the times of the four ordinary terms to be holden within that our realm from time to time, two days every week of the said term (that is to say) Wednesday and Friday or any other days and times when you or any two of you *[quorum as before]* shall think meet.

V. And further, We give unto you or any three of you ...full power to receive, hear and determine all bills, complaints...*[etc.]*concerning any...offences committed... within our said realm of Ireland, and the dependents and incidents upon the same, in such like manner...as such like offences are or heretofore have been used to be received, heard, ordered, and determined in the Court of Star Chamber within our realm of England.

VI. And we do also authorise and give full power unto you or any three of you...to award all ordinary process as well upon all the said bills which be exhibited for any the causes or offences afordsaid as also upon all contempts to be committed in any of the said matters in like manner as is used in our Court of Star Chamber within our realm of England....

VII. And we do also give unto you or any three of you...full power...to call and command before you into the said Court...all the misdoers and offenders that shall so be complained upon, and to proceed to the examination, discussion and determination of the said disorders *[etc.]* in the same manner and order as in our said Court of the Star Chamber here in England is used, and such as you shall find to be in fault to punish by fines to our use, imprisonment and otherwise after their demerits and according to your discretions....

VIII. And we do by authority of our royal prerogative grant and declare that all judgements, taxations, decrees and orders that shall be given, made and taken by you...shall be of the like force...and effect against the party or parties as any the judgements...given...in the Court of the Star Chamber within our realm of England are or ought to be.

83. *THE PLANTATION OF ULSTER:*

(a) ORDERS AND CONDITIONS FOR UNDERTAKERS, 1608.[1]

...Thirdly, His Majesty will reserve unto himself the appointment in what County every Undertaker shall have

---

reigns of Elizabeth and James I, (Oxford 1913) pp.150-153.
1. W. Harris. (ed.) *Hibernica...*, part 1.(Dublin 1747) pp.63-7.

his Portion. But to avoid Emulation and Controversy,
which would arise among them, if every Man should chuse
his Place where he would be planted; his Majesty's
Pleasure is, that the Scites or Places of their Portions
in every County shall be distributed by Lot....

ARTICLES concerning the English and Scottish Undertakers, who are to Plant their Portions with English and
Inland Scottish Tenants.
1. His Majesty is pleased to grant Estates in Fee-Farm to
them and their Heirs....
3. Every Undertaker of so much Land as shall amount to
the greatest Proportion of two thousand Acres, or thereabouts, shall hold the same by Knight's Service *in Capite*;[1]
and every Undertaker of so much Land as shall amount to
the middle Proportion of fifteen hundred Acres, or thereabouts, shall hold the same by Knight's Service, as of
the Castle of Dublin. And every Undertaker of so much
Land as shall amount to the least Proportion of a thousand Acres, or thereabouts, shall hold the same in common
Soccage: And there shall be no Wardship upon the first
discents of the Land....

83. (b) ORDERS FOR UNDERTAKERS, 1610.[2]
...The precincts are by name distinguished, part for
the English, and part for the Scottish, as appeareth by
the table of distribution of the precincts.

Each precinct shall be assigned to one principal undertaker and his consort, as will appear by the table of
assignation of the precincts.

The chief undertakers shall be allowed two middle proportions if they desire the same; otherwise no one undertaker is to be allowed above one great proportion.

They shall have an estate in fee simple to them and
their heirs.

They shall have power to create manors, to hold courts
baron twice every year and not oftener, and power to
create tenures in socage to hold of themselves.

They, their heirs and assigns, for the space of 7 years
next ensuing, shall have liberty to export out of Ireland
all commodities growing or arising upon their own land
undertaken, without paying any custom or imposition;
which shall not extend to any commodities transported by
way of merchandise....

...Every of the said undertakers shall hold the lands
so undertaken in free and common socage, as of the castle of Dublin, and by no greater service....

Every of the said undertakers before he be received to
be an undertaker, shall take the oath of supremacy,

---

1. There being few applications under these feudal terms, subsequent
orders in 1610 adopted a freehold tenure without any conditions for
service: [see below No.83 (b).]
2. *Bull., Inst. Hist. Research*,XII pp. 178-183. These provisions concentrated on the planting of the lands: undertakers were not granted
powers of legislation or jurisdiction as in a palatinate.

either in the chancery of England or Scotland, or before
the commissioners to be appointed for the establishment
of the plantation, and shall also conform themselves in
religion according to his Majesty's laws....

   [Undertakers or their agents had to present themselves in Ireland to the Lord Deputy before the following Midsummer day for
   the allocation of the lands assigned to them.][1]

83. (c) FORM OF A BOND FOR THE PERFORMANCE OF THE CONDITIONS OF
    PLANTATION BY BRITISH UNDERTAKERS, 1610.[2]

   The condicon of this obligacon is such: That...the
within Bounden, AB or his heirs within three yeares, to
be accompted from the feast of Easter last past, erecte
and build one dwellinge howse of Stone or bricke with a
stronge Cort or Bawne about the same in or uppon the porcon of land called the proporcon of C:, lyeinge within
the barony or precincte of D: in the Countie of E: And
shall also within the said three yeares plant or place
uppon the said proporcon of land 48 able men of the age
of 18 yeares or upwardes, being borne in England or the
Inland ptes of Scotland ... And shall alsoe duringe the
space of 5 Yeares after the feast of St. Michael tharch-
angell next ensueinge the date hereof, be resident himselfe in person uppon the proporcon; or place someother
person therupon as shalbe allowed as aforesaid; whoe
shalbe likewise resident uppon the same, untill thend of
the said five years; unlesse by reason of sickness or
other important cause to be licensed by the Lords of the
Councell of England or by the L: Deputie or cheef Governor of Ireland to be absent himself for a tyme....

84. ACT SECURING TITLES TO LANDOWNERS IN ULSTER (10 Car.I sess.3
                      cap.3), December 1634.[3]

   WHEREAS for the better government and security of
Ireland, sundry plantation have at several times been

---

1. Conditions for servitors and for natives who were to be allocated
lands were also laid down; they were to hold their lands in fee
simple by a *soccage* tenure for an annual rent and to till and husband 'after the manner of the English'.
2. Ulster Plantation Papers 1608-13. From MS.N.2.2., in the Library
of Trinity College, Dublin: *Analecta Hibernica no.8* (Dublin 1938).
pp.196-7. The concern was to secure a resident population, not absentee landlords: cf. the later 'deficiency Acts' in the West Indies
which sought to prevent among an overwhelming slave population the
reduction in the number of white resident planters.
3. As lord deputy Thomas Wentworth had obtained the king's authority
for calling an Irish Parliament. He attempted to secure an equal
balance between Catholics and Protestants. With some allies among
the native Irishry and the Norman Irish he sought for the benefit of
the peasants and smaller gentry to institute an inquiry into land
tenures and defective titles. For the benefit of the Ulster planters he secured this Act which assimilated land law to the English
model by bringing tenures directly under the Crown.

made in the several counties of...Tyrone, Armagh,...Fer-
managh...and Londonderry, grounded as well upon ancient
as recent title of your crown, declared as well by inquis-
itions, as other records and evidences...

 [and since many undertakers' of British birth', tradesmen and
 many'natives of best quality and condition' have been planted
 there and many improvements made; and since the king had indicated his wish that his subjects should 'proceed cheerfully' in
 their course of planting and civilising]

to the end also that all questions and doubts...for or
concerning your Majesty's title, or any other title to
all or any the said lands, tenements or hereditaments,
may be taken away:

 I. Your Majesty, your heirs and successors, shall be
rightly and by good, lawful and indefeasible title and
estate in fee simple, deemed and adjudged to be in the
actual and real possession and seisin, in right of your
imperial crown of England and Ireland, of all the castles, manors, lands, tenements, and hereditaments, lying
and being in the said several counties of Tyrone, Armagh,
...Fermanagh,...Londonderry,...or heretofore passed or
mentioned to be passed by letters patents to any British
under-taker or under-takers respectively, as plantation
lands, at such time or times whensoever any of the fore-
mentioned castles, manors, lands, tenements, or hereditaments, shall be within the space of five years next
ensuing the end of this present session of Parliament,
now passed, granted or confirmed, to any person or persons, bodies politique or corporate respectively, by
letters patents under the great seal of this Kingdom....

 [All grantees were to be free of all rents to the Crown.]

85. MEMOIR FROM THE DUKE OF ORMOND TO CHARLES II, CONCERNING HIS
  FINANCIAL RESPONSIBILITY IN OFFICE, 1675.[1]

 It is true, that a sum of money mentioned in the establishment, was, and ever had been allowed to the Lieutenant to dispose of upon emergent occasions. But his
warrants were of no force even in that small sum, without
the concurrent signature of a certain number of the Officers of State and revenue...It is likewise true, your
Majesty and you alone may add, alter and take from the
establishment, what and how you think fit;....

 But it may be, and I doubt not, has been objected,
that allowing what came in of your revenue, was not by
any of these ways misapplied; yet what was due was not
brought in as it ought, nor the improvable branches of it
improved as they might have been. And that this cannot

---

1. T. Carte, *Life of the Duke of Ormonde*,Vol.III (Letters) London,
1735. James Butler,first duke of Ormond [see No.60 (b) p.87] returned as the king's lieutenant to Ireland from 1661 to 1668 when he
had worked to reverse the Cromwellian settlement and had urged Charles
II to use his prerogative in Ireland's interest, particularly against
the anti-Irish commercial legislation of the English Parliament.

be denied, I have heard urged as demonstrable from the
undertaking of the Lord Ranelagh and his partners, upon
the State of the Irish revenue given in by the Lord Aun-
gier. By which undertaking, they obliged themselves upon
the condition contained in their proposals, to support the
growing charge of the Government in Ireland,not exceeding the establishment then on foot; to pay your Majesty's debts as set down in the aforesaid state; and in
two years after the expiration of their term, to pay your
Majesty eighty thousand pounds....
    That the undertakers have paid, either the arrears, or
growing pay of the Army at the times they undertook, I do
not think they have the confidence to affirm. That the
arrears of the Army, which by their contract should have
been fully paid without defalcation or composition, have
been compounded for, so that little more than seven shillings in the pound hath come to the soldiers, I suppose
will not be denied.

(b) WALES

   Still unconquered but torn by the mutually jealous principalities
of Gwynedd, Powys and Deheubarth and the many petty chiefs and war-
ring tribes, Cymru constituted a threat to the Norman conquest of
England on its western borders.   There three powerful Norman rivals
(the marcher lords of Chester, Shrewsbury and Hereford) – the count-
erpoise established by the Conqueror in the north, centre and south
to match the three Welsh principalities - meddled ambitiously in the
affairs of their feuding Welsh neighbours, and gradually had encroa-
ched upon Deheubarth and Powys, consolidating their power and colonising the 'marches' as somewhat unreliable dependencies of the
Norman kings.   Indeed, at Chester in 973 the Saxon king, Edgar, had
received the homage of all the Welsh princes.   In 1209 John inter-
vened to impose peace on the princes of the centre and the south and
accepted their homage at Woodstock.   But royal invasions had been
met by Welsh resistance and the independence of Wales had been maintained, particularly in the heartland of Snowdonia and Anglesey.
Henry II's invasion had failed in 1165, but on his way to Ireland
in 1171, he had confirmed the Lord Rhys as his 'justice' in south
Wales, content to leave local affairs in the hands of Welsh princes,
if they recognised his suzerainty - a form of indirect rule: But
this loyalty was personal only, not to the Crown of England: it
ceased with his death.   In the next century first Llywelyn ap Iorwerth of Gwynedd, and then his grandson, Llywelyn ap Gruffydd, gave
some temporary semblance to the unity of Wales.   But great as was
the extension of Welsh power from its northern mountain fastness,
Wales was as difficult a country to unite as it was to conquer.
When the future Edward I was given by Henry III the palatinate of
Chester and all the royal Welsh demesne, somewhat tactlessly he
extended the English system of shire, hundred and poll tax to these
lands by direct rule of his officials.   Llywelyn ap Gruffydd, assuming the title of 'Prince of Wales' in 1258 and supported by all the
Welsh magnates, challenged this anglicisation as the champion of
Welsh custom and unity.   This defiance, initially so successful, led

indeed to the undermining of Welsh independence and at last to the
surrender of Snowdonia. Union with, and tentative assimilation into,
the realm of England was a task left to the Welsh Tudors two· and· a·
half centuries later.

86. MAGNA CARTA, 17 June 1215.[1]
    56. If we have dispossessed or removed any Welshmen
from their lands or franchises or other things, without
legal judgment of their peers, in England or in Wales,
they shall immediately be returned to them; and if a
dispute shall have arisen over this then it shall be settled in the March by judgement of their peers, concerning
holdings of England according to the law of England, concerning holdings of Wales according to the law of Wales,
and concerning holdings of the March according to the
law of the March.[2] The Welsh shall do the same to us
and ours.

87. TREATY OF ABERCONWAY, 9 November 1277.[3]
     [Llywelyn agreed to pay £50,000 to purchase the royal grace and
     favour and to surrender claims to Edward I's conquests (apart from
     Anglesey). His own authority and jurisdiction as Prince of Wales
     was limited to Snowdonia. Edward I promised that, if Llywelyn
     wished to claim rights in land which others had occupied outside
     the *cantrefs* ceded to the king by the Treaty, he would show the
     prince full justice *'secundum leges et consuetudines partium ill-
     arum in quibus terra ille consistunt'* (art.2).]
13. Controversies and disputes moved or to be moved between the Prince and anyone whatsoever shall be determined
and decided according to the March law when they appertain to the Marches and according to Welsh law when they
arise in Wales.[4]

---

1. 1 Statutes of Realm 12.
2. John's treaty with Llywelyn ap Iorwerth, 1201, had permitted the
Prince of Wales to determine *'utrum causa illa tractetur secundum
legem Angliae vel secundum legem Walliae'*. The Treaty of Montgomery
in 1267 recognised Welsh law and custom within the principality of
Wales for which Llywelyn ap Gruffydd as Prince gave obedience and
homage to Edward I. (*Foedera* 1816 I.pp.84,474). Such law in North
Wales was based upon that of Hywel Dda (see A.Owen ed. *Ancient laws
and institutes of Wales*, 1841).
3. *Foedera* I p.545. The £50,000 was almost immediately remitted to
Llywelyn - a gracious and prudent act by Edward I.
4. But justices and judicial commissions of inquiry were often doubtful of the exact boundaries of Wales and its marches; and there was conflict between articles 2 and 13. In the *Arwystli* case Llywelyn claimed Welsh law since the lands and both claimant and defendant were
Welsh, and because every province in the king's *imperium* had its own
laws *'sicut Vasconienses in Vasconia, Scotici in Scocya, Ybernienses
in Ybernia, Anglici in Anglia'*etc. (J.Conway Davies, *The Welsh assize
roll* p.266). The defendant, Gruffydd ap Gwenwynwyn, on the other hand
demanded march law since he was a marcher lord subject to common law
and the law of the king himself as judge in the *curia regis* (so he

88. 'STATUTE OF WALES' MADE AT RHUDDLAN, (12 Edward I cap.17), 1284.[1]

I. Edward by the Grace of God King of England, Lord of Ireland, and Duke of Aquitain, to all his Subjects of his Land of Snowdon, and of other his lands in Wales, Greeting in the Lord. The Divine Providence, which is unerring in its own Government, among other gifts of its Dispensation, wherewith it hath vouchsafed to distinguish Us and our Realm of England, hath now of its favour wholly and entirely transferred under our proper dominion, the Land of Wales with its Inhabitants, heretofore subject unto us in Feudal Right, and all obstacles whatsoever ceasing; and hath annexed and united the same unto the Crown of the aforesaid Realm, as a Member of the same Body. We therefore, under the Divine Will, being desirous that our aforesaid Land of Snowdon and our other Lands in those parts, like as all those which are subject into our Power, should be governed with due Order,...and that the People or Inhabitants of those Lands who have thereunto so accepted, should be protected in security within our peace under fixed Laws and Customs, have caused to be rehearsed before Us and the Nobles of our Realm, the Laws and Customs of those parts hitherto in use: Which, being diligently heard and fully understood, We have, by the Advice of the aforesaid Nobles, abolished certain of them, some thereof We have allowed, and some we have corrected; and We have likewise commanded certain others to be ordained and added thereto; and these We will shall be from henceforth for ever stedfastly kept and observed in our Lands in those parts, according to the Form underwritten....

[II. Provision was made for the division of the principality into counties[2] and for their administration by sheriffs, coroners, bailiffs, *etc.* for inquiry and assize by jury *etc.*]

---

argued, though indeed the *curia regis* heard all kinds of law), Edward I seemed to quibble; and Llywelyn and his brother David, suspecting his determination to introduce English administration under guise of rejecting inconvenient laws as bad (*ibid.*232), were goaded into rebellion in 1282. English shire law had been introduced into the ceded counties and Edward I now consolidated his position by destroying the independence of the principality.

1. I Statutes of Realm 55. Edward I demonstrated in this code of law that, while he would observe Welsh law where it was just and reasonable and not derogatory of his prerogative, he was required by his coronation oath to root out bad, unjust or frivolous custom. This so-called 'statute' was really a charter given under the seal of the king as conqueror and drawn up from evidence collected by commissioners inquiring into Welsh usage, and on the advice of the king's council.

2. Wales had anciently been divided into three principalities or three provinces: each of which was subdivided into *cantrefs* which in turn consisted of two *commotes*. A *commote* was half a *cantref* (or hundred) and contained some fifty villages.

III. The Sheriff ought to execute his office in this Form, to wit: When any one shall have complained to him of any Trespass done to him against the Peace of the Lord the King, or of the taking and wrongful detaining of Cattle, or of an unjust taking, or of Debt or any other Contract not fulfilled and the like, either by Writ or without Writ, first let him take Pledges of prosecuting his Claim, or the party's Oath if he be a poor man, and afterwards make Execution as is more fully declared, in this manner....And for such Defaults a Penalty shall be incurred to our Lord the King, according to the Law and Custom of Wales....

IV. The Sheriff shall make his Turn in his several Commotes twice in the year, in some place certain to be therefore assigned: ie. at Michaelmas and at Easter. At which Turn all Freeholders and others holding Lands and dwelling in that Commote, at the Time of the Summons for holding the Turn, except Men of Religion, Clerks, and Women, ought to come thither. And the Sheriff, by the Oath of twelve Freeholders, of the most discreet and lawful, or more at his discretion, shall diligently make Inquire upon the Articles touching the Crown and Dignity of the Lord the King hereunder written....[1]

[The extent of the Sheriff's powers of jurisdiction and of the coroner, was defined. Provision was made for the forms of original writs, pleas, juries *etc.*]

XII. And whereas woman have not been endowed in Wales, the King granteth that they shall be endowed[2].... [And provisions for the law of dower were made.]

XIII. Whereas the Custom is otherwise in Wales than in England, concerning Succession to an Inheritance, inasmuch as the Inheritance is partible among the Heirs Male, and from Time whereof the Memory of Man is not to the contrary hath been partible, Our Lord the King will not have that Custom abrogated; but willeth that Inheritances shall remain partible among like Heirs, as it was wont to be, and Partition of the same Inheritance shall be made as it was wont to be made....

XIV. And Whereas the People of Wales have besought us that We would grant unto them, That concerning their Possessions immoveable, as Lands and Tenements, the Truth may be tried by good and lawful Men of the Neighbourhood, chosen by Consent of Parties; and concerning things moveable, as of Contracts, Debts, Sureties, Covenants, Trespasses, Chattels, and all other moveables of the same sort, they may use the Welsh Law,whereto they have been

---

1. This supervision by the sheriff, securing to the Crown a monopoly, was the chief instrument for the introduction of English criminal law. Appeals, however, did not lie to king's bench in England, but to the Prince of Wales.

2. Another provision (in §xiii)'contrary to the custom of Wales' was for women to inherit 'upon the failure of Heir Male'.

accustomed....We, for the common Peace and Quiet of our
aforesaid People of our Land of Wales, do grant the Premises unto them: Yet so that they hold not place in
Thefts, Larcenies, Burnings, Murders, Manslaughters, and
manifest and notorious Robberies, nor do by any means
extend unto these; wherein We will that they shall use
the Laws of England, as is before declared.[1]

And therefore We command you that from henceforth you
do steadfastly observe the Premises in all things; So
notwithstanding that whensoever and wheresoever and as
often as it shall be our Pleasure, we may declare, interpret, enlarge, or diminish the aforesaid Statutes, and
the several parts of them, according to our mere will and
as to us shall seem expedient for the security of us and
of our Land aforesaid....[2]

89. (a) ACT UNITING WALES WITH THE REALM OF ENGLAND (27 Hen.VIII
cap.26) 1536.[3]

Albeit the Dominion, Principality and Country of Wales
justly and righteously is, and ever hath been incorporated, annexed, united and subject to and under the Imperial Crown of this Realm, as a very Member and Joint of
the same, wherefore the King's most Royal Majesty of meer
Droit, and very Right, is very Head, King, Lord and
Ruler: (2) yet notwithstanding, because that in the same
Country, Principality and Dominion, divers Rights, Usages,
Laws and Customs be far discrepant from the Laws and Customs of this Realm, (3) and also because that the People
of the same Dominion have, and do daily use a Speech
nothing like, ne consonant to the natural Mother Tongue
used within this Realm, (4) some rude and ignorant People
have made Distinction and Diversity between the King's
Subjects of this Realm, and his Subjects of the said Dominion and Principality of Wales, whereby great Discord,
Variance, Debate, Division, Murmur and Sedition hath
grown between his said Subjects: (5) His Highness therefore of a singular Zeal, Love and Favour that he beareth
towards his Subjects of his said Dominion of Wales, minding and intending to reduce them to the perfect Order,
Notice and Knowledge of his Laws of this his Realm, and
utterly to extirp all and singular the sinister Usages

---

1. It might be noted that his compromise – the recognition of local
(i.e. Welsh) civil law but the insistence on English criminal law –
was that adopted in 1774 for Quebec.
2. The king's power as conqueror was thus reserved. An ordinance in
council at Lincoln in 1316 was made relating to Welsh custom, in
reply to petitions in Parliament.
3. By this statute the principality was annexed to the realm of England and incorporated into the kingdom. There had been signs of the
king's determination to deal with the break-down of law and order in
Wales and the marches. Statutes of 1534 and 1535 (26 Hen.VIII caps.
4,6,9 and 12, and 27 Hen.VIII caps. 5 and 7) concerned jurors in
Wales and the marches; abuses in the forests, and the appointment

and Customs differing from the same, and to bring the
said Subjects of this his Realm, and of his said Dominion
of Wales, to an amicable Concord and Unity, hath by the
deliberate Advice, Consent and Agreement of the Lords
Spiritual and Temporal and the Commons, in this present
Parliament assembled, and by the Authority of the same,
ordained, enacted and established, That his said Country
or Dominion of Wales shall be, stand and continue for
ever from henceforth incorporated, united and annexed to
and with this his Realm of England; (6) and that all and
singular Person and Persons, born and to be born on the
said Principality, Country or Dominion of Wales, shall
have, enjoy and inherit all and singular Freedoms, Liberties, Rights, Privileges and Laws within this his Realm,
and other the King's Dominions, as other the King's Subjects naturally born within the same have, enjoy and
inherit.

II. And that all and singular Person and Persons inheritable to any Manors, Lands, Tenements, Rents, Reversions, Services or other Hereditaments, which shall descend after the Feast of All-Saints next coming, within
the said Principality, Country or Dominion of Wales, or
within any particular Lordship, Part or Parcel of the
said Country or Dominion of Wales, shall for ever, from
and after the said Feast of All-Saints, inherit and be
inheritable to the same Manors, etc. after the English
Tenure, without Division or Partition, and after the Form
of the Laws of the Realm of England, and not after any
Welsh Tenure, ne after the Form of any Welsh Laws or
Customs; (2) and that the Laws, Ordinances and Statutes
of this Realm of England, for ever, and none other Laws,
Ordinances, ne Statutes....shall be had, used, practised
and executed in the said Country or Dominion of Wales,
and every Part thereof, in like Manner, Form and Order,
as they be and shall be had, used, practised, and executed in this Realm, and in such like Manner and Form as
hereafter by this Act shall be further established and
ordained; and Act, Statute, Usage, Custom, Precedent,
Liberty, Privilege, or other Thing had, made, used, granted or suffered to the contrary in any wise notwithstanding....

III. It is...enacted [because of the uncertainty of law
enforcement in the Marches] by the Authority aforesaid, That
divers of the said Lordships Marchers shall be united,
annexed and joined to divers of the Shires of England,
and divers of the said Lordships Marchers shall he united,
annexed and joined to divers of the Shires of the said
Country or Dominion of Wales....

[New shires were to be created as part of Wales; by §xxvi

---

of J.P's 'to the intent that one order of ministering of his laws
should be...used...as in other parts of England'. 27 Hen.VIII cap.5
also enabled the Crown to appoint magistrates in the palatine of
Chester as well as in Wales.

provision was made for their division into hundreds. Monmouth
however was to be detached and to be treated as an England shire.
At Brecon and Denbigh,'far distant from the city of London where
the laws of England be commonly... ministered', the king should
have a chancery and exchequer.]

X. And the Justice shall be ministered, used, exercised and executed into the King's Subjects and Inhabitants
in every of the said Shires of Brecknock, Radnor, Montgomery and Denbigh,according to the Laws and Statutes of
this Realm of England, and according to such other Customs
and Laws now used in Wales aforesaid, as the King our
Sovereign Lord and his most honourable Council shall allow and think expedient, requisite and necessary, by such
Justicer or Justicers as shall be thereunto appointed by
our said Sovereign Lord the King, and after such Form
and Fashion as Justice is used and ministered to the
King's Subjects within the three Shires of North Wales....
    [In Glamorgan, Carmarthen, Pembroke & Cardigan, Welsh Law was
    to be expressly forbidden and the judicial process was to be
    (as above) according to the English form as in North Wales.]
XV. [From 1 November, All Saints Day]...Justice shall be
ministered and executed to the King's Subjects and In-
habitants of the said County of Glamorgan, according to
the Laws, Customs and Statutes of this Realm of England,
and after no Welsh Laws, and in such Form and Fashion as
Justice is ministered and used to the King's Subjects
within the Three Shires of North Wales [i.e. Merioneth,
Anglesey, and Caernarvon; similarly with regard to the counties of
Carmarthen, Pembroke and Cardigan.]
XX. Also be it enacted by the Authority aforesaid,
That all Justices, Commissioners, Sheriffs, Coroners,
Escheators, Stewards, and their Lieutenants, and all
other Officers and Ministers of the Law, shall proclaim
and keep the Sessions Courts, Hundreds, Leets, Sheriffs
Courts, and all other Courts in the English Tongue; and
all Oaths of Officers, Juries and Inquests, and all other
Affidavits, Verdices and Wagers of Law, to be given and
done in the English Tongue; and also that from hence-
forth no Person or Persons that use the Welsh Speech or
Language, shall have or enjoy any manner Office or Fees
within this Realm of England, Wales, or other the King's
Dominion, upon Pain of forfeiting the same Offices or
Fees, unless he or they use and exercise the English
Speech or Language ....
    [Instead of marcher lords, sheriffs were now responsible for
the appearance in court of 'every misruled and suspect Person within
their Sheriffwick:' the lords were to be compensated for loss of
the forfeitures previously accruing to them.]
XXVII. The Lord Chancellor is to appoint a King's Commission to investigate and report to King in Council Welsh
laws and customs...and that upon deliberate Advice thereof
had and taken, all such Laws, Usages, and Customs as the
King's Highness and his said most honourable Council shall
think expedient, requisite and necessary to be had, used

and exercised in the before-rehearsed Shires, or any of
them, or in any other Shire of the Dominion or Country of
Wales, shall stand and be of full Strength, Virtue and
Effect, and shall be for ever inviolably observed, had,
used and executed in the same Shires, as if this Act had
never been had ne made;[1] any Thing in the same Act contained to the contrary in any wise notwithstanding.

XXVIII. And it is further enacted by the Authority
aforesaid, That for this present Parliament, and all
other Parliaments to be holden and kept for this Realm,
two Knights shall be chosen and elected to the same
Parliament for the Shire of Monmouth, and one Burgess
for the Borough of Monmouth, in like Manner, Form and
Order, as Knights and Burgesses of the Parliament be
elected and chosen in all other Shires of this Realm of
England, (2) and that the same Knights and Burgesses
shall have like Dignity, Preeminence and Privilege, (3)
and shall be allowed such Fees, as other Knights and
Burgesses of the Parliament have been allowed;

XXIX. And that for this present Parliament, and all
other Parliaments to be holden and kept for this Realm,
one Knight shall be chosen and elected to the same Parliaments for every of the Shire of Brecknock, Radnor,
Mountgomery, and Denbigh and for every other Shire within the Country or Dominion of Wales; (2) and for every
Borough being a Shire-town within the said Country or
Dominion of Wales, except the Shire-town of the foresaid
County of Mereoneth, one Burgess; (3) and the Election
to be in like Manner, Form and Order, as Knights and
Burgesses of the Parliament be elected and chosen in
other Shires of this Realm;....

[By § xxx the liberties and jurisdiction of the lords marcher
over their tenants were preserved.]

XXXI. Provided alway, That this present Act, nor any
Thing therein contained, shall take away or derogate any
Laws, Usages or laudable Customs now used within the three
Shires of North Wales; nor shall not deprive nor take
away the whole Liberties of the Duchy of Lancaster, but
that the said Liberties shall continue to be used in
every Lordship, Parcel of the said Duchy, within the
Dominion and Country of Wales, as the Liberties of the
said Duchy be used in Shire Ground, and not County Palatine, within this Realm of England....

XXXV. Provided alway, That Lands, Tenements and Hereditaments lying in the said Country and Dominion of Wales,
which have been used Time out of Mind, by the laudable
Customs of the said Country, to be departed and depart-
able among Issues and Heirs Males, shall still so continue
and be used in like Form, Fashion and Condition, as if

---

1. Therefore, on the recommendation of the commissioners, certain
Welsh customs might be retained and enforced by the Crown, despite
§ ii of this Act.

this Act had never been had or made; any Thing in this
Act to the contrary notwithstanding....
    [By § xxxvi the king might at his discretion suspend or revoke
    the Act within three years of the dissolution of Parliament, and
    every such suspension or revocation under the great seal shall be
    'as good and effectual to all intents and purposes as if the same
    had been done by authority of the present Parliament'.][1]

89. (b) ACT MAKING FURTHER PROVISION FOR THE INCORPORATION OF WALES
        WITH ENGLAND (34 & 35 Hen.VIII cap.26), 1543.[2]
    [Wales was to be divided into twelve shires together with Mon-
    mouth and various marcher lands. Existing divisions into hundreds
    were to be retained.]

---

1. (See also § cxx of 34 and 35 Hen.VIII cap.26: No.89 b) . By 20
Geo.III cap.42 § iii (1747) it was declared and enacted that references to 'England' in any statute would be deemed to include 'the
dominion of Wales and the town of Berwick-upon-Tweed'. From the
eleventh to the fifteenth century Berwick had been a shuttlecock between the kingdoms of England and Scotland, being captured and recaptured, ceded and receded in turn by English and Scots - sometimes
barely for weeks but often for several decades. In 1296 Edward I
had held a Parliament there; but in 1326 Berwick sent representatives to Bruce's Parliament in Scotland. Even before it was finally
ceded to Edward IV of England in 1482 and permanently enfranchised
by him and Parliament (22 Ed.II cap.8), Berwick would seem occasionally to have sent representatives to the English Parliament. According to Mansfield (L.C.J.) some English statutes, passed in the reign
of Henry VI (when the Scots held the town) were already and expressly
applied to Berwick and were regarded as binding (*Parl. Hist*.XVI.174).
In 1405 Boynton was tried in Berwick for treason to the English king.
The claim was made in 1759 in *Rex v. Cowle*(2 Burrow 834) that king's
bench had no jurisdiction over Berwick, a conquered town,which (it
was alleged) by charters from Edward I (1296) and other English kings
as well as by confirmatory statutes was governed by its own laws
originally deriving from Alexander III of Scotland. In April 1605,
for example, a royal charter was granted by James VI and I and was
also immediately confirmed by Parliament (see J. Fuller, *History of
Berwick*,1799: app.I-2 Jac.I cap.28). Mansfield in judgement held
that the king's rights as overlord in supreme jurisdiction extended
even over palatinates and dominions: Berwick was not a palatinate;
it had no *jura regalia* or superior courts of its own as Wales had
once had; but it was a free incorporate borough subordinate to the
realm of England as previously it had been to Scotland.
Certainly since 1482 many statutes explicitly named Berwick: for
example, in 1541 (32 Hen.VIII cap.49) the Act pardoning heresies referred to Berwick, the Channel Isles and Calais, together with the
realm of England and Wales, and in 1660 (12 Car.II cap.34) the Act
for forbidding the planting of tobacco [see No.253] mentioned Berwick.
But many other statutes which omitted such specific reference would
also seem to have been regularly applied there, even though in 1551
the Crown had named it a'free town'with some measure of local autonomy.
2. This is a second and final Act of Union. The marches were incor-

...IV. *Item*, That there shall be and remain a President
and Council in the said Dominion and Principality of
<u>Wales</u>, and the Marches of the same, with all Officers,
Clerks and Incidents to the same, in Manner and Form as
hath been heretofore used and accustomed; (2) which
President and Council shall have power and Authority to
hear and determine....such Causes and Matters as be or
hereafter shall be assigned to them by the King's Majesty,
as heretofore hath been accustomed and used .¹...

[There would be 'the King's great sessions of Wales' in the
shires twice a year; and the appointment of justices and limits
of their jurisdiction were detailed and their procedure enumerated. The stewards of manors were to hold courts and leets as in
England. The rights of the king to incorporate towns was reserved and officers of corporate towns might continue to exercise
jurisdiction provided 'they follow the Course, Trade and Fashion
of the Laws and Customs of the Realm of England,and not of any
Welsh Laws or Customs:' juries might be of six men as previously.
Circuits were to be provided; each shire was to have up to 8
J.P's comissioned under the great seal by the advice of the president and council of Wales and exercising their offices 'in like
manner as is used in England'. Sheriffs too (and coroners in
each shire) were 'to do all things for the Ministration of Justice and for the Conservation of the King's Peace...as Sheriffs
of England.....within the Realm of England.' All Welsh officials
and subjects (§ lxv) 'shall be always obedient, attendant and
assisting to the said President, Council and Justices of Wales'.]

...LXXXVI And albeit the same Act as yet was never put
in Execution for any of the said Offences heretofore done
or committed within any of the said three Shires of North
Wales, that is to say, the counties of Anglesey, Caernar-
van and Merioneth, be it now declared and enacted by the
Authority aforesaid, That the said Act, and every Article therein contained, shall from henceforth take Effect,
and be executed in all Points for and concerning any of
the said Offences perpetrated and done, or that hereafter shall be perpetrated or done, within the said County of Merioneth, to be enquired of, heard and determined
within the County of Salop, in like Manner and Form as
commonly is and hath been used for any of the same or
like Offences committed or done within any other County
of South Wales: and Matter or Cause heretofore risen or
grown to the contrary thereof notwithstanding....

XCI. *Item*, that all Manors, Lands, Tenements, Messu-
ages and other Hereditaments, and all Rights and Titles

---

porated into the shires and deprived of much of their own power,
and the administrative procedures in Wales were assimilated to those
in England.
1. Though originally resting (like the council of the North) on the
king's commission, the council of Wales acquired statutory authority
from this section. Its jurisdiction was terminated by statute in
1641 (16 Car.I cap.10)[see No.18n.]

to the same, in any of the said Shires of Wales, descended to any manner Person or Persons [since 24 June 1542] or
that hereafter shall descend, be taken, enjoyed, used,
and holden as English Tenure, to all Intents according
to the common Laws of this Realm of England, and not to
be partable among Heirs Males after the Custom of *gavelkind* , as heretofore in divers Parts of Wales hath been
used and accustomed....[1]

    [Similarly in Monmouth and the marches, mortgages and disposals
    of land were to be according to English laws and statutes. Lib-
    erties, franchises and customs of the lords marcher were to be as
    regulated by statute (27 Hen.VIII cap.24).]

    CX.*Item*, That all the King's Subjects and Residents
in Wales shall find at all Parliaments hereafter to be
holden in England, Knights for the Shires, and citizens
and Burgesses for Cities and Towns[2], to be named and
chosen by Authority of the King's writ under the Great
Seal of England, according to the Act in that case provided, and shall be charged, and chargeable to all Subsidies and other Charges to be granted by the Commons of
any of the said Parliaments,...

    CXIII. *Item*, That all Errors and Judgements before
any of the said Justices at any Time of the great Sessions, in Pleas real or mixt, shall be redressed by Writ
of Error, to be sued out of the King's Chancery of England, returnable before the King's Justices of his Bench
in England, as other Writs of Error be in England. And
that all Errors in Pleas personal shall be reformed by

---

1. This was further affirmed in § cxxviii. The Statute of 1536 had
prescribed English common law in Wales, but had provided (§.XXVII)
for commissioners to recommend continuing tolerance for certain
Welsh customs.
2. Apart from 1322 and 1327 when Welsh representatives came to
Parliament, the first M.P.'s for Wales were elected as provided by
the statute of 1536. (For more than a century there had been four
Welsh bishops in the Lords). Though hitherto unrepresented, Welsh-
men were liable to be taxed 'as they have been accustomed heretofore'.
Previous statutes exempting Wales from particular parliamentary taxation had often been passed because Wales had made special *mises* of
its own to the king, and therefore further taxation was unnecessary
and unfair. However, in 1535 by 27 Hen.VIII cap.14 - i.e., prior to
the Act of Union and to the grant of representation - Parliament had
legislated to deal with the avoidance of customs duty on leather exported from Wales, Cheshire and Cornwall and to enforce the duties
as paid in London: that was, 4s.9d a dicker for strangers; 4s.1d for
denizens : [see p.9n.].
A further Act (35 Hen.VIII cap.11) provided for payment of Welsh M.P's
In seeking to make Parliament representative of dependencies of the
Crown, a statute (5 Hen.VIII cap.1) enfranchised Tournai and it returned an M.P. in 1513. Similarly Calais by 27 Hen.VIII cap.6.3 was
granted representation which it enjoyed till its loss by the English
Crown in 1558.

Bills to be sued before the said President and Council
of Wales, from Time to Time, as the Party grieved will
sue for the same.

CXIX. *Item* , It is further enacted by the Authority
aforesaid, That the King's most Royal Majesty shall and
may, at all Times hereafter from Time to Time, change,
add, alter, order, minish and reform all manner of Things
afore rehearsed, as to his most excellent Wisdom and Discretion shall be thought convenient; and also to make
Laws and Ordinances for the common Wealth and good Quiet
of his Dominion of Wales and his subjects of the same,
from Time to Time, at his Majesty's Pleasure;...Anything
contained in this Act... [or other Acts] to the contrary
notwithstanding.

CXX. And all such alterations of the premises or any
part thereof, and all such laws and ordinances to be hereafter made, devised and published by authority of this
Act of the King's Majesty in writing under his Highness'
great seal shall be of as good strength, virtue and effect as if they had been had or made by authority of Parliament.[1]

(c) SCOTLAND

The kingdom of Scotland succeeded in maintaining its separate
identity and autonomy, if not always its sovereign independence,
until the Union with England in 1707. Through the Norman and Ange-
vin periods its boundaries with England remained undetermined. Under
David I in the middle of the twelfth century the Scottish Crown had
some valid claim to lands southward to the Tyne and Tees on the east
of the Pennines and through Northumberland to Lancaster on the west.

---

1. Since the legislative power of the king in council antedated that
of king in parliament and since Parliament had not yet secured supremacy over the prerogative, it would be anachronistic to term this
as 'delegated' legislation. But it should be noted that the Crown
was being permitted a discretion to modify statute law, at least on
the distant frontier: [see also § xxxvi of the Act of Union ,p.133].
In 1539 by the Statute of Proclamations (31 Hen.VIII cap.8) when the
king in council had been empowered to legislate by proclamations which
again would have the same force as if they had been enacted in Parliament, that power was limited by the provision that such proclamations could not affect common law, lives or property, 'any lawful and
laudable customs of the realm' or existing statutes. This was to
prove a distant precedent for the so-called 'Henry VIII clause' in
the late nineteenth and twentieth centuries when, with increased government interference and greater (and specialised) detail in law and
administration, 'delegated legislation' became a new and important
dimension in government. In the Local Government Act of 1888 and
other statutes the 'Henry VIII clause' gave to the executive authority 'as if enacted in the Act' to modify and supplement the Act
itself; it was a phenomenon of constitutional development which
featured in evidence before the Donoughmore Committee on ministers'
powers in 1932 and thereafter tended to fall into disuse.

Not till 1237 was there some general acceptance of the Cheviot-Tweed border.

The relationships of this northern kingdom with England were variable and ambiguous. In 973 the king of Scotland had done homage to the Saxon king, Edgar, at Chester. William the Conqueror had found it necessary in 1072 to tackle the uncertainties on the northern borders by invading Scotland: he had received the homage of Malcolm III at Abernethy and obtained acceptable terms for a treaty. This homage was renewed in 1092 to Rufus and again in 1097 when Edgar, son of Malcolm and Margaret, ascended the Scottish throne as the declared vassal of the English king, a dependency he acknowledged to his death in 1107. Meanwhile, the Scottish court and neighbouring districts on the lowlands, under the influence of Queen Margaret, had become significantly anglicised.

It was David I who, though long living in England and by marriage an English earl, reversed this process: his court was Norman and his realm was feudalised. Following the excessive, ruthless barbarities of his devastating invasion into England, he had succeeded in consolidating the Scottish realm. Though the extensions of his dominions southwards did not long survive his death in 1153 and his successor, Malcolm IV, did homage at Chester four years later, nevertheless he had established a country which proved just strong enough to defy Edward I and indeed, in Bruce's victory over Edward II at Bannockburn, to retain its effective independence.

90. TREATY OF VALOGNES, 1174.[1]

This is the treaty and settlement which William, king of Scotland, has made with his lord, Henry, king of the English, son of the Empress Matilda. William, king of Scots, has become the liegeman of the king against all men, for Scotland and for all his other lands and has sworn fealty to him as his liege lord in like manner as his other men are wont to do to him....

[The Scottish king and magnates[2] swore fealty to Henry II on behalf of themselves and on behalf of those not present at the treaty making.]

---

1. P.R.O. E. 162/2f.166. Trans. from Latin. William the Lion, who had succeeded his brother, Malcolm IV as king of Scotland, was prisoner of Henry II and therefore under coercion. *Foedera 1*.31 has 'at Falaise' and often this is called the Treaty of Falaise.
2. This direct homage by the Scottish magnates to the English king was waived at Canterbury in 1189, in return for 10,000 marks, by Richard I who was in need of money for his Crusade. The relationship between the two countries was to be as it had been in the reign of Malcolm IV. It remained debatable whether this homage was for Scotland, or Lothian, or merely for his English lands, though it is probable that it meant that William continued to accept the suzerainty of the English king as his predecessors had done. When Alexander III did homage and swore fealty at Westminster in 1270 (see *Foedera* I ii.563), it seems that, according to other versions, it was only for his lands in England, and the kingdom of Scotland was expressly excepted.

91. DRAFT TREATY OF BRIGHAM, 18 July 1290.[1]

[In the event of Margaret, Queen of Scotland, becoming the wife of his son, Edward I promised to recognise that Scotland would remain separate and distinct (*severez e devis*) with its own laws, liberties and customs and without any subjection to the realm of England, though always saving the rights of the English king as overlord.]

...And that no one of the realm of Scotland for contract or trespass made in the same realm, nor in any other point of law, will be called to answer outside the same realm contrary to the laws and customs of the same realm, in so far as they have been observed as reasonable in the past....

[The rights, power and regalities of the Scots Crown were not to be diminished.]

And that no parliament will be held outside the realm and the marches of Scotland on those matters which concern that realm or the marches or the state of the inhabitants in that realm; and that no tallages, aids, levies or maletotes will be exacted by the aforesaid King or will be imposed on the people of that same realm, unless for the common need of the realm and in the manner in which kings of Scotland were wont to ask for such[2]....

92. (a) EDWARD I's ASSERTION OF HIS OVERLORDSHIP, 10 May 1291.[3]

Our[4] lord the King has observed the peace of the realm of Scotland to be disturbed by the deaths of King Alexander[5] and of his descendants who were kinsfolk of our lord the King...and in his desire to do right to all those who can make any claim to the inheritance of the kingdom of Scotland and in order to keep the peace among the people, he has asked you, the good people of the

1. J. Stevenson, *Documents illustrative of the history of Scotland* (1870) I, p.162 ff. Trans. from French. The petition of the Scottish magnates to the king-in-parliament for such a treaty (on condition that dispensation for the marriage would be granted) is in *Foedera* I (1816 ed.) 730.
2. Since Margaret, 'the maid of Norway' died in the Orkneys on her voyage to England, this treaty, though confirmed at Northampton in August 1290, could have no effect. The struggle for the Scottish crown lay primarily between John Balliol and Robert Bruce, both with claims through William the Lion's brother. Both claimants, who were as much English barons as Scottish princes, appealed to Edward I who seized this opportunity as arbitrator to demand recognition of his overlordship. This was accepted in June 1291 (*ibid*. 755) and in June and July 1292 (*ibid*.765, 774). The abortive Treaty of Brigham was formally cancelled by John Balliol in June 1293.
3. Printed in E.G.L. Stones, *Anglo-Scottish relations*, (1970) pp. 51-2. Trans. from French. The statement was made at Northam.
4. The speaker may have been Roger Brabazon (J), making the claim for the king.
5. Margaret's grandfather had had a fatal riding accident in March 1286.

realm, to come here....He himself has come hither from
a distant place in order that, by virtue of the overlordship which belongs to him, he may do justice to everyone
and after all disturbances have been quelled may restore
settled peace to the kingdom of Scotland....
    [He promised to respect all rights and liberties and to act
    justly 'as sovereign'.]
    Our lord the King asks for your kind agreement and
for recognition of his overlordship and wishes to act on
your advice in doing and in executing justice.[1]

93. (b) REPLY OF THE SCOTTISH MAGNATES, 2 June 1291.[2]
    [In the interregnum Edward I had claimed that he was overlord,
    that Scotland was held to him in chief, and that he would main-
    tain Scots law.]
    Sire, to this statement the good people who have sent
us here make answer that they do not in the least believe
that you would ask so great a thing if you were not convinced of your sound right to it. But they have no knowledge of your right, nor did they ever see it claimed and
used by you or your ancestors;[3] therefore they answer
you, as far as in them lies, that they have no power to
reply to your statement, in default of a lord to whom
the demand ought to be addressed and who will have power
to make answer about it....But the good people of the
realm earnestly desire that he who shall be king in the
aforesaid kingdom shall do to you whatsoever reason and
justice may demand, for he and no other will have power
to reply and to act in the matter[4]....

---

1. Again, in June 1291(*Foedera* I pp.763-5) Edward I declared that he
had no intention of imposing new duties or of diminishing Scottish
liberties. He was concerned only with his right to do justice, to
hear evidence and to receive appeals by virtue of his superior and
direct overlordship over the realm of Scotland. This was accepted
then (*ibid.* I p.765), and again a month later at Berwick(*ibid.* I p.
774).
2. Printed in E.L.G. Stones in *Scot.Hist.Rev.* XXXV (1956) pp.108-9.
See also E.L.G. Stones and G.G. Simpson, *Edward I and the throne of
Scotland, 1290-6* (1978).
3. It had certainly been 'claimed' within living memory, if not 'used'.
4. During the vacancy of the throne the Scottish magnates and claimants agreed at Northam a few days later to resign Scotland into the
custody of Edward I as sovereign lord. The English king promised for
his part to restore the realm immediately to the successful claimant
and to demand nothing but rights incident to homage. When after lengthy discussion of Scots law and interrogation of Scottish assessors,
Balliol at the end of 1292 swore fealty, was crowned and did homage,
Edward I continued to claim the right to hear appeals from his vassals
in the Scottish Parliament both in the court of king's bench and in
Parliament in England as a right of that homage. At Berwick in 1296
a 'union' parliament heard Scottish appeals and dealt with Scottish
legislation. The English Parliament as court of the overlord was supreme, but the overlord, of course, had other courts - in Scotland as

93. EDWARD I TO POPE BONIFACE VIII, 7 May 1301.[1]
   [He wrote to set the pope's mind at rest, instructing him in
   the history of the English Crown's ancient claim to homage from
   Scotland. This derived from Brutus, the Trojan hero, who conquered the whole island of Albion and divided his realm between his
   three sons - into England, Wales and Scotland. To King Arthur
   and later to Saxon kings, Scottish kings had done homage: so,
   too, Malcolm III to William I, Duncan to William II, David to
   Matilda, William the Lion to Henry II, *etc*. Previous popes, including Gregory IX,had urged Scottish recognition of English overlordship. John Balliol had done homage and then had rebelled
   (in 1296), invading England, 'slaying children in the cradle and
   women lying in childbirth', and 'small children of tender years
   learning their first letters they burned'.]
We mobilised the resources of our power against John
and the Scottish people as the law allowed us, and proceeded against them as notoriously contumacious traitors
and as our open enemies. So the realm of Scotland, publicly admitting before us and the magnates of our realm
the above treasons and crimes, rendered into our hand
freely completely and absolutely the realm of Scotland,
so far as he had *de facto* possession of it....
   [Since when the prelates, magnates and communities of Scotland
   had offered homage and fealty to Edward I as lord[2] and had acknowledged that the realm of Scotland belonged to him 'of full right
   by reason of property no less than of possession'.][3]

94. ORDINANCE FOR THE GOOD ORDER OF SCOTLAND, September 1305.[4]
   ...With regard to the laws and customs for the govern-

in Ireland or Gascony.   1. *Foedera* I ii 932ff. Trans. from Latin.
2. At Parliament in Berwick in August 1296. Anxious to have Edward's
support against the French king, Boniface let himself be convinced by
these arguments.
3. Edward I presumably intended to establish Scotland as a dependent
kingdom on the same basis as Ireland. Instructions for the collection of the new customs in Scotland were sent in 1304; a 'union'
Parliament, including Scottish representatives, met in 1305, and legislated for government by lieutenant, council and assembly in Scotland. But Bruce's rebellion, Edward I's death and the defeat of the
English at Bannockburn removed the threat of subordination and preserved Scotland's independence. But while Edward II in 1327 seemed to
acknowledge that Scotland was 'free quit and entire' without any kind
of subjection, it was also clear that Bruce's success was personal and
demands for homage (and English intervention),made but rejected, continued till Elizabeth I formally abandoned them in 1560. The English
Parliament continued to legislate occasionally for Scotland; e.g. no
man or woman 'of England nor Ireland nor Wales, nor of our Sovereign
Lord the King's Power in Scotland' should wear cloth other than that
made in the same territories (11 Ed.III cap.2) and no foreign-made
cloth was to be imported into England, Ireland, Wales or Scotland
(11 Ed.III cap.3).
4.*Rotuli parliamentorum* I. 268a.Trans. from French. In the Lent of
1305 the king in Parliament at Westminster (the royal administration

ment of the land of Scotland, it is ordained that the
custom of the Scots and the Brets henceforth be forbidden.
And it is also ordained that the King's Lieutenant, at
the moment when he will come into the land of Scotland,
shall cause the good people of the land to meet in a
certain place which shall seem convenient, and that there,
in the presence of him and the people which have assembled there, may be read the laws which King David made and
also the amendments and additions which have since been
made by the Kings. And the King's Lieutenant in concert
with the council which he shall have, composed as well
of Englishmen as of Scots, shall reform and amend the
laws and customs which are openly displeasing to God and
reason as well as they can do in so short a time and
going as far as they may without the assent of the King....
     [Matters which he could not, or dare not, alter without the
  king's assent must be dispatched in writing to the king at Westminster. The Lieutenant and the Scots chosen by the people of
  the commonalties of that realm to go to Westminster would have
  power to confirm what would be ordained.]

95. DECLARATION OF ARBROATH, 6 April 1320.[1]
     [The assembled Scots clergy and barons denounced the usurping
  claims of Edward I to overlordship and rejoiced that they had
  now an independent sovereign.]
   By reason of his desert as of his right, by the providence of God, by the lawful succession and by our common

---

having been at York between 1298 and 1305) had ordered the Scots to
elect 10 representatives to come to the next Parliament. In their
presence this ordinance was made. Though the chief officer in Scotland would be English, the local authority in Scotland was to be
shared by Scots and English. The prospects for peace seemed good,
but in February 1306 Bruce slew Red Comyn and the Scots revolt began.
1. Acts,Parl. Scotland I pp.474-5. Trans. from Latin. This declaration of Scottish independence was made by the two estates in their
appeal to Pope John XXII for his support, in the name of the nobles,
clergy and the 'commonalty of Scotland'. This was a formal letter to
the pope (whose predecessor, Clement V, had excommunicated Bruce for
murdering Comyn) and was probably drafted by Bernard, abbot of Arbroath, as an expression of the 'national' feeling which had been
aroused and stimulated by Bruce - at least among some barons and
clergy. Not till 1326 did the third estate appear with any regular-
ity; and not till the mid-fifteenth century were burgesses normally
present. The Scottish Parliament, indeed, remained a static and subordinate assembly: a judicial and administrative body rather than a
representative legislature. The reluctance of the Commons to attend
led in 1367 to the nomination of a standing sub-committee to deal
with business: a procedure which became normal and developed into
the management of Parliament by the 'Lords of the Articles' who controlled the initiation and drafting of legislation, and virtually
superseded the 'Three Estates'. Though for long periods the 'Lords'
were nominated by the king, the Parliament assembled merely to ratify
decisions of an executive council - sometimes (e.g. 17 June 1617) in

and just consent we have made him *[Robert]* our King because through him our salvation has been wrought. Yet
even him, if he yielded our cause to England, we would
cast out as the enemy of us all and choose another king
who would defend us, for so long as a mere handful of us
live we will never surrender to the dominion of England.

    Not for glory nor for wealth nor honour do we fight,
but for freedom only, which no true man will lose, surrender, but save with his life....

96. (a) JAMES I's SPEECH TO HIS FIRST ENGLISH PARLIAMENT, 22 March
                                           1604.[1]

    [The king expressed his gratitude for his rapturous welcome by
    the people of England. The first blessing of the union of Crowns
    was peace, internal and external. But a union of kingdoms would
    bring greater strength, harmony and stability.]

    Do we not yet remember that this Kingdom was divided
into Seven little Kingdoms besides Wales? And is it not
now the stronger by their Union? And hath not the Union
of Wales to England added a greater Strength thereto?
Which, 'tho it was a great Principality, was nothing com-

---

a single day. This royal control of the legislature is the Scottish counterpart of the procedure of Poynings' Law in Ireland.
With such restriction on its initiative, and with the members of the
Commons chosen by an *elite* of tenants-in-chief, the General Assembly
of the Church became a much more representative body of Scottish
opinion than was Parliament.
1. I. C.J. pp.142. In a similarly enthusiastic speech to the third
session of his first Parliament on 18 November 1601 (*ibid*. pp.314-5),
he answered certain objections, particularly that relating to Scotland's poverty and underdevelopment. On 31 March 1607 (*ibid*. pp.357-
363) he was more restrained, reasonable and persuasive: English
common law was 'the best in the world': it was right to consider a
statutory assimilation of the laws of both kingdoms to the criterion;
but it would need preliminary preparation - the love-play before
marriage. Union would 'advance the Greatness of your Empire seated
here in England' with its metropolis in London; Scotland would have
to be wooed to sacrifice her identity 'in the sweet and sure bond of
love'. He saw little likelihood of Scots leaving home and swarming
south: more likely would English be attracted to opportunities in
waste lands in the north.
The king had not advocated complete assimilation in the laws and
legal systems, only some uniformity: Castile and Aragon had been
united without legal union; so too had Navarre with France. But
Scots law was an untidy assortment of principles and traditions,
and union might facilitate some reform of undesirable features .
Calvin's case [see above No.20], however, settling the issue of
naturalisation without a union of laws, removed from the Scots any
real incentive for subsequent legal union, and in face of English
parliamentary prejudice, James had to be content with that judicial
decision: assuring a uniform status to subjects not only in the realms,
but subsequently in all dependencies.

parable, in Greatness and Power, to the ancient and famous Kingdom of Scotland. But what should we stick upon
any Natural Appearance, when it is manifest that God, by
his almighty Providence, hath pre-ordained it so to be....
    [We lived in our island surrounded by one sea and separated by
    no rivers or mountains, 'only by little small Brooks or demolished
    little Walls', and so indivisible that 'Borderers themselves on
    the late Borders cannot distinguish' the boundaries. By the union
    of Crowns it had 'become like a little world within itself, being
    intrenched and fortified round about with a natural and yet admir-
    able strong Pond or Ditch'. The two nations had no longer any
    distracting impediment to greatness overseas by need of 'keeping
    sure their Back-door'.]
    What God hath conjoined then let no man separate. I
am the Husband and all the whole Isle is My Lawful Wife....
I hope therefore no Man will be so unreasonable as to
think that I that am a Christian King under the Gospel
should be Polygamist and Husband to Two Wives; that I,
being the Head should have a divided and monstrous Body;
or that being the Shepherd to so fair a Flock, whose Fold
hath no Wall to hedge it but the Four Seas, should have
my flock parted in Two....
    For even as little Brooks lose their Names by their
running and Fall into great Rivers...so by the Conjunct-
ion of divers little Kingdoms in one are all those private Differences and Questions swallowed up....

96. (b) ACT IN RECOGNITION OF THE UNION OF CROWNS, (1 Jac.I cap.1)
                                              1604.
    [Parliament expressed its pleasure and thanksgiving at 'the
    Union of two mightily famous and ancient kingdoms (yet currently
    but one) of England and Scotland under one imperial crown in your
    most royal person'. They besought the king]
    that... it may be published and declared in this high
court of Parliament and enacted by authority of the same,
That we (being bounden thereunto both by the laws of God
and man) do recognise and acknowledge (and thereby express our unspeakable joys) That immediately upon the
dissolution and decease of Elizabeth, late Queen of England, the imperial Crown of the realm of England and of
all the kingdoms, dominions and rights belonging to the
same, did by inherent birthright and lawful and undoubted
succession descend and come to your most excellent Majesty
as being lineally, justly and lawfully next and sole heir
of the blood royal of this realm as is aforesaid...and
that by the goodness of God Almighty and lawful right of
descent under one imperial crown, your Majesty is of the
realm and kingdoms of England, Scotland, France and Ireland the most potent and mighty King and by God's goodness more able to protect and govern us your loving subjects in all peace and plenty than any of your noble
progenitors[1]....

1. This was the limit to which the English Parliament were prepared

96. (c) PROCLAMATION FOR THE UNION OF THE CROWNS OF ENGLAND AND
SCOTLAND, 20 October 1604.[1]

[The king expressed his gratitude to God for 'the blessed Union,
or rather Reunitinge' of the two kingdoms under one imperial Crown.
The island was divided by 'none but imaginarie Boundes of Separation': 'a little world within itselfe' with similarities of
mind, martial prowess, language and religion. Union, the work of
God and nature, was now possible, not by conquest but by descent.
Commissioners of the Parliaments of both realms would discuss the
details,[2] but as a 'First Stone of the Worke', the king as head
of both peoples proclaimed a unity of name as 'significant Pre-
figuration' of what would be forthcoming.]

Wherefore We have thought good to discontynue the dev-
yded Names of England and Scotland out of our Regall Stile

---

to go towards union in their first session. In the discussions of
March and April 1604 (I C.J. pp.171-188 *passim*.) the Commons found
many objections and inconveniences in the king's plans for a united
kingdom. They opposed his suggestion of the use of the title of
Great Britain and even resolved (*ibid*. p.179) that there should be
'no union of name before a union of government'. In May the discussion of a union was delegated to commissioners of Parliament who were
named but not yet appointed; and in June a bill authorising the commissioners to consider terms was passed (1 Jac.I cap.2). At this
point (*ibid*. p.243) James seemed to accept their cautious approach
and to declare his general satisfaction.
1. *Foedera* (1615 ed.).XVI 603. In his eagerness for a union of his
realms, James I issued this proclamation. Though strongly opposed
in both kingdoms, he tried to enforce the use of the new title in
Scotland.
2. The English commissioners had been appointed on 15 September 1604
(I C.J. p.256). They met the Scots for the first session on the very
day the king issued this proclamation, but did not complete their
discussions nor agree on the terms they would recommend to both Parliaments till 6 December 1604. It was almost two years before the
English Parliament began to consider them (*ibid*. pp.320-24). While
the Commons were ultimately prepared to repeal hostile acts (*ibid*.
p.377) and even to accept reciprocity in trade provided there were
guarantees that Scots would be subject to English duties and law,
they refused to declare naturalisation but were prepared (under certain conditions) to enact it (*ibid*. pp.350,355). The cause of union
then became involved in the question of legal assimilation. The Commons wanted a union of law - on English lines,of course - to make
the union 'perfect'; they were particularly concerned with the differences in criminal procedures and were firmly opposed to any change
in English law (*ibid*. pp.378.388). This would mean lengthy discussion, codification, legislation - and further delay; and the king
argued that the better should not be an enemy of the good — that the
imperfect should not reasonably be considered an absolute impediment
to the perfect union. He agreed that preparation was necessary to
make a union perfect, but in a sense a full and absolute union was
in his person already (*ibid*.pp.364-8). In December 1607 however he
seemed to think that a union of law could easily be accomplished:
three days' work by the Scottish Estates would bring Scots law into

and doe intend and resolve to take and assume to Us...
The Name and Stile of King of <u>Great</u> <u>Brittaine</u>, including
therein, according to the Truth, the whole Islande....
    [There could be no personal vainglory in this new name, which
    indeed reduced the enumeration of his many dominions; and 'Great
    Britain' was a true and ancient name long recognised by chronicl-
    ers and map-makers.]
    Upon all which Considerations Wee do...by force of our
Kingly Power and Prerogative assume to Ourself by the
cleernes of our Right The Name and Stile of King of Great
Brittann, Fraunce and Ireland, Defender of the Faith &c...
in our just and lawful Title and doe hereby publish, promulge and declare the same to th' ende that in all our
Proclamations, Missives Forraine and Domesticall, Treaties,
Leagues, Dedicatories, Impressions and all other Causes
of like nature, the same maye be used and observed....

97. ORDINANCE FOR THE UNION OF ENGLAND AND SCOTLAND, 12 April 1654.[1]
    His Highness the Lord Protector of the Commonwealth
of England, Scotland and Ireland, etc. taking into consideration how much it might conduce to the glory of God
and the peace and welfare of the people in this whole island, and after all those late unhappy wars and differences, the people of Scotland should be united with the
people of England into one Commonwealth and under one Government, and finding that in December 1651, the Parliament
then sitting did send Commissioners into Scotland to inv-
ite the people of that nation unto such a happy Union, who
proceeded so far therein that the shires and boroughs of
Scotland, by their Deputies convened at Dalkeith, and

---

conformity with the English! In February 1609 the English Commons
were still finding objections to, and inconveniences in, Union (*ibid.*
p.392).
1. S.R. Gardiner (ed.) *Constitutional Documents of the Puritan rev-*
olution (1906) pp. 418-422. Following his victory over the Scots
Royalists and Covenanters at Dunbar in 1650, Cromwell established a
firm and efficient military control in Scotland. In 1653 the Instrument of Government [see above No.62] inaugurated a United Common-
wealth.Though in the administration of justice Cromwell's commissioners were notably honest and impartial and even successful in extending law and order, the government was alien, insensitive and authoritarian, based (as it was) on garrisons of occupation: it was also a
crushing financial burden. 'As for the embodying of Scotland with
England, it will be (said Robert Blair) as when the poor bird is embodied with the hawk that hath eaten it up'.
The Union was based on force and did not survive the Commonwealth.
Cromwell had provided what was an appropriate epitaph: 'Whatever we
get by treaty will be firm and durable; it will be conveyed to posterity. That which you have by force I look upon as nothing'. With
the Restoration the Scottish Parliament met once more, and in 1663
the Lords of the Articles were also restored with a procedure of selection by the Estates whereby the clergy elected 8 nobles and the
nobility 8 clerics, while together these chose 16 commoners. The

again at Edinburgh, did accept of the said Union, and
assent thereunto; for the completing and perfecting of
which Union, be it ordained, and it is ordained by his
Highness the Lord Protector of the Commonwealth of England, Scotland and Ireland, and the dominions thereto
belonging, by and with the advice and consent of his
Council, That all the people of Scotland, and of the Isles
of Orkney and Shetland, and of all the dominions and territories belonging unto Scotland, are and shall be, and
are hereby incorporated into, constituted, established,
declared and confirmed one Commonwealth with England;
and in every Parliament to be held successively for the
said Commonwealth, thirty persons shall be called from
and serve for Scotland.

    And for the more effectual preservation of this Union,
and the freedom and safety of the people of this Commonwealth so united, be it ordained, and it is ordained by
the authority aforesaid, That all the people of Scotland
and of the Isles of Orkney and Shetland, and of all the
dominions and territories belonging unto Scotland, of
what degree or condition soever, be discharged of all
fealty,[1] homage, service and allegiance [to the issue of
Charles Stuart]....

    And it is further ordained by the authority aforesaid,
that the said office, style, dignity, power and authority
of King of Scotland, and all right of the three Estates
of Scotland to convocate or assemble in any general Convocation or Parliament, and all conventional and Parliamentary authority in Scotland, as formerly established,
and all laws, usages and customs, ordaining, constituting
or confirming the same, shall be and are hereby and from
henceforth abolished and utterly taken away and made null
and void....

    [There would be free trade between England and Scotland and
    within any part of the Commonwealth or dominions thereof.]

    And be it further ordained by the authority aforesaid
that all cesses, public impositions and taxations whatsoever, be imposed, taxed and levied from henceforth prop-
ortionably from the whole people of this Commonwealth so
united ....

    [All dominions of tenures and superiorities importing servitude
    and vassalage in Scots law were abolished.]

98. ACT FOR UNION OF THE TWO KINGDOMS (5 Anne cap.8), 1707.[2]
    Most gracious Sovereign, Whereas Articles of Union were

Scots Parliament accordingly remained a docile instrument of government for a further period.
1. The Commonwealth Parliament abolished feudality, but heritable
jurisdictions were restored in 1660, were confirmed in 1707 and were
not finally abolished till after the 'Forty-Five'.
2. The union of Crowns had proved a frustrating relationship - the
yoking of unequals. England's dominance - due to greater power ,
resources and prosperity - rankled in Scotland: Scotland's depend-

agreed on, the twenty-second day of July, in the fifth
year of your Majesty's reign, by the Commissioners nominated on behalf of the Kingdom of England, under your
Majesty's Great Seal of England, bearing date at Westminster the tenth day of April then last past, in pursuance of an Act of Parliament made in England, in the
third year of your Majesty's reign, and the Commissioners
nominated on the behalf of the Kingdom of Scotland, under
your Majesty's Great Seal of Scotland, bearing date the
twenty-seventh day of February, in the fourth year of
your Majesty's reign, in pursuance of the fourth Act of
the third session of the present Parliament of Scotland,
to treat of and concerning an Union of the said Kingdoms:[1]...

---

ency, impotence and poverty were continually demonstrated. With
Stuart kings in England, Scotland was taken for granted, her national
interest was overlooked and policy as conceived in London was imposed. Scotland had no separate diplomatic representation, little
trade, no empire: her ministers were chosen and dismissed in London.
This imbalance in the relationship was a characteristic later advoc-
ates of co-ordinate status between the realm and the dominions (as
in America) did not notice. But just as power caused England to
become dominant in the twelfth-century Norman empire, so too in the
seventeenth-century union of the English and Scottish Crowns.
The badness of the relations between the sister kingdoms – not least
their imperial and commercial jealousies – led to the Union of the
kingdoms: that, and hard logic. The Scots Parliament, though still
unrepresentative, had found new independence and initiative since
1690 when the paralysing influence of the Lords of the Articles (in
the words of the Claim of Right, a 'great grievance') was finally
removed. In the matter of securing the succession after Queen Anne
there was ample scope for mutual blackmail between the two kingdoms.
The Scots Parliament deprived the sovereign of executive power relating to (anent) peace and war, and threatened a separation of
Crowns when Anne died; while the English Parliament replied with an
Aliens Act (3 and 4 Anne cap.7, see above pp.45-6n). The alternatives seemed to be either increased hostility leading perhaps to war
and conquest, or a union by consent which would eschew uniformity
and respect mutual differences (e.g. in Church and law). The English
wanted the acceptance of the Hanoverian succession north of the Border; the Scots wanted to exploit expanding opportunity for trade
and colonisation. Commissioners were appointed on behalf of both
kingdoms to negotiate a Treaty of Union: the articles of which were
then further confirmed in statute form by both Parliaments.
1. It was to be an incorporating, not a federal, union. The fashion
for federal government was in the distant future, though many Scots,
perhaps without much clear knowledge, preferred it. The frictions
and frustrations in the Swiss and Dutch models were far from attrac-
tive. Moreover, it is probably impossible to work federal government based upon only two units (c.f. Pakistan in the 1950's and
1960's). Similar difficulties would certainly face such a federation
in Sri Lanka between Sinhalese and Tamils, or in Cyprus between Greeks
and Turks. The normal tensions in federal-provincial relations would
become polarised on national or racial lines.

[and whereas the Scottish Parliament had approved the Articles
by statute and the Queen had assented to a complementary Act securing the Protestant religion and Presbyterian church government
as a fundamental and essential condition of the Treaty of Union][1]

ARTICLE 1.
THAT the two Kingdoms of England and Scotland shall upon
the first day of May, which shall be in the year one thousand seven hundred and seven, and for ever after, be
united into one Kingdom by the name of Great Britain....
[The crosses of St. George and St. Andrew were to be conjoined.
The Hanovarian succession to the monarchy of the 'United Kingdom
...and of the dominions thereto belonging'was affirmed. There
should be one and the same Parliament for the United Kingdom.]

ARTICLE IV.
   That all the subjects of the United Kingdom of Great
Britain shall, from and after the Union, have full freedom and intercourse of trade and navigation to and from
any port or place within the said United Kingdom, and
the dominions and plantations thereunto belonging; and
that there be a communication of all other rights, privileges, and advantages, which do or may belong to the
subjects of either kingdom; except where it is otherwise
expressly agreed in these Articles....
   [Scottish ships were to be accepted as British ships under the
Acts of Trade which were confirmed as applying to England and

---

1. The Treaty was confirmed by statutes in both Parliaments, one of
which was certainly not omnicompetent nor sovereign, the other still
doubtfully so (see Finch in *Clarendon's* trial [6 Howell St.T. p.328,
1667] and Holt (C.J.), quoting *Bonham's* case [8 Coke 118a] in the
City of London v.Wood [12 Modern 687, 688; 1702] on the limitations
of the powers of the English Parliament). The Treaty was therefore
the source for, and superior to, the statutes. This created difficulties in law when subsequently the British Parliament with unlimited
sovereign powers sought to amend the terms of the Treaty. How could
a legislature unilaterally amend a treaty which in international law
could be done only by bilateral agreement between the original treating powers which the Union itself had destroyed? How could a post-
Union legislature claim greater powers than its constituent elements,
the pre-1707 Parliaments? In *MacCormick v. Lord Advocate* (1953) the
court of session was called upon to consider an alleged violation of
the fundamental law of the Treaty. It rejected the distinctively
English theory of Parliament's unlimited sovereignty and denied that
the British Parliament could lawfully vary any conditions of the
Treaty by ordinary legislation. It did not, however, assert its testing right to declare such a statute *ultra vires*: nor did it state
categorically whether the International Court of Justice would be
competent to give an advisory opinion in a 'domestic' matter. The
British Parliament indeed could alter the articles of the Treaty if
it were of 'evident utility' to the Scots and were ratified by acquiescence; but it was not necessary to regard such a statute as
a legitimate use of Parliament's constitutional powers.

Scotland. There was to be no discrimination in trading advantage
or restriction, or in custom or excise. Scotland was not to be
liable for any other duties previously imposed by the English Parliament, 'except those consented to in this treaty', and since it
'cannot be supposed that the Parliament of Great Britain will ever
lay any sort of burdens upon the United Kingdom but what they shall
find of necessity at that time for the preservation and good of
the whole and with due regard to the circumstances and abilities
of every part of the United Kingdom', future taxation and exemption was left for the British Parliament to determine (Art.xiv).
Taxation was to be uniform but concessions were made to Scotland
relating to window tax, stamp duties, land tax etc.The English
exchequer would pay £398,085/10/0 to its Scottish counterpart
as the 'equivalent' for the share of the National Debt which Scotland was to shoulder, and over half that sum was to be used to pay
off the shareholders and creditors of the Darien Company.[1] While
public law should be uniform in the United Kingdom, no alteration
in Scots law relating to private right was to be made 'except for
evident utility' of the Scots.][2]

ARTICLE XIX.
   That the Court of Session, or College of Justice, do
after the Union, and not withstanding thereof, remain in
all time coming within Scotland, as it is now constituted
by the laws of that Kingdom, and with the same authority
and privileges as before the Union, subject nevertheless
to such regulations for the better administration of .jus-
tice, as shall be made by the Parliament of Great Britain:... [Similarly the courts of justiciary and admiralty.]
and all other courts now in being within the Kingdom of
Scotland do remain, but subject to alterations by the
Parliament of Great Britain; and that all inferior courts within the said limits do remain subordinate, as they
are now, to the supreme courts of justice within the
same, in all time coming; and that no causes in Scotland
be cognoscible by the Courts of Chancery, Queen's Bench,
Common Pleas, or any other court in Westminster Hall;[3]
and that the said courts, or any other of the like nature,
after the Union, shall have no power to cognosce, review,

---

1. These financial terms were generous and politic, helping to ease
the acceptance of union in Scotland. The Darien shareholders recovered their capital and a 5 per cent annual interest,and debts of the
Scottish government to nobles and officials were paid off.
2. Scots law (an amalgam of feudal, Celtic, Norman and Roman civil
law) differed considerably from English law in procedure, interpretation and rule (e.g. in marriage and succession). In Scots law the
king could do wrong and could answer in court for it.
3. There was no mention of appeals, and the house of lords did not
sit in Westminster Hall. Two years later, in *Greenshields' Case*,
appeal was taken from the court of session to the house of lords,
which in 1711 declared its own appellate jurisdiction and asserted
the principle of toleration for the episcopalian church of Scotland.

or alter the acts or sentences of the judicatures <u>within</u>
Scotland, or stop the execution of the same; and that
there be a Court of Exchequer in Scotland after the union,
for deciding questions concerning the revenues of customs
and excises there, having the same power and authority in
such cases, as the court of Exchequer has in England; and
that the said court of Exchequer in Scotland have power
of passing signatures, gifts, tutories, and in other
things, as the court of Exchequer at present in Scotland
hath; and that the court of Exchequer be settled by the
Parliament of Great Britain in Scotland after the Union;
and that after the Union, the Queen's majesty, and her
royal successors, may continue a Privy Council in Scotland, for preserving of publick peace and order, until
the Parliament of Great Britain shall think fit to alter
it, or establish any other effectual method for that
end[1]....

> [The rights and heritable jurisdictions, the private courts of
> the nobles, and the privileges of royal burghs in Scotland were
> confirmed. 16 representative Lords were to be elected by the
> Scottish peers for each Parliament, and 45 M.P's.[2] were to be
> elected by the same process as previously to the Edinburgh Parl-
> iament: this manner was 'ingrossed in this treaty'. There was
> to be one great seal for Great Britain, and the 'Honours of Scot-
> land' were to be kept in Scotland.]

ARTICLE XXV.

That all laws and statutes in either Kingdom, so far
as they are contrary to, or inconsistent with the terms
of these Articles, or any of them, shall, from and after
the union, cease and become void, and shall be so declared to be, by the respective Parliaments of the said
kingdoms

*As by the said Articles of Union, ratified and approved by the
said Act of Parliament of Scotland, relation being thereunto had, may
appear.2. And the tenor of the aforesaid Act for securing the Prot-
estate Religion and Presbyterian Church Government within the Kingdom of Scotland, is as follows:....*

> [The essential complementary Scottish Act, securing the Protest-
> ant religion and Presbyterian church government within Scotland
> was annexed and re-enacted now in a statute of the English Parli-
> ament.]

---

1. This section was expressly made liable to variation by subsequent
British legislation: by 6 Anne cap.6, an Act for rendering the union
of the two kingdoms 'more intire and compleat', the two privy councils were replaced by a single one for Great Britain: J.P's were to be
appointed in every shire and stewartry of Scotland, and procedures
for the election of 45 Scots M.P's were laid down for the guidance
of sheriffs and stewarts.
2. This was a compromise: on a basis of representation by population
(i.e. Scotland about one-eighth of England) Scotland could claim 85
seats; but on representation by wealth and resources (i.e. Scotland
about one-fortieth of England) the claim would be for 13 seats.

5. And it is hereby statute and ordained, That this Act of Parliament, with the establishment, therein contained, shall be held and observed in all time coming, as a fundamental and essential condition of any Treaty of Union to be concluded betwixt the two Kingdoms, without any alteration thereof, or derogation thereto in any sort for ever:....[1]

[The Parliament of England might provide similarly for the security of the Anglican Church in England, and by rehearsing earlier statutes, did so. English and Scottish Acts relating to church governments were declared 'in all times coming as a fundamental and essential condition' of the Treaty without any alteration 'in any sort for ever', so too the Scottish Act relating to the election of the 16 peers and the 45 M.P's (30 by shires and stewartries, and 15 by boroughs named). Candidates and electors were to be over 21, protestant and freeholders previously entitled.]

(d) THE PALATINATE OF DURHAM

The palatine bishopric on the Scottish border was a device, like that of the marcher lords in Chester, Shrewsbury and Hereford, to secure some supervision to the king of England on a remote frontier. The 'grant to Saint Cuthbert' was regarded as the origin of this great dominion of the bishop of Durham. It was an immunity protected by geography, saintly vengeance and the royal charters. Distant from the metropolis, the bishop had been delegated more power and discretion than an ordinary feudal lord. The grant *jura regalia* - those rights and privileges within the palatine which the king had in the realm - provided him with considerable personal authority

---

1. The Scots had surrendered *de jure* independence which was unreal, but they retained their Church, their law and their judiciary. Perhaps the loss of a Parliament with no great tradition was a small sacrifice; but as the lord chancellor said when the Honours of Scotland were borne out for the last time, it was 'the end of the auld sang'. For long periods and on many issues, even in Scottish affairs, the Scots M.P's and peers carried little weight at Westminster: but at other times and occasions their influence on English and Welsh concerns was considerable. The Parliament at Westminster by a statute (6 Anne cap.2) repealed the Scottish Act 'anent peace and war' and another refusing (unless conditions which recognised Scotland's autonomy were met) the succession of the Hanoverians.
The Treaty was a courageous departure from the obsessions of contemporary theorists: the commercial exclusiveness of the English was given up without reserve; and the superstition of '*cuius regio, eius religio*' was broken when the coexistence of two churches was tolerated within a single state.
But Scottish colonists in British settlements took English common law, not Scots civil law, with them, though perhaps the latter would have been a more convenient export in Viscount Stair's recently compiled and handy *Institutions of the law of Scotland* (1681, 1693) or Sir George Mackenzie's compendium of the same name (1684). English

and local autonomy to maintain 'the bishop's peace': not till 1536
was the king's peace extended by statute to Durham. Of course,
though bishops might often exaggerate their independent powers of
self-government (particularly when kings were weak or preoccupied
elsewhere), in the last resort the privileges of the bishop's franchise depended *de jure* on the gift of the king and *de facto* on the
king's power, tolerance or temper: '*scio te tamen magnum feodum
habuisse, et inde te judicavimus* '(see E.H.R. LXXXI No.320 pp.449 -
73).

The bishop could delegate powers, appoint officials (including
sheriffs), create corporations and boroughs, claim wardships, mint
coinage, and forfeit lands escheated for felony. He could grant
pardon and was immune to action in his own courts. By 1330 his
court had exclusive possession of all pleas of the Crown, though of
course a final appeal to the king was always a *de jure* possibility.
For his part the king would often respect the bishop's immunities
circumspectly. In April 1340, for example, Edward III,'being unwilling to prejudice' the bishop's liberty in relation to a suspected
traitor apprehended within the palatinate,ordered the warden of
Berwick to restore the suspect to the bishop's jurisdiction (*Register of de Kellawe* IV p.240). By his frequent negotiations with the
Scots the bishop indeed could play a virtually semi-independent role
in foreign affairs. The bishop's *council*,the entourage of a *seigneur*, included his officials (steward, sheriff, chancellor and receiver general), magnates and clergy as advisers. The *assembly*, a
shire court of barons, tenants and freemen of the bishopric, had
both administrative and rudimentary legislative functions. Though
statutes of the realm applied unless Durham were expressly excluded,
the bishop could sometimes suspend their effect within the palatinate. As early as 1302 the assembly had a right to consent to taxation - even a small limited control over appropriation. By the end
of the fourteenth century its assent to taxation was a retrospective
formality which Parliament in 1449 dispensed with altogether. Thereafter Durham was liable to taxation by Westminster, though not till
1672 was it granted representation in Parliament. Under the palatinate, the commonalty,indeed, could best exercise some limited curb
on the bishop by allying with local magnates or with the king who
after all appointed the bishop and indeed for long periods might
keep these palatine powers in his own hands (see G.T.Lapsley, *The
County Palatine of Durham* (1900) *passim.*)

It might be noted that palatine powers were also granted in Ireland, for example, by Edward III on 5 June 1372, of the Liberty of
Tipperary to James le Butler with the exercise of royal rights 'as
within a palatine county' - a grant upheld on 23 April 1586 (see
E. Curtis, ed., *Calendar of Ormond deeds* VI (1943) pp.33-5).

Powers 'as ample...as any bishop of Durham within the bishoprick
or county palatine of Durham...ever have had' were granted to some
of the priorietors of plantations in America later[see: e.g. Nos.
153, 154].' What the King has without 'ran the old adage, 'the
Bishop has within '.

---

common law lacked such a digest. Of course, a Scottish colony under
the Scottish Crown would enjoy Scots law [see No.152].

99. CHARTER FROM HENRY II TO THE BISHOP OF DURHAM 1153.[1]

Henry...to the archbishop of York and the bishop of
Lincoln and his Justices, barons, sheriffs, and all his
faithfull subjects,both French and English, of Yorkshire
and Lincolnshire and of Northumberland, greeting. Know
that I have granted to God and Saint Cuthbert, and the
church of Durham and Hugh the bishop, all the lands, customs, laws and immunities of which the said church was
seised on the day when William,[2] the first bishop of that
name died: and if the church has been deseised of the
said things, it is to be swiftly reseised. I also command that the said Bishop Hugh of Durham[3] is to hold them
in the most favourable and free conditions of which Bishop William and Bishop Runulph ever previously held them
for a day or a night.[4]

100. AGREEMENT BETWEEN THE BISHOP AND THE COMMONALTY OF THE
        FRANCHISE OF HIS PALATINATE, July 1303.[5]

This treaty was rehearsed before our said Lord the
King, in the presence of the parties, satisfied and ass-

---

1. *Historiae Dunelmensis Scriptores Tres.* ed. J.Raine (Surtees Soc.
publ. 1839) App.XXXI Trans. from Latin. Sometimes this charter was
called 'the grant to Saint Cuthbert' - the seventh-century bishop of
Lindisfarne subsequently buried in Durham cathedral.
2. William of St. Calois (1081-96).
3. Hugh Pudsey.
4. This charter was confirmed by letters patent of Richard II, Henry
IV and V,and Elizabeth I, There were also four other charters from
Henry II, between 1154 and 1175 (*Hist. Dunelm.Script. Tres.*App.XXII -
XXXV). The king informed the nobles and justices in Northumberland
that he had granted to the bishop 'all the liberties and free customs
and immunities' which the bishop's predecessors had had since Henry
I's time (XXXII). He told the justices and sheriffs of Northumberland
and Yorkshire that 'with the advice of my barons and with the consent
of the Bishop' he had sent his justice on assize 'into the land of
St. Cuthbert' to deal with brigands, murderers and robbers: as a
matter of urgent necessity, not as a precedent for royal interference
with acknowledged 'ancient liberties'. (XXXIII) He exempted 'all the
land and men of St. Cuthbert' from attendance at shire courts etc.
and from assisting sheriffs, and he confirmed their possessions in
sac and *soc*,*etc.*and all their customs on the most favourable and
free conditions under which they have ever enjoyed them'. (XXXIV) He
commanded sheriffs and justices to respect the jurisdiction of the
bishop's court: 'that his men shall not plead...anywhere but in the
Bishop's Court, provided that the said Bishop does not stray from
right'. (XXXV) : a privilege which clearly hints at <u>royal</u> supervision
of what <u>was</u> right. Five hundred years later in *Jennet v. Bishopp*
(1 Vernon 184) 1683, it was decided that Chancery could hear no appeal from a palatinate, like Chester. By a statute of 1363, however,
an appeal did lie to Chancery from the duchy court of Lancaster.
5. *Register of Richard de Kellawe*, 1311-16,ed.T.D,Hardy (1875) III
pp.61-7. This agreement was made before Edward I by Anthony, lord
palatine and bishop, and the commonalty.

enting, in the following form....
    [Since complaints had been made against the bishop's bailiff for
    contravening existing custom and statutes regarding arrest and
    imprisonment]
the Bishop grants that no man be imprisoned by his bailiffs within his franchise otherwise than is used elsewhere
in the realm, and that inquests be taken by the coroners
of the bishopric, as is used elsewhere in the realm according to the form of the statute....Whereas the men of
the commonalty feel themselves grieved in that the Bishop
causes lands which are held of others by knight service
to be seized and held in his wardship by reason that these
same tenants have held of him by knight service, the Bishop said that he ought to have wardships by his prerogative of the lands which these same tenants held of others
by knight service, between Tyne and Tees, just as the King
has them elsewhere in England. And the King granted that
the Bishop should have it,as he himself has it elsewhere
in England. And whereas no free man of the bishopric
should be impleaded except in the free court of the Bishop, the bailiffs of the Bishop came and caused them to
be impleaded in the *halimotes*[1] and amerced them along with
the villeins, contrary to the common law of the realm....
And the Bishop grants that none of his ministers shall
seize other lands or chattels into his hand, without writ
of warrant from the Chancery, unless it be after the death
of an ancestor who holds of him in chief... and that no
land or chattel be seized into his hand, otherwise than
has been used in the times of his predecessors ....
    [The bishop promised to desist from demanding purveyance except
    in time of war 'then as the King and other lords do in such a
    case'. Furthermore he would observe the due procedures of the for-
    est laws of the realm itself.]

101. EDWARD II's REQUEST TO THE BISHOP, May 1311.[2]
    When we asked the knights, freemen and commons of the
several counties of our realm for a footsoldier, a strong
man able to defend himself and well equipped with the proper arms, to be provided from each *vill*[3] in the said counties for the aid of our expedition against Scotland,to
come to the land of Scotland in the said expedition...We,
having a particular trust in your good will and in the hope
that you would be good enough to take thought for and assist the things which can effect the desired outcome of the
enterprise which, blessed be the Most High is already pro-
spering, request and require you with all earnestness to
be kind enough to consent, as far as it concerns you, to
the said *vills* giving us such aid in this occasion....We
wish too, that any such assistance which the men of the
said *vills* may decide, of their own free will and with
your assent, should be given to us, should not tend to
your prejudice or theirs, or that of your heirs or theirs

---

1. The court of the lord of the manor: a court baron.
2. Rot. Scot 4 Ed.II m3d. *Register of Richard de Kellawe* I p.16-7
3. A feudal unit of territory similar to a tithing or parish.

or to be used as a precedent hereafter, and, for their
safeguard, we send to them our letters patent in this
matter....

102. (a) TERMS OF APPOINTMENT FOR RICHARD MARMADUKE TO THE BISHOP'S
COUNCIL, October 1311.[1]
    Witness that the said Master Richard has remained of
the council of the said bishop one year next following
after the making of this indenture and has granted that
he will counsel and help the said bishop well and loyally
in all matters concerning him and his church of Durham
and will well and loyally help to maintain, keep and govern the peace in the franchise of Durham between the
waters of Tyne and Tees; and will help, according to the
law of the land, to restrain and try malefactors in the
said franchise every time he is required or ordered so to
do. And for doing all these aforesaid things well and
loyally, the said bishop will give to the said Mr. Richard 20 silver marks to be taken from the exchequer of the
said bishop of Durham.

102. (b) COMMISSION TO SIR RICHARD MARMADUKE AS STEWARD OF THE
PALATINATE, December 1314.[2]
By the present letters we appoint you our Seneschal and
entrust to you the Wardship of our royal liberty of Durham and Sadberg,[3] giving you full power to call together
the people of the said liberty to provide for their own
safety, whenever you think it opportune, and to compel
their assembly, to impose and levy money, to coerce any
who rebell against or oppose what is ordained for the
common advantage, to expel from the said liberty those
who are notoriously suspect of breaking the peace, to
give instructions and commands to our lower bailiffs in
matters relevant to the said guarding and of doing everything else which its wardens have been used to do. Therefore we strictly enjoin and command all our faithful subjects in the said liberty to be ruled by you in all that
has been set out above and in any other matters which you
may decide to ordain for the common advantage....

103. MANDATE FROM EDWARD II FOR THE OBSERVANCE OF HIS CHARTERS
February 1316.[4]
    Edward,...to all to whom the present letters may come,
greeting. Know that, since we have granted and confirmed

---

1. *Register of Richard de Kellawe* I pp.9-10. The bishop palatine of
course appointed the members of his council, and they were paid.
2. *Register of Richard de Kellawe* II p.686. His powers included the
summoning of an assembly for the palatinate.
3. A parish between Stockton and Darlington.
4. *Register of Richard de Kellawe* II pp.1116-7. The king affirmed
that the charters of the realm were to be enforced within the palatinate.

and renewed by a charter of our own, the Great Charter
of the Lord Henry,[1] formerly the King of England, our
father, together with the Charter of the Forest and have
commanded that these charters are to be valid in each
one of their articles and are to be strictly observed,
We wish and grant, on our own behalf and that of our
heirs, that if any statutes shall be contrary to the said
charters or to any article contained in those same charters, they shall be corrected in due form by the common
council of our realm, or even annulled.[2]

104. THE BISHOP'S CLAIM TO ALL ROYAL LIBERTIES WITHIN THE PALATINATE,
1316.[3]

For he said, first, that he himself has all the royal
privileges in his said liberty so that no servant of the
Lord King, an escheator, that is, or any other, may enter
the said liberty to perform any office there.

That the Bishop and his predecessors, the bishops of
Durham, have held the said liberty with these privileges
from time out of mind.

That the Bishop and his said predecessors have had
from time our of mind their Chancellor and their own seal
in the said liberty for the service of their people in
that liberty in those matters that concern the keeping
of the peace, pleas of land, and every thing else which
concerns the governance of the people. Likewise no writ
of the King runs in that liberty or has been used to run
from time immemorial. As long as the said castle and
manors are in the King's hand the people is deprived of
lawful governance in as much as the said Bishop cannot
command or judge the King or the King's bailliffs for
the said places....Such a royal liberty cannot be divided:
the Bishop, therefore, should have it in its entirety
since he has done no wrong to the Lord King.

105. EDWARD III's REQUEST TO THE BISHOP, February 1338.[4]

The King to the venerable father in Christ, Richard,
by the same grace, Bishop of Durham, greeting. Since
the prelates, earls, chief men and magnates, and commons
of our Realm in our present Parliament which was summoned at Westminster on Candlemas Eve last [1 February] considering how arduous are our affairs which affect in
many ways the defence of our realm and of the holy Church
of that realm and of our other lands and places and also

1. i.e. the revised version of Magna Carta, issued by Henry III.
2. By contrast with the rule of repugnancy in later charters [e.g.
Nos, 150,151] and subsequently in the Colonial Laws Validity Act
(1865), statutes were not yet regarded as a superior form of law and
could be amended or avoided if they conflicted with the charters.
3. *Register of Richard de Kellawe* III p.5. The king's mandate seemed
to encroach upon the immunities of the palatinate and a strong bishop
might protest effectively against a weak king.
4. *Register of Richard de Kellawe* IV.pp.225-8. Parliament had made

the rights of our Crown, and for the sake of which and
for their transaction we must of necessity pour out money
in vast sums, have freely granted to us one half of the
clipped wool in their possession up to a fixed number of
sacks as a subsidy for supporting the burden of the said
affairs - provided that adequate security is given to
them that the wool will be made good to them at a reasonable price and provided that they are able, as is proper,
to market the rest of the wool and...since it is the
bounden duty of each and every man of our Realm to set
his hand to helping in the defence of the realm and its
holy Church against invasion by the enemy, we request
and command you to summon before you the prelates, abbots,
priors, earls, barons, knights and others who ought,to
your knowledge, to be summoned, as well as the commons of
your liberty of Durham,...and effectually to persuade
them on our behalf and to rouse them with all the diligence you can to grant us one half of the wool which has
been clipped and is in their possession within the said
liberty, just as the other men of our said kingdom have
of their good will made us such a grant. At the same
time you are to inform the said men who are to be summoned before you that, should they refuse to join the
other inhabitants of the realm in assisting in the defence and preservation of the said Realm, we shall stretch
forth our hand further in order to require help from them
in such an emergency.

106. THE RIGHTS OF THE BISHOP WITHIN HIS PALATINATE, c.1350.[1]
     In such places where libertie royall is, there the
Kinges writte renneth not, nor noon of the Kinges officers nor ministers can or may, be the Kinges writte, nor
other commaundment, entre, doo ony office, or sease on
landes by way of eschets or forfautre. *Ergo*, except it
bee by the auctoritie of Parliament, as abowe, thy cannot
within libertie Royall medell with forfauture of werre....
     In all cases of forfautures fallen by the course of
the commune lawe, and without it be expressly otherwise
provided by auctoritie of Parliament, the Lorde seaseth
within hys libertie royall, as the King doth without....
     ...upon an Acte *etc.* , the first yere of king Edward
the thryde, it was ordeneyd that the same bisshop shuld
have hys libertie of forfauture of werre as he had be the
patent of king Henry the thryde, *etc:* and that the king
shuld ammove hys handes of all landes being in hys handes
by forfauture of werre being within the same liberties,
etc....

     [Precedents were given of the rights to forfeiture being exerc-
     ised by the bishop and accepted by the king.]

its grant to the king: the assembly of the palatinate was requested
to do the same under threat of royal intervention.
1. *Register of Durham Palatine* f.43. *Historiae Dunelmensis Scriptores
Tres*. App. CCC/II. This is an undated statement of the immunity of
the bishop's liberty and *jura regalia*.

107. CHARTER FROM EDWARD III TO THE PALATINATE, 1377.[1]
   Know that...the men of the Liberty of Durham, considering the greatness of our need and of the burden which
our people bore, granted to us of their free and spont-
aneous will such a subsidy...to be raised from them
within the said liberty...In our wish graciously to take
thought for the future immunity of the said men from such
payments so that such a grant which was made to us as of
grace, or the raising or payment of the said subsidy
shall not tend to their prejudice or that of their heirs,
We have granted...[on our own behalf and that of our heirs] to
these men and their heirs, that the granting or imposition, the levying or payment, of the said subsidy [as was
said above] shall not in future be brought as a precedent
or example. But it is our wish, and We grant it to these
men, that they themselves and their heirs should be from
now on as free as they were before the said grant and
imposition, and that they should have their liberties
and privileges in full and hereafter enjoy and use them
freely, provided that the rights due to us as King or as
suzerain and the other rights of our Crown are always
preserved to us and our heirs.

108. (a) SIR JOHN FORTESCUE ON A DIFFERENCE BETWEEN THE PALATINATES
                              AND WALES, 1458.[2]
   ...for there are different sort of franchises. One
is Wales where the King's writ does not run; for if the
precipe quod reddat is brought here [i.e. in the royal courts
concerning land]in Wales and if recovery is awarded on it,
then it is void and *coram non judice*, for it is no part of
the realm of England and therefore the court has no jurisdiction there, save concerning advowsons, for *quare
impedet* can be brought here [i.e. in the royal courts]concern-
ing a church in Wales and it *[the writ]* will be sued in
the adjoining *[English]* county because the justices do not
obey any man there. Another franchise is a county palatine, as Durham or Chester, which is of another nature
than Wales is, for if a man vouches to warranty another
man in Chester, *[the writ] summoneas ad auxiliandum* shall not
issue into the county palatine, but a special issue will

1. Carts.III f.228. *Historiae Dunelmensis Scriptores Tres* (Surtees
Soc. publ. 1839) App.CXXV.
2. 36 Hen.VI f.33 Sir John Fortescue, chief justice in king's bench
from 1442 until attainted by Parliament in 1461, became tutor to the
Prince of Wales, for whom-together in exile-he probably wrote *De
laudibus legum Angliae* and later *On the governaunce of the kingdom
of England*,both useful descriptions of legal government institutions.
Deriving from natural law, the king's rights were governed by it; the
state was compounded of various parts or communities, each regulated
in a mixed dominion by law and custom, which the king was bound to
respect, though with their approval he might vary or change.That the
king should govern within the law was ever the British way: Brutus
of Troy had founded the realm on such a basis:[see p.140 above].

issue to the lord of the franchise to make process to
summon him, *etc.* ; and in this way *[i.e. by this means]* a judgement will be awarded here on lands to the value of
those in the county palatine; and this cannot be done
with land in Wales.[1]

108. (b) SIR EDWARD COKE (C.J.) ON THE POWERS OF A PALATINE, c.1628.[2]
  [He gave an account of the county palatine of Lancaster which
  had been created by statute in a full Parliament by Edward III
  in 1363.]
     It is called *comitatus palatinus*, a county palatine...
because the owner thereof, be he duke or earl &c. hath
in that county *jura regalia* as fully as the King hath in
his palace from whence all justice, honors, dignities,
franchises and priviledges as from the fountain at the
first flowed....The power and authority of those that had
county palatines was king-like, for they might pardon
treasons, murders, felonies and outlawries thereupon.
They might also make justices of eire, justices of assize
of gaol delivery and of the peace....
  [All writs and processes were in the palatine's name and were
  all against his peace, not the king's. Forfeitures of land and
  goods for high treason were his also. The king's writ had not
  run in a palatinate. By contrast with Lancaster, the palatinate
  of Durham had been created by the prerogative in the time of William I. It had been challenged and questioned particularly in 1433,
  but 'in the end the judgement was given in Parliament for the
  Bishop' and the case brought by the king's attorney against the
  bishop's powers had failed. Bishop Bek[3] had, under Edward I,
  'state and greatness as never any bishop was, Wolsey except'.
  Bishops palatine had their own courts of chancery with appeals in
  the first instance to the bishop: only thence on error to king's
  bench.]

109. ACT FOR RECONTINUING OF CERTAIN LIBERTIES AND FRANCHISE HERETO-
     FORE TAKEN FROM THE CROWN (27 Hen.VIII cap.24) 1536.[4]
     Where divers of the most ancient prerogatives and auth-
orities of justice appertaining to the imperial Crown of
this realm have been severed and taken from the same by

---

1. In *Jennet v. Bishopp* (1 Vernon 184) the high court of chancery
held that no appeal lay to Chancery from a decree in a county palatine: 'if any appeal lies it must be to the King himself'. Until
1536 [see No.109],all writs from the Crown (save of in error) were
excluded.
2. *Fourth Institute of the Lawes of England* (1797 ed,) pp.204,216.
3. Anthony Bek was bishop of Durham from 1284-1311:[see above No.100].
4. The task of consolidating the realm and extending royal authority
into liberties and franchises granted by earlier kings in the frontier palatines and marches required legislative action, most conveniently and impressively by Parliament. By succession the other palatines of Chester and Lancaster had already been united to the Crown.
But Durham had retained a considerable amount of self-government.

sundry gifts of the King's most noble progenitors, kings
of this realm, to the great diminution and detriment of
the royal estate of the same and to the hindrance and
great delay of justice; For reformation whereof Be it
enacted...That no person or persons, of what estate or
degree soever they be of, from the first day of July
which shall be in the year of our Lord God 1536, shall
have any power or authority to pardon or remit any treasons, murders, manslaughters, or...felonies...or any outlawries for any such offences afore rehearsed, committed,
perpetrated, done, or divulged, or hereafter to be committed, done or divulged, by or against any person or persons in any parts of this realm, Wales, or the marches of
the same; but that the King's Highness, his heirs and
successors Kings of this realm, shall have the whole and
sole power and authority thereof united and knit to the
imperial Crown of this realm, as of good right and equity
it appertaineth; any grants, usages, prescription, Act or
Acts of Parliament, or any other thing to the contrary
thereof notwithstanding.

II. And be it also enacted...That no person or persons,
of what estate, degree, or condition soever they be,...
shall have any power or authority to make any Justices
of Eyre, Justices of Assize, Justices of Peace, or Justices of Gaol Delivery, but that all such officers and
ministers shall be made by letters patents under the
King's great seal in the name and by authority of the
King's Highness...in all shires, counties, counties palatine, and other places of this realm, Wales, and marches
of the same or in any other his dominions,[1] at their
pleasure and wills, in such manner and form as Justices
of Eyre, Justices of Assize, Justices of Peace, and Justices of Gaol Delivery be commonly made in every shire of
this realm; any grants, usages, prescriptions, allowances, Act or Acts of Parliament, or any other thing or
things to the contrary thereof notwithstanding.

III. And be it further enacted...That all original
writs and judicial writs, and all manner of indictments
of treason, felony, or trespass, and all manner of process to be made upon the same in every county palatine
and other liberty within this realm of England, Wales and
marches of the same, shall...be made only in the name of
our said Sovereign Lord the King,...and that every person
or persons having such county palatine or any other such
liberty to make such originals, judicials, or other process of justice, shall make the teste[2] in the said original writs and judicial in the name of the same person or
persons that have such county palatine or liberty,...
whereby it shall be supposed anything to be done against
the King's peace, shall be made and supposed to be done

1. Presumably this statute therefore applied outside the realm.
2. i.e., the last clause in a royal writ.

only against the King's peace,...and not against the
peace of any other person or persons, whatsoever they be;
any Act of Parliament, grant, custom, usage, or allowance
in eyre before this time had, granted, or used to the
contrary notwithstanding....
    [Justices in the county palatine of Lancaster would be commiss-
    ioned 'under the King's usual seal of Lancaster' as previously.]
    XIX. Provided alway and be it enacted, that Cuthbert,[1]
now Bishop of Durham, and his successors Bishops of Durham,and their temporal Chancellor of the County Palatine
of Durham for the time being, and every of them, shall
from henceforth be Justices of Peace within the said
County Palatine of Durham, and shall exercise and use
all manner things within the same County Palatine that
appertaineth or belongeth to any Justice of Peace within
any county of this realm of England to do, exercise, and
use, by virtue and authority that they be Justice of
Peace, in as ample and large manner as any other Justices
of Peace in any county within this realm have or might
do, exercise, or use; any thing or things in this Act
contained to the contrary notwithstanding.[2]

---

1. Cuthbert Tunstall, who, after Wolsey's fall, had been briefly
president of the Council of the North, the jurisdiction of which did
not include Durham till this Act and the subsequent reform of 1537.
2. The insurrections in the northern counties following the dissolution of the lesser monasteries - 'the Pilgrimage of Grace' - and
Henry VIII's determination to suppress the larger religious houses
enforced his purpose to make England a unitary state under the Crown.
In 1537 the Council of the North was strengthened by lawyers and
professional administrators: still under the presidency of the bishop of Durham, but now with a jurisdiction over the palatinate as
well, which previously had been excluded. (Councils for Wales and
for the West were also established to expedite the king's justice
and a subsidy in 1540 (32 Hen.VIII cap.50) was gratefully made to
meet increased administrative costs.) In his *Fourth Institute* Coke
pointed out that the Council of the North had been set up by royal
commission under the great seal, but when such authority was questioned as being against law, royal instructions were given instead
which were private and 'not enrolled in any court whereunto the subject might have resort': the privacy of royal instructions was of
course an issue in the colonies later. On advice by the judges of
common pleas, James I ordered instructions for the Council of the
North to be enrolled and thereby enabled the subject to know the law.
As for Durham, though it continued in certain formal ways to remain
an anomaly and to maintain an independent judicial system, the king's
writ now ran there and the system was in his name. The bishop lost
his powers of pardon, appointment of the judiciary, fines *etc.*; and
gradually the Council of the North drained life out of the palatinate's autonomy.
In 1543 by 34 and 35 Hen.VIII cap.13 parliamentary representation
was granted to Chester, as it had been in 1536 to Wales. The Act of
1543 stated that the residents of the palatine of Chester 'have
always hitherto been bound by the Acts and Statutes' of Parliament

110. ACT FOR A SUBSIDY AND TWO FIFTEENTHS AND TENTHS BY THE TEMPOR-
ALITY, (1 Eliz, I cap.21) 1559.[1]
[In thanks for the queen's accession and the restoration of the
realm and the imperial Crown thereof 'lately so sore shaken', and
as a 'small gift' towards the 'great costs and inestimable charges' of government, Parliament granted a 'present' of two whole
fifteenths and tenths to be paid on moveables by all shires, cities and boroughs; and a subsidy in two instalments of 2s. 8d. in
all, of every pound to be paid by every subject, by guilds and
communalties; and at other rates by aliens *etc.*]
XXVII. Provided also that this present Act of subsidy
nor anything therein contained, extend to any of the English inhabitants in any of the counties of Northumberland, Cumberland, Westmoreland, the town of Berwick, the
town of Newcastle upon Tyne and the bishopric of Durham,
for any lands, ...goods, chattels or other moveable substance which the same inhabitants...have within the said
counties *[&c.]*....

111. INSTRUCTIONS FOR THE PRESIDENT AND COUNCIL OF THE NORTH,
22 July 1603.[2]
XLV. And further our pleasure is that, when any persons in the counties of Northumberland, Westmoreland, Cumberland, and the bishopric of Durham, or the towns of
Newcastle, Carlisle or Berwick, shall disobey any process directed from our said Council or any their orders
and decrees...and cannot conveniently be apprehended or
taken by the sheriffs or their officers, then the said
Lord President and Council shall write letters or direct
process to the Lords Wardens of the Marches or to the
Bishop of Durham or to his officers or to the chief officers of the towns and castles of Newcastle, Carlisle and
Berwick...for the apprehension and order of the said
persons....
XLVI. And our pleasure is that the Lord President
shall admonish and give in charge to the Lords Wardens
of the Marches of England against Scotland and all the
justices of peace in the counties of Northumberland, Westmoreland, Cumberland and Durham, to foresee that the
towns, villages and farms be not there decayed or wasted,
nor the lands converted from tillage to pasture, nor so
taken from the houses that the tenants and farmers thereof cannot be able to keep horses or geldings for service
and defence of the frontiers there as heretofore in times

but had often felt 'grieved' by legislation in which they had representation neither of knights nor of burgesses. Similarly in 1513 after
capturing Tournai, Henry VIII had ordered Sir Edward Poynings, his
governor there, to enfranchise the town. Jean le Sellier, indeed,
took his seat as M.P. But in 1519 Tournai was restored to Francis I.
1. Durham could still be exempt from parliamentary taxation, and
therefore was expressly named in this statute.
2. State Papers (Domestic): James I vol.2 No.74. Lord Sheffield was
the president, and the instructions were signed by Robert Cecil as
secretary of state.

past they have been, for, that being suffered, the frontiers shall be much depopulated and made weak; Wherefore
our pleasure is that the same shall not be permitted, and
that, if any such defaults have been within forty years
past, the same to be amended and reformed with all speed
and at the furthest within one year; and the Council
shall for that purpose direct forth Commissions   at all
times convenient, and not cease until some reformation be
had according to one statute made in the 23rd year of
Queen Elizabeth *[23 Eliz.4]*.[1]

112. ACT FOR THE REPRESENTATION OF THE COUNTY AND CITY OF DURHAM IN
                          PARLIAMENT (25 Car.II cap.9) 1672.[2]
     Whereas the inhabitants of the County Palatine of Dur-
ham have not hitherto had the liberty and privilege of
electing and sending any knights and burgesses to the
High Court of Parliament, although the inhabitants of the
said County Palatine are liable to all payments, rates
and subsidies granted by Parliament equally with the inhabitants of other counties, cities and boroughs of this
Kingdom who have their knights and burgesses in the Parliament and are therefore concerned equally with others
the inhabitants of this Kingdom to have knights and burgesses in the said High Court of Parliament of their own
election to represent the condition of their county as
the inhabitants of other counties, cities and boroughs of
this Kingdom have...Be it enacted That from time to time
...the said County Palatine may have two knights for the
same County and the City of Durham,two citizens to be burgesses for the same city, forever hereafter to serve in
the High Court of Parliament to be elected and chosen by
your Majesty's writ to be awarded by the Lord Chancellor,
or Lord Keeper of the Great Seal...to the Lord Bishop of
Durham...and a precept to be thereupon grounded and made
by the Lord Bishop...to the Sheriff of the County.

---

1. Other statutes too had legislated for the northern shires and the
palatine of Durham - e.g., 43 Eliz.I cap.13. In 1646 the palatine was
formally abolished by Parliament, and though there were protests and
petitions in favour of the continuance of the local courts, Commonwealth legislation put Durham in 1654 on the same judicial base as
other counties.
2. It should be noted that here,as in the statute of Henry VIII's
reign (34 and 35 Hen.VIII cap.13) granting parliamentary representation to the palatine of Chester, it was expressly because the palatine
was already bound by statute and taxation before they were represented
that this concession was made as equitable. Similarly Berwick and Calais were taxed by statutes of Henry VI a century before they were enfranchised under Henry VIII. Lord Camden was in error when in 1766 he
declared 'taxation and representation are inseparably united'. (Parl.
Hist. XVI.169). If the clergy had argued with some success under Richard II that they alone could grant taxes on their property, tolerance
of that doctrine was due to fear of the power of pope Boniface, not
to legal principle. If palatines had been required by writ to tax

[Elections would be 'made by the greater number of freeholders
of the county and by the major part of the mayor, aldermen and
freemen' of the city,and returns would be made by the sheriff.
Those elected were to have the same authority and enjoy the same
liberties and privileges as other members of the house of commons.]

(e) THE ISLE OF MAN

The Isle of Man had been a fief of the kings of Norway before its
cession in 1266 to Scotland. When Edward I claimed the overlordship
of Scotland, it became a disputed dependency; and, though temporarily
reconquered by Bruce, in 1346 the Scottish kings had virtually given
up attempts to recover the island from English domination. In the
late fourteenth century the English Crown granted or sold its custody to several Englishmen. When Lord Scrope, who had bought the
island, forfeited his possessions for high treason in 1399, Henry
IV granted Man to the earl of Northumberland; but when the Percy
lands were declared forfeit by statute for his rebellion in 1405,
the island was granted as a fief to Sir John Stanley, first on 4
October 1405 for his lifetime,then on 6 April 1406 for his heirs and
successors. Two hundred years later, however, an English court cast
doubt on the legality of the grant because it had preceded the actual
bill of attainder against Northumberland; but in 1610 Man was regranted to the Stanleys, both by the Crown and by parliamentary authority.

The title of 'King of Man' was given up in 1550 for that of *Lord* '
though it is probable that Thomas Stanley, the second earl of Derby,
who succeeded in 1504, had never used the royal style, believing that
a great lord had more claim to fame than a petty king. Nevertheless,
the proprietors still retained all the prerogatives and regalities.
The Lord of the Isle appointed as his representative a *Captain* or
Governor: he (or his representative) chose his officials and court-
the *Tynwald* - of officials, elders, and '*deemsters*' chosen from the
people as authorities on local customary law; and he had the right
to call(or dismiss)the additional 24 members of the *House of Keys* to
Tynwald. He exercised the right of pardon, initiated what legislation there was, and imposed customs duties. (See James Gell, ed.,
An abstract of the Laws...of Man,Manx Soc. publ. XII.1867; and J.F.
Gill, ed., *The Statutes of...Man*, 1883).

What the Crown had granted,it could of course revoke, as Elizabeth
I did for a period after 1594; and from case law Coke argued in his
Fourth Institute (1797 ed. caps.69,282) that English parliamentary
statutes would apply there, if Man were expressly named. After the
Isle was re-invested in the Crown in 1765 by statute (to overcome
certain restrictions in the Crown's powers in the previous Act of
1610), local custom continued to be recognised by the courts even on
appeal in the privy council; and though the law officers reported

themselves, it was because it was administratively more convenient
to permit that method. Such were the arguments put by Mansfield in
reply to Camden during the same debate [see Volume II].

on 10 November 1802 that 'no doubt' could be entertained of 'the
legal competency of Parliament to make laws to bind the Isle of Man'
[P.P. 1805 V.pt.ii (79)] , British statutes rarely applied.

113. LETTERS PATENT FROM HENRY IV TO SIR JOHN STANLEY, 6 April 1406.[1]
...We have conceded to the said John, the Castle, the
Pele and Lordship aforesaid, and all the islands and said
lordships to the same island of Man belonging, which were
possessed by the aforesaid earl,[2] who against us and our
allegiance traitorously rose up; and which appertained
to us both by confiscation, as well as by reason of the
forfeiture of the same earl. To have and to hold to the
same John for the term of his life, all the island, castle, pele, and Lordship aforesaid, together with the royalties [etc.] ...as fully, freely, and entirely as the
beforesaid earl or any other lord of the same island of
Man...and inasmuch as the said John has restored to us
our said letters recorded in our chancery [i.e. those of 4
October 1405] to be cancelled, we...have given and conceded
to the same John, the island, castle, pele and lordship
before said, and all the islands and lordships to the
same island of Man belonging, not exceeding the value of
four hundred pounds per annum, to have and to hold to the
same John, his heirs and assigns...together with the royalties [etc.]...and all other profits, commodities, and emoluments,..in anywise pertaining or belonging to it; together with the patronage of the bishopric of the said
island of Man [etc.]...of us and our heirs, forever, for
the homage, allegiance, and service of rendering to us
two Falcons, on one occasion only, namely, immediately
after making homage of this kind,[3] and rendering to our
heirs, future Kings of England, two Falcons on the days
of their coronation, in lieu of all other services, customs, and demands, as freely, fully and entirely as the
said William, or any other lord of the island aforesaid
...we willing nevertheless, and conceding that whensoever
the said John or his heirs or their assigns shall happen
to die, whether of full age or under, then those heirs
existing immediately after the death of the said John, his
heirs or assigns, from time to time forever shall succeed,
namely, whichever of them immediately after the death of

1. J.R. Oliver (ed.) *Monumenta de insula Manniae II*(Manx Soc. publ.
VII 1861) pp.232-6. Sir John Stanley had been deputy in Ireland twenty years previously and was to return there as lord lieutenant. He
was being rewarded for his loyalty to Henry IV during the rebellion
in the north. His great-grandson, Thomas, evading support of Richard
III and action on Bosworth Field, placed the crown on Henry Tudor's
head, and was created first earl of Derby.
2. Henry de Percy, earl of Northumberland, who had rebelled against
the king in the previous year.
3, The grants to Scrope and Northumberland had been by knight service
in capite.

him to whom by hereditary riqht, or any other manner shall
succeed to the islands,...shall successively enter upon
and peacefully hold possession for himself, his heirs and
assigns, of us and our heirs, by the homage and allegiance....[1]

114. CLAIMS OF THE KEYS, 1581, 1608 and 1704.[2]
   (a) But now the 24 Keys are called the representatives
of the country because, when any new law is made, they
doe represent the Body of the country and were by the
ancient Constitution chosen by the Country out of the
Sheadings of this Isle, and noe Law is binding on the
people (one part of the Legislative power being in them).

---

1. In Stanley's constitution for Man in 1407 the closing words were
'And without the Lord's will none of the XXIV Keys to be'. Early
proprietors construed this to mean that the Lord alone had the right
to choose the twenty-four members for the Keys; but already by 1430
the Keys were assuming a representative role - 'six men from every
shedding...chosen by the whole commons'. However , very infrequently
before 1866 were they directly elected.
Recently the clause in the 1407 grant was retained in the form that
'without the Governor's will no session of the Keys can take place'.
2. MMS of John Parr, deemster, (fl.1690) quoting *Lib. Cancell*, and
Knowsley *Muniments* I: A.W. Moore, *A History of the Isle of Man* (1900)
II, pp.766, 769,776. Under Norse and Celtic systems of government the
king of Man had consulted his chiefs and announced his decisions in
an assembly of freemen. The Tynwald was primarily a judicature, declaring or interpreting law, and it remained predominantly so at least
until the end of the sixteenth century. (For the form and procedure
of the sessions of the Tynwald court in 1417, see *Statutes of the
Isle* ed. J.F.Gill (1883) p.3). From 1265 the Keys (originally *taxiaxi*,
then *Yn- Kiare-as-Feed*) were summoned by the king occasionally for
advice or support, but had no share in decisions. These 24 Keys were
chosen to represent *sheadings*,hundreds or parishes at different times
and in various ways. Sometimes they were named by the proprietor -
frequently so for judicial purposes; at others they were elected by
the tenants; while at still others they were a self-perpetuating
group, themselves filling vacancies as they occurred. By 1581 their
presence at the Tynwald had become recognised as a normal part of the
legislative process, though indeed for the most part they did little
but endorse the orders of the proprietor. The formula for law-making
at the beginning of the seventeenth century was 'It is, by the general consent of the lieutenant, officers and *deemsters* and the twenty-
four Keys of this Isle in Tynwald assembled, enacted for law...' and
laws were 'proclaimed upon Tynwald Hill in due process of law'. By
1601 the Keys were claiming certain privileges and a jurisdiction
over contempt: a critic had said they 'never did good to the Isle and
they were buostin-belly churles' (*Statutes* I p.69). For long they remained largely a self-chosen oligarchy: they would select two candidates for any vacancy from whom the proprietor (or governor) would appoint the new member, though usually he named the candidate with the
more votes. In 1866 (29 Vict. cap.23), in return for surrender to
the Tynwald of control of the revenues,surplus to the agreed civil

[Parr's interpolation] without their consents.[1]   *[1581]*.
   (b) [It was declared by the Keys and four men from each parish]
That the earl with the consent of the 24 Keys, the representatives of the Commons there, have alwaies and may
raise,or diminish these impositions at their pleasure.[2]
                                                  [1608]
   (c) [The House petitioned the proprietor] that it may be
enacted as a Law That no orders of public concern, touching either the Government of the Island or the punishing
and fining of your people, which are not warranted by the
Lawes already made or to be made, may be of any force or
be put in execution but be declared void and of no effect
till the same receive the concurrence and allowance of
your people's representatives, the 24 Keys: that so all
umbrage of arbitrary Government may be removed and your
people have knowledge of the rule of their obedience.
                                              [1704].[3]

115. THE CASE OF THE STANLEY INHERITANCE (Trinity Term), 1598.[4]
     [Henry IV had granted the Isle of Man to Sir John Stanley by

---

list, the British government insisted that the house of keys should
be directly elected.
1. The distinction was being stressed between the Keys as a court
selected by the governor and as a legislature chosen by the islanders.
2. This claim was premature – the king in England was still claiming
to impose taxes without parliamentary consent. The right of the Keys
to a share in fixing taxation was admitted in 1637 and 1645,and to
a primacy in financial matters in 1711 and 1714; but it was not
till 1958 that a British statute empowered the Tynwald to impose customs duties (without the necessity for parallel legislation in Parliament) and to secure control of the public purse.
From 1609 the council and the Keys formed a joint legislature and
until 1704 (when they divided into two Houses) they debated matters
together. In 1737 the Keys demanded co-ordinate authority with the
council in ordinary legislation.
3. It would seem that the proprietor disregarded this petition, though the Keys certainly took part in legislating the customs Acts
both of 1711 and of 1714. Indeed, following the English revolution
of 1688 the house of keys did more frequently challenge the arbitrary acts of the proprietor and consolidated their powers; but their
petition for liberties in 1719, their summary of grievances in 1723
and their appeal to the king and privy council in 1726 against the
Derby regime were all unsuccessful.
The oath the Keys took in this period (c.1710) required them to give
fidelity to the proprietor, to aid and assist the *deemsters* 'in all
doubtful matters', to maintain the ancient laws of Man, to keep secret the deliberations in Tynwald, to deliver their opinions justly
and to do right without fear or favour: (Manx Soc. publ. XXVI p.169).
4. 2 And.LX.116. Trans. from French. See also E. Coke,*Fourth part
of the Institutes of the Law of England* (1797) cap.69. 283. On the
death of Ferdinando, the fifth earl of Derby and eighth Lord of Man
in 1594, there was a conflict between the claims of his daughters as
heirs general and of his brother, the sixth earl, as heir male. There

letters patent under the great[1] seal of England in which 'it was
ordained that the law in the island should be according to the
common law of the land'. The judges agreed that the Isle of Man
was 'an ancient kingdome of itselfe and no part of the kingdome
of England'.]

And in this case it was argued that this island did
not descend to Henry IV, for the island was not parcel of
the Realm of England, but it came to the King by conquest,
as was proved before the lords *etc*. and as for this it
was agreed by them that it passed by letters patent under
the great seal; for the King, as for this, did not grant
any inheritance in Berwick, Calais or any other part of
the Realm of England by any other means than if there were
a special Act of Parliament made for it ....

[Coke stated in his precis that these judges also affirmed the
judgement in a case brought by the dowager countess of Derby in
1520-3 (11 Hen.VIII) claiming her dower overseas in the English
Chancery when the king had the wardship; but that it was resolved
by the justices and all the king's council in 1523 that 'the office was meerly void because the Isle of Man was no part of the
Realm...nor was it governed by the law of this land, but was like
to Tournai[2] when it was in the hands of the king and to Normandy
and to Gascony which were meerly out of the jurisdiction of Chancery which was the place and had the authority to endow the widow
of the king *etc*. But the Isle of Wight was made part of the country
of the South by statute, and Wales and Ireland are parts of the
Realm, so a writ of error lies to England from an erroneous judgement made in Wales and Ireland, in Man, in Gascony or in Calais,
for they are not parts of the Realm'.[3] The plea for dower by the
countess was therefore turned down: the widow of a deceased king
could not have the dower of sovereignty.]

---

was also some fear that Man might become a Spanish base. The Crown
of England thereupon took possession of the island and of the Lordship till the issue was settled, and it appointed a governor. At the
queen's command the case was heard by Egerton, the lord keeper, the
chief justices of queen's bench and common pleas and the chief baron
of the exchequer.
1. According to Oliver's *Monumenta,* the patent was issued 'by writ of
privy seal'.
2. Tournai was captured by Henry VIII in 1513 and restored to Francis
I six years later:[see p.162n.]
3. Keilway 202. Trans. from French. The date indeed, was probably
1523 (14 Hen.VIII). Coke commented later that 'though the King's writ
runneth not on the Isle of Man, yet the King's commission extendeth
thither for redress of injustice and wrong'; but the commissioners
must proceed according to the peculiar laws and customs of the Isle.
Their judges (*deemsters*),he said, were elected and complicated cases
still went to the Tynwald. Coke's *First part* cap.3 affirmed from this
1598 case that the Isle would descend by English common law, but his
Fourth part cap.69 stated that justice must be done for wrongs within
the Isle according to the law of Man: *secundum legem et consuetudines
partuum illarum* (20 Ed.I Pat.Rolls.).*Deemsters* became virtually hereditary authorities, though they were supposed to represent the peo-

And another point was made whether the statutes of
the Parliament of England might bind that island without
special mention of it, the matter and the manner how;
and it was said by the counsel for the Earl, and affirmed
by the counsel for the other party, that none on that island has inheritance in that island nor in the lands there
(except the Earl and the Bishop) and that they are and
have been wont to be governed by no other laws than the
laws of the land and they produced the record of the laws
they had.

And after many things moved relating to this point, it
was held by all those attending that [the Statutes of Westminster II *de donis conditionalibus*, the Statute of 27 Hen.VIII
of Uses and the Statutes of Wills (32 and 24 Hen.VIII)] did
not bind the said island nor the inheritance thereof by
any statute whatever made in England without special and
express ordinance for them[1] and that it is in the same
case as Ireland where the people are governed by the laws
and Acts of the Parliament of their land and not by any
other law of this land, unless an Act of Parliament which
ordaines a law expressly as for those of Ireland and
Wales....

> [The judges held that the king could seize and regrant lands by
> commission under the great seal. They further resolved that a
> fee simple in Man under the patent to the Stanleys was descendable
> 'according to the course of the common law [of England]: for the
> grant itself by letters patent is warranted by the common law in
> this case and therefore, if there be no other impediment, the Isle
> in this case shall descend to the heirs general and not to the
> heir male,[2] as the grand seignories and *commotes* in Wales were
> impleadable at common law, but the lands were held of them by the
> customs of Wales'.][3]

116. (a) LETTERS PATENT FROM JAMES I TO HIS SUBJECTS IN MAN,
                                        1 April 1609.[4]
Whereas by our Royal Prerogative and the Laws and Cus-

---

ple's (or folk) interest rather than that of the king, or the proprietor, of Man.
1. See also W.D. Lewis (ed.) *Blackstone's Commentaries* I, p.92.
2. In feudal law, it was argued, the male would succeed.
3. But the Stanley girls were minors, and in February 1609 they agreed for their successful claim to be bought out by the sixth earl and
they surrendered it to the Crown for regrant to the male line. Six
times between 1605 and 1610, however, James I had granted leases (one
of 40 years) to different individuals as administrators for a rent or
homage. On 2 May 1610 he granted Man to the earl of Derby to be held
'as of our Manor of East Greenwich in Kent in fealty only, in free
and common soccage, and not in chief or by knight's service'. This
grant in *male tail* was confirmed by a private parliamentary statute
(8 Jac.I cap.4). See J. Parr, *An abstract of the laws* (1867 Manx publ.
XII ed. James Gell pp.61-4. Man was evidently subject to the Crown and
to the English Parliament.
4. J.Parr, *op.cit*.p.44. These letters patent under the privy seal con-

toms of our Kingdom of England, it wholly appertains to
us from the fulness of our power at our free will and Royal pleasure, from time to time, to make, declare and ordain in all such Territories, Countries and Places which
have been acquired or conquered by the force of our arms,
such Ordinances and Laws which all our Subjects residing
in those parts and have lands of inheritance or goods or
chattels there may use, enjoy, hold and be obliged to
observe,... [the king granted to all subjects and residents] That
they and every of them may for the future transfer, alien,
grant and devise as well the whole island or any part
thereof...and that such grant...shall be good, firm,valid
and effectual in Law...[any law, custom or statute of England or
Man notwithstanding].

116. (b). PRIVATE ACT FOR THE ASSURING AND ESTABLISHING OF THE ISLE
                OF MAN (8 Jac.I cap.4) , 1610.[1]
     ...And be it enacted...That your said subjects, William
Earle of Derbie, and the said Lady Elizabeth his wife, for
and during their lyves and the longer liver of them, and
after their deathes the said James Lord Stanley and the
heires males of his body lawfully begotten...and after his
death without such issue, the heires males of the body of
the said William Earle of Derbie...and for default of such
issue, the right heirs of the said James, Lord Stanley,
shall and may forever hereafter have, hould, and quietly
enjoye freely and cleerly against your Majesty...against
Thomas, Lord Ellesmere...the Ladie Alice, Countess of Derbie his wife, late the wife of Ferdinando, late Earle of
Derbie deceased, and against Henry, Earle of Huntingdon,
and...his wife, Grey, Lord Chandoys and...his wife...
[and various heirs of the aforementioned] ...all the said Isle,
Castle, Peel and Lordship of Man... [the rights attached were
enumerated] And the revercion and revercions,remaynder and
remaynders of all and singuler the P'misses ...thereof...
[and rents, liberties, etc. mentioned in grants of 1609 and 1610]
to hould the said Isle, Castle, Peele, and Lordshipp of
Mann, and all the singuler the premisses of your Highnes
...and under the severall tenures, rents and services in
and by the said severall letters patents [i.e. those of 7
July 1609 and 2 May 1610] severally and respectively reserved....
     And be it further enacted...That neither the said James,
Lord Stanley, nor any of the heires males of his body lawfully begotten... [nor those of Robert Stanley or William, Earl
of Derby] shall have any power authoritie, or libertie to
give, graunt, alien, bargaine, sell, convey, assure, or
doe away the said Isle, Castle, Peel, and Lordship of
Manne...lands [etc.]... and other the premisses in this Act
mencioned...but that the same shall remayne and continewe

---

firmed rights in property.
1. J. Parr, op.cit. pp. 61-4.

to the said James, Lord Stanley... *[etc.]* as before by
this Act is appointed...; Saving nevertheless that it
shall and may be lawfull for them...·to make such estates
of such several parties thereof as by the lawes and customs of the said Isle is usuall, and to make such leases
and demises of such parts and parcells thereof as tenante
in taile by the statute made in the two-and-thirtieth
yere of the raigne of King Henry the Eigth, may lawfully
do within this your Highnes realmeof England .... [Letters
patent 17 March 1606 to Leigh and Spencer, granting lands for 40
years were to be upheld.]

117. *THE CASE OF WILLIAM CHRISTIAN*, 5 August 1663.[1]
    [The opinion of all the judges in the privy council was]
    ...That the Act of General Pardon and Indemnity did,
and ought to be understood to, extend into the Isle of
Man as well as into any other of His Majesty's Dominions
and Plantations beyond the Seas; that, being a Publique
General Act of Parliament, it of right ought to have
been taken notice of by the Judges in the Isle of Man,
although there were no Proclamation made thereof: His
Majesty, being therefore deeply sensible of this great
violation of his Act of General Pardon, whereof His Majesty...doth expect and require that all His Subjects in
all his Dominions and Plantations shall enjoy the full
benefit and advantage of the same... [ordered full restitution of Christian's properties to his heirs and the trial of the
two *deemsters* by king's bench.][2]

---

1. W. Harrison, *Illiam Dhone and the Manx rebellion, 1651* (1877) p.
55. Christian had taken a lead in the revolt against the Lord proprietor and in the surrender of the Isle to the Commonwealth forces;
the Lord proprietor was executed in 1651 as a Royalist and his estates were confiscated. When the Stanleys were restored with Charles
II, Christian was arrested and tried. In December 1662 he appealed
to the king to be tried 'by your Majesty's laws of England where
he had many years lived and hath an estate', but the two *deemsters*
and others 'pretending themselves to be a Court of Justice' in Man
found him guilty and he was executed before the privy council received his plea. On appeal by his son the members of the Manx Court
were summoned to the privy council where the chief justices were
present. The Lord proprietor claimed that, though Parliament could
legislate for Man, the island was not mentioned by name in the Act
of Indemnity, as Ireland, Wales and the Channel Islands were, so the
Act did not apply. The sixth section of this Act of 1660 (12 Car.
II cap.11) had however, stated 'That all and every the Subjects
of these his Majesty's Realms of England and Ireland, the Dominion
of Wales, the Isles of Jersey and Guernsey and the Town of Berwick
upon Tweed *and other his Majesty's dominions'* and other corporate
bodies, should be acquitted and pardoned for all treasons etc.
2. For trial of Manx cases in England, see Nos. 115, 118 and 121.
But normally justice was administered by the Tynwald and *deemsters* ;
and appeals to the Crown were indeed rare.

118. *CHRISTIAN v. CORREN*, 13 July and 4 November 1716.[1]
   Before a Committee of Council at the Cockpit. Appeal from a decree in the Isle of Man. The subject cannot be deprived of his right to appeal by any words in the King's grant to that purpose, much less if the grant be silent in that particular.

The Earl of Derby, King of the Isle of Man, made a decree in that island concerning lands there; and the person, against whom the decree was made, appealed hither.

One (and indeed the principal) question was, whether an appeal did lie before the King in Council; there being no reservation in the grant made of the Isle of Man by the Crown, of the subject's right of appeal to the Crown.

And it was urged for the appeal by myself[2] (who alone was of counsel with the appellant), that it appearing, in this case that Hen. IV had granted the Isle of Man to the Earl of Derby's ancestors, to hold by homage and other services, though there was no reservation of the subject's right of appeal to the Crown, yet this liberty was plainly implied.

For that such liberty of appeal lay in all cases where there was a tenure of the Crown; that it was the right of the subjects to appeal to the sovereign to redress a wrong done to them in any court of justice; nay, if there had been any express words in the grant to <u>exclude</u> appeals, they had been void; because the subjects had an inherent right, inseparable from them <u>as subjects</u>, to apply to the Crown for justice. And on the other hand –

The King as the <u>fountain of justice</u> had an inherent right, inseparable from the Crown, to distribute justice among his subjects; and if this were a right in the subjects, no grant could deprive them of it; the consequence of which would be, that in all such cases, *viz.* where there were words exclusive of such right of appeal, the King would be construed to be deceived, and his grant void, also precedents were cited in point.[3]

---

1. Peere Williams 329–331. In 1706 the Lord proprietor had deprived William Christian of an estate possessed by the family for 80 years and had given it to John Corren. Christian appealed to the privy council. The law officers advised (P.C 2/85 p.231) that a right of appeal to the king in council was inherent in the Crown, though not explicitly reserved in feudal grants. The Lord proprietor had regulated appeals to himself and to the Tynwald in 1666, as the Tynwald itself did in 1737. After the Crown was reinvested with the Isle in 1765, appeals undoubtedly lay to the privy council, but were soon limited to civil cases.
2. Peere Williams who collected this volume of law reports.
3. John Comyns, counsel for Corren, had argued that Man was no part of the realm of England and was governed by its own customs, not by the laws of England, and that no express reservation of appeals was provided for in the letters patent of 1406 or the statute of 1610. Man was comparable with Scotland [presumably before 1707], a distinct kingdom with different laws from England. Subordinate jurisdiction

Lord Chief Justice <u>Parker</u>, who assisted at Council upon
this occasion, thought that the King in Council had necessarily a jurisdiction in this case, in order to prevent
a failure of justice, and took notice, that if a copy-
holder should sue by petition in the lord's court, upon
which the lord should give judgement, though no appeal
or writ of error would lie of such judgement, yet the
Court of Chancery would correct the proceedings, in case
any thing were done therein against conscience.

Whereupon their Lordships proceeded in this appeal,and
determined in favour of the appellant; and it is observ-
able, that Lord Derby also, at length, rather than that
some things in the grant made by the Crown to his ancestors should be looked into, chose to submit, and express
his consent, that the matters in question on the appeal
should be examined by the King in Council.

119. ACT FOR THE IMPROVEMENT OF HIS MAJESTY'S REVENUES OF CUSTOMS,*ETC*.
(12 Geo.I cap.28), 1725.

[There had been widespread evasion of 5 Geo.I cap.11, and the
duties on tea, coffee, brandy and rum by smuggling *etc*. The Isle
of Man is particularly mentioned as a base for such disregard of
the law. Measures are to be taken to enforce the Customs Acts.
No goods other than its own produce may be imported from Man into
Great Britain and Ireland: (§ xxi)].

XXV. And for the better enabling his Majesty to prevent
the said frauds and abuses, in the exporting or importing
of goods and merchandizes to and from the Isle of Man,
be it further enacted by the authority aforesaid, That it
shall and may be lawful to and for the Commissioners of
His Majesty's Treasury now or for the time being, or any
three or more of them, or the Lord High Treasurer for the
time being, on the behalf of His Majesty,his heirs and
successors, and also to and for the Right Honourable James,
Earl of Derby, his tenants or assigns, *[etc.]*...and all or
any other person or persons claiming or to claim by, from
or under the said Earl or any of his ancestors, to rent,
contract, or agree for the absolute purchase or sale, release or surrender, to or for the use of His Majesty,...
of all or any estate, right, title, or interest, which he
the said Earl...may have or claim in or to the said Island
or Lordship of Man, or in or to all or any regalities,
powers, honours, superiorities, jurisdictions, rights,
privileges, duties, customs, revenues, profits, or other
advantages whatsoever in, over, or about the said Island
of Man, or its dependencies, for such sum or sums of money,
or upon such other terms or conditions as they shall think

---

without appeal to the king in counsel, he argued, existed in J.P's,
the commissioners of excise, colleges and the Cinque ports. No appeal other than that in 1663 [No.117] had ever been entertained from
Man – and that had been an executive intervention rather than a
judicial appeal : such was the case Comyns presented unsuccessfully
against Christian's appeal.

fitting....[1]

120. OATH ADMINISTERED TO THE PROPRIETOR'S GOVERNOR, c.1740.[2]
   [His allegiance to the king being reserved, he was to swear fealty to the proprietor.]
   You shall take the advice and consent of the rest of the Lords Councill of the said Isle, or so many of them as shall be present within the Isle, in all matters that concern the State and Government of the said Isle and houses.
   These and all other things appertaining to the Governor of this Isle, his office and place, you shall, according to the purport and extent of your commission, and the laws of the said Isle do and perform, so far as in you lyeth.

121. *EARL OF DERBY v. DUKE OF ATHOLL*, (Trinity Term) 15 July 1751.[3]
Argued by counsel for Derby
   [The Act of 1610 invested the Isle in Lord Derby and his male heirs and, failing such issue, an express clause restrained and avoided any grant or conveyance to the contrary: this Act virtually extended the principles of *de donis conditionalibus* to Man and was a breach with Manx custom.]
   Acts of the Parliament of England did not indeed extend to Man without particular express words, but that rule must be confined to disputes relating to private property in the Isle by the inhabitants which are to be governed by another law [a mixture of Norse, Scots and English law]: the extent of that rule will not take in the question of the property and disposition of the entire Isle itself because it is the subject matter of a grant by the Crown under the Great Seal and consequently passes as an instrument framed in the language and manner of the laws of this country and should not therefore be construed

---

1. In 1736 James Murray, duke of Atholl, succeeded through the female line to his cousin's Lordship of Man, and the following year he assented to a charter of liberties for his new subjects: this included trial by jury. On 20 August 1764 he wrote to the Treasury that if the Crown took over, 'between thirty and forty thousand inhabitants must still have a right to their constitutions, laws, administration of justice and interior trade and commerce; and it would be in the case of Guernsey, Jersey, Sark and Alderney, where imports and exports are governed by their own laws, as much as if they were under feudatory lords'. When in 1765 the British Parliament was engaged in discussing a further bill against evasions ('The Mischief Act', 5 Geo.III cap.39) the duke protested, then gave way, and named his price for the surrender of the proprietorship before information about its revenues were available. Among those to whom in the interim he had leased lands in the island was the future Lord Mansfield, William Murray, in November 1737.
2. *The Constitution of the Isle of Man*, (ed. R. Sherwood) Manx Soc, publ. XXXI p.251.
3. Also *The Bishop of Man v. Earl of Derby:* 2 Vesey sen. 337-352. Also in P.P. 1805. V.pt.ii (79), p.42. The case in chancery (not in

different from them [as indeed in the *commotes* of the Welsh border where the king's writ also did run]...Though a right and title
was gained by conquest, that makes no alteration; the laws
of Man still continued the rule of their property.[1] So it
is in Jamaica according to Blankard;[2] so notwithstanding
the conquest of King William I which introduced several
Norman customs, yet the old customs remained [in England].
So of Wales and Ireland. But this isle was both by
forfeiture and conquest....

   [The grant in 1610 was expressly in common soccage, not by knight
   service. Why should not the law of Man be a mixture of common
   and statute law? This would argue for the heirs male.]

Argued by counsel for Atholl

   [Man was a feudal principality of the King and was not devisable.
   The Statute of Wills did not apply to Man; nor was the Act of
   1610 a 'virtual extension' of *de donis conditionalibus*.]

   ...If the Crown of England conquers a country and
leaves the people to enjoy it, the conquered keep their
own laws until the conqueror declares the contrary, *a
fortiori* where he declares they shall. An English colony
[*sic*]carrys with them all the laws of the Crown in being
at the time of planting it which are adapted to the situation, not all others; but no statute made after binds
without naming them. This isle belonged to the Crown
before any Act of Parliament: they are then to hold all
their lands and no statute in England can extend to them.
On the common law which never tolerated wills and which
part of the feudal law was received in England, it could
not be devised....

   [The rights of the heirs general to the dominion and lordship
   were not avoided by the private Act.]

Hardwicke (L.C.).

   [Both parties had admitted that]... Man is not part of the
realm of England, parcel only of the King's crown of England: a distinct dominion, now under the King's grants
and so ever since from a long time past granted; held as
a feudatory dominion by liege homage of the Kings of England [as previously of Norway and Scotland]: the laws of England
therefore as such extend not to it, neither the common nor
the statute law, unless expressly named or some necessary
consequence resulting from it. But notwithstanding that
it was an estate and dominion in the King of England, not

---

the privy council) concerned the claim by Derby contesting the inheritance of the Lordship and lands in Man by Atholl through the female
line.
1. In 1879 the Manx *Attorney-General v. Mylchreest* (4 A.C. 294) the
privy council decided that the laws of the Isle had permitted tenants
to remove clay and sand regardless of whether the Crown had rights to
them as mineral deposits. This usage grew up with the consent of the
Lords of Man and the privy council accepted it as established custom.
2. i.e. *Blankard v. Galdy* (1693); see Volume II.

parcel of his realm, but of his Crown which he could
grant under his great seal and (as said Anderson[1]) could
be granted by him in no other manner because the great
seal of England operates in all the dominions not only
parcel of the realm but of the Crown. The King therefore can grant lands in Ireland and the plantations, Jersey and Guernsey under the great seal of England because
part of the Crown....

> [Man was held of liege homage of the King in 1405 and the ten-
> ure was in free soccage. The Stanleys could not alienate it with-
> out a regrant and new licence from the Crown in 1610. Moreover a
> statute was passed to confirm it. Since 1610 the Stanleys]

...have not power to alien[ate] by any method of conveyance
whatever, this isle and dominion without licence of the
Crown, and that by direct consequence of the tenure created by letters patent; and it was enacted that all those
persons should hold by that tenure, for though it is in
socage it is *in capite* of the King and is of the most
honorable kind not only in the feudal law but the common
law of England....

> [A subordinate feudatory kingdom, tenant *in capite* in soccage,
> could not be alienated without the king's licence either by feu-
> dal or by common law.
>   The private Act of 1610 did not make Man alienable against the
> heirs general. Though it might be argued that on the analogy of
> appeals to the king from the *commotes* and marches, cases might
> go to the privy council, Hardwicke reaffirmed[2] that judgement on
> the title to the Isle (as indeed to Sark) could be determined in
> Chancery in England. The suit of the earl of Derby therefore
> failed.]

122. 'THE REINVESTING ACT' FOR EXECUTING A CONTRACT BETWEEN THE
      TREASURY AND THE PROPRIETOR (5 Geo.III cap.26), 1765.
      [The duke and duchess of Atholl and their trustees had signed a
      contract of 7 March 1765 for 'the absolute Purchase' of the Isle
      of Man at the price of £70,000.]
  And whereas the said Contract and Agreement cannot be
effectually established and carried into Execution, without the Authority of Parliament:[3] Be it enacted...That

---

1. See above No.115
2. Vesey noted that the question concerning the right or title to
the Isle of Man to be determined in chancery had been held in *Derby
v. Atholl*,1749 (1 Vesey sen.204): otherwise it was said that it would
be permitting those who claim the seigniory of the Isle to judge in
their own cause; it was further declared that it must be shown what
other court has jurisdiction, if not chancery.
3. Because of the restraints in 8 Jac.I cap.4 against alienation of
the Isle, a re-investing statute had to be passed to accept the terms
agreed between the duke of Atholl and the British Treasury for the
Crown's resumption of the grant. The preamble contains a detailed
account of the various vicissitudes of the proprietorship. The Act
enabled the Crown to purchase the island and take possession by proclamation on 21 June 1765. A royal governor was appointed.

from and immediately after the Payment into the Bank of
England by his Majesty, his Heirs or Successors, in the
Names of the said John, Duke of Atholl, and Charlotte,
Duchess of Atholl his Wife, Baroness Strange, Sir Charles
Frederick, and Edmund Hoskins, [their trustees]... of the
Sum of seventy thousand Pounds of lawful Money of Great
Britain,[1] free and clear of all Taxes, Impositions, Fees
Rewards, and other Deductions whatsoever...the said Island,
Castle, Pele, and Lordship of Man, and all the Islands and
Lordships to the said Island of Man appertaining together
with the Royalties, Regalities, Franchises, Liberties, and
Sea Ports, to the same belonging, and all other the Hereditaments and Premises comprized, mentioned, and granted,
in the said Letters Patent [i.e. 6 April 1406 to 2 May 1610,
together with the statute (8 Jac.I cap.4)]... and every or any of
them (except as herin-after is excepted) shall be, and
they are hereby, unalienably vested in his Majesty,...
freed and discharged, and absolutely acquitted, exempted,
and indemnified, of, from, and against, all Estates, Uses,
Trusts, Intails, Reversions, Remainders, Limitation, Charges, Incumbrances, Titles, Claims, and Demands whatsoever,
from, by, or under, the said Letters Patent and Act of
Parliament....

IV. Nothing in this Act contained shall extend, or be
construed to extend, to vest in his Majesty...the Patronage of the Bishoprick of the said Island of Man...[2]

---

1. Though the Atholls sold the proprietorship and sovereignty, they
retained their estates. A generation later, however, in 1791, their
heir, the fourth duke, petitioned against this contract on the
ground that the third duke in 1765 had acted precipitately, without
adequate knowledge of the potential value of the island, its revenues and its trade, which had increased since. The matter was considered by a commission, by the privy council and by the law officers.
The law officers reported (10 November 1802) that 'On the first question viz. the legal competency of the British Parliament to make laws
to bind the Isle of Man, we think it a question upon which no doubt
can be entertained'; all authorities and precedents were 'clear and
precise upon the subject' and proved that Parliament had exercised
this right whenever it considered it necessary; but though lawful,
the right to introduce legislation without sufficient compensation
was not necessarily justifiable. In the case of Man, they said, the
quantity of illicit trade had made it difficult to assess the proper
value of legitimate returns and would argue against any compensation.
Having determined, in March 1804, that there was no sufficient ground
for reconsideration, in July the privy council promised the duke a
proportion of the increased revenues by rent charge. [P.P. 1805 V
pt.ii (79)]. By 45 Geo. III cap.113, the duke acquired an annuity
of one quarter of the customs. In 1825 (6 Geo.IV cap.34) this annuity was finally compounded.
2. Further British statutes applying to the Isle were passed, for
the most part imposing customs duties, e.g. 20 Geo.III cap.42, 28
Geo.III cap.63, 45 Geo.III cap.99, 50 Geo.III cap.42 and 6 Geo.IV
cap. 105.

[or any ecclesiastical temporalities. The bishop of Sodor and
Man was to continue to hold them of His Majesty at an annual rent
of £101-15s-11d. and two falcons on coronation days.]

(f) THE CHANNEL ISLANDS

The Channel Islands were dominions of the duke of Normandy before
William I invaded England in 1066 to take the English crown: therefore the islanders could regard themselves as conquerors of the realm
of England, not dependents on it. The islands were, however, separated from Normandy by the French conquest of the Duchy in 1204 and
were ultimately acknowledged as domains of the English king by the
treaty of Brétigny in 1360 (*Foedera* III pt.i p.487). But a century
and half earlier, by a generous grant of local autonomy, John had
bid for, and bought, the allegiance of the islanders. By charter
he recognised their right to their own systems of ancient Norman
(and often very uncertain) island custom and to their own *Cour
Royale* of the bailiff and *jurats*, a self-perpetuating oligarchy of
seigneurs, as interpreters of them.   The rights of Englishmen and
indeed more - quittance from tolls in England and from military service - were also later granted to them. Furthermore, charters of
Edward VI, Elizabeth I and Charles II granted the islanders a remarkable privilege of neutrality in war [see No.132].

The seigneurs of the Channel Islands therefore enjoyed substantial home rule, though in their skirmishes with the king's governors
they claimed to acknowledge that the king himself as *Duke* had the
sole right to initiate taxation [see No. 141(a)]. The king indeed
did from time to time demonstrate his solicitation for their security - 'farthest remote from the rest of our domynions' in James I's
words [see No.137 (b)] 'thereby most exposed to the daunger of
invasion' - by requiring taxes for defence. But, if the islanders
protested their respect for the prerogative royal, they also argued
that 'the Lord King of England has nothing in these islands save the
status of Duke' and therefore parliamentary statutes did not, they
said, automatically extend to islands never annexed to the realm.
Three conditions had, they asserted, to be fulfilled: the islands
must be expressly named in an Act; the king must have ordered registration of the Act in the *Cour Royale*:and the *Cour Royale* must
have done so. Since islanders were not represented in Parliament,
they argued, such exemplification was necessary to secure the general 'cognisance of new measures' locally.

Attorneys general in England did not accept these conditions: a
general reference to the 'plantations' or 'dominions' was sufficient
for a Act to extend to the Channel Islands: registration by the
Cour Royale was only a convenient, not a legally necessary procedure.
The Navigation Act of 1660 did not, indeed, name the Channel Islands
generally or specifically in section XVII, but in other sections
(e.g. III, IV, VI and XIV) did enumerate both Jersey and Guernsey;
however, though never registered, it was observed - as least as
effectively as in Massachusetts.

Some enterprizing'home rulers'argued that, since the Act of 1542,
restraining the use of crossbows and handguns, expressly excluded

the Channel Islanders [see Section I No.7], Parliament had recognised
that it could not legislate without the consent of their island legislatures, *the States*; but surely such express mention in the Act would
argue that Parliament had to make positive exemption if the statute
were not to apply: in the context it is clear that islanders along
with the others exempted were regarded as frontiersmen who would be
the first line of 'home guard' defence against hostile invasion.
Though there is little legal doubt about the right of Parliament to
legislate for the Channel Islands even by 'necessary intendment'
(i.e. without express words), in practice Parliament left legislation
to the king-in-council and to the island States.

The most important contribution of the Channel Islands to later
imperial history, however, concerned appeals to the privy council.
In 1641 by 16 Car.I cap.10 the Long Parliament abolished prerogative
jurisdiction (including the Star Chamber and the councils of the
North, of Wales and of the marches), but section iii, with its reference specifically to 'this kingdom' and its acknowledgement of
'the ordinary course of law', in effect limited such abolition to
the realm itself. Appeals had,indeed, come to the privy council
from the Channel Islands by the ordinary course of law, at least
(it was claimed) since the fourteenth century. They continued to be
heard by the Council in England during the Protectorate. When Charles II sought to assert royal supervision over the American plantations in the 1670s, the continuing existence of appeals overseas
from Jersey and Guernsey proved both the precedent and the pretext
for a regular system of appeals from the colonies to the privy
council : [See below III C.]

123. JERSEY: CHARTER FROM JOHN, c. 1204.[1]
First, he appointed twelve *jurats* of the Crown to hold
pleas and maintain the rights belonging to the Crown.
II. He also granted and established for the security
of the Islanders that henceforth the Bailiff might try
without writ, under the supervision of the said *jurats* of
the Crown, pleas of *novel disseisin* made within a year of
the act, of *mort d'ancestor* within a year of the ancestor's
death, of dower similarly within a year of the husband's
death *[etc.].*....
III. These *jurats* of the Crown must be chosen from the
natives of the Islands by the servants of the Lord King
and by the chief men (*optimates*)of the country; that is, at
the death of one of them or for another legitimate cause,
another worthy of trust must be appointed in his place.
IV. Those elected must swear unconditionally to maintain and preserve the rights of the Lord King and of the

1. P. Falle, *Account of the island of Jersey* (1837) pp.222-3. Trans.
from Latin. The original charter is lost, but the Inquest of Henry
III recited and confirmed these terms granted by John when he was losing the mainland territories of Normandy to the French king and, by
a generous gesture of local self-government, hoped to prevent the
further loss of the offshore islands of the Duchy: a gamble which was
notably successful.

inhabitants ....
[The twelve, in the absence of the justices, must judge all
cases and assess fines unless they were too difficult. The Lord
King might ask for the record of any trial. Inhabitants were not
obliged to do homage to the Lord King until he came himself or
appointed a deputy expressly for that purpose.][1]

124. LETTERS PATENT FOR THE WARDENSHIP OF THE ISLANDS, 4 December
                                                    1229.[2]
    Know that the Lord King grants to Richard de Gray and
John de Gray his brother the custody and the revenues of
Jersey, Guernsey and all the islands in those parts for
4 years from the feast of Saint Martin of the fourteenth
year *[of our reign]* ...and they are to govern and rule the
inhabitants of the islands justly and according to their
laws and customs ....
    [The king promised not to alienate the custody of the islands
    before the end of the stated period.]

125. (a) PATENT FROM HENRY III FOR ASSIZES, 17 February, 1219.[3]
    Philip de Alban is ordered to undertake the assizes
of the Islands of Jersey, Guernsey, Sark and Alderney in
those same islands without letters from the Lord King in
case of half a knight's fee or less. But he is not to
take assizes involving more than half a knight's fee without letters from the Lord King ....
    [He was also to collect *fouage* (hearth money) due to the king
    according to Norman custom.][4]

125. (b) WRIT TO THE WARDEN OF THE ISLANDS, 10 June 1233.[5]
    Mandate to the Warden of the islands of Jersey, Guern-

---

1. As late as 1866 the attempt by a minority of ratepayers in Jersey
to secure reform of the *Cour royale* of bailiff and *jurats* by separat-
ing judicial and legislative functions, and by replacing the *jurats*
by paid judges was frustrated by reference to this charter (*In re the
Jersey Jurats:* 3 Moore.P.C. (N.S.) 457). At that time the *jurats* were
elected on a property qualification and, although on several occasions
(as in 1833) the rateable qualification had been modified, were chosen
for life. Together with 12 rectors, 12 mayors and 14 deputies elected by ratepayers for a 3 year term, *jurats* were also members of the
States. Though, in the lord chancellor's words, the justical committee of the privy council were convinced that 'a complete change' of
the Royal Court was 'absolutely necessary for the welfare of the island', there was no immediate prospect of improving the present constitution by prerogative action; and they advised against the use of
the 'undoubted rights' of the Crown against the wishes of an overwhelming majority of electors, who were opposed to democratic reform.
2.*Cal.Pat. Rolls.* 1225-32. p.330. Trans. from Latin.
3. *Documents historiques relatifs aux Iles de la Manche* 1199-1244
(1879) p.15. Trans from Latin. P. d'Aubigny was the Warden (*custos)*
of the Islands.
4. In addition, annual services and rents were paid by seigneurs who
held *in capite* from the king.
5. *Cal. Pat. Rolls.* 1232-47 p.18. Trans. from Latin.

sey, Sark, Alderney and Herm to cause to be summoned before him at a certain day and place all assizes and pleas
which have been moved in the said islands by the King's
precept to do justice therein according to law and the
custom of the same islands.

126. GUERNSEY: THE FRANCHISES OF THE KING OF ENGLAND AND OF THE
ISLANDERS, 1274.[1]
   These are the franchises of our Lord, the King of England in the island of Guernsey. First, he has the lordship over all and his franchises as Lord and his writs
and all things which appertain to the Crown....
   [He had the right to hold assizes every three years, to collect
   dues, customs, £70 worth of aid three times a year, and to hear
   chief pleas of inheritance and forfeitures.]
   These are the franchises of the people of Guernsey.
First, for seventy pounds of aid which our Lord the King
takes for all the island of Guernsey, they ought to be
quit from military service and from cavalcade and from
tallage [etc.]...[and have]right of trial within the country
[Guernsey] by the judgement of twelve jurors without going
out of the country....[2]
   [They also enjoyed rights regarding fish, flesh, corn and mills,
   which were defined.]

127. JERSEY AND GUERNSEY: PLEAS IN ANSWER TO *QUO WARRANTO*, 1309.[3]
   (a) *Jersey*, 9 June.
   The commonalty of this island being asked what law they
use and by what law they claim to be governed, - that is,
whether by the law of England or of Normandy or by special
customs granted to them by Kings *etc.* - say, By the law of
Normandy, except that they have certain customs used in
this Island from a time whereof memory runneth not, differing nevertheless from the laws of the Normans as appears
more fully in a certain schedule which they have delivered....
   [The law was, they said, interpreted in the Royal Court by the
   bailiff and 12 local-born *jurats*, who had also been relied upon
   for advice by the itinerant justices. The king's attorney said
   it was manifest that, though all the islands were under one Norman
   law and custom, the islanders of Jersey had assumed laws and customs 'which altogether disagree with the laws and customs of other
   islands' in inheritance, dower, and weights and measures. The
   commonalty affirmed that 'their ancestors have used such customs
   as they now claim'.]

---

1. *Jersey Prison Board III*,p.881. Trans. from French. This contemporary statement by the Royal Court summed up the rights and duties
of the duke of Normandy and his people in Guernsey.
2. In 1234 Henry III referred in a letter to the Warden at Jersey to
an inquest by a jury of 24 according to the custom of that island:
Docs. hist. rel. aux Isles de la Manche 1205-1327 ed. W. Nicholle
p.31.
3. *Jersey Prison Board II*,p.111 and *III*,p.885. Trans. from French.

(b) *Guernsey*, 8 July.
      The Commonalty of this Island...say, Neither by the
law of England nor of Normandy, but by certain customs
used in this Island from a time whereof memory runneth
not....
      [The king's attorney questioned their variable use of ancient
      custom and asserted that 'in these islands there ought to be one
      law and one custom'.]

128. CHANNEL ISLANDS: CHARTER FROM EDWARD III, 10 July 1341.[1]
      ....Know that we, recalling with pleasure the loyalty
and bravery of the dear and faithful inhabitants of our
islands of Jersey, Guernsey, Sark and Aurigny *[Alderney]*
have always shown till this day in their attachment to
our royal person and to that of our ancestors, Kings of
England,...grant all privileges, liberties, immunities,
exemptions and customs respecting their persons, their
goods and their moneys and the other things that they
lawfully enjoy by virtue of concessions made to them by
the Kings of England, our predecessors,..Above all we
desire to inform ourselves more completely on the extent of these privileges and customs in order to confirm
more particularly all which appears to us good and
just....

129. CHANNEL ISLANDS: CHARTER FROM RICHARD II, 28 July 1394.[2]
      [In consideration of their good deeds and great loyalty, the
king granted to the islanders]That they and their heirs and
successors may in perpetuity be free and have acquitance
in all cities, boroughs, market towns and ports within
our realm of England of all manner of tolls, exactions
and customs in such wise and in the same manner as our
faithful liege subjects in our aforesaid realm enjoy.

130. GUERNSEY: PRECEPT OF ASSIZE, 1441.[3]
      ...They, the inhabitants and persons dwelling on the

1. *Jersey Prison Board II* P.156. Trans. from Latin. This charter is
an amplified confirmation of the 'Extent' of 30 July 1331 which *inter
alia* recognised the privileges of the Islands to their 12 *jurats* and
to the local settlement of all local cases, except the three offences
previously reserved to the Crown's decision.
2. *Jersey Prison Board* II, p.158. Trans. from Latin. In 1309 a letter
from Edward II had granted that the islanders would not be regarded
as aliens in England.
3. J. Warburton,*Treatise on the history, laws and customs...of Guernsey* (1822) pp.148-9. Trans. from French. This 'Precept' was the report
of the king's itinerant justices, Sir Robert de Northon, Sir William
de la Rue and others on the liberties, usages and customs of Guernsey,
and gave a fuller and more detailed account of them than there had
been in the 'Extent' of 1331. By order in council of 23 October 1783
the particular Guernsey versions of Norman custom were ratified. This
was known as the 'Approbation des Lois': it was virtually an updated
interpretation of chartered rights.

said island and their predecessors, have had the usage
and ancient custom of appointing and electing from among
themselves twelve men , the most notable and discreet,
wise, loyal and rich...who are sworn in by the King's
Bailiff then exercising the said office, and take oaths
- namely, that they shall well and loyally record and judge
according to their consciences each and every case and
cause whatsoever which shall be determined in law before
the said Bailiff and themselves, the which above mentioned
are called *Jurats* of the court of our said Lord the King,
and are judges *mesne* between our said Lord the King and
his men dwelling in the said island, and they have cognizance, jurisdiction, precognition and judgements in the
company of the said Bailiff of all manner of causes, civil
and criminal, occurring in the said island whensoever, as
is clearly declared in the Extent[1] of our said Lord the
King: Provided always that, according to the ancient custom of the said island, the punishment of three certain
cases, if they befall there, is especially reserved to the
Crown alone; *namely*, cases of treason, the second is of
coiners, and the third is of putting and laying hands in-
juriously upon the person of the said Bailiff or of any
of the said jurats in the performance and exercise of their
duties, of which cases the cognizance belongs there and
the punishment to the said Crown....

   [All liberties, usages and customs enjoyed since the conquest
of England and ratified by English kings were detailed and confirmed.][2]

131. (a) JERSEY: ORDER IN COUNCIL, 3 November 1494.[3]
   [Complaints had been made against the Captain and Governor,
Matthew Baker, by the islanders. The king in council ordered
that]
   ...from now henceforth *[no Captain]* ...shall name, or
present, institute, or create any Dean or Bailiff in our
said Island of Jersey, and we have retained and do retain
the nomination...to be provided by us and not by others
whenever the case shall arise[4] and that our said Captains

_____

1. After inquiry this 'Extent' had been accepted in 1331 as an authentic statement both of the king's revenues and prerogatives, and of
the rights of islanders and duties of office-holders.
2. The Extent, the Precept, and (later) the Approbation were regularly
adduced by the States in their assertion of local autonomy: for example, in their protest against the governor's proclamation of
martial law in 1607 and in their rejection of Star Chamber writs in
1639.
3. *Jersey Prison Board* II p.176. Trans. from French.
4. Later by order in council 27 May 1674, Charles II endorsed the
opinion of Heneage Finch,lord keeper of the seal, that in relation
to Guernsey, 'there is no right in the Governor to name the Bayliffe',
though, 'sometymes the Governors have been trusted with the nominations; nor is it reasonable it should be claymed as a Right'.

and Governors...shall not have any jurisdiction... [eccles-
iastical or secular in the island against or between islanders] but
we do will order and command that they be moved, instituted, and pursued in our ordinary Jurisdiction of our
said Island of Jersey before our Bailiff and *Jurats* thereof....

    [Conflicts between the Captain and the courts were to be deter-
    mined in the privy council. Islanders were to enjoy free move-
    ment from Jersey into 'our other countries and dominions'.]

131. (b) JERSEY: ORDER IN COUNCIL, 17 June 1495.[1]

    [Provision was made for the safety of the island, the loyalty
    of the Captain-general, and the trial of treasons by the king in
    council. Tenants *in capite* were to assist the Captain in defence
    according to 'the ancient customs' of the island. The king was
    to be paid customs.]

Neither the Captain nor the *Jurats* of the island may
impose or levy any *taille* or imposition on the people
of the island without the knowledge and commandment of
the King, save it may be for such pursuits as shall be
done at the good grace of the King for the common good
and the defence of the said island.

The King shall have the right to nominate the Bailiff... [the Dean and other officials], and the Captain and
Jurats shall not interfere in any way in their appointment....

    [The Captain and *jurats* should have no power to pardon. Pro-
    cedure for sealing and registering decisions by the *jurats* was
    laid down.]

In case of any debate or dispute between the Captain
and the *Jurats* the use of forcible action of one against
the other is forbidden; but each of the parties shall
have recourse to the good grace of the King to give direction as the case may require.

132. GUERNSEY: CHARTER FROM ELIZABETH I, 15 March 1561.[2]

    [The islanders had by several charters enjoyed rights and priv-
    ileges locally and within 'the realm and dominions'.]

4.   ...we do by these presents give and grant, to the
said Bailiff and *Jurats* of our island of Guernsey...and
Alderney and Sark that they...be, for ever exempted and
acquitted,...within our Kingdom of England; and within
all our Provinces, Dominions, Territories, and other
Places under our Subjection, within our Realms, or beyond the Seas, from all Tributes,...and Exactions whatsoever that may be due...to ourselves...in any Manner, by
Virtue of any Charters, Grants, Confirmations and Princ-
ely-Writs, of our said Progenitors, formerly Kings of
England and Dukes of Normandy, or others, or by virtue
and by Reason of any legal or reasonable Usage, Prescrip-

---

1. *Jersey Prison Board* II p.185. Trans. from French.
2. *Jersey Prison Board* I pp.35ff; II pp.216ff. Also *The Charter* (n.
p.o.d.) pp.2-8.Trans. from Latin. A similar charter was granted to

tions or Customs ....
    [Various other privileges granted by her predecessors were con-
    firmed, among which it was affirmed that]
    ...in time of war the merchants of all nations and oth-
ers, as well aliens as inhabitants, as well enemies as
friends, may freely legally and with impunity come go and
frequent the said islands and coastal regions with their
trading vessels, merchandise and goods as well to avoid
storms as to carry on there their other lawful business...
and they shall be...free of molestation either to their
merchandise or in their persons not only around the said
islands...but also indeed in an area on all sides distant
from them as far as the sight of man *(usque ad visum homini)*:
that is as far as the sight of the eye can follow[1]....
    [The custom and laws of the Island were confirmed. So too was
    the jurisdiction of the bailiff and *jurats*.]
7... That, for the time to come, none of them be cited, or
summoned, or drawn in any Law-suit, or forced in any Manner
by any Briefs, or Writs, issued from any of our Courts of
the Kingdom of England, to appear and answer before any
Judges, Courts, or other Officers of Justice, out of any
of the said Island...touching or concerning...any Thing,
dispute, cause or matter of controversy...arising, or
emergent, in the said Island;...
9.   Saving always entire and without detriment, the Regal
and Sovereign-Power, Dominion and Empire of our Crown of
England, as to what may concern the Allegiance, Subjection and Obedience of the said Islanders,...and also as to
what may concern the Regalities, Prerogatives, Incomes,
Revenues, Tributes and other Rights...anciently due *[to
us]* ...by our Royal-Prerogative, as Kings of England, or
the Prerogative of the Duchy of Normandy....

133. (a) JERSEY AND GUERNSEY: ORDER IN COUNCIL, 22 July 1565.[2]
    Where heretofore for a good tyme past humble sute
was made to the Lordes on the behalf of th'inhabitants of
the Isles of Jersey and Guernzeye who found themselves
moche greved that divers of the same Isles, contrary to
their auncient Charters and Lyberties, were called to answer here by processe awarded against them owt of sundrye
of the Queen's Majesty's Coortes of Record here and after
Judgements given in the same Isles appealls made hither

Jersey on 27 June 1562.
1. This 'privilege of neutrality' had been granted to the Channel
islanders in 1483 by the pope. It was confirmed for the first time
in the charter of Edward VI, 6 March 1549 (J.P.B. II pp.203-6). It was
finally abolished by royal proclamation in 1689. Perhaps some Acad-
ian of Nova Scotia, having known of this privilege, lived in hopes
of securing similar liberties in the forty years after 1713: [see
Volume II.]
2. *Jersey Prison Board* I p.40; II p.234. If cases in the first instance were to be tried locally, nevertheless appeals would under conditions, lie to the privy council.

unto the said Coortes,...
    [the Lords of the privy council had asked the solicitor-general
    to consult with the lord chief justice and Sir Hugh Paulet, Captain
    of Jersey, regarding local chartered rights. The council now ord-
    ered that]
    ...from henceforthe all sutes commenced there alredye
or hereafter to be commenced between any subjects of these
Isles should be heard,ordered and adjudged in the same
Isles and not within this realm... [similarly too where one
party was resident in England and the other an islander.]
    And further their Lordships resolved that no appeles
should be made from any sentence or Judgement given in
the same Isles hither but only according to the words of
their Charters *Au Roi et son Counsaill* which agreeth as Sir
Hugh Powlett allegith with such order or forme as hath
heretofore ben acustomed with their Lordshippes' determy-
nacions.

133. (b) JERSEY: ORDER IN COUNCIL, 13 May 1572.[1]
    Where certeine peticions have bin exhibited to my Lor-
des of the Counsell by Helier de Carteret, Lord of St.
Owne in the Isle of Jersey, one of the *Jurats* and Justices
there, as well in his owne name as in the name of the
reste of the *Jurats* and Justices of that Isle, for the
reformacion of certeine inconveniences risinge in some
pointe of the lawes of that Isle, and the maner of prosec-
utinge the same; the said Lordes recommending the same
peticions to be considered by the Quenes Majesties' Attorney Generall, with the Judge of thadmoraltie or some
others lernid in the Civill Lawes,It was commaunded by my
said Lordes That an order touching those peticions, and
for reformacion in those cases to be hadd, should be
written downe in the Counsell Booke in maner and forme
followinge:...Firste, That no appeals be admitted or allowed from any sentence or judgement in any matter or cause
not excedinge the value or somme of seven poundes ster-
linge or currant English money.
    That no appeale in any cause or matter, great or smale,
be permitted or allowed before the same matter be fullie
examined and ended by diffinitive sentence, or other judgement having the force and effect of a sentence diffinitive.
    That everie appeale shall be prosecuted within three
monthes next ensuinge the sentence or judgement given
therein, excepte there be just cause of lett or impediment to be proved before their Lordships, being the Judges
of Appeale, and by their Lordships allowed.
    That no appeale be hereafter received without the cop-
pie as well of the sentence or judgement, as also of the
whole processe of the cause closed together under the
Seale of the Isle; and that there may be no lett to the
appelaunte in having thereof: It is ordered by the said

1. P.C. 2/10.

Lords That the Bailif and *Jurats* of the Isle from whome
the appeale shall be made, shall, uppon requeste made to
them, deliver, or cause to be delivered, to the said partie appelaunte the said coppie within eight daies after
such requeste.

133. (c). GUERNSEY: ORDER IN COUNCIL, 9 October 1580.[1]
   ...Whereas they complain that they were restrained
from appeales, It is ordered That it shal be lawfull for
anie of the Inhabitants of that Isle and all other finding themselves greived with anie judiciall decree, sentence or Judgement made or given by the Bailyffe and *Jur-*
ats of that Isle to appeale from the same to Her Majesty
and the Lords of Her Privy Counsell, so as the same be
made at the time of such a decree, *etc.* ...Provided that
is shall not be lawfull to appeale to anie cause criminal,
or of correction, nor from the execucion of any order
taken in their Court of Chief Pleas, nor in cries of
Haro[2], nor for any matter moveable, not exceeding the somme of ten pounds Sterling of England....

134. ARTICLES TO BE CONSIDERED BY THE PRIVY COUNCIL, c.1568.[3]
   The Isles of Jersey and Guernsey are part of the duchy
of Normandy governed by the laws spiritual and temporal
of the same Duchy, and so long as the Queen holdeth the
said isles, governed as aforesaid, her Highness is not
out of possession of the said Duchy, but may by the laws,
usage and customs of Normandy maintain just claim and
title to the Duchy, the ancient inheritance of the Crown
of the realm.
   The spiritual government in Normandy, namely in the
diocese of Coustances, *[Coûtances]*, is reformed,[4] and therefore it is to be considered whether that order of reformation may, with the aforesaid orders of this realm, be
tolerated in the said isles, parcel of the said diocese,
which reformation of Coustances differeth nothing in doctrine from this realm and agreeth best in rites and ceremonies with the reformation of life, manners and language of the isles.[5]

---

1. *Jersey Prison Board*, III p.915.
2. A Norman process at law, initiated by an outcry in alarm or distress for help: *'haro'*. If called out three times on one's knees, denouncing someone threatening house or property, it instituted a legal
process. The exclamation was improbably an invocation of Rollo , duke
of Normandy : Chaucer in the Miller's (100) and the Reeve's (151) Tales
had similar usage for 'harrow'.
3. H.M.C.*Salisbury MSS* XIII App. p.23; an unsigned and undated note.
These Articles were presented by certain petitioners from Guernsey.
4. The argument is that the Huguenot Church was *de facto* established
in the mother diocese. Norman protestantism was Presbyterian, not
Anglican.
5. By the order in council of 7 August 1565, though the Anglican mode
of worship was to be used elsewhere on the islands, Calvinism was

The temporal government of Guernsey having of long
time been abused, is by good and grave advice to be reformed and reduced to the ancient laws, usages and customs of
Normandy, and the Justiciars [*Wardens, captains or lieutenants*],
abusers thereof by erroneous judgements, privy conspiracies *&c*, punished by fine or otherwise to replace them by
such as will in the fear of God minister justice, *&c*....

That henceforth no money be levied upon the Commons of
Guernsey without public assembly of the *States* of the isle
consenting together and the Captain agreeing thereto; nor
that no procurations pass in the said isles for the public
affairs of the same but by like assembly consent and
agreement....

135. JERSEY: ALLEGED ORDINANCES OF ROYAL COMMISSIONERS, 3 April
1591.[1]

Whereas it appears from evidence that this island of
Jersey being part or member of the Duchy of Normandy without having ever at any time been disjoined or separated
from under the continual true and lawful subjection to
Her Majesty and her noble ancestors as well Dukes of Normandy as afterwards Kings of England, the inhabitants thereof have...not only always remained and continued in the
enjoyment of their ancient laws, customs and liberties,
but also from time to time [*these same*] have been increased
[by royal charters granted since the 'unnatural revolt of the rest
of the Duchy' from true obedience] ....And also forasmuch as
from all time whereof memory is not to the contrary, the

---

permitted in the two main churches of St. Helier and St. Peter Port.
In June 1568 the privy council informed the Guernsey petitioners that
the bishop of Winchester, not of Coûtances, would be in charge; and
by the order in council of 11 March 1569 the island churches
were formally separated from the diocese of Coûtances.
The Channel Islands were being permitted to be protestant in their
own way: in remote dependencies non-confirmity might be tolerated
(cf. the Crown's acceptance of liberty for consciences in the Rhode
Island charter of 1663). With the active co-operation of the lieutenant governors, the tacit acquiescence of the queen, and finally the
formal consent in 1603 of James I, Calvinism was established. However James I soon realised he had acted impulsively and indicated
his desire for conformity to the Church of England. In Jersey by 1623,
when a dean had been appointed and new ecclesiastical canons were
accepted (printed in *Jersey Prison Board* I pp.217-9), his policy was
successful, largely as a result of a division between ministers and
congregations over the quarrels of the bailiff (Hérault) and the
lieutenant; but the dean was soon in conflict with the powerful de
Carterets. In Guernsey,however, where there were no such divisions,
Calvinism persisted much longer, even against the efforts of archbishop Laud.
1. *Jersey Prison Board* II, p.241. Trans. from French. The commissioners, Dr. T.Pyne and R.Napper, were appointed to investigate the charges made by de Carteret against the captain general, Sir Anthony Paulet. They found no truth in them; and with the consent of the bailiff,

Bailiff and Jurats of the said Island have had jurisdiction over and concerning all matters of justice in that island and likewise have managed affairs of great importance
with the assistance of the common council commonly called
the States...with the express consent of the Captain or
Governor, who in all causes which touch and concern the
royal estate, government, or prerogative of Her Majesty
in this island, represents her royal person; which is a
very high and honourable office and has been established
in the said island since the time of the revolt above mentioned as well for the defence thereof...as for the maintenance and securing of the said inhabitants in their due
and rightful obedience to Her Majesty....

   [Such a chief magistrate had been proved necessary to avoid dissensions and the breakdown of law and order, as by the recent
   events since the death of Sir Amyas Paulet. The right of the
   bailiff and *jurats* to determine all cases, save treason and actions between the Captain and *jurats*, was affirmed. Appeals to the
   privy council were also further regulated by limiting its jurisdiction to civil cases involving £10 or over.]

136. (a) JERSEY: LETTER FROM ELIZABETH I TO THE ROYAL COURT PROVIDING
         FOR LOCAL DEFENCE, 17 April 1597.[1]
   [The queen's council had learnt that they had done nothing for
   fortifying the island or for paying money promised for the purpose.
   This was conduct 'worthy of sharp reprehension'.]
   For these respects We do now more earnestly will and
require of you that you shall make present payment of the
sum before mentioned unto Sir Anthony Paulett, Knight, to
Her Majesty's use. And in case you shall make default We
have given directions unto him to deliver into the hands
of one of the messengers of Her Majesty's Chamber those
that have been causes of the deferment of this payment
that they may answer the dealing in that sort before Us....

   [They were enjoined to assist the governor in seeing that the
   island was furnished for defence.]

136. (b) GUERNSEY: ORDER IN COUNCIL, 9 June 1605.[2]
   ...Moreover to the motion they [the inhabitants in their

___

jurats and States, drew up these ordinances, but they were never formally sanctioned in the privy council nor registered in the Royal
Court or States.
1. *Jersey Prison Board* II p.273. In August 1350,Edward III, by letters
patent in the council, directed the Warden to collect forthwith a custom duty in Guernsey for building a wall round St.Peter Port. Those
who objected on the ground that this was a tallage, from which they
claimed exemption, were to be imprisoned (*ibid.* III,p.913) for it was
not for the king's use, but for the common defence of Guernsey.
2. *Jersey Prison Board*,III, p.922. A special sub-committee of the
privy council to hear appeals from the Channel Islands was named
(e.g. in the order in council of 12 June 1635 where appeals in civil
cases were to concern sums of over £1).

petition] make for some order to be prescribed towching
the charge there may be occasion for the better guard, defence, and preservacon of the Isle...and as the Captaine is
by His Majesty trusted with the charge and Government of
the whole Island so in all those matters that concerne the
preservacon and defence of the Isle the cheefe order and
direction dependeth upon the care and commaundement of the
Governor or Captaine...So their L*[ordships]* do not think it
fitt that he shall impose any assesment or Taxe thereby
to charge the Inhabitants for the said provisions, without conference had with the Bailiffe and Jurats and by
their consent and agreement....

    [A commission was to be sent to examine and report to the privy
council on the Book of Extents of his Majesty's revenues.]

Lastlie, whereas it is desired that some convenient
course may be sett downe for prevention and remedie of
the intollerable charge and trouble in the prosecution of
Appeales: for answer hereunto the best remedy that can
be yealded for the present is that it be ordered, and so
it is ordered by the Lordes, That from henceforth no Inhabitant...shall bring any Appeale hither concerning imm-
ovables (that is concerning the question of landes) under
the value of ffortie shillings sterling of yearlie rent
nor concerning moveables (that is in goods and chattells)
under the value of ffortie pounds sterling.

137. (a) GUERNSEY: COMPLAINT BY PARISHES AGAINST MARTIAL LAW, 1607.[1]

We think it not fit or convenient, that the Governor
should exercise any martial jurisdiction to the impeachment of the ordinary course of justice, except it be in
time of war or hostility, or for the suppressing or supp-
rising of robbers and pirates, or for the avoiding of imminent danger, otherwise like to ensue unto the Island;
which for the better satisfaction of the inhabitants of
the Isle, we wish not to be done without advice taken
thereof with the Bailiff, and Jurats, who best understand
the common style and general strength of the Island;....

    [They complained against such interference with the ordinary
internal jurisdiction of the bailiff and *jurats* and with the king's
personal prerogative. They objected to the governor's attempt to
restrain trading with foreign countries, and to require inhabitants to keep watch and ward at the Castle,*etc.*]

---

1. *Documents relatifs a L'Ile de Guernsey* (1814) No.1 p.6. The parishes were alarmed at the establishment of martial law by the governor, Sir Thomas Leighton, 'of his own authority'. In reply two commissioners of inquiry, Gardiner and Hussey, were sent to the islands.
The commissioners were to inquire into all complaints, all controver-
ces between royal officials and the islanders and the defects in local
laws and customs. See also *Extente de L'Isle de Jersey*, 1607 - Jac-
ques 1 : Soc. Jersiaise, publ. 5me. (1880) pp.1-2. Several such commissions were sent out in the next forty years.

137. (b) COMMISSION TO GARDINER AND HUSSEY REGARDING THE LAWS AND
CUSTOMS OF THE ISLANDS, 1607.[1]

[The king expressed his particular solicitude for the Islands
- 'a porcon remayneing as yet unto us in possession of our aunc-
iente Duchie of Normandie' - on account of their proven loyalty
and because they were 'in respect of their scituacon farthest remote from the rest of our saide domynions...thereby most exposed
to daunger of invasion'.]

...Manie controusies haue happened,and doe yet depend
aswel betwene some of our Officers and chiefest persons
of authority and Governmente in those Isles, as alsoe betweene sondrie other private persons and particular parties
there one againste annother whereof manifolde complaintes
and appeales haue been made and broughte unto us and our
privie Counsell...wee...[therefore] doe give full power and
aucthoritie unto you aswell to enquire and to take knowe-
ledge of all such defectes, ambiguities and imperfeccons
as are to be founde in the lawes Customes and Governmente
of the saide Isles....

137. (c) GUERNSEY: MESSAGE FROM PRIVY COUNCIL TO ROYAL COURT,
September 1628.[2]

We have bin informed by the Deputies of the Isle of
Guernsey, that the commission lately sent thither, concerning Martiall Law, hath startled the people, and raised
some doubtes in their minds of His Majestie's wonted good
affection towards them. For the cleering whereof wee are
commanded by His Majestie to lett you know, That he int-
endeth not on any thing to diminish or abrogate the ancient liberties and privileges you have enjoyed in the
tymes of his Royall Progenitors, so long as you continue
his dutifull and loyal subjects as you have don, whereof
we make no doubte. And as concerning the Commission for
Martial Law, you shall understand that His Majestie had
no other intent nor end in it, but onely for the better
regulating and governing of the 200 soldiers in His Majestie's pay in theise doubtfull and troublesome tymes, and
is well pleased that whatsoever hath been already don by
vertue of the said Commission shall be voide and of none
effect as to any other of the inhabitants of the same
Isle, and that the further power and execution thereof
shall cease until His Majestie's pleasure shall be otherwise signified....

138. JERSEY: ORDER IN COUNCIL, 15 June 1618.[3]
It is ordered first That the Bailiff shall in the

---

1. *Extent de l' Ile de Jersey*,1607. pp.i-ii.
2. *Actes des Etats de Guernesey* I (1851) p.115. Another commission had
recently been sent to the island and the king was now annulling the
order for martial law because of protests.
3. *Jersey Prison Board* II.pp.331-4. This followed the report of the
commissioners, Sir E. Conway and Sir W. Bird, on civil and military
administration in the island, and the claims of the bailiff against

cohue[1] and seat of justice and likewise in the assembly of
the *States* take the seat of precedence as formerly, and
that in all other places and assemblies the Governor take
place and have precedence which is due unto him as Governor without further question.

And forasmuch as the Governor is trusted by His Majesty with the charge and government of that Island as may
best suit with the safety of the place and His Majesty's
service otherwise;

It is ordered That he be called and known by the name
and title of *Governor* according to the style contained in
his letters patent and not by the name of Captain; and
there be no assembly of the States in that Isle without
the consent of the Governor or of his lieutenant in his
absence. In which it is to be understood that the Governor, or his lieutenant in his absence, have a negative
voice, to the end it may be provided that no ordinance be
agreed upon prejudicial to His Majesty's service or the
interest of the people....[2]

And for the better ordering and government of the ecclesiastical charge in that Isle, it is ordered That a
Dean be erected there...[The king was to appoint one from a
list of those named by the governor and the *States*.]

Whereas they[3] desire that in regard the poverty of the
greatest number of the inhabitants is such as they are
not able to provide themselves of such sorts and quantity
of armour and munitions nor to contribute to such fortifications as are necessary for His Majesty's service and
the safety of the country, having otherwise no public
purse whereby they may ease the people upon such occasions,
His Majesty will be pleased to grant unto them power and
authority to levy *in perpetuum* a *sou tournois*[4] upon every pot
of wine of the measure of that island which shall be
henceforth sold by retail in all the taverns of the same,
to be employed for the use aforesaid, it is ordered That
their petition be granted....[5]

---

the governor.
1. Crush, or mob.
2. By the order in council of 29 July 1619 (*ibid.* II pp.335-6) the
power of the governor to delay calling the States was limited to 15
days. So too was his veto on legislation, since 'acts as are made in
their Assembly are but provisional ordinances and have no power...
until they be confirmed by us'.
3. Petitions to the commissioners had been made by de Carteret, seigneur of St. Ouen, and other justices in the name of the States.
4. a *sou* was a twentieth part of a *livre*. A *sou* coined in Tours was
valued at one fifth less than one minted in Paris.
5. By the order in council of July 1619 this power was granted to
the bailiff and *jurats* (not the States) to levy and appropriate for
defence and other specified purposes. The power does not, however,
seem to have been used, as the islanders resented indirect taxation
even if imposed locally.

[and the inhabitants furnished with modern 'serviceable arms' and
Castle Elizabeth fortified. Authority was also given to levy a
petty custom *in perpetuum* upon imports, to build and to maintain
a harbour. Their request for an exemption from customs duties on
exports into England would be considered.]

139. GUERNSEY: REPORT BY THE COMMISSIONERS TO THE COUNCIL OF STATE,
February 1649.[1]
1. *Concerning the Bailliffe and Justices and Subordinate Officers
of the Court.*
   ...That whereas the custome hath beene that the King
had the power to nominate the Bailiffe, and the Governor
executed that power, it is desired that the said Bailiffe
may be chosen by the Countrey, i.e. by the voyces of all
the housekeepers of the Island, which doe not take almes,
or have not been convinced *[convicted]* of crimes.
                    The reasons for it
   (i) Because the Bailiffe, being the Governor's creature, joynes for the most part with the particular interest of the Governor against the common good..., It is
desired that the Countrey may have liberty...to choose
a new Bailiffe and a new choice of all the 12 *Jurats*;
and the Bailiffe and Justices to continue but for 3
yeares, at the end of which time that a new choice be
made....[Some bailliffs 'whoe have not had the French tongue' had
been appointed in the past.]
   *Reasons why there should be a new Bailiffe and a new choice of
the 12 Jurats.*
   (ii) Because the Bench doth determine things arbitrarily, not observing in their sentences the lawes of the
Island,... *[and]*
   (vi) Because that the Justices joyned with the Governor in setting and leavying of many taxes upon the people
in a way contrary to the lawes and liberties of the people, (for taxes used to be layd by the Constables and
Douzeniers of the parishes) but the Justices, joyning with
the Governor, did lay upon particular men what they pleased, and in case of their refusing to pay what was soe
arbitrarily layd, the goods of some men were seized....
IV. It is complained concerning the Lawes by which this
Island is governed that it is Norman law, and locall
customes of this Isle; the first of which is full of
intricacy, and in some things of contradiction,...and
sometimes the Court goes by the old, and sometimes by
the new lawes: and as for the locall customes, they are
partly written, and partly in the brest and at the will
of the Bailiffe and *Jurats*,.... It is therefore desired
that there may be a Commission made...to review the Norman lawes and the customes of this Countrey, and then to
digest into one body of law soe much as shall be judged
meete and convenient to make an ample and cleare rule

---
1. *Actes des Etats de l'Isle de Guernsey*, vol.I (1851) pp.357-65.

for the administrating of justice and judgement....
VIII. *Concerning Appeales*.

That whereas by the graunt of Queene Elizabeth and
afterwards of King James the inhabitants of this Isle
had liberty to appeale to England from the sentence of
the Court of Guernezy, provided that it should not be
allowed in case of judgement given in criminal cases,and
that such appeale be limited to 15 dayes after the sentence, and that it be made onely to the King and his Councell, It is desired, since the King and his Councell be
taken away, that the Parliament be pleased to appoint in
what Court their appeale should now be heard;....[1]
IX. For the Government of this Isle we make this humble
proposition, that it be changed: and that instead of a
Governor constantly residing here, that there be three or
five of the well affected gentlemen of this Isle constituted Governors, and 2 or 3 of England appointed Commissioners by Parliament to goe once a yeare to that Isle, to
see all things in good order and the Parliament's commands
to be followed and obeyed, and for these reasons;-
1. From the president which the Parliament hath made in
governing the Isle of Wight, which is, by appointing Commissioners to goe sometimes thither to see that all things
be in order.
2. From the experience of such a government in this Isle;
for the power of this Isle was for five months in the
hands of some commissioned gentlemen of the Country (immediately before Colonel Russell's being sent hither) and
then this Island saw its best dayes for matter of government.
3. By this means the islanders will be out of danger to
have their liberties and estates invaded, as of old it
hath beene, through the tyranny and covetousness of their
governors, that were strangers: in soe much that noe
place of England's dominion hath beene soe oppressed and
burdened with usurpations and extorsions as these Isles
have beene of a long time.
4. And principally the necessity of affaires requires
this, for by this means the State revenue will defray
almost the whole charge of this government, which will
also put England to considerable expence of Treasure
yearly: and wee conceive that England is not in case to
beare preter-necessary burdens.

140. JERSEY: ACT OF STATES, 24 July 1669, REGISTERING LETTERS PATENT
OF 14 April 1669.[2]
   [The king had granted to the bailiff and *jurats* power to levy

---

1. When the Act for regulating the privy council and for abolishing
the star chamber and all prerogative jurisdiction (16 Car.I cap.10)
was passed in 1641, section iii which confirmed 'the ordinary course
of the law' was interpreted as allowing appeals from the Channel Islands to continue. This became a precedent for the assertion of a right
of the privy council to hear appeals from the plantations at the Restoration [see below IIIC].   2. See p.195 n.1.

money for, and to appropriate it to, certain public buildings,
and he had instructed the *States* to register this order in council forthwith. The *States* were ready to comply, but asserted
their ancient privileges:][1]

...that they neither consent nor intend that, in virtue
or under colour of this registration, the said duties be
ever diverted wholly or partially to any other uses than
those in consideration of which they have been this day
received...nor that the said duties and small custom or
toll subsist longer than the aforesaid causes of their
issue may require...Forasmuch as the said duties and
small custom or toll might occasion umbrage and fear that
in future times they should become a charge on the inhabitants to the peril of their ancient liberties, charters and privileges...although the new duties to be levied may produce pecuniary advantages...it is moreover
expressly promulgated and registered.

141. (a) JERSEY: ORDER IN COUNCIL, 21 May 1679.[2]
[A petition had complained that chartered privileges had recently been violated: orders in council and Acts of Parliament
including the Navigation Act (12 Car.II cap.18) had been executed by the governor without being registered in the Royal Court.
The king had been asked to grant redress. It was therefore declared to be H.M.'s pleasure that previous privileges be confirmed[3]
and]

...That for the future, all Orders, Warrants, or let
ters, of what nature soever they be, which shall be sent
into the said Island, either from his Majesty or from

---

1. *Jersey Prison Board* II,p.393. Trans. from French. In the presence
of the governor, Edward de Carteret, the bailiff, the *jurats*, the
royal officials, the dean, rectors and constables (who had been expressly charged to collect and report the views at parish meetings
so that proceedings would be with the suffrage of the whole people)
the order in council (*ibid*.I p.64) transmitted to the States, was
accordingly registered. For similar registrations of letters patent
in the Royal Court (9 April 1663) relating to the appointment of
loyal *jurats* and in the States (10 June 1669) dealing with judicial
procedures see *ibid*.II pp.375,379. The latter required *jurats* to deliver their opinion not arbitrarily but 'according to the lawes and
customs of that isle as neare as may be'.
2. P.C. 2/68 pp.43-4. Also *Jersey Prison Board* II pp.411-3. Governor
Thomas Morgan had by-passed the Royal Court and had levied money on
exports. He had seized ships without the authority of the Royal Court
and had exacted duties from French vessels under the Navigation Act,
though Jersey was not (the petitioners asserted) named in it (see No.
252). Despite their charters Jersey goods had been taxed in English
ports.
3. Charles II had confirmed the privileges granted by his predecessors '*quondam regis Angliae et duces Normanie*' on 10 October 1662. These
included free commerce with the enemy in time of war, immunity from
taxation, trial of all cases inside the island ('saving only the supreme royal power, dominion and empire') and right of appeal to the

this Board, or from any other of his Majesty's officers, or ministers, shall not be henceforward put in Execution by any person or persons whatsoever in the said Island, untill they be first presented unto his Majesty's Royall Court there in order to be Registred, and published. And in Case any of the said Orders, Warrants or letters be found to infringe the Petitioners said ancient Lawes, Charters, & Privileges so confirmed unto them, his Majesty is graciously pleased to order, That his said Royall Court may suspend the Registring & publishing the same, and the execution thereof, untill upon their representation, his Majesty's pleasure be further knowne therein,[1] And concerning Acts of Parliament wherein the sd. Island is named, and thereby obliged to give obedience to so much thereof as they are concern'd in: His Majesty is further graciously pleased to order, That forasmuch as the Petitioners have no representatives in Parliament, all such Acts of Parliament before they be put in Execution in the said Island, shall be exemplified under his Majesty's great Seale of England, and sent to his Royall Court there, to be Registred & published, to the end the Petitioners may have Cognizance thereof, to conform themselves thereunto, and avoyd the transgression thereof[2]....

---

king in council.

1. The formula in the Jersey Code of 1771 was almost identical to this. The Royal Court would seem to have in the last resort no option whether or not to accept orders in council; 'if the Crown thereupon does not give way, there is no legal alternative but to register the Order'. (P.P. 1860 XXXI p.v.) Whether this procedure applies to orders made under the authority of a British statute remains doubtful since such orders, now common, were virtually unknown when the Code was enacted in 1771. The question of the power of the privy council (as council of the duke of Normandy) to legislate for Jersey without concurrence of the States was raised (but not determined) in the *Jersey Prison Board Case* in 1894. In practice conflicts (and challenge in the privy council) are avoided by mutual consultation before any extension of laws.

2. Again the Code of 1771 prescribed the same procedure for extending statutes to Jersey. Presumably this was a convenient means of publicising the extension of parliamentary Acts, not the necessary prerequisite for such an extension to be lawful, The commissioners in 1861 reported (P.P. 1861 XXIV (2761) p.vi.) that 'the competency of Parliament to legislate for Jersey is unquestionable, but the interference of the British legislature(except in matters of a fundamental nature e.g. for regulating the succession to the Crown, etc. or upon other subjects universally applicable to the whole Empire ...)would be viewed by the Islanders generally with dissatisfaction'. Where an Act expressly mentioned the Island, or more generally 'the dominions' it would be 'obligatory by its own force without registration' though registration would be convenient for promulgation (see also question 6167 and pp. 505 ff). But 'the ordinary legislature of Jersey consists of the Sovereign in Council and the Island States. Acts of Parliament do not apply there, unless such an intention distinctly appears'.

[There would be no seizure of ships or goods without order from
H.M.'s Royal Court, no duties on French shipping to the island,
and no customs on goods from Jersey in English ports.][1]

141. (b) JERSEY: REMONSTRANCE OF THE ROYAL COURT TO THE PRIVY
COUNCIL, 1679.[2]
    ...It is a maxime of State that noe authority whatso-
ever under yours can leavye or impose any kind of Taxe
or Import,noe not for once onely (some very fewe necessarye cases excepted) without your expresse Command signifyed under your Great Seal; and that the leavying of
any such tax is a Prerogative Royall essentially adhering to your Crowne, which to violate is felony....
    [Consequently the governor clearly had no right to levy duties
    'of his sole authority without the least pretence of permission
    from your Majesty upon these your subjects as well upon strangers'.
    They gave details of such customs and duties imposed and exacted.
    They further asserted the order in council of 21 May, obtained
    without the governor's knowledge, did not limit his acknowledged
    powers or deprive him of his just dues,nor the Crown of its pro-
    per revenues. The Royal Court should have been consulted in many
    matters, such as the granting of passports to ships for foreign
    ports: Acts of Parliament 'which shall concern this Island shal-
    be sent over hither exemplifyed under the Great Seal before it
    be executory.]
There is a Maine Priviledge belonging to these Islands
acknowledged at all hands, even by foraign writers as
well as domestick and by our neighbouring Princes, of
greate antiquity; which Priviledge hath been confirmed
by the Charters of your Majesty's Predecessors down to
your Majesty's owne time, to witt the Priviledge of commerce in time of warre; by which the Subjects of other
Princes and States as well as your owne, may securely
come and trade with us, without trouble or molestation
of any your officers by sea or land, and to be protected
by them in theire coming and going '*per visum oculi*' as
farre from the said Islands as a man's eye can discerne.

The 1771 Code referred to those Acts where the Island is named and
'*dans lequel elle est intéressé*';so the extension of an Act could be
implied by necessary intendment (see P.P. 1847 XV (865) p.xi). There
is a convention that Parliament does not tax the Channel Islands.
For centuries immunity from English customs was provided for Island
produce in their charters,but it is now dealt with by the Customs
Consolidation Act of 1876 (39 & 40 Vict. cap.36 § clvi).
1. Section xvii of 12 Car.II cap.18 prescribed duties to be paid by
French vessels trading with 'England, Ireland, Wales or the town of
Berwick upon Tweed', thus making no specific mention of the Channel
Islands; but other sections of the same statute (e.g. iii,iv, vi,
and xiv) did name the Islands.
2. *Jersey Prison Board* II p.428. The governor , Thomas Morgan, had
suspended the order in council of 21 May 1679 and they were here listing their grievances over his impositions and his usurpations of
royal prerogative.

Which Priviledge was derided and slighted by the late
Governor and hath been sundry wayes violated by other
Governors to the great prejudice of this Island.

141. (c). JERSEY: REPORT FROM COMMITTEE OF PRIVY COUNCIL AMENDING
          ORDER IN COUNCIL, 17 December 1679.[1]
     In Obedience to Your Majesty's Order in Council of the
31st of October last Referring unto Us the Consideration
of the differences between Sir John Lanyer[2], Knight Governour of Your Majesty's Island of Jersey, and the Bayliffe & *Jurats* of that Island, touching certain Priviledges granted unto them by an Order of Your Majesty in
Councill of the 21st of May last, Wee...doe find, That
the sayd Order was obtained at this Board, without consulting either the Governour of the sayd Island, or the
Officers of Your Majesty's Customes, And that severall
parts thereof (if put in execution) would be prejudiciall
both to Your Majesty's Authority there, And to the Revenue of your Customes, and the Trade of this Kingdome:
So that it is our humble Opinion, That the sayd Order be
recalled, and instead thereof, that Your Majesty would be
pleased to Command, That all Warrants, or Letters from
Your Majesty or this Board, which are to be a Standing
Rule for their Proceedings, Be registered in the Royall
Court of that Island before they be putt in Execution,
And that there be a Clause in every such Order, Warrant,
or Letter, requiring the Registring thereof accordingly,
Nevertheless as to such other Warrants, Letters, or Orders, as Your Majesty or this Board shall send, or Judge
fit to be executed without Registry, No Registry shall
be thereof without speciall Direction in that behalfe.
     And as to Acts of Parliament, wherein that Island is
named, or any wayes concerned, That Your Majesty will be
pleased to direct, That such Acts of Parliament, so soon
as they are printed, be transmitted to that Island,
with an Order of Your Privy Councill annexed, directing
the Registering, and publication thereof....
          [Duties prescribed under the Navigation Act were to be imposed
       on French shipping in Jersey and the revenues were to be used on
       the Castle, the prison and the harbour, not for the governor's
       own gain. The governor's right to summon the *States* and to exer-
       cise a veto was reaffirmed.]
     His Majesty was pleased to approve thereof, and did
Order that the same be effectually put in Execution in
all its severall parts.

142. GUERNSEY: JOHN WARBURTON ON THE ORGANISATION OF THE STATES,1682[3]
     The assembly of the *States* is composed of the bailiff

---

1. P.C. 2/68 pp.320-2. An order in council was issued and registered
under protest by the States on 19 March 1680. On 8 August 1689 it was
affirmed that the king could not dispense with provisions made by the
Act.
2. Lanyer had replaced Morgan, but the differences had continued.
3. J. Warburton,*Treatise on the history, laws and customs of the is-*

and *jurats*, the ministers of each parish, and the constables, who represent the rest of the inhabitants of their parish, and give their votes as such representatives; the bailiff and *jurats* and so the ministers, voting for themselves only. These States are not to be assembled but by authority from the Governor; and it is not usual to call them together, but upon some extraordinary occasions, such as the making an address to the King, upon some public grievance which they desire to have redressed, or the raising a sum of money by way of tax or imposition, for some public use, to which, at least the Governor's assent must be had, and if they should agree to such an imposition as would be of any long continuance, the King's allowance would be expedient to be had likewise.

143. (a) JERSEY: OPINION OF SIR THOMAS TREVOR (A.G.),1698.[1]
   [The privy council had asked him whether the registration in
   the Royal Court of an English statute wherein Jersey and Guernsey
   were named was required to make such an Act legally binding in
   the island. He declared his answer to be]
   That the registering of an Act of Parliament made in
England wherein the Island of Jersey is expressly named
is not necessary in point of law to make it obligatory
there; and such registry is only for the convenience of
the islanders that they may have notice of what Acts are
made in England to bind them.[2]

---

land of Guernsey (first published 1822) pp.52-4. Warburton was Somerset herald to Charles II.
1. *Jersey Prison Board* I, p.76. A petition from Jersey had asked for the Navigation Act (12 Car.II cap.18) to be suspended, and argued that, for it to be legally enforceable it should have been registered in the island. Trevor was later chief justice in common pleas.
2. An order in council was issued on 8 September 1698 declaring the council's approval of the attorney general's opinion that the Navigation Act could be enforced without registration. (This Order was not registered either). A similar ruling was given in *A.G. v. Le Marchant* (1772). In 1832 it was held that the Habeas Corpus Act (31 Car.II cap. 2) though never registered in the Island had force there on the authority of the privy council alone (P.P. 1861 XXIV (2761) p.273). In 1854 the States of Guernsey protested against the extension of the Merchant Shipping Act (17 & 18 Vict. cap.194) to the island, claiming their right 'to be governed by Her Majesty in Council alone' as a fundamental principle. Moreover, in 1906 the law officers strongly endorsed a memorandum written by Sir Almeric Fitzroy (*Memoirs*,1925,I, pp.296-7) for the lord president of the council, asserting an 'indefeasible right of Parliament to enforce such laws as it chooses' in the Channel Islands. Fitzroy's memorandum was prompted by the president of the board of trade's answer (*Hansard* 4th series, CLIX,775) to a question from Sir W.J. Collins asking for the introduction of a new clause into the Merchant Shipping Bill to make it expressly applicable to the Channel Islands; Lloyd George had in fact misleadingly said that 'We could hardly legislate for the Channel Islands. We do not legislate for the Colonies. We approach them, if necessary, to bring

143. (b) GUERNSEY: ANSWER OF *JURATS* TO PRIVY COUNCIL,
10 January 1737.[1]

We never pretended to be invested with the power and
authority of making laws, and it is what neither we nor
our predecessors before us, ever assumed; but we beg to
acquaint your Lordships that this Court has always, as
well by the nature of our constitution as by virtue of
sending charters from the Crown and other express orders
in Council, deemed itself authorised and empowered to
make regulations and set down rules and methods as were
necessary for enforcing and putting in due execution the
laws of the Island.[2]

143. (c). JERSEY: ORDER IN COUNCIL, 20 April 1774.[3]
...His Majesty, taking the said Report into consider-

---

their legislation into line with our own'.
1. P.P. 1847-8 XXVII (945) p.xii. The *jurats* had been asked to define
the powers of the Royal Court.
2. i.e. that their powers were executive rather than legislative. The
commissioners in 1848 (*ibid*.p.xi-xii) commented that the Royal Court
in Guernsey, acting in *Chefs Plaids*,had 'very limited' legislative
functions. It had the initiative and could alone submit proposed Acts
to the States which would require confirmation by the privy council.
Its temporary directives, or *Ordonnances*, had force without confirmation by the States, the governor or the privy council, but it was
incapable of passing *ordonnances* 'which militate against any Order
in Council' or any other superior authority. As for the States, though
they performed no continuous or indispensable legislative functions,
they were probably 'constituted on the model of the *Trois Etats* in
Normandy:the bailiff and *jurats* corresponding with the *noblesse*;the
rectors...answering to the clergy; and the *douzaines*,an elected
body in each parish, representing the *tiers état*'. In Guernsey however the Royal Court continued to have some legislative powers and
did not lose them to the States.
By contrast commissioners in 1860 (P.P. 1859-0 XXI pp.38-9) found the
Royal Court in Jersey had been long regarded as 'the only legislative
body'. At first the king as duke made laws without consulting anybody;
thereafter he seems sometimes to have consulted bailiff and *jurats*;
at others also the rectors and constables in the States. Since the
end of the sixteenth century 'laws were passed sometimes by the Royal
Court and sometimes by the States, both kinds being deemed of equal
authority if sanctioned by the Sovereign in Council and duly registered in the Island'. By-laws, or *reglements*, however, operative for
up to three years, could be passed without approval of the privy council. The Code of 1771 removed the legislative power in Jersey from
the Royal Court and gave it to the States.
2. *Jersey Prison Board*, II, p.531. Petitions had been received complaining against the levying of certain duties by the Jersey States.
The law officers had been asked for their opinion and the council
now made this declaration in accordance with their report.
3.An order in council of 4 July 1777 directed the States of Jersey to
impose taxes for the maintenance of service widows and orphans,and to
register the order forthwith. (*ibid*. p.534).

ation, was pleased, by and with the advice of His Privy
Council, to approve thereof and accordingly to declare
That the States of the said Island of Jersey have no authority to pass any Act or Law imposing the said duties and
taxes mentioned in the said Acts for laying a duty on rum
and gin imported into the said island, without application having been made to His Majesty for that purpose and
His Majesty's consent and approbation being first had and
obtained; and His Majesty is hereby pleased to declare
the said Acts imposing the several duties and taxes...to
be null and void in themselves and to order that the Bailiff and *Jurats* of the Royal Court...do cause the said Acts
to be erased out of the records of the said Island; and
that none may pretend ignorance of His Majesty's pleasure
hereby signified, the said Bailiff and *Jurats* are to cause
this order to be forthwith registered and published in
due form in the said Island.

143. (d) JERSEY: REPRESENTATION AND PETITION OF THE STATES, 17
July 1830.[1]
   [They protested against an order in council of 28 June 1830
   which imposed fines on members of the *States* for non-attendance.
   This was a precedent which might undermine 'their very existence
   as the legislative body of this Island'.]
   The *States* with all due deference and respect conceive
that it would be highly dangerous to their ancient rights
and liberties that the existing laws might be changed or
new ones enacted on the private suggestion from the Lieutenant-Governor without the knowledge or intervention of
the assembly of the States who are the constitutional
representatives of the inhabitants of this Island. The
States would by this means be deprived of the initiating
power which they have hitherto possessed and the Lieutenant-Governor invested with it. The *States* while they most
dutifully acknowledge the supreme and controlling power
of His Most Excellent Majesty-in-Council with respect to
all laws and ordinances whatsoever concerning this Island
do humbly crave permission to claim as one of their most
ancient precious privileges, the rights of originating
and discussing all Laws intended to be made for the Government of the Island previous to their receiving the
Royal Sanction ....
   [This had been confirmed in the order in council of 28 March
   1771.]

143. (e) *IN RE THE STATES OF JERSEY*,30 November 1853.[2]
   [The *States* under the presidency of the bailiff had protested
   against the orders in council of 1852 that]...the *States* of

1. *Jersey Prison Board* II p.703. The Lord Lieutenant was recalled.
2. 9 Moore P.C. 185. The question concerned whether the Crown by
order in council, sent in 1852 to the Lieutenant Governor of Jersey
by the Secretary of State for the Home Department, could without concurrence of the States of Jersey, make law.

Jersey have from time immemorial existed as a legislative
body and have been recognised as such by innumerable Charters and Orders of Her Majesty's royal predecessors. The
legislative powers of the *States* of Jersey have...been
regarded as of the most ample description, in so far as
concerns laws which were to take effect in the Island;
the right to initiate which has been left to the *States*
as the body most likely to be conversant with the wants
and customs of the people of Jersey. The power of self-
government under the superior control of the Sovereign
in Council has not only constantly been recognised, but
the confidence thus reposed in them has ever been met by
the inhabitants of Jersey with feelings of gratitude and
unfailing loyalty. That the *States* would further observe
that, while one of the most important privileges of the
Island is that of not being subject to be taxed by the
Imperial Parliament in which it is unrepresented, no tax
can be imposed upon the people of Jersey, except with the
consent of the *States* by whom they are represented....

 [No record of taxation without previous consent of the *States*
was known; the property qualification for the franchise was low
enough to enable a much larger proportion of inhabitants to vote
than in comparable English boroughs; the right of the *States* to
initiate legislation had been confirmed by orders in council,
e.g. 28 March 1771; and frequently, instead of expressly applying
a British statute, the *States* had been invited to legislate along
similar lines. The orders concerning a new police force and new
judicial procedures, which they rejected, would subvert their
political and municipal institutions and impose taxation, unsol-
icited by the inhabitants of Jersey. The proximity of France meant
sufficiently heavy tax burdens on the islanders for defence anyway.

 Counter petitions had asked not only for the Crown to insist
on its orders, but also for reforms of the Island's constitution,
judiciary and administration. They argued that the *States* had
acted unlawfully in refusing to register the orders in council.
They stated that, by an order in council of 17 December 1679,
Acts of Parliament, which expressly named the Island, could be
sent to Jersey to be registered and published forthwith.[1] The
States, they said]
...are not a legislative body, but only a Common Council,
having never been incorporated by Royal Charter, and therefore did not possess any inherent right to originate law,
or impose taxes or to exercise any legislative functions
whatsoever save except when Her Majesty might be pleased
from time to time to grant them permission to enact a law
on a special application made to Her Majesty for that
purpose, defining beforehand the purport of the law or
tax they might wish to enact.....[They affirmed that] the
whole legislative authority, both initiative and final,
on all matters and things left unprovided for by Act of

---

1. Normally Parliament empowers the Crown to negotiate for the extension of its laws to the islands.

Parliament, was vested in Her Majesty in right of Her
Majesty's sovereignty ....
    [The States had replied that they had been a legislature from
time immemorial and adduced a letter of Edward III (1351), charters of Henry VII (1495) and Elizabeth (1561), various patents,
ordinances, orders in council and history books on early German,
French and English Parliaments.
    In judgement the privy council advised that, though the orders
in council were well calculated to improve the administration of
justice in Jersey, yet there were serious doubts whether, without
the assent of the States, the queen's prerogative could validly
legislate, at least in a matter involving taxation; and therefore
it recommended that the queen should approve, in place of the orders, the six Acts passed by the States in August 1852.][1]

(g) GUILDS

    As well as establishing subordinate jurisdictions within the realm
of England and the dominions, the medieval Crown delegated substant-

---

1.Similarly in *In re the States of Guernsey*,14 Moore P.C. 368 in April
1861, the amalgamation of the offices of *Controle de la Reine* and
Procureur de la Reine by the Home Secretary without sanction of the
States of Guernsey was held legal only by order in council with local
registration.
The question of the validity of an order in council for the Channel
Islands without the consent of their own States has not been expressly decided.
The States had claimed – on the basis of the 1679 order, the 1771 code
and even earlier precedents – that registration of an order-in-council
was substantive and not merely procedural: it implied necessary consent. When on 27 June 1891 an order appointed the lieutenant-governor
as chairman of the Jersey Prison Board, this assertion of the Crown's
authority to enhance the position of its representative at the expense
of the bailiff was challenged as an attack upon 'immemorial constitutional rights': the States had sought to limit the function of the
lieutenant-governor strictly to military affairs and to secure all
civil responsibilities for the bailiff, but recently in 1890 had suffered a setback in their attempt to block the royal pardon for Marie
Daniel. In the *Prison Board case* before the judicial committee of
the privy council, the attorney-general for Jersey, putting the argument for the Crown's legislative powers, denied the claims of the
States to limit them: the States were not a provincial parliament,
but only 'a municipal corporation or common council' with limited powers to make provisional ordinances only. The J.C.P.C. however did
not decide on the general point of the Crown's right to legislate
without registration, but advised the Crown to recall the 1891 order
in council which had materially altered the previous arrangements for
the Prison Board. There is a strong presumption that, if the J.C.P.C.
had had to decide on the main constitutional issue, it must have affirmed the Crown's right to legislate, but by avoiding that decision
it permitted a continuing evolution of the island's autonomy.

ial powers of self-administration to a variety of lesser subordinate
bodies - to boroughs and to colleges,for example. Four are represented in this volume; guilds and corporations in this section: the
Calais Staple and the Merchant Adventurers above in Section I A (2).
In each case the Crown granted powers which, though extensive, were
strictly limited in that the rules made by these bodies must not be
repugnant to statute, the prerogative or the common law. The Crown
had extended its protection to guildsmen, granting them a monopoly,
the right to exclude interlopers, and the privilege of making their
own conditions of trade. When merchants ventured abroad they sought
to secure from the rulers of foreign countries within which they
traded,'*capitulations*' - heads of agreement - which might, for example, authorise them to establish staples, depots or factories in
which their resident agents would enjoy a jurisdiction or self-
government under their own laws [see for example, the rights permitted to merchants in the Turkish and Chinese empires, and the preamble
to the Foreign Jurisdiction Act (53 & 54 Vict. cap.37, 1890)]. The
importance of these corporate bodies to the theme of this book is
that in the sixteenth century the Crown used the common elements in
the charters they had granted as a model for the grants of authority
made first to chartered trading enterprises, and then to chartered
colonizing companies.   The constitutional status of at least the
corporate American colonies (as distinct from those granted in fief)
thus had a double parentage: principles established in relation to
the dominions of the Crown within the British Isles and those relating to chartered corporate bodies. Some of the later confusion
concerning the precise constitutional rights of the colonists stemmed
from this dual parentage: were colonies provinces like Ireland, or
municipalities like London, or companies like the Muscovy Company?

   In general therefore the organisation of colonial governments
overseas later owed much to the precedents provided first by the
guilds and then by the chartered companies: the classical triptych
of governor, council and assembly developed from the director, assistants and the general court of shareholders (see F. Madden 'Not
for export' in *The first British Commonwealth,*ed. Hillmer and Wigley
1980).

   In particular the limitation that by-laws made by guilds would be
valid only if they were not <u>repugnant</u> to the law of England and ·
could be declared null and void by the courts if they were, was incorporated as a matter of routine in the grants to companies and
proprietors later. The ambiguity of the phrase remained until the
Colonial Laws Validity Act (28 & 29 Vict. cap.63) of 1865: did 'the
law of England' mean parliamentary statute, or Crown legislation or
instruction, or the decisions in English courts? Did it include
them all?

144. ACT RESTRAINING UNLAWFUL ORDERS MADE BY GUILDS (15 Hen.VI
                        cap.6) 1437.[1]
   Item, since the masters, wardens and men of several
gilds, fraternities and other companies incorporate dwelling in divers parts of the realm, often under guise of

---

1. The preamble to this Act was in identical terms with a petition
from municipal officials who found (as, indeed, in 1376 predecessors

rules and regulations and other terms in general words to
them granted and confirmed by charters and letters patent
of the ancestors of our Lord the King, make among themselves sundry unlawful and unreasonable ordinances as
well of such things whereof the cognizance, punishment
and correction appertain solely to the King, to the lords
of franchises and other persons, and whereby our said Lord
the King and others are deprived of their franchises and
profits, as well of the things which oftentimes in confed-
eracy are made for their own profit and the general disadvantage of the people. Even so, our Lord the King, with
the advice and consent of the Lords spiritual and temporal
aforesaid, and at the prayer of the aforesaid Commons, has
ordained by the authority of the same Parliament That the
masters...between now and the feast of St. Michael next
coming, bring all their letters patent and charters and
have them entered on record before the chief governors of
the cities, burghs and towns where such gilds, fraternities and companies are. And has also ordained and has
prohibited, by the authority aforementioned, the making
or executing henceforth by any such masters...of any ordinance leading to the disinheritance or diminution of the
franchises of the King or others, or against the common
profit of the people, or of any other ordinance or charge
unless it be discussed and approved as good and reasonable by the justices of the peace or chief governors aforesaid and before them entered on record and by them subsequently revoked and repealed if it be found and proved
by them unlawful or unreasonable... [on pain of losing the
legislating powers conferred in their charter, and a fine of £10 for
each conviction of *ultra vires*.]

145. CHARTER FROM EDWARD IV INCORPORATING THE BARBER-SURGEONS OF
                                   LONDON, 1462.[1]
    [London barber-surgeons were undergoing various difficulties,
    and the 'ignorance, negligence and stupidity' of unskilled barbers
    had meant that many of the king's liegemen have 'gone the way of
    all flesh'.]

---

had complained) that grants and immunities given in charters hindered
them in the performance of their duties.
The later Statute of Liveries, 1504 (19 Hen.VII cap.7) recited this
complaint of 1437 and referred to the unlawful behaviour of the guilds
in fixing prices, though no evidence has been found, either before or
after this Act, of ordinances claiming to regulate prices on guild
authority alone. The Act of 1504 enacted that guild by-laws should
be 'examined and approved' by the chancellor, the treasurer of England and the chief justices: in many boroughs, however, endorsement
of such by-laws continued to be by municipal authorities, local governors and J.Ps. rather than by the royal officers of state and
chief justices.
1. S. Young,*Annals of the Barber-Surgeons*, (1890) pp. 56-7.

We...have, at the humble request of our aforesaid beloved, honest and freemen of the said Mystery of Barbers in
our said city, granted to them That the said Mystery, and
all men of the Mystery aforesaid, may be in deed and name
one body and one perpetual Community, and That two Princip-
als of the said Community may, with the consent of twelve
persons, or at least eight of the said Community who are
best skilled in the Mystery of Surgery, every year elect
and make out of the Community two Masters or Governors of
the utmost skill, to superintend, rule and govern the Mystery and Community aforesaid and all men of the said Mystery,
and of the businessmen of the same for ever....
    [They might have a common seal and hold property in fee and per-
    petuity *etc.*]
And that the said Masters or Governors and Community...
may lawfully and honestly assemble themselves, and make
statutes and ordinances for the wholesome government, superintendence, and correction of the said Mystery, according to the exigency of the necessity, as often and whenever it may be requisite, lawfully and unpunishably, without leave or hinderance of us...or servants of us...:
Provided that such statutes or ordinances are not in any
ways contrary to the laws and customs of our Kingdom of
England[1]....
    [The Masters were to superintend all City surgeons, *etc.*]

146. ACT CONFIRMING LETTERS PATENT OF HENRY VI TO ORMOND AND OTHERS
        TO FOUND A GUILD OF SHOEMAKERS IN DUBLIN, 4 December 1465.[2]
    [At the prayer of Robert Nervyle, Master of the Guild of the
    Blessed Virgin Mary, and other shoemakers who had asked for a
    parliamentary confirmation of the licence granted by Henry VI to
    the lord lieutenant, James, Earl of Ormond, and others of the
    King's Irish council to found a guild.]
    ...it is ordained, established, and enacted by author-
ity of the said Parliament...that the letters patent, the
tenor whereof hereinafter follows...be accepted, approved,
ratified and confirmed in all points, granting...That...
they may have and hold use and enjoy freely, quietly and
with impunity all and every grant, free gift, liberty and
privilege, according to the tenor, form and effect of the
said patent for ever; any statute...to the contrary not-

---

1. This provision, which was also included in grants to merchant adventurers overseas, became the rule of repugnancy: that is, that colonial law would be invalid if considered repugnant to the law of
England. This rule was limited by the Colonial Laws Validity Act,1865
(28 & 29 Vict. cap.63) to statutes of Parliament which by 'express
words and necessary intendment' applied to a colony, and was made
inapplicable to the laws of the Dominions by the Statute of Westminster, 1931 (22 Geo.V cap.4).
2. H. F. Berry (ed.) *Statutes* (Ed.IV) pp. 333–41. For greater assurance the Lancastrian letters patent to the shoemakers were confirmed
in the Irish Parliament: Ormond, a Lancastrian supporter, had been
executed, and the earl of Desmond was now deputy.

withstanding ····

[The letters patent were recited to the effect that Henry, King of England and France and Lord of Ireland had] ...granted and given licence to them...as far as in us lies, that they or those of them who shall survive, to the glory of God and the Blessed Virgin Mary, a Fraternity or Guild of the Art of Shoemakers of our city of Dublin....And that the brethren of the fraternity or guild aforesaid so begun, founded, commenced and entered into, may every year have two Masters from among themselves who shall be of the Art of Shoemakers, for the rule, government and superintendence of such Fraternity or Guild....

[The guild might make ordinances, acquire land, and punish defaulters.]

...And that such Masters for the time being, by the advice of the more reputable Brethren of the Art aforesaid, shall have full power to elect, ordain and successively constitute, other Masters from year to year, to have the rule, government, and superintendence of such Fraternity or guild, and of the Art aforesaid...And them and each of them from time to time, when it shall be needful and necessary, from the aforesaid offices, to remove and exonerate, and others of the Art aforesaid in their place...to substitute. And that they may have and use a common seal to be employed for the business and acts relating to the said Fraternity or Guild, which seal shall remain under the custody of the said Masters for the time being. And also that the Masters aforesaid and their successors, Masters, who for the time shall be, for that Fraternity or Guild, and for the lands, tenements, rents, services, possessions, goods and chattels of the said Fraternity or Guild, in whatsoever actions, causes, plaints, demands and pleas, as well real and personal as mixed, of whatsoever kind or nature they be, by the name of the Masters of the Fraternity or Guild of the Blessed Virgin Mary of Dublin, before secular and ecclesiastical judges whatsoever, may implead and be impleaded, and also to answer and be answered, shall be able and in duty bound...And that the Masters and Brethren of the said Fraternity o r Guild may meet...to make lawful and honest ordinances, to the glory of God and honour of the Blessed Virgin Mary, for the good government of the said Fraternity or Guild from year to year and from time to time; ...Masters of the Fraternity or Guild aforesaid, may have full cognizance of all manner of pleas, trespasses, debts, accounts, contracts, agreements, deceits, falsities and misprisions, between shoemaker and shoemaker, shoemaker and his servant or apprentice, and between any other person and any person of the Art of the shoemaker aforesaid ····

[They were empowered to hear complaints and to impose fines: 'the amercements accruing in this behalf'were to be levied and collected by the officials of the guild 'for the use and profit of the Fraternity or guild'.]

147. CHARTER FROM ELIZABETH I TO THE CLOTHIERS OF WORCESTER, 23
September 1590.[1]

....whereas by the humble petition of our wellbeloved of
the Misteryes or Faculties of weavers, walkers, and clothiers of our citty of Worcester, We are given to understand that the trade and affaires of the said Misteries
and Faculties, through default of good and provident government, oversight, and correc'con, are many tymes insuf-
fitiently done, as well to our prejudice as also in dec-
eipt of our lieges and subjects, We being very unwilling
to meete with such prejudice and deceite to come or be
hereafter...doe will, graunt, and ordaine by these presents, for us, our heirs and successors, That the said
Misteries and Faculties of weavers, walkers, and clothiers, within our said citty of Worcester and the liberties
thereof...for ever hereafter shall be, and may bee, in
deede, fact, and name, one body corporate and politick
really and fully in all things....
      [They were granted corporate legal rights, a seal *etc*. The
    first master, four wardens and thirty assistants were named.]
      ...it shall and may be lawfull to the said Master,
Wardens, and comonalty...to have, retaine, and appoint a
certaine Councellhouse within the presinct and jurisdicc'-
ons of the said citty; and that the same Master, Wardens,
and Assistance (*sic*) or the greater parte of them for the
time being, as often as to them it shall seeme fitt and
necessary, may and shall have by these presents for ever,
full power and authority, from tyme to tyme, to call within the said house a certaine Court or convocation of the
same Master, Wardens, and Assistants...to treate, debate,
consult, and diserne of the statutes, lawes, articles,
and ordynances of the said Misteryes and Faculties aforesaid, and the good order, state and government thereof,
touching and concerning, according to their sound discretions of the greater parte of them for the time being assembled: and thereupon from time to time to frame, constitute, ordaine, make, and establishe such Lawes, Statutes, Ordynances, and Constitutions, soe as they be not
repugnant nor contrary to the laws and statutes of our
realme of England, as unto them...shall seeme to be good,
holesome, profitable, honest and necessary, as well for
the good order and government of the said Master, Wardens,
and comonalty, as for the publick good and com'on utyli-
tie of the said misteryes and faculties, or any of them,
as for the direccon and declaracon why and in what manner
and order the said master and wardens, assistants and
comonalty, for the time being, in their offices, functions, misteryes, causes, and busines, shall bear, behave,
and use themselves.... [Powers of punishment were alsc granted.]
All which Lawes, statutes, ordynances, and constitutions
...We will to be observed, under the paynes and penalties
therein conteyned, so as not-withstanding that they be not

---

1. V.Green,*History and antiquities...of Worcester* (1796)II App. pp.
lxxi - lxxv.

repugnant nor contrary to the lawes and statutes of our
realme of England....
    [Master, wardens and assistants were to elect annually the
    Master and wardens for the ensuing year. 'Corporall oaths' were
    to be administered. Municipal officials were to be 'in all things
    aiding and assisting' to the Master and wardens.]
    We will and graunt...that these our letters patents be
in and by all things good, firme, forceable, and effectuall in the law, according to the true intent thereof:
the Statute...in the XIXth year of the raigne of...Henry
VIIth...or any other statute, ordaynance, priviledges,
proclamac'ons, or restraints, concerning the premisses,
or any parcell thereof, or any other thing, cause, or
matter to be contrary thereof made, ordayned, provided,
or proclaymed, in any wise notwithstanding.[1]

148. *THE CASE OF THE TAILORS OF IPSWICH* (Mich.12 Jac.I), 1614.[2]
    [The Masters and Guild of the Tailors had brought an action for
    debt against William Sheninge, claiming that the royal charter
    had empowered the guild with full power to make reasonable laws
    and impose fines, and that 19 Hen.VII cap.7[3] had enacted procedure
    for such legislation and restricted it only if 'contrary to the
    King's prerogative and to the common profit of the people'. Shen-
    ing had practised the trade of tailor, though not admitted by the
    guild and not having paid the admission fee. It was resolved]
1.   That at the common law no man could be prohibited from
working in any lawful trade, for the law abhors idleness,
the mother of all evil...and especially in young men who
ought in their youth (which is their seed time) to learn
lawful sciences and trades which are profitable to the
commonwealth...and thereby [5 Eliz.I cap. 4][4] it appears
that without an Act of Parliament none can be in any manner restrained from working in any lawful trade....
2.   That the said restraint of the defendent for more than
the said Act of 5 Eliz. has made, was against law; and
therefore foreasmuch as the Statute has not restrained him,
who has served as an apprentice for seven years, from exercising the trade of tailor, the said ordinance cannot prohibit him from exercising his trade...for these are against
the liberty and freedom of the subject...and all this is
against the common law and the commonwealth: but ordinances for the good order and government of men of trades and

---

1. In granting the court of the company such power in complete disregard of the Statute of Liveries (19 Hen.VII cap.7), the Crown was certainly endowing it with considerable privilege and powers of self-
government.
2. 11 Coke Repts. 53b. The necessity for approval of by-laws by royal
officials and chief justices did not prevent courts declaring them null
and void if repugnant to English law.
3. See above, footnote 1.
4. This Act prohibited the practice of a craft or mystery without an
apprecticeship of seven years; but Sheninge had served such a period
of apprenticeship.

mysteries are good, but not to restrain any one in his lawful mystery....

4.   It was resolved that the statute of 19 Hen.VII cap. 7 doth not corroborate any of the ordinances made by any corporation which are so allowed and approved as the statute speaks, but leaves them to be affirmed as good, or disaffirmed as unlawful by the law.[1]

---

1. See similarly *Guild of the stationers of London versus Salisbury* (Comb. 221.) in 1694 where a by-law of the guild, even signed by the lord chancellor, was challenged, though the decision was inconclusive, the king's bench 'inclining' for the defendant but advising him to submit to the company.
Cf. the issue relating to delegated legislation 'as if enacted in the Act', in *Lockwood v. the Patent Agents*, 1894 A.C. 347.

(B) THE ESTABLISHMENT OF COLONIES AND OTHER ENTERPRISES OVERSEAS BEFORE 1641

(1) THE ROYAL PREROGATIVE AS

A SOURCE OF AUTHORITY

The special feature which distinguished English colonization before 1760 from much that followed later was that all the early American colonies were established by authority of the Crown, not of Parliament. Prerogative grants in this first period took one of two forms, both deriving from practices and precedents that have been illustrated in Section A above: grants in fief, or corporate charters. The pattern of American colonial government as it existed until 1776 was largely determined by the nature of these instruments delegating the Crown's authority to proprietors or corporate bodies.

(a) GRANTS IN FIEF

The delegation of an authority to explore, annex and govern distant dependencies demanded increasing care and sophistication during this period. The favoured individuals were vassals of the Crown: until the grant to Baltimore 1632 (when there was a change to freehold tenure : No.154) they owed the king homage and knight's service *in capite*. The Crown was interested in, and hopeful for, some return for its favours over and above the token of vassalage (white horse, arrows, falcons etc.): the ever-expected discovery of gold and silver in the New World, even on the shores of Newfoundland. In granting 'ample powers' on the frontiers of empire as on the Scottish borders to those it was hoped were trustworthy, the kings followed consciously the precedent of the palatinate of Durham. Moreover, the delegation of a power of law-making to proprietors was limited by the rule of repugnancy derived from borough and guild [see Section I A (4)g.] and the association (in some form and time at the proprietor's discretion) of representative local consent from colonial freeholders.

149. LETTERS PATENT FROM HENRY VII TO JOHN CABOT, 5 March 1496.[1]
Be it knowen that We have given and granted,...to our welbeloved John Cabot citizen of Venice, to Lewis, Sebast-

---

1. Printed in F.N. Thorpe,*Federal and State Constitutions* Vol.I pp. 46-7. Giovanni Caboto of Genoa, and then of Venice, had failed to obtain support for a search for the North-West passage in Lisbon and

ian, and Santius, sonnes of the sayd John, and their
heirs...full and free authority, leave, and power to saile
to all parts, countreys,and seas of the East, of the West,
and of the North, under our banners and ensignes, with
five ships of what burthen or quantity soever they be,
and as many mariners or men as they will have with them
in the sayd ships, upon their owne proper costs and charges, to seeke out, discover, and finde whatsoever isles,
countreys, regions or provinces of the heathen and infidels whatsoever they be, and in what part of the world soever they be, which before this time have bene unknown to
all Christians:[1] We have granted to them,...and have
given them licence to set up our banners and ensignes in
every village, towne, castle, isle, or maine land of them
newly found. And that the aforesayd John and his sonnes,
or their heires and assignes may subdue, occupy and possesse all such townes, cities, castles, and isles of them
found, which they can subdue, occupy and possess, as our
vassals, and lieutenants, getting unto us the rule, title,
and jurisdiction of the same....Yet so that the aforesayd
John...be holden and bounden of all the fruits, profits,
gaines, and commodities growing of such navigation, for
every their voyage, as often as they shall arrive at our
port of Bristoll (at which port they shall be bound and
holden onely to arrive) all manner of necessary costs and
charges by them made, being deducted, to pay unto us in
wares or money the fift[h] part of the capitall gaine so
gotten. We giving and granting unto them...that they
shall be free from all paying of customes of all and singular such merchandize as they shall bring with them from
those places so newlie found.
     And moreover, we have given and granted to them,...that
all the firme lands, isles, villages, townes, castles and
places whatsoever they be that they shall chance to finde,

Seville. He had come to England (where indeed he may have been born)
and had become associated with the merchant adventurers in Bristol
where he settled. With this patent from Henry VII which granted him
rights of discovery, annexation and monopoly, but cautiously involved
the king in no contribution towards the expenses of the venture, he
sailed westward in 1497 with support from the Bristol merchants and
made a landfall in the region of Newfoundland or Cape Breton Island.
The charter from Henry VII, in effect repudiated the bull of Alexander VI, 1493, which purported to divide the unknown world between
Portugal and Spain. Cabot was made vassal of the Crown, paying in
token a share of any net profit to the king.
1. While Christian princes were expected to respect the contemporary
rules of international law (*jus gentium*) relating to their own (and
others) territorial possessions *inter se*, this respect and forbear-
ance did not extend to pagans and infidels who were assumed to be in
a state of permanent warfare with Christendom. This assumption made
in *Calvin's Case* [see No.20] was repudiated by Mansfield (C.J.)in
Campbell v. Hall (1774) as an exception no longer tolerated; 'in
all probability' he declared, it 'arose from the mad enthusiasm of
the Crusades', [see Vol.III].

may not of any other of our subjects be frequented or
visited without the licence of the foresayd John and his
sonnes, and their deputies, under payne of forfeiture as
well of their ships as of all and singular goods of all
them that shall presume to saile to those places so
found....

150. LETTERS PATENT FROM ELIZABETH I TO SIR HUMFREY GILBERT,
11 June 1578.[1]

...we have given and granted, to our trustie and welbeloved servaunt Sir Humfrey Gilbert of Compton, free libertie and licence from time to time to discover, finde,
search out, and view such remote, heathen and barbarous
lands, countreys and territories not actually possessed of
any Christian prince or people, as...shall seeme good: and
the same to have, hold, occupie and enjoy to him...for
ever, with all commodities, jurisdictions and royalties
both by sea and land: and the sayd sir Humfrey and all such
as from time to time by licence of us, our heires and successours, shall goe and travell thither, to inhabite or
remaine there, to build and fortifie at the discretion of
the sayde sir Humfrey...the Statutes or Actes of Parliament
made against Fugitives, or against such as shall depart,
remaine, or continue out of our Realme of England without
licence, or any other Acte, Statute, lawe, or matter whatsoever to the contrary in any wise notwithstanding. And
wee doe likewise...give full authoritie and power to the
saide sir Humfrey...that hee...shall and may...have, take,
and lead in the same voyages, to travell thitherward, and
to inhabite there with him...such and so many of our subjects as shall willingly accompany him and them...with
sufficient shipping, and furniture for their transportat-
ions, so that none of the same persons...shall be specially
restrained by us, our heires and successors. And further,
that he the said Humfrey,...shall have, hold, and occupy
and enjoy...for ever, all the soyle of all such lands...
so to be discovered or possesses...and of all Cities, Castles, Townes and Villages, and places in the same, with

---

1.R. Hakluyt, *The principle navigations, voyages, traffiques and discoveries of the English nation* (1903) VIII pp.17-23. <u>Gilbert</u> had been
an early advocate of plantation in Ireland and had become converted
by the enthusiasm of Dr. John Dee, Richard Hakluyt and others to a
project for the search for a North-West passage and for a settlement
in America; a claim to which on behalf of Britain the strange vis-
ionary Dee had justified, on grounds of a legendary Arthurian empire
in the west. Gilbert sailed west to Newfoundland, raised the English
flag on the shores of St. John's harbour, and was drowned on his way
home. Despite his impetuous zeal, it is doubtful whether St. John's
was to be more than a resort for fishermen or a haven for privateering
against Spanish convoys. There were poor planning and material for a
colony. His half brother, Ralegh, took over his colonising schemes
with a new patent from the queen in almost identical terms (dated
25 March 1584). Though he sought parliamentary confirmation, it only

the rites, royalties and juridictions, as well marine as
other, within the sayd lands or countreys of the seas
thereunto adjoyning, to be had or used with ful power to
dispose thereof, and of every part thereof in fee simple
or otherwise, according to the order of the laws of England, as nere as the same conveniently may be...to any
person then being...within the allegiance of us...paying
unto us for all services, dueties and demaunds, the fift
part of all the care of gold and silver, that from time
to time, and at all times after such discoverie, subduing
and possessing shall be there gotten all which lands,...
shall for ever bee holden by the sayd Sir Humfrey,...of
us, our heires and successours by homage, and by the sayd
payment of the sayd fift part before reserved onely for
all services....

   [Gilbert was empowered to defend himself against unlicensed
   settlers and merchants within 200 leagues of any site occupied
   within the next 6 years]

And for uniting in more prefect league and amitie of such
countreys, landes and territories...with our Realmes of
England and Ireland, and for the better encouragement of
men to this enterprise: We doe by these presents graunt,
and declare, that all such countreys so hereafter to bee
possessed and inhabited as aforesaid, from thenceforth
shall be of the allegiance of us...And wee doe graunt to
the sayd sir Humfrey...and to all and every of them, and
to all and every other person and persons, being of our
allegiance, whose names shall be noted or entred in some
of our courts of Record, within this our Realme of England,
and that with the assent of the sayd sir Humfrey...shall
nowe in this journey for discoverie, or in the second
journey for conquest hereafter, travel to such lands...
that they...being either borne within our sayd Realmes of
England or Ireland, or within any other place within our
allegiance, and which hereafter shall be inhabiting within
any the lands...with such licence as aforesayd, shall, and
may have, and enjoy all the privileges of free denizens
and persons native to England, and within our allegiance:[1]
any law, custome, or usage to the contrary notwithstanding.
   And forasmuch, as upon the finding out, discovering,
and inhabiting of such remote lands...it shall be necessarie for the safetie of all men that shall adventure themselves in those journeys or voiages, to determine to live
together in Christian peace and civill quietness each with
other...Wee...doe give and graunt to the sayd sir Humfrey

passed the Commons. By 1587, at a second attempt a 'true colony' of
settlers was temporarily founded at Roanoke Island in 'Virginia' but
it had disappeared by 1590. The successful planting of the wilderness
required hope, resolution and time. As Francis Bacon wrote in *Of
Plantations* 'planting of countries is like planting of woods; for you
must make account to lose almost twenty years' profit and expect recompense in the end'. Most hopes of profit from empire indeed began
and ended in expectation and little more. 1.Settlers would take the
'rights of free-born Englishmen' with them: [see also No.19].

...That he shall and may from time to time for every hereafter within the sayd mentioned remote lands and countreys,
and in the way by the Seas thither, and from thence, have
full and meere power and authoritie to correct, punish,
pardon, governe and rule by their...good discretions and
policies, as well in causes capitall or criminall, as
civill, both marine and other, all such our subjects and
others, as shall from time to time hereafter adventure
themselves in the sayd journeys or voyages habitative or
possessive, or that shall at any time hereafter inhabite
any such lands...or that shall abide within two hundred
leagues of any the sayd place or places, where the sayd
sir Humfrey...shall inhabite within six yeeres next ensuing the date hereof, according to such statutes, lawes
and ordinances, as shall be by him the said sir Humfrey
...devised or established for the better government of
the said people as aforesayd: so always that the sayd
statutes, lawes and ordinances may be as neere as conveniently may, agreeable to the forme of the lawes and
pollicy of England:[1] and also, that they be not against
the true Christian faith or religion now professed in
the church of England, nor in any wise to withdraw any
of the subjects or people of those lands or places from
the allegiance of us...as their immediate Soveraignes
under God ....

   [The privy council might grant licences to sir Humfrey to import from the realm goods and necessaries, any Act to the contrary
   notwithstanding.
   If Gilbert and his associates antagonised any foreign Christian
   prince and failed to make restitution, then they should be considered 'out of our protection and allegiance, and free for all
   Princes and others to pursue with hostilitie as being not our
   Subjects'.]

151. NEWFOUNDLAND: LETTERS PATENT FROM JAMES I TO SIR GEORGE CALVERT
                         FOR 'AVALON',7 April 1623.[2]
   ...Whereas our Right Trusty and well beloved Councillor, Sir George Calvert Knight, our Principal Secretary
of State, being excited with a laudable and pious Zeal, to
Enlarge the Extents of the Christian World and therewithall of our Empire and Dominion Hath heretofore to his

_____

1. For this rule of repugnancy see also, for example, Nos. 145,148
and subsequent grants to Calvert *etc.* Nos. 151,153,154,155.
2. Public Record Office: Colonial Office 195/ 1 pp.1-10. Some landed
proprietors in England saw land overseas as a more highly regarded
investment than trade. Though undergoing substantial changes, the
countryside and society of contemporary rural England were manorial:
the lords of the manor still exercised jurisdiction and administration,
and service tenures were not finally abolished till 1660. Calvert had
already purchased lands from the London and Bristol Company in Newfoundland and had sent out colonists to settle at Ferryland. By this
charter from the king he was confirmed in his purchase and his 'palatinate' extended to Placentia in the west and Conception Bay in the
north. His dislike of the climate when he visited 'Avalon' led him

great Cost purchased a certain Region or Territory hereafter described in a Country of ours situate in the Western parts of the world commonly called <u>Newfoundland</u>, not
yet husbanded or planted, though in some parts thereof
inhabited by certain Barbarous people wanting the Knowledge of Almighty God. And intending now to transport
thither a very great and ample Colony of the English
nation,Hath humbly besought our Kingly Majesty to Give,
Grant and confirm all the said Region with certain Privileges and Jurisdictions requisite for the good Government
and State of the said Colony and Territory to him, his
Heirs and Assigns for ever...
     [the king specified the geographical limits of the land granted,
     adjacent islands, fisheries and mines *etc*.] ...together with
all and singular the like, and as ample Rights, Jurisdictions, privileges, prerogatives, royalties, liberties, Immunities and Franchises whatsoever, as well by Sea as by
Land, within the Region, Isles and Limits aforesaid. To
have, exercise, use and enjoy the same as any Bishop of
Durham within the Bishopric or County Palatine of Durham,[1]
in our Kingdom of England hath at any time heretofore had,
held, used or enjoyed or of Right ought, or might have had,
held, used or enjoyed.
     And him the said Sir George Calvert, his Heirs and
assigns, We do by these presents, for us, our heirs and
Successors, Make, Create and Constitute, the true and
absolute Lords and Proprietors of the Region aforesaid,
and of all other the premises Saving always unto us, our
Heirs and Successors, the Faith and Allegiance due to us.
     To have, hold,possess, and enjoy the said Region, Isles
and other the premises unto the said Sir George Calvert,
his Heirs and Assigns, to the Sole and proper use and
behalf of him the said Sir George Calvert, his heirs and
Assigns for ever, To be holden to us, our Heirs and Successors, Kings of England *in Capite*, by Knights Service.
And yielding therefore yearly unto us our Heirs and Successors a White Horse, whensoever, and as often as, it
shall happen that we, our Heirs and Successors shall come
into the said territory or region...
     [and one fifth of precious metals. The territories were to be
     erected by 'the fullness of our royal power and prerogative', into
     a province to be called *Avalon*.]
     ...Know Ye therefore moreover, That We for us, our
Heirs and Successors, reposing special Trust and confidence in the Fidelity, Wisdom, Justice and provident circumspection of the said Sir George Calvert, Do Grant free
full and absolute Power, to him and his Heirs for the good
and happy Government of the said Province to Ordain, make,
enact and under his and their Seals to publish any Laws
whatsoever appertaining either unto the public State of
the said Province, or unto the private Utility of particular Persons according unto their best discretions, by

---

to seek openings for colonisation further south [see No.154].
1. See Section 4 (d).

and with the Advice, consent and approbation of the Freeholders, of the said Province or the greater part of them,
whom for the enacting of the said laws, when and as often
as need shall require, We will that the said Sir George
Calvert and his Heirs, shall Assemble in such sort, and
form, as to him shall seem best ....

[The proprietor was authorised to appoint judges and magistrates
with such powers as seem 'most convenient' to him, to pardon all
offences 'whether before Judgement or after', and to exercise the
usual judicial powers.]

Which Laws so as aforesaid to be published, Our Pleasure is, and so we Enjoin, Require and Command, shall be
most absolute and available in Law....Provided nevertheless that the said Laws so stand with reason, and be not
repugnant, nor contrary, but as near as conveniently may
be agreeable to the Laws, Statutes and Customs of this
our Kingdom of England ....

[Emergency powers were granted to the proprietor to legislate
without the consent of the assembled freeholders; except in matters relating to personal and freehold property].

And that all, and singular the Subjects and Liege
people of us, our Heirs and Successors, transported or to
be transported into the said Province and their Children
there already born or hereafter to be born, Be and shall
be Denizens, and Lieges to us, our Heirs and Successors,
and be in all things held, treated, reputed and esteemed,
as Liege and Faithful People of us, our Heirs and Successors born within our Kingdom of England or other our
Dominions, may purchase, receive, take, have, hold buy
or possess and them to occupy and enjoy, give, sell, alien
and bequeath,

As likewise all Liberties, Franchises and privileges
of this our Kingdom of England, freely, quietly and peaceably have and possess, occupy and enjoy as our Liege
people, born or to be born within our said Kingdom of
England, without the Let, Molestation, vexation, trouble
or offence of us, our Heirs and successors whomsoever; Any
Statute, act, Ordinance or Provision to the contrary hereof notwithstanding....

[The powers of self-defence necessary in 'so remote' a country
among savages, 'enemies, pirates and robbers' were entrusted to
Calvert 'as fully and freely as any other Captain General had ever
had:' this included 'full power and authority to exercise the Law
Military' in the event of rebellion or mutiny.

Other matters referred to included the proprietor's right 'to
confer Favour, rewards and Honours'on deserving settlers.]

152. NOVA SCOTIA: PROCLAMATION FOR THE INSTITUTION OF THE ORDER OF
BARONETS, 30 November 1624.[1]

Our Soverane Lord, being formarlie gratiouslie pleased

---

1. D. Masson (ed.) *The register of the privy council of Scotland*
(1896) XIII pp.649-651. The Crown of Scotland was hereby granting
favours to encourage a Scottish colony under Scots law. This proclam-

to erect the heritable honnour and title of ane Baronet,as
ane degree, state, and place nixt and immediatlie following
the younger sones of Vicounts and Lordis Baronis of Parliament, as ane new honnour whairwith to rewaird new meritis;
haveing conferrit the same honnour, place, and dignitie
upoun sindrie of the knights and esquhyiris of England and
Ireland, to thame and thair airis maill for ever, in con-
sideratioun of thair help and assistance toward that happie
and successfull Plantatioun of Ulster in Ireland, to the
grite strenth of that his Majesties Kingdome, increase of
his Hienes revenues, and help to manie of his Majesties
goode subjects; and Quhairas our said Soverane Lord, being
no les hopefull of the Plantatioun of <u>New Scotland</u> in the
narrest pairt of America, alreadie discovered and surveyed
be some of the subjects of his Majesties Kingdome of Scotland...and for that conceaving that manie his Majesties subjects of this his ancient Kingdome ...will not be deficient
in anie thing quhilk may ather advance his Majesties royall
intentioun towards that plantatioun...the samyn being ane
fitt, warrandable, and convenient means to disburding this

---

ation was made at the Mercat Cross, Edinburgh and elsewhere on St.
Andrew's Day. <u>Sir William Alexander</u>, Scots poet and friend of James
VI, spent much of his time in England, but was an enthusiast for Scottish colonisation. Though previously he had failed with his 'Fife
Adventurers' in an attempt to plant and pacify the Hebrides, he received in September 1621 a grant under the great seal of Scotland for
'Nova Scotia'. This patent, full of the legal pedantry of old Scots
feudal tenures which were to be exported to the colony, made Alexander
hereditary lieutenant-general with powers similar to those of other
proprietors; and settlers' children were granted the same liberties
which they would have had in Scotland or other dominions (presumably
including 'New England') as if they had been born there. The grant
ignored the superior French claim and actual occupation of a small
part of the area: it was moreover extensive, for it included what was
later Cape Breton, Prince Edward Island, New Brunswick and Gaspé as
well as the peninsula of Nova Scotia. (Indeed Cape Breton and P.E.I.
were detached from Alexander's proprietary and transferred as the
barony of Galloway to Robert Gordon in 1622). The first attempts
to colonise - Alexander was particularly anxious to provide opportunities for 'borderers' - were not successful: reconnoitring the coast-
line, but little else. Then,to restore the finances of the adventure,
recourse was made,with the approval of the Scottish privy council, to
the institution of baronets which had previously been used to plant
Ulster. It was proposed that those subscribing 3000 marks and providing six men would be granted hereditary titles and grants of land extending three miles along the coast and ten miles inland. (The provision of six men was later made commutable by a further payment and the
subscription was reduced to 1000 marks). Details of administration and
the organisation of a colony with provinces, diocese, baronies, *etc.*,
were approved by the Scottish privy council when Charles I conferred
a new grant on Alexander in 1625. In three years a colony was planted
at Poutrincourt's previous site, Port Royal, in Acadia, and very briefly a smaller one on Cape Breton under Lord Ocheltree. In 1630 after

his Majesties said ancient Kingdome of all such younger
brether and meane gentlemen, quhois moyens ar short of
thair birth, worth, or myndis, who otherwayes most be
troublesome to the houssis and freinds from whence they
are descendit[1] (the common ruynes of most of the ancient
families) or betak thameselffis to forren warrs or baisser
chifts...gif transplantit to the said cuntrey of New Scotland...to be governed by the laws of this his ancient Kingdome of Scotland; and our said Soverane Lord being most
willing and desyreous that this his said ancient Kingdome
participate of all such otheris honnouris and dignities as
ar erected in anie of his Majesties other kingdomes, to
the effect that the gentrie of this his Hienes said ancient Kingdome of Scotland may both haif there dew abroad
amongs the subjects of otheris his Majesties kingdomes,
and at home amongs thameselffis according to thair degree
and dignitie; as alsua his Majestie, being most gracious-
lie pleasit to confer the said honnour of Heretable Baronet as ane speciall mark of his Heighnes princelie favour
upoun the knights and esquyires of principall respect for
thair birth, worth and fortouns, togidder with large pro-
portionis of landis within the said countrey of New Scotland, who salbe generouslie pleasit to set furth some men
in his Heines royall colonie nixt going thither for that
plantatioun; Thairfore...it is his Majesties princelie
pleasure and express resulutioun to mak and creat the
nomber of ane hundreth Heretable Baronettis of this his
Hienes Kingdome of Scotland be patentes under his Majesties grite seale thairof, who and thair airis maill sall
haif place and praecedencie nixt and immediatlie after
the youngest sone of the Vicounts and Lordis Barouns of
Parliament, and the additioun of the word Sir to be prae-
fixed to thair propper name, and the style and the title
of Baronet subjoyned to the surname of everie ane of thame
and thair airis maill[2]....

153. THE CARIBBEES: LETTERS PATENT FROM CHARLES I TO THE EARL OF
CARLISLE, 2 July 1627.[3]

[Carlisle had expressed a desire to found a colony in the Cari-

---

a brief joint venture with David Kirke, Alexander conveyed his rights
to a French protestant, de la Tour. Two years later by the Treaty of
St. Germain-en-Laye Charles I restored the territory (along with Quebec) to France.

1. An early example of the desire to export misfits from a metropolitan society. See later the transportation of convicts and the 'shov-
elling out of paupers'.

2. The lands of the baronets were to be held in *seisin* of the esplan-
ade of Edinburgh Castle. Sir W. Alexander, earl of Stirling, held his
grant of the king as of the Crown of Scotland. Similarly in 1634 Sir
Edmund Plowden obtained from Strafford as Irish lord chancellor a
grant on the Delaware as of the Crown of Ireland. But Plowden's palatinate in 'New Albion' proved as brief and insubstantial as Alexander's was in 'Nova Scotia'.

3. C.O. 29/1 pp.1-11. In the West Indies there was much confusion of

bbee islands].
   ...Now he hath humbly requested, That that whole Region
or Countrye [of the Caribees listed] should be indued with
certaine Priviledges and Jurisdictions, and sound Govern-

---

claims between rival colonisers, merchants and noble patrons, Thomas
Warner, who had made temporary settlements in St. Christopher in 1622
and 1624, was granted a royal commission on 13 September 1625 as governor of four Leeward islands (St. Kitts, Nevis, Montserrat and Barbados) but with no title to the land itself. Meanwhile, since Sir
William Courteen and his associates - a private company without a
charter - had begun (their petition for a royal grant in the *terra
australis* of South America having failed) to colonise Barbados, Warner
sought through the necessary mediation of a noble middleman this patent which the king instead granted to the spendthrift earl of Carlisle, James Hay, for a proprietary palatinate in the Caribbees. It
enumerated the islands beginning with St. Kitts and expressly included both Barbados and the barren rock of Barbuda with which it might
have been (and possibly had been) confused. Thus deprived of a title
for his colony, Courteen obtained, similarly through the good offices
of the earl of Pembroke, a patent dated 25 February 1628 which included Barbados together with the Windward islands of Trinidad and
Tobago. Following the investigation by the lord keeper and a suit
in Chancery, however, Carlisle's patent (which had been amplied on
7 April 1628 by a grant of all customs for ten years) was confirmed
a year later and firmly included Barbados under four different spel-
lings. Though the Courteen group in the island seized the Carlisle
governor, Charles Wolverston, and temporarily reinstated John Powell
as their own, by 1630 Carlisle had apparently triumphed both in
Whitehall and in Barbados.
Proprietary rule was arbitrary, oppressive and lawless: from Barbados
and St. Kitts the proprietor received revenues and provided the mal-
administration and defence (not least of the charter itself). When
Carlisle died dix years later, heavily in debt, the intrigues continued afresh as the earl of Warwick, later Parliamentary governor-in-
chief for all plantations, purchased the rights in the Pembroke charter of 1628. One by-product of this struggle, strangely at the hand of
the tyrannical governor Hawley, was the calling in 1639 of an assembly of elected representatives in Barbados in place of the previous
public meetings of freeholders. The assembly, at first advisory
only, then soon fully legislative, was indeed exported from Barbados
by settlers moving to the off-islands of Nevis, Antigua and Monserrat
where colonists were for the most part jealously self-governing and
independent both of Barbados and king, Parliament and proprietor in
London. Carlisle had appointed Warner as governor for life in St.
Kitts delegating to him authority 'to do all things for the advancement and establishing the public good' of St. Kitts and, gradually
as his strong rule brought reasonable tranquillity, he became as much
a local leader as a proprietor's man - indeed his successor was
elected locally. But the English colony, sandwiched between two French
ones, shared the island fitfully and sometimes amicably with the French
until the cession of French rights in 1713. The English colony was
formally separated from Barbados in 1671 when Sir Charles Wheler was
appointed governor of St. Kitts and the other Leeward islands [see
below No.340].

ment belonging to the state of a Colony. This of our Regal
Authority is given and granted to him, ...Moreover, We do
give...to the said James Earle of Carlisle...all and every
one of the aforenamed Islands, both great and small, And
all other Iles, and Islands within twenty degrees of the
Aequinoctiall Line from the Northward of ye same Region....
[He was granted]priviledges, Jurisdictions, prerogatives,
Royalties, Liberties, Freedoms, Regall Rights and Franchises whatsoever, as well by Sea as Land within the Limits
of the said Islands: To have, use, exercise and enjoy as
any Bishopp according to the Customs·of Duresme [*Durham*]
within the said Bishopprick, or the County Palatine of
Duresme in our Kingdome of England ever before hath had,
held, used, or enjoyed, or of right could or ought to have,
hold, use, or enjoy.

    And the same Earle of Carlisle of the aforesaid Region
we do create, and ordaine, absolute Lord, as He to whom
the propertie doth belong, keeping true Faith, and Allegiance to Us, our Heires, and Successors. To have, hold,
keepe, possesse, and enjoy the aforesaid Region, Islands,
and all other the premisses, to thaforesaid Earle of Carlisle his Heires and Assignes for ever, to beholden, of
Us our heires, Successors, Kings of England *in Capite* by
Knights Service....

    [He was also to pay a yearly rent of £100 and one-fifth of
    precious metals, and to provide a white horse if there were a royal
    visit].

    ...We...have intended to advance thaforesaid Islands
into a Province, therefore we do erect and incorporate them
with fullnesse of power and Regall Prerogative, into a
reale Province for us our Heires and Successors, and name
them *Carlisle* or the *Islands of Carlisle Province*....

    Whatsoever Lawes, whether for the publique state of the
province, or the private Utility of every man are appointed, must be with consent of Councill, and approbation of
the free Inhabitants of the same Province containing the
same to be approved.

    Now for the makeing of Laws, when as often as it shalbe
needfull, the said James Earle of Carlisle, We have appointed to erect, make and sett forth such Laws in such
forme, as shall seeme best to him[1]...and also to be Sealed
with the Signett of the said James Earle of Carlisle....
And that ye said James Earle of Carlisle...by himselfe, or
by his Judges, Justices, Magistrates, Officers and Ministers in place appointed shall...truelie execute Justice
in what causes soever, or with what power soever in such
order as the said James Earle of Carlisle or his Heires
shall thinke fitt to be best....So as notwithstanding the
said Laws be agreeable as neere as conveniently may be to
the Laws, Statutes, Customs, and Rights of our Kingdome of

---

1. The lord proprietor therefore had the right to initiate legislation
and there is <u>in this section</u> no reference to any need for the consent
of council or freemen to the laws he might deem necessary in an emergency.

England, and not repugnant thereunto and to Reason....
The said James Earle of Carlisle and his Heires, by himself
and his Magistrates and Officers in those parts lawfully
preferred may make Decrees and Ordinances both fitt and
profitable...as well for the keeping of the peace, as for
ye better Government of the people...Which Ordinances...so
farr as possible may be agreeing to the Laws and Statutes
of our Kingdome of England, And...extend not themselves
either to the hurt or discomodity of any person or persons,
or the binding, constraining, burthening, or takeing away
either their Liberties, Goods or Chattels.

Wee will also...That the said Province be of our Allegiance. And that all and every Subject and Liege proper of
us, brought or to be brought to their Children, whether
there borne or afterwards to be borne, shalbe Natives and
Subjects of Us, our Heires and Successors, to be as free
as they that were borne in England...And also freely quietly and peaceably to have and possesse all the Liberties,
Franchises and Priviledges of this our Kingdome, and them
to enjoy as Liege people of England whether borne or to
be borne....

...We...have given and graunted to the said James Earl
of Carlisle...by himselfe, Captaine, Deputy, or other officers by him or them authorised, In case of suddaine rebellion, tumult, or sedition if any be...to use the Law of
Armes against any delinquent, in as ample manner and forme
as by any Generall Commander or Commissioners of this our
Realme of England is used to be done virtue of their place
....

[The proprietor might confer honours and incorporate boroughs and
cities, and might import into England and Ireland free of duties
for 10 years].

...That the said James Earle of Carlisle...shall have
and enjoy from time to time all and every Subsidy, Custom
and Imposition of all Goods and Merchandises to be landed
or inladen in the Ports Harbours, or other places of Shipping within the said Province.

...We...in no time to come shall impose...any Imposition
Custome or Tax whatsoever either upon the Inhabitants,[1]
Lands, Goods, or Chattells, or Merchandises of the said
Province whether to be Loaded, or to be unloaded.[2]

154. MARYLAND: LETTERS PATENT FROM CHARLES I TO BARON BALTIMORE,
                                             2 June 1632.[3]

[The new Lord Baltimore 'treading in the steps of his father'
wished to establish 'by his own Industry and Expence a numerous

---

1. The patent presumably left to the lord proprietor the right to
impose taxes and there is no mention of any need for consent by the
freeholders.
2. By the second patent of 7 April 1628 Carlisle obtained the grant for
10 years of all customs on imports and exports, payable both in English
and island ports.
3. W. MacDonald (ed.),*Select charters...* (1899) pp.53-9. Cecil Calvert,

Colony of the English Nation in America' on lands 'hitherto uncultivated'[1] and partly occupied by pagan savages].
    We ...do give, grant, and confirm, unto the aforesaid
Caecilius, now Baron Baltimore, all that Part of the Peninsula, or *Chersonese*... [and adjacent territories and islands
whose boundaries were carefully defined].
    And furthermore the Patronages, and advowsons of all
Churches which (with the increasing Worship and Religion
of Christ) within the said Region...hereafter shall happen to be built, together with Licence and Faculty of
erecting and founding Churches, Chapels, and Places of
Worship, in convenient and suitable Places, within the
Premises, and of causing the same to be dedicated and
consecrated according to the Ecclesiastical Laws of our
Kingdom of England, with all, and singular such, and as
ample Rights, Jurisdictions, Privileges, Prerogatives,
Royalties, Liberties, Immunities, and royal Rights, and
temporal Franchises whatsoever, as well by Sea as by Land,
within the Region...aforesaid, to be had, exercised, used,
and enjoyed, as any Bishop of Durham, within the Bishoprick
or County Palatine of Durham, in our Kingdom of England,
ever heretofore hath had, held, used, or enjoyed, or of
Right could, or ought to have, hold, use, or enjoy.
V.   And We do by these Presents...Make, Create and Constitute him, the now Baron of Baltimore, and his Heirs,
the True and Absolute Lords and Proprietaries of the Region
aforesaid, and of all other Premises (except the before
excepted) saving always the Faith and Allegiance and Sovereign Dominion due to US...; To hold of us...as of our

---

son of Sir George, was now Lord Baltimore. Sir George had been to
Virginia, but, since he was now a Catholic and was unable to take
the oaths of supremacy and allegiance, he returned to England to secure a new charter from the king. However, he had died just before
the patent, opposed by the hostility of the defunct Virginia Company,
was - in its fourth draft - finally issued. His object had been to
provide a refuge for his co-religionists, but Maryland was not to be
exclusively Catholic: from the beginning toleration was granted to
all who believed in the Trinity. He had asked for a grant on the same
model as his previous one for Avalon: he obtained one of wide powers
and few obligations where the proprietor was free to organise a society of manorial lords, freeholders and servants, where writs ran in
his name, and where in appeals and in law-making he had the powers
of the king. Despite a further legal challenge by the Virginia Company, he was confirmed in full possession of the patent, and in 1634
a selected group of settlers, Anglican and Catholic (some of whom had
avoided taking the necessary oaths) was sent to Maryland. Baltimore
himself had to stay at home to supervise, govern and provide for his
colony and to defend his charter.
Though Baltimore tried to curb the Jesuits and to secure some impartial balance between Catholics and Protestants, internal dissensions
grew. Between 1655 and 1658 Puritan rule ousted that of the proprietor.
Proprietary rule was confirmed by Charles II in 1660, but lapsed again
between 1691 and 1716: [see No.330].
1. Claiborne's plantation at Kent Island was not 'uncultivated'. But

Castle of Windsor, in our County of Berks, in free and
common soccage, by Fealty only for all Services, and not
in capite , nor by Knight's service, yielding therefore unto
us...two indian arrows of those Parts, to be delivered at
the said Castle of Windsor, every Year, on Tuesday in
Easter-Week: And also the fifth Part of all Gold and
Silver Ore, which shall happen from Time to Time, to be
found within the aforesaid limits.
VI.   Now, That the aforesaid Region,...may be eminently
distinguished above all other Regions of that Territory,
and decorated with more ample Titles, Know ye, that We
...do...erect and incorporate the same into a Province,
and nominate the same *Maryland*....
VII.   And forasmuch as We have above made and ordained
the aforesaid now Baron of Baltimore, the true Lord and
Proprietary of the whole Province aforesaid, Know you therefore further, that We...do grant unto the same now Baron
...for the good and happy Government of the said Province,
free, full, and absolute Power, by the tenor of these
Presents, to Ordain, Make, and Enact Laws, of what kind
soever, according to their sound Discretions, whether
relating to the Public State of the said Province, or
the private Utility of Individuals, of and with the Advice, Assent, and Approbation of the Free-Men of the same
Province, or of the greater Part of them, or of their
Delegates or Deputies, whom We will shall be called together for the framing of Laws, when, and as aften as Need
shall require...and to constitute and ordain Judges, Justices, Magistrates and Officers, together with the usual
jurisdictions, legal powers, *etc*...So nevertheless, that
the Laws aforesaid be consonant to Reason and be not
repugnant or contrary, but (so far as conveniently may
be) agreeable to the Laws, Statutes, Customs and Rights
of this Our Kingdom of England.
VIII. And forasmuch as, in the Government of so great a
Province, sudden Accidents may frequently happen, to
which it will be necessary to apply a Remedy, before the
Freeholders of the said Province, their Delegates, or
Deputies, can be called together for the framing of Laws;
...the aforesaid now Baron of Baltimore; and his Heirs,
by themselves, or by their Magistrates and Officers,...may,
and can make and constitute fit and wholesome Ordinances
from Time to Time, to be kept and observed within the Province aforesaid, as well for the Conservation of the Peace,
as for the better Government of the People inhabiting
therein, and Publickly to notify the same to all Persons

it did not legally belong to Virginia either, though it was represented in the assembly there by two burgesses. The Crown did not recognise the royal colony of Virginia as having inherited all the property of the company, and in 1638 the Laud Committee affirmed Baltimore's absolute right to it.
1. This change of tenure from that in Avalon was prompted by Sir George's experience. He had made a similar change in his Irish estates.

whom the same in any wise do or may affect...; so that the
same Ordinances do not, in any Sort, extend to oblige,
bind, change, or take away the Right or Interest of any
Person or Persons, of, or in Member, Life, Freehold, Goods
or Chattels ....

[The proprietor might enjoy import and export duties, and impose
taxes.]

XVIII. And furthermore...We...do give...unto the aforesaid
now Baron of Baltimore, his Heirs and Assigns, full and
absolute Licence, Power, and Authority... *[to]* assign,
alien, grant, demise or enfeoff so many such, and propor-
tionate Parts and Parcels of the Premises, to any Person
or Persons willing to purchase the same, as they shall
think convenient; to have and to hold...in Fee-simple,
or Fee-tail, of for Term of Life, Lives, or Years; to
hold of the aforesaid now Baron of Baltimore, his Heirs
and Assigns, by...such...Services, Customs and Rents of
this Kind. as to the same now Baron Baltimore, his Heirs
and Assigns, shall semm fit and agreeable, and not immediately of Us....

XIX. We also,...do...grant Licence to the same Baron of
Baltimore, and to his Heirs, to erect any Parcels of Land
within the Province aforesaid, into Manors, and in every
of those Manors, to have and to hold a Court-Baron, and
all Things which to the Court-Baron do belong; and to have
and to keep View of Frank-Pledge, for the Conservation of
the Peace and better Government of those Parts, by themselves and their Stewards, or by the Lords, for the Time
being to be deputed, of other of those Manors when they
shall be constituted, and in the same to exercise all
Things to the view of Frank-Pledge belonging.[1]...

[The freeholders were not to be subordinate to the government
of Virginia or any other colony, but to be immediately subject to
the Crown of England.]

155. NEWFOUNDLAND: LETTERS PATENT FROM CHARLES I TO THE MARQUIS OF
HAMILTON AND OTHERS, 13 November 1637.[2]

[The neglect of charter obligations granted to earlier proprietors had necessitated some new provision for 'our poor subjects...
living without Government'.]

...Wee therefore, taking it into our princely consider-

---

1. For every 20 able-bodied and armed men transported, it was proclaimed in 1641 by Baltimore that an adventurer would be provided with
2000 acres as a manor with the customary privileges belonging to manors in England:H.B. Adams (ed.) *Johns Hopkins Studies* (1883)VII pp.19-20.
2. C.O. 195/1 pp.11-27. The king presumed that all the patentees had
deserted their grants and gave the whole island away to Hamilton ,
Kirke and their associates. Baltimore, however, challenged these letters patent, and brought an action against Kirke, the governor, for
dispossion of his house and rights. In 1662 by order of Charles II
he was re-possessed of his estate and jurisdiction but, failing to
re-establish a colony, his proprietary lordship ended after 1675.

ation of what great consequence it is to us and our Subjects, that the Plantacion in our Dominions of Newfoundland aforesaid should be by our Royall power and authority be cherished, and speedily promoted...Wee, by the
advice of the Lords and others of our Privy Councill, and
at the humble Petition of our right trusty and right well
beloved Cousins and Councillors, James,Marquisse of Hamilton,...Philip, Earle of Pembrook and Mountgomery,...
and Henry, Earle of Holland,...and of our well beloved
servant Sir David Kirke Knight,[1]...Doe give and grant to
...[the aforesaid] for ever all that whole continent Island,
and Region aforesaid,commonly called or knowne by the
name of *Newfoundland*, bordering upon the continent of
America between Forty-six, and Fifty-three degrees of
Northerly Latitude more or lesse, and every part and parcell thereof being divided from the said Continent of
America by an Arme of the Sea,,,[and its adjacent islands,
fisheries, mines, etc, as 'true and absolute Lords and Proprietors'.]

[The inhabitants] shall not fell...any trees, or woods
whatsoever, Nor make, erect, or build any House or houses
whatsoever, Or plant, or inhabite within six miles of the
Sea shore, or of any part of Newfoundland aforesaid...
Nor within or upon any Island lying or being within tenne
Leagues of the Sea shore[2]....

Save only that the planters and Inhabitants shall have
like Liberty of Fishing there, and takeing and Cutting
of Wood for theire use about Fishing, as other our Subjects have to enjoy, And also shall and have full power
and Liberty to Build any Fort and Forts, and any place
or places within the said Limmits for the Defence of the
said Country and Fishing... And also that the Inhabitants,
or Residents of Newfoundland aforesaid, or any of the Islands adjoyneing shall not at any tyme hereafter appropriate to themselves...or take up before the arrivall of
the Fishermen aforesaid the best or most convenient Beaches, or places for Fishing, [or damage boats and stages left
by the fishermen]....

And that all, and every the Subjects of us, our Heires
and Successors, borne or to be borne within our Kingdome of England, or in any other our Kingdomes, or Dominions...shall...enjoy, the Freedome of Fishing in any the
said Continent, or Island of Newfoundland As fully, freely,
Liberally, effectually and beneficially, as at any tyme
heretofore hath been accustomed.

To have and to hold, possesse and enjoye the said Con-

---

1. Kirke had been involved with Alexander in Nova Scotia and had captured Quebec in 1629 on behalf of the Company of Adventurers to Canada. When Charles I restored Canada to France in 1632 Kirke turned
his attention to Newfoundland. He went as governor in 1638 to Newfoundland but, sued by Baltimore and out of favour with the Commonwealth government, died in prison in 1654.
2. This prohibition on settlement was a new concession to the exclus-

tinent Island, or Region of Newfoundland, and all and
Singular other ye premisses aforesaid, with their and
every of their Rights, Members, Jurisdictions, Prerogatives, Royaltyes, and appurtenances, whatsoever (except
before excepted) to them the said James Marqŝ. of Hamilton *[etc.]*...To hold of us, our Heires and Successors,
Kings of England in Cheife by Knights Service [yielding
2 white horses when necessary, and annually one-fifth of gold and
silver ore, gems and precious metals.]

Know yee further, that Wee...Doe...give and grant full
and free Liberty, power & authority to them...for the good,
happy, and peaceable Government of Newfoundland aforesaid,
and the Inhabitants thereof, To erect, make and enact, any
lawes whatsoever, eyther for the publick Estate of ye said
Continent or Island, or the private proffit of the Inhabitants aforesaid according to their good Discretions together with the common Assent and approbacon of the Freeholders of the Continent or Island aforesaid, or the Major
part of them [with power to enforce laws and punish infringements.]

Saving and Excepted alwayes, and our Will and pleasure
is that the said Lawes and Penaltyes...shall not Extend,
to any Fishermen, Mariners, or others our Subjects, whatsoever, that shall come thither to Fish, according to the
Liberty before by these presents given. But that all such
persons, and all matters and things concerning the said
persons, and Fishing shall be from tyme to tyme for ever
hereafter, free from the power, authority, Government and
Punnishment of ye said Lords and Inhabitants of the said
Newfoundland, and be Subject unto, and immediately under
the Order, Rule, and Government of us, our Heires, and
Successors, and ye Lords of our Privy Councill of England, or such Commissioners or Councillors for forreigne
affaires or otherwise, as wee, our Heires and Successors,
shall from tyme to tyme appoint, and Direct, and unto the
Lawes, Orders, and Directions made in the nynth yeare of
our Reigne.[1]

Which Wee hereby declare and ordaine shall be inviolably
kept and observed by the said Fishermen, and the said Lords
and planters and all other our Subjects Inhabiting in the
Newfoundland aforesaid untill the same shall be altered or
revoked by Us, our Heires, or Successors. [And power to appoint magistrates and enforce justice.]

Which said Lawes, and every of then Wee Will, enjoyne,
and by our Regal authority...doe strictly Charge and Comm-
and to be firmely, and inviolable kept observed and performed, of all the Subjects and Leige People of Us...res-
ideing and inhabiting within ye same...,

So as the said Lawes be not repugnant or contrary to
the Lawes, statutes, Rights and Customes of this our
Realme of England, and so as the same be not contrary, or
repugnant, or doe not extend to any of the persons or

ive monopoly of the western fishermen. [For the 'Western charter' see
No.166.]

1. The proprietors with an assembly of freeholders had neither right
of legislation nor of jurisdiction over fishermen.

places or Restraint and prejudice of the Liberties of
Fishing, and other the Libertyes and Powers excepted,and
Reserved to our Subjects in those presents ....
  [Proprietors might make laws alone in times of crisis, but not
  such as would be injurious to freeholders or prejudicial to fishing. Newfoundland was to be for ever within the allegiance, and
  its inhabitants regarded for all purposes as natural-born subjects.
  They might take goods to Newfoundland free of customs charges.
  The proprietors had the powers of a general in dealing with pirates
  and other enemies, and might use martial law in cases of internal
  'rebellion or tumult'. Merchants might import goods into England
  at the same rate of duties as English merchants.]
  And because that all other Kings, Princes and Potentates
...may knowe and acknowledge our Just and undoubted Right,
and interest in, and to the said Continent Island, and
Region of Newfoundland, and to all and every the Islands,
Seas, and places to the same belonging, and...within thirty
Leagues thereof, Our Will and pleasure is, and Wee doe
hereby...Constitute, ordaine and appoint, that there shall
bee for ever from and after the Feast of the Birth of our
Lord God next ensuing the date hereof Leavyed, and taken
to the use of Us...and from all and every Stranger...which
shall...make use of any the Grounds or Beaches within any
Ports, or Harbours eithin Newfoundland aforesaid erected
or to be erected, or within any other Islands within
thirty Leagues of the Island of Newfoundland aforesaid
...after the rate and proportion of Five Fishes, out of
every hundred Fish in the Seas, Rivers, or places aforesaid, to be had or taken within ye Terme hereafter mentioned, 51 years accounting after the number of five-Score
Fishes, to every hundred respectively,... [Also 5% on fishes,
oils *etc*. bought in Newfoundland.]
  Moreover, Wee takeing into our royall Consideration,
that very great will be the Danger, and the charge excessive, which must of necessity be undergone, and expended,
before a Plantation of such an Extent...can be brought to
perfection, eyther to maintaine, or Defend itself...Wee
...doe demise, grant, and confirme unto them...th'aforesaid
Quantety or summe of Five Fishes out of every hundred
Fishes...upon the said Strangers...to be sett, imposed,
demanded, and taken from tyme to tyme, from all and every
Stranger, and Strangers, which shall at any tyme or tymes
hereafter, make use of any the Grounds and Beaches aforesaid...and on oils etc. To have and to hold...for and
during the Terme and tyme of One and fifty yeers from
henceforth next ensuing....Yeilding and paying therefore
...unto us...yeerly...the full, and entyre tenth part,of
all and singular ye Benifitt proffit, and Commodity, Summe
and Summ of money whatsoever which shall or may from tyme
to tyme, grow, arise, or be payable out of all and Singular
the Imposts, Customes, and payments aforesaid, and every or
any of them....
  [They were granted the sole trade of Newfoundland, except the
  fishery. No taxes would be imposed, apart from duties payable on

imports into England. Ships and seamen were to be free from being pressed for 51 years except 'in case of inevitable danger, and necessity, for the safety, preservation and guarding of our Kingdomes of England, Scotland, and Ireland, or any of them, from Hostility, Incursion or Invasion.']

And to the end that God Almighty may give his Blessing to this Plantation, and that the Inhabitants thereof may live in peace and prosperity and that none may thither resort to inhabite that are not of that true Christian Faith, whereof on earth it is our cheifest happynesse to be Professor and Defender, Our Will and pleasure is, that every person and persons of the age of twelve yeeres, or upwards, eyther before hee or they shall Leave this our Kingdome of England, or Dominion of Wales, or any other our Dominions, or at his or their arrivall into the Island of Newfoundland, or any other the Island thereunto belonging or appertaining...Shall upon the holy Evangelist, take the severall and respective Oaths of Allegiance and Supremacy ... [before the proprietors, or their deputies.

'The Orthodox Religion publicly professed and allowed in our Church of England'was to be established.]

(b) GRANTS TO COMPANIES

Grants to groups of merchants, companies and guilds within the realm and to those adventuring overseas had been made by the Crown in earlier centuries (see, for example, Nos. 14, 145-47). Now in the wake of new discoveries and with the 'expansion of Europe', other enthusiasts - nobles, knights, gentry, aldermen - were prepared to take risks in the hope of elusive profit and to probe overseas for an increase of the nation's trade - and their own wealth. At first these associations were 'regulated' companies rather than joint-stock corporations. But as in Calais previously, rights of self-government and self-regulation were delegated to them in their royal charters.

156. CHARTER FROM PHILIP AND MARY FOR A MUSCOVY COMPANY, 6 February, 1555.[1]

[Whereas lords Winchester, Arundel, Bedford, Pembroke and Howard of Effingham 'at their owne adventure, costs and charges'had fitted out ships to discover new lands to the north not before frequented by the English or any friendly Christian prince, and where-

---

1. R. Hakluyt, *Principal Navigations* (1903 ed.) II pp.304-16. Sir Hugh Willoughby had set out to rediscover the route north of Norway to Russia in 1553 in an attempt to open direct trade with India, China and the East. Richard Chancellor, one of his captains, had received from the Tsar, Ivan the Terrible, encouraging promises of privileges for English merchants at Archangel. When in 1581 the Muscovy Company gave up its concern with the overland route to the East, a Levant Company received a charter from Elizabeth I. Two years previously the Sultan of Turkey had granted the first *'capitulations'* to English merchants: 'heads' of concessions which *inter alia* gave to consuls, appointed by the English ambassador at the Porte, the jurisdiction in disputes, criminal and civil, between Englishmen within the Turkish dominions. (*ibid.* V pp.169 ff. with Zuldon Murad Can's

as such enterprise was 'as well for the glorie of God, as for the
illustrating of our honour and dignitie royall, in the increase
of the revenues of our Crowne, and generall wealth of this and
other our Realmes and Dominions and of our subjects of the same',
Philip and Mary granted that they should be henceforth]

...one bodie and perpetuall Fellowship and Communaltie of
themselves, both in deede and in name, and them, by the
names of Marchants Adventurers for the discoverie of lands,
territories, Iles and seignieries unknowen,...We doe incorporate, name, and declare by these presents, and that the
same fellowship or communalty from henceforth shalbe, and
may have one Governour of the saide fellowship, and communalties of Marchants Adventurers.

And in consideration that one Sebastian Cabota hath bin
the chiefest setter forth of this journey or voyage, therefore we make, ordeine, and constitute him the said Sebastian
to be the first and present *Governour* of the same Fellowship and Communaltie, by these presents. To have and enjoy
the said office of Governour, to him the said Sebastian
Cabota during his naturall life, without amoving or dis-
missing from the same room.

And furthermore, we graunt unto the same fellowship and
communaltie and their successors, that they the saide fellowship and communaltie, and their successors, after the
decease of the saide Sebastian Cabota, shall, and may freely and lawfully in places convenient and honest, assemble
themselves together, or so many of them as will or can
assemble together, as well within our citie of London, or
elsewhere, as it shall please them, in such sort and maner,
as other worshipfull corporations of our saide citie have
used to assemble, and there yeerely name, elect and choose
one Governour or two, of themselves, and their liberties,
and also as well yeerely during the natural life of the
said Sebastian Cabota now Governour, as also at the election of such saide Governour or governours before his decease, to choose, name and appoint eight and twenty of the
most sad, discreete, and honest persons of the said fellowship, and communaltie of Marchant Adventurers, as is above
specified, and 4 of the most expert and skilfull persons
of the same 28 to be named and called *Consuls*, and 24 of
the residue to be named and called *Assistants* to the said
Governour, and Consuls for the time being, which shal remaine and stand in their authorities for one whole yeere....

[The four consuls and 24 assistants were named by the Crown for

letter to the queen; VI pp. 79-92 for the 1592 charter incorporating
the Levant company). English merchants were 'to use their own customs'. This early grant of 'foreign jurisdiction ' was extended during
the next 250 years by further *'capitulations'*. Only when the Levant
Company was wound up in 1826 were some legal doubts expressed about
the continuation of such extra-territorial jurisdiction by the Crown.
A review by Hope Scott in a minute of 18 January 1843 led to such jurisdiction being placed upon a statutory basis (6 & 7 Vict. cap.94) :
the first Foreign Jurisdiction Act :[see Volume III].

the first year.] And further, we...wil and graunt by these
presents unto the saide Governour, Consuls, Assistants,
Fellowship and Company of Marchants Adventurers aforesaid,
and to their successors, that the said Governour or governours, 4 Consuls, & 24 Assistants, that now by these
patents are nominated and appointed, or that hereafter be
by the saide fellowship and communaltie of Marchants Adventurers, or the more part of them, which shalbe then present,
so from time to time to be chosen, so that there be 15 at
the least wholy agreed thereof [The necessary composition of
such a *quorum* was defined. They] shal and may have, use and exercise ful power and authority to rule and governe all and
singuler the Marchants of the said fellowship and communalties, and to execute and doe full and speedie justice to
them, and every of them, in all their causes, differences,
variances, controversies, quarrels, and complaints, within
any our realmes, dominions and jurisdictions onely moved,
and to be moved touching their marchandise, traffikes, and
occupiers aforesaid, or the good order or rule of them or
any of them....

    [The company was granted a common seal, might purchase and grant
    lands etc., of limited annual value 'the statutes provided against
    alienation into *mortmain* ... notwithstanding'. They might bring
    and answer suits 'in as ample manner and forme as any other cor-
    poration of this our Realme may doe'.]

The saide Governour, or Governours, Consuls and Assistants,
and their successors, in maner, forme, and number afore
rehearsed, shall have full power and authoritie from time
to time hereafter, to make, ordein, establish and erect
all such statutes, actes, and ordinaunces, for the government, good condition, and laudable rule of the said Fellowship and communaltie of Marchants Adventurers, aforesaid,
as to them shall bee thought good, meete, convenient and
necessarie, and also to admit unto the saide Corporation
and fellowship to be free of the same, such as many persons, as to them shal bee thought good, meete, convenient
and necessarie.... [The governor and company had full powers to
enforce and punish breaches of their own regulations.] So alwayes,
that the saide Actes, statutes and ordinances bee not
against our prerogative, lawes, statutes, and customes of
our realmes and Dominions, nor contrary to the severall
duetie of any our subjects towards us, our heires and successours, nor contrarie to any compacts, treaties or leagues, by us or any our progenitours heretofore had or made,
to or with any forreine Prince or potentate, nor also to
the prejudice of the corporation of the Maior, Communalties and Citizens of our Citie of London, nor to the prejudice or any person or persons, bodie politique, or corporate, or incorporate, justly pretending, clayming, or
having any liberties, franchises, priviledges, rights or
preheminences, by vertue or pretext of anie graunt, gift,
or Letters patents, by us, or anie our Progenitours, heretofore, given, granted, or made....

[Merchants of the company might sail and trade anywhere 'unknowen' and 'not...commonly frequented under our banner (etc.)' and they might plant 'our banners (*etc*.)' in 'newly found' lands 'as our vassals and subjects' and might 'acquire and get Dominion, title and jurisdiction of the same'.]

And furthermore, whereas by the voyage of our subjects in this last yeere attempted by Navigation, towards the discoverie and disclosure of unknowen places, Realmes, Islandes, and Dominions by the seas not frequented, it hath pleased Almighty God to cause one of the three shippes by them set foorth for the voyage, and purpose above mentioned, named the *Edward Bonaventure*, to arrive, abide, and winter within the Empire and dominions of the high and mightie Prince our cousin and brother, Lord John Basilivich, Emperour of all Russia,[1] Volodomer, great duke of Muscovie, &c. Who, of his clemencie, for our love and zeale, did not onely admitte the Captaine and marchants our subjects into his protection and Princely presence, but also received and intertained them very graciously and honourably, granting unto them by his letters addressed unto us, franke accesse into all his Seigniories and dominions, with licence freely to traffique in and out with all his Subjects in all kinde of Marchandise, with divers other gracious priviledges,liberties,and immunities specified in his sayde letters under his Signet: [*We*] ...doe give and graunt unto the same Governours, Consuls, Assistants, fellowship, and communalty above named, and to their successours, as much as in us is, that all the mayne landes, Isles, portes, havens, creekes, and rivers of the said mighty Emperour of all Russia, and great duke of Mosco, &c ... [and those of other rulers of unknown and unfrequented lands in the North,] by sea shall not be visited, frequented, nor hanted by any our subjects, other than of the sayd company and fellowship, and their successours without expresse licence, agreement and consent of the Governour, Consuls, and Assistants of the said fellowship and communaltie above named, or the more part of them, in manner and number aforesayd, for the time being, upon paine of forfeiture and losse, as well of the shippe and shippes, with the appurtenances, as also of all the goods, marchandises, and things whatsoever they be....[2]

[Merchants might defend themselves against any interlopers who might infringe the monopoly of the company.]

---

1. Ivan the Terrible.
2. In 1566 they obtained privileges and protection from the Shah of Persia. The same year their rights as a corporate company were confirmed by statute (8 Eliz. I cap.1). They were now renamed 'the Fellowship of English merchants for discovery of new trades' and their monopoly was extended to include Armenia, Persia and the Caspian Sea. The reason given for parliamentary enactment included loss of trade through interlopers who were making use of the trade opened up by their enterprise in Asia Minor and beyond. Trade in English goods was to be 'onely in English ships and...for the most part with English

157. CHARTER FROM ELIZABETH I FOR A GUINEA COMPANY, 3 May 1588.[1]

[A group of merchants from the West country and London were anxious, with the encouragement of 'certain Portugals resident within our Dominions', to establish 'an orderly trafique and trade of marchandize' with those parts of the Guinea coast between the Senegal and Gambia rivers.]

...We have therefore thought it convenient, that our said loving subjects...for the better incouragement to proceede in their saide adventure and trade in the said Countreis, shall have the sole use and exercise thereof for a certaine time.   In consideration whereof...We doe give and graunt unto the said William Brayley, [and others named] ...that they and every of them by themselves or by their servants or Factors and none others, shall and may for and during the full space and terme of tenne yeares next ensuing the date of these presents, have and enjoy the free and whole trafique, trade and feat of marchandise ...And for the better ordering, establishing, and governing of the said societie and Company in the said trade and trafique of marchandizes, and the quiet, orderly and lawfull exercise of the same...give and graunt full license and authoritie unto the said William Brayley [and his associates] ...that they or the most part of them shall and may at all convenient times at their pleasures, assemble and meete together in any place or places convenient, aswell within our citie of Exeter, as elsewhere within this our Realme of England, or other our dominions, during the said terme of ten yeare, to consult of, for, and concerning the saide trade and trafique of marchandize, and from time to time to make, ordaine, and stablish good, necessary, and reasonable orders, constitutions, and ordinances, for, and touching the same trade [and to enforce, amend and repeal them.] ...So alwayes, as the same orders, constitutions and ordinances, be not repugnant or contrary to the lawes, statutes, and customes of this Realme of England, nor any penaltie to exceede the reasonable forme of other penalties, assessed by the Company of our Marchants, named Adventurers....

[They were empowered to seize the ships of interlopers and were exempt from customs duties for 10 years. The Crown reserved its right to revoke this grant at six months' notice.][2]

---

mariners' on penalty of a £200 fine. English dressed and dyed woollens were also protected.
1. R. Hakluyt, *op.cit.* IV pp.443-0. The patent was granted to eight adventurers for ten years and the company was not incorporated. At first they traded in ivory, palm oil and cotton; later, of course, in slaves. In 1618 a new venture, the 'Gynney and Bynney' Company, was incorporated and granted a monopoly southward to the Cape of Good Hope which was renewed in 1631 for 31 years. The Royal Adventurers into Africa was a somewhat haphazard group, formed in 1660 and obtained a new charter in 1663 but within five years was dormant, crippled and practically bankrupt. In 1672 the Royal African Company was incorporated and received a charter:[see No.257] . 2. For example, on 2

158. CHARTER FROM ELIZABETH I FOR AN EAST INDIA COMPANY,
                                    31 December 1600.[1]
[The Earl of Cumberland and some 217 others - knights, aldermen
and burgesses - had petitioned for the right to make 'one or more'
ventures to the East Indies.]
We greatly tendering the Honour of our Nation, the
Wealth of our People, and the Encouragement of them, and
others of our loving Subjects in their good Enterprizes,
for the Increase of our Navigation, and the Advancement of
lawful Traffick, to the Benefit of our Common Wealth,...
go give and grant unto our said loving Subjects,...That
they and every of them from henceforth be, and shall be
one Body Corporate and Politick, in Deed and in Name, by
the Name of *The Governor and Company of Merchants of London, Trading into the East-Indies*,...capable in Law to
have, purchase, ...and retain, Lands, Rents, Priviledges,
Liberties, Jurisdictions, Franchises and Hereditaments of
whatsoever Kind, Nature and Quality so ever they be...And
also to give...and dispose Lands...and to do and execute
all and singular other Things....[2] And that they and their
Successors ...may plead and be impleaded...in whatsoever
Courts and Places...in such Manner and Form as any other
our liege People of this our Realm of England....And that
The said *Governor and Company*...may have a Common Seal,
to serve for all the Causes and Business of them and their
Successors...And further, we will...that there shall be

Dec. 1614 James revoked the charter to the Merchant Adventurers, and
on 12 August 1617 restored it: G. Cawston and A.H.Keane, *The early
chartered companies* (1896) pp.296-304.
1. J.Shaw, *Charters relating to the East India Company* (1887) pp.1-15.
Private missions to the East (by Fitch and Lancaster, for example) to
open direct communications for trade and spices had been taking place
for some twenty yeare before John Mildenhall, a Levant merchant,in
1603 arrived at the court of the Moghul emperor, Akbar, claiming to
be the queen's envoy to negotiate commercial privileges. The tradit-
ional route for spices had been through the dominions of the 'Grand
Turk' and concessions ('*capitulations*') made by the Sultan in 1579 had
led to the queen's granting of a charter for the Levant Company in
1581. The growing power of the Dutch monopoly east of the Cape of Good
Hope - the alternative route - and the collapse of the Portuguese monopoly caused many in the Levant Company to petition for the right to
form an association - a regulated company - to trade direct to the
Indies. The sub-continent of India was only a second best, clutched
at when the Dutch effectively excluded the English from the spice islands. Elizabeth made this grant in the first instance for fifteen
years. In 1613 the first 'factory' was opened at Surat; in 1616 Sir
Thomas Roe was sent as an embassy to secure a commercial agreement
with the Moghul emperor; and in 1640 Fort St. George was erected at
Madras with the company's jurisdiction extending to the surrounding
district, held as a feudatory of the Hindu Sultan of Golconda. The company paid half the customs duties to him as a quit rent. The volume of
trade was small; the produce of India was much less profitable than were
spices; and the company was faced by many European and Indian rivals,
including other English 'interlopers'.
2. No sovereignty over newly discovered lands was assumed. Factories

from henceforth one of the same Company to be elected and
appointed... which shall be called *The Governor of the
said Company*,and that there shall be from henceforth
Twenty-Four of the said Company, to be elected and appointed...which shall be called *The Committees of the said
Company*, who, together with The *Governor*...shall have the
Direction of the Voyages, of or for the said Company, and
the Provision of the Shipping and Merchandizes thereto
belonging and also the Sale of all Merchandizes returned
in the Voyages...and the managing and handling of all other
Things belonging to the said Company....

    [Sir Thomas Smith[1] was named as first governor, and 24 members
of the first Committee were listed; and the Court (or general assembly) might elect the deputy governor. Future governors and committees would be elected annually[2] by governor and company and would
take a 'corporal oath', and an oath of fealty to the Crown. They
would manage the voyages. The governor might be removed by the Court.]

    And further we do...will and grant unto The said *Gover-
nor and Company*...that they, and all that are or shall
be of the said *Company* and every of them, and all the
Sons of them, and every of them, at their severall Ages
of One and Twenty Years or upwards: And further, all such
the Apprentices, Factors, or Servants of them and of every
of them, which hereafter shall be employed, by The Said
Governor and Company,in the said Trade of Merchandize, of
or to the *East-Indies*,beyond the Seas, or any other the
Places aforesaid, in any Part of the said East-Indies, or
other the Places aforesaid, shall and may, by the Space
of Fifteen Years, from the Feast of the Birth of our Lord
God last past, before the Date thereof, freely traffick
and use the Trade of Merchandize, by Seas, in and by such
Ways and Passages already found out and discovered, or
which hereafter shall be found out and discovered, as
they shall esteem and take to be fittest, into and from
the said East-Indies, in the Countries and Parts of Asia
and Africa, and into and from all the Islands, Ports,
Havens, Cities, Creeks, Towns, and Places in Asia and
Africa, and America, or any of them, beyond the Cape of
Bona Esperanza *[Good Hope]* to the Streights of Magellan,

---

could be established with the permission of local rulers.
1. He was already governor of the Levant Company. Later he became
treasurer of the Virginia Company and governor of the Bermuda Company, and had interests in the plantation of Ulster.
2. In 1619 the question of election by ballot became a matter of dispute in the court when Sandys and Warwick sought to oust Smith from
power. But by August 1621 the ballot box was accepted for elections
and 'in all ambiguous and weighty matters and in all gratuities
over £10 '.(Calendar State Papers, East Indies, *1617-21* V, VI. Nos.
700, 1066, 1072). Similarly vote by ballot was adopted by the allied
Virginia and Bermuda Companies.

where any Trade or Traffick of Merchandize may be used or
had, and to and from every of them, in such Order, Manner, Form, Liberty and Condition, to all Intents and Purposes, as shall be, from Time to Time, at any publick
Assembly or Court...limited and agreed, and not otherwise, without any Molestation, Impeachment or Disturbance,
any Statute, Usage, Diversity of Religion or Faith, or any
other Cause of Matter whatsoever, to the Contrary notwithstanding: So always the same Trade be not undertaken,
nor addressed to any Country...already in the lawful and
actual Possession of any such Christian Prince or State,
as at this present is, or at any Time hereafter shall be
in League or Amity with us, our Heirs or Successors, and
who doth not or will not accept of such Trade, but doth
overtly declare and publish the same, to be utterly
against his or their Good-Will and Liking, AND further
our Will and Pleasure is, and by these Presents, for us,
our Heirs and Successors, we do grant unto The said Governor and Company...and to their Successors, that it shall
and may be lawful, to and for The said Governor and Company, and their Successors, from Time to Time to assemble
themselves, for or about any the Matters , Causes, Affairs, or Businesses of the said Trade, in any Place or
Places, for the same convenient, during the said Term of
Fifteen Years, within our Dominions or elsewhere, and there
to hold Court for the said Company, and the Affairs thereof; and that also it shall and may be lawful,to and for
them or the more Part of them...to make, ordain and constitute such, and so many reasonable Laws, Constitutions,
Orders and Ordinances, as to them, or the greater Part
of them, being then and there present, shall seem necessary and convenient, for the good Government of the same
Company,..

[and to execute, revoke and enforce by punishment(including
minor fines and imprisonment) such regulations;[1] provided these
laws and punishment 'be reasonable and not contrary or repugnant
to the Laws, Statutes or Customs of this our Realm'. Goods exported on the first four voyages were to be free from duty: import
duties during the 15-year period might be paid in half-yearly instalments. Procedure was outlined for the re-export of the expected surplus of East Indian goods 'in English bottoms'. Licence to
take up to £30,000 in silver coin was granted, any English law
not withstanding[2]; on subsequent voyages they might use in trade
any silver they have acquired abroad up to £30,000 value. They
might conduct their trade by armed convoy of six ships and six
pinnaces, though the Crown might commandeer these - with their
crews - if necessary for the defence of the realm.]

1. The legislative power granted here was much more limited than that
granted to Gilbert or to Massachusetts Bay [Nos.150,165],for example.
The company's policy was expressly opposed to conquest and colonisation.
2. The East Indian trade was from the first suspected of being a drain
on bullion. Thomas Mun in *A discourse of trade* (1621) argued that the

And, further we...do grant unto the said Governor and Company...and their Successors, that they and their Successors, and their Factors, Servants and Assigns, in the Trade of Merchandize, for them and on their Behalf,and not otherwise, shall, for the said Term of Fifteen Years, have, use and enjoy, the whole entire and only Trade and Traffick,and the whole entire and only Liberty, Use and Privilege of trading and trafficking, and using Feat and Trade of Merchandize, to and from the said East-Indies, and to and from all the Islands, Ports, Havens, Cities, Towns and Places aforesaid, in such Manner and Form as is above-mentioned....

And by virtue of our Prerogative Royal, which we will not in that Behalf have argued, or brought in Question, we straitly charge, command and prohibit...all the Subjects of us...that none of them, directly or indirectly, do visit, haunt, frequent or trade, traffick or adventure, by way of Merchandize, into or from any of the said East-Indies, or into or from any the Islands, Ports, Havens, Cities, Towns or Places aforesaid, other than The said Governor and Company...and such particular Persons as now be, or hereafter shall be of that Company, their Agents, Factors and Assigns, during the said Term of Fifteen Years, unless it be by and with such Licence and Agreement of the said Governor and Company... [on pain of forfeiture and imprisonment].

And further, for the better Encouragement of Merchants, Strangers or others, to bring in Commodities into our Realm, we...do grant unto The said Governor and Company... that they and their Successors, may, from Time to Time, for any Consideration or Benefit, to be taken to their own Use, grant or give Licence, to any Persons or Person, to sail or traffick, into or from any of the said East-Indies....[1]

[The Crown would not grant licences to others without the company's approval. It reserved its right to revoke the patent with two years notice. It might also renew the grant, provided that it would 'not be prejudicial or hurtful to this our Realm'.[2]]

---

real value of the trade was the profit which would be obtained on the re-sale of East Indian goods to other countries [see No.163 (b).]
1. The company was a 'regulated', not a joint stock, one: that is, each merchant ventured his own capital for each separate voyage but was subject to certain common regulations.
2. In May 1609 (J. Shaw *op. cit.*pp.16-31) the charter was made perpetual (subject to three year's notice of revocation by the Crown) since the trade was not only of great honour' but also in many respects profitable to Us and our Common Wealth'; and in 1612 the several separate ventures were merged in a joint stock, though still only for a series of voyages. In 1623 the company was further empowered to hold trials by jury for crimes committed by its servants on Indian soil. Though Charles I in 1635 gave a patent to a rival association of merchants (which included Courteen) and Cromwell in 1655 seemed to encourage interlopers, the charter of 1657 (renewed in 1661) granted to the company the privilege of exclusive trade on a permanent joint stock

159. THE VIRGINIAS: FIRST CHARTER FROM JAMES I FOR TWO COLONIES,
10 April 1606.[1]

[Whereas Sir Thomas Gates and others were anxious to establish
colonies in the American mainland and adjacent islands between
34°N and 45°N]

II.And to that End, and for the more speedy Accomplish-
ment of their said intended Plantation and Habitation
there, are desirous to divide themselves into two several
Colonies and Companies; The one consisting of certain
Knights, Gentlemen, Merchants, and other Adventurers, of
our City of London and elsewhere, which do desire to begin
their Plantation and Habitation in some fit and convenient
Place, between four and thirty and one and forty Degrees
of the said Latitude, alongst the Coasts of Virginia and
Coasts of America aforesaid; And the other consisting of
sundry Knights, Gentlemen, Merchants, and other Adventurers, of our Cities of Bristol and Exeter, and of our Town
of Plimouth, and of other Places, which do join themselves unto that Colony, which do desire to begin their
Plantation and Habitation in some fit and convenient Place,
between eight and thirty Degrees and five and forty Degrees of the said Latitude, all alongst the said Coast of
Virginia and America, as that Coast lyeth,..

    [the king, concurring in their desire to glorify his Majesty,
    to propogate Christianity, and to bring'the Infidels and Savages,
    living in those Parts, to human Civility, and to a settled and
    quiet Government', granted these letters patent.]

IV. And do therefore, for Us,...grant and agree, that the
said Sir Thomas Gates, Sir George Somers, Richard Hackluit, and Edward-Maria Wingfield, Adventurers of and for
our City of London, and all such others, as are, or shall
be, joined unto them of that Colony, shall be called the
first Colony;And they shall and may begin their said
first Plantation and Habitation, at any Place upon the
said Coast of Virginia or America, where they shall think
fit and convenient, between the said four and thirty and
one and forty Degrees of the said Latitude; And that
they shall have all the Lands, Woods, Soil, Grounds, Havens, Ports, Rivers, Mines, Minerals, Marshes, Waters,

---

basis. (W.R.Scott, *The constitution and finance of English, Scottish
and Irish joint-stock companies to 1720.* (1910) p.128). The charter
of 1657 seems lost.
1. W. MacDonald (ed.) *Select charters*...(1899) pp.1-11. Sir John Popham (L.C.J.) representing the London interest and Sir Ferdinando Gorges on behalf of the Plymouth interest, had taken a lead in petitioning the king for a patent for two companies for 'Virginia' - one for
the London adventurers in the south of the North American coast, the
other for the Plymouth group in the north. Gates, Somers and Hakluyt
were among those associated with them. When James I made this grant,
its terms relied very considerably on the draft Popham had prepared
with the assistance of the law officers, Coke and Dodderidge. The
London company succeeded in planting a precarious but enduring colony
at James-town in May 1607. The Plymouth Company failed and withdrew
from Sagadahoc.

Fishings, Commodities and Hereditaments, whatsoever, from
the said first Seat of their Plantation and Habitation by
the Space of fifty Miles of English Statute Measure, all
along the said Coast of Virginia and America, towards the
West and Southwest, as the Coast lyeth, with all the Islands within one hundred Miles directly over against the
same Sea Coast; And also all the Lands [etc.]...from the
said Place of their first Plantation and Habitation for
the space of fifty like English Miles, all alongst the
said Coast of Virginia and America, towards the East and
Northeast, or towards the North, as the Coast lyeth, together with all the Islands within one hundred Miles, directly over against the said Sea Coast; And also all the
Lands, [etc.] ...from the same fifty Miles every way on
the Sea Coast, directly into the main Land by the Space
of one hundred like English Miles; And shall and may inhabit and remain there; and shall and may also build and
fortify within any the same, for their better Safeguard
and Defence,according to their best Discretion, and the
Discretion of the Council of that Colony; And that no
other of our Subjects shall be permitted, or suffered, to
plant or inhabit behind,or on the Backside of them, towards
the main Land, without the Express Licence or Consent of
the Council of that Colony, thereunto in Writing first had
and obtained....

   [A similar grant was made to T. Hanham, R. Gilbert, W. Parker
   and G. Popham of the West Country for a *second colony* between
   38ºN abd 45ºN, provided that the two colonies were separated by
   at least 100 miles.]

VII. And we do also ordain...that each of the said Colonies shall have a Council which shall govern and order all
Matters and Causes, which shall arise...within the same
several Colonies, according to such Laws, Ordinances, and
Instructions, as shall be, in that behalf, given and signed with Our Hand or Sign Manual, and pass under the Privy
Seal of our Realm of England; Each of which Council shall
consist of thirteen Persons, to be ordained, made, and
removed, from time to time, according as shall be directed and comprised in the same instructions; And shall have
a several Seal, for all Matters that shall pass or concern
the same several Councils....

VIII. And that also there shall be a Council established
here in England, which shall, in like Manner, consist of
thirteen Persons, to be, for that Purpose, appointed by
Us...which shall be called our *Council of Virginia*; And
shall, from time to time, have the superior Managing and
Direction, only of and for all Matters, that shall or may
concern the Government[1]... [both of the two colonies and of the

---

1. This royal council in England was an assertion of the Crown's continuing control and supervision, and of the king's reserve power to
change membership of the colonial councils, to issue overriding instructions, and to grant land and pardons. James I was unlikely to deprive
himself of such rights in so vast a domain, as Popham well knew. For

region between 34°N and 45°N] Which Council shall, in like
Manner, have a Seal, for Matters concerning the Council
or Colonies....

> [One-fifth of precious metals and one-fifteenth of any copper
> found in the colonies and their hinterlands were reserved for
> the Crown.]

X. And that they shall, or lawfully may, establish and
cause to be made a Coin, to pass current there between
the People of those several Colonies, for the more Ease
of Traffick and Bargaining between and amongst them and
the Natives there, of such Metal, and in such Manner and
Form, as the said several Councils there shall limit and
appoint....

> [The companies were permitted to take out of the realm all vol-
> untary colonists and supplies necessary 'for their Use and Def-
> ence' and to eject unauthorised settlers. They might also impose
> fines of 2½% on traders caught interloping if they were within
> the king's allegiance; of 5% of the value of their goods, if
> aliens. This money was appropriated for the first 21 years to
> the use of the colonies; thereafter to the use of the Crown. For
> seven years the companies were free from excise duties on necess-
> aries imported into the colonies.]

XV. Also we do, for Us...declare...that all and every the
Persons, being our Subjects, which shall dwell and inhabit within every or any of the said several Colonies
and Plantations, and every of their children, which shall
happen to be born within any of the Limits and Precincts
of the said several Colonies and Plantations, shall have
and enjoy all Liberties, Franchises, and Immunities, of
free denizens and natural subjects within any of our other Dominions, to all Intents and Purposes, as if they had
been abiding and born, within this our Realm of England,
or any other of our said Dominions....[1]

> [Goods exported without licence from any dominion and intended
> for sale abroad would be forfeited. Colonists committing offences
> against the subjects of a friendly Christian prince were to make
> due restitution on pain of outlawry after proclamation made in
> any convenient English port.]

XVIII. And finally, we do, for Us, our Heirs and Successors Grant and agree, to and with the said Sir Thomas
Gates, Sir George Somers, Richard Hackluit, and Edward-
Maria Wingfield, and all others of the said first Colony,
that We, our Heirs, and Successors, upon Petition in that
Behalf to be made, shall, by Letters-patent under the
Great Seal of England, give and grant unto such Persons,
their Heirs and Assigns, as the Council of that Colony,
or the most Part of them, shall, for that Purpose nominate
and assign, all the Lands, Tenements, and Hereditaments,

---

the royal instructions of 20 November 1606,see No.167.
1. Common lawyers, like Popham and Coke, were preserving the claim
of Englishmen beyond the realm to retain their rights (trial by jury,
law of inheritance *etc.*) in America. Colonists were not beyond the
law, but took the law,and their subjecthood,with them.

which shall be within as is aforesaid, to be holden of Us,
our Heirs, and Successors, the Precinct limited for that
Colony, as of our Manor at East-Greenwich in the County
of Kent, in free and common Soccage only, and not *in
Capite:* [1] ....

    [A similar grant of freehold tenure was made to Hanham and com-
    pany for the northern colony. Allocation of lands among the under-
    takers for each plantation would be a matter for the council of
    each colony.] [2]

160. NEWFOUNDLAND: CHARTER FROM JAMES I FOR A COMPANY, 2 May 1610. [3]

    Know ye whereas divers our loving and well-disposed
subjects are desirous to make plantation to inhabit and
establish a colony or colonies in the southern and eastern parts of the country and isle or islands commonly
called Newfound Land, unto the coast and harbours whereof
the subjects of this our Realm of England have for the
space of fifty years and upwards yearly used to resort in
no small numbers to fish, intending by such plantation
and inhabiting both to secure and make safe the said trade
of fishing to our subjects for ever, and also to make some
commendable benefit for the use of mankind by the lands
and profits thereof which hitherto from the beginning (as
it seemeth manifest) hath remained unprofitable, and for
better performance of such their purpose and intentions
have humbly besought our regal authority and assistance.
    We, being well assured that the same land or country

---

1. That is, that this remained king's land held as of a royal manor
in freehold tenure, not - as a feudal-service tenancy - direct from
the Crown.
2. On 23 May 1609 a second charter for Virginia, prepared by Sandys
and the law officers, Hobart and Bacon, separated the two corporate
companies, replaced the royal council by the company council, and
vested control of the colony in the treasurer and council of what
was now a joint stock company. The powers of shareholders in the
general court were increased in the third charter three years later:
[see below No.171].
3. C.T. Carr (ed.) *Select Charters* (Selden Soc. 1913: vol.XXVIII) pp.
51-62. A strong plea for planting Newfoundland 'to increase our great
shipping' had been made by Hakluyt in his *Discourse on Western planting* (1584) 'for it is the long voyages...that harden seamen'. John
Guy and Bristol adventurers had petitioned for this patent to enable
them to form a joint stock company on the Virginia model of 1609. It
gave them a monopoly of trade, not of fishing. Guy founded a colony
near Conception Bay, but it gradually languished into a seasonal fishing settlement. Calvert's colony later at Ferryland in Avalon seemed
to show greater powers of endurance, but he became interested in the
Maryland venture, and Kirke, who was granted a patent for the island
took over Ferryland and became involved in litigation over his charter. One difficulty in colonising Newfoundland was the fierce opposition of the fishermen of the Western ports who obtained royal
approval and recognition for their ancient rights by charter in 1634
and by parliamentary affirmation too:[see No.166)].

...remaineth so destitute and so desolate of inhabitants
that scarce any one savage person hath in many years been
seen in the most part thereof...and being so vacant is as
well for the reasons aforesaid as for many other reasons
very commodious for Us and our Dominions, And that by the
law of nature and nations We may of our royal authority
possess our selves and make grant thereof without doing
wrong to any other prince or state, considering they cannot justly pretend any sovereignty or right thereunto in
respect that the same remaineth so vacant and not actually possessed and inhabited by any Christian or any other
whomsoever, and therefore thinkinge it a matter and action
well beseeming a Christian king to make use of that which
God from the beginning created for mankind, and thereby
intending not onlie to work and prove the benifit and
good of many of our subjects, but principally to ourselves
to increase the knowledge of the omnipotent God and the
propogation of our Christian faith have graciously assented of their intention and suit,..

[the king therefore granted to the earl of Northampton, Sir
F. Bacon, J. Guy and others named and to be appointed, the right
to be 'one body or communalty perpetual' as 'The Treasurer and
Company of Adventurers and Planters...of London and Bristol for
the Colony or Plantation of Newfoundland'. Within the limits of
the grant (which were defined) their powers were to be as ample
as any which the Crown had ever heretofore granted to any company
'body politic or corporate, or to any adventurer or adventurers'
in any foreign part whatever. The existing fishing rights of
Englishmen and aliens, however, were not to be impaired. The
Treasurer and company were to hold their lands 'as of our manor
of East Greenwich...in free and common socage and not *in capite*'
and to pay to the Crown one-fifth of any precious metals.]

And forasmuch as the good and prosperous success of the
said plantation cannot but chiefly depend, next under the
Blessing of God and the support of our royal authority,
upon the provident and good direction of the whole enterprise by a careful and understanding Council, And that it
is not convenient that all the Adventurers shall be so
often drawn to meet and assemble as shall be requisite for
them to have meetings and conferences about their affairs,
Therefore We do ordain establish and confirm That there
shall be perpetually one Council consisting of twelve persons here resident in London which shall govern and order
all matters and causes which shall arise, grow or happen
by reason of the said plantation, or which shall or may
concern the government of any colony or colonies to be established in any the said territories or countries of Newfound Land before limited or any the precints thereof....

[The first treasurer and council were named. Subsequent vacancies were to be filled by a majority vote of those adventurers present. They were further granted the right to make coin for use in
Newfoundland.]

And further *[We]* grant full power and authority to the
said Council here resident...from time to time to nominate

...and likewise to revoke...all and singular governors,
officers and ministers which hereafter by them shall be
thought fit and needful to be made or used for the government of any colony or plantation in Newfoundland...And
also to make...all manner of orders, laws, directions,
instructions, forms, and ceremonies of government and
magistracy...not only within the precincts of the said
colony...but also upon the seas in going or coming to and
from the said colony...as they in their good discretions
shall think to be fit for the good of the adventurers and
inhabiters there....

[All officials and residents were to be subject to the government appointed by the council. The consent of a *quorum* of five
councillors was necessary for the admission of new members of the
company, and that of a majority of the general-assembly for the
ejection of existing members. The company might take out of
the realm and dominions such subjects (and strangers who wished
to become subjects) as were willing to become settlers, together
with supplies necessary 'for the use and defence and trade' there.
For seven years such necessaries were free from export duties and
for 21 years from import duties, save a 5% merchant tax. The company's governor might eject unauthorised settlers and impose a
fine of 5% on unlicensed traders if subjects; and of 10% if
aliens. For 21 years the company might use the money for the
benefit of itself or its plantation; thereafter the Crown would
take it. Colonists and their posterity born there would have
all the liberties of free Englishmen.]

And forasmuch as it shall be necessary for all such
our loving subjects as shall inhabit within the said territories or precincts of Newfound Land aforesaid to determine to live together in the fear and true worship of
Almighty God Christian peace and civil quietness each with
other, whereby every one may with more safety pleasure
and profit enjoy that whereunto they shall attain without
great pain and peril, We...do give and grant to the said
Treasurer and Company and their successors and to such
governors, officers, and ministers as shall be by the
said Council constituted and appointed according to the
natures and limits of their offices and places respectively, That they shall and may from time to time for ever
hereafter within the said territories or precincts of
Newfound Land or in the way by the seas thither and from
thence have full and absolute power and authority to correct, punish, pardon, govern, and rule all subjects of
Us, our heirs and successors, as shall from time to time
adventure themselves in any voyage thither, or that shall
at any time hereafter inhabit in the precincts and territories of the said land called Newfound Land aforesaid,
according to such orders, ordinances constitutions, directions and instructions as by the said Council as aforesaid shall be established, and in defect thereof in cause
of necessity according to the good discretions of the said
governors and officers respectively as well in cases

capital and criminal as civil: So always as the said
statutes, ordinances, and proceedings as near as conveniently may be shall be agreeable to the laws statutes government and policy of this our Realm of England.

And We do further...grant declare and ordain That such
principal Governor or Governors as from time to time shall
duly and lawfully be authorised and appointed in manner
and form in these presents heretofore expressed, shall
have full power and authority to use and exercise martial
law in cases of rebellion or mutiny in as large and ample
manner as our Lieutenants in our counties within our Realm
of England have or ought to have by force of their commission of Lieutenancy:...

[Goods fraudulently exported from any of 'our Kingdoms' to a
foreign country on the pretext of intending to land them within
the territories now granted would be forfeited.]

And further our will and pleasure is that in all questions and doubts that shall arise upon any difficulty of
construction or interpretation of any thing contained in
these our Letters Patents, the same shall be taken and interpreted in most ample and beneficial manner for the said
Treasurer and Company and their successors and every member thereof:...

[The names of the company's adventurers were to be enrolled in
a record book which would be proof that their privileges were as
full and absolute as if they had been named in these letters patent. To prevent the extension of the Church of Rome, the oath of
supremacy was to be administered to all going to settle there.
Offences against friendly Christian princes by colonists, however,
were to be punished by outlawry, if after proclamation 'within
any part of the realm of England commodious for that purpose', restitution had not been made within a set time-limit.]

161. BERMUDA: CHARTER FROM JAMES I FOR A COMPANY, 29 June 1615.[1]
[The history of the Virginian charters, of the sale of the islands to Sir William Wade and others in November 1612 and of their

---

1. J.H. Lefroy, *Memorials of the discovery...of the Bermudas,1515-
1685*. (1877) Vol.I p.90. The Bermuda (or Somers Isles) Company was
incorporated after the purchase of the islands - Prospero's'still-
vex'd Bermoothes' - from the Virginia Company by which, as a result
of the shipwreck there of Sir Thomas Gates and Sir George Somers in
1609, they had been claimed as 'discoveries': the Virginia charter
of 12 March 1612 had extended the company's claim over islands 300
leagues from the mainland.
A colony was founded on St. George's Island and divided into 'families', , 'tribes' and'hundreds'; and by 1620 the settlers had an
assembly of the resident governor, council, and elected representatives for the purposes of levying taxes and making laws. But the main
control remained at the company's headquarters in London, Sir Thomas
Smith had been chosen as the first governor of this company as he remained also the executive head (treasurer) of the parent Virginia Company. But since the earl of Warwick had been the prime mover in obtaining this Bermuda charter from the Crown, he resented Smith's

surrender to the Crown in November 1614 was recounted. The islands
were now regranted to the earl of Southampton, Sir Thomas Smith,
Sir Edwin Sandys and others.   The Company was incorporated in
England and Wales and their lands were to be held 'as of our Mannor of East Greenwich in free and Common Soccage and not in Capite' with one-fifth of any gold and silver to be reserved to the
Crown. The organisation of the company by governor and 24 elected
assistants in general court of assembly was laid down.[1] The governor and a *quorum* of seven assistants would deal with the executive business concerning the plantation and the Company; and the
governor and a majority vote of those present might legislate
provided their laws 'bee not contrary to the Laws and Statutes of
this our Realme of England'...]
     ...And our will and pleasure is, and hereby wee do est-
ablishe and ordeyne That once euerie yeare, namely the last
Wednesday in Easter Terme, the place of Gouernor, Deputy
and Assistants of the said Company and all other officers
of the said Company here residinge shalbee void and shalbee then in the general Court to bee holden for that day
newly chosen for the yeare ensuinge by the greater parte
of the voices of the said Company then present and except
for death, sickness or absence or any other importante
occasion, the said Companie shalbee drawne to nominate and
elect the said Governour or deputy or other officers at any
other tyme: In which cases it shalbee lawfull for them to
proceede to a new eleccon according to their discretons....
     [The letters patent specified that] ...a just and equall
division of the said Islands and of the landes and other
comodities, profitts and hereditaments therein conteyned
shall be made by the said Governor and Company in some
great and generall Quarter courte assembled, whereof one
parte not exceedinge a fourth-part of the said Islands
shall be allotted and reserved to the said Governour and
Company in comon for the maintenance and defraying of generall and publique charges from tyme to tyme. And the remaine and the profitts of the said landes and other Hereditaments, soe to be allotted in comon, after the said publique charges defrayed shalbee yearely devided amongst the
severall members of the said company according to the proporcon of each Mans severall shares or parts....
     [The rest of the islands was to be divided into eight 'tribes',
each of 50 shares; public lands and profits were not to be alien-

---

pluralism and, in alliance with Sir Edwin Sandys, sought to unseat
him. Sandys was indeed elected treasurer of the Virginia Company in
1619, but Smith, perhaps with the aid of the device of the ballot box
borrowed by Sandys from the East India Company practice, was re-elected governor of the Bermuda Company.
In 1673 the assembly was suspended when the elected representatives
attempted to sit apart from the governor and council in Bermuda. In
1684 the company was dissolved and Bermuda became a royal colony.
1. The royal council of the Virginia Charter of 1606 had been abandoned in their second charter of February 1609.

ated unless with the Company's consent. No man was to hold more than 10 shares without court's consent, or more than 15 under any circumstances. No one might have a voice in the Court unless he owned at least one share.]

162. LETTERS PATENT FROM JAMES I FOR THE COUNCIL FOR NEW ENGLAND,
3 November 1620.[1]
[The patent recited the Virginian charters of 1606, and of 1609 (when the London and Plymouth companies had been separated). Sir Ferdinando Gorges and others now intended to establish a 'fishery, trade and plantation' within the limits of the northern territory: some of whom had indeed already 'taken actual possession' in the king's name 'as Sovereign Lord thereof' and 'have settled' people there. They therefore petitioned for incorporation and for the grant to them of the usual rights and privileges in the area between 40° and 48°N on grounds that it was not 'actually in possession' of a Christian prince and 'deserted' by 'its naturall inhabitants', the Indians, through plague and savage warfare. Therefore in order to convert the heathen, to secure civil order, to enlarge his dominions and to improve the fortune of the adventures,]

...Wee therefore...do...grant...that all that circuit, continent, precincts, and limitts in America, lying and being in breadth from fourty degrees of northerly latitude, from the equinoctiall line, to fourty-eight degrees of the said northerly latitude, and in length by all the breadth aforesaid throughout the maine land, from sea to sea, with all the seas, rivers, islands, creeks, inletts, ports,and havens, within the degrees...of the said latitude and longitude, shall be the limitts...of the second collony to be called *New England*...For the better plantac-

---

1. F. W. Thorpe, *The federal and state constitutions* (1909) III pp. 1827-40. The moribund Virginia Company of Plymouth had virtually expired in 1608 after the failure and repatriation of the brief colony at Sagadahoc in Maine. Gorges – like Gilbert and Ralegh a landed gentleman rather than a merchant– sought to reorganise the company on proprietary, not commercial lines: a board of landed proprietors, – without the normal organisation of general courts and voting by shareholders – to distribute estates in America, perhaps with semi-feudal fiefs and the manorial institutions familiar in Devon. This patent, however, was primarily for a land company: unlike the Massachusetts Bay Company charter [see below No.165] – it was not granted full powers and authority to rule and administer all plantations set up within its dominion.That the grant was delayed some eight months was due partly to the opposition to its exclusive right to fish in northern waters.   One result of the delay was that the Pilgrim Fathers, unwilling to wait any longer – sailed from Plymouth without a patent from this Council, which they would have preferred, and resolved to make do with the patent they had – that to Peirce and 'his associates – from the London Company, hoping to establish themselves as a distinct plantation and 'civil community' within the government of 'Virginia'.

ion, ruling and governing of the aforesaid New England,
Wee...ordain that from henceforth there shall be...in our
Towne of Plymouth, in the County of Devon, one body polit-
icque and corporate, which shall have perpetuall succession, which shall consist of the number of fourtie persons,
and no more, which shall be, and shall be called and knowne by the name, *the Councill established at Plymouth in
the County of Devon for the planting, ruling, ordering,
and governing of New-England, in America....*
    [The first council was named. Its members included Buckingham,
    Salisbury, Warwick, Ferdinando Gorges, Thomas Gates and Rawleigh
    Gilbert. The council was empowered to fill vacancies, to elect
    a President, to own property, to sue and be sued as a corporate
    body.]
    And Wee do further...grant...that it shall...be law-
full...for the said Councill...in their discretions...to
admitt such...persons to be made free and enabled to
trade...unto...New-England...and unto every part and
parcell thereof, or to have...any lands or hereditaments
in New-England...as they shall think fitt, according to
the laws, orders, constitutions, and ordinances by the
said Councill and their successors from time to time to
be made....
    [The council was invested with full powers of appointment and
    dismissal of officials and of 'government and magistracy', pro-
    vided any orders they make were 'not contrary to the laws and
    statutes of the realm'. The governor might exercise martial law
    in case of insurrection.]
    And Wee do further...absolutely give, grant and con-
firm unto the said Councill...all the aforesaid lands,
waters, fisheries, mines *[etc.]* ...and singular other commodities, jurisdictions, royalties, privileges, franchises
and preheminences...to be holden of Us...as of our manor
of East Greenwich in our County of Kent in free and comon
soccage and not *in capite*, nor by Knight's Service....
    [The council was empowered to manage and allocate these lands.
    It might defend its territories from unlicensed interlopers and
    enemies and might enforce its contracts with its servants, sailors
    and labourers. It might send out emigrants, together with goods
    'necessary for the said Plantacion'.]
    And Wee grant unto the said Councill...that the said
territoryes...shall not be visited, frequented or traded
unto by any other of our subjects...either from any the
ports and havens belonging or appertayning...unto Us...
or to any forraigne state, prince or pottentate whatsoever. And therefore Wee do hereby...charge...all the
subjects of Us to what degree and quality soever they be,
that none of them directly or indirectly presume to vissitt,
frequent, trade or adventure or traffick unto or from the
said territories...unless it be with the license and consent of the said Councill and Company first had and obtained in writing under the Common Seal....
    [on pain of displeasure, imprisonment and forfeiture.[1] Those

---

1. As fishing could not be carried on without access to the land,

servants who broke their contracts or who were brought back to
England for 'notorious misdemeanours', were liable to arrest by
the President, examination before the Council, and punishment
either by being bound over according to the English practice, or
by being sent back to New England to be dealt with by the Company.
English settlers and their children would have all the rights of
natural born Englishmen, but no one might emigrate thither without
first taking the oath of supremacy. For seven years the Council
was freed from customs duties and for 21 years from impositions.
The Crown promised to amplify and extend the powers granted, should
these prove inadequate.]

163. *PUBLIC DEBATE OVER MONOPOLIES IN AMERICA AND THE EAST*, 1621:
     (a) DEBATES ON FISHING RIGHTS OF THE NEW ENGLAND COUNCIL, 25
          April, 2 May, 24 May, 20 November, and 1 December 1621.[1]
25 April 1621 (H.C.)
     Sir Edw. Sands: Moveth...a free liberty for all the
King's subjects for fishing there. That the taking of
timber and wood *[was]* no prejudice to the colony. A beneficial fishing *[might be]* hoped for on the south of America. *[It would be]* pitiful, *[if]* any of the king's subjects
should be prohibited, sithence Dutch and French *[were]* at
liberty; who come, and will fish there, notwithstanding
the colony....
     Mr. Secretary *[Sir George Calvert]*[2] doubteth. The fisher-
men *[were]* the hinderers of the plantation, That they burn
great store of woods,and choak the havens. *[He]* will
never strain the King's prerogative against the good of
the commonwealth, *[It was]* not fit to make any laws here
[i.e. in Parliament] for those countries which *[were]* not as
yet annexed to this crown.
     Mr. Guy:[3] If this House have jurisdiction to meddle with
this bill, *[he]* would consent to the proceeding thereof,
That there are divers patents....That the king hath already
done, by his great seal, as much as can be done here by
this Act....

---

this section gave to the Council a fishing monopoly in northern waters. The Virginia Company of London objected strongly to its exclusion from these fisheries [see No.163 (a)] and, though the privy council confirmed the monopoly (Acts of the Privy Council I No. 65),oppos-
ition in the Commons to Gorges' grant continued until Charles I dispensed with Parliaments in 1628.
1. By the provisions of this bill debated in the Commons, all British
subjects were to have free right of fishing on the shores of America,
and to select their places for curing fish according to priority of
arrival, with liberty to take wood for fuel and repairs (Hist.MSS.Comm.
Third *Rept.*, App.,p.21).The bill, which passed in the Commons but which
was not sent to the Lords, was a protest against the monopoly of fishing rights granted in November, 1620, to the Council of New England.
2. Calvert received a grant for his colony in Newfoundland in 1623
[see pp.215-7].
3. He had been resident governor of Newfoundland, 1610-12, after the
grant of the charter from James I [see No.160];and the mayor of
Bristol, 1618-9.

Mr. Brooke: That we may make laws here for Virginia;
for, if the king give consent to this bill, passed here,
and by the Lords, this will controul the patent. The case
[was] diverse for Gascoigne, *[Aquitaine,etc.]* which *[were a]*
principality of themselves. *[His vote was]* to commit it.
    Sir Edw. Sands: That Virginia *[was]* holden of the manor
of East Greenwich. *[i.e. he was arguing that Parliament in which
Greenwich was represented therefore could legislate for North America.]*

2 May [1]
    I was present at the comittee in Chequer. A business
it was of 3 partes:
1. Appered Mr. Gwy *[Guy]* for Newfoundland, offerynge his
provisoe which was rejected, yet not very unreasonable, in
respect of his preterite paines and cost.
2. Two mercuryes, Sir Ferd *[inando]* Gorges and Sir Jo *[hn]*
Bowser *[Bourchur]*. who brought incantations in their mouthes
by their elegant speeches. And theis would monopolize
[i.e. support the monopoly of] fishinge. Offered it was by
Mr. Chidleigh[2] in their behalfes *[i.e. the Western Adventurers]*
to have from them liberty, if we[3] take it in curtersy:
which was to accept of my birthright in curtesy from a
subject, when also God and nature, by right of creation,
had made the sea free. And theis men which are the northern plantation or New England, have not one man there, in
theis 70 years. They would reny *[i.e. refuse]* liberty of
wood and tymber for stages to dry fish: and to repair or
make botses, and whereas to destroy wood (in those vast
cuntryes all woodes for 1000 of myles), it a benefit, and
to preserve wood is a manifest mischeefe to the planter,
whose far greatest labor is to cleere ground and destroy
wood, 9 partes of 10 of his labors: and theis New England
men will nether plant themselfes, nor suffer others, ney-
ther eate hay themselfes, nor suffer the laborynge oxe:
like coles'dog: or as bests, - like my next neighbor's
signe of St. George, that is ever redy on horsbacke , but
never rydeth forwardes, *nec movet, nec promovet*.
    The 3 was the Virginia Company, who wish all to be free,
and geve leave to all men freely on their coasts: and assented willingly to the bill: a company that undergoeth all
care, labor, and charges out of their privates, for a generall one, and publicke good of the common welth: who can

---

1. The draft bill was committed to a subcommittee of Sandys, the burgesses of London, York and port towns in the Exchequer Chamber to meet
on 2nd May. This account of the proceedings written by John Smyth of
Nibley, M.P. for Midhurst, is undated. (Add. MSS 34121 ff.11-12).
2. George Chidleigh (or Chudley), representing Lostwithiel, was also
named in the patent as one of the councillors of New England.
3. It would seem that John Smyth was opposed to the New England monopoly and that these remarks constitute his own comments on Chudley's
suggestion. He appears to continue with an attack on what he regarded
as the 'dog-in-the-manger' attitude adopted by the planters towards
the fishermen.

never looke for any benefit by dyvidend....
Whereupon consideringe the benefitt which Virginia prom-
iseth (and so touch it somewhat at large) conclude, that
Sith this bill aymeth at the help towards that plantation,
that it is a good bill, and wish it to passe for a laws.
24 May
 Mr. Earle reporteth the bill of fishing upon the coast
of America, with the amendments, which twice read....
 Mr. Secretary: That this bill not proper for this
House because concerneth America.[1]
20 November
 Mr. Glanvyle moveth, to speed the bill of fishing upon
[the] coasts of America; the rather, because Sir Fer*[din-
ando]* Gorges hath executed a patent sithence the recess.[2]
Hath, by letters from the Lords of the Council, stayed
the ships ready to go forth.[3]
 Mr. Neale, accordant. That Sir Ferd.hath besides threatened to send out ships, to beat them off from their free
fishing; and restraineth the ships, *ut supra*. Moveth
the House to take consideration hereof.
 Sir W. Heale:That this was true; but my Lord Treasurer *[Sir Lionel Cranfield]* hath given order, that the ships
shall go forth presently, without stay.
 Sir Edw. Coke: That the patent may be brought in. And
 Sir Tho. Wentworth: That the party may be sent for.

1 December
 *An act for the freer Liberty of fishing, and fishing voyages, to
be made and performed in the sea-coasts and places of New-found-
land, Virginia, New England, and other the sea-coasts and ports of
America.*
 Mr. Guy: That this bill taketh away trade of fishing
from those which are inhabitants of Newfound-land. Tender-
eth a proviso, *[presumably to preserve the interests of the Newfoundland patentees]* in parchment which twice read.
 Mr. Neale, against this proviso, That the choice of
the first place in every harbour, which desired by it,
restraineth all liberty of free fishing.[4]

---

1. That is, presumably, that it was a matter for the king and that
overseas dominions were not the concern of parliament.
2. On 4 June Parliament had adjourned to 14 November. On 1 June the
Council for New England issued to John Peirce a patent through which
the Pilgrims obtained a legal right to make a settlement in New England.
Sir Ferdinando Gorges was for many years governor of Plymouth, Devon.
He had long been interested in colonisation of North America and had
taken a lead in reorganising the Plymouth 'Virginia Company' and the
Council for New England in 1620.
3. On 28 September the privy council, in a letter addressed to the
mayors of certain seaport towns,merchants, and owners of ships, forbade, under threat of punishment, trade with New England, to the prejudice of that plantation, and without respect to the government or
orders established for the public good.
4. The first arrival in the fleet from the West country each season

[He referred to 13 Eliz I cap.11 which permitted the free export of herring and fish 'to any place out of the Dominions' and
the free import of cod and ling by English subjects. In the debate
of 17 April he had cited 2 Edw. VI cap.6 which enabled merchants
and fishermen trading with Iceland, Newfoundland and Ireland' to
practise and use the same trade of Merchandise and Fishing, freely
without any such Charges or Exactions as is before limited' to
promote the supply of fish for England in greater quantities and
'at more reasonable Prices'.]
That they may take the first place now, if can get it;
but the thing desited, is a choice place in every harbour: and not only for themselves, but for their company.
   Mr. Secretary, contra. That plantations fit to be
cherished, *[would be]* overthrown by this will, without the
proviso. That this bill giveth priority of the *[landing]*
stage to those, that come; *[i.e. the fishing fleets]* and
may put out those, which plant and inhabit there. Doubt-
eth, without this proviso, the bill will never pass the
royal assent.[1]

163. (b) THOMAS MUN: A DEFENCE OF THE EAST INDIA TRADE, 1621.[2]
   The trade of Merchandize, is not onely that laudable
practize whereby the entercourse of Nations is so worth-
ily performed, but also (as I may terme it) the verie
Touchstone of a kingdomes prosperitie, when therein some
certen rules shall be diligently observed....
   And therefore, as it is most plaine, that proportion
or quantitie, must ever be regarded in the importing of
forren wares; so must there also be a great respect of
qualitie and use; that so, the things most necessarie be
first preferred; such as are foods, rayment, and munition

---

took the best mooring; in Newfoundland the first captain became 'admiral' [see Vol.II: also p.260n.] .
1. The bill without Guy's proviso was passed by the Commons, but was
never sent to the Lords.
2. From Thomas Mun, *A discourse of trade from England to the East
Indies, answering to diverse objections which are usually made against
the same* (1621). A London merchant, Mun also wrote *England's treasure by foreign trade, or The balance of our foreign trade is the rule
of our treasure* (published by his son in 1664) which considered the
increase of English exports and the decrease of English reliance on
foreign goods. He analysed the characteristics, knowledge, and abilities necessary for a merchant as the 'steward of the kingdom's stock
...a work of no less reputation than trust which ought to be performed
with great skill and conscience that so the private gain may ever
accompany the publique good'. Foreign trade was, he argued, 'the
great revenue of the King, the honour of the kingdom, the noble profession of the merchant, the school of our arts, the supply of our
wants, the employment of our poor, the improvement of our lands, the
nurcery of our mariners, the walls of the kingdoms, the means of our
treasure, the sinnews of our wars, the terror of our enemies'. He considered the East India trade the most profitable for the realm. Of
course his pamphlets were promotional, the substance of things hoped

for warre and trade; which great blessinges, when any
countrie doth sufficiently enjoy; the next to be procured are wares, fitting for health, and arts; the last,
are those, which serve for our pleasures, and ornament.
    Now, forasmuch, as by the providence of almightie God,
the kingdome of England, is indowed with such aboundance
of rich commodities, that it hath long enjoyed, not onely
great plentie of the things before named, but also,through
the superfluitie, hath been much inriched with treasure
brought in from forren parts; which had given life unto
so many worthy trades, amongst which that unto the East
India by name; the report whereof, although it is already
spread so famous through the world; yet notwithstanding,
heere at home, the clamorous complaints against the same,
are growne so loude and generall....
The first Objection. *It were a happie thing for Christendome (say many men) that the Navigation to the East-Indies,
by way of the Cape of Good hope, had never bene found out,
For in the fleetes of shippes, which are sent thither
yearely out of England, Portingall, and the Low countries;
The gold, silver, and Coyne of Christendome, and particularly of this Kingdome, is exhausted, to buy unnecessarie
wares.*
The Answere. The matter of this Objection is very waighty,
and therefore, it ought to be answered fully; the which
that I may the better performe, I will divide the same
into three parts. 1. In the first I will consider, the
necessarie use of the wares, which are usually bought out
of East-India into Europe; namely, Druggs, Spices, Raw
silke, Indicoe, and Callicoes, 2. In the Second; I will
intimate the manner and meanes, by which the said wares
have beene heretofore, and now are brought into Europe.
3. In the Third and last; I will prove, that the Treasure
of England, is not consumed, but rather greatly to be increased by the performance of the said Trade....So that
by the substance, and summes of these accompts, it doth
plainely appeare, that the buying of the said quantitie
of Rawsilkes, Indico, and Spices, may be performed in the
Indies, for neare one third part of the ready moneyes,
which were accustomed to be sent into Turkey to provide
the same; So that there will be saved everie yeare the
value of £953,543 4s. 4d. sterling of readie moneyes,
that heretofore hath beene exported out of Christendome
into Turkey;...but I conceave I have sayd sufficient, to
shew how the trade of the East Indies hath bene, and now
is brought into Christendome generally: what money is
yearly sent out; by whom; and the possibilitie, or meanes which they have to performe it. I will therefore in
the next place, satisfie the Objectors; that it is not
the East-India Trade, which wasteth the Gold, and Silver,
Coyne, or other treasure of this kingdome in particular.
    For first, who knoweth not, that gold in the East-
Indies hath no ratable price with Silver? Neither hath

---

for, not necessarily secured.

the Silver coyne of England any equally value with the
Spanish Rialls according to their severall prizes here;
Besides that, his Majestie hath not authorized the East-
India Companie, to send away any part of this kingdomes
Coyne either Gold, or Silver; but onely a certaine limited summe of forren Silver yearlie; which as they dare
not exceede, so never have theyas yet accomplished the
same. For it doth plainely appeare in their bookes; that
from the originall and first foundation of the Trade, in
Anno. 1601. untill the moneth of July, Anno. 1620. they
have shipped away onely £548,090 sterling in Spanish Rialls, and some Dollers; whereas, by licence, they might
have exported in that time £720,000 sterling. Also, they
have laden away in the same tearme of xix yeares, out of
this Kingdome £292,286 sterling in Broad-clothes, Kersies,
Lead, Tinne, with some other English and forren commodities; which is a good Addition, and vent of our wares, into
such remote places; where heretofore they have had no
utterance at all....

And now (omitting much matter which might be written
touching the discoveries of other Trades from one Kingdome or port to another, in the Indies: with the commodities thereof, whereby the imployment of our shippes, together with the stocke of money and goodes which is sent
out of England in them, may be much increased) I will
draw to a conclusion of the point in hand; and shewe,
that whatsoever Summes of forren readie monyes are yearely sent from hence into the East-Indies, His Majestie in
the letters Patents graunted to that Company, hath notwithstanding with singular care provided, that the brethen of
the Company shall yearely bring in as much silver, as they
send forth; which hath beene alwayes truly performed,
with an overplus, to the increase of this Kingdomes treasure: Neither is it likelie, that the money which is thus
contracted for, by the Companie at certaine prices, and
to be delivered them at times appointed, would bee otherwise brought into England, but onely by vertue and for performance of the said cotracts; for, without this assurance of Vent, together with a good price for the said
monyes, the Merchants would undoubtedly make their returnes
in other wares; the use and extraordinarie consume whereof, would be found lesse profittable to the Commonwealth,
when the matter should be duly considered, as I shall yet
further endeavour to demonstrate....For if the rule be
true, that when the value of our commedyties exported doth
overballance the worth of all those forraigne wares which
are imported and consumed in this kingdome, then the rem-
aynder of our stock which is sent forth, must of necessitie
returne to us in Treasure. I am confident that upon a
diligent and true inquiry it will be found, that the overballance of all our other Trades together will not amount
unto so greate a summe of money as the East-India Trade
alone doth overballance in this kinde....And to make the
matter yet more plaine, whereas it is already said that

£100,000 in money exported may import about the value of
£500,000 sterling in wares from the East-Indies, wee must
understand that part thereof to bee properly called our
importation that this Realme doth consume, which is about
the value of £120,000 sterling yeerely. So the remainder
being £380,000 is matter exported unto forraine partes in
the nature of our Cloath, Lead, Tinne, or any other native
commodities, to the great increase of this kingdomes
stocke, and that also in so much Treasure, so farre as
the East-India Trade can be rightly understood to subsist
in this particular....

The second Objection. *The timber, Plancke, and other mat-*
erialls, for making of shipping, is exceedinglie Wasted,
and made dearer, by the building of so many great Shippes,
as are yearely sent to Trade in the East-Indies; and yet
the State hath no use of any of them upon occasion; For
either they are not here; or else they come home verie
weake, and unserviceable.

...Do they not knowe that trees doe live and growe;
and being great, they have a time to dye and rot, if
opportunitie make no better use of them? and what more
noble or profitable use then goodly Shipps for Trade and
warre? are they not our barnes for wealth and plentie,
serving as walles and Bulwarkes for our peace and happ-
ines ? Doe not their yearely buildings maintaine many
hundred poore people, and greatlie increase the number
of those Artesmen which are so needfull for this commonwealth? ...the East-India companie are well prepared at
all times, to serve his Majestie and his Kingdomes,with
many warlike provisions,which they alwayes keep in store;
such as Timber, Plancks, Ironworkes, Masts, Cordage,
Anchors, Caske, Ordinance, Powder, Shot, Victualls readie
packed, Wine, Sider, and a world of other things, fitting
the present building, repairing and dispatch of Shippes
to Sea;...[1]

The third Objection. *The voyages to the East Indies doe*
greatly consume our victuals, and our Marriners: leaving
many poore Widdowes and Children unrelieved; Besides,
that many Ships are yearely sent forth to the East Indies,
and few we see as yet returned; Also, this Trade hath
greatly decayed the Traffique and shipping, which were
wont to be imployed into the Streights: And yet the said
Trade to the East Indies, is found very unprofitable to
the Adventurers: Neither doth the Common-wealth finde
any benefit by the cheapenesse of Spice and Indico, more
then in times past.

...Thus doth it plainely appeare, that these revolutions
of Trades, have and doe turne to the good of the Commonwealth; neither hath the affayres of the East Indies
impaired or decayed any other Trade, Shipping or Marriners of this Realme; but hath mightily increased them
all in it selfe. Wherefore let us now take a view of
this noble addition of the kingdomes strength and glory....

1. Clearly Mun's expectations were exaggerated.

The fourth Objection. *It is generally observed that his Majesties Mint hath had but little imployment ever sithence the East India Trade began; wherefore it is manifest, that the onely remedie for this, and so many evils besides, is to put downe this Trade: For what other remedie can there be for the good of the Common-wealth?*
...And that the pretended evill which many with malice chase, is that great good, which other Nations seeke by pollicie and strength to keepe, and likewise to obtaine; In which proceedings, it concerneth us, especially to observe the diligences and practises of the Dutch; who with more gladnesse would undertake the whole Trade to the East Indies, then with any reason we can abandon that part thereof, which we now enjoy; neither can our restraint from the Indies keepe our Silver from thence, as long as the Dutch goe thither: for we know, that devices want not to furnish such dessignes; and when their Ships returne from India, shall not our Silver out againe to helpe to pay a double price, or what they please, for all those wares which we shall want for our necessities?...
   Neither is this importation meant otherwise than concerning those wares, which are consumed in this Realm: for the comodities which are brought in, and after carried out unto forren parts again, canot hurt but doe greatly help the comonwealth, by encrease of his Majesties Customes and Trades, with other imployments of the subjects; by which particulars I might yet set foorth the glory of the East India Trade, which hath brought into this Realme in fifteene moneths space, not onely so much Spice, as hath served the same for the sayd time; but also by the superfluitie thereof, there hath beene exported into forraine parts for about £215,000 sterling. So then let all men judge, for what a great value wee may hope hereafter to export yearely: when unto these spices we may (by God's assistance) add the infinite worth of Rawsilkes, Indicoes, Callicoes, and some other things: All which are to bee issued in the nature of Cloth, Lead, Tinne, or any of our owne Merchandize to the enriching of this Kingdome by encrease of the Common-stocke. So then to conclude the point, we ought not to avoid the importation of forraine wares, but rather willingly to bridle our owne affections to the moderate consuming of the same: for otherwise, howsoever the East India Trade in particular is an excellent meanes greatly to encrease the stocke of mony which we send thither yearely, by returning home five times the value thereof in rich commodities all which (in short time) may be converted into Treasure,...Yet notwithstanding, if these Indian wares thus brought home, cannot be spared to serve for that purpose of Treasure; but must be sent forth together with our owne native commodities: and yet all little enough to provide our excesse and extraordinary consume of forraine wares: then is it likewise as certaine that the generall Trade of this Kingdome doth hinder and divert the comming in of the said

Treasure by over-ballancing the value of our wares exported; with the importation and immoderate consume of
forraine Commodities....

164. VIRGINIA: JAMES I TO THE SPEAKER, 28 April 1624.[1]
    Whereas Wee have taken notice that some of the Virgin-
ia Compagnie have presented a petition to our House of
Commons [which was likely to renew the discords the king had sought to calm] We doe signify to our House of Commons, That
wee hold it very unfitt for the Parliament to trouble
themselves with those matters, which can produce nothing,
but a further increase of schisme, and faction, and dis
turbe the happy and peaceable proceeding of the Parliament which wee hope your cares (as hitherto they have done)
shall concurr with ours to bring to a good issue. As for
these businesses of Virginia, and the Barmudoes, ourself
have taken them to heart, and will make it our own worke
to settle the quiet, and wellfare of those plantations,
and will bee ready to doe anything that may bee forthe
reall benefitt, and advancement of them.
Comment by Sir Francis Nethersole, May 1624.[2]
    ...In this strayteness of time as it was apprehended
there was not withstanding a motion made for the hearing
of the late differences in the Virginia Company...the
contentyons and factions occasioned by them being growne
so great...thereupon though with much unwillingness the
matter was entertayned in our house, and a Committee of
the whole house appoynted to heare the cause....But...
came a letter from the King dyrected to the Speaker of
our house by which his Majesty talking of this business
in very fayre termes, forbad the house to proceede any
further therein as having beene by him specially recommended to his Councill who had already taken much paynes
to quiet those troubles in the sayd Company, which his
Majesty feared might be stirred agayne by our meddling
with them and other among ourselves by occasion thereof.
This was assented unto by a general silence, but not without some soft mutterings that by this meanes and example,
my Lord Treasurers business or any other might be taken
out of the Parliament.

165. MASSACHUSETTS: FIRST CHARTER FROM CHARLES I FOR A COMPANY,
                                        4 March 1629.[3]
    [The charter began with a recital of the patent of 1620 to the
New England Council, and confirmed the subsequent grant by that

---

1. State papers (Domestic) : James I vol.CLXIII, No. 71.
2. Cal. State Papers (Colonial) 1574-1660 p.62:he was M.P. for Corfe.
3. *Records of the Governor and Company of the Massachusetts Bay*,I
pp. 3-19. A New England Company was formed in 1628 as a venture to
plant a 'bible commonwealth' in the area round Cape Ann where both
a New Plymouth out-colony and a Dorchester enterprise had failed to
establish a resident fishery plantation. The Rev. John White, rector
of Dorchester, and his associates, used Rosewall, the high sheriff

body on 19 March 1628 to Sir Henry Rosewall and others. The territorial limits of the grant were defined together with mineral and
fishing rights, provided that these lands were not actually possessed by another Christian prince or within the bounds of any English colony already established. Lands were to be held in free
and common soccage 'as of our manor of East Greenwich' on payment
of one-fifth of gold and silver ore. The company was incorporated
- 'one body politique and corporate in deed, fact and name' with
the usual legal rights and obligations.]
   ...And wee doe hereby...graunte, That...there shalbe
one Governor, one Deputy Governor, and eighteene Assistants...to be from tyme to tyme...chosen out of the freemen of the saide Company, for the tyme being, in such manner and forme as hereafter in theis presents, is expressed.
Which said officers shall applie themselves to take care
for the best disposeing and ordering of the generall buy-
sines and affaires of...the said landes and premisses...
and the plantacion thereof, and the government of the
people there....
   [The names of the first governor, Mathewe Cradocke, his deputy
   and assistants were listed. The governor was empowered to call
   assemblies of the Company.]
   And that the said Governor, Deputie Governor, and Assistants...shall or maie once every moneth, or oftener at
their pleasures, assemble, and houlde, and keepe a Courte
or Assemblie of themselves, for the better ordering and
directing of their affaires.... [Any seven assistants with the
Governor or deputy should constitute a 'sufficient court or assembly'
to conduct business.] ...and that there shall or maie be held
...upon every last Wednesday in Hillary, Easter, Trinity,
and Michas termes respectivelie for ever, one greate, generall and solempe Assemblie, which foure Generall Assemb-

---

of Devon and other influential patrons to secure a grant somewhat
covertly from the earl of Warwick, president of the Council for New
England. But whether that grant of 19 March 1628 was made by him officially as president, or privately as a recipient of a grant 'in the
Massachusetts' on 31 May 1622, is not clear. He may indeed have re-
assigned that petty fief which he held of the king in common soccage
to the New England Company. (That original grant was taken to New
England for safety and greater independence, and may well have been
amended and amplified to suit the company's needs; it was certainly,
and perhaps prudently,lost). The voluntary joint stock company sent
John Endicott forthwith to found a religious community at Salem; but
doubts about the previous grant to Robert Gorges on that coast in 1623
prompted the New England Company to petition, again somewhat secretly,
for incorporation by royal patent. This charter transformed the company into the Massachusetts Bay Company on the model of the Virginia
patent of 1612. Probably by oversight the place of residence of the
company was omitted: a fact which enabled the puritans to seek to
build their commonwealth in the American wilderness, quite independent of external authority, whether of company, king, Parliament or
New England Council in London.

lies shalbe stiled and called the *Foure Greate and Generall Courts of the saide Company:* in all and every or any of which saide Greate and Generall Courts soe assembled, Wee doe...graunte...That the Governor,or, in his absence, the Deputie Governor...and such of the Assistants and freemen...as shalbe present, or the greater nomber of them soe assembled, whereof the Governor or Deputie Governor and six of the Assistants, at the least to be seaven,[1] shall have full power and authoritie to choose, nominate, and appointe such and soe many others as they shall thinke fitt, and that shall be willing to accept the same, to be free of the said Company and Body, and them into the same to admitt, and to elect and constitute such officers as they shall thinke fitt and requisite for the ordering, mannaging, and dispatching of the affaires of the said Governor and Company...and to make laws and ordinances for the good and welfare of the said Company and for the government of the...plantation...so as such laws be not contrary or repugnant to the laws and statutes of this our realm of England....

> [The election of a governor, deputy and assistants was to take place annually in the general court on the last Wednesday in Easter term. All officials were required to take an oath for their faithful performance of their duties. The Company was exempt from all taxes and customs in New England for seven years and for 21 years on imports from England. All settlers and their children were 'to enjoy all liberties and immunities of free and natural subjects within any of the dominions of us...as if they were born within the realm of England'.]

...and wee doe...graunt...That it shall...be lawful to and for the Governor or Deputie Governor and such of the Assistants and Freemen of the said Company...as shalbe assembled in any of their Generall Courts aforesaide, or in any other Courtes to be specially summoned and assembled for that purpose, or the greater parte of them....from tyme to tyme to make, ordeine, and establishe all manner of wholesome and reasonable orders,lawes, statutes, and ordinances, directions, and instructions, not contrarie to the lawes of this our realme of England, aswell for setling on the formes and ceremonies of government and magistracy fitt and necessary for the said plantation and the inhabitants there,... [and the control of official appointments and elections, the administration 'such oathes warrantable by the lawes and statutes' of England, and the imposition of penalties] according to the course of other corporations in this our realme of England, and for the directing, ruling, and disposeing of all other matters and thinges whereby our said people, inhabitants there, maie be soe religiously, peaceablie, and civilly governed, as their good life and orderlie conversation maie wynn and incite the natives of *[that]* country to the knowledg and obedience of the onlie true

---

1. Whether such a body of seven with such full powers constituted a *quorum*, or had an effectual veto was ambiguous, and became the basis for the assistants' claim to a 'negative voice'.

God and Savior of mankinde, and the Christian fayth, which,
in our royall intention and the adventurers free profession, is the principall ende of this plantation....Provid-
ed also...That theis presents shall not in any manner
enure, or be taken to abridge, barr,or hinder any of our
loving subjects whatsoever to use and exercise the trade
of fishing upon the said coast in any the seas thereunto
adjoyning, or any armes of the seas or saltwater rivers
where they have byn wont to fishe....

166. NEWFOUNDLAND: CHARLES I's COMMISSION FOR THE WELL-GOVERNING OF
     HIS SUBJECTS INHABITING NEWFOUNDLAND, 10 February 1634.[1]
     ...Whereas, the region or country, called Newfoundland,
hath been acquired to the dominion of our progenitors,
which we hold, and our people have many years resorted to
those parts,where, and on the coasts adjoining, they emp-
plyed themselves in fishing, whereby a great number of
our people have been set at work, and the navigation and
mariners of our realm have been much increased; and our
subjects resorting thither, one by the other, and the
natives of those parts were orderly and gently entreated,
until of late some of our subjects in the realm of England planting themselves in that country, and there residing and inhabiting, have imagined that for wrongs or
injuries done there, either on the shore or in the sea
adjoining, they cannot be here impeached; and the rather
for that we, or our progenitors, have not hitherto given
laws to the inhabitants there, and, by that example, our
subjects resorting thither injure one another and use all
manner of excess, to the great hindrance of the voyage
and common damage of this realm: for preventing such inconveniences hereafter, we do hereby declare in what manner our people in Newfoundland and upon the seas adjoining,
and the bays, creeks, and fresh rivers there, shall be
guided and governed....
1st. If any man on the land there shall kill another, or
if any shall secretly or forcibly steal the goods of any
other in the value of forty shillings, he shall be forthwith apprehended and arrested, detained, and brought prisoner into England the crime committed by him shall be made
known to the Earl Marshal of England for the time being,

---

1. L.A. Anspach, *A history of the island* (1809) pp.498-503. This is
the so-called 'first Western charter' subordinating the interests of
the colonists to those of the fishermen. It was confirmed and enlarged in 1661 and 1670. A royal commission to the lord treasurer and
others in December 1630 had required them to establish the fishery as
a nursery of seamen, and negotiations had been proceeding towards a
legal recognition of the long standing privileges, customs and prejudices of the West country fishermen. This charter was virtually
a reaffirmation of 'Guy's laws' of 1611 and of their other existing
regulations; it accepted their opposition to a resident governor
and left other enforcement of the law on the island to the mayors of
the Western seaports, who would be the associates and friends of the

to whom the delinquent shall be delivered as prisoner;
and the said Earl Marshal shall take cognizance of the
cause; and if he shall find by the testimony of two witnesses or more that the part had there killed a man, (not
being at that time first assaulted by the part slain, or
that the killing were by misadventure), or that he had
stolen such goods, the delinquent shall suffer death, and
all the company shall endeavour to apprehend such male-
factor.
2nd. That no ballast, presstones, or any thing else hurtful to the harbours, be thrown out to the prejudice of
the said harbours; but that it be carried on shore, and
laid where it may not do annoyance.
3rd. That no person whatever, either fisherman or inhabitant, do destroy, deface or any way work any spoil or
detriment to any stage, cook-room, flakes, spikes, nails,
or any thing else that belongeth to the stages whatsoever,
either at the end of the voyage, when he hath done and
is to depart the country,or to any such stages as he
shall fall withal at his coming into the country; but
that he or they content themselves with such stage or
stages only as shall be needful for them; and that, for
the repairing of such stages as he or they take, they
shall fetch timber out of the woods, and not do it with
the ruining or tearing of other stages.
4th. That, *according to the ancient custom*[1], every ship,
or fisher that first entereth a harbour in behalf of the
ship, be Admiral of the said harbour, wherein, for the
time being, he shall receive only so much beech and flakes or both, as is needful for the number of boats that he
shall use, with an overplus only for one boat more than
be needeth, as a privilege for his first coming; - and
that every ship coming after content himself with what
he shall have necessary use for, without keeping or detaining any more to the prejudice of others next coming;
- and that any that are possessed of several places in
several harbours shall be bound to resolve upon which of
them they choose, and to send advice to such aftercomers
in those places, as expect their resolution, and that
within eight and forty hours, if the weather so serve,
in order that the said after comers may likewise choose
their places, and so none receive prejudice by others
delay....

---

fish merchants and sea captains. This attempt to provide for the protection of persons and property, and the maintenance of order in the
island was therefore inadequate.
1. The 'fishing admiral' system was certainly a custom more than a
century old. The captain of the first ship to enter a harbour at the
beginning of a new fishing season became 'Admiral' and was the arbiter
to whom disputes among the very cosmopolitan fishermen were referred.
The effectiveness of his law clearly depended on his personal authority, strength and respect, and his interest in settling quarrels
rather than catching fish.

10th. That no person do set up any tavern for selling of wine, beer, or strong waters, cyder, or tobacco, to entertain the fishermen; because it is found that by such means they are debauched, neglecting their labours, and poor ill-governed men not only spend most part of the shares before they come home, upon which the life and maintenance of their wives and children depend,but are likewise hurtful in divers other ways, as by neglecting and making themselves unfit for their labour, by purloining and stealing from their owners, and by making unlawful shifts to supply their disorders, which disorders they frequently follow since these occasions have presented themselves.

Lastly, That, upon the Sundays the company assembled in meet places, and have divine service to be said by some of the masters of the ships, or some others; which prayers shall be such as are in the Book of Common Prayer. And because that speedy punishment may be inflicted upon the offenders against these laws and constitutions, we do ordain that every of the mayors of Southampton, Weymouth, and Melcombe-Regis, Lynn, Plymouth, Dartmouth, East Low, Foyle, and Barnstable for the time being, may take cognizance of all complaints made against any offender against any of these ordinances *upon the land* and, by oath of witnesses, examine the truth thereof, award amends to the parties grieved, and punish the delinquents by fine and imprisonment, or either or them, or of their goods found in the parts of Newfoundland, or on the sea, cause satisfaction thereof to be made, by warrants under their hands and seals. And the Vice-Admirals in our counties of Southampton, Dorset, Devon, and Cornwall, upon complaint made of any of the premises committed upon the *sea*, shall speedily and effectually proceed against the offenders.

Also we will and ordain, that these laws and ordinances shall stand in force and be put in due execution until we shall orderwise provide and ordain; and we do require the Admirals in every harbour in this next season ensuing, calling together such as shall be in that harbour, publicly to proclaim the same on shore.[1]

(2) THE MEANS OF METROPOLITAN CONTROL

Although the basic assumption of the Crown, as shown in the vari-

---

1.The grant of this charter to the Western Adventurers was clearly a victory for the fishing interests. But their powers to enforce it were inadequate. Moreover, David Kirke, who had captured Quebec and been concerned with Alexander's settlement in Nova Scotia, had come to Newfoundland with some Scots settlers when Canada and Acadia were restored to France in 1632. In 1637 [see above p.225] he, Hamilton and others received a proprietary grant for the whole island, not just the Avalon peninsula. By this patent they were expressly permitted to engage in fishing which they had to do to survive; but this sharpened the conflict between settlers and the migratory fishermen which led to Kirke's failure.

ous grants and charters above, was that each new colony or overseas trading enterprise should be autonomous in certain respects, it was also intended that the Crown should retain general control. The privy council was theoretically the instrument of this royal super- vision, but from 1606 a subordinate and specialized council was set up with specific power to control the Virginian settlements, paral- lel with similar regional councils in England, such as the Council of the North. This council does not seem, however, to have had much, if any, control over the colonies, and most colonial matters were dealt with by the privy council.   A second attempt at delegating a control over colonial affairs was made when the Commission under Archbishop Laud was set up in 1634 [No. 170 below], and one aim was clearly to stamp out religious heterodoxy. This commission aroused much resentment in America and it ceased to exist during the Civil War. With the abrogation of the Virginian charter in 1624 [No.168], a new problem arose: how a colony which no longer had a chartered company in charge should be governed. The solution was to make Virginia a 'royal' colony whose governor, council and senior offic- ials were directly appointed by the Crown of England. This became the normal procedure,whenever responsibility for an overseas poss- ession was given up by its owners; and by the mid-eighteenth cent- ury all but five of the American colonies (three chartered and two proprietary) were royal provinces with substantially uniform insti- tutions.

167. THE VIRGINIAS: INSTRUCTIONS FROM JAMES I FOR THEIR GOVERNMENT,
20 November 1606.[1]
    Articles, Instructions and Orders made...*for the good Order and Government of the two several Colonies and Plan- tations to be made by our loving subjects, in the Country commonly called Virginia and America, between thirty-four and forty-five degrees from the aequinoctial line....* Wee according to the effect and true meaning of the same letters pattents, *[i.e. 10 April 1606]* doe by these presents, ...establish and ordaine That our trusty and well beloved Sir William Wade, *[and 12 others named]*...shall be our councel for all matters which shall happen in Virginia or any the territories of America, between thirty-four and forty-five degrees from the aequinoctial line northward, and the Is- lands to the several collonies limitted and assigned, and that they shall be called the *King's Council of Virginia*, which councel or the most part of them shal have full power and authority, att our pleasure, in our name, and under us...to give directions to the councels of the several collonies which shal be within any part of the said coun- try of Virginia and Emerica...for the good government of the people to be planted in those parts, and for the good ordering and desposing of all causes happening within the same, and the same to be done for the substance thereof, as neer to the common lawes of England, and the equity

---

1. W. Hening, *Virginia Statutes at large* (1809) I pp 67-75. For the first charter, see No.159.

thereof, as may be, and to passe under our seale, appointed for that councel; which councel, and every or any
of them shall, from time to time be increased, altered
or changed, and others put in their places att the nomination of us, our heires and successors, and att our and
their will and pleasure....

   [The King's Council of Virginia would name the members of the
   council for each of the two colonies. These colonial councils
   would annually elect a president. Any person attempting to sed-
   uce the king's subjects from their due allegiance to him 'as their
   immediate soverayne under God' would be arrested, imprisoned and,
   if necessary, brought to England for punishment.]

And moreover Wee doe hereby ordaine and establish for us,
our heires and successors, That all the lands, tenements,
and hereditaments to be had and enjoyed by any of our
subjects within the precincts aforesaid, shal be had and
inherited and enjoyed, according as in the like estates
they be had and enjoyed by the lawes within this realme
of England; and That the offences of tumults, rebellion,
conspiracies, mutiny and seditions in those parts which
may be dangerous to the estates there, together with murther, manslaughter, incest, rapes,and adulteries committed
in those parts within the precincts of any the degrees
above mentioned (and noe other offences) shal be punished
by death, and that without the benefit of the clergy,
except in the case of manslaughter, in which clergie is
to be allowed; and That the said several presidents and
councells, and the greater number of them, within every
of the several limits and precincts, shall have full power and authority, to hear and determine all and every the
offences aforesaid, within the precinct of their several
colonies, in manner and forme following, that is to say,
by twelve honest and indifferent persons sworne upon the
Evangelists, to be returned by such ministers and officers as every of the said presidents and councells, or the
most part of them respectively shall assigne, and the
twelve persons soe returned and sworne shall, according
to the evidence to be given unto them upon oath and according to the truth,[1] in their consciences, either convict
or acquit every of the said persons soe to be accused and
tried by them....

   [The president and council had powers of judgement and reprieve.
   The right of pardon was reserved to the king. Civil jurisdiction
   was also vested in the president and council. For the first five
   years the adventurers should 'trade together all in one stocke or
   divideably (but in two or three stocks at the most)'.]

   Alsoe our will and pleasure is, and Wee doe hereby
ordain, That the adventurers of the said first colony and
plantation, shall and may during the said terme of five

---

1. This might seem to imply that juries would not judge only on the
evidence given in court. The argument of *vicinage* was of course not
finally repudiated in Britain until *Rex v. Sutton* (1816) when a judge's
recommendation of such local (and personal) evidence, not known to the
court, led to a retrial.

years, elect and choose out of themselves one or more
companies, each company consisting of three persons att
the least who shall be resident att or neer London, or
such other place, and places, as the councell of the colony for the time being, or the most part of them, during
the said five years shall think fitt, who shall there from
time to time take charge of the trade....
   [A similar provision was made for the northern colony, the company for which would be resident at Plymouth. All colonists must
   take 'the usual oath of obedience' and the one recently prescribed
   (1605) by Parliament.]
...the said President and Councell of each of the said
colonies, and the more part of them respectively shall
and may lawfully from time to time constitute, make and
ordaine such constitutions, ordinances, and officers, for
the better order, government and peace of their several
collonies: Soe alwaies as the same ordinances, and constitutions doe not touch any party in life or member,
which constitutions, and ordinances shall stand, and continue in full force, until the same shall be otherwise
altered, or made void by us, our heires, or successors,
or our, or their councel of Virginia: Soe always as the
same alterations, be such as may stand with, and be in
substance consonant unto the lawes of England, or the
equity thereof....
   [The members of the king's council of Virginia were to take the
   same oath as members of the privy council.]

168. VIRGINIA: PROCLAMATION BY CHARLES I FOR ESTABLISHING ROYAL
                         GOVERNMENT, 13 May 1625.[1]
   *A Proclamation for Settlinge the Plantation of Virgin-
ia, 1625.*
   Whereas the Collonie of *Virginia,*planted by the handes
of Our most deere Father of blessed Memorie, for the Propogation of Christian Religion, the Increase of Trade, and
the inlarging of his Royall Empire, hath not hetherto prospered soe happiely as was hoped and desired, a greate
Occasion whereof his late Majestie conceived to bee, for
that the Government of that Collonie was comytted to the
Companie of *Virginia,*incorporated for a Multitude of Persons of severall Dispositions, amongst whome the Affaires
of greatest Moment were and must be ruled by the greater
Number of Votes, and Voyces,[2] and therefore his late Majestie...did desire to resume that Popular Government, and
accordingly the Letters Patent of that Incorporation

1.*Foedera*(1748ed.) VIIIp.52.Personal differences, particularly between Sandys and Warwick in the General Court had plagued the Virginia
Company in the previous five years while the colony suffered from
lack of food, support, money or guidance. Though Sandys tried to bring
the matter before Parliament as a political issue,James I insisted on
hearings before the privy council. It became clear that the company
could not fulfil its obligations and the privy council took over the
direction – an arrangement at first temporary, then permanent.
2.See pp.235-6,245 and 271n.

were, by his Highnes Direction, in a legal Course questioned,[1] and thereuppon judicially repealed and adjudged
to be voyd, wherein his Majestes ayme was onlie to reduce
that Government into such a right Course as might best
agree with that Forme which was held in the rest of his
Royall Monarchie, and was not intended by him to take aw-
aie or impeach the particuler Interest of anie private
Planter or Adventurer, nor to alter the same otherwise
then should be of Necessitie for the Good of the Publique....
    And therefore Wee doe by these Presents publish and
declare to all Our lovinge Subjectes, and to the whole
World, that Wee hould these Territories of *Virginia* and
the *Summer Islandes*,[2] as alsoe that of *Newe England*, where
Our Collonies are alreadie planted, and within the Lymit-
tes and Boundes whereof Our late deere Father, by his Letters Patents under his Greate Seale of England remayninge
of Record, hath given Leave and Libertie to his Subjects
to plant and inhabite, to be a parte of Our Royall Empire
discended uppon Us and undoubtedlie belonginge and apperteyninge unto Us, And that Wee hould Our Selfe as well
bound by Our Royall Office to protecte, maynteyne and
supporte the same, and are soe resolved to doe, as anie
other Parte of Our Domynions; And that Our full Resolution is, that there maie be one uniforme Course of Government in and through all Our whole Monarchie; That the
Government of the Collonie of *Virginia* shall ymediately
depend uppon Our Selfe, and not be commyted to anie Companie or Corporation, to whome itt maie be proper to trust
Matters of Trade and Commerce, but cannot bee fitt or safe
to communicate the ordering of State Affaires be they of
never soe meane Consequentes....Wee doe hereby declare
that We are resolved, with as much convenyent Expedition
as Our Affaires of greater Importance will Leave, to establish a Counsell consisting of a fewe Persons of Under-
standinge and Qualitie, to whome Wee give Trust for the
ymediate Care of the Affaires of that Collonie, and whoe
shall be answerable to Us for their Proceedings, and in Matters of greater Moment shall be subordinate and attendant
unto Our Privie Counsell heere; And that Wee will alsoe
establishe an other Counsell to be resident in *Virginia*,
whoe shalbe subordinate to Our Counsell here for that Collonie; and that att Our owne Charge We will maynteyne
those publique Officers and Mynisters, and that Strength
of Men, Munition and Fortification as shalbe fitt and nec-

---

1. In May 1623 James I had ordered the privy council to appoint a commission of inquiry into the company's use of their charters. By the
end of July the law officers, having considered the report of the
inquiry and examined the charters, declared that the king might justly
resume the government of the colony. When the court of the company attempted to refuse such a surrender, the attorney general applied for a
quo warranto writ in king's bench. On 24 May 1624 the charter was
declared void.   2. i.e. Bermuda.

essarie for the Defence of that Plantation, and will, by
anie course that shalbe desired of Us, settle and assure
the perticuler Rights and Interests of every Planter and
Adventurer in anie of those Territories which shall desire the same, to give them full Satisfaction for their
quiet and assured enjoying thereof....
    [The Crown would buy at reasonable prices the tobacco crop,
    'which is the only present meanes of their subsistinge'.]

169. VIRGINIA: REPORT OF COMMISSIONERS TO THE PRIVY COUNCIL RECOM-
     MENDING A TRADE MONOPOLY, 14 August, 1633.[1]
     [The commissioners appointed to meet the chief planters of
     Virginia reported]
     ...That this plantation hath beene maintained and sup-
ported for many yeares by the Planters and Adventurers
of the Virginia Company; And they have lately petitioned
his Majesty for renewinge their Antient Charter, And do
hope his Majesty wilbe Gratiously pleased to Graunt it
unto them, forbiddinge all others. And it hath beene
often moved into your Lordships by us, That the Trade
should be carryed wholly by the English, and the retournes to be made wholly into England only....
Whereof it will follow that: His Majesty's Customes and
duties shalbe wholly receaved. Our owne men and shipp-
inge Imployed. The Navigation of the kingdome increased.
The plantation duly and sufficiently supplyed. Our Merchants and Planters benefitted and encouraged by the transportation of that surplus which now Strangers carry to
their owne Marketts. All of which benefitts to his Majesty's kingdome and people are wholly loste if strangers
be permitted to trade and transporte the Comodities of
that plantation into fforraigne parts, as now they do.
    And for the same reasons (as we Conceave) in all the
king of Spaines Plantations in the West and East Indies,
all strangers are probitted to trade and transporte, and
their owne subjects constrained to make all retournes into
Spaine and Portugal only.[2]

170. LETTERS PATENT FROM CHARLES I ESTABLISHING A COMMISSION FOR
     THE GOVERNMENT OF FOREIGN PLANTATIONS, 28 August 1634.[3]
     [The commission was directed to Archbishop Laud and eleven
     others.]
     Whereas very manie of our Subjects...with great indus-
try and expenses have caused to be planted large Colonies

1. C.O. 1/6 No.80 p.207. The commissioners had been instructed to consider the petition from Virginia and to discuss it with a deputation
of planters.
2. Tucker, one of the commissioners, argued strongly against the Dutch
in particular. If the Dutch continued to trade freely with Virginia,
not only would customs duties, and trade, but the whole plantation
would be lost to the Crown. Their own colony at New Netherlands was
already a threat.
3. W. Cunningham, *The growth of English industry and commerce in modern times* (1903) II app. C pp.909-12.

of the English nation in divers parts of the world altogether unmanured and voyd of Inhabitants or occupied of
the Barbarous people that have no knowledge of divine worship, Wee being willing gratiously to provide a remedy
for the tranquility and quietnes of those people...have
constituted you the aforesaid Archbishop of Canterbury...
and anie five or more of you our Commissioners; and to
you and anie five or more of you Wee doe give and commit
power for the Government and safeguard of the said Colonies...to make lawes, constitutions and ordinances pertaining either to the publike State of those Colonies or
to the private proffit of them, And concerning the lands
goods debts and succession in those partes, And how they
shall demeane themselves against and towards forraigne
Princes and theire people, or how they shall beare themselves towards us and our subjects as well in anie forraigne parte whatsoever or on the Seas in those parts or
in theire retorne sailing home, Or which may appertaine
to the maintenance of the Clergi government or the Cure
of Soules amongst the people living and exercising trade
in those partes by designing out congruent porcions ariseing in Tithes, oblations and other things there, according to your sound discretions in politicall and Civile
causes. And by haueing the advise of two or three Bishops for the settling , makeing and ordering of the business for designing out necessarie Ecclesiasticall and Clergi portions, which you shall cause to be called and taken
to you. And to make provision against the violators of
those lawes, constitutions and ordinances by imposing of
penalties and mulcts, imprisonment if therebe cause, and
that the qualitie of the offence do require it by depriv-
ation of member or life to be inflicted. With power also-
our assent being had-to remove and displace the Governors
or Rulers of those Colonies for causes which to you shall
seeme lawfull and others in theire steed to constitute.
And to require an accompt of theire Rule and Government....
      [The commissioners might punish incompetence and negligence in
governors 'according to the quantitie of the fault'.]
And to constitute Judges and magistrates politicall and
civile for civile causes and under the power and forme
which to you five or more of you shall seeme expedient.
And to ordaine Judges, Magistrates and Dignities to causes
Ecclesiasticall...And to ordaine Courts Pretorian and Trib-
unall as well ecclesiasticall as Civile of Judgements To
determine of the formes and manner of proceedings in the
same and of appealing from them in matters and causes as
well criminall as Civile personall reale and mixt, and
to the seats of Justice what maie be equally and well-
ordered and what crimes, faults, or excesse of contracts,
or injuries ought to belong to the Ecclesiasticall Courts
and what to the Civile Court and seats of Justice.
      Provided, neverthelesse, that the lawes, ordinances
and constitutions of this kinde shall not be put in execution before our assent be had thereunto in writing under

our signet signed at least. And this assent being had and
the same publikly proclaimed in the Provinces in which they
are to be executed, Wee will and command that those lawes,
ordinances and constitutions more fully to obtaine strength and be confirmed, shalbe inviolably observed of all
men whome they shall concerne. Notwithstanding it shalbe
lawfull for you five or more of you...to change revoake
and abrogate them and other new ones in forme aforesaid
from tyme to tyme to frame and make as is aforesaid And to
new evills arising or dangers to applie new Remedies as
is fitting so often as to you it shall seeme expedient.
Furthermore,you shall understand that we have constituted
you...our Commissioners to heare and determine according
to your sound discretions all manner of Complaintes,either
against those Colonies or their Rulers or governors at
the instance of the partie greived or at the accusation
brought concerning injuries from hence or from thence to
be moved betweene them and theire members, and to call the
parties before you and to the parties or theire procurat-
ors from hence or from thence being heard The full compl-
ement of Justice to be exhibited....

   [Cases of proven complaint misdemeanour or disaffection by governor or any colonist were to be tried in England before the
   commission.]

Morevoer, Wee doe give unto you or anie five or more
of you Power and speciall command over all the charters,
letters Patents, and rescripts Royall of the Regions,
provinces, Islands, or Lands in forraigne partes graunted
raising colonies To cause them to be brought before you
and the same being reviewed If aniething surreptitively or
unduly have bin obtayned, or that by the same privilege,
Liberties, or Prerogatives hurtfull to us or our Crowne or
to forraigne Princes have bin preiudicially suffered or
graunted The same being better made knowne unto you five
or more of you To command them according to the lawes and
customs of our Realme of England to be revoaked....

(3) COLONIAL SELF-GOVERNMENT

   The theme of this section is the evolution of the various systems
of internal government in the colonies. Although, as is clear from
the documents in section B (1) above and in the first document in
this section, the Crown always intended that the colonies should run
their own affairs within the framework laid down by the royal grant
or charter, it was very soon clear that the colonists were interpreting this concession far more widely than the Crown had intended. In
the special case of New Plymouth and the three charter-less offshoots
of Massachusetts (Connecticut, New Haven and Rhode Island) government
was from the start set up by the colonists along their own chosen lines
and without royal regulation,because none of these possessed a charter
or grant. But in Massachusetts, which had a charter, the settlers
similarly assumed virtually complete freedom to decide how to run
their own affairs,ignoring the terms of their charter and English legal principles alike. This was the starting point of a process of autochthonous constitutional development in the Americas which was common

to all colonies,irrespective of their formal constitutional status;
whose long-term result was that no two colonies had precisely the
same constitutional system and that even royal colonies such as Virginia claimed a degree of autonomy not intended,nor welcomed, by the
English authorities.

(a) VIRGINIA

171. THIRD CHARTER FROM JAMES I, 12 March 1612.[1]

[The limits of the Company's grant were extended to include
islands within 300 leagues of Virginia. The Company might hold
weekly a court and assembly for routine business and quarterly
a great and general court. Since the failing and non-payment of
subscriptions had hindered the progress of colonisation, those
who in writing had engaged to make payment might be sued, and
judges were instructed to favour claims by the Company for sums
promised.]

...Now, forasmuch as it appeareth unto us, that these
Insolences, Misdemeanors, and Abuses, not to be tolerated
in any civil Government, have, for the most part, grown
and proceeded, in regard our Said Council have not any
direct Power and Authority, by any express Words in our
former Letters Patents, to correct and chastise such Offenders; We therefore, for more speedy Reformation of so
great and enormous Abuses and Misdemeanors, heretofore
practised and committed, and for the preventing of the like
hereafter, do...give and grant to the said Treasurer and
Company, and their Successors for ever, that if shall and
may be lawful for our said Council for the first said Colony in *Virginia*,or any two of them (whereof the said Treasurer, or his Deputy..., to be always one) by Warrant under
their Hands, to send for, or to cause to be apprehended,
all and every such Person and Persons, who shall...mis-
behave themselves, in any the Offences before mentioned
and expressed....

[Abusive or insolent behaviour before the council during such
  trials might be punished by the council or any two of them who]
shall and may have full Power and Authority, either here
to bind them over with good Sureties for their good Behaviour, and further therein to proceed, to all Intents and
Purposes, as it is used, in other like Cases, within our
Realm of England, Or else, at their Discretions, to remand

---

1. W.H. Hening (ed.) Virginia,*Statutes at large* (1809) I pp.98-110.
This third charter was granted to include Somers' Island (Bermuda)
within the company's patent and, in view of the defaulting of many
adventurers in the payment of their voluntary subscriptions, to secure for the company greater powers of control. By 1612 the company
had outgrown its experimental forms and needed a regular organisation
for the conduct of business, and a more secure common joint stock fund
for the development of the colony. The greater power vested in the
shareholders of the general court led to factions and enabled Sandys
and Warwick to oust Smith as treasurer. The Bermuda Company received
a separate patent in 1615 [see above No.161].

and send back, the said Offenders, or any of them, into
the said Colony in Virginia, there to be proceeded against
and punished, as the Governor, Deputy or Council[1] there
...shall think meet; or otherwise, according to such
Laws and Ordinances, as are and shall be in Use there,
for the Well-ordering and good Government of the said
Colony....
    [Authority was granted for lotteries to raise funds and for
    the appointment of receivers, auditors, surveyors and commission-
    ers.]
XX. And further Our will and pleasure is That in all questions and doubts that shall arise upon any difficulty of
construction or interpretation of any thing contained in
these or any other our former letters patent, the same
shall be taken and interpreted in most ample and beneficial manner for the said Treasurer and Company, and their
successors and every member thereof.

172. ORDERS AND CONSTITUTIONS BY THE VIRGINIA COMPANY FOR THE BETTER
    GOVERNING OF THE COMPANY IN ENGLAND, 19 June 1619.[2]
    [There were to be quarterly sessions of the general court (of
    treasurer, council and company) for making laws, disposing lands
    and settling the trade of company and colony. In addition there
    were to be fortnightly meetings of an ordinary court for routine
    administration. Elections, legislative functions and land dis-
    tribution[3] were reserved for the general court only. Officers
    would be elected annually in Easter term.]
    The Treasurer, in the beginning of the Court at the
giving up of his office, shall declare by word or writing the present estate of the colony and planters in Virginia, and deliver into the Court a booke of his accounts
for the year past, examined and approved under the Auditor's
hands: declaring withall the present estate of the case....
    At the choice of each officer, the persons nominated
for the election shall withdraw themselves till the party
chosen be publiquely so pronounced, and generally no man
shall be present in the Court whilest himselfe or his
matter passeth the judgement of the Court....
    For the avoiding of divers inconveniences, it is thou-
ght fit that all elections of principal officers in or
for Virginia, as also of the Treasurer and deputy here,

---

1. The council in Virginia had been absolute and self perpetuating.
But by order of the company on 28 February 1610 all authority was
vested in the governor who virtually appointed his successor: Gates
and Dale were autocrats and succeeded in putting the colony on a firm
and sound footing. Their councils were advisory only.
2. S. M. Kingsbury (ed.)*The records of the Virginia Company* (1933)
III pp.340-65.
3. Sandys as treasurer had been responsible for a change in policy,
distributing company land to private owners in return for quitrents
and creating a society of freeholders,indentured servants and later
negroes. In 1624 monthly county courts were established under plantation 'commanders', and in 1634 eight shires with J.P.s exercising
local legislative, judicial and executive functions.

be performed by a ballating box, as in some other Companies.[1]...
     [The responsibilities of the treasurer and deputy were prescr-
     ibed. He was to deliberate with his council on all important iss-
     ues. Councillors alone were to be appointed for life, though they
     might be removed by the general court. To preserve 'that reputat-
     ion which is fit for their place and imployment none hereafter
     under the degree of a Lord,or principal magistrate,shall be chosen
     for the Council'. In the making of laws 'the policy and forme of
     England is to be followed as neere as may be'. A committee of 16
     annually elected, was to carry out the decisions and deal with the
     routine business of the court. The governor and officers for the
     colony of Virginia were to be elected by ballot in the quarterly
     court: the council in Virginia might be elected by a show of hands.
     Laws would be drafted and examined in the committee, would be pres-
     ented to the council, and would be finally approved in the general
     court.] [2]

173. PROCEEDINGS IN THE FIRST ASSEMBLY, 30 July 1619.[3]
     ...At the reading of the names of the Burgesses, except-
ion was taken against Captaine Warde, as having planted
here in Virginia, without any authority or comission from
the Treasurer, Counsell and Company in Englande. But considering he had bene at so great chardge and paines to aug-
mente this Colony, and had adventured his owne person in
the actions, and since that time had brought home a good
quantity of fishe, to relieve the Colony by waye of trade;
and above all because the comission for authorizing the
General Assembly, admitteth of two burgesses out of every
plantations without restraints or exception. Upon all

1. e.g. the East India Company , [see above No.158n.].
2. Many of the orders for the Bermuda Company presented 6 February
1622 were copied *verbatim* from these. There was to be a ballot for
governor, sheriff and secretary, but other officials could be chosen
by show of hands. The council consisted of the sheriff, ministers,
secretary, two captains and the overseer of public land, but might
include those who had served in such posts (and others) at the discretion of the general court; resolutions would be determined by a
majority of votes,but the governor had two original votes and a casting vote. Courts were to administer justice 'according as far as possible to the equity of the lawes of England'. There was a somewhat
complex system of meetings. Of the quarterly courts two would include
6 representatives of each 'tribe' and 12 for the common land. Every
two years a general assembly of governor, council (each with a veto),
representative ' tribesmen' and occupiers of common land would meet.
This body alone could tax and make laws subject to confirmation in
the quarterly court. Every three years the quarterly court could send
commissioners to inquire into the actions of officials in the islands:
L. H. Lefroy, *Memorials*...(1877) I pp.182-228.
3. *Coll.*New York Hist. Soc. (2nd ser.) III pp.336-8,344. This was from
the proceedings of the first day. The assembly of 22 men elected in
June met in the church at Jamestown and sat for six days. All males
over 16, even servants under indenture, voted openly, though no doubt

these considerations, the Assembly was contented to admitt
of him and his Lieutenant (as members of their body and
Burgesses) into their Society. Provided that the said
Captain Warde with all expedition...should procure from
the Treasurer, Counsell, and Company in England a Comission lawfully to establishe and plant himselfe and his
Company, as the Chieffs of other plantations have done.
And in case he doe neglect this, he is to stande to the
censure of the nexte generall assembly[1]....

> [On objection to the burgesses from Captain Martin's plantation
> at Martin's Brandon,[2] they argued that Captain Martin's patent
> from the company in 1617 exempted him, his tenants and servants,
> from the general laws of the charter, and from the laws to be made
> in the General Assembly. On 2 August 1619 Martin reaffirmed that
> he would not surrender this privilege of exemption, 'Whereupon it
> was resolved by the Assembly, that his Burgesses should have no
> admittance'.][3]

174. ORDINANCE ESTABLISHING A COUNCIL AND GENERAL ASSEMBLY, 24 July
1621.[4]

> [In order to settle an equitable and beneficial form of govern-
> ment which would administer justice, carry out executive functions
> and make provision for future contingencies and economic develop-

---

leaders in the several plantations influenced the election. All males
over 16 too had to pay one pound of tobacco towards the expenses of
the assembly. As this extract shows, the assembly immediately assumed
the right to determine its own membership.
1. Warde had settled at Wardes Plantation without patent from the company. He promised to rectify this omission and did so by the next year.
2. Martin had been in Virginia for long periods since 1607. He was
the only remaining (and privileged) member of the company's original
resident council. On his appealing to the company against the assembly's decision, the company ordered him to take out a new patent without any special exemptions. He had claimed 'to enjoy his lands in as
large and ample a manner...as any lord of any manors in England'; but
the assembly asserted that it was 'impossible' for them to know the
prerogatives of all English manors. The company complied with their
plea for the uniformity, and equality, of grants and laws.
3. Two sub-committees of the assembly scrutinized the company's charter of privileges. Their deliberations showed concern for land titles,
distribution and inheritance, for the price of tobacco,and for the
erection of a university. They passed laws on gaming, dress, drunkenness, immorality, crops, Sabbath observance, Indian trade and Indian
education. On 4 August they apologised to the company for sending
'titles rather than laws, propositions rather than resolutions, attempts than achievements', and petitioned for the right to disallow
company orders as they recognised the company could disallow their
laws: they also requested that their laws could be enforced before
the company's pleasure were known - i.e. that the veto would not avoid
them *ab initio*.They also imposed the taxation for the payment of officers of the assembly. Soon they were claiming taxation as their exclusive right.
4. W.W. Hening, *op. cit.* I pp.110-3. An ordinance authorising Gover-

ment in the colony,]

II. We therefore, the said treasurer, council, and company, by authority directed to us from his Majesty under the great seal, upon mature deliberation, do hereby order and declare, That from hence forward there shall be two supreme councils in Virginia, for the better government of the said colony aforesaid.

III. The one of which councils to be called the Council of State (and whose office shall chiefly be assisting with their care, advice, and circumspection, to the said governor) shall be chosen, nominated, placed, and displaced, from time to time, by us, the said treasurer, council, and company, and our successors....

[The first council which included the governor (Sir Francis Wyatt)[1], Sir George Yeardley, John Berkeley, George Sandys and John Rolfe[2], was named.]

Which said councillors and council we earnestly pray and desire, and in his Majesty's name strictly charge and command, that (all factions, partialities, and sinister respect laid aside) they bend their care and endeavours to assist the said governor; first and principally in the advancement of the honour and service of God, and the enlargement of his kingdom against the heathen people; and next, in erecting of the said colony in due obedience to his Majesty, and all lawful authority from his Majesty's directions; and lastly, in maintaining the said people in justice and Christian conversation amongst themselves, and in strength and ability to withstand their enemies; And this council to be always, or for the most part, residing about or near the governor.

IV. The other council, more generally to be called by the governor once yearly, and no oftener but for very extraordinary and important occasions, shall consist, for the present, of the said Council of State, and of two burgesses out of every town, hundred, or other particular plantation, to be respectively chosen by the inhabitants; which council shall be called the General Assembly, wherein (as also in the said Council of State) all matters shall be decided, determined, and ordered, by the greater part of the voices then present; reserving to the governor always

---

nor Sir George Yeardley to call an assembly was made by the treasurer, council and London company in 1618. This has been lost, but it is presumed that this ordinance of 1621 is substantially the same as the earlier one. The idea for the establishment of such a body was probably Sandys' and was certainly novel. The right to vote was certainly not o n e which belonged to 'natural-born Englishmen'. The proposed institution of a general assembly was probably an imitation of the quarterly general court in the metropolitan government of the company. The council and elected burgesses sat together with the governor (who had a veto) and made decisions by majority vote.

1. Wyatt was nephew by marriage to Sandys, and remained governor till 1626.
2. He had been secretary and recorder of the colony and the husband

a negative voice. And this General Assembly shall have
free power to treat, consult, and conclude, as well of
all emergent occasions concerning the public weal of the
said colony and every part thereof, as also to make, ordain, and enact such general laws and orders for the behoof
of the said colony, and the good government thereof, as
shall, from time to time, appear necessary or requisite.
V. Whereas, in all other things we require the said General Assembly, as also the said Council of State, to im-
itate and follow the policy of the form of government,
laws, customs, and manner of trial, and other administration of justice used in the realm of England, as near
as may be,[1] even as ourselves, by his Majesty's letters
patent, are required.
VI. Provided, that no law or ordinance,made in the said
General Assembly, shall be or continue in force or validity, unless the same shall be solemnly ratified and confirmed in a general quarter court of the said company
here in England and so ratified, be returned to them
under our seal; it being our intent to afford the like
measure also unto the said colony, that after the government of the said colony shall once have been well framed
and settled accordingly, which is to be done by us, as by
authority derived from his Majesty, and the same shall
have been so by us declared, no orders of court afterwards, shall bind the said colony unless they be ratified
in like manner in the general assemblies.[2]

175. STATUTES RELATING TO TAXATION AND PRIVILEGE (21 Jac.I) March
1624.[3]

(a) (Act *VIII*) That the governor[4] shall not lay any taxes

---

of Pocohontas, who had died in 1617 off Gravesend.
1. A Virginia Act of 1670 indicated that English practice had not
been closely followed. The franchise, for example, had been far too
liberal and had not been restricted to men of property with a stake
in the 'public good'.
2. The provision was the company's compliance with the request of the
first general assembly of 1619. They had asked that laws passed might
become operative at once though the company might subsequently disallow them; and that they might not be bound by the company's laws
until they had ratified them as suitable for the best interests of
the colonists.
3. W. Hening *op. cit.*I pp. 124,125: the general assembly was prompt
to claim the sole right to impose taxes and to assume certain parliamentary privileges. These two statutes were frequently re-enacted.
In early Virginia it appears to have been the custom to declare all
previous acts void and then to legislate anew (*ibid*. pp.177.179.204,
240). By March 1660 however repeal was not total; 'Whereas by the frequent reviews and alterations of the lawes of this countrey there may
be some contrarieties happen and some of the precedent lawes be adverse
to the lawes enacted this Assembly and especially to the power now
'established',only such laws or parts of Acts contrary to the present
form of law and government'were made 'void and null.' (*ibid*.p.531).
4. By Act III of March 1643 the governor and council were denied pow-

or ympositions upon the Colony, their lands or comodities
other way than by the authority of the General Assembly
to be levyed and ymployed as the said Assembly shall
appoynt.[1]
(b) (Act *XI*). That no burgesses of the General Assembly
shall be arrested during the time of the assembly, a week
before and a week after, upon pain of the creditor's forfeiture of his debt and such punishment upon the officer
as the court shall award.

176. GOVERNOR HARVEY TO CHARLES I, 1629.[2]
    ...That his Majesty wilbe pleased gratiously to extend
his favour to the planters, for a new confirmation of
their lands and goods by charter under the great seale of
England, and therein to authorize the Lords to consider
what is fit to be done for the ratifying of the privilid-
ges formerly granted, and holding of a general assembly,
to be called by the Governor upon necessary occasions,
therein to propound laws and orders for the good government of the people, and for that it is most reasonable
that his Majesty's subjects should be governed only by
such laws as shall have their original from his Majesty's

---

ers to tax (*ibid*. p.244) cf. the 8th article of the Articles of Surrender 1652 [see No.225].
1. By Act XXXIII of 1624 (*ibid*.p.128) a tax of 10 pounds of tobacco
'upon every male head above sixteen years of age' was levied. It
varied over the years (*ibid*.p.229, 279), but in 1645 was temporarily
abolished as being 'insupportable' for the poor, and was replaced
by a property tax (*ibid*.p.305). In October 1648 however a poll tax
was reimposed.
Quit rents at 2 shillings per 100 acres after the first seven years
were provided for in January 1640 (*ibid*.228). In 1645 by the king's
express bounty the proceeds were applied to the payment of the colonial treasurer and any surplus was appropriated by the assembly
(*ibid*. p.307). But it is also clear that there was general neglect
in collection and payment (*ibid*. p.351).
2. *Virginia Magazine of History and Biography*,VII pp.369-0. The company had now been dissolved: Sir Francis Wyatt was the last governor of the company and first of the royal government. Though special
assemblies had been summoned, even informally, by the king's governors since 1624 they had exercised few legislative functions. The
king had not yet indicated whether such a representative body of burgesses was an acceptable or regular instrument of government in a
royal province. Neither in the instructions to Sir George Yeardley
in April 1626 nor those to Sir John Harvey in March 1628 was there
any mention of a house of burgesses - only of a council which had
joint authority with the governor and tended to become a dominant
influence. Full power was granted 'to you and the greater number of
you respectively', the governor and councillors named, 'to execute
and perform' all the functions of government. The governor was bound
by the majority in council and had no longer a veto: it seemed that
as governor he was only *primus inter pares* on the council whether in
its executive, judicial or legislative sessions. Harvey's struggle

royal approbation, it be therefore so ordered that those
lawes, so there made, only stand as propositions until
his Majesty shalbe pleased, under his great seale or privy
seale, or by the Lords of his noble privy councell to ratify the same....

177. ACT ESTABLISHING MONTHLY COURTS, February 1632.[1]
    (Act *XXXIII.*) To all to whom these presents shall come,
I, Sir John Harvey, Knight, governor and captayne general
of Virginia, send greeting in our Lord God everlasting.
Whereas for the greater ease of the inhabitants in diverse
parts of this colony and for the better conservation of
the peace, and due execution of such lawes and orders as
are or shall be established for the government of the
people and the inhabitants of the same - The governor and
councel together with the assembly have thought fit and
accordinglie ordered and appoynted that theire shall be
monthlie corts, and oftener uppon extraordinarie causes
requiring and agreed uppon by the maior part of the commissioners, held and kept in some of the remote plantations.... [Commissioners were appointed 'to do and execute whatever
the justice of the peace, or two or more justices may doe'.] Provided always that it shall and may be lawful for the plaintiff or defendant in such suite before the sayd commissioners dependinge either before or after judgement, if
it be before execution awarded, to appeal to the corts
of James Citty, there holden by the governor and counsell.
···· [The oath for commissioner ran thus: 'You shall doe equal right
    to the poore and to the rich after your cunninge, wit and power
    and after the lawes and customes of this colony and as neere as
    may be after the lawes and customes of the realme of England and
    statutes thereof made....']

178. GOVERNOR HARVEY TO SIR FRANCIS WINDEBANK, December 1634.[2]
    ...my power heere is not greate, it being limited by

---

with the council led to his temporary 'thrusting out' in 1635. When
the king sent him back, a new commission did give the governor nominally more authority.
1. W. W. Hening, *Statutes at large...Virginia* (1823) I p.169. In March
1624 monthly courts had been established for two districts to deal
with petty offences and minor suits. In 1634 sheriffs were appointed
for the counties. In March 1643 trial by jury was made available at
request in civil cases in these county courts: juries were to be
of 'able men'. Grand juries were introduced in 1645 but were dispensed with in 1659 as a failure. (*ibid.* p.521).
2. W. H. Barnes (ed.) *Proceedings of the Council of Maryland*, 1636-
37 (1885) p.30. John Harvey, governor of Virginia, had been asked
by the king to furnish the Maryland settlers with all possible help.
By doing so, he increased his own unpopularity in Virginia. There
he had attempted to assert his own power, to reduce that of the dominant council, and to avoid the claims of the assembly, by legislating by proclamation. Council and assembly combined to depose him in
1635, and, though the king briefly reinstated him, he was then re-

my Commission to the greater number of voyces at the Councell Table, and there I have almost all against me in
whatever I can propose, especially if it concerne Maryland; and these proceedings of the Councell do so embol-
den others that, notwithstanding the obligation of Christianity and his Majestie's commands to be assisting to
them in their first beginning, many are so averse as that
they crye and make it their familiar talke that 'they
would rather knock their Cattell on the heads then sell
them to Maryland'. I am sorry its not in my power to rule
these exorbitant courses [but 'for their present accommodation'
he had sent some of his own cows. Letters from England to Matthews,[1]
Claiborne, and other councillors had stirred up 'a notable combination' against Maryland and himself. On reading one letter Matthews 'the patron of disorder...threw his hatt upon the ground,
scratching his head and in a fury stamping, cryed "A pox upon
Maryland".]

(b) NEW PLYMOUTH

179. PROPOSED GOVERNMENT FOR NEW ENGLAND, c.1620.[2]
   ...For they proposed to comit the management of their

---

placed by Wyatt who had been governor in 1624 at the demise of the
Company and had continued to call informal assemblies in the interim.
Windebank was secretary of state.
1. Samuel Matthews, sent in 1623 by the privy council as one of the
commissioners to inquire into the state of Virginia, had stayed
there after the recall of the charter. A councillor, at first favoured by Harvey, he became his chief critic, taking a lead in his expulsion: 'Sir, the people's fury is up against you and to appease it is
beyond our power, unlesse you please to goe to England and there to
answer their complaynts'. During the Commonwealth he was elected governor. William Claiborne had been granted by the Scottish Crown in
1631 a patent for a company trading over much of N.E. America from
his base on Kent Island, which, though not 'hitherto uncultivated'
[see p.223] fell within the Maryland proprietary: which, as an anti-
Catholic, he strongly opposed. To recover his property, forfeited in
1638 by a Maryland bill of attainder, he espoused the parliamentary
cause, maintaining his attacks on Baltimore and Berkeley, and in 1652
as a parliamentary commissioner secured Virginia's submission:[see
No.225].
2. Coll.Mass.Hist.Soc. (2nd ser.) V p.85.[For the charter for the
Council of New England see above No.162]. This is an extract from
Hubbard's History of New England probably written about 30 years
later.The council, despite Gorges' energy,proved to be somewhat uncertain and indecisive:perhaps because it saw its role as a distrib-
utor of land rather than a provider of government. Not till 1623-4
were officials sent to the northern colony and these included Gorges'
son, Robert, as lieutenant governor over all England,with a fief at
Massachustack held by knight service. Whereas in Virginia the establishment of a general government had preceded grants for particular
plantations,in New England the proliferation of indentures for scattered plantations (and the Pilgrims' settlement at New Plymouth) existed before any effective attempt was made at a general government.

whole affairs to a general government, assisted by so
many of the patentees as should be there resident upon the
place, together with the officers of state, as Treasurer,
Admiral, Master of the Ordnance, Marshall, with other persons of judgement and experience, as by the President and
Council then established, for the better governing those
affairs should be thought fit, resolving also, (because
all men are wont most willingly to submit to those ordinances, constitutions, and orders, themselves have had a
hand in the framing of,) the general laws whereby the
state should have been governed, should be first framed,
and agreed upon by the General Assembly of the states of
those parts, both spiritual and temporal....

180. WILLIAM BRADFORD'S ACCOUNT OF THE MAYFLOWER COMPACT,
11 November 1620.[1]
    I...begin with a combination made by them before they
came ashore; being the first foundation of their government in this place. Occasioned <u>partly</u> by the discontented
and mutinous speeches that some of the strangers[2] amongst

Though in 1623 and again in 1635 the domain of New England was divided by lot among the patentees,only Gorges for his Province of Maine
had his grant confirmed by royal charter in 1639 as a palatinate.
1. From Bradford's *Of Plymouth plantation* ed. S.E. Morison (1952)
pp. 75-81. Bradford, who in 1621 was elected governor and remained
so for some 30 years, was a member of the congregation which had left
Scrooby for Holland in 1607 to retain its 'Separatist' identity. After
ten years' exile the 'Pilgrims' sought 'removal to some other place',
and began to negotiate with the Virginia Company for a patent, at the
same time, in the Leyden agreement (1618), assuring the king of their
loyalty and orthodoxy. Though James I however refused to protect them
and promised only not to molest them, some of them went ahead and
through the good offices of Sandys obtained grants from the Virginia
Company [see No.181n.] which seemed to enable them as a group of
undertakers to retain their identity as a distinct locally self-
governing plantation under their own leaders, though subject generally to the government of Virginia. Moreover Thomas Weston, acting
in the name of 'John Peirce and his associates', was ready to provide
financial assistance, and a voluntary partnership of adventurers and
Pilgrims was formed, of which one part would remain in England and
the other go to America. Weston and the adventurers hired the *Mayflower*, a vessel previously employed in the Mediterranean wine trade.
On 16 September 1620 it sailed from Plymouth, overcrowded and over-
laden, and on 9 November, making landfall at Cape Cod,it turned southward towards Virginia; but, wearying of the rocks and shoals to the
south, it returned and anchored in the bay behind Cape Cod two days
later. Families did not, however, go ashore to live until Christmas.
2. Presumably these were from among the passengers who were not of
the 35 Leyden 'Separatists' and who had come from Southampton and
London.   Friction between the 'Separatists' and the other planters
was already apparent.

them had let fall from them in the ship: 'That when they
came ashore they would use their own liberty, for none
had power to command them, the patent they had being for
Virginia, and not for New England which belonged to another government with which the Virginia Company had nothing to do.' And <u>partly</u> that such an act by them done,
this their condition considered, might be as firm as any
patent and in some respects more sure.

The form was as followeth: In the name of God, Amen.
We, whose names are underwritten, the loyal subjects of
our dread Sovereign Lord King James, by the grace of God
of Great Britain, France and Ireland, King, Defender of
the Faith, [& c]., Haveing undertaken for the glorie of
God and the advancement of the Christian faith and honour
of our King and countrie, a voyage to plant the first
colonie in the northerneparts of Virginia, doe, by these
presents, solemnly and mutually in the presence of God
and one of another, covenant and combine ourselves togeather unto a civill body politick for our better ordering
and preservation and furtherance of the ends aforesaid;[1]
and by vertue hereof to enact, constitute and frame such
just and equall lawes, ordinances, acts, constitutions
and offices from time to time as shall be thought most
meete and convenient for the generall good of the colonie,
unto which we promise all due submission and obedience.
In witness whereof we have hereunder subscribed our names
at Cape Codd,[2] the 11th of November in the year of the
raigne of our Soveraigne Lord King James of England,France
and Ireland the eighteenth and of Scotland the fiftie
fourth. *A.D. 1620.*

181. INDENTURE FROM NEW ENGLAND COUNCIL TO JOHN PEIRCE AND OTHERS,
                                        1 June 1621.[3]

[The president and council of New England would grant 100 acres

---

1. Some provision for the administration of the plantation was imper-
ative. Being within the domain of 'New England' without chartered
authority, they had no legal right to exercise civil government and
secure law and order. But in Separatist churches authority was vested
in the members of the congregation themselves. Hence this solemn,
autochthonous, social contract: a civil version of their church government. By this sacred covenant they sought to knit themselves into
a corporate, locally self-governing community. N.B. The Pilgrims affirmed their loyalty to the king.
2. Only 41 of the 149 passengers and crew, signed: 19 from Leyden, 16
from London, 4 servants and 2 sailors. They were a minority among the
planters but were dominant by reason of their clear firmness of purpose and sense of covenant with God. Though freer and more sympathetic
than the puritans of neighbouring Massachusetts, they asserted a strong moral discipline and prospered. The single plantation of New Plymouth developed as other towns and congregations grew up. Finally in
1691 the plantation was absorbed into Massachusetts.
3. W. Bradford, *History of Plymouth plantation* (1912 ed.) I p.246.
<u>John Peirce</u>, a London clothmaker, was ostensibly acting for the Ply-

of land for every person transported within 7 years, and 1500 acres
to each undertaker to be used for public purposes. The location
of the grant, otherwise undefined, was not to be within 10 miles
of any other English settlement. The president and council furthermore promised that they]

...shall also at any time within the said terme of Seaven Yeeres, upon request under the said President and Counsell made, graunt unto them, the said John Peirce and his
Associates, Undertakers and Planters...Letters and Grauntes
of Incorporation by some usual and fitt name and tytle
with liberty to them and their successors from time to
time to make Orders, Lawes, Ordynaunces and Constitutions
for the rule, government, ordering and dyrecting of all
persons to be transported and settled upon the landes
hereby graunted...and of the said Landes and Profitts
thereby arrysing. And in the meane tyme until such graunt
be made, it shall be lawfull for the said John Peirce [etc]
... by consent of the greater part of them to establish such
Lawes and Ordynaunces as are for their better government,
and the same by such Officer or Officers as they shall by
most voyces elect and choose put into execution...[1]

-mouth Pilgrims. When they were exiled in Leyden, a patent for a
private plantation had been obtained on their behalf, in the name of
the Rev. John Wyncop, from the Virginia Company on 19 June 1619
(S.M.Kingsbury ed. *op. cit.* I pp.221,228). Again, on 20 February 1620
another London merchant, Thomas Weston, obtained a patent on behalf
of John Peirce 'and his associates' from the Virginia Company (*ibid.*
p.249); and on 2 February 1621 (*ibid.* p.303) Peirce himself had a
grant from the company permitting them to make temporary orders 'provided they were not repugnant to the laws of England'; but since the
Pilgrims settlement was already by then 'seated...within the lymite
of the Northerne Plantacion', the grant was revoked on 16 July 1621
by the Company (*ibid.* p.515).
On 20 April 1622 Peirce surrendered this patent to the New England
Council and obtained a new ampler one in the form of a 'deed poll'
for himself, attempting to convert his trust into a proprietorship.
But his ventures miscarried and on 23 March 1623 the council assured
the Pilgrims that 'they, the Associates, [were] to receive and enjoy
all that they doe and may possesse by vertue' of this 1621 indenture.
Once more on 13 January 1630 the council confirmed this grant to Bradford and the Pilgrims, and in March 1641 it was assigned to the freemen of New Plymouth. But at no time did the Crown grant them a royal
charter.
1. Clearly this was simply a grant of land with only limited and temporary legislative powers. How the council could grant further permanent powers of local self-government and effect incorporation without a royal charter is not clear. The plantation at New Plymouth
rested on the Compact, enforced by this indenture, confirmed to Bradford and 'his associates' by a patent from the New England Council
under Warwick on 13 January 1630 which defined boundaries and guaranteed land titles. This latter instrument was known as the 'Old Charter' ; but it gave no legal, civil or governmental powers. W. Bradford was the government, with 'assistants elected annually by the

182. COURT ORDERS, 1 January 1632.[1]
It was enacted by publick consent of the freemen of
this society of New Plymoth, That if now or heereafter
any were elected to the office of Governour, and would
not stand to the election, nor hold and execute the office for this yeare, that then he be amerced in twenty
pounds sterling fine; and in case *[it was]* refused to be
paid upon the lawful demand of the ensuing Governour,
then to be levied out of the goods and chattels of the
said person so refusing.
It was further ordered and decreed, That if any were
elected to the office of Councell, and refused to hold
the place, that then he be amerced in ten pownds sterling
fine; and in case *[it was]* refused to be paid, to be
forthwith levied.
It was further decreed and enacted, That in case one
and the same person should be elected Governour a second
yeare, having held the place the foregoing yeare, it
should be lawful for him to refuse without any amercement;
and the company to proceed to a new election, except they
can prevaile with him by entreaty.
At this Court...*[names given]* ...were admitted into the
freedome of this society, and received the oath.
At the same court Edward Wynslow was chosen Governour,
and held and was sworne to administer justice in that
place for the yeare to come.   [William Bradford, temporarily
wishing not to be elected as governor, was chosen with others for
the council.]   Peeter Browne was amerced in 3 ss. fine
for not apearing at the same court.
Act 2. And whereas our ancient worke of fortification
by continuance of time is decayed...It is further agreed
by the court aforesaid, That a worke of fortification
bee made about the said fort in March or April next ensuing, by the whole strength of men able to labour in the
colony; and that the governour and cowncell measure the
worke, and appoint the whole their joynt and several parts
of labour...
Act 3. In regard of our dispersion so far asunder and
the inconveniency that may befal, it is further ordered,
That every freemen or other inhabitant of this colony provide for himselfe, and each under him able to beare armes,
a sufficient musket, and other serviceable peace for war
...and other apurtenance....
Act 5. An action tryed between John Washburne,plaint-
iffe, and Edward Dowty, defendant, about an hog the defendant had taken wrongfully from the plaintiffe, as hee
alledged; but the jewry, Robert Heeks being foreman,
fownd the plaintiffe to be faulty, and acquitted the def-

freemen' and with two representatives similarly elected from each
town sitting in a general court on the Massachusetts model.
1. N. B. Shurtleff (ed.) *Records of the colony of New Plymouth* (1855)
I pp.5-7.

endant. According to this verdict judgement pronounced
against the plaintiffe.
   Will Bennet complained of Edward Dowty for divers injuries, which was referred to the councell to be ended by
them.

183. 'GENERAL FUNDAMENTALS', 4-5 October, 1636.[1]
   The ordinances of the colony and corporation being read,
divers were fownd worthy the reforming, others the rejecting, and others fitt to be instituted and made. It was
therefore ordered and agreed, that four for the towne of
Plymouth, two for Scituate, and two for Duxburrow, should,
as committees for the whole, be added to the Governor and
Assistants, to rectefie and prepare such as should be
thought most convenient, that, if approved, they may be
put in force the next Generall Court....[The assistants were
named.]
1. Wee, the Associates of the Colony of New-Plimouth, coming hither as free born Subjects of the Kingdome of England, Endowed with all and singular the Priviledges belonging to such: Being Assembled, Do Enact, Ordain and
Constitute; That no Act, Imposition, Law or Ordinance be
Made or Imposed upon us at present or to come, but such
as shall be Enacted by consent of the body of Freemen or
Associates, or their Representatives legally assembled;
which is according to the free Liberties of the free born[2]
People of England.
2. And for the well Governing this Colony: It is also
Resolved and Ordered, That there be a free Election annually of Governour, Deputy Governour and Assistants, by
the Vote of the Freemen of this Corporation.
3. It is also Enacted, that Justice and Right be equally
and impartially Administered unto all, not sold, denied
or causelesly deferred unto any.
4. It is also Enacted, that no person in this Government
shall suffer or be indamaged, in respect of Life, Limb,
Liberty, Good Name or Estate, under colour of Law, or countenance of Authority, but by Virtue or Equity of some
express Law of the General Court of this Colony, or the
good and equitable Laws of our Nation, suitable for us, in
matters which are of a civil nature (as by the Court here
hath been accustomed) wherein we have no particular Law
of our own. And that none shall suffer as aforesaid, without being brought to answer by due course and process of
Law.
5. And that all Cases, whither Capital, Criminal, or between man and man, be Tried by a Jury of twelve good and
lawful men, according to the Commendable customs of Eng-

---

1. W. Bradford, *History of Plymouth Plantation* (1912) II p.237. These
were revised in 1671, and how far they were modified before 1671 cannot
be clearly determined.
2. This was their title to self-government and their separate exist-
ance.

land, except where some express Law doth referre it to
the judgement of some other Judg or Inferiour Court where
Jury is not; in which Case also, any party agrieved, may
Appeal and have Trial by a Jury ....
  [Jurymen could be challenged. No sentence could be delivered
  without '2 sufficient witnesses or other sufficient evidences
  or circumstances equivalent thereunto'.]
8. That whereas the great and knowne end of the first
Comers in the year of our Lord, 1620, leaving their dear
Native Country, and all that was dear to them; transporting themselves over the vast Ocean, into this remote
wast Wilderness,and therein willingly conflicting with
Dangers, Losses, Hardships and Distresses, some, and not
a few, Was, that without offence, they under the protection of their Native Prince, together with the enlargement
of his Majesties Dominion, might with the liberty of a
good Conscience enjoy the pure Scriptural worship of God,
without the mixture of humane inventions and impositions;
and that their Children after them might walk in the Holy
wayes of the Lord: And for which end they obtained leave
from King James of happy Memory, and His Honourable Council: with farther Grants from His Gracious Majesty,
Charles the I and His Honourable Council, by Letters
Patents for sundry Tracts of Land, with many Priviledges
therein contained for their better Encouragement to proceed on in so Pious a Work, which may especially tend to
the propagation of Religion, etc as by Letters Patents
more at large appeareth.[1]...
  [The churches were to be protected and ministers were to be
  provided for.]
9. And finally, It is Ordered and Declared by this Court
and the Authority thereof, that all these aforegoing Orders and Constitutions are so Fundamentally Essential to
the just Rights, Liberties, Common Good, and Special End
of this Colony, as that they shall and ought to be inviolably preserved.[2]

---

1. In 1671 the revised Fundamentals referred to the 'further assurance of the continuance of our liberties and priviledges' given by
Charles II. 'And whereas by the good hand of our God upon us, many
others since the first comers, are for the end come unto us, and sundry others rise up amongst us, desirous with all good Conscience, to
walk in the Faith and Order of the Gospel, whereby there are many
Churches gathered amongst us, walking according thereunto: And whereas (by the Grace of God) we have now had above sixty Years experience
of the good consistancy of these Churches,with Loyalty to our Prince,
civil Peace and Order, and also with spiritual Edification, together
with the welfare and tranquility of the Government'.
2. Certain offences which in England were under the jurisdiction of
ecclesiastical courts and punishable there by fine, confession or
penance,were punishable by death according to New Plymouth laws.

184. FORM OF THE DEPUTATION OR COMMITTEESHIP GRANTED BY THE GOVERN-
     MENT FOR THE DISPOSAL OF LAND FOR THE ERECTION OF A PLANTATION,
     NEIGHBOURHOOD, COLONY, TOWNSHIP OR CONGREGATION WITHIN THIS
     GOVERNMENT.   12 February 1639.[1]

Whereas our souveraign lord the King is pleased to betrust us,[2]...*[initials]* ...with the gouvernment of so many
of his subjects as doe or shalbe permitted to live within
this gouvernment of New Plymouth, and that it seemeth good
unto us to begin, set up, and establish a neighbourhood,
or plantacon, at a place called — being bounded —and
lying — miles westward from the said towne of New Plymouth;
And whereas, by reason of the distance of place, and our
many weighty occasions, we cannot so well see to the rec-
eiveing in of such persons as may be fitt to live together
there in the feare of God, and obeydyence of our said souveraigne lord the King,in peace and loue,...Wee haue thought good to betrust our welbeloued...*[initials]*...with receiving in such people unto them as may make good our desires before expressed, and therefore require of the said
...*[initials]*...That all and every of them be conscionably
faythfull, and carefull as well to receive in peacable
and faythfull people, according to their best discerning,
as also faythfully to dispose of such equall and fitt porcons of lands unto them, and euery of them, as the severall estates, rancks, and quallities of such persons, as
the Almighty in his prouidence shall send in amongst them
shall require, that so we may comfortably retifye and confirme such said porcons of land as they shall allot and
set forth in our behalf...Provided alwayes, that the said
...*[initials]*...reserve for our disposall, at least—acres
of good land, with meaddow competent in place convenient,
and be lyable from tyme to tyme, and at all tymes to receiue and folloe such good and wholsome instruccons as they
shall receiue from the gouverment about the disposall of
the said lands, and the well ordering of their heighbour-
hood, and conformitie to such good and wholsome lawes,
ordinance, and officers as are or shalbe established under
our souveraigne lord the King, within this said gouverment
of New Plymouth .

185. COMMISSION FOR DECIDING THE CONTROVERSY BETWEEN PLYMOUTH AND
     MASSACHUSETTS BAY CONCERNING BOUNDARIES,   4 June 1639.[3]

Whereas for the avoiding and preventing of all differen-

1. N.B. Shurtleff (ed.) *op. cit.* I pp. 113-4.
2. The loyalty of the Pilgrims to the king had been expressed in the
Compact, and it was frequently affirmed. The king also sent occasional letters to the plantation expressing thanks, approval and promises.
These royal letters read in the general court seemed to imply a qualified recognition of this anomalous 'colony', but their attempt to
secure a royal charter in 1629 had been bungled and had failed.
3. N.B. Shurtleff (ed.) *op. cit.* I pp. 127-8. Boundary disputes between colonies were frequent: few so ostensibly amicable as the general court of New Plymouth here.

ces and controversies that might arise about or concerning the extent and limit of the patent of New Plymouth and
Massachusetts Bay, and for the continuance and maintenance
of the ancient love and amity we, the inhabitants of the
government of New Plymouth, have always most zealously desired to hold observe and keep well our neighbours, the inhabitants of the said Massachusetts Bay, Know you that we,
the Governour, Counsell of Assistants and the rest of the
whole cominaltie and body of freemen of the said government of New Plymouth, being this day in publike Court sum-
oned and assembled together, haue, with mutual and joynt
assent and consent made, constituted, deputed, assigned,
and authorised our right trusty and welbeloued William
Bradford, gent, and our Governour, and Edward Winslow,
gent., our joynt...deputies, agents, and comissioners, to
solicite, conferr, comune, and entreate with the depties,
agents, and comissioners, deputed, constituted, authorised,
and appoynted by the government and inhabitants of the
said Massachusetts Bay appoynted for the like purpose on
their parts and behalf, and finally to finish, determine,
and sett forth the extents, limmitts, and boundaries of
the lands betwixt the two said pattents and governments,
so as they may remayne and bee forever hereafter unalterable and invyolable perpetually without any further question, contention, countroversie, debate, or difference
whatsoever. And whatsoever our said deputies, agents, and
comissioners, shall doe, conclude, determine, and finish,
or cause to be donne, concluded, determined, and finished,
in, about, and concerning the said premisses, shalbe, and
euer taken to bee, as ample, authinticall, and effectuall
to all the said ends, intents, and purposes as if the
same had beene done and performed by the whole body and
cominalty of the Gouvenour, Counsell of Assistants, and
freemen of the gouverment and corporacon of Plymouth
aforesaid in theire owne persons, and so to remayne absolutely without any controdiccon or question whatsoever hereafter, and to be entered upon record at the next General
Court after the returne of our said Comissioners &c...[1]

(c) MASSACHUSETTS

186. PROCEEDINGS OF THE COMPANY RELATING TO THE TRANSFERENCE OF
     GOVERNMENT TO NEW ENGLAND, 28 July - 20 October 1629.[1]
(a) General Court, 28 July 1629.
     ...a letter of the 27th of May from Mr. John Ende-

---

1. The fact of its separate existence as a corporate 'colony' over
twenty years was recognised when New Plymouth was invited to join the
New England Confederation in 1643 [see No.249].
2. N. B. Shurtleff (ed.) *Records of the governor and company of Massachusetts Bay* (1853) I pp. 48, 51, 56, 58-9: Massachusetts Hist. Soc.
Proceedings LXII pp.279-0. These documents illustrate the transformation of the organisation of a normal London trading company into the
government of an unprecedented New England Puritan Commonwealth. The

cott[1] was now read, wherein, amongst other things, hee
complaines of the profane and dissolute living of divers
of our nation, formerly traders to those parts, and of
their irregular trading with the Indians, contrary to
his late Majesty's proclamacon, desiring that the Company
would take the same into their serious consideracon and
to use some speedy means heere for reformacon thereof.
Whereupon the proclamacon made in Anno 1622 was read;[2]
and it is thought fitt that suite bee made to his Majesty
or the Lords for renewing thereof, with addicon of such
benfitiall clauses as shalbe needful for reforming so
great and unsufferable abuses.... Lastly, Mr. Governor
Cradock read certaine proposicons conceived by himself,
viz., that for the advancement of the plantacon,the ind-
ucing and encouraging persons of worth and qualitie to
transplant themselves and famylyes thither, and for other
weighty reasons therein contained, to transfer the government of the plantacon to those that shall inhabite
there, and not to continue the same in subordinacon to
the Company heer, as now it is.[3] This business occasioned
some debate; but by reason of the many great and considerable consequences thereupon depending, it was not now
resolved upon; but those present are desired privately
and seriously to consider hereof, and to sett downe their

---

deterioration and worsening outlook for religion in England prompted
many puritans to contemplate emigration. John Winthrop, Suffolk squ-
ire and J.P., fearing the wrath of God would descend upon England,
sought with others to create a new world for the 'saving remnant' of
God's Elect, and confident of divine purpose and protection, planned a new colonising experiment of an organised self-governing community - a new Zion - free from all dependence on England, either on
Crown or on Parliament.
1. John Endecott, son-in-law of Mathew Cradock, was acting governor
in the colony at Salem. He had taken charge of the settlement there
and had exercised a firm, if ruthless government. He had, moreover,
contrary to the original intentions of the company, established in
Salem an independent congregational church similar to that of the
Pilgrims at New Plymouth. His action in deporting two members of
his council, because they were Anglicans alarmed Rev.J.White and the
moderate Puritans in the company. Unlike the Pilgrims, these puritans were repudiating allegiance to the king [ct. No.193(a)], but
were loyal to the Anglican church, hoping to reform it from within.
2. A royal proclamation in 1622 had forbidden traders to sell arms
to the Indians.
3. Cradock was attempting to strengthen the government in the plantation at the expense of the London company. It was feared that since
the corporation was open to all stock holders, the puritans might be
swamped by those who did not share their vision of Zion. But soon
the discussion moved to exporting not only the governing powers,
but the whole company and its charter to New England. There was no
express words in the charter requiring the corporation to be residenced in England.

particular reasons in wryting *pro* and *contra* , and to produce the same at the next General Court;...
(b) The Agreement at Cambridge, 26 August.[1]
   Upon due consideration of the state of the plantation
now in hand for New England, wherein wee (whose names are
hereunto subscribed) have engaged ourselves: and having
weighed the greatness of the worke in regard of the consequence, God's glory and the churches good: As also in
regard of the difficultyes and discouragements which in
all probabilityes must be forecast upon the execution of
this businesse: Considering withall that this whole adventure growes upon the joint confidence we have in each
others fidelity and resolution herein, so as no man of
us would have adventured it without assurance of the rest:
Now, for the better encouragement of ourselves and others that shall joyne with us in this action, and to the
end that every man may without scruple dispose of his estate and afayres as may best fitt his preparation for this
voyage, it is fully and faithfully agreed amongst us, and
every of us doth hereby freely and sincerely promise and
bind himselfe in the word of a Christian and in the presence of God who is the searcher of all hearts, That we
will so really endeavour the execution of this worke, as
by God's assistance we will be ready...in our persons,
and with such of our several familyes as are to go with
us, and such provision as we are able conveniently to
furnish ourselves withall, to embarke for the said plantation by the first of March next,...at such port or ports
of this land as shall be agreed upon by the Companie, to
the end to passe the seas (under God's protection) to
inhabite and continue in New England: *Provided always*,
that before the last of September next the whole government together with the patent for the said plantation be
first by an order of court legally transferred and established to remain with us and others which shall inhabite
upon the said plantation....And we do further promise
every one for himselfe, that shall fayle to be ready
through his own default by the day appointed, to pay for
every day's default the sum of £3 to the use of the rest
of the Companie who shall be ready by the same day and
time.
(c) General Court, 29 August.
   [The arguments for and against the transfer were discussed.][2]
After a long debate, Mr. Deputie Goffe put it to the
question, as followeth: 'As many of you as desire to have
the pattent and the government of the plantacon to bee
transferred to New England, soe as it may be done legally,
hold up your hands: Soe many as will not, hold upp your

_____

1. This agreement was made by a dozen of the company (including Dudley,
Vassall, Humfry, and Winthrop, hitherto not a stockholder) who were
now concerned to move the company to America - with the charter, if
that could legally be done. But secrecy seems to have prevented them
taking any legal advice.
2. They were not, however, written down in these minutes.

hands'.

Where, by erecoon of hands, it appeared by the general consent of the Company, that the government and pattent should be setled in New England, and accordingly an order to bee drawne upp.[1]

(d) Court of Assistants, 16 October.

This Court was appointed to treat and resolve, that upon the transferring of the government to N. England, what government shalbe held at London, whereby the future charge of the joynt stock may bee cherished and preserved, and the body politique of the Company remaine and increase.

What persons shall have the charge of the managing of the joynt stock,both at London and in N. England; wherin it is conceeved fitt that Captain Endecott continue the government there, unless just cause to the contrarie. These and other things were largely discussed; and it was thought fit and natural that the government of persons be held there, the government of trade and merchandises to be here....But for that there is a great debt owing by the joynt stock,it was moved that some course might be taken for cleering thereof, before the government bee transferred;...[2]

(e) 19th October 1629.

The occasion of this meeting being to resolve of the alteracon of the government, and therein to consider how the debts upon the joynt stock shalbe first discharged, and how the same shalbe hereafter managed; and herein what was formly treated on, was againe related, and for that divers questions will arise to bee determined in this business, which will take upp much tyme, and cannot bee soe convenyently done at a Court, it was thought fitt That certaine comittees bee appointed on either part to meete and make proposicons each to other.... And to this purpose, articles betweene the planters and adventurers for performance of what shalbe determined, was now drawne by Mr. Whyte, the councillor, read and approved, and are to be presented to morrow at a Generall Court, to be ratyfyed, and then sealed; and at that court the Governor and Assistants to be chosen for the Government in N. England....

(f)General Court, 20 October.

Mr. Governor acquainted those present, That the espetiall occasion of summoninge this Court was for the electon of a new Governor, Deputie, and Assistants, the government being to bee transferred into New England, according to

---

1. Only 27 of the 125 freemen of the company however, were present, and the Cambridge signatories virtually secured control.
2. The intention of the Cambridge agreement had presumably been the complete extinction of the company as a merchant corporation in London. However, it was decided by a sub-committee between October and December 1629 to have a subordinate body in England to manage the trading stock and the debts.

the former order and resolucon of the Company. But before
the Court proceeded to the said eleccon, certaine articles
of agreement, conceived at a meeting yesterday between the
adventurers heere at home and the planters that are to goe
over, aswell for the mannaging and setling of the joynt
stock as for reconcilinge of any differences that may happen upon this change of government, was now read and recommended to the Court for their approbacon, and for the nom-
inacon and appointment of a competent nomber of committees
to meete and treat and resolve of thses businesses....
[Sub-committees representing planters and adventurers were appointed.]
Mr. Winthrop was, with a generall vote and full consent of
this Court, by eraccon of hands chosen to bee Governor for
the ensuing yeare, to begin on this present day;...[1]

187. PROCEEDINGS OF THE FIRST COURT OF ASSISTANTS IN THE COLONY,
                                            23 August 1630.[2]
    [It was proposed that there should be monthly sessions of the
    court of assistants, and that the General Court should sit quart-

---

1. According to the charter,elections were to be held at the end of
Easter term, not in October. This infringement of the charter was
only the first of many. Winthrop held office initially for eighteen
months, ruled with 'assistants' (magistrates) only, and summoned no
general court till 19 October 1630 in Boston. This was evidently a
mass meeting: where, stangely perhaps, the decisions were made by
the generality (i) that the governor and deputy would be elected by
the assistants alone and (ii) that legislation and selection of executive officials would be only by governor and assistants. The puritan leaders believed that the charter could be re-shaped as they (and
God) desired into a frame of government for a Commonwealth. The sea-
change transformed a radical puritan opposition into an authoritarian
oligarchy.
In May 1631 Winthrop was re-elected Governor for the year 'by the general consent of the Court according to the meaning of the patent'. He
was convinced that government should be, not by the people, but by
the elect and godly few. 'Democracy', he said, of which there was
'no such government in Israel' was 'among civil nations accounted the
meanest and worst of all forms of government'. So power was concentrated under his own dominant control. Until conflict in 1644 over
ownership of a sow led to division into two houses, assistants and
deputies (elected freemen) sat together in the general court. Thereafter, decisions requiring agreement by both houses, the assistants
lost their 'negative voice' (veto) but they remained for a further
period effectively the standing council of government when deputies
were not summoned or sitting.
2. N.B. Shurtleff (ed.) *op. cit.*I p.74. This session took place in
Charlestown. The general court had been held at Goffe's house in
London on 19 February 1630. Governor and assistants had met in Southampton, just before the *Arbella* sailed with Winthrop's 'saving remnant' to set up the city of God in the American wilderness. Since the
officials of the company voyaged with the colonists, there were no
hiatus in its government; and the leaders proved as resolute as they
were resourceful in pursuit of the frame of government for a puritan

erly.]

It was ordered, that, in all civill accons, the first
process or summons by the beadle or his deputy shalbe directed by the Governor or Deputy Governor, or some other
of the Assistants being a justice of the peace; the next
process to be a *capias* or *distringas*,at the discrecon of
the Court....

It was ordered, that the Governor and Deputy Governor,
for the tyme being, shall alwaies be justices of the peace,
and that Sir Richard Saltonstall, Mr. Johnson, Mr. Endicott, and Mr. Ludlowe shalbe justices of the peace for
the present tyme,in all things to have like power that
justices of peace hath in England for reformacon of abuses
and punishing of offenders; and that any justice of the
peace may imprison an offender, but not inflict any cor-
porall punishment without the presence and consent of
some one of the Assistants....

188. ORDERS OF THE GENERAL COURT RELATING TO ASSISTANTS AND FREEMEN,
18 May 1631.[1]

For explanacon of an order made the last Generall Court, holden
the 19th of October last, it was ordered nowe, with full
consent of all the commons then present, That once in
every yeare att least, a Generall Court shalbe holden,
att which Court it shalbe lawfull for the commons to pro-
pounde any person or persons whome they shall desire to
be chosen Assistants, and if it be doubtfull whether it
be the greater parte of the commons or not, it shalbe
putt to the poll. The like course to be holden when they,
the said commons, shall see cause for any defect or mis-
behavour to remove any one or more of ye Assistants...
and to the end the body of the comons may be preserved
of honest and good men, it was likewise ordered and agreed that for time to come no man shalbe admitted to the
freedome of this body polliticke, but such as are members
of some of the churches within the lymitts of the same.[2]

189. ACTS OF GENERAL COURT, 1632-4. [3]
(a) 9 May 1632.

It was generally agreed upon by the erection of hands,
That the Governor, deputie governor and assistants should
be chosen by the whole Courte of governor, deputie governor, assistants and freemen, and that the governor shall
alwaies be chosen out of the assistants....[4]

---

state which they erected on the basis of a trading charter.
1. N.B. Shurtleff (ed.) *op. cit.* I p.87.
2. This arbitrary restriction of the franchise (which violated the
charter) was prompted by Winthrop's stern criteria for puritan worth
and fear of a broad suffrage. It recognised the narrowly religious
base of the government, restricting citizenship probably to about one
ninth of adult males in the colony.
3. N.B. Shurtleff (ed.) *op. cit.* I pp. 95, 117-9.
4. Presumably as a consequence of the exclusive requirements of the

(b) 14 May 1634.[1]
[A new oath to be taken by all freemen was agreed.]
Further, it is agreed, That none byt the Generall
Courte hath power to choose and admit freemen: That none
byt the General Courte hath power to make and establishe
lawes, nor to elect and appoint officers as governor,
deputy governor, assistants, treasurer, secretary, captains, ensigns, lieutenants or any of like moment, or to
remove such upon misdemeanour or also to set out the duties and powers of said officers, That none but the Generall Courte hath power to rayse moneyes, and taxes and to
dispose of lands, *viz.* to give and confirm proprieties....[2]
It was further ordered, That the constable of every
plantacon shall, upon process receaved from the Secretary,
give tymely notice to the freemen of the plantacon where
hee dwells to send soe many of their said members as the
process shall direct to attend upon publique service. And
it is agreed That noe tryall shall passe upon any for life
or banishment, but by a jury soe summoned, or by the Generall Courte.
It was further ordered, That it shalbe lawful for the
freemen of every plantacon to choose two or three of each
towne before every Generall Courte to conferre of and
prepare such public business as by them shalbe thought
fitt to consider of att the nexte Generall Courte; and
That such persons as shalbe hereafter soe deputed by the
freemen of *[the]* several plantacons to deale in their behalf in the publique affayrs of the Commonwealth, shall have
the full power and voyces of all the said freemen deryving
to them, for the makeing and establishing of lawes, granting of lands *etc.,* to deale in all other affayrs of the Commonwealth wherein the freemen have to doe: the matter of
election of magistrates and other officers onely excepted,

previous May [see No.188], the puritans leaders had now sufficient
confidence in the godly character of the freemen to permit them to
choose officials. The charter of course did not limit the election
of the governor in this way - i.e. only from among the assistants.
1. At this meeting Winthrop was by ballot replaced temporarily as
governor by Thomas Dudley for his arbitrary conduct. He later commented that 'the best part' of a community 'is always the least, and
of that best part the wiser is always the lesser'.
2. A public meeting at Watertown had petitioned that taxation by the
court of assistants was a violation of the charter. Winthrop had replied that, since the colony had become a commonwealth and no longer
a corporation, the elected court of assistants had become a parliament. This Act by the general court is their reply to Winthrop's
championship of the assistants' case. It is significant of the earlier changes of May 1632 that it was the general court which claimed
this exclusive authority, though the assistants continued to impose
taxes contrary to this Act. The freemen themselves were now increasingly a limited and privileged minority; but nevertheless taxes and
forced labour were imposed on those who were not represented by the
deputies. Only in the town meeting did such non-freemen have any voice.

wherein every freeman is to give his owne voyce....[1]

190. (a) ORDERS OF GENERAL COURT RELATING TO DEFENCE AND TAXATION,
3 March 1635.[2]

It is ordered, that the present governor, deputy governor [the other members of this sub-committee were named]...whoe
are deputed by this court to dispose of all millitary affaires whatsoever, shall have full power and aucthority to
see all former laws concerneing all millitary men and
munition executed, and also shall have full power to ordeyne or remove all millitary officers, and to make and
tender to them an oathe suteable to their places, to dispose of all companyes, to make orders for them...and to
see that strickt dissipline and traineings be observed,
and to command them forth upon any occasion they thinke
meete, to make either offensive or defencive warr, as
also to doe whatsoever may be further behoofefull, for
the good of this plantation, in case of any warr that may
befall us, and also that the aforesaid comissioners or
the maior parte of them, shall have power to imprison or
confine any that they shall judge to be enemyes to the
commonwealth, and such as will not come under commaund
or restrainte, as they shalbe required, it shalbe lawfull for the said comissioners to put such persons to
death....

It is ordered, there shalbe £300 levyed out of the
several plantations, according to the last rate of townes, to be paide to the Treasurer before the 6th of May
nexte.

It is ordered, that the constable of every plantation
shall deliver to the deputyes to be chosen for the nexte
General Court a coppy of their towne rates, to be considered of by them, to the end that those townes which have
bene over rated in the £900 levy, may in the nexte levy,
receave equal satisfaction for the tyme past and to come.

190.(b) ORDERS OF GENERAL COURT RELATING TO JURIES, 4 March 1635.[3]

...It is ordered, that there shalbe two grand juryes
summoned every yeare, the one to informe the Court in March, the other to informe the Court in September, yearely,
of the breaches of any order, or other misdemeanors, that
they shall knowe or heare to be committed by any person or
persons whatsoever within this jurisdiction, or to doe any
other service of the Commonwealth that they shalbe enjoyned.

1. i.e. the whole body of freemen were required at the May meeting
for elections; but towns would elect deputies for ordinary government business and administration at the other three meetings of the
general court.
2. N.B. Shurtleff (ed.) *op. cit.* I p. 138.
3. N.B. Shurtleff (ed.) *op. cit.* I p.143. Juries had been empanelled
from the first days of the colony (see *ibid.* pp.77-8). In Connecticut
the party losing a case paid each juryman sixpence (J. H. Thumbull

191. ACTS CONCERNING THE POWERS AND DELIBERATIONS OF MAGISTRATES
     AND DEPUTIES, 3 March 1636 and 7 March 1644.[1]
(a) 3 March 1636.

Further ordered this present Court, that the Generall
Court to be holden in May nexte for eleccon of magistrates
and soe from tyme to tyme as occacon shall require, shall
elect a certain number of magistrates for tearme of their
lyves as a standing counsaile not to be removed but upon
due conviccon of crime, insufficiency, or for some other
waightie cause; the Gouvernor for the tyme being to be
always president of this counsaile and to have such further power out of Court as the Generall Courts shall from
tyme *[to tyme]* indue them withall.[2]...

> [Quarterly county courts should try all civil cases concerning
> debt or damage not in excess of £10, and all criminal cases not
> involving life, dismemberment or banishment. Appeals would be
> heard in the next great quarter court of governor and assistant
> in Boston. Since reorganisation of business had made it unnecess-
> ary to hold so many general courts, they should meet in future
> twice a year (May and October) instead of quarterly.]

And whereas it may fall out that in some of these Generall Courts, to be holden by the magistrates and deputies, there may arise some difference of judgement in doubtfull cases, it is therefore ordered, That noe lawe, order
or sentence shall passe as an act of the Court, without
the consent of the greater parte of the magistrates on the
one parte, and the greater number of the deputies on the
other parte; and for want of such accorde, the cause or

(ed.) *Public Records...Connecticut* (1850) p.9).
1. N.B. Shurtleff (ed.) *op. cit.*I p. 167,169; II p.58: supplemented
by *Charter and general laws of Massachusetts Bay* (1814). These general courts met in Newtown (Cambridge) and Boston respectively.
2. According to John Cotton's sermon two years before, the strength
of the 'commonwealth' lay in the concurrence of magistrates, ministers and people. But, with the support of ministers and elders, the
magistrates had in 1635 asserted their dominant authority and sought
to check that of the deputies by acting as a standing council in the
intervals between sessions of the general court. [c.f. the standing
defence committee No. 190(a)]. Now they were attempting to establish
an oligarchy of life councillors chosen from among themselves. The
deputies were naturally jealous and resentful, and in June 1639 (I p.
264) succeeded in getting an Act making it clear that no new order
of magistrates had been created contrary to the charter and that life
councillors had no more than the ordinary powers of magistrates. The
need for a standing council was, however, vindicated (II p.21), and
in 1644 the deputies proposed as a compromise a commission of seven
magistrates, three deputies and Rev. Nathaniel Ward as its members.
The magistrates objected to this 'overthrow of the foundation of our
government' and asserted the right of the court of merchants in a
patent to act as the standing council. The opinion of the church elders was sought and their judgment, delivered by John Cotton, supported
the magistrates' claim (J. Winthrop, *History* II pp.205, 251-6):[see
also No.197.]

order shall be suspended, and if either partie thinke it
soe materiall, there shalbe forthwith a committee chosen,
and one halfe by the magistrates, and the other halfe by
the deputyes, and the committee soe chosen to elect an
umpire, whoe togeather shall have power to heare and determine the cause in question....[1]
(b) 7 March 1644.
I. It is hereby declared that the generall court consisting of magistrats and deputyes is the chief civil power
of this commonwealth; which onely hath power to rayse
money and taxes upon the whole country and dispose of land,
viz. to give and confirm proprieties appertaining to and
immediately desired from the country; and to act on all
affaires of this commonwealth according to such power
both in matters of counsel, making of lawes and matters
of judicature by impeaching and sentencing any person or
persons according to the law and by reviewing and hearing
any complaynts orderly presented against this person or
court[2]....
2. Forasmuch as, after long experience, wee find divers
inconveniences in the manner of proceeding in courts by
magistrates and deputies sitting together[3] and accounting
it wisdome to follow the laudable practice of other states who have layd groundworks for government and order in
the issuing of business of greatest and highest consequence, It is therefore ordered, first, that the magistrates may sit and act business by themselves, by drawing
up bills and orders which they shall see good in their
wisdome, which haveing agreed upon, they may present them
to the deputies to bee considered of,how good and wholesome such orders are for the country, and accordingly to
give their assent or dissent; the deputies in like manner siting apart by themselves, and consulting about such
orders and lawes as they in their discretion and experience shall find meete for common good, which agreed upon
by them, they may present to the magistrate, who, accord-

1. This Act virtually enabled the magistrates to negative the decision of the deputies who could by weight of numbers have outvoted them.
2. This declaration was similar to that of the elders, *ibid.* II p.225.
3. Magistrates and deputies had championed opposing claimants to the
ownership of Mrs. Sherman's sow, and this deadlock led to the division of the general court into two houses. The issue also raised the
question of the 'negative voice' which Winthrop and the magistrates
had claimed was fundamental for the welfare of the commonwealth. When
deputies had been first elected in 1634 they had asked to see the
charter and they claimed all rights were vested in the general court.
Winthrop, however, had ruled that they should put any recommendations
and grievances to the court of assistants, and that the assistants
should have exclusive power to originate laws, The division of the
general court in 1644 may have 'determined' the issue of the 'negative voice', but it also might seem to confirm control by the
magistrates.

ing to their wisedome, haveing seriously considered of
them, may consent unto them or disalow them; and when
any orders have passed the approbation of both magistrates
and deputies, then such orders to be ingrossed, and in the
last day of the court to bee read deliberately, and full
assent to bee given; Provided, also, that all matters of
judicature which the Court shall take cognisance of either civill or criminal such a case shall be determined
by a major vote of the whole court met together.

192. ACT OF GENERAL COURT RELATING TO TOWNSHIP GOVERNMENT,
3 March 1636.[1]
Whereas particular towns have many things which concern only themselves, and the ordering of their own affairs, and disposing of businesses in their own town, it
is therefore ordered That the freemen of every town, or
the major part of them, shall only have power to dispose
of their own lands and woods with all the privileges and
appurtenances of the said towns not repugnant to the laws
and orders here established by the General Court; as
also to lay mulcts and penalties for the breach of these
orders, and to levy and distrain the same, not exceeding
the sum of twenty shillings; also to choose their own
particular offices as constables, surveyors for the highways, and the like; and because much business is like to
ensue to the constables of several towns by reason they
are to make distresses and gather fines, therefore that
every town shall have two constables where there is need,
that so their office may not be a burden unto them, and
they may attend more carefully upon the discharge of their
office, for which they shall be liable to give their accounts to this court then they shall be called thereunto.

193. (a) PETITION TO THE LORDS COMMISSIONERS AGAINST RETURN OF THE
CHARTER, 6 September 1638.[2]
Whereas, it hath pleased your Lordships, by order of

---

1. N.B. Shurtleff (ed.) *op. cit.* I p.172. This Act is the first of a
series of laws which established the characteristically Massachusetts
system of local government – the town meeting. See similarly the Body
of Liberties in 1641 (§ 12, 56,66,74.): [see No.198].
2. R.C. Winthrop, *Life and letters of J. Winthrop* (1869) II pp.226-8.
Gorges' ambitions for the grant of a new feudal principality for himself over all New England (instead of the corporate charter under the
revised patent for the Virginia Company of Plymouth, now the New England Council [see Nos. 162-5]) were thwarted by the failure of his
son's proprietary at 'Massachustack' and by the existence of the
Massachusetts Bay Company. He had been seeking to have their charter
annulled, and to bring their colony under a new New England government. The privy council, however, in January 1633 had reported in
favour of the company not on legal or ecclesiastical grounds, but
largely on its benefit to the realm; though new instructions, issued
a year later, showed concern by requiring oaths of allegiance and
supremacy for all emigrating to New England. With the establishment

the 4th of April last, to require our patent to be sent
unto you; We do here humbly and sincerely profess, that
we are ready to yield all due obedience to our Sovereign
Lord the King's Majesty, and to your Lordships under him,
and in this mind we left our native country, and according
thereunto hath been our practice ever since: so as we are
much grieved that your Lordships should call in our patent,
there being no cause known to us for that purpose, our
government being settled according to his Majesty's grant,
& we not answerable for any defect in other plantations.
This is that which his Majesty's Subjects do believe and
profess, and therefore we are all humble suitors to your
Lordships, that you be pleased to take into further consideration our condition and to afford unto us the liberties
of subjects, that we may know what is laid to our charge
and have leave and time to answer for ourselves before we
be condemned as a people unworthy of his Majesty's favour
or protection. As for the *quo warranto* mentioned in the
last order we do assure your Lordships that we were never

---

of the Lords commissioners for regulating foreign plantations under
Laud in April 1634 with powers to supervise the colonies and even to
revoke their charters [see No.170],the threat to Massachusetts and
the opportunity for Gorges' wider dominion had increased. The moribund New England Council divided up their lands the following year
in preparation for surrender of their charter in June 1635. The
king was ready to appoint Gorges as governor general of New England
(and his partner, Mason, as vice admiral over the seas, even to
California and Nova Albion). Massachusetts was accused of framing
'new concepts' in religion and government, amounting to rebellion
(Am.Ant. Soc. *Proc.*1867 **pp.**123-5); and a writ of *quo warranto* was issued against the Massachusetts Company. It proving difficult to serve,
and to require attendance, it was not till May 1637 that the king's
bench gave judgement for the king to recover powers granted, for
the charter to be cancelled, and Cradock to be arrested. Gorges obtained his governor generalship only to find it a paper victory; he
managed to salvage only the proprietary of Maine from his ruined
hopes. Charles I, entangled in difficulties in Scotland and then in
England, could not help Gorges enforce the judgement. In reply to
the demand on 4 April 1638 for the immediate surrender of the patent,
the general court in Massachusetts resolved not to return it, to
resist the governor general, and to make excuses in this petition
to the Lords commissioners. Above all they resolved 'to avoid and
protract': a policy in defence of their autonomy they pursued with
skill and resource for half a century [see Nos. 284, 291].Already
colonists had realised that distance from the metropolis could enable
them to resist, procrastinate, side-step, manipulate, neglect or
modify the orders of the legitimate imperial authority. Royal officials on the spot and local leaders (expatriate and indigenous) who had
needs, ambitions, pressures, priorities and estimates of their own
'frontier' interest, different from those in London, could thwart
metropolitan intention and milk the imperial factor for their own
ends.

called to make answer to it, and if we had, we doubt not
but that we have a sufficient plea to put in....
    [They had emigrated under the king's charter, encouragement and
    favour. To abrogate their charter would render them 'runagates
    and outlaws'; they would be exposed to ruin; their lands would
    be exposed to occupations by French and Dutch and lead to the
    dissolution of all English plantations in America.]
    3. If we should lose all our labour and cost and be
deprived of those liberties which his Majesty hath granted
us and nothing laid to our charge,nor any failing to be
found in us in point of allegiance (which all our countrymen do take notice of and we justify our faithfulness on
this behalf) it will discourage all men hereafter from
the like undertakings upon confidence of his Majesty's
royal grant.
    Lastly, if our patent be taken from us, (whereby we
suppose we may claim interest in his Majesty's favour
and protection,) the common people here will conceive that
his Majesty hath cast them off, and that hereby they are
freed from their allegiance and subjection, and thereupon
will be ready to confederate themselves under a new government, for their necessary safety and subsistence, which
will be of dangerous example unto other plantations, and
perilous to ourselves, of incurring his Majesty's displeasure, which we would by all means avoid. Upon these
considerations we are bold to renew our humble supplic-
ation to your Lordships, that we may be suffered to live
here in this wilderness, and that this poor plantation,
which hath found more favour with God than many other,
may not find less favour from your Lordships, that our
liberties should be restrained, when others are enlarged:
that the door should be kept shut upon us, while it stands
open to all other plantations; that men of ability should
be debarred from us, while they have encouragement to
other colonies. We do not question your Lordships' proceedings, we only desire to open our griefs where the
remedy is to be expected. If in any thing we have offended his Majesty and your Lordships we humbly prostrate
ourselves at the footstool of supreme authority....[1]

193. (b) RESOLUTION OF THE GENERAL COURT, 7 September 1638.[2]
    ...It was agreed that whereas a very strict order was

---

1. The threat to the patent made it politic for the general court to
protest their loyalty in hope of the king's protection. Some indeed,
considered it'perjury and treason' to appeal thus to the king, while
others were firmly denying any wish 'to erect a seminary of faction
and separation', as the New England Council had affirmed. (P. Force,
Tracts pp. 14,44. and T. Hutchinson,*History* I p.87).
2. J. Winthrop. *Life and letters* II p.223: an extract from his
journal. Mathew Cradock had been ordered in 1635 to get the charter
returned for inspection at Westminster: and on 4 April 1638 the attorney general reported to the Lords Commissioners that a *quo warranto*
writ had been issued but no one had appeared to answer it. The privy

sent from the Lords Commissioners for the plantations for
the sending home our patent upon pretence that judgement
had passed against it upon a *quo warranto*, a letter
should be sent to the Governor in the name of the court
to excuse our not sending of it: for it was resolved to
be best not to send it, because then such of our friends
and others in England would conceive it to be surrendered,
and that thereupon we should be bound to receive such a
governor and such orders as should be sent to us, and
many bad minds and some weak ones among ourselves would
think it lawful, it not necessary, to accept a general
governor.[1]

194. A QUESTION OF JURISDICTION AND APPEAL, June 1638.[2]

Four servants of Plimouth ran from their masters, and
coming to Providence they killed an Indian...Being discovered, they fled and were taken to the Isle Aquiday
[Rhode Island] . Mr. Williams gave notice to the governor
of Massachusetts and desired advice. He returned answer
that, seeing they were of Plimouth, they could certify
Plimouth of them, and, if they should send for them, to
deliver them; otherwise seeing no English had jurisdiction in the place where the murder was committed, neither
had they at the Island any government established, it
would be safest to deliver the principal, who was certainly
known to have killed the party, to the Indians his friends
with caution that they should not put him to torture, and
to keep the other three to further consideration. After
this, Plimouth men sent for them (but one had escaped) and
the governour there wrote to the governour here[3] for advice,
especially for that he heard they intended to appeal to
England. The governour returned answer of encouragement
to proceed notwithstanding, seeing no appeal did lie, for
that they could not be tried in England and that the whole
country here were interested in the case and would expect
to have justice done.

---

council then tried to secure the delivery of the letter and writ, and
warned that the king would 'reassume into his hands the whole plantation'. Winthop now pleaded that they had never previously received
a summons to answer the writ.
For the difficulty of delivering a *quo warranto*, and the preference
therefore for a *scire facias*, see below Nos. 284,291.
1. There was a continuing fear that a general royal governor over all
New England would be sent *(ibid.* p.222: see also No.292). Gorges of
course had been pressing for such a large 'dominion', proprietary
not royal, for many years, though the New England Council had felt
constrained to parcel out its lands among its members – in 1623 and
1625. Only the grant to Gorges was confirmed by the Crown: the province
of Maine in 1639, which was annexed by Massachusetts in 1652.
2. J. Winthrop, *The history of New England* (1853 ed.) I p.321.
3. John Winthrop.

195. A BOSTON QUARTER COURT: CRIMES AND PUNISHMENTS, 3 September 1639.[1]

...John Stacy, Junior, for being distempered with drinke, was set in the stocks...John Neale, for runing away and stealing, was censured to bee severely whiped, and comitted to his master to bee kept chained...Thomas Bushrode, being accused of defaming the government, was comited and fined 6.13s.4d., which paying, to bee discharged ...Marmaduke Peirce, being accused of suspition of murther, and the matter not appearing cleare, it was refered until the next Quarter Court, and the jewry was enjoyned then to appeare...John Kempre, for filthy, uncleane attempts with three yong girles was censured to bee whiped both heare, at Roxberry, and at Salem, very severely, and was comitted for a slave to Leist Davenport...Mathewe Edwards, for puting his hand under a girles coates, was censured to be whipped. Thomas Knore. for selling a pot full of strong water without license, was fined 5sh. Nicholas Davison, for swearing an oath, was ordered to pay 20sh. which hee consented unto...John Joanes, for defileing his wife before marriage, was fined 20sh. Mr. Thomas Lechford for going to the jewry and pleading with them out of court, is debarred from pleading any mans cause hearafter, unlesse his owne, and admonished not to presume to meddle beyond what hee shalbee called to by the courte.

196. JOHN WINTHROP: TWO DIFFICULTIES IN FRAMING A BODY OF LAWS, November 1639.[2]

One was want of sufficient experience of the nature and disposition of the people, considered with the condition of the country and other circumstances, which made them conceive, that such laws would be fittest for us which would arise *pro re nata* upon occasions *etc.* and so the laws of England and other states grew, and therefore the fundamental laws of England are called customs, *consuetudines.*   2. For that it would professedly transgress the limits of our charter which provide we shall make no laws repugnant to the laws of England and that we were assured we must do. But to raise up laws by practice and custom had been no transgression.

197. REV. JOHN COTTON: DRAFT ABSTRACT OF THE LAWS, 1641.[3]
    Chapter I: *Of Magistrates*
    [All magistrates were to be chosen by freemen out of those ablest and best qualified noblemen or gentlemen: Ex.XVIII.21; Eccles. X.17: Jer. XXX 21.]

1. N.B. Shurtleff (ed.) *op. cit.* I pp.268-0.
2. J. K. Hosmer (ed.) *John Winthrop's Journal...* (1908 ed.) I pp.388-9.
3. Mass. Hist. Soc. *Collections* 1st.V: pp.173-4. *Hutchinson Papers,* I pp. 184-6; P. Force, *Tracts* III no.9. Repudiating all external authority, whether of king or Parliament, the Massachusetts Commonwealth had asserted its freedom to shape government according to their convictions of God's plans for them. In close combination with church

II. The Governor hath joynt power with the assistants to
governe the whole country according to the lawes established hereafter mentioned: He hath power of himselfe,
and in his absence the deputy Governor, to moderate all
publique actions of the commonwealth.
(1) As first, to send out warrants for the calling of the
General Courts (except that of elections). Josh.XXIV.1.
(2) To order and transact all actions in the courte where
he sitteth, as to gather suffrages and votes, and to pronounce sentence according to the greater parts of them.
III. The power of the governour with the rest of the
councellours is: Num.XI.14 - 16.
(1) To consult and provide for the maintenance of the
state and people   Exo. XVIII. 22.
(2) To direct in all hard matters wherein appeale is made
to them from inferior courts.   Deu. XVII. 8,9
(3) To preserve religion   Exo. XXXIII.27and
                                             XXV.40.
(4) To oversee the fortes and munition of the country, and
to take order for the protection of the country from forraigne invasion or intestine sedition, and as need shall
require, with consent of the people, to enterprise warrs.

2 Chr.XIX.11; 2 Kings. XX.13; 2 Chr.XXXII.21; Cor.XIX.32;
XXIII.6; Prov.XXIX.5.
IV. And because these great affaires of the state cannot
well and sufficiently be attended, nor wisely administered,
if they be often changed, therefore the councellors are
to be chosen for life, unlesse they give just cause of
removal, which if they doe, then they to be removed by
the general court.

Exo. XVII.9; Pro.XXIV.6; I Kings. XII.6; Pro.XXVIII.2;
Exo.XVIII.22.
V. The power of the Governour sitting with the Councellours and Assistants, is to hear and determine all causes,
whether civil or criminal, which are brought before him,
through the whole commonwealth, yet reserving liberty of
appeale from him to the General Courte.   Deu.1.XVI.17
VI. Every towne is to have judges within themselves,
whose power shall be once in the month, or in three months

---

elders, the dominant group of governor and assistants sought to reconcile the law of God with the rights of Englishmen. But the freemen and
their deputies wanted a body of liberties to curb the harsh and arbitrary power of the assistants. Cotton had been asked to produce such
a code in 1636, 'agreeable to the word of God which may be the fundamentals of this commonwealth'. (N.B. Shurtleff (ed.) *op.cit.* I pp.174-
5), but this so-called 'model of Moses his judicials' presented to
the general court the following year, though it was based largely on
English common law with supporting Old Testament texts, was not adopted. Nor was this, his second attempt, which had been asked for in
1639. In the meantime magistrates would proceed according to such laws
as were established and 'where there is noe lawe, then as neere to
the lawe of God as they can'(p.175).

at the furthest, to heare and determine civil causes and
pleas of lesse values, and crimes also which are not capital, yet reserving liberty of appeale to the courte of
Governor and Assistants.   Exo.XVIII.21,22.
VII. For the better expedition and execution of justice,
and of all affaires incident upon every courte, every
courte shall have certaine officers, as a secretary to
inrolle all the acts of the courte and besides, ministers
of justice to attach and fetch and set persons before the
Magistrate , and also to execute the sentences of the
courts upon offenders; Jer.XXXVI.10,11 and 12; 2 Sam.XX
24,25. And for the same end it shall be lawful for the
Governor, or any one or two of the Councellors or Assistants, or Judges to give warrant to an officer to fetch
any delinquent before them, and to examine the cause, and
if he be found culpable of crime, to take order, by sureties or safe custody, for his appearance at the courte.
John VII.32,45; Acts V.26,27 and Lev.XXIV.12; Num.XV.34.
    And further, for the same end to prevent the offenders
lying long in prison, it shall be lawful for the Governor,
with one of the Councell, or any two of the Assistants, or
Judges, to see execution done upon any offenders for any
crime that is not capital, according to the lawes established, yet still reserving a liberty of appeale from
them to the courte, and from an inferior courte to an
higher courte.
    Chapter II: *Of the free burgesses and free inhabitants.*
1. First, all the free burgesses, excepting such as were
admitted men before the establishment of churches in the
country, shall be received and admitted out of the members
of some or other of the churches in the country, such
churches as are gathered or hereafter shall be gathered
with the consent of other churches already established and
such members as are admitted by their own church unto the
Lord's table....
    [Burgesses had power to choose from among themselves local judges
    and deputies. The general court was empowered to call governor
    and assistants to account, to legislate, to impose taxes, and to
    hear appeals. The law providing for defence, for inheritance, for
    commerce and for trespass was defined. Blasphemy, perjury, sab-
    bath profanation, treason, rebellion, murder and adultery were to
    be capital crimes. Non-capital crimes included theft, rape, for-
    nication[1] and slander. Punishments and procedures (e.g. trial by
    jury[2]) were laid down.]
    The Lord is our judge, The Lord is our law giver, The
Lord is our King: He will save us (Isiah XXXIII,22.).

---

1. Rape and fornication were at times to be 'punished' by marriage (viii).
Rebellious children were to be executed (vii).

2. Juries were to be chosen not by the magistrates but by the free
burgesses 'who are least obnoxious to suspicion of partiality.'
(ix).   For juries, see below pp.654-660.

198. *'THE LIBERTIES OF THE MASSACHUSETTS COLLONIE IN NEW ENGLAND'*
December 1641.[1]

The free fruition of such liberties, immunities, and
priviledges as humanitie, civilitie, and Christianitie
call for as due to every man in his place and proportion,
without impeachment and infringement, hath ever bene and
ever will be the tranquillitie and stabilitie of Churches
and Commonwealths: And the deniall or deprivall thereof,
the disturbance, if not the ruine of both.

We hould it therefore our dutie and safetie whilst we
are about the further establishing of this Government to
collect and express all such freedomes as for present we
foresee may concerne us, and our posteritie after us, And
to ratify them with our sollemne consent. Wee doe therefore this day religiously and unanimously decree and confirme these following rites, liberties, and priveledges
concerning our Churches,and civill state to be respectively
impartiallie and inviolably enjoyed and observed throughout our jurisdiction for ever.

1. No mans life shall be taken away; no mans honour
or good name shall be stayned; no mans person shall be
arested, restrayned, banished, dismembred, nor any wayes
punished; no man shall be deprived of his wife or children; no mans goods or estaite shall be taken away from
him, nor any way indammaged under coulor of law, or countenance of authoritie: Unlesse it be by vertue or equitie
of some expresse law of the country warranting the same,
established by a Generall Court and sufficiently published, or in case of the defect of a law in any partecular
case by the word of God. And in capitall cases, or in
cases concerning dismembring or banishment, according to
that word to be judged by the General Court.

2. Every person within this jurisdiction, whether Inhabitant or forreiner, shall enjoy the same justice and
law, that is generall for the plantation, which we constitute and execute one towards another, without partial-
itie or delay.

3. No man shall be urged to take any oath or subscribe
any articles, covenants or remonstrance, of a publique and
civill nature, but such as the Generall Court hath considered, allowed and required....

---

1. W. MacDonald (ed.) *op. cit.* pp. 73-91. This *'Body of Liberties'*
was based upon the draft submitted by the Rev. Nathanial Ward. There
was some reluctance,particularly among the 'assistants', to an absolute
commitment to a code of laws which both might be restrictive in unknown contingencies in the future and might seem to accept the charter's criterion of repugnancy to the laws of England. These 'liberties'
were to operate for a trial period of three years; but many deputies
remained dissatisfied and it soon became clear that there would be
considerable revision. A new moral code was enacted in November 1646
(N.B. Shurtleff, *op. cit.*II pp.98-104) and a new *'Body of Laws and
Libertyes'* was accepted in May 1648, the general court having previously required the insertion of scriptural and other references in

[Impressment for public work or service must be by order of the general court: the physically incapable and mentally unsound were exempt. Purveyance and commandeering too must be authorized by the general court: reasonable hire and recompense were to be paid.]

7. No man shall be compelled to goe out of the limits of this plantation upon any offensive warres which this Commonwealth or any of our freinds or confederats shall volentarily undertake. But onely upon such vindictive and defensive warres in our own behalfe, or the behalfe of our freinds, and confederats, as shall be enterprized by the Counsell and consent of a Court generall, or by the Authority derived from the same....

[Monopolies would be granted only briefly. No fines on alienation, escheats and forfeitures would be imposed. Any man would have the right to ask questions or present motions at any court, council or town meeting (§ 12). All should have the liberty to depart from the colony.]

Rites, Rules and Liberties concerning Juditiall proceedings.

18. No mans person shall be restrained or imprisoned by any Authority whatso ever, before the law hath sentenced him thereto; If he can put in sufficient securitie, bayle, or mainprise, for his appearance, and good behaviour in the meane time, - unless it be in Crimes Capitall, and Contempts in open Court, and in such cases where some expresse act of Court doth allow it.

19. If in a generall Court any miscariage shall be amongst the Assistants when they are by themselves that any deserve an Admonition or fine under 20 sh., it shall be examined and sentenced amongst themselves: If amongst the Deputies when they are by themselves, It shall be examined and sentenced amonst themselves; If it be when the whole Court is togeather, it shall be judged by the whole Court, and not severaillie as before....

29. In all Actions at law it shall be the libertie of the plantife and defendant by mutual consent to choose whether they will be tryed by the Bench or by a Jurie, unlesse it be where the law upon just reason hath otherwise determined. The like libertie shall be granted to all persons in Criminall cases....

31. In all cases where evidence is so obscure or defective that the Jurie cannot clearly and safely give a positive verdict, whether it be a grand or petit Jurie, It shall have libertie to give a *non Liquit*, or a spetiall verdict, in which last, that is in a spetiall verdict, the Judgement of the cause shall be left to the Court, and all Jurors shall have libertie in matters of fact if they cannot finde the maine issue, yet to finde and present in their verdict so much as they can; If the Bench and Jurors

shall so differ at any time about their verdict that either of them can not proceed with peace of conscience, the case shall be referred to the Generall Court, who shall take the question from both and determine it....

[Appeals might be made to the court of assistants; 'and everie man shall have libertie to complaine to the Generall Courte of any injustice done him in any court of assistants or other' (§ 36). Criminal cases must be heard at the next court. No man should be twice sentenced for the same offence. Torture was not to be employed until after a man was found guilty of a capital offence: then such torture to elicit names of other confederates must not be barbarous.]

50. All Jurors shall be chosen continuallie by the freemen of the Towne where they dwell.

51. All Associates selected at any time to Assist the Assistants in Inferior Courts, shall be nominated by the Townes belonging to that Court, by orderly agreement amonge themselves.

Liberties more peculiarlie concerning the free men.

58. Civill Authoritie hath power and libertie to see the peace, ordinances and Rules of Christ observed in every church according to his word, so it be done in a Civill and not in an Ecclesiastical way....

60. No church censure shall degrade or depose any man from any Civill dignitie, office, or Authoritie he shall have in the Commonwealth....

62. Any Shire or Towne shall have libertie to choose their Deputies whom and where they please for the General Court, So be it they be free men, and have taken their oath of fealtie, and Inhabiting in this Jurisdiction....

66. The Freemen of everie Towneship shall have power to make such by-laws and constitutions as may concerne the wellfare of their Towne, provided they be not a Criminall, but onely of a prudentiall nature, And that their penalties exceede not 20 sh. for one offence. And that they be not repugnant to the publique laws and orders of the Countrie. And if any Inhabitant shall neglect or refuse to observe them, they shall have power to levy the appointed penalties by distresse.

67. It is the constant libertie of the freemen of this plantation to choose yearly at the Court of Election out of the freemen all the General officers of this Jurisdiction. If they please to discharge them at the day of Election by way of vote, They may do it without shewing cause.   But , if any other generall Court, we hould it due justice, that the reasons thereof be alleadged and proved. By Generall officers we meane, our Governor, Deputie Governor, Assistants, Treasurer, Generall of our warres. And our Admirall at Sea, and such as are or hereafter may be of the like generall nature.

68. It is the libertie of the freemen to choose such deputies for the Generall Court out of themselves, either in their owne Townes or elsewhere as they judge fitest; And because we cannot foresee what varietie and weight of

occasions may fall into future consideration, And what
counsells we may stand in neede of, we decree That the
Deputies (to attend the Generall Court in the behalfe of
the Countrie) shall not any time be stated or inacted, but
from Court to Court, or at the most but for one yeare;
that the Countrie may have an Annuall libertie to do
in that case what is most behoofefull for the best wel-
faire thereof.

69. No General Court shall be desolved or adjourned
without the consent of the Major parte thereof.

70. All Freemen called to give any advise, vote, verdict, or sentence in any Court, Counsell, or Civill Assembly, shall have full freedome to doe it according to
their true Judgement and Consciences, So it be done orderly and inofensively for the manner....

74. The freemen of every Towne or Towneship shall have
full power to choose yearly, or for lesse time, out of
themselves a convenient number of fitt men to order the
planting or prudentiall occasions of that Towne, according to Instructions given them in writeing; Provided nothing be done by them contrary to the publique laws and
orders of the Countrie, provided also the number of such
select persons be not above nine....

[Members of a minority in court, council or assembly might have
their contra-remonstrance recorded in the rolls, but not the reasons for their dissent 'for the avoiding of tediousness'. Freemen
had a right to abstain from a positive or negative vote. The liberties of women, children, servants and animals were defined. Capital offences would include idolatry, witchcraft, adultery, blasphemy, murder, kidnapping and false witness. The rights of Christians and of the Churches were defined (§ 95): these included the
means whereby ministers and elders prevented error and preserved
truth.]

96. How so ever these above specified rites, freedomes,
Immunities, Authorities and priveledges, both Civill and
Ecclesiasticall are expressed onely under the name and
title of *Liberties*, and not in the exact forme of Laws,
or Statutes, yet we do with one consent fullie Authorise,
and earnestly intreate all that are and shall be in Authoritie to consider them as laws, and not to faile to inflict condigne and proportionable punishments upon every
man impartiallie, that shall infringe or violate any of
them....

[These 'liberties', unless altered or repealed, should be enforced for three years and should be read and considered at each
general court in that period. The general court had the final
power to interpret them.]

(d) MARYLAND

199. (a) CONDITIONS FOR PLANTATIONS,8 August 1636.[1]
[The terms for previous years were confirmed: for example, for

---

1. W. H. Browne (ed.) *Archives of Maryland: Proceedings...* (Balt.1885)

every five men aged between 16 and 50 whom adventurers brought in
1633 they had been promised 2000 acres at a yearly rent of 400 lbs.
weight of wheat.]

And we doe further will and authorise you that every
2000 acres, and every 3000 acres, and every 1000 acres of
land so to be passed or granted as aforesaid unto any adventuror or adventurors, be erected and created into a
Manor to be called by such name as the adventuror or adventurors shall desire, and we doe hereby further authorise
you, That you cause to be granted unto every of the said
adventurors within every of their said manors respectively
and unto his or their heirs, a Court Baron and Court Leet,
to be from time to time held within every such manor respectively and to the end you may the better be informed
in what manner to pass every such grant court and courts
as aforesaid, according to our intention, we have sent
unto you under our hand and seal a draught of a grant of
a manor Court Leet, and Court Baron, and a grant of a
freehold, which presidents you are to follow changing only
the adventurors' names, the rents and conditions of plantation as the case shall require, for doeing whereof
this shall be your sufficient warrant, so we bid you heartily farewell.

199. (b) RECORD OF COURT LEET OF ST. CLEMENT'S MANOR, 8 September,
1670.[1]

Presentments: Wee present that Barthollomew Phillips
his land was not layd out according to order of Court
formerly made, wherefore he is fined one hundred pounds
of tobacco and caske to the Lord....We present that John
Stanley and Henry Neale killed three marked hogs upon the
Lords Manor which Captain Gardiner received, which hogs
were not of Captain Gardiner's proper marke: which is
transferred to the next Provinciall Court, there to be
determined according to the Law of the Province....We
present that the Lord of the Mannor hath not provided a

III p.47-8. These terms for land grants were sent by Baltimore to his
brother Leonard Calvert, the lieutenant-general of the proprietary.
The large land grants dictated a colony of scattered country estates.
Baltimore had certainly always desired to see his palatinate composed
of manors held of him, and paying quit rent to him. Leonard Calvert
had led the first settlers to Maryland in March, 1634: the Lord Proprietor's estates at home and the threat to his charter at court prevented his ever seeing his colony.
1. J. Johnson, *Old Maryland Manors* (Johns Hopkins Univ. Stud. VII
1883). A patent of 3 November 1639 from the Lord proprietor had made
Thomas Gerard, Lord of the Manor, with rights to hold Court Leet and
Baron with all powers, rights and profits as the law and custom in
England. The <u>Court leet</u> of freeholders, leaseholders and tenants, under the steward and with a jury, concerned itself with felonies and
the making of by-laws. The <u>Court baron</u> of freeholders dealt with
rents, debts, tenancies and trespass. From the few surviving records
of these manorial courts, this day's work illustrates their operation.

paire of stocks, pillor, and Ducking Stoole Ordered that
these instruments of justice be provided by the next Court
by a generall contribution throughout the Manor....We
present Richard Foster to be Constable for this Manor for
the years ensuing who is sworne accordingly....We present
Mr. Thomas Notly, Mr. Justinian Gerard and Captain Luke
Gardiner, freeholders of this Manor: for not appearing
to do their suit at the Lords Court wherefore they are
amerced each man 50 lbs. of tobacco to the Lord.

200. COMMISSION TO GOVERNOR CALVERT AND COUNCIL, 15 April 1637.[1]
   ...Know ye that Wee, takeing into our serious consid-
ercon the necessity of makeing a Governor, appointing a
council and other officers, and establishing of laws proper
and convenient for preservation of the peace and support
of the common weale of our Province of Maryland, and likewise calling to mind the faithfull and laudable service
done by our dear brother, Leonard Calvert Esq., as well
in the adventure of his person in the first discent and
settleing our colony there, as in the ordering and advanc-
eing the same by his personal residence within the same
our said province, wherein he hath manifested to the satisfaction of ourself and of our colony there, such wisdom,
fidelity, industry, and other virtues, as render him capable and worthy of trust hereby by us intended to be
reposed in him, and for divers others good causes and
considercons us thereunto especially moveing, have nominated, constituted, ordained, authorised and established,
and by these presents doe nominate, constitute, ordain,
authorise, and establish the said Leonard Calvert in the
absence of us and our heirs, our Lieutenant Generall,
Admirall, Chief Captain and Commander as well by sea as
land of our said Province of Maryland and the islands to
the same belonging....
   And We doe further by these presents make constitute
and ordain and establish the said Leonard Calvert to be
our Chancellor, Chief Justice, and Chief Magistrate within our said province, untill we or our heirs shall signifie the contrary under our hand and seal, and from time
to time to appoint and constitute officers and ministers,
for the preservation of the peace, administracon and execucon of justice, and for doeing and executing of all
other things whatsoever, which belong to the establishing
and governaunce of a good and happy comonwealth within our
said province; and we doe further give and grant to him
our said Lieutenant, Chancellor, Chief Justice, and Chief
Magistrate, full and absolute power and authority to
assemble the freemen of our said province or their deput-

St. Clements (now Blakiston) was where the settlers in 1634 had first
landed.
1. W. H. Browne (ed.) *op. cit*, III pp.49-55. Leonard Calvert had received full instructions from his brother before this, but probably
no commission. This document from the Lord proprietor with such remarkably amply powers (even the *jura regalia* in his palatinate) deleg-

ies, at St. Maries within our said province upon the five
and twentieth day of January next ensueing the date hereof,
and then and there to signifie to them that we doe disassent unto all the laws by them heretofore or at any time
made within our said province, as we doe hereby declare
them to be voyd.[1] And further to shew unto them the draught or coppy of all such laws and ordinances for the good
government of our said province, as we shall before that
time transmit to them our said Lieutenant under our hand
and seal, with our assent for enacting of the same. And
likewise if the said freemen or their deputies soe assembled shall approve of and consent unto all the said drau-
ghts or coppies of the said laws and ordinances, in manner
as we send the same over, to publish the same as laws under
the Great Seal of our province, that the people and inhabitants of our said province may take the better notice
thereof. And we doe further by these presents give and
grant unto him our said Lieutenant like absolute power and
authority after the said Assembly soe called as aforesaid,
shall be by him dissolved, at all or any other time or
times, when and as often as he shall think fit, and call
and summon one or more General Assembly or Assemblys of
the freemen within our said province, and to propond and
prepare other wholesome laws and ordinances, for the government and well ordering of the said province, and people
within the same, to be by us assented to and confirmed, if
upon view and mature consideracon had of the same we shall
in our judgment approve thereof. And we doeby these presents give and grant full power and authority unto our said
Lieutenant to adjourn and dissolve the said Assembly soe
authorised to be called on the five and twentieth day of
January next ensueing the date hereof as aforesaid and all
other Assemblys by him hereafter to be called at his pleasure. And forasmuch as the calling of a Generall Assembly
of the said freemen and the consulting about, and enacting
of laws, will require long time and much consultation, and
many times sudden, and other necessary occasions may happen or fall out which require a speedy remedy, We doe
therefore give and grant unto our said Lieutenant full power and authority to make constitute,ordain and publish in
our name such reasonable and profitable ordinances, edicts
and proclamation with reasonable pains and penalties therein to be expressed and to be duly inflicted on all offenders against the same, as he our said Lieutenant in his dis-

---

ated to his deputy a generous discretion and centralised all government
and tenure of office in his hands.
1. Clearly there had been some sort of assembly previously, Now the
Lord proprietor was asserting his right to initiate laws and to send
drafts for legislation by the assembly. The assembly meeting in 1638
consisted of prominent men summoned by individual writs, and of the
freemen summoned by a general writ. From 1639 it was composed of councillors (exclusively lords of manors) and of delegates elected by
hundred or manor.

cretion shall think fit, Provided that such penalties doe
not extend, to the takeing away the right or interest of
any person or persons of or in their life members, freeholds, goods, or chattells, all which ordinances, edicts
and proclamations shall stand in force only and until we
or our heirs shall signifie the contrary to him our said
Lieutenant General and the people thereof, or that he our
said Lieutenant shall in his discretion think fit to
repeale the same....

    [The lieutenant governor was empowered to choose suitable places
for ports and markets, to pardon offenders, to grant land etc. Hawley, Cornwallis and Lewger were appointed to be the Council. Cases
were to be tried according to the laws of the province,or in default of such according to the laws and statutes of England as
near as the governor 'may or can judge'.]

201. RETURN OF THE BURGESSES OF KENT, 15 February, 1639.[1]

    Know all men by these presents both present and to come
that We the freemen of the Isle of Kent whose names are
hereunder written have elected and chosen our Loving Friend, Nicholas Brown, Planter to be our Burgess or deputy
during the next General Assembly at St. Marys...in our
names to assent to all and only such things as our Burgess
shall think fit thereby giving as free and full consent
unto all laws and matters whatsoever within the said Assembly shall be agreed and concluded of as if we our selves
in person had consented thereunto. *[24 signatures]*

202. ACTS RELATING TO THE SUMMONING, POWERS, AND LAWS OF THE ASSEMBLY,
February 1639.[2]

    (a) Be it enacted by the Lord Proprietarie of this pro-
vince of and with the advice and approbation of the freemen of the same That from henceforth for ever everyone
being of the Council of this province and any other gentleman of able judgement and quality summoned by writ and
(the Lord of every Mannour within this province after man-
nors be erected) shall or may have his voice, seat and
place in every General Assembly to be hereafter called in
this province, and shall be called by summons or writ
[and when such writ] shall isue for the calling or summoning

---

1. W. H. Browne (ed.) *op. cit.* I p.30. Kent Island was the plantation
where Claiborne, Baltimore's arch-enemy, had his headquarters. Claiborne disputed that Kent Island was part of Maryland since it was not
uncultivated territory (*hactenus inculta*) at the time of the grant to
Baltimore. But in 1638 the Laud commissioners had decided in favour
of Baltimore and the Maryland assembly had passed an Act of Attainder
against Claiborne [see p.277n.].
2. W. H. Browne (ed.) *Proceedings and acts of the General Assembly of
Maryland* (1883) I pp.74-5, 81-2. The assembly of the palatinate of
Durham consisted of a joint meeting of the bishop's council (household
and palatinate officials) and all freeholders. It is improbable that
at any time there had been elected representatives. [see Section 4
(d)].

a General Assembly of the freemen of this province the
Commander...high Constable...or...Sheriff of the county
shall within every hundred summon all the freemen inhabiting within every hundred...to...elect and chuse some one,
two or more able and sufficient men for the hundred...to
come to every such General Assembly...and every Act and
ordinance made in such General Assemblies by persons so
called elected and chosen as aforesaid or the major part
of them and assented to by the Lord Proprietarie or his
heirs Lords and proprietaries of this Province or by his
or their Leiutenant General...shall be judged, deemed and
taken to be of as good force and strength and as effectual
to all intents and purposes as if the Lord Proprietarie
himself and all the freemen within the said province had
been personally present at such General Assemblies and had
consented to and approved of the makeing and enacting of
such laws and ordinances Provided that all acts approved
by the freemen and by the Leiutenant General in the name
of the Lord Proprietarie as aforesaid shall be of force
until the Lord Proprietarie shall signifie his disassent
to the same under the great seal and no further or longer.

(b) Be it enacted by the Lord Proprietarie of this province of and with the assent and approbation of the freemen of the same That from and after this General Assembly
shall be dissolved a General Assembly of the freemen of
this province shall be called and summoned once in every
three years at the least to consult of the affairs and
publique good of this Province and for the enacting of
laws and ordinances for the better government of the same
and that the said freemen so assembled shall from and
after the summoning of such Assembly and Assemblies until
the dissolution of the same have the like power, priveledges, authority, and jurisdiction in all causes and matters
arriseing or to arrise or happen within this province as
the House of Commons within the Realme of England at any
time heretofore assembled in that kingdom have had used,
or enjoyed, or of right ought to have used or enjoyed in,
about, or concerning any matters things and causes whatsoever which have at any time happened or risen within the
Realme of England.[1]

(c) Whereas the Kings Majestie by his letters pattents
hath given and granted full free and absolute power and
authority to the Lord Proprietary of this Province to make
and ordeine any laws apperteining to the state of this
Province by and with the advice, assent and approbation
of the freemen of the same or of the greater part of them
or of their deligates or deputies and to that end to assemble the said freemen or their deligates or deputies in
such sort and forme as to the said Lord Proprietarie should
seem best - By vertue wherof several writts or summons have
been directed to certain gentlemen to appear personally at

---

1. An early claim to Commons' privileges.

this Assembly and to the rest of the freemen inhabiting
within the several hundreds of this colony and the Isle
of Kent to elect their delegates or deputies in their
names and steads to be present at the same; and accordingly all the freemen of the said several hundreds and
of the Isle of Kent (some few excepted) have elected
certain persons to that end and the same their election
have subscribed and returned upon record and their said
dellegates and deputies are now assembled accordingly,
Be it therefore enacted and ordeined,by the said Lord
Proprietarie by and with the advice, assent, and approbation of the freemen and of the delegates and deputies assembled at this present Assembly That the said several
persons so elected and returned as aforesaid shall be and
be called Burgesses and shall supply the places of all the
freemen consenting or subscribing to such their election
in the same manner and to all the same intents and purposes as the burgesses of any burrough in England in the
Parliament of England useth to supply the place of the
inhabitants of the burroughe whereof he is elected burges,
and that the said gentlemen and burgesses and such other
freemen (not haveing consented to any the elections as
aforesaid) as now are or shall be at any time assembled
or any twelve or more of them (whereof the Leiutenant
General and Secretary of the province to be allwaies two)
shall be called the House of Assembly; and that all Acts
and ordinances assented unto and approved in the said
House or by the major part of the persons assembled and
afterward assented unto by the Leiutenant General in the
name of the said Lord Proprietary and all the freemen of
this Province were personally present and did assent to
and approve the same. Which bill being read and passed
by all the gentlemen and freemen present they did consent
it should be underwritten by the secretary in these
words.... [The freemen had assented to this bill that it should be
engrossed and published under the greate seal .] Then the Leiu-
tenant-General, Leonard Calvert Esq. being demanded by
the secretary whether he did assent to the said bill for
and in the name of the Lord Proprietarie; answered yea,
and willed that his assent should be underwritten to it
in these words:

'The Leiutenant Generall in the behalf of the Lord
proprietarie willeth that this be a law'.

203. (a) ACT ERECTING A COURT OF ADMIRALTY, February 1639.[1]
    Be it enacted by the Lord Proprietarie of this prov-
ince by and with the advice and approbation of the freemen of the same That all causes and matters whatsoever
maritime determinable in any Court of Admiraltie shall
be fineally heard and determined within this Province
by and before such judge and judges as the said Admirall

1. W. H. Browne (ed.) *op. cit.* I pp.46-7.

shall authorize to hear and determine the same or by and
before such Commissioner or Commissioners as (in defect or
vacancie of an Admiral) the Lord Proprietarie of this
Province shall authorize under the great Seal to hear and
determine the same: which said Admirall or cheif Commissioner shall or may appoint a Register for recording all
matters belonging to that office and the said Admirall
Cheif Judge or cheif Commissioner for the time exerciseing
that office and the said Register shall be a court of record and shall be called the Court of Admiralltie, and the
said Court shall or may enjoy use and exercise all or any
the same or the like powers, priveledges, authorities and
jurisdictions within this province as the high Court of
Admiraltie in England enjoys or may enjoy, use and exercise within the Realm of England (except where it is otherwise provided by any Law of this Province)....And such
summary formes of proceedings shall be used and observed
in the Court as the said Admirall, cheif Judge or cheif
Commissioner shall approve or appoint to be used.

   And all causes civill shall be tried and decided by
the said Admirall, Judge or Judges, Commissioner or Commissioners and all causes crimminall shall be tried by a
jury of five or more merchants marriners or other freemen
of the Province as their number shall be appointed upon
the writ, the said jury to be returned by the Marshall or
Officer of the Court and conviction shall be the said
Jurors agreeing in their verdict....

   And such judgement shall be given...as is most agreeable to the laws of the Province or (in default thereof)
to the judgements...by the custom or Law Merchant of England or in the Admiraltie Court of England....

203. (b) ACT FOR THE APPOINTMENT OF TITHMAN, CONSTABLE AND SHERIFF,
                                           February 1639.[1]
   Be it enacted by the Lord Proprietary of this Province
of and with the advice and approbation of the freemen of
the same That the Lord of every Mannour within this province (after any mannour shall be erected) shall yearly at
the first Court Baron held after Michaelmas in any year
nominate and appoint some inhabitant of the mannour (not
being of the Councill) to be tithman of that mannour who
shall execute all precepts and warrants to him directed and
shall in all things have the like power within the said
mannour as a tithman hath or ought to have in any mannour
in England by the law or custom of England....The Lieutenant Generall of the province for the time being shall yea-

----

1. W. H. Browne (ed.) *op. cit.*I pp.54-5. The tithingman was concerned
with domestic regulations and family affairs in a manor; the constable
held 'ward' over parish or township, apprehending, collecting fines
and rates, and carrying out punishments; the sheriff had responsibility for the keeping of the peace in the shire, the administration of
justice as directed by the courts, the execution of writs, the conduct
of elections &c.

ly at the first hundred court in every hundred held after
Michaelmas in any year nominate and appoint some inhabitant of the hundred (not being of the Councill) to be high
Constable of that hundred who shall execute all precepts
and warrants to him directed and shall in all things have
the like power and authority within the said hundred as
a high Constable of any hundred in England...At the first
County Court held after Michaelmas the Cheif Judge of the
said court shall nominate and appoint any inhabitant of
the county (not being of the Councill) to be Sheriff and
Coroner of the county who shall execute or cause or oversee the execution of all writts and warrants to him directed and shall in all things have the like power and
authority and shall be chargeable with the same duty
and office within the county as a Sherrif or Coroner of
any shire in England....

204. ACT FOR THE GOVERNMENT OF KENT ISLAND, March 1639.[1]
    Be it enacted by the Lord Proprietary of this Province
at and with the advice and approbation of the same That
the island commonly called the Isle of Kent shall be
erected into a hundred and shall be within the County of
St. Maries (until another county shall be erected of the
eastern shoare and no longer) and shall be called by the
name of Kent hundred, and the Commander of the said island from time to time appointed by the Lord Proprietary
or his Leiutenant Generall shall be a justice of peace
within the said hundred dureing such time as he is Commander, with all power and authority to a justice of
peace belonging by the laws of this Province, and the said
Commander shall appoint some one to be clerk or register
for the recording of all matters perteining to that office, and the said Commander the Register for the time
being shall be a Court of Record and shall be called the
hundred Court of Kent.
    And all matters and causes whatsoever civil or crimin-
al (except wherein the said Commander is a partie), happening o r ariseing by or between any inhabitants of the
said island or wherein any inhabitants of the said island is default and detirminable in the County Court,
shall or may be heard and determined by and before the
said Commander in the said hundred court and the said
court shall have power to use and exercise all the same
and the like powers and jurisdictions and to issue and
award all processe necessary for the bringing of any
cause to a trial and executing of judgement therein as
may be used and exercised, issued or awarded by or out
of the County Court.

1.W.H. Browne (ed.) *op. cit.* I pp.55-6. Similarly at Act (*ibid.* p.62)
appointed three 'conservators of the peace' for Kent Island with powers as J.Ps in England and authority to summon a court leet.
For Kent Island, see above pp.272,309,311.

(e) THE CHARTERLESS PLANTATIONS

Virginia, Massachusetts, Maryland and other corporate and proprietary colonies had in their charters from the Crown a firm legal
basis for their local self-government. Even New Plymouth had the
ostensible pretext of a patent of 1619 (unused as the Pilgrims landed too far north) to Peirce and his associates from the Virginia
Company, and of another (subsequently in 1621) from the New England
Council for the assignment of land, but not for its government which
the king alone could give. But several of the other plantations in
New England - refugees in search of greater freedom from the arbitrary rule of Massachusetts - had no grant or legal sanction whatever.
Therefore, just as the Pilgrim Fathers had sought to remedy their
lack of civil power by a mutual social contract - the Mayflower
Compact of 1620 - covenanting to make and to obey regulations for
the common good, so too plantations and townships hiving off from
Massachusetts into Connecticut, New Haven and Rhode Island sought
to establish their independent commonwealths by voluntary autochthonous (self-rooted) initiatives within their scattered communities.
Lacking any delegation of power from the Crown, they necessarily
assumed a power to constitute a form of government from themselves.

205. CONNECTICUT: FUNDAMENTAL ORDERS, 14 January 1639.[1]
Forasmuch as it hath pleased the Allmighty God by the
wise disposition of his divyne providence so to Order and
dispose of things that We, the Inhabitants and Residents

---

1. *Connecticut Colonial Records* I pp.20-25. The fertile lands on the
Connecticut river had been an area in which both New Plymouth and New
Amsterdam had taken an early active interest some years before groups
of Massachusetts settlers from Watertown, Dorchester and Newtown came,
with the approval from the Bay authorities, to make rival claims to
lands there. Unlike the Rhode Islanders, the majority were not seeking a new religious freedom, though certainly some of their leaders -
Ludlow, Hooker and Haynes - did wish to secure a broader based form
of government than that in Massachusetts. A grant by Warwick as president of the New England Council to Lord Saye and Sele and others for
a plantation west of the Narragansett river was endorsed by the Bay
government as honest broker between the patentees and the settlers.
In a commission on 3 March 1636 John Winthrop's son was confirmed as
governor, and individual commissioners in the scattered Connecticut
settlements of Hartford, Windsor and Wethersfield were authorised to
exercise authority and to convene in general court a meeting of 'the
inhabitants of the towns'. This presumably meant all freeholders who
were Christians; but in practise of course, the elected magistrates
ruled and made regulations, and no one was admitted to membership of
the commonwealth without the general court's consent. There seem to
have been 'admitted inhabitants' who took part in town affairs and
'freemen' who were eligible for the general court and office in the
commonwealth itself. Despite Massachusetts' endorsement of the commission of 1636, Connecticut spokesmen firmly asserted that it derived
from their own authochthonous authority alone and repudiated 'any
claymes of the Massachusetts' jurisdiction over them'. Connecticut

of Windsor, Herteford and Wethersfield, and now cohabiting
and dwelling in and uppon the River of Conectecotte and
the Lands thereunto adjoyneing; And well-knowing where
a people are gathered togather the word of God required
that to mayntayne the peace and union of such a people
at all seasons as occation shall require, doe therefore
assotiate and conjoyne our selves to be as one Publike
State or Commonwealth; and doe, for our selves and our
Successors and such as shall be adjoyned to us att any
time hereafter, enter into Combination and Confederation
togather, to mayntayne and preserve the liberty and purity
of the gospell of our Lord Jesus which we now professe, as
also the disciplyne of the Churches, which according to
the truth of the said gospell is now practised amongst
us; As also in our Civell Affaires to be guided and governed according to such Lawes, Rules, Orders and decrees
as shall be made, ordered and decreed, as followeth:-
      1. It is Ordered, sentensed and decreed, That there
shall be yerely two generall Assemblies or Courts....*[in
April and in September]* the first shall be called the *Courte
of Election*,wherein shall be yerely Chosen from tyme to
tyme soe many Magestrats and other publike Officers as
shall be found requisitte: Whereof one to be chosen Governour for the yeare ensueing and untill another be chosen, and noe other Magestrate to be chosen for more than
one years; Provided allwayes there be six chosen besids
the Governour; which being chosen, and sworne according
to an Oath recorded for that purpose, shall have power to
administer justice according to the Lawes here established,
and for want thereof according to the rule of the word of
God; which choise shall be made by all that are admitted
freemen and have taken the Oath of Fidellity, and doe co-
habitte within this Jurisdiction, (having beene admitted
Inhabitants by the major part of the Towne wherein they
live,) or the mayor parte of such as shall be then present....[1]
      2. It is Ordered, sentensed and decreed, That the Elec-
tion of the aforesaid Magestrats shall be on this manner:
every person present and qualified for choyse shall bring
in (to the persons deputed to receave them) one single
paper with the name of him written in yt whom ye desires
to have Governour, and he that hath the greatest number of
papers shall be Governour for that yeare. And the rest
of the Magestrats or publike Officers to be chosen in
this manner: The Secretary for the tyme being shall first
read the names of all that are to be put to choise, and
then shall severally nominate them distinctly, and every
one that would have the person nominated to be chosen

---

was, however, a plantation without royal charter, and in these Fundamental Orders the leaders set out a written constitution, a frame of
government, for themselves.
1. The second court in September was for legislative, administrative
and judicial business. These provisions of course were modelled upon
the Massachusetts Company charter.

shall bring in one single paper written uppon, and he
that would not have him chosen shall bring in a blanke:
and every one that hath more written papers than blanks
shall be a Magistrat for that yeare; which papers shall
be receaved and told by one or more that shall be then
chosen by the court and sworne to be faythfull therein;
but in case there should not be sixe chosen as aforesaid,
besids the Governor, out of those which are nominated,
then he or they which have the most written papers shall
be a Magestrate or Magestrats for the ensueing yeare, to
make up the foresaid number,...

   [To prevent hasty elections, names of candidates for the magistracy nominated by towns and by the court itself must be announced
in a General Court prior to the Court of election. The governor
who must be 'a member of some approved congregation, and formerly
of the magistracy within this jurisdiction' might not be elected
in two successive years. He might summon special general courts
with the approval of the majority of the magistrates.]

   7. It is Ordered, sentensed and decreed That after there
are warrants given out for any of the said Generall Courts, the Constable or Constables of each Towne shall forthwith give notice distinctly to the inhabitants of the same,
in some Publike Assembly or by goeing or sending from howse
to howse, that at a place and tyme by him or them lymited
and sett, they meet and assemble them selves together to
elect and chuse certain deputyes to be att the General
Courte then following to agitate the afayres of the commonwelth; which said Deputyes shall be chosen by all that
are admitted Inhabitants in the severall Townes and have
taken the oath of fidellity; provided that none be chosen
a Deputy for any Generall Courte which is not a Freeman of
this Commonwealth.... [The method of electing deputies to the
General Court was specified.]

   8. It is Ordered, sentensed and decred, that Wyndsor,
Hartford and Wethersfield shall have power, each Towne, to
send fower of their freemen as their deputyes to every
Generall Courte; and whatsoever other Townes shall be hereafter added to this Jurisdiction, they shall send so many
deputyes as the Courte shall judge meete, a resonable proportion to the number of Freemen that are in the said Townes being to be attended therein; which deputyes shall
have the power of the whole Towne to give their voats and
alowance to all such lawes and orders as may be for the
publike good, and unto which the said Townes are to be
bownd.

   9. It is ordered and decreed, That the deputyes thus
chosen shall have power and liberty to appoynt a tyme and
place of meeting togather before any Generall Courte to
advise and consult of all such things as may concerne the
good of the publike, as also to examine their owne Elections, whether according to the order, and if they or the
gretest parte of them find any election to be illegal, they
may seclud such for present from their meeting, and returne
the same and their resons to the Courte; and if yt prove

true, the Courte may fyne the party or partyes so intrud-
ing and the Towne, if they see cause, and give out a warrant to goe to a newe election in a legall way, either in
parte or in whole....

10. It is Ordered, sentensed and decreed, that every
Generall Courte, except such as,through neglecte of the
Governor and the greatest parte of Magestrats,the Freemen
themselves doe call, shall consist of the Governor, or
some one chosen to moderate the Court, and 4 other Magestrats at lest, with the mayor parte of the deputyes of the
severall Townes legally chosen; and in case the Freemen
or mayor parte of them, through neglect or refusall of
the Governor and mayor parte of the magestrats, shall call
a Courte, it shall consist the supreme power of the Commonwelth, and they only shall have power to make lawes or
repeale them, to graunt levyes to admitt of Freemen, dispose of lands undisposed of, to severall Townes or persons, and also shall have power to call either Courte or
Magestrate or any other person whatsoever into question
for any misdemeanour, and may for just causes displace or
deale otherwise according to the nature of the offence;
and also may deale in any other matter that concerns the
good of this Commonwelth, excepte election of Magestrats,
which shall be done by the whole boddy of Freemen....

[The governor should preside, grant freedom of speech and exercise a casting vote. No court 'shall be adjourned or dissolved
without the consent of the major parte of the Court'.]

11. It is ordered, sentenced and decred, that when any
Generall Courte uppon the occasions of the commonwelth
have agreed uppon any summe or sommes of mony to be levyed
uppon the severall Townes within this Jurisdiction, that
a Committee be chosen to sett out and appoynt what shall
be the proportion of every Towne to pay of the said levy,
Provided the Committees be made up of an equall number
out of each Towne.

206. NEW HAVEN: FUNDAMENTAL AGREEMENT AND PROCEEDINGS, 4 June and
25 October, 1639.[1]

(a) *4 June 1639.*
The 4th day of the 4th moneth called June 1639, all the

---

1. C. J. Hoadly (ed.) *Records of the colony and plantation of New
Haven from 1638 to 1649* pp. 11-12, 13, 15, 20-21. In April 1638 a
party of emigrants led by Rev. John Davenport and Theophilus Eaton,
a London merchant, had settled at New Haven on Long Island sound,
south-west of the Connecticut plantations. Davenport had left England in 1636 because of the Laudian repression and had been concerned
with the Massachusetts Bay Company. Eaton had managed the company's
affairs at home and, on coming to Massachusetts, had been disappointed
with the opportunities of expanding commerce - and shipbuilding in
particular - and had begun to seek better harbours in the Quinnipiac
region. There, without charter from the Crown or indeed, it seems,
from Warwick, on land bought from the Indians,they came to establish
a plantation separate from Massachusetts and for a year lived under

free planters assembled together in a general meetinge to
consult about settling civill Gouvernment according to
God, and about the nomination of persons that mighte be
founde, by consent, of all fittest in all respects for
the foundation worke of a church which was intend *[ed]* to
be gathered in Quinipieck....For the better inableing them
to discerne the minde of God and to agree accordingly concerning the establishment of civill order, Mr. John Davenport propounded divers *quaeres* to them, publiquely praying them to consider seriously in the presence and feare
of God the weight of the business they met about, and not
to be rash or sleight in giveing their votes to things
they understoode not, but to digest fully and throughly
what should be propounded to them, and without respect to
men, as they should be satisfied and perswaded in their
owne mindes to give their answers in such sort as they
would be willing they should stand upon records for posterity.

This being earnestly pressed by Mr. Davenport, Mr.
Robert Newman was intreated to write in carracters and to
read distinctly and audibly in the hearing of all the people what was propounded and accorded on that it might
appeare that all consented to matters propounded according to words written by him.

Quaere 1. Whether the Scripturs doe holde forth a
perfect rule for the direction and government of all men
in all dueties where they are to performe to God and men
as well in the gouvernment of famylyes and commonwealths
as in matters of the church.

This was assented unto by all, no man dissenting as
was expressed by holding up of hands. Afterward it was
read out to them that they might see in what words their
vote was expressed. They againe expressed their consent
thereto by holdeing up their hands, no man dissented....
[The plantation covenant made on their first landing at New Haven
was still to bind them.]

Quaere 4. All the free planters were called upon to
express whether they held themselves bound to establish
such civill order as might best conduce to the secureing
of the purity and peace of the ordinances to themselves
and their posterity according to God. In answer hereunto
they expressed by holding up their hands twice as before,
that they held them selves bound to establish such civil
order as might best conduce to the ends aforesaid.

Then Mr. Davenport declared unto them by the scripture
what kinde of persons might best be trusted with matters
of gouvernment and by sundry arguments from scripture
proved that such men as were discribed in Exod.XVIII 2:
2.Deut.I.13 & XVII.15:and 1.Cor.VI 1 to 7 ought to be in-

a corporate covenant. A year later in a large barn belonging to
Robert Newman these 'fundamental articles of agreement' were accepted.
The influence of Cotton, with whom Davenport had lodged in Boston,is
evident.

trusted by them,seeing *[they]* were free to cast themselves
into that mould and forme of Common wealth which appeareth
best for them in reference to the secureing of the pure
and peaceable injoyment of all Christ his ordinances *[in]*
the church according to God, whereunto they have bound
themselves as hath beene acknowledged. Having thus said
he satt downe, praying the company freely to consider
whether they would have *[it]* voted at this time or not.
After some space of silence Mr. Theophilus Eaton answered
it might be voted, and some others allso spake to the same
purpose, none at all opposeing it. Then it was propounded
to vote....
    [One man alone dissented to the article that 'free burgesses
    shall be chosen out of church members' alone. He proposed that
    all God-fearing men should be eligible and was opposed to the
    free planters giving power 'out of their hands'. But he received
    no support. All were convinced that the article represented 'the
    minde of God'.] [1]
All haveing spoken their apprehensions, it was agreed
upon, and Mr. Robert Newman was desired to write it as
an order whereunto every one that hereafter should be admitted here as planters should submit and testefie the
same by subscribeing their names to the order, namely that
church members onely shall be free burgesses, and that
they onely shall chuse magistrates and officers among themselves to have the power of transacting all the publique
civill affayres of this Plantation, of makeing and repealing lawes, devideing of inheritances, decideing of differences that may arise and doeing all things or businesses
of like nature....
    [This was agreed by a show of hands as 'a fundamental agreement
    concerning civil government'. As for the establishment and organ-
    ization of the church, twelve men were selected who chose seven
    'pillars of the community' from among themselves who named nine
    others in addition to themselves to form a general court. A man
    who had overcharged for corn confessed both his repentance and res-
    titution.]
    (b) *25 October 1639*.
    ....And this charge was given and accepted by them [i.e.
the newly admitted members of the church] If you shall know any
person or persons which intend, plott, or conspire any
thing which tends to the hurt of prejudice of this Jurisdiction, or the civill gouvernment here settled, you shall
forthwith discover it to the magistrates, or to one or
more of the Deputies who shalbe chosen and intrusted in
the publique occasions of the same, you shall assist and

---

1. A breakaway community at Milford was established in 1639 with officials and freemen not restricted only to church members. Another
group hiving-off at Guilford, however, confined such political privileges to members of their own church alone. Other plantations at Stamford and Southold seem to have been much less independent of New
Haven.

be help full thereunto with body, minde and goods, in any
thing which may concerne the safety or promove the peace
and welfare thereof, as God shall give abillity and opp-
ertunity. And you shall be subject to all lawes and orders which according to God shall be made by the court, to
the uttmost of your power....
    [After a reading of Deut. I 13 and Exod. XVIII 21 by Davenport,
    Theophilus Eaton was chosen magistrate and four others were elec-
    ted as his deputies.][1]
    It was further agreed that there should be a renewing
of the choyce of all officers every year at the Generall
Court to be held for this plantation the last weeke in
October yearely. And that the worde of God shall be the
onely rule to be attended unto in ordering the affayres
of government in this plantation.

207. RHODE ISLAND: COVENANT AT PROVIDENCE PLANTATION, 27 August 1640.[2]
    Wee, Robert Coles, Chad Brown, William Harris, and
John Warner, being freely chosen by the consent of our
loving friends and neighbours the Inhabitants of this
Towne of Providence, having many differences amongst us,
they being freely willing and also bound themselves to
stand to our Arbitration in all differences amongst us to
rest contented in our determination; being so betrusted,
We have seriously and carefully indeavoured to weigh and
consider all those differences, being desirous to bringe
to unity and peace, although our abilities are farr short
in the due examination of such weighty things, yet so
farre as we conceive in laying all things together we
have gone the fairest and equalist way to produce our
peace.
    II *Agreed*. We have with one consent agreed that for
the disposeing of these lands that shall be disposed belonging to this towen of Providence to be in the whole
Inhabitants by the choise of five men for generall dis-
poseall of lands and also of the towne Stocke, and all
Generall things, and not to receive in any six dayes any

_____

1. Eaton remained governor and virtually dictator till his death
in 1658. He was largely responsible for the rejection of trial by
jury at New Haven.
2. J. R. Bartlett (ed.) *Records...of Rhode Island* (1856) I pp.27-31.
In 1635 Roger Williams was banished from Massachusetts Bay by order
of the general court for advocating greater religious liberty, for
denying the competence of civil magistrates in matters of conscience,
and for questioning the validity of the Crown's right by charter to
give away Indian lands. On lands bought from the Indians he had the
next year established on Narragansett Bay a settlement, named 'Providence', which became a refuge for those 'destitute especially for
conscience's sake'. By a form of social compact 'a town fellowship'
on 20 August 1636, (*ibid*.p.14) heads of families had agreed freely
to accept obedience to the will of the majority until a charter
could be obtained from the king: such obedience was, however, characteristically limited to civil matters only. This later covenant in

townesmen, but first to give the Inhabitants notice to
consider if any have just cause to shew against the receiving of him as you can apprehend, and to receive none
but such as subscribe to this our determination. Also,
we agree that if any of our neighbours doe apprehend himselfe wronged by these or any of these 5 disposers, that
at the Generall towne meeting he may have a tryall.

Also wee agree for the towne to choose, beside the other
five men, one or more to keepe Record of all things belonging to the towne and lying in Common.

We agree, as formerly hath bin the liberties of the
town, so still, to hould forth liberty of Conscience.

III. *Agreed*, that after many Considerations and Consul-
tations of our owne State and alsoe of States abroad in
way of government, we apprehend no way so suitable to our
Condition as government by way of Arbitration. But if
men agree themselves by arbitration, no State we know of
disallows that, neither doe we: But if men refuse that
which is but common humanity betweene man and man, then
to compel such unreasonable persons to a reasonable way,
we agree that the 5 disposers shall have power to compel
him to choose two men himselfe; or if he refuse, for them
to choose two men to arbitrate his cause, and if these
foure men chosen by every partie do end the cause, then
to see theire determination performed and the faultive to
pay the Arbitrators for theire time spent in it.... [Furth-
er provision was made for the eventuality of a non-settlement of an
issue.]

IV. *Agreed*, that if any person damnify any man, either
in goods or good name, the person offended follow not the
cause uppon the offendor, that if any person give notice
to the 5 Disposers, they shall call the party delinquent
to answer by Arbitration....

V *Agreed*, for all the whole Inhabitants to combine
ourselves to assist any man in the pursuit of any party
delinquent, with all best endeavours to attack him: but
if any man raise a hubbub, and there be no just cause,
then for the party that raised the hubbub to satisfy men
for their time lost in it.... [39 signatures, including Roger
Williams.]

1640 illustrates further the autochthonous form of mutual arbitration
they devised.
For the patent from the earl of Warwick and the parliamentary commissioners in 1643, see No.208 (b).

II. THE FORMATIVE PERIOD OF EMPIRE, 1641–88

By 1641 the first phase of English overseas colonization was complete. There were settlements in the Caribbean, in Bermuda, and along the littoral of continental North America from Virginia to Maine and Newfoundland. There were also trading bases in India and Sumatra. 1641 forms a watershed because the Civil War and the Commonwealth which followed broke the continuity of constitutional practice. Hitherto the Crown, which had monopolized the granting of charters etc., had assumed that colonization would always be undertaken by private groups or individuals at their own expense. Despite some attempts to assert royal control, metropolitan super- vision had been slight and there had been no resolute assertion of uniformity in any field. Even control of colonial trade had been limited to royal proclamations demanding that certain colonial goods (notably tobacco) should be exported direct to England. From 1649, however, there is a new trend. First, the Commonwealth government from 1649 to 1653 felt it necessary to asume effective control of all the colonies and then took the firm step in 1651 of passing an act regulating colonial trade by Act of Parliament. After 1660, the Restoration government, influenced by the current of mercantilist opinion then common throughout western Europe, evolved a broad policy of attempting to treat the multiple American colonies as part of a single English commercial empire. This involved creating cen- tral agencies of control, first as part of the privy council, then from 1696 as a separate advisory Board of Trade; establishing Eng- lish control over the internal government of the colonies; and fin- ally attempting to consolidate some of the smaller colonies into more rational and governable units. True, a number of new colonies were established during this period by individuals or groups which were given grants or charters along conventional lines; and this represents a contrary trend. But increasingly, as these grants or charters became ineffective, the colonies became royal provinces on the model of Virginia. This process was by no means complete by 1688, or even by 1776. But by the 1690s the general shape of the colonial empire was becoming clear as it was to remain until the American Revolution. On the one hand principles and institutions purported to integrate the colonies into a single economic and pol- itical system, controlled primarily in the interest of the realm, which (it was argued) was also that of dependencies, thus protected from foreign rivals: while on the other hand a mass of local inter- ests and traditions continued to reflect the diverse origins and autonomous attitudes of the colonists, who aspired to imitiate (where convenient) the successes of the Commons over the Crown's prerogative, to assert their equality with the realm, and to expand their self-government to the edge of independence. The schism in the empire in the 1770s with the secession of the American colonies ultimately stemmed from the latent conflict between these two traditions, already present in the period before 1688.

(A) THE CIVIL WAR AND INTERREGNUM, 1641-60

(1) METROPOLITAN POLICY AND LEGISLATION

During the period of the Civil War and the Interregnum Parliament asserted its right to supervise and to control trade and plantations - by commissions, grants, instructions, orders and 'Acts'.

208. (a) ORDINANCE FOR THE GOVERNMENT OF PLANTATIONS IN THE WEST INDIES ETC.,2 November 1643.[1]

Whereas many thousands of the natives and good subjects of this Kingdom of England, through the oppression of the prelates and other ill-affected ministers and officers of state, have of late years, to their great grief and miserable hardship, been inforced to transplant themselves and their families into several islands, and other remote and desolate parts of the West Indies, and having there, through exceeding great labour and industry (with the blessing of God), obtained for themselves and their families some competent and convenient means of maintenance and subsistance, so that they are now in a reasonable well-settled and peaceable condition... [but fearing for the security of their estates many had petitioned to have parliamentary confirmation of their governments,] The Lords and Commons...have thought fit, and do hereby constitute and ordain Robert,Earl of Warwicke, Governor in Chief and High Lord Admiral of all those islands, and other plantations inhabited, planted or belonging to any his Majesty's the King of England's subjects, or which hereafter may be inhabited...within the bounds and upon the coasts of America: and, for the more effectual, speedier, and easier transaction of this so weighty and important a business which concerns the well-being and preservation of so many of the distressed natives of this and other his Majesty's dominions,the Lord and Commons have thought fit, that Phillip,Earl of Pembroke [and 16 other peers and M.P.s] shall be Commissioners, to join in aid and assistance with the said Earl of Warwicke, Chief Governor and Admiral of the said plantations; which Chief Governor, together with the said Commissioners or any four of them,

---

1. C.H. Firth and R.S. Rait (ed.) *Acts and ordinances of the interregnum* (1911) I pp.331-3. Embroiled in its struggle with Charles I, Parliament was also concerned to assert its powers of supervision over the colonies: the commissioners under the earl of Warwick assumed the powers of the king and his privy council overseas.

shall hereby have power and authority to provide for,
order, and dispose, all things which they shall from time
to time find most fit and advantageous to the well-governing, securing, strengthening, and preserving of the true
Protestant religion amongst the said planters and inhabitants....And, for the better advancement of this so great
work, it is hereby further ordained, by the said Lords
and Commons, that the aforesaid Governor and Commissioners shall hereby have power and authority...to call unto
their advice and assistance therein any other of the aforesaid planters,owners of land, or inhabitants of the said
islands and plantations, which shall then be within twenty
miles of the place where the said Commissioners shall then
be; and shall have power and authority to send for, view,
and make use of, all such records, books and papers, which
do or may concern any of the said plantations....It is
hereby further ordained and decreed, that the said Robert
Earl of Warwicke, [and the commissioners named] shall have
power and authority, from time to time, to nominate, appoint, and constitute, all such subordinate governors,
counsellors, commanders, officers and agents, [and to fill
vacancies and dismiss all such governors *etc.*, and to delegate any
power or authority to govern and preserve plantations from disturbance.]

208(b) PATENT FROM PARLIAMENTARY COMMISSIONERS FOR PROVIDENCE
                         PLANTATIONS, 14 March 1644.[1]
    Whereas by an Ordinance of the Lords and Commons, now
assembled in Parliament, bearing Date the Second Day of
November, Anno Domini 1643, Robert, Earl of Warwick, is

1. J.R.Bartlett (ed.) *op.cit.*I pp.143-6. Within a few years of the
founding of Providence there were several separate communities in its
vicinity: opposed to the rigours of the Massachusetts puritanism,but
mutually disputatious over doctrine and divided over personal leader-
ship – Williams in Providence; Coddington first in Portsmouth and
then (after the Hutchinsons' take-over there) in Newport; and similarly Gorton, after the Arnolds had won the support of his settlement at Pawtucket for a pro-Massachusetts policy (which he deplored),
finally at Warwick . But threats from Indian tribes, claims of Massachusetts' expansion, and moves towards New England confederation
prompted Williams to seek some closer union between these petty commonwealths to mitigate their sturdy isolationist and opinionated independence. So he obtained this patent from Warwick's commission for
an incorporation of three of the plantations around Rhode Island. It
did not grant land, but seemed to confirm purchase from the Indians.
It empowered the towns with rights of civil government. Since Portsmouth and Newport were already united,the incorporation was not put
into effect till 1647; and again between 1651 and 1653 a separate
commission to Coddington as lifelong governor of Portsmouth and Newport meant separation between mainland and islands until Williams
secured parliamentary confirmation of this patent of 1644. On 8
July 1663 a new charter from the Crown was granted to Rhode Island
with express recognition of the right to freedom of conscience[No.271].

constituted, and ordained Governor in Chief, and Lord High
Admiral of all those Islands and other Plantations inhabited or planted by, or belonging to any His Majesty the
King of England's Subjects, (or which hereafter may be inhabited and planted by, or belonging to them) within the
Bounds, and upon the Coasts of America... [and other peers and
members of the Commons who were named as parliamentary commissioners.
They were empowered to appoint governors, councillors and officials
'fit for the better governing and preserving'of the plantations to
the advantage and security of the colonists.]
... And whereas there is a Tract of Land in the Continent
of America aforesaid, called by the Name of Narraganset-
Bay; bordering Northward and Northeast on the Patent of
the Massachusetts, East and Southeast on Plymouth Patent,
South on the Ocean, and on the West and Northwest by the
Indians called Nihigganneucks, alias Narragansets; the
whole Tract extending about Twenty-five English Miles unto
the Pequot River and Country.
    And whereas divers well effected and industrious Eng-
lish Inhabitants of the Towns of Providence, Portsmouth,
and Newport in the tract aforesaid, have adventured to
make a nearer neighborhood and Society with the great
Body of the Narragansets, which may in time by the blessing of God upon their endeavours, lay a sure Foundation
of Happiness to all America. And have also purchased, and
are purchasing of and amongst the said Natives, some other
Places, which may be convenient both for Plantations, and
also for building of Ships, Supply of Pipe Staves and other
Merchandize... [Accordingly the Earl of Warwick and the parliamentary commissioners] do...give, grant, and confirm, to the
aforesaid Inhabitants of the Towns of Providence, Portsmouth, and Newport, a free and absolute Charter of Incorporation, to be known by the Name of the Incorporation of
Providence Plantations, in the Narraganset-Bay, in New
England - Together with full Power and Authority to rule
themselves,and such others as shall hereafter inhabit
within any Part of the said Tract of land, by such a Form
of Civil Government, as by voluntary consent of all, or
the greater part of them, they shall find most suitable to
their Estate and Condition; and, for that end, to make
and ordain such Civil Laws and Constitutions, and to inflict such punishments upon Transgressors, and for Execution thereof, so to place, and displace Officers of Justice, as they, or the greatest part of them, shall by
free consent agree unto. Provided nevertheless, that the
said Laws, Constitutions, and Punishments, for the Civil
Government of the said Plantations, be conformable to the
Laws of England, so far as the nature and constitution of
the place will admit. And always reserving to the said
Earl, and Commissioners, and their Successors, Power and
Authority for to dispose the general Government of that,
as it stands in relation to the rest of the Plantations
in America as they shall conceive from Time to Time, most
conducing to the general Good of the said Plantations,the

Honour of his Majesty, and the Service of the State....

209. REPORT TO THE PARLIAMENTARY COMMITTEE, 28 February 1647.[1]
   ...That in pursuance of the said power, the said Government in Chief and Commissioners did, about November, 1643
pass several Acts under their hands and seals, for exempting the inhabitants of *The Charibee Islands* from all taxes
and common charges, other than what should be necessary
for the support of the government, and defraying the public occasions of the islands; as also for the authorizing
of them to choose their respective governors (with reference to their approbation by the said Governors in Chief
and Commissioners) and to oppose the admittance of any
other governor, not authorized by the said Governor in
Chief and Counsellors, that should be obtruded upon them,
or that should exact any taxation other than what is before mentioned...

210. ORDINANCE FOR A COMMISSION TO THE CHANNEL ISLANDS, November 1647.[2]
   The Lords and Commons in Parliament, assembled taking
notice of the great sufferings of the well-affected inhabitants of the towne and island of Guernzey, and the adjacent isles of Alderney and Sarke, for their adherence to
the Parliament, against the open and avowed enemies thereof, and likewise of their oppressions and grievances, by
reason of malignant and disaffected persons in places of
judicature, office, and authority; - for remedy therein,
doe order and ordaine...That Edmond Ludlow   [and three other
M.P.s]...are hereby constituted and appointed Commissioners,
and are authorised to heare and examine the complaints and
grievances of the said inhabitants...and examine witnesses
on either part upon oath.

211. (a)'ACT'CONSTITUTING A COUNCIL OF STATE, 13 February 1649.[3]
     [The Council was named. They were to take all steps to suppress
     the claim of the late king's sons to 'the Crowne of England or Ire-
     land, the Dominion of Wales, or to any of the dominions or territ-
     oryes to them or eyther of them belonging'.]

---

1. Lords Journals, IX 51a.
2. *Actes des Etats de L'ile de Guernsey* (1851) I pp.306ff.Some of the
Channel Islands had become nests of Royalists. Prince Charles took refuge for a time with the De Carterets in Jersey and was proclaimed king
in February 1649. A year later Parliament authorised the reduction of
Scilly, Man and the Channel Islands to submission, and Admiral Blake's
victories led to Jersey's surrender. Cromwell insisted on appointing
the *jurats* himself and the people of Jersey were fined heavily for
their rebellion against Parliament. For the report of these commissioners in 1649,see above No.139.
3. C. H. Firth and R. S. Rait (ed.) *op. cit*.pp.2-4. Similarly the Act
abolishing the monarchy on 17 March 1649 expressly discharged the islanders of Guernsey and Jersey from allegiance, as it did also 'the
people of England and Ireland and the dominions and territories thereunto belonging'. The subordination of the dominions to the realm in

You are hereby authorised and required to use all good
wayes and meanes for the reducing of Ireland, the Isles
of Jersey, Guernsey, Silly and the Isle of Man and all
other parts and places belonging to the Comonwealth of
England not yet reduced....
> [They were to care for and maintain the shipping of the Common-
> wealth, to encourage the trade of England and Ireland and 'the
> dominions to them belonging'; and to 'promote the good of all
> foreign plantations and factories belonging to this Commonwealth'.
> They were to conduct foreign affairs.]

211. (b).'AN ACT'DECLARING ENGLAND TO BE A COMMONWEALTH, 19 May 1649.
Be it declared and enacted by this present Parliament,
and by the authority of the same, That the people of England, and of all the dominions and territories thereunto
belonging, are and shall be, and are hereby constituted,
made, established, and confirmed, to be a Commonwealth
and Free State, and shall from henceforth be governed as
a Commonwealth and Free State, by the supreme authority
of this nation, the representatives of the people in Parliament, and by such as they shall appoint and constitute
as officers and ministers under them for the good of the
people, and that without any King, or House of Lords.

212. (a)'AN ACT'FOR PROHIBITING TRADE WITH THE BARBADOES, VIRGINIA,
BERMUDA, AND ANTEGO, 3 October 1650.[1]
Whereas in Virginia, and in the islands of Barbada's,
Antego, St. Christophers, Nevias, Mounsirat, Bermuda's,
and divers other islands and places in America, there
hath been and are colonies and plantations, which were
planted at the cost, and setled by the people, and by
authority of this nation, which are and ought to be subordinate to, and dependent upon England; and hath ever
since the planting thereof been, and ought to be subject
to such laws, orders and regulations as are or shall be
made, by the Parliament of England; and Whereas divers
acts of rebellion have been committed by many persons inhabiting in Barbada's, Antego, Bermuda's, and Virginia,
whereby they have most trayterously, by force and subtilty,
usurped a power of government, and seized the estates of
many well-effected persons into their hands, and banished
others, and have set up themselves in opposition to, and
distinct from this state and Commonwealth, many of the

---

this phrase [see also No.211 (b)] should be contrasted with the equality of 'realm and the dominions' in previous legislation, [e.g.
Nos. 10,11,12].Without the king's assent,these were not of course'Acts'.
1. Firth and Rait (ed.) *op.cit*.II pp.425-9.On the pretence of dealing
with the rebel 'royalist' colonies, this parliamentary legislation,
virtually the first Navigation Act of the Commonwealth, [but see also
No.2] asserted its imperial supremacy over trade to all English plantations in America. The Act sought to secure the dependence of Barbados,
Virginia, Bermuda and Antigua by prohibitions on their commerce and
foreign shipping.

chief actors in, and promoters of these rebellions having
been transported and carried over to the said plantations
in forein ships, without leave, licence or consent of the
Parliament of England: the Parliament of England...do
declare all and every the said persons...to be notorious
robbers and traitors, and such as by the law of nations
are not to be permitted any maner of commerce or traffique
with any people whatsoever; and do forbid to all maner
of persons, foreiners, *and others*[1], all maner of commerce,
traffique and correspondency whatsoever, to be used or
held with the said rebels in the Barbada's, Bermuda's,
Virginia and Antego, or either of them....
    And to prevent for the time to come, and to hinder the
carrying over of any such persons as are enemies to this
Commonwealth, or that may prove dangerous to any of the
English plantations in America, the Parliament doth forbid
and prohibit all ships of any forein nation whatsoever,
to come to, or trade in, or traffique with any of the
English plantations in America, or any islands, ports or
places thereof, which are planted by, and in possession
of the people of this Commonwealth, without license first
had and obtained from the Parliament or Council of State
....

> [Foreign ships trading without licence to any of the said plant-
> ations might be seized and be proceeded against 'in some port in
> this Commonwealth before the Court of admiralty'. The council of
> state was authorised to send commissioners to enforce obedience,
> settle plantations and grant pardons, and to make all provision
> for the government of the plantations; any previous letters pat-
> ent notwithstanding.][2]

212. (b) NAVIGATION ACT, (cap.22) 9 October 1651.
    For the increase of the shipping and the encouragement
of the navigation of this nation,[3] which under the good

1. i.e. a prohibition of all trade including that with England and
with other plantations.
2. For the commissions from the council of state sent to 'rebel' Royalist colonies see Nos.224-5, 240-1.
3.This so-called 'First Navigation Act' was a second step further to
secure English sea power and defence. Its primary concern was for
national security: the promotion of shipping and the increase of seamen, not for trade. But shipping was a necessary means for expansion.
In *Certain Proposals* (1652) Henry Robinson wrote somewhat over-
enthusiastically of the need to enlarge foreign plantations and 'to
get further footing in Barbarie, East and West Indies'. 'Not only
that wee may better provide our selves of Canvas for Sailes, Masts,
Timber, with all other things necessary for Shipping within our own
Dominians; but also in that a little spot of ground, as England is,
with its Dominions, if it doe not enlarge them, in future generations and (feare me) will be found inconsiderable in respect of Spain,
Portugall, the United Provinces, and any other European Nation which
shall have arrived to, and be armed with five or ten times a greater
strength, power and riches' from their colonies.

providence and protection of God is so great a means of
the welfare and safety of this Commonwealth: Be it enacted by this present Parliament...That no goods or commodities whatsoever of the growth, production or manufacture of
Asia, Africa or America, or of any part thereof; or of any
islands belonging to them...as well of the English plantations as others, shall be imported or brought into this Commonwealth of England, or into Ireland, or any other lands,
islands, plantations, or territories to this Commonwealth
belonging, or in their possession, in any ship or ships,
vessel or vessels whatsoever, but only in such as do truly
and without fraud belong only to the people of this Commonwealth, or the plantations thereof, as the proprietors
or right owners thereof; and whereof the master and mariners are also for the most part of them of the people of
this Commonwealth, under the penalty of the forfeiture
and loss of all the goods that shall be imported contrary
to this act; as also of the ship (with all her tackle,
guns and apparel) in which the said goods or commodities
shall be so brought in and imported....

    [one half to the Commonwealth, the other to the person who
    seized the goods and prosecuted. Similarly no European goods were
    to be imported into England, Ireland, or the plantations, save in
    ships of the Commonwealth, or in ships of the country where those
    goods were produced. Fish, oil and whalebone were to be imported
    and exported only in ships of the Commonwealth. Exceptions were
    to be made for English ships to carry goods from the East Indies
    and the Levant not produced in those countries, and from Spanish
    and Portuguese colonies.]

    Provided that this Act or anything therein contained,
shall not extend nor be construed to extend to any silk
or silk wares which shall be brought by land from any part
of Italy, and there bought with the proceed of English
commodities, sold either for money or in barter; but that
it shall and may be lawful for any of the people of this
Commonwealth to ship the same in English vessels from
Ostend, Nieuport, Rotterdam, Middelburg, Amsterdam, or any
ports thereabouts, the owners and proprietors first making
oath by themselves, or other credible witnesses, before
the Commissioners of the Customs for the time being or
their deputies, or one of the Barons of the Exchequer, that
the goods aforesaid were so bought for his or their own
proper account in Italy.

213. (a) COUNCIL OF STATE'S COMMISSION TO WILLIAM CODDINGTON,
                           3 April 1651.[1]
    The said Councel for the better incouragament of the

---

1. S.P. 25/65 pp.210-3. Coddington,a Quaker, had bought and planted
the Aquidneck and Conanicut islands and had sought a grant under the
protection and 'authority of this nation and state of England'. Though
with some reluctance he had accepted the establishment of the Rhode
Island confederation, he was concerned to keep his own plantations as

said adventurers, and...reposing confidence in the ability
and wisedom, faithfulnesse and good assertion of you, the
said William Coddington, doe by these presents make and
constitute you to bee Governour of the said ilands, hereby giveing and granting unto you, the said William Coddington, full power and authority to take upon you the office
and exercise of the government of the said ilands and to
cause equal and indifferent justice to bee duely administered to all the good people in the said ilands inhabiting, according to the law established in this land as far
as the constitution of those places will permit in the
name of the keepers of the libertyes of England by authority of Parliament, and to use and observe the same and
noe other forme or stile in all commissions, writings,
deputations, instructions and in all other legal and civil
proceedings, but according to the former directed by this
present Parliament since the abolishing of kingship and
alteration of government.

And you are further to raise forces for defence and
execute and doe all just things and use all lawful meanes
to settle improve and preserve the said ilands in peace
and safety until the Parliament shall take other or further order therein, unto whom or to this Council you are
to give an account of your proceedings from tyme to tyme,
and to present as things emerge what you conceive to bee
for the good of the said islands, and for the advantage
and interest of this Commonwealth in your well ordering
and disposing of the same. Moreover you, the said William Coddington, after yor entrance upon the government of
the said islands, are to call unto yor selfe for the
better discharge of yor office and government a Councel
consisting of persons rightly qualyfyed for judgment and
good affection, to the interest of this Common wealth, not
exceeding the number of six after the manner hereafter
set downe and exprest *viz*.

That the said persons shall bee nominated by such
freeholders of the towne of Newport and Portsmouth within
the said islands as shall bee well affected to the government of this Common wealth, according to yor instructions, and the Act in that case provided; and afterwards
chosen and confirmed by you the said Governor; which said
persons soe nominated and afterwards chosen by you the
said Governour as aforesaid or any three or more of them,
shall sit in councel and are to bee assisting unto you
in the affaires belonging to yor trust until that tyme
twelve monthes at which tyme a new election is to bee made

---

free and separate as possible.
This commission, which made him a feudal proprietor and life-long governor, presumably superseded the patent which Warwick's committee had
made to Williams in 1644. The council of state revoked Coddington's
commission in April 1652 when Williams successfully protested. Four
years later Coddington accepted this decision and submitted once more
to the confederation.

as aforesaid and soe annually.

And you have hereby power and are authorised to tender the engagement in these words 'I doe declare and promise that I will bee true and faithful to the Commonwealth of England, as it is now established without a Kinge or House of Lords'....

[This declaration was to be required of all councillors and electors. The council might temporarily elect his successor at his absence or death, until Parliament gave further orders.]

213. (b) COUNCIL OF STATE'S INSTRUCTIONS FOR JOHN TREWORGIE,
3 June 1653.[1]

...1st. You are hereby required and authorized to take care for the government and well ordering of the said country of Newfoundland and the people there inhabiting, and likewise the fishery according to such lawes and ordinaunces as are hereto annexed.

2nd. You are by yorselfe or such fit persons as you shall appoint to collect the imposition of fish due from and payd by strangers, and likewise the imposition of oyle, for the use of this Commonwealth, and adventurers aforesaid, until the supreame authority shall declare their further pleasure therein.

3rd, You are to use yor best endeavors to secure the fishery there against any that shall attempt to disturbe or interrupt it and to that end you have hereby full power and authority to command such ships and vessells as are upon that coast or in any of the harbors to keepe together or otherwise to dispose of themselves in such manner as may bee most for the common safety and to use such other meanes for the end aforesaid as you shall judge meet; and all captaynes of convoyes are hereby required to bee assisting to you in the execution thereof. And you are to consider in what manner any of harbors and bayes, belonging to the country may bee fortified for preservation both of the country and fishing....

[Kirke's property was to be restored, provided that the person he named to receive it promised to preserve it 'to the use of the Commonwealth'.]

You are upon the close of this summer's fishery to returne back into England and to repaire to the Councel or the supreme authority of this Commonwealth, and to give as well a just and true accompt of all such money and profitts as have come to yor hands due to the Commonwealth or adventurers, as of all your proceedings and in what condition you left all things there at yor coming away....

213. (c) INSTRUCTIONS TO THE COMMANDER OF A PROPOSED EXPEDITION AGAINST DUTCH SETTLEMENTS IN THE MANHATTOES, 1653.[2]

You are to...[with certain ships named] direct your course

1. Council of State; Order book (Apr.-July 1653) XCVII. Treworgie was hereby renewed, for the period of the summer fishery in Newfoundland, as commissioner to manage the interest of the Commonwealth there.
2. *Thurloe State Papers* (1742) I p.721. The end of the war with the

either to the Masachuset Bay in New England or to Pequott
Harbour, New Haven, or other good port, within any of
those united colonies...as Providence shall order the
wind and other occurrences, most conducing to the furtherance of the present design. Upon the arrival...in any of
the aforesaid harbours, you are immediately to deliver or
send away the letters committed to you, directed to the
several governours of the colonies of the Massachusets,
Plymouth, Conecticut, and New Haven....If upon return
from them you find an inclination and readiness in them
to joyn in the present undertaking for vindicating the
English right, and extirpating the Dutch...you are, without neglect of any opportunity, to address yourself to
the work, by ordering the ships for the Manhattoes [and
arranging a *rendezvous* with colonial soldiers]...If the Lord give
his blessing to your undertaking, that the forts and places be gained, you shall not use cruelty to the inhabitants, but encourage those that are willing to remain under
the English government, and give liberty to others to
transport themselves for Europe. Upon carrying of the
places, you shall, with the like advice, settle such
garrisons, and order affairs in such a manner, as what
is so gained, may be preserved for the English interest,
till further direction be given therein....
    [The charges for the expedition were to be borne by the fur
    trade.]
    In all your proceedings, you shall endeavour to hold
loving correspondence, and advise with the governors of
the English colonies, and such as they shall commit trust
to, for your assistance, that if possible no breach or
disaffection may appear in this undertaking, which is
only designed for the security of these plantations, with
the comfort of themselves and posterity. The aforementioned service being performed, if time permit, and opportunity be presented, you are to proceed to the gaining in
any other places from the enemy; which upon advice with
the Council of War may be judged feazible and conducive
to the settlement of the peace and safety of the English
plantations.

214. THOMAS MODYFORD: PAPER ON THE SPANISH ISLANDS AND MAIN, December
                                                              1654.[1]
    1. Because the islands are inhabited only with Spani-
ards, and by them very inconsiderably; so that if you go
there, you will find little more than land and trees, and
your business will be only to clear ground, build houses,
plant and make inclosures; a work of great toil, long time,

Dutch in 1654 postponed for a decade the capture of New Netherlands
till the eve of the second Dutch war [see No.273 and Section B 2 (f)
viii.]
1. *Thurloe State Papers* III pp.62-3.Modyford was one of those who
provided information for Cromwell. He clearly underrated the strength
of Spain in the Caribbean and favoured a direct attack on the mainland itself.

and excessive charge of which the old planters are very
sensible; whereas on the Main you will meet with good towns, well peopled, with a few Spaniards and many Indians,
whom they keep in slavery, and who very probably will be
faithful to milder masters.

2. The islands must be inhabited wholly by English,
(for the Spaniards will not serve under them;) which may
too much exhaust our native country of men, and render us
weak at home; but on the Main you have Indians to practise on, who, without dispute, will by politic and rational means be as so many hands gained to the Commonwealth.

3. The returns from the islands will be so small and
so slow,in regard they are to be produced by the labour of
the planter, that it will beget impatience in the adventurers, and perhaps a total desertion of the design; whereas from the Main you will presently be masters of gold,
silver, and pearl, besides hides and tallow, and the present commodities arising from the many settled plantations
there.

4. By settling the islands you provoke the Spaniard,
but do not at all disable him of his revenge; but by
settling on the Main you do not only take from him the
benefit of his pearl, and the mines of gold and silver
already open, but also hinder the passage of his treasure
from Peru, and lay Peru fairly open to an invasion.

5. By settling the islands you do not at all impede
his correspondence with his other colonies, so that he is
still free and at large to advise and execute all things,
as if you were not there; but by settling on the Main
you cut off his correspondence from Peru and all South
America, so that he cannot supply them from Spain; by
which means they must of necessity have all their commod-
eties from you; and how that may work and what intellig-
ences that may produce among them, may easily be imagined.

Lastly, it will be necessary, if the person who shall
command in chief of these forces, have a power to command
all the governors of the English in any part of America,
and that his Highnes's orders be directed to them to that
purpose: and though I verily believe, that every man will
be forward to embark on this design, yet it is wisdom to
have a power of pressing, which on some extraordinary occasions may be made use of.

215. INSTRUCTIONS TO GENERAL VENABLES FROM THE LORD PROTECTOR,
December 1654.[1]

[Robert Venables was appointed commander in chief of the forces
raised in England, Barbados *etc.* for the Western Design.]

---

1. B.M. Add. MSS 11410 f.41. Printed in C.H. Firth (ed.) *The narrative of General Venables* (Camden Soc.1900) pp.113-5. Cromwell's
Western Design was prompted partly by a sense of divine mission to
replace Catholic settlers by puritans; partly by a desire for revenge
upon Spaniards for their 'barbarities' at Tortugas, Santa Cruz and
Old Providence; and partly by a wish to consolidate English colonies

...The designe in general is to gain an interest[1] in
that part of the West Indies in the possession of the Spaniard, for the effecting whereof we shal not tye you up to
a method by any particular instructions, but only communicate to you what hath bin under our consideration. Two
or three wayes have bin thought of to that purpose....

> [One possibility would be to land on Hispaniola or St. John's
> Island as places which would 'become magazines of men and provis-
> ions for carrying on the designe on the mayne land' and to obstr-
> uct the Spanish plate fleet *en route* for Europe. Another would
> be to take Carthagena on the main land as 'the seat of the inten-
> ded designe': here houses and plantations already existed; the
> resources and spoils could be used to maintain the army and profit
> the Commonwealth. A third plan would be to reach Carthagena by
> way of St. Domingo or Porto Rico. Discretion was left to Venables
> and any two of the Commissioners to determine the best means of
> managing and executing the design. Penn, in charge of the fleet,
> was required to assist. He might 'keep for the use...of the Com-
> monwealth' such places as he may capture.]

6. You have hereby powre with the advise of the said
Commissioners, or any two of them, to place garrisons in
any such places as shall be taken in, and to appoint fit
governors thereof, and to give them commissions under your
hand and seale accordingly, and to slight the said garrisons, and remove the said governors, as you by advise aforesaid shal thinke necessary and for our service.

7. You have hereby power and authority by the advise
aforesaid to offer and give reasonable conditions to such
persons as will submit to our government and willingly
come under our obedience, and also to treate and conclude
for the surrendering of any fort, castle, or place, into
your hands, having in all your transactions care of preserving the interest of this Commonwealth.... [Dangerous enemies
must be rendered harmless by sending them as prisoners to Europe or
by other expedient means.]

10. Whereas all particulars cannot be foreseen, nor positive instructions for such emergencies so before hand
given but that most things left to your prudent and discreet management as occurrences may arise upon the place, or
from time to time fal out...

> [he was granted a wide discretion, provided he took special care
> to discharge 'that great trust' committed to him.]

---

in 'America', to prey on Spanish treasure fleets and thus ease the
Commonwealth's financial problems, and to secure increased trade for
the merchants of the city to whose demands he was becoming sensitive.
Venables' commission (9 December 1654) repudiated the papal division
of the world between Spain and Portugal,and proclaimed a crusade to
liberate America from 'miserable thraldom and bondage both spirituall
and civill'. (pp. 109–10). Venables had served with Cromwell in
Ireland.

1. A wide and undefined discretion.

216. (a) JAMAICA: ARTICLES OF PEACE, 17 May 1655.[1]

Imprimis, That all forts, arms, amunition, utensils and necessaries for war, of what kind or nature soever, (except what is hereafter exempted) and all kind of shipping that now is in any harbour of this island, with the furniture, sails, apparel, ammunition, ordnance etc. thereunto belonging; as also goods, wares, merchandizes, or what else is upon the said island, to be delivered up unto the right honourable General Venables, or whom he shall appoint, to receive the same for the use of his Highnes Oliver, the Lord Protector of the Commonwealth of England, Scotland, and Ireland, before the *[30th]* day of this instant month of May, *[i.e. twelve days]* without any deceit embezzlement, or concealment whatsoever.

Secondly, That all and every the inhabitants of the island (except the hereafter excepted) shall have their lives granted, and shall not be abused in their persons; and that those of them that shall desire to depart this island shall, with their wives and children be transported to some part of Nova Hispania, wind and weather permitting; or otherwise to some of the King of Spain's dominions in America, they providing their own provisions and victuals necessary for the voyage, the which they shall have the permission freely to do....

Thirdly [Officers might carry their swords.]

Fourthly, That liberty shall be given to all that shall depart according to the second article, to carry with them their wearing apparel and any books or writings they shall desire.

Fifthly, That all artificers and meaner sort of inhabitants who shall desire to remain on the island (except hereafter excepted) shall enjoy their freedom and goods (excepting slaves) they submitting and conforming to the laws of the English nation, and such others as shall be declared by authority to be put in use and exercised within this island....

[Household goods must remain in, or be returned to, the places where they belong. Hostages must be given to ensure the true execution of these articles, and details were set out for the promised transportation of families. A census of the island inhabitants, 'their names, titles, qualities, and occupations, together with the names of their wives, children, servants and slaves', was to be presented to the General, who might also grant concessions to

---

1. St. Iago de la Vega, *Interesting tracts relating to...Jamaica* (1800) p.34. Having failed to take Santo Domingo, Penn and Venables came to Jamaica and took Kingston and Villa de la Vega almost without opposition. The Spanish governor, Don Juan Ramirez, agreed to these terms insisted on by Venables; but they were repudiated by the Jamaican grandees, and guerilla warfare continued for five years. These articles were similar to those which the Spaniards had imposed when the English had surrendered Old Providence Island off the Nicaragua coast in 1641. Julian de Castilla's account of these terms [see below No.216 (b)] varied a little in detail.

slaves regarding their liberty.]
The commissioners for us were Major-General Fortescue,
Vice-Admiral Goodson, Colonel Richard Holdipe and Colonel
Edward D'Oyly.

216. (b) JULIAN DE CASTILLA'S ACCOUNT OF THE PEACE ARTICLES.[1]
[The articles] were to the effect that within twelve
days from their date every faithful Christian was to present himself to the general, or his deputies, with all the
money in gold, silver and copper he might have, jewels,
silverware, slaves, household effects, ranches, farms,
sugar estates, mills, arms, munitions and merchandise -
and there were other clauses so detailed that they read
like an inventory drawn up by heirs in disagreement. Artificers poor and rich, who might desire to remain in the island, might do so provided they agreed to live under the
government and laws of England. No priest nor book might
remain in the island. Each person was to bring his own
victuals for a month and present himself at the end of
twelve days. His Excellency would furnish ships to convey
them to lower ports, that is, to Honduras and Campeche,
allowing each person two shirts and one suit of clothes,
the military officers to retain their arms and insignia.

217. REPRESENTATIONS BY THE ARMY OFFICERS IN JAMAICA TO THE LORD
     PROTECTOR, July 1655.[2]
... That servants from Scotland or elsewhere may bee
sent to assist in planting, etc. for which the officers
out of their paie will make such allowance as his Highnesse
shall think fitte, and assigne them such proportions of
land, as his Highnesse shal direct at the expiration of
their respective termes....
That the allottment and distribution of land to the
respective regiments of the army allready approved of
by his Highnesse commissioners may bee ratified by his
Highnesse sanction....
That such encouragement, as his Highnesse shall thinke
fitt, may bee given and granted to such, as shall desire
to come from England, or aney other English collonies.
That for the better regulatinge and ordering this little commonwealth, and encouragement of such as desire to
live under a civill and settled government, his Highnesse
will please to make such constitutions and lawes, as his
Highnesse shall thinke meete for the government of this
place, or impower such in the place as his Highnesse shall
approve of, to make and constitute from time to time wholesome and necessary lawes, as shal bee most fitt for the
better ordering and government of thinges here; and to
erect court and courts of justice and equity for decideing
of controversies betweene party and party....

1. St. Iago de la Vega, *op. cit.* p.37.
2. *Thurloe State Papers*, III p.661. The army officers were asking for
help in establishing a plantation and for the powers of civil government.

[A court of admiralty and a commission to privateers were requested.]
That his Highnesse will please to allow that such marchant or marchants, as shal bee willing to advance the service and plantation of this island, may have all due encouragement....

218. ORDER OF THE PROTECTOR AND COUNCIL, 26 September 1655.[1]
[The following 'offer' was made to encourage emigrants from the New England colonies to settle in Jamaica: that if colonies of settlers transplanted themselves to Jamaica they would be granted land in free and common soccage, rent-free for 7 years and thereafter at no more than a penny an acre; that they should be free for 7 years to hunt and take horses and cattle not belonging to other planters.]
3. That his Highness will graunt them letters patent under the great seale of incorporation with as large priviledges and immunityes both for chooseing their officers and otherwise as are graunted to any city or towne corporate within the Comonwealth of England.[2]
4. That neither they nor their servants shall without their owne consent be drawn out into the warrs unles it be in case of invasion or rebellion and for the defence of the said island... [and that for 3 years they would be free of customs and excise duty on produce exported to Britain.]
6. That his Highnesse will take care and be oblidged to appointe from tyme to tyme such a Governor and comander in cheife of the said island and such persons to assist him in the management of the affaires thereof as shalbe men of integritye and feareing God, and that he will from time to tyme alert and constitute some from amongst them to be of that number who for their fidelitye, prudence, godliness and honestie may be fit for such trust. And that as speedy as may be a civil government shalbe setled agreeable to the word of God and as far as the condition of that place will admit to the lawes of England, where provisions shalbe made that the Churches of Christ shall have liberty and protection in all wayes of godliness and honestie.[3]

1. S.P. 76 P.305. This offer forms part of the instructions to Daniel Gookin. In encouraging colonisation, Cromwell was offering protection, land, freehold tenure and the privileges of Englishmen.
2. A proclamation of the Lord Protector, dated 10 October 1655 (C.S. P. 1675-6 p.229; E. Long, *History of Jamaica* I pp. 214-6) promised that 'all and every person and persons that shall hereafter happen to be borne within the said island shalbe...deemed and accounted to be free denizens of England and shall have and enjoy all and every such benefitte, priviledges, advantages and immunities whatsoever as any the natives or people of England borne in England now have and enjoy in England'.
3. The proclamation further indicated that 'the Churches of Christ' were presumed to be protestant.

7. That towardes the transportation of themselves their servants and estates his Highnes will furnish them with six shipps of convenient burden if they desire that number and alsoe a fitting convoy. They undertaking to victual shipps of burden from the tyme the said shipps shall arrive in their ports for the purpose aforesaid until they have performed their voyage.

8. As to the quantity and proportion of land to be appointed for them according to the first proposition, - You are authorized to expound that such quantity of land shalbe put forth as will answere the proportion of twenty acres for every male of twelve yeares old and upwards, and ten acres for all other male or female to be transported as aforesaid.

9. That the said quantity of land shalbe set forth unto them within six weeks after the agreement made for their transportation and signification of their desires on that behalfe to the commander in cheife or the commissioner intrusted for that purpose to whom you shall direct yourselfe or any other persone concerned herein in any of the premises or any part of them.

10. That they doe engage to transport the whole number of males for⁹ with twenty acres to each is to be set forth within two yeares after the aforesaid agreement and that they doe begin their worke of transporting sometymes before the end of September 1656....

219. MANIFESTO BY LORD PROTECTOR, 26 October 1655.[1]

...That the Spaniards themselves are the occasion of this war, will evidently appear to every one who considers how, as oft as they find opportunity, without any just cause, and without being provoked to it by any injury received, they are continually murdering, and sometimes even in cold blood butchering, any of our countrymen in America they think fit; while in the mean time they seize upon their goods and fortunes, demolish their houses and plantations, take any of their ships they happen to meet with in those seas...Nor do they pretend any other or better right for so doing, than a certain ridiculous gift of the Pope on which they rely, and because they were the first discoverers of some parts of that western region....

But such an imaginary title , founded on such a silly pretence, without being in possession, cannot possibly create any true and lawful right. The best right of possession in America is that which is founded on one's having planted colonies there, and settled in such places[2] as

1. J.A. St.John (ed.) *Prose works of John Milton* (1848) II pp.334-350. Milton probably obtained information from one of the clerks of the council, William Jessop, who had been secretary to the Providence Company. It is likely that Lord Saye and Sele also had a hand in drafting the manifesto.
2. The assertion of the right of 'effective occupation' against the bulls of demarcation between Spain and Portugal of Alexander VI and

had either no inhabitants, or by the consent of the inhabitants, if there were any; or at least in some of the wild
and uncultivated places of their country, which they were
not numerous enough to replenish and improve; since God
has created this earth for the use of men, and ordered
them to replenish it throughout....

The Spaniards will be found to hold their possessions
there very unjustly, having purchased all of them against
the will of the inhabitants....The English hold their possessions there by the best right imaginable...by the law
of nature and nations....'Such things as belong to none,
and such as are abandoned by their former possessors, become his property who first seizes them'....Since we have
settled our colonies in such places as were neither possessed by the natives nor the Spaniards, they having
left behind them neither houses nor cattle, nor anything
that could by any means keep up the right of possession,
the justness of our title to these places was so much the
more evident, and the injuries done us by the Spaniards
so much the more manifest....[1]

(2) COLONIAL CLAIMS TO AUTONOMY AND EQUALITY OF STATUS

(a) VIRGINIA

220. INSTRUCTIONS TO SIR WILLIAM BERKELEY, 9 August 1641.[2]

[He should take care to foster worship according to the forms
of the Church of England. He should require oaths of allegiance
and supremacy from all who intended 'to plant themselves in the
country'.]

3. That justice be equally administered to all his Majesty's subjects there residing and as near as may after the
form of this realm of England, and vigilant care to be
had to prevent corruption in officers tending to the delay or perverting of justice.
4. That you and the councillors, as formerly once a year
or oftener, if urgent occasion shall require, do summon
the burgesses of all and singular plantations there, which
together with the Governor and Council makes the Grand

Julius II and the treaty of Tordesillas 1494.
1. The losses of the Providence company seemed to loom large in this
apology, but many of Cromwell's friends had been hurt by them.
2. *Virginia Magazine of History and Biography* (1895) II pp.281-8. Sir
William Berkeley, courtier and playwright, had been appointed (with
William Alexander) one of the commissioners dealing with 'Canada' in
1632. It was February 1642 before Berkeley actually replaced Sir Francis Wyatt, who had been sent three years earlier to bring Governor
Harvey to account for his injustice and oppression. These instructions were substantially the same as those to Wyatt (*ibid*.XI. pp.54-
7) with the crucial provision for an annual Grand Assembly. Berkeley
proved in his first period as governor to be a popular planter governor - conciliatory, even liberal, but staunchly royalist. When Charles
I was executed, he offered the colony as a royalist asylum for the
new king, Charles II.

Assembly, and shall have power to make acts and laws for
the government of that plantation correspondent, as near
as may be, to the laws of England, in which assembly the
governor is to have a negative voice as formerly.[1]
5. That you and the Council assembled are to set down the
fittest months of the quarterly meeting of the Council of
State, whereas they are to give their attendance for one
and consult upon matter of council and state and to decide
and determine such causes as shall come before them and
that free access be admitted to all suitors to make known
their particular grievancies, being against what person
soever, wherein the Governor for the time being, as formerly, is to have but a casting voice if the number of the
councillors should be equally divided in opinion ....
    [The governor was impowered to summon emergency meetings of the
    council; offending councillors could be tried at the quarter cou-
    rts, or, if the safety of the state demanded speed, at an emerg-
    ency session of the council.]
7. For the ease of the country and quicker dispatch of
business, you, the Governor and Council, may appoint in
places convenient,inferior courts of justice and commissioners for the same, to determine of suits not exceeding
the value of ten pounds, and for the punishment of such
offences as you and the Council shall think fit to give
them the power to hear and determine ....
    [The governor was instructed to appoint all public officials
    to execute his orders, writs and the acts of the General Assembly.
    To recompense councillors for their time spent on public business,
    they (and 10 servants for each of them) were exempted from all
    taxation - 'a defensive war, assistance towards the building of
    a town or churches, or the minister's dues excepted'.]
11. To the end the country may be the better served against
all hostile invasions it is requisite that all persons from
the age of 16 to 60 be armed with arms, both offensive and
defensive,
    [though newcomers would be exempt from all but local defence dur-
    ing their first year in the colony. The governor was responsible
    for seeing that the obligations of the assize of arms was fully
    enforced by the muster master-general, that the colonists were
    properly trained, and that a garrison of ten was maintained at
    Point Comfort. To 'prevent the treachery of the savages', inter-
    course with Indians was to be strictly regulated under licence.
    A system of alarm by beacons *etc*. was to be organised. Special
    care should be taken to extirpate vice, to suppress drunkenness
    and to encourage religion and virtue; and attention given to the
    regulation of trade and industry, the planning of towns, the grant
    and use of land to ensure defence and cultivation and the divers-
    ification of crops (hemp, flax, tar, silk *etc*.,). Trade with the
    ships of foreign countries was forbidden, save'upon some extremity'
    and then under bond that such goods should be landed only at Lon-

---

1. The governor had had a veto in the last years of the company,
[see above No.172].

don. In the case of all exports from Virginia, bond had to be
given that they would be landed directly within 'his Majesty's
dominions and not elsewhere'.]

221. DECLARATION OF THE GRAND ASSEMBLY TO THE KING AGAINST THE
                                  COMPANY, 1 April 1642.[1]
...We, the Governor, Council and Burgesses of the Grand
Assembly, send greeting....
    [George Sandys, as agent of the assembly in exhibiting a petit-
    ion to the Commons for restoring the letters patent of the company,
    had mistaken his instructions; no such rechartering of the company
    was ever sought with their consent. After full debate they now
    contrasted their previous condition as 'intollerable' under the
    company but now 'comparatively happy' under the king. They had
    resented the monopoly the company had imposed on trade.]
    The present happiness is exemplified by the freedom of
yearly assemblies warranted unto us by His Majesty's gracious instructions and the legal trial *per* juries in all
criminal and civil causes where it shall be demanded....
    [And the king had also encouraged them freely to address their
    petitions direct to him, whereas 'of former times...private let-
    ters to friends were rarely admitted passage'. The restoration of
    the company would threaten their tenures and their privileges; it
    would spell ruin: and they threatened to depart.]
    For by such admission
Ist We shall degenerate from the condition of our birth
being naturalized under a monarchical government, and not
a popular and tumultuary government depending upon greatest numbers of votes of persons of several humours and
dispositions[2]....
    [They would breach their allegiance and religion to give up
    lands granted by, and held from the king for a return to depend-
    ence under the company. They feared too the end of their freedom
    of trade 'the blood and life of a commonwealth' - by the reimpos-
    ition of a monopoly.]

222. ACTS RELATING TO TAXATION, 1643-45.
    (a) 2 March 1643.[3]
(Act *III*). It is further enacted and confirmed, That the

---

1. W.W. Hening, *Statutes at large in Virginia* (1823 ed.) I pp.230-5.
When Berkeley became governor he sought to win over the support of the
assembly against moves in London to restore the old Company of Virginia. A remonstrance, dated later in 1 July 1642, summarised the benefits the colony had received from Berkeley: the repeal of the poll tax
from which the governor was paid his salary; their imitation of English laws; poor relief etc. He had also secured the status of the
royal province. Charles I replied to this declaration that he had not
'the least intention' to restore the company or 'to change a form of
government' which so contented his Virginian subjects.
2. A reference to the ballot box used by the company. Clearly the assembly had no love for democracy as they had known it.
3. W.W. Hening *op.cit.* I pp.244,279. Act I of this session had repealed laws of all former assemblies (save those reenacted) because 'the

Governor and Council shall not lay any taxes or impositions upon this collonie, their lands or comedities, otherwise than by the authoritie of the Grand Assembly to be leavied, and imployed as by the Assembly shall be appointed.

(Act *LXX*). It is enacted by the authoritie aforesaid, That there be leavied this present crop, nine pounds of tobacco per poll, for every tithable person throughout the collonie by the sheriffs as formerly, to be disposed of in the same manner and to such uses according to the order of this present Grand Assembly.

(b) 20 November 1645.[1]

(Act *XV*) Whereas the anncient and usual taxing of all people of this collony by the pole equally, hath been found inconvenient and is become insupportable for the poorer sorte to beare, This Assembly haveing taken it into consideration have for their releife hereafter thoight fitt to alter the same; Be it therefore enacted That all publique leavies and county leavies be raised by equal proportions out of the visible estates of the collony, The conformity of the proportions to be as followeth (*viz.*)

One hundred acres of land at	04 lb. tobacco
One cow 3 years old at	04
Horses, mares and geldings at	32 a peece.[2]
A breeding sheep att	04
A breeding goat at	02
A tithable person at	20

[A census of tithable persons and animals was to be made by the county courts annually.]

223. ACTS RELATING TO THE FRANCHISE, 1646-56.[3]

(a) 5 October 1646.

(Act *XX*). Whereas divers inconveniences are likely to ensue by disorderly and illegal election of burgesses, by subscribing of hands contrary to the warrant directed for the sayd election, by which means it alsoe happeneth that few or none doe appeare personally according to sumons, Be it therefore inacted, That noe election shall be made of any burgesse or burgesses but by plurality of voices, and that no hand writing shall be admitted: Be it alsoe further inacted That what freemen soever...that

---

many and sundry Acts and laws at former Grand Assemblies established in severall books and volumes digested have been found very prejudiciall to this Collony'. Act XXXIX gave Burgesses freedom from arrest for the session and ten days after dissolution: Act XLVII provided for them to be paid by county levies.

1. *ibid*.p.305. Act XVII provided that the revenues from quit rents were to be applied first to the treasurer's salary, and any surplusage was then to be at the disposal of the assembly.

2. i.e. each.

3. W.W. Hening *op.cit.* 333-4. 403, 412.

shall not make repaire accordingly, such person or persons
unless there be lawfull cause for the absenting himselfe
shall forfeit 100 lb. of tobacco for his non-appearance,
freemen being covenant servants being exempted from the
said fine....
(b) 31 March 1655
    (Act VII). All house keepers whether freeholders, lease
holders, or otherwise tenants, shall onely be capeable to
elect burgesses...provided that this word house-keepers
repeated in this Act extend no further than to one person
in a family.
(c) 31 March 1656
    (Act XVI). Whereas we conceive it something hard and
unagreeable to reason that any persons shall pay equal
taxes and yet have no votes in elections, therefore it
is enacted by this present Grand Assembly, That soe much
of the Act of chooseing burgesses be repealed as excludes
freemen from votes[1]: provided allwaies that they fairly
give their votes by subscription and not in a tumultuous
way.

224. DEFIANCE TO THE COMMONWEALTH BY GOVERNOR AND ASSEMBLY,
                                        17 March 1651.[2]
(a) Speech of Governor Berkeley.[3]
    Gentlemen, you perceave by the declaration that the
men of Westminster have set out...how they meane to deale
with you hereafter[4]....For the reason why they talk so
Magisterially to us is this, we are forsooth their wor-
ships slaves, bought with their money and by consequence
ought now to levy, or sell but with those they shall Authorize, with a few trifles to Coszen us of all for which
we toile and labour....The strength of their argument runs
onely thus: 'we have laid violent hands on your Land-lord

---

1. i.e. the Act of 1655. By an Act of 1670 the franchise was again
limited to householders and freeholders, not freemen : [see below
No.297].
2. *Virginia Magazine of History*, I pp.75-81; XI p.37. Governor and
assembly had given a clearly royalist answer to news of the king's
execution and acknowledged Prince Charles as Charles II: W.W.Hening
op. cit. I p.359.
3. Berkeley had been recommissioned as governor by'Charles II'in June
1650.
4. The Navigation Act of 3 October 1650 - this 'pretended Act of Parliament' as the assembly termed it - forbade all trade to or from the
'rebel' colonies of Barbados, Antigua, Bermuda and Virginia with England or any part of the world (see above p.327): a strong assertion
of parliamentary power over the 'dominions' with the threat of enforcement by the navy. The Virginians had encouraged Dutch merchants
(see Act XXVIII of 1643: W.W.Hening *op. cit.*I p.258). In April 1647
the assembly had heard rumours that Parliament intended to ban all
foreigners from the plantation trade and had renewed their invitation
to the Dutch to enjoy freedom of trade with Virginia. So now the assembly looked to Dutch ships to take off their tobacco.

[Charles I], possessed his Manner house where you used to pay your rents, therefore now tender your respects to the same house you once reverenced'...Surely we are more slaves by nature than their power can make Us if we suffer ourselves to be shaken with these paper bulletts.... You have heard under what heavy burdens the afflicted English Nation now groanes ....Consider yourselves how happy you are and have been, how the Gates of Wealth and Honour are shut to no man and that there is not here an Arbitrary hand that dares to touch the substance of either poore or rich. But that which I would have you chiefly consider with thankfulness: that God hath separated you from the guilt of the crying bloud of our Pious Souveraigne of ever blessed memory ....

(b) Declaration and resolution of the Assembly[1]

  [They reaffirmed their loyalty to Charles II and denounced the Commons as regicides. In the Act prohibiting trade with them, they have been branded as 'rebels'. In their protest against the measure, they repudiated such charges.]

And first whereas they say, That the plantations in America were seated at the cost, and established by the authority, of some in England and therefore ought to be governed by the laws of England....In reply we say, we were some of us sent, others permitted to come hither by the gratious favour of our pious Kings, sworne to governe and be governed (as farr as possible the place was capable of) by the lawes of England; which lawes we have inviolably and sacredly kept as farr as our abilityes to execute, and our capacities to judge, would permit us, and with reason; for these lawes onely in such times of tumults, storms and tempests can humanly prevent our ruines. These lawes often enjoyned us the oaths of allegiance and supremacy and they tell us that no power can absolve or manumit us from our obedience to our Prince and his lawfull successors. These lawes tell us that when we have don all we can to avoyd it, we may resist violence with force and in a lawful defence of our selves destroy any that shall endeavour to take away our lives or substance. These lawes we profess are our guides and do believe we deserve punishment and infamy if we willingly, or willfully deviate from them ....

  [They could not be expected to 'yield' passive obedience 'to whosoever possesse themselves of Westminster Hall where heads of divers factions and pretentions have presided and excluded one the other in quick succession'. Unlike Parliament they had not usurped the government, but had governed according to their constitution, the law of England and their allegiance without innovation or alteration. It ill became Parliament to bring such charges; if the Virginians had been guilty of such illegalities, 'what more likely patrons could we chuse to protect us than those who

---

1. This declaration was unanimously consented to by the governor, council and burgesses of the Grand Assembly.

accuse us?' A few interested persons in London were seeking to
exclude them 'from the society of nations which bring us necessaries for what our country produces'.]

Therefore of the whole matter we conclude: We are resolved to Continue our Allegeance to our most Gratious King,
yea as long as his gratious favour permits us, we will
peaceably (as formerly) trade with the Londoners and all
other nations in amity with our Soveraigne: Protect all
forraigne Merchants with our utmost force from injury in
the rivers; Give letters of Reprisall to any injured within our Capes: Allwais pray for the happy restoration of
our King and repentance in them who to the hazard of their
souls have opposed him.[1]

225.'ARTICLES AT THE SURRENDER OF THE COUNTRY', 12 March 1652.[2]

First, It is agreed...that the plantation of Virginia
and all the inhabitants thereof shall be and remaine in
due obedience and subjection to the Common Wealth of England according to the lawes there established. And that
this submission and subscription bee acknowledged a voluntary act, not forced nor constrained by a conquest upon
the countrey. And that they shall have and enjoy such
freedomes and priviledges as belong to the free borne people of England and that the former Government by the commissions and instructions be void and null.

2ndly, That the Grand Assembly as formerly shall convene and transact the affairs of Virginia, wherein nothing
is to be acted or done contrarie to the government of the
Common Wealth of England and the lawes there established.[3]

---

1. London shippers complained strongly that the Blockade Act was in-
juring their carrying trade rather than the rebel colonies. The
council of state, aware of the impossibility of enforcing a total blockade, sent commissioners to seek (if possible) a peacable submission
before resorting to force, and they interpreted their instructions in
a liberal way. When the commissioners arrived in the Chesapeake in
March 1652 Berkeley blustered but terms were soon agreed.

2. H. R. McIlwaine (ed.) *Journals of...House of Burgesses* pp.76-9; W.
W. Hening *op.cit.* I pp.363-8. The terms consisted of two agreements:
one (quoted above) with the province as represented in the grand
assembly, the other with governor and councillor to arrange a smooth
transition of power. The parliamentary commissioners took over the
government. A new assembly chose one of the commissioners, Richard
Bennett (who had left the colony during Berkeley's persecution of
dissenters) to be governor, and another, William Claiborne, to be
secretary.

3. It was a common feature of revolutionary government that the assembly should be the dominant institution and that the executive should
only exercise power delegated by it and be answerable on all matters
to it. The Burgesses became the chief instrument of government in
Virginia with the council of state having a veto - which it did not use.

[Full amnesty was granted for all acts and words against Parliament. The patent rights, especially relating to land titles, were confirmed, and the 'antient' boundaries of Virginia guaranteed.]

7thly. That the people of Virginia have free trade as the people of England do enjoy to all places and with all nations according to the lawes of that Common Wealth. And that Virginia shall enjoy all priviledges equall with any English plantations in America.[1]

8thly. That Virginia shall be free from all taxes, customs and impositions whatsoever and none to be imposed on them without consent of the Grand Assembly. And soe that neither forts nor castles bee erected or garrisons maintained without their consent.

9thly. That noe charge shall be required from this country in respect of this present fleet....

[All inhabitants were to subscribe to the engagement with Parliament within a year, or remove themselves from the colony.[2] The use of the Book of Common Prayer was permitted for a year in parishes where the majority wished to use it.]

226. PROTEST OF THE INHABITANTS OF NORTHAMPTON COUNTY, May 1652.[3]

Wee, the inhabitants of Northampton countie, doe complayne that from tyme to tyme wee have been submitted and bine obedient unto the payment of publiq taxacons. Butt after the yeare 1647, since the tyme we conceive and have found that the taxes were very weightie. But in a more espetiall manner...the taxacon of forty six pounds of tobacco per poll this present yeare.[4] And desire that the same bee taken off the charge of the countie. Furthermore, we alledge that after 1647, wee did understand and suppose our countie of Northampton to be disjoynted and sequestered from the rest of Virginia. Therefore that Lawe which requireth and injoyneth taxacons from us to bee arbitrary and illegal. Foreasmuch, as wee had neither summons for ellecon of Burgesses nor voyce in their assemblye during the time aforesaid but only the singular Burgess in September, ano: 1651. We conceive that wee may lawfullie protest against the proceedings in the Act of assembly for publiq taxacons which have relacon to Northampton countie since the year 1647.[5]

1. Significantly the council of state did not ratify and confirm this article. Nor indeed the following one, relating to taxation.
2. Neither Berkeley nor the councillors were compelled during the ensuing year to take a new oath of allegiance. Berkeley continued to reside in Virginia and his permit was extended.
3. J. C. Wise. *The early history of the eastern shore of Virginia*, p.139. Northampton county was over Chesapeake bay, remote from James Town and the other settlements of Virginia, and was showing a certain hostility to, and independence of, the colonial government. The grievances included this protest against taxation without representation.
4. The poll tax had been imposed by the parliamentary commissioners.
5. A year later the Virginia assembly took steps to prevent separatism in Northampton, but discontent continued there from a sense of

227. POWERS OF THE GRAND ASSEMBLY AND ITS RELATIONSHIP WITH GOVERNOR
AND COUNCIL, 1652 -8.[1]
(a) <u>30 April 1652</u>.
...(Act *I*)...And the said Governor, Secretary and Council of State are to have such power and authorities and
to act from time to time, as by the Grand Assembly shall
be appointed and granted to their severall places respectively for the time aforesaid.
(b) <u>5 May 1652</u>.
(Act *III*) It is agreed and thought best for the government of this country by the Governor, Council and Burgesses that the right of election of all officers of this
colony be and appertain to the Burgesses, the representative of the people....
(c) <u>6 May 1652</u>.
(Act *IV*) Whether the Governor and Council shall be
members of this Assembly or no: Generally voted they
shall be, taking the oath the Burgesses take.
(d) <u>2 April 1658</u>.[2]
We, the said Burgesses, do declare, That we have in
ourselves the full power of the election and appointment
of all officers in this country untill such time as wee
shall have order to the contrary from the supreme power
in England. All which is evident upon the Assembly records.
. That wee are not dissolvable by any power yet extant
in Virginia but our owne. That all former election of
Governor and Council be void and null.[3]

228. THE RESTORATION, 13 March 1660.[4]
(Act *I*) Whereas by reason of the late frequent distract-

isolation from the colonial capital. (*Virginia Magazine* II 2.289).
Some power was delegated locally on the county in 1656 to deal with
Indians and manufactures (W.W. Hening *op. cit.*I p.396).
1. W.W. Hening,I pp.371,2,3,&502. The Burgesses were to elect the governor, the councillors and all officials and these were only to have
such limited powers as granted by them. Virginia became virtually a
revolutionary republic.
2. The assembly resisted the claim of Governor Samuel Matthewes and
the council to dissolve it as 'not presidentall neither legall according to the lawes now in force'. Governor and council were prepared to
put the issue of dissolution to the Lord Protector, but the assembly
refused to be conciliatory: the governor and council must acknowledge
that their claim was illegal. They proceeded to declare the offices of
governor and councillors vacant. When the council of state in 1659
seemed to challenge the assembly's autonomy and to promote the powers
of the governor and council at their expense, the Burgesses reaffirmed
their rights.
3. S. Matthewes was, however, reelected as governor the same day.
4. W.W. Hening *op.cit.* I p.530. Somewhat curiously the assembly,having
asserted their absolute power , chose the most loyal of king's men
as governor, though with limited powers as their servant. When Berkeley demurred,affirming his royalism, the assembly insisted and Berk-

ions (which God in his mercy putt a suddaine period to) there being in England noe resident absolute and gen'll confessed power, Be it enacted and confirmed.

That the Supreme Power of the government of this country shall be resident in the Assembly. And that all writts issue in the name of the Grand Assembly of Virginia until such a comand and commission come out of England as shall be by the Assembly adjudged lawfull.

(Act *II*)...That the honourable Sir William Berkeley bee elected Governour and Captain Generall of Virginia and that he governe according to the auncient lawes of England and the established lawes of this country, and that all writts issue in the name of the Grand Assembly of Virginia, that once in two years at least he call a Grand Assembly or oftener if he see cause, that he have liberty to make choice of a Secretarie and Council of State with the approbation of the Assemblies and that he do not dissolve this Assembly without consent of the major part of the House.[1]

(b) MASSACHUSETTS

229. (a). ACT ASSERTING COLONIAL NEUTRALITY, 20 May 1644.[2]

WHEREAS the civil wars and dissentions in our native country, through the seditious words and carriages of many evil affected persons, cause divisions in many places of government in America, some professing themselves for the King, and others for the parliament, not considering that the parliament themselves profess that they stand for the King and parliament against the malignant papists and delinquents in that kingdom. It is therefore ordered that what person soever shall by word, writing, or action endeavour to disturb our peace, directly or indirectly, by drawing a party under pretence that he is for the King of England and such as join with him against the parliament, shall be accounted as an offender of a high nature against this commonwealth, and to be proceeded with, either capitally or otherwise, according to the quality and degree of his offence, Provided always, that this shall not be extended against any merchant strangers and shipmen that come

---

eley accepted temporarily, till a new authority, whether king or protector, emerged in England.
1. In July 1660 Berkeley received a new commission from the restored king. During this second period as governor, however, he proved more arbitrary, avaricious and irascible than previously. He dominated the council, managed the assembly and secured control of appointments in county courts and vestries. He thanked God there were no free schools nor printing in Virginia 'for learning has brought disobedience and heresy and sects into the world and printing has divulged them and libels against the best government'. (W.W.Hening *op.cit.* II p.517).
2. T. Hutchinson, *History of Massachusetts Bay* (1765) I pp 135-6. Hutchinson commented on this 'prudent' Act of the general court, 'We shall find that authority <u>here</u>, acquiescing under every change of government in England. When we consider the dependence of a colony upon its mother country, nothing less is ordinarily to be expected'.

hither merely for matter of trade or merchandize, albeit
they should come from any of those parts that are in the
hands of the King and such as adhere to him against the
parliament, carrying themselves here quietly and free
from railing or nourishing any faction, mutiny, or sedition amongst us as aforesaid.

229. (b). REASONS FOR RECOGNISING A PARLIAMENTARY COMMISSION,
                                          July 1644.[1]
   [Captain Stagg, with a commission from the earl of Warwick as
Lord High Admiral, had seized a British ship in Boston harbour.
This led to tumult and debate. Some of the elders and magistrates
in the general court at Salem argued that the commission could not
supersede a patent, and that the charter of the people's liberties
had been violated: they were 'subject to no other power but among
themselves'. But the majority reasoned differently and more circumspectly that it should be 'thought fit not to oppose' recognition
of Stagg's commission:]
1. Because this could be no precedent to bar us from opposing any commission or other foreign power that might
indeed tend to our hurt and violate our liberty; for the
parliament had taught us that *salus populi* is *suprema
lex*.
2. The King of England was enraged against us and all that
party and all the popish states in Europe: And if we
should now, by opposing the parliament, cause them to forsake us we could have no protection or countenance from
any but should be open as a prey to all men.
3. We might not deny the parliament's power in this case
unless we should deny the foundation of our government by
our patent; for the parliament's authority will take place
in all peculiar and privileged places where the King's
writs or commissions will not be of force as in the Dutchy
of Lancaster, the Cinque Ports &c; and in London itself the
parliament may fetch out any man, even the Lord Mayor
himself; and the reason is, because what the parliament
doth is done by themselves, for they have their burgesses
etc. there; nor need they fear that the parliament will do
any man wrong; and we have consented to hold our land of
the manor of E. Greenwich and so such as are burgesses or
knights for that manor are our burgesses also. This only
might help us, that the King giving us land which was
none of his, but we are forced to purchase it of the nat-

---

1. J.K.Hosmer (ed.) *J. Winthrop's Journal II* p.185. The pragmatism
of these arguments, the acceptance of the revolutionary doctrine of
salus populi, and the need for England's protection led the majority
of elders and magistrates not only into historical error (e.g. that
a parliamentary writ was more extensive than the Crown's) but to a dangerous argument for the future (e.g. that the burgesses for E. Greenwich'virtually represented'the colonists too). But they could still
employ the doctrine of *salus populi* against Parliament itself at
need.

ives or subdue it as *vacuum domicilium*, we are not bound
to hold that of him that was not his. But if we stand upon
this plea we must then renounce our patent and England's
protection which were a great weakness in us, seeing their
care had been to strengthen our liberties and not overthrow
them; and if the parliament should hereafter be of a malignant spirit *etc.*, then if we have strength sufficient we
may make use of *salus populi* to withstand any authority
from thence to our hurt....

    [They had already openly declared their affection to Parliament's
    cause.]
    It was objected by some that ours is *perfecta respublica*
and so not subject to appeals and consequently to no other
power, but among ourselves.[1] It was answered, that though
our patent frees us from appeals in cases of judicature,
yet not in point of state; for the King of England cannot
erigere perfectam respublicam in such a sense; for *nemo
potest plus juris in alios transferre quam in se habet:*
he hath not an absolute power without the parliament.[2]

230. *THE DEBATE OVER THE CHARACTER OF LAW AND GOVERNMENT:*
    (a) REMONSTRANCE AND PETITION OF DR. CHILD AND OTHERS TO THE GOV-
    ERNOR, ASSISTANTS AND DEPUTIES, 16 May 1646.[3]
    ...Whereas this place hath been planted by the incour-
agement, next under God, of letters patents given and granted by his Majesty of England to the inhabitants thereof,
with many privileges and immunities...Notwithstanding, we
cannot, according to our judgments, discerne a setled forme
of government according to the lawes of England, which may

---

1. This matter of appeals became a crucial issue later at the Restoration [see Nos.401 ff].
2. Thus in practice a passive benevolent neutrality on Parliament's
side in the Civil War was the policy adopted by the general court.
In 1644 they were exempted by Parliament from the payment of all English duties.
3. Prince Soc.Publ. *Hutchinson papers* (1865) I pp.216-0. Dr. Robert
Child, an ardent Presbyterian, an advocate of toleration and a friend
of the younger Winthrop, was concerned with the arbitrary aspects of
Massachusetts government. He and his associates attacked the local
élite who dominated church and state affairs as intolerant and tyrannical: they objected to the restriction of the franchise, the narrow-
ness of freemanship, and the want of English law as 'the enslavement
of freeborn Englishmen'.(J. Winthrop, *History* (1908) pp.297-0). Many
who paid taxes and performed military duties were debarred from citizenship. In asserting their right to appeal ·over the heads of the colonial government to the parliamentary authority, Child and his fellow
remonstrants (including Samuel Maverick who was the only freeman not
a church member) were not only denying the jurisdiction of the general
court (*ibid.*p.294) but they were invoking metropolitan supervision and
interference. The Massachusetts oligarchy feared a conspiracy to reduce the commonwealth to dependency on England: to question the authority of governor and assistants was clearly regarded as a crime.Child
was fined for the 'sin of Korah' (i.e. rebellion: *Numbers* XVI) and then

seem strange to our countrymen, yea to the whole world,
especially considering we are all English. Neither do
we so understand and perceyve our owne lawes or libertyes,
or any body of lawes here so established, as that thereby
there may be a sure and comfortable enjoyment of our lives,
libertyes, and estates, according to our due and naturall
rights, as freeborne subjects of the English nation. By
which, many inconveniences flow into plantations, *viz.*
jealousies of introducing arbitrary government, which
many are prone to beleeve, construing the procrastination
of such setled lawes to proceed from an overgreedy spirit
of arbitrary power (which it may be is their weaknes)
such proceedings being...at present a cheife cause of the
intestine warre in our deare country....

    [The scales of justice were 'unequally balanced': uncertainty
    caused fears and jealousies and meant the absence of 'a due and
    unbowed rule of law'.]

    Wherefore our humble desire and request is, that you
would be pleased to consider of our present condition and
upon what foundation we stand, and unanimously concurr to
establish the fundamental and wholesome lawes of our native
country,and such other as are no wayes repugnant to them,
unto which all of us are most accustomed; and we suppose
them best agreeable to our English tempers, and yourselves
obliged thereunto by the general charter and your oathes
of allegiance. Neither can we tell, whether the Lord hath
blest many of these parts with such eminent political
gifts, so as to contrive better lawes and customes than
the wisest of our nation have with great consideration
composed, and by many hundred yeares experience have found
most equal and just...And for the most strict and due
observation and execution of the said lawes by all the
ministers of justice, that there may be a setled rule for
them to walke by in all cases of judicature, from which
if they swerve there may be some power setled, according
to the lawes of England, that may call them to account for
their delingquences, which may be a good meanes to prevent
divers unnecessary appeales into England....

    We therefore desire that civil liberty and freedom be
forthwith granted to all truely English, equal to the rest
of their countrymen, as in all plantations is accustomed
to be done, and as all freeborne enjoy in our native country; (we hoping here in some things to enjoy greater liberties than elsewhere, counting it no small losse of liberty to be as it were banished from our native home, and
enforced to lay our bones in a strange wildernes) without
imposing any oathes or covenant on them, which we suppose
cannot be warranted by the letters patent, and seeme not
to concur with the oath of allegiance formerly enforced

---

he was seized and prevented from taking his petition to London
(*ibid.*pp.305,306,308,316,317) until the general court's agent, Edward
Winslow, had put their case. In the court's opinion Child and his associates had 'taken too much upon them' and 'meddled' in business not
theirs'.

on all, and later covenants lately imposed on many here present by the honourable houses of parliament, or at least to detract from our native country and lawes, which by some are stiled foreign, and this place termed rather a free state, than a colonie or corporation of England....

[All of them valued the privileges of their English heritage and glory that 'we may continue to write that we and ours are English'. They asked that they be not impressed, dispossessed, banished or taxed arbitrarily; and that 'no greater punishment be inflicted...than are allowed...by the laws of our native country'.]

230. (b). DECLARATION OF GENERAL COURT, 4 September 1646.[1]

...For our government itselfe, it is framed according to our charter, and the fundamental and common lawes of England, and carried on according to the same (takeing the words of eternal truth and righteousnes along with them, as that rule by which all kingdomes and jurisdict-ions must render account of every act and administration, in the last day) with as bare allowance for the dispropp-ortion between such an ancient, populous, wealthy kingdome, and so poore an infant thinne colonie, as common reason can afford....As for those positive lawes or statutes of England, which have been from tyme to tyme established upon the basis of the common law, as they have been or-dained upon occasions, so they have been alterable still upon occasions, without hazarding or weakening the found-ation, as the experience of many hundred yeares hath given proofe of. Therefore there is no necessity that our owne positive lawes (which are not fundamental) should be fra-med after the patterne of those of England, for there may be such different respects, as in one place may require alteration, and in the other not [2]....

[They protested their own lack of legal knowledge and skill, but set down in parallel columns the common laws and customs of England (beginning with Magna Carta) and the 'fundamentalls of Massachussetts', and how warranted by their charter.]

By this it may appeare that our politie and fundamentals are framed according to the lawes of England, and accord-ing to the charter; so that the petitioners (if they had not cast off all modesty) must needs be ashamed of this complaint, as also of those which follow, *viz.* arbitrarie government, the negative vote, illimited oaths, unjust taxes, illegal committments, etc. For the first we use to say, Rome was not built in a day:...Let them produce any colonie or commonwealth in the world, where more hath beene done in 16 yeares. Let them shew where hath beene more care and strife to prevent all arbitrarines, and to bring all judgments to a certaine rule, so far as may be. Let them confesse theire ignorance of the judicial pro-ceedings in England, or theire malice which setts them on,

---

1. *Hutchinson papers* (1865) I pp.226-7, 236.

to take up any thing to throw at us, though it cut theire
owne fingers, as the practise of England, (which they
would seeme so much to adhere unto) will most certainely
doe, if they looked into any of those courts of judicature
(except it be the common pleas) but especially the chauncery (which is the highest court of judicature) the court
of requests, the chauncery of the exchequer and of the
Dutchie, in which courts they are not tyed to the common
lawes or statutes of England, but doe judge arbitrarily
(*secundum aequum et bonum*) according to equitie....

230. (c) CHARGES MADE BY DR. CHILD AND OTHERS: ANSWERS AND REPLIES,
1646.[1]
  [Those who signed the Remonstrance were charged with false,
  scandalous and seditious allegations against the government of
  Massachusetts.]
...3. They charge us with manifest injury to a great part
of the people here, persuading them, that the liberties
and privileges in our charter belong to all freeborn Englishmen, inhabitants here; whereas they are granted only
to such as the governor and company shall think fit to
receive into that fellowship.
   4. They closely insinuate into the minds of the people,
that those now in authority do intend to exercise unwarr-
anted dominion and an arbitrary government, such as is
abominable to the parliament and that party in England,
thereby to make them slaves; and (to hide themselves)
they pretend it to be the jealousies of others, and
(which tends to stir up commotion) they foretel them of
intolerable bondage to ensue.
   5. They go about to weaken the authority of our laws,
and the reverence and esteem of them, and consequently
their obedience to them, by persuading the people, that
partly through want of the body of English laws, and partly through the insufficiency or ill frame of those we
have, they can expect no sure enjoyment of their lives
and liberties under them....
  [They had claimed to represent 'many thousands secretly discon-
  tended' with church discipline and civil government, who threatened to remove themselves to 'where they may live like Christians'.
  They had alleged that such a tyranny existed as made their brethren in England justly indignant. They had now appealed from the
  jurisdiction of this government - a proof of their disaffection.]
The answers of the accused and the replies of the General
Court.
Answer. To the fourth they answer as in their petition,
and a reason they give of their fear of arbitrary government is, that some speeches and papers have been spread
abroad for maintenance thereof, *etc.*, and that a body of
English laws have not been here established, nor any other
not repugnant thereto.

1. J.K.Hosmer(ed.) *Winthrop's Journal*, 'History of New England' (1908)
II pp.297ff.

Reply. To this it was replied, 1. That the constant care
and pains the court hath taken for establishing a body of
laws, and that which hath been effected herein beyond any
other plantation, will sufficiently clear our government
from being arbitrary, and our intentions from any such disposition ....
2. For the laws of England (though by our charter we are
not bound to them, yet) our fundamentals are framed according to them, as will appear by our declaration which is to
be published upon this occasion,[1] and the government of
England itself is more arbitrary in their chancery and
other courts than ours is, 3. Because they would make men
believe, that the want of the laws of England was such a
grievance to them, they were pressed to show, what laws of
England they wanted, and it was offered them, (before all
the assembly, who were desired to bear witness of it,) that
if they could produce any one law of England, the want
whereof was a just grievance to them, the court would quit
the cause, whereupon one of them instanced in a law used
in London, (where he had been a citizen,) but that was
easily taken away, by showing that that was only a bye-law,
or peculiar custom of the city, and none of the common or
general laws of England.
Answer. They answer negatively to the fifth, alleging that
they only commend the laws of England as those they are
best accustomed unto, etc., and therein they impudently and
falsely affirm, that we are obliged to those laws by our
general charter and oath of allegiance, and that without
those laws, or others no way repugnant to them, they could
not clearly see a certainty of enjoying their lives, liberties and estates, etc., according to their due natural rights, as freeborn English, etc.
Reply. To this it was replied, that they charge us with
breach of our charter and of our oaths of allegiance, whereas our allegiance binds us not to the laws of England any
longer than while we live in England, for the laws of the
Parliament of England reach no further,[2] nor do the king's
writs under the great seal go any further; what the orders
of state may, belongs not in us to determine. And whereas
they seem to admit of laws not repugnant, etc. , if by repugnant they mean, as the word truly imports, and as by the
charter must needs be intended, they have no cause to complain, for we have no laws diametrically opposite to those
of England, for then they must be contrary to the law of
God and of right reason, which the learned in those laws
have anciently and still do hold forth as the fundamental
basis of their laws, and that if any thing hath been otherwise established, it was an error, and not a law, being
against the intent of the law-makers, however it may bear
the form of a law (in regard of the stamp of authority set
upon it) until it be revoked....

---

1. See above pp. 352-3 [cf. pp.302-5]   2. Even when Parliament,
whose cause they 'affected', had just won the first civil war, they
were prepared to repudiate its authority.

[Dr. Child had attempted to prove] that we were subject to
the laws of England.   His argument was this, every corporation of England is subject to the laws of England; but
this was a corporation of England, *ergo*,. *etc.*,

To which it was answered, 1. That there is a difference
between subjection to the laws in general, as all that
dwell in England are, and subjection to some laws of state,
proper to foreign plantations, 2. We must distinguish between corporation within England and corporations of, but
not within, England; the first are subject to the laws of
England in general, yet not to every general law, as the
city of London and other corporations have divers customs
and by-laws differing from the common and statute laws of
England. Again, though plantations be bodies corporate,
(and so is every city and commonwealth) yet they are also
above the rank of an ordinary corporation,...

230. (d) ADVICE OF THE ELDERS ON THE REPLY TO THE COMMISSIONERS FOR
          FOREIGN PLANTATIONS, 4 November 1646.[1]
Concerning the question of our dependence upon England,
we conceive,

1. That as we stand in near relation, so also in dependence upon that state, in divers respects, *viz.* 1. We have
received the power of our government and other privileges,
derived from thence by our charter.2. We owe allegiance
and fidelity to that state. 3. Erecting such a government
as the patent prescribes and subjecting ourselves to the
laws here ordained by that government, we therein yield
subjection to the state of England. 4. We owe unto that

---

1.   J.K. Hosmer *ibid*.II pp.294-5 .   Opposition to the Massachusetts
oligarchy was particularly vocal in 1646. There was a questioning of
its competence under the charter (*ibid*. p.268) accompanied by demands
as 'freeborn subjects of England' for their liberties 'both in church
and commonwealth', for the law of England and even for liberty of conscience (p.274). Samual Gorton and others, who claimed that they were
being excluded from their lawful settlements in Narragansett Bay by the
Massachusetts government, petitioned Warwick, now governor in chief
and lord admiral, and his parliamentary Commissioners for Foreign
Plantations. Though Warwick had championed the Massachusetts Company,
their stern and arbitrary puritanism was losing his sympathy and in
May 1646 the commissioners ordered the governor and assistants to respect the rights of the Narragansett settlers (pp.333,334). This instruction raised the question 'in what relation we stood to the state of
England' (p.290). The assistants agreed that the charter was 'the foundation of our government', but some argued that since it derived from
England (as did their protection and naturalisation) and since it specified tenure as 'of East Greenwich', they were subordinate to Parliament; while others asserted that it granted absolute self-sufficient
and independent power just as Normandy and Gascony were independent
of the French government and the Hanse towns were of Germany, (p.291).
As for suing for a new charter from Parliament, it would not necessarily provide greater security and would grant more limited power as
in the Rhode Island patent of 1643 (see above pp.324-6). The question

state the fifth part of gold and silver ore that shall,
etc. 5. We depend upon the state of England for protection
and immunities of Englishmen, as free denization, *etc.*

2. We conceive, that in point of government we have
granted by patent such full and ample power of choosing
all officers that shall command and rule over us, of making all laws and rules of our obedience, and of a full and
final determination of all cases in the administration of
justice, that no appeals or other ways of interrupting
our preceedings do lie against us.

3. Concerning our way of answering complaints against
us in England, we conceive, that it doth not well suit
with us, now we are directly called thereto, to profess
and plead our right and power, further than in a way of
justification of our preceedings questioned, from the
words of the patent. In which agitations and the issues
thereof our agents shall discern the mind of parliament
towards us, which if it be propense and favorable, there
may be a fit season to procure such countenance of our
proceedings, and confirmation of our just power, as may
prevent such unjust complaints and interruptions, as now
disturb our administrations. But if the parliament should
be less inclinable to us, we must wait upon Providence
for the preservation of our just liberties ....

[4. They might recognise Warwick and the commissioners 'without
subjecting to them in point of our government'.]

230. (e) REMONSTRANCE OF THE GENERAL COURT TO THE COMMISSIONERS,
4 December 1646.[1]
[Petitions to the commissioners, by-passing the court were not
provided for in the charter and were therefore unlawful. The appeals of Child and his associates]
we have not admitted, being assured that they cannot stand

---

of the relationship with the realm, and any subjection to England
due to the 1629 charter was firmly answered by the court: the
charter had given them an absolute 'self-sufficiency' which excluded
need for 'a superior power, either general governor or *etc.* to compleat our government'. The petitioners had impugned 'the Christian
vigilancy' of church and government, asserting that by denying 'free-
born' rights to those not members of certain congregations they were
deprived of Englist law and enslaved under 'an arbitrary government'. The court repeated that they were not subject to Parliament's
law or writ when no longer in England:[see above p.354]. It was a
contempt to assert the charter gave them no more power than 'an ordinary corporation' of 'mechanic men': among Greeks and Romans 'colonies have been esteemed other than towns...for they have been the
foundations of great commonwealths'.The other question of how circumspectly they should reply to the commissioners and how far recognise
some supervisory jurisdiction was put to the church elders.
1. J.K.Hosmer, *History* II pp.309-15.Edward Winslow,a magistrate from
New Plymouth,was sent to London with this remonstrance and instructions
to answer Child's charges,and to resist the imposition of appeals and
of a parliamentary enquiry.Since he was able to arrive long before
Child, he obtained a favourable decision from the commissioners, if

with the liberty and power granted us by our charter, nor
will be allowed by your honors, who will know it would be
destructive of all government...if it should be in the
liberty of delinquents to evade the sentence of justice
and force us by appeal to follow them to England where the
evidence and circumstance of facts cannot be so clearly
held forth as in their proper place [as Parliament itself had
shown in excluding appeals to Rome.]   Beside, though we shall
readily admit the wisdom and experience of that Great
Council and of your honors as a part thereof are far more
able to prescribe rules of government and to judge of
causes than such poor rustics as a wilderness can breed
up, yet considering the vast distance between England and
these parts, your counsels and judgments could neither be
so well grounded nor so seasonally applied as might be so
useful to us [nor, if there were no interference, could England
be answerable 'in the Great Day of account' for their errors.]

231. ACT OF GENERAL COURT, 26 May 1647.[2]
    This corte, taking into consideration the usefull parts
and abilities of divers inhabitants amongst us which are
not freemen, which, if improved to public use, the affairs
of this commonwealth may be the easier carried an end, in
the severall townes of this jurisdiction, doth hereby declare that henceforth it shall and may be lawful for the
freemen within any of the said townes to make choyce of
such inhabitants, though non-freemen, who have taken or
shall take the oath of fidelity to this government to be
jury men, and to have their vote in the choyce of the selectmen for towne affairs, assessment of rates, and other
prudentials proper to the selectmen of the several towns;
provided still that the major part of all companies (of
selectmen be [ing] freemen) from time to time that shall
make any valide act, as also where no selectmen are to
have their vote in ordering of schooles, hearding of cattle, laying out of highwayes, and distributing of lands,

---

not on Gorton's settlement, at least on these two major matters of
the colony's immunity.
1.Though some part of Child's programme was secured in 1648 when,des-
pite the odd supporting scriptural texts, the *Body of Laws and Libertyes* was firmly based on the law of England:the delay of his mission to
London,and Winslow's advocacy there on behalf of the Commonwealth
meant that the Massachusetts government remained inbred,narrowly based and virtually independent.It negotiated directly with the French in
Acadia,coined its own money,and exercised what sovereign rights it
could, immune as it was from interference from England.In 1652
they enacted themselves into a 'free state': [see below p.360].
2.N.B.Shurtleff (ed.) *op.cit.*II pp.197.Since only church members,who
had taken the freemen's oath and been formally admitted as freemen,
could hold office and there were many more non-freemen than freeman,
it was necessary to spread the burden of official responsibility.This
reform was accordingly introduced. In the *Laws and Libertyes* the following year,non-freemen could attend court and town-meetings and present motions.They did not,however, have a general franchise or the
right to be elected to high office in the Commonwealth. In May 1658

any law, usage, or custome to the contrary notwithstanding;
provided also that no non-freeman shall have his vote untill he have attained the age of 24 years; provided also that
none that are or shalbe detected and convicted in any corte
of any evill carriage against the government, or commonwealth, or churches (it being intended to be immediately
done) shalbe capable to vote until the corte where he was
convicted or sentenced hath restored him to his former liberty.

232. THE CAMBRIDGE 'PLATFORM OF DISCIPLINE', August 1648.[1]

...Church government stands in no opposition to civil
government of commonwealths, nor any intrencheth upon the
authority of civil magistrates in their jurisdictions, nor
any whit weakneth their hands in governing, but rather
strengtheneth them and furthereth the people in yielding
more hearty and conscionable obedience unto them....

   [The kingdom of Christ and the government of princes 'both stand
   together and flourish, the one being helpfull to the other, in their
   distinct and due administrations'.]

The power and authority of Magistrates is not for the
restraining of churches, or any other good workes, but for
helping in and furthering thereof; and therefore the consent and countenance of magistrates when it may be had, is
not to be sleighted, or lightly esteemed; but on the contrary; it is part of that honour due to christian magistrates to desire and crave their consent and approbation
therein: which being obtayned, the churches may then proceed in their way with much more encouragement, and comfort....

   [Church officers and magistrates should not intermeddle in each
   other's affairs. Moses and David, both princes and prophets, were
   exceptional.]

   6. It is the duty of the magistrate, to take care of
matters of religion, and to improve his civil authority
for the observing of the duties commanded in the first,
as well as for observing the duties commanded in the second table.

   7. The objects of the powr of the magistrate, are not
things meerly inward, and so not subject to his cognisance
and view, as in unbeliefe, hardness of heart, erronious

this Act was somewhat modified, requiring non-freemen to be rated at
£20 estate (*ibid.* IV: p.336).
1. Printed in H.S.Commager (ed.) *Documents* (1947 ed.) p.30. Soon
after the challenge of Dr. Child's petition, William Vassall and others had renewed demands for the removal of civil disabilities suffered
by non-members of the church. The general court asked a synod of clergy to consider the drafting of a uniform plan of government and discipline and the relations of the civil and church authorities. This
statement of the close alliance of church and state, prepared at Cambridge in 1648, was not finally approved by the congregations and the
general court until 1651. In effect it confirmed the Massachusetts
theocracy and the full power of the magistrates to enforce the rule

opinions not vented; but only such things as are acted
by the outward man: neither is their powr to be exercised,
in commanding such acts of the outward man, and punishing
the neglect thereof, as are but meer inventions, and devices of men; but about such acts, as are commanded and
forbidden in the word; yea such as the word doth clearly
determine, though not always clearly the judgement of
the magistrate or others, yet clearly in it selfe. In
these he of right ought to put forth his authority, though
oft-times actually he doth it not.

    8. Idolatry, blasphemy, heresy, venting corrupt and
pernicious opinions, that destroy the foundation, open
contempt of the word preached, prophanation of the Lords
day, disturbing the peaceable administration and exercise
of the worship and holy things of God, and the like, are
to be restrayned, and punished by civil authority.

    9. If any church one or more shall grow schismaticall,
rending it self from the communion of other churches, or
shall walke incorrigibly or obstinately in any corrupt
way of their own, contrary to the rule of the Word; in
such case, the magistrate is to put forth his coercive
power, as the matter shall require. The tribes on this
side Jordan intended to make war against the other tribes,
for building the altar of witness, whom they suspected to
have turned away therin from following of the Lord.

233. MASSACHUSETTS INDEPENDENCE, 1652.[1]

    ...As a mark of sovereignty they coin money, stamped
with inscription Mattachusetts and a tree in the center
on the one side, and New England with the year 1652 and
the value of the piece on the reverse.

    All the money is stamped with these figures 1652, that
year being the aera of the commonwealth, wherein they enacted themselves into a free state, enlarged their dominions, subjected the adjacent colonies under their obedience and sommoned deputies to sit in the general court
which year is still commemorated on their coin....

(c) MARYLAND

234. COMMISSION TO GOVERNOR CALVERT, 4 September 1642.[2]

    And we doe further by these presents make constitute
ordeine and establish the said Leonard Calvert to be our
Chancellor Cheife Justice and cheife Magistrate within
our said province until we or our heires shall signifie
the contrary under our hand and seale; and we doe hereby
give him power from time to time to appoint and constitute

and judgements of their clergy in matters of morality, heresy and
freedom of thought and worship.

1. *Hutchinson papers II* (1865) pp.213-4. This statement to the Lords
of Trade in 1676 was in Edward Randolph's *Narrative*. Hutchinson commented that this was a misrepresentation: the money continued to be
coined, but the date was not altered.

2. W.H. Browne (ed.) *op.cit.* III p.110: the lord proprietor acting
as king.

officers and ministers for the administration and exequu-
tion of justice, and for doing and exequuting of all other
things whatsoever which belong to the establishing and government of a good and happy commonwealth within our said
province.

And we doe further by these presents grant unto him
our said Lieutenant Chancellor, Cheife Justice and cheife
Magistrate full and absolute power and authority when and
as often as he shall think fit to call and summon one or
more general assemblie or assemblies of the freemen of
our said province or their deputies at such place or places within our said province as he shall think fit, for
the consulting[1], preparing, and enacting of wholesome lawes
and ordinances for the government and well ordering of
the said province and people within the same to which
purpose we doe hereby grant full power and authority unto
our said Lieutenant General ...from time to time in every
general assembly to be summoned by him in the said Province of Maryland in our name, steed and place to give assent and consent unto all such lawes and ordinances as he
our said Lieutenant General, Chancellor, Cheife Justice, and
cheife magistrate shall think fit and necessary for the
good government of the said Province of Maryland, and
which shalbe consented unto and approved of by the freemen of the said province or the major part of them or
their deputies to be assembled by him the said Lieutenant
General...there from time to time for the enacting of
lawes within that province: Provided that the said lawes
so to be assented unto by him our said Lieutenant General
...there in our name be as neare as conveniently may be
agreeable and not contrary to the lawes of England.

235. ACT CONCERNING RELIGION, 21 April 1649.[2]

Forasmuch as in a well governed and Christian common
wealth matters concerning religion and the honor of God

---

1. This might seem to be a yielding of the proprietor's claim to sole
initiative. The assembly was asserting itself and the charter was in
danger in England from Parliament's growing strength, so some concession was politic. However Claiborne was soon to seize a chance of revenge and, with Richard Ingle, to reduce Maryland to disorder. Only
with the help of Governor Berkeley of Virginia was Leonard restored
to his governorship.
Though in practice both houses initiated legislation, the lord proprietor insisted for many years on his legal right: in his commission
to his son, Charles, in 1666 (*ibid.*XV p.10)general assemblies were
required to give 'advice' assent and approbation to laws ordained by
him and 'all such lawes or acts as you shall hereafter receive from
us'.
2. W.H. Browne, (ed.) *op.cit.*I pp.224-7. Though for a period the
Jesuits had been the only clergy in Maryland, toleration had existed
there in practice from the beginning. It was a policy to attract
settlers, but in 1648 Baltimore determined to secure his proprietory
from the charge of being a catholic colony and, in legislating toler-

ought in the first place to bee taken into serious consideration and endeavoured to bee settled: Be it therefore ordered and enacted by the Right Honorable Cecilius Lord Baron of Baltemore, absolute Lord and Proprietary of this province with the advise and consent of this General Assembly, That whatsoever person or persons within this province and the islands thereunto belonging shall from henceforth blaspheme God, that is curse him, or deny our Saviour Jesus Christ to bee the sonne of God, or shall deny the holy Trinity the father sonne and holy Ghost, or the Godhead of any of the said three persons of the Trinity or the unity of the Godhead, or shall use or utter any reproachfull speeches words or language concerning the said Holy Trinity, or any of the said persons thereof, shalbe punished with death and confiscation or forfeiture of all his or her lands and goods to the Lord Proprietary and his heires [1] ...

[Fines, imprisonment and banishment were punishments for blasphemy of the Virgin Mary and the apostles.

It was a punishable offence to reproach any other settlers as 'heretick, Scismatick, Idolator, puritan, Independent, Presbyterian, popish priest, Jesuite, Jesuited papist, Lutheran, Calvinist, Anabaptist, Brownist, Antinomian, Barrowist, Roundhead, Separatist' and to profane the Sabbath by disorderly recreation or work.]

And whereas the inforceing of the conscience in matters of religion hath frequently fallen out to be of dangerous consequence in those commonwealthes where it hath been practised, and for the more quiet and peaceable government of this province, and the better to preserve mutual love and amity amongst the inhabitants thereof. Be it therefore also by the Lord Proprietary with the advise and consent of this Assembly, ordeyned and enacted (except as in this present Act is before declared and set forth) that noe person or persons whatsoever within this province, or the islands, ports, harbors, creekes or havens thereunto belonging professing to beleive in Jesus Christ shall from henceforth bee any waies troubled, molested or discountenanced for or in respect of his or her religion nor in the free exercise thereof within this province or the islands thereunto belonging nor any way compelled to the beleife or exercise of any other religion against his or her consent, soe as they be not un-

_____

ation for the many puritan settlers, to protect the catholics also: he had firmly opposed making the Catholic Church the established one. He had recently had to recover his proprietory from the hands of Claiborne and others who sought to undermine his authority. He replaced a catholic governor by William Stone, a protestant supporter of the parliamentary cause, and sent out certain draft laws, including this one.
1. This harsh provision, added by the puritans in the assembly, seems never to have been enforced.

faithfull to the Lord Proprietary,or molest or conspire
against the civil government established or to bee established in this province under him or his heirs....
    [Penalties were prescribed for those who molest such professing
    Christians.][1]

236. ACT DIVIDING THE ASSEMBLY INTO TWO HOUSES, August 1649.[2]
    Be it enacted by the Lord Proprietor with the advise
and consent of the Counsell and Burgesses of this province
now assembled: That this present assembly during the continuance thereof bee held by way of Upper and Lower howse
to sit in two distinct roomes as part, for the more convenient dispatch of the busines therein to bee consulted
of....
        [Governor, councillors and secretary were to form the upper hou-
    se: the burgesses and clerk were to constitute the lower house.]
    And all bills that shall bee passed by the said two
howses or the major part of both of them, and enacted or
ordered by the Governor shall bee lawes of the province
after publicacion thereof, under the hand of the Governor
and the Great Seale of the said province as fully to all
effects in law as if they were advised and assented unto
by all the freemen of the province personally.

237. PROCEEDINGS OF THE ASSEMBLY, 10–11 April 1650.[3]
    (a) 10 April 1650.
    The Report was read and sent in to the Upper howse. The
Burgesses likewise delivered a petition to the Upper howse
by their Speaker, desyring vindication of their honors for
certaine harsh speeches uttered by Mr. Thomas Greene[4]
against them, taxing them with injustice for expelling Mr.
Thomas Mathews out of the howse, refusing to take the oath
of secrecy, and for their taking the said oath in that manner.
    Uppon debate of which it being conceived impertinent

---

1. The Act was passed in an assembly, possibly the majority of whom
were catholics.Between 1654 and 1658 when puritans were temporarily
in control, as parliamentary commissioners had successfully ousted
the authority of Baltimore and Governor Stone, the protection for catholics was withdrawn. But when Cromwell's council of state reported in
Baltimore's favour in 1656 and required the reenactment of this Act
concerning religion, the way was open for the restoration of the lord
proprietor and the revival of toleration.
2. W.H.Browne (ed.) *op.cit.*I pp.272–3. Until 1670 the assembly represented all freemen in the colony, not merely the freeholders. See Weston's Case *ibid.*I p.170.
3. W.H. Browne (ed.) *op.cit.*I pp.275–6. The Houses were debating a
report on the Body of Laws detailing the rights of the lord priorietor
and the liberties of the people.The Act concerned the'recognition' of
Baltimore's title, powers and jurisdiction by all freemen in the province.
4. As deputy governor in Stone's temporary absence,in November 1649
he had proclaimed Charles II without the wish or knowledge of Baltimore.

for the Burgesses to take the oath of secresy in the
Lower howse unlesse the same were likewise taken by the
Counsell in the Upper howse, which said order was brought
into the Lower howse *viz.* whether such members in the
Upper howse, refusing to take the oath of secresy, as
the Burgesses, shall have liberty or vote in the said
howse, and the howse assented that they should not have
vote or seate in the said howse, during the Assembly, unlesse they assent, and take such oath. And further that
once reading bee adjudged sufficient for such orders for
the speedy dispatch of the counties busines, notwithstanding the former order for 3 several readings *etc.* and the
Governor told the Speaker that hee should have an answer
of the petition the next day after the 2nd. vote uppon
that bill.

(b) 11 April 1650.
Touching the Act of Recognition now in dispute some
were of opinion that they could not passe it as a perpetual law, but for some time only. And have liberty to
repeale it, when they shall find their liberties or consciences infringed by it.[1]

238. (a) PETITION BY PARLIAMENTARY COMMISSIONERS AGAINST LORD
BALTIMORE 'S PATENT, 1656.[2]
The province of Maryland, in that state wherein it
stood under the Lord Baltimore's government, had more
need of reducing than any English plantation in America
for these reasons, *viz.*

1. The covenant, laws and platform of government established in England, declare the suppression and extirpat-
ion of popery, to which his Highness oath tends; but the
Lord Baltimore's government declared and swears the up-
holding and countenancing thereof, both by the officers
and people.

2. The Lord Baltimore exercised an arbitrary and tyrannical government, undertook a princely jurisdiction,

---

1. The puritans,gaining strength in the assembly, were already res-
tive also about the Toleration Act. In 1654 the assembly declared the
Act of Recognition null and void,and repealed the Toleration Act.
2. *Thurloe State Papers* (1742) V pp.482-6. Claiborne and Bennett as
commissioners had in March 1652 'reduced' Maryland to obedience to
Parliament's authority. But popular disapproval caused them to rein-
state Governor Stone and Baltimore forthwith instructed his governor
to reassert his proprietary rights: whereupon Claiborne and Bennett
again in 1654 deposed Stone.In January 1656 Baltimore complained to
Cromwell, and Bennett and Mathews (Claiborne having become secretary
of Virginia) presented these objections against his patent. After
consultation and deliberation in the council of state, Baltimore
was in November 1657 confirmed in his full powers as proprietor -
with nominally more absolute prerogatives than the king had exercised
at home: royal powers were acceptable if on a distant American frontier and not exercised by a Stuart.The following document [No.238 (b)]
detailed the objections.

stiles himself absolute lord and proprietor, constituted
a privy council, most of Papists,and rest sworn thereto.
This privy council must be the legislative power, that is
to put in execution, such laws, the laws which the Lord
Baltimore himself makes and imposeth; and he makes what
laws he pleaseth. The people are indeed called to assemblies, but have neither legislative power nor of judicature,
that being appropriated to the privy council or upper-house;
so that what is determined by them, admits of no reference
or appeal.
    3. The Lord Baltimore's grants of land are made to the
end that the grantees might be the better enabled to do
him and his heirs all acceptable service; for the tenure
is for all service to which they must all swear, before
they have any grants, without any relation to,or mention
of the supreme authority of England, either in this or
any thing else that passeth there....
    [Baltimore had issued writs in his own name. Charles Stuart was
    proclaimed king in Maryland. Baltimore had termed the parliament-
    ary 'reducement' rebellion, and had instructed his officials
    (including the governor) to disobey the commissioners, and carry
    on government in his name. His patent unjustly disseized Claiborne
    at Kent Island.]

238. (b) OBJECTIONS AGAINST LORD BALTIMORE'S PATENT, AND REASONS WHY
        THE GOVERNMENT OF MARYLAND SHOULD NOT BE PUT INTO HIS
        HANDS, 1656.
    1. By the patent he was to have no land, but such as
was uncultivated and inhabited by pagans only; but Maryland was inhabited, and part of it possessed and cultivated
by the English in Virginia, *viz.* the Isle of Kent and that
long before the name of Maryland was ever heard of.
    2. By the patent it is provided, that he made laws with
the advice and consent of the inhabitants and freemen; and
by the practice of the Lord Baltimore and his officers
there the people have no law, but what he allows and consents unto.
    3. He is enjoined to make laws agreeable to the laws of
England; but several of the laws made there were different
from and disagreeable to the laws here, as appears by the
report of the committee of the navy....
    [The oaths of fidelity to Baltimore, of 'recognition' of his
    powers and of defence of the free exercise for the catholic relig-
    ion were obstacles to Parliament's powers. The 'reduction' of 1652
    and the reinstatement of His Highness the Lord Protector's power
    in 1654 were narrated.]
    And it is humbly conceived, that his Highness will not
think fit to re-establish the Lord Baltimore in such an
absolute and unlimited power as he pretends there, for the
considerations, and for these further reasons *viz.*
    1. In respect of the dissatisfaction and malignancy of
the said Lord Baltimore and his governors from time to time
against the parliament and their interests namely, several
commissions gotten from the late king at Oxford, taking

Captain Ingle's ship, and tampering with the seamen, to
carry her for Bristol, which was then in the king's hands,
proclaiming Charles II *etc*.
   2. In respect of the many petitions and complaints of
the inhabitants of Virginia and Maryland against a popish
monarchical government, so contrary unto and so inconsistent with his Highness's interest and the liberty and freedom of his subjects; it being also contrary to the known
laws of this land, and particularly of the instrument or
platform of government.
   3. In order to peace and the common good of those
plantations which mainly consist in uniting and keeping
them under one government; whereby dissensions, quarrels
and cutting of throats, likely continually to arise between such near neighbouring plantations, will be prevented,
his Highness's authority (will be) established, trade
encouraged, the excessive planting of tobacco restrained,
so making way for more staple commodities, as silk etc.
to be raised; the running away of delinquents and persons
indebted from one place to another taken off, and the
whole strength the common enemy the Indian, or any other
enemy, the more readily conjoined upon all occasions;
besides that old, great, sad complaint of seducing the
poor ignorant Protestants, and Papists to bear rule over
the free-born subjects of this nation, will be likely
hereby in some measure to be taken off, and yet those
of the Popish persuasion not debarred of any lawful liberty and freedom either in relation to civil things, or
the exercise of their conscience.

(d) THE CARIBBEES - BARBADOS

239. RICHARD LIGON ON ISLAND GOVERNMENT, c.1650.[1]
   They governe there by the lawes of England for all
criminall, civill, martiall, ecclesiasticall and maritime
affairs. This law is administered by a governour and ten
of his councill, forr courts of ordinary justice in civill
causes which divide the land in four circuits; justices of
the peace, constables, churchwardens and tithing men: five
sessions in the year for tryall of criminall causes and
all appeals from inferior courts in civill causes, and all
appeals from inferiour courts in civill causes. And when
the governour pleases to call an assembly for the supream
court of all, for the last appeales, for the making of new
lawes, and abolishing old - according to occasions, - in

---

1. R. Ligon, *A true and exact history* (1657) pp.100-1. His observations relate to Barbados in the period between 1647 and 1650 when he
was there: he had come to the island with Modyford. Amid the confusion of grant, re-grant, claim and counter-claim in the Caribbean, the
proprietorship of Carlisle had been finally enforced in Barbados against his rivals. But in the feuding of factions there had been reigns
of terror and savagery in the island, and in the 1640s by claiming
a strict neutrality between king and Parliament and uncertain of the

the nature of the Parliament of England, and accordingly
consists of the governour as supream, his councill in the
nature of the peers, and two burgesses chosen by every
parish for the rest.[1] The island is divided into eleven
parishes. No tithes paid to the minister but a yearly allowance of a pound of tobacco upon an acre of every mans
land besides certain church-duties of marriages, christenings and burials.[2] A standing commission there was also
for punishing adultery and fornication, though rarely put
into execution.[3]

240. DECLARATION OF AUTONOMY BY LORD WILLOUGHBY, COUNCIL AND ASS-
                                 EMBLY, 18 February 1651.[4]
    The Lord Lieutenant-General, together with the lords
of this council and assembly, having carefully read over
the said printed papers, and finding them to oppose the
freedom, safety, and well-being of this island, have
thought themselves bound to communicate the same to all
the inhabitants of this island; as also their observation

---

fate of the proprietary after Carlisle's death Barbados virtually had
'home-rule'.
1. The first assembly had been called by Governor Hawley in 1639. It
consisted of 11 councillors and 24 representatives. Not till 1641 did
it claim any right to initiate.
2. Sugar was already a better and more profitable crop than tobacco
and within ten years was virtually the only staple and the medium of
payments. This resulted in considerable social and economic changes,
for tobacco could be produced successfully on small holdings, but sugar
seemed to require large plantations and abundant labour.
3. Some contemporary accounts would, however, seem to indicate that
they were rife. Ligon himself escaped being eaten by the crew on his
return to the debtor's prison in England.
4. Printed in N.D. Davis, *The Cavaliers and Roundheads in Barbados*
(1887) pp.197-200. This is their answer to the Act of Parliament of
30 October 1650 forbidding trade with Barbados, Virginia, Bermuda and
Antigua. The parliamentary commissioners under Warwick had in 1643
invited the inhabitants of the Caribbees to submit to Parliament: St.
Christophers had instead admitted the authority of the Earl of Marlborough in opposition to Parliament, while the rest of the islands
'remained at least neutral' (*Lords Journals* IX p.51). In Barbados in
1646 'a general declaration subscribed by every parish' had refused
any alteration of government until 'God shall be merciful unto us as
to unite the King and Parliament'. The proprietorship was virtually
nominal and the planters practically independent and self-governing
under Governor Bell. Both royalists and parliamentarian sympathisers,
appealing to the 'liberties of free-born Englishmen', were opposed to
inferference from England. Francis Lord Willoughby had taken lease of
the proprietary rights for 21 years from Michaelmas 1646 and, coming
to Barbados in May 1650 as the Earl of Carlisle's lieutenant, had proclaimed Charles II and thus placed the island in open revolt to the
Commonwealth Parliament. He had been granted 4% on all goods exported
by the merchants and 2% on those exported by the planters (C.O. 1/11
No.66). In January 1652 Willoughby capitulated to Ayscue's terms [see

and resolution concerning it, and to proceed therein after
the best manner, wherefore they have ordered the same to
be read publickly.

Concerning the abovesaid Act, by which the least capacity may comprehend how much the inhabitants of this
island would be brought into contempt and slavery, if the
same be not timely prevented.

First – They alledge that this island was first settled
and inhabited at the charges, and by the esspecial order
of the people of England, and therefore ought to be subject to the same nation. It is certain, that we all of us
know very well, that wee, the present inhabitants of this
island, were and still be that people of England, who with
great danger to our persons, and with great charge and
trouble, have settled this island in its condition, and
inhabited the same, and shall wee therefore be subject to
the will and command of those that stay at home? Shall
we be bound to the government and lordship of a Parliament
in which we have no representatives, or persons chosen by
us, as also to oppose and dispute all what should tend to
our disadvantage and harme? In truth, this would be a
slavery far exceeding all that the English nation hath
yet suffered. And we doubt not but the courage which hath
brought us thus far out of our own country, to seek our
beings and livelihoods in this wild country, will maintain
us in our freedoms; without which our lives will be un-
comfortable to us.

Secondly – It is alledged that the inhabitants of this
island have, by cunning and force, usurped a power and
government....

[If the inhabitants could have answered such allegation, they
would testify that] the government now used amongst us, is
the same that hath always been ratified, and doth every
way agree with the first settlement and government in
these places; and was given us by the same power and
authority that New England hold theirs; against whom the
Act makes no objection.

And the government here in subjection, is the nearest
model of conformity to that under which our predecessors
of the English nation have lived and flourished for above
a thousand years. Therefore we conclude, that the rule
of reason and discourse is most strangely mistaken, if the
continuation and submission to a right well- settled government be judged to be an usurping of a new power, and
to the contrarie, the usurpation of a new government be
held a continuation of the old.

Thirdly – By the above said Act all outlandish nations
are forbidden to hold any correspondency or traffick with
the inhabitants of this island; although all the antient
inhabitants know very well, how greatly they have been
obliged to those of the Low Countries for their subsist-

---

below pp.369–0].Daniel Searle was appointed governor, and Willoughby
was banished.

ence, and how difficult it would have been for us, without
their assistance, ever to have inhabited these places, or
to have brought them into order [but the islanders are 'dayly
sensible of their dependence upon the Dutch and for the cheapness of
their goods and in gratitude will never deny them freedom of commerce'.][1]

Fourthly - For to perfect and accomplish our intended
slavery, and to make our necks pliable for to undergo the
yoake, they got and forbid to our own countrymen, to hold
any correspondency, commerce,or traffick with us, nor to
suffer any to come at us, but such who have obtained particular licences from some persons....As likewise that no
inhabitants of this island may send home upon their own
account any island goods of this place, but shall be as
slaves to the Companie, who shall have the abovesaid licences, and submit to them the whole advantage of our labour and industry.

Wherefore, having rightly considered, we declare, that
as we would not be wanting to use all honest means for
the obtaining of a continuance of commerce, trade, and
good correspondence with our country, so wee will not
alienate ourselves from those old heroick virtues of true
English men, to prostitue our freedom and privileges, to
which we are borne, to the will and opinion of any one;
neither do we thinke our number so contemptible, nor our
resolution so weake, to be forced or persuaded to so
ignoble a submission, and we cannot think, that there are
any amongst us who are soe simple, and soe unworthily
minded, that they would not rather chuse a noble death,
than forsake their ould liberties and privileges.

241. ARTICLES OF CAPITULATION, 11 January 1652.[2]
    1. That a liberty of conscience in matters of religion
be allowed to all except such tenents as are inconsistent
to a civil government....
    2. That the courts of justice shall still continue and
all judgements and orders therein be valid until they be
reversed by the form of law.
    3. That no taxes, customs, imports, loans or excise
shall be laid, nor levy made on any of the inhabitants of
this island without their consent in a General Assembly....
    [No man was to be imprisoned or deprived of land or property

---

1. Later they were to affirm that such trade was indispensable and
to protest against the alternative, a monopoly in the English market,
as totally inadequate.
2. R.H. Schomburgk, *A history of Barbados* (1848) pp.280-3. These
articles of surrender (rendition) were agreed by Lord Willoughby and
the commissioners for the Commonwealth of England who included Modyford and Searle. Admiral Ayscue with his fleet had been sent to secure the submission of the royalist island and offered generous terms
to them.

'without the due proceedings according to the known laws of England and the statutes and customs of this island in the courts of
justice here first held'.   No one was to be compelled to go to
England to defend his title without consent of the General Assembly. An Act of Indemnity was to be passed by Parliament to pardon
all inhabitants and the Act of October 1650 declaring them 'traitors' would be removed from the records.   All inhabitants were to
have sequestered lands in the island and in England, Scotland and
Ireland restored.   A special provision guaranteed to Willoughby
the restoration of his lands in England, Surinam, Ireland and
Antigua, and in Barbados.[1]
   9. That all port-towns and cities under the Parliament's
power shall be open unto the inhabitants of this island in
as great a freedom of trade as ever, and that no companies
be placed over them, nor the commodities of the island be
ingrossed into private men's hands; and that all trade be
free with all nations that do trade and are in amity with
England....[2]
   19. That the government of this island be by a governor,
council and assembly, according to the ancient and usual
customs here: that the governor be appointed by the States of England, and from time to time received and obeyed
here, the council be by hime chosen, and an assembly by
a free and voluntary election of the freeholders of this
island in the several parishes; and the usual custom of
the choice of the council be represented by the commissioners to the Parliament of England, or to the Council of
State established by authority of Parliament, with the
desires of the inhabitants for the confirmation thereof
for the future....[3]

242. JOHN BAYES TO THE COMMITTEE FOR FOREIGN AFFAIRS, 4 February, 1653[4]
   Ther is a high faction carrieing on by persons in the

---

1. This article was broken when Willoughby was banished by an assembly,
elected under Ayscue's direction - for their Commonwealth loyalties.
2. Though Ayscue explained that this was subject to parliamentary limitation, the Barbadians interpreted the article literally, and, with
Searle's connivance, ignored Parliament's injunctions. They continued
to petition for repeal of the 'Navigation Act' claiming that if mother
country and dependency were indeed subject to one authority, then both
should have the same privileges and restrictions. If Barbados were an
integral part of the Commonwealth they had a right to enjoy the trade
with foreign nations which England had.
3. Parliament ratified these articles on 18 August 1652 .
4. C.O. 1/12 No.2 pp.7-8. Bayes, a notorious agitator, was not exactly an impartial witness. He had a grudge against the council and
assembly, for they had dismissed him as treasurer. Searle's commission from the parliamentary council of state did not delegate to him
the right of veto or the power to nominate councillors. A new commission in June 1653, however, granted him power to choose and control
his council.

Island of Barbadoes, who are nowe very prevalent, to lessen the power and authority of the governor, and to make that island...a free state (as they put it) to choose their owne governors, establish their owne laws, and to have a freedom of trade with any nation, whether in amity with England or not, this in my hearing quite oft bin pleaded.

As to the first for the choyce of their governor they use this argument, that every corporation in England has liberty to elect an annuall magistrate and why should not they have the same priviledge, sayeing that to appoint governors over them is not freedome but king-like.

To the second, being nowe of trade with the Dutch, they say their articles are not kept, which allowed...freedom of trade, and why should they not have trade as formerly considering the distance of the island from England, hence it cannot be supplyed at all times,[1] though this last yeare I affirme it was as well supplied by our owne nation with every thing as ever it was any time this twenty od yeares that I have known it.

These things frequently disputed will (if not prevented) in a short time alienate the affections of these people, from that due obedience which they are bound to yield to the supreme authority of this Comonwealth by so much acquiring the sole power in and amongst themselves, and are nowe at a great height, haveing constituted a kind of parliamentary power, and chosen themselves a speaker, and ...soe eclipst the governor's power, that at present he signifies little,only his title, haveing not the fifth part of that power which all former governors have had.

That your honours will please to consider it expedient to give the governor a latitude in his commission who is a prudent faithfull man, and one that doth endeavour to uphold yor interest as much as in him lyeth....

That you would pledge to continue him for some time, he is one well understanding the interest of that plantation and one who is well respected....

That he may, by your comission, be sole governor in that place and none other to cooperate with him in equal authority, while you are pleased to continue him there.

That he may be empowred to make any be of his council, and to comissionate all officers both civil and martial throughout the island, for as he is now...he can not remove any, though never soe ineffective, nor impower any, though of knowne faithfullness, without a full consent of those who challenge power with him....

243. COLONEL THOMAS MODYFORD TO JOHN BRADSHAW, 16 February 1653.[2]

...This place, Sir, hath now the happiness to have a

---

1. One crucial difficulty about the 'navigation system' as it developed was that there was not enough authorised shipping to carry all that the planters could produce.
2. C.O. 1/11 No.41. Many Barbadians desired one of themselves as gov-

share in your freedomes and the inhabitants are now fully
satisfied that they fought for their bondage and layd
downe their armes for their liberties...you knowing soe
well the nature of our country men, can best judge how
they ought to be governed, the same freedomes, the same
formes of government, the same friends, and the same enemyes you have, the same wee desire may be ours. The great
difficulty is...How wee shall have a representative with
you in your and our parliament. To demand to have burgesses with you to sit and vote in matters concerning England may seeme immodest, but to desire two representatives
to be chosen by this island to advise and consent to matters that concerne this place, I presume may be both
right and necessary, for if lawes bee imposed upon us
without our personal or implyed consent, wee cannot be
accounted better than slaves,which as all Englishmen
abhor to bee, soe I am confident you detest to have
them....

244. (a) GOVERNOR SEARLE TO THE COUNCIL OF STATE, 19 September 1653.[1]
     ...A demand was by the assembly of freeholders pres-
ented to mee, that a law maight here forthwith be made
by which this assembly of the people, styling them sellfs
the representative body of the Island of Barbadoes intrusted (say they) with this peoples lives, liberties,
and estates and of the government and authority of the
island, maight bee established and confirmed by a law for
one whole yeare, and so from time to time yearly successive representatives from each parish to be chosen by a
free and voluntary election of this people, theis new
representatives to sit before the old body be dissolved
(a power and authority which yet they never enjoied in
this littell island.)
     To which an answer was made. I know of noe other rep-
resentatives of the nation of England in what parte soe

ernor – not one (like Searle) appointed from England,   Thomas Modyford, who had been a royalist moderate, was ambitious for the post,
ingratiated himself with Bradshaw the regicide, became speaker of
the assembly in 1654, and intrigued to have Searle recalled. Only
in April 1660 did he obtain the appointment from the council of
state. But his triumph was short-lived. Charles II discarded him
and made a compromise agreement with Willoughby as governor, but
not proprietor.
1. C.O. 1/12 No.12. pp.29–30. Empowered with his new commission,
Searle had failed to secure a majority in the new assembly: indeed
there were too few 'Commonwealth men' to run the government. The
Barbadian home-rule (or 'free state') party, encroaching further on
the governor's powers, now demanded a permanent representative government. The assembly was now making taxes available only for short
periods,was controlling and scrutinising appropriations and contracts
(especially in public works by sub-committees), and appointing the
treasurer.

ever of the Comon wealth they are in intrusted with the
lives, liberties, and estates of the peoples, but the supreame authority which God had established and sett over
them, and that I should not by any power in my comission
without betraying that great trust comitted unto mee, give
up the interest of the state in this island into the hands
of an assembly of the people...by a law to constitute them
a body or representative with the peoples lives, liberty
and estates, which if so I humbly conceive were in effect
to establish them a free state independant to the Comonwealth only to remaine under Englands protection, but not
to owne England's jurisdiction....The usual custome in
haveing the freehoulders, two from a parish, as an assembly called when any law...regulating this collony is necessary to be made, is still amongst us and, haveing concluded on what was necessary to be donn, are dismissed.
But some restless and unquiet spirits, I doubt unsattis-
fied with the constitution of England's government (who
are heare amongst us) would model this littel limbe of the
Comonwealth into a free state of themsellfe, since they
cannot be what otherwise they would be ....

[Those who had sent to England a remonstrance against the assembly were threatened by them with dismissal from public employment. The assembly would also seek control of the militia. The
governor had accordingly dissolved them.]

244. (b) PETITION FROM THE ASSEMBLY TO THE LORD PROTECTOR,
September 1653.[1]

Wee humbly pray...That, in regard wee are English men
of as clear and pure extract as any, wee may enjoy our
part of liberty and freedome equal with the rest of our
country-men, and bee made proportionable sharers of all
those blessings which our good God by you his instrument
hath bestowed on our nation.

2. That noe misinformation (which some bold insinuating
persons at this distance may attempt to give you) may induce your Excellency to receive any other character of
our hearte than what appeares in this our address...

3. That your Excellencies protection against all forraigne foes may bee extended to us, and wee included in
all leagues and treaties which your Excellencie shall
contract with forraigne states.

4. That...you would please to enjoyne all persons which
are or shall be entrusted by you here precisely to observe
our articles and allow us the freedomes and liberties
thereby given us, and equally to distribute justice according to the rule of the knowne lawes of our nation....

1. C.O. 1.12 No.12 (11) pp.33-4. Searle and his council had considered the petition and asked the assembly to give details of their
complaints: what privileges had not been enjoyed, what injustices
committed or not redressed, what articles of the island's surrender
had not been respected. No reply is recorded.

245. GOVERNOR SEARLE TO THE LORD PROTECTOR, 1 June 1655.[1]
...Dureing the time of General Venables being heare,
came to my hands a pattent from your Highnes;...which haveing communicated to the councell and assembly of freeholders of this island, much allackraty and demonstrations
of chearfull obedience to your Highnes and to the power
and authority therein given appeared in them, as allsoe
for that your Highnes was therein pleased to confirmed
unto them theire former and ancient priviledge for the
election of free-holders, as the representative of this
island, to give theire consents heare, in the makeing such
constitutions, ordinances, and by-lawes (not repugnant to
the lawes of the commonwealth) as may be thought fit for
the good and well-being of this collony....
   By former commissions and powers to mee given, as well
from your Highnes as from the Parliament, the former supreame authority, I have exercised the government of this
place from the time of its surrender, as well in the military as civil authority...and doe humbly judge and conceive your Highnes commands on mee by vertue of saide pattent is of noe lesse extent....
      [Unfortunately General Venables claimed authority over the island
      militia, granted his own commissions under collateral powers from
      Cromwell, and made void all those granted by the governor. The
      division of civil and military authorities had caused disputes. A
      meeting of councillors and freeholders had requested that since
      the direction of their defence was an internal Barbadian matter,
      the management of the militia should be settled in Barbados 'as
      from the first settlement of this collony hath bin donne'.]
   It is humbly conceived, your Highnes pattent to my
sellfe and councell chosen, is full and ample authority
and power for us to continue to act by, as well in the
military as to the civil authority.

246. THOMAS MODYFORD TO THE LORD PROTECTOR, 20 June 1655.[2]
   We hear by a letter from Middleton, that the king of

1. *Thurloe State Papers* (1742) III pp.499-500. Cromwell's Western Design was very unpopular in Barbados. Venables' army had consumed provisions, confiscated arms and recruited nearly 4000 servants and labourers:
a new rival sugar colony was feared. Furthermore Venables,by appropriating the excise duties, virtually imposed a special tax on the Barbadians since such duties were normally sufficient for public expenses.
A new commission from Cromwell had just arrived, appointing Searle for
three more years; and Searle, with support of council and assembly,
voiced the discontent with a divided civil and military authority. They
further demanded of Cromwell that 'our government be under no command,
but immediately his'. They knew of course that he had no time free to
manage all the business of Barbados,but wanted to be left to rule themselves without interference by any of his appointed deputies. Modyford
had written fulsomely to Cromwell in support of the Venables expedition, setting out his reasons against burdening Cromwell with all executive decisions for Barbados (*ibid*. III pp.565-6).It was fitting that
he should be appointed governor of Jamaica at the Restoration.
2. *Thurloe State Papers* III pp.565-6. (1742).

Spain is gone to St. Lucar, and is forming a great army
and fleet for these parts. Truly, if he should attempt
Barbados, he will find us in an unsettled condition; for
though we have men enough, and some number of horse, and
they pretty well armed, yet they want conduct, and a mind
to reduce us to unity; such ugly divisions are nourisht
and underhand fomented amongst us, that you would, were
you here, wonder at it; and all grounded upon that malicious apprehension they have against this settlement in the
Indies, fearing (forsooth) it will make sugar cheap, and
thin this island of people, which when the wood is gone
(and that cannot be very long first) must fall of itself.
From hence the militia fixt and settled by the commissioners is opposed, and levies and perfection of it infin-
itely impeded, upon pretence that none but their own governor must appoint their militia, and that not without
consent of the assembly, that his power and authority is
eclipsed by this way. These have a party in the assembly,
and there voted Bayes(the old firebrand) to go home with
a petition to his Highnes, chiefly desiring that our governor may receive orders from no man but immediately from
his Highness, against which Francis Raynes, William Vassall, Peter Kent and myself have drawn our dissent, and
shewed our reasons, and do hope they will prevail. The
party is so much countenanced, that the governor's council have joined with them. One of them told John Colliton,
the reason was, because General Venables said, they were
a company of geese. I know no way to help this evil, but
some smart orders from his Highness, confirming what his
commissioners have done, requiring a strict obedience to
it.
    Since the writing of the above we have met in the ass-
embly; and being they could not carry their petition, and
desires as they would, they made a motion, that the assembly had sat long enough, being twenty two months, and
therefore desired the governor would dissolve it, which
(every man being willing of his ease) was consented to,
and the desire allowed of by the governor; so as now
there is no assembly in the Barbados. I thought good
to enclose a copy of our reasons.
    Reasons why we whose names are underwritten cannot
consent to the instruction and desire, whereby his Highness is to be requested, that no commands should be laid
on our governors, but such as come immediately from himself.
    1. Because they think it unfit to circumscribe or limit
the supreme magistrate in a matter of so great a consequence, and so high a nature as this is, *viz.* to confine
him to a single person, seeing his liberty and undoubted
prerogative is to employ whom God shall please to direct
him....
    2. [He should not be restricted from employing such men as the
occasion should require.

3. His Highness could not dispatch all business himself, therefore must delegate to others.]
4. The subscribers conceive that this will be looked on
rather as a bold capitulation, than as an humble request;
and so may be a means to give his Highness displeasure,
whereby a jealousy may be begot to the bringing of some
curb on this place.
5. This will be a great hinderance to his Highness's
affairs in these parts,in begetting some difficulties in
procuring the assistance, which we may without prejudice
yield to his Highness's ministers; and therefore to prevent the great prejudice, which this desire may bring on
this country, they, according to the trust reposed in them,
utterly dissent from the same; thereby desiring to be adjudged free of the ill consequences of the same. In witness whereof they have hereunto set their hands.
The dissolving the assembly hindred the progress of this
debate; but I believe they will find such an one as will
agree to send it; for I find them so much inclined, that
I am resolved not to be of it.

247. PETITION OF THE ASSEMBLY TO PARLIAMENT, 11 December 1659.[1]
1. That wee may enjoy and have confirmed...by a law
etc: antient libertys, priviledges, customes, constitutions, and laws, fixed in the primary settlement and wherein our...interests are onley dependant, together with, our
articles made on the Rendition of this Island, to this
authority according to a letter from the Council of State,
dated the 14th of October 1652.
2. That no offices whatsoever relating to this Island
(except the Governor) may be imposed on us, by gift, grant,
patent, commission, or otherwise, howsoever, but bee and
remaine to the government here, to bee nominated, chosen
and dependant thereon,...
3. That in case wee may be thought worthy to be obliged
by any principal freedome you may reasonably condiscend
unto: that we may have a confirmation of liberty here (by
a law, or your commission) for the representative body of
the people to choose a governor out of the freeholders of
this island and one out of every parish to bee his assistant and joyne with him in the execuson of government: and
in case of the governor's death to elect a new governor
and councill, or if otherwise that the representation of
this island may bee expressed and nominated in your commission to be a parte of the government joyntly and equall
with the governor.
4. That in regard the generality of the people here, are
poore and the necessary defense of this place is required
in this remote parte, might exhaust the very uttmost gaine
and profit of theire labours, that all fines, mulcts, amercements., fellons goods, forfeitures, whatsoever may bee
and remaine to the disposing of the government here, for

1. Egerton MSS 2395 p.182. The resignation of Richard Cromwell and the
recall of the Rump encouraged the Barbadian home-rulers to press their

publicke and necessary use to the defense of the place.

5. That in regard wee are English Men, and should bee reputed to the Comonwealth, no other than as one of her ports (as of Bristol to London) that all customs on goods exported, from England to this colony may bee taken of, and that wee may bee enfranchised with all trade generally, equal with any people of England. And that no monopolizes, companyes, societyes, or other incroachments bee continued or permitted in any trade relating to this island, but in regard the necessary existence of this place requires some more than ordinary freedome in order to its producton. That all nations in amity may bring us provisions, servants, horses, slaves, mares, or cattle, whether of theire growth, or not, and that the Act made in October 1650 restrayning all manner of trade with us bee repealed.

6. That forasmuch as great prejudices have befallen us, by the presumptiousnes and refractiousness of comanders of men or war, victuallers, and other vessells , that it bee confirmed to us that all comanders of shipps arriving here may conform to the lawes and customes of this place, by entry of bonds, not to carry of any debitors, servants, slaves, but submit to the government here, on seizures or other business here transacted, as finally as at any port of England.

7. That in all treatyes forraingne, this colony may bee comprized...that all advantages may attain to us as a good member of the Comonwealth, equal with other the partes, or people of the English nation.

8. That the government here, by governor, councel and assembly may have power to make such necessary lawes for the good of this place and people, as intrench not, or repugne any penal law, or statutes of this nation, or derogatory to this authority and government of the Comon wealth of England.

9. That wee may have power to appoint a little minthouse within this island for coyning of money, equal with New England and Jamaica, and to raise all forreigne money.

10. That you will be pleased to accept these our desires as singly fouoht for, in reference to the best and real good of this island, and not out of any disrespect to the person of our governor, at present confirmed over us, whose integrity to your Honours hath beene ever very eminent amongst us.

248. COMMISSION TO THOMAS MODYFORD FROM THE COUNCIL OF STATE,
24 April 1660.[1]
...We doe by these presents give and grant unto the

---

claims. But, if this petition was ever presented, the Long Parliament was now so close to dissolution that it was never considered.
1. C.O. 31/1 pp.13-14. Though the right of electing a governor was not granted, Modyford was a planter governor and the council itself was now to be elective, each parish selecting a member. But such a

said Collonell Thomas Modiford full power and authority
from time to time at his pleasure to choose such and soe
many fit and discreet persons as to him shall seem expedient (not exceeding the number of ten) to bee at his Councell, and to bee assistant to him in the execution and
discharge of the trust hereby reposed in him the said
Collonell Thomas Moddyford and wee doe further by these
presents give and grant power and authority unto him the
said Collonell Thomas Moddyford and his Councell and assistants by and with the advice and consent of the freeholders of the said isle or islands, or their representatives being in that behalfe, and for such purpose duely
chosen according to the course and manner of eleccon as
hath been used and practised there, to make and ordeyne
such reasonable constitucons, ordinances and by lawes, not
repugnante to the lawes of England, as to them shall seem
meet, for the better peaceable, and quiet government of
the people of the said isle or islands....

(3) CONSOLIDATION IN COLONIAL SELF-GOVERNMENT

(a) NEW ENGLAND

249. ARTICLES OF CONFEDERATION BETWEEN MASSACHUSETTS, NEW PLYMOUTH,
   CONNECTICUT AND NEW HAVEN, 19 May 1643.[1]
   Whereas we all came into these parts of America, with
one and the same end and ayme, (namely, to advance the
Kingdome of our Lord Jesus, and to enjoy the liberties
of the Gospel,) in purity with peace; and whereas in our
settling we are further dispersed upon the sea-coasts,
and rivers, than was at first intended, so that we cannot

---

new constitution was still-born. On 4 April the exiled Charles had
already made the Declaration of Breda; on 25 April the newly-elected
Parliament met; and within a month Charles II was back in England.On
hearing of the Restoration, Modyford remembered his royalism and proclaimed the king. It was too late to secure his governorship in Barbados.
1. W. MacDonald (ed.) *op.cit.*pp.94-101. This remarkable experiment
in closer association, the New England Confederation, had some success in the middle years of the century. Though a few meetings of commissioners were held until the cancellation of the Massachusetts
charter in 1684, its effectiveness ceased with the Restoration. But
even in the 'forties and 'fifties, it was too loose a union of unequals; Massachusetts with superior resources being able virtually
to veto decisions of the other confederates, and even to impose duties on their goods. The idea of such a confederation had been raised
in a synod at Newtown (Cambridge) in 1637, partly in emulation of the
Dutch United Provinces, partly in fear of Dutch expansion and Pequot
belligerence, partly in suspicion of the plans of Gorges and the king.
It was to be a league of mutual help 'a consoliation' - wherein the
general courts of the colonies retained all powers and were subject
to no new supreme authority. Mutual jealousies, however, frustrated

(according to our desire) with convenience communicate in
one government and jurisdiction; and whereas we live en-
compassed with people of severall nations[1], and strange
languages, which hereafter may prove injurious to us, and
our posterity: And forasmuch as the natives have formerly
committed sundry insolences and outrages upon severall
plantations of the English, and have of late combined
against us,[2] And seeing by reason of the said distractions
in England, which they have heard of, and by which they
know we are hindred both from that humble way of seeking
advice, and reaping those comfortable fruits of protection
which, at other times, we might well expect, We therefore
doe conceive it our bounden duty, without delay, to enter
into a present Consotiation amongst our selves, for mutuall help and strength in all our future concernments, that,
as in nation, and religion, so in other respects, we be,
and continue, One, according to the tenour and true meaning of the ensuing Articles.
     I. Wherefore it is fully agreed and concluded by and
between the parties, or jurisdictions above named, and
they doe joyntly and severally by these presents agree
and conclude, That they all be, and henceforth be called
by the name of, *The United Colonies of New England.*
     II. The said United Colonies for themselves, and their
posterities doe joyntly and severally hereby enter into
a firm and perpetuall league of friendship and amity, for
offence and defence, mutuall advice and succour, upon all
just occasions, both for preserving and propogating the
truth, and liberties of the Gospel, and for their own mutual safety, and wellfare ....
     [The several colonies should retain each its 'peculiar juris-
     daction'. No new plantation should be admitted to the Confederat-
     ion, 'nor shall any of the confederates joyne in one jurisdiction
     without consent of the rest.'][3]
     IV. It is also by these Confederates agreed, That the
charge of all just wars, whether offensive, or defensive,
upon what part or member of this Confederation soever they
fall, shall both in men, provisions, and all other disbursements, be born by all the parts of this Confederation,

---

successful negotiations for six years. Though Rhode Island in 1644
and 1648 requested admission, it was refused unless the island accepted merger with Massachusetts or New Plymouth.
1. Notably the Dutch and the French.
2. The ruthless policy of Connecticut towards the Pequot Indians in
1637 had increased the danger of a counter-attack.
3. In May 1662 the royal charter for Connecticut, however, included
the territory of New Haven without such consent. It was two and a
half years before the general court of New Haven accepted its fate
and capitulated to its absorption - 'as from a necessity brought upon
us' - by Connecticut. By then the stubbornly exclusive theocracy of the
New Haven general court was becoming unpopular and many preferred the
'Christless' rule of Connecticut under the grant of the new liberal
charter.

in different proportions, according to their different
abilities... [and to the numbers of the male populations between
sixteen and sixty years old.]

V. It is further agreed, That if any of these jurisdictions, or any plantation under, or in combination with
them, be invaded by any enemy whomsoever, upon notice,
and request of any three magistrates of that jurisdiction
so invaded. The rest of the Confederates, without any further meeting or expostulation, shall forthwith send ayde
to the Confederate in danger....

[Massachusetts, providing 100 armed men, the other 45 each-until
the commissioners for the confederation met to assess the need.
Each plantation was to appoint two commissioners,and if six of
the eight did not agree on any matter, then the issues were to be
referred back to the several general courts. Commissioners were
to meet, apart from extraordinary meetings, once a year in September in turn at Boston, Hartford, New Haven and Plymouth. They
should appoint a president from among themselves. He was not to
be invested with any special power of vote or veto.]

VIII. It is also agreed, That the Commissioners for
this Confederation hereafter at their meetings, whether
ordinary or extraordinary, as they may have Commission or
opportunity, doe endeavour to frame and establish agreements and orders in generall cases of a civil nature, wherein all the plantations are interested, for preserving
peace amongst themselves, and preventing (asmuch as may
be) all occasions of war, or differences with others,
as about the free and speedy passage of justice in each
jurisdiction to all the Confederates equally, as to their
own, receiving those that remove from one plantation to
another, without due certificates, how all the jurisdictions may carry it towards the Indians, that they neither
grow insolent, nor be injuried without due satisfaction,
least war break in upon the Confederates, through such
miscarriages....[1]

[Commissioners were also to concern themselves with the return of
runaway servants, fugitive offenders, Indian affairs and judicial
proceedings. Any breach of these articles by any of the confederates would be considered by the commissioners for the others, so
that the confederation might be preserved.][2]

250. NEW HAVEN: FRAME OF GENERAL GOVERNMENT FOR THE UNITED TOWN-
SHIPS, 27 October 1643.[3]

[Save in the exceptional case of Milford, only members of one
of the approved churches in New England might be burgesses, or

---

1. The commissioners were thus a legislative and executive body with
equality in voting for each of the confederate colonies. In New Haven
and New Plymouth the governor was one of the two commissioners.
2. Since the representatives of New Plymouth lacked authority to sign
the articles,ratification by that colony did not take place until the
commissioners' first meeting in September 1643.
3. *New Haven Colonial Records* I pp.112-6. The proliferation of townships from New Haven and the admission of New Haven to the New England
Confederation (see pp.378-0) prompted this reorganisation of the gov-

vote, or hold office. Elected magistrates in the several town
courts would judge by majority vote, minor civil and criminal
cases. Appeals 'would be heard by the Court of Magistrates for
the whole jurisdiction'.]

3. All such free burgesses through the whole jurisdiction, shall have vote in the election of all magistrates,
whether Governor, Deputy Governor, or other magistrates,
with a Treasurer, a Secretary and a Marshall, *etc.*, for
the jurisdiction....

['For the ease of those free burgesses, especially in the remote
plantations', proxy votes sealed up in their presence might be
counted.]

4. All the magistrates for the whole jurisdiction shall
meete twice a yeare att Newhaven, namely, the Munday immediately before the sitting of the two fixed Generall Courts
hereafter mentioned, to keep a Court called the Court of
Magistrates, for the tryall of weighty and capitall cases,
whether civill or criminall, above those lymitted to the
ordinary judges in the particular plantations, and to receive and try all appeales brought unto them from the aforesaid Plantation Courts, and to call all the inhabitants,
whether free burgesses, free planters or others, to account for the breach of any lawes established, and for other misdemeanours, and to censure them according to the
quallity of the offence....

[Four would constitute a *quorum*. Absentees would be fined. Appeals
from the Court of Magistrates would be to the General Court.]

5. Besides the Plantation Courts and Court of Magistrates, their shall be a Generall Court for the Jurisdiction,
which shall consist of the Governor, Deputy Governor and
all the Magistrates within the Jurisdiction, which Deputyes shall from time to time be chosen against the approach
of any such Generall Court, by the aforesaid free burgesses,
and sent with due certifficate to assist in the same, all
which, both Governor and Deputy Governor, Magistrates and
Deputyes, shall have their vote in the said Court. This
Generall Court shall alwayes sitt att Newhaven (unless upon
weighty occasions the General Court see cause for a time
to sitt elsewhere) and shall assemble twice every yeare,
namely, the first Wednesday in Aprill, and the last Wednesday in October, in the later of which Courts, the Governor,
and Deputy Governor and all the magistrates for the whole
jurisdiction with a Treasurer, a Secretary and Marshall,
shall yearely be chosen by all the free burgesses before
mentioned, besides which two fixed courts, the Governor,
or in his absence, the Deputy Governor, shall have power

---

ernment of the New Haven plantations and the superimposition of a
colonial jurisdiction over the towns. Previously the general court in
New Haven was a town meeting of 'admitted' free burgesses. In future
it was the representative body, partly judicial but predominantly legislative, for a loose confederation of the townships of New Haven,
Guilford, Milford, Stamford, Southold and Branford.

to summon a Generall Court att any other time, as the
urgent and extraordinary occasions of the jurisdiction
may require, and att all Generall Courts, whether ordinary or extraordinary, the Governor and Deputy Governor,
and all the rest of the magistrates for the jurisdiction,
with the Deputyes for the severall plantations, shall sitt
together, till the affayres of the jurisdiction be dispatched or may safely be respited...which Generall Court,
shall, with all care and dilligence provide for the maintenance of the purity of religion, and shall suppress
the contrary, according to their best light from the
worde of God, and all wholsome and sound advice which
shall be given by the elders and churches in the jurisdiction, so farr as may concerne their civill power to deale
therein.
    Seconly, they shall have power to mak and repeale
lawes, and, while they are in force, to require execution of them in all the severall plantations.
    Thirdly, to impose an oath upon all the magistrates,
for the faithful discharge of the trust comitted to them,
according to their best abilityes, and to call them to
account for the breach of any lawes established, or for
other misdemeanors, and to censure them, as the qullity
of the offence shall require.
    Fowerthly, to impose and [an] oath of fidelity and due
subjection to the lawes upon all the free burgesses, free
planters, and other inhabitants, within the whole jurisdiction.
    5ly to settle and leivie rates and contributions upon
all the severall plantations, for the publique service
of the jurisdiction.
    6ly, to heare and determine all causes, whether civill
or criminall, which by appeale or complaint shall be orderly brought unto them from any of the other Courts, or
from any of the other plantations, In all which, with
whatsoever else shall fall within their cognisance or
judicature, they shall proceed according to the scriptures, which is the rule of all righteous lawes and sentences, and nothing shall pass as an act of the Generall
Court butt by the consent of the major part of magistrates, and the greater part of Deputyes.[1]

1. But amid the encircling ambitions of the Dutch and of rival New
Englanders in Massachusetts and Connecticut, the attempt to expand
on the Delaware exhausted the resources of New Haven. Hemmed in and
failing to develop as a trading and shipping centre, the colony did
not prosper: indeed, Cromwell tried to persuade the settlers to mig-
rate to Ireland or Jamaica. When Connecticut received a royal charter in 1662, the colony of New Haven was too poor to send an agent
to plead its cause and the confederation began to break up, Branford
alone remaining with the township of New Haven to the end. Connecticut demanded the submission of New Haven and, as a result of the
grant of New Amsterdam in 1664 to the Duke of York and the dispatch
of a royal commission of inquiry into the New England governments,

251. FEDERATION OF RHODE ISLAND TOWNSHIPS, 21 May 1647.[1]
    [A majority of the plantations of Providence being present, the
    assembly had full 'power to transact'.]
    Forasmuch as we have received from our noble lords and
honoured governors, and that by virtue of an ordinance of
the Parliament of England, a free and absolute charter of
civil incorporation, *etc.*, we do jointly agree to incorporate ourselves, and so to remain a body politic by the authority thereof, and therefore do declare to own ourselves
and one another to be members of the same body, and to
have a right to the freedom and privileges thereof by subscribing our names to these words, following:
    We, whose names are hereunder written, do engage our-
selves to the utmost of our estates and strength, to maintain the authority and to enjoy the liberty granted to us
by our charter, in the extent of it according to the letter, and to maintain each other by the same authority, in
his lawful right and liberty.
    And now since our charter gives us power to govern
ourselves and such other as come among us, and by such a
form of civil government as by the voluntary consent, etc.,
shall be found most suitable to our estate and condition.
    It is agreed, by this present assembly thus incorporate,
and by this present act declared, that the form of government established in Providence Plantations is democratical;
that is to say, a government held by the free and voluntary consent of all, or the greater part of the free inhabitants.
    And now to the end that we may give, each to other (not-
withstanding our different consciences, touching the truth
as it is in Jesus, whereof, upon the point we all make mention) as good and hopeful assurance as we are able, touching each man's peaceable and quiet enjoyment of his lawful
rights and liberty, we do agree unto, and by the authority
above said, enact, establish, and confirm these orders
following.
                    Touching Laws
    1. That no person in this colony shall be taken or im-
prisoned, or be disseized of his lands or liberties, or be
exiled, or any other otherwise molested or destroyed, but

New Haven was, following a vote in its general court, absorbed by
Connecticut in January 1665.
1. J.R. Bartlett (ed.) *op.cit.* I pp.156–160. A general assembly was
called at Portsmouth to organise a government and draw up a body of
laws under the 1644 patent. It was composed of freemen from four towns
(Warwick now being included and Pawtuxet being firmly, by its own wish,
excluded). Towns retained corporate rights in municipal matters, but
had neither political nor legal supremacy. President, four assistants
and officials were to be elected yearly in the full assembly of freemen (later after 1650 by 6 deputies from each town). Such assemblies
were judicial as well as legislative in function. Towns could initiate
legislation, and measures before enactment were referred to the towns-
people for approval.

by the lawful judgment of his peers, or by some known
law, and according to the letter of it, ratified and confirmed by the major part of the General Assembly lawfully
met and orderly managed.

2. That no person shall (but at his great peril) presume to bear or execute any office that is not lawfully
called to it and confirmed in it; nor though he be lawfully called and confirmed, presume to do more or less
than those that had power to call him, or did authorize
him to do.

3. That no Assembly shall have power to constitute any
laws for the binding of others, or to ordain officers for
the execution thereof but such as are founded upon the
charter and rightly derived from the General Assembly,
lawfully met and orderly managed.

[The bill of rights restated others from English precedents.][1]

And now, forasmuch as our charter gives us power to
make such laws, constitutions, penalties, and officers
of justice for the execution thereof as we, or the greater part of us shall, by free consent, agree unto, and
yet does premise that those laws, constitutions, and penalties so made shall be conformable to the laws of England, so far as the nature and constitution of our place
will admit, to the end that we may show ourselves not
only unwilling that our popularity should prove (as some
conjecture it will) an anarchy, and so a common tyranny,
but willing and exceedingly desirous to preserve every
man safe in his person, name and estate; and to show ourselves, in so doing, to be also under authority, by keeping within the verge and limits prescribed us in our charter, by which we have authority in this respect to act;
we do agree and by this present act determine, to make
such laws and constitutions so conformable etc. or rather
to make those laws ours, and better known among us; that
is to say, such of them and so far as the nature and constitution of our place will admit.

Touching the Common Law

It being the common right among common men, and is
profitable either to direct or correct all, without exception; and it being true which that great doctor of the
Gentiles once said, that the law is made or brought to
light, not for a righteous man, who is a law unto himself,
but for the lawless and disobedient in the general, but
more particularly for murderers of fathers and mothers,
for manslayers, for whoremongers, and those that defile
themselves with mankind; for menstealers, for liars and
perjured persons, unto which, upon the point, may be reduced the common law of the realm of England, the end of
which is, as is propounded, to preserve every man safe
in his own person, name, estate; we do agree to make, or
rather to bring such laws to light for the direction or

---

1. Reference was given almost invariably to the English statute
book.

correction of such lawless persons, and for their memories
sake to reduce them to these five general laws or heads....
    [Which crimes were included under the laws of murder, manslaugh-
    ter, whoremongering, theft and perjury were defined. A detailed
    statement of the laws followed, together with that of judicial pro-
    cedure and administration.]

(B) ATTEMPTS TO ASSERT METROPOLITAN AUTHORITY, 1660–88

After the confusion caused by the civil war and the opportunity this had given to the colonists to claim far more autonomy than their original constitutions envisaged, the Restoration government faced the need to redefine and establish effective imperial authority over the colonies. The policies adopted took three main forms. First, as regards the commercial relations between colonies and mother country, the Crown adopted and extended the monopolistic principles contained in the Commonwealth's Navigation Act of 1651. Significantly parliamentary legislation rather than prerogative instruments was used to give these regulations the greatest possible force; and by 1673 most of the restrictive rules that controlled imperial trade had been enacted in the form they were to retain until the mid-nineteenth century, though not all of them were yet (or ever) effectively implemented. Second, there was a continuous process of experiment in the institutions of metropolitan control. The privy council remained at the centre of imperial administration, acting through a succession of subordinate councils or committees. Here can be seen the genesis of a permanent professional imperial secretariat in London, which later reached a climax with the creation in 1696 of the Board of Trade, even though this was not part of the privy council and did not possess executive authority. (It was only after 1700, when the board gradually declined into a political rather than a bureaucratic body, that this trend was reversed, with important consequences during the eighteenth century). Finally, the Crown attempted, with considerable determination though limited consistency, to strengthen central control over the domestic affairs of individual colonies. This aim is reflected in the new commissions and instructions to colonial governors, in the creation of new imperial agencies in the colonies, in the rejection of the more extreme claims made by local assemblies to control colonial governments and policies, and in the attempt to extract perpetual Crown revenues from royal colonies – successful in the Leeward Islands but unsuccessful in Virginia and Jamaica. The case of Jamaica is a particularly important one, in this and other matters since this was a newly-acquired colony that had been conquered from Spain by Cromwell's forces in 1655; and for this reason the Crown inherited initially an unlimited authority there, by contrast with its constitutionally restricted power in the other American colonies which had been acquired by settlement. It is clear that in the 1670s the Lords of Trade made a considerable attempt to establish more effective royal control over finance and legislation in Jamaica than the Crown possessed in any of the other colonies; but they were eventually forced

to climb down as a result of doubts expressed by the law officers in
1680 as to whether the Crown could reverse concessions previously made
to English settlers even in a conquered colony. This issue was finally
settled by Lord Mansfield's judgement in the case of *Campbell v. Hall*
(1774) concerning Grenada. Between 1660 and the mid-1670s this policy of centralization was partly offset by the Crown's continuing to
grant extensive powers to the proprietors of new colonies and to issue
further colonial charters. But the 'exclusion crisis' of 1679 - 81
marked a turning point. Thereafter it seems to have been considered
policy to revoke existing charters (though not necessarily proprietary
grants), leading to the revocation of all the New England charters and
the establishing of the'Dominion of New England'in 1685. In 1688,
therefore, the omens suggested that metropolitan control would continue
to be made effective and that in due course all colonies would become
royal rather than chartered or proprietary. The Revolution Settlement
of 1688/9 reversed this trend and ultimately led to the lax inefficiency - or 'salutary neglect'- which characterized British colonial
government in the period 1714-63.

(1) PARLIAMENTARY LEGISLATION ON COMMERCE

The authority of Parliament was invoked to secure the regulation
and dependence of colonial trade in the interest of the realm: an
agreed 'national' policy adopted not only by England but by her European rivals. England should enjoy a monopoly of colonial produce in
return for providing her colonies with a monopoly in the home market:
colonial goods must be brought direct to an English port; and to build
up the navy and mercantile marine, England should secure the carrying
trade in English ships crewed by English mariners. Earlier Acts had
been concerned to promote the navigation of England,and the powers and
jurisdiction of admirals had been placed on a statutory basis. When
horizons became no longer limited by feudal lordship, borough, commonalty or march, and Western European nations entered into competition
for trans-oceanic commerce and empire, English merchants looked to
Parliament for greater protection and aid, not least against the Dutch.
So during the Commonwealth and the Restoration, on the basis of principles already laid down, the commercial policy of England was defined,
refined and consolidated in statutory form - the Laws of Trade.

252. NAVIGATION ACT (12 Car. II cap.18), 1660[1]
    *For the increase of shipping and encouragement of the
navigation of this nation, wherein, under the good providence and protection of God, the wealth, safety and strength
of this kingdom is so much concerned:* Be it enacted that...

---

1. This Act 'for the encouragement and increasing of shipping and
navigation' was passed in 1660 by the'Convention Parliament'when at
the Restoration the 'Act' of 1651 had ceased to have effect: it was
confirmed by the 'Cavalier Parliament' a year later. The first seventeen sections of the Act endorsed and elaborated the Commonwealth
Act. Its avowed purpose was mastery at sea; for, as the Speaker's
address claimed in September 1660 (C.J.VIII pp.174-5) 'so long as
your Majesty is master at sea, your merchants will be welcome wherever they come; and that is the easiest way of conquering, and the
chiefest way of making whatsoever is theirs, ours, and when it is

no goods or commodities whatsoever shall be imported into
or exported out of any lands, islands, plantations or territories to his Majesty belonging or in his possession, or
which may hereafter belong unto or be in the possession,
of his Majesty, his heirs and successors, in Asia, Africa
or America in any other ship or ships, vessel or vessels
whatsoever, but in such ships or vessels as do truly and
without fraud belong only to the people of England or Ireland, dominion of Wales or town of Berwick upon Tweed, or
are of the built of and belonging to any the said lands,
islands, plantations or territories, as the proprietors
and right owners thereof, and whereof the master and three
fourths of the mariners at least are English[1]...[under penalty of forfeiting goods and vessel. No alien could be a merchant or
factor in the plantations, upon pain of forfeiture of his goods.]
II...And all governors of the said lands, islands, plantations or territories,and every of them, are hereby strictly required and commanded, and all who hereafter shall be
made governors of any such islands, plantations or territories, by his Majesty, his heirs or successors, shall
before their entrance into their government take a solemn
oath, to do their utmost that every the aforementioned
clauses, and all the matters of things therein contained,
shall be punctually and *bona fide* observed according to
the true intent and meaning thereof[2]...[on pain of recall.]
III. And it is further enacted...That no goods or commodities whatsoever, of the growth or manufacture of Africa,
Asia, America, or of any part thereof, or which are described or laid down in the usual maps or cards of those
places, be imported into England, Ireland, or Wales, islands of Guernsey and Jersey, or town of Berwick upon
Tweed, in any other ship or ships, vessel or vessels whatsoever, but in such as do truly and without fraud belong
only to the people of England or Ireland, dominion of Wales, or town of Berwick upon Tweed or of the lands, islands,

---

ours, your Majesty cannot want it'. The general policy of encouraging
shipping was of course, centuries old [see above pp.5-6]. See also R.
Hakluyt's *Discourse on Western Planting* (1584): 'No enterprise can be
devised more fit to increase our great shipping than this Western
fortifying and planting'.
1. The 1651 Act [No.212 (b)] had only specified *'for the most part'*.
Scots seem to have been regarded as English for since 1603 they had
been H.M.'s subjects [see *Calvin's case* No.20]. Even after the Statute of Frauds of 1662 (see p.389) excluded Scots (together with Manxmen and Channel Islanders), Scots, permanently residing in England or
the colonies could enjoy, with English subjects, most of the benefits
of the Acts.
2. The colonial governors were increasingly made, by statute and instruction, to bear the main responsibility for executing the laws of
trade. By 7 and 8 Will. III cap.22 § iv, this oath was to cover all
Acts relating to the plantations, on pain of recall and fine of
£1,000 [see Volume II].

plantations or territories in Asia, Africa or America, to
his Majesty belonging, as the proprietors and right owners
thereof, and whereof the master, and three fourths at least
of the mariners are *English*....
IV. And it is further enacted...That no goods or commodities that are of foreign growth, production or manufacture,
and which are to be brought into England, Ireland, Wales,
the islands of Guernsey and Jersey or town of Berwick upon
Tweed in English-built shipping, or other shipping belonging to some of the aforesaid places, and navigated by English mariners, as aforesaid, shall be shipped or brought
from any other place or places,country or countries, but
only from those of the said growth, production or manufacture, or from those ports where the said goods and commodities can only, or are, or usually have been,[1] first shipped for transportation, and from none other places or countries...,

[Certain fish, not caught in the owners' ships themselves, could
be imported only at double custom duty. No alien was to engage in
the English coastal trade. Three quarters of a crew must be English if the ship's cargo was to receive the reduction in rate due
to an English-built vessel. Provision was made to prevent frauds
by certificate and oath.][2]

XVII. Provided also, and it is hereby enacted, That every
ship or vessel belonging to any the subjects of the French
King, which from and after the twentieth day of October in
the year of our Lord one thousand six hundred and sixty
shall come into any port, creek, harbour or road of England, Ireland, Wales or town of Berwick upon Tweed,[3] and
shall there lade or unlade any goods or commodities, or
take in or set on shore any passengers, shall pay to the
collector of his Majesty's customs in such port, creek,
harbour or road for every ton of which the said ship or
vessel is of burthen, to be computed by such officer of
the customs as shall be thereunto appointed, the sum of
five shillings current money of England....
XVIII...No sugars, tobacco, cotton wool, indicoes, ginger
fustick, or other dying wood, of the growth, production
or manufacture of any English plantation in America, Asia

1. This phrase seems unnecessarily vague and led to evasions.
2. The Statute of Frauds (13 & 14 Car.II cap.11) in 1662 attempted to
prevent abuses and defined these provisions more explicitly. There
were to be oaths taken at customs houses, searches of vessels and
supervision of unloading. No foreign-built vessel, though owned and
manned by Englishmen was to enjoy the benefits of an English ship;
and now 'English' was to mean 'only H.M.'s subjects of England, Ireland and the plantations', so presumably Channel Islanders, Manxmen
and Scots were excluded.There was a sizable increase in their involv-
ement in smuggling. Scottish Parliament had passed in 1661 a retalia-
tory Act on the model of 12 Car.II cap.8.
3. There are doubts whether the omission of the Channel Islands in
this section (ct. § § iii and iv) was significant[see above pp.195,
197].

or Africa] shall be shipped, carried,conveyed or transported from anv of the said English plantations to any land,
island , territory. dominion, port or place whatsoever,
other than to such other English plantations as do belong
to his Majesty, his heirs and successors, or to the Kingdom of England, or Ireland, or principality of Wales, or
town of Berwick upon Tweed, there to be laid on shore....
XIX...That for every ship or vessel...which shall set sail
out of or from England, Ireland,[2] or town of Berwick upon
Tweed, for any English plantation in America, Asia, or
Africa, sufficient bond shall be given with one surety to
the chief officers of the custom-house of such port or
place from whence the said ship shall set sail, to the
value of one thousand pounds, if the ship be of less burthen than one hundred tons; and of the sum of two thous-
and pounds, if the ship be of greater burthen; that in
case the said ship or vessel shall load any of the said
commodities at any of the said English plantations, that
the same commodities shall be by the said ship brought to
some port of England, Ireland, Wales, or to the port or
town of Berwick upon Tweed, and shall there unload and put
on shore the same, the danger of the seas only excepted;...

[The governors were to take bond of all ships coming to plantations, that all goods would be carried to England, *etc.* or to
some other English plantations.]

253. ACT PROHIBITING THE PLANTING OF TOBACCO (12 Car.II cap.34),1660.[3]
     Your Majesty's loyal and obedient subjects, the lords
and commons in this present parliament assembled,consider-
ing of how great concern and importance it is, that the
colonies and plantations of this kingdom in America, be
defended, protected, maintained, and kept up, and that all
due and possible encouragement be given unto them; and
that not only in regard great and considerable dominions
and countries have been thereby gained, and added to the
imperial crown of this realm, but for that the strength
and welfare of this kingdom do very much depend upon them,
in regard of the employment of a very considerable part
of its shipping and seamen, and of the vent of very great
quantities of its native commodities and manufactures, and
also of its supply with several considerable commodities

---

1. This 'enumeration' of colonial exports as a monopoly for English,
Irish and Welsh ports alone was not in the 1651 Act, though it had
been foreshadowed in an order in council of 1621 for exports from
Virginia. The list here is very selective and since fish, grain and
timber were not enumerated, this section had little effect in any but
the tropical plantations and islands. The list of goods enumerated was,
however, considerably increased in future Acts to increase customs
revenues and to safeguard employment in England.
2. See section xi of 22 & 23 Car.II cap.26 below,No.255.
3. The prohibition was as much in the interest of the Crown's customs
revenues as a concession to the plantations in return for restrictions
on their trade.

which it was wont formerly to have only from foreigners, and at far dearer rates; (2) and forasmuch as tobacco is one of the main products of several of those plantations, and upon which their welfare and subsistence, and the navigation of this kingdom, and vent of its commodities thither, do much depend; and in regard it is found by experience, that the tobaccoes planted in these parts are not so good and wholesom for the takers whereof; and that by the planting thereof, your Majesty is deprived of a considerable part of your revenue arising by customs upon imported tobacco;...*it is hereby enacted*...that no person or persons whatsoever shall...set, plant, improve to grow, make or cure any tobacco, either in seed, plant or otherwise, in or upon any ground, earth, field, or place within the kingdom of England, dominion of Wales, islands of Guernsey or Jersey, or town of Berwick upon Tweed, or in the kingdom of Ireland,under the penalty of the forfeiture of all such tobacco....

   [Sheriffs and J.P.s might destroy any such tobacco planted.
   Private and physic gardens were excepted.

254. STAPLE ACT (15 Car.II cap.7) 1663.[1]
   Forasmuch as the encouraging of tillage ought to be in an especial manner regarded and endeavoured; and the surest and effectuallest means of promoting and advancing any trade, occupation or mystery, being by rendring it profitable to the users thereof; (2) and great quantities of land within this kingdom for the present lying in a manner waste, and yielding little, which might thereby be improved to considerable profit and advantage (if sufficient encouragement were given for the laying out of cost and labour on the same) and thereby much more corn produced, great numbers of people, horses and cattle imployed, and other lands also rendred more valuable....

   [It was enacted that, when the price did not exceed certain
   specified rates, corn might be exported to, and imported from,
   'any parts beyond the seas'.]
V...in regard his Majesty's plantations beyond the seas are inhabited and peopled by his subjects of this his kingdom; for the maintaining a greater correspondence and kindness between them, and keeping them in a firmer dependence upon it,[2] and rendring them yet more beneficial and advantagious unto it in the further imployment and increase of English shipping and seamen, vent of English

---

1. This Act 'for the encouragement of trade' made the realm of England (with Wales) a 'staple'for colonial imports: it was a device to increase, and to facilitate the collection of customs duties. With a few exceptions (section vii) all European goods, intended for the English colonies would first be imported, unloaded and re-loaded in English ports.
2. This attempted subordination of the colonies to the realm was a feature of Restoration imperial policy,as it had been of the Commonwealth [see No.211 (b).].

woolen and other manufactures and commodities, rendring
the navigation to and from the same more safe and cheap,
and making this kingdom a staple, not only of the commodities of those plantations, but also of the commodities
of other countries and places, for the supplying of them;
and it being the usage of other nations to keep their
plantations trade to themselves.[1]
VI. Be it enacted...That...no commodity of the growth,
production or manufacture of Europe, shall be imported
into any land, island, plantation, colony, territory or
place to his Majesty belonging...in Asia, Africa or America, (Tangier only excepted) but what shall be *bona fide*,
and without fraud, laden and shipped in England, Wales,or
the town of Berwick upon Tweed,[2] and in English built shipping [or foreign ships bought and registered before Oct.1622] ...
and whereof the master and three fourths of the mariners
at least are English, and which shall be carried directly
thence to the said lands [*etc*.]....[Penalties were prescribed.]

---

1. In *A Discourse about Trade* (published in 1690 but written soon
after 1666) Josiah Child argued that, if the trade of the plantations
was not confined solely to 'Mother Kingdoms', the latter were damaged
by having them. 'The Danes keep the Trade of Izland to themselves:
the Dutch, Surrenham and all the Settlements in East India: the French
St. Christopher's and their other Plantations in the West Indies: The
Portugeeze, Brazil and all the Coasts thereof: the Spaniards, all
their vast Territories upon the Main in the West Indies and many Islands there; and our own Laws seem to design the like, as to all our
Plantations in New England, Virginia, Barbadoes &c although we have
not yet arrived to a compleat and effectual Execution of those Laws':
(p.vi). He was concerned that 'the People of New England, by vertue of
their Primitive Charters being not so strictly tied to the observation
of the Laws of this Kingdom, do sometimes assume a liberty of Trading,
contrary to the Act of Navigation': many American goods, especially
tobacco and sugar, were exported directly to Europe 'without being
landed in England or paying any Duty to his Majesty which is not only
loss to the King and a prejudice to the Navigation of Old England;
but also a total exclusion of the old English Merchant from the vent
of those Commodities in those Ports where the New English Vessels
trade'; since the New English merchants paid no customs, they could
sell cheaper and dominate the market(p.x). He thought no colony 'better
apt' for ship building than New England, 'nor none comparably so qualified for the breeding of Sea Men' by reason of their natural industry and their cod and mackerel fisheries: yet there was nothing 'more
prejudicial' and 'more dangerous' to Old England than an increase in
colonial shipping.
2. The omission of Ireland in this and other sections (e.g. viii-x,
xii-xiv) appeared to have been intentional [see below No.255].
Ireland was seen as a commercial rival of England: though English
merchants in Ireland claimed that England and Ireland were integrated
as 'one body', merchants in England were indeed strongly opposed to
any concessions whatever to their rivals in Ireland.

VII Provided always...That it shall and may be lawful to
ship and lade in such ships, and so navigated, as in the
foregoing clause is set down and expressed, in any part of
Europe, salt for the fisheries of New-England and Newfoundland, and to ship and lade in the Madera's wines of the
growth thereof, and to ship and lade in the Western islands of Azores wines of the growth of the said islands,
and to ship and take in servants or horses in Scotland
or Ireland, and to ship or lade in Scotland all sorts of
victuals[1] of the growth or production of Scotland, and to
ship or lade in Ireland, and the same to transport into
any of the said lands, islands, plantation, colonies, territories or places: and things in the foregoing clause to
the contrary in any wise notwithstanding ....

 [To prevent evasion, all importers and ship masters had to deliver within 24 hours a full inventory of all goods and certificates
that the ship was English-built and English-manned, under pain of
confiscation of goods and vessel. Before leaving for his colony
a governor had to take an oath to execute the laws of trade, under penalty of recall, and a forfeit of £500 to the Crown and £500
to the informer.]

IX. And it is hereby further enacted, That if any officer
of the customs in England, Wales or town of Berwick upon
Tweed, shall give any warrant for, or suffer any sugar,
tobacco, ginger, cotton-wool, indigo, specklewood or Jam-
aica-wood, fustick or other dying-wood of the growth of
any of the said lands, islands, colonies, plantations,
territories or places, to be carried into any other country or place whatsoever, until they have been first unladen *bona fide* and put on shore in some port or haven in
England or Wales, or in the town of Berwick;   that every
such officer for such offence shall forfeit his place, and
the value of such of the said goods as he shall give warrant for, or suffer to pass into any other country or place,
the one moiety to his Majesty, his heirs and successors;
and the other moiety to him or them that shall inform or
sue for the same in any court of record in England or
Wales, wherein no essoin, protection or wager in law shall
be allowed....

 [Foreign coin and bullion might be exported 'foreasmuch as
several considerable and advantagious trades cannot be conveniently driven and carried without' and experience had shown that they
were 'carried in greatest abundance (as to a common market) to such
places as give free liberty for exporting the same'. Furthermore
'Whereas a very great part of the richest and best land of this
kingdom...cannot so well be otherwise employed and made use of as
in the...fattening of cattle', penalties were temporarily prescribed for the importation of all (but Scottish) foreign cattle and
sheep. Similarly penalties were authorised for fish imported in
non-English ships. There was a further tightening of the law

---

1. It was reported that there were ingenious attempts to increase the
scope of this exemption by listing soap and candles as 'provisions'.

against tobacco growing, since 'the penalties prescribed...by the
law were so little' a deterrent.]

255. ACT PROHIBITING TOBACCO PLANTING AND REGULATING THE PLANTATION
                          TRADE. (22 & 23 Car.II cap.26)1671
     [Despite legislation in 1660 and 1663 tobacco planting in England
     had increased 'to the apparent loss of H.M.'s customs and the dis-
     couragement of H.M.'s plantations in America' *etc.*, J.P's were to
     order all constables *etc.* to make regular search for the tobacco
     crops and to destroy all plants. Penalties were prescribed for
     all constables who failed in this duty. Sections V and VI of the
     Staple Act of 1663 were recited.]

XI. Notwithstanding which, some persons taking advantage
of the not mentioning the repealing of the word Ireland[1]
in one clause in an act of parliament made in the twelfth
year of his Majesty's reign,[2] intituled, An act for the
encouraging and increase of shipping and navigation; where
bonds are directed to be taken for all ships that shall
lade any sugar, or other commodities therein particularly
mentioned, in any of the said plantations, That the same
commodities shall be by the said ship brought to some port
of England, Ireland, Wales, or town or port of Berwick and
shall there unlode, and put the same on shore, the said
persons having either refused to give bond for the return
of their ships in such case to England, Wales, or town
or port of Berwick only, or having given such bond have
nevertheless gone with their ships to Ireland; by which
means (although this kingdom hath and doth daily suffer a
great prejudice by the transporting great number of people[3]
thereof to the said plantations, for the peopling of them)

---

1. Between 1663 and 1670 the bonds (issued in the form prescribed in
the 1660 Act) permitted Ireland to trade while the statute of 1663
had forbidden it. But the positive exclusion of Ireland in this section of the 1671 Act at the request of the Treasury and Customs,was
operative only till 1680 when this Act expired and was, given the
English merchants fear of Irish competition, surprisingly not renewed
at once.
2. 12 Car.II cap.18 sect.xix
3. Josiah Child had argued in *A discourse* that 'Plantations being at
first furnished, and afterwards successively supplied, with People
from their Mother Kingdoms and people, being Riches, that loss of people to the Mother Kingdoms, be it more or less, is certainly a damage,
except the employment of those People abroad do cause the employment
of many more at home in their Mother Kingdoms, and that can never be,
except the Trade be restrained to their Mother Kingdom which will not
be doubted by any that understands the next Proposition, *viz.* That the
Dutch will reap the greatest advantage by all Colonies issuing from
any Kingdom in Europe, whereof the Trades are not so strictly confined
to their proper Mother Country'. 'Where the market is free, they shall
be sure th have the Trade that can sell the best pennyworths, that buy
dearest and sell cheapest (which Nationally speaking) none can do but
those that Money (*sic*) at the lowest rate of Interest and pay the least
Customs which are the Dutch'. Before the Navigation Act there were ten

yet that the trade of them would thereby in a great measure be diverted from hence, and carried elsewhere, his
Majesty's customs and other revenues much lessened, and
this kingdom not continue a staple of the said commodities
of the said plantations, nor that vent for the future of
the victual and other native commodities of this kingdom;
Be it therefore enacted, That the word Ireland, shall be
left out of all such bonds which shall be taken for any
ship or vessel which shall set sail out of or from England, Ireland, Wales, or town of Berwick upon Tweed, for
any English plantation in America, Asia, and Africa; [under
pain of forfeiture if a vessel from Ireland traded direct for such an
English plantation.][1]
XII. And whereas many complaints have been made of shipping
and vessel's belonging to some of his Majesty's colonies
in America, that contrary to the intent and meaning of
this and other afore-mentioned laws, they have brought
and transported the said commodities to divers parts of
Europe, and there unloaded the same: Be it further enacted, That the governors, or their commanders in chief,

---

Dutch ships to Barbados for one English, (vi-vii).
1. When in 1685 this Act, after a lapse, was renewed, the Lord lieutenant and the commissioners of Irish revenue prompted by 'some merchants of Ireland' made representations against any further exclusion
of Ireland. The commissioner of English customs asserted on 29 March
1686 (C.O. 324/4) that it was 'the true interest of England and the
usage of all Nations to keep their Plantation Trades to themselves'
and that there were strong reasons for keeping plantations 'in a
firm dependence upon England...by making this Kingdom the only staple
for all colonial trade.' Irish provisions were cheap and had an
advantage in a permitted direct trade (15 Car.II cap.7 § vii); and
if 'permitted to trade thither upon equall terms with England' the
Irish would 'in great measure robb this Kingdom...of this Beneficial
flourishing Trade'. On 22 April the commissioners of Irish revenue
again argued that 'it looks very hard that the Inhabitants of Ireland,
who are subjects of England and live under the Protection of the same
King and yield Obedience to his Laws and quietly pay their Dues for
the support of his Government, should be debarred that Trade' because
of the selfish fears of English merchants. The commissioners of English customs, however, did not relent. On May 12 they declared to
the lord high treasurer that they saw no case for concession. The
Irish commissioners had also urged that the plantation duty on tobacco was best collected in Ireland 'which...seems to Reflect upon
our managery in England, we shall not take any notice of'. Moreover,
they pointed out firmly to the lord treasurer that they, the commissioners of English customs, have responsibility for 'the whole
body of Plantation Laws' and were the sole line of communication between the lord treasurer and the governors and officials in the plantations. They could not preserve 'one constant uniform method' or
'give due Account of their Managery if so great and so near a Kingdom
as Ireland be freely let into the Trade thereof' and be allowed to
import enumerated goods direct.   This principle of Ireland's exclusion was affirmed permanently in the Act of 1696(C.O.324/49:[seeVol.II].

of his Majesty's respective plantations, do once a year at least make a return to his Majesty's officers in the port of London, or to such other person or persons as his Majesty shall appoint to receive the same, a list of all such ships or vessels as shall lade any of the said commodities in such plantations respectively, as also a list of all the bonds taken by them: (3) and in case any ship or vessel belonging to any of his Majesty's plantations, which shall have on board her any sugars, tobacco, cotton-wool, indicoes, ginger, fustick or other dying-wood, shall be found to have unladed in any port or place of Europe, other than England, Wales, or the town of Berwick upon Tweed: That such ship or vessel shall be forfeited, with all her guns, tackle, apparel, ammunition, furniture and lading, to be recovered and divided as aforesaid.

256. PLANTATION DUTIES ACT (25 Car.II cap.7), 1673.[1]
    ['Foreasmuch as the whale-fishing is a very considerable and profitable trade, giving imployments to great numbers of seamen and shipping'; liberty was given to all His Majesty's subjects in England and Wales to trade with Greenland directly without payment of customs duties, but if in colonial ships, then duties were prescribed.
    Whereas the freedom to ship sugar, tobacco, cotton, *etc.*. from the plantation of their growth to other plantations]
V...but contrary to the express letter of the aforesaid laws, have brought in to divers parts of Europe great quantities thereof, and do also daily vend great quantities thereof, to the shipping of other nations who bring them into divers parts of Europe, to the great hurt and diminution, of your Majesty's customs, and of the trade and navigation of this your kingdom; (4) for the prevention thereof...Be it enacted...That...if any ship or vessel which by law may trade in any of your Majesty's plantations, shall come to any of them to ship and take on board any of the aforesaid commodities,[2] and that bond[3] shall not be first given with one sufficient surety to bring the

---

1. This Act was concerned to regulate the trade of colonial merchants and to prevent evasions of the Act of 1660 by making unprofitable a direct trade in enumerated goods from a colonial port to Europe. The increasing demand for tobacco, for example, had led to an increase in smuggling. A plantation duty, 'an ingenious device', was to be charged if such goods were not shipped direct to England from the colony of origin. The privilege of free trade between colonies had been abused, for goods had been sent to another colony first and then to Europe. What remained uncertain, however, until the Act of 1696, was whether, if the captain or merchant paid the duty required by this Act of 1673, he could still trade direct to Europe: an obscurity not removed by the attorney-general's opinion in 1676 (C.O.5/903.p.106)
2. i.e. those commodities enumerated in 12 Car.II cap.18.
3. This bond - deposited with the governor, naval officer or collector that if he did not unload his cargo at some colonial port he would take the goods to England - was a distinguishing feature of this 'new Navigation Act: it tightened the control of the mercantile system.

same to England or Wales, or the town of Berwick upon
Tweed, and no other place, and there to unload and put the
same on shore, (the danger of the seas only excepted)that
there shall be answered and paid to your Majesty, your
heires and successors, for so much of the said commodities
as shall be laded and put on board such ship or vessel,
these following rates or duties:...
    [The prescribed rates for customs duties (for example, a penny
    a pound of tobacco, £112-5-0 for a hundredweight of white sugar;
    a halfpenny a pound on cotton wool,*etc*) were to be collected by
    officials to be appointed in the plantations.]
VI. For the better collection of the several rates and
duties aforesaid imposed by this act...it is hereby further enacted...That this whole business shall be ordered
and managed, and the several duties hereby imposed shall
be caused to be levied by the commissioners of the customs
in England now and for the time being, by and under the
authority and directions of the lord treasurer of England
or commissioners of the treasury for the time being....[1]

(2) THE CROWN AND THE COLONIES

    The detail of colonial administration remained the concern of the
Crown. There was need to improve metropolitan supervision: beginning
haltingly [see Nos.167ff], it had been rendered virtually ineffective
by the civil war. There were tentative experiments (as experience
increased) in amending and enlarging the form and content of commissions and instructions for governors. It was necessary to secure
accountability to the Crown of its servants, officials, agents and
patentees to whom had been delegated the use of royal power.

(a) THE CREATION OF PREROGATIVE AGENCIES

    With the Restoration there was urgent need to establish a new
committee or council, linked with the privy council, to deal with colonial business: the royal council for Virginia, the Laudian and Warwick commissions, and the council of state had in turn attempted some
general supervision during the previous half century. There were several new agencies created during the next fifteen years. In 1675 a
sub-committee of privy councillors - the 'Lords of Trade' - took direct charge.

257. COMMISSIONS AND INSTRUCTIONS FOR THE COUNCILL APPOINTED FOR
     FORRAIGNE PLANTATIONS, 1 December 1660.[2]
(a) *Commissions*...Haveing taken into our Princely consid-

---

1. By this Act the main structure of the'Navigation system'was now completed, and in 1675 the newly appointed lords of trade showed a fresh
determination to enforce the Acts. A proclamation was issued on 24
November 1675 to command the obedience of all H.M.'s subjects to the
Acts of Trade and to require all governors to compel everyone to aid
the collectors of customs in their duties. The lords of trade suspected governors of conniving at evasion: they drafted a more rigid form
of oath and required more frequent reports of their efforts at super
vision and control.
2. C.O. 1/14 No.59. Within a few weeks of the Restoration (4 July

eration and provided for the general State and condition
of the Trade Naviqation and Forraigne Context of our Severall Kingdomes and Dominions, Wee are not without a particular eye and regard to the many Colonies and Forraigne
Plantations which have beene settled and carried on by
the Comissions and encouragements of our Royal Predecessors, Wee have thought fitt therefore to drawe those our
distant Dominions and the severall Interests and Governments thereof into a nearer prospect and consultation,
haveing to our abundant satisfaction observed that the
industrie and adventures of our good Subjects, with the
Supplies and assistances which have beene drawne from here
have verie much inlarged the power, growth and improvements thereof, they being now become a great and numerous
people whose plentifull trade and commerce much imployes
and increaseth the Navigation and expands the Manufactures
of our other Dominions and exchanges them for comodities
of necessary use, And brings a good accesse of Treasure
to our Exchequer for all customs and other duities. In
consideration whereof and for divers other causes...Wee
have judged it moot and necessary that so many remote
Colonies and Governments, so many wayes considerable to
our Crowne and dignitie and to which we doe bear soe good
an esteeme and affection, should now no longer remain in
a loose and scattered condition but should be collected
and brought under such an uniform inspetton and conduct,
that wee may the better apply our Royall Councills to
their future regulation, security and improvement...WEE
THEREFORE... ordaine you to be a *Standing Councill*, hereby giveing and granting unto you, or five or more of you
full power and authoritie to take into your consideration
...the present and future State and condicon of our severall Forraigne Plantations and to consult and proceed
therein, according to the powers confirmed in these our
Comission and such other Instruccons as are hereunto annexed, or according to any further Instruccons which you

---

1660) an order in council had appointed a committee of the lord
chamberlain, the lord treasurer and others to deal with petitions
from merchants trading to the plantations and islands of America,
and 'to use prudential means for rendering these dominions useful to
England and England helpful to them'. There had of course been an
attempt to establish a more vigorous administrative control in the
last years of the Protectorate. Lord Willoughby, Thomas Povey, Martin
Noell and other merchants had urged the need of a council to obtain
information about the colonies, to secure the dependence of officials,
to reduce the proprietaries and to make the colonies realise they
were 'part of the embodied Commonwealth whose head and centre is here'.
Such proposals were now being put into practice. A council for trade
had been commissioned on 7 November and this similar council a month
later. However, they proved somewhat unwieldy bodies. A reorganisation of the privy council established in February 1668 a joint council
for trade 'under whose consideration is to come whatever concerns
H.M.'s Forraine Plantations as also what relates to his Kingdoms of

shall from time to time receive from us. And you are hereby further required and impowered to receive and prosecute all such propositions and overtures as shalbe offered
unto you by any other persons and as you shall judge to be
for the benefitt or improvement of any of our said Forraine
Plantations. And to view and make use of all such bookes,
Records or other writings...for your better Information
...And wee doe hereby require all and everie our Governors or any other person or persons that by vertue of any
Comission or Graunt from us or any of our Royall Predecessors doth, doe or shall exercise any power, Jurisdiction
or authoritie upon any of our said fforraine Plantations
... [and all officials, ministers, merchants, planters and seamen]
who shall receive any summons, order or other direction
or appointment from the said Councill of Forraigne Plantations...that they do forthwith yeild a ready conformity
thereunto....
Instructions.[1]
3. You shall informe your selves by the best wayes and
meanes you can of the state and condition of forraigne
Plantations And by what Comissions or authorities they
are and have been governed....
4. You are to order and settle such a continuall correspondence that you may be able as often as you are required
thereunto to give up to us an account of the Government of
each Colonie. Of their Complaints, their wants, their

Scotland or Ireland' and to hear appeals from the Channel Islands
(P.C. 2/60 pp.176-7). In 1672 there was a new joint council for trade
and plantations under Shaftesbury with John Locke as secretary.
1. These instructions were modelled upon the *Overtures* prepared by
Thomas Povey in 1660 and were elaborated from his proposals of 1654:
see C.M. Andrews, *British committees* etc. (J. Hopkins Univ. stud.XXVI
1908) pp.69-74. He had been chairman for the committee for the West
Indies in 1657, was treasurer to the Duke of York from 1660 to 1668,
and in 1661 was also appointed receiver-general for the plantation
rents and revenues.
When in September 1672 the ineffective council for trade and more
efficient council for foreign plantations were united under Shaftesbury, he and Locke prepared, on the basis of Carolina and Bahamas
experience, a more detailed set of instructions which served as a
basic comprehensive model for future imperial government (*ibid*.pp.107-
9). The joint council was to be concerned with the obstacles and opportunities for English trade, to encourage the search for new staples
and increase the sale of manufactures, and to consider a more open
trade than that offered by monopoly corporations. As for the foreign
plantations, the council was to know the general state of all colonies,
to seek full information about councils, assemblies, courts, statutes,
laws: about defence works, boundaries, mines, raw materials, spices,
manufactures, fisheries, ports; about the numbers of settlers, servants, negroes, births and deaths; about dues, duties and revenues;
about treaties, agreements and charters. They were accordingly to
keep in regular correspondence with the governor.

abundance, their growth...that...the true condition of
each part and of the whole may be thoroughly understood
whereby a more steady judgement and ballance may be made
for the better ordering and disposing of Trade...that soe
each place within itselfe and all of them being collected
into one...views and management here may be regulated and
ordered upon Comon and equall grounds and Principles.
5. You are to applie your selves to all prudentiall meanes
for the rendering those Dominions usefull to England and
England helpful to them And for the bringing the severall
Colonies and Plantations within themselves, into a more
certaine civill and uniform waie of Government and for the
better ordering and distributing of publique Justice among
them....

   [They were to consider how other countries governed their colonies.]

8. You are to take especiall care and enquire into the
strict exicution of the late Act of Parliament entituled
an Act for the encouragement increasing of Shipping and
Navigation that as much as in you lyes none of those good
ends and purposes may be disappointed for which the said
Act was intended and designed....

11. You are lastly required...to advise, order, settle and
dispose of all matters relating to the good Government
Improvement and Management of our fforaine Plantations
or any of them with your utmost skill and prudence. And
in all cases wherein you shall judge that further powers
and Assistants shall be necessary you are to addresse
yourselves to us our Privy Council for our further pleasure....

258. COMMISSION TO JAMES, DUKE OF YORK, AS HIGH ADMIRAL,
                                  27 February 1662.[1]
   We give and grant...to James, Duke of York, the office
of High Admiral of Dunkirk, New England, Jamaica, Virginia,
Barbados, St. Christopher, Bermuda, and Antigua in America,
of Guinea, Binney and Angola in Africa, and Tangiers...
We grant to him all jurisdictions, authority, liberties,
offices, emoluments and privileges of that office of High

---

1. C.O. 29/1 pp.74-5. Trans. from Latin. The duke's appointment as
lord high admiral had been confirmed by order in council on 4 July
1660. Lord Berkeley, Sir George Carteret and Sir William Penn were
with Samuel Pepys on the navy board. No commissions for the erection
of vice-admiralty courts in the colonies were issued till 1697, though
prize cases were dealt with locally by governors who had vice-admirals'
powers: e.g. Willoughby's commission for the Caribbees in June 1663
(C.O. 1/17 p.113). 'Wee doe by these presents authorize and ordeyne
the said Francis Lord Willoughby to be our Vice Admirale in all the
seas and coasts within the places and limits aforesaid' and to hear
'all marine and other causes'. Willoughby also had a commission direct
from the duke in January 1667 (C.O. 29/1 pp.88-91) and was instructed
in July 1672 to take orders as vice-admiral from the duke. (C.O. 29/1
p.145).

Admiral for life including jurisdiction over treason,
arson, homicide, felony [*etc.*] ....

259. INSTRUCTIONS FROM THE LORDS COMMISSIONERS OF THE TREASURY TO
      GOVERNORS, 22 September 1667.[1]
   Yet his Majesty, minding to have the said Acts fulfilled as much as possible the affairs of the tyme would permit, did extend and limit the said license and dispensation only to the kingdom of England and not to any other
place whatsoever. And his Majesty well considering of
what importance it is to the welfare of this nation in
general as well as to his Majesty's revenue in particular
that these laws be duly and strictly observed; and finding that notwithstanding all the penalties against the
transgressors thereof, several ships have been permitted
or taken the liberty to trade or convey goods and merchandize between the said plantations and other parts of his
Majesty's dominions, *viz*. Scotland, Ireland and Tangier
and also into foreign countries contrary to the true and
express meaning of the said Acts: which his Majesty cannot
but in great measure impute to the neglect of duty in his
Governors of the said Plantations who have not been so
careful as they ought in debarring all trade with such
ships as have come without certificate from England; nor
in taking bond from such as are permitted to trade from
other Plantations and returning the same to the chief
officers of the custom[2] in London as is particularly directed....

      [The king did not wish to execute the penalties of the law
      against such governors without warning or exhortation against such
      'disservice to his revenue and contempt to the lawes and his auth-
      ority'. He required them to be 'punctual' in enforcing the law
      and in prosecuting offenders.]

260. ORDER IN COUNCIL APPOINTING THE LORDS COMMITTEE OF THE PRIVY
      COUNCIL FOR TRADE AND PLANTATIONS, 12 March 1675.[3]
Whitehall. Present:- Lord Keeper, Earl of Bridgewater,
                      Earl of Craven, Earl of Carbery,
                      Lord Maynard, Lord Berkely, Mr.
                      Secretary Williamson.
Committee of Trade and Forraine Plantations to have the
Intendency of all affairs formerly under the care of the

---

1. Treasury 11/1 pp.49-57. The Lords commissioners had been appointed
in May. The Acts of Trade had proved difficult to enforce; licences
and dispensations had been granted; even foreign shipping had been
admitted in wartime. In the West Indies, French and Dutch ships were
regularly trading without interference. Now all dispensations were
being revoked.
2. Until September 1671 the customs were farmed out, but a board of
commissioners to manage customs was then appointed.
3. J.R. Brodhead (ed.) *Documents relating to the colonial history*...
New York (1856) III pp.229-0. The privy councillors themselves now
took over direct charge of these affairs - the 'Lords of Trade'. They

Council of Trade.

The Right Honourable The Lord Keeper of the Greate Seale of England this day acquainted the Board of his Majestie's Command that his Majestie, haveing been pleased to dissolve and Extinguish his late Councill of Trade and Forraine Plantations whereby all matters under their cognizance are left loose and at large, Had thought fit to commit what was under their inspection and management to the Committee of this Board appointed for matters relating to Trade and Foreign Plantations [The lord treasurer, and 20 others were named]... and did particularly order that the Lord Privie[1] Seale, the Earl of Bridgewater, Earl of Carlisle, Earl of Craven,Viscount Fauconberg, Viscount Halyfax, Lord Berkeley, Mr. Vice Chamberlain, and Mr. Chancellor of the Exchequer should have the immediate care and intendency of those affairs, in regard they had been formerly conversant and acquainted therewith, And therefore that any five of the last named Lords should be a quorum of the said committee, And that their Lordshipps meet constantly at least once a weeke, and make report to His Majestie in Councill of their results and Proceedings from time to time, And that they have power to send for all Bookes, papers and other writing concerning any of His Majestie's said Plantations, in whosoever Custody they shall be informed the same do remayne; And his Lordshipps further signifyed his Majestie's pleasure that Sir Robert Southwell do constantly attend the said Committee. J. Nicholas.

261. PATENT FROM CHARLES II TO WILLIAM BLATHWAYT FOR THE OFFICE OF
     SURVEYOR AND AUDITOR GENERAL, 19 May 1680.[2]
   ...Wee, of our royall care of good government and direction of our affaires in the remoter parts of the world and particularly taking into our princely consideration how necessary it is for us to settle our revenue arising within and from our several foreign dominions, islands, colonies, and plantations, in America; and how much it would tend to the advantage of our service, and benefit of our subjects, to make some better provision for the due payment to us, our heirs and successors, of our said revenues; and for the due and orderly taking, examining and stating, the accounts of all and every collectors, receivers, auditors, treasurers, sub-collectors, and other

---

were determined to take a firmer and more vigorous part in colonial business. 1. Anglesey: Nottingham was keeper and Danby treasurer. 2. N.B. Shurtleff (ed.),*Records of the governor and company...Massachusetts Bay* (1853) V pp.52–6. This appointment was part of the lords of trade's attempt to strengthen royal control over colonial revenues, and to prevent mismanagement and misappropriation. Blathwayt was a reliable and conscientious official, dedicated to the task of securing to the Crown a firm and careful supervision of colonial affairs: Randolph was appointed his deputy in October 1681. In 1683 William Dyer was appointed as the first surveyor general of customs with a roving commission to inspect the books of collectors – which he did not appear to carry out.

inferior officers, ministers, and persons, to whom it shall
or may appertain or belong, to act or intermeddle in or
with the collecting. levying, or receiving, of any of the
sums of money...payable, unto us, and accruing within our
said dominions and colonies:...by these presents, for us
our heirs and successors, do create, erect, and establish,
an office of generall inspeccion, examination,and auditt
of all and singular accompts...of any of our foreign dominions, colonies, and plantations, in America; and the chief
officer thereof shall be stiled and called the Surveyor
auditor-general of all our revenues arising in America....
    [W. Blathwayt was appointed surveyor auditor-general 'during good
    behaviour']
And we do hereby,...command all governors, deputy governors, councils...and all other officers and persons whatsoever, of, in, or appertaining to, our said colonies and
dominions in America, from time to time, to observe, ful-
fill, and obey, our will and pleasure in all things concerning the premises, and to be aiding, assisting, and
favouring, to the said William Blathwaite, his deputy or
deputies, in the due execution thereof:...these our letters
patent or the enrollment or exemplification thereof, shall
be good and effectual in the law, and shall as well in all
courts of record or elsewhere within our realm of England,
as also within any of our said islands, plantations, territories, and dominions, whatsoever....
    [He was to be paid £100 a year from the revenues of Virginia,
    £150 from those of Barbados, £100 from the Caribbees, and £150
    from Jamaica. He was to obey instructions from the lord high trea-
    surer, the chancellor of the exchequer and the commissioners of
    the treasury.]

(b) THE CROWN GOVERNORS AND OTHER ROYAL OFFICIALS

262. COMMISSION TO LORD WINDSOR AS GOVERNOR OF JAMAICA, 2 August 1661.[1]
    ...Wee...by these presents doe assigne, constitute and
appoint you, the said Thomas Windsor, Lord Windsor, to be
our Governor in and upon our said Islands of Jamaica and
to doe and execute all things in due manner to the said
Government and office apperteyninge...to the...good Government of the said Island...and doe give power and authoritye...by this present commission graunted unto you, and
such Instructions as shall from tyme to tyme be given unto
you by us under our Signet and Signe manuall and according
to such good right and reasonable lawes customs and constitutions as are exercised...in our other...plantations, to
make such Lawes as shall upon mature advice and consideration be held most right and proper for the good government...of our said Island of Jamaica, provided they be not

---

1. C.O. 1/15 No.76. Contrary to many expectations, the Crown resolved
at the Restoration to retain Jamaica, to end martial law and to establish civil government there. In commissions the Crown delegated certain
named prerogative powers to the governors; in instructions the Crown

repugnant to the Lawes of England but agreeing thereto as
neare as the condition of affayres will permitt. And for
the better administration of justice and management of affayres upon our said Island you...shall forthwith take unto
you a Councill consisting of twelve persons to be elected
as shalbe appointed in our said Instructions[1] and by the
advice of any five or more of them you shall erect and constitute such and soe many civill Judicatures with power to
administer any oathes as by yor selfe or said Councell
shalbe holden necessarye... And we doe hereby give full
power and authority to you...to muster, command and [?]
all the militarye forces of the said Islands...And for the
better suppression of...Insurrections...you... doe putt in
execution the lawe Martiall upon all notorious offenders.
And to the end that the industrye of our good people may
have all possible encouragement and their professions...
may be better provided for, wee doe by these presents give
and grant to you...with the advice of your said councill
...power and authoritye to give one or more comission or
comissions unto one or more of our subjects...for the finding out of which trades shall be most necessarey to be
undertaken for the good and the advantage of the inhabitants of our said Island....[2]

263. *PROPOSALS FOR A REVISED COMMISSION FOR SIR JONATHAN ATKINS AS
      GOVERNOR OF BARBADOS AND THE WINDWARDS*, 1673-74:

(a) Memorandum of alterations and additions, December
                                              1673.[3]

Alteracon -- He is constituted Governour of Barbados, St.
Lucia, St.Vincent's, Dominico, which three last were not
in my Lord Willoughby's Commissione expressly mentioned.

---

indicated more fully how such powers were to be used. This commission for Lord Windsor to succeed D'Oyley was prepared by a special Jamaica committee of the privy council on which Clarendon served: his
subsequent instructions [see below No.348] gave him considerable discretion to meet unforeseen eventualities: indeed, in 1664 Modyford's
gave him power 'to act in all things not mentioned in these instructions'. (C.O. 1/18 No.26). In the next decade, however, the Crown attempted to centralise and to tighten its control - e.g. over colonial
laws, councillors, patentees and appeals.
1. Seven months later in Windsor's instructions there was no such indication of any method of 'election' or 'appointment', but since now
an elected assembly was conceded, Windsor nominated his council. As he
was present in the privy council when discussions were held, it was
presumably what was intended.
2. In February 1664 when Modyford was brought over from Barbados with
a new commission it was substantially of his own devising.
3. C.O. 1/30 No.92. The privy council had asked for a paper showing
the changes proposed in the new draft for Atkins' commission. The
council of trade and foreign plantations was determined to control
forceful, persuasive, wayward governors, who did as they pleased and
justified themselves by alleging the council did not understand local
conditions. The presence of a Crown-nominated council in the colonies,

Alteracon -- The persons who are to be of the Councell
at Barbadoes appointed and named by his Majesty and Sir
Jonathan's Commission; but my Lord Willoughby had in his
the choice of them left to himself, in this Island as well
as in the others.
Addition --That in case of a Vacancy in any of the Councells of the respective Islands...Sir Jonathan is to certify his Majesty thereof by the first opportunity that
his Majesty may appoint others in their place under his
Signet and Signe manual, which was not in my Lord Willoughby's Commission.
Addition --But in case lesse than nine remains in any of
the said Councells, Sir Jonathan hath power out of the
principall inhabitants to make up the full number of the
Councell to be nine... which was not in my Lord's Commission.
Alteracon --Sir Jonathan hath power to suspend or expell
any of the Members of the said Councills with the advice
and consent of the said respective Councills, which Power
my Lord Willoughby had absolutely without such advice.
Alteracon -- As often as mention is made of doing anything with the advice of the Councill, it is expressed
in Sir Jonathan Commission, 'With the advice and consent
of the said Councill'; but in my Lord Willoughby's 'With
the Advice and Consent of any 7 or more of the Members of
the said Councill'.
Alteracon --Upon occasion of receiving Instructions from
the Lord High Admirall of England; instead of His R.
Highnesse in my Lord Willoughby's Commission, Sir Jonathan
hath 'Our Commissioners for executing the office of Lord
High Admirall of England, or from Our High Admirall of
England for the time being'.
Addition -- Sir Jonathan Atkins hath Power (which is not
mentioned in my Lord Willoughby's Commission) in the Vacancy of any office in the King's Gift, to put in one to
officiate till it be disposed of by His Majesty.

263 (b) <u>John Locke to Lord Arlington</u>, 6 January 1674.[1]
    The Nomination of the Councill reserved in his Majesty
here for these Reasons;
1. Because the Government would thereby more immediately
depend upon his Majesty and so the Island be better secured under his Obedience.
2. It would prevent the great inconveniences that would

---

immediately dependent on the king and not on a local popular autocrat,
might help to secure obedience to metropolitan authority. For the commission to <u>Atkins</u>,[see No.342]. He was governor till 1680.
1. C.O. 1/31 No.2. <u>John Locke</u>, as secretary to the council for trade
and plantations, was replying to the secretary of state who had asked
for the reasons for altering the terms of the commission to Atkins of
3 December 1673 as compared with those to Lord Willoughby. The commission to Willoughby in 1672 had already asserted the king's right to
appoint to patent offices, and had ruled that laws not confirmed within
2 years would lapse.

follow upon the Councills being too much at the Governors
devotion which they are like to bee, when depending upon
his pleasure, whereby making up but one Obedient Vote,
they serve onely to confirme and justify any Errors...he
may fall into; but are not likely to be restrained or
amend them, which is their proper business.
3. It prevents the mischeife which certainly followes
from having men in debt of the Councill who for the security they enjoy by sitting at that Board will undoubtedly
vote any thing the Governor will direct, the inconveniences whereof were very much felt in Barbados, and complained
of, by the Inhabitants in the time of former Governors....
4. The Government of the Plantations would be hereby sui-
ted to that which hath been allwaies observed in Ireland[1]
and long experience had approved of there, where the nom-
inacon of the Councill was not thought fitt to be trusted
to his Majesty's Lord Lieutenant though a person alway of
eminent dignity, wisdom and loyalty and estate, and though
Ireland be neere at hand, and so all miscarriages capable
of a more timely remedy.
5. That the Governor might be hereby preserved from those
animosities which often arise upon the placeing and dis-
placeing of men in the Councill, whereby the Governor is
often unavoidably embroyld and his Majesty's Affaires prejudiced. These, as I remember, were some of the reasons
that lead the Councill to this Alteration without the
least reflection on Sir Jonathan Atkins,[2] but merely out
of their Care of his Majesty's Service and the generall
consideration of human frailty;and therefore if I mistake
not, they intend to give his Majesty the same advice in
all his Plantations soe often as they shall have occasion
to consider the Comission of any Governor his Majesty
shall please to send to any of them.[3]

---

1. The Irish model of government clearly had attractions to privy
councillors in the 1670's: [see below No.358ff.].
2. Atkins vehemently objected to the curtailment of his necessary
patronage as a slight to his honour and integrity: he was being
'laden with fetters' before he ever arrived in Barbados - 'The Governor will be a puppet ' (C.O. 1/30 No.84). As for the Crown's nomination of all the councillors, 'they seem rather to be ordeyned to
be my governors than I theirs'. (C.O. 1/37 No.22).
3. In his instructions on 28 February and 11 May 16741 Atkins was
precisely ordered to scrutinize the assembly's laws; he must no longer re-enact automatically laws as they expired; only in great emergency should a law be re-enacted which the Crown had not confirmed.
His proclamation of martial law must now have the consent of council
and assembly. He must not remove judges and magistrates, or leave
offices vacant to collect their fees.
In March 1674 Carlisle's commission as governor of Jamaica, which he
had passed on to Lord Vaughan, contained both a similar nomination
of the entire council of Jamaica by the king, and these provisions
against re-enactment.

264. *THE CROWN'S CONTROL OVER PATENTS*, 1674-77:

(a) <u>Additional Instruction to Governor Atkins</u>, 11 May 1674.[1]
...You are, by and with the advice of the council, to
take care that good and sufficient deputies be put in for
the executing of all places in Barbados which are granted
under the great seal of England; and if it shall happen
that any deputy shall be found to be unfit for the discharge of any such office and upon intimation it be not
amended, you are by the first opportunity to represent it
to us by one of our secretaries of state and to our Council
of Trade and Foreign Plantations....[2]

(b) <u>Additional instructions to Governor Vaughan</u>, 3 December 1674.[3]
...Whereas wee have thought fitt to dispose of severall
offices and places in our said Island of Jamaica by Letters Patents under our Great Seale of England, Our will
and pleasure is that you take care that the said severall
offices and places bee freely and without any molestation
enjoyed and held, by the respective persons to whom granted, or their sufficient Deputies, and in case any of the
said patentees, or their deputees shall misbehave themselves in the Execution of any of the said Offices, Our
will and pleasure is that you only suspend them from the
Execution of the same till you shall have represented the
whole matter unto us, and received our pleasure and determination thereupon, taking care that those who shall be,
in the meantime, appointed by you to execute any of the said
Offices give security to be answerable for the profitts of
the same to the respective Patentees....

(c) <u>Henry Coventry to Governor Atkins</u>, 21 November 1677.[4]
...Whatsoever your Opinion is that it is prejudiciall

---

1. C.O. 1/31. In his commission on 19 December 1673 [see below No.342]
Atkins had been forbidden to dispose of any office previously granted
under the great seal. In Willoughby's instructions of 10 June 1672
there had been a similar injunction.
2. On 22 October 1680 a new clause was suggested for Governor Dutton's
instructions which voided all patents (save that of secretary and marshal) unless the office holders resided in the island, and put all
other places (save that of secretary and marshal) at the governor's
disposal (C.O. 29/3). But nevertheless the king's own warrant on 11
March 1681 required Dutton to admit certain royal patentees to office:
just as, for example, the king later granted Nell Gwynne, revenues
from the logwood duties for 21 years from September 1683.
3. C.O. 1/31 No.82.
4. B.M. Add. MSS.25120 f.120. <u>Coventry</u> as secretary of state had argued that unless it could be shown that the king had positively deprived
himself of the right to appoint to an office, Atkins could not dispute
and exclude a royal patent. Now he was acknowledging the final submission of the Barbadians to the king's patent for the clerkship of
the markets, previously in the governor's gift. To secure the 'proper
use' of the 4½% duty for island purposes, and maybe a temporary ease-
ment from a burden which (with the additional expenses of internal gov-

to Government to have Officers nominated here his Majesty
and Councell are of other opinion: That it concerneth
his Majesty to be a little better acquainted with those
that beare Offices in his Plantations than of late he hath
been, for till some later orders of the Councill his Majesty hardly knew the Laws or Men by which the plantations
were governed...His Majesty was resolved to let them know,
they are not to govern themselves, but be governed by him.
     [He warned that the 'late stubborn carriage' of planters would
     occasion strict inquiry and advised Atkins to co-operate, not
     obstruct. Indeed, no Lord Lieutenant of Ireland had protested
     against patents under the great seal: and surely Ireland might
     'pretend a little before Barbados'.]

265. *THE GOVERNOR AND THE NAVAL OFFICER*, 1676-84:

(a) Governor Vaughan to the Lords of Trade, 26 June 1676.[1]
     ...your Lordships may please to observe, the Care I
have taken for the Erecting and Establishing of the Navall
Office, that the Acts of Trade and Navigation might bee
strictly observed, wherein I have faithfully done my
duty, and been very Exact my self in the Entrys of all
Ships, and in January had sent unto the Comissioners of
the Customs a List of all the Vessells that had since my
Arrivall to that time, entered into Bond here, or brought
Certificates they had given in in England. I pursued
exactly what the Act made in the 12th Yeare of his Majesty's Reign does enjoyn also, and...use my utmost endeavours, That all the Acts concerning Trade and Navigation
may bee effectually put in Execucon....

(b) Patent to Abraham Langford, 5 May 1676.[2]
     ...Wee...by these presents Doe Give and Graunt unto
our Trusty and Well beloved Abraham Langford, Gent. the

---

ernment and the Dutch War) they could ill-afford, and to obtain freer
trade, if not home rule, the planters had adopted a policy of passive resistance against the king's nominations: Bridge as councillor
(though he was not a freeholder); Stede as provost marshal ; and
Wyatt as clerk of markets. When Wyatt died in 1679, the king again
nominated his successor.
1. C.O. 1/37 No.12. Though such a post as 'naval officer', who would
be responsible to the governor for the execution of the Navigation
Acts, was implicit in the Act of 1663, it seems that the first such
officer was appointed by Governor Vaughan for Jamaica in 1676. There
was often friction between the naval officer and the collector of customs. Vaughan's instructions emphasised the naval officer's accountability to the governor who bore ultimate responsibility. Vaughan was
governor from 1675 to 1678.
2. C.O. 1/41 No.107. By granting this patent as naval officer for
Barbados under the great seal, the king was disregarding the governor's responsibility under the Act of 1663 and invading his patronage.
Langford petitioned the king against Atkin's refusal to recognise
his authority and denying him the right to arrest - 'one of the chiefest perquisites of the office'. The lords of trade in August 1677

Office and Place of Clerke of the Navall or Navy Offices
in our Island of Barbados...To have, Hold, Exercise and
Enjoy the said Office and Place...by himselfe or his sufficient Deputy or Deputies Dureing our Pleasure. Together
with all fees, Rights, Privilledges, Perquisites and Advantages whatsoever thereunto belonging or in any wise
apptaining in as Large and ample manner to all intents
and purposes whatsoever as William London or any other
Person or Persons heretofore Exercising or Enjoying the
said Office or Place have had or Received in or for the
Exercise or Execution thereof.   Although Expresse mencon
of the true yearely Vallue or certainty of the premisses
or of any of them or of any other Guifte or Graunts by
us or by any of our Progenitors or Predecessors heretofore
made to the said Abraham Langford in these presents is
not made....

(c) The Governor and Company of Massachusetts Colony to the Naval
Officer, 17 March 1682.[1]
Whereas you are chosen and appointed Naval Officer for
the service of His Majesty in the severall parts of the
Massachusetts colony during the pleasure of the Governor
and Company, These are in His Majestie's name to authorise
and require you diligently and faithfully to attend to
that service by taking entries of all ships and other
vessels outward and inward bound by taking bonds and receiving and granting cirtificates for their clearing,
keeping faire bookes of all entries, cirtificates and
bonds once in six months, returning foure copies of all
such bonds with the Governor for the time being, according to the lawes of this jurisdiction[2] made in pursuance
of the Acts of Parliament for the encouragement and increase of trade and navigation, and to observe all such
orders and instructions as you shall receive from the
Governor and Company relating to the execution of the said
office....

(d) Governor Lynch's instructions to the Naval Officer, 20 June 1684.[3]
Whereas you are Constituted Navall Officer by his Majestie's Comission under the Great Seale of England, you
are hereby required to Execute the said Office diligently

reported that 'the Warrants of arrest was always belonging to the
Naval Office' in Barbados; and Atkins was unable to maintain that his
commission excluded any subsequent prerogative grant by the king [see
below No.343].
1. N.B. Shurtleff (ed.) op.cit.V p.338. By the act of the general
court, naval officers were appointed to Boston, Salem and Newbury.
Randolph was angry at this method of complying with the intention of
the Navigation Acts: but there was no power of disallowance reserved
to the Crown under the 1629 charter. Simon Bradstreet was governor
from 1679 to 1686.
2. Acts of Parliament, it was claimed, must be re-enacted by the general court to be valid in the colony:[see below Nos.313,320].
3. C.O. 1/49 No.7.Lynch had been governor of Jamaica 1663-4 and again
1671-5, and was now in his third tour 1682-4.

and faithfully that you may doe soe, you are to have and
Carefully to use all the Lawes and Statutes Concerning
Navigation, Trade and Customs...of the King or what other
Acts there is or Orders you shall have from his Majestie,
Lords of the Treasury or others your Superiors relating
to Trade Customs or Navigation. In the Exact performance
whereof You are to be Exceeding Carefull, Here being like-
wise a Collector (But at Present noe surveyor) for the
Extra and Plantacon Dutyes by Act of the King, you shall
Advise me if the said Collector does not do his Duty that
I may inform the Comissioners of the Customs of England
and for that the said Collector may better performe his
Duty - You shall shew him all the Enteries, Certificates,
Bonds *etc*....,
　　You are every 6 Months to send the Comissioners of the
Customs in England Coppyes of all Entrys, Bonds, Certific-
ates *etc* ....
　　You are Likewise to keep Due Entryes of all shipps,
Goods, Passengers, Servants, Negroes *etc*. Imported into
this Island whence and of what Number and Quality, and
likewise of all Goods Emported in what shipps, Quantity,
and of what Nature and to what Place, of all which you
shall twice a year give Account to our Auditor Generall,
William Blaithwaite Esq., for the Lords of his Majesties,
Councill and Treasury...as Navall Officer to *[?see]*the Collector and receiver take due Entryes and that his Majestie's
Customes for Wine *etc*.., be faithfully Collected, and if he
or any Waiter or under Officer Neglect the faithfull Performance of their Duty you shall Informe me [or the council.]

266. THE GOVERNOR AND THE MILITIA, 1679:
(a) <u>Report of the Committee for Trade and Plantations</u>, 28 May 1679.[1]
　　We have, in obedience to your Majesty's commands, ent-
ered into the consideration of the present state of your
Majesty's island of Jamaica....
Ist...they are unsatisfied with a clause in the militia
bill, whereby it is provided, that the governor may upon
all occasions and emergencies act as captain general and
governor in chief, according to and in pursuance of all
powers and authorities given unto him by your Majesty's
governor...It is not without the greatest presumption that
they go about to question your Majesty's power over the
militia in that island, since it hath been allowed and

---

1. C.O. 138/3 pp.294 ff. By his commission the governor was captain
general of all military forces in the colony: with the council's assent he could build forts and declare martial law. But Militia Acts
in Jamaica from 1664 sought to limit the governor's powers by laying
down rules and conditions: they had challenged in 1673 his right to
commandeer slaves. In 1675 and 1677 Governor Vaughan had attempted
to include in militia bills a clause asserting his prerogative power,
neither diminishing nor increasing it. This led indeed, to the controversy in April and May 1677 over the 'Bill of privileges' and the
Act declaring the laws of England to be in force [see below No.356].

declared, even by the laws of this your kingdom, that the sole supreme government, command, and disposition, of the militia, and of all forces by sea and land, and of all forts and places of strength, is residing with your Majesty, within all your Majesty's realms and dominions.

(b) <u>Reply of the Jamaican Assembly to Governor Carlisle</u>, 23 November 1679.[1]

...no act of England gives your Majesty the like power over the militia as ours doth; for, on any apprehension of danger, the general with his council of officers, have power to put the law martial on foot for what time they please, and to command us in our own persons, our servants, negroes, horses, even all that we have, to your Majesty's service,...

267. *DISCUSSIONS ON DRAFT COMMISSION AND INSTRUCTIONS TO SIR RICHARD DUTTON FOR BARBADOS AND THE WINDWARDS*, 1680:

(a) <u>Recommendations by the Lords of Trade</u>, 6 August 1680.[2]

...Their Lordships agree that five Councillors shall make a Quorum according to his Majesty's Orders lately signified to Sir Jonathan Atkins.

As for the power of Enacting Laws, It is thought fit That the method of Biennial Laws bee laid aside and that they continue in force untill they bee disallowed by his Majesty pursuant to the directions of the Lord Francis and William Willoughby their Commissions.[3] And that it bee strictly provided That all Laws of what nature and

---

1. Journ. Jam. Ass. I p.52. The Jamaican assembly had contemplated the revolutionary step of ignoring the Crown and petitioning the house of commons instead. They were trying to curb in Jamaica a prerogative limited in England, presumably in the way the Militia Acts of 1662 and 1663 had done, though the Act of 1661 (13 Car.II Stat.1 cap.6) had declared that by the laws of England the 'sole' command was the king's. Later Parliaments had indeed attempted to interfere with the king's command but without success. Samuel Long, the Jamaican Speaker, contended that to accept the governor's proposed clause would make it impossible to challenge any increase in his powers: 'if this *proviso* pass they would make everything in the Commission commanded to be lawful'. 'His Majesty's commission was no law to them and...there might be that which was unlawful in such commissions'. (C.O. 1/140 p.194:*Cal. State Papers* 1677-80 No.270).
2. C.O. 391/3 pp.184-6. The commissions and instructions in their final form were approved by the lords of trade on 22 October and were dated 30 October (C.O. 29/3 pp.37 ff). In the same week, they were sent to the privy council as suitable for Jamaica, the Poynings' experiment having failed [see No.366].
3. Previously, under the last commission to Willoughby for the Windwards in 1672, to Wheler for the Leewards in 1671 and to Lynch for Jamaica in 1670, all laws not confirmed by the Crown within 2 years had been deemed to have expired. Now laws would be invalid when disallowed, but would continue to be in force until the Crown made such a decision.

duration soever bee transmitted under the Seal of the
Island within three months or sooner after their being
enacted...the Governor shall incurr the forfeiture of that
yeares salary wherein hee shall upon any pretence whatsoever, omit to send over the Laws within the time limited....

[The governor had to take an oath to observe his commission and
instructions.]

Their Lordships, taking notice that Laws are made in
Barbados for raising a Publick Revenue out of Liquors
imported and otherwise wherein the King's Name is not mentioned, It is thought fit That Sir Richard Dutton bee directed in his Instructions not to pass any Law upon any
occasion whatsoever for raising money, unless the stile
bee made agreeable to the Laws of England, whereby all
money is said to bee given to the King's most Excellent
Majesty for the support of the Government or some particular use, as the Instructions to the Earl of Carlisle, and
Lord Culpeper direct.

And there having been formerly clauses inserted by the
Assembly whereby the Impost on Liquors and other Publick
Moneys are made accountable to the Governor and Council
and Assembly and to such other persons as they shall appoint and to no other person whatsoever, It is now thought
fit That Sir Richard Dutton bee instructed not to admit
of or pass any Clause whereby the said Revenues shall not
become accomptable to the Treasury here or the Excheqyer
and that it bee particularly directed That the money shall
bee disposed of by Warrant from the Governor with the advice of the Council and not otherwise. But the Assembly
may bee nevertheless permitted to view the Accompts of
money disposed of by virtue of such Laws as they shall
make.[1]

And whereas the Impost on Liquors has been raised for
very short termes whereby the King's Service has received
great prejudice Provision is to bee made That noe Law for
raising an Imposition on Liquors shall continue for less
than one yeare. And that in generall all Laws may bee
made indefinit and without Limitation of time, except the
same bee for a temporary end which may expire and have its
full effect within a certain time....

...the Governor doe not erect or dissolve any Courts
or Offices of Judicature not before erected or established,
without his Majesty's especial orders; and that therefore
hee doe transmit, with all conveneint speed after his arrival, an account of all Establishments of Courts, Offices

---

1. This instruction was further strengthened on 15 December 1682. The
liquor duty (apart from the 4½% duty whose revenues the king had appropriated to his own use) provided the sole permanent resource for the
expenses of the islands' government at the disposal of the governor,
council and assembly. In 1685 the Barbadian legislature passed an
Act to pay £6000 annually to the king for 11 years to buy out the
4½% duty, to which Dutton assented,but which (on the advice of the
customs commissioners) was disallowed,for the yearly revenues from
the duty exceeded that sum.

etc to the end hee may receive his Majesty's especial orders therein....

...the Governor is to have an Instructions not to remit
any fine or forfeiture either before or after Sentence
untill hee shall have given his Majesty an account thereof
and receive his Directions thereupon....[An attorney general
was to be employed.]

(b) Sir R. Dutton's additional proposals for his commission, 11 September 1680.[1]

...That an Article of the Commissions formerly graunted
by the Lords Francis and William Willoughby may be inserted in my Comission as necessary to support his Majesty's
Authority in the Government, The words are as followeth
'And because such Assemblies of Freeholders as is hereafter expressed cannot bee soe suddenly called as there
may bee occasion to require the same, We doe therefore by
these presents give and graunt unto the sayd Francis Lord
Willoughby full power and authority by and with the advice
of the sayd Councill, or the Major part of them from tyme
to tyme upon emergent occasions to make and ordeine fitt,
and wholsom ordinances and orders within the Islands and
Places aforesayd to bee kept and observed, as well for the
keeping of the Peace as for the better Government of the
People there abiding and to publish the same to all whom
it may concerne.

Which Ordinances wee doe by these presents streightly
charge and comand to bee inviolably observed within the
Islands and Places aforesayd under the penalty therein
expressed. Soe as such Ordinances bee reasonable and not
repugnant or contrary but as nere as may bee considering
the nature and constitution of the People and the Place
agreeable to the Lawes, or Statutes, of this our Kingdom
of England. And soe as the same Ordinances doe not extend
to the binding, charging or taking away of the Right or
interest of any person, or persons in their Freeholds,
goods, or Chattels whatsoever.'

That thereas som Persons formerly putt out of the Councill have thereupon procured favour enough with the People
to bee chosen into the Assembly, where they have much opposed his Majesty's Interest, there may bee therefore added
to this Comission a Clause like unto that in the Comission
to the Earle of Carlisle *viz*: 'That every Member of the
Councill suspended by the Governor or displaced by his
Majesty may be incapable during such suspention and after

_____

1. C.O. 1/46 No.6. Sir Richard Dutton proved an authoritarian adventurer whose ostentatious confrontations with the assembly proved counter-
productive to the Crown's attempts to secure greater control. After
attempting to defraud his deputy, Sir John Witham, he was finally recalled in 1686.In his commission the power to legislate by governor
and council alone was not revived, but the promise to put the disposal
of offices (other than those of secretary and marshal) in the governor's hands was nominally conceded [see above No.264 (a) n.]

being so displaced of being elected into the Generall Assembly.'
   That the Governor may be impowered (as the Lords William
and Francis Willoughby were) to Administer the Oaths of
Allegiance and Supremacy to all such Persons as hee shall
think fitt.
   That as all Lawes in Barbados are to bee made as nere
as conveneiently may bee to the Lawes of England by reason
of the different constitution of the Place, soe the Articles of Warr may bee allsoe directed to bee made as nere
as conveniently may bee to those formerly in use in England.
   And it is further offered to yor Lordshipps in relation
to the Government of Barbados that his Majesty may bee
moved not to appoint any Councellor without the recomendat-
ion, or Participation of the Governor who will bee allwayes
ready and best enabled by his Personall knowledge as to
present unto his Majesty the names of such as shall bee
best quallifyed for that trust, least Persons in debt ill-
affected to the Government, or otherwise unfitt, may happen to bee put into the Councill.
   That his Majesty may bee pleased to graunt no other
Patents for the future under the Great Seale of England
of any office not allready graunted, And that upon the
next vaccancie the Government may have the disposall of
all Places formerly graunted by his Predecessors except
that of Secretary and Provost Marshall which are the two
Principle Offices in the Island. And that for the future
noe Deputy may Officiate for a Patentee without a certificate from the Governor of his due quallification, or
approbation of his fittness to execute such Employment....
   [He further asked that he should not be obliged to disclose his
instructions to his council.]

(c) THE CROWN AND THE GRANT OF CHARTERS 1661-81

   This section shows how the restored king, despite an instinct to
strengthen and secure the Crown's own control overseas, nevertheless
continued in practice to do as his predecessors had done, yielding
impulsively to the importunacy of favourites, enthusiasts, creditors
and vested interests and granting away powers to them by royal charter: mortgaging future imperial control by buying temporary favour
or quietude through concession.

268. RENEWAL OF THE WESTERN CHARTER FOR THE NEWFOUNDLAND FISHERY,
                    26 January 1661.[1]
   [The provisions of the charter granted by Charles I in 1634 were
   repeated.]
   ...Moreover and further than as was ordained by the laws
of our said late father and for the encouragement of our

_____

1. C.O. 1/15 No.3. Also Dartmouth Corporation arch.:(Exeter); DD6/928.
Newfoundland had nominally experienced government by chartered company
(Guy and Kirke), by proprietor (Baltimore), and even by more direct
metropolitan rule - for Treworgie had been appointed governor with a

subjects in the said Newfoundland and in the seas adjoining and for the benefit of the said trade there, We do hereby straightly charge prohabit and forbit all and every one owners of ships trading in the said Newfoundland fishery, that they nor any of them do carry, or transport, or permit, or suffer any person or persons to be carried or transported in their or any of their ships to the said Newfoundland other than such as are of his or their own or other ships company or belonging thereunto, and are upon the said shipps hire and employment, or such are to plant and do intend to settle there....

269. CHARTER FROM CHARLES II FOR THE EAST INDIA COMPANY, 3 April 1661.[1]

[Earlier charters were confirmed].
...We do, for Us, our Heirs and Successors, grant to and with The said *Governor and Company of Merchants of London, Trading into the East-Indies*, and their Successors, that all Plantations, Forts, Fortifications, Factories or Colonies, where the said Company's Factories and Trade are or shall be in the said East-Indies, shall be immediately and from henceforth under the Power and Command of The said Governor and Company, their Successors and Assigns; and that the said Governor and Company..., shall have Liberty, full Power and Authority to appoint and establish Governors, and all other Officers to govern them: And that the Governor and his Council, of the several and respective Places where the said Company have, or shall have

commission over all settlers and fishermen by Cromwell and the council of state: [No.213 (b)]. Now once again the charter of 1634 was renewed, affirming absolute priority for the fishermen of the West country and the value of their migratory industry and trade to England. Indeed, until the 1780s the regular seasonal population of fishermen outnumbered the residents. But by the mid-seventeenth century some English settlement had gradually taken place in Avalon peninsula, while some French rivals were established in Placentia. Equipment – quays, stages,cookrooms – was no longer makeshift and expendable: it was worth while to arrange for some guarding and caretaking throughout the year. The fishermen came in large vessels, but the fishing was increasingly done by small 'bye-boats', many built in the island. This change was clearly not welcomed by those who advised the king: this additional clause to the Western charter was aimed at prohibiting the carrying of 'bye-boat' keepers. The fishery must be kept migratory and dependent on the West country. It must not become island-based. Nevertheless, the clause did permit those who intended permanently to settle to be taken there. So 'bye-boat' keepers continued to be carried: they could claim that they had intended to settle but had changed their mind. Amendments to the Western charter in 1671 forbade the transport of any passengers at all [see No.388].
1. J. Shaw, *Charters*....(1887) pp.32-46. Cromwell's charter, granting in 1657 to the Company the privilege of a trade monopoly on a permanent joint stock basis, had ceased to be valid at the Restoration. Charles II now gave them identical privileges.

any Factories or Places of Trade, within the said East-
Indies, may have Power to judge all Persons, belonging to
The said Governor and Company, or that shall live under
them, in all Causes, whether civil or criminal, according
to the Laws of this Kingdom, and to execute Judgment accordingly: And in case any Crime or Misdemeanor shall be
committed, in any of the said Company's Factories, in the
said East-Indies, where Judicature cannot be executed as
aforesaid, for Want of a Governor and Council there, then
in such case, it shall and may be lawful for the Chief
Factor of that Place, and his Council, to transmit the
Party, together with the Offence, to such other Plantation, Factory or Fort, where there is a Governor and Council, where Justice may be executed, or into this Kingdom
of England, as shall be thought most convenient, there to
receive such Punishment as the Justice of his Offence
shall deserve.[1]

And moreover...We do give and grant unto The said Governor and Company free Liberty and Licence...in case they
conceive it necessary to send either Ships of War, Men or
Ammunition, into any their Factories or other Places of
their Trade, in the said East-Indies, for the Security
and Defence of the same: And to choose Commanders and Officers over them, and to give them Power and Authority, by
Commissions under their Common Seal or otherwise, to continue to make Peace or War with any Prince or People,
that are not Christians, in any Places of their Trade, as
shall be most for the Advantage and Benefit of The said
Governor and Company, and of their Trade....

[The company could erect forts to defend themselves, and could
recompense themselves for injury and loss 'upon the goods, estate
or people of those parts'.]

And further Our Will and Pleasure is, and by these
Presents, for Us, Our Heirs and Successors, We do grant
unto The said Governor and Company...and to their Successors, full Power and Lawful Authority, to seize upon the
Persons of all such English, or any other Our Subjects,
in the said East-Indies, which shall sail in any Indian
or English Vessel, or inhabit in those Parts, without the
Leave and Licence of The said Governor and Company, in
that Behalf first had and obtained, or that shall contemn
or disobey their Orders, and send them to England; and
...shall be liable unto and suffer such Punishment, for
any Offences, by them committed in the said East-Indies,
and Parts before granted, as the President and Council
for The said Governor and Company there shall think fit,
and the Merit of the Offence shall require....

[Those sentenced could appeal to the company in England and
receive such punishment 'as the laws of this nation allow'. Under
no pretext could the company undertake trade to any place 'already
lawfully possessed by any Christian prince in alliance with the

---

1. Trials for offences in India could therefore be held in England.

King'.]

Provided also, that if it shall hereafter appear to Us,
Our Heirs or Successors, that this Grant, or the Continuance thereof, in the whole, or in any Part thereof, shall
not be profitable to Us, Our Heirs and Successors, or to
this Our Realm, that then, and from henceforth, upon and
after Three Years Warning, to be given to the said Company,
by Us, Our Heirs or Successors, under Our or their Privy
Seal, or Sign Manual, this present Grant shall cease, be
void and determined, to all Intents, Constructions and
Purposes....

270. CHARTER FROM CHARLES II FOR CONNECTICUT, 10 May 1662.[1]

Whereas, by the severall Navigations, discoveryes and
successfull Plantations of diverse of our loveing Subjects
of this our Realme of England, Severall Lands, Islands,
Places, Colonies and Plantations have byn obtayned and
setled in that parte of the Continent of America called
New England, and thereby the Trade and Commerce there hath
byn of late yeares much increased, And whereas, We have
byn informed by the humble Petition of our Trusty and welbeloved John Winthrop, John Mason [and 17 others] being Persons Principally interested in our Colony or Plantation
of Conecticutt in New England, that the same Colony or
the greatest parte thereof was purchased and obteyned for
greate and valuable considerations, And some other parte
thereof gained by Conquest and with much difficulty [and
expense] Now Know yee, that in Consideration thereof, and
in regard the said Colony is remote from other the English
Plantations in the Places aforesaid, And to the end the
Affaires and Business which shall from tyme to tyme happen
or arise concerning the same may bee duely Ordered and
managed, Wee have thought fitt, and att the humble Petition of the Persons aforesaid, and are graciously pleased
to Create and Make them a Body Pollitique and Corporate,
with the powers and Priviledges hereinafter mentioned;And
accordingly wee...Doe Ordeine, Constitute and Declare That
they, the said John Winthrop... [and the others named]...and
all such others as now are or hereafter shall bee Admitted
and made free of the Company and Society of our Collony of

---

1. Connecticut Hist. Soc.,_Coll_.I p.52; and Connecticut Colonial Records II p.3-11. At the Restoration John Winthrop had immediately put in
train negotiations to secure a royal charter for Connecticut. In May
1661 a petition from the general court was prepared to the king, and
Winthrop was sent as agent to seek a renewal of the probably non-
existent patent from the Warwick commissioners, and a new grant from
the king. (There was no reference to any Warwick patent in this charter
under the privy seal). Otherwise the liberal terms were those which
Winthrop had himself drafted - including the absorption of New Haven.
He had been instructed by the general court to see that the liberties
and privileges of Connecticut were not to be 'inferior or short' to
what had been granted to Massachusetts.

Conecticut in America, shall...bee one Body Corporate and
Pollitique in fact and name, by the Name of Governour and
Company of the English Colony of Conecticut in New England
in America...And further, wee...Doe declare and appoint,
that for the better ordering and manageing of the affaires
and business of the said Company and their Successors, there
shall be one Governour, one Deputy Governour and Twelve Assistants, to bee from tyme to tyme Constituted, Elected and
Chosen our of the Freemen of the said Company for the tyme
being in such manner and forms as hereafter in these presents is expressed....

   [Winthrop was appointed first and present governor 'and Mason his
   deputy' and 12 assistants were named for the first four months before the elections in October.   The governor should summon a general assembly of the company twice a year to consist of the assistants and no more than 2 freemen elected for each township. The
   general assembly was empowered to elect annually the governor and
   assistants and to appoint officials and admit freemen.   The boundaries were defined and included New Haven[1].]

271. CHARTER FROM CHARLES II FOR RHODE ISLAND AND PROVIDENCE PLANT-
                         ATIONS, 8 July 1663.[2]

   [John Clarke had presented a petition on behalf of Benedict Arnold, Roger Williams, William Coddington, Samuel Gorton and a score
   of others named from the various townships, who had committed themselves to a common cause and to the continuance of their colony as
   a single corporate unit.   In toil and hazard they had survived and
   prospered.]

   ...And whereas in their humble addresse, they have freely declared, that it is much on their hearts (if they may

---

1. Probably without the Crown's knowledge, for royal letters and
orders-in-council continued to be sent to New Haven in 1662 and 1663.
New Haven indeed had delayed proclaiming the king and had offered refuge to the regicides. Some townships resisted annexation to Connecticut
and appealed to the New England Confederation, but the grant of neighbouring New Netherland to the duke of York in 1664 hastened its submission in 1665. The commissioners of the New England Confederation had
agreed in the previous September that the Connecticut delegates represented New Haven too.
2. Rhode Island Colonial Records II pp.3–21. Anxious to secure a royal
charter guaranteeing its privileges, especially against aggressive
neighbours, the general court of Rhode Island in October 1660 had commissioned J. Clarke as its agent. On Roger Williams' urging, the plea
for 'freedom of conscience to worship the Lord their God as they are
persuaded' was a priority. The promptness of Rhode Island in proclaiming the king and the Crown's suspicion of Massachusetts favoured
Clarke's petition, and John Winthrop may have helped with the wording.
It gave legal status to a plantation virtually outlawed by the New
England Confederation because of its dangerous religious heresies and
anarchist political principles. The organisation of the settlements
remained loose; strength of individual consciences for liberty made
consensus (and consent to laws) difficult; and obscurity in the charters' definition of boundaries caused disputes lasting more than 70
years with New Plymouth (then Massachusetts) and Connecticut.

be permitted), to hold forth a livelie experiment, that a
most flourishing civill state may stand and best bee maintained, and that among our English subjects, with a full
libertie in religious concernements; and that true piet-
ye rightly grounded upon gospell principles, will give
the best and greatest security to sovereignetye,and will
lay in the hearts of men the strongest obligations to true
loyaltye: Now know yee, that wee beinge willinge to encourage the hopefull undertakeinge of oure sayd loyall and
loveinge subjects, and to secure them in the free exercise
and enjoyment of all theire civill and religious rights,
appertaining to them, as our loveing subjects; and to
preserve unto them that libertye, in the true Christian
faith and worshipp of God, which they have sought with
soe much travaill, and with peaceable myndes, and loyall
subjectione to our royall progenitors and ourselves, to
enjoye; and because some of the people and inhabitants
of the same colonie cannot, in theire private opinions,
conforme to the publique exercise of religion, according
to the litturgy, formes and ceremonyes of the Church of
England, or take or subscribe the oaths and articles made
and established in that behalfe; and for that the same,
by reason of the remote distances of those places, will
(as wee hope) bee noe breach of the unitie and uniformitie
established in this nation: Have therefore thought fitt,
and doe hereby publish, graunt, ordeyne and declare, That
our royall will and pleasure is, that noe person within
the sayd colonye, at any tyme hereafter, shall be any wise
molested, punished, disquieted, or called in question,
for any differences in opinione in matters of religion,
and doe not actually disturb the civill peace of our sayd
colony; but that all and everye person and persons may,
from tyme to tyme, and at all tymes hereafter, freelye
and fullye have and enjoye his and theire owne judgments
and consciences, in matters of religious concernments,
throughout the tract of lande hereafter mentioned.....[1]
And accordingely wee...ordeyne [that Arnold,Williams, Coddington, Gorton and the others named,and others to be admitted freemen
in the future] shall be from tyme to tyme and forever hereafter, a bodie corporate and politique in fact and name
by the name of *The Governor and Company of the English
Collonie of Rhode Island and Providence Plantations in
New England in America*...And further, we...doe declare
and apoynt that, for the better ordering and managing of
the affaires and business of the sayd Company...there
shall be one Governour, one deputie Governour and ten
Assistants to bee from tyme to tyme...elected...out of
the freemen of the sayd Company....
    [Benedict Arnold was appointed 'the first and present Governor',

---

1. This generous principle of toleration was the basis for Rhode Island's existence. Nevertheless it should be noted that it was granted
by the king when the Cavalier Parliament was engaged in asserting
Anglicanism and persecuting nonconformity in the 'Clarendon code'.

and the deputy and the 10 assistants were named for the next nine months before the elections in May. The governor should summon a general assembly twice a year to consist of the assistants and the freemen elected (up to 6 for Newport, 4 each for Providence, Portsmouth and Warwick, and 2 from each other place). A *quorum* of 7 of the governor, his deputy and assistants might appoint times and places for the general assembly to meet. When the assembly was not in session, the governor and assistants were empowered to appoint officials.   They were not to invade neighbouring colonies or to molest Indians. The boundaries were defined.]

And further our will and pleasure is that in all matters of publique controversy which may fall out between our Collonie of Providence Plantations and the rest of our Collonies in New England, itt shall and may bee lawfull to and for the Governour and Company of the sayd Collony of Providence Plantations to make their appeals therein to us, our heirs and successours, for redresse in such cases, within this our realme of England: and that itt shall be lawfull to and for the inhabitants of the sayd Collony of Providence Plantations, without let or molestation, to passe and repasse with freedome, into and through the rest of the English Collonies, upon their lawfull and civill occasions, and to converse, and hold commerce and trade, with such of the inhabitants of our other English Collonies as shall bee willing to admitt them thereunto, they behaveing themselves peaceably among them; any act, clause or sentence, in any of the sayd Collonies provided, or that shall be provided, to the contrary in anywise notwithstanding....

272. FIRST CHARTER FROM CHARLES II FOR CAROLINA, 24 March 1663.[1]
Ist. Whereas our right trusty, and right well beloved Cousins and Counsellors, *Edward*, Earl of Clarendon, our high

---

1. *Statutes at Large of S. Carolina* (1836) I pp.22 ff. Though the territory south of Virginia had been granted on 30 October 1629 as '*Carolana*' to Sir R. Heath (A.G.): (W.L. Saunders (ed.) *Records of N. Carolina* I pp.5 ff), that royal patent was declared void by the privy council in 12 August 1663 on the ground that 'no English whatsoever have...hitherto planted in the said Province' (it was also affirmed for the future that, if within a certain period no plantation were made, a grant would lapse - *ibid.* I p.42). The supposed attractions of this unused grant had prompted Lord Ashley, Sir W. Berkeley of Virginia and Sir J. Colleton of Barbados (and also of the African Company) to seek the backing of more influential courtiers for the charter as absolute proprietors of a palatinate: jointly, but not corporately, possessed of seignorial privileges. Venturers from New England and Barbados, seeking some sub-grant and separate identity, enjoyed little success; but under Sir W. Berkeley's protection and in continuing dependence on Virginia, a plantation in '*Albemarle*' with W. Drummond as governor of the province (later North Carolina) was established and left largely to its own devices. To the mid-south round 'Charles Town' where John Yeamans, armed with the liberal '*Concessions and Agreement*' of 1665 [see No.370] had been governor of the county of '*Clarendon*'

Chancellor of England... [Albemarle (Monck) captain-general; Lord Berkeley of the navy; Sir George Carteret, vice-chamberlain; Lord Craven; Lord Ashley, chancellor of the exchequer; Sir W. Berkeley and Sir J. Colleton] being excited with a laudable and pious zeal for the Propagation of the Christian Faith, and the Enlargement of our Empire and Dominions, have humbly besought leave of us by their industry and charge, to transport and make an ample Colony of our subjects, natives of our Kingdom of England, and elsewhere within our Dominions, unto a certain country hereafter described, in the parts of America not yet cultivated or planted, and only inhabited by some barbarous people, who have no knowledge of Almighty God.

2nd. And whereas the said Edward, Earl of Clarendon...and the seven others...have humbly besought us to give, grant and confirm unto them and their heirs, the said country, with Priviledges and Jurisdictions requisite for the good government and safety thereof: Know ye, therefore, that we, favouring the pious and noble purpose of the said Edward Earl of Clarendon...and others...by this our present Charter...do Give, Grant and Confirm unto the said Edward Earl of Clarendon...and others...all that territory or tract of ground, scituate, lying and being within our dominions of America, extending from the North end of the Island called Lucke-Island, which lieth in the Southern Virginia Seas, and within six and thirty degrees of the Northern Latitude, and to the West as far as the South Seas, and so Southerly as far as the river St. Matthias, which bordereth upon the coast of Florida, and within one and thirty degrees of Northern Latitude, and so west in a direct line as far as the South seas aforesaid....

3rd. And furthermore, the Patronage and Advowsons of all the Churches and Chapels, which...shall happen hereafter

---

and had even called a general assembly, the settlers had to be withdrawn in 1667. Nevertheless, a second charter, extending boundaries to north and to south, was obtained on 5 June 1665 (*ibid*.I pp.201 ff), and Ashley and Locke, his secretary, made in 1669 a new more energetic effort to establish a colony under Yeamans further to the south, which did precariously survive – amid internal dissensions, and Spanish claims and French ambitions. Though tenacious of their rights,the proprietors were for the most part not interested in the government of their palatinate: the forms of government were archaic, irrelevant, irritating; authority was diluted among the'eight' and on their deaths among their heirs; their attempts to supervise were futile and impotent, and their choice of governors bad. When Locke was encouraged to draft the elaborate *'Fundamental Constitutions'*in 1670 as a prospectus for their system of government, there was a vain effort to reproduce all the customs, privileges and jurisdictions of the bishops of Durham [see Nos.99 ff]. But the history of proprietary Carolina was largely dominated by the resistance of assemblies to the imposition of such *'Constitutions'* by the proprietors,who, though they might abbreviate them, remained wedded to their 'excellent modell' for over 30 years – however unpractical it might be for a thinly populated infant colony.

to be erected, together with license and power to build
and found Churches, Chappels and Oratories...and to cause
them to be dedicated and consecreted according to the
Ecclesiastical laws of our Kingdom of England, together
with all and singular the like, and as ample Rights, Jurisdictions, Priviledges, Prerogatives, Royalties, Liberties, Immunities, and Franchises of what kind soever, within
the Countries, Isles, Islets, and Limits aforesaid.
4th. To have, use, exercise and enjoy, and in as ample
manner as any Bishop of Durham in our Kingdom of England,
ever heretofore have held, used, or enjoyed, or of right
ought or could have, use, or enjoy. And them,the said
Edward Earl of Clarendon...and the seven others...their
heirs and assigns, We do by these Presents...make, create
and constitute, the true and Absolute Lords Proprietors
of the Country aforesaid, and of all other the premises;
saving always the faith, allegiance and sovereign dominion
due to us...for the same, and saving also the right, title,
and interest of all and every our subjects of the English
nation, which are now planted within the limits and bounds
aforesaid, (if any be)...to hold of us...as of our manner
of East Greenwich...in free and common soccage and not
in capite or by knight service, yielding and paying yearly
to us, our heirs and successors, for the same, the yearly
rent of twenty marks of lawful money of England, and also
the fourth part of all gold or silver ore, which, within
the limits aforesaid, shall from time to time happen to
be found....
    [That 'the province of Carolina' might be 'dignified...with as
    large titles and priviledges as any other part of our Dominions',]
We...do grant full and absolute power by virtue of these
presents, to them...for the good and happy Government of
the said Province, to ordain, make, enact, and under their
seals to publish any laws whatsoever, either appertaining
to the publick state of the said Province, or to the private utility of particular persons, according to their
best discretion, of and with the advice, assent and approbation of the Freemen of the said Province, or of the
greater part of them, or of their Delegates or Deputies,
whom for enacting of the said laws, we will that the said
Edward, Earl of Clarendon...and the seven others...shall
from time to time assemble in such manner and form as to
them shall seem best, and the same laws duly to execute
upon all people within the said Province and limits thereof....
6th. And because such assemblies of freeholders cannot
be so conveniently called, as there may be occasion to
require the same, we do, therefore...give and grant unto
the said Edward, Earl of Clarendon... [and the seven others]
... by themselves or their magistrates...full power and
authority, from time to time to make and ordain fit and
wholesome Orders and Ordinances, within the Province
aforesaid...and to publish the same to all to whom it
may concern; we do by these presents streightly charge

and command to be inviolably observed within the said
Province, under the penalties therein...so as such Ordinances be reasonable, and not repugnant or contrary, but
as near as may be, agreeable to the laws and statutes of
this our Kingdom of England, and so as the same ordinances do not extend to the binding, charging, or taking
away of the right or interest of any person or persons,
in their freehold, goods or chattels whatsoever....

    [The eight proprietors were granted exemption for 7 years from
    any custom duties on the produce of Carolina imported into any
    other dominion. They might impose duties, grant or sell land in
    fee-simple and fee-tail (the statute of 18 Edw. I cap.1 *Quia*
    emptores notwithstanding).]

13th. And because many persons born, or inhabiting in
the said Province, for their deserts and services, may
expect to be capable of marks of honour and favour, which,
in respect of the great distance, cannot be conveniently
conferred by us: ...we do... give and grant unto the said
Edward Earl of Clarendon...and the seven others...full
power and authority, to give and confer, unto and upon,
such of the inhabitants of the said Province, as they
shall think do, or shall merit the same, such marks of
favour and titles of honour as they shall think fit, so
as these titles of honour be not the same as are enjoyed
by, or conferred upon any the subjects of this our Kingdom
of England....

    [The eight proprietors were empowered to build forts etc to
    appoint governors, JP's and officials, [1] to incorporate towns,
    to licence markets and to erect manors.[2]

    The eight proprietors and all other tenants and inhabitants of
    Carolina were granted]

that the province and the tenants and inhabitants thereof,
shall not from henceforth be held or reputed a member or
part of any colony whatsoever in America, or elsewhere,
now transported or made, or hereafter to be transported
or made; nor shall be depending on, or subject to their
government in anything, but be absolutely seperated *[sic]*
and divided from the same; and our pleasure is, by these
presents, that they be seperated, and that they be subject
immediately to our crown of England, as depending thereof
forever; and that the inhabitants of the said Province,
nor any of them, shall at any time hereafter be compelled
or compellable, or be any ways subject or liable to app-

---

1. When the Crown appointed a collector of customs for the northern
colony of Albemarle in 1676, there was a revolt against the proprietors led by J. Culpeper who imprisoned the king's collector and assumed the office and revenues himself. Culpeper was tried in London
and found guilty, not of treason but of <u>riot</u>, since Albemarle did not
possess a regular government.
2. By the Fundamental Constitutions in July 1669, two-fifths of the
land would be held by the hereditary nobility (the Lord proprietors
as signiors;the 'landgraves' with baronies; and the 'caciques'); the rest
by commoners and freeholders (lords of the manor and yeomen). It was
a ponderous system for a frontier colony.

ear or answer to any matter, suit, cause or plaint whatsoever, out of the Province aforesaid, in any other of our
islands, colonies, or dominions in America or elsewhere,
other than in our realm of England, and dominion of
Wales....[1]
18th. And because it may happen that some of the people and
inhabitants of the said Province, cannot in their private
opinion, conform to the publick exercise of religion,acc-
ording to the liturgy form and ceremonies of the Church of
England, or take and subscribe the oath and articles, made
and establised in that behalf, and for that the same, by
reason of the remote distances of these places, will, we
hope, be no breach of the unity and uniformity established
in this nation; our will and pleasure therefore is, and
we do by these presents...give and grant unto the said
Edward, Earl of Clarendon and the seven others...full and
free license, liberty and authority, by such legal ways
and means as they shall think fit, to give and grant unto
such person or persons, inhabiting and being within the
said Province, or any part thereof, who really in their
judgements, and for conscience sake, cannot or shall not
conform to the said liturgy and ceremonies, and take and
subscribe the oaths and articles aforesaid, or any of them,
such indulgencies and dispensations in that behalf, for
and during such time and times, and with such limitations
and restrictions as they...shall in their discretion think
fit and reasonable;[2]... [provided such persons as were so indulged
should be loyal, obedient to the laws, and keep the peace.]

273. CHARTER FROM CHARLES II TO THE DUKE OF YORK FOR NEW NETHERLAND,
12 March 1664.[3]

[The king granted to his brother part of Maine, territory south
of 'the Canada river', all Long Island, Martha's Vineyard, Nantuc-
ket and all land from the west side of Connecticut river to the
east side of Delaware bay.]

...And all our estate, right, title, interest, benefit,
advantage, claim and demand of in or to the said lands...

---

1. Implicitly the right to appeal to the courts in the realm was guaranteed. A similar provision for dependence on the Crown of England was
in the charter for the Bahamas granted to six of these lords proprietors in 1670.
2. There was a similar power to grant dispensations in the Bahamas
charter.
3. J.R.Brodhead (ed.) *op.cit.* II pp.295-8. Pressures against the Dutch
from London merchants aided by Sir George Downing (late of The Hague)
won enthusiastic support from the duke, Lord Berkeley and Sir George
Carteret for the conquest of New Netherland (at the confluence of the
Hudson, Delaware and Connecticut rivers) on the pretext that the Dutch
had squatted on English territory there. This proprietary grant disregarded the claims not only of the Netherlands and the Dutch West
India Company,but also of the chartered boundaries of Massachusetts and
Connecticut whose assistance the duke sought in securing his province.
On 2 April the duke named Richard Nicolls as his deputy governor. On

together with the yearly and other the rents, revenues
and profits of all and singular the said premises...
[to be held of the royal manor of East Greenwich 'in free and common soccage and not *in capite*,nor by knights service'] and the said
James Duke of York doth...promise to yield and render
unto us our heirs and successors of and for the same
yearly and every year forty beaver skins when they shall
be demanded or within ninety days after. And we do further...grant unto our said dearest brother James Duke of
York...full and absolute power and authority to correct,
punish, pardon, govern and rule all such the subjects of
us our heirs and successors who may from time to time
adventure themselves into any the parts of places aforesaid or...hereafter inhabit within the same according
to such laws, orders, ordinances, directions and instruc-
ments as by our said dearest brother...shall be established.[1] And in defect thereof in cases of necessity according to the good discretions of his deputies, commissioners, officers or assigns respectively, as well in all
causes and matters, capital and criminal as civil, both
marine and others, so always as the said statutes, ordinances and proceedings be not contrary to but as near as
conveniently may be agreeable to the laws, statutes, and
government of this our realm of England. And saving and
reserving to us our heirs and successors the receiving,
hearing and determining of the appeal and appeals of all
or any person or persons of in or belonging to the territories or islands aforesaid in or touching any judgment
or sentence to be there made or given.[2] And further [he
was empowered] to nominate...by such name or names, stile or
stiles as to him or them shall seem good, and likewise to

---

27 August he secured the surrender of New Amsterdam without a shot's
being fired, [see No.373]. The property of a trading company thereby
became a proprietary domain of the king's brother. Unlike many of
the lord proprietors of Carolina, he was personally interested in
his colony, but his concern was largely financial.
1. There was no palatinate clause; but literally interpreted, the
powers - to make laws, to control appointments, to fix customs, to
erect courts etc. - were the duke's and were absolute. The duke had
discretion in all matters of government essential to the good of the
inhabitants. Significantly (in contrast with the Maryland and Carolina grants) there was no mention of an assembly and none was summoned until 1683. Governors had a council of advisers, chosen (according to the duke's instructions) for 'their abilities, integrity and
acceptability' to the inhabitants - and the 'Duke's laws' provided
for the afforcement of the council by magistrates in the court of
assizes [see No.400(i)]. Moreover the duke also had an advisory
'Council of Commissioners' in England - formally so-called in
1674: legal counsel without whom he seems not to have acted.
2. The reservation of appeals to the king was in accordance with the
new policy of the Crown. Allegiance was sworn to the king and writs
ran in his name.But governors found it impossible to serve three masters - to obey the king's instructions over the Navigation Acts, to
satisfy settlers' demands,and to fill the duke's purse.

revoke, discharge, change and alter[1]...all...governors, officers and ministers which hereafter shall be by him ...thought fit and needful to be made...And also...make, ordain and establish all manner of orders, laws, directions, instructions, formes and ceremonies of government and magistracy fit and necessary for and concerning the government of the territories and islands aforesaid....

274. CHARTER FROM CHARLES II FOR THE HUDSON'S BAY COMPANY, 2 May 1670.[2]
   [Prince Rupert and others had successfully organised a trading expedition to Hudson's Bay and now the undertakers had sought a commercial monopoly.]
   ...Now know ye that We...do give, grant, ratify and confirm unto our said cousin, Prince Rupert [and others named] that they and such others as shall be admitted into the said Society as is hereafter expressed, shall be one Body Corporate and Politique in deed and in name by the name of *The Governor and Company of Adventurers of England trading into Hudson's Bay*...and that the said Governor and Company...shall have perpetuall succession...and be capable to have and hold all lands [rents, privileges, jurisdictions, and franchises, to grant and dispose of land, to sue and be sued as a corporation, and to] have a common seal to serve for all the causes and businesses of them and their successors....
   [The affairs of the company were to be administered by a governor and a committee of seven, three of whom, with the governor or his deputy, would constitute a *quorum*. The names of the first appointees were given, Prince Rupert being the first governor. Appointments were valid for one year. The deputy governor was to be appointed at a public assembly of the company (or a majority of its members) called the Court General. Future governors and the committee members were to be elected annually in November by the assembled governor and company, or the greater part of them.]
   We...do give, grant and confirm, unto the said Governor

---

1. See Nicholls' proclamation of 12 June 1665 [see below No.372].
2. Printed in B. Willson, *The Great Company* (1900) II pp.318–336. Courtiers and London merchants had become interested in opportunities for trade in the Bay which had been pressed upon them by a Boston merchant, Z. Gillam and two French explorers, Radisson and Groseilliers. The king himself had lent a vessel to Prince Rupert for the preliminary expedition in 1668 when Gillam and Groseilliers had wintered in the Bay and returned with a valuable cargo of furs. Now Charles II granted a charter of incorporation to Prince Rupert, Ashley, Albemarle, Arlington, Carteret, Colleton, Craven and others with a monopoly of trade. (The duke of York had shown interest but was not named). The charter was comprehensive and perpetual. Though the company was to be concerned with trade, not settlement, it was a patent for a colony – Rupert's Land. It did not specify whether it was to be a joint stock company or not: for long it was a sort of investment trust for other companies. There were many setbacks and no regular dividend till 1713; but the superiority of English goods and ability to load ships direct enabled it to survive French rivalry. The charter,surrendered in 1870, was a grant of comprehensive power, rivalled only by that to the East India Company.

and Company...the sole trade and commerce of all those seas, straits, bays, rivers, lakes, creeks and sounds, in whatsoever latitude they shall be, that lie within the entrance of the straits, commonly called Hudson's Straits, together with all the lands and territories upon the countries,coasts, and confines of the seas, bays, lakes, rivers, creeks and sounds aforesaid, that are not already actually possessed[1] by or granted to any of our subjects, or possessed by the subjects of any other Christian Prince or State, with the fishing of all sorts of fish, whales, sturgeons and all other royal fishes, in the seas, bays, inlets and rivers within the premises, and the fish therein taken, together with the royalty of the sea upon the coasts within the limits aforesaid, and all mines royal, as well discovered as not discovered within the territories, limits and places aforesaid, and that the said land be from henceforth reckoned and reputed as one of our plantations or colonies in America, called *Rupert's Land*.

And further We do...constitute the said Governor and Company...the true and absolute lords and proprietors of the same territory, limits and places, and of all other the premises, saving always the faith, allegiance and sovereign dominion due to us...to have, hold, possess and enjoy the said territory, limits and places, and all and singular other the premises hereby granted as aforesaid, with their and every of their rights, members, jurisdictions, prerogatives, royalties and appurtenances whatsoever, to them the said Governor and Company, and their successors for ever, to be holden of us, our heirs and successors, as of our manner at East Greenwich, in our County of Kent, in free and common soccage, and not *in capite* or by Knight's service, yielding and paying yearly to us...for the same, two elks and two black beavers, whensoever and as often as we...shall happen to enter into the said countries, territories and regions hereby granted....[2]

We do grant...that it shall and may be lawful to and for the said Governor and Company...from time to time, to assemble themselves, for or about any the matters, causes, affairs, or business of the said trade, in any place or places for the same convenient, within our dominions or elsewhere,[3] and there to hold Court for the said Company and the affairs thereof;   and that also, it shall and may be lawful to and for them, and the greater part of them, being so assembled...whereof the Governor or his Deputy for the time being to be one, to make, ordain and constitute such and so many reasonable laws, constitutions, orders and ordinances as to them, or the greater part of

1. The principle of effective occupation had been the counter-argument in international law promoted by those countries like England excluded from the papal division of the world between Spain and Portugal.
2. These rents were paid in 1939 and 1959.
3. Express provision for the government to be transferred [ct.Massachusetts: pp.285-9].

them...shall seem necessary and convenient for the good
government of the said Company, and of all governors of
colonies, forts and plantations, factors, masters, mariners and other officers employed or to be employed in any
of the territories and lands aforesaid, and in any of
their voyages, and for the better advancement and continuance of the said trade or traffic and plantations, and
the same laws, constitutions, orders and ordinances so
made, and put in use and execute accordingly, and at their
pleasure to revoke and alter the same or any of them, as
the occasion shall require....

    [They had power to punish offences, provided that both the reg-
  ulations and the penalties were not repugnant to English law and
  custom.]

    And furthermore...We...do grant unto the said Governor
and Company...that they...shall forever hereafter have,
use and enjoy, not onely the whole, entire, and only trade
and traffic, and the whole, entire, and only liberty, use
and privilege of trading and trafficking to and from the
territory, limits and places aforesaid, but also the whole
and entire trade and traffic to and from all havens, bays,
creeks, rivers, lakes and seas, into which they shall
find entrance or passage by water or land out of the territories, limits and places aforesaid; and to and with
all the natives and people inhabiting...the territories,
limits and places aforesaid; and to and with all other
nations inhabiting any the coasts adjacent to the said
territories limits and places which are not already possessed as aforesaid, or whereof the sole liberty or privilege of trade and traffic is not granted to any other of
our subjects.

    And We...do grant to the said Governor and Company...
that neither the said territories, limits and places hereby granted as aforesaid, nor any part thereof...shall be
visited, frequented or haunted by any of the subjects of
us, our heirs or successors, contrary to the true meaning
of these presents, and by virtue of our prerogative royal
...unless it be by the license and agreement of the said
Governor and Company in writing first had and obtained,
under their common seal, to be granted upon pain that
every such person or persons that shall trade or traffic
into or from any of the countries, territories or limits
aforesaid...shall incur our indignation, and the forfeiture and the loss of the goods, merchandises and other
things whatsoever,which so shall be brought into this
realm of England, or any of the dominions of the same,
contrary to our said prohibition, or the purport or true
meaning of these presents, or which the said Governor and
Company shall find, take and seize in other places out of
our dominion, where the said Company shall trade...; and
one-half of all the said forfeitures to be to us...and
the other half thereof we do...give and grant unto the
said Governor and Company....And further...We...will not
grant liberty, license or power to any person, or persons

whatsoever...to trade, traffic or inhabit, unto or upon
any of the territories, limits or places afore specified
...without the consent of the said Governor and Company,
or the most part of them....

[Any member of the company who, having promised to supply money
for a voyage, failed to produce it, might be disfranchised and
deprived of his trading rights.]

And...it shall and may be lawful in all elections and bye-
laws to be made by the General Court of the Adventurers
of the said Company, that every person shall have a number of votes according to his stock, that is to say, for
every hundred pounds by him subscribed or brought into
the present stock, one vote, and that any of those that
have subscribed less than one hundred pounds, may join
their respective sums to make up one hundred pounds, and
have one vote jointly for the same, and not otherwise:
And further,...We do...grant to and with the said Governor
and Company of Adventurers of England trading into Hudson's Bay, that all lands, islands, territories, plantations, forts, fortifications, factories or colonies, where
the said Company's factories and trade are or shall be,
within any of the ports or places afore limited, shall
be immediately and from henceforth under the power and
command of the said Governor and Company, their successors and assigns; saving the faith and allegiance due to
be performed to us...and that the said Governor and Company shall have liberty, full power and authority to
appoint and establish Governors and all other officers
to govern them, and that the Governor and his Council of
the several and respective places where the said Company
shall have plantations, forts, factories, colonies or
places of trade within any of the countries, lands or
territories hereby granted, may have power to judge all
persons belonging to the said Governor and Company, or
that shall live under them, in all causes, whether civil
or criminal, according to the laws of the kingdom, and
to execute justice accordingly....

[If a crime was committed in a place where there was no means
of executing justice, the chief factor of that place and his council might take the culprit either to a governor or council, or to
England. The company were authorised to defend their possessions
and rights by force, and to seize interlopers and punish them.]

275. CHARTER FROM CHARLES II FOR THE ROYAL AFRICAN COMPANY,
27 September 1672.[1]

Whereas all and singular the regions...called or known
by the name...of Guinney, Binney, Angola and South Barbary

---

1. C.T. Carr (ed.) *Select Charters*...(1913) pp.186–92. Though it
granted powers for the government of a merchant company and for a
court and governors in Africa, this charter was primarily (and almost
solely) concerned with a trade monopoly – 'the whole entire and only
trade' along the western coast of Africa from Morocco to the Cape of
Good Hope. The 'Gynney and Bynney Company' granted a patent in 1618

in Africa...and the sole trade and traffic thereof, are
the undoubted right of Us...and have been enjoyed by Us and
our predecessors for many years past as in right of this
our Crown of England; and whereas the trade of the said
regions...is of great advantage to our subjects of this
Kingdom....

 [and whereas previous charters had proved ineffectual, accidents
 in the late wars had caused losses,[2] and powers previously granted
 had proved insufficient, new stock for a new company had been collected, and the Crown had accepted the surrender of their patent by
 the Company of Royal Adventurers.]

 We hereby grant...unto...James, Duke of York, [Ashley
(now Shaftesbury) Craven, and 21 others] all and singular the
regions and dominions beginning at the Port of Sally in
South Barbary[3] inclusive and extending thence to Cape de
Bona Esperanza with all islands near adjoining...during
the term of one thousand years: yielding and rendering
therefore to Us...and our successors two elephants, whensoever we...or any of them shall arrive, land and come into
the said dominions....Nevertheless, our will and pleasure
is...that our present grant and demise of the regions...
and all the benefit, commodity, profit and advantage made
...shall be interpreted to be in trust and for the sole
use, benefit and behoof of the Royal African Company, and
therefore we do...grant to...James, Duke of York [and to
over 200 names including Prince Rupert, Shaftesbury, Craven, Carteret,
Colleton, Arlington, Coventry, Childe and Gorges] that they and all
such other as they shall think fit to reserve into their
Company and Society to be traders and adventurers with them
...shall be one body corporate and politique and of themselves indeed and in name, by name of the *Royal African
Company of England*....

(*ibid*. pp.99ff.) had virtually only granted licences to individual merchants and had been unable to prevent interlopers. An interest in
gold on the West African coast had prompted Prince Rupert to secure in
1660 a charter for the 'Company of Royal Adventurers into Africa' (*ibid*.
pp.172 ff.) wherein he was one of the 36 assistants named. In 1663 when
another patent for a new 'Company of Royal Adventurers of England trading into Africa' replaced that earlier grant he was named as the first
governor (*ibid*.pp.177 ff.). In this charter to the Royal African Company granted after the necessary new capital of £110,000 had been subscribed, he was one of the many shareholders, but not a trustee. An
attempt to secure a parliamentary statute as well as a royal patent
failed in 1672, but there were renewed efforts especially after 1688.
In 1698 an Act (9 Will.III cap.26) opened the African trade to all English subjects, but left the maintenance of the forts in the company's
hands: [see Volume II].
2. The petition from the shareholders had mentioned losses during the
Dutch war, especially due to De Ruyter. The company of 1663 had been
almost bankrupt even before that war broke out. When in 1669 the king
asked whether it wished to continue trading it was suggested that new
stock should be sought unencumbered by debts. The general court accepted this, but the creditors refused a 40% repayment of debts until this
new charter forced them to accept. 3. Near Tangier.

[The king incorporated the company with perpetual succession and power to take and purchase lands, to enjoy manors, to plead and be impleaded, and to have a common seal 'engraven on one side with the image of H.M.'s royal person in parliamentary or royal robes, and on the other with an elephant bearing a castle supported by two negroes'. For the government of the company there would be a governor, sub-governor, deputy-governor and 24 assistants, and the Duke of York, Shaftesbury and John Buckworth from the 24 trustees were named respectively as holders of these offices. In the first three weeks of January officials and assistants would be annually elected.[1] The governor and the sub-, or deputy-, governor and 7 assistants as a *quorum* would manage the voyages, sales and appointments made by the company. An oath of loyalty to the king and the company and of respect for the company's rules and limits was prescribed. The governor and court of assistants had power to hold courts for managing business, for summoning general courts, for making reasonable laws, for imposing punishments by imprisonment or fine to the use of the company (provided the same were not repugnant to the laws of England), for removing any officials for misdemeanours, for assigning stock, for arming ships, for making explorations, *etc*.

The company was granted sole trade in those regions in gold, silver, negroes, redwood, elephants' teeth and all other produce. All H.M.'s subjects were forbidden under penalty to traffic into and to import from those regions without license from the company: ships and goods would be forfeited. To prevent clandestine trading customs officials would enforce the company's monopoly.]

We do...grant...that the said Governor, sub-governor, deputy governor and assistants...or any seven of them shall have the ordering rule and government of all such forts, factories, plantations as...shall be...settled...under the said Company within the parts of Africa aforementioned and also full power to make and declare peace and war with any of the heathen nations...that...are...natives ...

[of the regions.[2] The governor and assistants had power to appoint governors of such forts locally, who could raise military forces and execute martial law, according to the company's instructions and to H.M.'s sovereign right over all its plantations. Two-thirds of gold mined was reserved to the king.]

And for the more effectual encouragement of merchants ...we have thought fit to erect...a Court of Judicature to be held at such place or places...as the said Company shall ...direct and appoint....

[The court, consisting of a lawyer and two merchants, would determine forfeitures, bargains, contracts, mercantile and maritime cases according to the rules of equity, the customs of merchants,

---

1. This charter gave more control to the shareholders than those of 1660 or 1663: they could have a general court summoned to consider the conduct of company officials and dismiss them.
2. A similar provision was in the East India Company charter of 1683. This power and the assistance of the customs officials in enforcing the company's monopoly were not in the patents to the earlier African companies.

and any rules the king should lay down: it could confiscate property and impose fines. The company was granted all privileges in
the city of London as fully as any merchant company hitherto established by patent.]

276. CHARTER FROM CHARLES II FOR PENNSYLVANIA, 4 March 1681.[1]
...Whereas our Trustie and well beloved Subject, William
Penn, Esquire, sonn and heire of Sir William Penn, deceased,
out of a commendable desire to enlarge our English Empire
and promote such usefull comodities as may bee of benefitt
to us and our Dominions, as also to reduce the Savage Natives by gentle and just manners to the love of civill Societie and Christian Religion, hath humbley besought leave
of us to transport an ample colonie unto a cartaine Countrey
hereinafter described in the partes of America not yet cultivated and planted.   And hath likewise humbley besought
our Royall Majestie to give, grant, and confirme all the
said Countrey with certaine priviledges and Jurisdicons
requisite for the good Government and safetie of the said
Countrey and Colonie, to him and his heirs forever. Knowe
yee, therefore, that Wee,favouring the petition and good
purpose of the said William Penn, and haveing regard to
the memorie and meritts of his late father, in diverse
services...by this Our present Charter...Doe give and
grant unto the said William Penn, his heires and assignes
All that Tract or parte of land in America, with all the
islands therein conteyned....[The boundaries of the grant were
(somewhat vaguely) described.][2] Wee do, by this our Royall Charter...make, Create and Constitute the true and absolute
Proprietaries of the Countrey aforesaid, [always saving the
allegiance of Penn and all proprietors and inhabitants to the Crown,
and also retaining the 'sovereignty' to the Crown.] ...To bee holden to us, our heirs and Successors, Kings of England, as

---

1. *Charter and laws of Pennsylvania* (1879) pp.81–90. William Penn,
Quaker son of Cromwell's and Charles II's admiral, and lawyer campaig-
ner for civil liberties, had on 1 June 1680 petitioned for a grant of
land west of the Delaware. He wanted to establish a sanctuary in America for all Protestants including Quakers. The king owed the Penn
family a considerable sum, and he and the duke of York were among Penn's
friends. But the lords of trade were reluctant to advise the king to
grant this patent; and, when the king's favour was known, they saw to
it that (indeed, as Penn wanted) the feudal prerogatives of the proprietor were much reduced: defects in earlier grants in excluding the
power of the Crown were now apparent. Unfortunately precedent dictated
that such a grant had to be proprietory. Though there was no mention
of 'the palatinate of Durham', the charter granted Penn 'a province
and seignoirie' – a medieval concept curiously at odds with the new
devices for more central control by the Crown and with Penn's own design for a 'holy experiment' in justice, toleration and brotherly love.
It was a compromise: part feudal, part royal, part personal.
2. There were many conflicting claims, and many expert advisers with
inaccurate geographical knowledge.

of our Castle of Windsor, in our County of Berks, in free
and common socage by fealty only for all services, and
not *in Capite* or by Knights service, Yeelding and paying
therefore...two beaver Skins to bee delivered att our said
Castle of Windsor, on the first day of Januarie, in every
yeare; and also the fifth parte of all Gold and Silver
Oare, which shall from time to time happen to be found
within the Limitts aforesaid, cleare of all Charges, and
...wee doe hereby erect the aforesaid Countrey and Islands, into a Province and Seignoirie, and doe call it
Pensilvania[1]....

> [Penn as 'true and absolute proprietor' of all these lands and
> dominions was empowered to make laws not repugnant to the laws of
> England, and to raise money 'by the advice, consent and approbation
> of the majority of the freemen or their deputies'. Penn had the
> right to initiate laws, but was instructed 'in such sort and forme
> as to him...shall seeme best' to call an assembly. He had power
> to erect courts, to appoint judges and magistrates and to pardon
> (treason and wilful murder excepted).]

And Saveing and reserving to us, Our heirs and Successors,
the receiving, heareing and determining of the Appeale
and Appeales, of all or any person or persons, of, in or
belonging to the Territories aforesaid, or touching any
Judgement to bee there made or given....

> [In emergencies, the proprietor or his representatives might
> make ordinances agreeable to English law without the consent of
> the freemen.]

And our further will and pleasure is, that the Lawes
for regulating and governing of Propertie, within the said
Province, as well for the descent and enjoyment of lands,
as likewise for the enjoyment and succession of goods and
Chattells, and likewise as to felonies, shall be and continue the same as shall be for the time being,by the general course of the Law in our Kingdome of England, untill
the said Lawes shall be altered[2]by the said William Penn,
his heires or assignes, and by the freemen of the said
Province, their Delegates or Deputies, or the greater part
of them....

> [To prevent misconstruction or extension of powers granted which
> might 'depart' from faith and allegiance] Our further will and
> pleasure is, that a transcript or Duplicate of all lawes
> which shall be soe as aforesaid, made and published within
> the said provinces, shall within five yeares after the
> makeing thereof, be transmitted and delivered to the
> privy Councell, for the time being, of us...And if any
> of the said Lawes within the space of six months, after
> that they shall be soe transmitted and delivered, bee

---

1. 'The name the King would have given it in honour of my father'.
2. This is an explicit indication that colonial law, which was invalid if repugnant to English law, could validly be different from
it.

declared by us, ...in our ...Councell, inconsistent with
the sovereignety or lawfull prerogative of us,...or contrary to the faith and allegiance due to the legall Government of this realme, from the said William Penn, or
his heires, or of the Planters and Inhabitants of the
said province; from thenceforth such Lawes concerning
which such such Judgement and declaracon shall be made,
shall become voyd, otherwise the said Lawes soe transmitted, shall remaine and stand in full force according
to the true intent and meaneing thereof....[1]
    [Penn and his settlers were licensed to export their produce
    only to England,or within a year to reexport them to other countr-
    ies 'either of our Dominions or foreign', paying the appropriate
    duties and observing the Acts of Navigation. He could establish
    ports,] Provided, that the said William Penn and his
heires, and the Lietenants and Governors for the time
being, shall admitt and retaine in and about all such
ports, havens, Creeks and Keyes, all officers and their
Deputies, who shall from time to time be appointed for
that purpose, by the farmers or Commissioners of our customs, for the time being. And Wee doe further appoint
and ordaine...That he the said William Penn...may from
time to time forever, have and enjoy the Customs and Subsidies in the ports, harbours and other Creeks, and places aforesaid, within the province aforesaid, payable or
due for the merchandizes and wares, there to be Laded and
unladed, the said Customs and Subsidies to be reasonable
assessed, upon any occasion by themselves, and the people
there as aforesaid, to be assembled to whom wee Give
power, by these presents for us, our heires and Successors, upon just cause, and in a due portion, to assesse
and impose the same, Saveing unto us, Our heires and
Successors, such imposicons and customs as by Act of parliament are and shall be appointed: And it is further our
will and pleasure, that the said William Penn, his heires
and assignes, shall from time to time constitute and appoint an Attorney or Agent, to reside in or neare our
Citty of London, who shall make knowne the place where
he shall dwell or may be found, unto the Clerks of Our
privy Counsell, (for the time being, or one of them,) and
shall be ready to appeare in any of our Courts at Westminster, to Answer for any misdemeanors that shall be comitted, or by any wilfull default or neglect permitted by
the said William Penn, his heirs or assigns, against our
Lawes of Trade or Navigacon....[2]

1. The review of laws and the right of disallowance in proprietaries
had previously been reserved to the lord proprietor, not to the king.
It was North (C.J.) who insisted on the provision. The first Act so
disallowed was probably in 1699.
2. The lords of trade (and particularly Blathwayt who was opposed to
the Crown's granting away its power) were concerned to see that the
authority of the commissioners of customs was acknowledged. The provision of a colonial agent in London was a new feature of supervision

[The agent was to pay such fines and penalties for such default
or neglect as were prescribed by Act of Parliament. If no such
payment was made within a year] then it shall be lawfull for
us, our heires and Successors, to seize and Resume the
government of the said province or Countrey, and the same
to retain until payment shall be made thereof....
[Nevertheless no such resumption would affect the individual
property of the planters. Penn might not correspond with an enemy
prince,nor make war against any friendly one.]
That Wee...shall att no time hereafter sett or make,or
cause to be sett, any impossicon, custome or other taxacon, rate or contribucon whatsoever, in and upon the
dwellers, and inhabitants of the aforesaid province, for
their Lands, tenements, goods or chattels, within the
said province,or in and upon any goods or merchandize
within the said province, or to beladen or unladen within
the ports or harbours of the said province, unless the
same be with the consent of the proprietary, or chiefe
Governor and assembly, or by Act of Parliament in England....[1] [If 20 colonists asked for an Anglican preacher, the
Bishop of London[2] would send one.][3]

(d) THE CROWN'S ATTEMPT TO CONTROL, REORGANISE AND
    DISCIPLINE CHARTERED COLONIES, 1661-88.

This section shows how the Crown tried from time to time to repent
of its generosity,to curb the growth of colonial autonomy, to restrict the devolution of powers, and to take back those granted away.
It was no new instinct, for Charles I had expressed a wish for a
uniform system of colonial government. Nor did it cease to be a policy
after the revolution of 1688: indeed, for another eighty years it
was pursued with some consistency by the board of trade [see Volume
II]; but the want of resolution and lack of interest in the metropolis (by kings and Parliaments) enabled colonial self-government on
a distant frontier - already sturdy enough, fertile in expedient
and evasion, and determined to preserve its identity - to prevent
complete success. In this period before 1688, however, the policy
of the restored Stuarts culminated in the revocation of some of the
charters, particularly of the Massachusetts Bay Company, and on the
eve of the English revolution in the establishment of the Dominion
of New England.

---

and control - again at the suggestion of the chief justice.
1.A notable reservation of the right of king-in-parliament to impose
taxes on a colony.
2. This provision was made at the wish of the bishop of London, one
of the lords of trade.
3. Penn at once drafted an account of his province and its attractions which he circulated in England and on the continent. He wrote
a letter to prospective settlers in April,assuring them that they
would not be at the mercy of a governor 'who was come to make his
fortune great' and that they would be able to shape their own laws
and to live as a 'free people'. On 11 July 1681 he drew up his 'Conditions and Concessions' dealing with terms for land grants and plant-

277. RESOLUTION OF THE COMMITTEE OF THE PRIVY COUNCIL FOR FOREIGN
PLANTATIONS, 7 January 1661.[1]
Ordered that my Lord Treasurer bee requested to present
to his Majesty the humble desire and advise of this Councell to aggree with all such who have any of his Majesties
Forraine plantacons, and to take the same propriety into
his owne hands and that his Majesty will bee pleased to
prevent the same for the future.[2]

278. NEW HAMPSHIRE: Order in Council, 10 July 1679.[3]
Whereas your Majesty hath lately ordered in Councill
that signification should bee made to your Colony of the

---

ing, and with relations with the Indians.
1. C.O. 1/14 p.8. Charles I had in May 1625 [see p.65] stated his
wish to secure 'one uniforme course of government in and through all
our whole monarchie': but had yielded to pleas and pressures by enthusiastic promoters in a spate of often conflicting grants to individuals and companies. The struggle between king and Parliament had delayed, if not prevented, effective action, and colonies had been able
to secure a tradition of autonomy which could resist a distant metropolis effectively when it attempted to assert authority at the Restoration. In its commission [see No.257] the council for foreign plantations, urged by London merchants, had been given the responsibility
for a royal policy to bring the colonies under a 'uniform inspection
and conduct'. But the Restoration also saw the revival of proprieties;
and, in generosity and under pressure and debt, the king continued to
give power away.
2. The resistance to proprietary grants had been fitful and remained
so: a matter of intention, not practice (as the previous section
shows). But petitions for grants did not always succeed. At the Restoration Stirling failed to substantiate his claim(from the council
of New England)in Long Island; so did Hamilton in New Cambridge on
the Connecticut. The board of trade later in 1698 considered that
'the revival of all the dormant titles under the grants of the Council
of Plymouth would lead to unspeakable disturbance and confusion'.
3. C.O. 5/903 pp.360-4. This was a minor assertion of the authority
of the Crown: New Hampshire was removed from the jurisdiction of Massachusetts and made a royal province. The territorial claims of Gorges
and Mason had of course been infringed by the charter of Massachusetts
Bay, and the government in Boston had continued to encroach and to
interfere, not least with the work of the royal commissioners in 1664-
5 and of officials enforcing the Navigation Acts in the 1670s. John
Mason had received part of New Hampshire when the council of New England was surrendering its charter; but his claim to have received a
royal charter in 1639, which his heirs (unlike those of Gorges) could
not produce, was rejected by the chief justices in 1677: any Mason
rights were territorial, not governmental. The attorney general, Sir
William Jones, further declared that fifty years of undisturbed possession gave indisputable rights to the owners of the lands.
The lords of trade considered the question and recommended the assumption of responsibility for New Hampshire by the Crown. They told the
Massachusetts agents that the king 'took it ill' that Massachusetts had
brought out Gorges' valid claim to Maine, but that since New Hampshire

Massachusetts in New England That they forbear to exercise any Jurisdiction over the Townes of Portsmouth,
Hampton, Dover, Exeter or any other of the Townes or
Lands in the Province of New Hampshire...that your Majesty would take the same into your own care...Wee do humbly
propose to this end the method and regulation following:
1. That your Majesty do, by your Great Seale constitute
a President and Councill, to take care of the said Tract
of Land and the Inhabitants thereof.
2. That *[John Cutt]* bee President for the first year and
so long after as till your Majesty shall nominate another,
that there bee Six more named...to bee of the Councill,
and power left to them to swear in three others out of
the several parts of the Country being such as are most
fitly qualified. That these here named or any three administer to the President the Oaths of Allegiance and Supremacy, and then hee the same to all the rest; and that hee
out of the said number may name one for his Deputy to
preside in his absence, and the President or the said
Deputy and any five to make a *Quorum.*
3. That they meet to open their Commission at Portsmouth
and there choose officers, appointing time and place of
future meetings as the majority shall agree and to use
such Seale for their Orders as shall bee sent unto them.
4. That all Justice, civill and criminall, bee for the
present administered by the said Councill but in such ways
and methods as are suitable to the Laws of England so far
forth as the circumstances of the place will admitt. And
that every person who thinks himselfe aggrieved by Sentence given about Title of Land may Appeale to His Majesty
in Councill and ye like in any personall action above the
value of 501. and not under... [giving security in advance]
and in criminall punishments to bee inflicted if the same
rise to life or limb that either the party bee sent home
with the state of the Conviction, or execution respited,
till the Case bee here represented and orders sent therein (unless in Cases of murther) .].. [Provisions for the militia
and liberty of Protestant conscience were made.]
8. That for supporting the Charges of the Government the
President and Councill do continue the Taxes which are
now layd. That they levy and distribute the same to those
ends in the best manner they can, untill an Assembly shall
bee called and other methods agreed upon. That in three
months after the President and Councill are Established

---

remained 'without any lawful government' (with Massachusetts explicitly excluded from government and Mason with no right to govern) it
was necessary, to prevent 'distraction and violence', for the king
to take the province 'into his immediate care' (C.S.P. 1677-80 Nos.
352, 912). The lords of trade were opposed to new proprietary grants
[see e.g. No.282]. Robert Mason had agreed to the Crown's terms on
1 July 1679, and this order in council outlined the terms of settlement and government for the issuing of a commission under the great
seal.
1. The Crown was insisting on the right to hear appeals; but the ass-

they issue Writts for the Calling of a Generall Assembly,[1]
using therein such Rules, as to the persons who are to
choose their Deputies and the time and place of meeting
as they shall judge most convenient.
9. That the President of the Councill...may recommend
unto them the making of such Acts as may most tend to the
Establishing them in obedience to your Majesty's authority....That they consider of the fittest ways for the
raising of Taxes, and in such Proportion as may bee for
the support of that Government. That what Acts they do
make are to bee approved by the President and Councill
and thereupon to receive force untill your Majesty's
Pleasure bee known upon the same Acts as to their change
confirmation or disallowance, and therefore they are to
send over such Acts by the first Ships that depart for
England after their making. Also intimation is to bee
given unto them that Your Majesty is graciously pleased
that they nominate unto you 3 persons, out of which Your
Majesty will choose one to bee the President of that Councill and that they also nominate 18, out of which your
Majesty will choose 9 to bee the Members of the said Councill. And when any of them dye, the remainder of the
Councill are to elect a new Member for the time and to
send home his name and the names of 2 more that your Majesty may appoint which of the 3 you most approve...in the
Case of the death of the President, his Deputy shall for
the time succeed to that place of President and choose
his Deputy untill your Majesty's Pleasure bee finally known
therein. And wee further propose that your Majesty do
declare unto your Council that you incline to observe this
method of Grace and favour towards the Assemblies till by
inconveniencies arising from thence you shall see cause
to alter the same.

278 (ii) <u>Commission constituting a President and Council</u>, 18 September
1679.[2]
     Whereas, our Colony of the Massachusetts, at Massach-
usetts Bay, in New-England, in America, have taken upon
themselves to organize a government and jurisdiction over
the Inhabitants and Planters in the Towns of Portsmouth,
Hampton, Dover, Exeter, and all other the Towns and lands
in the Province of New-Hampshire, lying and extending from
three miles northward of Merrimack River, or any part
thereof, into the Province of Maine, not having any legall
right or authority so to do; which said jurisdiction...we
have thought fit, by the advice of our Privy Council, to
inhibit and restrain for the future....And whereas the

---

embly claimed to act as a court of appeal.
1. The first assembly met in March 1680, and following New England
tradition, confirmed the township system of local government and enacted some characteristically puritan criminal laws, quite incompatible
with English law. Robert Mason arrived with a warrant from the king
making him a counsellor; and in March 1682 Edward Cranfield was appointed governor.   2. *Documents and records relating to the province*

Government of the part of the said Province of New-
Hampshire, so limited and bounded as aforesaid, hath not
yet bin granted unto any person or persons whatsoever, but
the same still remains under Our immediate care and protection: To the end, therefore, that our loving subjects,
the planters Inhabitants within the limits aforesaid, may
be protected and defended in their respective rights, liberties and properties, and that due and impartiall justice may be duly administered in all cases, civill and
criminall and that all possible care may be taken for the
quiet and orderly government of the same, now Know ye,
that We...do erect, constitute and appoint a President and
Council to take care of the said Tract of land called *The
Province of New-Hampshire*,and of the Planters and Inhabitants thereof, and to order, rule and govern the same
according to such methods and regulations as are herein
after provisied and declared.   And for the better execution of Our Royall pleasure in this behalf, We do hereby
nominate and appoint Our trusty and well beloved subject,
John Cutt, of Portsmouth, Esq., to be the first President
of the said Councell, and to continue in the said office
for the space of one whole year next ensueing the date of
these presents, and so long after, untill We, Our heirs
and successors, shall nominate and appoint some other
person to succeed him in the same....

   [6 councillors were named from the inhabitants. The president
   and council were to nominate 3 others. The other recommendations
   of the order in council were to be put into effect. The council
   would meet within 20 days at Portsmouth, and choose officials,
   and administer oaths. The king's seal was to be used in administering justice. Taxes previously imposed were to continue until
   an assembly met.[1] Laws were subject to the assent of president
   and council and to be valid unless and until disallowed by the
   Crown.]

   And whereas the said province of New Hampshire, have
many of them bin long in possession of severall quantities of lands, and are said to have made considerable improvements there upon, having noe other title for the
same than what hath bin derived from the Government of
the Massachusetts Bay, in vertue of theire Imaginary line,
which titell as it hath by the opinion of our Judges in
England,[2] bin altogether set aside, soe the Agents from
the saide Colony have consequently disowned any rights,
either in the people or government thereof, from the three
mile line aforesaid; and it appearing unto us that the

---

of New Hampshire (1867) I pp.373-82.
1. A clause in Governor Cranfield's commission confirmed that until
the assembly made adequate provision, existing taxes and imposts would continue: a power he had to use - and abuse by extortion- because
of the resistence to him and to the Crown's policies, and the refusal
of revenues.In 1684 he resorted to collecting taxes which had not been
voted by the assembly.
2. On 12 June 1677: [see No.317].

ancestors of Robert Mason, esquire, obtained grants from
our greate Councill of Plimoth,[1] for the tract of Land
aforesaid, and wheare at very greate expence upon the
same, until molested and finally driven oute, which hath
occasioned a lasting complainte for Justice, by the said
Robert Mason, ever since our restoration; how ever, to
prevent in this case any unreasonable demands which might
be made by the said Robert Mason, for the right he claimeth in the saide soyle, we have obliged the said Robert
Mason, under his hand and seal, to declare that he will
demand nothing for the time paste, untill the 12th of
June last past, nor molest any in the possession for the
time to come, but will make out titles to them and theire
ayres forever, provided they will pay to him upon a fair
agreement, in Lieu of all other Rents, six pence in the
pound, according to the Juste and trew yearly value of
all houses builte by them, and of all lands, whether gardens, orchards, arribell or pasture, which have been improved by them, which he will agree shall be bounded out
unto every of the parties concerned, and that the residue maye remaine unto himself to be disposed of for his
best advantage.[2] But notwithstanding this overture from
the said Robert Mason, which semeth to be faire unto us,
[if] any of the Inhabitants of the saide province of New
Hampshire shall refuse to agree with the Agent of the said
Robert Mason, upon the terms aforesaid, our will and pleasure is that the president and Councell of New Hampshire
aforesaide, for the time being, shall have power and are
hereby impowered to Interfere and reconsile all Differences
if they can. That shall or maye arise between said Robert
Mason and the said Inhabitants; but if they cannot, then
we do hereby commande and require the said president and
Councill to send into England such coppies, fairly and
Imparsially stated, together with their one opinions upon
such cases, that we, our ayres and successors, with the
advice of our and their Councill may determine therein
according to equity; and lastly, our will and pleasure
is, that the said president and Councill for the time
being, doe prepare and send to England, such rules and
methods for their own proceedings, as may best suite with
the constitution of the saide prov. of New Hampshire.
     For the better establishing our authority there and
the government thereof, that we and our privie Councill
may examine and alter or approve the same, in witness
whereof, we have caysed these our letters to be made
patent....

---

1. i.e. the Council of New England.
2. It was unlikely that Mason would be able to collect any such quit
rents: but he could reimburse himself by selling the lands. In 1684
he surrendered to the Crown all fines and forfeitures and one-fifth
of his nominal rents and profits to support royal government in the
colony (C.S.P. 1681-5 No.1895).

279. BERMUDA: REPORT OF THE LORDS OF TRADE ON A PETITION AGAINST THE
                    COMPANY, 21 October 1679.[1]

[As for the petitioner's charge that the company had refused to
summon an assembly, it was clear that the Bermudians had 'no further rights to assemblys' than was given them by the company or
the governor who could 'best judge of the use of them'. As for
their charge that petitions to the king or the company for relief
required the consent of the governor and council, this did not
appear a denial of petitioning, since it was 'very fit' that the
opinions of the governor and council should always accompany their
petitions...for their better information'.]

...whereas the Inhabitants complain That the Company
debar them from the liberty of Appeals and Petitions unto
His Majesty particularly alleging That about five years
past the General Assembly had agreed on a Petition which
is now read to His Majesty, and sent it to the company to
be presented by them, but that they stifled the same returning hard language to such as brought it. The Company
confess the receipt of their Petition but deny their
having concealed the same out of any designe to obstruct
the relief to the Inhabitants, the effect thereof having
been laid before His Majesty in Council about three years
past, upon a hearing between the Company and Mr. Perient
Trott.

    Their Lordships doe hereupon agree to Report their
opinion that the Inhabitants ought to have absolute liberty to present their peticons and appeals unto His Majesty without any interposition or participation whatsoever....[2]

280. NEW PLYMOUTH: GOVERNOR WINSLOW'S ANSWERS TO THE LORDS OF TRADE
      ON THE STATE OF THE COLONY, 1 May 1680.[3]
1. Inquiry What Councills, Assemblys and Courts of Jud-

1.J.H. Lefroy, *Memorials...of the Bermudas*, 1515-1685 II pp.477-8.
The island of Bermuda, torn between royalist and parliamentary factions, had been pacified by the parliamentary fleet in 1654; but tension, disorder and sedition continued. The planters evaded the Navigation Acts and petitioned for free trade (Shaftesbury had written of
their 'aetheism,profaneness and drunckenness'). They had long been in
conflict with the Bermuda (Somers) Company, which, now dwindled to
a small remnant of shareholders, proved to be at once arbitrary and
powerless. The island assembly- the first to meet in the English American empire - had become irregular and met only once between 1669 and
1681. In 1679 the Bermudians petitioned against the company for non-
representative taxation and blocking their right to petition the king.
The lords of trade upheld these two charges and furthermore asserted
that the Adventurers of London had gone beyond the terms of their
charter in assuming the functions of a court of judicature. The conflict between the planters and the company was soon to lead to a successful *quo warranto* action against the charter.
2. The right of the Crown to hear appeals was insisted on in the Pennsylvania Charter of 1681 [see p.432] and was an instruction demanded
by Culpeper of the Virginian House of Burgesses in 1682 [see No.304 n.]
Culpeper was required to allow no appeals to the assembly: it was
'absolutely necessary that all our subjects may have liberty to appeal
to us'. 3. C.O. 5/94 pp.56-7. In a petition to the king on 1 July

icature are within your Government? and of what
nature and kind?

Answer   We have in the month of June annually a General
Court or Assembly at which, by vote of the freemen
our Governor and Magistrates are chosen; and Deputies from the severall Townes then meet and sitt
with the Magistrates to make and repeale Laws as
need requires; and att three other Courts of Assistants by the Governor, Magistrates and Jurys are
Tryalls of Actions and Causes Capitall and Criminall.

2. Inquiry. What Courts of Judicature relating to the
Admiralty?

Answer   Wee do not find Admiralty Jurisdiction granted
us, nor have presumed to erect a Court of Admiralty, though there hath sometimes been occasion
for it by reason of Prizes brought into Our Harbours (in which case Wee have taken Bond to Bring
the Cause to speedy Tryall at some Court of Admiralty by His Majesty granted in England or elsewhere.)

3. Inquiry. Where the Legislative and Executive powers of
your Government are seated, and by what Charter
the same are constituted?

Answer   The Legislative power is seated in the Governor,
Magistrates and freemen either personally appear-
ing or by the Deputys their representatives. The
Executive power in the Magistrate in such manner
as the Answer to the first Enquiry declares. Our
Magistrates have also the power of Justices of the
Peace. Wee have also Courts held in the severall
Townes for Tryall of small actions not above forty
shillings value. The severall Courts above ment-
ioned wee suppose are fairly constituted by Charter
obtained in the 5th year of the Reigne of Our late
Sovereigne Lord King Charles the first....[1]

1679 New Plymouth had prayed again for the continuance for their
civil and religious liberties and for a charter of incorporation and
government similar to that granted to Connecticut.The lords of trade
considered the petition on 15 September and asked a number of questions.
Joseph Winslow here replied to the secretary of state, Coventry,with
answers and protestations of loyalty. The king's reply on 1 June 1680
promised to enlarge their liberties and privileges, but gave no charter. The lords of trade had now given up hope of regulating Massachusetts without voiding its charter, and were moving towards a policy
of consolidating the New England colonies. But in February 1683 and
on several occasions [see No.283] before their final appeal in March
1691 the general court tried without success to secure a royal patent.
In 1686 New Plymouth was absorbed into the Dominion of New England and
in 1691, by the second charter [see Vol.II] to Massachusetts,became
annexed to that colony.
1. But, of course, not by the king, but by the council of New England
[see p.280]. Later in their loyal address of 4 June 1689 welcoming

281. MASSACHUSETTS: PETITION TO CHARTER II BY EDWARD RANDOLPH FOR
     THE VACATION OF THE CHARTER, 6 April 1681.[1]
     [All the New England colonies had submitted to the king's laws,
orders and instructions, save Massachusetts which continually resisted the Crown's authority and had no regard for royal commands.
Cases he has brought in Massachusetts courts against illegal traders had failed, and considerable damages had been given against
the Crown. The Massachusetts government had denied appeals to the
privy council, refused to publish royal proclamations relating to
Acts of Trade, have not yet sent agents as requested by the king,
continued to coin money, *etc.*]
     ...And forasmuch as the Charter by which this Corpor-
ation pretends to act is of the same constitution with
that of the Corporation of Bermodos against which Corporac-
ion your Majestie hath caused a Writt of *Quo Warranto* to
be brought (as formerly hath been done against the Government of Virginia) for misdemeanors committed by them, and
their refusall to submitt the regulation of their Government unto your Majestie.
     And whereas the Corporacion of the Massachusetts have
far surpassed them in their unparralell'd misdemeanors and
contempts and even in their daily arbitrary actings amounting to no lesse than High Treason, to the great oppression
and dissatisfaction of people inhabiting under their Government.
     The Petitioner therefore humbly prays your Majestie in
the name and behalfe of those your Majesties good Subjects
to direct your Majesties Attorney Generall to bring a Writt
of *Quo Warranto* against the Governor and Corporacon of the
Massachusetts Bay in New England (which your Majestie has
never refused in like cases for vacating their Patent,
there being noe kind of doubt but your Majesties Writt
will have its desired effect not only to the great releife

_____

William and Mary after 'the illegal and arbitrary government of Sir
Edmund Andros' (i.e. the Dominion of England),the general court of New
Plymouth explained how they had reverted to their 'wholesome' (pre-
June 1686) constitution and had at once 'proceeded to the election of
a governor and assistants, according to the form of our Old Charter
which we enjoyed for three score and six years without interruption,
and conceive we have good title to by prescription, according to Coke,
that oracle of the laws'. (C.S.P.1689-92 No.183;*Records of...New Plymouth* (1855) VI p.209, Usage,'the free liberties of the free-born people' [see General Fundamentals of 1636,No.183] and the royal recognition of their separate identity in king's letters had given them their
right to govern.
1. Printed in R.N. Toppan, *Edward Randolph* (1899) III pp.89-9. Randolph
now collector of customs in New England, had been making a strong case
since 1676 for action against the Massachusetts Bay for abuse of its
charter [see No.316].At home the challenge to municipal charters had
begun: errors and lapses in city and borough affairs were being discovered to justify forfeiture of patents. Evesham and Norwich were
among the early charters to be voided. In 1683 proceedings against the
city of London were undertaken on *quo warranto* writ in king's bench

of your Majesties oppressed Subjects and bringing that
government under their due allegiance, but to the certain
encrease of your Majesties Customs and Revenue here in
England....[1]

282. RESOLUTION OF THE LORDS OF TRADE, 16 September 1682.[2]
     We have in obedience to your Majesty's Commands consid-
ered the Petition of the Earl of Doncaster wherein he
prays your Majesty to grant unto him under the Great Seale
of England All the Tracts of Land in America called *Florida* and *Guiana* with such powers for the Government thereof
as are therein set forth; And wee have also examined the
Petition of Robert Barclay praying your Majesty to confirm
to the Proprietors their Interest in the Soile of *East New
Jersey* by Patent under the great Seale of England and thereby to grant to the Petitioner and his heirs the Government of the said Province; and in answer thereunto wee
humbly offer our opinions: That it is not convenient for
your Majesty to constitute any new Propriety in America
nor to grant any further powers which may render the
Plantations less dependent upon the Crown.

283. NEW PLYMOUTH: GOVERNOR THOMAS HINCKLEY TO WILLIAM BLATHWAYT,
                                                    1684-87.[3]
 (a) 16 March 1684.
     [He had sent an address and petition to Charles II by Randolph,
     together with a copy of their patent as requested.]

(Mich.33 Car.II in Cobbett's complete *Collection of State Trials* VIII
pp.1039-1358). It was argued there that where by charters so many
'independent commonwealths' and 'republics' had been established, the
king could for breach or lapse reassume what he had granted away: the
limits of the jurisdiction of the mayor and sheriff of London had been
set forth with penalties in 28 Ed.III cap.10; and other statutes including those of Gloucester and Westminster II had provided for a general
method of proceeding by *quo warranto* [see pp.14-5]. The bench gave
unanimous judgement that the franchise and liberty of London be taken
into the king's hands.
1. The lords of trade were instructed by the privy council to consider
this petition and to report.
2. C.O. 324/4 pp.84-5. Nevertheless, in March 1683 the Duke of York
legalised the sale of Carteret's share in East New Jersey to 24 proprietors by a deed of release which the king seems to have confirmed in
the following November.
3. Massachusetts Hist. Soc., *Coll.* 4th series V. p.123. Thomas Hinckley, previously a commissioner of the United Colonies, was elected governor of New Plymouth annually for ten years from 1681, apart from
the period of the existence of the Dominion of New England when he
was a member of Andros' council. William Blathwayt had been appointed
surveyor- and auditor-general of the king's revenues in America in
1680 [see No.261], was secretary to the lords of trade and in 1686
became officially (as he had been virtually) clerk to the privy council.
On 24 April 1685 Hinckley wrote similarly to the lords of trade, protesting the loyalty of New Plymouth and asking for royal confirmation

...Sir, I, having no better scribe then at hand did
presume to send said petition...under scribbling of my
own hand not so polished as might be fit for the eye of
so great a prince, yet hope my dutiful affection therein
will be graciously accepted of His Majesty and defects
pardoned; hoping to find grace in his sight, especially
as to the assurance of the continuation of our religious
liberties in the public worship of God, according to the
best light of our consciences - in all humility and with
peaceable and loyal minds- here professed and hitherto
enjoyed by us, through the high favor of our most gracious prince, under God, Which to enjoy without offence
to those worthy persons who were otherwise minded, was
the known end of the first undertakers into this then
desolate desert....Not that we would infringe the liberties of others of orthodox principles, much less such as
desire to walk in the exercise of their religion according to the way of the Church of England; and therefore
hope it will be no grief of heart another day, to those
reverend and other worthy persons who are contrary-minded
to us as to the manner of God's worship, that they do not
or have not instigated His Majesty against us to the free
exercise of our worshipping the most high God according
to the best light of our consciences and of his holy
word....It is the opinion of sundry wise men eminently
loyal to His Majesty that the rigid actings of some
gentlemen in New England, contrary to His Majesty's commission in his most gracious indulging all Protestants in
the liberty of their consciences, hath been a real dis-
service to His Majesty [promoting disquiet, complaint and dis-
loyalty to the king's regulations.]
(b) 28 June 1687.[1]

    [Expectations raised by Charles II's encouraging letter of 12
    February 1679 had been disappointed, and apprehensions were now
    rife.]
...Poverty is like to come upon us like an armed man,par-
tly by the way or rule of levying rates or taxes engrossed
and said to be sent to England for His Majesty's confirmation; which was for the substance of it, a law made
many years agone by the Massachusetts General Courts.[2]..

    [But the valuations of lifestock and horses, maybe just when
    first imposed, were certainly no longer so, and had brought extreme
    poverty and utter ruin. Since the *quo warranto* proceedings the

---

of its liberties. On 4 June 1685 and in October 1687 the general court
sent petitions and addresses to James II (*ibid*.pp. 137-8, 169-185)
with the same request. A small colony - 'the first English plantation
in this wilderness' of New England - which had always prized its
separation and emphasised its difference from Massachusetts,was
struggling to retain its independent identity.
1. *ibid*. p.153.
2. This was a Massachusetts Act for the continuation and establishment
of certain rates and duties.

levies were moreover no longer lawful. Furthermore it was neither just nor legal]
...to impose that law made by another colony on us in our colony which never had any hand in the making of it, nor never had any such use or custom amongst us to rate every head above sixteen years old at £20 (a thing formerly complained of amongst themselves as a grievance) nor to rate our houses, built only to sleep and shelter ourselves and occasionally our friends therein.... [They were seeking the royal grant] of some petty subordinate government or continuance of our ancient laws, not repugnant to the laws of England and the frame of government here set up (as His Majesty shall see fit), [particularly preserving its tradition for religious tolerance.]

284. MASSACHUSETTS: (i) OPINION OF SIR ROBERT SAWYER (A.G.) ON A
QUO WARRANTO WRIT, 13 May 1684.[1]

...The *Quo warranto* was brought against the present members of the Company, for usurpeing to bee a body politick and the processe directed in the ordinary forme and a letter sent from the Sherifes of London to the Master and members of the Company by Mr. Randoll , but the letter was not delivered till after the returne of the writ was out. The Sherifes principall objection why he could not returne A summons was because the notice was given after the returne was past. He did also make it a question whether he could take notice of New England being out of his balywick. Upon Advice with the Kings Councill I conceive the best way to reach them will bee by a *Scire facias* against the Company to repeale the patent and upon a *nihil* returned by the Sherife of London, a second speciall writ bee directed to Mr. Randoll*[ph]* or some other person who shall give them notice in time before the returne of the writ who may make returne thereof, which I humbly submit to theire Lordships consideration
....

(ii) DECREE CANCELLING THE COMPANY'S CHARTER, 13 October 1684.[2]
[The governor and company had been summoned to appear in chancery in Trinity term to show cause why the patent should not be cancelled. They had not come.]

1. R.N. Toppan, *op.cit.* III p.297-8. In June 1683 Thomas Jones had applied for a *quo warranto* as advised by Sir William Jones (*ibid.* pp.94,225), but the king's letter (C.S.P.p.128) was milder than the lords of trade advocated. Randolph had served the writ personally in Boston (Shurtleff V p.421) in November 1683; but since the time for trial was then past, the process was effectively blocked.
2. Mass. Hist. Soc. *Coll.* (4th ser.) II p.278. The difficulty of serving a writ from the sheriff of London to the Massachusetts Company had prevented successful action by *quo warranto* in 1681-83 (R. N. Toppan *op.cit.* III pp.89,235, 246, 275, 297, 308), and recourse was had now to a *scire facias* to repeal the patent. After a *nihil* had been twice returned and the defendants had not appeared in chancery

Whereupon the aforesaid Robert Sawyer, knight, the King's
attorney general, who prosecutes this cause for our Sovereign Lord the King, prayed judgement and that the said Letters Patents, soe as aforesaid to the said Governor and
Company made and granted, the inrollment of the same for
the reasons aforesaid forfeited; Be cancelled, vacated and
annihilated and restored into the Chancery of our said
Sovereign Lord the King, there to be cancelled. And the
said Governor and Company, the fourth day of the Plea of
eight daies of the holy Tranity above mencioned, before
the King in his said Chancery here, that is to say att
Westminster aforesaid, being solemnly called, did not
appeare but made default...Therefore by the said Court
here itt is adjudged that the aforesaid Letters Patent...
and the inrollment thereof be vacated, cancelled and annihilated and into the said Court restored there to be cancelled.[1]

(iii) REPORT OF THE LORDS OF TRADE ON ITS FUTURE GOVERNMENT,
8 November 1684.[2]
    The Earl of Sunderland having acquainted the Committee
with his Majesty's pleasure that the Charter of the Massachusets Bay being now Vacated upon a *Scire facias* their
Lordships should consider what Methods of Government may
bee fittest for His Majesty's Service in those parts, as
also that a Commission and Instructions bee prepared for

---

within the time allowed, the charter could be voided summarily in
default.
1 .The charges against the company had been selected from the many
alleged and repeated by Randolph (e.g.15 February 1681,3 April,28
May 1682, 4 June 1683; R.N.Toppan,*op.cit*,pp.123,130,191 and 229; T.
Hutchinson, *Papers* II p.266) and particularly the twelve Articles
of 12 June 1683 (*ibid.* pp.233 ff.): unlawful 'taxation without representation' of non-freemen and non-residents, the coinage of money, the
oath of fidelity instead of allegiance (*ibid.* pp.272-7). These were
probably the clearest breaches of the rights of a private corporation,
but from the point of view of the constitutional historian there was
probably more interest in other charges not used: repugnancy,denial
of appeals, evasions of the parliamentary laws of trade, persecutions
of Anglicans, the establishment of their own admiralty court (G.Chal-
mers, *Political Annals* (1780) pp.450 ff,462). The dissolution of the
company, after decades of delay and evasion, meant the end of the
general court. Had the corporation not transferred to Massachusetts,
the cancellation of the charter might not have meant the end of the
assembly (cf. Virginia, 1624). A new form of government had, however,
to be established afresh by a new grant or statute.
2. C.O. 391/5 pp.21-4. For several years the possibility of appointing
a general governor over all the New England colonies had been discussed.
With the final vacation of the Massachusetts charter the opportunity
for consolidation was taken. Such a union of the northern colonies
had of course been the ambition of Gorges half a century earlier.

Coll. Piercy Kirk whom His Majesty hath appointed Governor.[1] Whereupon their Lordships, taking notice that the
Government of the Province of New Hampshire being already
in His Majesty's hands,[2] are of the opinion that it bee
put under the Government of Coll. Kirk upon the Revocation
of Mr. Cranfield's Commission. And that the Colony of
New Plimouth, having no legal Charter or Constitution may
bee alsoe fit to bee annexed thereunto, together with the
Province of Main, which the Corporation of the Massachus-
ets-Bay lately bought of Mr. Gorges the Proprietor. But
because there remains some doubt whether the Propriety of
that Province,being placed in Trustees by the Corporation,
bee legaly devolved onto His Majesty upon their dissolution. It is ordered that this Case bee stated to Mr.
Attorney General, and if hee bee of the opinion that this
Province is devolved to His Majesty,it bee then annexed
to the Government of Coll. Kirk.[3]

Their Lordships doe likewise observe that the Colonys
of Rhode-Island and Conecticut are governed at present
by Charters granted by His Majesty in the year 1663 which
are not yet vacated by any Proceedings at Law....[4] It is
agreed that the Governor have a Council of twelve persons to bee chosen by the King, Five of whom are to bee
a Quorum, and that they bee suspended by the Governor as
hee shall see cause. And that, upon the death of the
Governor, the eldest Counsellor doe preside as in other
Plantations...And that an Assembly bee called when the
Governor shall see occasion[5]....

The Abstract of my Lord Howard's Commission for the
Government of Virginia is alsoe read and ordered to bee
the Rule and Model whereby the Commission to Coll. Kirk
is to bee prepared,with this Difference that, besides the
Exigencies wherein the Martial Law is to bee executed, it
extend alsoe to Soldiers in pay....

Their Lordships will take into further consideration
what Rule ought to bee set for Appeals, or Whether the
summe shall not exceed two hundred pounds or more.[6]

1.Kirke had served in Tangier, but was prevented from taking up his
post in Massachusetts by Monmouth's rebellion in the suppression of
which he played a notorious part.Randolph had thought it a bad appointment and succeeded in getting Joseph Dudley, an able and conciliatory New Englander, made president of a provisional government. He
himself was given the posts of secretary and registrar; but Dudley
did not prove to be merely his compliant tool.
2. See No.278.
3. The attorney general reported that,with the dissolution of the
corporation of Massachusetts, the proprietorship of Maine lapsed to
the Crown.
4. Such proceedings were instituted [see Nos.286-7].
5. In the debate in the privy council it was finally decided not to
require the governor and council to summon an assembly, and no mention was made of any in the commission to Sir Edmund Andros.
6. For the issue of appeals in the Virginia instructions see No.305.

As alsoe what Salary may bee requisite for the Governor,[1] And whether it may not bee fit to continue the present Taxes, untill the Assembly shall grant such as are necessary for the support of the Government.

(iv) INQUIRY BY THE LORDS OF TRADE OF THE KING'S PLEASURE ON REPRESENTATIVE GOVERNMENT, 26 August, 1685.[2]

The Rt. Honourable the Lord President is desired by the Lords of the Committee for Trade and Plantations, humbly to lay before his Majesty That their Lordships had, according to his Majesty's Directions, prepared the draught of a Commission for the temporary Government of New England till a Generall Governor be sent over. That their Lordships finde it necessary to receive his Majesty's pleasure concerning a Clause prepared touching Assemblyes to be called for making of Lawes and raising money, which is agreeable to the opinion of Mr. Attorney and Mr. Solicitor Generall who have Reported that notwithstanding the forfeiture of the Charter the Right did yet Remain in the Inhabitants to consent to such Lawes and Taxes as should be made or imposed in New England; Which clause nevertheless is so drawn that no Lawes are to be made without the Consent of the Governor and Councill nor to continue longer in force than it shall please his Majesty in whose power it remains to approve, alter or Repeale any Acts or publick Regulations of the Government.

285. BERMUDA: GOVERNOR RICHARD CONEY TO LORD SUNDERLAND, 6 June 1685[3]

...As to the Customs on Tobacco, they are so far from being willing to pay it, that they privately conveigh it

---

1. The reduction in the number of governors had been proposed as a means of cutting expenditure, but in 1681 (C.S.P. 1681-85 No.82) the lords of trade had reported that the salary of the general governor must be at the king's charge in order to secure obedience.
2. C.O. 5/904 No.251. The lords of trade, who had closer knowledge of colonial affairs and opinion, remained unhappy at the privy council's decision and at James II's resolve to avoid the inefficiency and procrastination which assemblies had caused. Randolph too favoured the summoning of an assembly.
3. C.O. 1/57 No.135. Since the petition of 1679 some of the planters, including Burghill, had indicated to the privy councillors their readiness to pay a 4½% duty (as in Barbados etc. see No.293) to the Crown to secure the extinction of the charter. The company decided to submit their charter to the test of *quo warranto* . The decision in 1684 went against them, and at the wish of some of the planters and the decision of the Crown the charter was annulled.
Colonel Coney had been sent out as governor in 1683 by the company — but also with the king's express consent — and had been instructed to summon an assembly. When in 1684 Bermuda became a royal colony under Crown government he was continued as governor much to the anger of Burghill and others who had hoped that they would be permitted to choose their own planter-governor. Robert, earl of Sunderland, was secretary of state.

in their owne Bottoms to other ports as New England, Barbados *etc.* pretending that from those ports it shall be
transported for Old England and if it must pay Customs
(say the people) lett it pay yonder, and the Better to
palliate the discovery they stow it in Caske lyned with
fish....In the long run none of this reaches the Custome
House in London or elsewhere, for from the above named
ports in the night it is handed into other Bottoms and
transported into forraigne Countrys. Untill I can call
an Assembly I can only desire them to bring their vessels
under my comand and make a due entry of what they ship
off or import in the Secretary's Office that hereafter
custome may be paid; but they refuse to come under my
Comand to be searched, saying it is an oppression of the
subject: the few that do come under my comand lie off
seven or eight leagues at sea till the boats bring out
the tobacco to them. This was a common fraud in the Company's time....

[It was reported that the island made annually 400,000 or 500,
000 weight. He had attempted in vain to get the cooperation of
his council in obtaining details of the estates, tenants, tenures
and values to see if 'their perquisites be sufficient for their
places' and to develop and use the land more effectively.]

Here is above thirty sayle of trading vessels; and
theyre owners are welthy and the most contentious; yett
they pretend poverty, each thwarting the Government and
enslaving the meaner sort of people who would gladly thrive under Government. Tymber is wholly destroyed what with
building vessells and selling them to foreigners with
other sort of wooded ware to forraigne parts, and when I
prohibit it, they they cry out 'What! are you sent hyther
to enslave us? We are a free borne people, our lands are
our owne and we will doe with our owne what we please, and
if we doe not like the King's Government we can desert
the country and live better elsewhere. The Company was
a Company of Rascalls and thought to have brought us under theyre comand; but now we find we are in a way to be
perfectly enslaved and ruyned.' This is theire frequent
discourse to me; for they esteeme all Government to be
slavery but as is of theire owne establishing and are now
ayming to chuse one Thomas Richards to be theire governor....

[He could get no information; there was a conspiracy of silence:
they were 'so allied' that they would not 'disturb each other in
any matter that concerns the King'. He had great need of powder
and shot. He had ordered Henry Bysshe home: he had been 'a great
incendiary...notwithstanding the King's Commission'. Coney had
not 'enjoyed two days of quiet' since Bysshe landed. He had seized Captain Henley, a privateer, who landed over £3,000 worth of
Dutch goods from a Dutch ship, but the islanders had forced him
to free him. The council and captains of militia would not support the governor nor would the sheriff lay his broad arrow on
the goods landed. The islanders appeared to wish to make Bermuda
'a pirate's refuge'. Coney named the chief ringleaders in oppos-

ition to the king's commission to him: they had all expected that
the king would have allowed them to elect their own governor and
government when the Company was dissolved.]

...None of his Majesty's affayres here move forward;
many Articles I suppose are sent to your Lordships against
me; the people are continually quarrelling with me, I am
dayly in danger of my life. Yett I have not wrongd any
man of a farthing. Bribes I never tooke, though Henly and
the Country offered me some hundreds of pounds....The offence they take against me, is, because I comply with my
duty, stand for his Majesty's Interest, and not conive
at defrauds.

They say they must and will be heard by his Majesty
and that he must doe them justice according to his sacred
oath at his coronation. Likewise his privy Councell as
they are bound to doe. In this manner time is consumed
and nothing is done but railing against my Commission
and government. Contrary to my Commission, whom they
please must sitt in Councell with me and this from the
Councell themselves whoe would impose unknowne oaths upon
me, but what those oaths are I know not. They would keep
my forts without Commission from me, and the magazine
they would comand. I must not imprison any man without
consent of my Councell and it is they that are to govern
and myself to subscribe what they shall order. Truely,
my lord, I am afrayd that the countrey is betrayed. All
would live upon the public lands but neither pay for them
nor do any duty at the Towne or Ports....The clamour of
the countrey is that I have no power to govern here but
by the Duke of York who is a Papist; and must a Papist
command this countrey? The forts they will keep until
they know better by what authority I command here. As to
the humble adresse to his Majesty, one hath been drawne
up but I durst not subscribe to it. It relishes more of
a petition, conditions and directions to his Majesty than
an adresse ....

    [They were seeking to get him sent aboard a ship for England on
    the pretext that he was in danger and 'timorous' and should desert
    his commission.]

286. RHODE ISLAND AND PROVIDENCE PLANTATION:
    ARTICLES OF HIGH MISDEMEANOURS EXHIBITED AGAINST THE GOVERNOR
    AND COMPANY OF THE COLLONY BY EDWARD RANDOLPH, 15 July 1685.[1]
1. They raise great summes of money upon the Inhabitants
of that Colloney and others by fines, taxes and arbitrary
imprisonment contrary to law and deny appeales to His
Majesty.

1.C.O.1/58 No.11 i. These articles Randolph had been asked by the
lords of trade to draw up to justify *quo warranto* actions against
Rhode Island and Connecticut.
James II was now clearly determined to put into practice the ideas,
long held but dormant, for a consolidation of the colonies in the
north: [see No.292] a   greater New York, then 'the Dominion of New

2. They make and Execute Lawes contrary to the Laws of England.
3. They deny His Majesty's Subjects the benefitt of the
Lawes of England and will not Suffer them to be pleaded in
their Courts.
4. They keep noe authentick records of their Lawes, neither
will they Suffer the Inhabitants to have Coppyes of them.
5. They raise and Cancell their Lawes as they please without the consent of the Generall Assembly.
6. Their Governor, Deputy Governor, Assistants, Deputyes
and other officers for the administration of Justice, as
well as juryes and wittnesses are under noe legall oaths.
7. They violate the Acts of trade and have taken from Francis Brinley Esqr. His late Majesty's Commission appointing
the said Brinley and others to administer an oath to the
Governor of that Colloney for his duely putting in Execution the Act of trade and Navigation made in the 12th
year of His Late Majesty's Reigne. The Governor of that Colloney not having taken the said oath these three or four
years last past as is required in the said Act.

287. CONNECTICUT:
        ARTICLES OF HIGH MISDEMEANOUR EXHIBITED AGAINST THE GOVERNOR AND
        COMPANY BY EDWARD RANDOLPH, 15 July 1685.[1]
1. They have made Lawes contrary to the Lawes of England.
2. They Impose Fines upon the Inhabitants and Convert them
to theire owne use.
3. They Inforce an Oath of fidelity upon the Inhabitants
without administering the Oath of Supremacy and Allegiance
as in their Charter is directed.
4. They Deny to the Inhabitants the Exercise of the Religion of the Church of England arbitrarily fineing those who
refuse to come to their Congregationall Assemblyes.
5. His Majesty's subjects Inhabiting other Coloneys cannot
obtain Justice in the Courts of that Coloney of Connectic-
ott.
6. They Discourage and Exclude from the Government all
Gentlemen of knowne Loyalty and keep itt in the hands of
the Independent Party in the Coloney.[2]

288. THE NEW JERSEYS:
        REPORT OF THE LORDS OF TRADE, 17 July 1685.[3]
        ...Wee likewise offer Our Opinions that your Majesty's

---

England'. *Quo warranto* writs could be a device to transform the whole
region into a royal domain. But the traditions of over half a century
of self-government proved too strong.
1. C.O. 1/58 No.11 ii.
2. The attorney general was instructed the same day to issue writs
against Rhode Island and Connecticut.
3. C.O. 324/4 pp.230-1. The lords of trade had been asked to report
on a letter from the mayor of New York and other city officials complaining against the proprietors of New Jersey and Delaware and asking the king to reunite those lands with New York and reclaim western

Attorney Generall may have Directions to consider the
Severall Grants and Proprietys of East and West New Jersey and of Delaware aforementioned and to Enter the like
Writts of Quo Warranto against the respective Proprietors
if he shall find Cause, it being of very Great and Growing Prejudice to your Majesty's Affaires in the Plantations and to your Customs here that such independent Government be kept up and maintained without a nearer and
more Imediate Dependance on your Majesty.

289. CONNECTICUT:
    EDWARD RANDOLPH'S ADDRESS TO THE COLONY, 27 May 1686.[1]
    ...I am now to address to the Consernes of your Colon-
ie - against which I have with me two Quo Warrantoes, as
also against Road Island. His Majestie intends to bring
all New England under one government and nothing is now
remaineing on your part but to think of an humble submission and a dutifull resignation of your charter - which
if you are so hardie [to] offer to defend at law whilste
you are contending for a shaddow you will in the first
place loose all that part of your colonie from Conecticot
to N. Yorke and have it annexed to that gouvernment - a
thing you are certainly enformed of already, and nothing

Connecticut. Their complaint was that the city had lost trade, and
the king had lost revenues, by the separation of those territories
from New York. The lords of trade were now to add Rhode Island and
Connecticut, and the privy council itself to put Maryland (threatened
since February 1682: A.P.C.II.Nos.64,193) and Pennsylvania (R.N.
Toppan op.cit.IV.p.189) on the list for the attorney-general to consider and to proceed against. Baltimore had returned to England to
defend his charter and had paid the king a fine for estimated loss
of customs revenue, but nevertheless a writ against Maryland was ordered. On 15 August Randolph was instructed to serve writs on Rhode
Island, Connecticut, the Jerseys and Maryland: on the same day new
instructions to the collectors of customs in America specifically
deprived Baltimore of his right to appoint his own collectors. Again,
on 30 April 1686 the attorney general was told to institute proceedings for the vacation of the charters of Rhode Island, Connecticut,
Maryland, the Jerseys and Delaware.
1. J.R. Brodhead (ed.) op.cit.III p.368. Armed with the writs and
the threat of proceedings against the charters, Randolph from Boston
was writing to seek the submission of Connecticut.Rhode Island had
submitted at once, but Connecticut resisted until a third writ had
been served and then indicated its submission in December 1686,
though not until the seal of the corporation. In Connecticut there
had been division between those who wanted union with New York and
those (including the council) who preferred New England. Since these
colonies had submitted and their charters had not been judged void
in law, the attorney general gave his opinion in August 1692 (R.I.
Col. Records III p.293-4) that Rhode Island and Connecticut remained
in possession of their powers and they could reassume them: by
agreement the charters were accordingly confirmed.

will prevent but your obviating so generall a callamitie
to all New England by a heartie and timely application
to His Majestie with a humble submission, with an annexed
petition: to grant libertie of conscience, a confirmation
and continuation to you of all the lands now under your
gouvernment and such other favours as your wants can best
dictate to you...A Court by this Government is ordered
shortly to be kep in the Narrangansit to assert the Authority graunted by His Majestie's Commission and to prevent
the Road Islanders further incursions. I expect not that
you trouble me to enter your Coonie as a herauld to den-
ounce warre; my freindship for you enclines mee to perswade an accomodacon and to that end desire you to send
me word whether you will favor yourselves so farr as to
come to me in Boston where you will be witnesses of our
peace and beleife of His Majestie's Government; not such
a scare crow as to afright men out of their estates and
liberties, rather than to submit and be happie...[1]

290. PENNSYLVANIA, CAROLINA AND THE BAHAMAS: ORDER IN COUNCIL,
                                              30 May 1686.[2]
    His Majesty having this day in Councill taken into
his Royall consideration the state of his Plantations in
America, was pleased to Order that Master Attorney Generall doe forthwith proceed by *Quo Warranto* against the
Charter granted to William Penn, Esquire of the Proprietie
of Pensilvania: and also against the Charters granted to
the Proprietors of Carolina, and to the Proprietors of the
Bahama Islands in America.

291. MASSACHUSETTS: EXEMPLIFICATION OF JUDGMENT AGAINST THE CHARTER,
                                              25 May 1686.[3]
    ...And whereas also we are given to understand that
the said Governor and Company of Massachusetts Bay assuming on themselves under Colour of the said Letters Patents,
power to assemble to make good and wholesome lawes and
ordinances not repugnant or Contrary to the Lawes and
Statutes of this Kingdom of England, and for the better
Governing and ruling of the Inhabitants within the Bounds
Limits and premisses aforesaid in the said Letters Patents
above specified and granted, They the said Governor and

---

1. Randolph had recommended not union, but a confederation (similar
to that in the Leewards) with 4 councils and 4 assemblies under a
single governor.
2. Acts of Privy Council I p.209.Action was not however taken against
Penn's charter: both he and the Carolina proprietors seem to have
made a sufficient defence.Shaftesbury protested:he was harmed by the
threatened action:the proprietors had spent considerable sums on their
colonies (C.S.P. 1685-8 No.767).
3. C.O.5/905 pp.69-74.This summary, made for the privy council by the
clerk,Pengry, was read to the provisional council of New England and
recirculated to and confirmed by William III's privy council three
years later, (C.S.P. 1689-92 No.525).

Company under Colour and pretext thereof, respecting only
their own private Gaine and Profitt contrary to the Trust
in the Body Corporate and politick by Us and the Lawes of
this Realm of England reposed, have assumed the unlawfull
and unjust power and authority to levy money of Our Subjects and Liege People to the use of them the said Governor
and Company of Massachusets Bay aforesaid under Colour of
Lawes or ordinances by them *de facto* ordained and established, without any Right, Title or authority whatsoever
and in prosecution and Execution of such illegall and unjust power and authority so by them usurped, They the
said Governor and Company in their generall Court or Assembly aforesaid held at New England aforesaid, to witt, at
Westminster aforesaid in the County of Middx. aforesaid,
did make and publish certain Lawes by them *de facto* Enacted for the Levying of Severall Summs of Money of all Our
Subjects and Liege People as well Freemen, as not freemen
of the said Company and other Strangers (meaning the places, Limits, Bounds and premisses aforesaid in the said
Letters Patents above expressed and granted), Inhabitants
and those that come to them, that is to say of every man
of the age of sixteen yeares there Inhabiting (excepting
the Magistrates and Elders of Churches) one shilling and
eight pence a Head yearly to be paid, and also for all
Goods, Merchandizes and Provisions of all Sorts (excepting Fish, Sheeps wooll, Cotton wooll, Salt and such other
things as By former Lawes are exempted or otherwise Provided for (meaning the Lawes and Ordinances by the Governor
and Company aforesaid made) which from any foreign part
or other Jurisdiction should be Imported, into any Ports
Shores or elsewhere within that Jurisdiction (meaning the
Places Limitts Bounds and premisses aforesaid in the said
Letters Patent above specified and granted)...And that the
said Governor and Company of Massachusetts Bay aforesaid
under Colour and pretence of the orders and Ordinances
aforesaid, So by them for the private Lucre and gain, illegally made and without any other Right Title or Authority
whatsoever for the Space of Seven yeares last past have
Exated divers great Summs of money in the whole amounting
to fifty thousand Pounds p. annum of all the Persons aforesaid Inhabiting and Trafficking within the Places, Limits,
Bounds and premisses, And the same money converted and
disposed to their own use, that is to say at Westminster
aforesaid, To the Subversion of the good Ruling and Government of the Company aforesaid, and to the great oppression and Impoverishing of Our Subjects Inhabiting and trafficking there....
     [They had erected a mint at Boston and made 12 penny, 6 penny and
  3 penny coins with Massachusetts and a tree on one side and 'New
  England'on the other[1], as the currency of 'that Common Wealth'.]
..And that the said Governor and Company of Massachusetts

---

1. See No.233.

Bay aforesaid held at New England aforesaid to witt at
Westminster aforesaid did make and publish one other Law
or ordinance by the *de facto* Enacted to the effect following, that is to say That no man should be urged to take
an Oath or Subscribe to any Articles Covenants or Remons-
trances of publick and Civell nature, but such as the
Generall Court (meaning the publick assembly aforesaid)
had considered allowed and required, And that no oath of
any Magistrate or other officer should binde him any for-
ther or longer than he was Resident or reputed an Inhabitant of that Jurisdiction...and forasmuch as divers
Inhabitants of that Jurisdiction who had long continued
amongst them receiving Protection from that Government
had, as they were informed, uttered offensive speeches
whereby their fidelity to that Government might justly
be suspected, and also that divers strangers of Forreign
parts did repair to them, of whose fidelity they had not
that assurance which was commonly required of all Governments, It was therefore ordered by that Court, and the
authority thereof that the County Court, or any one Magistrate out of Court should have power and were thereby
authorized to require the oath of Fidelity of all Settled
Inhabitants amongst them who had not already taken the
same, as also To require the Oath in the said Law or
Ordinance underwritten of all Strangers who after two
months had their abode there, and if any person should
refuse to take the respective oath he or they should be
bound over to the next County Court or Court of Assistants, where if he should refuse should forfeit five pounds a week for every week he should continue in that Jurisdiction...which said oath...follows in these words,
'You,A.B., do acknowledge your self Subject to the Lawes
of this Jurisdiction during your residence under this Government, and do here sweare by the Great Name of the
Everliving God and engage Your Self to be true and faithfull to the same and not to Plott, Contrive and Conceale
any thing that is to the hurt or detriment thereof'; And
that the said Governor and Company of Massachusetts Bay
aforesaid for the space of Seven Years last past have
Imposed and Cause to be Imposed, to witt at Westminster
aforesaid, without any other Right or authority in that
behalf had or obtained and against Our Will the said Oath
on all Inhabitants and Residents within the Places, Limits
Bounds and Premises in the said Letters Patents above
exprest and granted in contempt of Our Lawes of this Kingdom of England, and to the dispersion and apparent Loss
of Our Royall State, and Contrary to the tenor and effect
of the said Letters Patents, By reason whereof Our Service
of and for the keeping of Our Peace and good Rule and
Government of Our People there was and is much Impeded,
to the great damage of Our People residing there, and to
Our no small prejudice and Grievance, By reason whereof
the said Governor and Company of Massachusetts Bay aforesaid have forfeited the said Letters Patents, and because

wee are willing that Justice should be done therein, Wee therefore command you (as wee have otherwise commanded) that by honest and Lawfull men of Your Bayliwick You cause to be made known to the said Governor and Company of Massachusetts Bay in New England aforesaid, that they be before us in Our Chancery aforesaid in Eight dayes of the Holy Trinity next coming...to shew cause if they have or can why the said Letters Patents so as aforesaid to them the said Governor and Company made and granted and the Inrollment thereof for the reasons aforesaid, ought not to be cancelled vacated annihilated and restored into our said Court of Chancery there to be cancelled...[and no such appearance or defence being made, the charter had accordingly been voided.]

292. *THE DOMINION OF NEW ENGLAND*, 1685-88:

> (i) COMMISSION FROM JAMES II FOR A PRESIDENT AND COUNCIL IN
>   NEW ENGLAND, 8 October 1685.[1]

Whereas a writt of *scire facias* hath been issued out of our high court of chancery against the late governor and company of the Massachusetts-Bay, in New England, whereby the government of that colony and members thereof is now in our hands; and we being minded to give all protection and encouragement to our good subjects therein, and to provide in the most effectuall manner, that due impartiall justice may bee administered in all cases, civill and criminall, and that all possible care may be taken for the just, quiet, and orderly government of the same: Know ye, therefore, that we, by and with the advice of our privy councell, have thought fit to erect and constitute...a president and councill, to take care of all that our territories and dominions of New England, in America, commonly called and knowne by the name of our colony of the Massachusetts-Bay, and our province of New-Hampshire and Maine, and the Narraganset Country, otherwise called the King's Province, with all the islands, rights, and members thereunto appertaining, and to order, rule, and govern the same according to such methods and regulations as are herein after specified and declared, until our Chief Governor shall arrive within our said colonies.

And for the better executing of our royal pleasure in this behalf, we do hereby nominate and appoint our trusty and well-beloved subject, Joseph Dudley, Esq. to be the first president of the said councell, and to continue in the said office until we, our heirs, or successors shall otherwise direct....[The 17 councillors names included Stroughton, Bulkeley, R. Mason, and E. Randolph.] And our express will and pleasure is, that no person shall be admitted to set,

---

1. Mass.Hist.Soc.,*Coll*.1st V pp.244-5.Also in Rhode Is.Colonial Records III p.195.This provisional form of government substantially adopted Randolph's proposals.All the 17 councillors named (apart from Randolph) were New Englanders and were generally regarded as moderates.

or have a vote in the said council, until he hath taken
the oath of allegiance, and the oath hereafter mentioned,
for the due and impartial execution of justice, and the
faithful discharge in them reposed ····

> [The president and council could establish courts, appoint off-
> icers, hear appeals and provide for defence. The proceedings in
> courts must be 'consonant and agreeable to the lawes and statutes
> of this our Realme of England'. They were to see that existing
> taxes were collected[1] and freedom of conscience, especially for
> Anglicans, was guaranteed. Appeals to the privy council were prov-
> ided for.]

292. (ii) PROTEST BY THE GENERAL COURT TO THE ROYAL COMMISSION FOR A
         PRESIDENT AND COUNCIL, 20 May 1686.[2]

> [The king had addressed them not as governor and company but as
> the principal inhabitants of Massachusetts. They objected to the
> new constitution on two grounds:-]

Upon perusall wee finde, as we conceive, First, That
there is no certain determinate rule for your administration of justice and that which is seemes to be too arbitrary.
2ly. That the subjects are abridged of their libertyes as
Englishmen both in the matter of legislation and in the
laying of taxes and indeed the whole unquestioned priviledge of the subject transferred upon yourselves, there
not being the least mention of an assembly in the Commission ....

> [Nevertheless, though they did not consent to the change they
> intended to demean themselves as loyal subjects, while praying
> in the meantime for relief.]

292. (iii) COMMISSION TO SIR EDMUND ANDROS AS GOVERNOR IN CHIEF OF
          THE DOMINION OF NEW ENGLAND, 3 June 1686.[3]

Whereas the Government of that part of our Territory
and Dominion of New England...is now in our hands...We...

---

1. The president and council did not appear to be empowered to levy
new taxes,only to continue to collect old ones. There were however no
revenue acts on the statute book in 1685 for the general court, fearing the loss of their charter,had repealed them all in 1683. Dudley
had to resort to a revival of import duties.
2. N.B. Shurtleff (ed.) op.cit.V.p.516. The change in government had,
in Randolph's words, 'unhinged the Commonwealth'. There were of course
many in New England who welcomed the fact that the exclusive power of
the Puritan oligarchy was broken. The provisional government of president and council was strongly in favour of incorporating Rhode Island
and Connecticut.
3. Publ., Colonial Soc.Mass.,*Coll*.II pp.44-56. His instructions were
issued on 12 September 1686 (C.O. 5/904). Apart from the omission of
an assembly this commission was the same as that to Dongan in New York
a week later: more generally, the powers given and the limitations
prescribed were to conform with those in other royal colonies like
Virginia.
The attempt to unite these colonies in a 'Dominion' had strong argu-

doe constitute and appoint you...Sir Edmund Andros to be
our Captain Generall and Governor in Cheife[1] in and over
all our...Dominion of New England in America comonly called the knowne by the name of our Colony of the Massachusetts Bay, our Colony of New Plymouth and our Provinces of
New Hampshire and Maine, the Narragansett Country, otherwise called the King's Province....

[He was to take the oath of allegiance and administer it to all
councillors, judges and sheriffs. He was empowered to suspend councillors and to make temporary appointments to vacancies.]

Wee doe hereby give and grant unto you full power and
authority by and with the advice and Consent of our said
Councell or the major part of them to make constitute and
ordaine Laws Statutes and Ordinances for the publicque
peace welfare and good government of our said Territory
and Dominion [so long as such laws were 'as neare as Conveniently
may be agreeable to the Laws and Statutes' of England].... Provided
that all such Laws Statutes and Ordinances...be within
three months or sooner...transmitted unto us under our
Seale of New England for our allowance or disapprobacon....

Wee doe...give and grant unto you full power and authority by and with the advice and consent of our said Councell or the major part of them to impose and assesse and
raise and levy such rates and taxes as you shall finde
necessary for the support of the Government....

[He should continue to collect existing taxes and should authorise appropriations under his own warrant. He must supervise justice,
erect courts, secure appeals to the privy council, organise the
militia, execute martial law in time of war, set up a court of
admiralty, authorise fairs and markets, establish customs houses,
and secure toleration for all Christians, especially Anglicans.
All officers civil and military and all inhabitants were to aid
and assist him.]

And wee doe likewise give and grant unto you full power

---

ments of logic and economy in its favour: a reduction in the expenses
of maintaining small separate and often inefficient governments; a
union for defence against the French and their Indian allies; a firmer application of the Acts of Trade — such reasons justified centralisation. The lords of trade seemed to be attracted to the idea on
the anology of the French Dominion of Canada. The voiding of the
Massachusetts charter provided the opportunity for a move, long contemplated not only in Whitehall: the Crown had shown remarkable patience with the Puritan oligarchy: the establishment of the Dominion
as a royal province might seem punitive when it finally came about,
but it was also an inevitable consequence. The facts of seventeenth
century empire required either an acceptance of colonial dependence,
or the dangerous assertion of independence with exposure to foreign
rivals. The absence of an assembly, though understandable, was an
error which deprived the experiment of much goodwill and any chance
of success.

1. The Crown paid Andros' salary.

and authority by and with the advice of our said Councill
to agree with the Planters and Inhabitants of our said
...Dominion concerning such lands, tenements and hereditaments as now are or hereafter shall be in our power to
dispose of and then to grant unto any person or persons
for such Termes and under such moderate quitt Rents,[1]
Services and acknowledgements to be thereupon reserved
unto us as shall be appointed by us which said Grants
are to passe and be sealed by our Seale of New England
and...shall be good and effectuall in Law against us, our
Heires and Successors [2]....

292. (iv) COMMISSION TO GOVERNOR ANDROS, 7 April 1688.[3]
     [He had already been commissioned in June 1686 as governor in
  chief over Massachusetts, New Plymouth, New Hampshire, Maine and
Narragansett Country.]

---

1. Lands in New England had previously been granted by the townships
and had not been subject to quit rents. But such grants were illegal
since the company's charter had included no power to establish townships and corporations. Titles 'derived from Adam through Noah' had
no validity in law.In return for their legalisation,and since colonial
governments had to support themselves, it seemed desirable to secure
such a permanent revenue by quit rents in conformity with English
custom.When Dongan had been instructed to require them in New York,
he had reported 'general satisfaction' for it secured tenures and
titles to the planters and provided 'noe small' increase in revenue
for the government. (J.R.Brodhead *op.cit.*III p.401,412).But it was
unwise to require quit rents on old grants in New England, even if
the rent was small and the prosecutions very few.
2. Andros set about the introduction of an English judicial system
and the codification of the laws; but, despite the changes in quarter
sessions, common pleas, trial by jury and writs in the king's name,
there were substantially few differences in practice. With want of
communications and revenues, the administration of the Dominion was
overstretched: his was an impossible task, even granted his resolution and loyalty. Friction continued between rival colonies, sects
and classes, even in his council itself. Clearly he was empowered
with legislative, as with executive, initiative. He raised revenues
by rents, poll taxes and import duties; though taxes were lower and
more equitable than under the company, the boycott against 'unrepresentative taxation' grew, though for half a century it had been the
accepted norm in Massachusetts under the Puritan oligarchy and the
agitation for an elected assembly conveniently forgot the franchise
had been severely restricted by the congregational test. The religious clauses of his instructions were obnoxious to the old theocrats
who found themselves in opposition for the first time in Boston where
they had had exclusive power: Andros also sought to curb their power
locally in town meetings. Early in 1688 the Reverend Increase Mather
went as agent for the'old'theocrats to London.
3. C.O. 5/904 pp.381 -4. These new additions to the Dominion certainly over-extended and weakened it.

...And Whereas since that time wee have thought it necessary for our Service and for the better protection and
security of Our Subjects in these parts to Joyne and annex to our said Government the neighbouring Collonyes of
Rhode Island and Conecticut, Our Province of New Yorke
and East and West Jersey with the Territories thereunto
belonging as wee do hereby Joyne annex and unite to our
said Government and Dominion of New England, Wee therefore...appoint you the said Sir Edmund Andros to bee Our
Captaine Generall and Governor in Cheife...

> [over Massachusetts, New Plymouth, New Hampshire, Maine, Narrag-
> ansett Country, Rhode Island, Connecticut, New York, East and
> West Jersey 'and all that tract of land from 40° North to the
> River Saint Croix eastwards, thence northward to the River of
> Canada, and from the Atlantic coast on the east to the South Sea
> on the west (Pennsylvania and Delaware only excepted)'. Powers
> granted repeated those in his earlier commission. In addition
> Andros was to have a lieutenant-governor as his deputy[1], an ass-
> istant who was to exercise these full powers in Andros' absence
> or death. Were neither available to act, the administration and
> authority would be undertaken temporarily by the council, the
> first councillor presiding.]

(e) THE CROWN'S SEARCH FOR PERPETUAL REVENUES IN ROYAL COLONIES, 1663-88.

The Restoration saw a gradual strengthening of royal supervision
over the colonies: local 'home rule' by planters or independent governors was challenged by a determination to secure greater information about the many dependencies and to secure greater obedience from
them. In this the matter of finance was crucial: the salaries of
royal governors and officials could not be safely left to the whim,
favour, control or boycott of the assemblies. It seemed desirable
therefore to obtain a perpetual civil list, which would enable colonies to live of their own and to pay their own way, and would also
give stability to colonial governments and immunise them against
assemblymen who had discovered that the most accommodating administration was that which was starved of funds and kept on the verge of
bankrupcy. If a colonial government, however, had a perpetual revenue,
then there was less chance of the opposition asserting its claims
successfully by the refusal of supplies until the royal governor
capitulated and its conditions were met.

293. BARBADOS: AN ACT FOR SETTLING THE IMPOST ON THE COMMODITIES OF
      THE GROWTH OF THIS ISLAND, 12 September 1663.[2]
      [Under Carlisle's patent many lands had been granted, but these

---

1. Francis Nicholson was appointed and New York designated as his
residence.Just before Jacob Leisler's rebellion he was ordered to
take over the governorship there (C.S.P. 1689-91 Nos.121,307).
2.B.Edwards,*History...of the British West Indies* (1819ed.) I pp.335-9.
In the West Indies the confused and complex conditions in the 'Caribbees'and uncertainties in recently-conquered Jamaica called for urgent

grants had lacked certainty and warrant. Since the king had, on
12 June 1663, granted Francis,Lord Willoughby,full powers to confirm all titles]
    ...For a full remedy thereof for all the defects afore-
related, and quieting the possessions and settling the
tenures of the inhabitants of this island, Be it enacted
by his excellency Francis,Lord Willoughby of Parham,*etc.*
his council and gentlemen of the assembly...That, notwithstanding the defects afore-related, all the now rightful
possessors of lands, tenements, and hereditaments within
this island, according to the laws and customs thereof,
may at all times repair unto his Excellency for the full
confirmation of their estates and tenures, and then and
there shall and may receive such full confirmation and
assurance, under his Majesty's great seal for this island,
as they can reasonably advise and desire, according to the
true intent and meaning of the Act.   And be it further
enacted...That all and every the payments of forty pounds
of cotton per head, and all other duties, rents and arrears of rent which have or might have been levied, be from
henceforth absolutely and fully released and made void;
and that the inhabitants of this island have and hold
their several plantations to them and their heirs for
ever, in free and common soccage, yielding and paying
therefore, at the feast of St. Michael every year, if the
same be lawfully demanded, one ear of Indian corn to his
Majesty, his heirs and successors for ever, in full and
free discharge of all rents and services for the future
whatsoever. In consideration of the release of the said
forty pounds, and in consideration of the confirmation of
all estates in this island as aforesaid, and in acknowledgement of his Majesty's grace and favour in sending to and
appointing over us his said Excellency...And forasmuch as
nothing conduceth more to the peace and prosperity of any
place, and the protection of every single person therein,
than that the public revenue thereof may be in some measure proportioned to the public charges and expenses; and
also well weighing the great charges that there must be

---

attention. In the *'Caribbees'* it could not even be said that the writ
of the proprietor ran, let alone of the king. But the Crown might, in
extinguishing the proprietary, secure a bargain by way of a permanent
revenue. The planters there had been concerned to have their land
titles confirmed in freehold, and finally accepted Willoughby's advocacy of the king's demands for the perpetual export duty in return for
this. This Act, approved by an order-in-council, was not repealed
till 1838 [see Vol.III].It remained an irritating reminder of the
Crown's conditions for terminating the proprietary granted to Carlisle
in 1627.Unfortunately for the planters, the terms of the appropriation were too vague, and the king later expropriated the revenue;and what
the planters had 'provided for themselves' was 'shippt to England'
leaving the Barbadian government 'without any publique revenue'. In
1669 Sir Charles Wheler and others paid the king £7,000 a year for
farming this 4½% duty; but Blathwayt's investigation of the arrears,
errors and loss to the Crown was decisive in seeing that after 1684

of necessity in maintaining the honour and dignity of his
Majesty's authority here; <u>the public meeting of the sess-</u>
<u>ions, the often attendance of the council, the reparation</u>
<u>of the forts, the building of a sessions-house and a pri-</u>
<u>son, and all other public charges incumbent on the govern-</u>
<u>ment;</u>[1] do, in consideration thereof, give and grant unto
his Majesty, his heirs and successors for ever,...and Be
it enacted by his Excellency Francis, Lord Willoughby of
Parham, captain-general and chief governor of this island
of Barbadoes, and all the other the Caribbee Islands, and
by and with the consent of the council and the gentlemen
of the assembly, representatives of this island...that is
to say, Upon all dead commodities of the growth or produce
of this island, that shall be shipped off the same, shall
be paid to our Sovereign Lord the King, his heirs and
successors for ever, four and a half in specie for every
five score....[Any exports evading such a duty would be forfeit,
half to the king and half to the informer.]

And Be it further enacted by the authority aforesaid,
That one Act made the seventeenth day of January, one
thousand six hundred and fifty, intituled, an Act importing the customs imposed and granted by the council, and
gentlemen of the assembly, to the right honourable Francis
Lord Willoughby of Parham, Lord Lieutenant-General of the
Province of Carolina, and Governor of Barbadoes; as also,
his Lordship's confirmation of the rights of the inhabitants of this island to their several estates, with the
tenure and rent thereon created, be, and is from henceforth repealed, made void, frustrate, of none effect, to
all intents, constructions, and purposes whatsoever.

294. VIRGINIA: ACT FOR RAISING REVENUE FOR THE BETTER SUPPORT OF
GOVERNMENT (Act III), 8 June 1680.[2]

Whereas there is a great and continuall charge required
for the maintenance of the governor and severall other off-

---

the 'farm' was not renewed.
Later in 1664 Willoughby obtained from the other assemblies in the
Leewards assent to similar duties.
1. Though not explicit, this seemed to imply that the Crown would
spend the revenues derived on island administration and defence. It
would, of course, have made the governor entirely independent of the
assembly. The Crown, however, used the money for other purposes and,
though the assemblies naturally complained of this breach of the implied conditions of the 1663 settlement and the diversion of revenues
from the island, they secured thereby considerable control over the
penurious governor. When the lease expired in 1670, the king quietly
ignored the Carlisle creditors and kept the money.
2. W.W. Hening, *op.cit.* II p.466. This was one of the three draft bills
brought to Virginia by Culpeper. It secured to the Crown (and <u>not</u> at
the disposal of the assembly as previously) a <u>permanent</u> revenue. The
Burgesses demurred, jealous of their rights. Culpeper reprimanded them
for claiming powers which the Commons had not assumed, save during the
Interregnum. He also warned them that the king might rightly claim

icers and persons as alsoe for the fort and fortifications,
besides many other contingent expenses absolutely necessary for the support of the government of this colony, Bee
it therefore enacted and it is hereby enacted by the King's
most excellent Majestie by and with the consent of the
general assembly, That for every hogshead of tobacco that
shall at any time hereafter be exported out of this colony
by land or by water to any other place whatsoever, there
shalbe paid by the exporter two shillings of currant mony
of England, as also for every ffive hundred pounds of
tobacco exported in bulk or otherwise and soe proportion-
ably for a greater and lesser quantity, the same to be to
the King's most excellent majestie, his heirs and successors for ever, to and for the better support of the government of this his Majestie's colony of Virginia in such
manner as is herein before expressed, and to and for noe
other use, intent and purpose whatsoever....

295. JAMAICA: TWENTY-ONE YEAR REVENUE ACT, 18 October 1683.[1]
    Wee, his Majestie's most dutifull and loyall subjects
the Assembly of this his Majestie's Island, being duely
sensible of his Majestie's Extraordinary Grace and favour

---

arrears of quit rent not collected for many decades. The Burgesses
finally yielded and passed this Act.
1. Early Revenue Acts in 1661 [see No.346] and 1663, passed by the
governor and council in Jamaica,had been without any explicit time
limit; similarly the Act of 1672. The lords of trade were concerned
to secure a permanent revenue for support of colonial governments:
they wondered whether such Acts, especially that of 1672, could be
confirmed in perpetuity. The attorney-general thought not.Moreover,
in 1664 Revenue Acts [see No.350(b)] had appropriated moneys not to
the king or governor, but to officials responsible to the assembly.
When the king had appointed T. Martyn as receiver general in 1674
his patent, with the connivance of governor and council, was not recognised by the assembly; and the 1675 Act had put disbursement into
the hands of its own treasurer. A permanent revenue bill had been
included among Carlisle's model drafts: but the assembly found the
proposal of 'perpetuity' against the 'practice of this island'and 'the
interest of any young colony' (Journ.Jam.Ass.I p.29). They objected
since they feared assemblies would cease to be summoned regularly;
'they have no other way to make their grievances known to the King
and to have them redressed than by the dependence of the governor
upon the assembly which is preserved by passing temporary bills of
revenue'. (C.S.P. 1677-80 No.1540). But when the Carlisle experiment
was given up, North (C.J.) reported that the Jamaicans were 'prepared
to grant a perpetual bill for the payment of the governor and another
for seven years for the other charges of the government', provided
they were restored 'their ancient form' of law-making [see No.266
(g)].
Carlisle was thereupon instructed to secure such Revenue Acts: permanent if possible; certainly for not less than 7 years. Morgan,his
lieutenant-governor, in October 1681 accepted a 7-year Act with a
score of other Acts 'tacked' to it which the lords of trade refused

in restoring unto us our Antient forme of makeing lawes[1]
enact and ordeyn to apply not onely the Revenue by us now
intended to be raised, but even all his Majestie's quitt
rents ariseing from Lands granted or to be granted within
this Island, to the Support of the Government of this his
Majestie's Island and the Contingent Charges thereof and
to noe other use whatsoever; and wee, likewise takeing
into a serious consideration the great Expense his Majestie hath and may be at in and about the support of the
Government of this his Island and the Contingent Charges
thereof, as alsoe the great sumes of money required for
the Reparacon of his forts and fortifications now much
decayed and the apparent danger and Inconveniency that
may arrise by any longer neglect, have cheerfully and unanimously given...and doe hereby...grant unto his most
Excellent Majestie his heires and Successors for and towards the repaireing and building forts and fortifications
and for the Defraying of the many necessary and Contingent
Charges incurred about the Support of the Government of
this his Majestie's Island, a Certaine Impost on the severall Liquors and Goods hereafter mentioned, for one and
twenty years.... [viz] ...all and every person or persons
whatsoever in this Island which from and after the makeing of this Act shall have or receive from the Governor
or Commander in Chiefe of this Island a Lycence to sell
and retaile any strong liquors in any part of this Island
shall pay the said lycence and every yeare for renewing

---

to allow. When Lynch was at last appointed governor, he was armed with
a threat to apply the English Tonnage and Poundage Act to the colony
and was given a prime task to secure a perpetual revenue, to accept
no 'tack', but to offer approval of such other laws desired if the
assembly complied with a permanent grant. In October 1680 the lords
of trade had surrendered in perpetuity quit rents, wine licence fees,
and all levies to the upkeep of the island's government, in order to
induce the assembly to make concession:Lynch believed that, properly
collected, these would have been sufficient to pay the salaries of
governors and officials.However, Lynch's tact and the assembly's confidence in him produced a 7-year Act in October 1682, and a year later
this 21-year Act, approved by the privy council in April 1684. The
distinction between royal and colonial revenues disappeared with the
surrender in Jamaica – alone among the colonies – of quit rents to
local government;but collection and disbursement were in the hands of
royal officials.
The search for a permanent civil list continued: in October 1688 the
assembly granted a perpetual revenue, but such were the methods used
by the governor, the Duke of Albemarle, and the doubtful legality of
his council and the assembly involved in passing the Act, that it
could not be either disallowed or confirmed. Revenues continued to
be collected therefore under this 1683 Act [see also Volume II].
1. i.e. the return, after the Carlisle experiment, to the former
method of government': [see below Nos. 366 (h) and following documents.]

of the same the sume of five pounds Currant mony to our
Soveraigne Lord the King, his heires and Successors....
[which revenue] as well his Majesties Quitt rents ariseing
from Lands Granted or to be granted within this Island
and every part and parcell thereof, as alsoe all and every
part of the Revenue hereby granted or which hereafter
shall grow due by vertue of this Act or anything herein
contained, shall be applyed and appropriated and are hereby appropriated to the support of the Government of this
his Majestie's Island and the Contingent Charges thereof
and to noe other use intent or purpose whatsoever....
  [A sum of £1250 per annum would be appropriated for 21 years
  to repairing and rebuilding fortifications. Provision was made
  for taking £500 security from the receiver general; and no collector, receiver or deputy should pay the £1250 or any other sum
  of money] whatsoever arriseing from the quitt rents or
by vertue of this Act, unless he or they have or receive
for his or their authority a Warrant under the hand and
seale of the governor or Comander in Cheife[1]...with the
advice and consent of the councill expressing the sume
to be paid and the end and purpose wherein the same is
or shall be applyed....
  This present Act shall remaine and continue in force
for the terme of one and twenty yeares and noe longer.

(f) THE CROWN AND CLAIMS TO AUTONOMY
  Nevertheless, distant colonies continued to assert their claims
to govern themselves, at least in relation to all internal affairs;
and the Crown had insufficient power to prevent erosion of its rights.

(i) VIRGINIA
296. (a) ACT PERMITTING TAXATION BY GOVERNOR AND COUNCIL March 1661[2]
  (Act *XVII*). Whereas the necessary charge of the country
doth enforce the raysing of an annuall levy which, being
commonly done by an assembly, the charge of which doth

---

1. The governor's control was thus secured over all disbursements of
money.
2. W.W.Hening *op.cit.*II p.24. Governor Sir William Berkeley found
that this house of burgesses, elected in 1661, was one which he could
control, and he did not dissolve it for 14 years. But sessions were
expensive; and by this Act governor and council were empowered to
impose taxes without summoning the Burgesses. The council in 1680
hoped that the king by proclamation would revive this Act, but the
privy council hesitated to employ this prerogative power. Instead,
in 1683 the commission to Governor Lord Howard asked for the enactment of a similar measure to this of 1661 by the assembly, but the
Burgesses jealously refused.The governor reported in 1686 their
'total denyal that the Governor and Councell should have any power
to lay the least Levy to ease the necessity of soe frequent Assemblys'. This had followed the message from the Burgesses on 1 December
1685 that, whereas the governor had proposed an Act similar to that

most times equall *[if]* not exceede all the other taxes of
the countrey, Be it therefore enacted That the governor
and councell in September 1662 shall have power to raise
and proportion a levy to defray the country debts and salaries allowed by the assembly and such other debts also
as they shall find justly and necessarily due according
to the number of tith-ables, provided the whole amount
not to more than 20 pounds of tobacco per poll and this
Act to continue for three yeares [unless the assembly should
be called for some emergency in the meantime.]

296. (b) RESOLUTION OF HOUSE OF BURGESSES ON MONEY BILLS, 9 November
1666.[1]

The honourable Governour sent knowledge of his pleasure to the House that two or more of the Councell might
join with the House in granting and confirming the sums
of the levy. The humble answer of the House is, That
they conceive it their privilege to lay the levy in the
House, and that the House will admit nothing without reference from the honourable Governour and Councell unless
it be before adjudged and confirmed by Act or order and
after passing in the House shall be humbly presented to
their honours for approbation or dissent.... This is
willingly assented to and desired to remain on record for
a rule to walk by for the future, which will be satisfactory to all.

297. ACT RELATING TO THE FRANCHISE, 1662-70.
(a) 23 March 1662.[2]
(Act *LXXXIV)* Whereas the charge of assemblyes[3] is much

---

of 1661 permitting the governor and council to impose a levy not exceeding twenty or twenty five pounds per poll, 'This House duely and
seriously considering how far it may tend to the disadvantages of this
Country and how unacceptable as wel as inconvenient it will be to the
Inhabitants of this his Majesty's Dominion in general, whom this House
represent, doe humbly signifye unto your Excellency that they can noe
waies concede to, or comply with, that proposition without apparent
and signal violation of the great trust with them reposed:' (H.R.Mc-
Ilwaine (ed),*Journals of the Council,*I p.81).Indeed on 3 December they
had protested in similar language against fees for the use of the seal:
a device,they believed,of indirect taxation [see below No.305 (h) and
(i)].
1.W.W. Hening, *op.cit.* II p.254.The exclusive initiative to lay taxes
had been won by the house of commons in England during the period of
the Virginia Company:see W.Notestein, *The winning of the initiative
by the House of Commons* (1924). The house of burgesses recognised the
right of the governor and council to approve or reject money bills.
The house of commons was within the next decade to deny the right of
the Lords to amend such bills.
2. W.W.Hening *op.cit.* II p.106.Act L of 1662 imposed a fine on burgesses who did not vote.
3.In September 1663 the house of burgesses was styling itself the
'House of Commons' *ibid.* II pp.203-4.

augmented by the greate number of burgesses unnecessaryly chosen by several parishes, Be it enacted That hereafter noe county shall send above two burgesses who shalbe elected at those places in each county, where the county Courts are usually kept; provided always that James Citty, being the metropolis of the country, shall have the priviledge to elect a burgesse for themselves, and every county that will lay out one hundred acres of land, and people itt with one hundred tithable persons, that place shall enjoy the like priviledge.

(b) 3 October 1670.[1]

(Act III) Whereas the usuall way of chuseing burgesses by the votes of all persons who, haveing served their tyme, are freemen of this country who, haveing little interest in the country, doe oftener make tumults at the election to the disturbance of His Majesties' peace, that by their discretions in their votes provide for the conservasion thereof, by makeing choyce of persons fitly qualifyed for the discharge of soe greate a trust; And whereas the lawes of England grant a voyce in such election only to such as by their estates real or personall have interest enough to tye them to the endeavour of the publique good; *It is hereby enacted*, that none but the freeholders and housekeepers, who only are answerable to the publique for the levies, shall hereafter have a voice in the election of any burgesses in this country; and that the election be at the court-house.

298. THE APPOINTMENT OF A COLONIAL AGENT, 1666[2]

(a) Resolution of the House of Burgesses, 6 November 1666
Proposed, Whether upon the Governor's[3] Reasons communicated to the House, be it conceived that there is a necessity of an Agent to manage the Countries Affairs in England if an honourable person would be found fit to be entrusted. A Committee appointed to treat with the Governor and request his Honour to consider some Hon'ble persons that might be fit and would please to accept the Managing the Affairs of the Country in England.

(b) Resolution, 9 November 1666.
It was proposed that the Governor's Honour should be requested and Instructed to make Choice of an Agent, and to impower the person by his Honour made Choice of to Act as an Agent for this Country in England for the Ensuing Year and to proceed according to such instructions as his Honour shall find the Necessities of the Country's Affairs require.[4]

1.*ibid.* II p.280.This disenfranchisement of freemen who were not landholders in imitation (they said) of English practice was temporarily reversed in 1676 by Act VII of'Bacon's Laws'(*ibid*.p.356), but it was reaffirmed in Lord Culpeper's instructions in 1679.
2.H.R.McIlwaine (ed.) *Journals of the Burgesses*,1659-93 pp.38,43.
3. Sir William Berkeley.
4. Colonel Moryson had already been chosen.In some other colonies the agent was appointed by, and under the control, of the assembly:

299. PETITION OF THE COLONY'S AGENTS TO CHARLES II FOR A CHARTER,
23rd June 1675.[1]

1st Head: That Virginia may be enabled by the King's letters patents as a corporation by the name of 'governor,
council and burgesses' to purchase and hold the grant of
the Northern Neck...which had been conveyed to the earl
of St. Albans, Lord Culpeper and others....[2]

2nd Head: That the people of Virginia may be assured that
they shall have no other dependance but on the Crown, nor
be *cantonized* into parcels by grants made to particular
persons....

Explanation: Nothing more is intended by this Head
than that the people of Virginia should rely on the Crown
alone for protection. No unlimited power is asked for, nor
any grant which shall lessen the authority of the King....

[They asked for the confirmation of their land titles, and for
the requirement that the governor, his deputy and the councillors
should all reside in Virginia.]

7th Head: That there shall be no tax or imposition laid
on the people of Virginia but according to their former
usage, by the Grand Assembly and not otherwise.

Explanation: The agents hope that this request will
not be deemed *immodest* when it is considered that both
the acquisition and defence of Virginia have been at the
charge of the inhabitants; and that the people at that
time were at the expence of supporting not only the government but the governor, which occasioned their taxes
to be very high and which must every year encrease with
the growth of the country....

First -As to the point whether the Virginians are in reason to be assured under His Majesty's great seal that they
shall not be taxed without their own consent.[3] (1.) It is
humbly conceived that, if His Majesty deduce a colony of
Englishmen by their own consent (or otherwise he cannot)
or licence or permit one to be deduced to plant an uncultivated part of the world, such planters and their heires
ought to enjoy by law in such plantation the same liberties and priviledges as Englishmen in England: such plantation being but in nature of an extension or dilatation
of the realm of England....

[The charter to the company had guaranteed rights to planters
and descendants rights as if natural-born subjects of England.

[see also No.339 and pp.485-7,497 and 500].
1. W.W. Hening *op.cit.* II pp.523-8. Francis Moryson, the agent for the
colony, was assisted by two additional agents, Thomas Ludwell and
Albert Smith, in making these representations against the Arlington-
Culpeper patent.
2. The eighth head asked for 'a confirmation by <u>charter</u> of the authority of the Grand Council'.
3. In a subsequent protest against delay in granting the charter they
asserted it 'to be the right of Virginians as well as all other Englishmen...not to be taxed but by their consent expressed by their
representatives'. (*ibid.* p.535).

Other colonies had not been taxed but of their own consent. They
were freeholders in common as of the manor of East Greenwich. It
was their industry and defence, 'the blood and treasure' of the
planters, not of the Crown, which had secured the colony. They
knew how best to value and to tax an individual's industry.][1]

300. NATHANIEL BACON: MANIFESTO AND DECLARATION, 3 August 1676.[2]

   [He denied the charges of rebellion and treason made in Governor
Berkeley's Declaration and Remonstrance on 29 May.[3] He and his
'rebels' were asserting the principles of morality and justice
against corruption and oppression. He impugned the sinister 'cabal'
of 'grandees' who for their own advancement and for the benefit
of 'unworthy favourites and juggling parasites' had 'like sponges
sucked up the public treasure'.]
   ...Another main article of our guilt is our open and
manifest aversion of all, not only the foreign, but the
protected and darling, Indians. This, we are informed, is
rebellion of a deep dye for that both the governor and
council are by Colonel Cole's assertion bound to defend
the queen and the Appamatocks *[Pamunkeys]* with their blood.[4]

---

1. This petition was committed by the lords of trade to the law officers' investigation and report.On 19 October 1675 the law officers
reported their approval of every article including the incorporation
of 'the governor, council and commonalty', 'the immediate dependance'
of Virginians upon the Crown, the confirmation of the powers of the
grand assembly subject only to the royal veto, and even their sole
right to impose taxes (a parliamentary taxation on exports being alone
exempted from this general rule). A month later the king in council
also gave his sanction for such incorporation by letters patent.But
Bacon's rebellion intervening, the actual charter granted on 10 October 1676 did little but affirm the 'immediate dependance' of Virginia as a royal province (*ibid.* pp.532-3).
2. *Virginia Magazine* I pp.55-61. Nathaniel Bacon, only recently arrived in the colony, had won frontier support in punishing Indian
depredations and atrocities in April 1676: Berkeley had delayed taking
action and calling up the militia,lest after defeating the Indians
the armed men should demand redress of grievances. Voicing the protests of the frontiersmen, Bacon led a revolt against the corruptions
of Berkeley's second governorship. In June, during a temporary reconciliation with the governor, a newly elected assembly under Bacon's
influence passed a series of reforms. These included the restoration
of the freeman franchise, the annual rotation of the office of sheriff, the prevention of pluralities and excessive fees, the triennial
election of vestries, and the reduction of the control of the governor and council in local affairs and the assessment of county levies, (W.W.Hening *op.cit.*II pp.341 ff) 'Bacon's Laws'were repealed in
February 1677 (*ibid.*p.380), though later a few were reenacted.
3. Printed in Massachusetts Historical Society, *Collections*,4th
Series IX pp.178-181.
4. A Virginia Act of 1660 had secured these 'friendly' Indians in
their lands: W.W. Hening, *op.cit.*II pp.13-14.

Now, whereas we do declare and can prove that they have been these many years enemies to the King and country, robbers and thieves and invaders of His Majesty's right and our interest and estates, but yet have by persons in authority been defended and protested even against His Majesty's loyal subjects ....

[Even 'their firearms so destructful to us' have been restored to these 'barbarous outlaws' by the governor. He had permitted trade with these murderous enemies, whereas a 'main article of our guilt is our design not only to ruin and extirpate all Indians in general, but all manner of trade and commerce with them'. All Indians should be outlaws, being 'wholly unqualified for the benefit and protection of the law' since they could not be prosecuted and were not capable of making equivalent satisfaction or restitution according to the manner and merit of the offences, debts or trespasses.

'A Declaration of the People' listed their grievances against the governor: his unjust and heavy taxes; his wastful use of funds; his neglect of the colony trade and defence, especially of the menace of the Indians; indeed, the emboldening of the 'barbarous heathen' by weak appeasement; the abuse of justice etc. Berkeley and 19 councillors (including Claiborne, Cole, Chicheley and Lee) were named as guilty.]

These are therefore, in His Majesty's name, to command you forthwith to seize the persons above mentioned as traitors to the King and country, and them to bring to Middle Plantation,[1] and there to secure them till further order,and in case of opposition, if you want any other assistance, you are forthwith to demand it in the name of the people of all the counties of Virginia.[2]

301. ADDITIONAL INSTRUCTIONS TO GOVERNOR BERKELEY, 13 November 1676.[3]
    I. You shalbe noe more obliged to call an assembly once every yeare, but only once in two yeares, unless some

---

1. Berkeley once more having proclaimed Bacon as a rebel, the latter had called a convention of his supporters east of Jamestown at Middle Plantation, later Williamsburg: these styled themselves as 'the commons of Virginia'. Bacon now assumed the title of 'General by consent of the people' and insisted upon an oath which implied resistance not only to the Indians and the governor,but even (if need be) to the king.
2. The rebellion had some features of a colonial revolt against the Crown, but it collapsed with Bacon's sudden death. Berkeley regained control, hanged the other leaders and confiscated their property. A commission of inquiry under Colonel Jeffreys was sent with troops from England and Berkeley finally departed in reply to the king's summons. But Jeffreys as lieutenant governor was thwarted in his investigations by both council and assembly.
3. W.W. Hening op.cit.pp.424-6 (These were dated 13 October 1676 in C.S.P. 1675-6 No. 1068). Berkeley was also ordered to return to England and report while Colonel Jeffreys as lieutenant-governor was to act in his place (C.S.P. 1675-6 No.1132). The king had in October 1676 generously granted full pardon to the rebels, Bacon only excepted. (ibid. II pp.367,428).However, Berkeley's proclamation and the Act of

emergent occasion shall make it necessary, the judging
whereof wee leave to your discretion. Alsoe whensoever
the assembly is called fourteene days shalbe the time pre-
fixed for their sitting and noe longer unless you finde
goode cause to continue it beyond that tyme.

2. You shall take case that the members of the assembly be elected only by freeholders as being more agreeable
to the custome of England, to which you are as nigh as
conveniently you can to conforme yourselfe·····

[He was to make a good peace with the Indians. All laws passed
under Bacon's influence were to be declared void, and Bacon was
to be arrested and tried.]

302. REPORT OF THE ROYAL COMMISSIONERS TO THE LORDS OF TRADE,
6 December 1677.[1]

[They gave 'a true narrative humbly and impartially reported'
of the Indian rising, of Bacon's charges against the governor, and
of his rebellion. They recommended the restoration of property
seized and a general act of oblivion. They suggested that defence
expenses should be paid from quit rents and an excise duty on
imported liquors (as in Barbados) instead of the oppressive poll
tax. A general import duty would enable tithable property to be
relieved.[2] The independent settlements in Maryland and Carolina[3]
threatened ruin to Virginia.]

Therefore we propose that (with a salvo of right to
the Proprietors) the jurisdiction and power of government
[of the Carolinas] may so reside in your Majesty that they
may be obedient to all orders, rules and processes of
your Majesty and Council, else you will find you have not
only given away so much land but so many subjects also,
and the next generation will not know or own the royal
power if their writs, trial and processes be permitted
to continue in the name of the Proprietors and their oath
of fealty without any salvo of allegiance to your Majesty.
It not only ruins servants,but runaway rogues and rebels
fly to Carolina in the south as their common subterfuge
and lurking place and when we remanded some of the late
rebels by letters, we could not have them sent back to
us....

---

the assembly in February 1677 made many more exceptions. A more complete Act of Indemnity was brought in draft by Lord Culpeper in 1680,
but it did exclude certain individual rebels who had previously been
condemned by Berkeley.
1. C.O. 1/41:Virginia Magazine IV pp.117-154. Colonel Jeffreys, Sir
John Berry and Francis Moryson,(who had been agent for the colony)
were the commissioners appointed in 1676 to consider the circumstances and grievances behind Bacon's rebellion.They had concluded a treaty with the Indians which recognised their land titles and tribal
law in return for their allegiance.The lords of trade were anxious
for an Indian policy which should include other colonies too.The commissioners here declared their opinions strongly against proprietary
colonies. 2. This was accomplished in 1684. 3. Berkeley had been a
proprietor of Carolina and was also temporarily its first governor.

303. REPORT OF THE LORDS OF TRADE TO THE PRIVY COUNCIL, 14 March 1679[1]
     Wee have, in obedience to your Majesty's Comands signif-
yed unto Us by the Rt. Honorable Mr. Secretary Coventry
on the 14th of December last, prepared such a Comission
and Instructions as Wee humbly conceive may be fit for
your Majesty to give unto the Lord Culpeper,your Leiut-.
and Governor General of Virginia. And therein Wee have
pursued the same Method and Directions as your Majesty was
pleased to prescribe unto Us for the Dispatch of the Earle
of Carlisle unto Jamaica,both in relation to the making of
Lawes, and in other fundamentall parts of the Government
under your Majesty with such Alterations and Additions as
the Difference or Necessity of each Colony hath required;
Which neverthelesse Wee have not thought fit to present
to your Majesty without first receiving your Especiall
Order touching such points as have appeared unto Us of
greatest moment and difficulty....
     [They recommended that the king should revoke the grants made
     to the Earl of Arlington, Lord Culpeper and others[2] as he had pro-
     mised Virginian petitioners, and he should apply the quit rents
     to the public uses and support of the government of the colony.][3]
3...whereas by an Order in Councill touching Jamaica, your
Majesty thought fit that all members of your Councill there-
being displaced by your Majesty should be incapable after
being so displaced of being chosen unto the Assembly, wee
find the same to be a matter of no small difficulty besides the great discouragement it will occasion in the minds
of your subjects there....[4]

---

1. P.C. 2/67 pp.132/3. Thomas, Lord Culpeper, had been vice-president
of the lords of trade since 1672 and had been designated as Berkeley's
successor in 1675.
2.Berkeley had tried in vain to prevent the parcelling out of Virginia
as proprietaries among royal favourites. As early as 1649 the exiled
king had patented the Northern Neck to Hopton and others,but in February 1673 Charles II had granted the whole of Virginian lands, escheats, quit rents and regalities to Arlington and Culpeper for 31 years.
This patent threatened both the authority of the government in James-
town and the status of Virginia as a royal province. The assembly made
strong representations to Arlington and Culpeper who consented to rel-
inquish their grant if they could retain quit rents and escheated property. In 1681 Arlington made over his share to Culpeper;and in July
1684 the king instructed the governor, Lord Howard, that he had reassumed these rights and that quit rents etc. should be collected and
used for the support of the Virginian government. (W.W.Hening *op.cit.*
II pp.521–2).But the king sought to increase their value fourfold and
directed the repeal of an Act of 1661 which had fixed the payment in
tobacco at 2d. a lb.,and he required money instead.When the assembly
refused to repeal this Act, the king in August 1686 did so by proclamation.
3. All land belonged to the king;and from January 1640 the Crown could
require a rent of one shilling for every 50 acres, paid in tobacco.
4. After the Restoration the two houses of the Grand (or General)Ass-
embly normally sat apart; but,in order to secure the council's control

7...as a Mark of your Majesty's supreme and imediate Authority all Writs be issued in your Royall Name only throughout the whole Country, notwithstanding any former usage
to the contrary....
  [The commission and instructions for Lord Culpeper were to be
  finally prepared and sealed.]

304. COMMISSION AND INSTRUCTIONS TO LORD CULPEPER, 6 December 1679.[1]
(a) *Commission*
...4. And wee hereby give and grant unto you (with the
advice and consent of the said Council) full power and
authority, from time to time, to summon or call General
Assemblys of the Freeholders and Planters[2] within the
said Colony and Dominion, as hath been formerly practised
and used in the said Colony and Dominion.
5. And Our Will and pleasure is that the persons thereupon
duly elected (and having before their sitting taken the
Oaths of Allegiance and Supremacy which you shall commissionate fit persons under the Seal of Our said Colony and
Dominion to administer, and without taking which none
shall bee capable of sitting though elected) shall bee
called and held the General Assembly of the said Colony
and Dominion of Virginia, and shall have full power and
authority to agree and consent unto all such Laws, Statutes
and Ordnances for the public peace, welfare and good Government of the said Colony and Dominion and of the people
and Inhabitants thereof and such others as shall resort
thereunto, and for the benefit of Us, Our heires and
Successors, as having been by you (with the advice and
consent of the said Council) framed and transmitted unto
us, shall bee by us approved and remitted unto you, under
Our Great Seal of England, in order to bee there enacted,
by your giving Our Royal assent thereunto: Which said
Laws, Statutes and Ordinances are to bee by you framed
(as near as conveniently may bee) to the Laws and Statutes
of Our Kingdom of England.
6. And Wee doe hereby nevertheless authorize and impower
you, in case of Invasion, Rebellion or some very great
necessity to pass an Act or Acts (by and with the consent
of the General Assembly) without transmitting the same

---

of the house of burgesses, it had often been the custom of certain
councillors to sit in the lower house and to assist them in their
work. But the separation of the two houses became fixed practice under
the governorship of Culpeper's successor, Lord Howard of Effingham:
joint committees of both houses of course continued to be a convenient
means of organising business (e.g. H.R. McIlwaine (ed.) *Journals of
Council* I p.24).
1.C.O. 5/1355 pp.315,334. Thomas,Lord Culpeper, had first received a
commission as governor in July 1675 to take effect on Berkeley's death
or recall, and two years later after Berkeley's death he took his
oaths of office. He did not arrive in Virginia until May 1680.
2. see above Nos. 296 (a),299, and 301.

first to me, to raise Money within Our said Colony and
Dominion to answer to occasion arising by such urgent necessities....
(b) *Instructions*.

    [The members of the council were named. Names for any future vac-
    ancies filled by men ' of estates and abilities' had to be confir-
    med by the Crown.]

23. And whereas It is Our Will and pleasure that, for the
future noe General Assembly bee called without Our special
directions; but that, upon occasion, you doe acquaint us,
by letter, with the necessity of calling such an Assembly,
and pray Our consent and direction for their meeting, You
shall at the same time transmit unto us, with the advice
and consent of the Council, a draught of such Acts as you
shall think fit and necessary to bee passed, that wee may
take the same into Our consideration, and return them in
the form wee shall think fit they bee enacted in. And,
upon receipt of Our commands, you shall then summon an
Assembly and propose the said Laws for their consent[1]....

    [An Act of Indemnity, a naturalisation Act and a revenue Act[2]
    'framed by our Privy Council here and approved by us as necessary
    for the use and benifit of the said colony' were sent to Culpeper.]

You will likewise take care that the assembly called
by you from time to time do not sit any longer than you
shall find necessary[3]....

    [All revenue Acts had to be enacted 'by the King's most excellent
    Majestie by and with the consent by the General Assembly'.[4] A more
    equitable tax than the poll tax should be found.][5]

---

1. It is doubtful whether Culpeper ever disclosed to the assembly
these instructions which would have imposed on Virginia the procedure
of Poynings' Law and which the Jamaican assembly had just successfully
rejected. The Virginian assembly did, however, pass the three bills
Culpeper had brought with him from England.By a subsequent commission
Culpeper was simply granted power 'with advice and consent of our said
council and assembly' to make laws: the Irish model was quietly forgotten.
2.The Act of Indemnity related to Bacon's rebellion;the second Act
placed the naturalisation of aliens in the governor's hand;and the
third Act required a permanent revenue for the support of government.
3. cf. No.301 for biennial assemblies.
4.The usual formula had been 'by the governor, council and burgesses';
indeed this former phrase continued to be regularly used after 1680
and was sanctioned by the lords of trade: 'General' assembly now, however, replaced 'Grand'Assembly: Act III of 8 June 1680 (W.W. Hening
*op.cit.*II p.466).A general instruction that revenues should be granted
not to the governor, but expressly to the Crown 'according to the
style of enacting laws within our kingdom of England' was sent to Virginia, Barbados and Jamaica in 1682, to the Leewards in 1683 and to
Bermuda and New York in 1686: the receiver or treasurer should hold
the money 'until our royal pleasure shall be known therein'.
5.By the additional instruction of 27 January 1682 Culpeper was ordered 'not to admit or allow of any appeals whatsoever from the governor and councill into the assembly' since the Crown judged it 'absol-

305. *HOUSE OF BURGESSES AND ROYAL INSTRUCTIONS*, 1682-88:[1]

(a) <u>Address to Governor Chicheley from the House</u>,19 April 1682.[2]
[They pleaded that he would direct 'the sunshine of your owne cleere judgment' to an investigation of their complaints: the burdens of government, including the cost of assemblies, the necessity (nevertheless) for action <u>by</u> the assembly, the disastrous price of tobacco, the widespread distress, and the need for defence against the Seneca and Susquehannock Indians.]

...*Lastly*,That in the ordinary Course of Justice in matters of greatest import amongst many perticular persons,appeals have bin made and waighty causes otherwayes transmitted to the assembly held in anno 1679 and thence referred to that of June 1680 when by an express from his Excellency noe private matters were to come in debate dureing that session, since which time two yeares are well nigh now elapsed, and if noe assembly at present shall be holden, great inconveniencyes will ensure, if not a totall fayleur of Justice.

(b) <u>Address to Governor Lord Howard from the House</u>,29 April 1684[3]
...That, whereas by his Excellency's Answer to the ad-

---

utely necessary that all our subjects may have liberty to appeal unto us'. Appeal from the governor and council should be made to the privy council, provided the sum at issue exceeded £300, that the appeal was made within three weeks,and that security was given. (C.O. 5/1356).
1. Threats of greater royal control were challenged by the house of burgesses: in particular, they protested against royal instructions relating variously to a change in appeals, to the revision of their laws and invasion of their legislative rights by the prerogatives of disallowance, amendment and veto, and to the use of proclamations to revive laws repealed by the assemblies, and to revoke powers given (as, for example, to county courts). Furthermore, the king had instructed the governor to repeal by proclamation the Act regarding payment of quit rents in tobacco [see above No.303 n.]
2. H.R. McIlwaine (ed.) *Journals...of the Burgesses* (1659-93) p.159. <u>Sir Henry Chicheley</u> was deputy in Culpeper's absence: he had summoned an assembly briefly (without the approval of the king or council) when there was widespread agitation for a limitation of the overproduction of tobacco. Their address concluded with a plea for a prolonged session of the general assembly to deal with the backlog of appeals from the general courts. But Chicheley adjourned the house seven days later.
3. *ibid.* p.204. Additional instructions to Culpeper in 1682 had required him to seek the repeal of all acts permitting appeals to the general assembly from inferior courts and J.P.s.When Francis, <u>Lord Howard of Effingham</u> succeeded him as governor in 1683, he determined to effect this; appeals in matters of £100 or more would lie in future to the governor and council alone and thence to the privy council - a feature of royal control which the king was seeking to make general over all colonies and dependences on the precedent of the continuance of appeals from the Channel Islands.The house of burgesses protested that the king was seeking to remove an 'inherent right and priviledge' and 'antient practice of the country'. But the governor refused to disobey his instructions, though he was prepared to support a proposal to the

resse of this House and by his sacred Majesty's Instruccons comunicated to the House, It is thereby permitted for
any person being unsatisfied with the Judgment of the Generall Courte to appeal to his sacred Majesty in Council
from any such Judgment exceeding the Reall Value of one
hundred pounds, giveing security and performing what other
Injunctions the Instruccons doe require, Which Grace of
his sacred Majesty to us his loyal subjects, we cannot but
aprehend in the most dutiful sense....

   [They felt that the order which Mrs. Bland had secured to compel
   Colonel Codd to appear before the privy council was vexacious,
   ruinous and unjust, and that the grounds alleged for this appeal
   to the king[1] insufficient. Therefore they begged that the order
   should be suspended.]

   (c) Message from the Governor to the House, 5 May 1684.[2]
...His Majesty has been pleased by his Royal Instruction to command me, with the assistance of your Councell,
to take care that all Lawes, now in force, be revised,
considered and represented to his Majesty for his approbacon or disalowance of the same, which I shall accordingly
make my care to be drawn into one Compleat body against
the next Assembly....

   (d) Address to the Governor by the House, 6 May 1684.[3]
...We have, upon your Excellency's Returne about the
Revising our Lawes,diligently and consideratly examined
those severall Instruccons you were pleased to Communicate
to us and in them find nothing of the Revising of the Lawes,
and humbly offer that Alteration, addition or diminution
of any Law quite takes away the force and vigour thereof,
which is not againe to be Recovered but by the Legislative
power which His Majesty's Gracious favour is granted to be
in the General Assembly together with his Royall Allowance
thereto. Therefore we conceive That that Revising and consideration, which in itselfe implies Alteration and amendment, cannot be begun but by the Advice and Consent of the
whole Generall Assembly and after don and performed cannot
legally passe without their approbation, allowance and confirmation....[4]

---

king that £300 would be a more appropriate figure than £100 as originally suggested in those instructions or £500 as suggested by the
Burgesses (*ibid*. p.243).
1. See below No.305 (e): Address to the king, 16 May 1684.
2. *ibid*.p.210
3. *ibid*. p.212.
4. On 8 May Howard explained that royal instructions were to him as
king's governor; he was not to publish them all, only such parts as
were 'fit and necessary'; and the Burgesses could not therefore know
what was included and what was not. He asked again that the revised
laws should be presented for the approval, disallowance or confirmation by the king (*ibid*. p.216). The Burgesses,recognising their
legal similarity to the corporations in the realm [see their Address
to the king,p.477] were presumably in some ignorance of the royal
attack on charters [see pp.442-3].

(e) <u>Address to the King by the House</u> 16 May 1684.[1]
[Some appeals had been made not to the General Assembly, but
to the privy council 'for matters of *meum* and *tuum* arising here'.]
   ...We humbly beseech your sacred Majesty to take into
your Royal Consideracon How grievous and ruinous it will
be to your Subjects here for it seems almost Impossible
how sundry matters of facts ariseing here can there be
tried being exceeding difficult for a Case of Intricacy
to be soe stated and the proofes so sufficiently Certified,
but that other Matter may necessarily fall within the plea
and soe other fact arise to be Cleared up by the want
whereof the Cause is lost, the parties delayed and with
expences Ruined. And it hath not till now been presidenti-
all since the first setling this Colony as wee can find
that any such Causes have been thence remooved. The Course
through this Long series of time hath been by appeals from
County Courts to Generall Courtes and thence (if cause
were) to the Generall Assemblys consisted (as now it doth)
of your Majesty's Governor, Councell and Burgesses, the
highest Court in this colony....
   [They referred to the *Bland* case and suggested a minimum of £300
   at issue in any case going on appeal to London.[2] They asserted
   that it had been for the enlargment of the Crown's dominions and
   revenues that their ancestors had left their native soil and ventured 'into a barbarous and melancholy part of the world',deprived
   of the presence of the king and other comforts enjoyed in England.]
   And that all this, notwithstanding, [we]...doe not...at
this day participate soe much in your Royall Grace and
bounty as your Majesty is gratiously pleased to extend to
most of the lesser and most inconsiderable corporation within
your Majesty's Kingdom of England, for that even such corporation, by your Majesty's said grace and favour, have
power and authority to make and enact lawes, ordinances
and statutes for the Welfare, Advantage and good government of their Corporation (so they be not contrary to the
lawes of England) which Lawes and ordinances your Majesty
hath not been pleased to take power to yourselfe to recall
and make void. And which Grace hath by sundry commissions,
letters and instructions of your Majesty and your Royal
progenitors been indulged to us till of late some Acts
and statutes by your Majesty's Governor, Councell and
Burgesses in Generall Assemblies made have been Repealed
and declared voyd by proclamation, your Majesty's said
Generall Assembly not consulted contrary to the 88th Act
of our Lawes printed by allowance in England in the 13th
yeare of your Majesty's Raigne,[3] and contrary to the ant-

_____

1. *ibid.* p.228.
2. See above No.305 (b),the Address of 29 April.The house of burgesses
continued to protest strongly but in vain, even after the revolution
of 1688: e.g. in 1691: *ibid.* p.370.
3. Act LXXXVIII of 1662 provided that 'noe act of courte or proclamation shall upon any pretence whatsoever enjoyne obedience thereunto,
contrary to any Act of Assembly untill the reversall of that Act by

ient usage in that behalfe....
    [They pleaded for a return to, and continuance of, that ancient usage and begged that] all such Lawes, statutes and ordinances as by the authority of your Majesty's Governor, Councell and Burgesses of your Generall Assembly of Virginia shall be ordained for the welfare, advantage and good government of this your dominion, as neer as may be agreeable to your Majesty's Lawes of your Realm of England, may have the force of Lawes until they shall be declared voyd and repealed by the same authority of your Majesty's said Generall Assembly, or at least untill your Majesty's sacred Majesty doe receive the grounds and reasons for makeing those lawes from your Majesty's Governor, Councell and Burgesses of your Generall Assembly here.[1]
    (f) Speech by the Governor, 4 November 1685.[2]
    ...What I shall propose to you att present is, what was deferred by the desire of the last Assembly to this and what I have his Majesty's particular Commands for, that you will prepare a Law, whereby all County Courts and Parishes may have noe power to make Bye Lawes obligatory within their Counties and Parishes till first approved of by his Majesty's Governor and Councel.[3]
    Farther, Gentlemen, in the perusing your Lawes I have observed in very many of them, that fines and forfeitures are to be accounted for to the Publique (as then soe termed) - a name certainly most odious under a Regal Government and that which doth in name, soe in consequence, but little differ from that detestable one (Republick) which

---

a succeed[ing] Assembly': W.W.Hening op.cit.II p.108.
1. On 21 May 1684 Howard refused to send this address to the king: 'the same is soe great an entrenchment upon the Royal authority that I canot but wonder you would offer at it' (ibid. p.243).In a letter of 1 August 1686 (Hening op.cit.III p.40) James II indeed personally ordered Howard to dissolve the assembly - 'the first assembly...soe dissolved',and the governor told them he hoped 'the last that should deserve it'. The king also ordered the removal of Robert Beverley as clerk of the house and asserted the right of the governor to appoint to that office in the future. Beverley had, whether intentionally or not, omitted an amendment for the Ports Bill which the governor had at first signed and then (discovering the error) vetoed. The Burgesses complained that the governor had thereby claimed a 'double negative vote': the bill duly authenticated by their clerk and signed by the governor was law and could not be changed but by a subsequent assembly. When Howard refused to resign, the Burgesses withheld a bill for a general tax levy.
2. H.R.McIlwaine (ed.) Journals of Council. I p.66.
3. The assembly had informed Howard in April 1684 that they had insufficient time to consider legislation to give governor and council control over local government and by-laws. Now he failed once more to secure such a measure from the assembly, so by proclamation on 22 February 1686 he repealed Virginian Acts which had permitted county courts and parish officials to make their own by-laws.

I am very much persuaded you all so realy abhorr, that you
will remove any thing which in the least relates to it:
therefore I recommend to you that all those Clauses in
those several Lawes may be repealed and a Law passed that
all fines and forfeitures for the future be appropriated
to his Majesty's use for the benefit of this his Majesty's
Dominion.[1]
    (g) <u>The Governor's answer to the House,</u> 19 November 1685.[2]
    [Lord Howard pointed out that the king had for the benefit of
the colony bought out Lord Culpeper's grant 'at so great expence'.
He doubted whether there was still an Act fixing payment of quit
rents at 2d per pound in tobacco.]
    ...But if there be such a Law, I appeal to yourselves
whether any Law can extend so far as to prejudice or invade any man's property, much lesse his Majesty's,
    [but, if there proved to be difficulties in finding specie, then
he would permit sheriffs to collect the quit rents at the rate of
one penny a pound.][3]
    (h) <u>Addresses to the Governor from the House, 29 October 1686.</u>[4]
    (i)...That for many years before the happy Restauration
of his late Majesty of blessed memory and since such his
happy restauration by a law of this Country made anno 1661/
2 the quitt rents due to his Majesty for all lands in this
his Majesty's Colonie and Dominion of Virginia have been
paid and accepted in tobacco at the rate of 2d per lb,And
your Excellencie having been pleased publiquely to signifie
that for time to come, according to Instructions from his
Majesty to your Excellencie, your Excellencie would comm-
and and expect the same should every year be paid in Current English Monie, according to the tenor and at the times
and dayes mentioned in all Patents for land. And the Inhabitants of this Country not being possibly able so to

---

1. On December 2nd 1685 the committee of grievances reported that
they had 'a great detestation and abhorance to any other Government
but that of a monarchy' and agreed to change the form of appropriation
'to his Majesty's use' for the benefit of Virginia (*ibid*.p.82).In
practice,however, the objectionable form continued to be employed.
2. *ibid*.p.75. The king had directed Howard in June 1684 to obtain the
collection of quit rents at 2 shillings for every 100 acres in money,
not in tobacco.Act XXXVI of 30 March 1662 (W.W.Hening *op.cit*.II p.31)
had fixed payments at 2d a pound in tobacco, but tobacco prices had
slumped disastrously since then.Moreover, there was as always a lack
of sterling currency in the colony.
3.Even this tentative concession would have overpriced tobacco, probably more than doubled its current value.But on 3 December Howard having reminded them that it was the king who had asked for money payments, the house resolved unanimously that they could not 'recede
from their first response without breach of the great trust in them
reposed'. (*ibid*. p.85). In August 1686 therefore by proclamation
James II repealed the Act of 1662: for 'under pretence of an Act of
assembly' the king's service and government had been deprived of funds.
4. H.R. McIlwaine (ed.) *Journals of ... Burgesses* (1659-93) p.267.

doe, there being noe Specificall Monie in this Country
nor possibility of such to be procured from England (his
Majesty's Lawes forbidding the transportation thereof)
They have under the deep sense of that difficulty, most
humbly moved from the Respective Counties,[1] that your
Excellencie be intreated by a humble address to permit
and grant that the quit rents due for all lands be paid
and discharged by Tobaccoes at the prices and rates of
2d per pound,

> [they therefore pleaded on behalf of themselves and all free-
> holders that the governor would waive this new instruction and
> order the collection of rents as formerly.]

   (ii)...That the Seale, first made gratiously granted
to this Country by King James the first of blessed memory
and since by his Royall Successors on the humble addresses of the Inhabitants of this his Majesty's Dominions
to this time as gratiously confirmed, was both at its
first grant and severall confirmations afterwards procured and purchased at the proper charge and expence of
this Country and accordingly all along made use of as
[an] authentique attestations to all their patents, grants
etc without fee, reward or other imposition, until your
Excellencie in April Generall Court 1685 was pleased to
declare and speedily after to set forth your proclamation
comanding the payment of two hundred pounds of tobacco
for affixing the same....[2]

> [This imposed fee had prevented and deterred many from seeking
> and settling lands 'to the great prejudice of his Majesty's Rev-
> enues in quit rents' and it has been resented by the planters as
> 'a great pressure, innovation and grievance'. Accordingly they
> asked the governor to revoke the proclamation and remove the fee.]

   (i) Address to the Governor from the House, 12 November 1686.[3]

> [They acknowledged that the governor had asserted that a fee
> for use of the seal had precedents in England and in the other
> dominions,[4] but they replied]

1.The Burgesses had been petitioned by freeholders in many counties
to resist the new form of rent.Howard recognised that the scarcity
of specie was a strong argument against the new instruction and agreed that the quit rent could be collected in tobacco at 1d per lb.
2. In April 1685 Howard had proclaimed the imposition of a fee for
the use of the seal of Virginia on patents, grants and other public
instruments.This fee, imposed without the consent of the general assembly, was resented and suspected by the Burgesses as a new form of
prerogative taxation. They had made protests previously without success.
3. H.R.McIlwaine, Journals of the Council I pp.116-7.This address is
out of strict chronology to keep documents on the fee separate from
the general problem of legislation by proclamation to revive Acts
the assembly had repealed.
4.On 2 and 3 December 1685 the governor had stated that such a fee
was 'agreable to the custome of all nations and all other his Majesty's plantations':that the lord chancellor in England claimed payment of £12 sterling;that the fee was reasonable' - 'Tobacco not being

...That altho' We are unacquainted with the Lawes and practices of the rest of his Majesty's Plantations and Dominions, We are well assured that both they and all his Majesty's Subjects of this his Dominion have such a Right to and Inheritance in the Lawes of his Majesty's King of England and the Liberties and Priviledges Granted to his Majesty's Subjects of that Kingdom from which they are descended, That noe payment by the name of any fee, Duty or other Imposition can or may be Demanded, Leavyed or Raised upon Us but by and with Our Own Consent....

[They asked Lord Howard to take note that in Virginia there had been no such precedent for a fee in previous commissions which empowered governors to keep the seal to authenticate instruments, grants *etc*.:and that there was no power in the governor to demand any sum in money or tobacco 'under any colour or pretence whatsoever except the same be consented to by the Generall Assembly'. They entreated the governor to give strict order that 'noe fee be demanded or taken for affixing the Seale to any Instruments but such as either is or shall be appointed by Lawe'.][1]

(j) Address to the Governor from the House, 2 November 1686.[2]

[They affirmed] that they willingly acknowledge his Majestie's authoritie in repealing or declaring voyd any of the lawes or acts of Assembly made in this his Majesties Dominion of Virginia, not having the Royall assent, but cannot consent or allow that any act of Assembly which hath been repealed by the same authoritie, that gave it being can be revived or reinforced so as to have the force and strength of a law, by any order or proclamation whatsoever....

[They believed that the king's action had proceeded from some mistake or misinformation, for the king had promised to maintain the established government and secure their rights and liberties. They asked the governor to revoke his proclamation of 19 June 1684 which had reinstituted the Act relating to attorneys which they had repealed in 1683.]

(k) The Governor's answer to the House, 10 November 1686[3]

...I tell you Nothing can be more afflicting to me than to find his Majesty's subjects of this his Dominion...to question the bounds of Prerogative and especially in so unfit expressions as to say you can neither consent nor allow that any Act of assembly repealed by the same Authoritie which gave it being can be revived or reinforced

---

...worth five shillings per cent';and that he would promise not to increase the fee (*ibid.*pp.81,85).
1.On 17 November 1686 the house resolved that the fee was 'not only unpresidentiall here, but contrary to Law and oppressive'. In 1689 the privy council ordered the fee to be discontinued.
2. H.R. McIlwaine (ed.): *Journals of...Burgesses* p.270. An Act requiring the licensing of attorneys, passed in 1680 and repealed in 1683, had in June 1684 been revalidated by proclamation. Four other Acts had been repealed by the same proclamation.
3. *ibid.* p.277.

by Proclamation. In it you ought to have well considered
under what different circumstances his Majesty's subjects
of his plantations are to those of his home subjects of
his great Kingdom of England, and how that we are to be
governed from time to time by his Majesty's instructions,
and that his Majesty hath reserved to himselfe the Prerogative Right of Repealing Lawes by Proclamation,[1] which,
though you do seem to grant yet it is with such Reserves
that it is no other Right of the Prerogative than as you
thinke fit to grant....[The right of the assembly to make laws
was subject always to royal pleasure.]

(1) <u>Address to the Governor from the House</u>, 3 May 1688.[2]
[They referred to their previous address and Lord Howard's answer on 12 November 1686 that he could not show them the particular
royal instruction to repeal the Act about attorneys, because he
'left it at home'. They did not wish to dispute, contradict or
lessen the royal prerogative.]

...This House do not nor dare not go about to say what
is prerogative and what is not: it is a Subject they will
not touch upon....*[They]* do not draw it under question
whether his Majesty by his proclamation may repeal all or
any lawes that have not past the Royall Assent: but if
before his Majesty hath given his Royall Assent in an other
Session repealed and made void it is as if the same had
never been and a Law may as well Receive its beginning by
proclamation as such revivall, since his Majesty's Instructions on Such case would be, as this House humbly conceived *ex post facto*....

[They invited the council to join them in making representation
against dangers foreseen. Suppose 'so prudent a governor' as Lord
Howard were removed], some Governor may be sent to Govern
us who, under the pretense of the liberty he hath to con-
strue prerogative and stretch it as far as he pleaseth,
may by proclamation Revive all the Lawes that for their
great Inconveniences to the Country have been Repealed
through forty years since and this would be no more but
ex post facto.... [They asked for the annulment of the proclamation
of 19 June 1686.]

(ii) MASSACHUSETTS

306. CAPTAIN BREEDON TO THE COUNCIL FOR FOREIGN PLANTATIONS,
11 March 1661.[3]

...I do here in the first place present you which the

---

1. This seemed a considerable threat to the powers of the general assembly – government by royal instruction; but clearly the governor was
making somewhat exaggerated claims for the prerogative: for the privy
council itself had refused to revive by proclamation the Act permitting taxation by the governor and council [see above No.296 (a)].
2. *ibid.* pp.304–5.
3. N.Y. Hist. Soc., *Collections* 1869 pp.17–8. The Restoration posed
acute problems for the Commonwealth of Massachusetts, just as Massachusetts defiance was clearly one of the major problems which the new

Book of Laws for Massachusetts Colony, whereby your Honours may understand the Government thereof better than
my selfe,which Government they assert to be by patent
from the King: which patent I never saw, therefore cannot
tell how agreeable to their patent they act. What laws
are not mentioned in this Book are in the Magistrates brests to be understood; the distinction of freemen and non-
freemen, members and non-members, is as famous as Cavalers
and Roundheads was in England, and will shortly become as
odious, and I hope abandoned. The greivances of the non-
members who are really for the King, and also of some of
the Members are very many....It is not unknowne to you
that they look on themselves as a Free State, and how they
sate in Councell in December last, a weeke before they
could agree in writing to His Majestie, there being so
many against owning the King, or their having any dependance on England. Their petition I have not seene, but by
information understand they acknowledge their allegiance
to His Majestie. Upon which I quere: *(Firstly)*Why do they
not proclaim His Majestie? *(Secondly)*Why do they not act
in His Majestie's name? *(Thirdly)*Why doe they not give
the Oath of Allegiance to His Majesty but instead thereof
force an Oath of Fidelity to themselves and their Government?....

By the *Book of Laws* you may understand that none but
freemen, who will take the Oath of Fidelity, are capable
of bearing office in Military or Civill affaires, and tho'
the officers are freemen, yet 2 thirds of the soldjers
are non-freemen, who tho' at present they obey the command of their Officers, would, I am confident, be glad to
have officers by the King's Commission, and do desire and

---

councils for trade and for foreign plantations (re-established by
patent in November and December 1660) had to tackle: its pretensions
to autonomy and to free trade were dangerously notorious throughout
the colonies and in foreign countries. The theocracy attempted to
maintain its exclusive position: it sought from the king a confirmation of its charter which was regarded as a covenant implying purely
voluntary subjecthood. The general court had written an address on 19
December 1660 to Charles II, now 'King over your British Israel',
(N.B. Shurtleff ed. *op.cit.* IV i p.431), had argued that the killing
of Quakers was in self defence, and had instructed their agents to
see that no appeals to the Crown were provided for nor any superior
power imposed and to plead for freedom from customs duties – the special privilege granted in 1644 to New England to the envy of the other
colonies.Petitions from many with grievances against Massachusetts
were presented to the council: these included the Quakers, Mason,
Gorges, Breedon and Maverick. It was argued that the Massachusetts
government had neglected public responsibilities, had violated private
rights, and had contravened the powers granted in the charter.
After hearing Thomas Breedon and others in evidence,the council decided to reply 'with all possible tenderness' to avoid recrimination,
but to seek such compliance 'necessary' to 'an English Colony' which
'cannot subsist but by a submission to, and protection from'the Crown.
Breedon,a Boston merchant,was soon discredited when under false pret-
ences,he secured a commission as governor of Nova Scotia.

expect a Governor to be sent from the King: others fear
it, and say they will dye before they loose their liberties and priviledges; by which it may appeare how difficult
it is to reconcile monarchy and independency. There's many
also desires His Majestie may be proclaimed there, and to
be governed by the laws of England; but in the *Book of
Laws* page the 9th is enacted That Whosoever shall treach-
erously or perfidiously endeavour the alterations and
subvertion of their frame of policy or government fundamentally, shall be put to death; and if any speake for the
King's interest, they are esteemed as against their frame
of policy or government and as mutiners: under which pressures many groaned at my coming away, being as I may say
debarred of their allegiance by a law wherein their laws
are contrary to the laws of England. I leave to Your Honours to judge of how great concernment it is that there
should be a speedy course taken for setling and establishing this country in due obedience and subjection to His
Majestie may appeare, by the two Hectors, Whally and
Goffe,[1] dayly bussing in their ears a change of government
in England and also by the multitudes of discontented persons of their gang, going and sending their estates thither. What the effects will be is easy to be feared, unless a speedy course be taken; they being the key to the
Indies, without which Jamaica, Barbadoes and the Charibby
Islands are not able to subsist....I doe farther assert
that the French and Dutch trading into the English Plantations in America, is very much to the prejudice of England and to the loss of His Majestie, in respect to customs, many thousand pounds yearly. Now whereas there are
many ships and persons bound for New England suddainly
upon account of liberty and to secure estates, I leave it
to Your Honours wisdome, whether it may not be requisite
that the merchants of England that trade thither, and those
of New England, should not give security for their friends
allegiances in New England; or els whether it may not be
expedient to lay an imbargo on all shipping bound thither,
untill His Majestie shall conclude of sending over for
establishing the setling that country in firme peace and
due obedience....

307. THE COUNCIL FOR FOREIGN PLANTATIONS TO GOVERNOR ENDECOTT,8
April 1661.[2]

[The council announced their responsibility to review and manage plantation affairs. They ordered the colonies of New England

---

1. Regicide judges, who had taken refuge in the colony and had not
been arrested.
2. C.O. 1/14 no.59. The new council sent circular dispatches to New
England, Virginia and Barbados, enclosing the declaration of Breda and
the Act of Indemnity and Oblivion (12 Car.II cap.2), and asking for
detailed information about each colony. John Endecott,a stern, even
vindictive, puritan, had been named an 'assistant' in the charter and

expressly to proclaim the king and to be obedient to him.]
...And forasmuch as divers Representations and Complaints have been made to his Majestie and to this Counsell
that the Province of which you are Governor and the powers and Juricatories thereof have taken upon you of late
yeares to extend and exercise a Jurisdiction beyond the
limitts and Authorities which are originally graunted unto
you and contrary to the tenor and meaning thereof; by
which other of his Majesties Royall Graunts and Comissions
are suspended and divers of his loving Subjects are withheld from the right, which they pretend doth loyally and
properly belong to them; And that others are dispossessed
of their freeholds and other parts of their estates as
being overruled by power, and by that evill administration
of Publique Justice; And that there are certaine Rules of
Government among you which are repugnant to the Lawes of
England and to that Equitie and indifference which ought
to be exercised and weighed out with an impartiall hand
and an equall ballance, to all members of yor Collonye,
aswell in the matter of Religion and Conscience as in
other matters, which concerne their Civil Estate:- It is
therefore the desire and appointment of this Counsell That
you, together with those who are joyned and interested in
your Government, doe forthwith proceede to such consider-
atons and Counseels as may collect and drawe together...
Memorialls of the State and condition of New England....
And that you add also a Discription of the Modell and
frame of your Government, the extent of the Collonie and
the Numbers thereof, the nature of yor Trade and the Improvements you are endeavouring, That by a full and perfect Intelligence and Information given to us by your selves...Wee may be able to judge better of you in relation
to your selves as you are a distinct Body under particular
Lawes and Policies rendered fitt, and suitable to the nature and temper of your affaires, and as you are dependent
upon the Crowne of England....Because it wilbe difficult
for this Counsell to make any certaine Judgement of Affaires of such a varietie and at such a distance...you doe
appoint and instruct some prudent Persons as are knowing
and interested in your Affaires[1] who may be able to represent and agitate things so that now misunderstanding
may arise either with you concerning his Majestie's Coun-
csells or Resolusons in your Affaires, or with his Majestie...when any Concernments of New England shall be here
had in Consideration.

308. REPORT OF A COMMITTEE OF THE GENERAL COURT ON LIBERTIES AND ALL-
EGIANCE, 10 June 1661.[2]

I. *Concerning our liberties*
1. Wee conceive the pattent (under God) to be the first

had been elected governor several times, including 1652 [see also
p.286].
[1].The Crown was concerned to be able to have in England agents who
could give information about a colony and explain the policy of the
Crown (see also No.339).   2. N.B. Shurtleff (ed.) *op.cit.* IV ii.pp.

and main foundacion of our civil politye here by a Governor and Company according as is therein exprest.
2. The Governors and Company are, by the pattent, a body
politicke, in fact and name.
3. This body politicke is vested with power to make freemen.
4. These freemen have power to choose annualy a Governor,
Deputy governor, assistants and theire select representatives or deputies.
5. This government hath also to sett up all sortes of officers as well superior as inferior and point out theire
power and places.
6. The Governor, Deputy Governor, Assistants and select
representatives or deputies have full power and authoritie
both legislative and executive, for the government of all
the people heere, whither inhabitants or strangers, both
concerning eclesiasticks and in civils, without appeale,
excepting lawe or lawes repugnant to the lawes of England.
7. The government is priviledged by all fitting meanes
(yea, and if neede be, by force of arms) to defend themselves, both by land and sea, against all such person or
persons as shall at any time attempt or enterprise the
destruction, invasion, dettriment or annoyance of this
plantation or the inhabitants therein....
8. Wee conceive any imposicion prejudiciall to the country
contrary to any just lawe of ours, not repugnant to the
lawes of England, to be an infringement of our right.
II. *Concerning our duties of allegiance to our sovereign
    lord the King.*
1. Wee ought to uphold and to our power maineteine this
place as of right belonging to our soveraigne lord the
King,as holden of His Majestie's manor of East Greenwich
and not to subject the same to any foreign prince or potentate whatsoever,
2. Wee ought to endeavour the preservation of His Majesties royal person, realmes and dominions and so farre as
lieth in us to dicover and prevent all plotts and conspir-
ances against the same.
3. Wee ought to seeke the peace and prosperitie of our
King and nation by a faithfull discharge in the governing
of this people committed to our care.... [Whalley and Goffe,
the regicides, would be apprehended.]

309. LETTER FROM CHARLES II TO 'THE MASSACHUSETTS',28 June 1662.[1]
   ...Whereas wee have lately received an humble address

25-6.When the king's gracious answer to their first address arrived,
the committee of four magistrates, four deputies and four elders had
been appointed to consider what they judged 'most expedient' to define as the liberties and the duties of the colony.This was to be their
base for any negotiating with the Crown.
1. Hutchinson Papers II pp.100-4 (Publ.,Prince Soc. N.Y.,1865). The
general court had, contrary to the governor's protest, sent Simon
Bradstreet and the Rev. John Norton as agents to England with a humble

and petition from the generall court of our colony of the
Massachusetts in New England...Wee are therefore willing
that all our good subjects of that plantation do know that
Wee doe receive them into our gracious protection...and
that Wee will preserve, and doe hereby confirme the pattent and charter heretofore graunted to them by our royall
father of blessed memory...and that Wee will be ready to
renew the same charter to them, under our great seale of
England, whenever they shall desire it. And because the
licence of these late ill times hath likewise had an influence upon our colony, in which they may have swerved
from the rules prescribed, and even from the government
instituted by the charter, which we doe graciously impute
rather to the iniquity of the time than to the evill intents of the hearts of those who exercised the government
there. And Wee doe therefore publish and declare our
free and gracious pardon to all our subjects of that our
plantation, for all crimes and offences committed against
us during the late troubles.[1]...Provided always, and be
it in our declared expectation, that upon a review of all
such lawes and ordinances that are now or have been during
these late troubles in practice there and which are contrary or derogative to our authority and government, the
same may be annulled and repealed, and the rules and prescriptions of the said charter for administring and taking
the oath of allegiance be henceforth duly observed, and
that the administration of justice be in our name. And
since the principle and foundation of that charter was
and is the freedom of liberty of conscience, Wee do hereby charge and require you that that freedom and liberty
be duely admitted and allowed, so that they that desire
to use the booke of common prayer and performe their devotion in that manner that is established here be not denyed the exercise thereof, or undergoe any prejudice or
disadvantage thereby, they using theire liberty peacably
without any disturbance to others; and that all persons of
good and honest lives and conversations be admitted to the
sacrament of the Lords supper, according to the said booke
of common prayer, and their children to baptisme....

  [Quakers, however, 'Whose principles being inconsistent with
  any kind of government' were denied this indulgence, as by statute
  in England. The number of assistants was to be no less than 8 or
  more than 10.]

Wee assuring ourselfe, and obliging and commanding all
persons concerned that, in the election of the governor
or assistants, there be only consideration of the wisedome
and integrity of the persons to be chosen, and not of any
faction with reference to their opinion or profession, and

---

address and firm instructions to answer charges and to represent the
Commonwealth as loyal.The king here graciously pardoned all past breaches of the charter; but required the oath of allegiance and greater
freedom of worship.

1. Regicides, however, were excepted.

that all the freeholders of competent estates, not vicious
in conversations, orthodox in religion (though of different perswasions concerning church-government) may have
their vote in the election of all officers civill or military ....

[The next general court was required to publish this letter
that all subjects might know H.M.'s favour and protection.][1]

310. SAMUEL MAVERICK TO LORD CLARENDON, c. July 1662.[2]

[Clarendon had asked him to draw up 'the heads of what might
be thought requisite for those of the Massachuseets to condescend
unto, upon the Continewation of the Charter.' He proposed:]

That all freeholders may have voats in Election of
officers, civill and military.

That all persons inoffensive in life and conversation
may be admitted to the sacrament of the Lord's supper and
theire children to Baptisme.

That such lawes as are now in force there derrogatinge
from the lawes of England, may be repealed.

That the oath of allegiance may be administered, inst-
eade of that which they tearme the oath of fidelitie.

That they goe not beyond theire just bounds, even those
which for neare twentie yeares they were content with all.

That they admitt of Appeales on just and reasonable
grounds.

That they permitt such as desire it to use the Common
prayer.

That all writts *etc.*may be issewed out in His Majesties name ....

[He believed that the sending of commissioners was urgent.][3]

311. CHARLES II TO THE GENERAL COURT, 23 April 1664.[4]

...Having taken much to heart the welfare and advance-

---

1. The general court published this letter and ordered all legal processes to be issued in the king's name. But other action was delayed
from meeting to meeting of the general court:the old policy of 'avoid
or protract' advocated in April 1638 [see above p.296].
2. N.Y. Hist. Soc.,*Collections* for 1869 pp.42-3. This is one of many
undated letters from Maverick, who was in England at the Restoration,
to Clarendon as high chancellor.He had been longer resident in Massachusetts than Endecott or Winthrop,had signed the Child petition, and
had become an opponent of the theocracy and an advocate of stronger
royal control.This letter seems to present his views after the colony's agents (Bradstreet and Norton) had returned to Boston with the
charter confirmed.
3.He had further advocated the taking of New Netherland.He believed
that three-quarters of the settlers in Massachusetts would rejoice to
welcome a royal governor and commissioners (*ibid.*pp.27,73).Clarendon ,
as lord chancellor, declared in September 1662 that a commission would
be sent, and in April 1663 an order in council provided for the preservation of the charter and the dispatch of commissioners.The instructions were not ready till 23 April 1664. (J.R.Brodhead *op.cit.*IIIp.95)
4. J.R. Brodhead (ed.) *op.cit.*III pp.61-2. With no resident Crown

ment of those our plantations in America and particularly
that of New England which in truth hath given a good example of industry and sobriety to all the rest, whereby God
hath blessed it above the rest; and having in our royall
breast a tender impatience to make use of God's extraordinary blessing upon it and our subjects in those parts,
by the improving the knowledge of Him and of his holy
name, in the conversation of infidels and pagans (which
ought to be the chief end of all christian plantations)
Wee have thought fitt, since we cannot in person visit
those our so farr distant dominions, the good government
thereof and the due administration of Justice wherein,
we do notwithstanding know to be as much our duty as that
which concernes our nearest kingdom, to send such Commissioners thither as may in our name visit the same, and
after having taken a view of the good government there
and received full information of the true state and condition of that our plantation and of their neighbors on
all sides, and a due consideration of what farther additions of happinesse may be made by our royall grace and
favour to those our people, they may represent the same
at their returne to us....And wee have had this resolution

---

officials in New England, the king needed commissioners to report to
him, to seek reconciliation with the colonial governments, to settle
rival boundary claims and to assert royal control. Nicolls (the
first governor of New York),Carr, Cartwright and Maverick were appointed, and they were required to ascertain whether the king's commands of June 1662 had been obeyed.By their commission they were
given authority to hear appeals.The general court resented the intr-
usion;they protested against the appointment of Maverick and feared
that 'instead of being governed by rulers of our own choosing (which
is the fundamental privilege of our patent) and by lawes of our owne,
wee are like to be subjected to the arbitrary power of strangers'.
They pleaded poverty in advance, lest the commissioners should impose taxes, and they even threatened exodus to new lands, though they
admitted they had yet had 'but a little taste', or any evidence,of
how the commissioners would act.Before the commissioners arrived
their charter had been hidden away 'safe and secret for the country':
Massachusetts was resolved to adhere firmly to the charter 'so clearly obtained and so long enjoyed by undoubted right'. The charter
was their weapon against all outside intervention – including a royal
commission. They ended their reply to the king on 20 October 1664
with a flourish: 'Let our government live, our patent live, our
magistrates live, our laws and liberties live, our religious enjoyments live' so that they might continue to say 'let the King live
for ever'. (N.B. Shurtleff, *op.cit.* IV ii p.133). The commissioners
had been instructed to secure cooperation and avoid offence, and the
king persuaded himself to regard this premature protest of the general court as 'the contrivance of a few persons who had been too
long in power' and were (he hoped) unrepresentative of the many; a
judgment may be true,but – given the strength of the oligarchy in
Massachusetts government – difficult to prove.Only after twenty years'
evasion and procrastination did the Crown,long wishfully-thinking a
satisfactory change of mind imminent, act effectively.

and purpose ever since our first arrivall in England to
send Commissioners thither...so we have had many reasons
occurent since to confirme us in that resolution and to
hasten this execution thereof, some of which we think
fitt to mention to yow.
1. To discountenance and, as much as in us lyes, to sup-
presse and utterly extinguish those unreasonable jealous-
ys and malicious calumnies, which wicked and unquiet
spirits perpetually labour to infuse into the minds of
men, that our subjects in those parts do not submitt to
our government, but look upon themselves as independent
upon us and our laws, and that we have no confidence in
their affections and obedience to us: all which lewd
aspersions must vanish upon this our extraordinary and
fatherly care towards those our subjects manifested in
the severall instructions given to our Commissioners,
which shall by them be communicated unto you, and which
will exceedingly advance the reputation and security of
our plantations there, and our good subjects thereof with
all forreign Princes and States, when they shall hereby
plainly discerne that we do look upon any injury done to
them as done to our selfe, and upon any invasion of our
dominion in those parts, or of the priviledges of our
subjects thereof, and that we will resent and vindicate
the same accordingly.
2. That all our good subjects there may know, as we have
formerly assured them by our gracious letters, how farr
we are from the least intentions or thoughts of violating
or in the least degree infringing ye charter heretofore
granted by our Royal Father, or restraining the liberty
of conscience thereby allowed; which as we do acknowledg
to be granted by our said Royall Father of blessed memory,
with great wisdome and upon full deliberation, so we have
great reason to believe and to bee assured that the support and maintenance thereof is at present as necessary
as ever. And therefore that...we are very willing to confirme or renew the said Charter, and to enlarge the same
with such other and fuller concessions as...you judge
necessary or convenient for the good and benefit of that
our Plantation.

312. *RESTRICTIONS ON THE FRANCHISE*, 1664-78:
(a) Act of the General Court, 3 August 1664.[1]
In answer to that part of His Majesty's letter of
June 28, 1662 concerning the admission of freemen, This
Court doeth declare, That the law prohibiting all persons
except members of churches, and that alsoe for allowance
of them in any County Court, are heereby repealed.
And doe heereby alsoe order and enact, That from hence-

1. N.B. Shurtleff (ed.) *op.cit.*IV ii.p.118. The general court deemed
it prudent to be seen to make concession; but the limited enfranch-
isement estimated at 3 per cent of the adult male population did not
convince either the commissioners or Randolph.

forth all Englishmen presenting a cirtifficat under the
hands of the ministers or minister of the place where
they dwell, that they are orthodox in religion and not
vitious in their lives, and alsoe a certifficat under
the hands of the selectmen of the place or the major part
of them, that they are freeholders and are for their oune
propper estate (without heads of persons) rateable to the
country in a single country rate...to the full value of
tenne shillings, or that they are in full communion with
some church among us, it shallbe in the liberty of all
and every such person or persons being twenty-fower yeares
of age, householders and setled inhabitants in this jurisdiction...to present themselves and their desires to
the Court for their admittance to the freedome of this
Commonwealth [Such admission as a freeman would depend on a
majority vote].

(b) H.M.'s Commissioners to the General Court, 18 May 1665.[1]
   ...The end of the first planters coming hither was
(as was expressed in your address, 1660) the enjoyment
of the liberty of your own consciences, which the King
is so far from taking away from you, that by every occasion he hath promised and assured the full enjoyment of
it to you; we therefore admire[2], that you should deny
the liberty of conscience to any, especially where the
King requires it; and that upon a vain conceit of your
own, that it will disturb your enjoyments, which the King
often hath said it shall not.
   You have so tendered the King's qualifications, (as
in making him only, who pays ten shillings to a single
rate, to be of competent estate) that when the King shall
be informed , as the truth is, that not one English member in a hundred pays so much, and that, in a town of
a hundred inhabitants, scarce three such men are to be
found, we fear the King will rather find himself deluded,
than satisfied by your late act....

(c) Edward Randolph's report to the Lords of Trade, 18 April 1678.[3]
   ...His Majestie doth further enjoine That all Freeholders of Competent Estates, not vicious in their conversations and Orthodox in their Religion though of different
perswasions concerning Church Government, have their votes
in the Elections of all officers Military and Civill. Yet
their Law provides That no man shalbe admitted a Freeman
unless he be in full Communion in some Church amongst
them, thereby excluding the most and best affected to his
Majestie and the Church of England. And by an other Law
orders That all persons which refuse to attend the publick
worshipp of God their established, be made uncapable of
voting in all Civill Assemblies.
   That although his Majestie commanded that in their

---

1. Mass.Hist.Soc. *Collections* 2nd series VIII:*Danforth MS.* pp76-7.
2. i.e. stand in amazement.
3. R.N. Toppan,*Edward Randolph* (Prince Soc.) II pp.312-9.

Elections of G[overnors and] Magistrates there be only consideration had to the vertue and integrity of the persons
to be chosen and not of any Faction with reference to
their opinion and outward profession, Their Law directs
that all Freemen preferre in their Elections the former
Magistrates under penalty of Tenn pounds: by which means
the first Founders of the Common Wealth are still continued in the Magistracy, and none (Except by Death) removed,
how obnoxious soever: Mr. Leveret, who was in actual Armes
against his Majestie and turned out his Majesties Just-
tices of the peace in the province of Main, being present
Governor; Mr. Guggins (who after his Majesties Commands
of seizing the Murtherers of his late Majestie came to
that Government) harboured and protected Goffe and Whaley,
is the last year againe Elected a Magistrate; Mr. Haw-
thorne who beeing then a Magistrate was commanded by his
Majestie's Letters of 1666 to attend upon his Allegiance
at Whitehall but refused to appeare, is still in the Magistracy....

313. THE CROWN AND THE CHARTER (c.1664).[1]

   ...The King himselfe, if your intelligence mistake
not, hath reduced the question into a narrow pinch: *viz.*
whether the Pattent doth denie his sovereignty here? Or
as you relate it, whether he hath noe jurisdiction over
the inhabitants of the Massachusetts and soe his late
Commission seems a violation of their charter which he,
whose honor is the strongest obligation to performance,
professeth he would not in the least infringe; In refference to the question I have heard it strongly argued
both on the affirmative and negative, and the summ of
what I have heard discoursed the way I shall as sucsinckly
as I am able to relate unto you for your better satisfaction, and then leave you according to the exactness of
your owne judgment to draw the conclusion.
   One, the *affirmative:* its pleaded that those the Massachusetts are as much the naturall subjects of the King
of England as those that are borne in any other of his
dominions and territories, and that he hath as absolute
jurisdiction over them as to sovereigntye as over any
of his subjects notwithstanding the priviliges of the
Pattent....
   [The usual reasons were that the king's title derived from
   Cabot's discoveries and from effective occupation of pagan lands,
   that the Massachusetts Company was granted its charter by the
   king; that thereby the king did not divest himself of jurisdict-

1.Mass.Hist.Soc.,*Proceedings*,1912-13.,XLVI.pp.287-302.This anonymous
and undated discussion of the patent and the question of the relationship of Massachusetts with the Crown was probably written about 1664
when Charles II had sent commissioners to New England to assert his
authority.It is an early statement of the Crown's retaining an ultimate supervision over colonial governments, despite grant or delegation. Though it ignored the authority of king in parliament, it set

ion;that political theorists and lawyers, according to Jean
Bodin, and precedents from Gascony, Burgundy and Scotland, affirmed that the king had no power to abdicate any such sovereignty;
and that allegiance and subjecthood were retained in the charter.
For the *negative*]
1st. It is first alleaged that it was the intent of the
Pattentees to transplant them selves at their owne charge
that they might enjoy the free exercise of their religion
which cannot be secured to them and their successors unless suported by the Civil Authority and that in a way of
absolute power without allowance of appeale: otherwise
they say all the power granted them would stand them in
little stead to such an end if they should be lyable to
submitt their judgments and sentences to the alteration
of others, to whom authoratie might be derived from a
soveraigne power or jurisdiction to overrule all their
juditial proceedings, to disannull the best laws that
might be enacted for the benefite of the inhabitants
either eclesiasticall or civill, and to revoake the most
just sentences that had been passed by their rulers....
2ly. its objected by some that the people of Massachusetts
ought to be exempted from any jurisdiction besides their
own because they are at soe great a distance and that
there can be noe lawfull summons to call them to answer
in England because the common law is included within the
four seas and therefore noe writ of justice or civill
power can reach to any forreigne place. *To which its
replied* that it's great Pitty the King should loose a
Province for want of a law to govern it. But the truth is
some are willing to please themselves with shewes in stead
of solid reasons. A King may have several provinces and
distinct kingdomes under his jurisdiction all of which
may be governed by their nationall and distinct lawes
yet hath their soveraigne equall jurisdiction over them
all and a compleat right to govern them, though not by
one and the same law, the subjects of the King in Scottland have a Parliament and lawes and customes of their
own, the King of England as such cannot command them out
of Scottland, nor ought he to judge them for any offence
committed against him as he is King of Scotland by the
common or statute law of England, yet nevertheless he
would be adjudged unskilled in law and reason also that
should say that the King of England cannot by law require
any of his subjects in Scotland or Ireland to appear
before him in England and there answer for any offences
against his soveraignty and jurisdiction. In generall,
if the Massachusetts had been a distinct kingdom or state,
yet while the King of England is there King, they owe
obedience and subjection to him and are bound to repair
to his prescence into what part of his dominion soever
he should send them, for such an end the Massachusetts
have liberty to make lawes of their own and not sending

---

out arguments used a century later.

burgesses to the Parliament of England they ought not to
be under the lawes that are made there, nor to be judged
by them (say some) but by their common lawes: It would
have some weight had this countrey been ever erected into
a distinct kingdome or government of itselfe, but being a
collonie of naturall English subjects it may be doubted
whether they are not included in the legislative power of
the Parliament of England; but, if it should be granted
that so they be not, the objection would not be of any
force to conclude the negative of the question, for as
much as still the King within whose dominions the Massachusetts are seated would require subjection to his athoritie
and jurisdiction as King, and the denyall of it would be
crimen laesae majestatis. It is noe matter by what law he
would judge, whether the lawes of force in England or in
the Massachusetts, his right of jurisdiction must needs
be acknowledged absolute and intyre over all his subjects
here as well as in other of his dominions.
3ly. In the next place it is usually alleaged that they
are exempted and freed from all duties and services except
the payment of the 5th part of royall oare holding as of
the maner of east greenwitch in free and common socage.
To this it's by others replyed that both the King and many
other lords and gentlemen in England have many such tennants, yet are not the King's tennants freed therby from
the duty of subjects, but only from such services as by
other tenures they would be lyable unto, its one thing to
be a tennant to the King in this or that sort of tenures
according to ancient custome peculiar to severall persons
and another to be subjects to the King which is common to
all that are settled in any of his dominions and soe are
equaly under his jurisdiction, be they naturall subjects
by descent or necisary subjects by force of armes and constraint, or voluntary subjects by consent or agreement iff
any please themselves with such a distribution it comes
all to one pass, because, though obligation be stronger
in one sort of subject then in an other, yet the duty of
obedience and subjection is equall to all that are soe
related to the King as his subjects, the Massachusetts owe
the 5th part of gold and silver oare to Charles Stuart as
their landlord and lord of east greenwitch, and not as
King of England; and whosoever were lord of east greenwitch
as one was lately reported to be would justly claime the
5th part of the said oare in the Massachusetts though he
were not King of England; and the King of England iff he
exchange the manor of east greenwitch for some other,
would yet claime a right of jurisdiction over the Massachusetts, and fine expressions enough in the pattent relating
to him as soveraine as well as the other relating to him
as landlord which will fully enough and sufficiently warrant his claime, as those of protection and aleagiance allready mentioned proper only to King and subjects and never
claimed by land lords as such from their tennants of any
sort whatsoever: It would puzle all the logicians, lawyers,

and divines in Europe to find under what tropick to place
such kind of subjects as will allow none to have jurisdiction over them.

4ly. The objection which in the next place offers itselfe
to consideration is the liberty of making lawes with full
and absolute power to govern the people here religiously.
This might have proved a dangerous obstruction to the
King's soveraignty, iff it had not been prevented by the
restriction going alone therewithall as in part hath been
declared already; that there is a power of government
granted is beyond exeeption, but it is yet to prove that
the King in granting that power hath divested himselfe
of any parte of his soveraigne athority over his subjects.
Kings cannot be present in all parts of their dominions
and therefore had need of ministers and deputies to officiate under them, and by virtue of their athority in
appointing such they doe not divide their kingdomes or
set up other kings though they communicate their power
they doe it cumulative not privative as the schooles
speake they never abdicate their power from themselves:
The King may in any corporation or city in his dominions
where he comes exercise all the authoritie of the governor
of the place, he may and in case ought to call to account
and take notice of the complaints against his ministers
or deputies, and releive any of his subjects that are
oppressed by them by their abusing his athoritie, otherwise how could the King scatter away all evill from his
throne or be a terror to the wicked which are essential
to his office....

   [Such a devolution of government locally did not exclude or
   deny the king's right to supervise and hear petitions and complaints and to make redress.]

...many societies and corporations have power to make
orders and lawes yet the King may and frequently hath
called the judges to account and punished them for their
unrighteous administration; nor ever did any corporation
(and soe is the governor and company of the Massachusetts
sometimes styled in the Pattent) continuing in its allegeance dispute or question their King's athoritie over
them, corporations and families are related to the kingdome or common wealth as the parts to the wholl: in the
one there is a community civill, as there is in the other
a community natturall, and many such communityes allied
together and combined under a soveraigne power to make
one kingdome or common wealth it is made by some the
spefficall difference of a corporation that it is a lawfull community or society under a soveraigne power and
that nothing can be ordained by them contrary to the
statutes established by the supreame authoritie soe as
their ordenances cannot be repugnant or contrary to the
lawes and ordenances of the supreme power under whom
they are combined....

5ly. It is also pleded that liberty is graunted in the
Pattent to defend ours against any that shall goe about

to anoy us or seeke our detriment: that liberty its treu
is founded on the very law of nature yet is it necisary
it should be determined as to perticulers and expressed?
for else without commission from a soveraigne power or
orderly combination in a free people it might be looked
upon as piracie or disturbance of the publique peace to
take up necesary armes, but how this should be intended
or interpreted by armes to apose resist theKing's athoritie can never enter into the minds of sober men....
6ly. That which falls next under consideration is the security granted for any act done by the pattent an exemplic-
ication whereoff is said to be a sufficient discharge
against the King, his heires, or successors to which the
answer is given, that as it is saffe for us that the pattent should secure us from danger of law or the King's
displeasure soe it doth not in the least derogate from
the King's right of jurisdiction over his subjects whose
honor it is (as will be easyly granted) to preserve unto
them all the priviledges granted in his royall charter;
nor is it any dishonor to assert his owne right of Empire
over them both which may very well consist not withstanding the subjecions of the different minded to the controversy iff it had never been expressed in the pattent the
most soveraigne prince in a royall monarchy being obliged
to attend to the law as his rule of government that law
(which in the treu extent and meaning of it is *salus
populi*) had been a sufficient bulwarke against the exor-
bitancy of praerogative or absolute will in the ruler and
that which is in terms expressed doth but explicitely
declare what every christian prince is implicitely obliged
upon his entring upon the seate of government to maintaine
and cannot but owne himselfe soe to be....
7ly. That which I have heard in the last place objected
...is the danger they fear would arise to the inhabitants
of the Massachusetts should they be necessitated to own
their dependence upon the King soe farr as to acknowledge
his right of jurisdiction over them: For answer to this
grand scruple,I have heard it said first in generall that
fear and jealousy are observed alwaies to be the worst
councellors that can be advised withall in exigents attended with difficulties or danger....we may not admitt of
the least morall evill to provide for the greatest civill
good, where God hath made subjection a positive duty men
may not dispence with obedience upon the pretence of danger or inconvenience....

[As Calvin had shown, rulers - even tyrants - were subject and
accountable to God. That it would be a dangerous concession for
Massachusetts to make if they acknowledged the King's jurisdiction,
did not mean that it did not lawfully exist? Look at *Romans* XII.i;
Peter II 13;*Proverbs*XVI.14:*Eccles*.VIII.2. 'It would not be amiss
sometymes to make a virtue of necessity': better to accept rather
than to deny the supreme authority.]

314. H.M.'s COMMISSIONERS TO THE GENERAL COURT, 16 July 1665.[1]
     [They have received a letter 'so full of untruth and in some
     places wanting grammar construction' that they find it difficult
     to believe it was approved by the governor and council.]
     The duty which we owe to God, to the King and to all
his subjects constrains us to perswade you not to suffer
yourselves to be as much mislead by the spirit of independency. The King did not grant away his Soveraigntie over
you when he made you a Corporation. When His Majesty gave
you power to make wholesome laws and to administer Justice
by them, he parted not with his right of judging whether
those laws were wholesome or whether justice was administered accordingly or no. When His Majesty gave you authoritie over such of his subjects as lived within the limits of your jurisdiction he made them not your subjects
nor you their supream authoritie. This prerogative certainly His Majesty reserved for himself and this certainly
you might have seen if ambition and covetousness or something as ill had not darkened both your eyes....
     [Pardon was promised in the king's letter of 1662 on condition
     of obedience.]
     Striveing to grasp too much may make you hold but a
little. 'T is possible that the Charter which you so much
idolize may be forfeited until you have cleared yourselves
of those many injustices, oppressions, violences and bloud
for which you are complained against, to which complaints
you have refused to answer; or untill you have His Majesty's pardon which can neither be obtained by nor bee
effectuall to those who deny the King's supremacy....

315. REPORT OF H.M.'s COMMISSIONERS TO LORD ARLINGTON,
                                        14 December 1665.[2]
...The Colony of the Massachusetts was the last and hard-
lyest perswaded to use His Majestie's name in their forms

---

1. J.R. Brodhead (ed.) *op.cit.* III p.99. The general court had refused
cooperation with the commissioners and had forbidden the hearing of
appeals.
2. J.R. Brodhead (ed.) *op.cit.* III pp.110-3. The commissioners managed
to deal with the conquest and pacification of New Netherland, to fix
the boundary between Connecticut and 'New York', and to secure the
general compliance of Connecticut, Plymouth and Rhode Island (newly
granted a royal charter in 1663); but they found Massachusetts strongly opposed to any concession and determined to stand by their interpretation of their own chartered sovereignty. The commissioners believed that the only remedy was the revocation of that charter. In
April 1666 Charles II sent a circular, expressing approval of all
the New England colonies, except Massachusetts which appeared to have
regarded the Crown's appointment of commissioners as a violation of
the charter, to have denied the Crown's jurisdiction, and to have
prevented subjects appealing to the king's justice. The general court
was accordingly asked to send agents to Whitehall to answer questions.
They claimed to doubt the authenticity of this letter: it was not
from the king. (G. Chalmers, *Political annals.* p.390).

of Justice....
    [They had visited the other New England colonies first and hoped
    that reason and good example shown there would prevail in Massach-
    usetts. But instead the general court]
...proclaymed by sound of trumpet, that the Generall Court
was the Supreamest Judicatory in that Province; that the
Commissioners pretending to hear appeales was a breach of
their priviledges, granted them by the King's royall father and confirmed to them by His Majestie's owne letter;
and that they could not permit it. By which they have for
the present silenc't about thirty petitions which desired
justice against them, and were all lost at sea.
    To elude His Majestie's desire of their admitting men
civill and of competent estates to be free-men, they have
made an Act whereby he that is 24 years old, a house-
keeper, and brings one certificate of his civill life,
another of his being orthodox in matters of faith, and
a third of his paying ten shillings (besides head-money)
at a single rate, may then have liberty to make his desire
known to the Court, and it shall be put to the vote.
    The Commissioners examined many townshipps and found
that scarce three in a hundred pay 10s. at a single rate;
yet, if this rate was generall, it would be just, but he
that is a Church-member, though he be a servant and pay
not 22d, may be a Freeman....
    They have put many Quakers to death, of other Provin-
ces,...They have beaten some to jelly, and been (other
ways) exceeding cruel to others; and they say the King
allowes it in his letters to them. Indeed they have mis-
construed all the King's letters to theire owne sence....
    They have many things in their lawes derogatory to His
Majestie's honour; of which the Commissioners made a bre-
viat and desired that they might be altered; but they have
yet done nothing in it. Amongst others, who ever keeps
Christmas Day is to pay Five Pounds....
    They of this Colony say that King Charles the First
gave them power to make lawes and execute them, and granted them a Charter as a warrant against himself and his
successors, and that so long as they pay the fifth part
of all gold and silver oar which they shall get, they
are free to use their priviledges granted them, and that
they are not obliged to the King, but by civility....
    This Colony furnished Cromwell with many instruments
out of their Corporation and their Colledge; and those
that have retreated thither since His Majestie's happy
returne, are much respected and many advanced to be Magistrates. They did solicit Cromwell by one Mr. Wensloe to
be declared a <u>Free State</u>, and many times in their lawes
stile themselves this *STATE*, this *COMMONWEALTH*, and now
beleived themselves to be so.
    They demand what taxes they please, but their accompts
could never yet be seen....
    [There were many loyal subjects who wished to return to obedience,
    allegiance and harmony with the king, but they were threatened and

'overawed', even though their opponents, the oligarchy in the
general court were so few.][1]
    ...Their way of government is Common-wealth-like; their
way of worship is rude and called Congregationall; they
are zealous in it, for they persecute all other formes.

316. (a) EDWARD RANDOLPH TO CHARLES II: *A SHORT NARRATIVE TOUCHING*
     THE DELIVERY OF YOUR MAJESTIES LETTERS TO THE MAGISTRATES OF
     BOSTON IN NEW ENGLAND, 20 September 1676.[2]
[The Governor of Massachusetts] freely declared to me that
the laws made by your Majesty and your Parliament obligeth
them in nothing but what consists with the interests of
that colony;[3] that the legislative power is and abides
in them solely to act and make laws by virtue of a charter
from your Majesty's royal father; and that all matters in
difference are to be concluded by their final determination without any appeal to your Majesty; and that your Majesty ought not to retrench their liberties, but may enlarge them if your Majesty please; and said, your Majesty
had confirmed their charter and all their privileges by
your Majesty's letter of the 28th day of June 1662, and
that your Majesty could do no lesse in reason than to let
them enjoy their liberties, and trade, they having upon
their own charge and without any contribution from the
Crown made so large plantation in the wildernesse, and
that during the Dutch warrs your Majesty sent ammunition
to New York for that place,but sent them word they must
shift for themselves and make the best defence they could,
and that notwithstanding the colony had many enemies, yet
they did believe your Majesty to be their very good friend,
for that your Majesty had by several letters expressed
your kindnesse to them....
    [Randolph's request that a general court be assembled to answer
    the letters had met with no response.]

---

1. A petition in this vein was indeed presented to the general court.
It declared that the royal charter itself was a proof that Massachusetts was a dominion of the king and its inhabitants his subjects.
(C.S.P. 1661-8/ 421).
2. T. Hutchinson, *Collection* (Prince Soc.) II p.240.Complaints against
evasions of the Navigation Acts by Massachusetts had grown, and appeals of Mason and Gorges against that colony provided a possible
opportunity to bring it into a closer dependence on the Crown. Edward Randolph, a lawyer, later to be the collector of customs in Massachusetts, was chosen as the special agent of the king to take letters to the general court requiring them to send agents to the privy
council to answer questions about the colony, its government and
laws. John Leverett, now governor, treated the king's letter in the
council with curt contempt; he dismissed the contents as unworthy
of notice. So Randolph had demanded a private meeting.
3. Randolph had drawn the governor's attention to ships from Spain,
France and elsewhere in Europe in Boston harbour contrary to the
Navigation Acts.

316. (b). EDWARD RANDOLPH'S *NARRATIVE*, 12 September and 12 October, 1676.[1]
[In his First Enquiry, he had given an account of the legislative and executive powers of the government in New England, of
the governor and general court, magistrates, elections, franchise;
coinage,[2] commissions issued in the name, not of the king, but of
the governor, *etc*.]
Second Enquiry. What lawes and ordinances are now in force
their derogatory or contrary to those of England, and what
oath is prescribed by the government?
The lawes and ordinances made in that colony are no
longer observed than as they stand with their convenience.
The magistrates not so strictly minding the letter of the
law when their publick interest is concerned, in all cases
more regarding the quality and affection of the persons
to their government than the nature of their offence. They
see no eveill in a church member, and therefore against
him, tho' in the smallest matters.
No law is in force or esteeme there but such as are
made by the generall court, and therefore it is accounted
a breach of their priviledges and a betraying of their
liberties of their commonwealth to urge the observation
of the lawes of England or his Majestie's commands....
[He listed the laws 'most derogatory and contradictory' to those
of England as those punishing capital cases by dismemberment or
banishment; the use of the word of God where the law was defective; the non-observance of church holidays: the oath of fidelity
instead of allegiance *etc*.
In his Third Enquiry he reported on church membership, freemen,
planters, servants, occupations, prosperity; In his Fourth, on
members of foot and horse in the trained bands; in his Fifth forts
and castles; in his Sixth, the boundaries; in his Seventh relations with France and New York; in his Eighth the cause for Indian
wars; in his Ninth produce and the laws of trade; in his Tenth
taxes, rates and duties; in his Eleventh the general 'well affected' attitude towards England in contrast to the disobedient truculence of the magistrates, and in his Twelfth church government.]

317. ORDER IN COUNCIL, 20 July 1677.[3]
Whereas it hath been represented to his Majesty in
Councill, That the Corporation of the Massachusetts Bay

---

1. T. Hutchinson, *Papers* (Prince Soc.) II pp.213 ff. This is Randolph'a report to the lords of trade.
2. See above No.233; the coinage of 1652.
3. A.P.C. (Col. series) I(1908) pp.725-6. The general court had decided to comply with the king's request and sent Stoughton and Bulkeley as agents to London. but only with powers to discuss the Mason
and Gorges claims. Randolph 's charges against Massachusetts set out
in his *Narrative* were considered by the lords of trade in May 1677
and 'matters of law' had been sent to the chief justices and law officers and 'matters of state' to the privy council. Randolph had urged
that the colony should be converted forthwith into a royal province,
that a general pardon and liberty of conscience should be granted,

in New England to take upon them to make Laws contrary to
the Power given them by their Charter, and to cause the
same to be executed to the diminution of his Majestys
Royall Authority, and the great Greivance and Oppression
of his Subjects inhabiting those parts. It was there-upon
Ordered by his Majesty in Councill, That Sir Francis Winn-
ington, his Majestys Sollicitor Generall, do inspect the
Laws made by the said Corporation of the Massachusetts
Bay and examine how far they agree with the Powers given
them by their Charter, And what variations or Differences he shall find there - in to report to his Majesty
in Councill with his opinion thereupon,...[1] [The agents
for the corporation were ordered to attend with their charter and
the books of laws.]

318. CHIEF JUSTICES' OPINION ON THE VALIDITY OF THE CHARTER,
                                12 June 1677.[2]
   We, having considered these matters, do humbly conceive...that the patent of the 4th. Car.I is good, notwithstanding the grant made in the 18th Jac., for it
appeareth to us by the recital in the patent 4th. Car.
that the Council of Plymouth granted away all their interest in the lands a year before and it must be presumed
that they then deserted the government. Whereupon it
was lawful and necessary for the King to establish a
suitable frame of government according to his royal wis-

---

and that the general court should be replaced by a governor and council appointed by the Crown. The lords of trade agreed on 2 August.
1.The law officers reported on 2 August (C.S.P.1677-80 p.139-40;R.N.
Toppan *op.cit.*II pp.281 ff.)that many laws were defective and repugnant to English law:'offences were made capital by the word of God:
if by the word is meant the Mosaic law the obligation ceaseth and the
patent will not in many instances befit to be followed by Christians' (e.g. the death penalty for gathering sticks on the sabbath,
for heresy, for a 'stubborn son' etc.).They found no law for the administration of an oath of allegiance,nor for any treason 'save against the Commonwealth'.There were also objections to the disabilities
against Anglicans,the exclusive franchise of the freemen,the taxation of unrepresented subjects, the non-recognition of parliamentary
statutes etc. 'The patent confirms the right of soil and erects a
corporation: the common privilege of corporation is granted' with the
limitation against law repugnant to the law of England. The company
had not *jura regalia* yet by virtue of their patent have erected
courts'. The agents were told that the code must be revised, so that
inconsistences with English law would be removed, that the Acts of
Trade would be enforced, and that the minting of money would cease.
2. J.G. Palfrey,*History of New England* III p.307. The chief justices
of king's bench and of common pleas had been asked by the privy
council on 16 May to give their opinion on the patent of 1629. The
lords of trade in July decided not to destroy the charter, but to
negotiate a supplementary one. (R.N. Toppan,*op.cit.*II p.274,C.S.P.
(1677-80) p.136). The <u>chief justices</u> were Sir Richard Rainsford (K.B.)
and Sir Francis North (C.P.).

dom which was done by the patent of 4th. Car.I. *making
the adventurers a corporation upon the place.*[1]..
     [Neither Maine nor New Hampshire was , however, within the
patent.]

319. ABSTRACT OF RANDOLPH'S REPORT TO THE LORDS OF TRADE,
                                    18 April 1678.[2]
1. That the Government of the Massachusetts is guilty
of crimes and misdemeanors which I formerly exhibited in
my Articles against them, even by the confession of their
owne petition wherein they desire a pardon for the same.
2. That they have incroached upon the bounds of the Sou-
therne Colonies in New England.
3. That the fundamentall Lawes of the Government are repugnant to the Lawes of England.
4. That they doe not allow liberty of conscience nor the
Exercise of the Religion professed by the Church of England constraining all persons to be present at their
Meetings.
5. That they admitt none to have share in the Government
Except such as are in full Communion with them.
6. That they have acted contrary to their Charter and His
Majesty's commands in 1662 and others.

---

1. So the colony was legally chartered and its legality had not been
impaired by the transference of residence of the charter. The chief
justices however had not considered whether it had been voided by
quo warranto proceedings in 1635, though a brief of the prosecution
was tabled on 20 July:(C.S.P. 1677-80 p.131).Therefore the law
officers believed that the case had not been properly stated to the
judges, and in April and May 1678 the specific question whether the
charter had been voided was put: it was ruled that no *quo warranto*
had been delivered or judgement given to dissolve the company, [see
above pp.296-8]; but it was also agreed that if the misdemeanours
alleged were proved, there was sufficient reason to forfeit the
charter (C.S.P. p.251;R.N. Toppan *op.cit.*II p.288,297; III pp, 3 -
5). It was also reaffirmed that it was necessary to have a royal
governor in the colony.
2. R.N. Toppan, *Edward Randolph* (Prince Soc.) II pp.318-9. This was
Randolph's summary of the charges to which the lords of trade required answers from the colony's agents, Stoughton and Bulkeley. But
the agents prevaricated, denying there was any religious test for
the franchise, though as recently as 1672 an Act disenfranchising
all who did not worship at a congregational church had been re-
enacted; and also they somewhat weakly excused the general court's
claim that they had never previously been ordered to enforce the
Navigation Acts. The lords of trade, tired of these evasive tactics,
asked the attorney general in May 1678 to report whether the violat-
ions were sufficient to justify the forfeiture of the charter: it
was now generally agreed in the privy council that a royal governor
was necessary.
Meanwhile, in March 1678 Randolph had been sent to Boston as collector of customs where he met with such total obstruction that the
king,whose patience was increasingly becoming exhausted (C.S.P. 1677
-80. p.598; 1681-5 pp.128-0; 290-1),wrote in October 1681, requir-

7. That they have assumed powers not granted in their
Charter intrenching His Majesty's Prerogative.
8. That instead of oathes of Allegiance and Supremacy
they have lately an oath of Fidelity to be taken to the
Country.[1]
9. [That] They permit no Law of England nor Act of Parliament to be in force there Except first allowed and Enacted by them.[2]
10. That they falsely charged His Majesty and his Ministers of State.
11. That they have not proceeded to any amendment of their
Crimes and Misdemeanors confessed by them,although timely
admonished thereto.

320. PETITION OF THE GOVERNOR AND COMPANY TO CHARLES II,
                                 2 October 1678.[3]
    The humble petition of and address of the Governor
and Company of your Majestie's colony of the Massachusetts in New England, Humbly sheweth, That whereas you
said petitioners have, since your Majestie's most happy
restoration, upon their severall addresses in the yeares
1661, 62, *etc.* received many signall and gratious returnes
of favour...
      [their charter had been confirmed, their errors pardoned and
      the king's favour demonstrated against continuous misrepresentat-
      ion of their aspirations to independence. They had sent Stough-
      ton and Bulkeley as requested to deal with the Gorges and Mason
      claims.]
...as wee have beene informed, your Majestie hath declared
your pleasure as to the settlement of the bounds of our
patent, and our right of government therein according to
our charter, which is matter of great sattisfaction to
all your good subjects heere, it being their utmost ambition to enjoy, under your royall protection and allegiance, the knowne and declared ends of the first undertakers, which hath hitherto binn carried on at their owne
charge, both formerly and lately defended by a greater
expence of bloud and treasure than will easily be believed, whereof they cannot but desire to reape the fruites,
which they assure themselves, they may without any dimin-

ing the general court to give Randolph full support or 'wee shall
take such further resolutions as are necessary to preserve our authority from being neglected'.A *quo warranto* writ was threatened. It
was their last chance. (R.N. Toppan,*op.cit.* p.113).
1. This oath of fidelity had in defiance been confirmed by the
general court on 10 October 1677:N.B. Shurtleff *op.cit.*V p.154.
2. In 1655 Captain Leverett had been strongly censured by the general court for arresting a Dutch vessel in Boston. They declared that
the Navigation Acts would not be permitted 'without the consent or
allowance of authoritie heere established': N.B.Shurtleff,*op.cit.*
IV i p.229.
3.N.B. Shurtleff *op.cit.*V pp 196-201.The general court had now yielded on the matter of an oath of allegiance, on treason, and on the
dropping of the word 'Commonwealth',but were firmly against any other

ution of your Majestie's greatnes, dominion, or glory, which with your Majestie's pardon, wee are bold to affirme, will not be advanced by any innovation or alteration of our present setlement.

Wee humbly supplicate your Majestie that our messengers, having dispatched the business betrusted with them by us, and comanded to attend by your Majestie, may be at liberty to returne, and not be obliged to make answer to such complaints[1] as are made by unquiet spirrits, who seeke not your Majestie's but their owne advantage and our disrest; and what shallbe incumbent on us wee shall, with all dutyfullnes, attend as beccomes good Christians and loyall English subjects, and shall glory in giving your Majestie all just sattisfaction, not insisting on any *errata* that may have slipped us in forty eight yeares, especially in our infancy or in the times of the late confusions, for which (as we have had) wee againe most humbly implore your Majestie's gratious pardon, which will further obleige us for the future to be most observant of your royall pleasure as to your establishment of us according to the charter granted by your royall father, and confirmed by your royall selfe ypon several occasions. Lett your Majestie be pleased to accept from our messengers above-said an account of our ready obedience to your Majestie's command for taking the oaths of allegiance in the forme prescribed, and our repealing that lawe referring to the oath, so ill resented by your Majestie, with some orders Mr Attorney and Mr Sollicitor excepted against, as our messengers have intimated....

[They answered all the charges made by the law officers.]

Those deffects are supplyed by lawes made against high treason, and the oath of allegiance sent by his Majestie was cheerefully taken by the Court, and the Courts order gone forth for all his Majestie's subjects to take the same, on penalty.

To objection I. Where in our lawes wee use the word 'Commonwealth', it is neither in contempt of our opposition to royall authority, and hath not of late bin used, nor heareafter shallbe ....

[To the second objection, they answered that the Quakers had caused dangerous divisions and a challenge to authority. Milder penalties had failed, so an Act had been passed for their banishment and death. They were no more 'put to death for religion' than Jesuit priests in Elizabeth's or James I's reign. They

concessions.

1. They had been instructed expressly to answer questions relating to the Gorges–Mason claims only; but in the course of the investigations conducted by the privy council, the law officers and the judges, they were asked about the treatment of the royal commissioners, the disregard of the king's orders, and the laws and government of the colony. As for their not having full powers to answer general questions, the king declared that he 'did not think of treating with his own subjects as with foreigners'.

answered the other charges made by the lords of trade.]
...To <u>objection</u> 7. Your answer also therein being approved, the Court adds, *viz*.That for the Acts passed in
Parliament for incouraging trade and navigation, wee
humbly conceive, according to the usuall sayings of the
learned in the lawe, that the lawes of England are bounded within the fower seas, and doe not reach Americca.[1]
The subjects of His Majestie here, being not represented
in Parliament, so wee have not looked at ourselves to be
impeded in our trade by the, nor yett wee abated in our
relative allegiance to His Majestie. However, so soone
as wee understood his Majestie's pleasure, that those
Acts should be observed by His Majestie's subjects of the
Massachusetts, which could not be without invading the
liberties and propperties of the subject, untill the General Court made provission therein by a law, which they
did in October 1677, and shall be strictly attended from
time to time, although the same be a discouragement to
trade, and a great damage to His Majestie's plantation,
until wee shall obteyne His Majestie's gracious favour
for that liberty of trade, which wee are not without hopes
but that His Majestie will see just occasion to grant to
us for the encouraging of his good subjects in a wilderness and hard country ....

[God had prospered their shipbuilding and seamanship:the Navigation Acts would only reduce H.M.'s customs, not increase them.]

Wee speake not thus to capittulate with His Majestie
but humbly submitt the same to his royall clemency and
grace.

To <u>objection</u> 7. *[sic.]* About customes, *etc.* wee say,
that imposition upon goods imported from England is not
propperly any customs, but a rate upon such an estate, as
a penny on the pound, when it comes into the merchants
hands, as all other inhabitants pay for their catle and
other their estate that they have.

To <u>objection</u> 8. As for the lawes accounted repugnant
to the lawes of England, wee say, that they were not deemed so to be in the dayes of their making by those that
made them, but only some of them divers from them: wee
are upon examination of those objected against, and such
as shall so appeare, wee shall repeale with all convenient speed, and shall endeavour for the future that none
such be enacted without His Majestie's express and particular licence, except such as the repealing whereof will
make us to renounce the professed cause of our first
coming hither....[2]

---

1. Therefore, according to their theory, in order to give the Acts
of Trade validity in the colony, the general court had re-enacted
them.But the argument from non-representation was double edged:for
they were themselves legislating for and taxing four-fifths of the
colonists who had no vote.
2. As for the king's request for the agents to answer more fully, in
March 1682, Joseph Dudley and John Richards were instructed to go

321. CHARLES II TO THE GENERAL COURT, 20 May 1679.[1]
   [Stoughton and Bulkeley were being allowed to return with this
   letter. The king asked that other agents[2] be sent with power to
   answer fully questions relating not just to the Mason and Gorges
   petitions, but generally about the charter, the government and
   the laws.]
   ...That His Majesty was well satisfied to find that the
Inhabitants had soe readily taken the Oath of Allegiance.[3]
And that His Majesty doth expect that his Letter of the
8th of June 1662 bee complyed with, soe as that those who
desire to serve God in the way of the Church of England
bee made capable of Magistracy and that neither they nor
any other be subject to forfeiture or other incapacities
for the sake of their Religion.
   That there bee noe other distinction in making Freemen
than that they bee men of competent Estates valuable at
ten shillings according to the Law of the place and that
they bee alsoe made capable of the Magistracy.
   That His Majesty thinks fitt that the ancient number
of eighteen Assistants bee observed according to the
Charter.
   That none bee admitted to any privilege or Office without taking the Oath of Allegiance. And that all Military
Commission and proceedings of Justice may run in His Majesty's name.[4]

(iii) MARYLAND

322. THE LORD PROPRIETOR'S COMMISSION FOR A PRIVY COUNCIL,
                                16 February 1666.[5]
   ...Know yee that we have constituted assigned and appointed and doe by these presents constitute assigne and

(N.B.Shurtleff *op.cit.*V p.34) but were not commissioned for another
year (*ibid.*p.356,389).With more moderate leaders in power in Boston,
they were told to be conciliatory and to make apology, but to be
evasive, to show what orders had been carried out (e.g.those relating
to allegiance, and freeman), to prevent any infringement of the charter, and to oppose appeals as 'burdensome'.
1.R.N.Toppan *op.cit.*III p.44.A further letter to the general court
given in the king's presence on 20 June 1679 regretted the absence
of the charter in Massachusetts, but indicated that he was ready to
forgive past misdemeanors as faults 'of a very few in power'. (*ibid.*
p.50).
2.More than three years lapsed before new agents, Dudley and Richards,
arrived..
3.In obedience to the king's letter of 27 April 1678,on 20 October
the court had enacted that, as they had taken the oath,'so by their
example and authoritie they doe require and command that the same
oath be taken by all His Majesty's subjects within the jurisdiction
that are of sixteene yeares of age and upwards'.(N.B.Shurtleff ed.
*op.cit.*V p.193).
4.For the moves to annul or revoke the charter see Nos.281,282,284
and 291.
5. W.H. Browne (ed.) *Archives of Maryland.*XV p.7.The Restoration see-

appointe our deare brother Philip Calvert Esquire[1] our
Chancelour of our said province;our trusty and welbeloved
Richard Boughton Esquire our principal Secretary of our
said province; our trusty and welbeloved Jerome White,
Esquire our Surveyor General of our said province; our
trusty and welbeloved William Evans Esquire our Muster
Master General of our said province; our trusty and welbeloved Baker Brooke Esquire; Edward Lloyd Esquire;Henry
Coursey Esquire; and Thomas Truman Esquire to be our privy
Councellors and to be of our private secret and continual
councel to us and to our Leiuetennant General and Cheif
Governor for the time being of our said province, and to
his Deputy and Deputyes to be by him assigned for and in
relation to all affayres of state and for and in relation
to the making of peace and warre and the good governance
and order of all our affayres relating to our said province
during our pleasure ....

    [Three of this privy council (the chancellor or principal sec-
retary being one) would be a *quorum*: 'a full sufficient and compl-
eate councill for the ends and purposes aforesaid'.]

323. (a) PUBLIC GRIEVANCES PRESENTED BY THE LOWER HOUSE,
                                20 April 1669.[2]
    1. That there is no person authorized by the Lord Prop-
rietor to confirm our laws
    2. That it appears by the body of laws that the Lord
Proprietary did assent to these general laws,now dis-

---

med temporarily to bring much needed stability to Maryland. Cecilius,
the second Lord Baltimore,had been restored to the undiminished powers
of his palatinate in 1657,and four years later revived the oath of
fidelity to himself.But the lower house of the assembly had grown in
stature and self-assertion during the alarms and confusions of the
Commonwealth years when the Puritans had consolidated their control
in it:indeed in 1660 it had claimed exclusive powers to itself without governor and council.Thereafter for a period there was considerable harmony:the lower house did not cease to be jealous of its own
privileges and 'ancient customs'on the model of the house of commons,
but showed readiness to recognise the proprietor's rights as defined
in the charter.The proprietor's governor originated bills, called and
prorogued the assembly and influenced its membership.The proprietor
personally retained the right to confirm or disallow laws.
The council,however,was clearly identified with the proprietor's clan
- a more obvious and less sensitive target for the lower house. With
an additional seven who were lords of the manor - a colonial peerage
- the privy council here named formed the upper house.The tone of this
and other official documents from the proprietor was notably regal.
1.Philip had been secretary of the province and in 1660 had been appointed governor.The next year Charles, son of Cecilius, succeeded him
and in 1675 became lord proprietor himself.
2. W.H. Browne (ed.) *op.cit.*II p.168.While ostensibly accepting the
validity of the proprietor's charter, the assembly was complaining
about the actions of his local officials who had (they alleged) departed from his policy.

assented to by the Lieutenant – General, saying his Lordship doth will those to be laws, and so subscribed his name (vide the Book of Laws) and therefore the same ought not to be dissassented to without the consent of this House.

3. The raising of the last years levys was against the Lord Proprietor's charter, the laws of the province and without the consent of the freemen of this province.

4. That these privileged attornys are of one the grand grievances of the country.

5. The sherrifs taking away merchants and other inhabitants tobaccos upon pretence of seisure for publick debts.

6. That officers are erected which do take fees exceeding and contrary to the Acts of Assembly.

7. That vexatious informers is another publick grievance.

(b) REPLY OF THE UPPER HOUSE, 21 April 1669.[1]

...For that upon the whole matter we cannot but exhort you to desire the Lower House that sent you to proceed to the publick affairs of the province and to tell them from the honourable the Lieutenant and Chief Governour that if they do yet persist to call his Lordship's just rights of consenting or not consenting to laws in what manner he hath it by his Pattent, his power of erecting courts and officers and manner of proceeding in courts at his pleasure according to his Pattent, and his appointing them the said officers just and reasonable fees as Publick Grievances, and unless he will redress these grievances, that is part with his royal jurisdiction granted by his Pattent to the Assembly, they will not proceed to any business as they formerly voted, He desires them to call in all the members of the House and to put it to the question and upon their journal to enter every particular member's consent or dissassent to that vote, and let the vote be signed by the Speaker that he may if he find they are resolved to do no business make an end of this Assembly.

(c) FURTHER REPLY OF THE UPPER HOUSE, 29 April 1669.[2]

That at the conference [of the two houses] the Chancellour do remonstrate unto them the ruin that is coming upon these rash proceedings of theirs 1. By leaving the prov-

---

1. *Ibid.* II p.176. The upper house had answered the grievances *seriatim* and now concluded with this general statement. They defended the actions and rights of the proprietor as legally within his patent and argued that his concessions to their privileges were not of right, but by grace and favour. They, therefore, refused to make a joint petition to him, and asked the lower house to remove such 'seditious votes' from their journals.

2. *Ibid.* II p.178. The lower house declared they had no wish to call the proprietor's rights 'grievances'. ('God forbid') and somewhat surprisingly expressed their readiness to have their journal 'contradicted, expunged, obliterated, burnt, anything' so that the Grievances should be removed from the record (*ibid.* p.184).

ince without law. 2. The people discontented and jealous
that their just libertys are denied them, when in truth
we only vindicate that just power in my Lord which the
King hath given him by his charter and is no way commun-
icable to the people. 3. The province much in debt and
particular persons much damaged in Talbot and Somerset
countys especially for want of their pay from the publick,
all which they have as much as in them lyes hindered by
their vote relating to the last year's levy. 4. The hinderance of the raising this Assembly's charges.5. The hinderance of curbing the Indians.

Further to declare to them *[1]* that they are not to conceive that their privileges run paralell to the Commons
in the Parliament of England, for that they have no power
to meet but by virtue of my Lord's charter, so that if
they in any way infringe that they destroy themselves;
for, if no Charter, there is no Assembly; no Assembly no
privileges. 2. Their power is but like the common council
of the City of London which if they act contrary or to
the overthrow of the charter of the city run into sedition
and the person questionable.

324. PROTEST BY THE LOWER HOUSE, 28 March 1671.[1]

That this House,having reassumed the debate concerning
the writs sent for summoning several of the burgesses,
delegates, and deputys elected by the freemen of this province to serve in the present General Assembly, and being
informed that several of the countys according to the
writs of the sherriffs of the several countys ordering and
impowering the freemen of the said countys to elect and
make choice of the said delegates and deputys of this
House which said delegates and deputys were chosen according to the tenour thereof; This House, considering the
premisses, do humbly conceive that of right the whole number of delegates and deputys so chosen ought to have been
summoned to appear to serve as delegates, burgesses, or
deputys for their several countys whose representatives
are omitted to be summoned to appear and serve in this
Assembly.

325. *COMPLAINT FROM HEAVEN WITH A HUY AND CRYE* BY JOSIAS FENDALL AND
OTHERS TO CHARLES II, November 1676.[2]

[The 'platform of the Berkeley party in Virginia and the Baltim-
ores in Maryland'was for 'Pope Jesuit to overterne England' and,

---

1.W.H.Browne (ed.) *op.cit.*II pp.240-1.During Fendall's governorship
four delegates were to be chosen.When Philip Calvert was acting in
1660 he left the number to the discretion of the sheriff, while Charles (later in 1675 the third Lord Baltimore) had required 1 to 4 to
be elected.In 1670,however,allegedly to save expense,he had issued
writs for only two of the four deputies chosen for each county.More-
over,he disenfranchised many freemen by limiting the franchise to freeholders though the charter had referred to freemen (*liberi homines*).
2. W.H. Browne (ed.) *op.cit.*V.pp.134-0. Fendall, appointed by Baltim-

with the aid of Indians, Maryland papists and French Canadians,
to drive protestants into purgatory. The petitioners accused Baltimore of causing death, ruin, mischief, oppression, extortion, im-
pressment and fraud. He was a tyrant, pocketing the public revenues, and under cloak of the assembly's 'mealy-mouthed, affraighted'
compliance, converting the common good to his private ends'. Maryland was ruled by a family compact.]

Young child [of] Charles Baltimore about 9 or 10 years of age,[1]
Governor in England; chirugien Warden,[2] a son-in-law, Deputy Governor in Maryland; Philip Calvert, Pukly[3] Chancellor; William Calvert nephew, secretary; Brooks surveyor
general, kindsman, (besides the secret councel of priests
and Natlyes[4] with perhaps a son-in-law or kindred more)
stronge papists, besids Mr. Chew Taylor and... [MSS defective]
half ones, with som protestants for fashion sake, in number
easily overrated with Law-Brother loe all most forgot. Now
when any thing in the popish chamber is hatched that must
have a country cloack, warrants issue forth to every county to choose 4 men, which my Lord's officer sheriff binds
by 4 indentures to serve his turne: but at a day afterward
appointed, a writ coms but for 2 out of theas 4, pikt out
for his purpos, *viz.* either papists owne creatures and
familiars or *ignoramuses*.   These are called Delegates,
but the country calls them Delicats, for they gladly com
to sutch christenings at St. Mary's[5] where there is good
cheere made, and the poore country pays every time - one,
two, or more hundred thousand pounds of tobacco for it.
For there is many items: an item for chancellor's fees;
item, secretary fees etc: and the more Assemblies the oftner it goes about, all dae thy nothing els, but augment
fees upon fees, and continue temperary lawes, as they
call them.

Now when these are confined in a room together, they
are called the lower house, and the provintiall court men

---

ore in 1657,had proved an unreliable governor, for he led an abortive
rebellion against the proprietary in 1660. He had remained a trouble-
maker and (with John Coode) became a mouthpiece for the discontent
growing against Baltimore's patent, particularly in the frontier area
of Charles Country, infected from neighbouring Virginia with Baconian
agitation. What had been an acceptable delegation of prerogative power
in 1632 was a generation later no longer so. This *Complaint* was somewhat laboured and hysterical in style, and notably anti-catholic.
1.Benedict Leonard was nine when Charles Calvert left Maryland to
consult with Baltimore.He was named governor.
2. Presumably Jesse Wharton who was named deputy governor in charge:
a sort of regent protector.
3. Perhaps 'public',maybe 'weakly' or even 'disgusting'.
4. Presumably the relations and associates of Thomas Notley, speaker
of the last assembly and then deputy governor to Charles Calvert from
1677 to 1681 : [see also p.307].
5. First permanent settlement and where the assembly still met. In
1695 the seat of government moved to Annapolis.

in an other chamber, stiled themselves the upper house;
and prescribes what the lower house is to consent unto,
which if any grummeles at, then perswadinge spirits goe
forth, and if any stands out or up for the comon good,
frowns and treathnings scares them to be quieth, right
or wrong: and this they call Acts of Assembly, but the
country calls them Dissemblings, and abreptive procured
Acts. These Acts must bee first over and above send into
England to the proprietary there, (and why not then to the
King's Majesty?) and what hee then doth not relish is of
no force, but his selfe interest irrevocable and perpetual
which causes the Assembly now to act for the most part
temporary for 3 years or *[until]* the next Generall Assembly,
and this doeinge and undoeinge is the reason the country
can never com to any estability – the one not dareinge
trust the other. And now pray where is the liberty of the
freeborne subjects of England and owr priviledges in Maryland, the Lord Proprietary assums and attracts more royal
power to himselfe over his tennants than owr gratious
Kinge over his subjects in England, and therefore charge
the Lord Proprietary with breach of charter, who gives
him, noe warrant to deal with the King's Majesty's subjects
in Maryland so deceitfully, as further appeared by the
sheriffs, which my Lord puts in and out, when, whome and
howe long him pleased, contrary to the custom of England
and is direct repugnant, as it is also against two express
Acts of Assembly: *Anno* number 61 and 62, wherein the commissioners of every country were to present 7 persons every
Martch, out of which the Governor was to choose one every
year and no longer.

But it coms a greater consequence, the Proprietary, with
his familiars houlds forth, that hee is an absolute prince
in Maryland, with as absolute prerogative royal right and
power as owr gratious souveraigne in England, and according to that, they set their compass to steere by and governe by: but wee replye, that if it is not within the compass of treason, to saye so, sure it is to acte so, for
what els sygnifyed, that my Lord Baltimore puts himselfe
in equal computation with his coarts of armes next to the
King's Majesty in the great map of Virginia and Maryland,
prikkinge him selfe distinctly in, and the King's Majesty
out of Maryland? To what purpose els are his coarts of
armes put up in every court, and under that authority
onely justice administered, all writs and warrants issued
forth, and under or by their dominion all process and
other writings concluded; appeals to his royal Majesty
into England termed criminal and denyed? Nay what else
imports, an Act of Assembly caused to be made *Anno* 50 so
that all men shall swear allegiance and supremacy under
the tittle of fidelity to the Lord Proprietary and his
hyres and successors for ever, or shall be banished
the province, as by the said oath at large is to bee seen
upon which then the Seavorn fight [1] orriginated, and the

---

1. The battle of the River Severn in 1655 between Stone, Fendall and

Lord Proprietary lost the country by it, to which said
oath openly maintained, as if the King's Majesty in England hath nothing to doe there, which is wunderful strange,
consideringe New Yorke and all other provinces in America
honour the King's most excellent Majesty, with the Emper-
ial Armes and suppremacy of England....

Next, wee acknowledge Lord Baltimore our land lord proprietary and the inhabitants his tennants in Maryland by
fealty onely, payeinge for all manner of services the
yearly quit rent as by owr pattents wee are no otherwise
injoyned: but our souveraigne lord the Kinge, proprietor
over Maryland, and wee his onely subjects and liege freeborne people of England to whom wee owe alleageance and
fidelity and to no other, and to him wee will swear and
engage, to bee true and faithful under the conduct of the
Lord Proprietary as his Majesty's general and his lift-
tennant and governor and government established here not
repugnant to the laws and customs (without infringeinge-
inge uppon the liberties and priviledges) of the freeborne
subjects of England, and hereuppon we doe now appeal to
our gratious kinge and Parliament, if wee by Maryland
charter are otherwise obliged, and produce by the proprietary's first Comistione of plantations published,that wee
are not otherwise required nor invited and therefore by
an usurped power, they will make themselves absolute over
owr lives, fortunes and estates....

[Marylanders were deprived of the privileges and franchises of
free Englishmen and of appeal to the king 'with his Parliaments'.
The proprietor playing the part of king shut them off from allegiance to the king. In order not to be rebels against the king, they
must rebel against Baltimore. The king's charter had entrusted the
proprietor to be 'a good steward to the Reallm of England'; but,
'an inferiour Irish lord' and the'pope's privy agent', Baltimore
had abused that trust and subordinated his palatinate to the
pope.]

Unmask the vizard and you will see a young pope and a
new souveraigne pepe out of his shell, and all the popish
faction tents and points in that their old and first Acts
of Assemblys, and so it is carryed alonge and all arts and
devises used to perswade and create fit turne-coats to
bring their purpos step by step to pass, from one degree
to another....

[They had to expose the plot. Jesuits who walked the streets in
England 'apparelled as tradesmen' revealed ,'their *plus ultra* in
their chapples' when sent over to Maryland. Baltimore was to be
canonised.How could they be 'rebels' in appealing to the king
against a proprietor who deprived them of their rights as subjects
of the Crown? They appealed to Charles II to judge between his
loyal subjects and Baltimore and his favourites. They petitioned
him to take the government of Maryland into his own hands, to appoint protestant officialsto rule according to 'the custom of

the proprietor's party on one side and Fuller and the puritans on the
other. Fuller won a complete victory.

England' and to regulate taxation in the interests of the many, not the few. They also asked for a troop of good resolute Scots Highlanders to defend them against the Indians and the French.]

326. PROCLAMATION, 27 June 1681.[1]

Whereas by an Act of Assembly of this province, made at a General Assembly holden at the city of St. Maries the twentieth day of October Anno Domini one thousand six hundred seaventy eight (by several prorogations prorogued and continued thereto from the fifteenth day of May Anno Domini one thousand six hundred seaventy six) entituled *an Act directing the manner of electing and summoning delegates and representatives to serve in succeeding assemblies* it was enacted that four deputyes and delegates for each respective county should be chosen and called to sit in every General Assembly for the future. The inconveniency whereof in burdening every county with the charge of four delegates as aforesaid Wee haveing duely weighed and considered, and conceiveing that the true intent of the said Act was onely to assure the freemen of this our province that all persons by them elected for their delegates and representatives, should be called to sit and vote in our said General Assembly. And, wee haveing consulted and advised with our Council thereupon, wee doe, by and with their advice, consent and approbation, hereby proclaime, publish and declare our disassent to the said Act, and the same to be null and void to all intents and purposes, any clause thereof or any thing conteined to the contrary in any wise notwithstanding. And that (after the dissolution of this present General Assembly) for the future two delegates onely shall be elected and chosen for every county to sit and vote in succeeding assemblies.

And whereas our said General Assembly holden as aforesaid by several prorogations hath been prorogued and continued until the eleaventh day of October next ensueing, but several urgent and weighty occasions and affaires relating to the state and wellfare of this our province (now every alarmed by forreigne Indians) since interveeneing which requires the sooner and more speedy conveeneing and sitting thereof, Wee have, by and with the advice and consent of our Council, determined and ordeined, and Wee doe hereby fully resolve, determine and ordeine That the said General Assembly be held at our city of St. Maries on the sixteenth day of August next ensueing and therefore Wee doe hereby will and require as also strictly charge and command all and singular the sheriffes of this our province forthwith upon receipt hereof to make Proclamation hereof in the most publick and convenient places within their res-

---

1. W.H. Browne (ed.) *op.cit.* XV p.379. The reduction in the number of delegates ordered in 1676 had caused a prolonged controversy. Charles Calvert, now proprietor, had done this merely by issuing writs for 2 deputies. Now he issued this ordinance and proclamation.

pective counties and to give notice to all and singular
the delegates and deputyes by the freemen of their county
already elected and which are now liveing and resideing
within their said county, That, all excuses set apart, they
and every of the said delegates come and personally appeare
at the said city of St. Maries on the said sixteenth day
of August next ensueing to doe and consent to those thinges which then and there by the favour of God shall happen
to be ordeined by us, by and with the advice and consent
of our greate Councill of this our province, concerning
the state and wellfare of this our province, and also to
give notice to such of our Councill as inhabit in their
respective counties that, all excuses set apart, they also
be and appeare at the day and place aforesaid in the upper
house of our said General Assembly to the end and purpose
aforesaid.[1]

327. (a) RESOLUTION OF THE LOWER HOUSE, 7 November 1682.[2]
   This house taking into consideration a message from
the Upper house of the 4th November instant viz. that the
two houses legally represent the freemen of the province,
put to the question whether the Upper house as well as
the Lower house are the representatives of the freemen of
this province.
   Resolved *nemine contra dicente* That the deputies and
delegates chosen by the freemen of this province in a
General Assembly are the only representative body of the
freemen of this province. That was put to the question
whether the charge of the Upper house of assembly shall be
brought to the publick account, and so paid by the publick.
   Resolved That the publick ought not to be charged or
bear the charges or expenses of the members of the Upper
house.

   (b) REPLY OF THE UPPER HOUSE, 10 November 1682.[3]
   In answer to the message of the Lower house of the 7th
instant last night received, this House do say that they

1.This proclamation did not settle the matter.The upper house prepared
a bill for elections on these lines;the lower house drew up another
bill providing for up to 4 deputies.Neither house would accept the
bill of the other.
2.W.H. Browne (ed.) *op.cit.*VII p.373.
3. W.H.Browne (ed.) *op.cit.*VII p.377.For a further year and half the
two houses remained deadlocked, often to the neglect of other business - including defence.In April 1684 the new assembly seemed to accept the proprietor's ruling.The following month Baltimore had to return to England to answer charges made by Penn, particularly relating
to boundaries: he found he had further to defend his charter against
threat of *quo warranto*: charges concerned the interference with the
royal customs, the enforcement of the Navigation Acts and the murder
of a royal collector, Rousby, by the acting governor, Baltimore's
nephew.

intended not any thing by those words in their message
dated the 4th instant further then that *[they]* are a part
of the body politick of this province without whose assent no laws can pass and do now vote accordingly, and,
that they did expect directions from his Lordship in
relation to the bill for electing and summoning delegates
etc.,ere they would proceed therein that the two houses
might not loose their labour.

328. INSTRUCTIONS FROM THE COMMISSIONERS OF CUSTOMS, 10 August 1685.[1]
   8. Whereas we have been informed that a considerable
number of bonds taken in our Province of Maryland from
masters of ships trading thither in pursuance of the Act
of Navigation, and that counterfeit certificates of landing the plantation commodities in England have been produced in discharge of some of the said bonds tho' the
said commodities were carryed directly to other parts
than England, Wales or Berwick, when no such bonds have
been there really given: and moreover that several forged
and counterfeit cocquetts alledged to be granted in England have been accepted in Maryland, by colour whereof
great quantities of European goods have been there past
as coming directly from England, Wales or Berwick, when
as in truth the said goods were shipt and laden elsewhere
to the manifest prejudice of our customs and the trade
and navigation of this Kingdom, You are therefore to cause
a list of all the bonds taken and that shall be taken in
Maryland between Michelmas 1679 and Michelmas 1685 next
coming to be forthwith transmitted to the Commissioners
of our customes in England for the time being, therein
distinguishing which of the said bonds are discharged,
and which of them remain uncleared. You are also to cause
to be transmitted to the said Commissioners all the original certificates which have been produced in Maryland
during that time from the several Custom Houses of England, Wales or Berwick for the discharge of bonds given
in Maryland, and also the original certificates of bonds
given or pretended to be given in the several ports of
this Kingdom, together with all the original cocketts
which have been produced for European goods shipt or pretended to be shipt in the said ports, keeping abstracted
lists or accompts thereof, and taking a receipt from the
person to whom the same are delivered.
   9. And whereas for the better collection of the several
rates and duties imposed by the said Act of the 25th year
of his late Majesty's reign that whole business is to be

1.W.H.Browne (ed.)*op.cit.*V pp.450-2.These articles in a general circular to governors were those specially for Maryland.Nehemiah Blakes-
ton, the royal collector, found his authority disregarded or impeded
by Baltimore's officials within the proprietary.The lords of trade
were already contemplating a *quo warranto* against the Maryland charter as its independence was a 'growing prejudice' to the Crown and
the customs.

ordered and managed and the several duties there imposed
are to be caused to be levyed, by the Commissioners of
our Customs in England for the time being by and under
the authority and direction of the Lord Treasurer of England or Commissioners of our Treasury for the time being,
You are forthwith to require and command such of your
officers as have taken upon them the collection of the
said rates and duties to cease any further to act therein
and to render to the Commissioners an accompt of their
receipts and payments since the death of the late Collector[1] together with an account of their seizures and
other proceedings. And you are to give in charge that
they do not hereafter presume to collect our duties or
otherwise to concern themselves therein without the special appointment and directions of the said Commissioners
and both you and they and all others concerned are hereby
required to be aiding and assisting to the Collector and
other officers appointed or that shall hereafter be appointed by the said Commissioners by and under the authority and direction of the Lord High Treasurer of England
or Commissioners of the Treasury for the time being in
putting in execution the several Acts of Parliament before mentioned together with such orders and instructions
as they have or shall from time to time receive from the
said Commissioners[2]....

329. *PROCEEDINGS IN THE GENERAL ASSEMBLY*, 1688: [3]
    (a) Speech by Governor Joseph to both houses, 14 November 1688.
    It cannot be (or at least I hope it is not) unknown
to any the members of this honourable assembly, that the
unquestionable duty of every of us in particular and of
us all in general, is that we first render thanks and
praise to the Almighty for that it hath pleased the Divine Goodness thus to bless us in this (I hope) so good
and happy a meeting; nor ought we to be strangers to the
end and duty for which the Divine Providence hath ordered
us to meet, I say Providence hath ordered, for that there
is no power but of God and the power by which we are assembled here is undoubtedly derived from God, to the King,
and from the King to his Excellency the Lord Proprietary,
and from his said Lordship to us....
    [Laws were necessary to enforce the divine will as seen in God's
    commandments and in the king's commands.]
    The third part of the end and duty thereof I spoke is
that which by the blessing of God shall occur in referr-
ence to his Excellency, the Lord Proprietary of this

1.Christopher Rousby had been murdered in October 1684 (after Baltimore had departed to defend his charter) by George Talbot, the proprietor's nephew.
2. This instruction was a considerable blow to the prestige and powers of the lord proprietor : the Crown was trespassing on the palatinate to supervise the internal administration of parliamentary
statutes.
3. W.H.Browne (ed.)*op.cit.*XIII p.147. William Joseph, a strenuous

province.

Gentlemen, I hope there are not any (in this present General Assembly) so wicked as (by Machiavilian principles) shall go about to divide the interests of my Lord and his people which indeed are not two interests but one, for that whatsoever shall be for the good and welfare of his people is also the undoubted good and welfare of my Lord whose chief care and study is to encrease the wealth and ease to the inhabitants of Maryland wherefore who ever shall endeavour to divide the hearts of the people from my Lord, or my Lord from the people let him (by this assembly) be declared a traitor to our God,King, Lord and people.

My Lord, Gentlemen, desired nothing of us but that we provide well for the people, for that by so doing we provide as well for my Lord as my Lord desires.

He is not, gentlemen, the man that puts either the King or people to charge of or for government, but is one that really endeavours to promote the interests of both by all meanes to him possible, tho' there's nothing more certain then that his Lordship and his Lordship's ancestors of ever noble and happy memory have with the hazard of their lives buried a vast estate in the first subduement and since continued settlement of this province to the allegiance of our sovereign lord the King, to a far greater value than the profits of this province do (or are like to do) or amount to; nor is any thing more apparent, *[than]* if his Lordship's interests in America were to be disposed of that there's none would give (considering the charge of government) the tenth part of what they cost, wherefore as my Lord of his part never did (as he never will) burthen the people whereby to be reimbursed the said charge,so will it be an act of the highest ingratitude in the people if of their part they do not justly and freely pay what is or of right ought to be my Lord's dues. But as your care, gentlemen, to rectifie abuses (if any be) of this nature is no ways doubted, so I shall and do desist the further pressing of this point to the intent I may the sooner come to the fourth and last part of our duty which is -

That you take all due care of yourselves ····
[Members of both houses of the assembly must take the oath of fidelity to the proprietor.][1]

(b) <u>Resolution of the Lower House</u>, 15 November 1688.[2]
Upon reading the message of the Upper house dated the

---

advocate of both prerogative and proprietary, was sent out by Baltimore as president of the council and deputy governor in his absence.
1.The oath was nominally taken by all settlers in the province and normally not once more by the members of both houses.While protesting their loyalty to the lord proprietor, both houses expressed their resentment at this innovation.
2. *Ibid.*XIII p.157.

14 and 15 of November instant in answer to them say That
this House is very sorry that the Upper house has conceived so bad an opinion of the Lower house as though they
had forgotten their duty or been unfaithfull to his Lordship and his government, but this house do protest that
they are and will be always ready and willing to the utt-
ermost of their power to yeild a faire and ready comply-
ance in all matters relating to the honour of his Lordship
and wellfare of the people that it may in no ways intrench
upon the priviledges of this house believeing it to be one
especial point of their duty to leave to their posterity
what themselves have received and hope to enjoy, and whereas the said message of the 15th of November instant is
concerning the Oath of fidelity
    Resolved by this house That they are not impowered to
act with his Lordship or Upper House of Assembly in any
other qualification or under any other denomination then
as the representatives of the freemen of this province in
the Assembly.
    That this house will still comply with the desires of
the Upper house in a message from the Upper house dated
the 14th of this instant November and with their answer
to the same of this days date that they are willing to
take the aforesaid Oath of fidelity when the Upper house
please to let this house know of any Act of Assembly imposing the said Oath upon the Lower house of Assembly.

    (c) Governor Joseph's reply, 16 November 1688.[1]
    ...I am commanded to tell you that fidelity is alleg-
iance which by the laws of England may be proposed even
to the House of Commons in Parliament sitting, and the
refusers are excluded from being members or having any
vote in Parliament, as if they never had bin elected; and
by the laws of this province if you be within the province
you are bound to take the Oath of fidelity to the right
honourable the Lord Proprietary under pain of banishment,
fine and imprisonment at the discretion of the government;
and further I am to tell you that the refusing allegiance
implyes rebellion, and that you have no priviledge to
break, contemn or disobey laws, wherefore you are desired
to return to your House and consider of it, for that the
government will not permit this House to proceed to any
business whatsoever till you satisfie the law and government in this point, for, by how much the more you refuse
allegiance, by so much the more the government have cause
to suspect your loyalty.

330. (a) GRIEVANCES OF THE LOWER HOUSE, 22 November 1688.[2]
    Whereas by an Act of Assembly entituled *an Act for*

1.*Ibid*. p.159. Temporarily the deputies gave in and took the oath.
But clearly Joseph's extreme views exacerbated the situation in Mary-
land:like the king he regarded any discontent as seditious;but with
the flight of James II,the proprietary itself was doomed and forfeit.
2.W.H.Browne (ed.) *op.cit*.XIII pp.171-2. Before an answer arrived on

raising and providing a support for his Lordship the Lord Proprietary of this province during his natural life etc. made at a General Assembly begun and held at the city of St. Maries in the province of Maryland the 27th day of March 1671 and by other Acts since made confirming the same and now in force, It was thereby provided that his said Lordship, his Receiver or Receivers General for the time being shall receive good sound merchantable tobacco for his said Lordship's rents and fines for alienations of lands reserved upon the several and respective grants of land in this province at the rate of two pence per pound, any thing in his said Lordship's grants to the contrary notwithstanding. Nevertheless his said Lordship's Receivers and other officers appointed contrary to the said law have and do under colour of their said offices not only refuse to receive tobacco as by the said law is provided, but exact money sterling to the great agreivance and oppression of the good people of this province of which we humbly desire address and relief.

2dly. Whereas the honourable the Secretarys of this province do charge the people of this province with several fees which are not by law due, particularly in that for recording proceedings which they do take and extort by way of execution, the said fees being due and paid under another denomination of which we humbly desire redress and reliefe.

3dly. Whereas it is provided in the *Act for Advancement of Trade* that the right honourable the Lord Proprietary should before the last day of August 1685 for the quick dispatch of ships etc. appoint in Wicocomoco, St.Maries, Patuxent and Ann Arundel for the western side of this province, and in Talbot and Somerset Counties for the eastern shore, some fit officer or officers for the entring and clearing of ships in the said several and respective places, for want of which trade has been discouraged to the great grievance of the inhabitants of which they humbly desire redress and relief.

It being likewise very prejudicial to his Lordships interest and income.

4thly.Whereas it is not only a great agreivance to the present inhabitants of this province but also of fatal consequence to their posterity, that laws made and assented unto by his Lordship and the people of province should be dispenced withall by any other authority than by which they were first made, which we humbly desire to know if his Lordship do intend to annul that clause of the Act about bringing tobacco to towns without an Act of repeale.

5th. Whereas the Attorney General has often presumed upon his own authority as Attorney General to send out

---

the matter of the proprietor's confirmation or disallowance of these laws Baltimore had been deprived of his proprietary.He retained his rights in the soil but lost his powers of government.A small group of insurgents led by John Coode, previously an associate of Fendall's, secured the surrender of the deputy governor in August 1689 and an assembly petitioned for royal government.

precepts directed to the several sheriffs commanding them
to bring the bodys of several the inhabitants of this
province to the provincial courts to answer such things
as should be objected against them, by which means several
of his Lordship's good people have been taken into the
custody of the several sheriffs and brought to the provincial court being altogether ignorant of what should
be laid to their charge before they come upon their tryal,
contrary to the fundamental and known laws and to the
great agrievance and unsupportable charge and damage of
his Lordship's good people of which we humbly desire to
be relieved.

    [The requisitioning of supplies of food from civilians by bogus
militia officers in peace time, the adjournment of the provincial
court until January, and the exacting of a duty of three pence on
tobacco were all grievances for which redress was sought.]

330. (b) ORDER IN COUNCIL, 12 March 1691.[1]

Wee have thought fit to take our province of Maryland
under our immediate care and protection, and by letters
patents under the great seale of England to appoint our
trusty and well beloved Lionel Copely Esquire,of whose
prudence and loyalty we are well assured, to be our governor thereof, until whose arrival we do hereby authorise
and impower you to continue in our name the administration
of the government and preservation of the peace and property of our subjects there, willing and requiring you to
take care that one moiety of the impost of two shillings
for every hogshead of tobacco, exported from our said
province, be collected for the use and support of our
government there, and to permit the duty of fourteen pence
per tunn, and the other moiety of the said duty of two
shillings per hogshead to be collected and received for
the use of the Lord Baltimore as Proprietary of our said
province, by such as shall be appointed by him to collect
and receive the same ....[The murderers of the collector were
to be found and tried.]

(iv) BARBADOS AND THE CARIBBEES

331. FRANCIS, LORD WILLOUGHBY, TO CHARLES II, 1 October 1661.[2]

The Kings Majestie haveing declared his desire and

1.W.H.Browne (ed.) *op.cit.*VIII p.235-6. (For convenience this post-
1688 document is printed here).The attorney general had given his
opinion,after a hearing at which Baltimore and Coode were both present, that in such a time of emergency as existed the king could commission the governor of Maryland even though the charter was not ann-
ulled.Colonel Copley had been Baltimore's choice for governor, but
the commission now came from the Crown and Maryland became a royal
province.When in 1716 a Protestant Calvert was given back his powers
of government, they were no longer an absolute lordship.
2. C.O. 1/15 no.87.The Restoration would seem automatically to have

intention to drawe under his imediate authoritye and counsell all the several forreigne plantations that they maye
have the same dependance with the rest of his Majestie's
dominions, and haveing signified that it is his royal pleasure that the Lord Willoughbye of Parham should surrender
up to his Majestie certaine claimes which hee hath to several of the said foreigne plantations possessed by him
under a grant made unto the Earle of Carlisle by King
Charles the first; The Lord Willoughbye is ready to submit
all his right and title thereunto to the pleasure of his
Majestie out of an assurance that his Majestie will gratiously condiscend to the following overtures of the Lord
Willoughbye which hee hath collected and laid downe heere
humbly apprehending it to bee the sense of his Majestie
and his privie counsell.

1. That the Lord Willoughbye, haveing about six yeares
to ronne in his lease of twenty-one yeares from the Earle
of Carlisle, may for that tearme have his Majestie's commission to bee his Majestie's Leftenant General as amply
as hee was heretofore, to have care of, conduct, government and improvement of the said island with such further
powers and instructions as maye best advance his Majestie's
authoritye and revenue upon these plantations.

2. That, seeing the said lease doth conveye and assure
to the Lord Willoughby halfe the proffits which were to
arrise to the Lord Proprietor upon the said plantation,
and that the Lord Willoughby hath hitherto beene a sufferer
in his person and estate for serveing his Majestie there,
his Majestie will be pleased for the said tearme of six
yeares to confirme to the Lord Willoughbye and his assignes the moietie of such proffits and revenues as by Lord

---

re-established the proprietorship of the Caribbees – 'Cariola'.Francis
Lord Willoughby, planter and courtier, was not unpopular in Barbados,
but the reimposition of the Carlisle grant threatened to reduce the
planters once more to mere tenants-at-will.Though in July 1660 the
king had ordered Willoughby 'instantly to apply himself to take care
of the affairs and government' of Barbados and required the islanders to obey him as strictly as 'before the late interruption', Modyford's intrigues and Carlisle's debts delayed settlement. When in
March 1661 those advocating Modyford's appointment as a royal governor offered without authority a duty on exports to the king if he
assumed the proprietorship himself, the compromise became clearer.
The king made the palatinate of the Caribbees a royal province and
Willoughby was commissioned as his governor of Barbados and the Caribbees for the remaining seven years of the Carlisle lease. The king
was to attempt a more effective and more resourceful threat to Barbadian 'home rule' than the proprietor.Imitating Cromwell, the direct
appointment of his own nominees to vacant offices was a first step:
secretary and provost marshal in 1661, posts previously filled by
local patronage. As for Willoughby, the privy council invited him
to draft his own instructions:these were confirmed in September 1662
and the new patent was sealed in June 1663.

Willoughbye shall bee raised to your Majestie upon the said plantation.

3. That, in consideration of the allowance of the moiety to the Lord Willoughbye, hee shall by his industrye and experience advance and settle all his Majestie's interests in those places and shall have noe other reward or allowance for being his Majestie's Leftenant Generall and Governor there than what the said moiety shall reach to....[1]

332. HEADS OF ADDRESSES BY THE COUNCIL AND ASSEMBLY TO CHARLES II, 18 December, 1662.[2]

That a declaration bee by Act of parliament,touching the assurance of our titles to our lands.

Tenure *in soccage* to bee held of the King *etc.* , paying such an acknowledgement as the governor, councell and assembly shall agree unto.

That all our children bee declared freeborne of all his Majesty's Dominions.

That noe tax bee layd without the consent of the freeholders...[nor any customs imposed on exports from England, as none to Virginia or New England.]

That wee may have a free trade as England hath....

333. 'PETITION OF RIGHT' BY THE ASSEMBLY TO GOVERNOR LORD WILLOUGHBY, 8 July 1665.[3]

[Despite Magna Carta, islanders had been arrested and dispossessed] ...They doe therefore humbly pray yor Excellency, that none of his Majestie's subjects, may hereafter (in

---

1. So Willoughby had to bear all public expenses.The other half was to be used to pay off the Carlisle creditors.
2. C.O.31/1 p.77.Until Willoughby arrived with his commission and instructions as royal governor in the summer of 1663,his nominee as president of the council, Humphrey Walrond, had acted. Willoughby's first duty on arrival was to secure the permanent revenues promised as part of the compromise. He secured the Act granting the king a 4½% duty on exports on 12 September 1663. [see No.293].
3.C.O.1/19 no.78(1).Since the stormy session when the Act imposing 4½% duty was passed,Willoughby had broken island custom and called no assembly.But when the Crown refused him use of the 4½% revenues for defence against the Dutch, he had to resort to an election.Samuel Farmer, as Speaker, immediately drafted this petition. By ordinance, Willoughby had reduced the courts of common pleas from five to two,and had, in asserting the king's authority,acted sometimes in an arbitrary way.He dissolved the assembly and sent Farmer to England on a charge of high treason.Despite urgent danger the next assembly also procrastinated and truculantly refused a defence levy.Then they attempted to secure control by establishing a commission of three planters who would be responsible for all defence revenues and expenditures: an attempt by the legislature to control the executive. This bill Willoughby vetoed.

such manner as is before mentioned) bee imprisoned or det-
ayned, and that none may hereafter without judgment of his
peers, bee put out...of his possessions, or disseised of
his inheritance, nor exiled and banished without due course of law; and that none bee comanded to attend as wittnesses (upon theire owne costs) when they can say nothing
material against the offender; and that our courts may
retourne to bee kept in theire due and accustomed press-
incts, accordinge to the sayd Act[1],and that our statutes
heere, may not bee subverted by any ordinance of yor self
and counsell;...that the doings and proceedings to the
prejudice of his Majestie's subjects heere...shall not bee
drawne hereafter into consequence or example.[2]

334. GOVERNOR LORD WILLOUGHBY TO CHARLES II, 8 August 1665.[3]
    ...I am ashamed to thinke how unprofitable a servant
I have beene for yor Majesty. And yet I can say I have
beene honnest, for I have done nothing for myselfe. I did
by the last fleete send home to your Majesty one Farmer,
prisoner with articles aginst him for his high misdemeanors and contempts of yor Majestie's government. Hee was
one of the chiefe ringleaders and a very dangerous fellow;
a great magna-charta-man and petition-of-right maker, the
first that started up that kind of language here, which
tooke so with the people, as I thought it not safe to let
him remaine any longer upon this island, where hee had
set all the people into a flame, and brought them into
that opinion, as that they were not to bee governed by
yor Majestie's comission, nor anything but theire owne
lawes, or rather theire owne wills, for they were beginning to dance after the Long Parliament's pipe, assuming
to themselves the imitation of it by the stile and title
of 'the best of parliaments', which was the doctrine this
John Cade began to spread amongst the people, and had prevailed very far upon them; but I hope yor Majesty hath
been pleased before this tyme, upon the process and accusation I sent home against him, to have caused such order
to bee taken with the gentleman as that yor Majestie's
islands may bee troubled no more, with such kind of planters nor his disciples which are behind, have any incouragement from yor Majestie's lenity to him, to grow more
insolent and bold...the people of the Leewards,as they
are.neerer the sun, so they grow more productive of theire
ill-humours, and dangerous practises which drove them out
hither to seeke a livelyhood, when they could not bee admitted for the evills they had done to enjoy any beeing
elsewhere. There are many things in order to yor Majestie's right governing the people in these parts, which my

---

1.i.e. the Barbadian Act of 1661,establishing five courts of common
pleas.
2.Farmer defended himself by attacking Willoughby's authority which
(he claimed) tended 'to subvert and destroy' the king's powers and
just rights in Barbados.
3.C.O. 1/19 no.92. Farmer was remanded and finally released. He returned to Barbados with William, Lord Willoughby who had gained his

comission is short in, and by exercising it any longer, I
shall but instead of gayning your Majesty ground loose
[sic] what hath beene got, for my back is at the wall, and
I find good words and meeke carriage begette little but
contempt, where no other can bee used against a people,
who have beene rough bred, and not used to the yoake - No
money to bee raised,without theire owne consents, therefore nothing to bee done but what they please. I have tryed
all waies and used all meanes, but find the people grow
more and more full of rebellious humours and principles
and not to be governed with an easy hand. And therefore
doe suppose I may bee more capable of doeing yor Majesty
better service in the future, when yor Majesty have so
chastised the Dutch, as there bee no danger from them in
these parts.

335. DECLARATION BY THE ACTING-GOVERNOR,COUNCIL AND ASSEMBLY,
7 March 1667.[1]
    [To resolve doubts about the laws and government in Barbados]
...It is hereby published and declared by the governor,
council and assembly, That the government of this island
shall bee according to the lawes of England and of this
island, for better explanation whereof, it is further
hereby ordered That all and every the lawes and statutes
of this island that have passed, bin approved and confirmed at any time heretofore under the reigne of his gratious Majesty King Charles the First of ever blessed memory, or at any time in the reigne of his Majesty that now
is, that stand unrepealled, shall bee valid, and taken to
bee lawes and statutes in force for the government of this
island; and That all and every the inhabitants of the same
shall bee regulated and governed as heretofore hath bin
according to the lawes of England and constitution and
lawes of this island and not other wayes any thing heretofore signified and seeming to contrary notwithstanding.

336. 'AN ACT FOR THE BETTER ASCERTAINING THE LAWS OF THIS ISLAND',
22 March 1667.[2]
    [The Declaration of 7 March was quoted with approval]...And for
that nothing more conduceth to the good and quiet of any
place and people, than the assuring and ascertaining such
laws and statutes, as they are to be governed and regulated by; and to take off all pretence of ignorance of the
same for the future:
    It is therefore ordained and enacted, by the governor,
council and representatives of the inhabitants of this
island now assembled, That all such Acts and statutes, as
have been made and published in this island, or viewed,

---

friendship, in 1667.
1.C.O.31/1 p.110.William Lord Willoughby was commissioned on 3 January (C.O.1/20)and arrived in Barbados in late April 1667.
2.The Laws of Barbados, London (1875) I no.1.

corrected and confirmed by any governor and council, or
president and council, by virtue of any commission from
King James or Charles I, his now Majesty's royal grandfather and father, of ever blessed memory; or, by virtue
of any commission from his most gracious Majesty that now
is, either immediately from either of their said Majesties,
or 'mediately from them or either of them, by, from or
under the late Earl, or any former Earl of Carlisle, by
or with the assent or consent of the representatives of
this place, legally called and continued, which stands
unrepealed by any power and authorities aforesaid, be
hereby enacted and declared to be in full force and virtue
in this island; and That all laws, acts and statutes, made
or published in this island, by any other power or authority than as before expressed are utterly void, and of none
effect; any declaration,order or ordinance to the contrary
notwithstanding.

And it is hereby further enacted by the authority aforesaid That... [the named commissioners] do, with what convenient
speed they can, collect and compile all the Acts and statutes in force, as aforesaid; and them cause to be fairly
and distinctly entered and enrolled by the secretary of
this island, in one book entirely by themselves, without
being mixed or confused with any the laws, acts or statutes
made void as aforesaid; which acts and statutes so trans-
cribed, entered and enrolled, and none other, shall be,
and be taken and esteemed to be, the acts and statutes in
force made in this island; any declaration,order or ordinance to the contrary notwithstanding.

It is also ordained and enacted by the authority aforesaid, That in regard the public seal appointed by his Majesty that now is, to the right honourable Francis Lord
Willoughby of Parham, for this and the rest of the Caribee
Islands, cannot at present be had to affix to this Act,
according to the appointment of his sacred Majesty, in
his grant to the said Lord Willoughby, bearing the date
the twelfth of June, in the fifteenth year of his Majesty's
reign, the present governors subscribing their names to
this Act, shall be deemed as effectual, and of as full
force and authority, to all intents and purposes, as if
the said public seal were thereunto fixed.—Henry Willoughby, Henry Hawley, Samuel Barwick.[1]

337. PETITION FROM THE ASSEMBLY TO CHARLES II, 5 September 1667.[2]
    [The island's prosperity was crippled by the prohibitions on its
    trade and the dearth of labour.] ...And now that they may not

---

1.William, Lord Willoughby,Henry his nephew, and these two merchants
had been appointed as interim government until Francis' death in June
1666 was proved.
2.C.O. 1/21 no.102.Recruitment of settlers by Lord Windsor and Modyford for Jamaica,Willoughby's disastrous expedition in the Dutch war,
and the prohibition of trade with Scotland, whence industrious servants had come,had produced a labour shortage.

fail in their duty to let his Majesty know that they may
be best secured and encouraged against their watchful
enemy, they pray: 1.That whereas free trade is the best
means of living to any colony, of which these islands having for some years been debarred, the planters have been
so impoverished and the enemy's trade so advanced, that
the English to maintain a livelihood have been forced to
fish with the French nets; that they may have free trade
with the coast of Guinea for negroes, or else that the
Royal Company be obliged to supply them at the price mentioned in their first printed declaration (though that
too, like the canker of usury, will soon be the bane of
a laborious planter), for free trade with a supply of
servants from Scotland[1]....3.For export of commodities
to any place in amity with England, in English bottoms,
on paying customs either in Barbados or in England...This
liberty will accommodate the planters with many needfull
commodities and to great advantage at reasonable rates
wherein (since debarred in free trade) they have not been
supplied.

338. ADDRESS OF THE ASSEMBLY TO CHARLES II, 3 August 1668.[2]
...2. Wee humbly offer to yor Majesties consideration,
the heavy pressure and burden (with the unspeakable trouble of raising, and manner of paying) of the customs of
fower and halfe per cent in specie, for all goods exported hence, and therein wee humbly beg yor Majesties' princely and gracious consideration, of how greate a yoake,
the payment thereof must needs bee in these hard tymes to
the poore planter who, after much tyme of care and sorrow,
and many yeares laboure and expense are thereby drained

1.When the king granted them permission to buy servants from Scots
merchants the following year, it proved a meaningless concession for
he required that there should be no infringement of the Navigation
Act. Scots merchants would not bring servants if they could not fill
up their ships on the return voyage with colonial products.
2.C.O. 1/23 no.20.William, Lord Willoughby, had succeeded his brother
as governor-in-chief of the province of 'Cariola' intermittently for
the remaining three years of the lease: Francis had died on his expedition to St. Kitts in 1666.The new assembly was stubbornly hostile to
him and all external authority: they accused him of extravagance in
the St. Kitts expedition and wanted freedom from the Navigation Acts
and the buying out of the 4½% grant by a lump sum. After vindicating
himself against these charges, Willoughby was granted a new commission in 1670 by the king as governor-in-chief of the Caribbees in the
direct pay of the Crown and with no proprietary share in the revenues any longer since the lease was now exhausted. Though the assembly
with the assistance of a London committee of planters continued to
agitate, there was no new charter, no reversion of the 4½% duty to
its proper use,and no concession of freer trade.Willoughby's arguments perhaps helped the house of lords in 1671 to amend by reduction
the duties imposed by the Commons and to provoke the Commons to assert
their right to determine rates and taxes (IX C.J.235.239) and to deny
the Lords a right to amend, though <u>not</u> to reject, money bills.

of that recompense, which should ever sweeten all their
industries,and past extreamityes, and bee the encouragement of ingenious designes futurely. And concerneing this
it is fit wee let yor Majestie understand that the said
custome was imposed upon us by an assembly who were first
elected by a power from the Earle of Carlisle onely, and
illegally conveened and continued by the Lord Francis Willoughby[1] of Parham, upon his arrival here...wee shall not
now further urge there abouts to yor Majestie. Beeing led
by these loyal affections to submit in any things...to
yor Majestie rather than by a challenge of their right to
disapprove their natural dutyes or displease soe gratious
a prince, Wee therefore, your Majesties loyal subjects,
humbly propose and pray that yor Majestie will please to
condescend to the takeing of a certaine sume of money, for
the purchaseing of, and releaseing that dutye or custome
for ever after, and for the granting us a charter including the benefites hereby so granted.[2] And such other imun-
ityes as wee shall propose to yor Majestie which shall not
bee derogating to yor Majesties honnor, or of such things
as yor Majestie cannot legally grant, or shall not advantage yor Majesties interest here, and make the inhabitants
in these partes happy and prosperous. Or if that your Majestie shall not thinke fit to comply with, or answare our
desires herein, wee then humbly pray that the said dutye
may bee paid in England in money at some reasonable rate
per cent on Muscadoes, white sugars and the several spec-
ies accordingly....[3]

339. *THE NEED FOR A COLONIAL AGENT*, 1670-73:
    (a) Gentleman planters of Barbados in England to the deputy gov-
        ernor,council and assembly,14 December 1670.[4]
    The Parliament are laying a very heavy Imposition on
Sugars and are lyke to put the Rates in favour of the Portugall Sugars, and Refiners of England, which wee are Lab-

---

1. To avoid the delays of an election in securing the permanent revenues required in 1663,the governor had re-summoned the old proprietary assembly. Therefore, it was argued, the grant was illegal.
2.i.e. a charter constituting the Barbadians an independent corporation, presumably with palatinate powers as previously granted to Carlisle in 1627.
3.In the Crown's view, supported by Finch (A.G.) in 1670,the payment
of the 4½% duty was not conditional on its use for the support of the
island government, but was simply an annual tribute in return for the
king's grant of freehold titles to the planters.
4.C.O. 31/2 Journals of the assembly pp.15-16. The desirability of
having some official representative in London of a colonial government was a general one. From Massachusetts the Crown had asked for
spokesmen to be provided [see pp.485;505] Absentee planters in England
also felt the need for some agent to speak for them, to lobby and to
publicise the policy and needs of the island.But whom should such an
agent represent? The governor or the assembly? Colonial assemblies
later came to appoint committees of correspondence responsible for
instructing agents.

ouring to withstand, and besides our Constant personall
Attendance upon the Buisness, which is very Burthensome
unto us, wee are some of us alsoe at Great expense, and
how Longe wee shall thinke it our Interest at our particular
Charge and Labour to withstand a Generall Inconveniency,
wee Leave you to Judge, Wherefore wee humbly advise you
to Lodge some stock in England in the hands of such men
as you dare trust, for defraying the charges of this nature,...Wee doe also desire that you would allow a Sallary
to a person of some quallity who shall constantly attend
the sevarals Councells and from time to time give notice
to us what is an Agetation Relateing to Barbados and with
our Advice draw up and prepare such things as are necessary, keepe a Register of the Orders Drawne upon your treasury for money, and from time to time Remitt Coppyes of
them to you By which you will perceive how your monyes
are Disposed of and whether to the Advantage of the publique or noe. This Agent wee will bee ready to Countenance
and Assist with our presence upon any occasion, And doe
further Advise that he may be some one concerned in Barbados otherwise he may have distinct Interest from you And
be mischievous unto you, and for his sallary to settle
from yeare to yeare that he may have his whole Dependance
upon the Assembly and know itt is the People of Barbados
that Imploy him, which will prevent the haveing such an
officer Imposed upon you from hence Or by your Governor
which shall come there, who haveing generally distinct
Interest from the People and putting him in, may make him
promote his Interest and not the Islands....

    (b) Thomas Povey to Governor Lord Willoughby,15 March 1673.[1]

....I doe in the first place, laie it down for a ground
that whosoever shall bee engaged in such a distant Government as your Lordship now is, ought before hee adventures upon it, to secure to Himself as many as Hee can of
the Principall Ministers neare the King and as many of
the principall Persons whose Trade or busyness relate to
that Place; who may represent things heere to the best Advantage, and bee readie to encounter that Envie, and Malice
and Misreport, and Mistakes, which doe most certainly per-
secut forreigne Employments especially when a Populaice
is concerned in them. Nor will it bee enough to bespeak

1.British (Museum) Library:EgertonMSS.2395 ff.487-9.Thomas Povey, a
wealthy London merchant and barrister, had been influential in setting up the council for foreign plantations in 1660 and had been a
frequent attender at its sessions.He had been chairman of the committee for the West Indies and a promoter of the Navigation Acts.He
had clearly been attempting to secure his own appointment as agent
for Barbados where his brother was provost-marshal, but without success;and by 1673 he had lost much of his influence.His advocacy of a
colonial agency was however welcomed in many colonies: so was his
description of its duties - 'to stand sentry and bee watchfull'.
William,Lord Willoughby died in 1673.

the Favour, and Good will of men in Power, unless some
fitt Person bee selected, to make due, and seasonable applications, and to awaken, and stirr upp and bring to Action
that kindness, and adhearencie, which will bee, in a manner fruitless, if not minded and sollicited, and applyed
to the Occasion to which their   interposition is necessary. It being sufficient in them to Continue well inclin'd
but it is to bee the work of some other diligent Person
who is as it were to stand sentrie and bee watchfull, and
give the Alarm when their Assistance is oportune, and requisite...And surely the Discretion and Reputation of that
Man are verie lowe, who will adventure himself upon a
Trust, and appear to man Employment of that Nature, unless
such previous things be considered and putt into his hands,
as may prepare and qualify Him. Such as are Copies of
Comissions, Instructions, Orders, Letters of other materiall Papers, from England relating to the Government. Which
are to bee registered by him, that Hee may have a recourse
to them, as occasion calls for them.
     For his better Direction and Vindication it is necess-
arie that 2 or 3 particular Friends about Court and as
many in the Cittie, bee desired to receive Him, and advise
with Him, when any matter offers, which may require consideration and Councell. By whose consent and approbation,
Hee may adventure upon some things in which singly Hee may
too much distrust or perhaps Presume upon his own judgment
by either of which Affairs may suffer...,
     For his Continuall Information everie shipp that comes
homeward ought to bring Letters from the Governor or his
Secretarie to him: In which all the Transactions of the
Island are to bee conveyed, that Hee bee not a stranger
even to the least Things, as well as to the Greatest,
which are oftentimes better understood; and represented
by knowing former circumstances.
     He ought first to receive his Letters to which everie
Master of the Shipp should bee obliged as far as conveniently may bee; it tending not a little to the Disadvantage of the Governour, that the King, or his Ministers or
the Exchange, bee possessed or prejudiced by letters or
Suggestions of others before his own Letters, and such
as are intrusted by Him, bee first heard.
     And because the Temper of the Place may bee the better
understtod, It may bee fitt Hee should knowe at least
the names of such as are of the Councell, which of them
are Complying; which opposing; and what Correspondencies
they have on the Exchange. And who is speaker of the Assemblie, and who the most Popular and Troublesome upon the
Island. Which Motions will bee Necessaire, if any Complaints shall be made heere, against, or relating to the
Government.
     And nothing being more likely to occasion Complaints or
Discourse than the Matter of Money, Hee should knowe how
the farme of the 4 and $\frac{1}{2}$ p.cent is managed; and by whom;
How that Revenue is answered or Employed; And what Dir-

ections the Governour hath received thereupon; And by what
means and allowances the Government is supported....

340. COMMISSION TO SIR CHARLES WHELER AS GOVERNOR OF THE LEEWARDS,
25 January 1671.[1]
To our Trusty and Wellbeloved Sir Charles Wheler...
Whereas by our Comission and our Greate Seal of England
bearing date the 6th day of December in the 21st yeare of
our Reign 1669, Wee did constitute our Right trusty and
welbeloved William Lord Willoughby...Our Captain Generall
and Governor in Chiefe over all our Islands in America
called the *Caribbee Islands* with divers powers and authorities therein contained for and dureing our Pleasure.
And Whereas wee have found it necessary for our Service
and Security and advantage of our Subjects as well Planters as Traders in those parts to divide the Government of
those Islands, and to constitute a Governor in chiefe over
Our Islands comonly called the *Leewards Islands* not Subordinate to the Governor of Barbados. Wee therefore...doe
constitute and appoint you our said Sir Charles Wheler,

1.C.O. 1/26. Although the superior contacts of Carlisle in London had
prevailed in 1627 over other claims in the Caribbees,his government
had not been effective throughout the islands of his palatinate. Even
in Barbados there had at first been divisions between his 'Windward
men' and the 'Leeward men' of Courteen and Pembroke. Warner, who had
been granted a royal charter in 1626 retrospectively for his settlement in St.Kitts – not dependent on Barbados,– became subsequently,
by appointment from Carlisle,the governor of his colony which shared
the island with the French. In the mid-century in the struggles with
the French and the Dutch, the islands with their own governments were
virtually independent of external control. In 1664 Willoughby had
asserted the proprietorship in order to terminate it: he had secured
from the assemblies of the Leewards a $4\frac{1}{2}\%$ export duty, in lieu of
rents and dues owed to Carlisle, but without any clauses appropriating the revenues to public expenses. In the Dutch War Nevis had
(with Barbadian help) been retained; Antigua and Montserrat had been
recaptured; and by the Treaty of Breda (1667) St. Kitts was to be
returned by the French.
The opposition to Willoughby's overall governorship-in-chief from
Barbados had been growing.There was some influential Barbadian pressure for separation too, and a strong petition from Leeward islanders in 1667-particularly from St.Kitts-had urged divorce from an un-
interested, jealous and ineffective government in distant Barbados
(C.S.P. 1661-7 No.1597). Following a report on the petition (C.S.P.
1669-74 p.540)the privy council in December 1670 decided to separate
the Leewards from the Windwards;they accepted the strength of local
demand, the remoteness of Barbados, and the French delay in retroced-
ing St.Kitts. Sir Charles Wheler,who had helped to further the petition, was made governor.Ambitious, autocratic, ruthless, he secured
St. Kitts by some tact, courage and a 'small artifice'; but he made
a bad bargain which was repudiated and he was recalled.Sir William
Stapleton, lieutenant governor of the predominantly Irish colony of
Montserrat, was appointed governor of St.Kitts and the rest of the
Leewards in 1672 with an identical commission:later his official res-

Our Captain Generall and Governor in chiefe in and over
Our Islands of St. Christophers[1], Nevis, Montserret, Ant-
igo, Barbudo and Anguilla and all other the Carribbee
Islands lyeing to Leeward from Guardaloupe to the Island
of St. John De Porto Rico, which now are or hereafter
shalbe under Our Subjection or Government.

And wee doe hereby require and command you to doe and
execute all things in due manner as shall belong unto your
said comand....And according to such reasonable Lawes and
Statutes as now are or hereafter shalbe made and agreed
upon by you with the advice and consent of the Councills
and Assemblyes of the respective Islands and Plantations
under your Government.....

And wee doe hereby give and grant unto you full power
and authority to choose a Councill in each of the respective Islands under your Government out of the principall
Planters and Inhabitants of the same consisting of the
number of twelve persons who are to be assisting unto
you with their advice in the Management of the affaires
and concernes of the said Governments and Plantacons in
relation to our Service and the Good of our Subjects
there....

And wee doe hereby give and grant unto you full power
and authority with the advice and consent of any 7 or more
of the said Councills from time to time as need shall require to sumon or call Generall Assemblies of the freeholders and Planters within every of the respective Islands under your Government[2] in manner and forme according
to the Custome and usage of our other Plantations, And our
will and Pleasure is that the persons thereupon duely elected by the major part of the freeholders of the respective
parishes and places and so returned shall be called and
held the representatives of that Island or Plantation
wherein they shall be chosen And shall have full power
and authority with the advice and consent of yorselfe and
any seven or more of the said Councills to make constitute
and ordaine Lawes Statutes and Ordinances for the Publique
Peace welfare and good Government of the said Islands respectively....Which said Lawes Statutes and Ordinances are
to be as neere as conveniently may be agreeable unto the
Lawes and Statutes of our Kingdome of England.

And the said Lawes Statutes and Ordinances shall con-

---

idence was moved to Antigua from St.Kitts.
1. The Treaty of Breda in 1667 required the French to restore St.Kitts
to the English Crown:in that same year the planters there had petitioned for a government separate from Barbados.
2. Stapleton proved a popular, reliable and able governor. He used
the somewhat vague terms of this clause to call general assemblies
of the Leewards, probably in 1674, certainly from 1678. Each council
in the Leewards sent 2 members and each assembly was represented by
its speaker and one other member. Until 1681 the function of the general assembly was only consultative; in 1681 it became a legislature.
Stapleton was seeking legislative uniformity in the islands [see No.
344].

tinue and bee in force for the space of two yeares and noe longer, unless they shall be approved and confirmed by us within the time limitted as aforesaid. And to the end nothing may be passed or done by any of the said Councill as Assemblies to the prejudice of Us, Wee will and ordaine that you the said Sir Charles Wheler shall have and enjoy a negative voice in the making or passing of all Lawes Statutes and Ordinances as aforesaid.

And that you shall and may likewise from time to time as you shall judge it necessary dissolve all generall Assemblys or Representatives summoned as aforesaid And our will and Pleasure is that you shall and may use a publique Seale....

[In February 1671 two additional instructions were inserted here.]

And wee doe hereby further give and graunt unto you full Power and Authority from time to time (as need shall require) to constitute, and appoint Deputy Governours, in the respective Islands under your Command.

Unto all and every of which Deputy Governours, we doe hereby give and graunt full power and Authority, to doe and execute, whatsoever they and every of them respectively, shall be by you authorized and appointed in pursuance of and according to the Powers and Authorities hereby graunted unto you ....

[Authority was delegated to the governor, with the advice and consent of seven or more councillors in each island, to erect courts where necessary, to appoint J.P.'s and sheriffs, and to administer oaths to them; to pardon (treason and murder excepted) and to reprieve for one whole year until the King's pleasure were known; to levy arms and to execute martial law.]

Provided allwaies and Our will and Pleasure is that all Establishments of Jurisdiccons, Courts, Offices and Officers, Powers, Authorities, fees and Priviledges granted or settled by you as aforesaid be with all convenient speed transmitted unto us to be allowed or disallowed as Wee shall judge fitt....

And we doe hereby give and grant unto you full power and authority with the advice and consent of any Seaven or more of the said Councills to erect one or more Court or Courts of Admiralty within the said Islands under your Government for the heareing and determineing of Marine Causes and matters with all reasonable and necessary Powers, Authorities, fees and Priviledges...and to exercise all powers belonging to the place and Office of Our Vice Admirall of and in all the Seas and Coasts about Our said Islands, according to such Comission, Direction, and Instructions as you shall receive from Our Dearest Brother the Duke of York Our High Admirall of England[1]....in case you shall happen to dye...Our Deputy Governor of Nevis for the time being shall and doe take upon him the administration of the Government and execute this Comission

---

1. See No.258.

and the several Powers and authorities herein granted or
contained untill Our Pleasure shalbe knowne therein....

341. GOVERNOR WILLIAM LORD WILLOUGHBY TO THE LORDS OF TRADE,
7 March 1673.
...I am commanded by my commission to have twelve of
my councell, and of them, seaven to be of one mind in all
votes, and it is rare that I can procure seaven to meet,
for which cause the King's and the countrye's business is
much retarded, and when they doe meet, unless they be all
of one mind (as seldome such a number will) the major part
of those make not a councell as my commission and instructions are worded, unless they be seaven.
    In the 4th. paragraph of my instructions I am obliged
to administer the oathes of allegiance and supremacy, the
latter I did decline, else had not had a councell composed of such persons as directed, being obliged to continue
those I found councellors at my arrival I wish they be
all quallified as they ought to be, with this I have acquainted by Lord Chauncellor and Lord Arlington, and begged
their approbation or directions....[He would sent the 'names
and qualleties' of his councillors.]
There's a liberty pretended to tender consciences, but
doth not at all answer the end wee have use of in these
parts, having so many of different judgments, and those
that I call the right, many of them not fit for any employment and thought by this clause the oathes of allegiance
and supremacy are dispensed with; yet the oath of a judge,
a justice and a constable, I am obliged by my commission
to give, which you know many tender consciences will refuse, I shall instance in one I found heere; that was a
Quaker, and judge of a court, and as well approved of by
all his neighbors in the precinct where he serves, as any
of the rest, and administered oath and justice as impartially, but he refusing the oath of a judge, my councell
fell severe upon him, and he must quit his place, and I
be hard to it to find a fitter....

342. COMMISSION AND INSTRUCTIONS TO SIR JONATHAN ATKINS AS GOVERNOR
    OF BARBADOS AND THE WINDWARDS, 1673-74.
    (a) Commission,19 December 1673.[2]
    Wee, reposeing special trust and confidence in your

1.C.O. 1/30 no.11.In his royal instructions of June 1672 for Barbados
and the Windwards,William, Lord Willoughby was charged to ensure that
at least seven of his 12 councillors would be unanimous:he could appoint councillors but must submit to the secretary of state names and
opinions.He was finding it difficult in a small community to obey.
2.C.O. 1/30 no.92. The Leewards had been separated from Willoughby's
responsibility in 1671:[see No.340.]. When he died in 1673, Sir
Jonathan Atkins, a former governor of Jersey, was appointed his successor in Barbados and the Windwards. This commission demonstrated
the Crown's resolve to assert maximum supervision. Arlington and
Shaftesbury, urged by merchant interests, were determined to exercise

prudence, courage and loyalty, out of our special grace, certaine knowledge and meere motion - have thought fit to constitute and appoint...you the said Sir Jonathan Atkins, our captaine-general and governor in cheife in and over our island of Barbados, Sta. Lucia, St. Vincent, Dominico and the rest of our island collonies and plantations in America, comonly called or knowne by the name of the *Car-ibee Islands*, lyeing and being to windward off Guardaloupe, and which now are or hereafter shalbe under our subjection or gouvernment....

[He was to execute all matters with care, according to the powers delegated in his commission.]   And according to such reason-able laws and statutes as now are or hereafter shalbe made and agreed upon by you with the advice and consent of the councils and assemblyes of the respective islands and plantations under your gouvernment in such manner and forme as hereafter expressed....

[The 12 councillors for Barbados were appointed and named by the king:they included John Willoughby, Peter Colleton, Henry Walrond and Samuel Farmer.]

And whereas the other islands above named are not yet so well planted as to give us occasion to informe oursel-ves of the estates and ability of the present inhabitants, Wee doe hereby give and grant unto you, Sir Jonathan Atk-ins, full power and authority to choose a council in each of the other islands under your gouvernmente out of the principal freehold inhabitants of the same respectively, each council consisting of the number of twelve persons respectively.

And when it shall happen, that by death, departure out of the respective island, expulsion or suspension of any of the abovesaid councellors of Barbados, or any of the councellors of any of the other islands, or any other-wise, any place shall be vacant in any of the said res-pective councills, each of which it is our will and plea-sure should consist of twelve persons any seaven whereof wee doe hereby appointe to be a quorum, Wee doe hereby will and require you to certify us by your first opportun-ity of such a vacancy by the death, departure, expulsion, suspension or otherwise of any of the respective council-lors in any of our said islands, that we may under our signet and signe manual constitute and appointe others

---

a more efficient and direct control.From the first, Atkins chafed at these limitations on the governor's powers, complaining bitterly against the draft and making his own proposals.(C.S.P.1669-74 Nos. 1184,1185,1188 and 1189). The plea for another planter governor had been refused:the king believed that they were 'too much inclined to popular government already'.Atkins'protests, however, went unheeded, and he became a strong and fertile champion of the Barbadians in argument with the home government. In the commission to Lord Vaug-han for Jamaica three months later the Crown nominated all members of the council: [see No.353].

in their roome.[1]
   But that our affaires at that distance may not suffer
for want of a due number of councillors if ever it shall
happen that there are lesse than nyne persons remaining,
in any of the said respective councills, Wee doe hereby
give and grant unto you, Sir Jonathan Atkins, full power
and authority to choose as many persons out of the principal freehold inhabitants of our said respective islands
as will make up the full number of each council to be nyne
and no more which persons so chosen and appointed by you
shall be to all intents and purposes councellors in the
said respective islands till either they are confirmed by
us, or till by the nomination of other councellors by us
under our signe mannual and signet the said respective
councells have each of them above nyne persons in them.
   With power to you, the said Sir Jonathan Atkins, after
you shall have first taken an oath for the due execution
of the office and trust of our captain-general and governor in cheife in and over our said islands which the said
councills respectively, or any five of the number of each
council have hereby full power and authority and are required to administer unto you to give and administer unto
each of the members of the said councills and to your deputy governor respectively as well the oathes of allegiance
and supremacy as the oath for the due execution of their
places and trusts....
   [The governor,with the council's consent, might suspend or expel
   council members.The governor and councils might] summon or call
general assemblyes of the freeholders and planters within
every of the respective islands under your gouvernment in
maner and forme according to the custome and usage of
Barbados.[2]
   And our will and pleasure is that the persons thereupon
duely elected by the major parte of the freeholders of the
respective parishes and places, and so returned shall be
called and held the representatives of that island or plantation wherein they shall be chosen....
   [The governor and councils might make laws for the 'public peace,
   welfare and good government' of the islands, 'as neere as conveniently may be agreeable unto the lawes and statutes of our kingdome of England'.]
   And the said laws, statutes and ordinances shall continue to be in force for the space of two years and no
longer, unless they shall be approved and confirmed by us
within the time limited as aforesaid.[3]

1. In the commission to Sir Richard Dutton (22 October 1680) the quorum
in Barbados was reduced to 5 and the governor was given powers to appoint temporarily to vacancies if the number fell below 7:C.O.29/3 p.25:
[see No.267].
2. A recognition of an autochthonous institution. By contrast with the
commission for the Leewards there was no provision for a general assembly of the Windwards.
3. In Dutton's commission laws had to be sent to England within 3

And to the end nothing may be passed or done by any of the said councills or assemblyes to the prejudice of us, our heirs or successors, Wee will and ordaine that you, the said Sir Jonathan Atkins, shall have and enjoy a negative voice in the makeing or passing of all lawes, statutes and ordinances as aforesaid....

[The governor had power to dissolve assemblies; he might also use the Barbados public seal. The governor and councils might set up criminal and civil courts.]

And Wee doe hereby grant unto you full power and authority to constitute and appointe judges, justices of the peace, sheriffes and other necessary officers and ministers in all and every the said islands for the better administration of justice and putting the lawes in execution. And to administer such oath or oathes as are usually given for the due execution and performance of offices, places and charges, and for the cleering of the truth in judicial causes....

[Copies of all 'establishments of jurisdiction' and appointments must be sent to England for approval. The governor had power of pardon in criminal cases and in cases where fines have been imposed, except where treason and murder were concerned, for there the Crown must be consulted. The governor might also present to benefices; levy armed forces, and transport them to the American colonies if needed for defence against an attacker. He must execute the duties of captain-general as if in England.]

And also by and with the advice and consent of the said councills respectively to prepare and ordaine articles of war and put the same in execution in time of insurrection, rebellion or invasion upon souldiers in pay only....

[Articles of war must receive the Crown's approval. The governor and councils might build such towns and fortifications as they consider necessary, and set up courts of admiralty.]

And wee doe hereby authorize you to exercise all powers belonging to the place and office of our vice-admiral of and in all the seas and coasts about our said islands according to such commission, direction and instructions as you shall receive from our commissioners for executing the office of lord high admiral of England or from our high admiral of England for the time being....

[The governor and councils might dispose of such 'lands, tenements and hereditaments' as were in their power, including the rents and services. They might also allow fairs and markets, ports and customs houses.]

And our further will and pleasure is that you shall not at any time hereafter by colour of any power or authority hereby granted or mentioned to be granted take upon you to give, grant or dispose of any office or place within any of the island colonies or plantations under your government which now are or have been granted by us, or any of our royal officers under the great seale of England,

___

months, and only if <u>not</u> confirmed were to be void.

and farther than that you may upon the vacancy of any such
office put in any person to officiate in the interval till
the said place be disposed of by us, our heirs or successors under the greate seale of England....

[The inhabitants of the islands must obey Sir Jonathan Atkins.
The governor might appoint his deputy, who was then empowered to
act as the governor. If the governor should die, the council of
Barbados should take over the administration.]

342. (b) Instructions, 28 February 1674.[1]

[He was to summon the council nominated and communicate his instructions to them.]

...6. And our further will and pleasure is that the
members of the said Councills respectively shall and may
have and enjoy freedome of debates and votes in all affaires of public concern....

[Councillors must be men of good estates and abilities, not too
much in debt; but they might not act as judges while serving on
the councils. He was to transmit copies of all laws and to suspend
no judge or official without sufficient cause. Fees and salaries
were to be moderate.]

14. Our will and pleasure is, and wee doe hereby require and comand you, that noe man's life, member, freehold
or goods be taken away or harmed in any of the islands or
places under your government but by established and knowne
lawes not repugnant to but as much as may bee agreeable
to the lawes of our kingdome of England.

15. [In order to encourage settlers of different religions] you
shall dispense with the takeing the oathes of allegiance
and supremacy to those that beare any part in the government (except the members and officers of the councills and
all judges and justices to whom you are hereby particularly directed to administer the same) finding out some
other way of securing yourselfe of their allegiance to us
and our government there. And in noe other case you are
to suffer any man to be molested or disquietted in the
exercise of his religion....But Wee oblige you in your
owne house and family to the profession of the Protestant
religion according as it is practised by us in England.
And the recomending it to all others under your government, as far as it may consist with the peace and quiet
of the said island....

[He was to discountenance drunkeness, debauchery,swearing etc.,
and to admit no one 'whose ill-fame' might bring scandal into
public employment. All planters and Christian servants were to be
armed and trained. He was to make yearly accounts and returns.]

22. You are to give all due encouragement and invitation to merchants and others who shall bring trade unto
our said islands or any way contribute to their advantage
and in particular to the Royal Company of Adventurors
trading into Africa....[2]

1.*Ibid*.no.94.These instructions were in draft on 19 December 1673.
2.[See No.275]. The Royal African Company were burdened by debts of
well over a million pounds of sugar unpaid by the planters. The gov-

30. You are for the better administration of justice
to endeavour to get a law passed in the assembly wherein
whall be set the value of men's estates, either in goods
or lands, under which they shall not be capable of serving as jurors....
    [He was to restrain severity by masters over servants.]
    37. You are earnestly to endeavour to gett the assembly
of Barbados to re-enact that Law, whereby all lands seized
by process of Law for the satisfaccon of Debts should be
sold as formerly by Outcry.[1] And to this purpose Wee
would have you and the members of your Council aquaint
the Assembly how sensible We are, what great inconveniences and prejudices are brought upon the trade of that Island by the difficulty men find in recovering their just
debts: which if by good laws and a due execution of them
it be not timely remedied will draw certain ruien upon
the place....
    [He was not to encourage planting in other islands than Bar-
    bados.][2]

343. GOVERNOR ATKINS TO THE LORDS OF TRADE, 21 May 1680.[3]
    [He described the procedure for making laws in Barbados. He
    confessed his errors in assenting to an Act infringing the prer-

---

ernor was now instructed to support the company's monopoly, which
Barbadian 'freetraders' resented, and to prevent its defrauding by
planter debtors.
1.The Royal African Company was angry at the protection of their
debtors by Barbadian courts.An order in council in 1669 made lands
as well as goods in the island subject to be sold in payment. Under
protest the law protecting debtors was repealed.
2. Barbadian planters had, against the Crown's wishes, attempted to
plant St. Lucia.
3. C.S.P. 1677-80 p.534. The extension of Crown control, with its
attendant increase of royal patronage by patents direct to favoured
clients in England, was reducing the influence of the governors over
officials in the plantations. Sir Jonathan Atkins was particularly
incensed that his naval officer, a post designed to act as his 'eyes'
in matters relating to the Navigation Acts, was appointed by the
Crown. Atkins had governed energetically: he supported the assembly
in its opposition to the 'ruinous' policy of the Navigation Acts, and
to the king's appointment of officials by patent under the great seal.
Unfortunately his championship of Barbadian autonomy caused him to
fall foul of English merchants, the Royal African Company and the
lords of trade. In July 1680 he was recalled for his neglect of the
Crown's interest and for his evasive procrastinations. He was replaced by Sir Richard Dutton, a somewhat high-handed adventurer who
had asked for enlarged powers in his commission and instructions:
the king no longer named the councillors and laws remained valid
longer than 2 years unless disallowed. Money must be appropriated
to the king for prescribed purposes,and disbursement would be by
authority of the governor and council alone: [see above No.
267.]

ogative - one concerning the collection of the Crown's 4½% duty -
and also to certain temporary laws including an impost on liquors.
There was urgent need for money for defence. The assembly was in
complete control of all taxes and revenues.]
   ...The taxes once imposed, the Barbadians order the
collecting and disposing of the money. I never concerned
myself with any of the public moneys nor touched them. I
gave my orders as to repairs, new works, arms and other
matters of military defence, and they appoint their own
Treasurer and Receiver and Commissioners to see the work
done. In my Commission it is laid down that the laws to
which I am to assent should be 'made as near as may be to
the laws of England'....
   [He found it customary for temporary legislation to be passed.
   The lords of trade, knowing that many assemblies had met since he
   arrived as governor, had been suspicious that he had failed to
   send home all their legislation, as now specifically required to
   do in his instructions of 19 December 1673; but (he argued) few
   Acts had in fact been passed.]
   When the Legislature does sit, it seldom sits more than
a day and when Acts are sent up from the Assembly to the
Council, they sometimes lie under consideration for a
month or two, or are returned with amendments which delays
their passing still longer. I have often repeated to your
Lordships that by express law of the country the Assembly
can sit no more than a year....
   I have often complained of the great invasion of the
rights of the Government by the granting of patents [i.e.
by the king] for all the officers of this island, but as
yet without remedy. Now, however, that your Lordships
have called attention to this evil, I doubt not that you
will prevail with His Majesty to redress. It must needs
be very prejudicial to a place to have all the offices of
trust in the hands of strangers, most of them little accountable, and without exception acting only by a deputy
of as little credit as themselves....Notwithstanding the
King's Patent [his own commission] and a law of the country
that all offices of trust shall be disposed of by the
Governor, there is not the smallest office, though not
worth the expense of obtaining, but is under a patent.[1]...
   [In his commission only the offices of secretary and provost
   marshal were excepted as royal patents, not in the gift of the
   governor. But several offices - the clerks of the market, of the
   post office and of chancery - had been filled directly by the
   Crown.]
   The next Patent was obtained by one Abraham Langford
for the Naval Office[2] which certainly by the Acts of Parliament and of Navigation were never intended to be disposed of by any but the Governors of the Plantations, who
are solely accountable to and for the same....The Governor

1. See above Section II B 2 (b).
2. For the patent to Abraham Langford see above No.265 (b).

forfeits £1,000 and is declared incapable of serving the
King, yet still this man is imposed on me, and I have no
security from him and his deputy....
    [He gave other examples of incompetent patentees, deputies and
    pluralists.]
    For my part I never did nor ever will make profit out
of my office whatsoever, whereby the King's honour may
seem to be lessened and his interest converted into dis-
service, which must needs follow the diminution of the
Government's authority, for where there is no dependence,
obedience seldom follows....[1]

344. *THE GENERAL ASSEMBLY OF THE LEEWARDS*, 1681-83:
    (a) Governor Stapleton to the Lords of Trade, 26 July 1681.[2]
    ...One thing more I offer to your Lordship's consid-
eration - to have all the Acts for the Leeward Islands to
bee all alike, there being noe difference in nature or
constitution (except two Acts that is, the Acts for forfeiting and reinvesting the then present proprietours, by
reason of the French conquest with their cannibal and het-
hen assistance which may extend to all but this island).
All other Acts in my slender judgement should bee the
same in the same government....If there bee anything in
the Acts illegal or unsuetable with the Royal prerogative,
bee pleased to attribute it to all our ignorancies....

    (b) Governor Stapleton to the Lords of Trade, 16 August 1682.[3]
    ...In order to the passing the Acts alike in the respec-

1.On 6 September 1681 (C.S.P.,Col.1681-5 No.220,p.111), the lords of
trade agreed that the governor of Barbados should appoint 'such person as he judges best qualified' to be attorney-general.The same day
Lynch's request that no patent should pass for any place in Jamaica
without prior approval of the lords of trade was also accepted in
principle.The governor's right to appoint was confirmed in the 1696
Navigation Act,but thereafter it soon became customary to appoint the
naval officer in England.
2.C.O. 1/47 no.39. The lords of trade gave approval on 16 October 1682
to Stapleton's efforts towards securing the assimilation of all the
Acts of the Leewards.The island assemblies had been immersed paroch-
ially and fitfully, with small 'daily concerns'; and it had long
been difficult to obtain any complete copies of the laws they were
alleged to have passed. Though Wheler had contemplated a general assembly as early as December 1671, it was on Stapleton's initiative that
such an assembly was summoned tentatively in 1681.His authority to do
so was not questioned by the lords of trade and was explicitly confirmed in the commissions to his successors,N. Johnson and C. Codring-
ton. In 1705 the general assembly enacted its own quasi-federal constitution [see Volume II]. It was summoned for the last time in 1798.
But the federal idea persisted:in 1871 a British statute established
a Leeward Islands legislature with six subordinate island presidencies;and after long gestation following the Montego Bay conference in
1947, a wider British Caribbean Federation was established in 1957 but
was dissolved by order in council in 1962.
3.C.O. 1/49 no.26.By contrast with that of 1681,this general assembly

tive Islands, I shall, God willing, meet a General Assembly of two or three of the Councill and of the like number
of the representatives of each Island here or at Antego
in November next....I have had all ready a denyall of any
perpetuall law for the people loves to bee courted and to
have precarious government;[1] their reasons is for feare
of having any impositions begged, yet I shall not fail to
propose it in the Generall Assembly....

(c) Journal of Leeward Islands Assembly, 30 October 1683.[2]
The severall proposals made by his Excellency, Sir
William Stapleton...to the Generall Councell and Assembly
of the Islands...
1. I doe desire that all laws be alike in the respective Islands that His Majesty's subjects in one Island may
not be to seede [sic] for new measures in proceedings in
the other Islands, we being under one government and the
like constitutions and circumstances.
Answer. That we have diligently considered his Excellencie's first proposall concerning all the Islands to be
governed by generall Acts, which we conceive will not
stand with the advantage and profit of the Islands by
reason of the severall Acts made in each Island somewhat
different from the other, soe that we humbly pray that
his Excellency would be pleased to accept of the Acts as
they are made in each Island and that the same be sent
home by his Excellencie, according to his Majesty's present command, in order to obtain his Majesty's royall assent to the same.[3]
(v) JAMAICA
345. INSTRUCTIONS TO GOVERNOR D'OYLEY,8 February 1661.[4]
...You are forthwith to proceed to the electing[5]of a

was expressly elected to legislate.
1. For the Crowns attempts to secure perpetual revenue Acts, see Nos.
293-5.
2. C.O. 1/53 no.4.
3.The minutes of the St.Kitts council for 20 October 1683 had instructed their representatives to be 'excused from General Assemblyes
and from the laws enacted by the authority thereof...that we may be
governed by those lawes made by His Excellency the Council and Assembly here'. Islands made such laws as answered their individual needs
best, it was argued.
4.C.O. 1/15.Throughout the anarchy of Jamaica's early years under the
Commonwealth, Edward D'Oyley as commander, with resource and skill,
had precariously secured the conquered colony.But he had little authority or money and was pessimistic about the value of the island.Ind-
eed,it was uncertain whether England would wish to retain Jamaica.
Finally in 1661 royal commission and instructions made clear that the
Crown accepted its permanency as an English possession and a parliamentary Act annexed it to the Crown;it was formally ceded by Spain in
1670 by the treaty of Madrid.D'Oyley's position was temporarily regul-
arised by these royal instructions until a new royal nominee, Lord
Windsor, was appointed in June 1661.
5.There is no evidence of any elections or of how representation was
arranged. The government remained until Windsor's arrival still essen-

counsell to consist of twelve persons, eleven whereof to
be chosen fairly and indifferently by as many of the officers of the army, planters and inhabitants as by your
best and most equal contrivaunce may be admitted thereunto, whether at once or several places, which eleven
persons so chosen together with the secretary of the
said island whom we doe appoint always one of the counsel,
are to be a counsel as appointed by us to assist you in
all matters wherein the safety and improvement of our
said island or any of our subjects shall be concerned,any
five of which said counsel so elected shall be a sufficient quorum the whole number being to be warned and summoned to meet together as often as any extraordinary occasion shall so require....

346. (a) REVENUE ACTS, 22 June 1661.[1]
    Whereas the Governor and Council having taken it into
serious consideration, the great charge of the government
of this island and other public charges, it is therefore
thought fit by the Governor, with the advice and consent
of his Council, and it is hereby enacted and ordained by
the Governor and Council and by the authority of the same,
That all strong liquors that now are or shall be brought
into this island, are to be entered and shall pay the
rates, hereinafter mentioned; (that is to say) every tun
of Spanish or French wine four pounds sterling; for every
gallon of brandy or spirits sixpence per gallon; and for
every tun of beer twenty shillings and so after that rate
for a smaller or greater proportion....
    [Penalties were prescribed for defaulting ship masters, etc.]
And...that for the better collecting of the said excise
and true account to be taken of the same, a Clerk of Entries be appointed who is truly to receive and set down all
entries that shall be hereafter made, and the same safely
keep as a check whereby the Treasurer may receive a true
charge from him when he shall be called to account, also
a Treasurer to receive the same, the said Treasurer and
Clerk of the Cheque to be nominated and appointed by the
Governor and Council for the time being and convenient
salaries be appointed for them, which said Treasurer,
Clerk of either of them and such officers appointed for
them with the approbation of the Governor and Council had
thereunto....

---

tially military. Windsor in his two months in Jamaica did little,
but he did disband the army, and indicated that the garrison was to
be changed into a 'plantation'.
1. Printed in A. M. Whitson, *Constitutional development of Jamaica*,
(1929) pp.169–171. Despite this Act, Jamaicans were subsequently to
affirm that the islanders had never been taxed without the consent
of their representatives, implying of course participation by elected
men. Legislation under D'Oyley and Sir Charles Lyttelton (who acted
as deputy-governor for Windsor till 1664) was by governor and council.

(b) [A poll tax was to be collected.]...And be it further
enacted and ordained...That the constables of each respective parish do collect and levy the said taxes, and
if any such constable or constables shall be found neglig-
ent of the said levy and collection, he or they for such
their neglect shall forfeit the sum of £4 sterling to be
recovered in any of His Majesty's courts of judicature in
this island by bill, plaint or information wherein no
respite, protection or wager of law is allowed, the one-
half thereof be given to him or them that shall inform or
sue for the same, the other moiety to His Majesty for the
public use of this island. And it is hereby further enacted and ordained That Lewis Ashton Esq. and Samuel Long
Gent. be appointed and are hereby appointed treasurers for
receiving the taxes and levies aforesaid. And that the
said treasurers or one of them do at convenient time
issue out warrants under his or their hands to the respective constables of each parish to empower the said constables for levying the taxes aforesaid. And it is hereby
further enacted and ordained That each constable as aforesaid do make return to the said treasurers or any one of
them of their warrants together with the sum which he or
they have collected in their respective parishes within 4
days after every such last day of April.And it is further
enacted and ordained That each of the said treasurers do
bind themselves in the penal sum of £1000 sterling to be
from time to time accountable and responsible when they
shall be thereunto called by the Governor, Council and
Assembly....

347. PROCLAMATION CARRIED OVER BY LORD WINDSOR (13 Car.II).
14 December 1661.[2]
We, being fully satisfied that our island of Jamaica,
being a pleasant and most fertile soil, and situate comod-
iously for trade and commerce, is likely, through God's
blessing, to be a great benefit and advantage to this and
other our kingdoms and dominions, have thought fit, for
the encouraging of our subjects, as well such as are already upon the said island, as all others, that shall
transport themselves thither, and reside and plant there,

---

1. In addition to these two Acts, the same month saw an additional
Act for the 'speedy raising of a public revenue in this Island', an
Act for the speedy raising of a 'public treasure', an Act for the
raising of a public revenue 'out of all strong liquors imported into
this Island', and an Act mentioned above for issuing money out of the
public treasury (for salaries etc). In each case power was given to
the governor,council and assembly. (C.O. 139/1).
2.C.O.1/15.Printed in E.Long *History of Jamaica* (1774) I pp.217-8.The
king,having decided to retain Jamaica, wished to encourage settlement
by generous grants.Windsor published this proclamation in Barbados and
took several hundred planters with him to Jamaica in August 1662,(see
Declaration, 11July 1662: C.O. 1/16 No.72).

to declare and publish, and we do hereby declare and publish That thirty acres of improveable lands shall be granted and allotted to every such person,male or female,
being twelve years old or upwards, who now resides, or
within two years next ensuing shall reside, upon the said
island; and That the same shall be assigned and set out,
by the governor and council, within six weeks next after
notice shall be given in writing, subscribed by such planter or planters or some of them in behalf of the rest,to
the governor or such officer as he shall appoint in that
behalf, signifying their resolutions to plant there, and
when they intend to be on the place; and, in case they do
not go thither within six months then next ensuing, the
said allotment shall be void, and free to be assigned to
any other planter; and That every person and persons, to
whom such assignment shall be made, shall hold and enjoy
the said lands so to be assigned, and all houses, edifices,
buildings and enclosures thereupon to be built or made, to
them and their heirs for ever, by and under such tenure as
is usual in other plantations subject to us. Nevertheless,
they are to be obliged to serve in arms upon any insurrection, mutiny, or foreign invasion. And that the said
assignments and allotments shall be made and confirmed
under the public seal of the island, with power to create
any manor or manors, and with such convenient privileges
and immunities as the grantee shall reasonably desire and
require; and a draught of such assignment shall be prepared by our council learned in the law, and delivered to
the governor to that purpose; and that all fishing and
piscaries, and all copper, lead, tin, iron, coals, and
all other mines (except gold and silver), within such
respective allotments, shall be enjoyed by the grantees
thereof, reserving only a twentieth part of the product of
the said mines to our use. And we do further publish and
declare, That all children of our natural-born subjects
of England,to be born in Jamaica, shall, from their respective births, be reputed to be, and shall be, free
denizens of England, and shall have the same privileges
to all intents and purposes as our free-born subjects of
England;[1] and That all free persons shall have liberty,
without interruption, to transport themselves and their
families, and any their goods (except only coin and bullion), from any our dominions and territories to the said
island of Jamaica. And we do strictly charge and command
all planters, soldiers and others upon the said island,
to yield obedience to the lawful commands of our right
trusty and well-beloved Thomas lord Windsor, now our governor of our said island; and to every other governor
thereof for the time being: under pain of our displeasure,
and such penalties as may be inflicted thereupon.

---

1. This was not,of course, a declaration that the laws of England were
now to be introduced wholesale into Jamaica:a claim which sometimes,
depending on their convenience, Jamaicans would make.

348.INSTRUCTIONS TO GOVERNOR LORD WINDSOR, 21 March 1662.[1]
    ...2.You shall with all convenient expedition, settle
the government there, and appoint and constitute the council, according to your commission and instructions...[Oaths
of supremacy and allegiance were to be administered.]
    4. You shall, as soone as conveniently you may with
the advice of the council, settle such judicatories for
civil affaires, and for the Admiralty, as may be most
proper to keepe the peace of our islands, and determine
all matters of right, and controversy and all causes civil
and criminal,matrimonial, testamentary, and maritime, yet
so as no man's freehold,life or member be taken away or
harmed, but by established lawes (not repugnant but as
much as may be) agreeable to the knowne lawes of England.
    5. You shall appoint and commissionate under our pub-
lique seale for the island, judges,justices, sheriffes,
and other officers for the more orderly administration of
justice, and you are hereby authorized to allow and order
them, or such of them as you shall thinke fit, meete and
convenient salaries, to be paid after the manner of Barbados and Virginia, or one of them. And the said persons
so constituted shall have power to administer oaths, in
such tryalls and processes, and to summon and send for
witnesses, persons, papers and writings to hold courts of
judicature and keepe publique records of their proceedings
in the same. And finally to determine and give judgement
in all suites, controversies, and also to try, condemne,
sentence and execute malefactors unlesse you find good
cause to repreive any of them,and herein you are to observe as much as may be the practise, and proceedings of
our lawes of England ....
    [He was to have authority over the neighbouring islands ('Salt
    Islands, Goate Islands, Pidgeon Islands and Camaines Islands') as
    well as Jamaica.]
    7. You have hereby full power and authority to graunt
such commissions as to you shall seeme requisite for the
subduing of all our enemies by sea or land, within and
upon the coasts of America, according to your commission
and the instructions now given you herein, or which you
may hereafter receive from us, declaring whome we would
have treated and accompted as enemies to us. And you shall
cause courts of Admiralty to be held in places most convenient, by such judge, judges, or other deputed person
or persons as shall be commissionated for that purpose by

_____
1.C.O. 138/1 pp.13 ff.Windsor's commission eight months earlier on
2 August 1661 had envisaged an elected council and presumably no
assembly. Now, following these instructions (in the discussion of
which Windsor had been present), the council was assumed to be a
nominated body; and though the governor and council would seem to
have full legislative powers, in sections 4 and 20 settlers were
granted justice agreeable to English laws and an assembly might be
called.

our deare brother James Duke of Yorke, our high Admiral
of England... [only specially commissioned ships might attack enemy
vessels.]

8.You shall promulge our royal license by proclamation
in our neighbour colonies and plantations, for the trans-
planting of all such persons, goods and families, as are
willing to transport themselves to our island of Jamaica,
and for that purpose you may employ what vessells can at
any time be spared, for the fetching planters, or any
other persons from the neighbouring colonies.

And you shall use all meanes you may for the strengthening and peopling of our said island. And if you find it
be advantageous for the prosperity of our island of Jamaica to entertaine any commerce with the Spanish plantations in those parts, or with any other colony or places
of trade, to the benefit and advantage of our said plantation, notwithstanding any prohibition or graunt made to
the contrary, you are hereby authorized to entertaine the
same.

And you are to take care that such things as are necessary for that island, and whereof there is scarcity, be
not suffered through the greediness of trade and private
benefit to the merchants to be exported, so as to leave
our island destitute of its necessary support.... ·

10. You are, as often as you have opportunity to encourage our good subjects in our name, and from us, and
to assure them that we shall from time to time, give them
all necessary protection and assistance to their industry
and traffique, it being our royal intention and we requiring it from your selfe and the council, that all the
inhabitants of what quality soever be encouraged to plant
trade and improve the said island to the best advantage.

And the lands as you find to be already allotted, or
which shall be allotted by you, to the inhabitants of our
said island, you shall under our publique seale of the
island graunt, confirme and ratify to them, and their
heires for ever, in free and common soccage, reserving
to us such rents thereupon as may be thought fit by you
and the council....

[He was to order a survey of harbours and erect forts; and 'as
well for the bearing of such like expenses as for a mark of our
sovereignty' he was to set aside 400,000 acres as a royal demesne.
Planters were to be provided with arms. He might grant lands in
free and common soccage with the reservation of quit rents to the
king. Windsor might grant himself up to 50,000 acres. He was to
punish officials for drunkenness and debauchery, and to encourage
ministers of the Church of England. To stimulate trade and production, exports from Jamaica were to be free of customs duties for
seven years:[1] thereafter 5% to be paid. Markets and fairs were to
be established.]

1. The Crown presumably intended to impose some tax in Jamaica like
the 4½% duty in Barbados and the Leewards.

And whatsoever is graunted by the governour with the
advice of the council under the publique seale of the island shall be approved and held good and lawfull to all
intents and purposes, whereby the undertakers may have
full encouragement to prosecute their traffique, commerce,
trade and plantations without doubt or scruple of alteration, by succeeding Leiutenants or Governors... [Details
of defensive measures against the event of a Spanish attack were
given.]

17. And for the greater encouragement to men of parts
and interest to transplant and settle themselves in that
our island of Jamaica, our pleasure is that none be admitted to continue or enjoy more than one office at one time,
or to keepe any office which is not executed by himselfe,
or that shall leave the island without your license. And
all officers both civil and military upon misbehaviour and
unfaithfulnesse in discharge of their trust,you shall by
the advice of the council suspend or discharge as shall
appeare upon due examination most agreeable to justice....
[Accounts of planters and the needs of the island were to be sent.]

19. You have hereby power with the advice of the council to constitute corporations and to graunt mannours and
royalties, under the great seale of the said island, with
such charters, jurisdictions priviledges and immunities
as you and the council shall judge convenient, and agreeable to our lawes of England, provided no lordshipps or
mannours containe lesse than five hundred acres.

20. You shall have power with the advice of the council
to call assemblies togeather, according to the custome of
our plantation to make lawes, and upon eminent necessities
to leavy moneyes,[1] as shall be most conducable to the honour and advantage of our Crowne, and the good and welfare
of our subjects.

Provided they be not repugnant to any of our lawes of
England and that such lawes shall be in force for two yeares, and no longer unlesse they shall be approoved and
confirmed by us....[2] [Lands lawfully possessed by planters were
to be confirmed.]

22. Forasmuch as there are many things in so remote a
place which will be omitted and not foreseene, and necessarily must be left to the prudence of our lieutenant or
governor to use his best circumspection and care with the
advice of the council, wee reposing great trust and confidence in you, Thomas Lord Windsor, doe hereby authorize
you to act, doe and execute in all things within your
trust, as in your judgement shall be for the security and
enlarging of our interest in those parts of America, and
for the advantage and improovement of the same (although
we have not given you particular instructions therein) not
contradicting anything contained in our commission or these
instructions.

1.A <u>conquered</u> colony was thus being given the privileges of settled
plantations like Barbados and Virginia.
2. The complacent 'parliamentarianism' of dominant groups in the colony

349. ORDINANCE FOR ASSEMBLY, 23 October 1663.[1]
...Ordered that there be an assembly and that thirty
persons being free holders bee fairely and indifferently
chosen in the several quarters of this island and that
Lieutenant Collonel Linch[2] doe cause the same to bee effected at or before the 20th day of December next,....

350. (a) ACT CONFIRMING DIVERSE ACTS OF THE GOVERNOR AND COUNCELL
         AND FOR REPEALING ALL OTHER ACTS AND ORDERS, January 1664.[3]
    The Governor and Councell with the consent of the gen-
tlemen of the Assembly have thought fit to enact and it
is hereby enacted and ordained...
    [that certain regulations, made on 18 June 1661 by the governor
    and council, and relating to masters and servants, markets and
    courts were now confirmed 'to be in as full force,as if each res-
    pective Act or ordinance...had been executed by the Governor and
    Council with the consent...of this present Assembly'[4] ,but]
    ...all other Acts and ordinances heretofore made by
the Governor and Councell only and not herein confirmed
bee utterly voyd and for ever cease.... [but, if anyone who
had already acted under such Acts was prosecuted, the jury should find
for him.][5]

350. (b) REVENUE ACTS, January 1664.[6]
    ... Whereas they have further considered that the

---

seemed to require firm supervision.
1.C.O. 139/1 p.23.The assembly met on 20 January 1664.William Beeston
and Samuel Long represented Port Royal.
2.Thomas Lynch, later chief justice, lieutenant governor and governor.
3.C.O. 139/1 pp.40-2. The assembly was immediately insisting on its
rights in legislation.Previous Acts made by governor and council were
not binding 'for want of the consent of the people met in Assembly'.
In future the legislative power of governor and council could be only
temporary – until the next assembly met.
4. Significantly the revenue acts passed by O'Doyley and Lyttelton's
councils [see above No.346] were not confirmed.Fearful that the Crown
might legally impose taxes on the conquered colony, the assembly was
determined to secure its own right to tax.
5. In their opinion of 18 May 1724 on the extension of the laws of
England to the colonies,the law officers (Philip Yorke and Clement
Wearg)found this Act 'remarkable':'It appears that it was insisted
upon by the people of the Island at that time, that the Acts, or
ordinances of the nature of the laws which had been formerly made by
the governors and councils only were not binding laws but void in
themselves for want of the consent of the representatives of the people met in an Assembly'. Nevertheless, they noted that in Modyford's
commission (15 February 1664) he was granted express powers to choose
a council of 12 and to legislate with its advice: G. Chalmers,*Opinions*
(1814 ed.) I p.221: C.O. 137/14ff 331-42. [See Volume II].
6. C.O. 139/1 pp.43,47. The assembly resolved that 'no further or
other tax or levy or assessment whatever bé imposed or levied upon
the island or inhabitants or residents thereof without the assent of
the Governor, Council and Assembly'. The money was not granted to

just and equitable collection and disbursement of the same
will both advance the public interest and service of this
His Majesty's island and give satisfaction to those from
whence it's levied and collected...Be it enacted and ordained by the authority of the Governor and Council with
the consent of the gentlemen of the Assembly that the receivers, treasurers and collectors of all the money raised
and to be raised by custom, impost or other levy shall
from the first of March next ensuing the date hereof monthly and for every month pay into the two public treasurers or one of them which shall be commissionated by the
Governor for the time being, and approved of by the Governor, Council and Assembly all and every the sums of
money by them received, collected or levied, as also together with a fair and particular account of the said imposts and every part thereof which the same public treasurers (or one of them) shall immediately remit into the
hands of the Governor to be examined that all the omiss-
ions, neglects and frauds of all or any of the said receivers, collectors or treasurers may be the better prevented, discovered and punished. And that the said monies
may with the more expedition and less embezzlement be
employed to the uses for which it [sic] is raised and intended as is particularly declared by other Acts bearing
date with these presents or as shall be hereafter appointed
by the further Acts and considerations of the Governor,
Council and Assembly, it is therefore hereby further ordained and enacted by the authority aforesaid that the said
two public treasurers (or any one of them) shall have power
sufficient in the law to also demand and take account from
all or any the said receivers, collectors or treasurers
and also all other persons whatsoever that now have or
possess or hereafter may have or possess any lands, houses,
properties, rents or servants that do now belong or hereafter may belong to His Majesty or to this his island....

---

the king but for 'the use of the public service' of Jamaica. Its collection and disbursement was by officials approved by the assembly.
Such control over royal officials did not of course exist in England,
nor did the house of commons yet examine royal accounts nor specifically appropriate the detail of supplies. A further Act instructed
the treasurers to pay salaries to the governor,the receiver, the judges, the provost-marshal and themselves. That the appointment of
revenue officials and the supervision of raising and spending money
was the responsibility of the assembly was the strongly-held belief
of Long, one of the treasurers, but Lyttelton and the council also
seem to have had sympathy for Long's bills which asserted the role of
the assembly. Where the assembly could not secure the accountability
of the Crown's representative, servants and officials,it was probing
to discover means of taking over some crucial areas of executive government itself – as did executive committees in American assemblies
later. Such devices were repudiated by the house of commons: the
task of Parliament was to criticise but not to perform, execute or
administer. By means which certainly included power over the purse,
it was securing the responsiveness – ultimately the responsibility-
of the king's ministers – so much closer to hand in London than in
America.

350. (c) 'ACT DECLARING THE LAWS OF ENGLAND IN FORCE, 10 November 1664[1]
   Bee it declared by the governor, council and assembly
and by the authority of the same That all the laws and
statutes[2] heretofore made in our native country, the Kingdome of England, for the publique weale of the same, and
all the liberties, priviledges, immunities and freedoms
conteyned therein have allwayes bin of force and are belonging unto his Majesty's liege people within this island
as theyre byrthright and that the same ever were, now are,
and ever shall be deemed good and effectual in the law.
And That the same shall be accepted and executed within
this His Majesty's island of Jamaica in all points and at
all times requisite according to the tenour and true meaning of them (excepting onely such statutes and soe much of
them whereby any subsidies,loanes, aides and other impositions are graunted or made);[3] Provided nevertheless...
That the said lawes and statutes may at any time hereafter,
by the governor, councell and assembly, bee mittigated,
altered, lessened or enlarged according as the constitution of this place shall require and as it shall seeme requisite and necessary to the respective generall assembly
then in being.

351. LIEUTENANT-GOVERNOR LYNCH TO LORD ARLINGTON, 20 August 1671. [4]
   His Majesty is Sovereign Ld. and Proprietor of this

1.C.O. 139/1.p.65/Sir Thomas Modyford, who had arrived as governor
in June 1664, argued that, realising their 'weakness' in law-making,
the new assembly passed 'the like law Sir Edward Poynings made' in
Ireland to make them 'partakers of the perfectly incomparable law of
our own country': (C.O. 1/22)[see above No.57]. But the assembly was
concerned to claim the protective safeguards against the Crown's arbitrary actions and the limitations on the prerogative which English
laws did appear to provide. In the conquered colony of Jamaica the
rights to English law - which the Crown had not granted - seemed a
valuable protection for individual liberty. Modyford, whose instructions had given him a wide discretion 'to act in all things' not actually mentioned in them, only summoned this one assembly and rarely
called his council after his first year; but he remained a popular
'planters' governor - virtually autonomous of royal control, for
Whitehall left him much to himself.
2.Neither the proclamation of 1661 nor instructions to governors had
granted the laws of England to Jamaica: what had been mentioned as
inducements for settlers were the 'privileges' of free-born Englishmen, and 'the knowne laws of England' as a criterion for repugnancy
of any island-made law.All English statutes were known;many were wholly inappropriate.Reports of cases were not available, and few islanders had any knowledge of (let alone any training in)the law.Indeed
in 1674 a bill was introduced to suppress professional lawyers and
was 'tacked' on to a revenue measure to secure its passage.
3. A prudent exception.
4.C.O. 1/27 No.221. Sir Thomas Lynch had served in Jamaica under
D'Oyley, had been on Lyttelton's council, had been dismissed as chief
justice by Modyford, and had been appointed lieutenant-governor in

Island, amd in all writs, Comissions and Grants, is stiled
*King of England, Scotland, France, and Ireland, Defendour
of the Faith, and Lord of Jamaica.*
   The Governor has his Majesty's Authority and Represents
His Person, and is solely enabled to Govern by his Comission and Instructions, in his Absence or Disability the
Lt.-Governor comands, They are both Appointed by the King
during his Pleasure.
   His Majesty's present Lt-Governor is Comander in Chiefe,
and has according to his Instruccons a Counsell of about
14 of the Best Men in the Island....
   A more Particular Account and Character of this Counsell
is to bee given by the Governor to the Lords of the Counsell for Forrain Plantacons: on Misdemeanors or suspicion
They may bee suspended; But the Secretary and Lords of
Counsell must have an Account of it That They may judge
if it's Reasonable for the King's service.
   The Governor is obliged to receive Orders from Them and
to consult his own Counsell in all Affayres of Moment, for
they are what the Kings Counsell and House of Lords[1] are
in England.
   Besides the Counsell there is an Assembly which is a
kind of Parliament or Representatives of the People and
there are 18 of them in all (2 for each of 9 parishes).
   These are Chosen indifferently by the People, by Virtue
of the Governor's Writs directed to the Provost Marshall,
And these with the Governor and Counsell have the Legislative Power, They make Lawes that are sent for England,
and are of force for two years, and ever after if the King
sends them back with his Royall Assent.
   The People here looks on it as a Priviledge, and their
Magna Charta, and They shall bee Governed according to
these Municipall Lawes and those of England, and not have
any Thing imposed on Them, but by their own Consente, as
Barbados and the Caribby Islands have.
   Besides the Lieut. Governor, his Majesty has here a
Major-General, that the Militia may bee the Better Disciplined and looked after. Because this is a Frontier Col-
lony, and Remote, His Office resembles that of Muster
Master in one of the Provinces of England.
   Hee has his Comission from the King, and Instruccons
from the Commander in Chiefe to this Purpose....

352. MINUTE OF THE COUNCIL, 11 May 1672.[2]
   The Governor and Councill, haveing not only by an open

1670. Here he was giving the secretary of state, <u>Lord Arlington</u>, an
account of the Jamaican form of government.
1. A misleading statement,which confused the executive and advisory
privy council with the upper house of the legislature.
2. C.O. 140/1 pp.300-1. Lynch found an empty treasury. The assembly,
summoned on 1 February, had considered the public accounts and, in a
joint committee with the council, his proposals for raising money which
they embodied in a single Revenue Act,which incidentally had no time

conference with the Gentleman of the Assembly, but by severall other Messages, declared to them the Dangers that
are approaching, and that Port Royall ought to be forty-
fyed in the best manner it could, and haveing likewise
sent them the King's Letter, which gives them Warning of
the danger, and bids us prepare, but sayes, that what is
necessary he expects should be done at our own Charge:
Notwithstanding all the Assembly being of an opinion, That
to secure the Island it was not necessary to fortify Port
Royall, or if it were, the fort there was already sufficient; but admitt it were not, the Country was not able,
and ought not to be charged with any Tax towards the
repaireing of that, or building of more forts, Platforms,
or Breastworks, upon which the Governour and Councill unanimously made this following Declaration, and ordered
that is should be entered:-

That it is absolutely necessary for the security of the
Island and Trade to fortify Port Royall, as soon and as
well as we can:

That the fort ought to be made as strong and regular
as possible for the security of Men, Stores, and reputation of the Island.

That, it appears by a Survey, that the fort (as it is)
may beat it down, and that unless speedily prepared, it
will fall itself.

That this fort, A Platform at Bonham Point, a slight
one at the Prison, and one at the Breast Work to the Sea-
ward will be sufficient to secure the Harbour against considerable force.

Upon the Examination of the Treasurers *[sic]* and Collectors, it appeares the Quitt Rents, and Impost can do
nothing towards the building of forts, they being not enough, to discharge Salleryes and Contingentcyes.

---

limit. But they feared that some 4½% export duty might be negotiated
(as with the Caribbees) and took defensive action by appropriating
all royal quit rents (as the Burgesses in Virginia temporarily had
done) to island use. When Lynch, urged by the Crown, asked for additional revenues to strengthen defences against the Spaniards and the
Dutch, the assembly refused. Having deprived the Crown of all local
moneys, they declared its sole responsibility for defence. Even a
year later, in face of news of the imminent arrival of a Dutch fleet,
they again refused to make any grant lest it be appropriated to other
purposes: they even questioned the governor's power to commandeer
slaves to repair Port Royal. In 1674 when the assembly did vote another Revenue Act, they 'tacked' to it the Act for the suppression of
lawyers,which Lynch had to accept.
The issue of a colonial contribution to imperial defence was a perennial one and reappeared at intervals from the mid-seventeenth century
through the Stamp Act and 'Grattan's Parliament' to imperial conferences
in the twentieth century. The metropolitan government might recognise
its major responsibility to protect colonies, certainly in European
wars, but contended that colonies should make some reasonable contribution to their own defence.

That the Country may at this time raise as much mony as will do all that is necessary, by way of pish[1]levyes, which (according to our Calcull) will be insencible and yet sufficient.

353. INSTRUCTIONS TO GOVERNOR LORD VAUGHAN,3 December 1674.[2]
   ...2.And being arrived there you are to take upon you the execution of the place and trust wee have reposed in you, and forthwith to call together the council of that island in your commission nominated, and, with due and usual solemnity to cause our said commission under the great seale of England, constituting you our present captain general and governor in cheife as aforesaid to be then and there published....
   [He was to communicate his instructions to the council. The council might have freedom to debate and vote in public matters.
   'Men of estate' were to be chosen for public office.]
   7. And to prevent arbitrary removalls of judges and justices of the peace, you are not to express any limitation of time in the commissions which you are to grant with the advice and consent of your council to fit persons for those employments.
   8. And our will and pleasure is that none of the members of the said council shall be made judges so long as they shall serve in the said council.
   9. Our will and pleasure is that in case of suspension or expulsion of any of the members of the said council, you forthwith transmit unto us by one of our principal secretaries of state, and to our Council of Trade and Forreign Plantations, the reasons of your so doing, together with the charges and proofs against the said persons and their answers thereunto....[He was to send the names of councillors.][3]

---

1. Slight, trifling.
2. C.O. 138/3 pp.12.ff. The earl of Carlisle had been chosen to replace Modyford as governor in 1670, but Sir Thomas Lynch had been commissioned as lieutenant-governor in 1670 to enforce the Treaty of Madrid and put an end to the connivance at privateering which had marked Modyford's governorship. During Lynch's tenure the power of the assembly had grown under Long as Speaker, especially in regard to appropriation, privilege and jurisdiction over its own membership, with conscious imitation of Commons practice.
Again in March 1674 a commission was drafted for Carlisle as governor but John, Lord Vaughan, received it. These instructions, similar to those issued in February to Atkins as governor of Barbados (in that the councillors were named by the Crown and not by the governor), had been originally prepared for Carlisle: but the council of trade had made a close examination of Jamaican law and practice before putting these instructions into a final form. The intention was to reduce the governor's discretion and to secure greater metropolitan supervision.
3. The Crown had indeed already named the councillors in the commission of 31 March 1674: see also § 2.

11. You shall not displace any of the judges and justices sherriffs or other officers or ministers, within
the said island of Jamaica, and other the territories depending thereon, without good and sufficient cause, nor
execute your self or by deputy any of the said offices,
nor suffer any person to execute more offices than one by
deputy....

[Civil and military officers might be discharged upon misbehaviour. Care was to be taken to regulate salaries and exactions.
Members of government were exempt from the oath of allegiance, but
not councillors. Religious toleration was to be provided although
the governor was advised to observe Anglican protestantism himself. Drunkenness was to be punished; men might only be 'molested'
by due process of law, and the governor was to send an account of
the island as soon as possible.]

18. You shall not after the 29th of September next
reenact any law except upon very urgent occasions,but in
no case more than once, except with our express consent...[1]

[Laws were 'to continue and to be in force for two yeares (except in the meantime His Majesty's pleasure shall be signified to
the contrary),[2] but noe longer, unless confirmed by His Majesty
within the two yeares aforesaid'. The defence of the island was
to be provided for and an account of arms made: the governor was
to assist governors of other islands. No customs were to be levied in the island for 14 years. The governor was to encourage farming,*etc*. He was to observe peace treaties, and not to declare
war.]

50. Whereas wee have thought fit to dispose of several
offices and places in our said island of Jamaica, by letters patents under our great seale of England, our will
and pleasure is, that you take care that the said several
offices and places bee freely and without any molestation
enjoyed and held by the respective persons to whom granted, or their sufficient deputies. And in case any of the
said patentees, or their deputies shall misbehave themselves in the execution of any of the said offices, our
will and pleasure is that you only suspend them from the
execution of the same till you shall have represented the
whole matter to us, and received our pleasure and determination thereupon, taking care that those who shall be
in the mean time appointed by you to execute any of the
said offices, give security to be accomptable for the profits of the same to the respective patentees.[3]

1.The practice of re-enacting laws,which had previously [see No.348]
been valid for two years (though no longer,unless confirmed by the
Crown),had meant that the Jamaican assembly could legislate temporarily without Crown supervision and had therefore effectively frustrated the Crown's power of disallowance.Now by these instructions the
express approval of the Crown was necessary before laws would be re-
enacted once they had expired.
2.The king's right to disallow (as well as to confirm laws) was thus
asserted.These words in brackets were inserted on the advice of the
council of trade.
3. This article was not in the Carlisle draft instructions. It emph-

354. THE ASSEMBLY AND PARLIAMENTARY PROCEDURE, 1675-77.[1]
    (a) 15 May 1675.
    His Excellency and the Council being met, William Bee-
ston esquire[2] came from the Assembly and acquainted his
Excellency that the Act of the revenue was now passed in
their house according to their first vote, making his
Excellency's order the treasurer's warrant[3] and that all
the Acts having been read three times in their house, he
humbly prayed they might be presented to his Excellency
by their Speaker and signed *in their presence*, and the
custom of this place was urged as a precedent for it; to
which his Excellency answered he should guide himself according to the custom and usage of Parliaments in England.
    [The assembly thereupon threatened to withdraw their bill if
    the governor refused to sign in their presence. The governor rep-
    lied that he could not be witness to anything that he did 'by
    virtue of his negative voice' and their threat to withdraw their
    assent was 'unparliamentary'.]
    And that having passed the Acts three times in their
house their consents were bound and they were wholly dispossessed of them and could not consider them as any records belonging to them.
    (b) 19 April 1677.
    Colonel Theodore Cary and Major John Bourden brought
from the house four bills, but being read but twice they
were sent back to the house to be read three times, it

asised the Crown's decision to increase its control by reserving patronage in certain patents to itself and by immunising such officials
from obstruction:another indication of its desire to remove discretion from the governor and the local influences upon him which had been
so evident in Modyford's governorship in Jamaica and Willoughby's
in Barbados.The island governments were to be more 'immediately dependent' upon the Crown, not the local governor.Of course both governors and colonists resented these royal patentees as outsiders [see
No.343].
1.Journ.Jam.Ass.I pp.10,12.Governors had signed bills in the presence
of the council and assembly,but Vaughan pointed out that this was repugnant to the custom of Parliament:a criterion of crucial importance
to assemblymen who were aspiring to the privileges, status and procedure of the house of commons.
2.The assembly in 1664 claiming jurisdiction over its members had
imprisoned Beeston, member for Port Royal, for non-attendance.
3. The assembly,in anger at the appointment of a royal receiver-
general,had in the Revenue Act of 1675 returned to the 1664 policy
of appointing its own treasurer and collector and appropriating revenues not to the king but 'the public use' of the island. It declared
that the Act itself would be sufficient authority for the treasurer
to pay out money. Vaughan had insisted that an order from the governor must be the treasurer's only warrant. The assembly had now finally agreed. The Revenue Act imposed duties on wines, brandy, ale
and cider, on sugars and on European vessels. It also laid down
salaries for the governor and officials.

being declared by his excellency in council that, according to the constitution of the English Parliaments or assemblies, all bills ought to be read three times in the
house where they first began before the other house could
proceed upon them....

> [The assembly replied that it had been their custom to read
> bills twice only, but on 21 April agreed 'to follow the customs
> of the Parliaments of England'.]

355. GOVERNOR LORD VAUGHAN TO THE LORDS OF TRADE, 18 January 1676.[1]

> [A month previously he had received the only dispatch from their
> Lordships since he had assumed the governorship. He had already
> sent full information, accounts, and a body of island laws which
> awaited approval urgently.]

...The Body of Laws which I sent to Mr. Secretary Coventry,
I understand lyes before your Lordships. I hope when they
are perused, your Honors will approve of them and move
his Majestie to give his royal assent to them, the sooner
they are returned, it will be the better, not so much for
the governing of the people here, who are very respectful
and obedient unto authority, as for incouraging others to
come, when they know what laws they shall be governed by.
Besides, my Lords, since I am tyed up by me Instructions
not to reenact any, I know not what wee shall do unless
these are returned unto us confirmed, or his Majestie
make some particular signification of his pleasure as to
that point....

> [Trade and planting were improving and the settlers were healthy
> and prosperous.]

...By the advice of his Majestie's council[2]. I called an
assembly who reenacted and made a good Body of Laws; they
are municipal, and particularly adapted to the interest of
this place, soe cannot clearly be understood by those who
are strangers to it, and lye now before your Lordships
for his Majestie's royal confirmation....

356. (a) ASSEMBLY JOURNAL, April-May 1677.

> 10 April
> ...*The Act declaring the lawes of England in force*

---

1. C.O. 138/3 p.27.Delays and disregard of correspondence were regular
subjects of mutual complaint and exasperation for both the Crown's
ministers and colonial governors.Vaughan was told that attendance at
Parliament demanded the major share of their Lordships' time.In May
1675 he had sent some 45 Acts - nearly all re-enactments of laws previously assented to by Lynch but already questioned:the two-year limit
meant they would all expire in April 1677.Vaughan's plea for local
legislation to be left to local discretion,however,went unheeded:the
lords of trade were meanwhile concerned with an examination of the
laws of Jamaica,the claims of the assembly,and the challenge to the
prerogative.
2. Vaughan found himself frustrated not only by their Lordships, and
by the assembly, but also by his council which contained many 'old
standers' and Cromwellian veterans.'There is so little power in the
Governor and so much given the people that, when they will, they will

being read, it was thought fit that instead thereof an
Act should bee drawn in the nature of a Petition of Right,
and [it was] voted that a committee bee appointed for that
purpose namely George Nedham, Charles Atkinson, Samuel
Barnard, John Burden and Samuel Barry, Esquires and ordered to bring in their report at the next sitting after
the holy day....[1]

3 May
...The committee between the Councell and Assembly was
held and the Bill of Priviledges debated as followeth....
The Councell's committee urged that the statute and common
lawes doe not extend to the marine lawes which therefore
would bee excluded by this Act.

Butt it was replyed to them that statute and common
lawes did not exclude the marine lawes - the substance of
the Act having by the assembly been taken out of the statutes of England which never put any stop to the marine
law. The words ('bill' 'libel' etc.) by the councell desired to bee left out because they raise some scruples as
if they were intended to abridge thereby the power of the
chancellor and admiral. Whereto the house answered that
the words were taken out of an Act of Parliament of forty
yeares standing which had not any wise in all that time
obstructed either the power of the chancery or admiralty
and therefore the scruple was needless.

The Councel's committee said that the last provisoe
was to bee admitted of, it being the same verbatim as
had formerly been allowed of in the Act of the Militia.
The house replyed that it would continue more aptly in
that Act than bee inserted in this.

The Councel's committee replyed that his Excellency
scruples that provisoe as abridging his commission, and
that it can doe noe harm if inserted in this Act.

To which the house answered that what they doe is to
secure their own properties, not to thwarte his Excellency's commission. And that his Excellency has acted in all
matters mentioned in his commission and has been punctually obeyed, and that the King's prerogative cannot bee
thought to bee touched, seeing the whole bill is taken
out of the statuts of England.

Urged by the Councell that the King may seem to have a
greater power here than in England, and soe a clause may
bee admitted to secure his prerogative.

To which was answered by the house that his Majesty
had given us here the same priviledges as his subjects in
England....His Excellency declared that he had not a sufficient knowledge of the lawes and therefore would desire
that the Assembly might rather confirme their former Acts,

do what they please' (18 May 1677:C.O. 1/40.)
1. C.O. 139/1 p.143.Vaughan,having received no confirmation of the
many laws he had sent to the lords of trade,had had to call an assembly which drafted a bill declaring the laws of England to be in
force and a 'Bill of Privileges' attacking the prerogative.

especially that making the lawes of England in force,than
make new Acts as they had done hitherto, which would take
up much time to examine and occasion a long and tedious
sessions....
 The two following provisos[1] voted <u>not</u> to be inserted
in the bill....
 May 4th.
 The question was put whether the house should adhere
or not to their Bill of Priviledges and amendments as they
were sent to the councell this day and it was unanimusly
coted in the affirmative and thereupon the following message was sent to his Excellency and councell by Lieutenant
Collonel Coleback [and others named.]: The House adhere to
their own bill with such amendments as they themselves
have consented to and doe conclude That it is the just
rights and inherent priviledges of his Majesty's subjects
of this island that they ought to have the benefits and
immunities of the laws of England and therefore until
their Bill of Priviledges be made in to an Act[2] they think
fit not to proceed on any further business but intend to
adjorne for one monthe.
 To the above message the gentlemen brought back this
reply: that his Excellency would consult with his councell
and send back his answer to the house by the marshal....
 [The house met with the governor.]
 The Speaker and Assembly attending of his Lordship, his
Excellency told them that he perceived by their vote which
had passed in their howse for adhering to their owne bill
[that] thereby both they and the Councell, according to
the constant custom and order of all Parliaments were excluded, from receiving the same bill unless it were altered and put into another dresse; that they might reinact
at the first opening of this season he have recommended
to them the reinacting of their old laws, supposeing those
the best which had been long practised among us and were
known that new ones might bee not well understood, and
lawyers take an advantage to render them obscure therby
onely to get money; that they might likewise remember
nothing was offered to him that last session but what was
readyly passed; that now he should consent to any thing
that had passed both howses that the Councell were very
exact and circumspect but that his owne sence was not declared, and that he now spoke to them onely the sence of the
Councell: upon which the Speaker replyed that they had
already conferred with the Councell and should be ready
to enter into any further argument with them, realising
nothing was contained in this bill sent up but according
to the laws of England which we had a right to as Englishmen and the king's subjects: unto which his Excellency
answered that he did not know that was disputed and the

1.These two provisos [see No.356 (b)] were those in the bill which
Vaughan had encouraged the council to draft in reply to that of the
assembly.
2. The assembly's bill was rejected by the council.

Act that was passed the last session was rather more full
than this now presented; and that when it came to him he
should not dispute any thing that concerned our rights;
and that he should readyly himselfe spend all he was worth
in the defence of it; and that he declared he was not jealous of them as he could protest for himself he had no
jealousy they had any of him....[1]

356. (b) COUNCIL JOURNAL, 2 May 1677.[2]
   A bill declaring the rights, libertyes, and priviledges
of his Majesty's subjects of this island and territoryes
thereon depending was read at this board the third time
and past, and was ordered to be sent down to the Assembly,
with their own bill sent up to this board....
   [Alterations had been made to other bills. The council added
   various amendments to this bill:]
   The fourth paragraph to be totally omitted, and the
two following provisoes to be inserted word for word *viz.*
   Provided nevertheless, and it is hereby further declared and enacted, That where the lawes made in this island
give remedy, such laws in regard of their more easy and
speedy reliefe shall be put in use, and not the laws of
England, unless the lawes of England do particularly name
or relate to this island,[3] any thing herein or in any other
act seeming to the contrary notwithstanding.
   Provided also, and it is hereby further declared and
enacted That nothing in this or any other Act contained,
shall be construed, deemed, taken or adjudged to abridge,[4]
alter, infringe, abrogate or inlarge the power and authority of his Majesty's commission given to his Majesty's
Captain General and Governor in Chiefe of this island,
but that the said commission be and remain in the same
and in as full force and validity as the said commission
was before the making of this Act, any thing herein,or in
any other Act that may bee to the contrary in any wise
notwithstanding....
   [The bill with these amendments was sent down to the assembly.][5]

356. (c) A BILL DECLARING THE LAWS OF ENGLAND IN FORCE WITHIN THIS
   ISLAND,AND THE TERRITORIES THEREON DEPENDING, 16 May 1677.[6]
   Whereas the lawes and statutes, heretofore made, or

1.The assembly had been told by Vaughan two years before in May 1675
that parliamentary procedure sanctioned such obstructionist tactics
to secure its bill.But, as it happened,when the house sat once more
after an adjournment of five days,they were persuaded by Vaughan to
drop their Bill of Privileges in favour of another declaration,and
another Act [see No.356 (c)] that the laws of England were in force
in Jamaica.
2. C.O. 140/3 p.569.The provisos here were rejected by the assembly,
[see p.558.]
3. i.e.(presumably) that an Act should apply only, as the Colonial
Laws Validity Act asserted in 1865,'by express word or necessary intendment';[see p.206n].
4.The assembly objected strongly to this word.They were seeking not
merely to prevent any extension of the power of the governor, but also
to limit existing prerogatives of the Crown. 5. See p.558.
6. C.O. 139/5 p.11.This bill had been introduced on 9 April, was then

used in our native country, the Kingdome of England, for
the publique weale of the same, and all the liberties,
immunities, and priviledges, contayned therein, have ever
beene of force, and are belonging unto all his Majesty's
leige people within this island, as their birth right, and
that the same now are, ever were, and ever shall be deemed
good and effectual in the lawe, and to be pleased in all
courtes of this island, for, by and on behalfe of his Majesty's subjects inhabitants of the same.

Be it therefore declared and enacted by the governor
and council and representatives of the commons of this
island now assembled,...That noe freeman, inhabitant or
resident of this island, of what state, or condition soever heebe, may or shall be taken, imprisonned, or disseized of his freehold, goods, chattels, liberties, free
customes and hereditaments, or be touched, molested,har-
med or adjudges in life, member or estate, or be exiled,
outlawed, or distroyed in any manner whatsoever, but by
the lawes of the Kingdome of England, or the lawes of
this island, to be tryed in the ordinary courtes of justice, and according to the ordinary course of the said
lawes, and the due processe thereof; And That none of the
people of this island be compelled to give, grant, or pay
any loane, tax, ayd, benevolence, imposition, or other
such like charge, but by Act of Parliament in England,
naming the relating to this island, or by the common consent of General Assemblyes in this island, consisting of
governor, councel, and representatives of the commons of
the same assembled;[1] And that noe procedings to the contrary heretofore made in any of the premises to the prejudice of the people of this island, shall be taken or
drawne hereafter into any consequence or example.

357. MINUTE OF THE LORDS OF TRADE, 30 April 1677.[2]
    ...Upon the whole matter their Lordships think fit to

---

superseded by the 'Bill of Privileges', but was finally reintroduced
and passed by both houses and was signed by the governor in 16 May.
Vaughan considered this Act less objectionable than the Bill of Privileges which the assembly had dropped. He did not, however, secure
clauses he proposed – saving the council's prerogative, or even affirming that Jamaican laws might be more appropriate and expeditious
than English.
1. This forthright section was accepted by Vaughan with considerable
reluctance. It should be noted that the assembly acknowledged the
right of Parliament to legislate for, and even to tax, the colony.
2.C.O. 391/2 pp.10,27,42. The lords of trade, still brooding over
the laws which Vaughan had sent home for review, had called upon the
lords chancellor, the keeper and the treasurer to help advise them
in their protracted task.Thomas Lynch was also in attendance. They
now referred the laws to one of the law officers, Sir William Jones,
and asked him not only to consider the laws but to prepare a bill
limiting the legislative power in Jamaica: looking back as ever for
a suitable and handy precedent,hard-pressed administrators seemed to
think the Irish model of Poynings' Law [see No.69] provided an appropriate answer.

referr the whole body of these laws unto Mr. Attorney General, with the observations made by the Committee thereupon for his perusal and opinion how far they are fit to
bee allowed by his Majestie. And it is more particularly
recommended to Mr. Attorney to consider of the Act declaring the laws of England in force in Jamaica: how far
it is necessary and usefull to the island; how far consistent with the King's right of dominion and what qualifications are proper thereunto.

Their Lordships will likewise desire Mr. Attorney to
prepare a bill (like Poynings' Law in Ireland)[1] directing
the manner of enacting, transmitting and amending these
laws by his Majesty here in England....[2]

358. RECOMMENDATIONS OF THE PRIVY COUNCIL, 16 November 1677.[3]

...The first point that did occur, as most worthy to
be considered by us, was the power and manner of enacting
laws for the civil, military and ecclesiastical government,
and upon taking a view of what has been practiced since
your Majestie's happy restauration, in the legislature,
Wee find that the methods and authorities, for the framing
and ordaining the said laws, have been only such as were
directed by your royal commissions , unto your Majestie's
several governors, or prescribed by the instructions given
them from time to time, and that as the constitution and
exigency of affairs have often changed, so your Majestie
has thought fit variously to adapt your royal orders thereunto.[4] And by the last commission given unto the Lord
Vaughan, your Majestie was pleased to empower his Lordship
with the advice of your Majestie's Council from time to

---

1. See No.69.
2. On 10 May, the attorney general was instructed to consider the
laws and to prepare a bill 'like Poynings' Law in Ireland, directing
the manner of enacting laws in Jamaica, the transmitting them, and
how to be received after H.M.'s amendments and additions'. 'For the
future no general assembly was to be called without H.M.'s directions'.
Drafts of bills the governor deemed necessary to be passed had to be
transmitted to the king.The body of laws was to be prepared by the
attorney general to be considered and then to be offered to the next
assembly.The style of enactment was to be 'by the Kings most excellent
Majesty by and with the consent of the general assembly'.
3. C.O. 138/3 pp. 160–5. The lords of trade and the attorney general
had considered the laws, their enacting style, the appropriation of
money and the previous commissions and instructions. Charles Howard,
the earl of Carlisle, a member of the lords'committee himself, at last
prepared to go to Jamaica and to govern firmly; he favoured a return
to conciliar government. The privy council now approved the lords'
report and ordered instructions and commission to be prepared accordingly.
4. i.e. no statute was necessary to change the constitution of Jamaica.   The king could alter the powers he delegated to the governor.

time, to summon General Assemblies of freeholders, who
have authority, with the advice and consent of the government of the island; which laws are to be in force for
the space of two yeares (except in the mean time your
Majestie's pleasure be signifyed to the contrary) and no
longer unless they be confirmed by your Majestie within
that time. Having therefore directed our thoughts towards
the consequences and effects which have been produced, or
may arise from this authority derived unto the said freeholders and planters, which wee observe to have received
a daily encrease by the resolutions they have taken less
agreeable to your Majestie's intentions, Wee do most humbly offer our opinions that the laws, transmitted by the
Lord Vaughan, which are now under consideration in order
to be enacted by your Majestie, may be entrusted in the
hands of the Earl of Carlisle, who, upon his arrival in
the island, may offer them unto the next assembly, that
they may be consented unto as laws originally coming from
your Majestie. And that for the future no legislative assembly be called, without your Majestie's especial directions, but that, upon emergencies, the governor to acquaint
your Majestie by letters with the necessity of calling
such an assembly and pray your Majestie's consent and
directions for their meeting, and at the same time do
present unto your Majestie a scheme of such acts as he
shall think fit and necessary and that your Majestie may
take the same into consideration and return them, in the
forme wherein your Majestie shall think fitt that they be
enacted.
    That the governor,upon receipt of your Majestie's com-
mands, shall then summon an Assembly and propose the said
laws for their consent, so that the same method in legislative matters be made use of in Jamaica, as in Ireland,
according to the form prescribed by Poynings Law. And
that therefore the present style of enacting laws, *By the
governor,council and representatives of the commons assembled* be converted into the stile of, *Bee it enacted by the
Kings most excellent Majestie, by and with the consent of
the General Assembly*.
    Wee are farther of opinion that no escheats, fines,
forfeitures or penalties be mentioned in the said laws,
to be applyed to the publick use of the island, and that
your Majestie do instruct your governor to dispose thereof for the support of the government, as also that, in
all laws for levying of mony and raising a publick revenue,
the clauses whereby the said levyes are appropriated unto
the publick use of the island without any mention made of
your Majestie or unto your Majestie for the said publick
use, are so far derogatory to your Majestie's right of
soveraingty, that they ought to be, for the future, altered and made agreeable unto the stile of England....
    And whereas it has upon some occasions proved inconven-
ient that the members of the Council have been constituted
by your Majestie's commission, wee are of the opinion that

for the future they be only named in the instructions of
the governor for the strengthening of whose authority
under your Majestie wee do offer that hee may have power
to suspend any of the said members if hee see just cause
without receiving the advice and consent of the Council.
As also that none of the said members so suspended or by
your Majestie's order displaced from that trust may be
permitted to be received into the General Assembly....[1]

359. INSTRUCTIONS TO GOVERNOR LORD CARLISLE, 30 March 1678.[2]
    [The council was named. It included Sir Henry Morgan,Sir Francis
    Watson, Sir Thomas Modyford and Samuel Long.][3]
...14. And whereas, by Our Commission, we have directed
that for the future no General Assembly be called[4], without Our speciall directions, but that upon occasion you
doe acquaint us by letter with the necessity of calling
such an Assembly and pray Our consent and direction for
their meeting. You shall at the same time transmit unto
Us,with the advice and consent of the Councill, a Draught
of such Acts as you shall think fit and necessary to be
passed that wee may take the same into Our consideration,
and return them in the forme Wee shall think fitt they
be Enacted in. And upon receipt of our commands you shall
then summon an Assembly and propose the said Laws for
their consent.[4] And accordingly Wee have Ordered to be
delivered unto you herewith, a certain body of Laws for
the use of Our said Island, framed in pursuance of other
Laws transmitted unto Us by former Governors with such
alterations and amendments as Wee have thought fit

---

1. The preparation of Carlisle's commission and instructions was ordered by the privy council 'according to the tenor' of these recommen-
dations:Danby, Coventry and Finch (L.C.) were among those who signed.
The lords of trade were also instructed to prepare a draft bill for
a perpetual revenue in Jamaica, as such a measure had facilitated
government in Ireland since 1662 and the parliament in Dublin had
not met since 1666. The Jamaican treasury was empty and, if an assembly was to be dispensed with, some permanent provision for revenue
was vital. The Crown could 'tack' such a revenue bill to a body of
laws necessary for good government in the island: the new frame of
the Jamaican constitution.
2. C.O. 138/3 pp.222-3.
3. Carlisle had wanted to nominate his own councillors. The lords of
trade were not prepared,however, to surrender that patronage to him.
As a compromise the names were included in the instructions, a secret
document, not as previously in the commission.
4.In the draft instructions where was no provision for an assembly at
all. A return to government by governor and council alone and by royal instructions seemed to have been contemplated; presumably even
prerogative taxation in a conquered colony without a representative
assembly.Though at first it was thought that any such change could be
best made locally in the Jamaican legislature,it appeared to have
been assumed that the Crown could alter the constitution of Jamaica
by its own action [contrast the decision in *Campbell v.Hall*,1774;Vol.III].
5. Compare the instructions for Culpeper in Virginia in 1679[No.303].

with the advice of Our Privy Councill here, which upon
your arrival in Our said Island you shall offer unto the
next Assembly that they may be consented to and enacted
as laws originaly coming from us.

15. Wee are willing nevertheless that in case of invasion,
Rebellion, or some very urgent necessity you pass an Act
or Acts with the consent of the Generall Assembly (without transmitting the same first unto Us) to raise money
within the said Island and Territories depending thereon,
to answer the occasions arising by such urgent necessities.

16. And you shall take care that the present stile of
Enacting Laws, by the Governor,Councill and Representatives of the Commons assembled, bee converted into the
stile of *Bee it Enacted by the Kings most Excellt Majesty
by and with the consent of the Generall Assembly....*

360. ADDRESS BY THE ASSEMBLY TO THE GOVERNOR, 4 October 1678.[1]
      [They have considered and rejected the proposed bills[2]. This
      new method of law-making is 'impracticable' and will discourage
      loyal settlers much needed in the infancy of Jamaica's growth.The
      manifest inconveniences of the proposed system include]

1st. That the distance of this place renders it impossible
to be put in practice and does not in any manner fall under
the same consideration as Ireland does, from which we conclude the example is taken.

2d. The nature of all colonies is changeable, and consequently the laws must be adapted to the interest of the place
and must alter with it.

3d. It is no small satisfaction that the people by their
representatives have a deliberative power in the making of
laws; the negative and barely resolving power being not
according to the right of Englishmen and practised no
where but in those commonwealths where aristocracy pre-
vails.

4th. This manner of form of the government brings all
things absolute and puts it into the power of a governor
to do what he pleases, which is not His Majesty's interest
and may be a temptation for even good men to commit great
partialities and errors.

5th. The method which has been always used both in this
island and in all other Colonies in the making of laws
was a greater security to His Majesty's prerogative than
the present form; for a governor durst not consent to any
thing against his interest; and if he did, the signification of the King's pleasure determined the laws so that
His Majesty had thereby a double negative.

1.Journ.,Jam.Ass. I pp.36-7.
2.These draft bills were based on the acts passed in Jamaica since
1672 and were for the most part 'municipal'.They had been prepared
with care and concern for the island's interests,customs and usages.
They had been issued not by order-in-council but under the great seal
of England,and were brought to Jamaica by Carlisle to serve as a 'new

361. ORDERS AND REPORT OF THE LORDS OF TRADE TO THE PRIVY COUNCIL,
    4 April 1679.[1]
    Whereas the right honorable the Lords of the Committee
for Trade and Plantations did this day make report unto
his Majesty in Council:
    That having in pursuance of his Majestye's order con-
sidered the present state and constitution of Jamaica and
the government thereof, as it is setled by his Majesty's
commission, their Lordships see noe reason why any alteration should bee made in the method of making laws, according to the usage of Ireland. For which their Lordships
are preparing reasons to evince the necessity and legality
of the same. And that whereas a ship is now lying in the
Downs bound for that island, their Lordships advise that
the right honorable Mr. Secretarie Coventry doe, by this
conveyance informe the Earle of Carlisle of his Majesty's
pleasure herein, with directions that all things bee disposed to this end. And that, in the mean time, the present laws enacted by the Lord Vaughan bee continued by
proclamation, or otherwise until his Majesty's pleasure
bee further known. As alsoe that his Lordship doe, by
the first conveyance, send over an authentic copie of the
Act for a public impost, lately enacted there, according
to his Lordship's instructions for matters of that nature.
    His Majesty having thought fit to approve thereof was
pleased to order, as it is hereby ordered, that the right
honorable Mr. Secretary Coventry doe signify his Majestie's pleasure unto the Earl of Carlisle, according to
the said report.

362. REPORT OF THE LORDS OF TRADE, 28 May 1679.[2]
    [They had reviewed the issues arising from the assembly's ref-
    usal to pass the draft bills brought to Jamaica by Governor Car-
    lisle. The previous permission to the Jamaican legislature to pass
    bills valid only for 2 years, if not approved within that time by
    the Crown, had proved too inconvenient and uncertain; so the Crown
    had accordingly preferred to send bills it had previously approved,
    for legislation by the assembly. The assembly had listed its objec-
    tions to this procedure. The lords of trade now stated their rep-
    lies.]

model' for the island's government. The Revenue bill was of course
crucial, and the assembly realising the threat to its existence, laboured to find excuses for rejecting all the other measures too. Carlisle soon despaired of the new proposed constitution; temporary laws,
he felt, were required 'till the colony bee better grown'.
1. C.O. 138/3 pp.284-5. The Lords' committee was opposed to concession
as Carlisle now advocated, and would accept no alteration in their new
frame of government. But they were uncertain whether to govern (as
in D'Oyley's commission) by governor and council, and so they permitted the governor to extend Vaughan's laws by proclamation.
2. C.O. 138/3 pp.294 ff. The Jamaican assembly had detailed their
objections to the draft bills, and to the threat of absolute government.

1. It is not without the greatest presumption that they goe about to question your Majesty's power over the militia in that island, since it has been allowed and declared, even by the laws of this your kingdom, that the sole supreme government, command and disposition of the militia and of all forces by sea and land, and of all forts and places of strength, is residing in your Majestie within all your Majesty's realms and dominions.

2. The objection made against the bill for the public revenue hath as little ground, since its being perpetual[1] is noe more than what was formerly offered by them unto your Majesty during the government of Sir Thomas Lynch, in the same measure and proportion as is now proposed:nor can it bee diverted[2] since provision is therby expressly made that the same shall bee for the better support of that government. Besides that it is not sutable to the duty and modesty of subjects to suspect your Majesty's justice or care for the government of that colony whose settlement and preservation has been most particularly carried on by your Majestie's tender regards and by the great expence of your own treasure.

3. It cannot, with any truth,bee said that these laws contain many and great errors, nothing having been done therein but in pursuance of former laws at divers times enacted by the Assembly, and with the advice of your Majesty's Privy Council, as well as the opinion and approbation of your Attorney General upon perusal of the same.

4. To the fourth objection, it may bee answered that if any thing had been found of moment or importance in the last parcel of laws transmitted by the Lord Vaughan, your Majesty's tender care of your subjects' welfare would have been such as not to have sent those bills imperfect or defective in any necessary matter.

5. As to the distance of the place which renders, as they say, the present method of making laws altogether impracticable, your Majesty having been pleased to regulate the same by advice of your Privy Council according to the usage of Ireland, such care was then taken as that noe law might bee wanting which might conduce to the welbeing of the plantations, and that nothing might bee omitted which in all former governments had been thought necessary. Nor is it likely that this colony is subject to greater accidents than your kingdom of Ireland, soe as to require a more frequent and sudden change of laws in other cases than such as are already provided for upon emergencies or in other manner than is directed by your Majestie's commission; whereby the inhabitants have free access to make complaints to your governor and council of

---

1. i.e. without any explicit time limit. This was the 1672 Act.
2. The assembly had assumed that revenues would be 'diverted' to the Crown's use in England.

any defect in any old law, or to give reasons for any new
one, which being modelled by the governor and council into
form of law and transmitted unto your Majesty, if by your
Majesty and council found reasonable, may bee transmitted
back thither too bee enacted accordingly.

6. It was sufficiently apparent unto your Majesty that
laws must alter with the interest of the place, when you
were graciously pleased to lodge such power in that government as might not only from time to time with your Majestie's approbation and by advice both of your Privy Council here and of the governor and council there *[to]* enable
the Assembly to enact new laws answerable to their growing
necessities; but even, upon urgent occasions, to provide
by raising money for the security of the island, without
attending your Majesty's orders or consent.

7. It is not to bee doubted but the Assembly have end-
eavord to grasp all power as well as that of a deliberative voice in making laws; but how far they have thereby
intrenched upon your Majesty's prerogative and exceeded
the bounds of their duty and loyalty, upon this pretence,
may appear by their late exorbitant and unwarrantable
proceedings, during the government of the Lord Vaughan,
in ordering and signing a warrant unto the Marshal of the
Island your Majestie's officer of justice, for the stop-
ping and preventing the execution of a sentence, passed
according to the ordinary forms of law, upon a notorious
pirat and disturber of your Majestie's peace.[1] And they
have farther taken upon them, by vertue of this deliberative power, to make laws contrary to those of England,
and to imprison your Majestie's subjects. Nor have they
forborn to raise money by publick acts, and to dispose
of the same according to their will and pleasure, without
any mention made of your Majesty, which has never in like
case been practiced in any of your Majesty's kingdoms.
How far therefore it is fit to intrust them with a power
which they have thus abused and to which they have noe
pretension of right, was the subject of your Majestie's
royal consideration when you were pleased to put a restraint upon these enormities, and to take the reins of
government into your own hands, which they in express
words, against their duty and allegiance, have challenged
and refused to part with.

8. It cannot, with any truth, bee supposed that, by the
present form of government, the governor is rendred absolute, since hee is now more than ever become accountable
unto your Majesty of all his most important deliberations
and actions; and is not warranted to doe any thing but
according to law and your Majesty's comission and instructions given by advice of your Privy Council.

9. And whether your Majestie's prerogative is prejudiced

---

1. A reference to the case of James Browne in July 1677 when the
assembly had presumed to challenge the governor and council as a
court of revision.

by the present constitution, is more the concernment of
your Majesty and subject of your own care than of their
consideration.

Lastly, and in the general, wee humbly conceive, that
it would bee a great satisfaction to your subjects there
inhabiting and an invitation to strangers, when they shall
know what laws they are to bee governed by, and a great
ease to the planters not to bee continually obliged to
attend the Assembly to re-inact old laws which his Majesty
has now thought fit, in a proper form,to ascertain and
establish: whereas the late power of making temporary laws
could bee understood to bee of noe longer continuance than
until such wholsom laws, founded upon soe many years experience, should bee agreed on by the people and finaly enacted by your Majesty in such manner as hath been practised
in other of your Majesty's dominions, to which your English
subjects have transplanted themselves. For as they cannot
pretend to farther privileges than have baen granted to
them either by charter or some solemn act under your great
seale: soe having, from the first beginning of that plantation, been governed by such instructions as were given
by your Majesty unto your governor, according to the power
your Majestie had originaly over them and which you have
by noe one authentic act ever yet parted with; and having
never had any other right to assemblys than from the permission of the governors and that only temporary and for
probation, it is to bee wondred how they should presume to
provoke your Majesty by pretending a right to that which
hath been allowed them meerly out of favor, and discourage
your Majesty from future favors of that kind; when what
your Majesty ordered for a temporary experiment, to see
what form would best sute with the safety and interest of
the island, shall be construed to bee a total resignation
of the power inherent in your Majesty and a devolution of
it to themselves and their wills without which neither law
nor government, the essential incidents of their subsistance and wel-being, may take place among them....

Wee can only offer, as a cure for irregularities past
and a remedy against all farther inconveniences, that your
Majesty would please to authorize and impower your governor
to call another assembly and to represent unto them the
great convenience and expediency of accepting and consenting unto such laws as your Majesty has, under your great
seale, transmitted unto them. And that, in case of refusal,
his Lordship bee furnisht with such powers as were formerly
given unto Colonel Doyley,your first governor of Jamaica,
and since unto other governors,whereby his Lordship may
bee enabled to govern according to the laws of England,
where the different nature and constitution of that colony
may conveniently permit the same; and, in other cases, to
act with the advice of the council in such manner as shall
bee held necessary and proper for the good government of
that plantation, until your Majesty's farther orders[1]....

1. Once more the lords of trade contemplated a return to government

363. HENRY COVENTRY TO GOVERNOR LORD CARLISLE, 2 June 1679.[1]
...I heartily wish you will persuade them to accept
His Majesty's proposall, and not think the freedome of
Englishmen to be violated in being Governed in the same
manner that all His Majesty's English Subjects that are
in Ireland are, whose Estates and qualities are without
doubt much superior to any in Jamaica, and without doubt
are, and that reasonaly soe, as carefull to conserve
their liberty's as any in Jamaica can....

364. (a) GOVERNOR LORD CARLISLE'S SPEECH TO THE ASSEMBLY,
20 August 1679.[2]
...That when he issued out the writts for the Calling
of this Assembly he was in hopes he should have more for
them to doe, supposing by this time he might have received
advice from England, but hitherto he had only received a
letter from the councell of trade in which they signified
to him that they had received the address of the last Assembly but still were of opinion that the Modell of Ireland
was most fitt for this place and were providing reasons
to convince us[3] thereof: That now he had only two things
to propose to us; the one was the Continuing the act of
revenue which he desired might be made for eaighteen months, Because he had sent Sir Francess Wattson[4] into England to negotiate for us the antient form of makeing laws
and expected he would returne hither by Crissmas...and
that if Sir Francess could not effect it he would goe home
himselfe in March and endeavour it and hoped to be here
againe before the Eighteen months were out, soe that then
there would be no cause for calling an Assembly in his
absence....[5]

364. (b) RESOLUTION OF THE ASSEMBLY ON MONEY BILLS, 25 August 1679.[6]
The House, considering the return of the Committee

by governor and council and by royal instructions, if a new assembly
still refused to accept Carlisle's body of laws.
1.C.O. 389/6 p.298. Coventry was secretary of state for the southern
department from 1674 to 1680: previously he was at the northern dept.
2.C.O. 139/1 p.216. Carlisle had felt compelled, with the expiration of
the Impost Act, to call an assembly on his own initiative without
prior approval of the Crown.
3. Carlisle was now identifying himself with Jamaican grievances and
was advocating a return to the previous method of legislation.
4. Sir Francis Watson was lieutenant-governor.
5. Carlisle reported that the assembly was 'nettled and warm'. But
after prorogation he hoped that 'they would fall off of their heat'.
Nevertheless, they would 'never consent to make chains, as they terme
this frame of government, to their posterityes': 15 September 1679:
C.O. 1/43, 138/3.
5. Journ. Jam. Ass. I p.45. A committee of the assembly had been instructed to scrutinise the account books of Thomas Martyn, the receiver
general, a royal patentee. A message from the king and governor on
22 August had informed them that he was not obliged to show them to

ordered to inspect Mr. Martyn's accounts...did vote *nemine contradicente* That notwithstanding my Lord's answer...it was and is their undoubted and inherent right that as all bills for money ought and do arise in this House,[1] so they ought to appoint the disposal of it and to receive and examine all the accounts concerning the same.

365. (a) HUMBLE ADDRESS BY THE ASSEMBLY TO GOVERNOR LORD CARLISLE,
14 November 1679.[2]
    We, His Majesty's most loyal and obedient subjects... cannot without infinite grief of mind read the report made to His Majesty by the right honourable the Lords of the Committee for Trade and plantations wherein...they have represented us a people full of animosity-unreasonable, irregular, violent and undutyful ....
    [Since the establishment of civil government in Modyford's governorship, the island had been prosperous and loyal. Jamaican militia Acts intended no diminution of the king's prerogative.For the absence of reference to 'the King' in their revenue Acts, both governor and council must share responsibility, for both had 'negative voices' and failed to use them: the inclusion of 'the governor' in place of 'the King' was a Jamaican variant of the English parliamentary form. There had been no time limit in the Revenue Act passed during Lynch's governorship because by his instructions laws were not to be in force for more than two years. In the body of laws proposed by their lordships nothing whatever was stated about the use of English laws, civil or criminal, and this therefore left to the governor an unfettered, and intolerable, discretion.]
    And whereas their Lordships say we cannot be subject to more accidents than His Majesty's kingdom of Ireland: to that we object, That advice and answers thence may be had in ten or fourteen days and that kingdom is already settled, our plantation but beginning; but further, we

---

the assembly. When Martyn had received his patent from the king four years before, the assembly had appointed its own collector to secure their own control of revenues and he had become involved with the assembly in an attempt to assert his authority. Later, however, when in May 1680 William Blathwayt, the secretary to the lords of trade, was made inspector and auditor general of all colonial revenues,Martyn's lethargy and incompetence brought him into conflict with Blathwayt and Governor Lynch over the provision of his accounts and the collection of quit rents.
1. Cf. C.J. IX. 509 (3 July 1678) when the house of commons had asserted their right to determine aids and supplies granted to the Crown, the Lords being denied as in 1671 (C.J. IX.235) the right to amend money bills.
2. Journ. Jam. Ass. I pp. 52-3. (The date is given as 23 November 1679 in C.O. 1/43 No.157 II p.281.) The assembly had not 'fallen off of their heat', and, returning after prorogation, had once again rejected all the body of laws which Carlisle had brought

cannot imagine that Irish model of government was *in principio* ever intended for Englishmen ....

[Anyway Poynings' law was a law made by the Irish parliament itself for 'the preservation of the English against the Irish faction'.]

And there is not the same cause, so there is not the same reason, for imposing the same on us, unless we, as they did, do it ourselves who are all his Majesty's natural-born subjects of his kingdom of England which is the reason the Parliament gave, in all Acts concerning the plantations, for obliging us by them to which, and with whom, and in what manner we may trade and impose a tax on us here, in case of trade from one colony to another; and it is but equity then that the same law should have the same power of loosing as binding ....

[They never desired any power but what governors had assured them was 'their birthright'. They claim that they have been told that they have the rights of English subjects to English laws,'the authority to determine what will or will not benefit them, and the same power over their members as the Commons have.'Martyn, a member of the assembly, had instituted action in chancery against members of the council and assembly: in exercise of their jurisdiction over members they had imprisoned him. Their action over James Browne, they are prepared to admit, on reflection, was 'not justifiable', but they had acted in good faith. Planters, they declared, had been encouraged to come to Jamaica by guarantees made by Lord Windsor of 'the old model of government which was ordered so like his Majesty's Kingdom of England'[1].]

And whereas their Lordships are pleased to offer their advice to His Majesty to furnish his governor with such powers as were formerly given to Colonel D'Oyley and others in whose time the then accounted army was not disbanded, but so continued till Lord Windsor's arrival who brought over the King's royal donative[2] and order to settle civil government: We hope their Lordships intend not that we are to be governed by or as an army, or that the governor be empowered to levy any tax by himself and council: since His Majesty, having discharged himself and his Council by an Act of Parliament of any such power over any of his subjects of his kingdom of England as we undoubtedly are,[3] it will be very hard to have any imposition on us but by our own consents; for their Lordships will know that no derived power is greater than the primitive....

[If nevertheless the king insists upon the new model of government, they will submit only in the hope of an early return to the 'ancient' form.]

---

1. Of course no such guarantee had been given. 2. Gift, bounty.
3. Presumably a reference to the Petition of Right from both Houses on 7 June 1628: 'your subjects have inherited this freedom That they should not be compelled to contribute to any tax...not set by common consent in Parliament'. There was some doubt whether this was virtually a statute, as also whether it extended overseas.

365. (b) THE HUMBLE DESIRE AND JUSTIFICATION OF THE COUNCIL TO GOV-
       ERNOR LORD CARLISLE, 23 November 1679.[1]
   ...all though Your Majesty's perspicacitie and truely
Royall prudence is best able to determine what Government
is the fittest for your Subjects in this Island, yet withall due Summission, in all humility, Wee begg leave to
reprisent to your Majesty the great inconvenience attending the present Frame in transmitting our lawes home.
   The vast distance will of necessity require a great
Expence of time between the first framing our Lawes here,
and the transmitting and returne of them hither againe,
so that before they can bee passed into Lawes by the Consent of the Assembly here, there will probably, as great
cause arise to alter, as there was att first to make them.
   And withall due submission, Wee judge it even impossible to adapt Lawes to the present constitution, so, as
not to admitt of often, and great Alterations; for according to our Experience hitherto, Wee have found urgent
occasions to Alter, and Amend the Lawes, that have more
immediately concerned us here, att the least every two
yeares: and Wee canot forsee but wee shall lye under the
same necessity still; so that if Your Majesty graciously
please to take it into your Princely consideration, and
either restore to us our former power, and way, or method
of passing Lawes, or att least, remitt that part of the
present method of makeing Lawes, which onely concerne us
here, as they may pass without transmitting the same, Wee
hope by our present Submission and intire obedience to all
your Lawes here, Your Majesty wilbee a Glorious Prince
and your Subjects here a happy people....
     [The council repudiated responsibility for omission of the king's
     name in the Revenue Acts, and also denied complaining to the ass-
     embly of the governor's power, under royal authority, to suspend
     a councillor.]

366. (a) LORD VAUGHAN: ACCOUNT OF THE GOVERNMENT, December 1679.[2]
     [Jamaica differed from other colonies in that it had no privil-
     eges granted to the settlers by letters patent. There was no civil
     government until the Restoration when D'Oyley's commission permit-
     ted him to call a council chosen by the people. The first assembly
     was summoned by Lyttelton, as Windsor's deputy in 1661, and enacted
     a revenue law 'wherein the collection, disposal and accounting was
     appointed by the assembly which raised it'.]
   ...Sir Thomas Modiford succeeded,haveing a comission
differing somewhat from my Lord Windsor's, and had a coun-

_____

1. C.O. 1/43 No.157; C.O. 138/3 p.369. Carlisle enclosed this justification in his dispatch to the lords of trade on 23 November 1679.
The arguments derived largely from the Jamaican chief justice.
2. C.O. 1/43 No.175.Vaughan had been asked by Blathwayt on 15 December
to provide the privy council with an account of 'the rights,privil-
eges and usages' claimed by the Jamaicans in relation to their laws
and methods of government, particularly in the disposal of revenues.
He and Lynch attended the Lords' committee on 22 December to answer
questions.

cil named by his Majestie in the comission (most of them
the same persons whom my Lord Windsor had chosen to be
the council by virtue of his comission). Sir Thomas Modyford called an assembly and passed several lawes (among
which one of revenue) the lawes he made were much after
the manner of those he had lived under in Barbados; by
his instructions they were not to continue longer than
two years; however the two yeares expireing he did not
call another assembly but continued the same lawes five
yeares longer by an order onely of the council (there).[1]
    Next to him was Sir Thomas Lynch[2] made lieutenant gov-
ernor who had no comission under the great seale, but had
his authority and instructions under the King's signe
manual onely. He called two assemblyes and passed lawes
in both of revenue and others in like manner as before
and since.
    To whom I succeeded as governor with the like instruct-
ions save only with this difference in my comission, that
whereas the lawes passed by other governors, were to continue two yeares and no longer unlesse confirmed by his
Majestie, the lawes passed by me were to continue two
yeares unlesse his Majestie signified his pleasure to the
contrary. I called an assembly and passed all the lawes
which were offered by them and the council, among which
one of revenue, with an account to be given, which I did
not stick at, 1st because it was given only to defray the
charge of the island, 2ly because my predecessors had allwayes passed those bills in that forme, and 3ly in my instructions (number 25) his Majestie disallow[ed] that no
custome should be layd upon any goods there for 14 yeares
to be accounted from 1670, so what was raised by them in
the meane time was to be applyed to their owne benefit and
publick uses. After two yeares I called a second assembly
and, tho' I had no formal or publick notice that his Majestie did not like the forme of the revenue bill, but haveing private intimation to that purpose, I did passe all
the lawes tendred to me, save only that of revenue, to my
owne greate losse; for I never did nor shall feare any
losse so much as that of his Majestie's favor.... [He had
sent accounts and copies of the laws to England.]
    When I was there the general sense of the island seemed
to be that it was their right, at least it was their desire to be continued under the forme of passing lawes by
the governor, council and assembly (like the Parliament of
England); that the council and assembly should have a deliberative and a negative too upon each other, and the governor a negative upon both; and revenue bills to begin in

---

1. He came to the conclusion that he could govern better without any
assembly, and virtually claimed to have imposed a Poynings' procedure
on Jamaica since no one but he could frame a law.
2. As president of the Jamaican council he had acted as governor when
Lyttelton followed Windsor to England on learning that Modyford had
been appointed to Jamaica.

the assembly, who called themselves the representatives
of the island, and were so called in my comission.
   As to the matter at present under consideration; what
the assembly there doe clayme, appeares by their last addresse to my Lord of Carlisle, but what rights they or any
other Englishmen may lawfully clayme to have in places
acquired by conquest, or in any other their forreign plantations, are matters of law and of state, too high for
me to presume to give my opinion in, and are most proper
for your Lordships' greate judgment.

366. (b) REPORT BY SIR THOMAS LYNCH TO THE LORDS OF TRADE,
                                    18 December 1679.[1]
   [Lynch gave an account of the government of Jamaica in the period from 1661 until the arrival of Carlisle with his new frame of
government. He pointed out that there was, contrary to the Lords'
assertion, no precedent for a Revenue Act without a limitation of
time: his revenue act in 1672 had in fact been really for 2 years
only; it was only because that bill had neither been confirmed nor
disallowed that the assembly had been able to renew it every two
years since, until Vaughan had finally vetoed it. Now there was
no Revenue Act at all.
   Two years previously Carlisle 'was sent as governor with Lord
Vaughan's first laws and an Act for a perpetual revenue on the
English model, which Act (as I have heard) was not to be examined
by the Jamaican Council but passed by the Assembly entirely'. This
frame of government 'after the manner of Ireland' was found grievous and inconvenient. The king nevertheless had refused to change
his mind. The assembly, Lynch was convinced,would never allow any
of the laws approved by the lords of trade to pass.]
   I hear also in discourse that they will not give their
consent to Acts which they have not debated, their reason,
so far as I can gather, being :- 1. That, being English,
they think they have a right to be governed as such, and
to have their liberties and properties secured by the laws
of England, or others of their own making. 2. They believe
that the King, in the proclamation brought over by Lord
Windsor, [1661][2]granted them freedom, denizenation, and
encouragement to transplant. 3. The King has declared by
his several commissions that they shall be so governed,
which commissions are recorded, and the people have for
16 or 17 years been governed by the laws of England and
of their own making. 4. All other colonies have, and always have had, Assemblies and power to originate laws. 5.
The Irish system is tedious from the distance between Jamaica and England, and the frequent changes of local inter-

---

1.C.O. 1/43;C.S.P. (Col.) 1677-80. No.1234. Lynch had been asked by the
committee to advise them. He had served in Jamaica under D'Oyley, was
appointed provost-marshal for life, served on Lyttelton's council,
was dismissed by Modyford,and had been lieutenant-governor from 1670
to 1674.
2.It seems that the Lord's committee had overlooked this proclamation
till Lynch reminded them that it had granted a conquered colony some
of the privileges of settlement.

est. 6. The Irish system (they say) was desired by the
English to support them against the Irish, but in Jamaica
they are all English. 7. They fear the rumours of such a
change may drive settlers and trade from the Island. 8. If
Assemblies have been constituted in all other colonies
from their first settlement as a government most like that
of England, they hope that an exception may not be made
in their prejudice. If particular people have offended,
let them suffer and not the colony. 9. They hope the King
will consider that his interests and those of trade are
bound up with theirs, for the burden of improvement and
defence lies on the planters, and agreeable laws will make
them bear it. *Further considerations*. The Assembly will
probably reject the laws offered to them, yet the need
for revenue is urgent; the Council may join the Governor
to order the laws to be continued, but I verily believe
that they will not continue the Revenue Bill, for they
think that belongs to the Assembly.[1] If they do it, it
will not be without process, and I doubt the judges would
quit and the juries give constantly against the officers.[2]
It would be the same, or worse, if an order to that effect
were sent from England, and it would give strange umbrage
to the rest of the colonies, which are too much discouraged already by low prices and French competition.

366. (c) MINUTE OF THE LORDS OF TRADE, 22 December 1679.[3]
    Their Lordships, taking notice that the Assembly of
Jamaica have refused to pass an Act for Ordering the Militia transmitted by His Majesty, fearing lest thereby they
might make it lawfull for the Governor to execute whatsoever Instructions might be sent him, Are of opinion That
Mr. Attorney Generall be desired to alter the last Clause
in that Act, so that it may not seem to give any greater
Powers than are allowed by that Act or are belonging unto
His Majesty by the Laws of England.
    And whereas there is another law made in Jamaica where-
by all Ships arriving there are obliged to pay a certain
proportion of Powder per Tun according to the antient usage of The Plantations, Mr. Attorney is further desired
to examine and report to The Committee whether There be
any law in England which may hinder the levying the said
proportion of Powder pursuant to Acts made in the Plantations.
    The Clause in the Act of Militia is as followeth,

---

1. i.e. the council would not agree to continue the Revenue Act by
proclamation.
2. i.e. such an Act could not be implemented for the Jamaican courts
would refuse to decide in favour of the collectors of revenue.
3. C.O. 1/43 No.176. The Lords' committee seemed prepared at last to
pay attention to those who urged some compromise. They had heard Sir
Frances Watson and now asked the attorney general to consider amending the clause in Carlisle's draft Militia bill to which the Jamaican assembly had objected as giving the governor absolute powers.

Provided always, and 'tis hereby further enacted and
declared by the authority aforesaid That nothing in this
Act contained be expanded, construed, or understood to
diminish, alter, or abridge the power of the Governor or
Commander in Chief for the time being...but that[1] *he may
upon all occasions or exergencies act as Captain Generall
and Governor in Chief* according to, and in pursuance of
*all the powers and authorities given unto him by his Maj-
esty's Commission*, any thing in this Act, *or any other*
to the contrary in any wise notwithstanding.

366. (d) THE LORDS OF TRADE TO THE LAW OFFICERS, 11 March 1680.[2]
    The right honorable the Lords of the Committee for
Trade and Plantations, upon consideration of the affaires
of Jamaica, have stated the questions following viz:
    1. Whether, from the past and present state of Jamaica,
his Majesty's subjects inhabiting and trading there have
right to the laws of England as Englishmen, or [either] by
vertue of the King's proclamation or otherwise.
    2. Whether his Majesty's subjects of Jamaica claiming
to bee governed by the laws of England are not bound as
well by such laws as are beneficial to the king by appointing taxes and subsidies for the support of the government,
as by other laws which tend only to the benefit and ease
of the subject.
    3. Whether the subsidies of tonnage and poundage upon
goods, that may, by law, or shall bee directly carried
to Jamaica bee not payable according to law by his Majesty's subjects inhabiting that island or trading there
by vertue of the Acts made in England.[3]
    4. Whether wine or other goods once brought into Eng-
land and transported from there upon which the respective
abatements are allowed upon exportation according to law,
the same being afterwards carried to Jamaica and landed
there shall not bee lyable to the payment of the full duty
of tonnage and poundage, which it should have paid if consumed in England, deducting only such part of the said
duty as shall not be repaid in England upon exportation
of the said goods from thence.

---

1. There is an alternative inserted here in the minute: 'in all things
and upon all occasions he may act as fully and freely as Captain Generall or Chiefe Governor to all intents and purposes as if this Act
had never been had or made'.
2. C.O. 138/3 p.376. Their secretary, William Blathwayt, sent these
questions to the law officers desiring their answers. Jamaican merchants had given evidence of the uncertainties and discontents pre-
vailing as a result of the constitutional crisis, and news of the second refusal of Carlisle's draft laws by the assembly had now arrived.
3. The lords of trade were considering using the Jamaican claim to
the laws of England against the assembly. The English statutes might
provide for a revenue from Jamaica without the consent of the assembly [e.g. No.12]. Sir Creswell Levinz (who later applied for a
quo warranto writ against the Bermuda Company [see p.440]) was attorney general, and Heneage Finch, son of the L.C., was solicitor-general.

366. (e) ANSWERS OF THE LAW OFFICERS TO THE LORDS OF TRADE,
27 April 1680.[1]

Having reported that the four questions submitted to them respecting Jamaica were of such difficulty as to deserve the opinion of the judges, Mr Attorney delivered his opinion that the People of Jamaica have noe right to bee governed by the Laws of England, but by such Laws as are made there and established by his Majesty's authority. But whereas Mr Sollicitor General doth deliver his opinion that the word *Dominion* in the Act of Parliament for Tunnage and Poundage may seem rather to imply the Dominion of Wales and Berwick upon Twede only, than to extend to the Plantations, and more especially, as Mr Attorney alleges, since the Islands of Guernsey and Jersey are not concerned in that Act;[2] their Lordships order the two first Questions only to bee sent unto the Judges,[3] without any mention to bee made of the two last, which particularize the Act of Tunnage and Poundage.

366. (f) ORDER IN COUNCIL, 23 June 1680.[4]

[The law officers were directed to confer with the judges on the following question and to report back to the Lords' committee.]

Whether, by His Majesty's Letter, Proclamation,or Commissions annexed, His Majesty hath excluded himself from the power of establishing Laws in Jamaica, it being a conquered Country and all Laws setled by authority there, being now expired.

366. (g) THE ADVICE AND MEDIATION OF CHIEF JUSTICE NORTH,
14 - 27 October 1680.[5]

14 October

The Earl of Carlisle attends and produces an entry in the Council Book of Jamaica of a law passed by Sir Charles Littleton and the Council, being a supplemental Act to the former, both which are indefinite and not determined by the commissions of Colonel Doyley or my Lord Windsor, whose deputy Sir Charles Littleton was.

After which Colonel Long[6] and Mr. Ashurst are called in

---

1. C.O. 391/3 p.167: C.S.P. (Col.) 1677-80 No.1347.The replies of the law officers were somewhat evasive. The 'laws of England' was so vague a phrase.
2. See above Nos.12, 252 and p.197.
3. i.e. the judges were to be asked the questions relating to the laws of England.
4. C.O. 138/3 p.382.This question whether the Crown could continue to legislate for Jamaica after previous proclamation and commissions was substantially the same as that in *Campbell v. Hall* 1774 [see Volume III].
5.C.O. 391/3 p.214 ff.extract from the journal of the Lords of the committee for trade.Charles II was present on this occasion.Carlisle had returned to England without formal permission of the committee, both to present the Jamaican case and to bring charges against Long and Beeston for impeding royal government in the island. 6. Long had

(the other gentlemen of Jamaica being in the country) and
being asked why they are not willing that a perpetual bill
of revenue should pass in Jamaica; they make answer that
have noe other way to make their aggreivances known to the
King and to have them redressed than by the dependence
of the governor on the assembly which is preserved by
passing temporary bills of revenue: and that a perpetual
bill being passed, all the ends of the government would
bee answered and there would bee no further need of calling
assemblys; to which my Lord of Carlisle replys that notwithstanding an Act for raising an impost on liquors
should be passed in that manner, yet the necessitys and
contingencies of the government are such as to require
the frequent calling of assemblys for raising money by
other means and doing publick words, the present revenue
coming far short of the expence of the government.[1]

   Their Lordships tell Colonel Long that in case they
bee willing to pass the act of revenue indefinitely, the
King may bee induced to settle other perpetual[2] laws which
they shall propose as beneficial to them...,

   [The Lords then debated the issue. 'It is there alleged that
   the laws of England cannot bee in force in another country where
   the constitution of the place is different from that of England'.
   The Lords decided to ask North (C.J.)'s opinion on two questions:]

   1. Whether the King by His proclamation published during my Lord Windsor's government,[3] his Majesty's letter
dated the 15th of January 1673, or any other Act appearing
by the laws of England or any law of Jamaica or by his
Majesty's commission or instructions to his governors,
has divested himself of the power hee formerly had to alter the forms of government in Jamaica?

   2. Whether any Act of the assembly of Jamaica or any
other Act of his Majesty or his governors have totally
repealed the Acts made by Colonel Doyley and Sir Charles
Littleton for raising a publick revenue; or whether they
are now in force.

   20 October

   His Lordship *[North]* concluded that the Act of Revenue
made in 1663 by Sir Charles Littleton is yet in force, as
being not repealed by any subsequent Act which were limited to the term of two years by his Majesty's commissions....[4]

---

been brought over as state prisoner. He was now being treated as a
spokesman and negotiator.
1.i.e. the revenues from the liquor duties would not be sufficient
to meet government expences.
2. If the assembly passed an 'indefinite' revenue act, the king might
confirm other acts 'indefinitely' too.
3. The Lords' opinion was that Windsor's proclamation concerned the
settlement not of government, but of property in Jamaica.
4. North's answer, if any, to the first question was not recorded
in the journal.

[Colonel Long then objected that (a) Modyford's assembly made
void all Lyttelton's Acts, (b) that by Windsor's instructions legislation was limited to two years only unless confirmed by the
king,which had not been done before Modyford assumed the government, (c) that none of the laws made by D'Oylev or Lyttelton and
their councils were 'now in force since they had no express power
to make laws by their councils' and (d) that 'thev as Enalishmen
ought not to be bound by any laws to which they had not given
their consent'.[1] The Lords decided to refer these arguments to
North.[2]]

21 October
[The king's proclamation in Lord Windsor's time being read,
these questions arose:]
1. Whether upon the consideration of the commission and
instructions to Coloney Doyley and Sir Charles Littleton
and the constitution of the island thereupon, the acts of
council made by Colonel Doyley and Sir Charles Littleton
were perpetual laws binding to the inhabitants of the island.
2. Whether, supposing those laws good and perpetual,
any of the subsequent laws or the proclamation in my Lord
Windsor's time have taken away the force of those laws....
[The 'gentlemen of Jamaica', Beeston and Ashurst, were instructed to meet and consult with North to explain their 'chief wants
to him whereby they may be inclined to pass an Act for the revenue
to the end that matters may be brought to an accommodation'.][3]

27 October
My Lord Chief Justice North reports that hee has been
attended by the gentlemen of Jamaica who have declared
themselves willing to grant the king a perpetual bill for
the payment of the governors,and another bill for the payment of contingencies to continue for seaven yeares. Provided they may bee restored to their ancient form of passing laws and may be assured of such of the laws of England
as may concern their liberty and property.[4]

336. (h) THE COMPROMISE BETWEEN THE CROWN AND THE ASSEMBLY,
                    28 October - 1 November 1680.[5]
28 October
...Having considered...the letter from the Council of

1.The council in D'Oyley's time was 'elected' and presumably representative,and its laws were just as much 'consented to' as any subsequent acts, revenue or otherwise.
2. Blathwayt sent these objections to the chief justice the same day.
3.At this point it is clear that the Lords' committee were persuaded
that they must give way because they could not get firm legal justification for the Crown's introduction of the new frame of government. Where they had a stronger legal case as in Massachusetts, they
were still prepared to challenge a much more formidable and wayward
dependency - and to revoke its charter.
4.On the same day Long presented a Jamaican petition to the king,which
alleged that the Carlisle commission had brought a 'fatal stop' to the
island's prosperity,and that planters were leaving.They asked for a
restoration of 'the ancient form of government'.
5. C.O. 391/3 pp.222 ff:extract from the journal of the lords of trade.

Jamaica dated 20 May last...and having read the petition of the merchants and planters of Jamaica presented to Council...as alsoe a paper prepared by Mr Blathwayt concerning the manner of making laws in Jamaica, their Lordships upon full consideration and debate of what may best conduce to his Majesty's service, agree That the present method of making laws in Barbados as settled by the commission of Sir Richard Dutton bee proposed unto His Majesty in Council[1] and that powers bee drawn up for the Earl of Carlisle with instructions suitable to that scheme and with respect to the present circumstances of Jamaica.

...And that the assembly may bee the more easily induced to grant a revenue for the support of the government,their Lordships are of the opinion that his Majesty's quit-rents and the tax on wine licenses as well as all other levys which now are, or shall bee made bee appropriated to the support of the government and to noe other use whatsoever.

30 October
...Colonel Long and the other gentlemen of Jamaica attend and are acquainted with the resolutions of the committee to report to his Majesty that they may enjoy the same method of making laws as is now appointed for Barbados, with which the gentlemen express themselves very well satisfied.

1 November
...Colonel Long and the other gentlemen of Jamaica attend and are asked their opinion whether, in consideration of his Majesty's favor to the assembly of Jamaica in restoring to them the deliberative voice, they will not bee ready to grant his Majesty a perpetual bill of revenue, especially since his Majesty thinks fit to appropriate his quit-rents with the rest of the revenue to the support of the government. To which the gentlemen answer That they doe not believe that the assembly will grant the revenue for a longer time than seaven years: but that they may bee willing to grant soe much as will defray the governor's salary perpetual, and the rest for seaven years....

Their Lordships...are of opinion that the governor bee instructed to endeavor the passing the revenue bill perpetual, and if hee cannot obtain it indefinite, that then hee pass it for the longest term hee can, not under seaven years.

366. (i) POWERS GIVEN TO GOVERNOR LORD CARLISLE FOR LEGISLATION, 3 November 1680.[2]
...And whereas it is necessary that good and wholesome

1.This formula disguised the fact that Jamaica recovered its former constitution.In Dutton's commission on 22 October the king no longer directly named the councillors;assemblies might examine accounts; and laws could not specify any duration for their validity.
2.C.O. 138/3 pp.445-7. In restoring the ancient form of constitution, the king reserved the right of disallowance and the governor retained a veto.

Laws and Ordinances bee setled and established for the Government and support of Our Island of Jamaica; We doe hereby give and grant unto you full power and authority, with
the advice and consent of the said Council from time to
time as need shall require to summon or call General Assemblys of the ffreeholders and planters within the said
Island after the manner and form as is now practiced in
Jamaica. And Our Will and Pleasure is That the persons
thereupon duly elected by the major part of the ffreeholders of the respective parishes and places and soe returned (and having before their sitting taken the Oaths of
Allegiance and Supremacy which you shall Commissionate
fit persons under the Publick Seal of that Island to administer...) shall bee called and held the General Assembly of Our Island of Jamaica. And That they or the major
part of them shall have full power and authority, with
the advice and consent of your selfe and of the Council,[1]
to make, constitute and ordain Laws, Statutes, and Ordinances for the publick peace, Welfare, and good Government
of the said Island and of the people and Inhabitants thereof and such others as shall resort thereto, and for the
benefit of Us, Our heirs and Successors, Which said Laws,
Statutes, and Ordinances are to bee (as neer as conveniently may bee) agreeable unto the Laws and Statutes of
Our Kingdom of England: *Provided* that all such Laws,
Statutes and Ordinances of what nature and duration soever bee within three months or by the first conveyance
after the making of the same, transmitted unto Us under
the Publick Seale for Our allowance and approbation of
them...in case all or any of them shall at any time bee
disallowed and not approved and soe signified by Us, Our
heirs or Successors under Our or their Signe Manual and
Signet or by order of Our or their Privy Council unto you
the said Charles Earle of Carlisle, or to the Commander
in cheif of Our said Island for the time being, then such
...shall from thenceforth cease, determine and bee utterly
void and of none effect...Wee will and ordain that you the
said Charls Earle of Carlisle, shall have and enjoy a Negative Voice in the making or passing of all Laws, Statutes,
and Ordinances as aforesaid....[2]

---

1. The enacting style of legislation was therefore to be 'By governor,
council and assembly' and the Revenue and Militia Acts had been amended by this formula the previous day.
2. His new instructions required Carlisle to secure a revenue bill.
This was the first request he was to put to an assembly: he was to
persuade them how necessary it was to secure a permanent supply for
the support of government. The Crown would agree to assign its quit
rents to that purpose 'and to no other use whatsoever'. A private
instruction of the same date reemphasised the need for a revenue bill,
perpetual if possible - certainly not for less than seven years.
Thereafter he should avoid summoning an assembly until the Act expired.
Certain draft bills relating to courts and the administration of justice which Culpeper took with him were not to be enacted if the assembly refused at least the seven year revenue act. 'And you are in

367. INSTRUCTIONS TO GOVERNOR LYNCH, 8 September 1681.[1]
   [He was empowered to appoint and suspend his councillors.]
   ...9.And, in the choice of members of the said council
as alsoe of the great officers, judges, assistants,just-
ices and sherifs, you are always to take care that they
bee men of good life, and well affected to the government,
of good estates and abilities and not necessitous people
or much in debt.
   10. And our will and pleasure is that you doe neither
augment nor diminish the number of our said council as it
is hereby established, nor suspend any of the present members thereof without good and sufficient cause. And in
case of suspension of any of them, you are forthwith to
transmit unto us and to the Lords of our Privy Council
appointed a Committee for Trade and Plantations the reasons for your soe doing, together with the charges and
proofs against the said persons and their answer thereunto....
   [If councillors were absent without leave for two years, their
   places were to be void.[2] Councillors' names were to be sent to
   England.]
   13. You shall with all convenient speed after your
arrival, call a General Assembly and, at their meeting,
signify unto them our royal care and provision for their
good government by appointing them such a method for the
framing of laws as may be conducive to our service and
acceptable unto them. And you are thereupon to proceed to
the passing good and wholesom laws in such manner as by
the said powers you are directed.
   14. And, in the first place, you are to give them to
understand how necessary it is for their welfare and prosperity that a publick revenue bee raised for the support
of the government.[3] And you are to endeavor (by the best

_____

convenient time to insinuate our directions herein unto some members
of the assembly' to persuade them of the need of such compliance.
No money was to be issued save on his warrant: no law enacted could
be re-enacted without express consent of the Crown.The Jamaicans might
suppose that they had successfully asserted their liberties against
the threats from the Crown. But the Crown had recognised the weakness
of its legal case, not the strength of Jamaican protest. The lords of
trade and their successors were still resolved to maintain the prerogatives of the Crown and to secure a permanent revenue (see instructions,8 September 1681,and later 24 May and 14 August 1701,6 December
1702,25 February 1704,19 July 1722,30 July 1724,and 1 June 1725). [See
Volume II].
1.C.O. 138/4 p.17.Carlisle being reluctant to return to Jamaica,Lynch
was commissioned on 6 August 1681 and arrived as governor in May 1682
to take over from Sir Henry Morgan,the lieutenant-governor.
2. By order in council (28 July 1681) Lynch could inspect all patent
offices and might remove absentees with some law 'like unto that in
Ireland'.
3. Until such a Revenue Act was passed, he must veto all other laws
save acts dealing with naturalisation and suppressing piracy.

means and inducements you can) the passing of a publick
revenue in such terms as may render it perpetual and according to the draught herewith sent you...And you are by
noe means to suffer that the revenue bee mentioned to bee
raised otherwise than to us, our heirs and successors for
the support of the government in such manner as wee have
directed. And, to the end our good subjects may the better bee induced to pass the said Act, you may assure them
of our resolution to apply not only the revenue thereby
to bee raised but even our quit-rents to the support of
that our government and to noe other use whatsoever...
But in case you shall not bee able to procure the passing
of the said bill to perpetuity, you are to obtain it for
the longest terme of years you can persuade the assembly
to agree unto. Provided always that, for any reason whatsoever, the same bee not limited or restrained to a shor-
ter term than seaven years from the time it shall be enacted....[1]

19. And you are not to suffer any publick money whatsoever to bee issued or disposed of otherwise than by a
warrant under your hand. But the assembly may bee nevertheless permitted, from time to time, to view and examine
the accompts of money or value of moneys disposed of by
vertue of such laws as they shall make, which you are to
signify unto them as occasion shall serve...

27. You shall not displace any of the judges, justices,
sherifs or other officers or ministers within our said
island without good and sufficient cause signified to us
and to our Committee for Plantations. And to prevent arbitrary removals of judges and justices of the peace, you
are not to express any limitation of time in the commissions which you are to grant with the advice and consent
of the council to fit persons for those imployments. Nor
shall you execute your self or by deputy any of the said
offices; not suffer any person to execute more offices
than one by a deputy.

28. You shall not erect any court or offices of judicature not before erected or established, without our especial order....

31. And you are to permit a liberty of conscience to
all other persons (except Papists) soe they bee contented
with a quiet and peaceable enjoyment of it not giving offence or scandal to the government.

368. MINUTE OF THE LORDS OF TRADE, 8 November 1682.[2]
    ...The Assembly is to be acquainted that his Majesty

1.Lynch obtained in October 1682 a seven-year revenue act without the
'tacks' which Morgan had had - somewhat naively - to accept in October
1681 - the confirmation of a corpus of island acts, 'the laws of England'; and annual sessions of the assembly. A year later his tact,
courage and ability were further rewarded by a 21-year revenue act:
[see No.295].
2. C.O. 391/4 p.75:extract from the journal. The Lords' committee were

will not suffer any obligation to bee imposed upon him
either in Jamaica or in any other of his Dominions to let
the Assembly sit every year in such manner as they intend.

That his Majesty is desirous of the Act of Revenue and
other laws, only out of his great indulgence, and care of
them, the same being only for their security.

That if they will not consent to reasonable laws for
the support of the government, it is to bee insinuated to
them that the laws of England may then perhaps bee understood to bee in force in Jamaica and particularly the Act
of Tunnage and Poundage whereby an imposition is laid on
wines imported into England and the Dominions thereof.

369.'THE STATE OF JAMAICA UNDER SIR THOMAS LYNCH HIS MAJESTIE'S
PRESENT CAPTAIN GENERAL AND CHIEF GOVERNOR', 20 September 1683.[1]
...The government is constituted by a charter or commission under the great seal of England, which on change
of government is always publisht, and afterward recorded
because it may bee seen by all; for it contains the powers
granted to the governors, and the graces conceded to the
people, as calling assemblys, assimilating the laws to
those of England, being governed by known laws without
which noe man's liberty or freehold is to bee taken away.

The <u>governor</u> here commands during his Majesty's pleasure and has noe salary but what only is paid by his Majesty in the island, without donatives or presents from
the assemblys or particular persons, under the title of
Captain General and Cheif Governor. His Majesty has been
pleased to vest his governors with all his powers civil,
ecclesiastical or military, which they are to discharge
according to their laws and those powers and instructions
they have from his Majesty by the advice of his Majesty's
council in the island. On the governor's disability or
absence, the lieutenant governor succeeds. If there bee
none, then the council governs, and the first counsellor
presides till his Majesty's pleasure bee declared therein.

The <u>council</u> consists generaly of about 12 or 13 appointed by his Majesty. They inspect the revenue and give orders for the issuing of it out [and] advise in matters relating to the government. They think themselves limited by
the law, like the King's Council in England, soe meddle
not with property unless it comes by writ of error out
of the Grand Court or appeal out of the Admiralty judic-

<hr>

shocked by the receipt of the Revenue Act, which Morgan had accepted
and had even recommended as submissive and cautious. The lords were
angry at the bland assertion of the assembly's terms. If the assembly
believed that the Crown had been vanquished in 1680, the lords of trade
were determined to renew the fight. Hence the threat that the Tonnage
and Poundage Act would be used to secure a revenue. Lynch however secured a Revenue Act without any objectionable 'tacks'[see No.295.]
1. C.O. 138/4 p. 214 ff. Edward Long attributed this to Lynch himself. This was an early, misleading assumption that councils and
assemblies were *'umbras'* of Lords and Commons.

iary before them, which has seldom hapned. As the governor represents the king, soe doe they the House of Lords,
for by the commission and instructions they are joyned
with the governor and assembly to pass laws.... [The councillors were named.]

The King has been soe gracious to the inhabitants of
this island that all the governors have had commands and
directions to assimilate the laws and government as near
as possible to that of England, and has therefore, by his
instructions and charter of government constituted assemblys that are *umbras* of an English Parliament.... [Assembly
members were named.]   These are chosen indifferently by the
freeholders of the several parishes and precincts, by
vertue of writs issued out of the Chancery under the great
seal directed to the Provost Marshal as high Sheriff that
(after the manner of England) signifys the time and place
of election, there indents, afterwards makes returns etc.
All the methods and proceedings of this assembly resemble
the English Parliaments as much as soe little body may soe
great an one. In all, the governor has a negative, prorog-
ues, dissolves. The laws they make are generaly municipal,
proper only for the usage of the island, and are of force
for what time his Majesty pleases, as may appear by his
manner of passing them in the following book.

The King is here, as in England, Head of the Church,
his governors, as his substitutes or chancellors collate
all the benefices that are worth from £100 per annum to
about 40th part....

[The Bishop of London nominated ministers of religion whose
religious duties were listed.]

Ecclesiastical mulctuary laws are not of force here,
for his Majesty considering this as a fertile and large
island fit for a royal colony and not being willing his
subjects should all goe to proprietorships or to forreign
countrys hath, to draw them hither, permitted liberty of
conscience that has been confirmed to dissenters by divers
laws and the king's instructions ever since his happy restoration, of which grace they have always and doe now make
a modest use, being respectful to the government and ready
to comply with all civil and military dutyes.

For this or the like considerations his Majesty has
been graciously pleased to give liberty to all strangers
who may (on taking the oath of allegiance) demand a patent for naturalization that enfranchises them as a native
inhabitant, for it they pay a small fee as appears by the
Act in the following book made for that purpose.

(vi) CAROLINA

370. 'CONCESSIONS AND AGREEMENTS' OF THE LORDS PROPRIETORS OF CAROLINA
TO,AND WITH,THE ADVENTURERS OF BARBADOS AND THEIR ASSOCIATES,
7 January 1665.[1]
[The governor was empowered to choose 6 - 12 councillors to

1.W.L. Saunders (ed.) *op.cit.*I pp.75 ff: S. Carolina Hist.Soc.*Coll.*V

advise him: all officials were to swear allegiance to the king and
fidelity to the proprietors and would hold their posts 'during
good pleasure'.]

7. *Item*. That all persons that are or shall become subjects
of the King of England and swear or subscribe allegiance
to the King and faithfulness to the Lords, shall be admitted to plant and become freemen of the said Province and
enjoy the freedoms and immunities hereafter expressed....
8. *Item*. That no person qualified as aforesaid within the
said Province or all or any of the Countries...at any time
shall be any ways molested, punished, disquieted or called in question for any difference in opinion or practice
in matter of religious concernments who do not actually
disturbe the civil peace of the said Province...but that
all and every such person and persons may from time to
time and at all times, freely and fully have and enjoye
his and their judgments and containces in matters of religion,...any law...usage or custom of this realm of England...notwithstanding....
10. *Item*.That the inhabitants being freemen...do as soon
as this our commission shall arrive, by virtue of a writt
in our names by the Governor to be for the present (until
our seal comes) sealed and signed make choice of twelve
deputies or representatives from amongst themselves who
being chosen, are to join with the said Governor and council for the making of such laws, ordinances and constitution as shall be necessary for the present good and welfare
of the several counties aforesaid....

   [Elections in the counties were to be held annually. General
   assemblies were empowered to appoint their own meeting to adjourn,
   to erect courts, to legislate 'consonant with reason and as near
   as may be conveniently agreeable to the laws and customs of H.M.'s
   Kingdom of England, provided also that they be not against the
   interest of us the Lords Proprayators...nor any of these our present Concessions, espetially that they be not against the Article
   of liberty of contience above mentioned'.
   Laws were to be in force for no more than a year and a half,

---

(1897) *Shaftesbury Papers* p.33 ff. To encourage the Barbadian adventurers and other undertakers from England, New England and the Caribbees, who were planning plantations in Clarendon country, the Lords
Proprietors covenanted to observe the liberal terms of this prospectus.
The assembly was to be the dominant instrument of government; governor and council seem primarily responsible for seeing that laws and
decisions made in the assembly were executed .By marked contrast, the
'Fundamental Constitutions' of 1670 were feudal and oligarchic.
Such 'Concessions' and 'Fundamental Constitutions' were a new departure in proprietary government: Baltimore had issued promotional conditions to intending planters in 1633,1636,1642 and 1648; but they
concerned only the amount of land offered. Neither he nor Carlisle
had outlined any general or elaborate proposals for the systems of
government they intended for their palatinates, as the lords proprietors did here. Nor did the Duke of York.

unless confirmed by the proprietors. Assemblies were to have the power,]

4. *Item*....by act as aforesaid to ley equall taxes and assessments, equally to raise money or goods upon all lands...or persons within the several precints, hundreds, parishes, manors...to the better supporting of the publick charge of the said Government and for the mutual safety, defence and security of the Counties ....

[*Assemblies* were empowered further to erect baronies and manors with their courts, to divide counties unto hundreds and parishes, to raise forts, to incorporate towns, to organise train bands, to naturalise, to prescribe grants of lands to planters and servants, to make appropriations for the government's expenses and to collect rents for the proprietors.

The *governor and council* were to see that the courts established by the assembly performed their duties, to nominate officials, to commission military offices, to grant reprieves, to issue writs for elections and to seal grants of land. For the better security of the proprietors and all the inhabitants,]

1. *Item*...they are not to impose or suffer to be imposed any tax, customs, subsidy, tallage, assessment or any other duty whatsoever upon any culler or pretence upon the said County or Counties and the inhabitants thereof, other than what shalbe imposed by the authority and consent of the General Assembly and then only in manner as aforesaid.[1]...

[There were many detailed provisions for terms of planting, for grants to adventurers, freemen, free women and servants; for allocation, survey and rates on land: for boundaries and titles.][2]

371. 'FUNDAMENTAL CONSTITUTIONS' PROPOSED BY THE LORDS PROPRIETORS FOR CAROLINA, 21 July 1670.[3]

Our Sovereign Lord the King, having out of His royal

---

1. A month later Berkeley and Carteret published almost identical 'Concessions' for planters in New Jersey. (*Archives of N. Jersey* 1st.I pp.28–43). These were amplified in the 'Explanations' of 6 December 1672 which set out their 'true meaning' (*ibid.* I p.99).
2. On 30 June 1665 the king granted to the Carolina proprietors a second charter with enlarged boundaries.
3. W.L. Saunders (ed.) *op.cit.* I p.187 ff. Locke's draft was dated 1 March 1670. (S. Carolina Hist.Soc. *Coll.* V (1897) – *Shaftesbury Papers* pp.187 ff.). The proprietors were seeking to emphasise the feudal forms of the palatinate with powers concentrated in the proprietors and the nobility, and to 'avoid erecting a numerous democracy'. The 'Parliament' was now being reduced to formal and limited powers: but since it did vote taxes, it thereby held the purse strings.

On 1 November 1670 a grant was made by the king to Ashley, Berkeley, Carteret, Albemarle, Craven and Colleton as absolute 'lords and proprietors' of the Bahamas 'in free and common soccage of the manor of E. Greenwich' on similar terms to the charter to Carolina, paying the king one-quarter of all precious metals found, with power to erect manors, make laws, appoint governors and magistrates, grant land, organise defence, exercise martial law, to tax 'by consent of the free-

grace and bounty granted unto us the province of Carolina
with all the royalties, proprieties, jurisdictions and
privileges of a county palatine as large and ample as the
county palatine of Durham with other great privileges for
the better settlement of the government of the said place
and establishing the interest of the Lords Proprietors
with equality and without confusion; and that the government of this province may be made most agreeable to the
monarchy under which we live and of which this province
is a part; and that we may avoid erecting a numerous democracy: We, the Lords and Proprietors of the province
aforesaid, have agreed to this following form of government
to be perpetually established amongst us unto which we do
oblige ourselves, our heirs and successors in the most
binding ways than can be devised.

  1. The eldest of the Lords Proprietors shall be *Palatine:* and, upon the decease of the Palatine, the eldest of
the seven surviving Proprietors shall always suceed him.[1]

  II. There shall be seven other chief offices erected –
viz. the Admiral's, Chamberlain's, Chancellor's, Constables's, Chief Justice's, High Steward's and Treasurer's:
which places shall be enjoyed by none but the Lords Proprietors to be assigned at first by lot; and upon the vacancy of any of the seven great offices by death, or otherwise, the eldest proprietor shall have his choice of the
said place.[2]

  III. The whole province shall be divided into counties;
each county shall consist of eight signiories, eight baronies and four precincts; each precinct shall consist of
six colonies ....

   [Each signiory, barony and colony would consist of 12,000 acres,
   the 8 signiories being the share of the 8 proprietors, and the 8
   baronies of the nobles. These lands (two-fifths of the whole) being
   perpetually annexed to the proprietors and nobles, the remaining
   three-fifths were available for the people 'so that in setting out
   and planting the lands, the balance of the government may be preserved'. After 1671 proprietors could not alienate their proprieties
   which would descend on their male heir, or to the next landgrave
   or cacique descended of the next female heir: the method of filling vacancies in the proprietorship was prescribed.
   There should be the same number of landgraves as of counties and

men', *etc.* (*ibid.*pp.160,207,440).
The Bahamas had been included in the Heath grant of 1629,and also in
a Commonwealth grant to Lord Saye and the Eleutherian and New Province
Adventurers of 1649. Both these patents were superseded by this new
grant.Due in part to confusion over two brothers,it transpired that
the first governor,Wentworth,had been elected to that position by the
planters themselves: 'a style' of government, said one of the proprietors, fit 'for a republique' but not for a proprietary. The islands
prospered briefly and then became a nest for pirates.
1.Thereby,said Locke, the difficulties of the hereditary principle
were avoided.
2. These officers formed the Palatine's Court (see § xxviii).

twice as many caciques who would together be the heritary nobility and members of 'parliament'. Each landgrave would have 4 baronies; each cacique 2. The method for appointing these nobles was prescribed. In each signiory, barony and manor, the lord would hold court-leet with appeals to the county or precinct courts.

A manor would consist of between 3,000 and 12,000 acres. Limits were placed on leases, sales and inheritance.]

XXVIII. There shall be eight supreme courts. The first called the *Palatine's Court* consisting of the Palatine and the other seven Proprietors. The other seven courts of the other seven great offices shall consist each of them of a Proprietor and six counsellors added to him....

[Under each of these seven courts should be a college of 12 assistants: chosen 2 by the Palatine's Court, 2 by the Landgraves' chamber, 2 by the Caciques' chamber; and finally, 4 by the Commoners' chamber and 2 by the Palatine's Courts out of the M.P.'s, sheriffs, county justices, younger sons of proprietors or eldest sons of other nobles. Out of this college, the Palatine's Court would choose 6 counsellors, one out of each named 'estate' or class, to join each proprietor in his court. The Grand Council would consist of all 8 proprietors of the Palatine's Court together with all the councillors of the eight proprietors' supreme courts. The proprietors had inherent original rights which the Grand Council could not 'put out'.]

XXXII. All elections in the Parliament in the several chambers of the Parliament and in the Grand Council shall be passed by balloting ....

[The Palatine's Court had power to call 'parliaments', to pardon, to appoint officials, to dispose all money (except taxes granted by parliament) to veto all Acts and decisions of the 'Grand Council and Parliament'. The Palatine had power as general and proprietor. The chancellor's court dealt with land grants, Indian affairs, disturbance of the peace, press licences, liberty of conscience etc. The chancellor should preside in 'Grand Council and Parliament'. The chief justice's court heard appeals from all other courts. The constable's court determined all military matters; and the admiral's all maritime affairs. The treasurer's court took care of revenues. The high steward's court would concern itself with trade, communications, sewers, bridges, markets, survey of lands, planning of towns *etc*. The chamberlain's court had responsibility for ceremony, precedence, births, death and marriages, fashions, habits and sports.

The 12 assistants could attend these courts as observors, but not to intervene (unless their opinions were required) or to vote. Their task was to prepare business.]

L. The Grand Council shall consist of the Palatine and seven Proprietors and the forty-two councillors of the several Proprietor's Courts ....

[The grand council had power to adjudicate on conflicts of jurisdiction in and between the proprietors' courts, to make peace and war, and to issue orders for defence.]

LI. The Grand Council shall prepare all matters to be proposed in Parliament. Nor shall any matter whatsoever be proposed in Parliament, but what hath first passed the

Grand Council: which, after having been read three several
days in the Parliament shall by majority of votes be passed or rejected....

[The grand council had final appellate jurisdiction, would dispose of all money voted by parliament and would meet at least once
each month. There were provisions for resident deputies for the
lords proprietors. The structure of county courts, of precinct
courts, and of assize courts, was prescribed: the land qualification for sheriffs, stewards and juries were also laid down. It
was 'a base and vile thing to plead for money or reward' so no
man could plead another's cause unless he swore he would receive
no recompense.]

LXXI. There shall be a Parliament, consisting of the
Proprietors (or their deputies), and landgraves and cass-
iques, and one freeholder out of every precinct, to be
chosen by the freeholders of the said precinct respectively. They shall sit all together in one room and have
every member one vote ....

[The franchise qualification was 50 acres within the precinct;
the qualification for MP's was 500 acres. Parliaments would meet
every second year in November. Sessions would begin with the reading and subscribing to these Fundamental Constitutions. Procedures
for elections were prescribed. No Act of 'parliament' would be valid
unless ratified in open parliament by the Palatine (or his deputy)
and 3 of the other proprietors (or their deputies), nor would continue for more than 2 years unless so ratified again. If any Act
was challenged by a proprietor as being against these Fundamental
Constitutions, the parliament would divide into 4 chambers, one
for each estate: Proprietors, landgraves, caciques; and representatives chosen by the precincts; and if three of the four estates
found that the proposed Act did not agree with these Constitutions, it would not pass.

'To prevent multiplicity of laws which by degrees always change
the right foundations of the original government', all Acts would
expire after 100 years. Commentaries and expositions - 'which
serve only to obscure and perplex' - of these Constitutions and
other Carolina laws were prohibited. Registration of all lands,
births etc. was to be provided. Local government by mayor, aldermen and councillors was prescribed.]

XCV. No man shall be permitted to be a freeman of Carolina or to have any estate or habitation within it that
doth not acknowledge a God and that God is publickly and
solemnly to be worshipped....

[The Church of England,'the only true and orthodox and the natural religion of all the King's dominions', was alone to be the
established Church. But since the Indians were 'utterly strangers
to Christianity whose idolatry, ignorance or mistake gives us no
right to expel or use them ill'; since many planters would be
'unavoidably of different opinions' on religion and should not be
excluded; since 'Jews,heathens and other dissenters' should not be
'scared' off but have the opportunity of learning the truth,peace,
meekness of the gospel by living among Christians, any 7 members
might constitute a separate church. But all had to subscribe to
the terms in §XCV who wished to be a church or to take office.]

No one should abuse another church or religion. Slaves could be
as fully members of a church as freemen. Trial by jury was guaranteed. Rent of one penny an acre was to be paid to the proprietors:
three-tenths to the Palatine, one-tenth to each of the others.
All between 17 and 60 should be bound to bear arms. The oath was
prescribed for all over 17:]
...I - do promise to bear faith and true allegiance to our
Sovereign Lord King Charles the Second, his heirs and successors and will be true and faithful to the Palatine and
Lords Proprietors of Carolina, their heirs and successors
and with my utmost power will defend them and maintain the
government according to these Fundamental Constitutions.[1]...
    [The same oath would naturalise aliens and admit to any office.]
    CXX. These Fundamental Constitutions...shall be and
remain sacred and unalterable form and rule of government
of Carolina for ever....

(vii) NEW YORK

372. PROCLAMATION BY GOVERNOR RICHARD NICOLLS, 18 August 1664.[2]
    Forasmuch as his Majesty hath sent us (by commission
under his great seal of England) amongst other things, to
expell, or to reduce to his Majesty's obedience, all such
foreigners, as without his Majesty's leave and consent,
have seated themselves amongst any of his dominions in
America to the prejudice of his Majesty's subjects, and
diminution of his royal dignity;[3] We, his said Majesty's
commissioners, do declare and promise, That whosoever of
what nation soever, will, upon knowledge of this Proclamation, acknowledge and testify themselves to submit to
this his Majesty's government, as his good subjects, shall
be protected in his Majesty's laws and justice, and peaceable injoy whatsoever God's blessing, and their own honest
industry have furnished them with; and all other privileges, with his Majesty's English subjects. We have caused
this to be published, that we might prevent all inconveniences to others,if it were possible; however, to clear
ourselves from the charge of all those miseries, that may
any way befall such as live here, and will acknowledge his
Majesty for their Sovereign, whom God preserve.

373. ARTICLES OF CAPITULATION, 27 August 1664.[4]
    I. We consent, That the states general or the West-

1.Though individually those taking up land or office took this oath
including 'to government according to these Fundamental Constitutions',
assemblies in Carolina resisted continual pressure from the proprietors to adopt them as an Act.They certainly constituted a cumbersome
and top-heavy frame of government.
2.M.Kammen (ed.) *William Smith's History of the Province of New York*
(1972) p.30.
3.This prior claim was based upon that of Sir William Alexander,Earl
of Stirling.He had been granted Long Island by the Council for New
England, not by the king, in 1635.
4. *ibid.*pp.31-3.These terms were agreed between the duke's commission-

India Company,shall freely injoy all farms and houses
(except such as are in the forts) and that within six
months, they shall have free liberty to transport all such
arms and ammunition, as now does belong to them, or else
they shall be paid for them.
II. All publique houses shall continue for the uses
which they are for.
III.All people shall still continue free denizens, and
shall enjoy their lands, houses, goods, wheresoever they
are, within this country, and dispose of them as they
please.
IV. If any inhabitant have a mind to remove himself,
he shall have a year and six weeks from this day, to remove himself, wife,children, servants, goods, and to dispose of his lands here....
   [Any public official who wished might be transported free to
   England. Soldiers and merchants of the West India Company were
   guaranteed safe return to Holland. Dutch settlers and ships were
   free to continue to come to the colony and could trade with Holland,England and the English plantations.]
VIII. The Dutch here shall injoy the liberty of their
consciences in divine worship and church discipline....
   XI. The Dutch here shall injoy their own customs concerning their inheritances.[1]
XII. All publique writings and records, which concern
the inheritances of any people, or the reglement of the
church or poor, or orphans, shall be carefully kept by
those in whose hands now they are, and such writings as
particularly concern the States General, may at any time
be sent to them.
XVI. All inferior civil officers and magistrates shall
continue as now they are (if they please), till the customary time of new elections, and then new ones be chosen
by themselves, provided that such new chosen magistrates
shall take the Oath of Allegiance to his Majesty of England, before they enter upon their office.
XVII. All differences of contracts and bargains made
before this day by any in this country, shall be determined, according to the manner of the Dutch.
XX. If at any time hereafter, the king of Great Britain,
and the States of the Netherland do agree that this place
and country be redelivered into the hands of the said States, whensoever his Majesty will send his commands to re-
deliver it, it shall immediately be done.[2]

---

ers (including John Winthrop from Connecticut and the duke's governor,Richard Nicolls) and the Dutch burgher representatives in the
dutch governor,Pieter Stuyvesant's house.
1. A conquered colony retained its laws until they were changed by
the conqueror [see No.374].
2.In August 1664 England and the Netherlands were at peace, but war
soon broke out. By the treaty of Breda in 1667 English occupation was
confirmed,and,though in renewed war in 1673 New York was retaken by
the Dutch,by the treaty of Westminster in 1674 it was once more restored to the English and the duke of York was again confirmed as

XXI. That the town of Manhattans shall choose deputyes, and those deputyes shall have free voyces in all publique affairs, as much as any other deputyes....

374. PROCLAMATION BY GOVERNOR NICOLLS, 12 June 1665.[1]
[The patent to the Duke impowered him 'to change all the names, styles, formes or ceremonies of government'.][2]
...For the more orderly establishment of his Majesty's royal authority, as near as may bee agreeable to the lawes and customes of his Majestie's realme of England...I have thought it necessary to revoke and discharge...the forme and ceremony of government of this his Majestie's towne of New Yorke, under the name or names, style or styles of *Schout, Burgomasters* and *Schepens*[3]: as also, that for the future administration of justice by the lawes established in these the territoryes of his Royal Highnesse wherein the welfares of all the inhabitants and the preservation of all their due rights and priviledges, graunted by the articles of this towne upon surrender under his Majestie's obedience are concluded; I do further declare, that by a particular commission, such persons shall be authorized to put the lawes in execution...which persons so constituted and appointed, shall be knowne and called by the name and style of *Mayor, Aldermen* and *Sherriffe*, according to the custome of England in other his Majestie's corporations.

375. GOVERNOR NICOLLS TO LORD CLARENDON, 30 July 1665.[4]
...Your Lordship will alsoe be more fully informed that the late indenture made to my Lord Berkley and Sir George Carteret is to the manifest destruction of tne Duke's collony, for my Lord, the very name of the Duke's power heere, hath bine one great motive for weell affected men to remove hither out of other collonies, men well affected to monarchy, and have found that our new lawes are not contrived soe democratically as the rest[5], and when I was last in Boston,

---

proprietor by a royal patent.
1.E.B. O'Callaghan, *The documentary history of...New York* (1850) I p.389. This so-called 'charter' began the process of anglicising the town government of New York.
2. By right of conquest the conqueror had the right to change the law and to declare what other laws he pleased (see *Calvin's Case* pp. 30,33 and 36-37).[For 'The Duke's Laws'see No.400 (b) (i)].
3. The schout fiscal performed duties similar to those of a sheriff and attorney general. The burgomasters and schepens formed a municipal council of councillors and aldermen: they were chosen annually by indirect election by a body of nine elected by a general meeting of inhabitants.
4. New York Hist.Soc.,*Collections*...1869 (1870) *Clarendon Papers*,no. *xxix*, pp.75-6.The earl of Clarendon was lord chancellor.
5. The 'Duke's code' had consciously omitted certain Massachusetts laws: it avoided reference to 'freemen', which was the mainstay of the puritan theocracy, and established a board of elected constables

I did engage a hundred famillyes to remoove, and dispersed
printed papers for their encoragment, but good land is
none of the least arguments to a planter which was then
to bee found in the Duke's pattent, but now is wholly
given away....
    [The land was poor and barren and revenues hard to secure for
    public expenses.]
    I durst not endeavour to stretch their purses farther
in the infancy of this change, least their affections
should be perverted and we do not want ill neighbours to
doe us ill offices on such occasions....The first 3 sessions have bine held with good satisfaction to all the collony, in   [Septem]ber is held a general assizes the governour, councell, and justice upon the Bench, where the
lawes are againe to bee reviewed and amended, in case any
reasonable objections bee made, otherwise to bee confirmed
heere, and remitted over to his Royal Highnesse for his
royal hand, to make them authentick, and then if they were
printed and imediately sent over they would bee fully satisfactory to these parts, and of some consequence to his
Majestie's interest....

376. THE DUKE'S ORDER FOR ENFORCING AND AMENDING HIS LAWS,
                                    6 August 1674.[1]
    Whereas there are hereunto annexed certaine Laws estab-
lished by authority of His Majesty's Pattents graunted to
me and digested into one volume for the publique use of
all the territories in America under my government collected out of the several laws in other His Majesty's American Colonies and Plantacions, upon perusall and consideracion of which it appeares that there may be an occasion
to make some alteracion or amendments in some particular
clauses thereof; These are, therefore, to authorize and
require you to put in execucion the said laws, except such
as shall have apparent inconveniences in them and after
your settlement in New York, with the advice and helpe of
your Councell, carefully to peruse and consider the same,
and if you finde it necessary for the ease and benefitt
of the people and the good of my service to make any alter-
acions, addicions or amendments in the said laws, you are
with the first opportunity to represent the same unto me,

and overseers instead of a town meeting.It also adopted the religious
toleration of the Dutch for all protestant sects. The provision for
retirement of only half the overseers each year was also peculiarly
Dutch:so too was plural nomination of candidates for the governor's
choice of sheriff. The selection of jurors only from the overseers
of the towns was in part the adaptation of a Dutch custom for, while
there had previously been no jury system, magistrates and former magistrates had been called upon to advise in criminal courts and to
arbitrate in petty civil cases.
1.*Ibid*.III p.226-7.New York had been temporarily recaptured by the
Dutch in July 1673.The duke had received a new charter on 29 June
1674 in the same terms as previously.

to the end you may receave from me such orders and direc-
cions as shalbe necessary for authorizeing you to put the
same in execucion.

377. THE DUKE OF YORK TO GOVERNOR ANDROS, 28 January 1676.[1]
    ...I have formerly writt to you touching Assembleys in
those countreys and have since observed what severall of
your lattest letters hint about that matter. But unless
you had offered what qualificacons are usuall and proper
to such Assemblyes, I cannot but suspect they would be of
dangerous consequence, nothing being more knowne than the
aptness of such bodyes to assume to themselves many priviledges which prove destructive to, or very oft disturbe,
the peace of the government wherein they are allowed.
Neither doe I see any use of them which is not as well
provided for, whilest you and your Councell governe according to the laws established (thereby preserving every
man's property inviolate) and whilest all things that need
redresse may be sure of finding it, either at the Quarter
Sessions or by other legall and ordinary wayes, or lastly
by appeale to myselfe. But howsoever if you continue of
the same opinion, I shall be ready to consider of any prop-
osalls you shall send to that purpose....[2]

378. THE DUKE'S INSTRUCTIONS TO GOVERNOR DONGAN,27 January 1683.[3]
    [He was to summon his councillors (a few being named) and to
    administer oaths of allegiance to the king and of fealty to the
    lord proprietor. He might inform them of his instructions where
    appropriate,and could suspend any councillors temporarily till the
    duke had made his final decision.]
    ...You are also with the advice of my Councill with all
convenient speed after your arrival there in my name to
issue out writts or warrants of sumons to the severall
Sheriffes or other proper officers in every part of your

1.J.R.Brodhead (ed.) *op.cit.*III p.235. Major Edmund Andros,a Guernsey seigneur, had served in the West Indies.The duke's instructions
in 1674 to him had protested his concern for the prosperity and well-
being of the colonists, but he had demanded dutiful obedience from
his tenants. Andros and the council were to impose taxes and exercise
administration.The basic laws were 'the laws of 1665', but Andros
and the council might modify them. Andros was a loyal servant, but
warned the duke that there was some growing demand for an assembly.
2.James had not realised that it was not the redress of grievances
but the right to be involved in making laws and imposing taxes which
was the chief concern.When Andros returned to England, James was persuaded that he should make the concession of an assembly 'which H.M.'s
other plantations have'. In the instructions to Thomas Dongan, an
Irish Catholic and friend of the Stuarts, as governor the duke authorised the summoning of an assembly [see No.378].
3. J.R. Brodhead (ed.) *op.cit.*III pp.331 ff. Thomas Dongan proved an
able governor, energetic in defence of the colony. He stayed living
in New York when superseded by Andros as governor of the Dominion
of New England.

said government wherein you shall expresse that I have
thought fitt that there shall be a Generall Assembly of
all the Freeholders by the person who they shall choose
to represent them in order to consulting with yourselfe
and the said Councill, what laws are fitt and necessary
to be made and established for the good weale and government of the said Colony and its Dependencyes and all the
Inhabitants thereof.... [There should be no more than 18 writs
issued.]   And when the said Assembly soe elected shalbe
mett at the time and place directed, you shall let them
know that for the future it is my resolucon that the said
Generall Assembly shall have free liberty to consult and
debate among themselves all matters as shalbe apprehended
proper to be established for laws for the good government
of the said Colony...and that of such laws shallbe as
shall appeare to mee to be for the manifest good of the
country in generall and not prejudiciall to me, I will
assent unto and confirm them....

[The governor was empowered to withhold his assent to laws and
to have a veto: acts assented to would be sent to the proprietor
for ratification or disallowance. No revenue bill should be passed
unless 'express mencon be made therein that the same is levyed
and granted to me'. The duke warned against temporary legislation.]

379. ACT OF THE FIRST GENERAL ASSEMBLY, 30 October 1683.[1]

[To establish the government of New York and to secure that justice and right may be equally done to all, the governor, council
and assembly enacted:]
    ...That the Supreme Legislative Authority under His
Majesty and his Royall Highnesse James, Duke of Yorke and
Albany *etc*. and Lord proprietor of this said province
shall forever be and reside in a Governour, Councell and
the people mett in Generall Assembly....
    That the exercise of the chiefe magistracy and adminis-
tracon of the government over the said province shall be
in the said Governour, assisted by a Councell with whose
advice and consent or with at least four of them, he is
to rule and govern the same according to the Lawes thereof....
    That according to the Usage Custome and practise of the
Realme of England a sessions of a Generall Assembly be
held in this province once in three yeares at least.
    That every freeholder within this province and freeman
in any Corporacon shall have his free choise and Vote in

1.Laws of the Colony of New York I (1894) pp.111.ff.The first assembly had met on 17 October.This so-called 'Charter of liberties and
privileges' was indeed the first statute and was probably largely the
work of Matthias Nicols, the speaker and mayor of New York.The assembly,though allegedly 'mostly Dutch',were clearly imbued with a desire for English constitutional forms. The duke approved this law a
year later,but it was disallowed by the privy council in May 1686
when the plans for the Dominion of New England were becoming firm.

the Electing of the Representatives without any manner of
constraint or imposicon. And that in all Eleccons the
Majority of Voices shall carry itt, and by freeholders is
understood every one who is Soe understood according to
the Lawes of England....

    [The number of representatives for the city and counties were
defined. The general assembly would be the supreme and only legislative power under his Royall Highness. The representatives
would control their own meetings and adjournments and would judge
privileges, qualifications and disputed elections.]

That noe freeman shall be taken or imprisoned or be de-
sseized of his freehold or Libertye or free customes, or
be outlawed or exiled or any other ways destroyed, nor
shall be passed up, adjudged or condemned, But by the Lawfull Judgement of his peers and by the Law of this province. Justice nor Right shall be neither sold, denied or
deferred to any man within this province....[1]

That Noe aid, Tax, Tallage, Assessment, Custome, Loane,
Benevolence or Imposicon whatsoever shall be layed, assessed, imposed, or levyed on any of his Majesty's Subjects
within this province or their Estates upon any manner of
Colour or pretence but by the Act and Consent of the Governour, Councell and Representatives of the people in Generall Assembly mett and Assembled....

    [All trials would be by a verdict of 12 men 'as neere as may be
peers or equals'. No compulsory quartering of soldiers or sailors
would be suffered in peace time. There were provisions for inheritance and tenure and for tolerationof all Christians; and churches were guaranteed their privileges.]

380. JAMES II TO GOVERNOR DONGAN, 5 March 1685.[2]

Whereas, by the decease of the late King Our most dearly
Beloved Brother[3] and Our Accession to the Imperial Crown
of this Realm, Our Province of New York, the Propriety
whereof was, by Letters Patent of His said Majesty vested
in us, is now wholly devolved upon Our Royal Person and
annexed to Our other Dominions...

    [This conversion of the proprietary into a royal dominion was
ordered to be proclaimed in New York.[4] Those holding office were
to continue until further notice.]

Wee doe hereby charge and require you to pursue such
Powers and Instructions as wee have formerly given you
and such further Powers, Authority and Instructions as
you shall at any time hereafter receive under Our Royall
Signet and Sign Manual, or by Our Order in our Privy Council.

---

1. The 'Magna Carta clause'.
2. J.R. Brodhead (ed.) *op.cit.* III p.360. Thus automatically by the
accession of a lord proprietor to the throne, the number of royal
colonies dependent directly on the Crown was further increased.
3. A month before, on 6 February.
4. As it was on 23 April.

381. OBSERVATIONS OF THE LORDS OF TRADE ON THE NEW YORK *'CHARTER'*
3 March 1685.[1]

Charter   That the Inhabitants of New York shall be gov-
            erned by and according to the Laws of England.

Observation This Priviledge is not granted to any of His
            Majesty's Plantations;where the Act of Habeas
            Corpus and all such other Bills do not take
            Place.[2]

Charter   Sheriffs and other Officers of Justice to be
            appointed with like power as in England.

Observation This is not so distinctly granted or practiced
            in any other Plantation.

Charter   That the Supream Legislative Authority shall
            remain in the Governor, Councill and the People
            mett in a Generall Assembly.

Observation The words The People met in a General Assembly,
            are not used in any other Constitution in Amer-
            ica; But only the words :
            General Assembly

Charter   The Exercise of the Cheif Magistracy and Admin-
            istration of the government shall be in the
            Governor assisted by a Council; with whose
            advice and consent he shall and may govern and
            rule the said Province according to the laws
            established.

Observation If this oblige and restrain the Governor from
            doing anything without the Councill, it is a
            greater restraint than any other Government
            is subject to.

Charter   That according to the usage and practice of
            the kingdom of England there shall be a ses-
            sion of a General Assembly to be called to
            meet once in 3 Years or oftner.

Observation This is an Obligation upon the government
            greater than has been ever agreed to in any
            other Plantation, And the grant of such a
            privilege has been rejected elsewhere, not-
            withstanding a Revenue offered to induce it.

1.J.R. Brodhead ed. *op.cit.*III pp.357-9.
2. Again, the extension of English law to English colonies was not
regarded as in any way implicit in the general rule of repugnancy:
nor, save where convenient in particular cases, was it considered
desirable either by the Crown's ministers or by colonists eager for
local self-government.As a 'conquered' colony New York certainly had
no right to English law unless so granted as an act of grace by the
conqueror.It was later argued [see below Volume II:sect.V.(A);West's
opinion (1720),Memo. of privy council (1722), and Yorke-Wearg opinion
(1724) *etc.*],that British statutes did not apply overseas anyway after
a colony was first planted,unless an Act positively named the plant-
ations.The Habeas Corpus Amendment Act (31 Car.II cap.2) was passed
fifteen years after New York was conquered. The Act of course only
made statutory a common law writ; but the argument from common law
could not apply convincingly to a conquered or ceded colony.

Charter   Which Representatives of the Province with
the Governor and his Councill shall be the
supream and only legislative power of the said
Province.

Observation Whether this does not abridge the Acts of Par-
iament that may be made concerning New York.[1]

Charter   That all Bills agreed upon by the said Representatives shall be presented by them to the
Governor and Councill for the time being for
their Approbation and Consent.

Observation This seems to take away from the Governor and
Councill the power of framing Laws as in other
Plantations.

Charter   Which Bills so approved shall be deemed a Law
for the space of two years unless the Lord
Proprietor shall signify his dissent within
that time. That in case the Lord Proprietor
shall confirm the Laws within that time, they
shall continue in force until repealed by the
Assembly. That in Case of Dissent or Determination of two years they shall be voyd.

Observation This Term of years does abridge the King's
power, and has been thought inconvenient in
other Plantations, and is different from Colonel Dungan's Instructions....

382. COMMISSION TO GOVERNOR DONGAN, 10 June 1686.[2]

...And we doe hereby give and grant unto you full power
and Authority with the advice and consent of our said Council or the major part of them, to make, constitute and
ordain Laws, Statutes and Ordinances for the publick peace,
welfare and good Government of our said Province and of
the people and inhabitants thereof and such others as
shall resort thereto, and for the benefit of us, our heirs
and sucessors....

(viii) NEW JERSEY

383. INDENTURE BETWEEN JAMES,DUKE OF YORK, AND LORD BERKELEY AND SIR
GEORGE CARTERET FOR NEW JERSEY, 24 June 1664.[3]

[The Duke's charter of 12 March 1664 was recited]...Now this
indenture witnesseth That his said Royal Highness James,

---

1. A concern for the authority of Parliament.
2.*Ibid.* III pp.377-82.Dongan was now being commissioned as royal governor with legislative as well as executive power. The members of
the council, with whose advice Dongan exercised these powers, were
named in his instructions pp.369-75.
3. Archives of N. Jersey Ist I pp.10-14.The device of lease and release (established by 27 Hen.VIII cap.10 to change land use into possession) had become a normal means of conveying land in freehold. On
23 June 1664 the duke, possessed of the fee simple by his royal patent, leased for 10 shillings the lands between the Hudson and Delaware,with a symbolic peppercorn reserved to signify use only. The
next day,by this release, the grant was cleared of the duke's right

Duke of York, for and in consideration of a competent sum
of good and lawful money of England to his said Royal Highness...in hand paid by the said John Lord Berkeley and
Sir George Carteret before sealing and delivery of these
presents, the receipt whereof the said James Duke of York
doth hereby akcnowledge...doth grant, bargain, sell, release, and confirm unto the said John Lord Berkeley and
Sir George Carteret, their heirs and assigns for ever,
all that tract of land adjacent to New England...[to the
west of Long Island and Manhatten, and bounded by the main ocean on
the east and on the west by the Delaware, and to the north by 41°40'
on the Hudson.]
which said tract of land is hereafter to be called by the
name or names of *New Ceaserea* or *New Jersey*...with their
and every of their appurtenances in as full and ample
manner as the same is granted to the said Duke of York by
the before rented Letters patent [1] and all the estate,
right title interest, benefit, claim and demand of the
said James,Duke of York, of, in, and to the said tract of
land ....

    [All of which land was by indenture on 23 June sold by the Duke
    to Berkeley and Carteret for the term of one year at a peppercorn
    rent: so that Berkeley and Carteret were 'in actual possession'
    of the land and were 'enabled to take a grant and release thereof'
    and hold the land for ever, rendering the duke annually the sum
    of 20 nobles of English money if demanded at Michaelmas.][2]

---

of reversion (the peppercorn);and Berkeley and Carteret secured not
merely the use but the fee simple.
1.This was clearly a reference to profits from the land, not to taxes
or customs,for the indenture dealt only with a conveyance of land and
the duke had in his patent no power to devolve powers of government,
or to grant a sub-fief.It is true that in 1672 and 1674 king's letters
were procured exhorting the inhabitants of New Jersey to obey the
laws and government of the proprietors; but (though for Connecticut
a land grant from the New England Council in 1635 had been reinforced
by a royal patent in 1662) there was never such a charter for the
New Jerseys. Berkeley and Carteret,however,declared themselves to be
'true and absolute Lords Proprietors': and assuming that they had in
New Jersey powers identical with those they had as lords proprietors
for Carolina,they issued on 10 February 1665 the 'Concessions' prepared for Carolina a month before [see No.370], including freedom of
conscience,generous land grants,appeal over grievances and a general
assembly for legislation and taxation. They styled themselves 'Lord
Proprietors of the Province of New Ceasarea or New Jersey' and the
duke connived at this fiction without attempting to legitimise it.But
discontent grew over the oath of fidelity to the proprietors and the
exaction of quit rents.
2.The money did not have to be paid and (like the original 10 shillings for the lease) probably was not. This tract of territory granted
by the duke was divided in July 1674 when Carteret was confirmed in
the north and eastern half, and John Fenwick (to whom Berkeley had
in March conveyed his share in trust for Edward Byllynge) the western part. William Penn and other Quakers became involved in West New

384. 'CONCESSIONS AND AGREEMENTS'OF WEST NEW JERSEY, 3 March 1677[1]
[Commissioners were to administer the province till a general
assembly was summoned. The *Concessions of 1665* regarding land
grants quit rents and taxation only by consent of the general assembly were repeated.]
Chapter XIII. That these common law or fundamental
rights and privileges of West New Jersey, are individually
agreed upon by the Proprietors and freeholders thereof,to
be the foundation of the government, which is not to be
altered by the legislative authority, or free assembly
hereafter mentioned and constituted, but that the said
legislative authority is constituted according to these
fundamentals, to make such laws as agree with, and maintain
the said fundamentals, and to make no laws that in the
least contradict, differ or vary from the said fundamentals, under what pretence or alligation soever....
[To attempt to subvert such fundamental laws was treason. Liberty of faith and worship, security from arbitrary arrest, trial
by jury, due process of law, witness and evidence in open court
were guaranteed.]
Chapter XXXII. That so soon as divisions or tribes,or
other such like distinctions are made; that then the inhabitants, freeholders, and proprietors, resident upon the
said province, or several and respective tribes, or divisions or distinctions aforesaid, do yearly and every year
meet on the first day of October, or the eight month, and
choose one proprietor or freeholder for each respective
propriety in the said province, (the said province being
to be divided into one hundred proprieties) to be deputies,

Jersey through disputes between Fenwick and Byllynge: in July 1676
a redivision took place by the 'Quintipartite Deed' which formally
separated West New Jersey from the East. Penn's commitment to guarantees for civil liberty 'the rights of Englishmen' - was a strong
influence in the subsequent Concessions of 3 March 1677 [No.384].East
New Jersey was in March 1683 after Carteret's death shared among 24
ill-sorted proprietors in England as tenants in common: their 'Fundamental Constitutions' of 6 June 1683 (*ibid*.I pp.395 ff.) clearly demonstrated their incapacity for practical government. There was an
executive 'common council' of all the proprietors (or deputies) and
12 freemen (elected from the 'great council') which divided into spec-
ialist committees for art and education,for trade,and for plantation.
The 'great council' was the legislature of all the proprietors and
72 (later 144) elected freemen, where bills would pass only by a complex two-thirds vote.But in the colony these Fundamental Constitutions
were ignored. In 1688 both East and West New Jersey were absorbed
with New York into the Dominion of New England.
1. Arch. N. Jersey 1st I.pp.241 ff. Penn seems to have had a major
responsibility for drafting this remarkably liberal document, which
affirmed freedom of conscience,trial by jury, no taxation without
representation, annual elections of commissioners (the chief execut-
ives), treasurers, chief justices, sheriffs and collectors by the
assembly; and elections to be by ballot.

trustees, or representatives for the benefit, service and
behoof of the people of the said province: which body of
deputies, trustees or representatives, consisting of one
hundred persons, chosen as aforesaid, shall be the general,
free and supream Assembly of the said province for the
year ensuing and no longer....

Chapter XXXIII. And to the end the respective members
of the yearly assembly to be chosen may be regularly and
impartially elected, That no person or persons, who shall
give, bestow, or promise directly or indirectly to the
said parties electing, any meat, drink, money or money's
worth, for procurement of their choice and consent, shall
be capable of being elected a member of the said Assembly.
And if any person or persons, shall be at any time corrup-
tly elected, and sufficient proof thereof made to the said
free assembly, such person or persons...shall be reckoned
incapable to choose or sit in the said Assembly, or execute any other public office of trust within the said province, for the space of seven years thence next ensuing.
And also that all such elections as aforesaid, be not determined by the common and confused way of cry's and voices,
but by putting balls into balloting boxes, to be provided
for that purpose, for the prevention of all partiality,
and whereby every man may freely choose according to his
own judgment, and honest intention....

　　[The assembly could determine its time of meeting and adjourn-
　　ment. In all votes a two-thirds majority was required as 'determin-
　　ative.' Assemblymen should be paid a shilling a day.]

Chapter XXXVI. That in every general free Assembly,
every respective member hath liberty of speech; that no
man be interrupted when speaking; that all questions be
stated with deliberation and liberty for amendments; that
it be put by the chairman, to them to be chosen, and determined by plurality of votes. Also that every member has
power of entering his protest and reasons of protestations.
And that if any member of such Assembly shall require to
have the persons names registered, according to their
yea's and no's, that it be accordingly done: and that after
debates are past, and the question agreed upon, the doors
of the house be set open, and the people have liberty to
come in to hear and be witnesses of the votes, and the
inclinations of the persons voting.

Chapter XXXVII. And that the said Assembly do elect,
constitute and appoint ten honest and able men, to be
Commissioners of state, for managing and carrying on the
affairs of the said province, according to the law therein
established, during the adjournments and desolutions of
the said general free assembly, for the concervation and
tranquility of the same.

Chapter XXXVIII. That it shall be lawful for any person
or persons during the session of any General Free Assembly
in that province, to address, remonstrate or declare any
suffering, danger or grievance, or to **propose**, tender or
request any privilege, profit, or advantage to the said

province, they not exceeding the number of one hundred persons.

Chapter XXIX. To enact and make all such laws, acts and constitutions as shall be necessary for the well government of the said province, (and them to repeal) provided that the same be, as near as may be conveniently, agreeable to the primitive, antient and fundamental laws of the nation of England. Provided also, that they be not against any of these our Concessions and Fundamentals before or here-after mentioned....

[The assembly might establish all courts, appoint judges and choose magistrates, constables and officials. It might subdivide the province into hundreds and proprieties, establish ports and markets, and impose 'equal taxes and assessments'.]

385. ANSWER BY THE GOVERNOR AND COUNCIL TO THE DEPUTIES,
19 October 1681.[1]

The Pattent from the Duke of Yorke to the Proprietors upon which our Commissions are grounded setts forth the foundation of our Government as you have been confirmed under his Majesty's owne hand, and wee well hoped that none of the seed sowne by Sir Edmond Andross had taken soe deep a roote as that any of the Deputies of this Province should att this time question the foundation of our Gov-ernment....

(ix)NEW PLYMOUTH

386. H.M.'s COMMISSIONERS TO GOVERNOR PRENCE, 1664.[2]
...That the Articles of Confederation, when the four colonies entered into an offensive and defensive league,

1.J.R. Brodhead (ed.) op.cit.III p.293. The deputies had asked to be informed whether the indenture of 1664 from the duke was the found-ation of their government. The governor and council proposed a joint committee with the deputies 'to debate and remove these scruples'. Philip Carteret was governor of East Jersey from 1667 to 1682.
2. Mass.Hist.Soc. Coll.1798 Vol.V. (1812) p.192. The charterless plantation of New Plymouth had acknowledged Charles II and protested its loyalty. In their petition of 5 June 1661, the governor, Thomas Prence, and the general court had expressed their pleasure at his restoration: 'it is enough our Joseph (or rather) our Charles is yet alive'. They had asked for a confirmation of their privileges (C.O. 1/15 no.61) but had secured no royal charter.
The roval commissioners, writing from Rhode Island, were concerned to clarify the purpose of the New England confederation of 1643. They were told that they were misinformed if they believed it an alliance against England. Though the commissioners acknowledged the cooperation of New Plymouth in their report on 14 December 1665, they reported that the plantation was 'too poor' to secure a charter and, when off-ered one free if they would permit the king to choose as governor one of three names submitted by them every 3 - 5 years, they had indeed refused - with protestations of thanks and loyalty. The days of New Plymouth as a separate colony were already numbered. Thomas Prence

neither did, nor shall oblige you, to refuse His Majesty's
authority, though any one, or all the other three,should
do so: not that we have the least imagination of your denying your obedience to His Majesty, but that we might stop
some foul mouths in America, and that His Majesty may be
the more confirmed in his good opinion of your loyalty,
who was informed (as we were told) That, that union was a
war-combination made by the four colonies, when they had
a design to throw off their dependance on England....1

(x) PENNSYLVANIA
387. 'FIRST FRAME OF GOVERNMENT' 25 April 1682.2
     [Penn rehearsed his precepts and convictions on the origin,

---

had been elected governor in 1634 and in 1638 and regularly from 1657
till 1682.
1.For New Plymouth, see also Nos. 280,283.
2. F.N.Thorpe (ed.) *op.cit.*V pp.3144-69.This *'Frame'* was issued by
Penn after discussion of his preliminary draft with friends and prospective settlers:it was intended not merely to promote interest in
some ideal future goal,but actually to be implemented as fully as
possible.A Second Frame was presented by Penn and accepted by council
and assembly on 2 April 1683 in a revised and reduced form,with smaller council and assembly and with no triple vote for the .governor.
(Minutes of Provincial Council (1838) I pp.xxxiv ff.).There is no
evidence that these Frames were submitted to the king for approval
as the charter would seem to have required.
This First Frame was accompanied by a series of 'laws agreed upon in
England' (*ibid.*I pp. xxix ff.) to be amended (if so desired) by the
freemen.These included the acceptance of the Frame as 'for ever...
fundamental'; the provision of free elections without influence or
corruption; for taxation by law; for open and speedy justice with
plain language and self-pleading before juries; for moderate fines
and fees: for education 'in some useful trade or skill' for all
twelve-year-old children 'to the end none may be idle but the poor may
work to live and the rich, if they become poor,may not want'; for
prisons and workshops;for a land registry and a census of vital stat-
istics; for the duties and trust of office; for the prevention of
wrongful conviction, plurality, fraud and defamation;for the observance of the Sabbath;for the liberty of worship and conscience to all
who believed in God,and for all officials to be professing Christians.
These were passed by the first assembly in December 1682,with supplementary proposals by Penn, as the 'Great Law' of Pennsylvania: the
sections relating to profanity,blasphemy,adultery,fornication,rape,
theft,arson,drunkenness,gambling,cock-fighting,May games and stage
plays were considerably amplified (S.Hazard,*Annals*,pp.608ff).At the
same time the assembly passed an Act of Union and Naturalisation,
incorporating at their petition certain settlements with Penn's province, and admitting those (Swedes and Dutch),who swore allegiance to
the king and fidelity to Penn ,as eligible as freemen.Furthermore, an
Act of Settlement,expressing thanks to the proprietor for his Frame
and his courtesy, made certain amendments: 'the fewness of the people,
their inability in estate and unskillfulness in the matter of government' dictated smaller councils and general assemblies.

nature and purpose of civil government.[1] Freedom existed where laws ruled and the people were party to these laws: where good men were involved in executing good laws, for government depended on men and not men on government; and where a frame of government existed 'to support power in reverence with the people, and to secure the people from the abuse of power'. 'Liberty without obedience is confusion, and obedience without liberty is slavery'. But he recognised that it was impossible to devise a frame which would please all men or suit all periods and circumstances. 'I do not find a model in the world that time, place and some singular emergencies have not necessarily altered; nor is it easy to frame a civil government that will serve all places alike.'

For the well-being of his province and the encouragement of all the freemen and planters, he guaranteed these following liberties, franchises and 'property for ever.']

Imprimus. That the government of this province shall, according to the powers of the patent,consist of the Governor and freemen[2] of the said province in form of a Provincial Council and General Assembly by whom all laws shall be made, officers chosen and publick affairs transacted, as is hereafter respectively declared....

[The freemen were to meet on a day named to elect from among themselves 72 members 'of most note for their wisdom, virtue and ability'[3] to assemble on another day named and to act as the provincial council: 24 of whom would serve for 3 years, 24 for 2, and the remaining third for one.]

*Fourth.*That after the first seven years, every one of the said third parts that goeth yearly off, shall be incapable of being chosen again for one whole year following: that so all may be fitted for government and have experience of the care and burden of it....

[For legislation, appointment, and the establishment of courts and judgment of criminals, the *quorum* was fixed at 48 and decisions would be carried only with a two-thirds majority: for lesser matters the *quorum* was 24 and a simple majority would suffice.The governor would have a 'treble voice' in council. He and the council would initiate and publish draft legislation, should execute the laws diligently, should defend the province and prevent subversion of this Frame, should plan towns, ports, and markets, should inspect the management of the treasury, should establish schools and encourage useful inventions.

1.Penn believed strongly in the 'ancient and fundamental freedom' of England and of Englishmen – of ownership of liberty and property; of voting for all laws under which they were governed; and of their influence on, and share in, the judicial power.
2. The proprietor was governor,but appointed a deputy:William Markham, his cousin, had been sent out in April 1681.'Freemen' were freeholders: every settler who bought 100 acres and cultivated at least 10; every free servant who took up 50 acres and cultivated 20;and everyone who paid scot and lot. (Second Law: *Minutes* I p.xxix).
3. Penn had 'wisdom, virtue and integrity' in his draft. The substitution was significant, for 'ability' implied wealth and property.

The Provincial Council[1] would divide into 4 equal executive sub-committees to deal respectively with plantations, settlement and highways, with justice and safety, with trade and treasury, and with morals, manners, education and arts. The combined *quorum* of these sub-committees - 24 members - would act as the standing council.]

Fourteenth. And to the end that all laws prepared by the governor and Provincial Council aforesaid may yet have the more full concurrence of the freemen of the province, it is declared, granted and confirmed That at the time and place or places for the choice of a Provincial Council as aforesaid, the said freemen shall yearly choose members to serve in General Assembly as their representatives, not exceeding two hundred persons who shall yearly meet on the twentieth day of the second month in the year one thousand six hundred eighty and three following, in the capital town or city of the said province, where during eight days the several members may freely confer with one another;[2] and if any of them see meet with a committee of the Provincial Council (consisting of three out of each of the said committees aforesaid, being twelve in all) which shall be at that time purposely appointed to receive from any of them proposals for the alteration or amendment of any of the said proposed and promulgated bills; and on the ninth day from their so meeting, the said General Assembly after reading over the proposed bills by the clerk of the Provincial Council and the occasions and motives for them being opened by the governor or his deputy shall give their affirmative or negative which to them seemeth best in such manner as hereinafter is expressed. But not less than two-thirds shall make a quorum in the passing of laws and choice of such officers as are by them to be chosen.[3]..

[Laws were to be styled as 'By the Governor with the assent and approbation of the freemen in Provincial Council and General Assembly'. In the first year the general assembly would consist of all the freemen; thereafter of 200 elected, to be increased with the enlargement of the province (but not to exceed 500) on the 'proposal' of the provincial county and the 'resolution' of the general assembly. The governor and council should erect courts; the council

---

1. Clearly the council was the superior body: like the assembly, it was elected, but it had responsibility for preparing and initiating laws which were submitted to the assembly: it also had considerable executive power.
2. The elaborate detail and specific dating of this clause was characteristic of the Frame. A later clause dealt with the deferring of business to the next day if the day named proved to be the Lord's Day.
3. The assembly was subordinate to the governor and the elected council.Penn pointed out that the assembly had a 'negative voice - not a debating,mending,altering,but an accepting or rejecting power'. This limitation on its power became naturally one of the first targets for attack by assemblies, seeking to assert themselves in the government, noticeably not to widen the franchise.

should propose annually 'a double number' of persons to serve as
judges and treasurers, and the freemen of the county courts should
propose 'a double number' to serve as sheriffs, J.P.'s and coroners:
from which the governor should nominate for the next year.

But since the need for immediate action prevented 'so quick a
revolution of officers', Penn appointed such officials for the
first year at once. The general assembly would continue to sit
until the governor and council declared there was no further work
for them to do; but could be recalled at need. All elections,mot-
ions, laws, *etc.*, were to be decided by ballot: and 'unless on
sudden and indispensable occasions,no business in Provincial Council or its respective committees shall be finally determined the
same day that it is moved'. If the governor was a minor and no
guardians had been appointed by his father, the council could nominate up to 3 to act as such and to exercise the governor's powers.
Any amendment of the Frame would require the consent of the governor, and six-sevenths of the freemen in the council and in the
assembly.]
And lastly, That I, the said William Penn for myself,
my heirs and assigns, have solemly declared, granted and
confirmed to do hereby solemnly declare grant and confirm,
that neither I, my heirs nor assigns, shall procure or
do any thing or things, whereby the liberties in this charter contained and expressed shall be infringed or broken;
and if anything be procured by any person or persons, contrary to their premises,it shall be held of no force or
effect....[1]

(xi) NEWFOUNDLAND

388. REPORT OF THE COUNCIL FOR FOREIGN PLANTATIONS, 2 March 1671.[2]
    [A petition of the Western Adventurers had been presented.]
...And after due consideration, of the best wayes and

1.In the Second Frame of April 1683 the superior privileges of the
council (now reduced to 18 members) over the assembly (now numbering
36) were confirmed.Then in the period when the proprietorship was
temporarily replaced by royal government,Governor Fletcher in 1693
allowed the assembly to initiate legislation,and he personally nominated the councillors.After the restoration of Penn's proprietary, his
deputy-governor,Markham (who had also been lieutenant governor to
Fletcher) had been compelled – in order to secure defence aid for
New York – to agree to demands for a Third Frame in November 1696:
this accepted Fletcher's reforms and recognised the assembly as at
least equal in importance to the council. A final fourth Frame – the
Charter of Privileges – was exacted from Penn in 1701: [see Volume
II].
2.C.O. 195/1. The hope held in 1661 [No.268] that fishermen and settlers could live in amity had proved false, for an economic crisis
had hit the fisheries.The Western Adventurers were convinced that the
settlers were to blame. There could be no concessions to their security: no governor was necessary. All authority should be concentrated
in the 'admirals'; and all interests should be subordinated to that
of the fishery.

Meanes of Regulating Securing, and Improooveing the Fishing Trade in Newfoundland, Wee doe humbly offer unto your
Majesty as our opinion and Advice.

That you would be pleased to grant by way off Addition
to Your Majesties former charter, and Establishment of the
Powers, Rules and Orders for the Government of the said
Fishery,

1. That all the Subjects of your Majesties Kingdome of
England shall and may for ever heerafter, peaceably Hold,
and Enjoy the Freedome of takeing Bayte, and Fishing in
any of the Rivers, Lakes, Creeks, Harbours, or Roads in
or about Newfoundland, or in any of the Islands adjoyning
thereto with Liberty to goe on Shoare in any part of Newfoundland or the said Islands, for the Cureing, Salteing,
Dryeing, and Husbanding of their Fish [cutting trees, building
boats, stages, *etc.*.]....Provided always that they submitt unto
and observe all such Rules and Orders, as now are or hereafter shall be established by your Majestie, your Heires
or Successors, for the Government of the said Fishery in
Newfoundland.

2. That noe Alien, or Stranger be permitted to take
Baits, or Fish in any of the Rivers, Lakes, Creeks, Harbours, or Roads in Newfoundland, Between Cape Race, and
Cape Bona Vista, or in any of the Islands thereunto adjoining.

3. That according to the Establishment of your Majesty's
Father (of blessed memory) in the 13th year of his Reign,[1]
No Planter or Inhabitant in or upon the said Newfoundland
be permitted to fell, cut down, root up, Waste, burn or
destroy any Wood or Timber Trees, or erect or make any
houses, buildings, Gardens etc, or inhabit or plant within
Six Miles of the Sea Shore in any part of the said Newfoundland, between the Cape de Race lying in or about 46
degreed of North Latitude and the Cape Bona Vista lying
in or about 49½ degrees likewise of North Latitude, nor
upon any Island within ten Leagues of your Shore between
the said Capes.

4. That no Planter or Inhabitant in Newfoundland, do
take up or possess any of the Stages, Cook Rooms, etc,
berths or Places for taking Bait or fishing before the
arrival of the fishermen out of England and that they be
all provided.

5. That the clause in your Majesty's Charter of confirmation of the Rules and Orders for regulating of the Newfoundland fishery [of 20 January 1661]... concerning the transportation of Men thither may be altered and enlarged in
manner following: That is to say that no Master or Owner
of any Fishing ship do transport or carry any Seamen, fishermen or other persons in his ship to Newfoundland other
than such as are truly belonging to his, or other ships
Company, and such as are engaged in the Voyage and share

---

1.   i.e. the grant to David Kirke, *etc.* in 1637 [see p.225].

or shares, or hire of the said Ship...[1] [The number of persons that could be transported was limited to 60 for each 100 tons burden.]

8. That the Masters and Owners of all Fishing ships trading out of England to Newfoundland be enjoined (according to the number of Men in their respective Ships) to provide in England Victuals and other Necessaries, Salt only excepted, for the whole Voyage or fishing Season, for themselves and Company and to put them on ships board, before their going out of Port.

9. That it be likewise strictly commanded, That no fishing Ship or Company, do depart out of England, directly for Newfoundland, or any Fishing Voyage in any year, before the first day of March nor to the Isles of Cape de Verde intending from them to Newfoundland, before the fifteenth day of January.

10. That from *[- hours]*forward all Masters of Fishing Ships trading to Newfoundland shall yearly before the beginning of their Voyage give Bond in his Majesty's name to the Mayors for the time being of the Ports of Southampton, Poole, Weymouth, Melcombe Regis, Lyme, Exeter, Dartmouth, Plymouth, East Lowe, Fowey, Falmouth, Biddiford, Barnstaple and Bristol and all other Ports and Sounds, upon the coast of England respectively, according to the Port or place from where they shall set out, under the Penalty of One hundred Pounds, with condition that they shall not carry out any Seamen, Fishermen, or other Persons, other than such as are truly belonging to his, or their,or other ships Company, and such as are engaged in the Voyage, and share, or shares of hire of the said Ship or ships respectively.

And that they shall be bringing or cause to be brought back into England, all such Seamen, Fishermen and other Persons as they shall carry out, Mortality and danger of the seas excepted, And also such persons as shall be employed from the Newfoundland in English ships north fish for Market voyages....

11. That no Master of any Fishing Ship or others, do take up, or use, any Stage already built, in any Port, Harbour or Bay between Cape Race and Cape BonaVista with a less number of Men than Twenty-five, who are to be on entire Company.

12. That no Fisherman or Seamen carried out as aforesaid, be suffered to remain in Newfoundland in the Winter, after the Fishing Voyage or Season is ended.

13. That the Admirals, Vice Admirals and Rear Admirals

1.This prohibition of passengers was a blow to settlement.In 1663 Parliament for the first time had legislated for Newfoundland, probably (by removing the most obvious abuses in the fishery) to protect the latter from any action by a civil government there. But this Act by forbidding the taxation of cod effectively prevented the reestablishment of proprietary control or the introduction of any civil administration with a local revenue.

of, and in, every Port or Harbour in Newfoundland for
the time being, be authorised and required, to preserve
peace and good Government among the Seamen and fishermen
in their respective Harbours, as well as on the shores.

To see your Majesty's rules and Orders concerning the
Regulation of the Fishery duly put into execution, and to
cause all Offenders to be apprehended that they may be
punished - according to their demeritts.

14. That the Captains of the Convoys yearly appointed
by your Majesty for securing the fishery in Newfoundland
be strictly enjoined by their Instructions from the Lord
High Admiral That they do not take into their Ships or
transport into Newfoundland any Seamen or other person
except such as do truly belong to their own respective
ships.

15. That they be aiding and assisting unto the Admirals,
Vice Admirals and Rear Admirals of the respective Ports
and Harbours in Newfoundland, from time to time as need
shall require, in preserving of peace and good Government
among the Fishermen and Seamen there and in apprehending
of Offenders.

16. That they ply from Port to Port there and do not
go into any Port or Harbour except in case of necessity
or for security.

17. That they do not fish themselves, or suffer any of
their ships Company to take, cure, Salt or dry any Fish
in or about Newfoundland.

18. That they take an Account of the Names, Situations
and Distances of the several Ports, Harbours, Bays and
Islands in and about Newfoundland between Cape Race and
Cape Bona Vista....

21. That they do not take into their Ships, any sort
of Fish, either by way of Merchandise, freight or otherwise, except what shall be for their own use or spending.

22. That at their returns into England they deliver
copies of their Journals and Observations upon the Fishery
unto the Lord High Admiral of England.

23. That the Admirals, Vice Admirals and Rear Admirals
in the respective Harbours and Bays in Newfoundland may
according to the ancient Customs, be empowered to apprehend and secure all Offenders,for any Crime committed in
Newfoundland,on shore or at sea, and to bring them to
England... [and to see no one wintered to Newfoundland or remained
there after 31 October. They were to keep journals and records of
ships and crews for the Council of Foreign Plantations.]

26. That the several Recorders, or their Deputies , and
the Justices of Peace for the time being,of the respective
Ports, Towns and Places before named, and one neighbouring
Justice of Peace for the same County, may be joined in Commission with the Mayors of the said Ports, Towns and Places
respectively and any two or more of them be empowered to
take cognizance of all complaints made of any offenders
against the Laws, Rules and Orders established by your Majesty for regulating the Newfoundland fishery and to hear

and determine the same, according as is provided and directed to the respective Mayors alone, by your Majesty's
said Charter of Confirmation....
     [Fines could be imposed on masters and crews for breach of
     H.M. rules.]
     28. That the clause in your Majesty's Charter of Confir-
mation which concerneth the Powers of the Earl Marshal,in
the punishing of Felonies, Murders etc. committed in Newfoundland, may be reviewed, there being at present no such
Office or Court; and in Lieu thereof if your Majesty shall
think fit, That a certain way of Judicature may be established for the hearing and determining of Treasons, Felonies and Murders, and all criminal matters committed or
done in Newfoundland, on the shore or at Sea, according
to Law and Equity, and for the awarding of Execution thereupon, as the cause shall require.
     29. And Lasty, That encouragement may be given to the
Inhabitants of Newfoundland, to transplant themselves and
their families to Jamaica, St. Christophers, or some others
of your Majesty's Foreign Plantations....[1]

389. REPORT OF THE LORDS OF TRADE, 25 April 1675.[2]
     [They had perused all previous papers and orders and heard the
     evidence of the agents for the Western ports, 'some desiring a
     colony and governor, but many more against both'. The English fish-
     ery had lost the market in France to a thriving French fleet; the
     New Englanders by contrast enjoyed a prosperous fishery.]
     ...That for some late yeares the Fish has fayled in
Newfound Land, and Adventurers have lost many of their
Shipps in the late Warrs, especially in that with Spain,
and the late Warrs have much diminished the hands which
used to take fish. The Inhabitants and Planters, who
contrary to their old Charter live within Six Miles of
the Sea, have destroyed the woods, do continue to destroy
whatever the Adventurers leave yearely behinde; They possesse early the Places of greatest Conveniency before the
Adventurers returne, and which is very pernicious do most
of them sell wine and Brandy, whereby the Seamen are with-

---

1. The Western fishery had a strong lobby and survived the adoption
of these proposed amendments to their 'Western Charter' [see Nos.166,
268] by an order in council of 10 March 1671 (Acts Privy Council,
1613-80 § 915). More power was granted to the fishing admirals and to
the West-country magistrates.
2. C.O. 1/67. A petition from a Mr. Hinton for the appointment of a
governor had been sent to the lords of trade for investigation and
report. At this period there were some 1490 'permanent' settlers of
whom no less than 1286 were servants employed by the 'planters' and
bye-boat keepers and hired from the fishing crews, or direct from
England or Ireland for no more than a year or two. Few planters and
bye-boat men had brought their families and most looked forward to
retirement at home after a few years' hard work in exile,building up
an estate and fortune.

drawne from their Labor, and many seduced to stay in the
place, while their Familyes do thereby become Burthens
to their respective Parishes at home.

From all which Reasons 'twas easy to beleive there was
a decay of the Trade as to England, and that the Complaynts
thereof were very just. But as to Mr. Hinton's Proposall
for curing all by a Governor, We could not finde that a
Governor could cure any part.

1. Because the Planters who are now there in Number
Eight Hundred or One Thousand, do live scattered in Five
and Twenty severall Harbours betwixt Renouse and Bonavista,
which are allmost Eighty Leagues assunder.

2. That in all the Winter when the abuses are many of
them done, there is no passing by Sea or Land from One
Place to another, so that neere Forty Harbours could have
no Government though a Governor were in the Country.

3. That besides the Charge of Forts, and of a Governor
which the Fish Trade cannot support, 'tis needless to have
any such defence against Forreigners, the Coast being defended in the Winter by the Ice, and must in the Summer by
the resort of your Majesties Subjects, for that place will
allwayes belong to him that is superior at Sea;[1] So that
unlesse wee saw proper Reasons for a Coloney, We could see
none for a Governor; And against a Coloney there are not
onely the rigours of the Climate, and infertility of the
Land, which, as is alleaged, oblige all those who are
there all the Winter to Idlenes, and inclines them to
Debauchery,But they cheifely consume the Products of New
England, the Shipping of which Country fournish them with
French Brandy, and Madera Wines in exchange for their Fish,
without depending for any supply from hence; And We had
reasons to presume that if the Climate and Soyle could
favor a Colony, they would rather adhere to New England,
and in time tread in the same stepps[2], to the losse of
those many advantages, which at present, by the Method
things are in, we yet enjoy. For We could not hope for a
like Regulation on the Product of this Place, as on the
Products of your Majesties other Plantations, because Fish
cannot beare the Charge of comeing home,but must goe directly to the Marketts abroad....

[They could not find any reason in the way the French fishing
was managed to explain its prosperity.]

So that after Consideration of the whole Matter, We
had recourse unto those Rules which were formely on like
occasion setled in Councill by your Majesties Order of

---

1. Newfoundland became an English possession rather than Portuguese,
Spanish or French because of sea power. All produce had to come or go
by sea.
2. If the migratory fishery declined,Newfoundland would become another
New England - a fate the lords of trade in the mid-1670s could hardly
contemplate with equanimity, in view of their struggle with Massachusetts.

the 2nd of March 1671 and We found them all so proper,and
effectuall for the advantage of this Trade, as to need
onely some few Additions to make the Trade revive and
flourish, And those Additions We humbly propose to your
Majestie as followeth.

1. That all Plantation and Inhabiting in that Country
be discouraged; And in order hereunto, That the Commander
of your Majesties Convoy have Commission to Declare at his
goeing this yeare, your Majestyies will and pleasure to
all the Planters, that they come voluntarily away, and in
Case of disobedience, that your Majestie will beginn the
next yeare; and so from time to time as often as your Convoys are sent thither, to putt in execution the ancient
Charter, which strictly forbidds any planters to Inhabit
within six Miles of the Shore from Cape Race to Cape Bonavista;[1] and finding any of them within that District, to
Seize, bring away, or send them home as Offenders, to
Answer their Contempts, and the Mischeifs before recited,
which have been occasioned by such their Inhabiting contrary to the Charter; And in this single point (as We humbly
conceive) does consist the validity and good effect of
the whole Regulation.

2. We further humbly Offer that the Convoy who is now
goeing,[2] may have Instructions to help and assist those
in their Transportation who shall be desirous upon this
intimation of your Majesties pleasure to returne home;
And to declare, that in Case they shall rather chuse to
betake themselves to any of your Majesties Forreigne Plantations, That the Governors are now writ unto, and Commanded by your Majestie to receive them with all favor, and
afford particular help and assistance towards their setlement; And such Letters humbly propose to be speedily
sent unto the said Governors....

3. That your Majesties Councill Learned be directed
(as formerly they were) to enquire into and review the
Powers formerly given by your Majesties Charter of Confirmation for the Trying of Treasons, Felonies, Murthers
etc done in that place, and that if the same be in anything deficient, or Inconvenient, that they Report what
sort of Judicature would be convenient to be Erected for
the hearing and determining of such offences.

4. And when the same is Reported, and your Majestie
shall in Councill settle and determine into what hands
the administration of that Power shall be placed, That
then the Majors of the Westerne Ports be required to
Renew their Charter, with the additional Rules and Powers
above-mentioned. Also that the same Charter may be printed,
and a Proclamation Issue to enforce the observation of all

1.This again was the charter of 1637 [see p.225].
2.Convoys had escorted the fishing fleet to Newfoundland each season
and during the 1650s the captain of the convoy had exercised some powers of supervision over the admirals. In 1675 the captain had given
his opinion that a permanent base was necessary in the island.

that shall be established thereby, for the better exciting
of all persons to their Dutyes who are concerned therein,
or Obliged to take notice of the same.

390. CONFIRMATION OF THE WESTERN CHARTER,27 January 1676.[1]
      [The terms of the charter were reaffirmed with additional regul-
      ations about the manning of ships, the proportion of 'green men',
      the powers of the admirals to apprehend offenders for trial in
      England, the prohibition of seamen to remain after the 31st of
      October, the keeping of journals and statistics, the lodging of
      bonds with mayors for the return of the crews.]
      ...And lastly because there is at present no Court
Marshal in England, We do therefore further require and
Command that if any man in Newfoundland shall kill another
or of any shall Secretly or forceably steal the Goods of
any other to the Value of 40 shillings he shall forthwith
be apprehended and arrested, detained and brought prisoner into England and the Crime committed by him made
known to one of our Principal Secretaries of State to the
end that due Order may be given to punish such Offenders
according to Law.

391. ORDER IN COUNCIL, 14 April 1680.[2]
      Upon a debate this day had at the Boord concerning the
Fishery and Colony of Newfoundland, His Majesty was pleased to Order, and it is herby Ordered that...the Committee
...do signifie unto the Magistrates of such Townes in the
West of England as are cheifly concern'd in that Trade,
That his Majesty intending to settle a Governor and erect
a Fort in New found Land for the preservation of his Majestys soverainty and good of the Fishery, They do ther-
fore transmit unto the Boord their opinions in what manner
and under what Regulations such a Governor may be setled
in New found Land, And that they appoint such Agents or
Correspondents as they shall think fit, to attend the Committee...on the 10th of October next with their said Opinions or what else they can offer for the benefit, and security of that Trade.[3]

1.C.O. 1/67 p.135. The Western fishery was consolidating its position.
2. C.O. 195/1.The argument for recognising and even encouraging settlement was that, if it were prohibited,the French would take over
the whole island and the fishery would be lost to England. Lawlessness which discouraged trade might seem to demand a resident governor; but that might increase the number of settlers to the detriment
of the migratory fishery.
3. In fact no governor was sent. When a year later some settlers
asked why not, the answer was that the government did not 'at this
moment think it expedient'. The government saw the need to recognise
the need for a few settlers to substantiate English claims to sovereignty and to protect the equipment in winter. But the establishment
of a government would be expensive and would attract more settlers
than were necessary. Therefore the compromise was some very limited

(xii) EAST INDIA COMPANY

392. *EAST INDIA COMPANY v. SANDYS*, 1684.[1]

[Holt argued that: By law no English subject could trade with
infidels without royal licence and the king might prohibit such
trade since it was, according to *Calvin's Case*, with his 'perpetual
enemies'. Furthermore with foreign Christian countries the right
to trade would depend entirely upon the king's relations - of
treaty, amity or alliance - with the foreign prince.]

...The East India Company charter is a grant to a company that they and their children shall trade to the Indies, notwithstanding any statute or diversity of faith or
religion, and that they shall have the sole commerce and
trade there. There is a prohibition to any of the King's
subjects to trade there without licence. Now, my lord,
this grant I take to be good: for, my lord, though it may
not be lawful without the King's licence yet it is in the
power of the King to make it so. And for this reason can
the King make an alien a denizen....

[This grant was not open to objection that it was a monopoly;
for it did not restrict any freedom of trade which others enjoyed
previously, for they had no right lawfully to trade in the East
Indies. Nor at the time of the parliamentary attack upon monopolies[2] did any impugn the charter to the East India Company. It was
a trade permitted by the king on the broad ground of national advantage.]

---

settlement, but without any government.
For a further century or more (see V. Harlow and F. Madden *British
colonial developments*, 1774-1834 (1953) pp.369-372), orthodox opinion
in Britain considered Newfoundland, not as a colony with its attendant
problems of truculence or even secession, but as a large fish industry, seasonally moored off the Grand Banks, and thereby a 'nursery
of seamen', not of settlers. [see Volume II: section IV (2) (e) (i)].
1. 10 St.T. 371. The Company, having a monopoly patent from the
Crown by the charter of 1661 [No.269], were suing Thomas Sandys for
interloping, without licence, in East India trade. After lengthy arguments by Holt and Finch for the Crown and Treby and Pollexfen for
Sandys, the C.J.(Jeffreys) found in favour of the company with
arguments deriving firmly from this opinion of Holt. Unfortunately for
the company it had become identified, under Sir Josiah Child's governorship, with the royal prerogative, and the monopoly remained a
subject of attack in Parliament by individual 'interlopers' seeking
greater freedom of trade with the East. On 19 January 1694 a Commons
resolution declared that 'all the subjects of England have equal right
to trade to the East Indies unless prohibited by Act of Parliament'.
A rival English Company was then incorporated by statute (9 and 10
William III cap.44) but the 'old' London Company secured its position
as largest stock-holder in the 'new' company. By 1709, when the old
company surrendered its charters, a United Company of 'old' and
'new' had, indeed, been operating jointly for more than a decade -
since 5 September 1698. Sir J. Holt was chief justice (K.B.) 1688-1710.
2. i.e.1621-4: Mompesson's impeachment and the Act against monopolies
(21 & 22 Jac.I cap.3).

III. LAW IN THE COLONIES, 1606-88

From the many documents relating to the nature of the law and the procedures and practices in colonial courts, a few significant themes and examples have been selected.

(A) LAW IN SETTLED, CHARTERED AND ROYAL COLONIES

(1) DIVERSE APPROACHES TO LAW

These few extracts relating to Virginia, Massachusetts, Maryland, New Haven, Rhode Island and the Leewards illustrate the various sources used as inspiration or criterion for law in these colonies: the law of Moses or Christ; the law of England, written or unwritten, known or often unknowable in the absence of law reports. Of course there was also a parallel growth of local tradition in isolation and ignorance: in reliance on individual colonial custom and usage - local, subjective and autochthonous: a sort of rough-and-ready folklore among judges and magistrates and a natural preference for their own precedents - remembered or half-remembered. As Captain Breedon reported in 1661, 'what laws are not mentioned in this Book are in the magistrates' brests to be understood' [see No.306]. In Massachusetts there had been a remonstrance against Mosaic law by Dr. Child and others [see also No.230] and a challenge to the exclusive powers of magistrates (*assistants*) by the deputies.

(a) VIRGINIA

393. (i) INSTRUCTIONS FROM JAMES I, 20 November 1606.[1]
...The councel, or the most part of them, shal have full power and authority att our pleasure in our name and under us...to give directions to the councels of the several collonies...for the good government of the people to be planted in those parts...and the same to be done for the substance thereof as neer to the common lawes of England and the equity thereof as may be[2]...

___

1. W. Hening (ed.) *Statutes...of Virginia* I p.71.
2. This requirement that colonial laws should be, not identical but, generally similar (within the rule of repugnancy) to the laws of England was the common form of instructions, whether to a colony gover-

And moreover wee doe hereby ordaine...That all the lands, tenements and hereditaments to be had and enjoyed by any of our subjects within the presents aforesaid shal be had and inherited and enjoyed, according as the like estates they be had and enjoyed by the lawes within this realme of England....

[Verdicts would be given by twelve jurors in criminal cases.]

(ii) 'ARTICLES,LAWS AND ORDERS', 24 May 1610[1]

Divine and moral[2]

[Regular daily public worship was required from all settlers under pains of martial law. Death was the punishment prescribed for blasphemy, conspiracy, treason, murder,sacrilege, sodomy, rape- of 'woman, maid or Indian', adultery, false witness, fraud, or trading with the Indians.]

Everie man and woman duly twice a day upon the first towling of the bell shall upon the working daies repaire unto the Church to hear divine service upon pain of losing his or her dayes' allowance for the first omission, for the second to be whipt, and for the third to be condemned to the gallies for six months.[3] Likewise no man or woman shall dare to violate or breake the Sabboth by any gaining, publique or private abroad or at home, but duly sanctifie and observe the same, both himselfe and his familie, by preparing themselves at home with private prayer,

---

ned indirectly (as here) by a company or directly by the Crown: see the instructions to Wyatt in 1621 and to Berkeley in 1641 [No.220]. This rule of repugnancy derived from the delegation of legislative power as to the guilds [see Nos. 144-8; and *inter alia* pp.215,217, 221,227,231,236,244,325 *etc.]*
1. William Strachey, *For the Colony of Virginea Britannia; Lawes divine, Moral and Martiall* (1612) collected in P.Force, *Tracts and other papers* (1844) III No.2.Strachey was secretary to Governor Sir Thomas Gates in Virginia and published these laws first established by Gates and amplified by his deputy. Though the company in London made orders for its own organisation and officials [see No.172], it delegated law-making in Virginia to the governor or lieutenant general: the need for a strong hand and rigid discipline in a frontier-outpost precariously held in the early years of lawlessness and misrule - 'the starving time' - and settled largely by the 'idle scum' of jails, stews and slums,prompted the harsh severity of this code, and Gates was seen as the saviour of Virginia (see the Company's *A true declaration of the state of the colonie* (1610) in P.Force *op.cit.*III No.1 p.15, which optimistically contrasted the abundant riches and potential fertility of Virginia with the idleness, indiscipline and anarchy of the previous four years: 'every man overvaluing his own worth...a commander;every man sharked for his owne present bootie, but...altogether carelesse of succeeding penurie'.) But these laws were calculated to terrorize and indeed to be enforced: the extreme penalties however were probably not exacted, and were gradually moderated and withdrawn.
2.The laws summarised here occupy eleven pages; the *martial* laws over forty.
3. Soldiers, craftsmen and workmen were required to work all hours

that they may be the better fitted for the publique, according to the commandements of God and the orders of our
Church as also every man and woman shall repaire in the
morning to the divine service and sermons preached upon
the Saboth day, and in the afternoon to divine service and
catechising, upon pain for the first fault to lose their
provision and allowance for the whole weeke following; for
the second to lose the said allowance and also to be whipt;
and for the third to suffer death....

    And if any man die and make a will, his goods shall
bee accordingly disposed; if hee die intestate, his goods
shall bee put into the store, and being valued by two
sufficient praisers, his next of kinne (according to the
common lawes of England) shall from the Company, committees or adventurers receive due satisfaction in monyes,
according as they were praised by which meanes the colonie
shall be the better furnished; and the goods more carefully preserved for the right heire and the right heire
receive content for the same in England....[1]

> [There was strict provision for all stores from loss, theft
> or sale. Settlers trading with sailors in metal, tools,[2] clothes
> and food were to be punished by confiscation and whipping: sailors
> trading in provisions above prices fixed at the mast head would
> suffer death. No live stock would be killed without leave of the
> governor/lieutenant-general, under pain of death for the principal
> and loss of ears and whipping for any accomplices. Wilfully careless weeding or theft of plant, herb, flower, or crop would be
> punished by death. Whipping was prescribed for fornication, and for
> washing of unclean linen in the streets, the fouling of the precincts of the fort by 'the necessities of nature', and refusal of
> religious instruction. Washerwomen would be whipped for stealing
> linen; cooks and bakers would suffer loss of ears and galley service for fraud; and fishermen would be executed for trading privately with sailors.][3]

(iii) INSTRUCTIONS TO GOVERNOR SIR FRANCIS WYATT, 24 July 1621.[4]
    [He was instructed] to keep up religion of the church of
England as near as may be[5]; to be obedient to the King

---

between the beating of a drum,on pain of whipping and a year in the
galleys for disobedience.
1.Even under such a rigorous regime the English common law on inheritance was respected.
2.All edged tools were to be registered and their whereabouts known.
3.By the time Yeardley arrived as governor with commission for summoning an assembly, the harsher aspects of Virginian semi-military
government were less necessary and were disappearing.
4.W. Hening (ed.) op.cit. I p.114 [see No.174,175].
5.The first extant statutes seem exclusively concerned with promoting
a uniformity to the doctrines and disciplines of the Anglican church
(ibid. pp.120,124) and with defence against the Indians (ibid.pp.124,
127). Thereafter there was much legislation (often by proclamation
of governor and council in the 1620s, and then by Acts of the general
assembly) about the planting of tobacco.

and to do justice after the form of the laws of England[1];
and not to injure the natives, and to forget old quarrels
now buried....

(iv) STATUTES CLAIMING CERTAIN ENGLISH LAWS (7 Car.I) February 1632[2]
(Act *XXX*) The statutes for artificers and workmen (1 Jac.
I cap.6) are thought fitt to be published in this Colony.
(Act *XXXI*) And the lawes of England agaynst drunkards are
thought fitt to be published and dulie put into execution,[3]
that is to say, for every offence to pay five shillings to
the hands of the church wardens and further as it is conteyned in the statutes of 4th of kinge James and the 5th
chapter.

(v) DECLARATION OF THE GRAND ASSEMBLY, 17 March 1651.[4]
     We say we were...sworne to governe and be governed (as
farr as possible the place was capable of) by the lawes of
England; which lawes we have inviolably and sacredly kept
as farr as our abilityes to execute and our capacities to
judge, would permit us and with reason; for these lawes

1.Monthly courts in Charles City and Elizabeth City were established
in 1624 (*ibid.* p.125) to decide suits and controversies not exceeding the value of 100 pounds of tobacco and to punish petty offences:
appeals lay to the governor and council. In 1632 the number of these
courts was increased and a quarterly court authorised for James Town
[see p.276]. In 1647 appeals from these monthly (now since 1643 called
county)courts to the quarterly courts and to the general assembly were
regulated (*ibid.*p.345); and the appeal to the assembly was specially
reserved to consider and settle new points of law.
In September 1632 the commission for monthly courts required observation of all orders and acts of the general assembly 'and according to
the same and as neere as may be according to the lawes of the realme
of England' following the procedure and punishments administered by
English J.P.s (*ibid.*p.186). In April 1642 in the assembly's remonstrance they protested 'the near approach which we have made to the
lawes and customs of England in proceedings of the court and trials
of causes' (*ibid.*p.237): cf. also the instructions to Governor Berkeley, 9 August 1641 [p.339] - Justice was to be 'equally administered
...as near as may be after the form of this realm'; and the legislation was to be 'correspondent as near as may be to the lawes of England'.
2.W.Hening (ed.) *op.cit.*I p.167.In early Virginia a few English statutes were re-enacted by the assembly as law in Virginia. Sometimes
too the criterion of English 'custom' and 'manner' in pleas and judgments was established by statute : e.g. that accounts and contracts
should be made and kept in money, not tobacco (Act *IV* of 1633: *ibid.*
p.216).
3. In September 1632 the formula was 'Be it also enacted according to
the lawes of England' (Act *XXIX:ibid.* p.193).
4.Virginia Magazine I p.81.Under the provisional government established on 30 April 1652 after the surrender [see p.345] justice was to
be done according to the instructions from the Parliament of England
'and according to the knowne lawe of England and the acts of the assembly here established' (W.Hening *op.cit.* I p.372).

onely...can humanly prevent our ruines...These lawes we
professe are our guides and do believe we deserve punishment and infamy if we willingly or wilfully deviate from
them....

(vi) INSTRUCTIONS TO LORD CULPEPER, 6 December 1679.[1]
    And for a further mark of our supreme and immediate
authority we do hereby signify unto you our express commands that all writs within our said province be issued
in our name, notwithstanding any former usage to the contrary.[2]

(b) MASSACHUSETTS
394. (i) ORDER OF GENERAL COURT FOR JUSTICES OF THE PEACE, 23 August
    1630.[3]
    It was ordered That the Governor and Deputy Governor
for the tyme being shall alwaies be justices of the peace,
and that Sir Richard Saltonstall, Mr. Johnson, Mr. Endicott and Mr. Ludlowe shalbe justices of the peace for the
present tyme, in all things to have like power that justices of peace hath in England for reformacion of abuses
and punishing of offenders; and That any justice of the
peace may imprison an offender but not inflict any corporal punishment without the presence and consent of some
one of the assistants....

(ii) ORDER OF THE GENERAL COURT ON SEXUAL OFFENCES, 14 June 1642.[4]
    It is ordered by this Court and the authority thereof
That if any men commit fornication with any single women
they be punished either by enjoining marriage, or fine,
or corporal punishment, or all of these, as the judge of
the Court that hath cognizance of the cause shall appoint,
most agreeable to the Word.

(iii) ORDER OF THE GENERAL COURT ON SEXUAL OFFENCES, 27 May 1674.[5]
    This Court, accounting it their duty by all due means
to prevent appearance of sinn and wickedness in any kind,
doe order, That henceforth it shall not be lawfull for
any singlewoman or wife in the absence of hir husband to
entertaine or lodge any inmate or sojourner with the dis-

1.C.O. 5/1355.A similar instruction was sent to New York in 1686 on
the Duke of York's accession as king, to Massachusetts in 1691; to
Jamaica, Barbados,Bermuda and New Jersey in 1702; and to Maryland in
1703.
2.See,for example,the statute of March 1660 just prior to the Restoration when Berkeley had been elected governor by the assembly: writs
were then to be issued 'in the name of the Grand Assembly', which had
under the Commonwealth asserted its 'supreme power' over governor and
council, claiming the sole right to dissolve themselves and to appoint all officials [see p.347-8].
3.N.B.Shurtleff (ed.) op.cit.Ip.74.   4. ibid. II
p.21. These orders illustrate the puritan code relating to sexual
offences. By contrast with the harsh Virginian laws briefly enacted
in 1610 [see No.393(ii)],these were enforced over a long period.
5.ibid.V p.4.

like of the selectmen of the toune, or magistrate, or commissioners who may have cognizance thereof, on penalty of
five pounds per weeke, on conviction thereof before any
Court or magistrate, or be corporally punished, not exceeding ten stripes; and all constables are to take cognizance
hereof for information of such cases....

(iv) ANSWERS OF THE REVEREND ELDERS TO CERTAINE QUESTIONS PROPOUNDED
    TO THEM, 13 November 1644.[1]
A.*1* The Magistrates are by pattent and election of the
people the standing counsell of the Commonwealth in the
vacancie of the generall courte and [have power] accordingly
to act in all cases (pertaining to government) according
to the said pattent and the laws made by the said generall
courte of this jurisdiction....

    [This answer was grounded on several explicit passages in the
    charter, especially the provision for the assistants, with the
    governor or deputy, to constitute 'a sufficient court or assembly'
    to conduct business.]

We doe not find that by the pattent they are expressly
directed to proceed according to the word of God, but we
understand that by a law or libertie of the country they
may act in cases wherein as yet there is no expresse law,
soe that in such acts they proceed according to the word
of God....
A.*3*...the general Courte hath not power by pattent in all
cases to choose anie officers as commissioners either assistants or freemen, exempting that is excluding all others,
to give them commission to set forth theire power and places because it would then follow that the magistrates
might be excluded from all cases of constant judicature
and counsell which are their principall worke whereby alsoe
the end of the peoples election would be made frustrate....

    [In particular cases however the general court might appoint such
    a special commission.]

Q.1... Whether the deputies in generall courte have judiciall and magistraticall authoritie?

1.*Hutchison papers* (Publ.,Prince Soc.1865) I pp.205-13.The deputies
had once more challenged the entrenched power of the magistrates
(*assistants*). A standing council of magistrates had previously acted
in the intervals between sessions of the general court: when questioned by the deputies in 1635, the'elders'(ministers and teachers)
had supported the magistrates.Now the deputies had in their separate
house voted for a commission (4 magistrates, 3 deputies and 1 elder)
to govern when the general court was not meeting.This proposed power-
sharing with the deputies was however regarded by the magistrates as
an attempt 'to overthrow the foundations of government'.Winthrop and
other magistrates therefore, as in 1635, put questions to the elders
as umpires between them and the deputies. In their answers the elders
generally upheld the magistrates who by patent, election and divine
calling were invested with the responsibility for judicature and
administration.

Q.2. Whether by pattent the generall courte, consisting
of magistrates and deputies, as a generall courte, have
judiciall and magistratical authoritie?

A.1.The pattent in expresse words giveth full power
and authoritie, as to the governor and assistants soe to
the freemen alsoe assembled in generall courte, (p.11 of
the charter). *2ndly*, Whereas there is a 3 fold power of
Magistraticall authoritie, legislative, judicative, and
consultative or directative, of the publique affaires of
the commonwealth, for provision and protection. The 1st
of these, namely, *legislative*,is expressly given to the
freemen joyntly with the governor and assistants, (p.12).
Consultative or *directative* power of the publique affaires
of the commonwealth, for provision and protection is also
granted by the pattent unto the freemen as to the governor
and assistants, (p.13). But now for the *judicature*, if we
speak of the constant and usuall administration hereof,
we do not find that it is granted to the freemen or deputies in the generall courte, either by the pattent or by
the election of the people, or by anie law of the country.
But if we speake of the occasional administration thereof
we find the power of judicature administrable by the freeman joyntly with the governor and assistants, upon a double occasion:- *(1)* In case of defect or delinquency of a
magistrate we find the whole generall courte of governor,
deputy governor, assistants and freemen may proceed to
remove him, p.12.   *(2dly)*, If by the law of the countrey
there lye anie appeale to the general courte or any other
speciall causes referred to theire judgement, it will necessarily inferre that in such cases, by such laws, the
freemen joyntly with the governor and assistants have
power of judicature touching the appealeants and cause,
the appeale and those reserved cases. What we speake of
the power of freemen, and same may be said of deputies,
soe far forth as the power of the freemen is delegated
to them by order of law....

> [On the question of the judge's discretion to modify sentence
> since there were 'variable degrees of guilt' the elders, by ref-
> erence to the Mosaic code, demonstrated that the Lord prescribed
> a single penalty for theft (*Exodus* 22.1). But they accepted that
> circumstances varied: 'the strikeing of neighbour may be punished
> with some pecuniary mulct when the strikeing of a father may be
> punished with death...the gathering sticks of the Sabbath day may
> be punished with death when a lesser punishment might serve for
> gathering sticks privily and in some need'. A single lie might
> be less severely punished than one 'before the judgement seat'.
> Again there were first and habitual offenders, the 'enticed and
> the enticers', the principals and the accessaries, the witting
> and the unwitting. Just as 'Solomon mittigated the punishment of
> Abiathar for his service done to his father formerly (I *Kings* 2.
> 26,27)', so the general court 'with chief power' might modify 'the
> penalties of great crimes'.]

A.2. The generall courte, consisting of magistrates and
deputies, is the cheife civill power of this commonwealth,

soe as to prescribe the power of magistracy and to prescribe in a civill way lawes unto all, not repugnant unto
the lawes of God, nor to the pattent, nor to the fundamentall lawes and liberties established in this commonwealth,
and accordingly may doe all other acts which belong to
such a power, as namely, both Acts of counsell tending to
the provision and protection and wellfare of the whole
body, and alsoe Acts of judgement, soe far as (according
to our answer to the two former questions of our honoured
magistrates) is by the pattent or choice of the people or
lawes of the commonwealth reserved to them and seated in
them....

    A,*3*. Our government is not a meere aristocracy, but
mixt of an aristocracy and democracy, in respect of the
generall courte.[1] 2dly,Notwithstanding ...yet it followeth
not necessary thereupon That it should be mixt in all
courtes and administrations thereof, because our forme
(as all other formes of civill government) is the ordinance of man...free to make it mixed or simply soe alsoe
...mixed in the generall courte and united in others,
according to the pleasures of the ordeiners thereof.Acc-
ordingly our pattent, notwithstanding it hath made our
government mixed in respect of the generall courte, yet it
seemes to have instituted subordinate administrations of
justice to be aristocratically dispensed by the courte of
assistants; yet even in these courtes there is some place
for a democratical dispensation in respect of the jurors[2]...

(v) JOHN WINTHROP'S SPEECH IN THE *HINGHAM CASE*,3 July 1645.[3]
    ...The great questions that have troubled the country,
are about the authority of the magistrates and the liberty

1.For Winthrop's contempt of democracy see pp.289 and 291.
2.See No.411(b).As a compromise between magistrates and deputies, it
was agreed to prepare a code of lawes [see pp.350 ff.].
3.J.K.Hosmer (ed.) *Winthrop's Journal* (1908) IIpp.280-1. This statement on the accountability of magistrates (*'assistants'*) to God's laws
and those of Massachusetts related to the action between Lieutenant
Emes and Captain Allen of the Hingham militia: when magistrates supported Emes, their tried and trusted officer, against the newly elected commander, Allen, the issue became one for an attack on the magistracy by the elected deputies. Winthrop addressed the general court
asserting the authority of the magistrates.
Since 1634 the deputies had sought to limit the theocratic dominance
of the magistrates who claimed, with the advice (when asked) of the
clergy ('the elders'), the exclusive power to interpret the voice of
God and saw no place for majority government 'in the wise administration of a civil state according to God'. The magistrates saw themselves
as the sacrosant custodians of the 'right form of government in church
and state', accountable only to God, and as the chosen builders of
God's plans as revealed in the Old Testament and interpreted (if
necessary) with clerical advice.
To reduce the magistrates' authority, particularly in regard to the
'negative vote' which they had asserted in the general court for fourteen years, the deputies in 1644 secured a majority for a resolution

of the people. It is yourselves who have called us to this
office, and being called by you, we have our authority
from God, in way of an ordinance, such as hath the image
of God eminently stamped upon it, the contempt and violation whereof hath been vindicated with examples of divine
vengeance. I entreat you to consider, that when you choose
magistrates, you take them from among yourselves, men subject to like passions as you are. Therefore when you see
infirmities in us, you should reflect upon your own, and
that would make you bear the more with us, and not be severe censurers of the failings of your magistrates, when
you have continual experience of the like infirmities in
yourselves and others. We account him a good servant, who
breaks not his covenant. The covenant between you and us
[*i.e. the officials and magistrates*] is the oath you have taken
of us, which is to this purpose, that *we shall govern you
and judge your causes by the rules of God's laws and our
own, according to our best skill.* When you agree with
a workman to build you a ship or house, etc., he under-
takes as well for his skill as for his faithfulness, for
it is his profession, and you pay him for both. But when
you call one to be a magistrate, he doth not profess nor
undertake to have sufficient skill for that office, nor
can you furnish him with gifts, etc., therefore you must
run the hazard of his skill and ability. But if he fail in
faithfulness, which by his oath he is bound unto, that he
must answer for. If it fall out that the case be clear to
common apprehension, and the rule clear also, if he transgress here, the error is not in the skill, but in the evil
of the will: if must be required of him. But if the case
be doubtful, or the rule doubtful, to men of such understanding and parts as your magistrates are, if your magistrates should err here, yourselves must bear it....

    [As for the liberty of the people, there was a <u>natural</u> liberty
which was no more than animal license. But <u>civil</u> liberty required
a proper subjection to authority.][1]

(vi) SUMMARY OF THE REMONSTRANCE OF DR. CHILD AND OTHERS, 16 May 1646.[2]
  ...The principal things complained of by the petitioners

---

that they would sit separately from the magistrates - in two houses.
1.The tone of Winthrop's speech was firm and temperate, but he was
angry at the democratic demands of the deputies.In his journal (*ibid.*
II p.242) he had noted,and commented on,their extreme demands: that
the general court should become a people's court; that scandalous petitions against magistrates should be heard in the general court; that
no credit should be granted to the testimony of the chief officers of
the Commonwealth; that even if such petitions against the magistrates
were found false,there would be no reproof of the petitioners;that
seditious practices against authority should not be ensured; that
time was well used in agitation; that authority was incompatible with
the liberty of the Commonwealth,*etc*.
2. This summary was in T. Hutchinson's *History of...Massachusetts Bay*
(1765) pp.145-6. [For a fuller extract from the document itself see
pp.350-2].

were,

1st. That the fundamental laws of England were not owned by the colony as the basis of their government according to patent.

2nd. The denial of those civil privileges, which the freemen of the jurisdiction enjoyed, to such as were not members of churches and did not take an oath of fidelity devised by the authority here, although they were freeborn Englishmen of sober lives and conversation, *etc.*

3d. That they were debarred from Christian privileges, *viz.* the Lord's supper for themselves, and baptism for their children, unless they were members of some of the particular churches in the country, though otherwise sober, righteous and godly, and eminent for knowledge, not scandalous in life and conversation, and members of churches in England.

And they prayed, that civil liberty and freedom might be forthwith granted, to all truly English, and that all members of the church of England or Scotland, not scandalous, might be admitted to the privileges of the churches of New-England;...

(vii) *GIDDINGS v. BROWNE*, 22 June 1657.[1]

...I find in this case for the plaintiff [with damages and costs] ...I understand this to be about a fundamentall law and that a fundamentall law properly so called. It is such a law that God and nature have given to the people. So that it is in the trust of their governors in highest place and others to preserve, and not in their power to take away from there....

[Such fundamental laws included the right to elect supreme governors. In addition]

2. That every subject shall and may enjoy what he had a civell right or title unto, soe as it cannot be taken from him, by way of gift or loan, to the use or to be made the right or property of another man without his owne free consent.

3. That such lawes (though called *liberties*) yet more properly they may be called *rights* and in this sense there may be added as a third fundamental law, *viz.* That no custome or precedent ought to prevayle in any moral case that may appear to be sinnfull in respect of the breach of any law of piety against the first table or of the righteousnesse against the second....

1.T.Hutchinson papers II (Publ. Prince Soc) pp.1-25.In February 1655 the majority at a town meeting in Ipswich had voted £100 to help house the minister,Thomas Cobbet.The question was whether such a vote could bind the minority (including non-members without any vote) who refused to consent to such a levy.Edward Browne,the marshal,had entered the house of George Giddings (who had opposed and refused the tax) and in distraint had taken away several pewter platters as his compulsory contribution. Giddings brought this action for trespass before a local magistrate, Samuel Symonds, later deputy-governor of Massachusetts.

[He had written a statement[1] 'what doth more clearly and fully
tend to inlighten my judgment.'][2]

(viii) THE NOMINATION OF COURT ASSOCIATES, 27 May 1674.[3]

[Where there was a lack of magistrates available for the county
courts,it was necessary for 'persons of worth' to be nominated by
the freemen as *associates* to assist in the administration of justice.]

...This Court...do further declare and order, that in
all counties where associates are to be appointed, the
freemen shall make their nomination of such associates
at the same time yearly when they give in their nominations for magistrates, which votes for nomination of associates shall be carryed also by the same commissioners of
the several tounes, sealed up, to their sheere meeting;
there to be opened; and those fower persons that shall
have the most votes shall be certified under the hands of
three of the sajd commissioners, the shire commissioner
being one, to the Court of Election yearely for the confirmation and approbation of the said associates, which

---

1.In this supplementary account he affirmed that 'it is against a
fundamentall law in nature to be compelled to pay that which others
doe give....No man hath any certaynty or right to what he hath, if
it be in the power of others (by pretence of authority or without)
to give away (when in their prudence they conceive it to be for the
benefit of the owner soe to doe) without his owne consent'. It could
not be denied that in England men had often lost their estates by
force,fraud or pretence of law (shipmoney,*etc.*), but never by compulsory gift to another -'to take from Peter and give it to Paul'. It
was wrong - since it infringed 'the fundamental law of mine and thine'
- to interpret the Act of the general court requiring contributions
to church and commonwealth as an attack upon the individual's liberty: in practice contributions had been voluntary.Parliament could
legally tax the whole country for the benefit of all for that was its
constitutional role. 'Let us not (here in New England) despise the
rules of the learned in the lawes of England who have both great
helps and long experience': the rules of interpretation, of equality
(as opposed to doctrinaire *'Levellisme'*, which he thought a tyranny),
of damage,of equity and of moderation should be observed; and he considered precedents and judgements in the courts. Elsewhere in Massachusetts,even the housing of a surgeon in Ipswich,contributions had
been made voluntarily, he said.
2.Browne appealed against this judgment to the Salem court which reversed the decision. On appeal to the general court on 20 August the
two houses disagreed - the deputies agreeing with Symonds' judgement,
the magistrates supporting Browne. But arguments against taxation by
town meeting being binding on all were as powerful against taxation
by the general court, and in a few days the deputies changed their
minds.
3. N.B. Shurtleff (ed.) *op.cit.* V p.4. These 'associates' were elected to act in a similar capacity as magistrates in the county courts.

being obteined, the secretary shall certify the clarke of
the County Court thereof, who shall give notice to such
associates to appeare at their next County Court, there
to take their respective oathes.

(c) MARYLAND

395. (i) PROCEEDINGS IN ASSEMBLY, 29 January 1637.[1]

Then question being moved what lawes the Province should be governed by, it was said by some that they might
doe well to agree upon some lawes till we could heare from
England againe. The president denying any such power to
be in the House, Capt. Cornwalers propounded the lawes of
England. The president acknowledged that the Commission
gave him power in civill causes to proceed by the lawes
of England and in criminal causes likewise not extending
to life or member, but in those he was limited to the lawes
of the Province there could be no punishment inflicted on
any enormous offenders by the refusal of these lawes····

[Having examined the terms of the commission carefully and finding no power therein to punish by loss of life or member, they
therefore agreed for the moment to deal with such 'enormous' offences by martial law.]

(ii) AN ACT FOR ERECTING A COUNTY COURT, March 1639.[3]

[It was enacted by the Lord proprietor 'by and with the advice
and approbation of the freemen' that all civil appeals and criminal cases should be judged 'by the lawes of this Province or by
the common law of England'; usage would be 'as any of the King's
courts of common law in England useth within England' except where
otherwise provided by 'any law of this Province'; forms would follow
those 'observed in courts of common law in England as neer as the
judge...may well know them'; and judgements would be agreeable to
provincial law or in default of such law to those usual in similar
civil or common law courts in England 'as neer as the judge...
shall be able to determine',][4]

And all that questions and demurers in law in this
court shall be determined by the said Cheif justice, commissioner or commissioners. And in all pleas and matters
civill or criminall (in this or any other Court within the
Province) the Lord Proprietarie shall be allowed all the
same and like prerogatives and Royall rights as are usa-
lly, or of right, due or belonging to a Court Palatine
(saving allways the Soveraigne Dominion due to the King
of England).

1. W.H.Browne (ed.) *Archives of Maryland* I p.9. Justices of the peace
were established by an Act of 1639 (*ibid*.p.52).
2. See No.412 (c)(ii)n.
3. W.H.Browne (ed.) *op.cit.*I pp.47-9.[see also pp.306,311].
4. Another Act in the same session (*ibid*.p.51) repeated that forms
and proceedings in courts should be as similar as possible to those
in English courts. Other Acts at the same time prescribed the laws
of inheritance (*ibid*.pp.60,64).

(iii) AN ACT FOR THE RULE OF THE JUDICATURE, 2 August 1642.[1]

Right and just in all civill causes shall be determined
according to the law, or most Generall usage of the Province since its plantacion or former presidents of the same
or the like nature, to be determined by the Judge; And in
defect of such Law, usage or president, then right and
just shall be determined according to equity and good conscience, not neglecting (so far as the Judge or judges
shall be informed thereof and shall find no inconvenience
in the application to this Province), the rules by which
right and just useth and ought to be determined in England
in the same or the like cases; And all crimes and offences shall be judged and determined as in England in the
same or the like cases; And all crimes and offences shall
be judged and determined according to the law of the Province, or in defect of certain law, then they may be determined according to the best discretion of the Judge or
judges judging as neer as conveniently may be to the laudable law or usage of England in the same or like offences:
Provided that no person be adjudged of life, member or freehold without Law certain of the Province....

(iv) AN ACT CONCERNING PROCEEDINGS AT LAWE, 9 April 1662.[2]

Whereas severall differences doe arise within this Province wherein there is noe rule or lawe provided in the
Province whereby to determine such differences and to
leave too much to Discrecion is to open a Gapp to Corrup-
cion for the avoyding such Inconveniencyes, Be it Enacted
by the Lord Proprietary by and with the Consent of the
Upper and Lower howse of this present Generall Assembly,
That in all cases where the Lawe of this Province is silent Justice shall be administred according to the Lawes
and Statutes of England if pleaded and produced. This Acte
to endure for three yeares or to the End of the next Generall Assembly. *The Lower howse have assented* — William
Bretton, Clerk.

The Upper howse desires to be sattisfyed how the County
Courts shall be sattisfyed when the Lawe of England is
rightly pleaded and whether all Lawes of England how inconsistent so-ever with a plantacion shall be admitted here.[3]_
John Gittings, Councillor.

1.W.H.Browne (ed.) *op.cit.* I pp.147-8.This Act (as were many of these
early laws), was temporary - 'until the end of the next assembly'.
The next assembly enacted that 'all justice, as well civill as criminal,shall be administered by the governor or other chief justice in
court according to the laws of the province, and in defect of (such)
law, then according to the sound discretion of the said governor...
and such of the council as shall be present in court or the major part
of them'. The duration of this Act was not apparently limited.
2.W.H.Browne (ed.)*op.cit.* I p.435.Previously where the laws of Maryland
were silent,the judges had used their discretion in deciding whether
particular laws of England were relevant.The lower house now sought to
reduce that discretion.
3. Their argument was that many English laws were not appropriate to

The Courte to judge of the right of pleading and incon-
sistancy according to the best of their Judgement,skill
and Cunning, And the howse humbly desired this Acte be assented unto.— Wm. Bretton, Clerk.

The Sence of the Upper howse is that by this meanes of
leaveing all to the Breast of the Courts, All is again
left to Discrecion and soe the Act unnecessary as it lyes.
Voted that it passed.— J. Gittings, Councillor.[1]

(v) DOUBTS ABOUT APPLYING ENGLISH CRIMINAL LAW, 29 May 1674.[2]
...Mr. Tyler & Mr. Truman sent to desire the Lower house
to Consider of the dangerous Consequences which will of
necessitie happen by this house's Condescending that all
Lawes in England should be in force in this Province for
the tryall of Criminalls without some Reservacion to Consider of the Conveniences of this Province: The Lawes of
England,being in those Cases especiallie soe Voluminous &
often times are Repealed without our knowledge, Therefore
this House desires the Lower house to take into their serious Consideracion how unsafe it will be for the Judges of
this Province to Proceed against Criminalls by anie such
uncertaine Lawes, and Therefore it is the desire of this
House that the Lower house will Consider of soe manie of
the Lawes of England for the Proceedings aforesaid that
the Judges may be ascertained of such their Proceeding,
Besides the Consideracion of such Lawes as may be in force
which if unknowne to this Province may be of dangerous
Consequence[3]....

(d) NEW HAVEN

396. (i) AN ORDER FOR THE RULE OF THE JUDICATURE, 3 April 1644.[4]
...Itt was ordered,That the judiciall lawes of God,as
they were delivered by Moses, and as they are a fence to
the morall law, being neither typicall nor ceremoniall,
nor had any reference to Canaan, shall be accounted of

---

the colonies,were inconsistent,and were (in the absence of trained
lawyers and law reports) unknown,or even repealed.Twelve years later
they wanted an authorised list of English criminal laws which were in
force in Maryland (see *ibid.*II p.348) to be made by a joint committee
of both houses.
1.The next day there was concern about witnesses making declarations
instead of taking oaths.'The Assembly hath admitted and obliged the
Judges to proceed according to the law of England', but, 'Wee can take
noe man's life nor dispose of any man's Estate but by the oath of
lawful witnesses': a declaration did not bind a witness to truth as
did an oath sworn on the gospels (*ibid.*I p.437).
2. W.H. Browne (ed.) *op.cit.*II pp.374-5.
3. The lower house replied that such a fixed list was unnecessary because they held that the laws of England as a whole were (or ought to
be) in force in Maryland.Ten years later the Lord proprietor argued
that such a wholesome importation into the colony was dangerous for
it would tie them in their law-making and many England laws were undesirable and irrelevant.
For the continuing conflict between the lower house and the Lord proprietor over the extension of the laws of England into Maryland see
Volume II.
4.C.J.Hoadly (ed.) *Records of the Colony and Plantation of New Haven
1638-49*, (1857) pp.130-131.

morrall equity, and generally binde all offenders, and be
a rule to all the courts in this jurisdiction in their proceeding against offendors, till they be branched out into
perticulars hereafter.[1]
   Itt was ordered Thatt in case any of the magistrates in
the smaller plantations see need of help in some weighty
causes or difficulty knowtty cases, upon due notice and
request to the Governor, provision shall be made accordingly[2]....

(ii) *THE CASE OF ROBERT BASSET*, 22 March 1653.[3]
      [It was reported that at the town meeting on 7 March in Stamford
      Basset had asked the constable, Richard Law, why it had been sum-
      moned, and being informed that it was called to choose deputies
      to go to the general court in New Haven,]
   Robert Basset replyed they would obey no authority but
that which was from the State of England; the constable
answered this authority is the authority of England; that
he denyed and said, then let us have England's lawes, for
England doe not prohibbitt us from our votes and liberties, and here wee are, and wee are cut of from all appeales to England, and wee can *[have]* no justice here; further, he said, they were made asses of and their backs
are allmost broke and it is time for them to looke to
themselves and to throw their burden of, for they shall
be made very fooles; and he spake against the justice of
the authority of this jurisdiction...is that authority
just that makes what lawes they please, executes them as
they please, calls for rates when they please and never
so much as give them a reason....They were not so much
neighbours but bond men and slaves....
   Robert Basset was asked if he knew what liberty men
had in England in poynt of vote, he said no; hee was informed that many thousands in England of great estates

---

1.*The Laws of New Haven* are printed in *ibid.* II pp.571ff.Blasphemy,
murder,adultery,sodomy, masturbation,rape,incest, sedition,sabbath-
breaking and cursing parents were capital offences; divorce was prescribed for desertion,impotence and infertility;marriage,fine and whipping were punishments for fornication. The *Records* contained evidence
that these penalties were often exacted.
2.Two,three or four deputies from the freemen were chosen to assist
magistrates in inferior plantation courts which dealt with issues of
small value and with petty crimes. These were not jurors, but the verdict was by majority with the governor or chief magistrate having a
casting vote.
3.C.J.Hoadly (ed.)*op.cit.*I p.59-60.Government in the loose confederation of townships under Hew Haven was precarious and regularly there
were doubts raised about its legitimacy and many threats of secession
(e.g.*ibid.*p.185).Basset's complaint was that New Haven imposed arbitrary rates and provided no defence or security for Stamford,and permitted them no free votes in the choice of civil officers. His claim
to be governed direct from England, however, was(unlike Dr. Child's
plea for English law) based upon ignorance.

and good repute in other respects have no vote in such
elections ····
    [He was told he was a disturber of the peace both of the chur-
    ches and commonwealth to which he had taken oath of fidelity.
    Sometimes he seemed a parliament man; at others a royalist. He
    was imprisoned until the next meeting of the general court.][2]

(e) RHODE ISLAND

397. ACTS AND ORDERS FOR THE COLONY AND PROVINCE OF PROVIDENCE,
                                                May 1647.[2]
    ...And now to the end that we may give, each to other,
(notwithstanding our different consciences, touching the
truth as it is in Jesue, whereof,upon the point we all
make mention), as good and hopeful assurance as we are
able, touching each man's peaceable and quiett enjoyment
of his lawfull right and Libertie, we doe agree unto, and
by the authority above said,Inact, establish, and confirme these orders following:-
Touching Lawes
    [No person would be imprisoned, disseized, exiled or destroyed
    but 'by judgement of his peers or by some known law'.]
    And now, forasmuch as our Charter gives us power to
make such Lawes, Constitutions, Penalties and Officers
of Justice for the execution thereof as we, or the greater
part of us shall, by free consent, agree unto, and yet
does promise that those Lawes, Constitutions, and Penalties soe made shall be conformable to the Lawes of England,
soe far as the nature and constitution of our place will
admit, to the end that we may show ourselves not only unwilling that our popularity should prove (as some conjecture it will,) an Anarchie, and so a common Tyranny, but
willing and exceedingly desirous to preserve every man
safe in his person, name and estate; and to show ourselves,
in soe doing, to be also under authoritie, by keeping
within the verge and limitts prescribed us in our Charter,
by which we have Authoritie in this respect to act; Wee
do agree and by this present act determine, to make such
Lawes and Constitutions soe conformable, etc., or rather
to make those Lawes ours, and better known among us; that
is to say, such of them, and so farr, as the nature and
constitution of our place will admit
Touching the Common Law
    It being the common right among common men, and is prof-
itable eyther to direct or correct all, without exception;

1.At this trial in May 1654 fourteen months later, he confessed his
error, acknowledged 'that the way of government here setled is according to God' and gave bond of £100 to keep the peace in future.
(*ibid.*p.95).
2.J.R.Bartlett (ed.) *Records of...Rhode Island and Providence Plantations* I pp.156-9,190. The colony had received a patent from the Lords
and Commons through Warwick's influence in 1644 [see pp.324 ff.]. For
a fuller extract from this document setting up a federation of the
Rhode Island townships and drafting its code of laws, see pp.383-5.

and it being true, which that Great Doctor of the Gentiles
once said, that the Law is made or brought to light, not
for a righteous man, who is a Law unto himselfe, but for
the Lawless and disobedient in the Generall, but more particularly for murderers of Fathers and Mothers; for Manslayers, for whoremongers, and those that defile themselves with mankind; for Menstealers, for Lyars and perjured
persons, unto which, upon the point, may be reduced the
common Law of the Realme of England, the end of which is,
as is propounded, to preserve every man safe in his own
person, name and estate;...[The crimes were defined.] These
are the Lawes that concerne all men, and these are the
Penalties for the transgression thereof, which by common
consent are Ratified and Established throwout this whole
Colonie; and otherwise than thus what is herein forbidden,
all men may walk as their consciences perswade them, every
one in the name of his God. And lett the Saints of the Most
High walk in this Colonie without Molestation in the name
of Jehovah, their God for Ever and Ever, *etc.,etc.*

(f) THE LEEWARD ISLANDS

398. INSTRUCTIONS TO SIR CHARLES WHELER, 31 January 1671.[1]
...You are to take care that no man's life, member,
freehold or goods be taken away or harmed in the said
province under your government, otherwise than by established and knowne lawes, not repugnant to but as neer as
may be agreeable to the lawes of this Kingdoms....

(B) LAW IN CONQUERED COLONIES

This section attempts to illustrate,by contrast with the settled
colonies, the problem of law in colonies conquered from or ceded by
other European powers. It is of importance to the major issues later
interpreted in the Grenada case of *Campbell v. Hall* (1774) and is of
immediate relevance to Quebec, so recently ceded to the British
Crown by the treaty of Paris (1763), and to the status of the French
law of the 'new subjects' of the king in that conquered colony: so
too subsequently to Spanish law in Trinidad,Romano-Dutch in Guiana,
Cape Colony and Ceylon; or again of French law in Mauritius and the
Seychelles, *etc:* [see Volume III.]

(a) JAMAICA

399. (i) INSTRUCTIONS TO GOVERNOR EDWARD D'OYLEY, 8 February 1661.[2]
...5. You shall as soone as conveniently you may with
the advice of the Councill settle such Judicatories for
civill affaires and for the Admiralties, as may be proper

1.C.O. 1/26.Wheler had received a commission for the Leewards on 25
January [see No.340]. A similar instruction was given to William,
Lord Willoughby for Barbados on 30 April 1672;to Lord Culpeper for
Virginia in 1682,and to Sir Edmund Andros for New England in 1686.
2.C.O. 138/1 p.7. [see also Nos. 215 ff, 262,345 ff.].

to keepe the peace of the Island,and may determine all
matters of right and Controversy, according to Justice
and Equity, And you are to take care that all Judges and
other Officers and Ministers shall take the Oaths of Allegeance, and Supremacy, before you in the Councill.

(ii) PROCLAMATION OF GOVERNOR LORD WINDSOR, 11 July 1662.[1]
    For as much as his most Excellent Majestye, Charles
the Second...By his Proclamacion, hath published his Royall intentions for the encouragement of all his free subjects on his Kingdomes, Dominions, and Territoryes, and
doth thereby graunt...to all free persons, without inter-
upcion to transport themselves, their Familyes, and goodes
(except only Coyne and Bullion) from any of his Majesty's
Dominions and Territories to the sayd Island of Jamaica
....
    5. In all thinges Justice shall be Duely administred,
and that agreeable to the knowne Lawes of England, or such
other Lawes not Repugnant thereunto, as shall be Enacted
by Consent of the Free persons of the sayd Island.

(iii) INSTRUCTIONS TO SIR THOMAS LYNCH, 31 December 1670.[2]
    You shall examine carefully the constitution of such
judicatories for civil and criminal affairs as are established there, and if they be any way defective with the
advice of the said council cause them to be altered and
amended in such manner as may be most proper to preserve
the peace of that our island and determine all causes,
civil and criminal, matrimonial and testamentary, so as
no man's freehold, life or member be taken away or harmed
but by established or known lawes, not repugnant to but
as much as may be agreeable to the known laws of our kingdom of England.   You shall in like manner establish one
or more courts of admiralty as you see cause,according to
the power given by our dearest brother the Duke of York,
our High Admiral of England and of those dominions likewise....

(iv) ORDER BY THE LORDS OF TRADE, 6 July 1676.[3]
    [In relation to the questions raised by Governor Vaughan about
    the case of the *St. George,*]

1.C.O. 1/16 no.72. By an Act(no.$xiii$)of 1664 courts were established.
Juries seem to have been used from the first.
2. C.O. 1/25 No.107.
3.C.O. 391/1 pp.154-5. These extracts concerned the conflict between
admiralty jurisdiction and Jamaican statute law. Governor Vaughan had
reported that a pirate ship, the *St. George* with 300 slaves aboard
had been seized on his orders for infringing the Royal African Company's monopoly, but the judge in Admiralty had dismissed the case on
the plea that by a Jamaican Act the ship was in St. Dorothy's parish.
When Vaughan then took action in the common law court, the judgement
was again given in favour of the ship's owner since the Royal African
Company's patent was invalid under the English Statute against Monop-
opies (21 and 22 Jac.I cap.3).

...That the Lords may see how for the Jurisdiction of
the Admiralty does extend itselfe, and consider whether
this Proceeding in Jamaica, where the Triall of the Shipp
is removed from the Admiralty to the Common Law can be
justified, on pretence that his Majesty's Grant to the
Royall Company is a Monopoly, or that the said Shipp was
not seized *super altum mare*, but in the Port of Old Harbour
within the Parish of St. Dorothye, *intra corpus comitatus*,
according to a late Act made in Jamaica...touching the
bounds of parishes where a tract of water is made part of
the parish...and therefore not of proper cognizance of
the Court of Admiralty by reason of 13 Rich.II cap.5, 15
Rich. cap.3 and 2 Hen.IV cap.11.[1]

(v) REPORT TO, AND ORDER BY, THE LORDS OF TRADE, 13 July 1676.[2]
   [They had scrutinised the statutes relating to admiralty jurisdiction from the fourteenth century, the patents to the Lord High[3]
   Admirals, the King's proclamation to encourage Jamaican planters,
   and the charter to the Royal African Company.[4]The opinion of the
   attorney general had declared,]
   ...This I conceave is plain that by his Majesty's aquis-
ition of that country *[Jamaica]* he is absolute sovereign
and may impose what form of constitution both of government and of lawes he pleaseth[5]; and the inhabitants are
in no sort entitled to the laws of England or to bee governed thereby but by the meere grace and graunt of the
King[6]; and therefore untill it shalbe seen what the King
hath graunted, I do forbear to give any further direction....
   Dr. Lloyd's[7] Report Read, and the Lords after debate
order That my Lord Vaughan be written to, that he take
care to preserve the Jurisdiction of the Admiralty, and
that the King's prerogative be not called in question
concerning forfeitures etc. notwithstanding an Act of the
Island, dividing it into severall Parishes, which cannot
lessen the Lord High Admirall's Jurisdiction granted to
his Royall Highnes.

1.See above No.15.The matters were referred to the attorney general
and to Dr. Lloyd, the surrogate to the Admiralty,for their opinions
on the validity of Jamaican Acts, the extension of English statutes
to the island, and the jurisdiction of the Lord High Admiral.
2.C.O. 391/1.
3.14 December 1661 [No.347].
4. 27 September 1672 : [see No.275].
5. i.e. as a conquered or ceded colony: see *Calvin's Case* 1608 [No.
20].
6. The recent Jamaican Act declaring the laws of England to be in
force in Jamaica was considered by him as invalid: since only if the
king so declared could they be so. Nor did the Statute against Monopolies which expressly referred to 'this realm or the dominion of
Wales' extend to any colony.
7.Dr. Lloyd in his opinion had declared that a Jamaican Act could not
make the high seas part of a parish nor deprive the Lord High Admiral
of a prerogative jurisdiction long since granted and recognised.

(b) NEW YORK

400. (i) 'THE DUKE'S LAWS', 1 March 1665.[1]
   [The laws,grouped alphabetically, concerned Absence of J.Ps
   and constables, civil actions, inheritances, fines, witnesses,
   appeals, arrests and summons, bail, births, burials, capital
   crimes, duties of ministers and churchwardens, fields, inns,
   Indians, marriage, masters and servants, militia, wolves *etc.*]
                    Assizes
   The Court of Assizes shall be held but once in the
year on the last thursday in September at New York[2]....
                    Councell
   Any Person who shall be sworn of the Counsell to the
Governour shall in any place within this Government have
in all respects the Power of a Justice of Peace and in
any Court of Sessions may set as President
                Jurores and Juryes[3]
   That the Clerk of the Sessions shall have in convenient time before the sitting of the court give a certif-

---

1.New York Hist.Soc.,*Collections* (1811) I pp.307-401.These Laws were
published and approved on 1 March 1665 at a 'general meeting' of representative freemen specially summoned at Hempstead on Long Island,
where the settlers were largely English.(Of the seventeen towns represented,13 were English and 4 Dutch).The Laws formed a criminal and
civil code,regulations for local government by a board of 8 elected
overseers and a constable, and organisation of courts and militia:
they included some customs of the Dutch, and omitted some of the
New Englanders. There was considerable dissatisfaction and many amendments subsequently; but absolute power was vested in the proprietor
and governor.
2.There were town courts and courts of sessions in the ridings held
three times a year. This annual Court of Assizes consisted of the
governor and council together with the justices of the courts of
sessions: it was the supreme judicial body as well as being the closest approximation to a central assembly (see 'Lawes' and 'Votes')
apart from the governor and council. At its meetings laws could be
published or repealed, business transacted, and decisions announced.
Under the Dutch West India Company and the metropolitan control by
its'College of Nineteen' merchants, the director general and his
council in New Amsterdam had exercised executive, judicial and legislative powers. Though, from the 1640s there had been local moves
within New Netherlands by 'The Twelve', 'The Eight' and 'The Nine'
to limit the director general's power by some representative system
it had failed. Peter Stuyvesant, the director-general, remained a
paternal autocrat, summoning groups of representatives (*landtdag*)
only in crises on the eve of the English conquest. The *schout* (sheriff) and the *schepens* (J.P.s) were appointed by him, though latterly
from a longer list of elected names. The Duke's Laws did not create
anew this Court of Assizes, but Nicolls assumed its continuance from
the Dutch period: the presence of 2 J.P.s from each court of sessions
was an innovation which gave some local representation to the central consultative body of government.
3.The introduction of the jury was a step towards anglicisation,

icate to the sheriffe or under sheriff of what and how
many causes are entered for their hearing the next sessions to the end the sheriff or under sheriff may (and are
hereby required) immediately to issue forth warrants to
the constable of the several townes of the jurisdiction
of the court for jurymen proportionable to the causes with
regard to the equality of the number from each town and
according to the warrant the constable shall warn so many
of the overseers to attend as jurymen and return their
names to the under sheriff, and if such number of jurymen so required prove not sufficient for the carrying on
the business with dispatch to the sessions, the justices
may require the sheriffe or under sheriff to supply their
number with so many able and discreet men as shall either
attend the court upon other occasions, or shall happen
to be inhabitants of the towne where the court shall be
held.

All Juryes so chosen shall be empanelled and sworn
truly to try between party and party and shall find the
matter of fact with the damages and costs according to
the evidence; where upon the justices in the absence of
other superior officers, shall pronounce the sentence
directing the jury in point of law, and if there be matter of apparent equity upon the forfeiture of an obligation, breach of covenant without damage or the like,
the Bench shall determine such matters of equity.

Every juryman shall be allowed three shillings six
pence *per diem* for the charges of their attendance out
of the fees and profits arising in each court where they
doe service, or by the country if those fall short.

No jury shall exceed the number of seaven nor be under
six, unless in special causes upon life and death, the
justices shall thinke fit to appoint twelve.

In all cases wherein the law is obscure, so as the
jury cannot be sattisfied therein. They have liberty to
present a special verdict (*viz*) If the law be so in such
a point, we find for the plaintiffe, but if the law be
otherwise, we find for the defendant, in which case the
determination doth properly belong to the court, and all
juryes shall have liberty in matter of fact, if they cannot finde the maine issue, yet to find and present in
their verdict so much as they can.

Whensoever any jury or jurores are not clear in their
judgements concerning any case, they shall have liberty

---

though there was a concession (by the presence of overseers) to the
Dutch system of having the advice and assessment of *schepens* available in court. In the terms of surrender the Dutch had been guaranteed their own law and custom relating to inheritance and existing
contracts. They resisted English civil law (including primogeniture
and trial by jury), but showed less opposition to English criminal
law. The quasi-feudal 'patroonships' of the Dutch Company's proprietary regime had already lost some of their privileged rights before
the conquest.

in open court (but not otherwise) to advice with any particular man upon the Bench, or any other whom they shall think fit to resolve and direct them before they give in their verdict.

The verdict shall be given in, by the foreman of the jury.

A verdict shall be so esteemed, when the major part of the jury is agreed and the minor shall be concluded by the major without allowance of any protest by any of them to the contrary; except in case of life and death, where the whole jury is to be unanimous in their verdict.

The Bench is briefly to sum up the evidence by way of information to the jury.

To be father, brother, uncle, nephew, or cousen german to the party or parties concerned, shall be a lawful exemption against a jurore before he be sworn and not after.

Any one that shall presume to reveale the dissenting votes of a jury or arbitration, shall forfeit ten shillings for the first offence, and for farther breach of this law. The next Court of Sessions, or Assizes shall impose a greater fine on the offender according to the merits of the cause.

Justices of the Peace

The justices of the peace or sheriffe or either of them shall have power to issue out writs or warrants according to the nature of the plaint.

The warrants of any justice of the peace shall be of force and is to be executed by any inferiour officer in any of the Ridings, as fully and effectually, as if the justice were an inhabitant within that Riding, provided always that the plaintiffe, or cause of plaint do arise within the Riding where the justice doth dwell.   The like rule is to be observed in hue and cryes.

The eldest justice of the peace in the absence of the governor, deputy governor, or some one of the council, shall pronounce the decrees or sentence of the court , except in case of natural imperfections or agreement amongst the justices themselves, it be otherwise determined to any other person of them, in neither of which cases the justice shall refuse to do his office, or enter his desent to the prejudice of the court.

Any justice of the peace, may if he please, or see cause for it preside as cheife in any of the towne meetings within the jurisdiction where he dwells.

Lands

All lands and heritages within this government shall be free from all fines and licences, upon alienation and from all heriots, wardships, liveryes, primier seizins, year day and wast, escheats, and forfeitures upon the death of parents or auncestors natural, unnatural, casual, or judicial, and that for ever (cases of high treason only excepted).

To the end all former purchases may be ascertained to the present possessor or right owner, they shall bring

in their former grants, and take out new pattents for
the same from the present governoure in the behalfe of
his Royal Highness, the Duke of Yorke.[1]

All purchasores of implanted lands shall of their cost
and charge, cause a survey and draught thereof to be made
within one yeare after such purchases and deliver the
same into the Office of Records, whereby the bounds and
limits thereof may bee justly distinguished, and if the
purchasors shall not within three years after the survey
plant, seat or inhabit upon the said purchasse they shall
forfeit their right, title and interest therein.

Lawes

In regard it is almost impossible to provide sufficient lawes in all cases, or proper punishments for all
crimes, the Court of Sessions shall not take further cognizance of any case or crimes, whereof there is not provision made in some lawes but to remit the case or crime,
with the due examination and proof to the next Court of
Assizes, where matters of equity shall be decided, or pun-
ismnent awarded according to the discretion of the Bench
and not contrary to the known laws of England....

Publique Affaires

Whereas this government may in many occasions be disappointed of speedy and true information of publique affairs out of England, as well as out of our neighbours'
colonyes, to the remedy of such future inconceniences,
every constable to whom any letters shall come directed
to the governour attested on the backe side the letter
with the name of one of his Majestie's principal Secretaries of State, or with the name of any one of the governours of any of his Majestie's colonyes of New England;
or any letters sent from the governour to the sheriff or
any of the justices of York shire upon Long Island and
so attested as abovesaid, shall be dispatcht by every
such constable within three hours at the furthest, after
the receipt thereof to the next constable, and so forward
as the letter directs upon the penalty of forty shillings
for every hour's delay. And in such cases all constables
are impowered to press a sufficient horse and man to that
purpose allowing for the man and horse satisfaction six
pence for each mile's travel,which shall be discounted
to each constable in the publique rates....

Votes

All votes in the private affaires of particular townes
shall be given and determined by the inhabitants, freeholders, householders and in matters committed to arbitration or at Sessions, either as to juryes in all cases
or to justices on the Bench, where the law is not cleare
shall be carried by the major part of the suffrages, the
minor to be concluded by the vote of the major.

1.Former grants were renewed by the duke in freehold tenure and fee
simple, as provided in the paragraph on *Possession.*

Public Charges

That every Inhabitant within this Government shall contribute to all charges, both in Church and Colony, where
he doth or may reserve benefit....

[The annual levy was determined by the governor and council and
executed and assessed by the sheriff and constable upon all males
over 16 years old.]

(ii) GOVERNOR NICOLLS TO LORD CLARENDON, 7 April 1666.[1]

...My Lord, I have remitted for confirmation to his
Royall Highnesse the present Lawes of this Colony collected out of the Lawes of the other Colonyes, onely with
such Alterations as may revive the Memory of old England
amongst us, for Democracy hath taken so deepe a Roote in
these parts, that the very name of a Justice of the Peace
is an Abomination, wherefore I have upon due Consideration of his Majesties Interest layd the foundations of
Kingly Government in these parts so farre as is possible,
which truely is grievous to some Republicans, but they
cannot say that I have made any alteration amongst the
English for they had no setled Lawes, or Government before.

Tis not easily to be imagin'd what paines I have taken,
how much patience I have exercised towards a sort of
People of such refractory and peevish dispositions as
are not knowne in old England, yet for my Masters service
I can suffer much more, and to shew the Planters that
his Royall Highnesse intended rather the settlement of
his Majesties Authority in true English words and formes,
than his proffitt, I thought it a part of sound discretion to lay little or no burden upon their meane Estates;

These Lawes have beene put in practice the space of
one yeare with some Amendments upon Reviews, and such is
the unfortunate Condition of these parts, that some Points
of the Lawes must of necessity admitt of Alterations or
Abolitions yearely, and yet by the Dukes Instructions I
am narrowly bound up to the space of a yeare for his Highnesse Confirmation, otherwise the Law is voyd, By which
Instruction fully executed, wee should at this present
have no Law in force; I hope his Royall Highnesse will
give a larger Latitude to the next Governor in that point,
and dispatch this New body of Lawes in print without
Alterations....

(iii)*SOUTHAMPTON v. SOUTHOLD*, 2 November 1667.[2]

...The Attorney of the Defendants reades Southold deed

---

[1].N.Y. Hist.Soc.,*Coll.*(1869) *Clarendon Papers,xxxvii* p.118:[see also No.
375].Though, as representative of the 'conqueror', Nicolls had power
to'change' the forms of government and laws, he had indeed accepted
some elements of Dutch law and continued the court of assize.

2.B.Fernow (ed.) *Documents relating to the colonial history of* ...
New York new ser.III pp.601-2.Governor Lovelace was enforcing the
duke's territorial claims, jurisdiction and laws in Long Island over

with Severall Indyan Testimonyes in two other writtings.
The Deed is dated December 27th 1662.[1] The defendants
pleads their purchase, according to the Customs ordered
to bee used in all the Colonyes, It being done with the
approbacion of the Governor of New Haven, under which Government they then were, and that Captain Young made purchase of the Land in question for New Haven. Mr. Wells and
Barnabas Horsons deposicion read about their payment for
Aquebauke Land, to the Treasurer of New Haven by order of
their Court.

A Peticon from the Inhabitants of Southold to the Court
of New Haven, concerning this Purchase were also read.

Richard Howell Testimony of what hee heard a Skinnacock[2]
Indyan say concerning the Land in question: it was dated
December 17, 1662.

Thomas Stanton, an Interpreter of the Indyan Language,
testifyed upon oath before Robert Macon June 12, 1667 what
he had heard severall Indyans relate about this Land, they
being examined about it.

Another paper of June 4th 1667, of Indyan Testimonyes
brought in, amongst the which Uncachaag Sachem[3], was one,
It being urged by the plaintiffs that the Governor had
put a decision to this matter allready, when it was before
him upon Complaint of the Towne against Captain Tapping,
The Governor was pleased to declare that what hee did the
last yeare about the Matter in Controversy betweene Cap-

---

townships which resented this external interference with their autonomy and the absence of 'the rights of English subjects' in the proprietary colony. They claimed that Nicolls had promised these English
settlements (which had previously protested against the autocracy of
New Amsterdam) the privileges of the other English colonists in America. Nevertheless (as this case showed) the duke's courts did exercise jurisdiction over rival land claims between townships: Southampton were the plaintiffs and Southold the defendants: neither township had yet taken out a new patent for their lands from the duke,
and in 1669 refused to pay a levy imposed by the New York court of
assize.

1. There were deeds relating to lands made over by Indians to Dutch
settlers from the 1630s (*ibid*.pp.2ff.) The Dutch West India Company
had insisted that there must be payment for land occupied and had
forbidden purchase otherwise than under authority and licence from
the Company.Later English settlers moved into the area, especially
into Long Island, and the Duke's Laws followed the Dutch Company's
policy in acquiring land and in forbidding sale of liquor to Indians.
2. A Seneca; that is one of the Iroquois confederation of the 'Five
Nations' (Cayugas, Mowhawks, Oneidas, Onondagas, Senecas) which had
been formed a century before against the Algonquins and Hurons. The
Montauks were the dominant tribe on Long Island, where Nicolls had
established a board of commissioners for Indian affairs.
3. i.e. a principal chief. Ten *sachems* from each of the Five Nations
met in council to give some general, if loose, purpose to the con-
federacy.

tain Tapping and the Towne of South *[amp]*ton which was
then composed, Hee only Confirmed the Right that either
of them really had, but did not create any new Right in
either of them. Captain Young further alleadges that about
6 yeares agoe, when Captain Scott sold some Land neare :
this to Southton, hee reserved this very Land to himselfe,
and that then Southton made no pretence or Excepcion to
it. Mr. Pierson for the plaintiffs affirmed Shinnacock
Indyans were the Right Owners of the Land in question,
and no other.

Richard Howell sworne saith according as this Testimony in writing, That Southold southbounds went to a Certaine Creeke to Young's and no Further.

Mr. Ogden being Upon his oath further declares, that
about 8 yeares agoe hee employed severall Indyans to mark
out the Bounds of these Lands and that they were at Markt
Tree over the two Rivers at Peaconnock, which were the
Bounds betweene Sinnacock and Yeannecock Indians. Hee
further declares how hee came seized of the Land in question, that it was about the firemoney the Shinnocock Indyans being to pay a Certaine sume of money for the Mischiefe done by them. The Montauks Sachem being bound for
them tooke the Land in question into his possession, and
upon some Consideracion made it over to Mr. Ogden, and
Mr. Ogden saith all his Right is conveyed to Southton.
Mr. Woodhull further certifyes what hee heard from the
Vncheckaug Sachem That hee being desired to enquire of
him who were the Proprietors of Aquebauck Lands He mett
with him a fortnight since and asking of him, who they
were hee said hee knew not, but that hee remembers well
that a beare being killed there about the skin and greace
was caryed to the Skinnacock Indyans as an acknowledgement that it was their Land, There was also another Indyan that spake to the same purpose. Two deposicions of
Joshua Barnes and Edmond Howell were read, to prove the
plaintiffs possession by moweing of the Grasse there.

After a full debate on either parts, the matter was
referred to the Jury who brought in their Verdict for
the plaintiffs....

The defendants move the Court for an appeale and give
in their Reasons, whereupon this following order was issued forth....

The Defendants having appealed from the verdict of
the Jury to bee heard in Equity; This Court upon Consideracion, doth thinke fitt to allow of the Defendants appeale to bee heard, at the next Generall Court of Assizes
to bee held on the First Wednesday in October 1668 they
giving security according to Law. And doe order that as
to the Meadows in Controversy betweene the plaintiffs
and defendants they shall both have liberty to mowe Each
upon the one halfe thereof, at the season of the yeare
or for their Cattle to feed, thereupon in the meane time
untill the Title Shall bee decided in Equity, unlesse
they Shall otherwise agree amongst themselves, which the

Court doth recommend unto both partyes. The defendants
are to pay the Costs and Charges of the Court.

(iv) *GRAVESEND v. FRANCIS BROWNE ET AL.*, 3 November 1669.[1]
    ...Mr. John Ryder, Attorney for the Plaintiffs, puts
in a declaration. The matter in controversy was a certaine parcell of meadow ground. The originall Pattent from
Governour Keift[2] graunted to the Towne bearing date December 19th 1645 was produced and read. The Indian graunt
dated May the 7th 1654 was likewise read, together with
Governor Nicolls his order of February 8th 1664 for all
Townes or persons to bring in their claymes at the Generall meeting at Hempstead, and the order of the Generall
meeting concerning the difference betweene the plaintiffs
and the Towne of New Utrecht; as also Governor Nicolls
his letter concerning the difference betweene the plaintiff and defendant.
    Mr. John Sharp Attorney for the Defendant before he
reads his answer makes Exception against their plea of
holding their Land by vertue of any Dutch graunt or
Groundbriefe, It being against a clause in the Amendments and Additions in the Laws made at the Generall
Court of Assizes in the yeare of 1666, in that they have
not had their Pattent renewed.
    The Answer was notwithstanding ordered to be read.
The Attorney for the Defendant produceth Governor Nicolls
his Pattent of confirmacion, as also the Dutch Ground-
brief dated the...day of May 1843. *[sic.]* There being
also a precedent graunt made in the yeare 1639. The whole
case after debate was comitted to the Jury, who brought
in their verdict for the Defendant *viz:*
    'It is the Judgment and verdict of the Jury that Fran-
cis Browne shall injoye the full extent of his Pattent
graunted by the Honoured Generall Governor Nicolls by
vertue of Precedency of Pattent, and that Gravesend do
pay unto Mr. Browne all just costs and damages, and that
Mr. Browne pay unto Gravesend a valuable consideration
for what worke the Towne hath done upon meadowe that
falls within Mr. Brownes' Pattent'.
    The Attorney for the Plaintiffs moves the Court for
appeale from the verdict of the Jury to the present
Court *[of Assizes]* which was graunted and upon mature deliberation and consultation had hereupon the ensueing order
and judgment of Court was made - *viz.*
    The Inhabitants of Gravesend Plaintiffs, Francis Bro-
wne, als de Bruijne - Defendant In an appeale to the

---

1. B. Fernow (ed.) *op.cit.* III pp.629-0. An appeal to the New York
court of assize here reversed the decision of the jury. Gravesend,
an English township on the New England model, had been settled on
Long Island under Dutch rule and had been among those claiming equal
rights and protection from the Dutch government and demanding a representative assembly in 1653.
2.William Kieftt was the director general of New Netherland prior to
Peter Stuyvesant.

Bench.
   The Court, having taken this cause into serious consideration, do think fitt to order In regard the merritts
of the whole matter have been heard and examyned into
both by the Late and present Governor who have made severall orders thereupon which appeare very equitable and
favourable to both partyes, That what hath beene ordered
as to the division of either meadowe grounde or other
Land betweene the Plaintiffs and Defendant by the late
or present Governour do stand good, and that the Plaintiffs, though cast in this suite by the verdict of a
jury, shall have the benefit of those orders, if within
the space of 28 dayes after the date hereof they take out
their Pattent according to the Lawe, and the Defendant
shall be contented with what hath been formerly alotted
to him.[1] The verdict of the jury is hereby disannulled
and the inhabitants of Gravesend are to pay all costs
and charges of this suite both at Comon Law and equity.
By order of the Governor and Court of Assizes.

(v) RICHARD NICOLLS' ANSWERS ON THE LAW IN NEW YORK, c.1669.[2]
1st. The Governor and Councell with the High Sheriffe
and the Justices of the Peace in the Court of the Generall assizes have the Supreame Power of making, altering,
and abolishing any Laws in this Government. The Country
Sessions are held by the Justices upon the Bench, Particular Town Courts by a Constable and Right Overseers. The
City Court of N. Yorke by a Mayor and Aldermen. All causes tried by Juries.
3rd. The Tenure of lands is derived from his R.H.,[3] who
gives and grants lands to Planters as their freehold forever, they paying the customary rates and duties with
others towards the defraying of publique charges....
4. The Governour gives liberty to Planters to find out
and buy lands from the Indyans where it pleaseth best the
Planters, but the seating of Towns together is necessary
in these parts of America....
5. Liberty of Conscience is graunted and assured with
the same Provisoe exprest in the Querie....
7. All Causes are tried by Juries, no Lawes contrary to
the Lawes of England. Souldyers onely are tryable by a
Court Marshall, and none others, except in cases of suddaine invasion, mutiny or rebellion as his Majesties Lieutenants in any of his Countries of England may or ought
to exercise.
8th. As to this point there is no taxe, toledge, Impost

1.This requirement for new patents was refused,and some 50 residents
of Southampton signed a remonstrance, protesting that they did not
have the rights of representative government.
2.E.B. O'Callaghan, *Documentary history of...New York* (1850) I p.59.
The ex-governor of New York had been questioned about the law in
the duke's proprietary.
3. H.R.H. the Duke of York.

or Custome payable upon the Planters upon Corne or Cattle:
the Country at present hath little other product, the
Rate for publicke charges was agreed unto in a generall
Assembly, and is now managed by the Governour his Councell and the Justices in the Court of Assizes to that
onely behoofe.[1]

(vi) THE DUKE'S INSTRUCTIONS TO GOVERNOR EDMUND ANDROS, 1 July 1674.[2]
    ...As to the course of Justice, you are to take care
that it bee administered with all possible equallity without regard to Dutch or English in their private consernes,
it being my desire as much as may be that such as live
under your government may have as much satisfaction in
their condicon as is possible and that without the least
appearance of partiallity they may see their just rights
preserved to them inviolably.
    And as for the forme of justice, I thinke it best for
you to put in execution such Lawes, rules and orders as
you find have been established by Coll. Nicolls and Coll.
Lovelace and not to vary from them but upon emergent necessities and the advice of your Councell and the gravest
and experienced persons there....
        [Any such modification of a law would lapse if not confirmed
    within the year by the Duke. The governor was to choose no more
    than 10 councillors. There was provision for religious tolerat-
    ion. Taxes must not be farmed.]

(vii) GOVERNOR ANDROS' ANSWERS, 16 April 1678.
    1. The Governor is to have a Councell, not exceeding
tenn, with whose advice to act for the safety and good
of the country and in every towne, village or parish a
Petty Court; and Courts of Sessions in the severall precincts, being three on Long Island and Townes of New
Yorke, Albany and Esopus and some smale or poore Islands
and out-places; And the Generall Court of Assizes composed of the Governor and Councell and all the Justices
and Magistrates att New Yorke once a yeare. The Petty
Courts judge of five pounds, and then may appeale to
Sessions, they to twenty pounds; and then may appeale
to Assizes to the King from all said Courts as by Law.
    2. The Court of Admiralty hath been by speciall Com-
mission or by the Court of Mayor and Aldermen att New

1.Orders were issued every three years for the collection of the
duke's customs.But when in 1681 merchants in New York refused to pay
them since the authorisation of 1677 had lapsed, the council applied
for direct orders from the duke. This led to the concession of an
assembly in Dongan's instructions.
2.J.R.Brodhead (ed.) *op.cit.*III pp.216-9.After recapture of New York
by the Dutch in July 1673 and its second surrender the following
year, the duke's proprietary rule was being re-established by the
new governor, Major Edmund Andros.
3.*ibid.*III p.260. The governor was replying to queries about the
government and courts in New York.

Yorke.

3. The chiefe Legislative power there is in the Governor with advice of the Councell; the executive power of
Judgements given by the Courts is in the sheriffs and
other civill officers.

4. The law booke in force was made by the Governor and
Assembly att Hempsted in 1665[1] and since confirmed by his
Royall Highnesse....

(viii) GOVERNOR DONGAN'S REPORT TO THE LORDS OF TRADE, 22 February
1687.[2]

The Courts of Justice are most established by Act of
Assembly and they are:
1. The Court of Chancery, consisting of the Governor and
Council, is the Supreme court of this province to which
appeals may be brought from any other court.
2. The Assembly, finding the inconvenience of bringing
Justices of the peace, Sheriffs, Constables and other persons concerned from the remote parts of this government
to New York, did, instead of the Court of Assizes which
was yearly held for the whole Government of this province,
erect a Court of Oyer and Terminer to be held once every
year within each County for the determining of such matters as should arise within them respectively, the members of which Court were appointed to bee one of the two
judges of this province assisted by three justices of the
peace of that county wherein such court is held. Which
Court of Oyer and Terminer has likewise power to hear appeals from any inferior court.
3. There is likewise in New York and Albany a Court of
Mayor and Aldermen held once in every fortnight, from
whence there can be noe appeal unless the cause of action
bee above the value of Twenty Pounds, who have likewise
priviledges to make such by-laws for the regulation of
their own affairs as they think fitt, soe as the same be
approved of by the Governor and Council. Their Mayor, Recorders, town-clerks and Sheriffs are appointed by the
Governor.
4. There is likewise in every County twice in every year
(except in New York where it is four times and in Albany
where its thrice) Courts of Sessions held by the Justices
of the Peace for the respective countys as in England.
5. In every Towne with the Government there are 3 commissioners appointed to hear and determine all matters of
refference not exceeding the value of five pounds....
6. Besides there, my Lords, I finding that many great
inconveniences daily hapned in the management of his Majesty's particular concerns within this province relating
to his Lands, Rents, Rights, Profits and Revenues by reason of the great distance betwixt the Cursory settled

---

1. The Duke's Laws.

2. E.B. O'Callaghan, *op.cit.*I pp.95-7.

Courts and of the long delay which thereon consequently
ensued, besides the great hazard of venturing the matter
on country Jurors who over and above that they are generally ignorant enough and for the most part linked together
by affinity, are too much swayed by their particular hum-
ors and interests, I thought fit in Feb. last by and with
the advice and consent of the Council to settle and establish a Court which we call the court of Judicature [*Exchequer*]to bee held before the Governor and Council for the
time being, or before such and soe many as the Governor
should for the purpose authorize, comissionat and appoint
on the first Monday in every month at New York, which
Court hath full power and authority to hear, try and determine suits matters and variances arising betwixt his
Majesty and the Inhabitants of the said Province concerning the said lands, rents, rights, profits and revenues.
    [He recommended that his Majesty might be pleased to consider]
to add to this Government Connecticut and Rhode Island;
Connecticut being so conveniently situate in its adjacing
to us and soe inconvenient for the people of Boston by
reason of its being upwards of two hundred miles distance
from thence, Besides Connecticut as it now is takes away
from us almost all the land of value that lies adjoyneing
to Hudsons River and the best part of the river itself,
Besides as wee found by experience [*that*] if that place
bee not annexed to that Government it will bee impossible
to make any thing considerable of his Majesty's customs
and revenues in Long Island they carry away without entring all our oyles, which is the greatest part of what wee
have to make returns of from this place: And from Albany
and that way up the river - our Beaver and Peltry[1]....

(C) THE RIGHT OF APPEAL

    We have seen from the Statute of Westminster I (p.14) that app-
eals came to the Crown from the medieval dependencies in the Marches.
This appeal survived the abolition of the prerogative jurisdiction of
the privy council in 1641 in the particular context of the Channel
Islands [see IA (4)(f)]. At the Restoration this surviving appeal to
the Crown was extended by the privy council to all the colonies and
plantations.

401. ACT FOR REGULATING THE PRIVY COUNCIL AND ABOLISHING THE STAR
                    CHAMBER (16 Car.I cap.10) 1641.[2]
I. Whereas by the Great Charter many times confirmed in

1.i.e. furs.
2. Statutes of the Realm V.pp.110-2. Though this statute purported
to abolish the jurisdiction of the privy council in the realm, appeals to the council were still possible from the Chancellors of England and Ireland sitting in lunacy, from the Court of Stannaries in
the absence of the Duke of Cornwall, and from the Channel Islands.

Parliament, it is enacted that no freeman shall be taken,
or imprisoned, or disseized of his freehold or liberties
or free customs, or be outlawed or exiled, or otherwise
destroyed, and that the King will not pass upon him or
condemn him but by lawful judgment of his Peers or by the
law of the land...

> [and similarly in 5 Ed.III cap.9, 25 Ed.III St.5.cap.4., 28 Ed.
> III cap.3, 36 Ed.III cap.15, 42 Ed.III cap.5, 3 Hen.VII cap.1 and
> 21 Hen.VIII cap.20, respect was paid to franchises and liberties
> and concern was expressed for the due manner, form and process of
> law, the statute (3 Hen.VII cap.1) establishing the Star Chamber
> was therefore repealed, since it had extended its jurisdiction and
> increased its punishments so that its 'arbitrary' power had become
> 'an intolerable burden to the subjects': it had assumed 'a power
> to intermeddle in civil causes' and private suits 'contrary to the
> law of the land and the rights and privileges of the subject by
> which great...mischiefs...and more much uncertainty' had been
> caused. All matters might now have 'proper remedy and redress...
> by the common law'.
>
> Similarly the Councils of Wales, of the North, of the Duchy of
> Lancaster and the palatine of Chester were abolished, and no sim-
> ilar court would be established 'in the realm of England or domin-
> ion on Wales'.]

III. Be it likewise declared and enacted...That neither
his Majesty, nor his Privy Council have or ought to have
any jurisdiction, power or authority, by English Bill,
petition, articles, libel or any other arbitrary way whatsoever, to examine or draw into question, determine or dispose of the lands, tenements,hereditaments, goods or chattels of any the subjects of this kingdom; but that the
same ought to be tried and determined in the ordinary
Courts of Justice and by the ordinary course of the law.[1]

From two dominions of the Crown, Jersey and Guernsey, appeals to the
privy council (as council of the duke of Normandy) had lain as part
of accepted 'ordinary' process of law, possibly since the fourteenth
century, certainly since 1572 (Jersey) and 1580 (Guernsey) [No.133
(b) (c)]. The privy council had also considered petitions and complaints from the Islands;and in 1635 a special sub-committee of the
council had been established to deal with appeals from Jersey.
1. This phrase was crucial in permitting the privy council to retain
the right to hear appeals from the Channel Islands. During the Civil
War and Commonwealth a council continued to hear such appeals. At
the Restoration this precedent was the justification for the Crown to
assert its appellate jurisdiction over cases from without the realm
in the colonies and plantations. [Cf. Thomas Pownall in his *Administration of the Colonies* (1765) pp.80-3; 'The defect in most, and
actual deficiency in many,of the colonies of a court of equity does
still more forcibly lead to the necessity of a measure of some remedial court of appeal....The general apprehension of these defects occasioned that at the first planting of the colonies the King in Council
here in England was established as a court of appeals from the provincial judicatories. At the time of settling these colonies, there
was no precedent of a judicatory besides those within the realm,-

402. MASSACHUSETTS ACT RESPECTING APPEALS, 3 May 1654.[1]
I. It is ordered by this Court and the authority thereof,
That it shall be in the liberty of every man cast, condemned or sentenced in any inferior court to make his appeal
to the court of assistants; as also to appeal from the
sentence of the magistrates or other persons deputed to
hear and determine small causes unto the shire court of
each jurisdiction where the cause was determined.... [The
appellant had to enter certain securities.]

403. ORDER IN COUNCIL FOR REORGANISING THE COMMITTEES OF THE PRIVY
                      COUNCIL, 12 February 1668.[2]
    ...His Majesty haveing among other the Important parts
of his Affayres, taken into his Princely Consideration the
way, and Method of Managing Matters at the Councill Board,
And reflecting that his Councills would have more Reputation if they were putt into a more settled, and Established Course; Hath thought fitt to Appoynt certain Standing Committees of the Councill for severall Businesses,
together with Regular dayes and Places for their Assemb-
ling, in such sort as followeth.
    1. The Committee of Forraine Affayres...to which Com-
mittee his Majesty doth also hereby Referre the Corresponding with Justices of the Peace, and other his Majesty's
Officers and Ministers in the severall Countryes of the
Kingdome, Concerning the Temper of the Kingdome etc....
    2. Such Matters as Concerne the Admiralty and Navy, as
also all Military Matters, Fortifications etc. so farr as
they are fitt to be brought to the Councill Board, without
Intermedleing with what Concernes the Proper Officers
(unless it shall by them be so desired)....
    3. A Committee for the Business of Trade, under whose
_____
except in the cases of Guernsey and Jersey, the remnants of the duchy
of Normandy, and not united within the realm: according to the custom
of Normandy, appeals lay to the Duke in council; and upon this ground
appeals lay from the judicatories of these islands to the King here,
as Duke in council; and upon this general precedent (without perhaps
attending to the peculiar case of the appeal lying to the Duke of
Normandy and not to the King) was an appeal from the judicatories of
the colonies to the King in council settled'].Pownall erred in think-
ing appeals lay to the privy council from 'the first planting'.
1.*Charter and general laws of Massachusetts Bay* (1814). The court of
assistants had claimed, and exercised,final appellate jurisdiction
from all subordinate courts in Massachusetts, though as early as 1638
(N.B.Shurtleff *op.cit.*I p.239) they had initiated legislation which
imposed restrictions against their hearing petty cases. The assistants
resisted strongly the attempt by the Crown to assert its right to hear
appeals from H.M.'s subjects in the plantations.
2.P.C. 2/60 pp.176-7. On 31 January 1668 the king had resolved on
a reorganisation of his privy council. The separate councils for
trade and for foreign plantations were now abolished and a single
joint council now commissioned. It was dissolved on 21 December
1674 to make way for the'lords of trade'. (C.O. 391/1 No.1).

Consideration is to come whatsoever Concernes his Majesty's
Forraine Plantacons, as also what Relates to his Kingdomes
of Scotland or Ireland, in such Matters only Relating to
eyther of those Kingdomes, as properly belonge to the Cognizance of the Councill Board, the Isles of Jersey and
Guernsey, which is to Consist of the Lord Privy Seale,
Duke of Buckingham, Duke of Ormond, Earl of Ossory, Earle
of Bridgewater, Earle of Anglesey, Earle of Lauderdaill
Lord Arlington, Lord Holles, Lord Ashley, Mr. Comptroller,
Mr. Vice-Chamberlain, Mr. Secretary Morice, Sir William
Coventrye[2], the usuall day of Meeting to be every Thursday
in the Councill Chamber, And oftner, as he that Presides
shall direct. And hereof Three or more of them to be a
Quorum, And it is further Ordered, That this Committee
calling unto them his Majesty's Attorney-Generall, or
else his Majesty's Advocate, do from henceforth heare all
Causes that by way of Appeale come from the Isles of Jersey & Guernsey, the Orders whereupon being in due forme
prepared by the Clerke of the Councill; are before they
are signed to be read at the Councill Board, and there
Approved of, that so they may Receive the Approbation and
Authority of the whole Councill, which before used to
Passe distinctly from the Committee only, by a derivative
power from the Board.[1]
   4. A Committee to whom all Peticons of Complaint and
Greivance are to be Referred. In which his Majesty hath
thought fitt hereby particularly to prescribe, not to
meddle with Property, or what related to *Meum* and *Tuum*.
And to this Committee his Majesty is pleased that all Mat-
ters which Concerne Acts of State, or of the Councill be
Referred;...
   Besides which aforesaid Committees, if there shall
happen anything Extraordinary, that Requires Advice, of
any Mixt nature, other then what is afore determined. His
Majesty's Meaning and Intention is, That particular Committees be in such Cases Appoynted for them, as hath been
hitherto accustomed; And that such Committees do make their
Report in Writing, to be offered to his Majesty the next
Councill day following....

404. OPINION OF SIR HENEAGE FINCH (S.G.) ON *MIDDLETON v. CHAMBERLAIN*,
                          24 November 1669.[3]
...1. That in point of Law,Constant Silvester, the Trustee
of Middleton, had a cleare Title to the Inheritance of an
Hundred Acres devised to James by purchase from Elizabeth.
Relic of Robert Greene.
   2. That however he ought not to have been impleaded

1.On this anology the right of the privy council to hear appeals would
soon be pressed upon the plantations.2. The duke of York's secretary.
3.P.C.2/62 pp.49-50.Finch (later A.G.,lord keeper and L.C.) was solicitor general and was giving his opinion to the privy council on the
case between Thomas Middleton and Edward Chamberlain over an estate
in Barbados. Errors in form were considered insufficient cause for
reversing colonial judgments.

during the Life of Elizabeth but had unquestionable Right
to hold the same during her Life in which two points most
of the Lawyers, who were advised with upon the case, agreed.
    3. That Chamberlain as Guardian to George Greene the
Infant did against the true Right in Law recover against
Silvester by Verdict & Judgement.
    4. That yet the Errors assigned by Silvester were onely
in forme, & not sufficient to reverse that Judgement.
    5. Silvester brought a new Ejectment, and the Defendant
Chamberlain as Guardian to the Infant George Greene prayed
the Plea might stay till his full Age, In which Case &
Action, Age was graunted but against Law, as I conceive.
    6. New Errors assigned by Silvester, but not heard And
I conceive they were only Errors in forme, and ought not
to weigh, if they had been heard, it being impossible,that
the Pleadings and Entryes at Barbados should be so exact
in forme, as the Pleadings in Westminster Hall.
    7. Upon the whole matter, the true Right being in Sil-
vester, as Trustee for Middleton, I conceive a new Eject-
ment ought to be brought, and no Age allowed to the Infant,
but that his Guardians should defend it at their perill
upon the Merits of the Title.   *Heneage Finch*
...His Majesty upon consideration thereof, was pleased to
approve of the said Report and did order that the same be
transmitted to...Lord Willoughby of Parham, Captaine Generall and Cheife Governor of the Barbados and the other
Caribee Islands who is hereby required to communicate the
same to the judges of the said island....[1]

405. *INSTRUCTIONS TO GOVERNORS*, 1678 - 82:
        (a) ADDITIONAL INSTRUCTION TO LORD CARLISLE, 30 March 1678.[2]
        ...And Our pleasure also is that, for the better and
more equitable Administration of Justice in Our said
Island *[of Jamaica]* , Appeals be allowed in cases of errour
from the Superior Courts of Our Island to You Our Governor and our Council there....

        (b) ADDITIONAL INSTRUCTION TO SIR R. DUTTON, 30 October 1680.[3]
        ...And Our will and pleasure is that, upon your arrival
in Barbados you signify our disapprobation and disallowance of all lawes made and in force there whereby any hindrance or restraint is put upon the liberty of appealing
unto Us in Council, except in criminal cases, as also in
civil cases where the sum or value contended for shall not
exceede one hundred pounds sterling, and where security

1.The decision in a case before the privy council was given in the
form of an order in council.
2.C.O. 138/3 p.235. In 1679 a similar instruction was made to Governor Culpeper for Virginia and to President Cutt in New Hampshire.
3. C.O. 29/3 p.43. Dutton received a commission for Barbados the same
day. For earlier attempt to assert the right of appeal to the Crown,
see Dr. Child's petition in 1646, and the commission to New England
in 1664 [p .350].

shall not be first duly given by the appelant to answering such costs as shalbe awarded in case the first sentence be confirmed; and you are not to pass any lawe for the future contrary hereunto....

    (c) INSTRUCTION TO SIR THOMAS LYNCH, 8 September 1681.[1]

...Our will and pleasure is That appeals be permitted to be made in cases of error from the courts in our said island *[Jamaica]* unto the Governor and Councill in civil causes at the hearing of which appeals any three or more of the judges of the Supreme Court are to be present to inform and assist the Court, provided the sum or value appealed for doe exceed one hundred pounds sterling and that security be first duly given by the appellant to answer such charges as shalbe awarded in case the first sentence be affirmed. And if either party shall not rest satisfied with the judgment of our said Governor and Councill that then they may appeal unto us in Councill, provided the sum or value so appealed for unto us exceed five hundred pounds[2] and that security be also duly given by the appellant to answer such charges as shalbe awarded in cases the sentence of our Governor and Councill be affirmed so as execution be not suspended by reason of any such appeal unto us....

    (d) ADDITIONAL INSTRUCTION TO LORD CULPEPER, 1682.[3]

You are not for the future to admit or allow of any appeals to be made from the governor and council to the assembly; but whereas we judge it absolutely necessary that all our subjects may have liberty to appeal to Us in cases that deserve the same, Our will and pleasure is that if either party shall not rest satisfied with the judgment and sentence of our governor or commander in chief, they may then apply to Us in our Privy Council [provided the sum at issue exceeded £300, security were lodged, and the appeal were made within 2 weeks of the sentence.]

And inasmuch as it may not be fit that appeals be too frequently or for too small a value brought upon our governor and council,you shall therefore, with the advice of our council, propose a law to be passed wherein the method and limitation of appeals unto our governor and council may be settled and restrained in such manner as shall be found most convenient and easy to our subjects in our said province *[of Virginia].* [4]

1.C.O. 138/4.

2.To affirm this limitation on 25 July 1685 (C.O.391/5 p.170) the lords of trade resolved that in the draft instructions for Sir Philip Howard 'noe appeals to his Majesty bee admitted in Jamaica in any action under £500'.

3.C.O.5/1356,28 Virginia Magazine p.43. For the opposition of the House of Burgesses ,see pp.475ff.A similar instruction was included on 3 June 1686 for Governor Andros in New England, and on 10 June 1686 for Governor Dongan in New York: J.R.Brodhead (ed.) *op.cit.* III pp. 539,379.

4.Some Indians sought arbitration from colonial officials. Governor

406. OPINION OF SIR ROBERT SAWYER (A.G.), 30 May 1681.[1]
I. I am of opinion that the Plantation Acts being publique
Laws and the Plantations being particularly bound by them,
did bind them without any particular notice given on behalfe of the King; yet it hath been usuall in such cases,
to take away all colour of excuse to signifie the same by
some order in Councill under the Councille Seale which
will be sufficient.
II and III. There is no question but the Sovereignety remaining in the King, an Appeal doth lye to His Majesty in
Council as from Jersey and Guernsey. And His Majesty in
Council may give rules in which Cases Appeales may be
allowed and how prosecuted, and for what value, as hath
been done in the case of Jersey and Guernsey, with consideration had to the greater distance of the place; for it
would bee an infinite vexation to allow a Latitude of
Appealing in any Case or before His Majesty in Council
have settled Rules,unless it bee in some exorbitant Case,
which may have influence upon the Government.
IV. By the Charter of King James the Council [of New Eng-
land] were to reside in England and to manage by Deputies
and assignes in New England; but by the Patent 4 Car.I
their assigns are made a Body Corporate and the Government vested in them, and they may reside and act in New
England.

407 . ORDER IN COUNCIL, 23 January 1684.[2]
...It was this day Ordered by his Majesty in Councill That
no Appeales be for the future admitted at this Board from
any of his Majesties forreigne Plantations unlesse there

Hinckley of New Plymouth had been empowered to hear appeals from
'praying Indians'.He reported in 1685 that the Indians had several
courts: they'often desire my help amongst them at their courts and
often do appeal from the sentence of the Indian judges to my determination, in which they quietly rest. Whereby I have much trouble and
expense of time amongst them, but if God please to bless my endeavours to bring them to more civility and Christianity, I shall account
my time and pains well spent'. (Mass.Hist.Soc., *Collections* 4th Vp.134).
1.R.N.Toppan ed. *Edward Randolph* III pp.100-1. Sawyer had been asked
by the lords of trade to give his opinions on certain questions asked
by Randolph - whether New England should observe the Navigation Laws
as other plantations did; whether appeals lay to the king in council,
and how; and whether the removal of the Massachusetts Company from
England had vacated their charter.
2. P.C. 2/70 p.108. Appeals to the Crown had been limited in civil
cases to matters which exceeded £100 in value and security had been
given by the appellant [see instructions to Culpeper in 1682]. Randolph had raised the issue in his request to the lords of the treasury on 30 April 1681 (C.S.P. 1681- 92). The minimum limit of £500
was imposed on appeals from Jamaica in Sir Philip Howard's instructions on 25 July 1685 (C.O. 391/5 p.170).

be sufficient Security first given by the Appellants as
well at this Board as in the respective Plantations to
prosecute their Appeales effectually, and to Stand the
Award of his Majesty in Councill thereupon....

408. ADDITIONAL INSTRUCTIONS TO GOVERNOR SIR RICHARD DUTTON,
                                      3 May 1684.[1]
     ...And for the better preventing vexatious suits and
appeals which may otherwise be brought before us in Our
Privy Council, our will and pleasure is That no appeal be
permitted to be brought from that our Island, unless such
appeal be made within one fortnight after sentence and
good security given by the appellant that he will effectually prosecute the same and answer the condemnation, as
also pay such costs and damages as shall be awarded to
us....

409. COMMISSION TO GOVERNOR SIR EDMUND ANDROS, 7 April 1688.[2]
     And Wee do further hereby give and grant unto you full
power and authority with the advice and consent of our
said Councill to erect constitute and establish such and
so many Courts of Judicature and public Justice within
our said Territory and Dominion as you and they shall think
fitt and necessary for the determining of all causes as
well Criminall as Civill according to law and equity, and
for awarding of execution thereupon, with all reasonable
and necessary powers authorities fees and privileges belonging unto them...
     And wee do further by these presents will and require
you to permit Appeals to be made in cases of Error from
our Courts in our said Territory and Dominion of New England, unto you, or the Commander in Cheif for the time
being and the Councill, in Civill causes: Provided the
value appealed for do exceed the sum of one hundred pounds
sterling, and that security be first duly given by the
Appellant to answer such charges as shall be awarded in
case the first sentence shall be affirmed.
     And whereas Wee judge it necessary that all our subjects
may have liberty to Appeal to our Royall Person in cases
that may require the same: Our will and pleasure is that
if either party shall not rest satisfied with the judgement or sentence of you (or the Commander in Cheif for the
time being) and the Councill, they may Appeal unto Us in
our Privy Councill: Provided the matter in difference
exceed the value and summ of three hundred pounds sterling
and that such Appeal be made within one fortnight after
sentence, and that security be likewise duly given by the
Appellant to answer such charges as shall be awarded in
case the sentence of you...and the Councill be confirmed;
and provided also that execution not be suspended by reason

1.C.O.29/4.An order in council of 23 January 1684 (P.C. 2/70 p.108)
had determined that there should be no appeals without security being
given.   2. J.R.Brodhead (ed.) *op.cit*.III pp.539-40.

of any such appeal to us.
   And Wee do hereby give and grant unto you full power
where you shall see cause and shall judge any offender
or offenders in capitall and criminall matters, or for
any fines or forfeitures due unto us, fit objects of our
mercy, to pardon such offenders and to remitt such fines
& forfeitures,treason and willfull murder only excepted,
in which case you shall likewise have power upon extraordinary occasions to grant reprieves to the offenders
therein untill and to the intent our pleasure may be further known....

(D) JURIES

   This section tries to illustrate from several colonies the operation of, modification of, or rejection of an English jury system
in some of the plantations in the seventeenth century.

(a) VIRGINIA

410.(i) ACT RELATING TO PETITIONS FOR A JURY, March 1643.[1]
   (Act LVII)
   Whereas it was enacted at an Assembly in June 1642 that
if either plaintiff or defendant shall desire the verdict
of a jury for the determining of any suite depending within
any of the courts of this collony, he or they shall signifie therein their desire by petition under his or their
hands unto the said courts before the said cause had any
hearing upon the day of tryall if it be the desire of the
plaintiff and their petitions to be fyled in the Secretary's office and with the clarke of the monthly court; and
if the defendant shall desire it he or they shall signifie
the same upon the entry of his appearance in the Secretary's office which shall be inserted in a booke to be kept
in the office for that purpose,...[That Act was now reenacted.]

(ii) INSTRUCTIONS TO LORD CULPEPER, 6 December 1679.[2]
   And whereas we think it fit for the better administration of justice That a law should be passed wherein shall
be set the value of men's estate either in goods or lands
under which they shall not be capable of serving as jurors, you are to endeavour the passing of such a law (if
not already done) as soon as there shall be an opportunity   [and to send it to the Lords of Trade for the King's approval]....

1.W.Hening *op.cit.*I p.273.In November 1645 (ActX,*ibid.*p.303-4) there
was detailed provision for the selection of 'able' jurors and the conduct of a trial:'jurors were to kept from food and release till they
have agreed upon their verdict according to the custome practised in
England'.In March 1646 (*ibid.*p.314) there was provision for their pay-
ment.Juries for criminal cases had been provided for in the royal instructions of 1606 at the time of the first charter [see p.238].
2.C.O. 5/1355. A similar instruction was given in Jamaica in 1678, to
New Hampshire in 1682, and to New York and New England in 1686.

(b) MASSACHUSETTS

411. (i) ORDER OF GENERAL COURT, 14 May 1634.[1]

It was further ordered that the constable of every plantacion shall upon process receive from the Secretary give
tymely notice to the freemen of the plantacion where he
dwells to send soe many of their members as the process
shall direct to attend upon publique service, and it is
agreed that noe tryall shall pass upon any for life or
banishment, but by a jury soe summoned[2]....

(ii) ORDER OF GENERAL COURT, 14 June 1642.[3]

It is ordered that in all tryalls between party and
party the jury shall find the matter of fact with the
damages and costs according to their evidence, and the
judges are to declare the sentence of the lawe upon it,
or they may direct the jury to find according to the lawe.
And if there fall out to bee any matter of apparent equity,
as upon the forfeiture of an obligation, breach of covenant without damage or the like, the judges shall determine
such matter of equity....

(iii) RESOLUTION OF GENERAL COURT, 27 September 1642.[4]

Mr. Bellingham, Mr. Saltonshall, Mr. Symons, Mr. Haw-
thorne, Captain Jeanison, Goodman Johnson and Goodman
Heath are appointed a committee to consider whether in
tryall of causes to retaine or dismise juries, against
the Court of Elections....

(iv) ORDER OF GENERAL COURT, 27 May, 1652.[5]

It is ordered and enacted by this Court and the authoritie thereof That after the end of this present session,
all actions of a civil nature shall be tried in all courts
within this jurisdiction by the judges of the said court
without a jury, except it be desired by the playntife or
defendant in which case it shall be graunted, provided
that the party that shall desire a jury shall pay the
charges of the jury [*viz:* 20 shillings in the court of assistants and the county courts,*etc.*]

1.N.B.Shurtleff (ed.)*op.cit.*I p.118.Though there was mention of juries
during the first months of the colony in Massachusetts, the grand and
petty juries were not generally introduced till 1634.Clearly there
was doubt about their desirability and in one period in the middle of
the century they were briefly discontinued.[see (iv)].The questions
were whether they undermined the authority of the magistrates,and
whether the magistrates could direct them to return a specific verdict.
2.The deputy,Increase Nowell,added to the minute the additional words
'or by the Generall Court'.
3.N.B.Shurtleff (ed.) *op.cit.*II p.21.
4.*ibid.*II p.28.A temporary order was passed asserting that the jury
should 'find the matter of fact with damages and costs according to
the evidence,and the judges are to declare the sentence upon it or
they may direct the jury to find according to the law'.
5.*ibid.*III p.262.All civil actions were to be tried without a jury

(v) ORDER OF GENERAL COURT, 19 October 1652.[1]
   It is ordered...That the laws about juries is repealed
and juries are in force again....

(vi) ORDER OF GENERAL COURT, 6 May 1657.[2]
   [In all cases the court and jury had to be convinced that the
   affirmation of the plaintiff should 'be proved by suffycient evidence, else the cause must be found for the defendant, for in the
   eye of the lawe everyman is honest and innocent unlesse it be
   prooved legally to the contrary'.]
   ...All evidence ariseth partly from matter of fact and
partly from law and argument: the matter of fact is alwayes feizeable to be judged off as well by the jury as by
the court, and concerning the law and the poynt of law in
reference to the case in question it is more easy and generally knowne and more difficult to be discerned. The duty
of the jury is, if they doe understand the law to the
satisfaction of their conscience, not to put it off from
themselves but to find accordingly; but if any of the
jury doth rest unsatisfyed what is law in the case, then
the whole jury have liberty to present a speciall verdict:
viz., if the law be so and so on such a poynt we find for
the playntiff; but, if the law be otherwise, we find for
the deffendant in which case the determination is left to
the court....

(vii) ORDER OF GENERAL COURT, 15 May 1672.[3]
   This Court, being desirous to prevent all dissattisfac-
tion and inconveniences that may arise in the triall of
civil cases in inferior Courts, sometimes happening by
reason of disagreement between the bench and jury, formerly allowed by law, doe order and enact That henceforth in
all county courts, after that the bench have used all reasonable indeavours for clearing the case to the jury by
declaring the lawe and comparing the matter of fact and
damage prooved therewith, the virdict of the jury finally
given shall be accepted and judgment accordingly entered.
   [Similarly in the court of assistants; unless the jury gave a
   perverse verdict, corrupt or erroneous, when the jury could be
   attainted and presented before a new jury of 24; penalties were
   prescribed for the jurors who were convicted of such a perverse
   verdict, and for those who brought an unsuccessful action against
   a jury. The order allowing magistrates to refuse a jury's verdict
   was repealed.]

(viii)THE PRACTICE IN THE COURTS RESULTING FROM CONFLICT BETWEEN
      JUDGES AND JURIES, c.1681.[4]
   It was a very common thing for the court to refuse to

unless the parties indicated that they desired one and were prepared
to pay the charges.   1. *ibid.* IV (i) p.107.
2. *ibid.* IV(i)p.291.   3. *ibid.* IV (ii) p.508.
4.T. Hutchinson, *History*...I p.401. The jury in the trial of Penn and
Mead for tumultuous assembly at the Old Bailey had been directed by

receive the verdict of the jury and in this case the cause
was carried before the general court.

The Jury sometimes gave their verdict, That there were
strong grounds of suspicion, but not sufficient evidence
to convict. The Court would give sentence upon this verdict, and punish for many offences, which, by the evidence
upon triall, the party appeared to them to have been guilty
of, although he was not convicted of the particular crime
he was charged with, *Secumdum allegata et probata* was a
rule of proceeding to which they did not confine themselves...Mr. Hinkley, governour of Plymouth, writing to Mr.
Stoughton for advice, in 1681, he answers him, 'the testimony you mention against the prisoner, I think is sufficient to convict him; but in case your jury should not be
of that mind, then, if you hold yourselves strictly obliged by the laws of England, no other verdict but not
guilty can be brought in; but according to our practice
in this jurisdiction, we should punish him with some grievous punishment, according to the demerit of his crime,
though not found capital'....

(ix) ORDER OF GENERAL COURT, 11 September 1684.[1]
...Whereas it is found, by experience, that the provision made by the law, titled *Juries*, May, 1672, for releife
in case of apparent corruption or error in the jurys
giving in their virdict contrary to law and evidence, is
perverted to the burdening of the country with unreasonable trouble, the great wrong of parties concerned, with
unjust reflections made thereby upon the jurys, -

It is ordered by this Court and the authority thereof,
That in all attaints, before the entry or allowance thereof, that the party attainting shall give in writting, under
his hand, for what cause, and shew how the same doth appeare so to be; and in case, upon a due tryall as the law
provides, the virdict of the former jury be confirmed,
such party so attainting shall pay to the country, as a
fine for unnecessary trouble to the Court, tenn pounds
in money, and to the jurymen that gave in the former virdict forty shillings a peice; and in case...be for corr-

---

the recorder to convict the accused, but had found the two Quakers
not guilty: the jurymen had been imprisoned in Newgate, but in Bush-
ell's case,1670 [6 St.Tr.999] had been released by the chief justice
in common pleas since 'the judge can never direct what the law is in
any matter controverted without first knowing the fact [which it was
the jury's function to ascertain]: and then it follows, that without
his previous knowledge of the fact, the jury cannot go against his
direction in law, for he could not direct'. The immunity of the jury
was thereby established in English law: but it should be noted that
the transformation of the jury from a body of witnesses and neighbours
(*vicinage*) to judges of facts presented only in court was not yet
complete.
1.*ibid*.V pp.449-0.

uption, it shall be lawfull for the jury so reproached
joyntly or severally to prosecute their action of slander
as to them shall seeme meet; and the plaintiffe reproach-
ing shall also be liable to such further fine to the country as the Court shall judge meet.

Also, in all cases where the former virdict is confirmed, the party concerned shall have double costs, and also
double interest, for being detyned of his just debt according to former virdict....

(c) MARYLAND

412. (i) ORDER OF THE ASSEMBLY, 17 March 1637.[1]
It was declared that the court or judge should impose
the fine, and the jury could assess the recompence to the
partie.

(ii) (ii) ACT ERECTING A COUNTY COURT, March 1639.[2]
...And all issues of fact in this Court shall be tried
by the said Cheif justice commissioner etc and the Councell sitting in Court or the major part of them, if the
defendant shall chuse to be tried by the Court; or otherwise by a jury of seven or more freeholders of the county
to be returned by the Sherrif if the defendant shall chuse
to be tried by his country ....

  [The sheriff on receiving a writ from the colony's chancery
  was to return five or more freemen for a 'grand inquest'. A grand
  jury required at least twelve jurors for any cases of felony or
  treason.]

(d) CONNECTICUT

413. (i) ORDER OF THE COURT OF ELECTION, 13 April 1643.[3]
...Whereas, in regard of the diversity of mens judgements amongst Jurors, it falls out divers tymes that no
verdict is given in,or else with great difficulty; Wherefore it is thought meet and so Ordered That the Jurors
would with all dilligence attend the issue and evidence of
the Cause before them,to which they are sworne, and if in
that case they cannot agree after all reasons disputed,
but some remayne unsatisfied, their reasons are to be tendered to the Court, and to be answered, and then they are
to consult together agayne, and if as yet any cannot bring
their judgments to joyne with their fellowes in a joynt
verdict, the greater parte shall give it in by their voate,

1.W.H.Browne (ed.) *op.cit.*I p.22.The question had been asked whether
in criminal cases the jury was to assess the fine to the Lord proprietor as well as the damages to the plaintiff.On 24 March a grand jury
of 24 freemen considered the charges against William Claiborne for
holding a seditious meeting against the proprietor (*ibid.*p.23).
2.W.H. Browne (ed.) *op.cit.*I p.49. Another Act of March 1639 required
that a jury of twelve freemen should try 'enormous offences': a lord
of the manor would be tried by a jury of lords of the manor (*ibid.*
p.51).
3.J.H. Trumbull (ed.) *Public records of...Connecticut* (1850) I pp.84-5.

and it shall be deemed to all intends and purposes a sufficient and full verdict, uppon which judgement may be
entered and execution and other proceedings to be had
therein, as though they had all agreed; Provided also,
that if it fall out the case be so difficult that the Jury
are equally divided sixe *[to]* sixe, the Jurors are to tender it to the Court, with their reasons, and a spetiall
verdict is to be drawen thereuppon; and then the Court
are to appoynt a tyme to argue the same, and the voate of
greater number of Magistrats are to carry the same, and
judgement to be entered thereupon, and execution and other
proceedings as in case of a verdict by a Jury....

(ii) ORDER OF COURT OF ELECTION, 5 July 1643.[1]
   ...It is Ordered, there shall be a Grand Jury of 12
persons warned to appeare every Court yerely in September,
or as many and oft as the Governor, or Courte shall thinke
meet, to make presentment of the breches of any lawes or
orders, or any other misdemeanors they know of in the Jurisdiction....

(iii) ORDER OF COURT OF ELECTION, 5 February 1644.[2]
   Whereas some question hath rysen concerneing unnecessary tryalls by Jury and found by experience that many such
sutes might be prevented if arbitrations were attended in
a more privat way according to the nature of the differences which is recommended by the Court to all the Towns of
this Government. And for the regulateing of Juryes for
the future, It is Ordered That in all cases which are entered under 40s. the sute shall be lefte to be tryed by the
Court of Magestrats as they shall judge more agreable to
equity and righteousnes; And That, in all cases that are
tryed by Juryes, the Court and Magestrats shall have liberty if they doe not conceave the Jury to have proceeded
according to their evidence in their verdict given in, to
cause them to returne againe to a second consideration of
the case; and if they continue in their former opinion and
doe not in the judgement of the Court attend the evidence
given in Court, It shall be in the power of the Court to
impanell another Jury and commit the consideration of the
case to them.
   It is also lefte in the power of the Court in any case
of tryall to vary and alter the damages given in by the
Jury as they shall judge most equall and righteous....
   [The general court was empowered to hear appeals from any court
   and jury. Juries might consist of from 12 - 6 men; 8 and 4 being
   the necessary majorities for verdicts in these cases.]

1.*ibid.* I p.91.
2.*ibid.*   I pp.117-8. This order was incorporated into the Code of
Laws of May 1650. (*ibid.* I p.506).

(e) RHODE ISLAND

414. ORDER OF GENERAL COURT, 19 September 1642.[1]
   It is ordered That the freemen of the towne in their
towne meetings shall appoint the juries for the courts
and That they shall have powre as well to appoint the
inhabitants, as freemen, for that service by virtue of
the tenure and grant of their lands which is freehold....
       [There would be two general sessions of the courts in June and
   December and quarter sessions in March and September.]
   And further it is ordered That the jurors shall have
twelve pence a piece paid them for every cause upon issue
joyned[2]....

1.J.R.Bartlett (ed.) *Records of...Rhode Island* I p.124.
2. Later in 1658 jurors were fined for non-attendance (*ibid.*p.400).

INDEX

ABOUT THE EDITORS

FREDERICK MADDEN is now an Emeritus Reader in Commonwealth Government and was Professorial Fellow at Nuffield College, Oxford University. He is the author or coeditor of *Oxford and the Idea of Commonwealth, Australia and Britain, Imperial Constitutional Documents 1765-1965,* and *British Colonial Developments 1774-1834.* He has contributed chapters to the *Cambridge History of the British Empire, III, Perspectives of Empire, The First British Commonwealth,* and *Essays in British History.* A tribute in the *festschrift* on his retirement spoke of him as "the quintessential Commonwealth-imperial historian of his generation."

DAVID FIELDHOUSE, previously Beit Lecturer in Colonial History and Faculty Fellow of Nuffield College, Oxford University, is now Vere Harmsworth Professor of Imperial and Naval History—the senior chair at Cambridge University. With Frederick Madden he was historical consultant for the Time-Life series on the British Empire. He is the author of *The Colonial Empires, Economics and Empire, 1830-1914* and *Unilever Overseas,* which won the annual award of the Business Archives Council in 1980.